The SUTTANIPĀTA

THE TEACHINGS OF THE BUDDHA SERIES

The Buddha's Teachings on Social and Communal Harmony: An Anthology of Discourses from the Pāli Canon

The Connected Discourses of the Buddha: A Translation of the Saṃyutta Nikāya

Great Disciples of the Buddha: Their Lives, Their Works, Their Legacy

In the Buddha's Words: An Anthology of Discourses from the Pāli Canon

The Long Discourses of the Buddha: A Translation of the Dīgha Nikāya

The Middle Length Discourses of the Buddha: A Translation of the Majjhima Nikāya

The Numerical Discourses of the Buddha: A Translation of the Aṅguttara Nikāya

THE TEACHINGS OF THE BUDDHA

The Suttanipāta

An Ancient Collection of the

Buddha's Discourses

Together with Its Commentaries

Paramatthajotikā II
and excerpts from the *Niddesa*

Translated from the Pāli

by

Bhikkhu Bodhi

Wisdom

Wisdom Publications
199 Elm Street
Somerville, MA 02144 USA
wisdompubs.org

Library of Congress Cataloging-in-Publication Data is available.
LCCN 2016048003

ISBN 978-1-61429-429-0 ebook ISBN 978-1-61429-454-2

21 20 19 18 17
5 4 3 2 1

Design by Gopa&Ted2.
Set in TexGyrePagella 10/12.4.

Wisdom Publications' books are printed on acid-free paper and meet the guidelines for permanence and durability of the Production Guidelines for Book Longevity of the Council on Library Resources.

Printed in the United States of America.

Dedicated to the memory of two departed friends from my time in Sri Lanka

Ayyā Nyānasirī
(1932–2004)

An American Buddhist woman who lived in Sri Lanka from 1978 until her death in 2004. An editorial assistant for the Buddhist Publication Society, ordained as a ten-precept nun in 1987, an inspiration to many of the English-speaking Sri Lankan Buddhist women in Kandy and Colombo, she was a great admirer of the Suttanipāta who aspired to follow the muni ideal.

Bhikkhu Sumedha
(1932–2006)

A Swiss bhikkhu who lived in Sri Lanka from 1974 until his death in 2006, resident at the Manāpadassana Cave near Doolwala, Kandy district. A brilliant artist with paint, brush, and words, a Dhamma teacher with keen insight into the teachings, he was also a monk of deep compassion who served as spiritual guide to doctors and patients at the Peradeniya Teaching Hospital.

Wherever these two departed friends may now be dwelling, may they rejoice in the knowledge that this translation is dedicated to their memory.

Publisher's Acknowledgment

The publisher gratefully acknowledges the generous help of the Hershey Family Foundation in sponsoring the production of this book.

Contents

Elucidator of the Supreme Meaning (Paramatthajotikā II)
The Commentary to the Suttanipāta

Preface

This volume offers a new translation of the Suttanipāta together with its commentarial apparatus. The Suttanipāta is an anthology of discourses ascribed to the Buddha, included in the Khuddaka Nikāya, the Minor or Miscellaneous Collection, the fifth of the five *nikāyas* that constitute the Sutta Piṭaka (or Compilation of Discourses) of the Pāli Canon. The Suttanipāta sits in this collection alongside such popular works as the Dhammapada, the Udāna, and the Itivuttaka, and is itself a perennial favorite among followers of Theravāda Buddhism. Most of the discourses in the Suttanipāta are in verse, some in mixed prose and verse. None is entirely in prose. Several discourses in the Suttanipāta are found in the main collections—specifically in the Majjhima, Saṃyutta, and Aṅguttara Nikāyas—though most are unique to this anthology.

Linguistic and doctrinal evidence suggests that the Suttanipāta took shape through a gradual process of accretion spread out over three or four centuries. The anthology is unique to the Pāli Canon, though it contains discourses with parallels in other transmission lines among the schools of Early Buddhism. This implies that the Suttanipāta itself was compiled within the Pāli school from preexisting material. Several of its texts are considered to be among the most ancient specimens of Buddhist literature. Among these are two chapters, the Aṭṭhakavagga (chap. IV) and the Pārāyanavagga (chap. V), that are quoted in the Saṃyutta and Aṅguttara Nikāyas. These two chapters are, moreover, the subjects of a two-part expository text, the Niddesa, so old that it was included in the Khuddaka Nikāya. The Suttanipāta also contains discourses that have been absorbed into the common Theravāda monastic liturgy, among them the Metta Sutta and the Ratana Sutta, and popular discourses like the Parābhava Sutta and the Mahāmaṅgala Sutta that serve as the basis for Buddhist lay ethics. These suttas are often drawn upon by preachers of the Dhamma for their sermons to the laity.

The Suttanipāta has been previously translated into English at least six times: by Robert Chalmers, Viggo Fausbøll, E. M. Hare, Ven. H. Saddhātissa, K.R. Norman, and N.A. Jayawickrama. A German translation by Nyanaponika Thera is also available. A translation of the Aṭṭhakavagga by Bhikkhu Paññobhāsa has been published in a small printed edition, inclusive of the Pāli text. Several chapters and individual suttas are posted on the website Access to Insight, most translated by Ṭhānissaro Bhikkhu. Another translation of the Aṭṭhakavagga, this one by Gil Fronsdal (2016), was published too late for me to consult when preparing the present work.

My intention, in preparing this work, was not to offer still another translation that would improve on the work of my predecessors and shake up the world of Buddhist scholarship with bold, innovative renderings. Rather, it was to make the Suttanipāta available in an accurate and readable version along with its commentaries as preserved in the Pāli Buddhist tradition. This is, I believe, the first time that the entire Suttanipāta Commentary and substantial excerpts from the Niddesa have been published in translation.

I based my translation of the Suttanipāta on three editions. I relied primarily on the excellent Roman-script edition by Dines Anderson and Helmer Smith, published by the Pali Text Society (PTS), but I also consulted two other versions. One is the electronic edition of the Burmese Chaṭṭha Saṅgāyana Tipiṭaka, the Sixth Council compilation, published by the Vipassana Research Institute and available online (designated CST4). The other is the Sinhala-script Buddha Jayanti edition published in Sri Lanka, now available online as a PDF. Occasionally I preferred a reading in one or another (or both) of these editions to that in the PTS edition. When I do so, I have usually mentioned my preference in a note. My numbering scheme follows that of the PTS edition.

In preparing my translation of the Suttanipāta I regularly consulted the careful and precise translations by Norman and Jayawickrama and often refer to them in my notes. I also found

Norman's endnotes (which take up 300 pages of his 430-page volume, *The Group of Discourses*) particularly helpful in understanding the text from a philological perspective. Jayawickrama's monograph, "A Critical Analysis of the Suttanipāta," gave me insights into the work's historical and linguistic development. The two translations I consulted most often occasionally differ due to their divergent approaches. Norman's aim, as he expresses it in his preface, is "to give the meaning of the text as it was intended to be understood by the original speakers, or as it was accepted by the first hearers" (GD x). This is a tall order for one living so far from the culture and environment in which the Suttanipāta took shape, but Norman brought to the task his consummate knowledge of Middle Indo-Aryan languages. Jayawickrama, in contrast, leans heavily on the commentary and thus follows more closely traditional Theravādin exegesis.

In my translation I have tried to steer a middle course between the two. I sought to remain faithful to the words of the text when it is clear, simple, and straightforward. Since this is not always the case, I relied on the commentary to understand more difficult verses and obscure words and expressions. There were, however, places where I had to differ from the commentary, even when doing so created a dissonance between my rendering of the root text and the commentary. I have noted these discrepancies in the introduction (pp. 78–81), where I refer to the notes that explain my disagreements. Also, unlike Norman and Jayawickrama, I have composed my translation in free verse. Since I am not a poet, I did not aim at poetic elegance but simply at rendering the verses in a style that is more uplifting and less pedantic than a bare prose translation.

To keep the translation of the canonical text as trim as possible, I have relegated virtually all my notes dealing with matters of substance to the commentarial section, with verse and commentarial numbers correlated. The citation of lines in these notes refer to the Pāli text, not the translation. Thus, for example, **189**c means verse 189, third line of the Pāli. Because of the differences in syntax between the two languages, the line number of a Pāli verse is not always the same as that of the English rendering. The notes to the root text deal primarily with my choices among the readings in the three editions I consulted and with other minor linguistic matters. Occasionally too I cite the commentary in a note to clarify a reading. I have recorded parallels to the discourses in the Suttanipāta in two places: under the summary of each sutta in the Guide to the Suttas and in Appendix 1. I also refer to parallels when I discuss them in the notes to the commentarial section.

The commentary on the Suttanipāta is named *Paramatthajotikā*. Since the commentary on the Khuddakapāṭha, a short work in the Khuddaka Nikāya, is also named *Paramatthajotikā*, modern editors designate the Khuddakapāṭha Commentary "*Paramatthajotikā* I" and the Suttanipāta Commentary "*Paramatthajotikā* II." *Paramattha* means "supreme meaning" and *jotikā* "illuminator" or "elucidator." Thus I render the title "Elucidator of the Supreme Meaning." This commentary is traditionally ascribed to Ācariya Buddhaghosa, the Indian monk who came to Sri Lanka in the fifth century C.E., where he composed the *Visuddhimagga* ("Path of Purification"), a comprehensive treatise on Buddhist doctrine and meditation, and commentaries on the four main Nikāyas; he may also have been the author of still other commentaries as well. These commentaries—known as *aṭṭhakathā*—were based largely on older commentaries preserved in the ancient Sinhala language, which in turn, it is said, were translated from still older Indian originals brought to the island centuries earlier.

Buddhaghosa's authorship of the commentary to the Suttanipāta is disputed, and it is virtually impossible to settle the issue with certainty. What is clear, however, is that the author of the Suttanipāta Commentary, whoever it may have been, draws upon the same system of exegesis that Buddhaghosa used, the system that had evolved over the centuries at the Mahāvihāra, the Great Monastery in Anuradhapura, the ancient capital of Sri Lanka. *Paramatthajotikā* II thus belongs to the same body of *aṭṭhakathā* considered authoritative by the Theravāda school of Buddhism. These commentaries look at the canonical texts through the lens of exegetical analysis maintained by the elders of the Mahāvihāra, which often draws upon ideas and schemes of categories unique to the Pāli school.

I have translated the entire commentary, with a few minor omissions. I omitted portions of the "term explanations" (*padavaṇṇanā*) that merely define particular Pāli words in the canonical text by way of synonyms more familiar to readers in the age of the commentaries. To have translated these passages into intelligible English, I would have had to define common English words with other common English words, which would be redundant if my translation of the root text is sufficiently clear. I have omitted, too, translations of individual sentences here and there that deal with technical grammatical issues and other matters of protocol.

My translation of the commentary is based primarily on the PTS edition of *Paramatthajotikā* II, edited by Helmer Smith. I also consulted the Vipassana Research Institute's electronic version of the Chaṭṭha Saṅgāyana edition and the Sinhala-script Simon Hewavitarne Bequest edition. Smith omitted from his edition of Pj II the commentaries on three suttas that the Suttanipāta shares with the Khuddakapāṭha—the Metta, Ratana, and Mahāmaṅgala Suttas. He had already edited *Paramatthajotikā* I, and since the explanations of these discourses are almost identical in the two commentaries, he decided to avoid the repetition. I therefore translated the commentaries on these suttas from the PTS edition of Pj I, again while also consulting the Burmese and Sri Lankan editions of Pj II, which include them.

While the style of the *aṭṭhakathā* can be dense and ponderous, I believe it is important to have the commentaries on the canonical text available in English translation as a safeguard against arbitrary interpretations. Since the Suttanipāta is composed mostly in verse, and the stanzas are sometimes obscure and suggestive, it is tempting for writers on Early Buddhism to seize upon single suttas and even a few enigmatic stanzas as the building blocks for erecting their own personal theories about "Original Buddhism just as the Buddha intended it." Thus, based mainly on the Suttanipāta, claims are sometimes put forth that Buddhism was originally a premonastic movement made up of individualistic wandering hermits, or that the Buddha was a radical skeptic whose teaching had no room for such ideas as kamma, rebirth, saṃsāra, and transcendent liberation, but was aimed solely at inner tranquility through the relinquishment of all views and attachments. Such theories depend largely on selective citation in defiance of the weight of evidence bearing down from the great mass of Early Buddhist literature and stubborn facts about the history of Buddhism.

Reading the Suttanipāta in the light of the main Nikāyas and their commentaries should serve to correct such speculative theories. While the commentaries certainly represent the views of later generations of exegetes and may not capture the original intent of the work in all respects, to ignore or reject them is to dismiss the cumulative efforts of the early doctrinal masters to understand and explain the Word of the Buddha.

As mentioned above, two chapters of the Suttanipāta, the Aṭṭhakavagga and the Pārāyanavagga, along with the Khaggavisāṇa Sutta, were taken as the subjects of an expository work included in the Khuddaka Nikāya. This work, known as the Niddesa or "Exposition," is divided into two parts. The larger part, the *Mahāniddesa* or "Great Exposition," comments on the Aṭṭhakavagga; the *Cūḷaniddesa* or "Minor Exposition" comments on the Pārāyanavagga and the Khaggavisāṇa Sutta.

By necessity I have included only excerpts from the Niddesa. Given that the *Mahāniddesa* comes to 385 pages in the Chaṭṭhasaṅgāyana edition, and the *Cūḷaniddesa* to 275 pages, full translations of these texts would have swelled this volume far beyond serviceable size. I have selected what I consider the most illuminating passages of both parts of the Niddesa and interlaced them with the translation of Pj II. I have sometimes simplified my renderings of the Niddesa (for example, by shortening the chains of synonyms it typically employs) and have tried to avoid excessive repetition, which is hard to do with a work as repetitive as the Niddesa. Only occasionally did I include translations of the suttas from other sources that the Niddesa quotes to reinforce its explanations.

William Stede, in editing the PTS edition of the *Cūḷaniddesa*, reorganized the work in accordance with his own conception of it as "an aggregate of disconnected pieces or atoms." He arranges, in Pāli alphabetical order, the terms commented on by the *Cūḷaniddesa* and for each term provides the verse numbers where the terms occur and the relevant explanations. For this reason his edition was not suitable for my purpose, which requires that I follow the sequence of the verses. I have therefore used as my text the Vipassana Research Institute's electronic version of both parts of the Niddesa, the *Mahā* and the *Cūḷa* portions, included in their edition of the Pāli Tipiṭaka (CST4). Each complete excerpt from the Niddesa is marked off with ⁞▮ at the beginning and ▮⁞ at the end. The source for each excerpt is set in bold preceding the passage. Those who read Pāli can find the passage in the electronic version by comparing these numbers with the VRI page numbers at the bottom edge of the window.

The serious non-academic student of Early Buddhism might feel daunted by the amount of material presented in this volume and not know where or how to proceed. As a practical approach, I suggest initially reading the introduction and the Guide to the Suttas, and then the translation of the Suttanipāta itself. Read it slowly and reflectively, without being anxious to understand every verse and line on a first reading. After reading and digesting the root text to the best of one's ability, return to the text again, this time reading each sutta individually—or perhaps even each verse—along with the commentary on it. Skip over those parts of the commentary one finds dense, tedious, pedantic, or irrelevant to one's concerns, and focus on those parts that actually explain the text. Connections between the root text and the corresponding portion of the commentary are easy to make because both use the same numbering scheme. Thus, for instance, the commentarial explanation of stanza **18** can be located by finding the bold number **18** in the commentarial section. Lines and phrases from the root text being commented on, known as the lemma, **are set in bold** (as thus illustrated). This makes them easy to identify. Occasionally, when there are gaps in the numbering of the commentary sections, this is either because the commentary does not comment on the verse (since all the terms are already clear) or because it merely offers routine word glosses that I thought need not be translated.

By any merit I have acquired through this work, may the Three Gems of the Ratana Sutta long flourish in the world and may the peoples of the world live together in peace, guided by the ethics of the Parābhava Sutta, the values of the Mahāmaṅgala Sutta, and the sublime attitudes of the Metta Sutta. May seekers of liberation discard erroneous views and deviant practices, as advised by the Aṭṭhakavagga, and set their feet on the path to the goal pointed to by the Pārāyanavagga, the Chapter on the Way to the Beyond.

Acknowledgments

Bhikkhu Anālayo and John Kelly read the entire translation of the Suttanipāta alongside the Pāli text, as well as the translation of the commentary, and both made helpful recommendations. Ven. Anālayo also suggested additions to my concordance of parallels (Appendix 1). Bhikkhu Khemaratana read the translation of the Suttanipāta and made several suggestions regarding my terminology, drawing me back to the use of simple ordinary words rather than more elevated literary words.

At several points, when questions arose in my mind about terms and passages in the commentary, I posted them on the Yahoo Pāli Discussion Group and received quick replies from group members. I found particularly helpful the replies from Petra Kieffer-Pülz, Bryan Levman, and the late Lance Cousins.

I am thankful to the residents and staff of Chuang Yen Monastery, who allowed me the leisure to undertake this translation with minimal disturbances. I am also grateful to my lay students for their support.

As with their earlier volumes in the Teachings of the Buddha series, Wisdom Publications has done an excellent job of production. I am thankful to the editor, David Kittelstrom, for his editorial suggestions, to Megan Anderson for meticulous proofing, to the production team, and to the publisher, Timothy McNeill.

Bhikkhu Bodhi
Chuang Yen Monastery
Carmel, New York

Key to the Pronunciation of Pāli

The Pāli Alphabet

Vowels: a, ā, i, ī, u, ū, e, o
Consonants:

Gutterals:	k, kh, g, gh, ṅ
Palatals	c, ch, j, jh, ñ
Cerebrals	ṭ, ṭh, ḍ, ḍh, ṇ
Dentals	t, th, d, dh, n
Labials	p, ph, b, bh, m
Other	y, r, ḷ, l, v, s, h, ṃ

Pronunciation

a as in "cut"
ā as in "father"
i as in "king"
ī as in "keen"
u as in "put"
ū as in "rule"
e as in "way"
o as in "home"

Of the vowels, *e* and *o* are long before a single consonant and short before a double consonant. Among the consonants, *g* is always pronounced as in "good," *c* as in "church," *ñ* as in "onion." The cerebrals (or retroflexes) are spoken with the tongue on the roof of the mouth; the dentals with the tongue on the upper teeth. The aspirates—*kh, gh, ch, jh, ṭh, ḍh, th, dh, ph, bh*—are single consonants pronounced with slightly more force than the nonaspirates, e.g., *th* as in "Thomas" (not as in "thin"); *ph* as in "putter" (not as in "phone"). Double consonants are always enunciated separately, e.g., *dd* as in "mad dog," *gg* as in "big gun." The pure nasal (*niggahīta*) *ṃ* is pronounced like the *ng* in "song." An *o* and an *e* always carry a stress; otherwise the stress falls on a long vowel —*ā*, *ī*, *ū*, or on a double consonant, or on *ṃ*.

Abbreviations

I. Editions Used

Be	Burmese-script Chaṭṭha Saṅgāyana Tipiṭaka edition in Vipassana Research Institute's electronic version 4.0
Ce	Sinhala-script edition
Ee	Roman-script edition

II. Texts in Pāli and Other Indian Languages

Unless otherwise specified, references to Pāli texts are to the editions of the Pali Text Society. References to Vism followed by Ppn give first the page number of the PTS edition of the Visuddhimagga followed by the chapter and section number of Bhikkhu Ñāṇamoli's translation, *The Path of Purification*.

AN	Aṅguttara Nikāya
Ap	Apadāna
Ap-a	Apadāna-aṭṭhakathā
As	Atthasālinī
Bv	Buddhavaṃsa
Bv-a	Buddhavaṃsa-aṭṭhakathā
Cp-a	Cariyapiṭaka-aṭṭhakathā
Dhp	Dhammapada
Dhp-a	Dhammapada-aṭṭhakathā
Dhs	Dhammasaṅgaṇī (VRI ed.)
Dīp	Dīpavaṃsa
DN	Dīgha Nikāya
It	Itivuttaka
It-a	Itivuttaka-aṭṭhakathā
Ja	Jātaka-aṭṭhakathā

Mhv	Mahāvaṃsa
Mil	Milindapañha
MN	Majjhima Nikāya
Mp	Manorathapūraṇī (Aṅguttara Nikāya-aṭṭhakathā)
Mp-ṭ	Manorathapūraṇī-ṭīkā (Aṅguttara Nikāya-ṭīkā) (VRI ed.)
Nidd I	Mahāniddesa (VRI ed.)
Nidd I-a	Mahāniddesa-aṭṭhakathā
Nidd II	Cūḷaniddesa (VRI ed.)
Nidd II-a	Cūḷaniddesa-aṭṭhakathā
Paṭis	Paṭisambhidāmagga
Paṭis-a	Paṭisambhidāmagga-aṭṭhakathā
PDhp	Patna Dharmapada
Pj I	Paramatthajotikā I (Khuddakapāṭha-aṭṭhakathā)
Pj II	Paramatthajotikā II (Suttanipāta-aṭṭhakathā)
Pp	Puggalapaññatti
Ps	Papañcasūdanī (Majjhima Nikāya-aṭṭhakathā)
Ps-ṭ	Papañcasūdanī-ṭīkā (Majjhima Nikāya-ṭīkā) (VRI ed.)
Pv	Petavatthu
Śag	Śarīrārthagāthā (of the Yogācārabhūmi)
SN	Saṃyutta Nikāya
Sn	Suttanipāta
Sp	Samantappasādikā (Vinaya-aṭṭhakathā)
Sp-ṭ	Sāratthadīpanī-ṭīkā (ṭīkā on Sp) (VRI ed.)
Spk	Sāratthappakāsinī (Saṃyutta Nikāya-aṭṭhakathā)
Spk-ṭ	Sāratthappakāsinī-ṭīkā (Saṃyutta Nikāya-ṭīkā) (VRI ed.)
Sv	Sumaṅgalavilāsinī (Dīgha Nikāya-aṭṭhakathā)
Sv-ṭ	Sumaṅgalavilāsinī-ṭīkā (Dīgha Nikāya-ṭīkā) (VRI ed.)
Th	Theragāthā
Th-a	Theragāthā-aṭṭhakathā
Thī	Therīgāthā
Thī-a	Therīgāthā-aṭṭhakathā
Ud	Udāna
Ud-a	Udāna-aṭṭhakathā
Udāna-v	Udānavarga
Vibh	Vibhaṅga (VRI ed.)
Vibh-a	Vibhaṅga-aṭṭhakathā

Vin	Vinaya
Vism	Visuddhimagga
Vism-mhṭ	Visuddhimagga-mahāṭīkā (VRI ed.)
Vmv	Vimati-vinodanī (ṭīkā on Sp) (VRI ed.)
Vv	Vimānavatthu
Vv-a	Vimānavatthu-aṭṭhakathā

III. Texts in Chinese

DĀ	Dīrghāgama (長阿含經)
EĀ	Ekottarikāgama (增壹阿含經)
MĀ	Madhyamāgama (中阿含經)
SĀ	Saṃyuktāgama (雜阿含經)
SĀ²	Saṃyuktāgama (another translation; incomplete) (別譯雜阿含經)
SĀ³	Saṃyuktāgama (another translation; incomplete) (別譯雜阿含經)
T	Taisho edition

IV. Other Works

BL	*Buddhist Legends* (see Burlingame 1921)
CDB	*Connected Discourses of the Buddha* (see Bodhi 2000)
CMA	*A Comprehensive Manual of Abhidhamma* (see Bodhi 2007a)
GD	*The Group of Discourses* (see Norman 2006b)
NDB	*Numerical Discourses of the Buddha* (see Bodhi 2012)
Ppn	*Path of Purification* (trans. of Vism)

V. Reference Works

BHSD	*Buddhist Hybrid Sanskrit Dictionary* (see Edgerton 1953)
DOP	*A Dictionary of Pāli* (see Cone 2001, 2010)
DPPN	*Dictionary of Pāli Proper Names* (see Malalasekera 1937–38)
PED	*Pāli-English Dictionary* (see Rhy Davids and Stede 1921–25)
SED	*Sanskrit-English Dictionary* (see Monier-Williams 1899)

VI. Other Abbreviations

CST4	Chaṭṭha Saṅgāyana Tipiṭaka Version 4.0
PBR	Pāli Buddhist Review
PTS	Pali Text Society
Skt	Sanskrit
VRI	Vipassana Research Institute (Igatpuri, India)
n.	note
p., pp.	page, pages
*	before title: title is hypothetical reconstruction; before word: word not listed in dictionary; after word: wild character

Introduction

1. The Suttanipāta as a Collection

The Suttanipāta is an anthology of Buddhist discourses belonging to the Khuddaka Nikāya, the fifth collection in the Sutta Piṭaka of the Pāli Canon. The title of the work means a compilation (*nipāta*) of discourses (*sutta*). Several of these discourses occur elsewhere in the Sutta Piṭaka, but most are unique to this collection. The commentary to the work, *Paramatthajotikā* II, already recognizes its composite nature when, in its introductory verses, it says that "it is so designated [Suttanipāta] because it was recited by compiling suitable suttas from here and there."[1] It is sometimes claimed that the Suttanipāta is one of the most ancient Buddhist texts. This may be true of some of its contents, but it is not true of the collection as a whole. As an anthology that emerged from the oral tradition, the Suttanipāta is a multitextured, multilayered work that spans several phases of Buddhist literary activity. It includes material that belongs to the most ancient stratum, but it also contains other material which, while still representative of Early Buddhism, has to be assigned to a later period. Exactly when the anthology came into existence is not known, but since, as a collection, it has no parallel in the texts surviving from other Early Buddhist schools, it is likely to be unique to the Pāli school now known as the Theravāda.

The stratification of material in the Suttanipāta shows that as a collection it underwent a process of gradual growth and evolution as newer material was added to a more primitive core and the contents were rearranged until it arrived at its present shape. The growth of the Suttanipāta by the addition of new material does not necessarily mean that all the suttas inserted into the anthology at a later time were composed subsequent to those included earlier. It is likely that as the work took shape, older suttas and strings of verses that were floating freely in the oral tradition, without anchorage in any established textual collection, were absorbed into the Suttanipāta in order to provide them with a secure home.

An illustration of this point is the Uraga Sutta, the first discourse in the collection. Four versions of the Uraga verses in Indic languages are known, and from their common theme and method of arrangement it is clear the verses always existed as a set. The version transmitted in the Gāndhārī language was inserted into the Gāndhārī Dharmapada, at the end of the chapter on the bhikkhu (chapter 2, corresponding to chapter 25 of the Pāli Dhammapada). Another version, found in the Patna Dharmapada, has its own chapter (22), the last in the work. And still another version, in Sanskrit, is included in the bhikṣu chapter (32) of the Udānavarga, a work of the Dhammapada genre; several verses referring to flowers are included twice, in the bhikṣu chapter and the chapter on flowers (18). Obviously, these arrangements reflect decisions made by the transmitters of these traditions about the most suitable place to accommodate the verses. The transmitters of the Pāli tradition made a different decision. They assigned the verses not to its Dhammapada or some similar work but to another anthology unique to that tradition, the Suttanipāta. Although the verses are very early, their placement at the beginning of the chapter suggests they were added there at a relatively late time.

As it stands now, the Suttanipāta is divided into five chapters (*vagga*): the Uragavagga, the Cūḷavagga, the Mahāvagga, the Aṭṭhakavagga, and the Pārāyanavagga. The number of suttas they contain, respectively, is 12, 14, 12, 16, and 18; in the last case the introductory verses and the epilogue are counted separately along with the sixteen *pucchās*, or question sections, that make up the body of the chapter. Although the Cūḷavagga, the "Minor Chapter," has more suttas than the Mahāvagga, the "Great Chapter," the two differ in length and in the number of their verses. The verse distribution among the five chapters is respectively 221, 183, 361, 210, and 174. The Mahāvagga also contains several relatively long suttas in which the verses are embedded in prose.

It is generally recognized that the last two chapters of the

Suttanipāta, the Aṭṭhakavagga and the *pucchās* of the Pārāyanavagga, are extremely old. They are quoted in the Saṃyutta Nikāya and Aṅguttara Nikāya and evidently existed as collections in their own right before they were integrated into the anthology that became the Suttanipāta.

The Aṭṭhakavagga as a distinct collection is mentioned in an incident recorded twice in the Pāli Canon, in the Vinaya and in the Udāna. In the Vinaya Mahāvagga it is reported that Soṇa Kuṭikaṇṇa, a pupil of the Elder Mahākaccāna, traveled from distant Avantī to visit the Buddha at Jetavana in Sāvatthī. After his arrival the Blessed One asked him to recite some Dhamma. In response, he recited all the texts of the Aṭṭhakavagga (*sabbān'eva aṭṭhakavaggikāni sarena abhāsi*). At the end of the recitation, the Buddha applauded him with the words: "Excellent, excellent, bhikkhu! You have learned well, attended well, memorized well the texts of the Aṭṭhakavagga."[2] The Udāna version adds a further detail. It states that Soṇa recited *all sixteen* texts of the Aṭṭhakavagga (*soḷasa aṭṭhakavaggikāni sabbān'eva sarena abhaṇi*), and the Buddha mentions the figure in his word of appreciation: "Excellent, excellent, bhikkhu! You have learned well, attended well, memorized well the sixteen texts of the Aṭṭhakavagga."[3]

The Aṭṭhakavagga is also referred to in SN 22:3 (III 9–12). Here a householder named Hāliddakāni comes to Mahākaccāna, Soṇa's preceptor, and says: "Bhante, this was said by the Blessed One in the Questions of Māgandiya of the Aṭṭhakavagga" (*aṭṭhakavaggiye māgandiyapañhe*). He then cites verse **844** and asks for an explanation. Mahākaccāna explains the verse in detail and then recites it again at the end of his reply.[4]

The Pārāyana is mentioned six times elsewhere in the canon. In SN 12:31 (II 47) the Buddha addresses Sāriputta, saying: "This was stated in the Questions of Ajita of the Pārāyana." He then cites verse **1038** and asks Sāriputta to explain it. In the Aṅguttara Nikāya the Buddha refers to the Pārāyana in the following places:

AN 3:32 (I 133) refers to **1048** from the Questions of Puṇṇaka
AN 3:33 (I 134) refers to **1106–7** from the Questions of Udaya

AN 4:41 (II 45–46) again refers to **1048** from the Questions of Puṇṇaka

On each occasion, rather than introducing the verse at the beginning of a discourse, he cites the verse at the end, preceded by the phrase "And it was with reference to this, bhikkhus, that it was stated by me in the Pārāyana" (*idañca pana m'etaṃ, bhikkhave, sandhāya bhāsitaṃ pārāyane*).

At AN 3:61 (III 399) a group of elders are sitting together after their meal when one of them says: "This was said, friends, by the Blessed One in the Pārāyana, in the Questions of Metteyya." He then cites **1042** (with a slightly different reading of the first line) and asks his fellow monks how they understand it. Each offers his own interpretation, after which they go to the Buddha for clarification. The Buddha then repeats the verse (at AN III 401) and explains his intention. Finally, in AN 7:53 (IV 63), it is said that early one morning the female lay disciple Nandamātā recited the Pārāyana in a voice so pleasing that the divine king Vessavaṇa, passing nearby, stopped in his flight and congratulated her for her recitation.

It may be significant that these passages refer to the work as Pārāyana rather than as Pārāyanavagga. The suffix *–vagga*, "chapter," may have been added only after the Pārāyana became a chapter in the Suttanipāta. In the case of the Aṭṭhakavagga, however, the suffix seems always to have been part of the title, perhaps implying that the group of suttas formed a set, not necessarily a chapter in a larger work.

The antiquity of these two chapters—the Aṭṭhakavagga and the Pārāyana—as well as their importance for the Buddhist community, can be understood from the fact that each was made the subject of an ancient commentary, the Niddesa, which was incorporated into the Sutta Piṭaka. The larger section, the *Mahāniddesa*, comments on the Aṭṭhakavagga; the shorter section, the *Cūḷaniddesa*, comments on the Pārāyanavagga and the Khaggavisāṇa Sutta.

Circumstantial evidence for the early existence of several other texts presently included in the Suttanipāta is provided by the Bhabra Inscription of King Asoka, where he cites seven discourses on the Dhamma that he desires "many monks and nuns should hear frequently and meditate upon, and likewise laymen and laywomen." Three can be reasonably identified with texts now existing in Sn. The Munigāthā are almost certainly the verses of the Muni Sutta (I,12). The Moneyya Sutta is probably the Nālaka Sutta (III,11), excluding the introductory verses. And since Upatissa was the personal name of Sāriputta, the Upatisapasina—Upatissa's Questions—is probably the Sāriputta Sutta (IV,16), where Sāriputta asks questions of the Buddha.

In commenting on its respective source texts, the Niddesa often buttresses its points by quoting from other texts (not the Aṭṭhakavagga or Pārāyanavagga), usually prefaced with the remark: "For this has been said by the Blessed One" (*vuttaṃ h'etaṃ Bhagavatā*) or "Hence the Blessed One said" (*ten'āha Bhagavā*). Several of these texts are now included in Sn. The ones most often referred to are the Sabhiya Sutta (III,6) and the Padhāna Sutta (III,2). Verse **271** from the Sūciloma Sutta is cited several times, as well as **576–81** from the Salla Sutta; individual verses from other texts are also cited. The Niddesa does not refer to these works by their titles, though in its citations from the Sabhiya Sutta it includes the line where the Buddha addresses Sabhiya by name. These quotations testify to the existence of those discourses at the time the Niddesa was composed, though from this it cannot be determined whether they had as yet been incorporated into the anthology now called the Suttanipāta. The earliest known references to the Suttanipāta are in the Milindapañha (at 369, 385, 411, 413, and 414), but these are all in a section of that work recognized as relatively late.

The formation of the Suttanipāta can only be reconstructed through critical analysis of its texts with reference to their language, doctrinal content, and the social conditions they reflect. The most thorough attempt at such a reconstruction was made by N. A. Jayawickrama in his "Critical Analysis of the Suttanipāta."[5] Jayawickrama suggests that the suttas of the Aṭṭhakavagga, the *pucchās* of the Pārāyana, and the poems extolling the muni ideal are likely to be the oldest parts of Sn. At a subsequent phase, he conjectures, the work was enlarged by including other material. In this phase he puts the didactic poems of the first three vaggas, the two biographical discourses (the Pabbajjā and Padhāna Suttas), the older dialogues of the Mahāvagga, the dialogue poems of the Uragavagga, and the yakkha poems. He considers four of the popular discourses—the Maṅgala, Metta, Parābhava, and Vasala Suttas—along with the Cunda and Kokālika Suttas to be a little younger but still pre-Asokan. The youngest suttas he takes to be the Ratana, the Vijaya, and the Dvayatānupassanā, and the latest compositions to be the *vatthugāthā*, the introductory verses, which were added at a relatively later time to the Nālaka Sutta and the Pārāyana. I would qualify this, however, with the observation that while the Dvayatānupassanā itself might be relatively young, its verses likely stem from an older period and may have been brought into the sutta to give them a framework. Several of these verses are found elsewhere in the Aṅguttara, Saṃyutta, and Itivuttaka. Verse **728** is identical with **1050**ef–**1051** of the Pārāyana, from which it was evidently taken.

Jayawickrama ascribes the composition of the bulk of the poems roughly to the period 400–300 B.C.E. He delineates five stages in the evolution of the anthology. (1) First, there was "an early nucleus of more or less floating material" available for the creation of an anthology. (2) Next came an attempt at a collection by bringing together the Aṭṭhakavagga, the Pārāyana *pucchās*, the Khaggavisāṇa Sutta, and a few other suttas on the ascetic ideal. These became the foundation of the work. (3) This was followed by a transitional stage in which more suttas considered representative of the Buddha's teachings were selected and bundled along with the foundational texts. (4) As more material was amassed, the Culavagga and Mahāvagga were separated off, thus yielding the five chapters we have now. (5) The final phase, he suggests, "was marked by the prefixing of the Uraga, Ratana, and Pabbajjā (and Padhāna) Suttas to the three respective vaggas under the editorial hand of monastic redactors for the purpose of propagating the Dhamma."

2. Formal Elements of the Suttanipāta

The discourses of the Suttanipāta exhibit a variety of structures and forms. There are suttas delivered entirely in verse, as straightforward expositions of a particular topic. Others take the form of dialogues in verse. And still others present the verses embedded in a prose framework. The prose may merely establish the setting of the discourse, as is the case with the Parābhava and Maṅgala Suttas, or the prose may weave a more elaborate narrative that culminates in a conversation in verse, as we find in the Sabhiya and Sela Suttas. The table on p. 34 classifies the suttas by way of their formal structures. The classification is based largely on Jayawickrama (PBR 1977, 87–88). I have, however, made several changes. I classify the Rāhula Sutta (II,11) as didactic verse rather than as a discourse given in reply to a question, since the body of the discourse has no direct relation to the introductory question. I classify the Kalahavivāda Sutta (IV,11) as a conversation in verse, since there is a repeated exchange of questions and replies. I also reclassify the epilogue to the Pārāyana, which includes dialogue in the verse portion.

Whereas the verses of the Suttanipāta are cast in a variety of styles characteristic of different periods in the evolution of Pāli prosody, the prose passages are in the standard canonical style of the main Nikāyas. This suggests that the prose passages may have originally been an orally transmitted explanation of the background to the sutta, without a fixed and formalized wording. These sections may have been spoken extemporaneously by the reciter so that the listeners could grasp the situations that occasioned the verses. Over time, as the canonical texts assumed a more definite shape, the prose narratives were integrated into the sutta and acquired a fixed wording, cast in the style that prevails elsewhere in the Pāli Nikāyas.

This hypothesis may explain certain discrepancies we encounter between the prose and the verses. For example, the Sundarikabhāradvāja Sutta (III,4) relates a background story identical with that which begins a sutta of the same title in the Sagāthāvagga of the Saṃyutta Nikāya (SN 7:9, at I 167–68), yet, with a few exceptions, the verses in the two suttas are entirely different. Obviously, the Buddha did not speak to the same brahmin under the same circumstances on two different occasions, on each of which he spoke different verses. The difference in the verses can only be explained by assuming that there were groups of verses held together by a vague story of how the Buddha uttered them in a conversation with a brahmin who held brahmanical beliefs about recipients of offerings. When the two groups of verses were being collected

Forms of the Suttas in the Suttanipāta

I. Simple didactic verse (22)
- (I) 1, 3, 8, 11, 12 (5)
- (II) 1, 3, 6, 8, 10, 11 (6)
- (III) 8 (1)
- (IV) 1– 6, 8, 12, 13, 15 (10)

II. Dialogues entirely in verse (29)
- A. Conversation in verse (21)
  - (I) 2, 5, 9 (3)
  - (IV) 9, 11 (2)
  - (V) 1–16 (16)
- B. Discourse given in reply to a question, challenge, or request (8)
  - (II) 2, 9, 13 (3)
  - (III) 11 (1)
  - (IV) 7, 10, 14, 16 (4)

III. Didactic discourse or dialogue following a prose introduction (16)
- (I) 6, 7, 10 (3)
- (II) 4, 5, 7, 12, 14 (5)
- (III) 3–7, 9, 10, 12 (8)

5 pieces not classified:
I,4 and Epilogue to Pārāyana: prose and verse, mixed narrative with dialogue
III,1, III,2, and Vatthugāthā of Pārāyana: narratives in verse, with internal dialogue

---

and incorporated into suttas, they were each provided with the same background story, one that had been orally transmitted in relation to one group of verses but was now attached to both.

Occasionally we find in Sn lines in which the speaker is identified or the person being addressed is mentioned by name (or both). These lines, though included in the Pāli text, are metrically not part of the verse itself but additions; in modern editions they are therefore enclosed in parentheses. Thus verses **18–29** identify the speaker as either Dhaniya or the Buddha; **33** identifies the speaker as Māra and **34** as the Buddha; **153–63** identify which of the two yakkhas, Sātāgira or Hemavata, is the speaker; and in **169** the Buddha is said to be addressing

Hemavata. And so in a number of other verses. According to the commentary, in all cases these lines were added by the compilers (*saṅgītikārā*).[6] When I have added my own identification of a speaker, I put the name in brackets above the verse.

The additional lines that identify the person being addressed are to be distinguished from those in which the auditor is addressed by name within the verse itself. The contrast might be clearly seen by comparing **1062** with **1064**. Verse **1062** contains an additional line in which the Buddha is said to be addressing Dhotaka, *Dhotakā ti Bhagavā*. In **1064**, the vocative Dhotaka is part of the verse proper and conforms to the meter: *kathaṃkathiṃ Dhotaka kañci loke.*

3. Interlocutors and Auditors

The Suttanipāta depicts the Buddha teaching and conversing with people from different walks of life in the Indian society of his time: a herdsman, a farmer, brahmins, monks, wandering ascetics, and lay disciples. His ministry in the texts extends even beyond the human sphere to devas and yakkhas. In this respect the anthology resembles the Sagāthāvaggasaṃyutta, with which it shares several suttas. The Sagāthāvagga is classified according to the types of people and beings with whom the Buddha speaks. Though the inquirers and auditors in Sn are far less numerous, they fit into most of these categories.

The following list shows the types of interlocutors in Sn who meet the Buddha and the other auditors whom he addresses, along with the numbers of the discourses in which they appear. The list is based solely on information provided by the text of Sn itself or by reasonable inference from the text.[7] It does not take into account the background information related by the commentary, whose attributions may stem from a later narrative tradition.

Ascetic inquirer(s): III,6, III,11. Total 2.
Bhikkhu(s), unnamed: II,6, II,9, II,10, II,14, III,3, III,10, III,12, IV,15. Total 8.
Bhikkhu, specified: II,11, II,12, III,3, IV,7, IV,16. Total 5.
Brahmin(s): I,4, I,7, II,2, II,7, III,4, III,7, III,9. Total 7.
Brahmanic students: III,5, V,1–16. Total 17.

Deities: I,6, II,1, II,4. Total 3.
King: III,1. Total 1.
Layperson, specified: I,2, I,4, I,5, II,14, IV,9. Total 5.
Māra: III,2. Total 1.
Yakkha(s): I,9, I,10, II,5. Total 3.
Unspecified: II,13, IV,8, IV,10, IV,11, IV,12, IV13. Total 6.
None: I,1, I,3, I,8, I,11, I,12, II,3, II,8, III,2, III,8, IV,1, IV,2, IV,3, IV,4, IV,5, IV,6. Total 15.

In this scheme I distinguish suttas that make no mention of an interlocutor or auditor from those in which the interlocutor or auditor is left unspecified. Those that make no mention of an auditor also do not specify a speaker; the implication is that the speaker is the Buddha himself. The Uraga Sutta (I,1) and the Metta Sutta (I,8) are examples of discourses that fall into this category; taken on their own, without reference to the commentary, they appear to be straightforward didactic poems bereft of any dialogical or expository format. The Khaggavisāṇa Sutta can also be cited as an example of this type, though the commentary explains each verse as the utterance of a particular paccekabuddha.

Suttas with an unspecified interlocutor feature another voice that poses questions, which the Buddha answers. The other speaker either asks questions at the beginning of the sutta, which the Buddha responds to without interruption in the body of the sutta, or the other speaker and the Buddha engage in an alternating question-and-response exchange. The Sammāpabbājaniya Sutta (II,14) is an example of the former type; the Kalahavivāda (IV,11) and the two Viyūha Suttas (IV,12–13) follow the question-and-response format. The commentary explains that the inquirer in all six suttas without a specified interlocutor was a duplicate buddha that the Blessed One had mentally created for the purpose of asking these questions, which no one else was capable of posing in just the way the Buddha wanted. While this explanation might seem to exceed the bounds of credibility, the background narrative to several sūtras in the Chinese 義足經 (*Arthapada), a parallel to the Aṭṭhakavagga, provides a similar explanation. This suggests that the two spring from a common narrative tradition, one that goes back to a very early period.

Among the categories of interlocutors and auditors who are identified, it might seem that "brahmin students" (*māṇava*) constitutes the largest group. However, the number in this category is inflated by counting separately the sixteen students of the brahmin Bāvari, who visit the Buddha as a group and ask him the sixteen sets of questions that make up the body of the Pārāyanavagga. If we collapse these into one, the distribution per category would more faithfully reflect the actual number of separate interlocutors. Further, since these sixteen students seem to have adopted the lifestyle of celibate ascetics, they could also be reassigned to the category of "ascetic inquirer," which would then expand to eighteen.

The categories of interlocutors and auditors in the Suttanipāta roughly correspond to those of the Sagāthāvagga, though proportions and details vary. Two discourses are spoken to deities in response to questions, and a third can be added if we include the Ratana Sutta, apparently addressed to earth and sky deities. Three suttas involve yakkhas, including two parallels to suttas from the Sagāthāvagga. Only one discourse reports a conversation with a king, the Pabbajjā Sutta, where King Bimbisāra visits the future Buddha outside the city of Rājagaha. This contrasts with the Sagāthāvagga, where an entire chapter of twenty-five suttas is devoted to the Buddha's conversations with King Pasenadi. Māra, too, appears here only once, in the Pabbajjā Sutta, also assigned to the period prior to the enlightenment. In the Sagāthāvagga Māra, too, gets an entire chapter of twenty-five suttas. There are no discourses involving bhikkhunīs, though according to the commentary the Vijaya Sutta, on the repulsive nature of the body, was taught to two bhikkhunīs for the purpose of removing their attachment to their beauty. Among the distinct categories, brahmins claim a disproportionately large number. This may be indicative of the friction that existed between Buddhism and Brahmanism. It is telling that in five of these discourses the Buddha challenges tenets and practices of the brahmins prevalent during this period (see pp. 41–42).

When we take an overview of the Buddha's interactions with inquirers from the different groups, one consistent feature that stands out is his success in winning them over to his teaching. Among householders, Dhaniya (I,2) and Māgandiya

(IV,9), who both start off scornful of the Buddha, end up going for refuge and entering monastic life along with their wives, after which they attain arahantship.[8] The two ascetic inquirers, Sabhiya and Nālaka, leave behind their old loyalties and go forth under the Buddha. The three yakkhas not only take refuge but extol the Buddha with exuberant words of praise. With the brahmins, perhaps the most difficult challenge and potentially the biggest win, the Buddha always ends victorious. Three of the brahmins—Kasibhāradvāja, Sundarikabhāradvāja, and Sela—not only take refuge but enter the homeless life, while the others become lay disciples. The brahmin student Māgha becomes a lay follower, and the sixteen brahmin inquirers of the Pārāyana become monastic disciples. In the Vāseṭṭha Sutta, Vāseṭṭha and Bhāradvāja become lay disciples, but at the beginning of the Aggañña Sutta it is reported that they were living among the bhikkhus seeking to become bhikkhus themselves. They did so even in the face of sharp condemnation by their fellow brahmins (DN III 80–81).

These cases of conversion point to what might have been an underlying purpose behind the compilation of the Suttanipāta—perhaps not the sole or primary purpose but a major one: to show the Buddha in his role as the incomparable teacher of devas and human beings (*satthā devamanussānaṃ*). Even when faced with fierce resistance, he prevails. Even when confronted by hostile antagonists, he wins them over. His adversaries, despite their prestige and rhetorical skills, are no match for the Buddha. With his wisdom, patience, wit, and skillful means, he turns his opponents into ardent disciples some of whom even attain the final goal of the holy life.

4. Themes of the Suttanipāta

The discourses of the Suttanipāta span a wide range of topics in Early Buddhism. These include personal and social ethics, devotional praise of the Triple Gem, reflections on death and loss, the path of monastic training, discussions with brahmins about class status, and the nature of the spiritual ideal. The Thematic Guide (pp. 93–94) offers a broad overview of the topics dealt with in the work. Here I will discuss the more important of these topics.

It is worth noting at the outset that the Suttanipāta does not contain systematic discussions of Buddhist doctrine in the analytical style that prevails in the prose Nikāyas. Such topics as the four noble truths, the eightfold path, the three marks of existence, the five aggregates, and other doctrinal topics are seldom mentioned or totally passed over. The word *anicca*, for instance, does not occur at all in any of the poems, and there is only one mention of *anattā* (at **756**a). From such observations, some scholars have suggested that the unstructured teachings we find in Sn and kindred works represent the authentic and original teachings of the Buddha and that the doctrinal expositions of the prose Nikāyas are late developments, perhaps the product of monastic editors.

Such a suggestion, however, would have bizarre consequences. It would in effect reduce the Dhamma to a collection of poems and aphorisms with only the barest unifying structure. The plain fact is that the discourses of Sn have a different purpose than to provide a comprehensive overview of the Dhamma. As works mostly in verse, their primary purpose is to inspire, edify, and instruct rather than to provide systematic doctrinal exposition. While the exact diction and format of the prose suttas might have taken shape at the hands of monastic editors, without the light shed by these suttas it is virtually impossible to determine the purport of the verse collections and the vision that unifies them.

(1) Lay Ethics

The Suttanipāta contains five discourses, popular in character, that have served as sources of moral guidance for lay Buddhists through the centuries. These are the Parābhava, the Vasala, the Āmagandha, the Mahāmaṅgala, and the Dhammika Suttas.[9] The first four inculcate standards of conduct that are not exclusively tied to Buddhist faith in the narrow sense but reflect the moral values accepted as normative by Indian society from a very early period. These norms constitute "Dhamma" in the broad ethical sense, as the timeless law of righteousness and moral truth that classical Indian thought sees as the bedrock of the cosmic and social order. It is this concept of Dhamma that King Aśoka, in his Rock Edicts, commended to his subjects, knowing that such norms were affirmed by the many diverse religious systems prevailing in his empire.[10] The Dhammika Sutta (at **393–404**) prescribes a code of lay ethics built on the blueprint of the five precepts and thus one that is more distinctively Buddhist in character.

The Pāli commentaries distinguish two aspects of morality, the negative and the positive, prohibitions and injunctions, rules of abstinence and guides to virtuous conduct. The negative side is called *vāritta*, the positive side *cāritta*. Two separate discourses, both spoken in conversations with devas, can be seen to serve as paradigms for these two dimensions of morality, especially as they relate to laypersons. The Parābhava Sutta (I,6) deals with *vāritta*, the types of conduct to be avoided. This includes bad friendship, neglect of one's filial duties, false speech, miserliness, maligning ascetics, womanizing, drinking and gambling, and other types of dishonorable behavior. Such conduct is said to be the cause of a "downfall" in that it defiles one's character, ruins one's reputation, leads to loss of wealth, and brings a fall to subhuman realms of rebirth.

The positive side of morality is broadly covered in the Mahāmaṅgala Sutta (II,4), which sketches the actions and personal qualities that lead to individual moral progress and harmony in the community. The actions advocated include association with the wise, support for one's parents and other family members, earning one's living by a respectable line of work, and giving to those in need. The discourse extols such virtues as heedfulness, reverence, humility, patience, and devotion to religious practice. The last verses apply more specifically to monastic life, advocating austerity, celibacy, insight, and realization of nibbāna.

Such codes of conduct, in both their negative and positive aspects, have a significance that extends beyond personal purification. While they sustain individuals in their endeavors to fulfill the moral and spiritual good, they contribute to the formation of a society marked by mutual care, kindness, and respect. In simple words and phrases they reveal the kinds of socially responsible conduct treated more elaborately in the Sīgalovāda Sutta (DN 31), which explains the reciprocal duties of householders in their relations with other members of their household and the broader society.

In the living Theravāda tradition three discourses in the Suttanipāta—the Mahāmaṅgala, the Ratana, and the Metta Suttas—play a special role as *parittas* or protective suttas. Recited daily in the monasteries and on ceremonial occasions, these discourses are regarded as a source of spiritual blessings. Each makes its distinctive contribution to this end. The Mahāmaṅgala Sutta delineates the guidelines for success in both mundane and spiritual undertakings. The Ratana Sutta invokes the protection of the deities and extols the excellent qualities of the Buddha, the Dhamma, and the Sangha. And the Metta Sutta teaches the cultivation of loving-kindness, a virtue that resonates throughout the sentient cosmos and attracts the protective care of the deities.

(2) Brahmanism and the Social Order

The Suttanipāta contains seven discourses that depict the Buddha engaging in discussions with brahmins: I,4, I,7, II,2, II,7, III,4, III,7, and III,9.[11] Five of these—I,7, II,2, II,7, III,4, and III,9—challenge fundamental tenets and practices of Brahmanism. In mounting these challenges the Buddha makes use of strategies tailored to the case at hand. At times he bluntly rejects brahmanic observances that he considered contrary to the rule of righteousness. This approach is evident in the Brāhmaṇadhammika Sutta (II,7) where he condemns animal sacrifice, which the brahmins had been urging upon the rulers in order to increase their wealth. At other times, rather than simply reject a prevalent brahmanic belief, he tries to undermine it from within, for instance by redefining a concept to subtly transform its meaning. Thus in his discussion with the haughty brahmin Aggikabhāradvāja (I,7), he redefines the concept of outcast (*vasala*) so that it does not refer to people of inferior birth but to those of dishonorable conduct. The same method is employed in the Vāseṭṭha Sutta (III,9), where he ascribes a new meaning to the word *brāhmaṇa*, so that it comes to mean not one born into the brahmin caste but the truly holy person replete in clear knowledge and virtuous conduct. In the Sundarikabhāradvāja Sutta (III,4) the Buddha issues a rejoinder to brahmanic beliefs about who is worthy of offerings. In the Āmagandha Sutta (II,2), when the brahmin Tissa accuses the past buddha, Kassapa, of transgressing the moral norm by eating meat, Kassapa turns the tables on him by explaining "impure fare" in terms of behavior rather than diet.

(3) The Turn toward Renunciation

In the Pabbajjā Sutta, King Bimbisāra visits the future Buddha at his hillside cave and tries to persuade him to give up his quest in order to resume his role as an elite member of the khattiya caste. The youthful mendicant replies: "Having seen the danger in sensual pleasures, having seen renunciation as security, I will go for the purpose of striving: it is here that my mind delights" (**424**). This pithy statement makes renunciation the pivot point of the spiritual quest. For Early Buddhism, as exemplified by the Buddha's own career, the household life is "confinement, a basis for accumulation of dust," while the homeless life is free and open. Thus, to bring the spiritual quest to completion, at some point a step must be taken beyond the life of righteousness within the world, a step that brings one onto the stainless path that leads to emancipation from the world. The act that marks this transition is "going forth from home into homelessness."

The spur for taking this step is the clear discernment of the faults of mundane life and the faith that there exists a higher dimension of spiritual freedom that can only be won by turning away from the pleasures and rewards of life in the world. While the Suttanipāta does not explore the pitfalls of mundane life in a systematic way, it brings together suttas that highlight these faults from different angles. The Kāma Sutta (IV,1), for example, points out the drawback of sensual pleasures, highlighting their addictive quality and the suffering that inevitably lurks just below their surface. The Vijaya Sutta (I,11) strips away the veneer of beauty that covers the physical body, exposing to the inner eye its inherent repulsiveness, transience, and impersonal nature. The Salla Sutta (III,8) and Jarā Sutta (IV,6) offer sobering meditations on old age and death. And the Dvayatānupassanā Sutta (III,12) offers methodical contemplations on suffering and its origin, holding up nibbāna, the cessation of all conditioned things, as the imperishable truth and the highest happiness.

(4) The Monastic Training

For those who embark on the life of renunciation, a clear path of self-discipline is needed to bring the goal into view. The Suttanipāta does not offer a systematic model of the monastic training as found in such prose discourses as the Sāmaññaphala Sutta (DN 2), the Cūḷahatthipadūpama Sutta (MN 27), and the Dantabhūmi Sutta (MN 125), each of which describes in sequence the steps that proceed from the initial act of "going forth" to the attainment of arahantship. But what the text lacks in systematic arrangement is compensated for by the attention several of its suttas devote to the details of monastic training.

The Dhammika Sutta (II,14), for example, explains how the monk should conduct himself on alms round, how he is to converse with disciples, and how he makes proper use of the four material requisites. The Tuvaṭaka Sutta (IV,14) speaks about the need for wakefulness and heedfulness in all activities. It rejects certain types of wrong livelihood, points out the need to remain unmoved by praise and blame, describes the kind of speech a bhikkhu should avoid, and prescribes patience and equanimity in the face of difficulties. The Sāriputta Sutta (IV,16) instructs a bhikkhu to be free of fear; to patiently endure oppressive conditions such as illness, hunger, cold, and heat; to ward off anger and arrogance; and to vanquish discontent. It describes the deportment the monk should assume when wandering for alms, the kind of speech he should utter, and the need to resist the lure of enticing sense objects. Perhaps the only discourse in Sn that provides a structured picture of the training is the short Rāhula Sutta (II,11). Here, speaking to his son, the Buddha traces the main steps of the training, from the initial act of entering the homeless life through to the attainment of perfect peace.

(5) The Spiritual Ideal

The Suttanipāta uses several terms to describe the person who has realized the final goal. In the prose Nikāyas this type of person is the arahant, but in Sn the word "arahant" is mostly restricted to stock prose passages on the Buddha's epithets and the announcement that a particular monk became an arahant. The only place in the verses where the word is used as an acclamation is at **644**c, where the true brahmin, as the Buddha defines this term, is said to be "the arahant with influxes destroyed" (*khīṇāsavaṃ arahantaṃ*). Instead of arahant, Sn uses three other words to designate the ideal figure: *bhikkhu*, *brāhmaṇa*, and *muni*.

Bhikkhu

Since the best qualified practitioner of the Buddhist path, according to Sn, is the bhikkhu, this word is occasionally extended beyond its normal use, as designating an ordained monk, and employed to represent one who has realized the goal. In the Uraga Sutta (I,1) the bhikkhu is depicted as one who has removed anger, cut off lust and craving, swept away conceit, uprooted the unwholesome roots, and abolished the latent tendencies—all criteria of an arahant. In the Sammāparibbājaniya Sutta (II,13), when asked how "a bhikkhu might properly wander in the world," the Buddha describes the bhikkhu in terms normally applicable to an arahant. He is one utterly released from things that fetter, who has abandoned greed and existence, who no longer harbors latent tendencies, who has destroyed the influxes, and has eliminated conceit. These expressions, as used here, again establish a functional equivalence between bhikkhu and arahant.

Brāhmaṇa

The Vāseṭṭha Sutta contains a long passage (**620–47**), already referred to, in which the Buddha attempts to reconceptualize the word *brāhmaṇa* so that it no longer designates one born into a brahmin clan but rather one who embodies ultimate holiness. As described in these verses, the brahmin is one who has cut off all fetters, bears his final body, dropped lust and hatred, and reached the supreme goal. The Aṭṭhakavagga also employs the word *brāhmaṇa* in this way. Thus a brahmin is one who does not grasp any view as supreme (**795**), who "does not posit even a subtle notion about what is seen, heard, or sensed," who does not cling to any view (**802**). A brahmin "does not indulge in mental constructs," he is "not a pursuer of views," he "maintains equanimity while others grasp" (**911**). He has relinquished all and is called peaceful (**946**).

Muni

The word used most often in the Suttanipāta to represent the liberated sage is *muni*. While the word usually denotes an arahant, as a nontechnical term it has a more numinous ambiance of meaning than arahant, suggesting an ineffable depth of realization. Since no English rendering can quite capture the mystical feel of the word, I have left *muni* untranslated, and by the same token I render *moneyya* and *mona* as "munihood" rather than translate them as sagehood or sagacity.

Jayawickrama (PBR 1977, 32) draws a distinction between the bhikkhu and the muni, maintaining that "in addition to possession of all the characteristics of the bhikkhu, there appears something nobler and more positive about [the muni] than the bhikkhu." This distinction seems to me partly misleading. Both the fully dedicated practitioner and the accomplished sage, as depicted in Sn, are bhikkhus. For the sake of convenience, the word "bhikkhu" may be taken to primarily denote the disciple in training, the word "muni" one who has reached the goal. But this usage is not fixed and inflexible, nor does it imply that the accomplished muni is not a bhikkhu. The two words are used with a certain fluidity and ambiguity that varies according to the context. In places "bhikkhu" describes the liberated sage; in other places "muni" designates one still in training. The Nālaka Sutta describes the practice for attaining the state of a muni in terms appropriate to the most austere training of a bhikkhu. Verse **221** slides seamlessly from "bhikkhu" to "muni" as if they were synonymous.

The *Mahāniddesa*, the canonical commentary to the Aṭṭhakavagga, says that there are six kinds of munis (p. 1037): householder munis, homeless munis, trainees, arahants, paccekabuddhas, and the Buddha, whom it calls "the muni among munis." I do not know of any references to householder munis in Sn. When the text uses the word, it usually refers either to monks in training, arahants, or the Buddha.

The Nālaka Sutta is the best example of a text that uses the word "muni" to describe a monk in training. The theme of the discourse is the practice to attain *moneyya*, the *state* of a muni, yet the sutta also uses *moneyya* to describe the *practice* for attaining munihood. Accordingly the word "muni" here signifies one who, though still in training, has earnestly taken up this practice. With this sense in view, the discourse says "women try to seduce a muni," who must be on guard against temptation (**703**cd). The muni should resort to the woods and sit at the foot of a tree (**708**d). The muni should behave properly when going on alms round in the village (**711**). The muni is one who maintains self-control and does not speak much (**723**ab). Since such injunctions, often expressed with optative verbs, would be unnecessary in relation to the arahant, it is clear they are identifying the muni with one still walking the ascetic path, a bhikkhu who has adopted an austere life of solitary wandering and strict meditation for the purpose of winning the final goal.

The following is a sampling of lines from the Muni Sutta that describe the arahant-muni:

> **207**c: one without an abode and without intimacy (see too **844**b)
> **208**c: a solitary wanderer
> **209**cd: a seer of the final end of birth, who cannot be designated
> **210**b: one without greed
> **212**c: one freed from ties, not barren, without influxes
> **214**c: one devoid of lust, with well-concentrated faculties
> **219**ab: a seer of the supreme goal, who has crossed the flood and ocean

The Aṭṭhakavagga especially extols the muni for his aloofness from conflict. The muni "does not become involved in an arisen dispute" (**780**c); the muni "would not engage in contentious talk with people" (**844**d); "liberated by knowledge, the muni does not enter disputes" (**877**bc). Since he does not take sides in disputes, the muni "is peaceful among the restless, equanimous, without grasping while others grasp" (**912**cd).

Munis dwell detached not only from disputes but from all phenomena. They are untainted by possessions (**779**b), untainted by sensual pleasures and the world (**845**f). They are not dependent on anything, for they take nothing as pleasant or unpleasant (**811**b). Being free from the "swellings" of conceit, they do not think of themselves as superior, equal, or inferior to others (**855**). Just as the lotus is untainted by water and mud, so too "the muni does not cling to anything among the seen, heard, or sensed" (**812**).

"Muni" is also used as an epithet of the Buddha. He is directly addressed as muni at **508**c, **700**c, **838**b, **1058**b, **1081**e, and **1085**b. At **225**b he is extolled as Sakyamuni, one of the rare appearances of this term in the Pāli Canon. At **83**a and **359**a he is called "the muni of abundant wisdom" (*muniṃ pahūtapaññaṃ*). At **484**c and **540**c he is called "the muni possessed of munihood" (*muniṃ moneyyasampannaṃ*). At **541**c he is said to be "the muni, the fully enlightened one" (*munī'si sambuddho*). At **545**b (= **571**b) he is called "the muni, the conqueror of Māra" (*mārābhibhū muni*). Verse **211**, which from other sources we know refers to the Buddha, describes him as a muni who "has overcome all, all-knowing, very wise, untainted among all things, and liberated in the destruction of craving."

(6) The Repudiation of Views

The above description of the muni leads into another theme prominent in the Aṭṭhakavagga, namely, the rejection of adherence to views. Throughout this chapter, the Buddha is shown maintaining that views are a spiritual blind alley. One who adopts a view grasps it tightly, proclaims it as supreme, and thereby becomes embroiled in conflict with those who hold contrary views. When views are grasped, sincere inquiry gives way to dogmatism as rival thinkers reject the impartial search for truth in favor of frenzied attempts to bolster their own standpoint. Like a hunter caught in his own snare, the theorists become trapped in systems of their own devising.

The adherence to views, according to Sn, is bound up with conceit. Inflated esteem for one's opinions leads to an inflated opinion of oneself, so that the theorist becomes "intoxicated with conceit, thinking himself perfect" (**889**). In contrast to the disputatious theorist, the sage—the muni or real brahmin—does not stick to any views and thereby experiences peace and inner freedom. Having seen through the commonplace opinions, amid those who grasp the muni abides in equanimity (**911**). Having seen into views, not grasping any of them, the sage discovers peace within (**838**).

These admonitions against the adoption of views have to be interpreted cautiously. They should not be taken in isolation from other teachings of the Buddha and read as an injunction to jettison right view and the aspiration for consummate knowledge. Rather, they are best understood in the light of the prose passages of the main Nikāyas that expose the dangers in views and teach the proper attitude to adopt toward right view. The *Mahāniddesa* repeatedly glosses the word "views" in the Aṭṭhakavagga as the sixty-two views, the speculative views about the self and the world laid out in the Brahmajāla Sutta, which describes all such views as "the feelings of ascetics and brahmins who do not know or see, the agitation and vacillation of those who are immersed in craving."[12] The explanation of the *Mahāniddesa* accords with a coherent picture of the Buddha's teachings, unlike the position that all views should be discarded without qualification, which would lead to a dead end.

Right view, as a constituent of the path, is essential for all the other path factors to reach maturity. It may be just a plank in the raft for crossing over from "the near shore" to "the far shore," but without that plank the raft would sink (see MN I 134–35). Reading the Aṭṭhakavagga in the light of the prose discourses, its message would be: (1) discard wrong views, morally subversive views and speculative assertions about the self and the world, which are rooted in false assumptions; (2) do not engage in disputes over views, which merely generate dogmatism, conceit, self-righteousness, and indignation; and (3) adopt right view and use it correctly, not as an object to be cherished, not as a subject for debates, but as an instrument of self-cultivation.[13] The liberated one, the arahant or muni, no longer requires right view, but even after liberation the arahant possesses "the right view of one beyond training" (*asekhā sammādiṭṭhi*), the clear experiential knowledge of the truths realized along the path.[14]

The interpretation I offer here accords well with Steven Collins's thesis that the attitude toward views adopted in Early Buddhism is stretched out on "a continuum, along which all conceptual standpoints and cognitive acts are graded according to the degree to which they are held or performed with attachment."[15] At the lowest point on this continuum there is the attitude of the ignorant worldling, who adopts views out of sheer attachment. In the middle, there is the attitude of the disciple, who adopts right view as a guide to wholesome action and as an integral part of a training aimed at severing attachments and realizing the ultimate state of liberation. And at the highest point—actually beyond the continuum—there is the unconditioned freedom from views of the muni, who has overcome all attachment and thereby attained liberation, including liberation from the bondage of views. To use this third attitude, the one that transcends the continuum, to repudiate those that operate along the middle and upper reaches of the continuum is to discard the means that make that attitude possible.

(7) The Ultimate Goal

For the Suttanipāta, as for all the texts of Early Buddhism, the ultimate goal of spiritual training is said to be nibbāna. Exactly how the discourses of Sn understand this goal has been a matter of debate. The Dvayatānupassanā Sutta seems to take an ontological perspective on nibbāna. The sutta says that whatever is transient is of a false nature, but nibbāna, not being transient, is of a non-false nature. The noble ones realize this truth, and by doing so they are "fully quenched" (*parinibbutā*), with all defilements extinguished (**757–58**).

Some interpreters, however, see a tension between such statements and the position of the Aṭṭhakavagga. The Aṭṭhakavagga, it is said, does not describe the goal in terms suggestive of transcendent liberation but instead emphasizes the tranquility the illumined sage wins in this very life through freedom from attachment. Though the Aṭṭhakavagga is certainly shy about treading in metaphysical waters, it might still be rash to conclude from this that the text actually conceives the final goal of Buddhist spiritual endeavor as nothing other than the tranquility that comes from non-attachment. The core suttas of the chapter, those on freedom from views, hardly provide a comprehensive picture of the Buddha's teachings, and thus their particular slant on the ultimate goal should not be regarded as categorical and complete.

While it is hard to understand why references to nibbāna as a state of transcendent liberation are not found in the Aṭṭhakavagga, it would strain credulity to infer from this that the chapter takes the ultimate aim of the Dhamma to be simply a state of inner peace not so very different from the ataraxia—the calmness untroubled by mental or emotional disquiet—sought by the Pyrrhonic skeptics of ancient Greece. It is also hard to see how the rigorous self-discipline laid down for the bhikkhu in the last three suttas of this chapter could culminate merely in a state of cognitive agnosticism, even if that includes a tranquil abiding in the here and now. Surely there must lie behind these suttas a background of understanding that the compilers and reciters shared but did not think necessary to articulate.

Though not very much is said about it, references to nibbāna as the goal of endeavor are not entirely absent from the Aṭṭhakavagga. The inquirer at **915** asks the Buddha how a bhikkhu attains nibbāna, which is here qualified as "seclusion and the state of peace" (*vivekaṃ santipadaṃ*). At **940**cd the Buddha instructs the bhikkhu to "pierce through sensual pleasures" and "train for one's own nibbāna" (*sikkhe nibbānam attano*), and **942**cd states that "one whose mind is set on nibbāna should not persist in arrogance." Admittedly, these statements in the text come from suttas that seem to be less archaic than those on transcending views, but there is no reason to consider the two perspectives as antithetical and mutually exclusive.

While the Aṭṭhakavagga may have its reasons for remaining taciturn about the goal, other suttas in the collection uphold the established view of nibbāna as a state of transcendent liberation. Chief among these is the Pārāyana, whose very title, "The Way to the Beyond," leaves no doubt about its point of view. As with the prose suttas, the Pārāyana describes nibbāna as the negation of the factors responsible for bondage. It says that nibbāna is to be won by the abandoning of craving (**1109**cd). "The state of nibbāna, the imperishable" is the dispelling of desire and lust for all pleasant objects of cognition (**1086**). When Kappa asks the Buddha to point out to him "an island" in the midst of the flood of old age and death, the Buddha declares that the island is nibbāna, "the extinction of old age and death" (**1092–94**). While such expressions are suggestive rather than explicit, they point in the direction of a world-transcending liberation gained by ending the cycle of repeated birth and death.

Apart from actual occurrence of the word "nibbāna" in Sn, the text also uses metaphorical terms to convey some idea of the goal. This is fitting for a work mainly in verse, which aims at inspiration and edification more than at doctrinal explication. Perhaps the most striking metaphor used for the goal is that of "going beyond," an image that draws its meaning from the crossing of a river, a common experience in monsoon-prone India.

The following is a list of expressions in Sn that invoke the idea of going beyond, expressed in Pāli as *pāragata*, *pāragā*, and *pāragū*:

> gone beyond all phenomena: **167**c, **699**d, **992**b, **1105**c, **1112**c (said solely of the Buddha)
>
> gone beyond birth and death: **32**c (said of the Buddha)
>
> you will go beyond the realm of death: **1146**de (said of Piṅgiya)
>
> you have gone beyond suffering: **539**a (said of the Buddha)

Several verses simply speak of one "gone beyond" (*pāragata*) without specifying an object overcome. Thus at **210**d, the muni is described as one who "does not endeavor, for he has gone beyond." At **359**b, the Buddha is addressed as a muni "who has crossed over, gone beyond, attained nibbāna." And at **638**c, the Buddha praises the arahant, the true brahmin, as "a meditator who has crossed over, gone beyond . . . attained nibbāna through no clinging."

Another metaphor for the attainment of nibbāna is "crossing over," an expression that likewise draws upon the river imagery. The exact expressions used in the text ring the inflections of the verb *tarati*, "to cross," and its past participle, *tiṇṇa*. Variations on this expression with their sources are as follows:

> crossed over attachment to the world: **333**c, **857**d, **1053**d–**1054**d, **1066**d–**1067**d, **1085**d–**1087**d
>
> crossed beyond: **1059**d
>
> crossed over birth, old age, death: **355**c, **358**cd, **1045**e–**1046**e, **1047**d-**1048**d, **1052**c, **1060**d, **1079**f–**1080**f–**1081**g, **1119**d

crossed over doubt or perplexity: **17**b, **86**a, **514**b, **540**b, **1088**c–**1089**c

crossed the flood: **21**b, **173**ab–**174**d, **179**d, **183**ab–**184**ab, **219**b, **273**cd, **471**a, **495**b, **771**c, **779**a, **823**c, **1052**c, **1059**c, **1064**d, **1069**abd, **1070**b, **1081**e, **1082**g–**1083**g, **1101**b, **1145**d

crossed over greed and miserliness: **941**cd

crossed over sensual pleasures: **948**a

cross the tie: **791**b

"crossed over" without a specific object: **36**b, **515**c, **545**d (= **571**d), **638**c

Still another expression relevant to understanding the goal posited in Sn is *bhavābhava,* which I render as "various states of existence." The form *itibhavābhavataṃ* occurs at **6**b. The commentaries sometimes interpret this compound as combining a positive and a negative, that is, as *bhava* and *abhava,* representing the dichotomy of gain and loss, success and failure, merit and demerit; they also see it as establishing a contrast between eternal existence and annihilation. Usually, however, they explain it as meaning "existence upon existence, various states of existence," with the long middle vowel indicating mere repetition. It thus signifies the round of repeated becoming, saṃsāra. Since the text pinpoints craving for *bhavābhava* as a cause of suffering, it instructs the disciple to overcome craving for *bhavābhava* and praises the one who has removed such craving. This suggests that the goal is not merely a state of tranquility to be realized within this life but a state of world-transcendence: release from the beginningless series of existences to which ordinary people are bound by their craving and delusions. In Sn we find the expression *bhavābhava* in the following verses:

6b: a bhikkhu has transcended such and such states of existence

496b: those worthy of offerings have no craving for any state of existence here or beyond

776d: inferior people are not devoid of craving for various states of existence
786b: one who is cleansed constructs no view about states of existence
801ab: one has no wish for various states of existence here or beyond
877d: the wise one does not come upon various states of existence
901d: those who are dependent on various practices are not rid of craving for various states of existence
1060d: the wise man has loosened this tie to various states of existence
1068d: one should not create craving for various states of existence

5. The Buddha in the Suttanipāta

While the arahant—conceived as the muni or as the true brahmin—represents the spiritual ideal of the Suttanipāta, the spiritual hero is none other than the Buddha himself. Occasionally the text uses the word "buddha" in a generic sense to denote anyone who has attained the final goal, in which case it is equivalent to the arahant. Thus **517**cd says they call one a buddha who is "rid of dust, unblemished, purified, and has attained the destruction of birth." At **622**, "buddha" is used along with several metaphorical terms—"one who has cut the strap and thong, the reins and bridle-band, whose shaft is lifted"—to describe the true brahmin.

These occurrences of the word "buddha," however, are relatively infrequent. Far more often the word is used in the exclusive sense to signify the ascetic Gotama and others who have achieved the status of a *sammā sambuddha*, a perfectly enlightened one, such as Kassapa, the previous buddha, in II,2. A buddha is distinguished as such because "he has directly known what should be directly known, developed what should be developed, and abandoned what should be abandoned" (**558**). While arahants have also accomplished these tasks, they do so in dependence on a buddha, while it is the buddha alone who clears the obstructions to ultimate knowledge and makes the path to liberation known to others. Hence the Buddha is called "the dispeller of darkness, the universal eye" (**1133**a), "the supreme eye for humans" (**347**d), a wind that sweeps away the clouds covering the world (**348**), a maker of light (**349**a).

Several suttas in Sn treat the word "buddha" as if it were in circulation among the wise men of the time, even those who had no inkling that one of this stature was actually dwelling in the world. A learned brahmin, on hearing the word, exclaims: "Even this sound 'buddha' is rarely encountered in the world" (III,7). When a deity informs the brahmin Bāvari that a buddha has arisen, "having heard the word 'Enlightened One,' Bāvari was elated" (**994**ab). The prose introduction to III,7 relates the tradition about the two destinies open to one whose body bears the thirty-two marks of physical excellence: either he becomes a wheel-turning monarch who rules over the earth, or if he goes forth into homelessness, he becomes a perfectly enlightened buddha "whose coverings in the world are removed."

Already in the Suttanipāta the building blocks of the Buddha-biography have started to take shape. While it makes no attempt to construct a continuous biography, the text contains three suttas that highlight key events in the Buddha's life: his birth (III,11), his renunciation (III,1), and his struggle against Māra (III,2). Nevertheless, compared to later works like the Jātakanidāna, the Buddhacarita, the Mahāvastu, and the Lalitavistara, the treatment here is simple and restrained.

Whereas in the prose Nikāyas the Buddha is often hidden behind his teachings, in the Suttanipāta, as in the Sagāthāvagga, he appears in the open as part of the ancient Indian culture of itinerant spiritual teachers wandering homeless from town to town. The suttas featuring dialogue give us insights into the Buddha's pedagogical techniques, those strategies that came to be called his skill in means (*upāyakosalla*). We can detect at least four techniques that he uses to convince inquirers and win opponents over to the Dhamma. One is what I call *analogical rebuttal*. When applying this technique, the Buddha adopts an expression or image used by the adversary and explains it in a way that validates his own mission. An example of this is the Dhaniya Sutta (I,2), where each time Dhaniya praises the security and bliss of the household life, the Buddha picks up his terminology and bends it to his purpose by praising the superiority of the homeless life. Another example is the Buddha's reply to Kasibhāradvāja (I,4), who censures him for living off the bounty of the land, without plowing and sowing. The Buddha declares that he does in fact plow and sow, and then explains how he plows the hearts of people and sows the seeds that ripen in the deathless.

A second technique is *terminological redefinition*, which involves taking up a term in common use in the world and then reconceptualizing it in a way consonant with the Dhamma. The Buddha applies this technique to such concepts as brahmin, outcast, impure fare, and one worthy of offerings. His replies to the questions of Sabhiya, with their subtle word plays, might also be subsumed in this category. Still another method, used when dealing with yakkhas, is *solving riddles*. We see this method at work in the three yakkha suttas—I,9, I,10, and II,5—spoken respectively to Hemavata, Āḷavaka, and Sūciloma. The fourth technique is straightforward *exposition*, which in Sn tends to be concerned with practical rather than doctrinal matters.

The Buddha appears in Sn not only as a teacher but as an object of devotion. Like a delicate melody, a subtle current of veneration, awe, and adulation runs through the poems, lending to them a touch of inspirational fervor. The Buddha is praised by a variety of voices, both human and nonhuman, including his own. In a long passage extending from **467** to **478** he explains to a brahmin why "the Tathāgata is worthy of the sacrificial cake." At **561**, he declares: "I have become Brahmā, peerless, one who has crushed Māra's army. . . . I rejoice without fear from anywhere." At **646** he calls himself "the chief bull, the excellent hero, the great rishi whose victory is won, without impulse, cleansed."

Most often, however, it is others who are shown praising the Buddha. When the rishi Asita beholds the newborn Buddha, he exclaims, "He is the best of all beings, the foremost person, the chief bull of men, the best of all creatures," who will turn the wheel of the Dhamma, "roaring like a powerful lion" (**684**). The two yakkhas, Sātāgiri and Hemavata, discuss at length the excellence of the Buddha's conduct and knowledge (**153–67**), and after meeting him, they extol him in a paean of exceptional beauty (**176–77**). The poet-monk Vaṅgīsa uses similes, metaphors, and allusions to sound the Buddha's praises (**343–53**), as does the lay disciple Dhammika (**376–84**). The wanderer Sabhiya, whose tormenting doubts were resolved by the Buddha, calls him "the Teacher, the muni, the conqueror of Māra, the one who leads this population across" (**545**). He compares the Buddha to a lion, without fear and dread, and to a lovely white lotus not tainted by muddy water (**546–47**). The erudite brahmin Sela, teacher of three hundred pupils, calls the Buddha "one who has become Brahmā, incomparable, the one who has crushed Māra's army" (**563**).

The sages of the Pārāyana likewise praise the Buddha in various ways. When they first see the Buddha he is "like the glorious sun with a hundred rays, like the moon when it has arrived at fullness" (**1016**). They call him the seer of the root, a Veda-master, the great rishi, the universal eye, the cutter off of craving, the one without impulse, the one who has crossed the flood, the one gone beyond all phenomena. They reveal to him their perplexity, voice their anguish, and ask him to be their refuge, to provide an island of security amid the perilous flood of birth and death.

Perhaps the high point of devotional expression in the Suttanipāta comes at its very end, in the epilogue to the Pārāyana, where the aged brahmin Piṅgiya is conversing with another person, presumably his teacher Bāvari. Piṅgiya states that, having found the Buddha, he is like a bird that has left a small woods and settled in a fruit-filled forest, like a goose that has arrived at a great lake. When asked how he could dwell apart from the Buddha, he replies that he does not dwell apart from him even for a moment. "Night and day," he says, "I see him with my mind as if with my eyes. I pass the night paying homage to him; hence I do not think I am apart from him" (**1142**). His body is feeble, his health is poor, and thus he cannot travel to be with the Buddha physically. But, he declares, he is never separated from the Master: "I go constantly on a journey of thought, for my mind is united with him" (**1144**).

6. Special Terms Used in the Suttanipāta

The Suttanipāta employs a number of terms that, while not unique to this work, occur often enough there to shed light on Buddhist perspectives during a very early phase of Buddhist history. These terms take us back past the established vocabulary of the prose canonical texts to a period when the choice of words might have been freer and more fluid and thus more transparent as to the concerns and ideals of the emergent Buddhist community. We have already encountered several of these in the description of the spiritual ideal: *muni*, *pāragū*, *tiṇṇa*, and so forth. A brief look at a few others might also be illuminating.

(1) Aneja

Used as a description of the Buddha and the arahants, *aneja* is based on the verb *ejati*, "to move, tremble, shake." The noun *ejā* accordingly means "motion, disturbance, agitation, emotion" (DOP). As a negative, *aneja* might literally be rendered "one without emotion, one without agitation," but the word is not intended to depict the arahant as cold and emotionless. Nor does it explicitly point to the absence of fear and worry, as "one without agitation" might suggest.

The commentaries consistently explain *ejā* as a designation for craving (*taṇhā*; see pp. 532, 1006, 1059, etc.); thus one who is *aneja* is one without craving. But *ejā* is a metaphorical word, and in this respect, unlike *taṇhā* or *rāga*, its use is evocative rather than descriptive. *Ejā* perhaps suggests the impact of craving on the mind rather than the desire itself. It might be best understood as psychological drivenness, the propensity of one overcome by craving to engage in compulsive behavior. I have rendered *aneja* as "one without impulse," understanding *ejā* to be the impulse of craving that drives a person to pursue the objects of desire.

Aneja is used exclusively to describe a buddha or an arahant. Norman renders *aneja* as "without lust," which seems to me to miss the evocative tone of *ejā*. In this respect Jayawickrama's rendering, "with no turbulence (of craving)," is preferable. The second bhikkhu of the Cunda Sutta, the type who "explains and analyzes the Dhamma," is said to be "the muni who has cut off doubt, who is without impulse" (**87**c). A bhikkhu who would properly wander in the world is "a master of things, gone beyond, without impulse" (**372**b). Having known that suffering is conditioned by disturbance, a bhikkhu should wander mindfully, "having given up impulse . . . without impulse, without clinging" (**751**). Just as in the middle of the ocean no wave arises, so a bhikkhu "should be steady, without impulse" (**920**c). The muni, too, is "without impulse, everywhere the same" (**952**b). The brahmin, as understood by the Buddha, is "a meditator who has crossed over, gone beyond, without impulse and rid of doubt" (**638**cd). Again, the true brahmin is "without impulse, cleansed, enlightened" (**646**c). In the Pārāyana, the Buddha himself is addressed as "one without impulse" (at **1043**a, **1101**a, and **1112**b).

(2) Akiñcana

Kiñcana originally meant "something, anything," the implication being that *kiñcana* are things one owns. Since Early Buddhism conceives of ownership as a burden, the commentaries extend the meaning of the word to the things that drag one down: hence it is taken to mean "an impediment" or "defilement." An arahant, by eradicating lust, hatred, and delusion, is thereby *akiñcana*, which I render closer to the more literal meaning as "one who owns nothing, one who is ownerless." This development is based on the canonical statement: "Lust, friend, is a something/an impediment, hate is a something/an impediment, delusion is a something/an impediment. For a bhikkhu with influxes destroyed, these are abandoned, cut off at the root."[16]

Like *aneja*, the word *akiñcana* is applied solely to the Buddha and arahants. The yakkha Hemavata praises the Buddha as one "owning nothing, unattached to sensual pleasures and existence" (*akiñcanaṃ kāmabhave asattaṃ*, at **176**b). The Buddha himself uses the exact same phrase to describe the true brahmin (**1059**b) and the muni (**1091**d). When a haughty brahmin asks the Buddha about his "birth" or social class (*jāti*), he first replies, "I am not a brahmin, nor am I a prince. I am not a vessa or anything else." Then he describes himself as *akiñcana*, "one owning nothing" (**455**).

The brahmin student Dhotaka in the Pārāyana praises the Buddha as "a brahmin owning nothing, traveling about" (**1063**). In two places the Buddha declares "one who owns nothing, taking nothing" (*akiñcanaṃ anādānaṃ*) to be a true brahmin (**620**c, **645**c). He even extends the phrase from the personal to the impersonal, using it to describe nibbāna: "Owning nothing, taking nothing (*akiñcanaṃ anādānaṃ*): this is the island with nothing further. I call this 'nibbāna'" (**1094**). The word *akiñcana* thus suggests an ideal of total renunciation, of casting off. First, it signifies one who has cast off all external possessions so that one can wander freely, unencumbered by concern over things that drag one down. And second, in its extended meaning, it indicates one who has discarded the internal possessions—the defilements of the mind—which might impede even one who wanders freely.

When *akiñcana* is turned into an abstract noun it yields *ākiñcañña*, "nothingness." This word is used as the name of the third formless meditation, the base of nothingness (*ākiñcaññāyatana*). This was the meditative attainment that the Buddha, before his enlightenment, attained during his apprenticeship under Āḷāra Kālāma, as told in the Ariyapariyesana Sutta (MN 26). In Sn the term appears without explicit reference to the scheme of the four formless attainments. Thus Upasīva is told to contemplate *ākiñcañña* in order to cross the flood (**1070–72**). Posāla is instructed to see with insight the origin of *ākiñcañña* in order to gain "the real knowledge of the brahmin" (**1115**). From Sn, it seems that these words were part of the contemplative and ascetic culture to which the Buddha belonged and thus were readily understood across traditions. But while non-Buddhist contemplatives could attain the base of nothingness as a formless meditative state, only the arahant could be described as *akiñcana*.

(3) Tādī

In its origins, *tādī* was a simple term of reference, a demonstrative meaning "such a person, a person like that," referring to one previously described. Over time, however, the word acquired an elevated connotation, so that it came to imply, as DOP puts it, "(one) who is unaffected, immovable." This sense is ascribed to *tādī* as far back as the Niddesa, which gives five reasons why one might be called *tādī*: because one is impartial toward the desirable and undesirable; impartial because one has renounced; impartial because one has crossed over; impartial because one is freed; and impartial as a descriptive term (see pp. 1073–74). I believe this nuance of the word is not solely a commentarial innovation but can already be discerned in the canonical texts.

It is not always easy to determine in any particular instance whether *tādī* is being used with this elevated meaning or as a simple term of reference. In translating the texts, I have had to let intuition guide my judgment. In the lines cited just below I see the word bearing an elevated sense and thus I render it as "impartial one." I provide the context so the reason for my choice will be clear:

86d: the *tādī* is the conqueror of the path
154b, **155**b: the mind of the *tādī* is well disposed to beings
219b: a *tādī* has crossed the flood and ocean
712c: a *tādī* remains the same whether or not he gains food on alms round
803d: a brahmin who has gone beyond, who does not fall back, is a *tādī*
957a: the Buddha, unattached, is a *tādī*

Nevertheless, there are several places where this elevated meaning does not seem to fit. In these instances I understand it in the referential sense and render it "such a one." Those occurrences are as follows:

488d: *tādī* describes a generous householder
509b: *tādī* describes one devoted to charity
697a: the rishi Asita is called *tādī*

In each explanatory verse of the Sabhiya Sutta as well, I take *tādī* to mean "such a one." This was a difficult choice, since the commentary interprets it in the elevated sense, but the context seems to support understanding it in its simple referential function.

(4) Upadhi

This word, like *kiñcana*, straddles the divide between the internal and the external, the subjective and the objective. DOP defines *upadhi* as "worldly possessions or belongings, acquisitions; attachment to such possessions (forming a basis for rebirth)." Thus it means both things one owns and the internal claims of ownership.

The use of *upadhi* to refer to external belongings is seen in the exchange between the Buddha and Māra at **33–34**. Appearing out of nowhere, Māra praises ownership of children and cattle and declares that "acquisitions are a man's delight" (*upadhī hi narassa nandanā*). The Buddha turns his words around and describes the situation from a higher point of view: "acquisitions are a man's sorrow" (*upadhī hi narassa socanā*). The objective sense appears in other passages as well. Thus a bhikkhu who wanders properly is one who "does not find a core in acquisitions" because he has "removed desire and lust for things taken up" (**364**ab).

Elsewhere the subjective sense is more prominent. We see this at **728 (= 1050**cd–**1051**) where *upadhi* is said to be the basis for the origination of suffering; this sets *upadhi* in a close relationship to *taṇhā* or craving. At two points the stanza uses a curious expression that indicates that *upadhi* is not simply something one acquires but something one actively creates and thus something over which one can exercise control. The verse says that "the ignorant person creates acquisitions" (*avidvā upadhiṃ karoti*) and therefore encounters suffering again and again. The wise, in contrast, "should not create acquisitions" (*upadhiṃ na kayirā*) but should regard doing so as the genesis and origin of suffering.

The arahant or true brahmin is one without acquisitions (*nirūpadhi*). The true brahmin has "become cool, without acquisitions, a hero who has overcome the whole world" (**642**bc). The Buddha, "having attained the destruction of all kamma, is liberated in the extinction of acquisitions" (**992**ef). He is praised for having "transcended the acquisitions" (**546**a). He teaches the state that is *anūpadhikaṃ*, "without acquisitions" (**1057**b, **1083**b). In a stock formula, not found in Sn, nibbāna itself is described as "the relinquishment of all acquisitions" (*sabbūpadhipaṭinissaggo*, at MN I 167,37; SN I 136,15; etc.).

(5) Ussada

Among the meanings of *ussada* given in DOP are "mound (of flesh), thickness, swelling, abundance, prevalence." An indication of what the word suggests in ordinary usage is at Pj I 150,22–23, where it is said that through the merit generated by seeing ascetics, "for many thousands of births one has no illness of the eyes, fever, swellings, or pimples" (*anekāni jātisahassāni cakkhumhi rogo vā dāho vā ussadā vā piḷakā vā na honti*). As a term with doctrinal import, *ussada* occurs at **515**d, where an ascetic who is "gentle" (*sorata*) is defined as one "for whom there are no swellings." Pj II 425,29 explains this as the absence of the seven swellings: lust, hatred, delusion, conceit, views, defilements, and misconduct (*rāga-dosa-moha-māna-diṭṭhi-kilesa-duccarita*). The ideal brahmin is praised as "observant, of good behavior, without swellings" (**624**ab). Here Pj II 467,24 explains *anussada* simply as "the absence of the swelling of craving" (*taṇhāussadābhāvena anussadaṃ*).

When a bhikkhu does not boast of his good behavior, the skillful say "he has no swellings anywhere in the world" (**783**d). Nidd I 51 comments on this by way of the seven swellings, with "kamma" replacing "misconduct": "There are seven swellings: the swelling of lust, the swelling of hatred, the swelling of delusion, the swelling of conceit, the swelling of views, the swelling of defilements, and the swelling of kamma. One who does not have these is an arahant, one whose influxes are destroyed." One who "does not conceive himself to be equal, or superior, or inferior" is said to have no swellings (**855**). Nidd I 178 explains this in mechanical fashion as the absence of the seven swellings, but obviously in this case the swelling of conceit is more prominent than the others. *Ussada* apparently are not things that merely happen to one passively. They are states or conditions that one actively creates. Hence the Buddha says of the bhikkhu in training, in a verse that links *aneja* to the absence of *ussada*, that he should be "steady, without impulse, and should not cause a swelling anywhere" (*evaṃ ṭhito anej'assa ussadaṃ bhikkhu na kareyya kuhiñci*).

(6) Kappa

In several of the discourses of Sn, especially in the Aṭṭhakavagga, the word *kappa* plays a major role, occurring with a frequency and gravity not found anywhere else in the Nikāyas. The word has multiple meanings. Among those listed in DOP are: an eon (a cycle of the world's evolution and dissolution); a rule, ordinance, or proper proceeding; a false supposition or theory; a figment. *Kappa* also occurs as a suffix indicating "similar to, like," as in the line *eko care khaggavisāṇakappo*, "one should live alone *like* a rhinoceros horn."

While *kappa* might be ambiguous when used alone, the psychological nuances of the word can be seen in prefixed forms that are obviously connected with thinking: *saṅkappa*, intentional thought, purpose; *vikappa*, distinction, discrimination, classification; and *pakappati*, to plan, to intend. From this we can infer that in Sn the base form *kappa* also has a psychological significance. Here, however, *kappa* does not denote mental activity in a neutral sense; it does not signify thoughts that can be either wholesome or unwholesome, "right thought" or "wrong thought." Rather, in Sn *kappa* is invariably given a negative valuation. The Niddesa explains that there are two kinds of *kappa*, that due to craving and that due to views. *Kappa* thus underscores the constructive function of thought when it is driven by defiled propensities. It is thought that fabricates ideas and notions derived not from actuality but from the subjective imagination.

I struggled to find an adequate rendering for *kappa*, one that could match the simplicity of the Pāli. After experimenting with several alternatives, I found myself forced to settle for "mental constructs, mental construction." This lacks the simplicity and suggestiveness of the original and may stress the cognitive aspect of *kappa* at the expense of the emotive aspect. But as the Niddesa says, *kappa* can arise from craving as well as from views, and thus it is not exclusively concerned with matters of doctrine and theory. It seems *kappa* encompasses both the act of mental construction and the products of the act, the mental constructs. It is not always easy to differentiate the two and thus I vary the rendering in the way that I see better fits the context. Apart from the noun *kappa*, we also find the causative verb *kappayanti*, which I render "they construct," the optative *kappayeyya*, "one would construct," and still other forms.

The message repeatedly conveyed by Sn is that the sage—the muni or true brahmin—keeps aloof from *kappa*, does not create *kappa*, does not take up *kappa*. The verses, for instance, tell us that the sage has "overcome mental constructs about things past and future" (**373**ab). Whereas devas and ordinary people are prone to mental construction, the sage "does not enter upon mental constructs" (**521**cd). True brahmins "do not construct" and "have no preferences" (**794**a), and thus are free from the knot of grasping. The muni, who does not rank himself in relation to others, is "not given to mental construction and thus does not enter upon mental constructs" (**860**d). The disciple in training is advised: "one should not construct any view in the world" (**799**a).

A prefixed form of the word, *pakappita*, occurs several times in relation to views and other objects of thought. The word is a past participle, which I have rendered "formulated." Thus it is said of the true brahmin that "not even a subtle notion is formulated by him about what is seen, heard, or sensed here" (**802**ab). The sage "does not grasp any judgments that have been formulated" (**838**ab). The corresponding absolutive occurs in the statement that disputes arise as a consequence of "having formulated (*pakappayitvā*) reasoning about views" (**886**c). Another prefixed form occurs as an optative in the line *kenīdha lokasmiṃ vikappayeyya*, which is found twice (at **793**d and **802**d). In accordance with the explanation in the Niddesa, I render this: "How could anyone here in the world categorize him?"

This emphasis on avoiding *kappa* underscores the function of the Dhamma as a system of mental training that requires introspective awareness of one's own thought processes and the effort to train the mind to abolish wrong modes of thinking, particularly in this case those driven by craving, distorted conceptualization, and attachment to dogmatic beliefs. Behind all *kappa* lies the positing of things as "I" and "mine" (*ahaṃkāra* and *mamaṃkāra*), which creates the false sense of a substantial self and reinforces possessiveness.

(7) Mamāyita, Mamatta

In the prose Nikāyas, the contemplation of non-self usually proceeds through a three-term formula whereby the disciple sees all phenomena, such as the five aggregates and twelve sense bases, thus: "This is not mine, this I am not, this is not my self" (*n'etaṃ mama, n'eso'ham asmi, na m'eso attā*). The three terms here are given equal weight. Sn, however, makes only a couple of references to the view of self. One is the observation at **756** that the world conceives a self in what is non-self (*anattani attamāniṃ passa lokaṃ*); the other is the instruction to Mogharāja at **1119** to see the world as empty and uproot the view of self (*attānudiṭṭhiṃ ūhacca*). But these are exceptional. The focus in Sn falls instead on removing the attachment to things taken as "mine."

This emphasis might be thought to indicate that Buddhism in its primitive phase gave greater weight to abolishing craving than to seeing through conceptual views of self. This thesis, it might be said, is supported by the specification of craving rather than ignorance as the origin of *dukkha* in the Buddha's first discourse. Such a conclusion, however, would be premature. Most passages in Sn offering advice about overcoming "mineness" are addressed to bhikkhus, who in adopting the Buddha's teachings would have already rejected the views of self promulgated by non-Buddhist teachers. For them, the challenge was to overcome craving.

In any case, words indicative of possessiveness prevail in Sn. The two most important words (actually alternative forms of the same word) are *mamāyita* and *mamatta*, both nouns built upon *mama*, "mine." Both words, it seems, straddle the two domains, the subjective and objective, referring to both the inner act of appropriation by which things are taken as "mine" and the things themselves appropriated and claimed to be one's own.

As to *mamāyita* it is said (at **466**b) that those worthy of oblations "have abandoned things taken as 'mine.'" People in the world tremble and sorrow over things taken as "mine" (**777**a, **805**a). Therefore, a monk in training "should not take anything in the world as 'mine'" (**922**d). This attitude should extend not only to people and material possessions but to everything comprised in the physical and mental complex designated "name-and-form" (**950**ab). Having given up taking things as "mine," in this very life the wise "might abandon suffering: birth and old age, sorrow and lamenting" (**1056**).

As for *mamatta,* a wise person understands that whatever is taken as "mine" (*mama*) must be abandoned at death; hence a follower of the Buddha "should not incline to take things as 'mine'" (**806**d). Taking things as "mine" depends on desire, and when desire does not exist, there is no taking as "mine" (**872**c). One "not finding anything to be taken as 'mine' does not sorrow, thinking: 'It is not mine'" (**951**cd).

7. The Suttanipāta Commentary

Each of the books of the Pāli Canon has an authorized commentary, called an *aṭṭhakathā,* "Discussion of the Meaning." The function of the commentary is to explicate virtually every significant word, phrase, and idea in its root text. The major Pāli *aṭṭhakathā* were composed by the great Indian commentator Ācariya Buddhaghosa, who came to Sri Lanka in the fifth century C.E. expressly for the purpose of composing commentaries. Buddhaghosa based his commentaries on the old Sinhala *aṭṭhakathā* preserved for centuries at the Mahāvihāra, the Great Monastery in Anurādhapura, the ancient capital of Sri Lanka. The original Sinhala commentaries were purportedly translated from Indian originals brought to Sri Lanka by the earliest Buddhist missionaries to the island. Others, such as the famous *Mahā-aṭṭhakathā,* were likely composed in Sri Lanka. None of these Sinhala commentaries has survived.[17]

The Suttanipāta, too, has its commentary, the *Suttanipāta-aṭṭhakathā,* also known under the name *Paramatthajotikā*: "Elucidator (*jotikā*) of the Supreme (*parama*) Meaning (*attha*)."[18] Since the commentary to the Khuddakapāṭha is also named *Paramatthajotikā*, it is customary to title that one *Paramatthajotikā* I and the Suttanipāta Commentary *Paramatthajotikā* II.[19] In the colophon of Pj II, the author claims to be "the elder who bears the name Buddhaghosa conferred by his teachers," and he describes himself with the same chain of epithets as is found in the colophon to the *Visuddhimagga*, Buddhaghosa's great treatise on Buddhist doctrine and meditation.

Buddhaghosa's authorship of the Suttanipāta Commentary has been disputed by present-day scholars, but this ascription also has its defenders. The text of Pj II bears evidence that the author was acquainted with other Pāli commentaries traditionally ascribed to Buddhaghosa.[20] These references could be understood either as Buddhaghosa alluding to his own previous works or as another author alluding to the works of Buddhaghosa. It is not critical, however, to settle the question of Pj II's authorship with certainty, for the purpose of the work is the same as that which Buddhaghosa set for himself in his commentaries to the four Nikāyas: to explain the meaning of the text in accordance with "the doctrine of the elders resident at the Mahāvihāra."

The commentaries are works of exegesis intended to lay bare the meaning of the canonical text and to explain its words in relation to the established body of Buddhist doctrine. Occasionally the commentaries will saunter off and relate interesting background information and illustrative stories, but such excursions are always subordinate to the task of explication. In undertaking this task, the commentaries analyze and explain the texts through the lens of the complex exegetical apparatus that was maintained at the Mahāvihāra. This meticulous scholastic system often makes the commentaries seem dry and ponderous, but with patience they can also be found to be highly illuminating, lighting up layers of meaning not apparent on a cursory reading. To help readers navigate their way through the translation of the commentary I will briefly explore the pillars of this system as they relate to the *Paramatthajotikā*. I will discuss them under two headings, exegetical methodology and doctrinal interpretation.

(1) Exegetical Methodology

The exegetical methodology can be subsumed under two principal tasks undertaken by the commentary, *padavaṇṇanā* and *atthavaṇṇanā*, "explanation of terms" and "explanation of the meaning." These two facets of the commentarial approach to the text correspond to the canonical description of the Dhamma as *sātthaṃ sabyañjanaṃ,* "possessing meaning and possessing phrasing." The explanation of terms is intended to clarify the words used in the text, often taking up each word for examination. The explanation of the meaning is intended to bring out the purport of each passage and to relate the text to the overall architecture of the Dhamma, which, it is held, is intrinsically meaningful or beneficial (*atthasaṃhitaṃ*) and directed toward a goal (also *attha*), the deathless nibbāna.

Since the explanation of terms usually involves merely defining the Pāli words of the original text by means of other Pāli words more in line with the commentarial diction, I have occasionally omitted this portion from my translation. To translate such passages would have involved simply defining English words with other English words. The explanation of terms almost always precedes the explanation of the meaning. As the commentary advances, term explanations become increasingly briefer and more infrequent, limited only to terms not encountered earlier in the work. Thus it is not seldom that we come across a statement to the effect (as in the comment on **117**): "We will pass over the terms whose meanings are clear and merely comment on the terms that have not yet been explained." Often Pj II will comment on just a few new words and add, "As to the rest, the term meaning is clear" (*sesaṃ uttānapadatthameva*), or even more briefly: "The rest is already clear" (*sesaṃ uttānameva*).

The difference between a term explanation and a meaning explanation can be seen in the commentary on **143**, the first verse of the Metta Sutta. Pj II first takes up the term explanation, defining "one skilled in the good" as an expert in the good (a synonym), "the good" (*attha*) as anything beneficial to oneself, and so forth. When it comes to the explanation of the meaning, Pj II contrasts "one skilled in what is not good" with "one skilled in the good" and explains each by way of types of behavior considered unsuitable and suitable for those who have entered monastic life.

The difference between term explanation and meaning explanation is also seen in the commentary on **259**, the second verse of the Mahāmaṅgala Sutta. Here, after giving brief definitions of the terms "fools," "the wise," "associating with," "venerating," and "worthy of veneration," Pj II moves on to the explanation of the meaning, where it elucidates the structure of the passage, the nature of foolish people and wise people, the marks of those who deserve veneration, and the benefits of venerating those who are truly venerable. The explanations are embellished with stories and citations from other texts relevant to the topic. Occasionally, rather than explain the meaning at length, the commentator will provide a statement of "the concise meaning" (*saṅkhepattha*), as in commenting on **57**, **58**, **80**, and **229**. A "summary of the meaning" (*piṇḍattha*), which might wrap up an extended passage, is found in the comments on **234** and **259**.

To explain a word in the root text, the commentary sometimes cites the different meanings the word has in different contexts, quoting passages from elsewhere in the canon to illustrate those meanings. An example is the explanation of *brahmacariya*, "the spiritual life," at **32**.[21] Here the word is said to be "a designation for abstinence from sexual intercourse, the path, the ascetic's duty, the Teaching, and marital fidelity." Another analysis of *brahmacariya* is at **267**, where only four aspects are mentioned: abstinence from sexual activity, the duty of an ascetic, the Teaching, and the path. At **69** the word *jhāna* is explained in two ways, which are correlated respectively with the eight meditative attainments and with insight, the path, and fruits. At **182**, different meanings of the word *sacca*, truth, are brought forward, again supported by textual citations. At **222**, we find different meanings of *bhūta*, and in commenting on the prose preamble to the Mahāmaṅgala Sutta, Pj II cites different meanings of the words *kevala* and *kappa*, which are joined into the compound *kevalakappa*, meaning "entire." Often, after collecting these different meanings of a word, Pj II will select one and declare: "Here [just this] is intended" (*idha . . . adhippetaṃ*).

To clarify the meaning of a passage, the commentary usually seeks to determine its purport (*adhippāya*). The commentary may bring out the purport by paraphrasing the canonical text, expanding upon the original statement to make the implications clearer. In its exegesis of the Dhaniya Sutta, for example, Pj II draws out the purport behind each of the Buddha's succinct replies to Dhaniya, and at the end of the poem, it does the same with his reply to Māra. Often the commentator will pass over the explanation of terms and go directly for the purport, saying, for example at **49**: "The verse is clear with regard to the meaning of its terms, but this is the purport here." At the end of the Kasibhāradvāja Sutta (p. 522), when the brahmin praises the Dhamma with four similes, the commentary says, "This is the construal of the purport," and proceeds to elaborate on the similes. In commenting on **143**, it offers three alternative ways of understanding the purport of the opening lines of the Metta Sutta. In the exchange at **168–75**, it explains the purport of the yakkha's questions and the Buddha's replies.

Another exegetical method used by the commentary is the *yojanā*, which I render "construal." The purpose of the *yojanā* is to unravel the syntax of a verse (or series of verses), joining the lines of the root text together into a fuller and clearer statement that conveys the purport. Since in Pāli verse, word order is shuffled to fit the meter and normal sentence structure may be disregarded to create a heightened effect, the commentary will offer a prose paraphrase of the verse (or verses), reformulating the passage with the use of standard syntax. Examples of the construal of individual verses are at **5**, **47**, **67**, **90**, and **404**. The construal may also explicate the *anusandhi*, the sequence of ideas in a text, explaining why the Buddha passes from one topic to the next. This is done to demonstrate the coherence of the text, for "no explanation by the buddhas is ever incoherent" (*na buddhānaṃ ananusandhikā nāma kathā atthi*), that is, never without *anusandhi*.

Occasionally, at the end of a long discourse, the commentator will tie all the verses together by offering a paraphrase of the whole poem. An example is seen at the end of the Mahāmaṅgala Sutta (pp. 771–72). Alternatively, the commentator may offer the construal at the beginning of a series of verses, as at **849**, where he says: ". . . thus the construal should be understood here. This method applies everywhere, but from this point on, without showing the construal, we will only explain the unclear terms." At the end of the commentary on the Khaggavisāṇa Sutta, the commentator says that all the verses should be construed according to the method given, but "we did not construe them in every case from fear of too much elaboration."

The commentaries almost always offer explanations of the "origin" (*uppatti*) of a sutta, the background to the discourse. They distinguish four modes of origin: personal inclination (of the Buddha), the inclination of others, a particular incident, and a question.[22] The preamble to the Khaggavisāṇa Sutta (at p. 401) mentions the four together and cites examples of each from Sn. The commentary to any sutta begins with the question, "What is the origin?" (*kā uppatti*), and then provides the origin story. Often Pj II will relate a detailed background story to the discourse, drawing on the rich narrative tradition of Buddhism. To explain the origin of the Metta Sutta, for example, the commentary tells the story of the monks who were harassed by tree spirits. In explaining the origin of the Ratana Sutta, it starts with the beginnings of the Licchavi clan, the founding of the city of Vesālī, and the plagues that afflicted the city. To explain the origin of the Maṅgala Sutta, it relates the controversy that had broken out over all of Jambudīpa about the meaning of the word *maṅgala*.

Sometimes, when commenting on a sutta in verse that appears to be an integral work, Pj II will explain that each stanza was actually uttered separately on a different occasion in response to a specific incident. This is the case with its treatment of the Uraga Sutta, the Khaggavisāṇa Sutta, and the middle stanzas of the Muni Sutta. The commentary to the Khaggavisāṇa relates the stories of each paccekabuddha who supposedly uttered a verse, explaining how they became disenchanted with the world, went forth, and attained enlightenment.

These origin stories betray a tendency to what might be called "projective literalism." By this I mean the construction of a concrete story corresponding to a metaphor or simile in the canonical text, the story being then projected onto the verse in order to explain its origin. For instance, where stanza **2** compares the cutting off of lust to the plucking of a lotus in a lake, the commentary provides a background story of a monk observing boys diving into a lake and plucking lotuses. Where stanza **5** illustrates the coreless nature of existence with the simile of the *udumbara* tree, which bears no flowers, the commentary brings forth the story of a brahmin searching for flowers in such trees. The same procedure occurs in relation to almost every verse of the Khaggavisāṇa Sutta.

In describing the background to the Kasibhāradvāja Sutta, the commentary provides a detailed account of the Buddha's daily routine, documenting virtually his entire schedule from the predawn hours through the middle of the night. The passage also explains how the Buddha locates the potential recipients of his teaching. Before dawn, it is said, he "enters the meditative attainment of great compassion and surveys the world with the buddha eye" until there appears in his field of vision those with supporting conditions who are ripe enough to benefit from his teaching. When morning arrives he heads in their direction and creates the opportunity for a discourse. Examples of this procedure are found in the background stories to I,4 (p. 497), I,7 (p. 545), I,10 (p. 611), II,5 (p. 773), III,4 (p. 887), and IV,9 (p. 1105).

Another exegetical technique distinguishes whether a particular teaching is based on persons (*puggalādhiṭṭhāna*) or based on qualities (*dhammādhiṭṭhāna*). A teaching based on persons can be employed to teach about qualities; and conversely, a teaching about qualities can be employed to teach about persons. The beginning of the commentary to the Parābhava Sutta says, with reference to the words "One who succeeds is easily known," that the Buddha points out the cause of a downfall by way of a teaching based on persons. Here, the subject to be explained is a quality (*dhamma*), namely, the cause of a downfall (*parābhavamukha*); but the text demonstrates this quality by speaking of the persons who undergo a downfall. The commentary on the Āmagandha Sutta neatly highlights the contrast between these two modes of teaching. In **242**, when explaining "carrion," the text describes such qualities or actions as taking life, violence, fraudulence, and so forth, and thus the teaching here is one with "qualities as a basis." But the next two verses, **243–44**, illustrate carrion by means of *people* who act immorally; thus this is a teaching about qualities that has persons as a basis.

(2) Doctrinal Interpretation

The commentaries provide not only exegetical analysis of the words of the texts but expositions of their purport from a doctrinal point of view. The concepts employed in the commentaries demonstrate how over time Buddhist doctrinal inquiry became increasingly more complex and sophisticated. The doctrinal specialists did not merely transmit the texts but subjected them to rigorous analysis and investigation. In this respect the commentaries are extraordinarily consistent with one another and even their explanations are extremely uniform. The treatment of a concept in one commentary will often be repeated verbatim in other commentaries, though sometimes with minor differences.

The use of various explicative categories shows that the Pāli tradition did not remain static but had built up an intricate doctrinal framework that could be applied to any text to draw out its doctrinal significance. Signs of a movement in this direction are already evident in the Nikāyas. The "analysis" (*vibhaṅga*) suttas, for example, anticipate the analytical methods of the commentaries by taking up each major term in a formula and providing it with a formal definition. The Dasuttara Sutta (DN 34) carries this trend still further. Here Sāriputta classifies groups of doctrinal concepts ranging from single items to groups of ten, distinguishing each group according to ten categories: whether the factors are helpful, to be developed, to be understood, to be abandoned, lead to decline, lead to distinction, are hard to penetrate, should be aroused, should be directly known, and should be realized.[23] As the methods of doctrinal explication evolved in the Mahāvihāra lineage, they converged into a rigorous, meticulous, and remarkably consistent system. Here I can only briefly touch on some of the doctrinal concepts employed in Pj II, with examples of how they are applied to the root text.

A fundamental distinction the commentary makes, one that stands at the base of the entire commentarial system, is the dichotomy of the mundane (*lokiya*) and the world-transcending (*lokuttara*). Factors of experience, modes of practice, and the teachings that describe them are distinguished on the basis of this dichotomy. A clear example is the commentary on the Dvayatānupassanā Sutta (at p. 1000), where it is said: "Accurate knowledge is a designation for insight into things defined as twofold by division into the mundane and the world-transcending."[24] In each of the dyads, the first member (*dukkha* and its origin) is said to be mundane, while the second member (cessation and the means to cessation) is said to be world-transcending. At **31–32** Dhaniya and his family see the Buddha's Dhamma body (*dhammakāya* = nibbāna) with the world-transcending eye and his form body with the mundane eye. In explaining **84** Pj II says that trainees live on the world-transcending path, while the virtuous worldling lives on the mundane path. Discussions of wisdom at **76–77**, **176**, and **188** distinguish between mundane and world-transcending wisdom. Stanza **276** speaks of mundane and world-transcending good conduct. At **261**, discipline is said to be a means to mundane and world-transcending happiness. And the commentary on III,3 (p. 882) says that proper speech "brings mundane and world-transcending well-being and happiness."

The distinction between the mundane and the world-transcending corresponds to another distinction mentioned at several points in Pj II, that between the preliminary portion of the practice and the subsequent portion. The preliminary portion (*pubbabhāgapaṭipadā*) is the training in good behavior, concentration, and insight leading to the world-transcending path. The world-transcending path is itself the subsequent portion of practice (*aparabhāgapaṭipadā*). This distinction rests on the idea that the gradual and sequential practice undertaken by a practitioner culminates in a momentary breakthrough by which one discerns the ultimate truth of the Dhamma.

This breakthrough experience is designated "the path" (*magga*), a new usage of an old term that shifts its meaning in a technically systematic direction. The four paths are the four breakthrough experiences by which the disciple sees the truth of the Dhamma and thereby attains to one or another of the four noble fruits, from stream-entry to arahantship. Each path endures for a single mind-moment during which one penetrates the four noble truths, directly experiences nibbāna, and eliminates certain defilements. The path is followed immediately by several moments of fruition (*phala*), during which the disciple experiences the bliss of release from the defilements that have just been eradicated by the path. This conception of a single moment path-experience immediately followed by fruition is not discernible in the Nikāyas. It is derived from the Abhidhamma analysis of experience into discrete *cittas* or mind-moments. The *Visuddhimagga* gives a full account of the process (in chaps. 21–22), which is presupposed by the commentaries.

This picture of a sequential practice culminating in a world-transcending breakthrough governs the distinction between the preliminary portion and the subsequent portion. At **186**, the preliminary portion is said to consist in good conduct of body, speech, and mind, the subsequent portion in the thirty-seven aids to enlightenment. In the comment on **203**, a bhikkhu who contemplates the body is said to [tentatively] abandon the unwholesome roots in the preliminary portion of practice, and as he progresses he "eventually reaches the path of arahantship and can thereby expunge all desire and lust." In commenting on "having known the state, having penetrated the Dhamma" at **374**a, Pj II explains the first clause as knowing the four noble truths with the wisdom of the preliminary portion of the path, and the second as penetrating the Dhamma of the four truths with the four world-transcending paths.

Since the four noble truths are the core of the liberating Dhamma, Pj II sets out to demonstrate how a verse or group of verses can be interpreted as an exposition of these truths. This is not always obvious, for the four truths may not be mentioned at all in the actual text; rather, they have to be teased out from suggestive phrases. Thus Pj II takes up the Buddha's final verse to Dhaniya (**29**) and explicates it by way of the four noble truths, so that the "bed of the womb" becomes the truth of suffering, "the bonds" the truth of the origin, the "cutting of the bonds" the truth of cessation, and the method of cutting the bonds (which is only implied) the truth of the path. In its interpretation of the riddles posed by the yakkha Hemavata at **170**, Pj II relates them to the truths of suffering and the path, which entail the truths of the origin and cessation. When it takes up the Buddha's reply at **171–72**, it explains how each phrase signifies one of the four truths. Similarly, in explicating the Buddha's reply to the yakkha Sūciloma at **272–73**, Pj II maps its terms against the four truths. And virtually all the verses of the Dvayatānupassanā Sutta, according to Pj II, are oblique expressions of the four noble truths.

The commentary recognizes that each of the four noble truths is bound up with a particular task, as is already indicated in the Nikāyas. Thus in glossing the stock declaration of arahantship (at pp. 169–70), the statement "What had to be done has been done" is interpreted thus: "The sixteen functions have been completed by the four paths in relation to the four truths respectively by way of full understanding, abandoning, realization, and development." The total of sixteen is arrived at because each of the four paths executes the same four functions. Each path fully understands suffering, abandons its origin, realizes cessation, and develops the path. At **167**, where the Buddha is declared one who "has gone beyond all phenomena," Pj II explains this by way of direct knowledge (of the four truths), full understanding (of suffering), abandoning (of the origin), development (of the path), realization (of nibbāna), and attainment (of buddhahood).

A few other doctrinal developments in the commentary may be briefly noted in passing. When explaining the meaning of the first line in the first verse of the Uraga Sutta, Pj II picks up the word *uppatitaṃ*, "arisen," and gives a fourfold analysis of the notion of arisen as "what is actually occurring, what has occurred and gone away, what has made an opportunity, and what has gained ground." This is a difficult passage, and the commentary here is not as clear as it might have been. It may be unfortunate that the author employed this analysis so close to the beginning of the commentary, when it might deter the reader from continuing with the work.

The commentary goes on to explain the removal of defilements to occur in two ways, by restraint (*saṃvara*) and by abandoning (*pahāna*), and it analyzes each as fivefold, citing other canonical texts as illustrations (pp. 362–65). Three kinds of abstinence (*virati*) are explained at **264**, which sets various aspects of practice in their proper context. And in several places the commentary explains "full understanding" (*pariññā*) as a threefold process by which insight advances to successively deeper levels. At **202**, the three kinds of full understanding are related to the contemplation of the body. There are references to the three kinds of full understanding at **250, 455, 458, 473**, and **736–37**. At **778**, the root text speaks of fully understanding contact, which Pj II explains as "having fully understood, by the three kinds of full understanding, contact such as eye-contact and so forth, or all name-and-form concurrent with contact." Just below, at **779**, the text speaks of fully understanding perception, which Pj II explains: "Having fully understood not only contact but perception too by the three kinds of full understanding." Similarly, where **1082** speaks of the full understanding of craving, Pj II says "having fully understood craving by the three kinds of full understanding." These explanations of *pariññā* (based on the Niddesa) involve a reconceptualization of the word. In the Nikāyas *pariññā* is used solely in relation to the final comprehension achieved by an arahant, yet in the commentaries its scope is widened so that it comes to include the stages of preparatory insight culminating in full comprehension.

Finally, like other commentaries, Pj II occasionally cites and evaluates alternative opinions, which differ from those approved in the sources on which the commentator relied, presumably the old Sinhala commentaries of the Mahāvihāra. These opinions are usually prefaced by the phrase *keci pan'āhu*, "but some say." The commentary may either gently tolerate the alternative opinion or flatly reject it. Thus at **13** a view is cited different from the dominant view and the commentator says: "One may accept whatever explanation one prefers" (*yaṃ ruccati taṃ gahetabbaṃ*). In commenting on the prose preamble to I,4 (pp. 501–2), he says the same about alternative explanations of the word "Magadha." At **16**, however, the author rejects an explanation of *vanatha*, which he says is applicable to the Dhammapada verse but not to the Uraga verse. At **191**, where in the root text Āḷavaka declares that he knows the worthy recipient of gifts, Pj II paraphrases this as referring to the Buddha. However, it adds, "Some say he said this with reference to the Sangha," and he lets this go without comment. At **257**, he cites two alternatives to the established explanation of three terms—"the taste of solitude, peace, and rapture in the Dhamma"—but says, with reference to the established explanation: "The previous explanation alone is good." At **268**, he cites an explanation of "sorrowless" (*asokaṃ*) as referring to nibbāna but points out that this "does not agree with the earlier term," which is *citta*, and therefore he upholds the position that the word describes the mind of an arahant. In relation to **689**, where the commentary says that the parasol over the newborn Buddha was held up by devas, he adds, "Some say this is stated with reference to a human parasol," but in that case, he points out, "there is nothing exceptional with this statement." This is an implicit endorsement of the authorized view that the parasol was being held up by devas.

(3) Tensions Between My Translation and the Commentary

Although I have leaned heavily upon Pj II in understanding the Suttanipāta, inevitably I came across explanations with which I disagreed. Often these did not affect my translation. In such cases I simply recognized that the explanations I found questionable reflect the thought of the period in which the commentary took shape; if I had an alternative explanation to offer, I relegated it to a note. However, I did run into commentarial interpretations of lines in Sn that I considered contrary to the intended meaning of the original, and these put me, as a translator of both the root text and its commentary, in a bind. If I were to translate the root text out of deference to the commentary, I would then be going against my own judgment. If I were to translate the root text in accordance with my understanding, a dissonance would then emerge between my rendering of the text and the explanation of the commentary, including the lemma, the line from the root text cited in the commentary. In cases where my understanding and the commentary conflicted, I have generally chosen to follow my personal judgment, even though by doing so I risk finding myself in the company of those dissenters Pj II speaks of dismissively as *keci pan'āhu*.

The following are the passages where I confronted this dilemma and resolved it in a way that runs contrary to the commentary. There may be still more such passages that I failed to record. I refer the reader to the relevant notes for explanations of the reason for my disagreement with Pj II.

6b. having transcended such and such states of existence
itibhavābhavatañca vītivatto
See p. 1364, note 305, and p. 1475, note 1418.

49b. words of address or abusive speech
vācābhilāpo abhisajjanā vā
See p. 1379, note 466.

64b. like a pāricchattaka tree that has shed its leaves
sañchannapatto [*sañchinnapatto*] *yathā pārichatto*
See pp. 1382–84, note 503.

66c. having cut off affection and hatred
anissito chetvā sinehadosaṃ
See p. 1384, note 507.

131a. One here who speaks what is untrue
asataṃ / asantaṃ yo'dha pabrūti
See p. 1398, note 653.

143b. having made the breakthrough to that peaceful state
yan taṃ santaṃ padaṃ abhisamecca
See p. 1401, note 684.

270c. Having originated from what do the mind's thoughts
kuto samuṭṭhāya manovitakkā
See p. 1444, note 1108.

277cd. one does not know defilement as the path leading to hell
saṃkilesaṃ na jānāti, maggaṃ nirayagāminaṃ
See p. 1445, note 1122.

322d. those equipped with attentive ears as a supporting condition
sotāvadhānūpanisūpapanne
See p. 1451, note 1173.

330c. being settled in peace, gentleness, and concentration
te santisoraccasamādhisaṇṭhitā
See p. 1453, note 1185.

382ab. these brahmins given to debate, and also some who are elder brahmins
ye keci'me brāhmaṇā vādasīlā, vuddhā cāpi brāhmaṇā santi keci
See p. 1463, note 1292.

453cd. The good and the Dhamma, good people say, are established upon truth.
Sacce atthe ca dhamme ca, āhu santo patiṭṭhitā.
See p. 1470, note 1368.

454ab. the speech that the Buddha utters for the attainment of nibbāna, the secure
yaṃ buddho bhāsati vācaṃ, khemaṃ nibbānapattiyā
See p. 1470, note 1369.

468a. the same as the righteous, far from the unrighteous
samo samehi visamehi dūre.
See p. 1472, note 1392.

496b. for any state of existence here or beyond
bhavābhavāya idha vā huraṃ vā
See p. 1475, note 1418.

519 and following. such a one: *tādī*
See p. 1480, note 1459.

635c. arrived at firm ground in the deathless
amatogadhamanuppattaṃ
See p. 1494, note 1596.

787ab. One involved is embroiled in disputes about teachings;
but how, about what, could one dispute with one uninvolved?
Upayo hi dhammesu upeti vādaṃ, anūpayaṃ kena kathaṃ vadeyya?
See p. 1514, note 1803.

873a. How must one attain for form to vanish?
Kathaṃsametassa vibhoti rūpaṃ
874c. form vanishes for one who has so attained
evaṃsametassa vibhoti rūpaṃ
See p. 1529, note 1931.

916ab. By reflection, he should stop [the conceit] "I am,"
the entire root of concepts due to proliferation.
Mūlaṃ papañcasaṅkhāya, mantā asmīti sabbamuparundhe.
See p. 1536, note 1980.

1055cd. having dispelled delight and attachment to these,
consciousness would not persist in existence
etesu nandiñca nivesanañca, panujja viññāṇaṃ bhave na tiṭṭhe
See p. 1547, note 2089–90.

1065d. right here I would live, peaceful and unattached
idh'eva santo asito careyyaṃ
See p. 1549, note 2099.

1087b. quenched in this very life
diṭṭhadhammābhinibbutā
See p. 1552, note 2119.

1148cd. The Teacher is the end-maker of questions
for those in doubt who acknowledge this.
Pañhānantakaro satthā, kaṅkhīnaṃ paṭijānataṃ.
See p. 1557, note 2170.

7. The Niddesa

When Pj II arrives at chapter IV and the *pucchās* of chapter V, it provides little more than word glosses on new terms in the root text, and does so in a perfunctory manner, often abridging explanations with "and so forth" even more than is usual for a commentary. Pj II adopts this very constrained role because an ancient expository text on those chapters already existed at the time it was composed, a text given canonical status. The text, called the Niddesa, is included in the Khuddaka Nikāya of the Pāli Canon. It is divided into two parts, the longer one called the *Mahāniddesa* or "Great Exposition" and the shorter one the *Cūḷaniddesa* or "Minor Exposition." The former is an exposition of the Aṭṭhakavagga, the latter an exposition of the *pucchās* of the Pārāyanavagga together with the Khaggavisāṇa Sutta. The *Cūḷaniddesa* does not comment on the introductory verses (*vatthugāthā*) of the Pārāyana, which suggests that this section was either composed at a later time or not yet considered fully canonical.

The fact that these parts of the Suttanipāta are commented on by the Niddesa without reference to the work as a whole indicates that they originally existed as independent units and were later collected along with other discourses to form the anthology. The dedication of a commentary just to these texts underscores the high regard with which they must have been held by the early Buddhist community. The Niddesa is traditionally ascribed to Sāriputta, though this is far more likely to be an article of belief than a genuine historical fact. It is conceivable, however, that the Niddesa was composed by monks in the pupillary lineage stemming from Sāriputta, learned monks who, in the process of elucidating the texts, may have drawn on some of Sāriputta's oral explanations. Both parts of the Niddesa frequently cite passages from the Sutta Piṭaka, including lines from suttas (other than those in the Aṭṭhakavagga and Pārāyanavagga) that are now included in Sn. This suggests that those suttas, too, existed as independent units before they were collected into the anthology.

The Niddesa's date of composition has not been determined with any degree of certainty. Norman earlier wrote (1983, 86) that "the beginning of the third century B.C.E. would seem to be quite suitable as the date of its composition," but he later took a more cautious position (at GD xxxiii), stating that the date "cannot be later than the date of the fixing of the Canon." Since the suttas cited correspond to the versions of the texts found in the Pāli Canon (with very minor variations), this indicates that the Niddesa was a work solely of the Pāli school not shared by other schools of Early Buddhism. It also entails that the work was composed subsequent to the emergence of separate schools. The Niddesa mentions the Abhidhamma several times, alongside Sutta and Vinaya, which of course means that it must have been composed later than the Abhidhamma.[25]

Here I want to point out some of the main themes and highlights of the Niddesa. For ease of reference in the discussion to follow, I notate the text according to the page numbers in the blocks of excerpts that I have included rather than cite the precise page number from the VRI edition, which I cannot determine anyway from the electronic version.

In what follows I will briefly discuss some methodological features of the Niddesa and the contributions it makes to an understanding of the texts on which it comments.

(1) Definitions and Compendia

The Niddesa, somewhat like the Abhidhamma, employs the practice of defining terms with a fixed series of synonyms that is repeated verbatim for each occurrence of the term in the root text. It thus functions partly like a thesaurus. Terms defined in this way include, among others, craving (*taṇhā*), wisdom (*paññā*), suffering (*dukkha*), and ignorance (*avijjā*) or delusion (*moha*). The definitions may contain compounds formed from the primary term as well as metaphors taken from elsewhere in the Nikāyas. If a synonymous term occurs in the root text it may first be defined by the primary term, which is then followed by the whole series of synonyms.

Thus where the expression "attachment to the world" (*visattikaṃ loke*) occurs at **770**, Nidd I 7 first glosses attachment as "craving" and then introduces a hundred synonyms for craving, including such metaphors as seamstress, ensnarer, woods, and jungle, as well as compounds like "the river of craving, the net of craving, the leash of craving, the ocean of craving." At **945**, where greed is called "the great flood," Nidd I 319–20 defines greed as craving and then introduces the same string of synonyms, abridged in the printed editions.

When **770** states "The wise say life is short," Nidd I 32 explains "the wise" (*dhīrā*) as those who possess intelligence (*dhī*). It then glosses intelligence as wisdom (*paññā*) and segues into a long series of synonyms for wisdom, including such metaphorical compounds as "the light of wisdom, the radiance of wisdom, the lamp of wisdom," and such technical expressions as non-delusion, discrimination of phenomena, and right view. The same definition (abridged) is cited at Nidd II 27–28 for wisdom as it occurs in **1035**. Where **1048** uses the expression "having comprehended" (*saṅkhāya*), Nidd II 53 equates comprehension with knowledge (*ñāṇa*) and then, as a gloss on knowledge, introduces the formal definition of wisdom (abridged).

Suffering at **1033** is explicated by Nidd II 23–24 with a compendium of the different types of suffering, beginning with "the suffering of birth, old age, illness, and death" and continuing, through a long list of human miseries (including the many diseases that afflict the body, which I have abridged), to "loss of relatives, loss of wealth, loss through illness, loss of good behavior, loss of view." The compendium recurs several times later in the Niddesa when the word "suffering" occurs in a verse. Sometimes the passage mentions only the major manifestations of suffering.

Another type of list is used to delineate the principles that are to be understood with wisdom. This list, which we might call "the compendium of comprehension," first appears in relation to the phrase "having realized the Dhamma" at **792**, which Nidd I 67–68 explicates with the long series of principles that should be realized. These include the three characteristics, dependent origination in the orders of arising and cessation, the four noble truths, the pentad of origin, passing away, gratification, danger, and escape, and the insight that "whatever is subject to origination is all subject to cessation." The same list occurs at least nine times in Nidd II's comments on verses in the Pārāyana.

(2) Defilements

The Niddesa employs several modes of grouping together mental defilements, some apparently unique to itself. A set of seventeen defilements plays a fundamental role, first appearing at Nidd I 17 on **772**: lust, hatred, delusion, anger, hostility, denigration, insolence, envy, miserliness, hypocrisy, deceitfulness, obstinacy, vehemence, conceit, arrogance, vanity, and heedlessness.[26] From fear of missing anything, the passage continues by saying "all defilements, all misconduct, all disturbances, all fevers, all afflictions, all unwholesome volitional activities." The same series is repeated many times in both Nidd I and Nidd II. Māra's army is defined with this list at

Nidd I 68–69 (on **793**) and elsewhere—an increase over the ten armies of Māra in Sn itself at **436–38**.

Occasionally the goal of spiritual endeavor is expressed as the "quenching" or "stilling" of the items in this list. Thus when **1041** says that a bhikkhu is "quenched by having comprehended," Nidd II 38 first glosses comprehension with the formal definition of wisdom; it then explains "quenched"—*nibbuta,* which implies the attainment of nibbāna—as the extinguishing of the seventeen defilements along with all other defilements and unwholesome volitional activities. Where **1087** describes the mindful ones as "always peaceful" (*upasantā ca te sadā*), Nidd II 115–16 says that they are "continuously peaceful through the pacifying and extinguishing of lust, hatred, delusion . . . of all unwholesome volitional activities."

Another set of eight defilements appears peculiar to the Niddesa: lust, hatred, delusion, conceit, views, restlessness, doubt, and the latent tendencies. Since the "latent tendencies" is a group and not a single defilement, perhaps here it should be understood not as an addition to the list but as the proclivities to the previous seven defilements. Each of these is described as operating in a particular way, as on their first appearance where Nidd I 18, commenting on **772**, says that a person dwells "lustful because of lust, full of hate because of hatred, deluded because of delusion, bound down because of conceit, seizing wrongly by views, distracted because of restlessness, indecisive because of doubt, tenacious because of the latent tendencies." This set occurs, either explicitly or implicitly, multiple times in Nidd I, but only once in Nidd II. Six of these defilements—excluding restlessness and the latent tendencies—are included among the "seven darts" at Nidd I 306–11 (commenting on the word "dart" at **939**), where the seventh dart is sorrow. The passage provides formal definitions of the seven darts and explains how, when struck by them, a person "runs in different directions."

A pair of defilements used to explicate several important terms in the Aṭṭhakavagga is craving and views (*taṇhā* and *diṭṭhi*). Nidd I 69, having related the verb "categorize" (*vikappayeyya*) at **793** to the noun *kappa* (which I render "mental construct"), says there are two kinds of mental constructs: by way of craving and by way of views. The same two types, set in relation to either *kappa* or *pakappanā* ("mental formulation"), are at Nidd I 70, 183–84, 232, and 241–42. Other concepts explained on the basis of the dichotomy of craving and views are:

possessions (*pariggaha*): Nidd I 41–42 (on **779**), I 201–2 (on **872**)
dependency (*nissaya*): Nidd I 77–78 (on **800**), I 96 (on **811**), I 138–39 (on **839**), I 179 (on **856**), I 344–45 (on **957**)
preference (*purekkhāra*): Nidd I 70 (on **794**), I 81 (on **803**), I 155–56 (on **849**)
judgment (*vinicchaya*): Nidd I 194–95 (on **867**)
residence (*nivesanā*): Nidd I 78–79 (on **801**)

In proclaiming a path to liberation, the Suttanipāta stresses the need to renounce craving for sensual pleasures. A stock passage, introduced at Nidd I 1–2 (on **766**) and repeated throughout the Niddesa, distinguishes sensual pleasures (*kāma*) as twofold: *sensual objects*, which are the five sense objects and enjoyable commodities, and the *sensual defilement*, which is sensual lust, sensual desire, sensual craving, etc. The tie that binds beings to the round of rebirths is craving for existence, which is represented by a formula cited at Nidd I 34 (on **776**). It recurs at Nidd I 179 (on **856**), along with craving for nonexistence, and again at Nidd II 90 (on **1068**).

Since the relinquishment of views is a major topic in the Aṭṭhakavagga, the Niddesa often comments on views, spoken of either explicitly as *diṭṭhi* or implicitly as *dhammā*, which I render "teachings." Whether as views or as teachings, these constitute a domain from which the practitioner must keep aloof. The Niddesa glosses both words, *diṭṭhi* and *dhammā*, as the sixty-two views, with reference to the speculative views about the self and the world described in the Brahmajāla Sutta (DN 1). Occasionally the Niddesa mentions, along with the sixty-two speculative views, the twenty views about the self, the tenfold wrong view, and the ten extreme views, for instance at I 35–36 (on **777**) and I 80–81 (on **803**).

Nidd I 284–85 (on **929**) introduces an interesting stratification of defilements into the coarse, middling, and subtle levels, based on AN 3:101 (I 254). The subtle level is represented by a list of nine types of unwholesome thoughts, which recurs at Nidd I 379–80 and at Nidd II 112 and II 145. Nidd II 63–64 (on **1050**) explains the "acquisitions" (*upadhi*) from which suffering arises as ten kinds of *upadhi*, a wider scheme than the usual four *upadhi* of the commentaries.

The elimination of the defilements is usually signaled in the Niddesa by a fixed formula, which says that these or those defilements "have been abandoned, eradicated, allayed, tranquilized, made incapable of arising, burnt up by the fire of knowledge."[27] We find this formula used in Nidd I in relation to, among other things, the seven darts at I 42–43; the five or three kinds of barrenness at I 44–45; grasping at I 72; the sixty-two views at I 77–78; craving at I 78–79; anger at I 156–57; remorse at I 158–59. In Nidd II it is used in relation to disturbance at II 36–37 and II 53–55; craving at II 37; the "seamstress" at II 39–40; and anger, lust, hatred, and delusion at II 53–55. These are merely several examples of the use of this formula.

(3) Spiritual Practice

The Niddesa treats spiritual practice from the same monastic perspective that governs its root texts, emphasizing such ascetic values as renunciation, detachment, and meditation. The idea of renunciation is underscored by the comment on the word "alone" (*eka*, literally "one" or "singly"). "Alone" at **816** is said to be twofold at Nidd I 105–6: as the going forth and as separation from a group. The former is described as the act of entering upon the homeless life, the latter as resorting to remote lodgings suitable for meditation. At Nidd I 341–44 (on **956**) the Buddha is said to be "alone in the way designated the going forth; alone in the sense of being without a partner; alone in the sense of the abandoning of craving; alone as utterly devoid of lust, hatred, and delusion, as utterly without defilements; alone by having gone to the one-way path; alone by having awakened to the unsurpassed perfect enlightenment." In elaborating on this, mention is made of how, in the prime of life, he went forth with his parents weeping and by abandoning the "impediment" of wife and child. The paccekabuddha too, at Nidd II 210–12 (on **35**), is described in a similar way as solitary, except that he has awakened, not to perfect enlightenment, but to "the unsurpassed pacceka enlightenment."

The solitary lifestyle adopted by the act of renunciation leads to the practice of seclusion (*viveka*). The Niddesa proposes a sequence of three kinds of seclusion, introduced at Nidd I 19–20 (on **772**): bodily seclusion, mental seclusion (achieved through the jhānas, paths, and fruits), and seclusion from the acquisitions, which is the deathless nibbāna. In connection with mental seclusion, Nidd I 5–6 (on **768**) mentions two ways of avoiding sensual pleasures, by suppression and by eradication. The former takes place by reflecting on the dangers in sensual pleasures and by concentration; the latter takes place by attaining the four world-transcending paths. This distinction plays a prominent role in the commentaries, which expand the means of abandoning to five (as at pp. 362–65).

Proper motivation is necessary to give direction to the spiritual life, and the overriding motive for ethical and contemplative practice in Early Buddhism is the attainment of nibbāna. Commenting on the phrase "one should train for one's own nibbāna" at **940**, Nidd I 312–13 says "one should train in the higher good behavior, in the higher mind, in the higher wisdom, for the extinguishing of one's own lust, hatred, delusion." The same is said at Nidd II 80–81 commenting on **1061**. The Niddesa consistently explains the higher good behavior as restraint by the monastic rules, the higher mind by the formula for the four jhānas, and the higher wisdom as the insight into arising and passing away and the understanding of the four noble truths (as at Nidd I 28–29, commenting on **775**). Where **942** says one should have "a mind set on nibbāna," Nidd I 315–16 explains that one practices all virtuous deeds not for the sake of a blissful rebirth but "for the purpose of detachment, leaning toward nibbāna, inclining toward nibbāna, bent upon nibbāna." It reinforces this point with some inspired verses not found elsewhere in the Pāli Canon (pp. 1196–97).

Since the foundation of monastic training is virtuous behavior, the Niddesa fills in the root text with details about monastic discipline. Where stanza **852** describes the monk as "not a schemer" (*akuhako*), Nidd I 163–65 explains three types of "scheming" (*kuhanā*), modes of deceptive behavior used to win respect and offerings from laypeople. Since the same verse says that the monk should be courteous (*appagabbho*), that is, without impudence, Nidd I 166–68 offers a detailed explanation of three kinds of impudence, bodily, verbal, and mental. One who is courteous behaves in precisely the opposite ways. Nidd I 168–69 continues with an explanation of unrepulsive (*ajegucho*) by detailing the ways a monk is morally repulsive; by abandoning these he becomes unrepulsive. Where **854** says that the monk "does not train from a desire for gain," Nidd I 173 provides a detailed account of how a bad monk trains from a desire for gain while a disciplined monk trains "only for the sake of taming himself, for the sake of calming himself, for the sake of his attainment of nibbāna." Stanza **927** mentions the modes of livelihood that a monk should avoid, such as casting spells, fortune-telling, and astrology, which Nidd I 280–81 elucidates with examples of each.

Spiritual training requires the use of intelligence, which in the root text is indicated by the term *paṭibhāna*, "ingenuity." Where **853** says the monk should be "gifted with ingenuity," Nidd I 171 explains this by way of three kinds of ingenuity: in learning, that is, in study of the scriptures; in interrogation, the ability to skillfully reply to questions about the Dhamma; and in achievement, mastery over the various practices. The perfection of understanding comes by directly knowing the principles comprised under the sphere of comprehension, usually described by the fixed formula referred to earlier, ranging from the three characteristics to the insight that whatever originates is subject to cessation. However, other approaches to developing wisdom are suggested in the root text and expanded upon by the Niddesa. When an inquirer asks how consciousness ceases, the Buddha (at **1111**) says one should not seek delight in feeling. Nidd II 146–47 elucidates this with a long passage on the contemplation of feeling: not seeking delight in feeling internally, externally, internally and externally, and so forth, down to discerning feeling by way of its origin, passing away, gratification, danger, and the escape from it.

The canonical text recommends full understanding (*pariññā*) of various domains of knowledge: of contact (at **778**), of perception (at **779**), and of craving (at **1082**). The Niddesa—respectively at I 37–38, I 40, and II 109—explains each of these by way of the three kinds of full understanding mentioned earlier: full understanding of the known, full understanding by scrutinization, and full understanding by abandoning. This scheme, which plays an important role in the commentarial map of the practice, expands the idea of "full understanding" beyond its usage in the Nikāyas, where it is considered an exclusive achievement of the arahant, to the stages of insight even preceding stream-entry.

Commenting on the injunction "Look upon the world as empty" at **1119**, Nidd II 164–69 gives a detailed account of how to contemplate emptiness. It first states that one sees the world as empty on two grounds: by considering its occurrence as beyond mastery and by contemplating it as consisting of hollow conditioned things. With quotations from the Nikāyas, it then proceeds to explain how to see the world as empty in six ways, ten ways, and twelve ways.

(4) The Spiritual Ideal

As the spiritual ideal of the Suttanipāta, the arahant is variously described in the Niddesa. Nidd I 58–59, commenting on how the arahant no longer takes up and lets go (at **787**), says: "The arahant has overcome grasping and letting go, transcended growth and decline. He has lived the spiritual life, completed the practice, finished the journey, reached the goal; for him there is no more renewed existence with its wandering on in birth and death." Where the root text (at **795**) says that the brahmin no longer grasps anything, Nidd I 71 says that for the arahant "there is nothing grasped, seized, adhered to, clung to, resolved upon." Nidd I 82–83 explains how the arahant is *tādī*, "impartial," in five ways: "impartial toward the desirable and undesirable; impartial because he has renounced; impartial because he has crossed over; impartial because he is freed; and impartial as a descriptive term." Stanza **902** speaks of one "who has no passing away or rebirth," and Nidd I 232–33 identifies this person as "the arahant, one whose influxes have been destroyed, for whom there is no going or coming, no going in time, no various states of existence, passing away and rebirth, production and dissolution, birth, old age, and death; for whom these have been abandoned and burnt up by the fire of knowledge."

The Niddesa celebrates the arahant under other designations, the most prevalent being muni. Nidd I 41–42 (on **779**) gives a detailed explanation of this term, mentioning six kinds of munis: householder munis, homeless munis, trainee munis, arahant munis, pacceka munis, and the buddhas, the "munis among munis." Of these, it is the last three that represent the spiritual ideal. Nidd II 97–98 (on **1074**) has an illuminating passage that explains how the muni is liberated and cannot be designated. This continues into Nidd II 99–100 (on **1076**) with a statement of how the liberated one cannot be measured and has passed beyond all the pathways of speech. This same attainment is described more analytically at Nidd II 29–30 (on **1037**) with an account of how volitionally active consciousness ceases in stages with each of the successive path attainments, until finally, when the arahant attains the nibbāna element without residue remaining, all name-and-form utterly ceases.

As the supreme muni and discoverer of the path, the Buddha is extolled by the Niddesa in ways that refer back to themes in the Nikāyas and extend beyond them into new territory. Nidd I 104 (on **815**) offers a detailed explanation of the word *bhagavā*, "Blessed One," which plays on verbal roots and near-homonyms. Nidd I 344–45 (on **957**) gives an explanation of the word *buddha* that concludes by saying that "Buddha" is not a name given by others but "a name pertaining to the end of emancipation, a designation accruing to the buddhas, the blessed ones, along with realization, with the obtaining of the omniscient knowledge at the foot of the bodhi tree." The passage continues at Nidd I 345–46 with an explanation of how the Buddha is *tādī*, "an impartial one," commented on earlier in relation to the arahant. Nidd II 140–41 (on **1105**) states that the Buddha has "gone beyond all phenomena" through direct knowledge, full understanding, abandoning, development, realization, and attainment. An inquirer (at **915**) addresses the Buddha as *mahesi*, "great rishi," and Nidd I 250–51 explains this to mean that he sought, searched for, and pursued all great qualities culminating in the great supreme goal, the deathless nibbāna. The explanation involves a word play that takes *mahesi* to be derived from *mahantaṃ esi* rather than, correctly, as a Pāli formation of *maharṣi*.

The brahmin youth Mettagū (at **1049**) calls the Buddha a

Veda-master, and Nidd II 55–57 explains this brahmanic term by imposing on it a new meaning consonant with the Buddha's teaching: "It is the knowledge of the four paths that is called the Vedas. Through those knowledges, the Blessed One has gone to the end of birth, old age, and death, has reached the end, gone to the peak, reached the peak, gone to the limit, reached the limit . . . gone to the deathless, reached the deathless, gone to nibbāna, reached nibbāna." At **1059**, where the Buddha is actually called a brahmin, Nidd II 75–76 explains: "One is a brahmin because one has expelled bad unwholesome qualities that are defiling, that lead to renewed existence, that are troublesome, that result in suffering, and that lead to future birth, old age, and death."

In the Nikāyas, the Buddha is called *cakkhumā*, literally "one who has eyes," which I render as "the One with Vision." The suttas ascribe various kinds of vision to the Buddha: the divine eye, the eye of wisdom, and the buddha eye. He is also extolled with the epithet "universal eye." In Sn, at **921**, the Buddha is hailed as "one with opened eyes" (*vivaṭacakkhu*), and Nidd I 261–65 uses this as an opportunity to collect the Buddha's types of vision into a set of "five eyes": the fleshly eye, the divine eye, the wisdom eye, the buddha eye, and the universal eye. The passage explains the universal eye as "the knowledge of omniscience" (*sabbaññutaññāṇa*). Nidd I 130 (on **834**) extols the Buddha's omniscience in a passage that goes far beyond anything said in the Nikāyas: "Whether past, future, or present, all phenomena in all modes enter the range of the Blessed One's portal of knowledge. . . . Just as all fish and tortoises from the whales on down move around in the great ocean, so the world with Māra and Brahmā, this population with its ascetics and brahmins, its devas and human beings, moves around in the Buddha's knowledge."[28]

A Thematic Guide to the Verses of the Suttanipāta

Brahmins
- arahant as 519, 620–47, 790–95, 801–3, 911–14, 1059–60
- degeneration of 284–315
- pure food and 242–48
- who is a brahmin? 137–42, 594–656
- who is an outcast? 116–42

Buddha
- birth of 679–98
- going forth of 405–24
- plowman, as 77–80
- praises of 161–67, 176–80, 224, 233–34, 343–54, 376–84, 538–47, 548–53, 570–73, 955–57, 1131–45
- self-praise 18–29, 467–78, 558–61
- striving of 425–49

Craving 740–41, 776–78, 1085–87

Death and loss 574–93, 804–9

Debates and disputes 824–34, 862–63, 878–94, 895–910

Emancipation/liberation
- by non-craving 354–55, 1089
- by final knowledge 1105–7
- of mind and wisdom 725–27
- of perception 1071–74

Field of merits 463–78, 482–86, 487–509, 568–69

Four noble truths 724–27

Happiness and suffering 759–65

Hell 667–78

Lay ethics
- blessings 259–66
- downfall, causes of 91–115
- friendship 253–55
- lay disciple's duty 393–404
- misconduct 116–34, 242–48
- various 181–82, 185–89

Liberated one
- arahant, as 644

A Guide to the Suttas

I The Chapter on the Serpent (Uragavagga)

I,1 The Serpent (Uraga Sutta), verses 1–17

The Suttanipāta opens with a poem of seventeen four-line stanzas in each of which the second couplet is a refrain: "that bhikkhu gives up the here and the beyond as a serpent sheds its old worn-out skin." The bhikkhu compared to the serpent is one who eliminates a particular defilement or deluded mode of cognition and thereby attains the state held up as the goal of the practice, the giving up of "the here and the beyond." Each verse speaks of a double act of relinquishment, both components of which might be compared to the snake's shedding of its worn-out skin. First there is the discarding of the defilement or deluded cognition, and second the giving up of the here and beyond. The two stand in a causal relationship, which can be seen to mirror the middle two noble truths, the defilements and delusions representing the truth of the origin of suffering and their relinquishment the truth of cessation. The result is an experience of internal release here and now and ultimate release from the round of repeated existence.

The expression that recurs in the refrain *orapāraṃ*, "the here and the beyond," might be seen as problematic, for it is used here in a sense that differs from the way this dichotomy is typically depicted in the suttas. Generally, in the Nikāyas, the here (*oraṃ*) or "near shore" (*orimaṃ tīraṃ*) represents saṃsāra, the round of birth, aging, and death, and the beyond (*pāraṃ*) or "far shore" (*pārimaṃ tīraṃ*) represents nibbāna, the ending of the round. The near shore is described as risky and dangerous, the far shore as secure and free of danger, and the aim of the practice is to cross from the here to the beyond, from the near shore to the far shore, as in the famous simile of the raft (at MN I 134). This metaphor plays a prominent role in Sn as well, particularly in the Pārāyanavagga (chap. V), "The Way to the Beyond." In the Uraga Sutta, however, the giving up of "the here and the beyond" cannot mean that the liberated monk transcends the duality of saṃsāra and nibbāna, an interpretation that would be contrary to the whole tenor of the Nikāyas. "The here and the beyond" must be conceived in relation to the dualities found *within* the sphere of conditioned existence, "here" likely representing existence in this present world, "beyond" existence in future lives, or "here" representing existence in the desire realm, "beyond" existence in the realms of rebirth corresponding to the higher stages of concentration.[29]

The first seven verses speak in turn of giving up certain defilements—anger, lust, craving, conceit, and so forth. Verses **8–13** are constructed around the idea of "neither running too far nor running back." Verse **8** connects this idea to the overcoming of "proliferation" (*papañca*), a term that suggests the diversity of the world as well as the expansion of metaphysical speculation; verse **9** connects the motif to knowledge of the world as devoid of substantial reality (*vitathaṃ*), a word that Pj II carefully qualifies as meaning not that the world is nonexistent but that "it lacks a real nature in the way conceived by foolish people on account of the defilements, namely, as permanent or pleasurable or attractive or self." Verses **10–13** relate the insight into the world's unreality to mental purification: the absence of greed, lust, hatred, and delusion. The verses in the final group, **14–17**, return more directly to the idea of eliminating defilements. In this group we find several clusters of defilements that play prominent roles in the Nikāyas: in **14** the latent tendencies (*anusayā*) and unwholesome roots (*akusalā mūlā*), and in **17** the five hindrances (*pañcanīvaraṇā*).

The Uraga Sutta has parallels in texts stemming from other schools of Early Buddhism. Two such parallels are included in their respective Dharmapadas. The Gāndhārī Dharmapada includes the serpent verses at the end of its chapter on the bhikkhu[30] and the Patna Dharmapada in an independent chapter that concludes the work. The third parallel, the Udānavarga, a Sanskrit work of the Dharmapada genre, includes the verses in two chapters: six appear at the end of the Puṣpavarga and thirty-two at the end of the Bhikṣuvarga (among these are the six of the Puṣpavarga, which thus occur twice in this work).

The fact that the verses occur at the beginning of Sn and at the end of their respective chapters in the parallels suggests, first, that from an early period the verses constituted an integral group united by the refrain with its simile of the snake's skin; and second, that they were added to their respective collections at a relatively late date.[31] This, however, does not necessarily entail that the verses themselves are late. To the contrary, as Jayawickrama remarks, "an examination of the Uraga Sutta in the various aspects of language, meter, style, doctrine, and ideology shows that it is a comparatively old sutta."[32]

The four parallel versions have been collated and compared by Bhikkhu Ānandajoti.[33] By correlating the different versions, several tentative conclusions can be drawn about the composition of the Pāli Uraga verses. Since **6** and **10–13** of the Uraga Sutta have no counterparts in the parallels, it seems likely that they are later additions. The simplest version is that in Gāndhārī, which has only ten verses; the Udānavarga version is the most elaborate, with twenty-six unique verses, only eleven of which correspond to the Pāli version. On the premise that greater simplicity is a sign of greater antiquity, Ānandajoti concludes that "we have preserved in the Gāndhārī the original core of verses, out of which variations have arisen in the other versions through keyword substitution."

‖ Parallels from other traditions: GDhp 81–90; PDhp 398–414; Udāna-v 18.21 A–F, 32.55–80.

I,2 Dhaniya (Dhaniya Sutta), verses 18–34

This sutta is a dialogue entirely in verse between the Buddha and a herdsman named Dhaniya, who meet on the herdman's estate near the Mahī River. The syntax of the poem, according to Jayawickrama, "shows that its language belongs to an early stratum of Pāli" (PBR 1977, 152). The poem can be divided into four parts. The first, **18–29**, is a challenge-and-response dialogue between the two protagonists. In each challenge verse, Dhaniya praises the comfort and security of the household life, inviting the sky god to send down rain, perhaps to confirm his sense of security. Responding verse by verse, the Buddha adopts Dhaniya's images but reinterprets them to praise the superiority of the homeless life. Verse **30**, a transitional stanza, is an interjection by the narrator, who reports that a great cloud has unleashed a downpour of rain. In the third part, **31–32**, Dhaniya, perhaps shaken by the sudden downpour, yields to the Buddha. He and his wife go for refuge and ask to "lead the spiritual life" under the Blessed One, so that they might go "beyond birth and death" and make an end of suffering. The Pāli expression, *jātimaraṇassa pāragū*, harks back to the Uraga Sutta but uses the word *pāra* in the familiar way, as meaning the "far shore" beyond the sea of birth and death.

In the fourth part, **33–34**, Māra takes over the role of challenger and praises "acquisitions" (*upadhi*)—here children and cattle—as a source of joy. The Buddha responds by articulating the viewpoint of the renunciant, who sees acquisitions as a cause of sorrow. This exchange appears to be an interpolation, for the sutta would have been complete if it had ended with Dhaniya's act of going for refuge. The same exchange with Māra occurs in SN 4:8 (I 108). By reason of similarity of themes, it is possible the pair of verses was taken from that source (or from a floating store of verses) and inserted into the Dhaniya Sutta.[34]

I,3 The Rhinoceros Horn (Khaggavisāṇa Sutta), verses 35–75

Like the Uraga Sutta, this discourse is based on a simile comparing the ideal ascetic to an animal, or part of an animal. Again, like the Uraga Sutta, the refrain states this simile in each verse, with the exception of stanza **45**. The title, along with the word used in the refrain, is ambiguous and has been the subject of a long-standing debate. The Pāli word *khagga* (Skt *khaḍga*) has two meanings, "rhinoceros" and "sword."[35] If *khagga* is taken as "rhinoceros," then *khaggavisāṇa* is a *tappurisa* (dependent) compound meaning "the horn of a rhinoceros." If *khagga* is taken as a sword, the term is a *bahubbīhi* (possessive) compound meaning "that which has a sword for its horn," namely, the rhinoceros itself.

The commentaries to Sn, including the Niddesa, explain *khaggavisāṇa* as a *tappurisa* compound meaning "the horn of a rhinoceros."[36] In my translation I have followed this explanation. Modern scholars are split over the meaning of the expression. In his "Critical Analysis of the Suttanipāta" (PBR 1977, 22–23) Jayawickrama argued strongly in favor of taking *khaggavisāṇa* as the rhinoceros rather than its horn. But several decades later he apparently changed his mind, for in his translation of Sn he renders it "the horn of a rhinoceros." Norman (2001, 38), too, favors this interpretation, writing: "When the Pāli can be so translated [as 'the rhinoceros horn'], when the earliest interpretations take it that way, when the Jain tradition supports it, and when the Indian rhinoceros is unique among animals in India in having only one horn, it seems certain to me that the reference is to the single horn. . . ." Salomon (2000, 13), in contrast, suggests that the original expression may have been deliberately ambiguous: "Since both interpretations are well justified on linguistic and natural grounds . . . there is no conclusive way to decide which position is the correct one, and I prefer to solve, or perhaps avoid, the problem by declaring that they are both right and that the ambiguity is perhaps an intentional and creative one." Dhivan Thomas Jones (2014) also argues for the ambiguity of the original expression but apparently prefers taking it to refer to the animal itself.

In contrast to these scholars, I do not think the expression, in the older canonical texts, is ambiguous. While I do not take commentaries to be infallible, since an exegetical work as ancient as the Niddesa explains *khaggavisāṇa* as the horn of a rhinoceros, this to my mind is a powerful argument in support of this interpretation. The Jātakas, moreover, several times mention *khagga* as a kind of animal, presumably the rhinoceros.[37] The Milindapañha describes King Milinda, on encountering Nāgasena and his entourage, as "frightened, terrified, and agitated, like an elephant surrounded by rhinoceroses (*khagga*)."[38] The *Vedic Index of Names and Subjects* (Macdonell and Keith 1912, 1:214) indirectly supports my interpretation when it states: "Khaḍga is the reading in the Maitrāyaṇī Saṃhitā of the name of an animal which, in the text of the Vājasaneyi Saṃhitā, variously appears as Khaṅga and Khaḍga. The rhinoceros seems clearly to be meant."

Thus if *khagga* is the rhinoceros, then *khaggavisāṇa* is the horn of that animal. I see no particular problem with the verb *care*, "to live, to move, to wander," for the point of the simile is not that one should live solitary as a rhinoceros horn lives solitary (admittedly a bizarre idea) but that one should live solitary as a rhinoceros horn is solitary. Pāli verse can allow such oblique similes. In texts of a later period, like the Apadāna Commentary, *khaggavisāṇa* is explained to represent both the animal and its horn.[39] But this is not so in the canonical texts, which do not use *khaggavisāṇa* elsewhere to designate the animal.

Buddhist tradition ascribes the verses in this sutta to paccekabuddhas. Each verse, according to the commentary, was uttered by a different paccekabuddha, either as a joyous declaration on the occasion of his own enlightenment (*udānagāthā*) or as a declaration of his enlightenment to others (*vyākaraṇagāthā*). The commentary provides the background story to each paccekabuddha's renunciation and enlightenment. The Khaggavisāṇa Sutta itself *does not* ascribe the verses to paccekabuddhas, but this connection is made elsewhere in the Pāli tradition and in parallel texts of other Early Buddhist schools. The Apadāna, a verse collection in the Khuddaka Nikāya stemming from a somewhat later period than the older parts of the Sutta Piṭaka, includes all the verses of the Khaggavisāṇa Sutta in the section called Paccekabuddha-apadāna. An introductory verse says that when paccekabuddhas assemble, they declare to one another the dangers they realized, the circumstances that occasioned their dispassion, and how they attained enlightenment.[40] The "rhinoceros horn" verses are purportedly the record of these declarations.

The Apadāna version begins with several verses in which the Buddha states that paccekabuddhas "performed services to the buddhas of the past but did not gain liberation in the teachings of the conquerors. Motivated by a sense of urgency, even without the buddhas, through their very sharp wisdom, even on the basis of a trifling object, they attained pacceka enlightenment. Apart from me, in all the world there is none who equals a paccekabuddha."[41] After several more introductory verses, the Buddha recites the rhinoceros verses. These begin with a verse not found in the Khaggavisāṇa Sutta but which could easily fit in there.[42]

The paccekabuddha is a somewhat enigmatic figure rarely mentioned in the main Nikāyas. In the scale of holy beings, the paccekabuddha is generally placed below a sammā sambuddha but above the arahant disciple (see MN III 254; AN IV 394–

95). The Puggalapaññatti, an Abhidhamma treatise, defines a paccekabuddha as one who "on his own awakens to the truths but does not attain all-knowledge with respect to them or mastery over the powers."[43] In this respect, the paccekabuddha is contrasted with a perfectly enlightened buddha, who attains all-knowledge with respect to the truths and mastery over the powers. The commentaries explain that paccekabuddhas, contrary to a common stereotype, are not completely silent. They give brief teachings to others and even accept disciples. They do not, however, attempt to establish an institution to preserve and propagate their teachings, nor, it seems, do they present their teachings in any systematic form.

If we accept the traditional ascription of the Khaggavisāṇa Sutta to paccekabuddhas, the verses give us some insight into their character. They are wary of forming bonds of affection; they see peril in intimacy; they esteem renunciation of sensual pleasures; they call on those who share their aspiration to renounce even their wives and children; they prize freedom above companionship; they are willing to endure hardship in order to protect their freedom. Their ideal is to be like a lion not frightened by sounds, like the wind not caught in a net, like a lotus untainted by water.[44]

Alternatively, if the old tradition that these verses were spoken by paccekabuddhas is rejected, the poem might be seen as expressing the attitude that prevailed among a certain segment of Buddhist ascetics during an early phase of Buddhist history. Some scholars have even maintained that the poem—along with other suttas on the muni ideal—represents a premonastic phase of Buddhism. Jayawickrama, for instance (at 1976, 79), sees the poem as reflecting a stage of Buddhist history when there was "no organized monastic body; but on the contrary there were the *munayo* (ascetics in general) or the bhikkhus who were expected to lead the life of a muni." Saddhātissa, too, in the introduction to his translation of Sn (1994, ix), distinguishes four stages of Buddhist literary development. He calls the first "the ascetic stage," which he differentiates from the second, the "monastic stage." The ascetic stage, he says, was "embodied by the oldest strata of the Sutta-Nipāta," when the Buddha's teaching was "austere and stoical so as to lead to steadfastness of purpose and endeavor, which would culminate in the final release from the unsatisfactoriness of mundane life."

This position, however, has been criticized as flawed and contrary to well documented accounts of the history of Buddhism. Salomon, for example, writes (2000, 15) that "such conclusions seem somewhat simplistic, even naïve, in light of a more modern understanding of the history of Buddhism. . . . Indeed, there is no clear evidence that there ever was, in any meaningful sense, a 'premonastic period' of Buddhism." Salomon sees the verses as expressing not an alternative to monasticism but the attitudes prevalent in the ascetic tradition of forest-dwelling monks. I would see the verses as expressing the attitude adopted not among forest monks in general but by certain meditative monks who upheld a strongly individualistic approach to practice, rejecting communal life even in small hermitages in favor of unsettled wandering and complete solitude. Among the famous disciples of the Buddha, Mahākassapa may have been the foremost model for this way of life.[45]

This, however, does not entail that such a lifestyle was the preferred paradigm for Buddhist monasticism even in its earliest phase. If the canonical account of the early history of the Sangha, as recorded in the Vinaya Mahāvagga and parallel texts from other schools, is at all trustworthy, it is clear that the Buddha established a monastic community soon after he began his teaching career. Although the emphasis in monastic life may have shifted over time, from homeless wandering and rigorous meditation practice to learning and monastic discipline, a monastic order with a distinct identity and formal procedures of ordination seems to have been integral to the Buddha's mission from the outset.

There are two known parallels to the Khaggavisāṇa verses from other Early Buddhist traditions. The Mahāvastu, a work of the Lokottaravādins (a branch of the Mahāsāṃghikas), has twelve verses that are also ascribed to paccekabuddhas. A version inscribed on a birch bark scroll in Gāndhārī, recently discovered, has forty verses. It seems to have circulated as an independent text rather than as part of a larger collection (as indeed was likely the case with the Pāli version).[46] As with the Pāli version, the Gāndhārī verses are not ascribed to paccekabuddhas or to any other speaker.

Pāli parallel: Ap I 8–13 (90–131). Parallels from other traditions: Sanskrit: Mvu 357–59; Gāndhārī: Salomon 2000, 115–201

I,4 Kasibhāradvāja (Kasibhāradvāja Sutta), verses 76–82

This is another dialogue that takes the form of challenge and response, similar to the Dhaniya Sutta but here in a mixed prose and verse format. The dialogue takes place between the Buddha and a brahmin named Kasibhāradvāja, "Bhāradvāja the Plowman." It seems odd that a brahmin is engaged in plowing, but brahmins were given grants of land by the kings as a reward for their services, and it is possible this brahmin took to cultivating crops on land he received in such a way.

The sutta can be divided into two major sections. The first, which includes the prose introduction and verses **76–80**, relates Kasibhāradvāja's challenge and the Buddha's rejoinder. The second, which extends from the prose following verse **80** to the end, describes the brahmin's response to the Buddha's rejoinder and the subsequent events.

In contrast to the Dhaniya Sutta, in which verses alternate in a contest of wits, in this sutta the Buddha is challenged only at the beginning, when Kasibhāradvāja criticizes the Buddha for living as a parasite, expecting others to feed him when he does not "plow and sow." The Buddha rejects this charge, declaring that he does in fact plow and sow. When the brahmin expresses puzzlement at this remark, the Buddha uses the terminology of agriculture to describe his process of spiritual training, which has the deathless as its fruit (**77–80**).

At this point the brahmin is won over and offers the Buddha a dish of milk-rice. The Buddha refuses it on the ground that he does not accept "food over which verses have been recited." He instructs the brahmin to throw the food away, and its disposal is accompanied by wondrous displays that fill the brahmin with awe, apparently inspiring him with faith. The concluding prose paragraph tells us that he goes for refuge, requests monastic ordination, and becomes an arahant.

It is of interest to note that the Saṃyutta parallel, SN 7:11 (I 171–73), ends with Kasibhāradvāja merely taking refuge as a lay follower. This disparity in the conclusions of the two suttas shows how the prose framework of a text in verse was not fixed but could vary depending on the oral tradition through which the text was transmitted.

> Pāli parallel: SN 7:11. Parallels from other traditions: Chinese: SĀ 98 (T II 207a10–27b28); SĀ[2] 264 (T II 466b18–466c11); SĀ[3] 1 (T II 493a7–493b11)

I,5 Cunda (Cunda Sutta), verses 83–90

In the Pāli Canon, this discourse occurs only in the Suttanipāta. The interlocutor is Cunda the smith's son, who offered the Buddha his final meal (related at DN II 127). The sutta has a parallel in the Sanskrit Mahāparinirvāṇa Sūtra, which is preserved only in fragmentary form; a full translation is found in the Chinese translation of the Dīrghāgama and in individual Chinese translations of the sūtra. The conversation is not recorded in the Pāli Mahāparinibbāna Sutta, where the Buddha received his last meal from Cunda. The background story to the discourse as told briefly in the Skt version of the sūtra corresponds to the account in the Pāli commentary.

According to both sources, an "evil bhikkhu" misappropriated a golden dish on which Cunda had served the meal. Though the miscreant thought he was unobserved, Cunda had caught sight of him. He did not reproach the monk on the spot, but in the evening he went to the Buddha to inquire about types of ascetics. This gave the Buddha the opportunity to explain how there are monks who assume the appearance of ascetics while violating their discipline. Against this background, the Buddha must have considered it necessary to warn lay devotees not to assume that all who wore the ochre robe were worthy of reverence and support.

The sutta distinguishes four kinds of ascetics. The first (at **86**), "the conqueror of the path," is the Buddha himself. The next two verses (**87–88**) describe the monk who serves as a teacher of the path—by implication an arahant—and the "one who lives on the path," a category that includes trainees (*sekha*) and virtuous worldlings. The fourth type, denounced in **89**, is the corrupt monk, a "defiler of the path." The closing verse **90**, which seems fitted to the situation at hand, admonishes laypeople not to let their encounters with bogus monks destroy their faith in the Sangha.

Parallels from other traditions: Sanskrit: Mahāparinirvāṇa Sūtra §26 (Waldschmidt 1951, 252–64); Chinese: DĀ 2 (T I no. 1, 18b9–18c6); T I no. 5, 167c6–168a11; T I no. 6, 183b10–183b27; T I no. 7, 196c12–196c23 (part-parallel)

I,6 Downfall (Parābhava Sutta), verses 91–115

The Parābhava Sutta is one of several discourses in the Suttanipāta that describe the ethical life appropriate for householders. The discourse takes the form of a dialogue between the Buddha and an unnamed deity. It unfolds in a dramatic format through a sequence of question-and-response verses governed by a repetitive pattern. The deity asks about a cause of downfall, the Buddha responds; the deity asks about another cause of downfall, the Buddha responds again; and so forth until twelve answers have been given.

The ethical guidelines advocated in the sutta, while representative of the Buddha's teachings for lay followers, are not unique to Buddhism but epitomize the shared ethical values of ancient Indian culture. With a few exceptions they share a common platform with Jainism and mainstream Brahmanism. The norms of conduct they prescribe are the prerequisites for both personal and communal well-being, establishing an ethical foundation for a social order that exemplifies harmony, kindness, and respect for others. But their impact extends beyond the present life, for they operate within the matrix of the law of kamma, according to which bad actions lead to a bad rebirth and future misery, while good actions lead to a fortunate rebirth and future well-being. The causes of downfall mentioned in the sutta include associating with bad people, indolence, deceptive speech, miserliness, social pride, sexual promiscuity, indulgence in liquor, fondness for gambling, and so forth. The sutta ends on an affirmative note, declaring that the wise person who avoids these causes of downfall "passes on to an auspicious world" (*sa lokaṃ bhajate sivaṃ*).

I,7 The Outcast (Vasala Sutta), verses 116–42

This is the first of five discourses in the Suttanipāta that represent the Buddha's response to Brahmanism.[47] The prose introduction, which grounds the discourse, points to two areas of tension that pitted the Buddha and his followers against the brahmin traditionalists. One concerns the relationship between the brahmins and the *samaṇas*, the renunciant ascetics, whom the brahmins spurned because they rejected the authority of the Vedas and the brahmin claim to superior social status. The other was the attitude toward the caste system. While the brahmins regarded the ordering of society into four social classes (*varṇa*), with themselves at the top, as divine, ordained by the supreme god Brahmā, the Buddha considered the caste system a mere conventional arrangement which, in his time, had become morally pernicious, consigning a substantial portion of the population—the outcasts—to almost subhuman status. His meeting with the brahmin Aggikabhāradvāja gives him a chance to offer a fresh perspective on the meaning of outcast and to expose the moral contradictions of the caste system.[48]

Even without the background story, the verses offer a forceful challenge to the brahmanic concept of purity and the belief that birth was a valid determinant of personal worth. The moral faults that define the outcast in the Buddha's view are similar to those laid out in the Parābhava Sutta, but here they are more closely affiliated with the Buddhist code of precepts. Verses **117–18** pertain to the first precept; **119–21** to the second; **122**, **129**, and **131** to the fourth; and **123** to the third. Verse **135** refers obliquely to Pārājika 4 of the Pātimokkha, the rule that prohibits a monk from making false claims to spiritual attainment.

The Vasala Sutta goes beyond the denunciation of moral evils and explicitly addresses the issue of caste identity. With verse **136** it repudiates the brahmanic belief that one's social class defines one's moral worth. Instead it asserts that a person's moral worth is determined by one's action. Thus the Buddha here turns the words *brāhmaṇa* and *vasala* on their head, redefining them in terms of character and conduct. This subtly undermines the foundation on which the system rested, namely, the assumption that a person's spiritual worth was determined by birth.

> Parallels from other traditions: Chinese: SĀ 102 (T II 28b19–29b20); SĀ[2] 268 (T II 467b27–468b18)

I,8 Loving-Kindness (Metta Sutta), verses 143–52

The Metta Sutta (or Karaṇiyametta Sutta) is the most popular discourse in the Theravāda canon. It belongs to a group of three discourses—along with the Ratana and Mahāmaṅgala Suttas—considered "protective suttas" (*paritta*) and sources of blessing. The theme of the sutta, as is clear from the title, is the practice of meditation on loving-kindness. While this meditation is open to everyone, monastics and laypeople alike, the sutta describes the practice in the context of monastic life, as is clear from the virtues inculcated in the opening stanzas: humility, contentment, frugality, sense restraint, and courtesy toward lay supporters.

The verses can be divided into four sections. The first, which consists of **143**, **144**, and **145**ab, lays down the ethical prerequisites for the meditation on loving-kindness. The second section, from **145**cd through **147**, constitutes the thematic meditation on loving-kindness, summed up in the opening and closing benediction: "May all beings be inwardly happy." This benevolent wish is extended to beings of various sizes and shapes, and the good wishes continue into **148**, which seems to be an appendix to the meditation proper. The third section, **149–51**, describes the intensification and expansion of loving-kindness until it suffuses the whole world. The fourth section, **152**, states the benefit of the practice.

A technical system lies behind the apparently simple words of this final verse. The first couplet alludes to the qualities of a stream-enterer: not adopting wrong views, impeccable conduct, and insight into the four noble truths. The second implies that by using the meditation on loving-kindness as a basis for insight, the disciple abandons sensual lust and attains the stage of non-returner, thereby taking rebirth in the form realm and "never coming back to the bed of a womb."

|| Pāli parallel: Khp 9

I,9 Hemavata (Hemavata Sutta), verses 153–80

The Hemavata Sutta is the first of three suttas in which the Buddha engages in a discussion with yakkhas, demonic beings depicted as temperamentally violent but capable of spiritual realization. Unlike the other two (I,10 and II,5), this one is entirely in verse, and the two yakkhas who approach the Buddha are favorably disposed to him, unlike the belligerent yakkhas in the other two suttas. Sātāgira speaks like a well-informed devotee; his friend Hemavata speaks as a curious inquirer who seeks to ascertain the Buddha's credentials. Behind the façade of the mythical characters, we can detect a real-life scene in which a knowledgeable lay Buddhist is trying to convince a friend to come to the monastery and ask the monks about the Dhamma.

The sutta can be divided into four parts. In the first (**153–63**[B]), Hemavata asks Sātāgira about the Buddha's qualities and Sātāgira responds to each question in a way designed to win his friend's approval. This dialogue, affirming the Buddha's purity in bodily action, speech, and mind, serves almost as a catechism on basic Buddhist virtues. The second part has a transitional function. The yakkhas decide to visit the Buddha and ask him about "release from the snare of death" (**164–67**). The third part consists of Hemavata's questions and the Buddha's responses (**168–75**). The yakkha's questions, posed as riddles, elicit a teaching on the six sense bases that expresses the same message conveyed more elaborately by such prose discourses as SN 12:44 (II 73–74) and SN 35:28 (IV 19–20). And in the fourth part (**176–80**), they praise the Buddha, go for refuge, and proclaim their devotion to the teaching. The two paeans of praise are eloquent poetic expressions of religious devotion.

Several verses of the Hemavata Sutta are spread across the Devatāsaṃyutta and Devaputtasaṃyutta of the Saṃyutta Nikāya as follows:

165ab & **166**a–c = SN 1:30, v. 1a–e (I 16)
170d = SN 1:30, v. 1f
171 = SN 1:30, v. 2
168–69 = SN 1:70 (I 41), but with no ascriptions
173–75 = SN 2:15 (I 53), but with several differences in readings
177 = SN 1:45 (I 33)

While it is possible that the verses in the Saṃyutta Nikāya result from the dismemberment of an existent poem, it seems more likely that the Hemavata Sutta was composed by joining together scattered verses and providing them with a narrative setting. The verses themselves may have been drawn from the floating pool of Buddhist verse rather than directly from the

Saṃyutta.[49] Nevertheless, despite its uncertain origins, the Hemavata Sutta stands as a beautiful testament to early Buddhist spirituality displaying moral clarity, devotional fervor, and philosophical depth joined in a harmonious whole.

> Parallels from other traditions: Chinese: SĀ 1329 (T II 365c6–367b4); SĀ² 328 (T II 483c17–485a23); T IV no. 198, 183b16–184b2

I,10 Āḷavaka (Āḷavaka Sutta), verses 181–92

The Āḷavaka Sutta was probably placed immediately after the Hemavata Sutta to group together discourses about yakkhas; it is puzzling, though, that the Sūciloma Sutta was not included here to form a triad of yakkha suttas. The sutta begins with a prose introduction in which Āḷavaka tries to test the Buddha's patience. When the Buddha refuses to play his game, he threatens to drive the Buddha insane and hurl him across the Ganges unless he can answer certain questions, which like Hemavata's are cast as versified riddles.

The exchanges can be divided into three sets. The first (**181–82**) deals with matters that are of general applicability but are perhaps particularly relevant to the lay follower, whose life flourishes through such virtues as faith, good conduct, truthful speech, and wisdom. The second set (**183–84**) inquires about the qualities needed "to cross the flood," to win liberation, and thus pertains to the renunciant life. The third set (**185–89**) again addresses the concerns of a householder and recommends truth, self-control, generosity, and patience. These bring success in this life and a fortunate rebirth. Finally, the sutta ends with the yakkha's confession of faith and pledge to uphold the Buddha's Dhamma (**190–92**).

> Pāli parallel: SN 10:12. Parallels from other traditions: Chinese: SĀ 1326 (T II 364b21–365a23); SĀ² 325 (T II 482c8–483b3)

I,11 Victory (Vijaya Sutta), verses 193–206

The topic of this discourse is meditation on the body. Its purpose is indicated by its alternative title, Kāyavicchandika Sutta, "Discourse on Removing Desire for the Body." Following Pj II, the sutta can be divided into four sections. The first, verse **193**, is intended to induce a detached attitude toward the body by directing attention to the body's postures and movements. Such reflection shows that the body's activities occur merely through the interplay of bodily and mental factors without any agent in the background, a self or soul exercising control over the process.

The second section, **194–99**, highlights the repulsive nature of the living body by opening it up with the scalpel of thought to expose its impure constituents—its organs, tissues, fluids, and effluvia—which are normally obscured by our fascination with the signs of physical beauty. The third section, **200–203**, shifts the focus from the living body to the dead one, vividly reminding us that the body we cherish and identify with will share the same fate as the corpse. The last section, **204–6**, shows the benefit of meditation on the body and urges the disciple to dispel the pride and vanity that arise on the basis of bodily health and beauty.

I,12 The Muni (Muni Sutta), verses 207–21

The Muni Sutta is devoted to the ideal figure of the Suttanipāta, the muni or sage (see pp. 45–47). As previously noted, King Aśoka refers to the Munigāthās in his Bhabra Minor Rock Edict, and scholars concur that this is likely to have been the Muni Sutta. Since the edict does not quote from the sutta it is impossible to verify this, but the edict does suggest that the verses were recognized as a distinct text at a comparatively early time.[50]

The fifteen stanzas of the Muni Sutta fall into three groups distinguished by their structural and thematic differences: (1) **207–10**; (2) **211–19**; and (3) **220–21**. According to Pj II, the four stanzas in the first group form a single unit originating from a shocking incident recorded at AN 5:55 (III 67–68). A mother and son who had gone forth under the Buddha became infatuated with one another and engaged in sexual intercourse. The Buddha then spoke these verses to warn the bhikkhus and bhikkhunīs to keep a circumspect distance from members of the opposite sex.

Despite the testimony of the commentary, a connection between the muni verses and the incident is questionable. The AN sutta ends with a different set of verses which, while misogynist in tone, are clearer, more cautionary, and more directly tied to the incident. The viewpoint of the muni verses is closer to that of the Khaggavisāṇa verses, expressing an aspiration to avoid all entanglements, including those that might arise in a monastic community. The ideal extolled here—"the vision of the muni"—is the life of solitary wandering, of dwelling "without an abode, without intimacy."

The verses employ metaphorical ideas taken from agriculture, but with a different orientation, aimed at ending growth rather than nurturing it. Seeds sprouting in the soil represent the karmic tendencies of consciousness which, when moistened by craving, give rise to a new birth and a fresh round of suffering. Hence the muni "cuts off what has arisen," "comprehends the grounds," and "crushes the seed." The opaque metaphors employed in the poem speak more clearly when illuminated by such suttas as SN 22:54 (III 54–55), where consciousness is compared to seeds, the "four stations of consciousness" (the other four aggregates) to the earth, and attachment to moisture. Attachment to the aggregates nourishes consciousness and binds it to a fresh round of becoming. When attachment is cut off, "consciousness is unestablished, ungenerative, and not coming to growth, it is liberated."

The nine stanzas that follow, **211–19**, constitute another unit within the Muni Sutta. According to Pj II, each of these stanzas was spoken by the Buddha on a different occasion in response to a different incident, but this seems unlikely. This device of grounding each verse (or group of verses) in a different origin story may have been employed by Dhamma expositors to enhance the appeal of the text, which might otherwise have seemed dry. The verses in this set, however, display sufficient unity of vision to suggest they originally belonged together, constituting a coherent poem. This supposition is supported by the refrain that ends each verse in the series. Verse **211** has near-parallels elsewhere in the canon,[51] and thus it might have been inserted into the poem by replacing the last line with the refrain. The three similes in **213** may have been imported from the Khaggavisāṇa Sutta (**71**), which would explain why the stanza has seven lines instead of four. Such transpositions of lines are typical of oral literature and do not disprove the claim that the nine verses have an inherent unity.

The last two verses, **220–21**, have a different flavor than the others, as can be seen in the way they use the word "muni" in the general sense of a bhikkhu rather than as a specific designation for the Buddha or an arahant.[52] The two verses are unified in theme, both declaring the superiority of the monk practitioner to the householder.

II The Minor Chapter (Cūḷavagga)

II,1 Gems (Ratana Sutta), verses 222–38

As one of the three blessing suttas, the Ratana Sutta is extremely popular in the lands of Theravāda Buddhism and is known by heart by almost all devout Buddhists. The commentaries trace the sutta's origin to a time when the city of Vesālī, capital of the Vajjian confederation, was afflicted by three calamities: famine, evil spirits, and plague. An envoy of the Licchavis, the ruling clan, came from Vesālī to Rājagaha to invite the Buddha to visit their city in order to quell the plague. When the Buddha arrived, Sakka, ruler of the devas, came along with a company of devas, causing most of the evil spirits to flee. The Buddha recited the Ratana Sutta and asked Ānanda to walk around the city, sprinkling water while reciting the sutta. As Ānanda did so, the remaining evil spirits fled and the plague subsided. Because of the origin story, the Ratana Sutta is still recited as a protective discourse to ward off illness, bad luck, and evil spirits.

The origin story is shared among Buddhist traditions. The Dhammapada Commentary relates a similar background story to Dhp 291.[53] The Ratana Sutta has parallel verses in the Skt Mahāvastu, which also traces their genesis to the plague at Vesālī. This version of the story differs in minor details but the substance is the same.[54]

The opening two stanzas (**222–23**) are an invocation to the *bhūtas*, the spirits, asking them to listen to the discourse and imploring them to treat people with loving-kindness. The stanzas that follow constitute declarations of truth (*saccavajja*), each of which proclaims the virtues of one or another of the three gems—the Buddha, the Dhamma, or the Sangha—and declares the wish that by the truth of the utterance, safety will prevail.

Despite its status as a popular discourse, the sutta displays a high degree of doctrinal sophistication. The stanzas on the Dhamma (**225–26**), for instance, make the subtle distinction between the Dhamma Gem as the unconditioned nibbāna and the Dhamma Gem as the path, here identified with world-transcending right concentration, "the concentration without interval." This distinction seems to draw upon such suttas as AN 4:34 (II 34), where the path is declared foremost among all conditioned things but nibbāna foremost among all things, conditioned or unconditioned. The verses on the Sangha recognize the eight noble persons joined into four pairs (**227**); the unshakable confidence of a noble person, based on penetration of the four noble truths (**229**; see SN V 444,17–25); a stream-enterer's freedom from an eighth existence (in **230**; see AN III 439,7–8); their abandoning of the three lower fetters and freedom from rebirth in the bad destinations (in **231**; see AN I 231,33–232,2, etc.);[55] the six things they cannot do (also in **231**; see AN III 438–40); and a noble one's inability to conceal a wrongful deed (in **232**; see MN I 324,4–20). The final benedictions present an interesting departure from standard usage in that they apply the epithet *tathāgata* to all three gems rather than to the Buddha alone.

‖ Pāli parallel: Khp 6. Parallels from other traditions: Sanskrit: Mvu I 290–95

II,2 Carrion (Āmagandha Sutta), verses 239–52

This sutta records a dialogue assigned to the time of the previous buddha, Kassapa, who arose many thousands of years in the past. According to Pj II, the dialogue was recounted by the Buddha Gotama to a hermit critical of his eating habits. The hermit's indignation at the Buddha mirrored a similar incident that occurred during the time of Kassapa, when a brahmin named Tissa censured the Buddha for eating meat and fish.

According to Pj II, the first three stanzas were spoken by Tissa as a criticism of the Buddha; stanzas **242–50** were spoken by Kassapa as a rejoinder to that criticism; and the concluding stanzas **251–52** were added by the compilers. In these concluding verses, "the Blessed One" and "the muni" refer to Kassapa, and "the master of the sacred hymns" (*mantapāragū*) to Tissa, who went forth under Kassapa and became his chief disciple. The only indication in the verses themselves that the protagonist of the sutta is not Gotama is the mention of Kassapa at **240**d and **241**e. He is also addressed as *brahmabandhu*, "kinsman of Brahmā," at **241**b, an epithet for a brahmin. Since Gotama is known to have been a khattiya and Kassapa is said to have been a brahmin, this corroborates the traditional view, so the attributions are not a commentarial invention.

The theme of the discourse is meat-eating, which testifies to a type of criticism that Gotama himself faced during his lifetime. The Buddha did not make vegetarianism compulsory but permitted his monastic disciples to consume meat, on condition that the animal was not killed specifically for them.[56] There is also textual evidence that the Buddha himself ate meat. This custom provoked sharp criticism from other quarters, particularly the Jains, who insisted on strict vegetarianism. In the sutta, the brahmin Tissa accuses the Buddha of eating *āmagandha*. I render the word "carrion," but it literally means "raw odor," perhaps referring to the putrid smell of meat.

In the ensuing verses the Buddha uses a pedagogical technique similar to the one used in the Vasala Sutta. He takes a term that had acquired negative associations as a result of prejudice and flips the term back to his critic, imbued with a new ethical meaning. In this discourse he redefines "carrion" so that it does not mean abhorrent food but such immoral actions as "destruction of life, theft, false speech, fraudulence and cheating, resorting to the wives of others" (**242**) and such defiled mental states as "anger, vanity, obstinacy, recalcitrance, hypocrisy, envy, boastfulness, and haughtiness" (**245**).

II,3 Moral Shame (Hiri Sutta), verses 253–57

This sutta consists of five verses that apparently lack a unifying theme. The sutta derives its name from the word *hiri* occurring in the first line, but otherwise no further mention is made of this topic. The commentary explains the verses with reference to a background story in which a hermit comes to the Buddha and tries to test him by mentally asking four questions: "What kind of friend should one not associate with? What kind of friend should one associate with? To what kind of exertion should one apply oneself? What is the foremost of tastes?" The verses are the Buddha's response to these questions. The story, it seems, accounts for the unity of the verses, except that the same verses occur in Jātaka 363 (III 196), set against a different background story. In any case, the first three verses clearly explain the proper choice of friends, a subject dealt with in great detail at DN III 185–87. The other two verses are concerned with spiritual cultivation, devotion to solitude, and enjoyment of meditative bliss.

‖ Pāli parallel: Ja III 196,10–23

II,4 Blessings (Mahāmaṅgala Sutta), verses 258–69

The Mahāmaṅgala Sutta completes the triad of "protective discourses" that includes as well the Metta Sutta and the Ratana Sutta. The sutta has a background story in prose and the rest in verse. The sutta's popularity might be understood through its content, which offers what might be called a comprehensive groundplan for the good life. The discourse can be viewed as a positive counterpart to the Parābhava Sutta. Whereas the latter explains the causes of a person's downfall, the Mahāmaṅgala explains the means to success.

The word *maṅgala,* which I translate as "blessing," more precisely means what is auspicious or a foretoken of good fortune. Because of the peculiarities of English, neither "auspiciousness" nor "foretoken of good fortune" works well even in a non-metrical rendering of the verses, and thus I settle on "blessing," which serves the purpose as long as the meaning of the Pāli word is borne in mind. In Indian culture of the Buddha's time, as Pj II explains, *maṅgala* had a superstitious significance. People sought *maṅgalas* in sights, sounds, sensations, or events considered signs of future well-being. As in other areas, the Buddha redefined this concept so that *maṅgalas* were not to be sought outwardly but in a morally honorable way of life.

The commentarial tradition holds that the Maṅgala Sutta enunciates thirty-eight *maṅgalas*. These can be divided into several categories. We might see **259–61** as prescribing the preparatory steps for a meaningful life; **262–63** as listing different facets of a virtuous life that would have been respected by all Indian ethical traditions; **264** as marking a more determined commitment to a life governed by the Buddhist precepts; **265–66** as the cultivation of inner virtues and study of the Buddha's teachings; **267** as intensive practice of meditation, culminating in the realization of nibbāna; and **268** as describing the mind of the arahant, who dwells in the world free from stains and sorrows. The final verse affirms the protective power of the course of training articulated by all the verses of exposition.

> Pāli parallel: Khp 5. Parallels from other traditions: Chinese: T IV no. 211, 609a12–609b14

II,5 Sūciloma (Sūciloma Sutta), verses 270–73

This is the third of the three yakkha suttas. The sutta is also found at SN 10:3, with a Skt parallel of the verses found among the Śarīrārthagāthā of the Yogācārabhūmi (see Appendix 2). Like the Āḷavaka Sutta it opens with a prose background story in which the yakkha Sūciloma threatens to harm the Buddha if he fails to answer his riddle correctly. The riddle, in verse **270**, concerns the place where unwholesome thoughts originate. The answer given in **271**, the verse of reply, uses merely the word *ito*, "from this," which is far from clear. The following verse states more explicitly that they are "born from affection, arisen in oneself." Since the verse is in the Anuṣṭubh meter, unlike the other verses which are in Triṣṭubh, it may be a later insertion, added to clarify the intent of the opaque verse preceding it. The commentary explains the last verse as an implicit statement of the four noble truths.

> Pāli parallel: SN 10:3. Parallels from other traditions: Sanskrit: Śag 11.1–4; Chinese: SĀ 1324 (T II 363b29–364a1); SĀ[2] 323 (T II 481c15–482a15)

II,6 Righteous Conduct (Dhammacariya Sutta), verses 274–83

The sutta derives its name from the word *dhammacariya* occurring in the first line, but otherwise the theme with which it deals is quite the opposite: the conduct of certain monastics who deviate from the moral ideal. The commentary calls it the Kapila Sutta, with reference to the strange background story.

Moral recklessness seems to have become a growing problem in the Sangha during the later years of the Buddha's life, as increasing numbers of unprincipled men (and perhaps women) sought to take refuge in the robes to enjoy a life of leisure made more comfortable by generous support from the lay community. Thus the Bhaddāli Sutta speaks of how corruption enters the Sangha when it reaches "the acme of greatness, the acme of gains, the acme of fame, the acme of renown" (MN I 445). The Kīṭāgiri Sutta opens with an account of a group of monks who spurned the precept against eating at night and insisted on following their own wishes, even arguing against the Buddha himself (MN I 473–75). Further signs of corruption are seen in the background stories to the Vinaya rules, which multiplied to contain the damage.

The Dhammacariya Sutta likewise testifies to the moral depravity that had seeped into the ranks of the Sangha. It condemns monks who delight in quarrels and harass their companions, assigning such miscreants to a rebirth in hell. The last four verses (**279–83**) instruct the virtuous monks to come together and expel the transgressors, described as "non-ascetics who imagine themselves ascetics." These same verses occur in AN 8:10 (at IV 172,6–11), a discourse that denounces monks who are "just chaff and trash among ascetics." In AN 8:20 (IV 204–5) the Buddha refuses to recite the Pātimokkha because he sees a bogus monk sitting in the assembly, one who is not a celibate though claiming to be one. The Dhammacariya Sutta belongs to this same genre and reflects the troubled spirit of this period.

II,7 The Tradition of the Brahmins (Brāhmaṇadhammika Sutta), verses 284–315

As the longest discourse in the Cūḷavagga, this sutta would seem to fit better in the Mahāvagga (chapter III), but it was probably included here because of the affinity between its title and that of the Dhammacariya Sutta. Another reason may be the parallelism between their themes. Just as the Dhammacariya Sutta decries the corruption besetting the monastic order, the Brāhmaṇadhammika Sutta deplores the deterioration that had taken place among the brahmins. Its theme, however, is not the inequity of the caste system but the heinous cruelty of animal sacrifice, particularly of cattle. The sutta views this practice as a grave violation of the moral order that ushers in a multitude of physical and social ills.

The thirty-two verses of the sutta can be divided into four groups, which might be called "before the fall, the initial fall, the deeper fall, and after the fall." The period "before the fall" (**284–98**) describes an ideal period in the distant past when the brahmins were models of spiritual glory. They were self-controlled, austere, pious, and simple in their way of life, revered by the population. Some observed life-long celibacy (**293**), others emulated their practice (**294**), but even the least diligent among them lived "within the boundary," performing sacrificial services that did not involve animal slaughter (**297**). As a result, "this population happily flourished" (**298**).

With **299–305**, the initial fall takes place. Coveting wealth, cattle, and women, the brahmins composed hymns enjoining sacrifice, went to the kings, and persuaded them to hold sacrifices, which the brahmins performed in return for lavish rewards. Still not content, "their craving increased still more," and they descended into the deeper fall (**306–10**). They now composed hymns calling for the sacrifice of cattle and recited these to the kings, who initiated the slaughter of cattle. At this point the brahmins had completely abandoned their original heritage. The remaining verses (**311–15**) describe the aftermath of the deeper fall. Diseases afflicting humankind increase, marital relations become disharmonious, social conflict and disorder spreads, and the population falls into the grip of sensual craving.

Somewhat strangely, disregard for the doctrine of birth (*jātivādaṃ niraṃkatvā*) is included among the misfortunes that result from the slaughter of cattle. At **596**, "the doctrine of birth" is identified with the view that "one is a brahmin by birth" (*jātiyā brāhmaṇo hoti*), a doctrine clearly rejected by the Buddha. Yet here disregard for this doctrine is lamented as a sign of deterioration, presumably because it leads to intermarriage among people born into different castes. There seems to be here an incongruity between this line of the text and the view expressed elsewhere that caste distinctions are purely conventional.

‖ Parallels from other traditions: Chinese: MĀ 156 (T I 678a24–679a25)

II,8 The Boat (Nāvā Sutta), verses 316–23

This sutta is named after the simile in **321**, but if it is the word *dhamma* that draws together the preceding two suttas, it might also be the alternative title of this discourse, Dhamma Sutta, that explains its position in immediate succession to them. The sutta deals with the proper relationship between the teacher of the Dhamma and the student. The student, it says, should venerate the teacher "as the deities venerate Indra." When the student shows respect, humility, and eagerness to learn, the teacher should generously share the Dhamma. Having learned the teaching, the pupil should then practice as instructed.

The discourse issues stern warnings to both prospective students and aspiring teachers. The student must use discretion in selecting a teacher. If one resorts to a wrong teacher, "a petty fool who has not reached the goal," one will end in failure. The teacher too must be properly qualified. An unqualified teacher would be like a person who has stepped into a mighty river and, swept off by the torrent, is unable to cross himself, much less to help others across. But just as one who has entered a boat can carry others across, so one accomplished in the Dhamma, "learned and of unwavering character," can guide students who are attentive and willing to learn.

II,9 What Good Behavior? (Kiṃsīla Sutta), verses 324–30

According to the commentary, the questions posed in the opening verse of this sutta were asked by Sāriputta on behalf of a friend from lay life, a wealthy young brahmin who had gone forth but could not make progress. Sāriputta brought him to the Buddha and asked the questions in the hope the Buddha would provide suitable instructions. The discourse deals with the proper conduct a monastic pupil should adopt toward teachers and it thus serves as a short guide to monastic etiquette.

II,10 Arouse Yourselves! (Uṭṭhāna Sutta), verses 331–34

This short sutta of four stanzas sounds a stirring call for diligent effort. The commentary explains that the verses were spoken in connection with an incident reported at SN 51:14. At the time a number of young bhikkhus living on the ground floor of Migāramātā's mansion were dwelling heedlessly. The Buddha asked Mahāmoggallāna to stir up a sense of urgency in them, which he did by using his psychic powers to cause the mansion to "shake, quake, and tremble" by touching it with his toe. When the monks emerged, shocked and frightened, the Buddha spoke the verses to urge them to strive more diligently in their practice.

II,11 Rāhula (Rāhula Sutta), verses 335–42

This sutta is addressed by the Buddha to his son Rāhula, who became a novice during the Buddha's first return visit to Kapilavatthu in the first year after his enlightenment. The Pāli Canon contains three other discourses addressed to Rāhula, but this is the only one entirely in verse. A sentence at the end of the sutta, evidently added by the compilers, states: "In such a way the Blessed One often exhorted the Venerable Rāhula with these verses." This signifies that the verses were not recited only on a single occasion but were taught repeatedly during the period of Rāhula's training.

The sutta begins with two introductory verses (**335–36**). According to the commentary, the first was addressed by the Buddha to Rāhula and the second is Rāhula's reply. The expression "torchbearer of humankind" (*ukkādhāro manussānaṃ*) in the first verse raises suspicion that the verse was not actually spoken by the Buddha but by someone else. While the commentary says that the Buddha used this expression with reference to Sāriputta, the expression itself seems to better fit the Buddha, who elsewhere is compared to a man who brings a lamp into a dark room so people can see forms (see p. 1456, note 1195).

The six verses of instruction cover, with remarkable concision and elegance, the full range of monastic training, from the first steps to the final goal. Stanza **337** reminds Rāhula of the meaning of his act of renunciation, undertaken out of faith and for the purpose of making an end to suffering. Stanza **338** stresses the importance of good friendship, seclusion, and moderation in eating; **339–40**ab covers other aspects of moral discipline; **340**cd–**341** directs Rāhula to meditate on the unattractive nature of the body, which heightens the sense of disenchantment and brings one-pointed concentration. Stanza **342**a refers to the "markless state" (*animitta*), the concentration of insight knowledge that culminates in the breakthrough to the world-transcending path; **342**b speaks of the latent tendency to conceit, a subtle defilement that persists even in a non-returner; and **342**cd states that with the elimination of conceit one will "live at peace," as an arahant who has reached the end of suffering.

II,12 Vaṅgīsa (Vaṅgīsa Sutta), verses 343–58

Vaṅgīsa was declared by the Buddha the bhikkhu foremost in inspirational ingenuity (*paṭibhāna*). His field of expertise was the composition of poetry. In the Vaṅgīsasaṃyutta (SN chap. 8) he displays his skill in creating improvised verse. He also has seventy-one verses in the Theragāthā, the largest number in that collection. These include the verses of this sutta.

The prose introduction to this sutta explains how after his preceptor, Nigrodhakappa, died, Vaṅgīsa was plagued by doubt whether he had attained final nibbāna. To settle his doubt, he went to the Buddha, and as a poet, pleaded in verse for an answer. Apparently he spoke in the midst of the Sangha, for in the verses he refers to others present who are eager to hear. His verses display a high degree of poetic refinement, which sets them off from the unembellished style of most early Buddhist poetry. Vaṅgīsa addresses the Buddha with majestic epithets. He calls him the universal eye, the one of broad wisdom, the supreme eye for humans, one of perfect wisdom, and so forth. He also makes use of metaphors and similes: the Buddha is like Sakka among the devas (**346**d), like a wind dispelling clouds (**348**b); his voice is like the honking of a goose (**350**b); he himself is like a man afflicted by heat and the Buddha's words are like a downpour of rain (**353**cd). Finally, after an elaborate appeal for clarification, the Buddha tersely declares that Nigrodhakappa had indeed "crossed over birth and death entirely" (**355**). This was the answer that Vaṅgīsa had longed to hear, and he welcomes it with joy (**356–58**).

‖ Pāli parallel: Th 1263–79 (verses only)

II,13 Proper Wandering (Sammāparibbājanīya Sutta), verses 359–75

According to the commentary, this sutta was spoken at the Great Gathering (*mahāsamaya*) in response to questions posed by a mind-created buddha. The Great Gathering occurred when five hundred of the Buddha's relatives who had gone forth as monks attained arahantship. Half were paternal relatives, half maternal relatives. They came in immediate sequence on a full-moon night to report their attainment. As the Buddha sat in their midst, surrounded by the five hundred newly enlightened arahants, countless deities from ten thousand world systems came to visit the assembly, hoping to hear a discourse.

The Buddha realized that the mode of teaching that would be most beneficial to the deities would be one given in response to questions. However, he also saw that no one present was able to ask the right questions. He therefore used his psychic power to mentally create a duplicate of himself. The duplicate asked the questions and he himself responded.

According to the commentary, on this occasion the Buddha gave six discourses in the mode of question and response; each was intended for deities of a different temperament. Five are included in the Aṭṭhakavagga (chap. IV). The Discourse on Proper Wandering, intended for those of lustful temperament, was somehow placed in the Cūḷavagga.

The theme of the discourse is revealed in the question posed in the opening verse: "How should a bhikkhu who has renounced the household life properly wander in the world?" The Buddha's answer, the commentary says, explains the arahant's practice up to its culmination in arahantship. The verses seem to extend over two stages of development, path and realization. The path stage is the practice of a disciple training for the final goal. This stage is suggested by the use of optative verbs, such as "should remove lust" (*rāgaṃ vinayetha*) in **361**a, "should discard anger and meanness" (*kodhaṃ kadariyaṃ jaheyya*) in **362**b, and "should not be elated" (*na uṇṇameyya*) in **366**a. The stage of training is also indicated by the expression "aspiring for the state of nibbāna" (*nibbānapadābhipatthayāno*) in **365**c. The stage of realization is reached by the arahant, described by such expressions as "utterly released from things that fetter," "one who has no latent tendencies," "whose influxes have been destroyed," and "a purified conqueror who has removed the coverings." Strikingly, the word "muni" does not occur in the exposition but only in the opening address to the Buddha.

II,14 Dhammika (Dhammika Sutta), verses 376–404

The title of this discourse again suggests that several suttas with *dhamma* or *dhammika* in their titles were drawn together into a single chapter. With twenty-nine verses, this is the second longest sutta in the chapter. The sutta is named after the lay follower Dhammika, who is highly extolled by Pj II as a non-returner of good behavior, learned in the Tipiṭaka (a clear anachronism), and possessing psychic powers. He is the head of a retinue of five hundred lay followers, which suggests he is a man of influence. However, he is not referred to elsewhere in the Nikāyas.

In his opening verse (**376**) he asks the Buddha about the behavior of two kinds of disciples, the renunciant and the lay follower. This is followed by a series of effusive stanzas that eulogize the Buddha, with allusions to incidents recorded elsewhere: the visits of the nāga king Erāvaṇa and the deity Vessavaṇa Kuvera, and the Buddha's triumphs in debate over other ascetics and brahmins. The stanzas thus display literary artifice, presupposing that the listener is acquainted with the traditional lore about the Buddha.

The Buddha's reply can be divided into two parts. The first deals with the proper conduct of a bhikkhu (**385–92**) and the second with the householder's duty (**393–404**). The first verse in the reply is addressed not to Dhammika the inquirer but to the bhikkhus, suggesting a disjunction in the composition of the poem. The instructions given for a bhikkhu cover proper deportment, right behavior on the alms round, restraint and circumspection in speech, and proper use of the material requisites. The emphasis here is strikingly different from that of the Muni Sutta or the Sammāparibbājaniya Sutta, where the ascetic and contemplative elements are more prominent. Here the advice seems more appropriate for a monk in the initial stages of training.

The section on the householder's duty begins with the recognition that the layperson cannot be expected to fully emulate the practice of a renunciant. The first six stanzas of advice (**394–99**) expound on the five precepts. The stanza on the third precept recommends complete sexual abstinence as the ideal and sex within marriage as second best. Whereas the first four precepts are accorded only one stanza, abstinence from intoxicants receives two. Stanzas **400–402** deal with observance of the uposatha, **403** with the layperson's duty to feed the Sangha, and **404** with other householder duties such as support for parents and right livelihood. The discourse reflects a period when a sizeable lay community had constellated around the Buddha and it had become necessary for the Buddha to explain the specific responsibilities of monastics and laypeople both in their own domains and in their mutual relations.

III The Great Chapter (Mahāvagga)

III,1 The Going Forth (Pabbajjā Sutta), verses 405–24

The Pabbajjā Sutta and its sequel, the Padhāna Sutta, along with the introductory verses of the Nālaka Sutta, are the earliest attempts to narrate in verse major events in the Buddha's life. Since each revolves around a particular incident, it would be an exaggeration to say that they constitute a primitive biography of the Buddha, but they certainly provided material for the construction of such a biography.

The narrative portion of the Pabbajjā Sutta, according to the commentary, was spoken by Ānanda, but the centerpiece of the sutta is the dialogue between the future Buddha and King Bimbisāra at the Pāṇḍava Hill outside Rājagaha. According to the commentary, the Buddha went to Rājagaha soon after renouncing the household life. The Jātaka Commentary (I 65,29–30) says that after he arrived at Anupiya, he first spent a week enjoying the bliss of renunciation and then left for Rājagaha, completing the 200-mile trip in one day. From this it follows that the encounter with Bimbisāra took place before the Buddha became a pupil of Āḷāra Kālāma, as told in MN 26 (at MN I 164–65).

The style of the Pabbajjā Sutta is simple and unadorned, free of embellishments and extraneous accretions. The Buddha is referred to as "Buddha" even though the sutta is set prior to his enlightenment. He is not called a bodhisatta. Several times the Buddha is referred to as "the bhikkhu" (**411**d, **412**c, **416**a) and once as a muni (**414**b). When asked about his origins, he does not identify himself as the son of a king, as the later legend has it, but acknowledges that the Sakyan realm was a protectorate of Kosala.

There is a parallel to the Pabbajjā Sutta in the Sanskrit Mahāvastu and another parallel in Chinese in the Four-Part Vinaya (四分律) of the Dharmaguptaka school (T XXII no. 1428). This indicates that the story of a meeting between the future Buddha and Bimbisāra was shared by different schools of Early Buddhism. The story is not recorded elsewhere in the Nikāyas, but it is told in the Jātaka Commentary (I 66), which refers to the Pabbajjā Sutta. The two men met after the Buddha began his teaching mission (at Vin I 37). On that occasion the Buddha taught the Dhamma to Bimbisāra and his retinue, who all attained stream-entry.

Parallels from other traditions: Sanskrit: Mvu II 198–200; Saṅghabhedavastu (Gnoli 1:94–96); Chinese: T XXII no. 1428, 779c26–780a24

III,2 Striving (Padhāna Sutta), verses 425–49

Although the Pabbajjā Sutta ends with the Buddha saying, "I will go for the purpose of striving," the events of the Padhāna Sutta, on the theme of striving, could not have occurred in immediate sequence. The sutta describes the Buddha's exertion during his period of extreme ascetic practice. If we accept the testimony of the Nikāyas, particularly MN 36 (at I 240), before the Buddha took up self-mortification he mastered the formless meditative attainments under Āḷāra Kālāma and Uddaka Rāmaputta. It was only after he left them that he pursued the practice of self-mortification. This means that the events narrated in the two suttas of Sn are separated by a temporal gap.

The Padhāna Sutta also differs from its predecessor in its flavor. Whereas the Pabbajjā Sutta is plain and realistic, the Padhāna Sutta introduces myth and personification in a short epic of the spiritual hero struggling against the forces of metaphysical evil, here represented by Māra. At the time the story occurs, the Buddha has not yet taken his seat beneath the bodhi tree, determined to reach perfect enlightenment that very day. He is still engaged in his ascetic practices, intent on pursuing them to their limits. Thus Māra's dialogue with the Buddha precedes the assault he will launch when the Buddha discovers the middle way, regains his physical vigor, and makes the great determination.

The sutta is a powerful drama in which Māra adopts the guise of compassionate concern in his efforts to persuade the Buddha to give up his exertion and instead accumulate merits as a householder. The Buddha resolutely rejects this proposal and spurns the ten "armies of Māra." These are treated metaphorically, but in the later Māra legend, the armies become actual demonic troops goaded by Māra into a relentless effort to drive the future Buddha away from his seat beneath the bodhi tree. Included among the ten armies are sensuality, discontent, and craving, which become personified as the three daughters of Māra who try unsuccessfully to seduce the Buddha (see SN 4:25, I 124–26).

A temporal gap in the Buddha's life separates the last four stanzas of the poem, **446–49**, from the previous ones. These stanzas seem to have been appended to the original sutta, which would have achieved closure if it had ended at **445**. Since Māra says here that he has followed the Buddha for seven years, this would put them a year after the enlightenment. Stanza **446** may have found its way into this poem from the floating mass of oral verses describing different events in the Buddha's life. Stanzas **447–48** are found elsewhere (at SN I 124), as is **449**, which seems out of context at SN I 122. These verses may have been "borrowed" from their original sources and inserted here to demonstrate that in his battle with Māra the Buddha ultimately prevailed.

> Parallels from other traditions: Sanskrit: Mvu II 238–40; Lalitavistara 18:1–22

III,3 Well-Spoken (Subhāsita Sutta), verses 450–54

This short sutta in mixed prose and verse again gives Vaṅgīsa the opportunity to display his poetic skill, this time on well-spoken speech. In the prose passage the Buddha enumerates four constituents of well-spoken speech, which oddly include "well-spoken speech" as one factor among them. After he restates the same points in verse, Vaṅgīsa asks permission to speak, and when permission is granted, he recites verses that explain his understanding of well-spoken speech as words that cause no harm to oneself or others. He next goes a step further and declares truth to be the *dhammo sanantano*—the ancient principle on which both the good and the Dhamma are grounded. Since it leads to nibbāna, the supreme good, Vaṅgīsa extols the Buddha's word as "the supreme speech."

> Pāli parallel: SN 8:5. Parallels from other traditions: Sanskrit: Śag 20 (Sn 452 only); Chinese: SĀ 1218 (T II 332a8–332a29); SĀ[2] 253 (T II 462b19–462c8)

III,4 Sundarikabhāradvāja (Sundarikabhāradvāja Sutta), verses 455–86

This discourse—also known as the Pūraḷāsa Sutta, "The Sacrificial Cake"—has a part-parallel in the Saṃyutta Nikāya (SN 7:9, I 167–70). In both the interlocutor is the brahmin Sundarikabhāradvāja. The two have the same prose introduction and share several verses (**462–63**, **480–81**), but otherwise they go off in very different directions. This demonstrates how the compilers of the texts might have selected different sets of verses circulating among the communities of reciters and then provided them with the same prose framework, even though it is impossible that two different discourses could have been given on the same occasion and under the same circumstances. In this sutta the verse section seems confused in places, and it is even unclear whether certain lines (between **456** and **461**) should be understood as prose interjections or as unmetrical verse. The commentary tries to unravel the confusion but it seems the text itself has been partly corrupted.

The sutta, like several we have so far encountered, pits the Buddha against a brahmin, this time over the question of who is worthy to receive offerings. The brahmin, spotting a robed figure sitting near the site of his Vedic ritual, is about to offer him the sacrificial cake, but when he discovers that the intended recipient is not a brahmin but an ascetic, he pulls back, about to withdraw the offering. The Buddha, however, challenges the brahmin's assumption. He first completely dissociates himself from caste affiliations, denying (in **455**) even that he is a prince; instead he defines himself as a true "man of nought": "I am not a brahmin nor am I a prince; I am not a vessa or anything else." He denies that the merit of an offering is determined by the recipient's birth, insisting that the merit depends upon the recipient's moral and spiritual qualities. Someone from a low family may be "a steadfast muni" and thus may be the one most worthy of the offering (**462**).

In stanzas **463–66** the Buddha describes in general terms those who deserve to receive an oblation. They are those who have renounced sensual pleasures, are devoid of lust, wander in the world without attachments, and have abandoned taking things as "mine." Each verse ends in the refrain: "a brahmin who would sacrifice intent on merit should make a timely oblation to him." But with **467** he changes pitch and launches into a hymn of self-praise extending over eleven verses, each ending in the refrain: "the Tathāgata is worthy of the sacrificial cake." Almost all the terms used in this hymn would be applicable to any arahant and thus are still indicative of Buddhism in its early phase, before sharp distinctions were drawn that elevated the Buddha to heights above his arahant disciples.

Through the force of the Buddha's argument the brahmin is won over and states his wish to make his offering to the Buddha. The Buddha, however, refuses the offering. We here meet the verses encountered earlier (**81–82**), where the Buddha rejected an offering on the ground that "food over which verses have been recited is not to be eaten by me." It is in *this context* rather than the earlier one that the rejection makes sense, for the food was previously the object of the brahmanic ritual, consecrated by the recitation of brahmanic verses.

The prose passage that concludes the sutta ends in the familiar way. The brahmin abandons his reservations, goes for refuge, asks to go forth under the Buddha, and finally attains arahantship.

|| Pāli parallel: SN 7:9 (part only)

III,5 Māgha (Māgha Sutta), verses 487–509

The theme of this sutta is similar to the preceding one, but the questioner, a brahmin youth named Māgha, does not approach the Buddha as an antagonist but as a reverential inquirer. His question, as posed in the opening stanza, is: "Who are worthy recipients of gifts for householders in quest of merit?" The question is raised against the backdrop of the ancient Indian belief that gifts of food and other requisites create spiritual merit, wholesome kamma conducive to good fortune in future lives, with the volume of merit dependent on the virtues of the recipients.

The Buddha replies by describing those who are true fields of merit. He does not specifically refer to himself and his own disciples but describes the qualities of the ideal recipients in broad terms characteristic of all arahants. Several of the verses correspond to those of the preceding sutta and the tone throughout is identical. When Māgha asks about the best way to perform the sacrifice, the Buddha explains the threefold excellence, which the commentary explains as giving with a placid mind before, during, and after the presentation of the gift. In its original context, however, what was intended may have been the excellence of the giver, the recipients, and the gifts. It is noteworthy that Māgha asks only about the way to rebirth in the brahma world, and the Buddha responds at the level of the question, without attempting to reveal the path of insight that leads to liberation. This illustrates the Buddha's pedagogical technique of assessing the capacities of the listeners and framing the teaching in a way that corresponds to their aptitude and inclinations.

III,6 Sabhiya (Sabhiya Sutta), verses 510–47

The Sabhiya Sutta begins with a long prose narrative about a wanderer named Sabhiya who is told by a guardian deity that he should live the spiritual life under an ascetic or brahmin who can answer certain questions for him. He approaches the six heterodox teachers, the Buddha's rivals in the Magadha region, but not only do they fail to reply to his question, even worse "they displayed irritation, hatred, and displeasure, and they even questioned the wanderer Sabhiya himself." This portion of the sutta is remarkably similar to the opening narrative of the Sāmaññaphala Sutta, where King Ajātasattu tells of how he asked the six teachers about the fruits of the ascetic life without receiving a satisfactory reply (DN I 52–59). Finally, Sabhiya considers visiting the ascetic Gotama to ask these questions. At first he hesitates, because Gotama is much younger than the six teachers, but he then considers: "An ascetic should not be belittled or disparaged just because he is young. For even if an ascetic is young, he might be powerful and mighty." We can detect here echoes of the Buddha's reply to King Pasenadi on their first meeting (SN I 69,1–7). After a long journey, Sabhiya reaches Rājagaha, meets the Buddha, and relates the purpose of his visit.

Speaking now in verse, Sabhiya requests permission to ask his questions and the Buddha invites him to speak up, assuring him: "I'll answer you according to the Dhamma." The dialogue that ensues is entirely in verse, with prose passages inserted only to demarcate the sections. Sabhiya's questions all concern the meaning of various terms that must have been discussed by the ascetics of northern India. The terms describe the ideal spiritual figure of the contemplative quest, the type of person who embodies the supreme goal. The terms about which Sabhiya seeks clarification from the Buddha fall into five groups, which are divided merely as a matter of convenience and not by any difference in their subject matter: (1) bhikkhu, gentle, tamed, enlightened (*buddha*); (2) brahmin, ascetic, cleansed, nāga; (3) field-knower, skilled, pundit (*paṇḍita*), muni; (4) Veda-master, cognizant, heroic, thoroughbred; (5) scholar, noble, one of good conduct, wanderer. The word *saṃnyāsin*, the preferred term of later Indian monasticism, is not among them, and thus it is likely the word originated later or at least became widespread subsequent to the age of Early Buddhism. The same is true of *paramahaṃsa*, "supreme goose," the word used in Hindu contemplative circles to designate the accomplished sage.

The answers to the questions involve subtle word plays and edifying etymologies that are extremely hard to translate into English in ways that correspond to the term being examined. The explanations themselves, in fact, sometimes preserve their relevance only in the Middle Indo-Aryan dialects and become tenuous when the texts are transposed into Sanskrit, or even in partly Sanskritized Pāli. Thus, as Norman has pointed out (GD 258; see too Norman 2006a, 134), the edifying derivation of *brāhmaṇa* from *bāhetvā sabbapāpani*, "one who has expelled all evil," would have been discernible only in a dialect in which the word was pronounced *bāhaṇa*. With the partial Sanskritization of the Pāli texts, *brāhmaṇa* was adopted for *bāhaṇa* and the pun became opaque. But the playful derivation of *samaṇa*, ascetic (literally "striver"), from *samitāvi*, "peaceful one," remained intact in Pāli but lost its cogency in Sanskrit, where *śramaṇa* could not be easily connected to *śamitāvi*. In some places explanatory lines seem to have migrated from the place where they properly belong, creating gaps in the explanation. There is a Sanskrit parallel to the Sabhiya verses in the Mahāvastu and another parallel in the Chinese translation of the *Abhiniṣkramaṇa Sūtra. As is inevitable in a literature originally oral, their explanations differ in places from the Pāli.

After the Buddha has answered all his question, Sabhiya extols him in verses of lyrical beauty. He then pays homage to the Buddha, and—the prose conclusion reports—he goes for refuge, receives ordination, and attains arahantship.

> Parallels from other traditions: Sanskrit: Mvu III 394–401; Chinese: T III no. 190, 833b8–835b22

III,7 Sela (Sela Sutta), verses 548–73

The Sela Sutta is another conversion story, this time centered on the erudite brahmin Sela. The sutta has an exact parallel in Majjhima Nikāya 92. The sutta opens with the encounter between the Buddha and another teacher named Keṇiya, whose status is unclear. The text describes him as a *jaṭila,* a type of ascetic that wore matted locks. Elsewhere the jaṭilas are depicted as celibate and as guardians of the sacred fire (perhaps votaries of the god Agni), but Keṇiya is shown as living partly like a householder, with a large hermitage where he is surrounded by family and relatives. The Buddha twice rejects his offer to provide a meal, but when asked a third time he silently consents.

This sets the dramatic background to the discourse. When Keṇiya's teacher, the learned brahmin Sela, arrives along with his three hundred students, Keṇiya informs Sela that he has invited the Buddha for the next day's meal. The very word "buddha" causes a wave of astonishment and exhilaration in Sela, for, he says, "even this sound 'buddha' is rarely encountered in the world." Sela is described as a master of the Three Vedas and their auxiliary texts, which apparently include traditions about buddhas and their secular counterpart, the wheel-turning monarch—at least according to the sutta.

Sela then visits the Buddha to determine whether Keṇiya's report is true. He examines the Buddha's body for the thirty-two marks of a great man, which he had learned about through his study of brahmanic lore. When he ascertains that the Buddha possesses all thirty-two marks—including one mark that could only be perceived with the help of the Buddha's psychic power—he extols the Buddha in verse and questions him about his attainment. In verse **558** the Buddha gives the most concise definition of a buddha found in the Nikāyas: one who has known what should be known, developed what should be developed, and abandoned what should be abandoned. He asks Sela to suspend his doubts, assuring him that his teaching is "well proclaimed, directly visible, immediate."

Having overcome their doubts, Sela and his students go forth, withdraw into seclusion, and attain arahantship. On the eighth day after their ordination, they return to the Buddha and announce their attainment, praising the Buddha in verse. Two of the stanzas are exactly the same as those in Sabhiya's eulogy (**571–72** = **545–46**). Like Sabhiya, in the final stanza Sela asks the Buddha to extend his feet so that he and his pupils can worship them.

> Pāli parallel: MN 92; Th 818–41 (verses only). Parallels from other traditions: Chinese: EĀ 49.6 (T II 798a25–799c16)

III,8 The Dart (Salla Sutta), verses 574–93

This sutta seems out of place in this collection, for it is a simple didactic poem lodged in the midst of long discourses composed in mixed prose and verse and apparently designed to demonstrate the Buddha's success in converting his contemporaries among the ascetics and brahmins of the Indian spiritual scene. The poem is a homily on death whose themes have been the stuff of Buddhist sermons down the centuries. The "dart" in the title is grief over the death of loved ones. The poem reminds us that the arrival of death is unpredictable; there is no means to avoid death; none of our loved ones can protect us when death calls on us, and we are helpless to protect them; we are all like pots doomed to break or like cows heading for slaughter. The wise recognize this and do not grieve, for they understand that to grow old and die is the way of the world. When facing loss, sorrow and lamentation are useless, for they cannot bring the dead back to life, while grieving only brings harm to oneself. Thus the wise extract the dart of grief, attain peace of mind, and dwell free of sorrow.

III,9 Vāseṭṭha (Vāseṭṭha Sutta), verses 594–656

This long discourse returns to the topic of the caste system with specific reference to the question: "How is one a brahmin?" Two brahmin students take opposing views on the topic. Bhāradvāja espouses the orthodox brahmanic view that one is a brahmin by birth. Vāseṭṭha represents the opposing view, which corresponds to that of the Buddha, that one is a brahmin by reason of one's good behavior. Unable to settle their differences, they decide to seek illumination from the Buddha.

A similar background story lies behind Dīgha Nikāya 13, the Tevijja Sutta, where the same two young brahmins differ about the way to the brahma world and ask the Buddha to adjudicate in their dispute.

Resorting to verse, the Buddha offers a sustained argument in which he addresses not only the meaning of the word "brahmin" but the entire system of human biology and divisive social institutions. He demonstrates first that while generic divisions separate other types of living beings, human beings are all biologically alike: "there are no distinctive marks produced by their particular birth" (**607**). He then argues that social distinctions are entirely a matter of convention: "Classification among human beings is spoken of by designation" (**611**). This means that human beings are designated as being this or that because of their activities (**612–19**). Finally he comes to the marks of a brahmin, where he employs the technique that I have called terminological redefinition to propose a reconceptualization of the nature of a brahmin. A true brahmin, for the Buddha, is not one who can claim a particular genealogy and maternal origin but one who embodies holiness in human form. In the long series of verses **620–47**—found also in the Dhammapada (chap. 26) and which may have been imported into the discourse from another source—he describes the brahmin as the arahant. At **648** he returns to the idea that "name and clan" are mere designation originating by convention and at **650** confirms the position of Vāseṭṭha in his debate with his friend: "One is not a brahmin by birth, nor by birth a non-brahmin. By action one becomes a brahmin, by action a non-brahmin." At **655** he describes the kind of action by which one becomes a brahmin. The same verse is recited by the Buddha at Th 631, affirming that Suṇīta, a former outcast, had attained arahantship and thus become a brahmin in the supreme sense.

Pleased with the Buddha's discourse, the two brahmin students go for refuge and declare themselves lay followers, as they also do at the end of the Tevijja Sutta. At DN III 80,4–6 it is reported that the two were living among the bhikkhus and preparing for ordination.

‖ Pāli parallel: MN 98; Sn 620–47 = Dhp 396–423

III,10 Kokālika (Kokālika Sutta), verses 657–78

The Kokālika Sutta occurs three times in the Nikāyas, in the Saṃyutta, the Aṅguttara, and here. This raises the question why it should have been included in the Suttanipāta. If we look at this anthology as serving, at least in part, a pedagogical purpose, the sutta may have been included here to illustrate the grave consequences of maligning the innocent, particularly the ariyans, the noble ones. The prose portion of the sutta relates the background. Kokālika was a monk who envied the chief disciples, Sāriputta and Moggallāna, for the esteem in which the Buddha held them. Out of spite, he tried to drive a wedge between the Buddha and the chief disciples by accusing them of having evil motives. Though the Buddha told him to stop, he continued to malign them and as a result—a "directly visible fruit" of that kamma—his body broke out in boils, which grew in size and caused his death. He was reborn in the Paduma hell, one of the hells with the longest life spans. The rest of the sutta continues in verse.

Where the other two versions end at the equivalent of **660**, with a statement about the duration of life in hell for those who slander the noble ones, the present version continues with a detailed account of the torments of hell. Pj II ascribes these additional verses to Mahāmoggallāna. This more elaborate version indicates relative lateness. The descriptions correspond to those in the Devadūta Sutta (MN 130). It is possible that one influenced the other, or that both drew upon a common source. The sutta ends with two verses that Pj II says were not commented on in the Great Commentary (Mahā-aṭṭhakathā) and thus may have been added by later editors.

> Pāli parallel: SN 6:10, AN 10:89. Parallels from other traditions: Chinese: SĀ 1278 (T II 351b12–352a13); SĀ[2] 276 (T II 470a14–470b20); EĀ 21.5 (T II 603b2–603c17)

III,11 Nālaka (Nālaka Sutta), verses 679–723

The Nālaka Sutta consists of two distinct sections joined by a unifying thread. The two sections are the introductory verses (*vatthugāthā*) and the body of the poem, which is about the practice for achieving the state of a muni. The introductory verses tell the story of the rishi Asita's visit to Kapilavatthu to see the infant Buddha, whose birth into the world he learned about from the deities. This poem perhaps constitutes the earliest record in verse of the encounter of Asita with the newborn Buddha. We find here the sole occurrence in Sn of the word *bodhisatta* (**683**a), and it seems to presuppose the more ornate perspective on the Buddha's life that we find in such suttas as MN 123 and texts of a similar genre. The incidents described in these verses have become mainstays of the familiar Buddha biography. We learn of Asita's sojourn among the deities, his hasty departure for Kapilavatthu, his prediction of the Buddha's destiny, his joy that an Enlightened One has been born into the world, and his grief that he himself will soon die and thus miss the opportunity to hear the liberating Dhamma.

The thread that connects the *vatthugāthā* with the body of the poem is the advice he gives his nephew Nālaka, mentioned at the end of the background story (**695-98**). He tells Nālaka that when he hears that the Buddha has begun his mission, he should seek him out and lead the spiritual life under him. At this point the background story gives way to the body of the discourse, which must be set at least thirty-five years later, after the Buddha has attained buddhahood. Now Nālaka meets the Master face to face and asks for an explanation of munihood.

On the basis of language, style, meter, content, and external evidence, Jayawickrama holds that the *vatthugāthā* are considerably later than the discourse to Nālaka, which he takes to be the archaic core of the sutta. He contends (PBR 1978, 17) that "the two parts of the sutta known as the Nālaka Sutta in Sn are in reality two independent poems differing in age, brought together at a subsequent date which, most probably, coincided with that of the final collation of Sn." The *vatthugāthā* certainly show signs of lateness. Their language is more ornate and they abound in metaphor, simile, and poetic conceits in a way that distinguishes them from the more vigorous and plainer verse style of the older canonical poems. However, while as a literary document the *vatthugāthā* may be younger than the body of the poem, the connection between Asita and Nālaka could well have been historical and thus the *vatthugāthā* could have a factual root. Texts from other schools of Early Buddhism also testify to the relationship between Asita and a younger nephew whom he advised to visit the Buddha, and while names and details may differ between diverse accounts, the correspondence between them on the core issue suggests they spring from a common source. This could have been an oral narrative that told about the actual relationship between the aged sage who prophesied the newborn infant's attainment of buddhahood and the younger nephew he advised to become his disciple. When introducing himself to the Buddha (at **699**), Nālaka refers to Asita, which establishes a connection between the body of the sutta and the background story.

When Nālaka finally meets the Buddha, he does not simply ask to become a monk but frames his question as an inquiry about *moneyya*, the state of a muni, and the practice to attain the state of a muni. In response the Buddha explains in detail the practice prescribed for a bhikkhu intent on winning the goal in this very life. In the light of the distinction made above (pp. 45–46) between aspirant munis and accomplished munis, the course of practice described is that of an aspirant muni training to become an accomplished muni. The training is quite different from the more gradual process the Buddha generally suggests to newly ordained monks. The guidance must have been intended for a disciple of mature spiritual faculties ready to make the steep ascent toward the peak of realization.

Hence at the outset the Buddha warns Nālaka that he is about to describe a training that is "hard to practice and hard to master," one for which "you must brace yourself and be firm" (**701**). The verses instruct the ascetic to maintain equanimity whether insulted or venerated, to remain on guard against the lure of attractive women, to conduct himself properly on alms round, to eat in moderation, to look impartially on what he receives, and to resort to solitary places suitable for meditation. The poem specifically recommends living in the woods and staying at the foot of a tree (**708**). It does not insist on vows of strict silence—the idea that *moneyya* (or *mauna*) conveys in later Indian tradition—but it does inculcate restraint in speech, for "creeks flow on noisily, but silently the great rivers flow" (**720**).

Parallels from other traditions: Sanskrit: Mvu III 386–89; Saṅghabhedavastu (Gnoli 1:52–55, *vatthugāthā* only)

III,12 Contemplation of Dyads (Dvayatānupassanā Sutta), verses 724–65

This is the only strictly doctrinal discourse in the whole of the Suttanipāta. Jayawickrama (PBR 1976, 161) regards it as one of the youngest suttas in the work, along with the Vijaya and Ratana Suttas. Apart from its language and content, he sees a sign of its lateness in its position at the end of the Mahāvagga, since late accretions to a chapter tend to be placed either at its beginning or its end. It is also the only sutta in Sn that unambiguously mentions the teaching of non-self under its familiar name, *anattā*. Elsewhere the need to free oneself from assumptions of self are expressed as injunctions to stop grasping upon things as one's own, to put an end to *mamāyita* and *mamatta* (see pp. 65–66), without an explicit doctrinal underpinning.

The sutta takes up sixteen topics of Buddhist doctrine, each of which it bifurcates for the purpose of contemplation. The method of dividing a given topic into pairs is what accounts for the title. The text is composed in mixed prose and verse, with the alternation of prose passages and verses conforming to a fixed format. After the first section, which follows directly from the announcement of the theme, the Buddha raises the question in the prose portion whether there is another way of contemplating things arranged in dyads. He then answers positively and explains the particular dyad. This is followed by the verse portion, which treats the same topic in a more inspirational and edifying way. The verses usually occur in pairs, to match the two sides of the dyad, though in some sections more than a single verse is needed to adequately articulate how to contemplate that side of the dyad.

The first section takes up the four noble truths, which it divides according to whether they pertain to the origination of suffering or to its cessation. The first two truths are subsumed under the first portion, the second two truths under the second. The next section frames the dyad in terms of acquisitions (*upadhi*), a word with several nuances. Although the commentary identifies *upadhi* here with kamma, I think it more likely refers to either the defilements or the five aggregates. All suffering, the text states, is conditioned by acquisitions; with the cessation of acquisitions suffering does not arise.

The same pattern is employed for seven factors in the familiar twelvefold series of dependent origination. Since the verses on the last factor, clinging, speak of existence, birth, and death, altogether they comprise ten factors of the series. The only two that are missing are name-and-form and the six sense bases. Pj II offers an explanation, which is not fully convincing, and this raises the suspicion that two sections could have been lost in the process of oral transmission. Unfortunately, there is as yet no known parallel of this sutta from other traditions against which to check it.

Several more sections follow that do not directly fall under the formula of dependent origination. The first is about "instigations" (*ārambha*), a term Pj II defines as "energy associated with kamma," but which I would conjecture here probably means endeavors motivated by craving. This is followed by nutriment, disturbance or agitation (*iñjita*), dependency, form and formless states, truth and falsity, and happiness and suffering. In the verses on truth and falsity (**756–58**), it is said that the world conceives a self in what is not-self (*anattani attamāniṃ*), imagining name-and-form to be true. The noble ones, in contrast, know nibbāna to be truth, of an undeceptive nature (*amosadhammaṃ nibbānaṃ, tadariyā saccato vidū*).

IV The Chapter of Octads (Aṭṭhakavagga)

The Aṭṭhakavagga, as was stated earlier, existed as a separate collection before it became part of the Suttanipāta. It is mentioned in the texts of other schools of Early Buddhism. There is a Chinese parallel titled 義足經, "The Discourse of Verses on Meaning," which is assumed to be a translation of a Skt title, *Arthapada Sūtra. An English translation is available (Bapat 1951), which also cites parallel verses from Sn. Another Skt form of the title, mentioned in other works, is Arthavargīya. The difference in titles between the Pāli and the Skt stems from an original ambiguity. The Skt word *artha* can be rendered into a Prakrit like Pāli either as *attha*, which means "meaning, good, benefit," or as *aṭṭha*, which can mean either "meaning" or "eight." The suffix *–ka* turns the simple number into a group number. The Chinese version was evidently based on an original that construed the sense as *artha*, "beneficial, meaningful." The Pāli tradition took the sense as *aṭṭhaka* or "eights," since four of the suttas in the chapter contain eight stanzas.[57]

The order of the first nine suttas is the same in both the Pāli and Chinese versions; it is only the last seven that differ slightly in position. The relationship is as follows, with the Pāli followed by the Chinese: 10 = 15; 11 = 10; 12 = 11; 13 = 12; 14 = 13; 15 = 16; 16 = 14. The two also differ in that the verses of the Chinese version are embedded in prose background stories, whereas the Pāli tradition has assigned the background stories to the commentary. This difference sheds some light on other suttas in mixed prose and verse in Sn, where the background story may originally have been an informal oral narrative that was later absorbed into the sutta.[58]

The chapter consists of sixteen suttas, composed entirely in verse. The number of stanzas in each sutta increases progressively from six in the first to twenty-one in the last. Several of these suttas differ only in nuance, treating the same topic from slightly different angles. Since their motifs and phrasing overlap and reverberate from one to the others, rather than summarize each individually I will discuss them collectively, drawing out their common nucleus.

The unifying theme behind these discourses is the detached stance the sage takes toward debates and doctrinal views. The following suttas articulate this theme:

IV,3 The Octad on the Hostile (*Duṭṭhaṭṭhaka Sutta*), verses 780–87
IV,4 The Octad on the Pure (*Suddhaṭṭhaka Sutta*), verses 788–95
IV,5 The Octad on the Supreme (*Paramaṭṭhaka Sutta*), verses 796–803
IV,8 Pasūra (*Pasūra Sutta*), verses 824–34
IV,9 Māgandiya (*Māgandiya Sutta*), verses 835–47
IV,12 The Smaller Discourse on Deployment (*Cūḷaviyūha Sutta*), verses 878–94
IV,13 The Greater Discourse on Deployment (*Mahāviyūha Sutta*), verses 895–914

Sutta IV,11 begins on a similar note and thus partly belongs to this group, but it unfolds in accordance with a trajectory peculiar to itself that calls for separate treatment.

The suttas in this class take a critical attitude toward the dogmatic adherence to philosophical views. Their message dovetails with the prose suttas in the main Nikāyas in which the Buddha refuses to endorse any of the speculative views circulating among the thinkers of his time. In the Cūḷamāluṅkya Sutta (MN 63), he says that such views are not connected with the fundamentals of the spiritual life. In the Aggivacchagotta Sutta (MN 72), he calls such views a thicket, a wilderness, a contortion, and a fetter. In the Vacchagottasaṃyutta (SN chap. 33) and the Avyākatasaṃyutta (SN chap. 44), he explains that such views arise because of a failure to understand the true nature of the five aggregates and the six sense bases. The Brahmajāla Sutta (DN 1) weaves a net of sixty-two speculative views, which the Buddha declares to be vain imaginings arisen from craving and ignorance. At stream-entry, the first stage of the path, the disciple eradicates the latent tendency to views, the fetter of personal-entity view, clinging to views, the knot of dogmatic adherence to views, the flood of views, and the yoke of views. Hence the critical stance on views characteristic of the Aṭṭhakavagga is in no way unique to that collection but an expression of the same attitude found in the prose suttas, but here delivered in the heightened and evocative language of verse.

The Aṭṭhakavagga depicts an era when intense debates were held among rival ascetics and brahmins, who would vie with one another in the debate arena in the hope of proving the superiority of their own doctrines and thereby winning converts. The discourses in this chapter sometimes describe how the disciple in training should act in relation to such debates; sometimes they describe the outlook of the accomplished sage, the muni or enlightened brahmin. For the disciple in training the discourses have a prescriptive force, urging one who aspires for sagehood to avoid debates over views. For the sage, such discourses are descriptive, depicting one who naturally avoids wrangling over views. Stanzas that pertain to both can be found in the same poem, and sometimes verses are ambivalent about their subject.

The Buddha's critical perspective on debates over views can be considered from two angles, one epistemological and the other psychological. The epistemological critique stems from the fact that although "truth is one," without a second, few recognize the unitary truth. Those who fail to understand the truth fall back on their raw perceptions in their efforts to understand the nature of reality. Since their perceptions are tainted by subjective biases, their convictions about truth reflect their predilections. Having fallen into the duality of "true" and "false" (**886**), the proponents of views spar over their conflicting standpoints, advancing their own views and attacking those of their opponents. This, however, inevitably draws them into an epistemological impasse. Each considers his own opinion to be true and the views of his opponents to be false; each considers the opponents to be fools, and each takes himself to be wise. However, since they are each in the same position relative to the others, it follows that their opinions would be either all true or all false, that the disputants would be either all fools or all sages (**880–82**; see too **903–4**).

The disputants do not merely cherish elevated opinions about the validity of their views. Even more, they *personally identify* with their views, staking their identities and self-esteem on their convictions about the truth. It is from this personal investment in their positions that the psychological danger in views becomes manifest. The danger erupts when theorists engage in debate. The Pasūra Sutta depicts this situation with a delicate touch of humor. It sketches the stages through which a disputant passes as the debate progresses, from the self-confidence with which he enters the arena through the turmoil he experiences as his arguments falter: "Wishing for praise, he becomes anxious. If his assertion is rejected, he feels humiliated. Upset by blame, he seeks a flaw" (**826**). Even success is no guarantee against a fall; for the pride that comes with victory is the ground of his distress (**830**a).

Beyond the personal anguish that comes from debates—the exaltation from winning, the dejection from losing—there is a more profound reason the Aṭṭhakavagga cautions against adherence to views. Views are symptomatic of a deeply rooted sense of insecurity and a compulsive need to establish a base of security to allay the anxiety. This is particularly the case regarding the content of the kind of views the Buddha was most concerned with: the self and its objective counterpart, the world. Since the self is actually a fiction, a mere mental construct, views about the self are always trailed by an inseparable shadow of agitation—anguish that the inner absence of selfhood might come to light. The agitation is kept at bay by adhering to views and indulging in craving. Because they suppress the underlying agitation, views create a dependency (**877**). It is for this reason that attachment to them "is not easily overcome" (**785**a). If one view proves inadequate, one drops it and takes up another view. As the text says: "They grab hold and let go, like a monkey grasping and letting go of a branch" (**791**cd).

Recognizing the danger, the muni "does not create a dependency even by knowledge" (**800**b). He has no dependencies, no craving for existence or nonexistence (**856**). Hence "the muni does not become involved in an arisen dispute" (**780**c). Instead of entangling themselves in views, the wise "loosen the knot of grasping, and they do not form desires for anything in the world" (**794**cd). "A brahmin"—a true sage—"does not take up mental constructs; he is not a pursuer of views nor a kinsman of knowledge" (**911**ab). Thus "he maintains equanimity while others grasp" (**911**d); he is "peaceful among the restless, equanimous, without grasping while others grasp" (**912**cd). Aloof from all such convictions, the sage "sees security everywhere" (*khemaṃ passati sabbadhi*, **953**d).

Since one ranks oneself in relation to others on the basis of one's views, attachment to views is closely bound up with conceit (*māna*), with positioning oneself in terms of the three discriminations: as superior, equal, or inferior. Those who think in this way, the text says, engage in disputes. The wise, in contrast, do not "shake among these three discriminations" (**842**). Since the muni does not proclaim himself superior, equal, or inferior, "he is peaceful, without miserliness, and does not take, does not reject" (**954**).

The basis on which views arise, according to the Aṭṭhakavagga, is said to be "the seen, heard, and sensed, good behavior and observances" (*diṭṭha, suta, muta, sīlabbata*). Elsewhere the first three terms are accompanied by a fourth, "the cognized" (*viññāta*), to represent the entire objective domain of experience: the objects of sight, hearing, the other senses, and inner reflection.[59] In the Aṭṭhakavagga, where only the three terms are used, it seems "the sensed" includes the cognized.[60] *Sīlabbata* comprises all the modes of conduct and observances that brahmins and ascetics adopted as part of their disciplines. The expression *sīlabbata* occurs among the ten fetters and four kinds of clinging to be eradicated along the path to liberation. The term probably includes the rites and sacrifices of the brahmins as well as the types of self-mortification pursued by ascetics.

The Buddha advocates detachment toward these objective bases of views. A bhikkhu in training "should not be attached to the seen, the heard or sensed, or to behavior and observances" (**798**cd). The sage "does not speak of purity by the seen and heard, by behavior and observances, by the sensed" (**790**ab); rather, he keeps "remote from all phenomena, from whatever is seen, heard, or sensed" (**793**ab) and "does not posit even a subtle notion about what is seen, heard, or sensed here" (**802**ab).The Aṭṭhakavagga thus teaches not only a pragmatic refusal to engage in debates about views but a radical rejection of views themselves, declaring: "One should not construct any view in the world by means of knowledge or good behavior and observances" (**799**ab). The wise "do not fall back on any view at all" (**800**d); even *dhammas*, the teachings, "are not embraced by them" (**803**b).

Such statements, taken out of context, can be misconstrued to mean that the practitioner must be ready to give up all views, including those usually identified as Buddhist. If all views are an impediment, it might be said, this must be true of Buddhist views as well, which are just a more refined type of clinging. Consistency therefore requires a suspension of conviction even about those teachings described elsewhere under the rubric of "right view": the views about kamma and rebirth, the three characteristics, the four noble truths, and other matters outside the range of immediate empirical observation.

If such arguments were correct, the Buddha would wind up advocating a complete agnosticism regarding the possibilities of super-sensory cognition. In that case the goal of his teaching would hardly differ from that of the ataraxia of Pyrrhonic skepticism: the tranquility that can be attained by suspending all attempts to arrive at epistemic certainty. Such arguments, however, fail to properly understand the nature and function of right view in the Buddha's path. Right view is "right" because it articulates matters seen and understood as true by the Buddha and accomplished sages. These matters are not merely of speculative interest but have a profound bearing on human well-being and happiness. As the tenth wholesome course of kamma, right view illuminates the moral lawfulness of the universe, showing how our actions eventually rebound upon us either for our benefit or our harm. As the first factor of the noble eightfold path, right view reveals the principles that must be penetrated with wisdom in order to realize the ultimate goal.

Right view differs from the kind of views repudiated in the Aṭṭhakavagga in that it is offered not as an object of intellectual consent but as a guideline to experiential insight. Right view serves a pragmatic function, disclosing truths relevant to our genuine well-being, both temporal and ultimate. The Buddha compares the Dhamma to a raft, which is for the purpose of crossing over, not for the purpose of grasping.[61] Right view is a component of that raft, the compass that guides the traveler to the other shore. The raft is not to be carried around on one's head, but it has to be used to get across. In a similar vein, the Aṭṭhakavagga subjects right view to a subtle dialectic. On the one hand, it says, purity is not to be achieved by view, learning, knowledge, and good behavior; on the other, it adds, purity cannot be achieved "without view, without learning, without knowledge, without behavior, without observances" (**839**). Right view and all its accessories are like carriages for arriving at the goal; they are not the goal itself (see MN I 149–50). Thus the enlightened sage, unlike the philosophical skeptic, is not committed to a perpetual aporia. What distinguishes the munis of the Aṭṭhakavagga is that, having fulfilled the function of right view, they *do not grasp upon views* and thus they abide in peace and equanimity.

The suttas of the Aṭṭhakavagga that lie outside this group concerned with the relinquishment of views may be summarized very briefly.

IV,1 Sensual Pleasures (Kāma Sutta), verses 766–71
This is a simple homily on the dangers in sensual pleasures, urging the disciple to avoid them "like a serpent's head with the foot."

IV,2 The Octad on the Cave (Guhaṭṭhaka Sutta), verses 772–79
This sutta begins almost as a sequel to its predecessor, reiterating its message that sensual pleasures are a source of suffering. At **776**, the discourse drops to a deeper level, moving from attachment to sensual pleasures to a more tenacious type of craving, "craving for states of existence." This is coupled with the habit of grasping upon things as "mine" (**777**), because of which people tremble like fish in a dried-up stream. To win freedom, one must stop taking things as "mine" and discard attachment even to existence. Release comes through insight into the process by which attachment is created. By fully understanding contact one is freed from greed (**778**b); by fully understanding perception one crosses the flood (**779**ab).

IV,6 Old Age (Jarā Sutta), verses 804–13
This sutta begins with a reflection on the transience of life and the inevitable separation from everyone and everything one loves. Since there are no permanent possessions, it says, one should not live the household life (**805**cd). In **807–8**, the poem moves from material possessions to loved ones, who vanish from one's sight at death like images seen in a dream; all that remains of them is their name. At **809**, the poem turns into a eulogy of the muni, who takes the message to heart and abandons possessions. Stanza **810** uses the word "bhikkhu" in place of muni, showing that in some contexts the two are interchangeable. Stanza **811** compares the muni to a lotus leaf and stanza **812** to the lotus flower, for he remains untainted by things seen, heard, and sensed just as the lotus remains untainted by mud.

IV,7 Tissa Metteyya (Tissametteyya Sutta), verses 814–23
This is a diatribe on indulgence in sexual intercourse, spoken in response to the question of a bhikkhu named Tissa Metteyya. The teaching here, it seems, is intended for a renunciant who reverts from celibacy to the enjoyment of sexual pleasures. At

821, it turns into another acclamation of the muni, who lives alone, indifferent to sensual pleasures, and thereby crosses the flood (**823**).

IV,10 Before the Breakup (Purābheda Sutta), verses 848–61

The commentary explains that this sutta and the five that follow—the Kalahavivāda, the Cūḷaviyūha, the Mahāvyūha, the Tuvaṭaka, and the Attadaṇḍa—were taught at the Great Gathering, like the Sammāparibbājaniya Sutta (II,13). Each of these discourses, says the commentary, was intended for a different group of deities and was taught in response to questions asked by a mind-created buddha. The Purābheda Sutta was delivered for the sake of devas who had given rise to the thought: "What should be done before the dissolution of the body?" The Early Buddhist traditions are not unanimous about this account. In the origin story behind the parallel version in the Chinese Arthapada, the questions are asked by the Buddha's father, the Sakyan Suddhodana. In any case, the discourse makes perfect sense as the response the Buddha might have given to questions asked by any inquisitive bhikkhu.

The question that inspires the discourse asks about the knowledge and conduct of the supreme person (*uttamaṃ naraṃ*), one who dwells at peace (*upasanto*). The reply offers a description of the muni, who is "a seer of seclusion in the midst of contacts" and thus free from defilements.

IV,11 Quarrels and Disputes (Kalahavivāda Sutta), verses 862–77

This sutta follows an alternating question-and-response pattern, where the questioner poses one verse and the respondent answers. The next question picks up on the response and carries the inquiry further. The sequence unfolds in a chain that proceeds from the more manifest level of effects to the more subtle level of conditions. The series thus constitutes an application of the principle of dependent origination to a process different from that described by the familiar twelvefold formula.

The sutta begins with a question about the origin of quarrels and disputes and proceeds to trace back the chain of conditions. Allowing for some oversimplification, the series from **862** to **872** might be depicted as follows: quarrels and disputes ← what is dear ← desire ← the pleasant and unpleasant ← contact ←

name and form. At this point, the respondent says, "When form has vanished, contacts do not touch one," which elicits a question about the attainment where form vanishes (**873**). There follows a cryptic stanza (**874**), probably intended as a riddle, about the attainment where form vanishes. The questioner then asks whether this is "the foremost purity of the spirit" and points to an alternative thesis about "an attainment without residue remaining." Though this phrase is ordinarily used to describe the ultimate dimension of nibbāna, here the respondent rejects both positions as "dependencies," probably to underscore that the two sides are taken up as views. He then states that the liberated muni does not enter disputes and does not encounter various states of existence (**875–77**).

IV,14 Quickly (Tuvaṭaka Sutta), verses 915–34

The questioner asks the Buddha: "How, having seen, does a bhikkhu attain nibbāna?" In response, the Buddha explains the contemplative practice of a bhikkhu, urging him to check the conceit "I am" and remove craving (**916–20**). From this high level the questioner reverts to a more rudimentary stage of training and asks the Buddha to speak about monastic discipline and concentration. The Buddha (starting at **922**) responds with a detailed account of the bhikkhu's training, describing his deportment, his attitude toward food and clothes, his mental cultivation, his livelihood, and his speech.

IV,15 One Who Has Taken Up the Rod (Attadaṇḍa Sutta), verses 935–54

While the commentary, in its introduction to the Purābheda Sutta (Pj II 548), says that the Attadaṇḍa Sutta was spoken to the deities at the Great Gathering, in its introduction to the Attadaṇḍa it says the discourse was taught by the Buddha to the Sakyans and the Koliyans, who were preparing to wage war over the water of the Rohini River, which both states needed to irrigate their crops. The Chinese Arthapada gives still a different origin story, relating it to the massacre of the Sakyans by Virūḍhaka, the rogue king of Kosala.

The sutta seems to be constituted by two sections that sit loosely together. The opening five stanzas are a testament of conscience expressing revulsion at the horrors of mass violence. According to the commentary, these verses were spoken by the Buddha with reference to the time he was a bodhisatta, when he could still experience agitation and distress. The speaker says that he was stirred by a sense of urgency (**935**), experienced fear (**936**), and was overcome by inner disorientation (**937**). At **940**, a voice interrupts, saying "There the trainings are recited," at which point the stanzas that follow (**940–45**) describe the training of a bhikkhu in familiar ways. Then at **946** the poem launches into an extended praise of the muni, which continues to the end of the discourse.

IV,16 Sāriputta (Sāriputta Sutta), verses 955–75

The commentary explains that this sutta was initiated by the chief disciple Sāriputta when the Buddha returned to the human world after spending the rains retreat among the devas. The first two verses sing praise of the Buddha, after which Sāriputta announces that he has come with a question; the commentary explains that he is asking on behalf of his pupils. From **958–62** he actually asks not one question but a multitude of questions pertaining to the training of a bhikkhu. In the remainder of the sutta (**962–75**) the Buddha explains the various aspects of monastic training: the fears a bhikkhu must overcome, the afflictions he must endure, his moral conduct, his cultivation of mind, how he should deport himself, and how he should investigate the Dhamma.

‖ Parallels from other traditions: see Appendix 1

V The Chapter on the Way to the Beyond (Pārāyanavagga)

Like the Aṭṭhakavagga, the Pārāyanavagga once existed as an independent collection before it was incorporated into the Suttanipāta, and like the Aṭṭhakavagga, it is alluded to a number of times in the main Nikāyas (see pp. 29–30). The chapter is divided into three major sections: the *vatthugāthā* or introductory verses, the *pucchās* or questions (inclusive of the Buddha's replies), and an epilogue, partly in prose and partly in verse. Some of the stanzas in the epilogue display the same style as the *vatthugāthā* and must have been added by the compilers; others are composed in the more archaic style of the *pucchās* and are probably integral to the original work. The commentary uses the word *sutta* to designate the sixteen sections with the questions and replies, but the canonical text merely calls each one a *pucchā*, "a question."

The *vatthugāthā* (**976–1031**) purport to narrate the background story to the *pucchās*. The central figure of the story is a brahmin named Bāvari who had established a hermitage in the south. One day, after supervising a sacrifice, he returned to his hermitage to find that a seedy-looking brahmin had arrived. The brahmin asks Bāvari for money. When Bāvari tells him that he had distributed all his wealth at the sacrifice, the brahmin becomes angry and curses him, declaring that in seven days his head will split into seven pieces. Bāvari believes the swindler and becomes despondent. Just then a benevolent deity appears to him and tells him that the visitor was a charlatan and that the only one who knows about heads and head-splitting is the Buddha, who is living in far-off Sāvatthī. Bāvari, however, is too old and weak to travel the distance to meet the Buddha himself, so he dispatches his sixteen pupils, who, the commentary says, are each accompanied by their own retinues. Traveling north, passing through city after city, they finally catch up with the Buddha at the Pāsāṇaka Cetiya near Rājagaha. After testing the Buddha to ascertain that he is the Enlightened One, the leader of the group, Ajita, asks the question about heads and head-splitting, which the Buddha answers to their satisfaction. The Buddha then invites the sixteen students of Bāvari to ask about any matters that perplex them, at which point the *vatthugāthā* give way to the *pucchās*.

It is widely recognized by scholars that the *vatthugāthā* stem from a considerably later period than the *pucchās*. One piece of evidence for this is the *Cūḷaniddesa*, the canonical commentary on the Pārāyanavagga. Though all editions of the *Cūḷaniddesa* include the *vatthugāthā* in the full text of the Pārāyana at the beginning of the work, the expository section does not comment on the introductory verses but only on the *pucchās*. This suggests either that the *vatthugāthā* did not exist at the time the *Cūḷaniddesa* was composed or the author(s) of the exposition did not consider this portion canonical.[62]

Though the text of the Suttanipāta that has come down joins the *vatthugāthā* and the *pucchās* into an integral whole, the two are not indissolubly bound together. It is possible that the story of Bāvari originated as a legend that was later attached to the *pucchās* as the preamble to a well-known collection of discussions between a group of ascetics and the Buddha on "the way to the beyond." The quaintness of the story stands in stark contrast to the simplicity and sobriety of the *pucchās*. Following the *vatthugāthā* Bāvari is not explicitly mentioned again, and the inquirers seem to come from a contemplative tradition quite different from that of a brahmin devoted to sacrificial rites. Among the inquirers, only one, Puṇṇaka, asks about sacrifice, a brahmanic concern.

Nevertheless, several of the verses in the *pucchās* use the word *brāhmaṇa* in a favorable sense. At **1059**a the word is conjoined with *vedagū*, another brahmanic term, to describe a liberated sage. Dhotaka calls the Buddha a brahmin (**1063**b), and the Buddha addresses Jātukaṇṇī in the same way (**1100**b). In his discourse to Posāla, the Buddha speaks of the real knowledge of the brahmin attained by insight (**1115**f). Moreover, in the epilogue Piṅgiya, conversing with an unnamed inquirer (whom Pj II identifies as Bāvari), addresses him as *brāhmaṇa* three times (**1140**b, **1142**b, **1144**d). Thus, while the colorful background story may have been added to awaken interest in the poems to follow, there seems no compelling reason to reject the tradition that sixteen students of a brahmin named Bāvari came to see the Buddha to inquire about the "way to the beyond."

Bāvari himself may have been not a ritual specialist but a contemplative brahmin of the kind described at AN III 224–25 as "one who is like Brahmā." In that case, his pupils would have been similar, celibates dedicated to the meditative life. It is possible, too, that his pupils included both khattiyas and brahmins, like the sages of the Upanishads.[63] It is conceivable that Bāvari even had a connection with Āḷāra Kālāma, the Buddha's first meditation teacher. While the text of the Pārāyana does not give any direct indication of this, it does drop two inconclusive clues. When Upasīva asks the Buddha how he can cross the flood, the Buddha tells him to contemplate nothingness supported by "there is not" (**1070**ab). Again, the inquirer Posāla asks about the knowledge of one for whom form has vanished, "who sees 'there is nothing' internally and externally." The Buddha replies that one knows the origin of nothingness and then sees it with insight (**1113–15**). It was under Āḷāra that the Buddha mastered the meditative attainment of the base of nothingness. If Bāvari knew that the Buddha was Āḷāra's former student, as news about the Buddha and the success of his ministry spread among the ascetic circles of the time, he might have sent his own pupils, several attainers of the base of nothingness, to go meet the Buddha to find out what he had realized and to clarify their own doubts about the way to the beyond. Aware of their meditative experience, the Buddha might have drawn on this to guide them a few steps further to the final goal. While this hypothesis is purely speculative, it seems far more plausible than what the narrative story tells us, that learned brahmins would have traveled a long distance to see the Buddha just to ask about head-splitting.

The *pucchās* themselves inquire into profound matters relating to bondage and liberation. The unifying theme, as indicated by the chapter title, might be summed up in the question: "What is the way to the beyond?" In the verses, the expression "going to the beyond" appears less often than the cognate expression, "crossing over": crossing the flood, crossing over birth and old age, crossing over attachment to the world (see pp. 51–52).

Each *pucchā* section poses its own questions. There are, however, affinities and resonances among the questions asked by the different inquirers. The questions might be concisely summarized as follows:

> V,1 Ajita (1032–39): By what is the world shrouded? What is its great peril? What is the blocking and closing off of the streams (of craving)?
>
> V,2 Tissa Metteyya (1040–42): Who is contented in the world? Who transcends the seamstress (craving)?
>
> V,3 Puṇṇaka (1043–48): For what reason do people perform sacrifices to the deities? Who in the world has crossed over birth and old age?
>
> V,4 Mettagū (1049–60): From where does suffering arise? How do the wise cross over the flood of birth and old age, sorrow and lamenting?
>
> V,5 Dhotaka (1061–68): Instruct me in the state of seclusion so that I can live peaceful and unattached. How can one cross over attachment to the world?

V,6 Upasīva (1069–76): Declare to me a basis by which I might cross this flood. Does one who has gone out cease to exist or does he remain through all eternity?

V,7 Nanda (1077–83): Is a muni one who has knowledge or one following a particular way of life? Who in the world has crossed over birth and old age?

V,8 Hemaka (1084–87): Declare the destruction of craving, having understood which one can cross over attachment to the world.

V,9 Todeyya (1088–91): What is the emancipation of one in whom craving is not found?

V,10 Kappa (1092–95): Declare an island for those standing in the midst of the stream, oppressed by old age and death.

V,11 Jatukaṇṇī (1096–1100): Speak about the state of peace as it actually is.

V,12 Bhadrāvudha (1101–4): Explain matters well to the people here who desire to hear your word.

V,13 Udaya (1105–11): What is emancipation by final knowledge, the breaking up of ignorance? By what is the world fettered? What must be abandoned to attain nibbāna?

V,14 Posāla (1112–15): What is the knowledge of one for whom perception of form has vanished, who sees "there is nothing" internally and externally?

V,15 Mogharāja (1116–19): How does one look upon the world so that the King of Death does not see one?

V,16 Piṅgiya (1120–23): Declare the abandoning here of birth and old age.

The Pārāyana ends with an epilogue in mixed prose and verse. Here an inquirer (who the commentary says was Bāvari) asks the elderly Piṅgiya why, when he has met the Buddha and accepted his Dhamma, he does not constantly follow him. Piṅgiya replies, in devotional verses of great beauty, that although he is separated from the Buddha physically, he is always united with him in mind (*mano hi me tena yutto*).

Parallels from other traditions: Sanskrit: 1034–41 = Śag 39.1–6, 9–10; 1112–13 = Śag 39.7–8

The Suttanipāta

Homage to the Blessed One,
the Worthy One,
the Perfectly Enlightened One

I The Chapter on the Serpent
Uragavagga

1 The Serpent (Uraga Sutta)

[1] 1. One who removes the anger that has arisen
as one removes with herbs a snake's spreading venom:
that bhikkhu gives up the here and the beyond
as a serpent sheds its old worn-out skin. (1)

2. One who has entirely cut off lust
as if plucking a lotus growing in a lake:
that bhikkhu gives up the here and the beyond
as a serpent sheds its old worn-out skin. (2)

3. One who has entirely cut off craving,
having dried up its fast-flowing stream:
that bhikkhu gives up the here and the beyond
as a serpent sheds its old worn-out skin. (3)

4. One who has entirely swept up conceit
as a great flood does a fragile bridge of reeds:
that bhikkhu gives up the here and the beyond
as a serpent sheds its old worn-out skin. (4)

5. One who finds no core in states of existence,
as one seeking flowers in udumbara trees finds none:
that bhikkhu gives up the here and the beyond
as a serpent sheds its old worn-out skin. (5)

6. One who has no irritations inwardly,
having transcended such and such states of existence:

that bhikkhu gives up the here and the beyond
as a serpent sheds its old worn-out skin. (6) [2]

7. One whose thoughts have been burned out,
entirely well excised internally:
that bhikkhu gives up the here and the beyond
as a serpent sheds its old worn-out skin. (7)

8. One who has neither run too far nor run back,
who has transcended all this proliferation:
that bhikkhu gives up the here and the beyond
as a serpent sheds its old worn-out skin. (8)

9. One who has neither run too far nor run back,
having known about the world, "All this is unreal":
that bhikkhu gives up the here and the beyond
as a serpent sheds its old worn-out skin. (9)

10. One who has neither run too far nor run back,
devoid of greed, [knowing] "All this is unreal":
that bhikkhu gives up the here and the beyond
as a serpent sheds its old worn-out skin. (10)

11. One who has neither run too far nor run back,
devoid of lust, [knowing] "All this is unreal":
that bhikkhu gives up the here and the beyond
as a serpent sheds its old worn-out skin. (11)

12. One who has neither run too far nor run back,
devoid of hatred, [knowing] "All this is unreal":
that bhikkhu gives up the here and the beyond
as a serpent sheds its old worn-out skin. (12)

13. One who has neither run too far nor run back,
devoid of delusion, [knowing] "All this is unreal":
that bhikkhu gives up the here and the beyond
as a serpent sheds its old worn-out skin. (13)

14. One who has no latent tendencies at all,
whose unwholesome roots have been uprooted:

that bhikkhu gives up the here and the beyond
as a serpent sheds its old worn-out skin. (14)

15. One who has no states born from distress
as a condition for returning to the near shore:
that bhikkhu gives up the here and the beyond
as a serpent sheds its old worn-out skin. (15)

16. One who has no states born from desire,
causes for bondage to existence:
that bhikkhu gives up the here and the beyond
as a serpent sheds its old worn-out skin. (16) [3]

17. Having abandoned the five hindrances,
untroubled, crossed over perplexity, free of darts:
that bhikkhu gives up the here and the beyond
as a serpent sheds its old worn-out skin. (17)

2 Dhaniya (Dhaniya Sutta)

18. "I've boiled my rice, I've milked the cows,"
(said the herdsman Dhaniya).[64]
"I dwell with my family near the bank of the Mahī.
My hut is thatched, the fire is kindled:
so if you wish, pour down, O sky god!" (1)

19. "I don't boil with anger, I'm rid of barrenness,"
(said the Blessed One).
"I dwell one night near the bank of the Mahī,
my hut open, my fire extinguished:
so if you wish, pour down, O sky god!" (2)

20. "No gadflies or mosquitoes are found,"
(said the herdsman Dhaniya).
"The cows roam in the meadow lush with grass.
They can endure the rain when it comes:
so if you wish, pour down, O sky god!" (3)

21. "I made a raft that is well constructed,"
(said the Blessed One).

"I have crossed, gone beyond, escaped the flood.
I have no more need for a raft:
so if you wish, pour down, O sky god!" (4) [4]

22. "My wife is obedient, not wanton,"
(said the herdsman Dhaniya).
"Living together with me long, she is agreeable,
and I do not hear any evil about her:
so if you wish, pour down, O sky god!" (5)

23. "My mind is obedient, liberated,"
(said the Blessed One).
"It's been long nurtured and well tamed;
further, no evil is found in me:
so if you wish, pour down, O sky god!" (6)

24. "I am employed by myself,"
(said the herdsman Dhaniya),
"and my children, living close by, are healthy;
I do not hear any evil about them:
so if you wish, pour down, O sky god!" (7)

25. "I am not employed by anyone,"
(said the Blessed One).
"I wander in all the world by what I've earned.
I have no need at all for wages:
so if you wish, pour down, O sky god!" (8)

26. "There are cows and suckling calves,"
(said the herdsman Dhaniya).
"There are cows with calf and breeding cows;
there is also a bull, chief of cattle, here:[65]
so if you wish, pour down, O sky god!" (9)

27. "There are no cows or suckling calves,"
(said the Blessed One),
"no cows with calf or breeding cows. [5]
There's not even a bull, chief of cattle, here:
so if you wish, pour down, O sky god!" (10)

28. "The stakes are planted, unshakable,"
(said the herdsman Dhaniya).
"The muñja grass halters are new and well shaped;
not even the sucklings can break them:
so if you wish, pour down, O sky god!" (11)

29. "Like a bull I have cut through the bonds,"
(said the Blessed One).
"Like an elephant I have sundered the rotten creeper.
I will never again come to the bed of the womb:
so if you wish, pour down, O sky god!" (12)

30. Filling the lowland and highland,
at once a great cloud poured down rain.
Having heard the rain falling,
Dhaniya spoke about this matter: (13)

31. "It is indeed no small gain for us,
that we have seen the Blessed One.
We approach you as a refuge, One with Vision:
be our teacher, great muni. (14)

32. "My wife and I, obedient, would lead
the spiritual life under the Fortunate One.
Gone beyond birth and death,
we would make an end of suffering." (15) [6]

33. "One who has sons delights because of sons,"
(said Māra the Evil One).
"One with cattle delights because of cattle.
For acquisitions are a man's delight;
without acquisitions one does not delight." (16)

34. "One who has sons sorrows because of sons,"
(said the Blessed One).
"One with cattle likewise sorrows because of cattle.
For acquisitions are a man's sorrow;
without acquisitions one does not sorrow." (17)

3 The Rhinoceros Horn (Khaggavisāṇa Sutta)

35. Having put down the rod toward all beings,
not harming a single one among them,
one should not desire a son, how then a companion?
One should live alone like a rhinoceros horn. (1)

36. For one who has formed bonds, there is affection;[66]
following on affection, this suffering arises.
Discerning the danger born of affection,
one should live alone like a rhinoceros horn. (2)

37. Sympathizing with friends dear to one's heart,
with mind attached, one forsakes the good.
Seeing this peril in intimacy,
one should live alone like a rhinoceros horn. (3)

38. As widespread bamboo becomes entwined,
just so is concern for wives and sons. [7]
But like a bamboo shoot, not getting stuck,[67]
one should live alone like a rhinoceros horn. (4)

39. As a deer unbound in the forest
goes off to graze wherever it wants,
so a wise person, looking out for freedom,
should live alone like a rhinoceros horn. (5)

40. One is addressed in the midst of companions,
whether resting, standing, going, or traveling.
Looking out for the freedom that is not coveted,
one should live alone like a rhinoceros horn. (6)

41. There is play and delight in the midst of companions,
and affection for one's sons is vast.
Averse to separation from those who are dear,
one should live alone like a rhinoceros horn. (7)

42. At home in the four directions, unrepelled,
contented with anything whatsoever,
enduring obstacles, fearless,
one should live alone like a rhinoceros horn. (8)

43. Even some monastics are hard to please;
so, too, householders living at home.
Being unconcerned about others' sons,
one should live alone like a rhinoceros horn. (9)

44. Having discarded the marks of a layman
like a koviḷāra tree whose leaves are shed,[68] [8]
having cut off a layman's bonds, the hero
should live alone like a rhinoceros horn. (10)

45. If one should find a judicious companion,
a fellow wanderer, of good behavior, resolute,
having overcome all obstacles, one should
live with him, satisfied and mindful.[69] (11)

46. But if one does not find a judicious companion,
a fellow wanderer, of good behavior, resolute,
like a king who has abandoned a conquered realm,[70]
one should live alone like a rhinoceros horn.[71] (12)

47. Surely, we praise the excellence of companionship:
one should resort to companions one's equal or better.
Not obtaining these, as one who eats blamelessly
one should live alone like a rhinoceros horn. (13)

48. Having seen radiant [bracelets] of gold,
skillfully fashioned by a goldsmith,
clashing together in pairs on the arm,
one should live alone like a rhinoceros horn. (14)

49. Thus if I had a partner, I would incur
[fond] words of address or verbal friction.
Looking out for this peril in the future,
one should live alone like a rhinoceros horn. (15)

50. Sensual pleasures are colorful, sweet, delightful,
but in their diversity they agitate the mind.
Having seen danger in the strands of sensual pleasure,
one should live alone like a rhinoceros horn. (16)

51. "This is adversity, a boil, disaster,
an illness, a dart, and peril for me":
having seen this peril in the strands of sensual pleasure,
one should live alone like a rhinoceros horn. (17) [9]

52. Cold and heat, hunger, thirst,
wind, the hot sun, gadflies, and serpents:
having patiently endured all these,
one should live alone like a rhinoceros horn. (18)

53. As an elephant that has abandoned the herd—
with massive back, lotus-like, eminent—
may live in the forest as he pleases,
one should live alone like a rhinoceros horn. (19)

54. It is impossible that one who delights in company
might attain even temporary liberation.
Having attended to the word of the Kinsman of the Sun,
one should live alone like a rhinoceros horn. (20)

55. "I have transcended the contortions of views,
reached the fixed course, obtained the path.
I have aroused knowledge, I'm not to be led by others":
one should live alone like a rhinoceros horn. (21)

56. Without greed, without scheming,
without thirst, not denigrating,
with stains and delusion blown away,
without wishes for anything in all the world,
one should live alone like a rhinoceros horn. (22)

57. One should avoid an evil companion,
who shows what is harmful, one settled in
unrighteousness.
One should not freely associate
with one who is intent and heedless;
one should live alone like a rhinoceros horn. (23) [10]

58. One should resort to the learned, a bearer of
Dhamma,
an eminent friend gifted with ingenuity.
Having known the benefits and removed doubt,
one should live alone like a rhinoceros horn. (24)

59. Having found no satisfaction in the world
with play, delight, and sensual pleasures,
not taking any interest in them,
refraining from ornaments, a speaker of truth,
one should live alone like a rhinoceros horn. (25)

60. Having abandoned children and wife,
father and mother, wealth, grain, and relatives,
sensual pleasures according to the limit,
one should live alone like a rhinoceros horn. (26)

61. "This is a tie, the happiness here is slight,
giving little gratification; the suffering here is more,
this is a hook": having known thus, a thoughtful person
should live alone like a rhinoceros horn. (27)

62. Having sundered the fetters,
like a fish in the water that has broken a net,
like a fire not returning to what has been burnt,
one should live alone like a rhinoceros horn. (28)

63. With downcast gaze, not footloose,
with guarded faculties, with protected mind,
unpolluted, not feverish with passion,
one should live alone like a rhinoceros horn. (29)

64. Having cast off the marks of a layman
like a pāricchattaka tree that has shed its leaves,[72] [11]
clothed in ochre robes, having renounced,
one should live alone like a rhinoceros horn. (30)

65. Not arousing greed for tastes, not hankering for them;
not nourishing others, walking for alms without
skipping houses;

with a mind unbound to this or that family,
one should live alone like a rhinoceros horn. (31)

66. Having abandoned the five obstructions of mind,
having dispelled all mental defilements,
independent, having cut off affection and hatred,
one should live alone like a rhinoceros horn. (32)

67. Having left behind pleasure and pain
and previously [discarded] joy and dejection,
having gained purified equanimity and serenity,
one should live alone like a rhinoceros horn. (33)

68. With energy aroused to attain the supreme goal,
with unsluggish mind and robust practice,
firmly persistent, equipped with strength and power,
one should live alone like a rhinoceros horn. (34)

69. Not neglecting seclusion and jhāna,
always acting in accordance with the teachings,
having explored the danger in states of existence,
one should live alone like a rhinoceros horn. (35)

70. Yearning for craving's destruction, heedful,
intelligent, learned, mindful,
having comprehended the Dhamma,
fixed in destiny, vigorous in striving,
one should live alone like a rhinoceros horn. (36) [12]

71. Like a lion unalarmed among sounds,
like the wind not caught in a net,
untainted like a lotus by water,
one should live alone like a rhinoceros horn. (37)

72. Like the lion, king of beasts,
who has fangs as its strength,
who lives by attacking and overpowering,
one should resort to remote lodgings;
one should live alone like a rhinoceros horn. (38)

73. At the right time pursuing liberation by
loving-kindness,
equanimity, compassion, and altruistic joy,[73]
not antagonized by the whole world,
one should live alone like a rhinoceros horn. (39)

74. Having abandoned lust, hatred, and delusion,
having sundered the fetters [that keep one bound],
not terrified at the extinction of life,
one should live alone like a rhinoceros horn. (40)

75. They resort to you and serve you for a motive;
friends without motive are today very rare.
Impure people are wise about their own good:
one should live alone like a rhinoceros horn. (41)

4 Kasibhāradvāja (Kasibhāradvāja Sutta)

Thus have I heard. On one occasion the Blessed One was dwelling among the Magadhans [13] at Dakkhiṇāgiri near the brahmin village Ekanālā. Now on that occasion five hundred plows had been yoked for the brahmin Kasibhāradvāja at the time of sowing.

Then in the morning the Blessed One dressed, took his bowl and robe, and went to the place where the brahmin Kasibhāradvāja was working. Now on that occasion the brahmin Kasibhāradvāja's food distribution was taking place. The Blessed One then approached the food distribution and stood to one side. The brahmin Kasibhāradvāja saw the Blessed One standing for alms and said to him: "I plow and sow, ascetic, and having plowed and sown, I eat. You too, ascetic, must plow and sow, and having plowed and sown, you can eat."

"I too, brahmin, plow and sow, and having plowed and sown, I eat."

"But we do not see Master Gotama's yoke or plow or plowshare or goad or oxen, yet Master Gotama says this: 'I too, brahmin, plow and sow, and having plowed and sown, I eat.'"

Then the brahmin Kasibhāradvāja addressed the Blessed One in verse:

76. "You claim to be a plowman,
but we do not see your plowing.
When asked, tell us about your plowing,
so that we can understand your plowing." (1)

77. "Faith is the seed, austerity the rain;
wisdom is my yoke and plow.
Moral shame is the pole, mind the yoke strap,
mindfulness my plowshare and goad.[74] (2) [14]

78. "Guarded in body, guarded in speech,
controlled in food and belly,
I use truth for weeding,
and gentleness is my release. (3)

79. "Energy is my beast of burden
carrying one toward security from bondage;
it goes ahead without turning back
to the place where one does not sorrow. (4)

80. "In such a way this plowing is done
which bears the deathless as its fruit.
Having plowed with this kind of plowing,
one is released from all suffering." (5)

Then the brahmin Kasibhāradvāja had milk rice poured into a large bronze dish and presented it to the Blessed One, saying: "Let Master Gotama eat the milk rice! You are a plowman, since you plow with a plowing that bears the deathless as its fruit."

[The Blessed One:]
81. "Food over which verses have been recited is not to be eaten by me;
this, brahmin, is not the principle of those who see.
The buddhas reject food over which verses have been recited;
there being such a principle, brahmin, this is their conduct. (6)

82."Serve with other food and drink
the consummate one, the great rishi,

one with influxes destroyed, with regret stilled,
for he is the field for one seeking merit." (7) [15]

"Then, Master Gotama, should I give this milk rice to someone else?"

"I do not see anyone in this world, brahmin, with its devas, Māra, and Brahmā, in this population with its ascetics and brahmins, its devas and humans, who could eat and properly digest this milk rice except the Tathāgata or a disciple of the Tathāgata. Therefore, brahmin, discard the milk rice where there is little vegetation or dispose of it in water where there are no living beings."

Then the brahmin Kasibhāradvāja disposed of that milk rice in water where there were no living beings. When the milk rice was thrown into the water, it sizzled and hissed and gave off steam and smoke. Just as a plowshare, heated all day and then placed in water, sizzles and hisses and gives off steam and smoke, so too that milk rice, when thrown into the water, sizzled and hissed and gave off steam and smoke.

Then the brahmin Kasibhāradvāja, agitated, with hair bristling, approached the Blessed One, prostrated himself with his head at the Blessed One's feet, and said to the Blessed One: "Excellent, Master Gotama! Excellent, Master Gotama! Master Gotama has made the Dhamma clear in many ways, as though he were turning upright what had been overturned, revealing what was hidden, showing the way to one who was lost, or holding up a lamp in the darkness so those with good eyesight can see forms. I go for refuge to Master Gotama, [16] to the Dhamma, and to the Sangha of bhikkhus. May I receive the going forth under Master Gotama, may I receive full ordination."

Then the brahmin Kasibhāradvāja received the going forth under the Blessed One, he received full ordination. And not long after his full ordination, dwelling alone, withdrawn, heedful, ardent, and resolute, the Venerable Bhāradvāja soon realized for himself with direct knowledge, in this very life, that unsurpassed consummation of the spiritual life for the sake of which clansmen rightly go forth from the household life into homelessness, and having entered upon it, he dwelled in it. He directly knew: "Finished is birth, the spiritual life has been lived, what had to be done has been done, there is no more coming back to any state of being." And the Venerable Bhāradvāja became one of the arahants.

5 Cunda (Cunda Sutta)

83. "I ask the muni, one of abundant wisdom,"
(said Cunda the smith's son),
"the Buddha, lord of the Dhamma, rid of craving,
supreme among bipeds, the most excellent of trainers:
how many ascetics are there in the world? Please tell me this." (1)

84. "There are four kinds of ascetics; there is no fifth,
(Cunda," said the Blessed One). [17]
"Being asked in person, let me explain them to you:
the conqueror of the path,[75] the teacher of the path,
the one who lives on the path, and the defiler of the path." (2)

85. "Whom do the buddhas call a conqueror of the path?"
(said Cunda the smith's son).
"How is one without equal as a shower of the path?[76]
Being asked, tell me about one who lives on the path,
and explain to me the defiler of the path." (3)

86. "One who has crossed over perplexity, free of inner darts,
delighted with nibbāna, without any greed;
the guide of this world together with its devas:
the buddhas call the impartial one a conqueror of the path. (4)

87. "One here who, having known the supreme as supreme,
explains and analyzes the Dhamma right here,
the muni who has cut off doubt, without impulse,
is the second bhikkhu,[77] whom they call a teacher of the path. (5)

88. "The one on the well-taught trail of the Dhamma
who lives on the path, controlled and mindful,
resorting to blameless ways of conduct,
is the third bhikkhu, whom they call one living on the path. (6)

89. "Having taken on the dress of the disciplined,
one who is brazen, a corrupter of families, impudent,
hypocritical, uncontrolled, chaff,
living as a dissembler: he is the defiler of the path. (7)

90. "When a householder who is learned, wise,
a noble disciple, has penetrated these, [18]
since he knows, 'They are not all like him,'[78]
on seeing such, he does not forsake his faith.[79]
For how could one equate them:
the undefiled with the defiled, the pure with the impure?" (8)

6 Downfall (Parābhava Sutta)

Thus have I heard. On one occasion the Blessed One was dwelling at Sāvatthī in Jeta's Grove, Anāthapiṇḍika's Park. Then, when the night had advanced, a certain deity of stunning beauty, having illuminated the entire Jeta's Grove, approached the Blessed One, paid homage to him, stood to one side, and addressed the Blessed One in verse:

91. "We ask Gotama a question
about a person in a downfall.
We have come to ask the Blessed One:
What is the cause of a downfall?" (1)

92. "One who succeeds is easily known,
one who falls down is easily known.
One who loves the Dhamma is successful;
one who detests the Dhamma falls down." (2)

93. "Thus we understand this;
that is the first case of a downfall.

Tell us the second, Blessed One:
What is the cause of a downfall?" (3)

94. "The bad are dear to him;
he does not treat the good as dear;
he approves of the teaching of the bad:
that is a cause of a downfall." (4)

95. "Thus we understand this;
that is the second case of a downfall.
Tell us the third, Blessed One:
What is the cause of a downfall?" (5) [19]

96. "If a person is lethargic, gregarious,
and does not make an exertion,
indolent, one who displays anger:
that is a cause of a downfall." (6)

97. "Thus we understand this;
that is the third case of a downfall.
Tell us the fourth, Blessed One:
What is the cause of a downfall?" (7)

98. "If one who is able does not support
his mother or his father
when they have grown old, their youth gone:
that is a cause of a downfall." (8)

99. "Thus we understand this;
that is the fourth case of a downfall.
Tell us the fifth, Blessed One:
What is the cause of a downfall?" (9)

100. "If one deceives with false speech
a brahmin or an ascetic
or some other mendicant:
that is a cause of a downfall." (10)

101. "Thus we understand this;
that is the fifth case of a downfall.

Tell us the sixth, Blessed One:
What is the cause of a downfall?" (11)

102. "If a person with abundant wealth,
endowed with bullion and food,
eats delicacies alone:
that is a cause of a downfall." (12)

103. "Thus we understand this;
that is the sixth case of a downfall.
Tell us the seventh, Blessed One:
What is the cause of a downfall?" (13)

104. "A person proud because of social class,
proud because of wealth, proud because of clan,
looks down on his own relative:
that is a cause of a downfall." (14)

105. "Thus we understand this;
that is the seventh case of a downfall.
Tell us the eighth, Blessed One:
What is the cause of a downfall?" (15)

106. "A womanizer, one fond of liquor,
addicted to gambling,
dissipates whatever he has gained:
that is a cause of a downfall." (16) [20]

107. "Thus we understand this;
that is the eighth case of a downfall.
Tell us the ninth, Blessed One:
What is the cause of a downfall?" (17)

108. "One not content with his own wives
is seen[80] among prostitutes,
seen among the wives of others:
that is a cause of a downfall." (18)

109. "Thus we understand this;
that is the ninth case of a downfall.

Tell us the tenth, Blessed One:
What is the cause of a downfall?" (19)

110. "When a man past his youth
marries a girl with *timbaru* breasts,[81]
he does not sleep from jealousy over her:
that is a cause of a downfall." (20)

111. "Thus we understand this;
that is the tenth case of a downfall.
Tell us the eleventh, Blessed One:
What is the cause of a downfall?" (21)

112. "If one places in authority
a debauched woman, a spendthrift,
or a man of similar nature:
that is a cause of a downfall." (22)

113. "Thus we understand this;
that is the eleventh case of a downfall.
Tell us the twelfth, Blessed One:
What is the cause of a downfall?" (23)

114. "If one of little wealth and strong craving
is born into a khattiya family,
he aspires to rulership here:[82]
that is a cause of a downfall. (24)

115. "Having examined these cases
of downfall in the world, a wise person,
noble, endowed with vision,
passes on to an auspicious world." (25) [21]

7 The Outcast (Vasala Sutta)[83]

Thus have I heard. On one occasion the Blessed One was dwelling at Sāvatthī in Jeta's Grove, Anāthapiṇḍika's Park. Then in the morning the Blessed One dressed, took his bowl and robe, and entered Sāvatthī for alms. Now on that occasion, at the residence of the brahmin Aggikabhāradvāja, a fire had been kindled and an oblation had been prepared. Then the Blessed

One, while walking for alms without skipping any houses, approached the residence of the brahmin Aggikabhāradvāja. The brahmin Aggikabhāradvāja saw the Blessed One coming in the distance and said to him: "Stop right there, you shaveling! Right there, you low ascetic! Right there, you outcast!" When this was said, the Blessed One said to the brahmin Aggikabhāradvāja: "But do you know, brahmin, what an outcast is or the qualities that make one an outcast?"

"I do not know, Master Gotama, what an outcast is or the qualities that make one an outcast. Please teach me the Dhamma in such a way that I might come to know what an outcast is and the qualities that make one an outcast."

"In that case, brahmin, listen and attend closely. I will speak."

"Yes, sir," the brahmin Aggikabhāradvāja replied. The Blessed One said this:

116. "A man who is angry and hostile,
an evil denigrator,
deficient in view, a hypocrite:
you should know him as an outcast. (1)

117. "One here who injures a living being[84]
whether once-born or twice-born,
who has no kindness toward living beings:
you should know him as an outcast. (2) [22]

118. "One who strikes or attacks
villages and towns,
notorious as an oppressor:
you should know him as an outcast. (3)

119. "Whether in the village or in the forest,
one who takes what has not been given,
stealing the belongings of others:
you should know him as an outcast. (4)

120. "One who, having taken out a loan,
flees when pressed [to pay it back],
saying, "I am not indebted to you":
you should know him as an outcast. (5)

121. "One who, from desire for some item,
strikes a person traveling along a road
and takes away the item:
you should know him as an outcast. (6)

122. "A person who for his own sake,
for the sake of others, and for the sake of wealth,
speaks falsely when questioned as a witness:
you should know him as an outcast. (7)

123. "One who is seen transgressing
with the wives of his relatives or friends,
whether by force or through endearment:
you should know him as an outcast. (8)

124. "If one who is able does not support
his mother or his father
when they have grown old, their youth gone:
you should know him as an outcast.[85] (9)

125. "One who strikes or verbally abuses
his mother or father,
his brother, sister, or mother-in-law:
you should know him as an outcast. (10)

126. "One who, when asked about the good,
instructs others in what is harmful,
who gives advice in an obscure way:
you should know him as an outcast. (11)

127. "One who, having done a bad deed,
wishes: 'May they not find out about me,'
a person of concealed action:
you should know him as an outcast. (12)

128. "One who, when visiting another's family,
enjoys there a meal of fine food,
but does not return the favor to his host:
you should know him as an outcast. (13)

129. "If one deceives with false speech
a brahmin or an ascetic
or some other mendicant:
you should know him as an outcast.[86] (14) [23]

130. "If, at the meal time, one verbally abuses
a brahmin or an ascetic that has arrived[87]
and does not give him [any food]:
you should know him as an outcast. (15)

131. "One here who speaks what is untrue,[88]
enveloped by delusion,
seeking to obtain something for himself:
you should know him as an outcast. (16)

132. "One who extols himself
and despises others,
inferior because of his own conceit:
you should know him as an outcast. (17)

133. "One who provokes anger, stingy,
of evil desires, miserly, deceitful,
without moral shame or moral dread:
you should know him as an outcast. (18)

134. "One who reviles the Buddha
or who reviles his disciple,
whether a wanderer or a householder:
you should know him as an outcast. (19)

135. "One not actually an arahant
who claims to be an arahant,
a thief in this world along with Brahmā:
this indeed is the lowest outcast.
I have explained to you
these outcasts that are spoken of. (20)

136. "One is not an outcast by birth,
nor by birth is one a brahmin.

By action one becomes an outcast,
by action one becomes a brahmin. (21)

137. "Understand that in this way, too,
according to this example of mine,
the caṇḍāla son, Sopāka,
famed [under the name] Mātaṅga. (22) [24]

138. "Mātaṅga attained supreme fame,
which is so very hard to obtain;
many khattiyas and brahmins came
to perform service for him. (23)

139. "He ascended the deva road,
the dustless great path;
having expunged sensual lust,
he passed on to the brahma world.
His social class did not prevent him
from rebirth in the brahma world. (24)

140. "Those born into a family of reciters—
brahmins who specialize in the sacred hymns[89]—
are often seen involved
in actions that are bad. (25)

141. "They are reprehensible in this present life
and have a bad destination in a future life;
their social class does not prevent them
from a bad destination or reproach. (26)

142. "One is not an outcast by birth,
nor by birth is one a brahmin.
By action one becomes an outcast,
by action one becomes a brahmin." (27)

When this was said, the brahmin Aggikabhāradvāja said this to the Blessed One: "Excellent, Master Gotama! Excellent, Master Gotama! Master Gotama has made the Dhamma clear in many ways, as though he were turning upright what had been overthrown, revealing what was hidden, showing the way to one who was lost, or holding up a lamp in the darkness so those with good eyesight can see forms. [25] I go for refuge to Master Gotama, to the Dhamma, and to the Sangha of bhikkhus. Let Master Gotama consider me a lay follower who from today has gone for refuge for life."

8 Loving-Kindness (Metta Sutta)

143. This is what should be done by one skilled in the good,
having made the breakthrough to that peaceful state:
he should be able, upright, and very upright,
amenable to advice and gentle, without arrogance. (1)

144. [He should be] content and easily supported,
of few duties and a frugal way of living;
of peaceful faculties and judicious,
courteous, without greed when among families. (2)

145. He should not do anything, however slight,
because of which other wise people might criticize him.
May all beings be happy and secure;
may they be inwardly happy! (3)

146. Whatever living beings there are
whether frail or firm, without omission,
those that are long or those that are large,
middling, short, fine, or gross; (4) [26]

147. whether they are seen or unseen,
whether they dwell far or near,
whether they have come to be or will come to be,
may all beings be inwardly happy! (5)

148. No one should deceive another,
nor despise anyone anywhere.
Because of anger and thoughts of aversion
no one should wish suffering for another. (6)

149. Just as a mother would protect her son,
her only son, with her own life,
so one should develop toward all beings
a state of mind without boundaries. (7)

150. And toward the whole world
one should develop loving-kindness,
a state of mind without boundaries—
above, below, and across—
unconfined, without enmity, without adversaries. (8)

151. Whether standing, walking, sitting,
or lying down, as long as one is not drowsy,
one should resolve on this mindfulness:
they call this a divine dwelling here. (9)

152. Not taking up any views,
possessing good behavior, endowed with vision,
having removed greed for sensual pleasures,
one never again comes back to the bed of a womb.
(10) [27]

9 Hemavata (Hemavata Sutta)

153. "Today is the fifteenth, the uposatha,"
(said the yakkha Sātāgira);
"a celestial night has arrived.
Come, let us see Gotama,
the teacher of perfect name." (1)

154. "Is the mind of the impartial one,"
(said the yakkha Hemavata),
"well disposed toward all beings?
Has he mastered his intentions
toward the desirable and undesirable?" (2)

155. "The mind of the impartial one,"
(said the yakkha Sātāgira),
"is well disposed toward all beings.
He has mastered his intentions
toward the desirable and undesirable." (3)

156. "Does he avoid taking what has not been given?"
(said the yakkha Hemavata).
"Is he self-controlled in regard to living beings?
Does he keep far from heedlessness?
Is he not devoid of jhāna?" (4)

157. "He does not take what has not been given,"
(said the yakkha Sātāgira),
"and is self-controlled in regard to living beings.
He also keeps far from heedlessness.
The Buddha is not devoid of jhāna." (5)

158. "Does he avoid speaking falsely?"
(said the yakkha Hemavata). [28]
"Is his way of speaking not rough?
Does he not say anything destructive?
Does he not speak idle chatter?" (6)

159. "He does not speak falsely,"
(said the yakkha Sātāgira),
"and his way of speaking is not rough.
He does not say what is destructive.
With reflection, he speaks what is meaningful." (7)

160. "Does he have no lust for sensual pleasures?"
(said the yakkha Hemavata).
"Is his mind unsullied?
Has he overcome delusion?
Does he have the vision of phenomena?" (8)

161. "He has no lust for sensual pleasures,"
(said the yakkha Sātāgira),
"and his mind is unsullied.
He has overcome all delusion;
the Buddha has the vision of phenomena." (9)

162. "Is he endowed with clear knowledge?"
(said the yakkha Hemavata).
"Is he also pure in conduct?
Have the influxes been destroyed by him?
Is there for him no renewed existence?" (10) [29]

163. "He is endowed with clear knowledge,"
(said the yakkha Sātāgira).
"He is also pure in conduct.
All the influxes have been destroyed by him;
for him there is no renewed existence." (11)

[Hemavata:]

163[A.90] "The muni's mind is accomplished
with respect to action and way of speech.
In accordance with the Dhamma you praise him,
one accomplished in clear knowledge and
conduct."[91] (11A)

[Sātāgira:]

163[B.] "The muni's mind is accomplished
with respect to action and way of speech.
In accordance with the Dhamma you rejoice over
one accomplished in clear knowledge and
conduct. (11B)

164. "The muni's mind is accomplished
with respect to action and way of speech.
Come, let's go see Gotama,
one accomplished in clear knowledge and
conduct." (12)

[Hemavata:]

165. "Come, let's go see Gotama,
the muni meditating in the woods,
with antelope calves, slender, a hero,[92]
eating little, greedless. (13)

166. "Having approached the nāga,
who is like a lion, wandering alone,
indifferent to sensual pleasures,
let's ask about release from the snare of death." (14)

[Sātāgira and Hemavata:]

167. "Let us ask Gotama,
the expounder, the instructor,
one gone beyond all phenomena,
the Buddha who has overcome enmity and
peril!" (15)

168. "In what has the world arisen?"
(said the yakkha Hemavata).
"In what does it form intimacy?
Having clung to what is the world
afflicted in regard to what?" (16) [30]

169. "In six the world has arisen,
(Hemavata," said the Blessed One).
"In six it forms intimacy;
having clung to six, the world
is afflicted in regard to six." (17)

170. "What is that clinging
in which the world is afflicted?
When asked about the outlet, tell:
how is one released from suffering?" (18)

171. "Five strands of sensual pleasure
with mind as sixth are declared in the world:
having expunged desire for these,
one is thereby released from suffering. (19)

172. "This outlet from the world
has been expounded to you just as it is.
This is what I declare to you:
one is thereby released from suffering." (20)

173. "Who here crosses the flood?
Who here crosses the sea?
Who does not sink in the deep,
which is without foothold, without support?" (21)

174. "One always accomplished in good behavior,
endowed with wisdom, well concentrated,
inwardly reflective, mindful,
crosses the flood so hard to cross. (22)

175. "One who has abstained from sensual perception,
who has overcome all fetters,
who has utterly destroyed delight and existence—
he does not sink in the deep." (23)

176. "Behold him of deep wisdom,
the one who sees the subtle meaning,
owning nothing, unattached
to sensual pleasures and existence.
Behold him, everywhere released,
the great rishi treading the divine path. (24)

177. "Behold him of perfect name,
the one who sees the subtle meaning,
the giver of wisdom, unattached
to the lair of sensual pleasures, [31]
all-knowing, very wise,
the great rishi treading the noble path. (25)

178. "Today indeed we have had a good sight,
a good morning, a good arising,
since we have seen the Enlightened One,
one without influxes who has crossed the flood. (26)

179. "These thousand yakkhas
possessing psychic potency and fame
all go to you for refuge:
you are our unsurpassed teacher. (27)

180. "We will wander from village to village,
from mountain to mountain,
paying homage to the Enlightened One
and to the excellence of the Dhamma." (28)

10 Āḷavaka (Āḷavaka Sutta)

Thus have I heard. On one occasion the Blessed One was dwelling at Āḷavī, in the abode of the yakkha Āḷavaka. Then the yakkha Āḷavaka approached the Blessed One and said to him: "Get out, ascetic!"

"All right, friend," the Blessed One said, and he went out. "Come in, ascetic." – "All right, friend," the Blessed One said, and he went in. A second time . . . A third time the yakkha Āḷavaka said to the Blessed One: "Get out, ascetic!" – "All right, friend," the Blessed One said, and he went out. "Come in, ascetic." – "All right, friend," the Blessed One said, and he went in.

A fourth time the yakkha Āḷavaka said to the Blessed One: "Get out, ascetic."

"I won't [32] go out, friend. Do whatever you must do."

"I'll ask you a question, ascetic. If you won't answer me, I'll drive you insane or split your heart or grab you by the feet and hurl you across the Ganges."

"I do not see anyone in this world, friend, with its devas, Māra, and Brahmā, in this population with its ascetics and brahmins, its devas and humans, who could drive me insane or split my heart or grab me by the feet and hurl me across the Ganges. But ask whatever you want, friend." The yakkha Āḷavaka then addressed the Blessed One in verse:

181. "What here is a person's best treasure?
What well practiced brings happiness?
What is really the sweetest of tastes?
How lives the one whose life they say is best?" (1)

[The Blessed One:]

182. "Faith is here a person's best treasure;
the Dhamma well practiced brings happiness;
truth is really the sweetest of tastes;
living by wisdom, they say, one's life is best." (2)

[Āḷavaka:]

183. "How does one cross the flood?
How does one cross the sea?
How does one overcome suffering?
How is one fully purified?" (3) [33]

[The Blessed One:]

184. "By faith one crosses the flood,
by heedfulness one crosses the sea.
By energy one overcomes suffering;
by wisdom one is fully purified." (4)

[Āḷavaka:]

185. "How does one gain wisdom?
How does one find wealth?
How does one achieve acclaim?
How does one bind friends?
When passing from this world to the next,
how does one not sorrow?" (5)

[The Blessed One:]

186. "Placing faith in the Dhamma of the arahants
for the attainment of nibbāna,
one gains wisdom from a desire to learn
if one is heedful and astute. (6)

187. "Doing what is proper, dutiful,
one with initiative finds wealth.
By truthfulness one wins acclaim;
by giving, one binds friends.[93] (7)

188. "The faithful seeker of the household life
who possesses these four qualities—
truth, *dhamma*, steadfastness, generosity—
does not sorrow when he passes on. (8)

189. "Come now, ask the others as well,
the many ascetics and brahmins,
whether there exists here anything better
than truth, self-control, generosity, and patience." (9)

[Āḷavaka:]

190."Why now should I ask
the many ascetics and brahmins?
Today I have understood
the good pertaining to future lives. (10)

191."Indeed, it was for my sake
that the Buddha came to stay at Āḷavī.
Today I have understood
where what is given bears great fruit. (11)

192."Now I will travel about
from village to village, from city to city,
paying homage to the Enlightened One
and to the excellence of the Dhamma." (12) [34]

11 Victory (Vijaya Sutta)[94]

193. When one is walking or standing,
sitting or lying down,
when one bends and stretches—
this is the motion of the body. (1)

194. Bound together by bones and sinews,
plastered with skin and flesh,
covered by the epidermis,
the body is not seen as it really is— (2)

195. as filled with intestines,
filled with the stomach,
with the liver and bladder,
the heart, lungs, kidneys, and spleen; (3)

196. with snot and saliva,
with sweat and fat,
with blood and oil of the joints,
with bile and grease. (4)

197. Further, from its nine openings
impurity flows constantly:
muck from the eyes,
wax from the ears, (5)

198. snot from the nostrils;
and from the mouth one sometimes
vomits bile and vomits phlegm;
sweat and dirt flow from the body. (6)

199. Then its hollow head
is filled with the brain.
Led on by ignorance, the fool
conceives it as beautiful. (7)

200. And when it is lying dead,
bloated and discolored,
cast off in a charnel ground,
the relatives are unconcerned with it. (8)

201. Dogs then devour it,
as do jackals, wolves, and worms;
crows and vultures devour it,
and whatever other beings there are. (9) [35]

202. Having heard the Word of the Buddha,
a bhikkhu possessing wisdom here
fully understands it,
because he sees it as it really is: (10)

203. "As this, so that;
as that, so this":
internally and externally
one should expunge desire for the body. (11)

204. That bhikkhu possessing wisdom here
who has expunged desire and lust
has attained the deathless, peace,
the imperishable state of nibbāna. (12)

205. This two-footed body,
impure and foul-smelling, is cherished,
though filled with various kinds of filth
and oozing here and there. (13)

206. One who, because of such a body,
would think to exalt himself
or who would disparage others—
what is this due to but lack of vision? (14)

12 The Muni (Muni Sutta)

207. From intimacy peril has arisen;
from an abode there arises dust.
Without an abode, without intimacy:
this truly is the muni's vision. (1)

208. One who, having cut off what has arisen,
would not foster what is arising or nurture it—
they call him a muni living alone:
that great rishi saw the state of peace. (2) [36]

209. Having comprehended the grounds, having crushed
the seed,
he would not nurture it with moisture.
Truly, that muni, a seer of the final end of birth,
having abandoned thought, cannot be designated. (3)

210. Having known all residences,
not desiring any one of them, he who is
truly a muni, devoid of greed, greedless,
does not endeavor, for he has gone beyond. (4)

211. One who has overcome all, all-knowing, very wise,
untainted among all things,

who has cast off all, liberated in the destruction of
craving:
he is one the wise know as a muni. (5)

212. One with the power of wisdom,
equipped with good behavior and observances,
concentrated, delighting in jhāna, mindful,
freed from ties, not barren, without influxes:
he, too, is one the wise know as a muni. (6)

213. Living alone, a muni, heedful,
not swayed by blame and praise—
like a lion not alarmed among sounds,
like the wind not caught in a net,
like a lotus not tainted by water,
a leader of others, not by others led:
he, too, is one the wise know as a muni. (7) [37]

214. One who remains steadfast like a pillar at a ford
when others speak provocative words about some matter;
who is devoid of lust, with well-concentrated faculties:
he, too, is one the wise know as a muni. (8)

215. One who is inwardly firm, straight as a shuttle,
disgusted with actions that are evil,
who investigates the uneven and the even:
he, too, is one the wise know as a muni. (9)

216. One self-controlled does nothing evil;
when young and middle-aged, the muni is restrained.
Irreproachable, he does not scold anyone:
he, too, is one the wise know as a muni. (10)

217. Whether from the top, the middle, or the remainder,
whatever food an alms-collector may receive,
he does not think to praise it or disparage it:
he, too, is one the wise know as a muni. (11)

218. The muni who lives abstinent from sexual union,
who even in youth is not bound anywhere,

abstinent from vanity and heedlessness, fully released:
he, too, is one the wise know as a muni. (12)

219. Having known the world, a seer of the supreme goal,
an impartial one who has crossed the flood and ocean, [38]
whose knots are cut, unattached, without influxes:
he, too, is one the wise know as a muni. (13)

220. The two are dissimilar, their dwelling and conduct far apart:
the layman supporting a wife and the ascetic owning nothing.
The layman is unrestrained in harming other beings,
while the muni, ever restrained, protects living beings. (14)

221. Just as the blue-necked peacock, flying in the sky,
never approaches the speed of a goose,
so the layman is no match for the bhikkhu,
a muni meditating secluded in the woods. (15)

II The Minor Chapter
Cūḷavagga

1 Gems (Ratana Sutta)

222. [39] Whatever beings are gathered here,
whether of the earth or in the sky,
may all beings indeed be happy
and then listen carefully to what is said. (1)

223. Therefore, O beings, all of you listen;
show loving-kindness to the human population,
who day and night bring you offerings;
therefore, being heedful, protect them. (2)

224. Whatever treasure exists here or beyond,
or the sublime gem in the heavens,
there is none equal to the Tathāgata.
This too is the sublime gem in the Buddha:
by this truth, may there be safety! (3)

225. Destruction, dispassion, the deathless, the sublime,
which Sakyamuni, concentrated, attained:
there is nothing equal to that Dhamma.
This too is the sublime gem in the Dhamma:
by this truth, may there be safety! (4)

226. The purity that the supreme Buddha praised,
which they call concentration without interval— [40]
the equal of that concentration does not exist.
This too is the sublime gem in the Dhamma:
by this truth, may there be safety! (5)

227. The eight persons praised by the good
constitute these four pairs.
These, worthy of offerings, are the Fortunate One's
disciples;
gifts given to them yield abundant fruit.
This too is the sublime gem in the Sangha:
by this truth, may there be safety! (6)

228. Those who strived well with a firm mind,
who are desireless in Gotama's teaching,
have reached attainment, having plunged into the
deathless,
enjoying perfect peace obtained free of charge.
This too is the sublime gem in the Sangha:
by this truth, may there be safety! (7)

229. As a gate post, planted in the ground,
would be unshakable by the four winds,
similarly I speak of the good person
who, having experienced them, sees the noble truths.
This too is the sublime gem in the Sangha:
by this truth, may there be safety! (8)

230. Those who have cognized the noble truths
well taught by the one of deep wisdom,
even if they are extremely heedless,
do not take an eighth existence.
This too is the sublime gem in the Sangha:
by this truth, may there be safety! (9)

231. Together with one's achievement of vision
three things are discarded: [41]
the view of the personal entity and doubt,
and whatever good behavior and observances there are.
One is also freed from the four planes of misery[95]
and is incapable of doing six deeds.
This too is the sublime gem in the Sangha:
by this truth, may there be safety! (10)

232. Although one does a bad deed
by body, speech, or mind,

one is incapable of concealing it;
such inability is stated for one who has seen the state.
This too is the sublime gem in the Sangha:
by this truth, may there be safety! (11)

233. Like a woodland thicket with flowering crests
in a summer month, in the first of the summer,
just so he taught the excellent Dhamma,
leading to nibbāna, for the supreme welfare.
This too is the sublime gem in the Buddha:
by this truth, may there be safety! (12)

234. The excellent one, knower of the excellent,
giver of the excellent, bringer of the excellent,
the unsurpassed one taught the excellent Dhamma.
This too is the sublime gem in the Buddha:
by this truth, may there be safety! (13)

235. The old is destroyed, there is no new origination,
their minds are dispassionate toward future existence.
With seeds destroyed, with no desire for growth, [42]
those wise ones are extinguished like this lamp.
This too is the sublime gem in the Sangha:
by this truth, may there be safety! (14)

236. Whatever beings are gathered here,
whether of the earth or in the sky,
we pay homage to the thus-gone Buddha,
venerated by devas and humans: may there be safety! (15)

237. Whatever beings are gathered here,
whether of the earth or in the sky,
we pay homage to the thus-gone Dhamma,
venerated by devas and humans: may there be safety! (16)

238. Whatever beings are gathered here,
whether of the earth or in the sky,
we pay homage to the thus-gone Sangha,
venerated by devas and humans: may there be safety! (17)

2 Carrion (Āmagandha Sutta)

[The brahmin Tissa:]

239. "Wild millet, grains from grasses, highland pulses,
green leaves, tubers, and squashes:
eating these, righteously obtained, the good
do not speak lies, desiring sensual pleasures. (1)

240. "But eating food well prepared, well flavored,
given by others, presented with respect, delicious, [43]
enjoying a dish of fine rice,
you eat[96] carrion, O Kassapa! (2)

241. "You said, O kinsman of Brahmā,
'Carrion is not proper for me,'
yet you are enjoying a dish of fine rice,
well prepared with the flesh of fowl.
I ask you about this matter, Kassapa:
what do you take to be carrion?" (3)

[The Buddha Kassapa:]

242. "Destruction of life, beating, mutilating, binding;
theft, false speech, fraudulence and cheating,
studying useless subjects, resorting to the wives of others:
this is carrion, but not the eating of meat. (4)

243. "People here uncontrolled in sensual pleasures,
greedy for tastes, mixed up with impurity,
who hold the nihilist view, warped, stubborn:
this is carrion, but not the eating of meat. (5)

244. "Those who are rough, violent, backbiters,
betrayers of friends, cruel-hearted, arrogant,
miserly, who do not give to anyone:
this is carrion, but not the eating of meat. (6) [44]

245. "Anger, vanity, obstinacy, recalcitrance,
hypocrisy, envy, and boastfulness,

haughtiness, and intimacy with the bad:
this is carrion, but not the eating of meat. (7)

246. "Those ill behaved, debt-evaders, slanderers,
crooked in their dealings, dissemblers here;
vile men who here commit wicked deeds:
this is carrion, but not the eating of meat. (8)

247. "Those people here uncontrolled toward living beings,
who steal from others, intent on inflicting harm,
immoral, cruel, harsh, disrespectful:
this is carrion, but not the eating of meat. (9)

248. "Those who are greedy toward these, hostile, transgressors,
ever intent, who are heading for darkness after death,
beings who fall head first into hell:
this is carrion, but not the eating of meat. (10)

249. "Neither [avoiding] fish and meat nor fasting,
nor nakedness, a shaven head, matted locks, dirt, or rough antelope hides,
nor tending the sacrificial fire,
or the many austerities in the world aimed at immortality,
sacred hymns, oblations, sacrifices, and seasonal penances,
purify a mortal who has not overcome doubt. (11) [45]

250. "One guarded over the sense doors
should live with sense faculties understood,[97]
firm in Dhamma, delighting in honesty and mildness.
A wise one who has overcome the ties,
who has abandoned all suffering,
is not tainted by things seen and heard." (12)

251. Thus the Blessed One repeatedly explained this matter;
the master of the sacred hymns understood it.

The muni, free of carrion, unattached, hard to lead,
elucidated it with variegated verses. (13)

252. Having heard the Buddha's well-spoken word,
which was free of carrion, dispelling all suffering,
humble in mind [Tissa] venerated the Tathāgata,
and right there declared he would go forth. (14)

3 Moral Shame (Hiri Sutta)

253. One flouting moral shame, despising it,
who says, "I am your friend,"
but does not do what can be done:
one should know of him: "He is not my [friend]."[98] (1)

254. The wise understand this one
who utters endearing speech to his friends
without following it up [with deeds]
as one who speaks without acting. (2) [46]

255. He is not a friend who is always alert
in suspecting dissension, observing only one's fault.
But he on whom one relies, like a son on [his father's]
breast,
who cannot be divided by others, is truly a friend. (3)

256. One develops a state productive of joy,
happiness that brings praise,
[expectant of] its fruit and benefit,
carrying out one's personal duty. (4)

257. Having drunk the taste of solitude
and the taste of tranquil peace,
one is without distress, without evil,
drinking the taste of rapture in the Dhamma. (5)

4 Blessings (Mahāmaṅgala Sutta)

Thus have I heard. On one occasion the Blessed One was dwelling at Sāvatthī in Jeta's Grove, Anāthapiṇḍika's Park. Then, when the night had advanced, a certain deity of stunning beauty, having illuminated the entire Jeta's Grove, approached the Blessed One, paid homage to him, stood to one side, and addressed the Blessed One in verse:

258. "Many devas and human beings
have reflected on blessings,
longing for safety,
so declare the highest blessing." (1)

259. "Not associating with fools,
associating with the wise,
and venerating those worthy of veneration:
this is the highest blessing. (2)

260. "Residing in a suitable place,
merit done in the past,
and directing oneself rightly:
this is the highest blessing. (3) [47]

261. "Much learning, a craft,
a well-trained discipline,
and well-spoken speech:
this is the highest blessing. (4)

262. "Serving one's mother and father,
maintaining a wife and children,
and an honest occupation:
this is the highest blessing. (5)

263. "Giving and righteous conduct,
assistance to relatives,
blameless deeds:
this is the highest blessing. (6)

264. "Desisting and abstaining from evil,
refraining from intoxicating drink,
heedfulness in good qualities:
this is the highest blessing. (7)

265. "Reverence and humility,
contentment and gratitude,
timely listening to the Dhamma:
this is the highest blessing. (8)

266. "Patience, being amenable to advice,
the seeing of ascetics,
timely discussion on the Dhamma:
this is the highest blessing. (9)

267. "Austerity and the spiritual life,
seeing of the noble truths,
and realization of nibbāna:
this is the highest blessing. (10)

268. "One whose mind does not shake
when touched by worldly conditions,
sorrowless, dust-free, secure:
this is the highest blessing. (11)

269. "Those who have done these things
are victorious everywhere;
everywhere they go safely:
theirs is that highest blessing." (12)

5 Sūciloma (Sūciloma Sutta)

Thus have I heard. On one occasion the Blessed One was dwelling at Gayā at the Ṭaṃkita Bed, the abode of the yakkha Sūciloma. Now on that [48] occasion the yakkha Khara and the yakkha Sūciloma passed by not far from the Blessed One. Then the yakkha Khara said to the yakkha Sūciloma: "He is an ascetic."

"He is not an ascetic; he is a sham ascetic. I'll soon find out whether he is an ascetic or a sham ascetic."

Then the yakkha Sūciloma approached the Blessed One. Having approached, he leaned toward the Blessed One. The Blessed One drew back. Then the yakkha Sūciloma said to the Blessed One: "Are you afraid of me, ascetic?"

"I'm not afraid of you, friend. It is just that your touch is bad."

"I'll ask you a question, ascetic. If you won't answer me, I'll drive you insane or split your heart or grab you by the feet and hurl you across the Ganges."[99]

"I do not see anyone in this world, friend, with its devas, Māra, and Brahmā, in this population with its ascetics and brahmins, its devas and humans, who could drive me insane or split my heart or grab me by the feet and hurl me across the Ganges. But ask whatever you want, friend." The yakkha Sūciloma then addressed the Blessed One in verse:

270. "What is the source of lust and hatred?
Where are born discontent, delight, and hair-raising terror?
Having originated from what do the mind's thoughts
toss one around as boys toss up a crow?"[100] (1)

271. "Lust and hatred have their source here;
from this are born discontent, delight, and hair-raising terror.
Having originated from this, the mind's thoughts
toss one around as boys toss up a crow. (2) [49]

272.[101] "Born from affection, arisen from oneself,
like the trunk-born shoots of the banyan tree,
manifold, attached to sensual pleasures,
like a māluvā creeper stretched across the woods. (3)

273. "Those who understand their source,
they dispel it—listen, O yakkha!—
they cross this flood so hard to cross,
uncrossed before, for no renewed existence." (4)

6 Righteous Conduct (Dhammacariya Sutta)[102]

274. "Righteous conduct, the spiritual life:
they call this the supreme treasure.
But if one who has gone forth
from home to homelessness, (1)

275. "is of scurrilous character,
a brute who delights in harassing others,
one's way of life is worse;
one stirs up dust for oneself. (2)

276. "A bhikkhu who delights in quarrels,
cloaked by the state of delusion,
does not know what has been declared,
the Dhamma taught by the Buddha. (3)

277. "Harassing one who is self-developed,
led on by ignorance,
one does not know defilement
as the path leading to hell. (4)

278. "Having entered the lower world,
going from womb to womb,
from darkness to darkness,
such a bhikkhu meets suffering after death. (5)

279. "As there might be a cesspit,
full to the brim, many years old,
such a one would be similar,
for one who is blemished is hard to purify. (6)

280. "When you know one like this,
bhikkhus, one attached to the home life,
of evil desires, evil intentions,
evil conduct and resort, (7) [50]

281. "having come together in harmony,
all of you should shun him.
Cast out the trash!
Expel the depraved fellow! (8)

282. "Then sweep the chaff away, non-ascetics
who imagine themselves ascetics!
Having blown away those of evil desires,
of evil conduct and resort, (9)

283. "let the pure, ever mindful,
make their dwelling with the pure.
Then, harmonious and judicious,
you will make an end of suffering." (10)

7 The Tradition of the Brahmins (Brāhmaṇadhammika Sutta)

Thus have I heard. On one occasion the Blessed One was dwelling at Sāvatthī in Jeta's Grove, Anāthapiṇḍika's Park. Then some affluent brahmins of Kosala—old, aged, burdened with years, advanced in life, come to the last stage—approached the Blessed One and exchanged greetings with him. When they had concluded their greetings and cordial talk, they sat down to one side and said to the Blessed One:

"Master Gotama, are the brahmins presently seen observing the brahmanical tradition of the ancient brahmins?"

"Brahmins, the brahmins are not presently seen observing the brahmanical tradition of the ancient brahmins."

"Please let Master Gotama speak about the brahmanical tradition of the ancient brahmins, if it would not be an imposition."

"In that case, brahmins, listen and attend closely. I will speak."

Those affluent brahmins replied: "Yes, sir." The Blessed One said this:

284. "The rishis of the past
controlled themselves and were austere;
having abandoned the five strands of sense pleasures,
they practiced for their own good. (1) [51]

285. "The brahmins did not own cattle,
nor did they keep bullion and grain.
They had study as their wealth and grain;
they guarded a divine treasure. (2)

286. "Whatever was prepared for them,
such food was placed at their doors.
People thought what was prepared in faith
should be given to those who sought it. (3)

287. "With cloths dyed various colors,
with bedding, and with dwellings,
[those from] prosperous provinces and realms
paid homage to those brahmins. (4)

288. "The brahmins were inviolable,
unconquerable, protected by Dhamma.
No one at all obstructed them in any way
at the doors of their homes. (5)

289. "For forty-eight years they observed
the spiritual life of virginal celibacy.
The brahmins in the past pursued
the quest for knowledge and conduct. (6)

290. "The brahmins did not marry outside,
nor did they purchase a wife.
Having united through affection,
they agreed to dwell together. (7)

291. "Apart from that occasion,
after her fertile season was over,
the brahmins never went to her
for sexual intercourse during the interval. (8)

292. "They praised the spiritual life
of celibacy and good behavior,
rectitude, mildness, and austerity,
gentleness, harmlessness, and patience. (9) [52]

293. "He who was supreme among them—
the brahmin firm in his exertion—
did not engage in sex,
even in a dream. (10)

294. "Training in accordance with his practice,
others here of intelligent disposition
praised the spiritual life of celibacy
as well as good behavior and patience. (11)

295. "Having requested rice,
bedding, clothes, ghee, and oil,
having righteously collected them,
they then performed sacrifice.
But at the sacrifice that was arranged,
they did not slaughter cattle.[103] (12)

296. "Like a mother, father, brother,
or any other relatives,
cows are our supreme friends,
since medicines are produced in them. (13)

297. "They give food and strength,
and so too beauty and happiness.
Having recognized this benefit,
they did not slaughter cattle. (14)

298. "Delicate, with large bodies,
handsome, and glorious, the brahmins
were keen on what was to be done and not done
according to their own traditions.
As long as these continued in the world,
this population happily flourished. (15)

299. "But an inversion took place in them:
having [previously] seen the slight as slight,
they saw the splendor of the king
and lavishly adorned women, (16)

300. "chariots yoked with thoroughbreds,
well made, with colorful coverings,
abodes and residences that were
designed and measured in proportion. (17)

301. "The brahmins then coveted
abundant human wealth
accompanied by herds of cattle,
and groups of resplendent women. (18)

302. "Having composed hymns to that end,
they then approached Okkāka and said: [53]
'You have abundant wealth and grain.
Sacrifice, you have much treasure;
sacrifice, you have much wealth.' (19)

303. "And then, convinced by the brahmins,
the king, lord of charioteers,
had these sacrifices performed:
the horse sacrifice, the man sacrifice,
the *sammāpāsa*, *vācapeyya*, and *niraggaḷa*.
He then gave wealth to the brahmins: (20)

304. "cattle and bedding and clothes
and lavishly adorned women;
chariots yoked with thoroughbreds,
well made, with variegated coverings; (21)

305. "residences that were delightful
and well designed in proportion.
Having filled them with various kinds of grain,
he gave this wealth to the brahmins. (22)

306. "Having obtained wealth there,
they agreed to store it up.
As they fell under the control of desire,
their craving increased still more.
Having composed hymns for this purpose,
they again approached Okkāka and said: (23)

307. "'Like water and the earth
like bullion, wealth, and grain,
just so are cattle [useful] to people,
for they are requisites of living beings.
Sacrifice, you have much treasure;
sacrifice, you have much wealth.' (24)

308. "And then the king, lord of charioteers,
convinced by the brahmins,
had many hundreds and thousands of cows
slaughtered in sacrifice. (25)

309. "They did not harm anyone in any way—
not with their feet or their horns.
The cows were as mild as lambs,
giving buckets of milk.
But having grabbed their horns,
the king slew them with a knife. (26) [54]

310. "Then the devas and the fathers,[104]
Indra, the asuras, and rakkhasas,
cried out, 'How unrighteous!'
because the knife struck a cow. (27)

311. "Formerly there were three illnesses:
desire, hunger, and old age.
But because of the slaughter of cattle,
there came to be ninety-eight. (28)

312. "This unrighteousness by violence
has come down as an ancient custom.
They kill the harmless creatures;
the sacrificers fall from righteousness. (29)

313. "In such a way this mean practice,
though ancient, is censured by the wise.
Wherever they see such a thing,
people censure the sacrificer. (30)

314. "When the Dhamma had thus been lost,
suddas and vessas were divided.
Numerous khattiyas were divided;
the wife despised her husband.[105] (31)

315. "Khattiyas and Brahmā's kinsmen,
and others protected by their clan,
disregarding the doctrine of birth,
have come under the control of sensual pleasures." (32)

When this was said, those affluent brahmins said this to the Blessed One: "Excellent, Master Gotama! Excellent, Master Gotama! Master Gotama has made the Dhamma clear in many ways, as though he were turning upright what had been overthrown, revealing what was hidden, showing the way to one who was lost, or holding up a lamp in the darkness so those with good eyesight can see forms. We now go for refuge to Master Gotama, to the Dhamma, [55] and to the Sangha of bhikkhus. Let Master Gotama consider us lay followers who from today have gone for refuge for life."

8 The Boat (Nāvā Sutta)[106]

316. A person should venerate the one
from whom he would learn the Dhamma,
just as the deities venerate Indra.
Being venerated, the learned one,
pleased with him, reveals the Dhamma. (1)

317. Having attended and listened to it,
practicing in accordance with the Dhamma,
a wise [pupil] who heedfully follows such [a teacher]
becomes intelligent, incisive, and astute. (2)

318. But if one resorts to a petty fool
who has not reached the goal and is full of envy,
not having discerned the Dhamma right here,
one meets death still immersed in doubt. (3)

319. It is like a man who might enter a river,
a torrent roiling with a swift current:
being swept away, flowing with the stream,
how could he help others to cross? (4)

320. Just so, without having discerned the Dhamma,
without attending to the meaning under the learned ones,
not understanding it oneself, immersed in doubt,
how can one get others to perceive it? (5) [56]

321. But as one who has embarked on a strong boat,
equipped with an oar and a rudder,
skillful, thoughtful, knowing the method there,
might thereby convey many others across, (6)

322. just so, a knowledge-master, self-developed,
learned and of unwavering character,
understanding it himself, might get others to perceive it—
those equipped with attentive ears as a supporting condition. (7)

323. Therefore one should follow the good person,
one who is intelligent and learned.
Having known the meaning, practicing along,
one who has understood the Dhamma can obtain bliss. (8)

9 What Good Behavior? (Kiṃsīla Sutta)

324. "Having what good behavior,
having what sort of conduct,
fostering what kind of actions,
can a person be properly settled
and attain the highest goal?" (1)

325. "One should be respectful toward elders, without envy;
one should know the proper time for seeing one's teachers.
When a Dhamma talk is occurring, one who knows the occasion
should listen carefully to well-spoken words. (2)

326. "One should go to teachers at the proper time,
having dropped one's pride, with a humble manner. [57]
One should recollect and practice the meaning,
the Dhamma, self-control, and the spiritual life. (3)

327. "Delighting in the Dhamma, delighted with the Dhamma,
firm in the Dhamma, knowing how to judge the Dhamma,
one should not engage in talk that corrupts the Dhamma
but should be guided by genuine well-spoken words. (4)

328. "Having abandoned laughter, chatter, lamenting,
annoyance, hypocritical deeds, scheming, greed, conceit,
stubbornness, crudeness, blemishes, infatuation:
one should live free from vanity, inwardly firm. (5)

329. "What is understood is the core of well-spoken words;
concentration is the core of what has been learned and understood.[107]
Wisdom and learning do not grow
for a person who is impetuous and heedless. (6)

330. "Those who delight in the Dhamma taught by the noble ones
are unsurpassed in speech, mind, and action.
Being settled in peace, gentleness, and concentration,
they have reached the core of learning and wisdom." (7)

10 Arouse Yourselves! (Uṭṭhāna Sutta)

331. Arouse yourselves, sit up!
What good to you is sleeping?
For what sleep can there be for the afflicted,
for those injured, pierced by the dart? (1) [58]

332. Arouse yourselves, sit up!
Train vigorously for the state of peace.
Do not let the King of Death, having caught you heedless,
delude you who have come under his control. (2)

333. Cross over this attachment
by which devas and human beings,
full of need, are held fast.
Do not let the opportunity pass you by;
for those who have missed the opportunity
sorrow when they arrive in hell. (3)

334. Heedlessness is dust always,[108]
dust follows upon heedlessness.

By heedfulness, by clear knowledge,
draw out the dart from oneself. (4)

11 Rāhula (Rāhula Sutta)

Introductory verses

335. "Do you not despise the wise man
because of constantly living with him?
Is the torchbearer of humankind
always respected by you?" (1)

336. "I do not despise the wise man
because of constantly living with him.
The torchbearer of humankind
is always respected by me." (2)

[The instruction]

337. "Having given up the five strands of sensual
pleasure,
so pleasing and delightful to the mind,
having renounced the home life out of faith,
be one who makes an end to suffering. (3)

338. "Associate with good friends,
and resort to a remote lodging,
secluded, a place with little noise;
be moderate in eating. (4) [59]

339. "Do not give rise to craving
for these—a robe and almsfood,
requisites and a lodging:
do not come back to the world again. (5)

340. "Be restrained by the Pātimokkha
and in the five sense faculties.
Let your mindfulness be directed to the body;
be full of disenchantment [toward the world]. (6)

341. "Avoid the mark [of sensual objects],
which is beautiful and connected with lust.
Develop your mind on the unattractive;
[make it] one-pointed, well concentrated. (7)

342. "And develop the markless state,
discard the latent tendency to conceit.
Then, by breaking through conceit,
you will live in tranquil peace." (8)

In such a way the Blessed One often exhorted the Venerable Rāhula with these verses.

12 Vaṅgīsa (Vaṅgīsa Sutta)[109]

Thus have I heard. On one occasion the Blessed One was dwelling at Āḷavī, at the Aggāḷava Cetiya. Now on that occasion the Venerable Vaṅgīsa's preceptor, the Elder Nigrodhakappa, had recently attained final nibbāna at the Aggāḷava Cetiya. Then, while the Venerable Vaṅgīsa was alone in seclusion, the following reflection arose in his mind: "Did my preceptor attain final nibbāna or not?"

In the evening, when he emerged from seclusion, the Venerable Vaṅgīsa approached the Blessed One, paid homage to him, and sat down to one side. [60] Seated to one side, the Venerable Vaṅgīsa said to the Blessed One: "Here, Bhante, while I was alone in seclusion, the following reflection arose in my mind: 'Did my preceptor attain final nibbāna or not?'"[110] Then, having risen from his seat, he arranged his upper robe over one shoulder, reverentially saluted the Blessed One, and addressed the Blessed One in verse:

343. "We ask[111] the teacher of perfect wisdom,
the cutter-off of doubts in this very life:
a bhikkhu passed away at Aggāḷava,
one well known, famous, inwardly quenched. (1)

344. "Nigrodhakappa was his name,
which you, Blessed One, gave to the brahmin.
Energetic, he lived intent on release,

paying homage to you, the one who shows the
durable. (2)

345. "O Sakya, we too all wish to know
about that disciple, O universal eye.
Fully attentive, our ears are ready to hear;
you are our teacher; you are unsurpassed. (3)

346. "Cut off our doubt! Tell me this:
announce he attained nibbāna, you of broad wisdom.
Speak up in our midst, O universal eye,
like thousand-eyed Sakka among the devas. (4)

347. "Whatever knots are here, paths of delusion,
factions of ignorance, bases of doubt, [61]
on reaching the Tathāgata, they no longer exist;
for he is the supreme eye for humans. (5)

348. "If no man would ever dispel the defilements
as a wind might dispel a mass of clouds,
the entire world would be enshrouded, utter darkness,
and even brilliant men would not shine. (6)

349. "But wise men are makers of light.
I consider you, O hero,[112] to be such a one.
Knowing, we come to one endowed with insight:
in the assemblies, disclose to us [the fate of] Kappa. (7)

350. "Quickly send forth your lovely voice, O lovely
one![113]
Like a goose that has stretched out, gently honk
with your rounded voice, well-modulated.
We are all upright: let us hear you! (8)

351. "He has abandoned birth and death entirely;
having pressed the pure one, I will make him speak the
Dhamma.
For worldlings cannot act on their wishes,
but for the tathāgatas, action is based on
comprehension. (9)

352. "This excellent declaration of yours
has been accepted [as coming] from one of upright wisdom.
This last reverential salutation is offered.
Knowing, do not delude us, you of perfect wisdom. (10)

353. "Having understood the noble Dhamma from top to bottom,
knowing, do not delude us, O one of perfect energy. [62]
As one afflicted by heat in summer longs for water,
I long for your word: so pour down the sound![114] (11)

354. "Was the beneficial spiritual life
that Kappāyana led not lived in vain by him?
Did he attain nibbāna or did a residue remain?
Let us hear just how he was liberated." (12)

355. "He cut off craving here for name-and-form," (said the Blessed One),
"the stream of the Dark One that had long lay dormant.
He crossed over birth and death entirely."
Thus spoke the Blessed One, chief of the five. (13)

356. "Having heard your word,
I am pleased, O best of rishis.
Indeed, my question was not in vain;
the brahmin did not deceive me. (14)

357. "The Buddha's disciple was one
who acted in accordance with what he said.
He cut through the net of Death,
extended tightly by the Deceiver. (15)

358. "Kappiya, O Blessed One,
saw the origin of clinging.
Kappāyana, indeed, overcame
the domain of Death so hard to cross." (16) [63]

13 Proper Wandering (Sammāparibbājanīya Sutta)

359. "I ask the muni, one of abundant wisdom,
who has crossed over, gone beyond, attained nibbāna,
inwardly firm:
having renounced the home life and discarded sensual
pleasures,
how would that bhikkhu properly wander in the
world?" (1)

360. "When he was uprooted [concern with] blessings,"
(said the Blessed One),
"with portents,[115] dreams, and lucky signs,
when he has abandoned the defects of blessings,
that bhikkhu would properly wander in the world. (2)

361. "A bhikkhu should remove lust for sensual
pleasures,
for pleasures both human and celestial;
having transcended existence, having penetrated the
Dhamma,
he would properly wander in the world. (3)

362. "Having put behind him divisive words,
a bhikkhu should discard anger and meanness;
when he has abandoned attraction and repulsion,
he would properly wander in the world. (4)

363. "Having abandoned what is pleasing and
displeasing,
without clinging, not depending on anything,
utterly released from things that fetter,
he would properly wander in the world. (5)

364. "He does not find a core in acquisitions,
having removed desire and lust for things taken up;
not dependent, not to be led by others,
he would properly wander in the world. (6) [64]

365. "Not hostile by speech, mind, and deed,
having rightly understood the Dhamma,
aspiring for the state of nibbāna,
he would properly wander in the world. (7)

366. "A bhikkhu should not be elated, thinking, 'He venerates me,'
and though insulted, he should not nurture resentment;
he should not be intoxicated over food gained from others:
he would properly wander in the world. (8)

367. "Having abandoned greed and existence,
a bhikkhu refraining from wounding and binding,
who has overcome perplexity, without darts:
he would properly wander in the world. (9)

368. "Having understood what is suitable for himself,
a bhikkhu would not injure anyone in the world;
having understood the Dhamma as it is,
he would properly wander in the world. (10)

369. "One who has no latent tendencies at all,
whose unwholesome roots have been uprooted,
who is wishless, without expectations:
he would properly wander in the world. (11) [65]

370. "One with influxes destroyed, with conceit abandoned,
who has transcended the entire pathway of lust,
tamed, quenched, inwardly firm,
he would properly wander in the world. (12)

371. "Endowed with faith, learned, a seer of the fixed course,
a wise one who, among partisans, does not take sides,
having removed greed, hatred, aversion,
he would properly wander in the world. (13)

372. "A purified conqueror whose coverings are removed,
a master of things, gone beyond, without impulse,

skilled in the knowledge of the cessation of conditioned
things,
he would properly wander in the world. (14)

373. "One who has overcome mental constructs
about things past and future,
having overcome, wise about purity,
released from all the sense bases,
he would properly wander in the world. (15)

374. "Having known the state, having penetrated the
Dhamma,
having seen clearly the abandoning of the influxes,
with the utter destruction of all acquisitions,[116]
he would properly wander in the world." (16)

375. "Surely, Blessed One, it is just so:
one who dwells thus is a tamed bhikkhu [66]
and has transcended all the things that fetter:
he would properly wander in the world." (17)

14 Dhammika (Dhammika Sutta)

Thus have I heard. On one occasion the Blessed One was dwelling at Sāvatthī in Jeta's Grove, Anāthapiṇḍika's Park. Then the lay follower Dhammika, together with five hundred lay followers, approached the Blessed One, paid homage to him, and sat down to one side. Seated to one side, the lay follower Dhammika addressed the Blessed One in verses:

376. "I ask you, Gotama, one of broad wisdom:
How does a good disciple act,
whether one who has gone from home to homelessness
or those lay followers who live at home? (1)

377. "For you know the course and destination
of the world together with its devas.
There is none equal to you, one who shows the subtle
meaning,
for they say you are the excellent Buddha. (2)

378. "Having directly experienced all knowledge,
you reveal the Dhamma, taking compassion on beings.
Your coverings are removed, you are the universal eye;
stainless, you shine radiantly in all the world. (3) [67]

379. "Erāvaṇa, the nāga king, came into your presence
when he heard you are 'the Conqueror.'
Having consulted with you, he departed[117]
[saying] "Excellent," delighted to have heard [your words]. (4)

380. "King Vessavaṇa Kuvera also approached you,
inquiring about the Dhamma.
When questioned, you answered him, O wise one,
and he too, having listened, was delighted. (5)

381. "Adherents of other sects given to debate,
whether Ājīvikas or Nigaṇṭhas,
all fail to overtake you in wisdom,
as one standing cannot overtake one walking swiftly. (6)

382. "These brahmins given to debate,
and also some who are elder brahmins,
are all dependent on you for the meaning,
as are others who think themselves debaters. (7)

383. "For this Dhamma, subtle and blissful,
has been well proclaimed by you, O Blessed One.
All wish to hear that alone: when asked,
declare it to us, supreme Buddha.[118] (8)

384. "All these bhikkhus sitting together
and the lay followers as well [wish] to hear it.
Let them hear the Dhamma realized by the stainless one
as the devas listen to Vāsava's well-spoken words."[119] (9)

385. "Listen to me, bhikkhus, I will proclaim to you
the cleansing Dhamma; all retain it in mind.[120] [68]
A thoughtful person, seeing the good,
should adopt that deportment proper for a monk. (10)

386. "A bhikkhu should not wander at the wrong time;
but at the proper time he should walk to the village for alms.[121]
For ties stick to one given to untimely wandering;
hence the buddhas do not wander at the wrong time. (11)

387. "Forms and sounds, tastes and odors,
and tactile objects drive beings mad.
Having removed desire for these things,
at the proper time one should enter for the morning meal. (12)

388. "Then, having obtained alms on the occasion,
having returned alone, one should sit down in seclusion.
Reflecting inwardly, one should not let one's mind
wander outside but should keep oneself collected. (13)

389. "If he should converse with a disciple,
or with anyone else, or with a bhikkhu,
he should speak about the sublime Dhamma;
he should not slander or criticize others. (14)

390. "For some contend in debate,
but we do not praise those of slight wisdom.
Ties from here and there stick to them,
for they send their minds far away. (15)

391. "Alms, a dwelling with bed and seat,
and water to wash the dirt from his cloak:
having heard the Dhamma taught by the Fortunate One,
a disciple of the one of excellent wisdom
should use these reflectively. (16)

392. "For in regard to almsfood, a lodging,
and water to wash the dirt from his cloak, [69]
a bhikkhu will not cling to these things,
as a water drop does not cling to a lotus leaf. (17)

393. "Now let me tell you the householder's duty,
how one should act to become a good disciple.

For this entire duty of a bhikkhu
cannot be carried out by one with possessions. (18)

394. "Having put down the rod toward all beings,
toward those in the world both firm and frail,
one should not kill living beings or cause to kill,
nor should one approve of others who kill. (19)

395. "Next, a disciple should not knowingly
take anything not given anywhere.
One should not cause stealing or approve of theft;
one should entirely avoid taking anything not given. (20)

396. "A wise person should avoid impure conduct
as one would avoid a blazing pit of coals.
But if one is incapable of the celibate life,
one should not transgress with another's spouse. (21)

397. "One who has entered a council or an assembly
should not speak falsely to anyone.
One should not make others lie or approve of false speech.
One should entirely avoid speaking untruth. (22)

398. "A householder who espouses this Dhamma
should not indulge in intoxicating drink.
He should not make others drink or approve of drinking,
having understood that this ends in madness. (23)

399. "Because of intoxication, foolish people do evil deeds,
and they make other heedless folk do such deeds. [70]
One should avoid this basis of demerit,
delightful to fools, causing madness and delusion. (24)

400. "One should not kill living beings or take what is not given;
one should not speak falsely or drink intoxicants.
One should abstain from sex, from impure conduct;
one should not eat at night [and] outside the prescribed time. (25)

401. "One should not wear garlands or apply perfumes;
one should sleep on a bed or a mat on the ground.
For this, they say, is the eightfold uposatha observance
taught by the Buddha, who has reached the end of suffering. (26)

402. "Hence confident in mind, having observed
the uposatha complete with its eight factors
on the fourteenth, fifteenth, and eighth of the fortnight
and during special periods, (27)

403. "in the morning the wise person
who has observed the uposatha,
rejoicing with a confident mind,
should distribute food and drink
to the Bhikkhu Sangha in a fitting way. (28)

404. "One should righteously support mother and father;
one should engage in a righteous business.
A heedful layperson, observing this practice,
reaches the devas called self-luminous." (29) [71]

III The Great Chapter
Mahāvagga

1 The Going Forth (Pabbajjā Sutta)

405. [72] I will tell of the going forth,
how the One with Vision went forth,
how, while investigating,
he approved of the going forth. (1)

406. "This home life is confinement,
a basis for dust;
the going forth is like[122] an open space":
having seen this, he went forth. (2)

407. Having gone forth, he avoided
evil deeds with his body.
Having abandoned verbal misconduct,
he purified his livelihood. (3)

408. The Buddha went to Rājagaha,
[the city] Giribbaja of the Magadhans.
Adorned with the excellent marks,
he walked for alms [in the city]. (4)

409. While standing in his palace,
Bimbisāra caught sight of him.
Having seen him endowed with the marks,
he uttered this statement: (5)

410. "Sirs, look at him,
handsome, stately, pure;

endowed with good conduct,
he looks a mere yoke's length ahead. (6)

411. "With downcast eyes, mindful,
it seems he is not from a low family.
Let the king's messengers run out.
[Find out] where the bhikkhu will go." (7)

412. The messengers sent by the king
followed closely behind him,
[thinking:] "Where will the bhikkhu go?
Where is his dwelling place?" (8)

413. Walking on alms without skipping houses,
his sense doors guarded, well restrained,
clearly comprehending, ever mindful,
he quickly filled up his bowl. (9) [73]

414. Having walked on alms round,
the muni departed from the city.
He ascended Mount Paṇḍava:
"His dwelling place must be here!" (10)

415. Having seen that he had entered his dwelling,
the messengers then[123] approached;
but one messenger returned
and informed the king: (11)

416. "Great king, this bhikkhu
lives on the eastern side of Paṇḍava.
He sits in a mountain cavern
like a tiger, a bull, or a lion." (12)

417. Having heard the messenger's report,
the khattiya set out in a fine vehicle.
Hurriedly, he departed
in the direction of Paṇḍava Mountain. (13)

418. Having gone along the ground for vehicles,
the khattiya descended from his vehicle;

having approached on foot,
he arrived and entered. (14)

419. Having sat down, the king greeted him
and then made polite conversation.
When the courtesies were finished,
he then uttered this statement: (15)

420. "You are young, a lad,
a youth in the prime of life,
endowed with beauty and stature,
like a well-born khattiya. (16)

421. "I will give you wealth—enjoy it
while shining at the head of an army,
accompanied by a troop of bull elephants.
Being asked, tell me your birth." (17)

422. "There is, O king, a country straight ahead,
on the slope of the Himalayas,
abounding in wealth and energy,
[ruled] by one native to the Kosalans. (18) [74]

423. "I am by clan an Ādicca,
by birth I am a Sakyan.
I have gone forth from that family, O king,
not longing for sensual pleasures. (19)

424. "Having seen the danger in sensual pleasures,
having seen renunciation as security,
I will go for the purpose of striving:
it is here that my mind delights." (20)

2 Striving (Padhāna Sutta)

425. "When, resolved upon striving,
I had gone to the Nerañjarā River,
as I was meditating very strenuously
to attain security from bondage, (1)

426. "Namucī approached me,
speaking compassionate words:
'You are thin, pale;
you're on the verge of death. (2)

427. "'A thousand parts belong to death,
one fraction of your life remains.
Live, sir, life is better!
While living, make merits! (3) [75]

428. "'While you are living the spiritual life
and performing the fire sacrifice,
abundant merit is stored up.
Why devote yourself to striving? (4)

429. "'Hard to travel is the path for striving,
hard to practice, hard to achieve.'"
Speaking these verses, Māra stood
in the presence of the Buddha. (5)

430. When Māra had spoken in such a way,
the Blessed One said this to him:
"Kinsman of the heedless, Evil One,
you have come here with a purpose. (6)

431. "I do not have any need
even for the slightest merit.[124]
It is fitting for Māra to speak
to those who have need of merits. (7)

432. "I have faith and energy too,
and wisdom exists in me.
When I am so resolute,
why do you ask me to live? (8)

433. "This wind might dry up
even the streams of the rivers,
so why, when I am resolute,
should it not dry up my blood? (9)

434. "When the blood is drying up,
the bile and phlegm dry up.
When my muscles are wasting away,
my mind becomes even more serene,
and my mindfulness and wisdom
and concentration become more firm. (10)

435. "While I am dwelling in such a way
I have experienced extreme pain,
yet my mind does not turn to sensual pleasures:
behold the purity of the being! (11) [76]

436. "Sensual pleasures are your first army;
the second is called discontent.
Hunger and thirst are the third;
the fourth is called craving. (12)

437. "The fifth is dullness and drowsiness;
the sixth is called cowardice.
Doubt is your seventh;
your eighth, denigration and pride. (13)

438. "Gain, praise, and honor,
and wrongly obtained fame [is ninth];
[the tenth is when] one extols oneself
and looks down at others. (14)

439. "This is your army, Namucī,
the squadron of the Dark One.
A weakling does not conquer it,
but having conquered it, one gains bliss. (15)

440. "I wear muñja grass;
wretched would life be to me.[125]
It's better that I die in battle
than live on defeated. (16)

441. "Some ascetics and brahmins,
engulfed here, are no longer seen.
They do not know the path by which
the disciplined ones travel. (17)

442. "Having seen the bannered army all around,
[and] Māra with his vehicle ready,
I will go out to meet him in battle:
may he not dislodge me from my place! (18)

443. "Though the world with its devas
cannot overcome that army of yours, [77]
I will destroy[126] it with wisdom,
like a fresh clay bowl with a stone. (19)

444. "Having gained mastery over my intention,
and with mindfulness well established,
I will wander from realm to realm,
guiding many disciples. (20)

445. "Heedful and resolute,
those practitioners of my teaching,
against your wishes, will go
to the state where one does not sorrow." (21)

446. "For seven years I followed the Blessed One,
[trailing him] step by step,
but I have not found an opening
in the Enlightened One, who is mindful. (22)

447. "There was a crow that circled around
a stone that looked like a lump of fat:
'Perhaps we'll find something tender here;
perhaps there may be something tasty.' (23)

448. "But finding nothing tasty there,
the crow departed from that place.
Just like the crow that attacked the stone,
we leave Gotama disappointed." (24) [78]

449. So much was he stricken with sorrow
that his lute fell from his armpit.
Thereupon that saddened spirit
disappeared right on the spot. (25)

3 Well Spoken (Subhāsita Sutta)

Thus have I heard. On one occasion the Blessed One was dwelling at Sāvatthī in Jeta's Grove, Anāthapiṇḍika's Park. There the Blessed One addressed the bhikkhus thus: "Bhikkhus!"

"Bhante!" those bhikkhus replied. The Blessed One said this:

"Bhikkhus, when speech possesses four factors, it is well spoken, not badly spoken, and it is blameless and irreproachable by the wise. What four? Here, a bhikkhu speaks only what is well spoken, not what is badly spoken. He speaks only Dhamma, not non-Dhamma. He speaks only what is pleasing, not what is displeasing. He speaks only what is true, not lies. When speech possesses these four factors, it is well spoken, not badly spoken, and it is blameless and irreproachable by the wise."

This is what the Blessed One said. Having said this, the Fortunate One, the Teacher, further said this:

450. "Well-spoken speech is best, the good say;
speak Dhamma, not non-Dhamma—that is second.
Speak what is pleasing, not displeasing—that is third;
speak the truth, not lies—that is fourth." (1) [79]

Then the Venerable Vaṅgīsa rose from his seat, arranged his upper robe over one shoulder, and having reverently saluted the Blessed One, said to him: "An inspiration has come to me, Blessed One! An inspiration has come to me, Fortunate One!"[127]

The Blessed One said: "Then express your inspiration, Vaṅgīsa."

The Venerable Vaṅgīsa then extolled the Blessed One to his face with suitable verses:

451. "One should utter only such speech
by which one does not torment oneself
nor cause injury to others:
that speech truly is well spoken. (2)

452. "One should utter only pleasant speech,
speech that is gladly welcomed.

One should speak words that bring nothing bad,
[speech] that is pleasing to others. (3)

453. "Truth, indeed, is deathless speech:
this is an ancient principle.
The good and the Dhamma, good people say,
are established upon truth.[128] (4)

454. "The speech that the Buddha utters
for the attainment of nibbāna, the secure,
for making an end to suffering,
is indeed the supreme speech." (5)

4 Sundarikabhāradvāja (Sundarikabhāradvāja Sutta)[129]

Thus have I heard. On one occasion the Blessed One was dwelling among the Kosalans on the bank of the river Sundarikā. Now on that occasion the brahmin Sundarikabhāradvāja was offering a fire sacrifice and performing the fire oblation on the bank of the river Sundarikā. Then, after he had offered the fire sacrifice and performed the fire oblation, the brahmin Sundarikabhāradvāja rose from his seat and surveyed the four directions all around, wondering: "Who might eat the remains of the offering?"

The brahmin Sundarikabhāradvāja then saw [80] the Blessed One sitting nearby at the foot of a certain tree with his head covered. Having seen him, he took the remains of the offering in his left hand and the waterpot in his right hand and approached the Blessed One. With the sound of his footsteps, the Blessed One uncovered his head. Then the brahmin Sundarikabhāradvāja, thinking, "This worthy one is shaven-headed, this worthy one is a shaveling," wanted to turn back. But it occurred to him: "Some brahmins here are also shaven-headed. Let me approach him and inquire about his social class."

Then the brahmin Sundarikabhāradvāja approached the Blessed One and said to him: "What is the worthy one's social class?" The Blessed One then addressed the brahmin in verses:

455. "I am not a brahmin nor am I a prince;
I am not a vessa or anything else.
Having fully understood the clan of worldlings,
owning nothing, with reflection I live in the world. (1)

456. "Clad in my cloak, homeless I wander,
with my head shaved, fully quenched within.
Since I am unattached to people here,
it is unfitting, brahmin, to ask me about my clan." (2) [81]

[The brahmin Sundarikabhāradvāja said:] "Brahmins, sir, ask other brahmins: 'Is the worthy one a brahmin?'"[130]

[The Blessed One:]

457. "But if you say you are a brahmin,
and say I am not a brahmin,
let me ask you about the Sāvittī,
with its three phrases and twenty-four syllables."[131] (3)

[The brahmin:]

458. "On what ground have many rishis, men, khattiyas,
and brahmins
here in the world performed sacrifices to the deities?"

[The Blessed One:]

"If an accomplished one, a Veda-master, at the time of
sacrifice,
gains an offering from anyone, it succeeds for the donor,
I say." (4)

[The brahmin:]

459. "Surely, this offering of his must succeed,"
(said the brahmin),
"since we have seen such a Veda-master.

It is because we have not seen those like you
that other people eat the sacrificial cake." (5)

[The Blessed One:]

460. "Therefore, brahmin, as you seek the good,
approach me here and ask your question.
Perhaps you may find here one at peace,
smokeless, untroubled, desireless, and very wise." (6)

[The brahmin:]

461. "Master Gotama, since I delight in sacrifice
I wish to hold a sacrifice but do not understand.
Let the worthy one instruct me: [82]
please tell me where an offering succeeds." (7)

[The Blessed One:]

"In that case, brahmin, lend an ear. I will teach you the Dhamma.[132]

462. "Ask not of social class but ask of conduct:
fire indeed is produced from any wood.
Though from a low family a steadfast muni
is a thoroughbred restrained by moral shame. (8)

463."One tamed by truth, endowed with taming,
who has reached the end of the Vedas,
one who has lived the spiritual life:
a brahmin who would sacrifice intent on merit
should make a timely oblation to him. (9)

464. "Those homeless ones who have abandoned sensual pleasures,
who are well self-controlled, straight as a shuttle:
a brahmin who would sacrifice intent on merit
should make a timely oblation to them.[133] (10)

465. "Those devoid of lust, with well-concentrated faculties,

freed like the moon from the grip of Rāhu:
a brahmin who would sacrifice intent on merit
should make a timely oblation to them. (11)

466. "Those who wander in the world without
attachments,
always mindful, having abandoned things taken as
'mine':
a brahmin who would sacrifice intent on merit
should make a timely oblation to them. (12)

467. "Having renounced sensual pleasures, faring
triumphant,
he who has known the end of birth and death, [83]
who has attained nibbāna, cool as a lake:
the Tathāgata is worthy of the sacrificial cake. (13)

468. "The same as the righteous, far from the
unrighteous,[134]
the Tathāgata is one of boundless wisdom,
untainted here or beyond:
the Tathāgata is worthy of the sacrificial cake. (14)

469. "He in whom there is no hypocrisy and conceit,
devoid of greed, with no sense of 'mine,' desireless,
with anger dispersed, inwardly well quenched,
that brahmin has abandoned the stain of sorrow:
the Tathāgata is worthy of the sacrificial cake. (15)

470. "He who has abandoned the residence of the mind,
who has no possessions at all,
clinging to nothing here or beyond:
the Tathāgata is worthy of the sacrificial cake. (16)

471. "He who is concentrated, who has crossed the flood,
and has known the Dhamma with the supreme view,
whose influxes are destroyed, who bears his final body:
the Tathāgata is worthy of the sacrificial cake. (17)

472. "He whose influxes of existence and caustic speech
are burnt up, vanished, and no longer exist,

that Veda-master in every way released:
the Tathāgata is worthy of the sacrificial cake. (18)

473. "He who has overcome the ties, for whom there are no ties,
who among those held by conceit is not held by conceit, [84]
who has fully understood suffering with its field and ground:
the Tathāgata is worthy of the sacrificial cake. (19)

474. "He who is not dependent on desire, a seer of seclusion,
who has overcome the view made known by others,
for whom there are no bases of any kind:
the Tathāgata is worthy of the sacrificial cake. (20)

475. "He who has penetrated phenomena far and near,
for whom they are burnt up, vanished, and no longer exist,
who is peaceful, liberated in the destruction of clinging:
the Tathāgata is worthy of the sacrificial cake. (21)

476. "He who has seen the destruction
and end of the fetters and of birth,
who has entirely dispelled the pathway of lust,
pure, faultless, stainless, flawless:
the Tathāgata is worthy of the sacrificial cake. (22)

477. "He who, by himself, does not perceive a self,[135]
concentrated, upright, inwardly firm,
who is without impulse, not barren, free from doubt:
the Tathāgata is worthy of the sacrificial cake. (23)

478. "He for whom there are no delusions within,
and whose knowledge sees into all phenomena,
who bears his final bodily form,
and has attained enlightenment—unsurpassed, auspicious—
to this extent there is purity of the spirit:
the Tathāgata is worthy of the sacrificial cake." (24) [85]

[The brahmin:]

479. "Let my offering be a truthful offering,
since I have found such a Veda-master.
Brahmā himself has been made manifest:
let the Blessed One receive it from me;
let the Blessed One enjoy my sacrificial cake."[136] (25)

[The Blessed One:]

480. "Food over which verses have been recited is not to be eaten by me;
this, brahmin, is not the principle of those who see.
The buddhas reject food over which verses have been recited;
there being such a principle, brahmin, this is their conduct. (26)

481. "Serve with other food and drink
the consummate one, the great rishi,
one with influxes destroyed, with regret stilled,
for he is the field for one seeking merit." (27)

[The brahmin:]

482. "Please [tell me], Blessed One, so that I might understand
who should eat the offering of one like me
seeking someone at the time of sacrifice,
after having met your teaching?" (28)

[The Blessed One:]

483. "One in whom aggression has disappeared,
whose mind is unsullied,
who is freed from sensual desires,
who has dispelled dullness; (29)

484. "one who has removed the boundaries,
who is skilled in birth and death,

a muni possessed of munihood,
one like that who has come to the sacrifice. (30)

485. "Having removed the frown,
pay homage to him with reverential salutation.
Venerate him with food and drink:
in such a way the offerings flourish." (31) [86]

[The brahmin:]

486. "The honorable Buddha deserves the sacrificial cake,
he is the unsurpassed field of merit,
the receptacle of sacrifice for all the world:
what is given to the worthy one brings great fruit." (32)

Then the brahmin Sundarikabhāradvāja said this to the Blessed One: "Excellent, Master Gotama! Excellent, Master Gotama! Master Gotama has made the Dhamma clear in many ways, as though he were turning upright what had been overthrown, revealing what was hidden, showing the way to one who was lost, or holding up a lamp in the darkness so those with good eyesight can see forms. I go for refuge to Master Gotama, to the Dhamma, and to the Sangha of bhikkhus. May I receive the going forth under Master Gotama, may I receive the full ordination."

Then the brahmin Sundarikabhāradvāja received the going forth under the Blessed One . . . [as at I,4] . . . became one of the arahants.

5 Māgha (Māgha Sutta)

Thus have a heard. On one occasion the Blessed One was dwelling at Rājagaha on Mount Vulture Peak. Then the brahmin student Māgha approached the Blessed One and exchanged greetings with him. When they had concluded their greetings and cordial talk, he sat down to one side [87] and said to the Blessed One:

"Master Gotama, I am a donor, a lord of giving, bountiful, devoted to charity. I seek wealth righteously, and having done so, from my wealth righteously gained, righteously acquired,

I give to one person, I give to two, three, four, five, six, seven, eight, nine, ten people; I give to twenty, thirty, forty, fifty people; I give to a hundred people and even more. When I give thus, Master Gotama, when I sacrifice thus, do I generate much merit?"

"Surely, student, when you give thus, when you sacrifice thus, you generate much merit. Student, one who is a donor, a lord of giving, bountiful, devoted to charity, who seeks wealth righteously, and having done so, from his wealth righteously gained, righteously acquired, gives to one person . . . gives to a hundred people and even more, generates much merit."

Then the brahmin student Māgha addressed the Blessed One in verse:

487. "I ask Master Gotama, the bountiful one,"
(said the brahmin student Māgha),
"wearing an ochre robe, wandering homeless:
when a householder devoted to charity, a lord of giving,
wanting merit, sacrifices intent on merit, [88]
by giving food and drink to others here,
in sacrificing, how[137] is his offering purified?" (1)

488. "When a householder devoted to charity, a lord of giving, (Māgha," said the Blessed One),
"wanting merit, sacrifices intent on merit,
giving food and drink to others here:
such a one succeeds through those worthy of offerings." (2)

489. "When a householder, a lord of giving, devoted to charity," (said the brahmin student Māgha),
"wanting merit, sacrifices intent on merit,
giving food and drink to others here:
describe, Blessed One, those worthy of offerings." (3)

[The Blessed One:]

490. "Those who wander unattached in the world,
owning nothing, consummate, self-controlled:

a brahmin who would sacrifice intent on merit
should make a timely oblation to them. (4)

491. "Those who have cut off all fetters and bondage,
tamed, liberated, untroubled, desireless:
a brahmin who would sacrifice intent on merit
should make a timely oblation to them. (5)

492. "Those who are released from all fetters,
tamed, liberated, untroubled, desireless:
a brahmin who would sacrifice intent on merit
should make a timely oblation to them. (6)

493. "Those who have abandoned lust, hatred, and delusion,
whose influxes are destroyed, who have lived the spiritual life:
a brahmin who would sacrifice intent on merit
should make a timely oblation to them. (7)

494. "Those in whom there is no hypocrisy and conceit, [89]
who are devoid of greed, with no sense of 'mine,' desireless:[138]
a brahmin who would sacrifice intent on merit
should make a timely oblation to them. (8)

495. "Those who have not fallen prey to cravings,
who, having crossed the flood, wander with no sense of 'mine':
a brahmin who would sacrifice intent on merit
should make a timely oblation to them. (9)

496. "Those who have no craving for anything in the world,
for any state of existence here or beyond:
a brahmin who would sacrifice intent on merit
should make a timely oblation to them. (10)

497. "Those homeless ones who have abandoned sensual pleasures,
who are well self-controlled, straight as a shuttle:
a brahmin who would sacrifice intent on merit
should make a timely oblation to them. (11)

498. "Those devoid of lust, with well-concentrated faculties,
freed like the moon from the grip of Rāhu:
a brahmin who would sacrifice intent on merit
should make a timely oblation to them. (12)

499. "Those who are at peace, devoid of lust, not irritated,
for whom there are no destinations, having abandoned them here:
a brahmin who would sacrifice intent on merit
should make a timely oblation to them. (13)

500. "Those who have entirely cast off birth and death,
who have overcome all perplexity:
a brahmin who would sacrifice intent on merit
should make a timely oblation to them. (14)

501. "Those who wander in the world as islands in themselves,
owning nothing, in every way released:
a brahmin who would sacrifice intent on merit
should make a timely oblation to them. (15)

502. "Those here who know this just as it is:
'This is the last life, there is no renewed existence':
a brahmin who would sacrifice intent on merit
should make a timely oblation to them. (16) [90]

503. "A Veda-master, delighting in jhāna, mindful,
attained to enlightenment, the refuge of many:
a brahmin who would sacrifice intent on merit
should make a timely offering to him."[139] (17)

[Māgha:]

504. "Surely my questions were not asked in vain;
the Blessed One has described for me those worthy of offerings.
You know this matter just as it is;
for this Dhamma has been thus understood by you. (18)

505. "When a householder devoted to charity,"
(said the brahmin student Māgha),
"a lord of giving, wanting merit, sacrifices intent on merit,
giving food and drink to others here, declare to me,
Blessed One, the excellence of the sacrifice." (19)

[The Blessed One:]

506. "Undertake sacrifice, and when sacrificing,
(Māgha," said the Blessed One),
"make the mind placid in every way.
For one sacrificing, the sacrifice is the basis:
established upon this, one discards faults. (20)

507. "One devoid of lust, having removed hatred,
developing a measureless mind of loving-kindness,
constantly heedful day and night,
pervades all directions measurelessly." (21)

[Māgha:]

508. "Who is purified, freed, and bound?
By what means does one go to the brahma world?[140]
Since I do not know, O muni, please tell me when asked.
The Blessed One is Brahmā made manifest, seen by me today, [91]
for in truth you are like Brahmā to us.
How is one reborn in the brahma world, O luminous one?" (22)

[The Blessed One:]

509. "One who performs a sacrifice with the threefold excellence, (Māgha," said the Blessed One),
"such a one should accomplish it with those worthy of offerings.
Having sacrificed thus, one rightly devoted to charity
is reborn in the brahma world, I say." (23)

When this was said, the brahmin student Māgha said to the Blessed One: "Excellent, Master Gotama! . . . [as at I,7] . . . Let Master Gotama consider me a lay follower who from today has gone for refuge for life."

6 Sabhiya (Sabhiya Sutta)

Thus have I heard. On one occasion the Blessed One was dwelling at Rājagaha in the Bamboo Grove, the squirrels' feeding ground. Now on that occasion a deity who had formerly been a blood relation of the wanderer Sabhiya had briefly recited a number of questions to him, saying: "You should lead the spiritual life, Sabhiya, under the ascetic or brahmin who answers these questions for you." Then, having learned those questions from the deity, the wanderer Sabhiya approached those ascetics and brahmins who were leaders of sanghas, leaders of groups, teachers of groups, well known and famous, ford-makers, [92] considered holy by many people; that is, Pūraṇa Kassapa, Makkhali Gosāla, Ajita Kesakambali, Pakudha Kaccāyana, Sañjaya Belaṭṭhiputta, and the Nigaṇṭha Nātaputta. He asked them those questions, but they did not reply. Not only did they fail to reply, but they displayed irritation, hatred, and displeasure, and they even questioned the wanderer Sabhiya himself.

Then it occurred to the wanderer Sabhiya: "Now these worthy ascetics and brahmins are leaders of sanghas, leaders of groups, teachers of groups, well known and famous, ford-makers, considered holy by many people; that is, Pūraṇa Kassapa . . . the Nigaṇṭha Nātaputta. When I asked them those questions, they did not reply. Not only did they fail to reply, but they displayed irritation, hatred, and displeasure, and even questioned me about them. Let me now revert to the lower life and enjoy sensual pleasures."

Then it occurred to the wanderer Sabhiya: "Now this ascetic Gotama, too, is the leader of a sangha, the leader of a group, the teacher of a group, well known and famous, a ford-maker, considered holy by many people. Let me approach the ascetic Gotama and ask him these questions." But it then occurred to him: "Those worthy ascetics and brahmins who are leaders of sanghas, leaders of groups, teachers of groups, well known and famous, ford-makers, considered holy by many people, are old, aged, mature, advanced in life, come to the last stage; they are elders, of long-standing, who have long gone forth; that is, Pūraṇa Kassapa . . . [93] . . . the Nigaṇṭha Nātaputta. Yet when I asked them those questions, they did not reply. Not only did they fail to reply, but they displayed irritation, hatred, and displeasure, and even questioned me about them. How then could the ascetic Gotama reply to those questions, when he is young in years and just newly gone forth?"

But it then occurred to him: "An ascetic should not be belittled or disparaged just because he is young. For even if an ascetic is young, he might be powerful and mighty. Let me then approach the ascetic Gotama and ask him these questions."

Then the wanderer Sabhiya set out on tour in the direction of Rājagaha. Wandering on tour, in stages he arrived at Rājagaha, at the Bamboo Grove, the squirrels' feeding ground, and approached the Blessed One. He exchanged greetings with the Blessed One, and when they had concluded their greetings and cordial talk, he sat down at one side and addressed the Blessed One in verse:

510. "Perplexed and full of doubt,"
  (said Sabhiya),
"I've come desiring to ask questions.
Please put an end to them for me.
Being asked questions by me in sequence,
answer me in accordance with the Dhamma."[141] (1) [94]

511. "You have come from afar,
  (Sabhiya," said the Blessed One),

"desiring to ask questions.
I will put an end to them for you.
Being asked questions by you in sequence,
I'll answer you in accordance with the Dhamma. (2)

512. "Ask me, Sabhiya, your questions,
whatever you wish in your mind.
For you I will put an end
to each of those questions." (3)

Then it occurred to the wanderer Sabhiya: "It is indeed wonderful! It is astounding! The other ascetics and brahmins did not even give me permission, but I have been given permission by the ascetic Gotama." Then pleased, jubilant, elated, full of rapture and joy, he asked the Blessed One a question:

513. "What has he attained, the one they call a bhikkhu?"
(said Sabhiya).
"In what way is one gentle, and how do they call one
tamed?
How is one said to be enlightened?
When asked by me, Blessed One, please answer."
(4) [95]

514. "When by the path practiced by oneself,
(Sabhiya," said the Blessed One),
"one has attained nibbāna, crossed over doubt,
abandoned nonexistence and existence,
lived [the spiritual life],
finished with renewed existence: he is a bhikkhu. (5)

515. "Equanimous toward everything, mindful,
one who does not injure anyone in all the world,
an ascetic who has crossed over, unsullied,
for whom there are no swellings: he is gentle. (6)

516. "One whose faculties have been developed,
internally and externally, in all the world,
having pierced through this world and the next,
one developed who awaits the time: he is tamed. (7)

517. "Having examined all mental constructs,
[and] saṃsāra, both passing away and rebirth,
rid of dust, unblemished, purified,
one who has attained the destruction of birth:
they call him enlightened." (8)

Then, having delighted and rejoiced in the Blessed One's statement, being pleased, jubilant, elated, full of rapture and joy, the wanderer Sabhiya asked the Blessed One a further question:

518. "What has he attained, the one they call a brahmin?"
(said Sabhiya).
"In what way is one an ascetic, and how is one bathed?
[96]
How is one said to be a nāga?
When asked by me, Blessed One, please answer." (9)

519. "Having expelled all types of evil,
(Sabhiya," said the Blessed One),
"he is stainless, well concentrated,[142] inwardly firm;
having gone beyond saṃsāra, consummate,
unattached, such a one is called a brahmin.[143] (10)

520. "One who is peaceful, having abandoned merit and
evil,
dustless, having understood this world and the next;
who has transcended birth and death,
such a one is truthfully called an ascetic. (11)

521. "Having washed away all types of evil,
internally and externally in all the world,
among devas and humans given to mental construction
he does not enter upon mental constructs:
they call him one who is ritually bathed. (12)

522. "One who does not commit any crime in the world,
having discarded all yokes and bondages,
who is not tied down anywhere, liberated:
such a one is truthfully called a nāga." (13)

Then . . . the wanderer Sabhiya asked the Blessed One a further question:

523. "Whom do the buddhas call a field-knower?"
(said Sabhiya).
"In what way is one skillful, and how is one wise? [97]
How is one called a muni?
When asked by me, Blessed One, please answer." (14)

524. "Having examined all the fields,
(Sabhiya," said the Blessed One),
"the celestial, the human, and the brahma field,
freed from the bondage that is the root of all fields,
such a one is truthfully called a field-knower. (15)

525. "Having examined all stores,
the celestial, the human, and the brahma store,
freed from bondage that is the root of all stores,
such a one is truthfully said to be skillful. (16)

526. "Having examined both translucencies,
internal and external, wise about purity,[144]
who has transcended the dark and bright,
such a one is truthfully said to be a pundit. (17)

527. "Having known the nature of the bad and good,
internally and externally, in all the world,
having escaped the tie and the net, he is a muni
worthy of veneration by devas and humans." (18)

Then . . . the wanderer Sabhiya asked the Blessed One a further question: [98]

528. "Having attained what do they call one a Veda-master?" (said Sabhiya).
"In what way is one cognizant, and how is one heroic?
How does one get to be called a thoroughbred?
When asked by me, Blessed One, please answer." (19)

529. "Having examined all the Vedas,
(Sabhiya," said the Blessed One),
"those that exist among ascetics and brahmins,
one rid of lust for all feelings,
having transcended all Vedas, is a Veda-master. (20)

530. "Having known proliferation [and] name-and-form,
internally and externally, as the root of illness,
freed from bondage, the root of all illness,
such a one is truthfully said to be cognizant. (21)

531. "One who has abstained from all evils here,
having transcended the suffering of hell,
an abode of energy,[145] heroic, keen in striving,
such a one is truthfully said to be a hero.[146] (22)

532. "One whose bonds have been cut off,
internally and externally, the root of ties,
freed from bondage, the root of all ties,
such a one is truthfully called a thoroughbred." (23)

Then . . . the wanderer Sabhiya asked the Blessed One a further question:

533. "Having attained what do they call one a learned
scholar?" (said Sabhiya). [99]
"In what way is one noble and how well conducted?
How does one get to be called a wanderer?
When asked by me, Blessed One, please answer." (24)

534. "Having learned and directly known all phenomena
in the world, (Sabhiya," said the Blessed One),
"whatever there is, blameworthy and blameless,
a conqueror, rid of perplexity, liberated,
untroubled everywhere: they call him 'a learned
scholar.' (25)

535. "Having cut off influxes and attachments,
that wise one does not return to the bed of the womb.
Having dispelled the threefold perception [and] the mire,

he does not enter upon mental constructs:
they call him 'a noble one.' (26)

536. "One here accomplished in good types of conduct,
always skillful, who has understood[147] the Dhamma;
one not tied down anywhere, liberated,
for whom there are no aversions, is well conducted. (27)

537. "Whatever kamma there is that ripens in suffering,
above, below, or across in the middle,[148]
having avoided it,[149] a practitioner of full understanding,
one terminates hypocrisy and conceit,
greed and anger, and name-and-form:
they call that accomplished one a wanderer." (28)

Then, having delighted and rejoiced in the Blessed One's statement, being pleased, jubilant, elated, [100] full of rapture and joy, the wanderer Sabhiya rose from his seat, arranged his upper robe over one shoulder, reverentially saluted the Blessed One, and extolled the Blessed One to his face with suitable verses:

538. "There are sixty-three approaches
based on the proclamations of ascetics,
O you of broad wisdom,
based on perception and perceptual labels,
which having removed, you went over the dark flood.[150]
(29)

539. "You have reached the end, gone beyond suffering;
you are an arahant, perfectly enlightened;
I think you are one whose influxes are destroyed.
Luminous, intelligent, abounding in wisdom,
end-maker of suffering, you led me across. (30)

540. "When you understood my perplexity,
you led me across doubt: homage to you!
O muni, accomplished in the ways of munihood,
not barren, Kinsman of the Sun, you are gentle. (31) [101]

541. "Where previously I was full of perplexity,
you answered me, One with Vision!
Surely, you are a muni, an enlightened one:
for you there are no hindrances. (32)

542. "And for you all states of anguish
have been dispersed and cleared away.
You have become cool, you are tamed,
steadfast, with truth as your endeavor. (33)

543. "When, O nāga, you, the nāga,[151]
the great hero, are speaking,
all the devas rejoice [in your teaching],[152]
including both Nārada and Pabbata. (34)

544. "Homage to you, thoroughbred of men!
Homage to you, supreme among men!
In this world together with its devas
you have no counterpart. (35)

545. "You are the Buddha, you are the Teacher,
you are the muni, the conqueror of Māra.
Having cut off the latent tendencies,
crossed over, you lead this population across. (36)

546. "You have transcended the acquisitions;
you have sundered the influxes.
You are a lion, without clinging,
you have abandoned fear and dread. (37)

547. "Just as a lovely white lotus
is not tainted by the water,
so too you are not tainted
either by merit or by evil.
Extend your feet, O hero:
Sabhiya pays homage to the Teacher." (38)

Then the wanderer Sabhiya, having prostrated himself with his head at the Blessed One's feet, said to the Blessed One: "Excellent, Bhante! . . . I go for refuge to the Blessed One, to the Dhamma, and to the Sangha of bhikkhus. May I, Bhante, receive the going forth under the Blessed One, may I receive [102] full ordination."

"Sabhiya, one formerly belonging to another sect who desires the going forth and full ordination in this Dhamma and discipline lives on probation for four months. At the end of the four months, if the bhikkhus are satisfied with him, they give him the going forth and full ordination as a bhikkhu. But individual differences are recognized by me."

"If, Bhante, one formerly belonging to another sect who desires the going forth and full ordination in this Dhamma and discipline lives on probation for four months, and if at the end of the four months the bhikkhus, being satisfied with him, give him the going forth and full ordination as a bhikkhu, then I will live on probation for four years. At the end of the four years, if the bhikkhus are satisfied with me, let them give me the going forth and full ordination as a bhikkhu."

Then the wanderer Sabhiya received the going forth under the Blessed One, he received full ordination . . . [as at I,4] . . . And the Venerable Sabhiya became one of the arahants.

7 Sela (Sela Sutta)

Thus have I heard. On one occasion the Blessed One was traveling on tour among the Aṅguttarāpans together with a large Sangha of bhikkhus, with [103] 1,250 bhikkhus, when eventually he arrived at a town of the Aṅguttarāpans named Āpaṇa.

The jaṭila Keṇiya heard: "The ascetic Gotama, the son of the Sakyans who went forth from a Sakyan family, traveling on tour among the Aṅguttarāpans together with a large Sangha of bhikkhus, with 1,250 bhikkhus, has arrived at Āpaṇa. Now a good report about that Master Gotama has circulated thus: 'That Blessed One is an arahant, perfectly enlightened, accomplished in clear knowledge and conduct, fortunate, knower of the world, unsurpassed trainer of persons to be tamed, teacher of devas and humans, the Enlightened One, the Blessed One. Having directly known and realized on his own this world with its devas, Māra, and Brahmā, this population with its ascetics and brahmins, its devas and humans, he makes it known to others. He teaches a Dhamma that is good in the beginning, good in the middle, and good in the end, with meaning and phrasing; he reveals a spiritual life that is perfectly complete and pure.' Now it is good to see such arahants."

Then the jaṭila Keṇiya approached the Blessed One and exchanged greetings with him. When they had concluded their greetings and cordial talk, he sat down at one side. As he sat there, the Blessed One instructed, encouraged, inspired, and gladdened him with a talk on the Dhamma. Then, having been instructed, encouraged, inspired, and gladdened by the Blessed One with a talk on the Dhamma, the jaṭila Keṇiya said to the Blessed One: "Let Master Gotama together with the Sangha of bhikkhus consent to accept tomorrow's meal from me."

When this was said, the Blessed One told him: "The Sangha of bhikkhus is large, Keṇiya, [104] consisting of 1,250 bhikkhus, and you place full confidence in the brahmins."

A second time the jaṭila Keṇiya said to the Blessed One: "Although the Sangha of bhikkhus is large, Master Gotama, consisting of 1,250 bhikkhus, and although I place full confidence in the brahmins, still let Master Gotama, together with the Sangha of bhikkhus, consent to accept tomorrow's meal from me." A second time the Blessed One told him: "The Sangha of bhikkhus is large, Keṇiya. . . ."

A third time the jaṭila Keṇiya said to the Blessed One: "Although the Sangha is large . . . still let Master Gotama together with the Sangha of bhikkhus consent to accept tomorrow's meal from me." The Blessed One consented in silence.

Then, knowing that the Blessed One had consented, the jaṭila Keṇiya rose from his seat and went to his own hermitage where he addressed his friends and companions, his relatives and family members thus: "Hear me, my honored friends and companions, relatives and family members. I have invited the ascetic Gotama together with the Sangha of bhikkhus for tomorrow's meal. Take care of the preparatory work for me."

"Yes, sir," his friends and companions, relatives and family members, replied. Then some dug out ovens, some chopped wood, some washed dishes, some set up a water jug, some prepared seats, while the jaṭila Keṇiya himself set up a pavilion.

Now on that occasion the brahmin Sela was staying at Āpaṇa.

[105] He was a master of the Three Vedas with their lexicon and rules of ritual, with their phonology and etymology, and with historical lore as the fifth; being skilled in philology and grammar, he was fully versed in natural philosophy and in the marks of a great man, and he was teaching the recitation of the hymns to three hundred brahmin students.

Now at the time the jaṭila Keṇiya had placed full confidence in the brahmin Sela. Then the brahmin Sela, while walking and wandering around for exercise attended by his three hundred brahmin students, came to Keṇiya's hermitage. There he saw some jaṭilas of Keṇiya's hermitage digging out ovens, some chopping wood, some washing dishes, some setting out water jugs, some preparing seats, and the jaṭila Keṇiya himself setting up a pavilion.

When he saw this, he asked the jaṭila Keṇiya: "Is Master Keṇiya to hold a marriage or a giving in marriage? Or is a great sacrifice in preparation? Or has King Seniya Bimbisāra of Magadha been invited with his troops for tomorrow's meal?"

"I will not be holding a marriage or a giving in marriage, Master Sela, nor has King Seniya Bimbisāra of Magadha been invited with his troops for tomorrow's meal, but I am preparing for a great sacrifice. The ascetic Gotama, the son of the Sakyans who went forth from a Sakyan family, while wandering on tour among the Anguttarāpans together with a large Sangha of bhikkhus, with 1,250 bhikkhus, has arrived at Āpaṇa. [106] Now a good report about that Master Gotama has circulated thus: 'That Blessed One is . . . the Enlightened One (Buddha), the Blessed One.' He has been invited by me for tomorrow's meal together with the Sangha of bhikkhus."

"Did you say 'Buddha,' Keṇiya?"

"I said 'Buddha,' Sela."

"Did you say 'Buddha,' Keṇiya?"

"I said 'Buddha,' Sela."

Then it occurred to the brahmin Sela: "Even this sound 'buddha' is rarely encountered in the world. Now the thirty-two marks of a great man have come down in our hymns, and the great man who is endowed with them has only two possible destinies, no other. If he lives the home life, he becomes a wheel-turning monarch, a righteous king who rules by the Dhamma, a ruler of the four quarters, victorious, who has attained stability in his country and possesses the seven gems. He has these seven gems: the wheel gem, the elephant gem, the horse gem, the jewel gem, the woman gem, the steward gem, and the governor gem as the seventh. His sons, who exceed a thousand, are brave and heroic and crush the armies of others. He rules over this earth bounded by the ocean, having conquered it by means of the Dhamma, without a rod, without a weapon. But if he goes forth from the home life into homelessness, he becomes an arahant, a perfectly enlightened buddha, whose coverings in the world are removed."

[He then asked:] "My good Keṇiya, where is Master Gotama, the arahant, the perfectly enlightened one, now living?"

When this was said, the jaṭila Keṇiya extended his right arm and said to the brahmin Sela: [107] "There, by that green line of the grove, Master Sela."

Then the brahmin Sela together with the three hundred brahmin students approached the Blessed One. He addressed the brahmin students: "Come quietly, sirs, treading step by step; for these Blessed Ones are hard to approach, like lions that wander alone. And when I am speaking with the ascetic Gotama, do not break in and interrupt me, but wait until our talk is finished."

Then the brahmin Sela approached the Blessed One and exchanged greetings with him. When they had concluded their greetings and cordial talk, he sat down to one side. He then looked for the thirty-two marks of a great man on the Blessed One's body. He saw most of the thirty-two marks of a great man on the Blessed One's body, except two; he was perplexed and doubtful about two of the marks, and he could not decide and make up his mind about them: about the male organ being enclosed in a sheath and about the largeness of the tongue.

Then it occurred to the Blessed One: "This brahmin Sela sees most of the thirty-two marks of a great man on me, except two; he is perplexed and doubtful about two of the marks, and he cannot decide and make up his mind about them: about the male organ being enclosed in a sheath and about the largeness of the tongue."

Then the Blessed One performed such a feat of psychic potency that the brahmin Sela saw that his male organ was enclosed in a sheath. [108] Next the Blessed One stuck out his tongue, and with it he repeatedly touched and stroked both ear holes and both nostrils, and he covered the whole of his forehead with his tongue.

Then the brahmin Sela thought: "The ascetic Gotama is endowed with the thirty-two marks of a great man; they are complete, not incomplete. Yet I do not know whether he is a buddha or not. However, I have heard aged brahmins advanced in years, the teachers of teachers, say that those who are arahants, perfectly enlightened ones, reveal themselves as such when their own praises are spoken. Let me extol the ascetic Gotama to his face with fitting verses."

Then the brahmin Sela extolled the Blessed One to his face with fitting verses:

548. "You are perfect in body, delightful,
well born and lovely to behold.
O Blessed One, golden is your color,
your teeth so white, you are full of vigor. (1)

549. "The features possessed
by a well-born man are all
to be found on your body,
these marks of a great man. (2)

550. "With clear eyes, bright face,
stately, erect as a flame,
amid this group of ascetics
you shine like the sun. (3)

551. "A bhikkhu so lovely to look on
with skin of a golden sheen—
why do you, one of supreme beauty,
adopt the state of an ascetic? (4)

552. "You are fit to be a king,
a wheel-turning monarch, lord of charioteers,
a victor in all the four quarters,
lord of the Jambu Continent. [109] (5)

553. "With khattiyas and great princes
all devoted to your service,

as king above kings, as a ruler of people,
you should exercise rulership, Gotama." (6)

554. "I am already a king,
(Sela," the Blessed One said).
"I am the unsurpassed king of the Dhamma,
I turn the wheel by means of the Dhamma,
the wheel that cannot be turned back." (7)

555. "You claim to be an enlightened one,"
(the brahmin Sela said).
"You say, Gotama,
'I am the unsurpassed king of the Dhamma.
I turn the wheel by means of the Dhamma.' (8)

556. "Who is your general, that disciple
who follows after the Teacher?
Who is it who helps you turn
this wheel that you set in motion?" (9)

557. "The wheel set in motion by me,
(Sela," the Blessed One replied),
"the unsurpassed wheel of Dhamma,
Sāriputta, the Tathāgata's offspring,
helps to keep turning. (10)

558. "What should be directly known is directly known,
what should be developed has been developed,
what should be abandoned has been abandoned:
therefore, brahmin, I am a buddha. (11)

559. "So remove your doubt about me
and be convinced, brahmin!
For it is rare to gain the sight
of the enlightened ones. (12) [110]

560. "I am one whose appearance
is rarely encountered in the world.
I am the Enlightened One,
brahmin, the unsurpassed surgeon. (13)

561. "I have become Brahmā, peerless,
one who has crushed Māra's army.
Having mastered all my enemies,
I rejoice, without fear from anywhere." (14)

562. "Sirs, hear this," (said Sela),
"as the One with Vision has spoken,
the surgeon, the mighty hero,
who roars like a lion in the forest. (15)

563. "Who having seen him, even one of dark birth,
would not place confidence in him,
the one who has become Brahmā, incomparable,
the one who has crushed Māra's army? (16)

564. "Whoever wishes may follow me;
who does not wish to may depart.
Here I will go forth under him,
this man of excellent wisdom." (17)

565. "If, sir, you now approve of the teaching
of the Perfectly Enlightened One,
we too will go forth under him,
this man of excellent wisdom." (18)

566. "There are three hundred brahmins here
who implore you, making salutations.
Let us live the spiritual life
under you, O Blessed One." (19)

567. "The spiritual life is well proclaimed,
(Sela," said the Blessed One),
"directly visible, immediate,
where the going forth will not be barren
for one who trains heedfully." (20)

Then the brahmin Sela and his assembly received the going forth under the Blessed One, and they received the full ordination.

Then, when the night had ended, the jaṭila Keṇiya had good

food of various kinds prepared in his own hermitage [111] and had the time announced to the Blessed One: "It is time, Master Gotama, the meal is ready." Then, in the morning, the Blessed One dressed, and taking his bowl and outer robe, he went with the Sangha of bhikkhus to the hermitage of the jaṭila Keṇiya and sat down on the seat made ready. Then, with his own hands, the jaṭila Keṇiya served and satisfied the Sangha of bhikkhus headed by the Buddha with various kinds of good food. When the Blessed One had eaten and had put aside his bowl, the jaṭila Keṇiya took a low seat and sat down on one side. Thereupon the Blessed One expressed appreciation with these verses:

568. "Fire offerings are the best of sacrifices,
Sāvittī the best of Vedic hymns.
The best of human beings is a king,
the sea the best for flowing rivers. (21)

569. "The moon is the best of celestial bodies,
the sun the best of things that shine.
For those desiring merit, the Sangha
is best for those who sacrifice." (22)

When the Blessed One had expressed his appreciation with these stanzas, he rose from his seat and departed.

Then, the Venerable Sela and his assembly, dwelling alone, withdrawn, heedful, ardent, and resolute, before long [112] realized for themselves with direct knowledge, in this very life, that unsurpassed consummation of the spiritual life for the sake of which clansmen rightly go forth from the household life into homelessness, and having entered upon it, they dwelled in it. They directly knew: "Finished is birth, the spiritual life has been lived, what had to be done has been done, there is no more coming back to any state of being." And the Venerable Sela together with his assembly became arahants.

Then the Venerable Sela together with his assembly approached the Blessed One. Having arranged his upper robe on one shoulder, extending his hands in reverential salutation toward the Blessed One, the Venerable Sela addressed him with verses:

570. "This is the eighth day, One with Vision,
since we went to you for refuge.
In these seven nights, Blessed One,
we have been tamed in your teaching. (23)

571. "You are the Buddha, you are the Teacher,
you are the muni, the conqueror of Māra.
Having cut off the latent tendencies,
crossed over, you lead this population across.[153] (24)

572. "You have transcended the acquisitions,
you have sundered the influxes.
You are a lion, without clinging,
you have abandoned fear and dread.[154] (25)

573. "Here these three hundred bhikkhus stand
saluting you with reverence.
Extend your feet, O hero:
let these nāgas pay homage to the Teacher." (26)

8 The Dart (Salla Sutta)

574. Without a sign, unknown
is the life of mortals here—
it is difficult and short,
and conjoined with suffering. (1) [113]

575. For there is no way by which
those who have been born will not die.
Death occurs also when one has reached old age:
for such is the nature of living beings. (2)

576. Just as when fruits have ripened,
there is always fear of their falling;[155]
so for mortals who have taken birth,
there is always fear of death. (3)

577. Just as the clay pots
produced by a potter
all finally end up by breaking,
such is the life of mortals. (4)

578. Both the young and the old,
both the foolish and the wise,
all go under the control of death;
all have death as their destination. (5)

579. When those overpowered by death
are going from here to the next world,[156]
the father cannot protect his son,
nor can one protect one's relatives. (6)

580. Even as the relatives are looking on
and wailing profusely,
see how each of the mortals is led away
like a cow to be slaughtered. (7)

581. Thus the world is stricken
by death and by old age;
therefore the wise do not sorrow,
having understood the way of the world. (8)

582. You who do not know the path
by which he has come or gone,
not perceiving either end,
yet lament without purpose. (9)

583. If while he is lamenting,
a bewildered person, injuring himself,
could derive some benefit,
a wise person too would do the same. (10)

584. It is not by weeping or sorrowing
that one attains peace of mind.
One's suffering arises still more
and one's body is harmed. (11) [114]

585. One becomes thin and pale,
and one inflicts injury upon oneself.
The departed are not thereby sustained;
thus lamentation is useless. (12)

586. Without abandoning sorrow,
a person incurs still more suffering.
Bemoaning the one who has died,
one comes under the control of sorrow. (13)

587. Behold others, too, about to depart,
people who fare according to their kamma:
living beings just trembling here,
having come under the control of death. (14)

588. In whatever way they conceive it,
it turns out otherwise.
Such is separation:
see the way of the world! (15)

589. Even if a person were to live
for a hundred years or longer,
there is separation from one's group of relatives
when one abandons life here. (16)

590. Therefore, having heard it from the arahant,
one should stop lamentation.
Having seen that he has departed and died,
realize, "I cannot [bring the dead back to life]."[157] (17)

591. Just as, if one's shelter were blazing,
one would extinguish the fire with water,
so too a sensible person—
wise, learned, skilled—
would quickly blow away arisen sorrow,
as the wind does a tuft of cotton wool. (18)

592. [Blow away] lamentation and muttering,
and one's own dejection:
seeking happiness for oneself,
one should draw out the dart from oneself. (19)

593. With the dart drawn out, unattached,
having attained peace of mind,
having overcome all sorrow,
sorrowless, one is quenched. (20) [115]

9 Vāseṭṭha (Vāseṭṭha Sutta)

Thus have I heard. On one occasion the Blessed One was dwelling at Icchānaṅgala, in a woodland grove near Icchānaṅgala. Now on that occasion a number of very well-known affluent brahmins were staying at Icchānaṅgala, that is, the brahmin Caṅkī, the brahmin Tārukkha, the brahmin Pokkharasāti, the brahmin Jāṇussoṇi, the brahmin Todeyya, and other very well-known affluent brahmins.

Then, while the brahmin students Vāseṭṭha and Bhāradvāja were walking and wandering for exercise, this chance conversation arose between them: "How, sir, is one a brahmin?" The brahmin student Bhāradvāja said: "When one is well born on both his maternal and paternal sides, of pure descent as far back as the seventh generation of ancestors, unassailable and impeccable with respect to birth, then one is a brahmin." The brahmin student Vāseṭṭha said: "When one is of good behavior and proficient in the observances, then one is a brahmin." But Bhāradvāja could not [116] convince Vāseṭṭha, nor could Vāseṭṭha convince Bhāradvāja.

Then the brahmin student Vāseṭṭha addressed the brahmin student Bhāradvāja: "Good[158] Bhāradvāja, the ascetic Gotama, the son of the Sakyans who went forth from a Sakyan clan, is dwelling at Icchānaṅgala, in the woodland grove near Icchānaṅgala. Now a good report about that Master Gotama has circulated thus: 'That Blessed One is . . . the Enlightened One, the Blessed One.' Come, good Bhāradvāja, let us go to the ascetic Gotama and ask him about this matter. As he answers, so we will retain it in mind." – "Yes, sir," the brahmin student Bhāradvāja replied.

Then the brahmin students Vāseṭṭha and Bhāradvāja went to the Blessed One and exchanged greetings with him. When they had concluded their greetings and cordial talk, they sat down to one side. The brahmin student Vāseṭṭha then addressed the Blessed One in verses thus:

[Prologue][159]

> 594. "We are both acknowledged to possess
> the knowledge we claim of the Three Vedas,
> for I am Pokkharasāti's pupil
> and he is a pupil of Tārukkha. (1)

595. "We are consummate in what is taught
by the experts in the Three Vedas;
skilled in philology and grammar,
in recitation we are like our teachers. (2) [117]

596. "A dispute has arisen between us, Gotama,
over the doctrine of birth:
Bhāradvāja says thus:
'One is a brahmin by birth,'
but I say one is such by action.
Know thus, One with Vision. (3)

597. "Since neither of us was able
to convince the other [of our view],
we have come to ask you, sir,
widely famed to be enlightened. (4)

598. "As when the moon becomes full
people salute it with reverence,
so in the world, venerating you,
they pay homage to Gotama. (5)

599. "So now we ask Gotama,
the eye arisen in the world:
Is one a brahmin by birth
or is one such by action?
Explain to us who do not know
how we should understand a brahmin." (6)

[The inherent distinctions among other living beings]

600. "I will explain to you both,
(Vāseṭṭha," said the Blessed One),
"in proper sequence, as they are,
the generic divisions of living beings;
for their kinds differ from one another.[160] (7)

601. "Know the grass and trees as well,
though they do not even make any claims:
their distinctive mark is produced by birth;
for their kinds differ from one another. (8) [118]

602. "Next come the moths and butterflies
even through the various kinds of ants:
their distinctive mark is produced by birth;
for their kinds differ from one another. (9)

603. "Then know the four-footed beings,
those both small and large:
their distinctive mark is produced by birth;
for their kinds differ from one another. (10)

604. "Know those whose bellies are their feet,
that is, the serpents, those long-backed creatures:
their distinctive mark is produced by birth;
for their kinds differ from one another. (11)

605. "Know too the fish that dwell in water,
whose range is the liquid depths:
their distinctive mark is produced by birth;
for their kinds differ from one another. (12)

606. "Next know the birds,
who fly with their wings in the sky:
their distinctive mark is produced by birth;
for their kinds differ from one another. (13)

[Humans are not intrinsically different from each other]

607. "While among these many kinds of beings,
their distinctive marks are determined by birth,
among humans there are no distinctive marks
produced by their particular birth. (14)

608. "Not by the hairs or the head,
not by the ears or the eyes;
not by the mouth or the nose,
not by the lips or the brow; (15)

609. "not by the neck or the shoulders,
not by the belly or the back;
not by the buttocks or the breast,
nor by the anus or genitals; (16)

610. "not by the hands or the feet
nor by the fingers or nails;
not by the knees or the thighs
nor by their color or voice:
birth does not make a distinctive mark
as it does for the other kinds of beings. (17) [119]

611. "Separately among human beings
nothing distinctive is found in their bodies.[161]
Classification among human beings
is spoken of by designation. (18)

[How human differences are conventional]

612. "The one among humans
who lives by husbandry,
you should know, Vāseṭṭha:
he is a farmer, not a brahmin. (19)

613. "The one among humans
who earns his living by various crafts,
you should know, Vāseṭṭha:
he is a craftsman, not a brahmin. (20)

614. "The one among humans
who lives by trade,
you should know, Vāseṭṭha:
he is a merchant, not a brahmin. (21)

615. "The one among humans
who lives by serving others,
you should know, Vāseṭṭha:
he is a servant, not a brahmin. (22)

616. "The one among humans
who lives by stealing,
you should know, Vāseṭṭha:
he is a thief, not a brahmin. (23)

617. "The one among humans
who earns his living by archery,

you should know, Vāseṭṭha:
he is a warrior, not a brahmin. (24)

618. "The one among humans
who lives by priestly service,
you should know, Vāseṭṭha:
he is a priest,[162] not a brahmin. (25)

619. "The one among humans
who rules over village and realm,
you should know, Vāseṭṭha:
he is a king, not a brahmin. (26)

[The marks of a true brahmin]

620. "I do not call someone a brahmin
based on genealogy and maternal origin.
He is just a pompous speaker
if[163] he is impeded by things.
One who owns nothing, taking nothing:
he is the one I call a brahmin. (27)

621. "One who has cut off all fetters,
who is not agitated,
who has overcome all ties, detached:
he is the one I call a brahmin. (28) [120]

622. "One who has cut the strap and thong,
the reins and bridle-band as well,
whose shaft is lifted, enlightened:
he is the one I call a brahmin. (29)

623. "One who, without hatred,
endures insults, attacks, and bondage;
whose power is patience, a powerful troop:
he is the one I call a brahmin. (30)

624. "One who is without anger,
observant, of good behavior, without swellings,
tamed, bearing his final body:
he is the one I call a brahmin. (31)

625. "Like water on a lotus leaf,
or a mustard seed on the point of an awl,
one who does not cling to sensual pleasures:
he is the one I call a brahmin. (32)

626. "One who understands right here
the destruction of suffering for himself,
whose burden is lowered, detached:
he is the one I call a brahmin. (33)

627. "One of deep wisdom, intelligent,
skilled in the path and the non-path,
who has reached the supreme goal:
he is the one I call a brahmin. (34)

628. "One who does not form bonds
with either householders or homeless ones,
who wanders without abode, of few desires:
he is the one I call a brahmin. (35)

629. "One who, having put down the rod
toward all beings frail and firm,
does not kill or make others kill:
he is the one I call a brahmin. (36)

630. "Not hostile among the hostile,
quenched among those who take up the rod,
not taking among those who take:
he is the one I call a brahmin. (37)

631. "One from whom lust and hatred,
conceit and denigration have dropped away,
like mustard seeds from the point of an awl:
he is the one I call a brahmin. (38) [121]

632. "One who utters no rough speech,
whose speech is articulate and truthful,
by which he does not hurt anyone:
he is the one I call a brahmin. (39)

633. "One here[164] who does not take
anything in the world not given,
long or short, subtle or gross, fine or plain:
he is the one I call a brahmin. (40)

634. "One in whom there are no yearnings
for this world and the next,
without desire,[165] detached:
he is the one I call a brahmin. (41)

635. "One in whom there are no attachments,
who, through knowledge, is rid of doubt,
who has arrived at firm ground in the deathless:
he is the one I call a brahmin. (42)

636. "One who here has transcended ties,
as well as both merit and evil,
who is sorrowless, dustless, and pure:
he is the one I call a brahmin. (43)

637. "One who is, like the moon,
stainless, pure, clear, and limpid;
for whom delight in existence is destroyed:
he is the one I call a brahmin. (44)

638. "One who has passed beyond this swamp,
the mire, saṃsāra, delusion,
a meditator who has crossed over, gone beyond,
without impulse and rid of doubt;
who has attained nibbāna through no clinging:
he is the one I call a brahmin. (45)

639. "One here who has abandoned sensual
pleasures,
who wanders without a home,
with sensual desire and existence destroyed:
he is the one I call a brahmin. (46)

640. "One here who has abandoned craving,
who wanders without a home,

with craving and existence destroyed:
he is the one I call a brahmin. (47)

641. "One who has discarded the human bond
and transcended the celestial bond,
fully detached from all bonds:
he is the one I call a brahmin. (48)

642. "One who has discarded delight and discontent,
become cool, without acquisitions,
a hero who has overcome the whole world:
he is the one I call a brahmin. (49) [122]

643. "One who completely knows
the passing away and rebirth of beings,
unstuck, fortunate, enlightened:
he is the one I call a brahmin. (50)

644. "One whose destination they do not know—
whether devas, gandhabbas, or humans—
an arahant with influxes destroyed:
he is the one I call a brahmin. (51)

645. "Before, after, and in the middle—
one for whom there is nothing at all,
one who owns nothing, taking nothing:
he is the one I call a brahmin. (52)

646. "The chief bull, the excellent hero,
the great rishi whose victory is won,
without impulse, cleansed, enlightened:
he is the one I call a brahmin. (53)

647. "One who knows his past abodes,
who sees heaven and the plane of misery,
who has reached the destruction of birth:
he is the one I call a brahmin. (54)

[Distinctions are based on deeds]

648. "For the name and clan ascribed to one
are a designation in the world.
Having originated by convention,
they are ascribed here and there. (55)

649. "For those who do not know this,
wrong view has long been their tendency.
It is just not knowing that they say:
'One is a brahmin by birth.' (56)

650. "One is not a brahmin by birth,
nor by birth a non-brahmin.
By action one becomes a brahmin,
by action one becomes a non-brahmin.[166] (57)

651. "One becomes a farmer by action,
by action one becomes a craftsmen.
One becomes a merchant by action,
by action one becomes a servant. (58)

652. "One becomes a thief by action,
by action one becomes a soldier.
One becomes a priest by action,
by action one becomes a king. (59) [123]

[The world goes round by action]

653. "So that is how the wise
see action as it really is—
seers of dependent origination,
skilled in action and its result. (60)

654. "By kamma the world goes round,
by kamma the population goes round.
Sentient beings are fastened by kamma,
which is like the linch pin of a moving chariot. (61)

655. "By austerity, by the spiritual life,
by self-control and by inner taming—
by this one becomes a brahmin;
this is supreme brahminhood. (62)

656. "One possessing the three clear knowledges,
peaceful, for whom renewed existence is finished:
know him thus, Vāseṭṭha,
as Brahmā and Sakka for those who understand." (63)

When this was said, the brahmin students Vāseṭṭha and Bhāradvāja said to the Blessed One: "Excellent, Master Gotama! . . . [as at I,7] . . . We now go for refuge to Master Gotama, to the Dhamma, and to the Sangha of bhikkhus. Let Master Gotama consider us lay followers who from today have gone for refuge for life."

10 Kokālika (Kokālika Sutta)[167]

Thus have I heard. On one occasion the Blessed One was dwelling at Sāvatthī in Jeta's Grove, Anāthapiṇḍika's Park. Then the bhikkhu Kokālika approached the Blessed One, [124] paid homage to him, sat down to one side, and said: "Bhante, Sāriputta and Moggallāna have evil desires; they have come under the control of evil desires."

When this was said, the Blessed One said to the bhikkhu Kokālika: "Do not say so, Kokālika! Do not say so, Kokālika! Be pleased with Sāriputta and Moggallāna, Kokālika. Sāriputta and Moggallāna are virtuous."

A second time the bhikkhu Kokālika said to the Blessed One: "Bhante, although the Blessed One has my faith and trust, still [I say] Sāriputta and Moggallāna have evil desires; they have come under the control of evil desires." And a second time the Blessed One said to the bhikkhu Kokālika: "Do not say so, Kokālika! . . . Sāriputta and Moggallāna are virtuous."

A third time the bhikkhu Kokālika said to the Blessed One: "Bhante, although the Blessed One has my faith and trust, still [I say] Sāriputta and Moggallāna have evil desires; they have come under the control of evil desires." And a third time the Blessed One said to the bhikkhu Kokālika: "Do not say so, Kokālika! . . . Sāriputta and Moggallāna are virtuous."

Then the bhikkhu Kokālika rose from his seat, paid homage to the Blessed One, and departed, keeping him on his right. Not long after the bhikkhu Kokālika left, his entire body became covered with boils the size of mustard seeds. Having been the size of mustard seeds, these then grew to the size of mung beans; then to the size of chickpeas; then to the size of jujube pits; [125] then to the size of jujube fruits; then to the size of an *āmalaka* fruit;[168] then to the size of unripe *beḷuva* fruits; then to the size of ripe *beḷuva* fruits.[169] When they had grown to the size of ripe *beḷuva* fruits, they burst open and oozed pus and blood. Then, because of that illness, the bhikkhu Kokālika died and, as a result of harboring animosity toward Sāriputta and Moggallāna, he was reborn in the Paduma hell.

Then, when the night had advanced, Brahmā Sahampati, of stunning beauty, illuminating the entire Jeta's Grove, approached the Blessed One, paid homage to him, stood to one side, and said to him: "Bhante, the bhikkhu Kokālika has died and, as a result of harboring animosity toward Sāriputta and Moggallāna, he was reborn in the Paduma hell." This is what Brahmā Sahampati said. Having said this, he paid homage to the Blessed One and, keeping him on his right, he disappeared right there.

Then, when the night had passed, the Blessed One addressed the bhikkhus: "Bhikkhus, last night, when the night had advanced, Brahmā Sahampati approached me and said to me: 'Bhante, the bhikkhu Kokālika has died and, as a result of harboring animosity toward Sāriputta and Moggallāna, he was reborn in the Paduma hell.' Having said this, he paid homage to me and, keeping me on his right, he disappeared right there."

When this was said, a certain bhikkhu [126] said to the Blessed One: "Bhante, how long is the life span in the Paduma hell?"

"The life span in the Paduma hell is long, bhikkhu. It is not easy to count it and say it is so many years, or so many hundreds of years, or so many thousands of years, or so many hundreds of thousands of years."

"Then is it possible to give a simile, Bhante?"

"It is possible, bhikkhu. Suppose there was a Kosalan cartload of twenty measures of sesamum seed. At the end of every hundred years a man would remove from it a single seed. That Kosalan cartload of twenty measures of sesamum seed might in this way be depleted and exhausted more quickly than a single Abbuda hell would go by. Twenty Abbuda hells are the equivalent of one Nirabbuda hell; twenty Nirabbuda hells are the equivalent of one Ababa hell; twenty Ababa hells are the equivalent of one Ahaha hell; twenty Ahaha hells are the equivalent of one Aṭaṭa hell; twenty Aṭaṭa hells are the equivalent of one Kumuda hell; twenty Kumuda hells are the equivalent of one Sogandhika hell; twenty Sogandhika hells are the equivalent of one Uppalaka hell; twenty Uppalaka hells are the equivalent of one Puṇḍarīka hell; and twenty Puṇḍarīka hells are the equivalent of one Paduma hell. Now, as a result of harboring animosity toward Sāriputta and Moggallāna, the bhikkhu Kokālika has been reborn in the Paduma hell."

This is what the Blessed One said. Having said this, the Fortunate One, the Teacher, further said this: [127]

657. "When a person has taken birth
an axe is born inside his mouth
with which the fool cuts himself
by uttering wrongful speech. (1)

658. "One who praises a person deserving blame,
or blames a person deserving praise,
collects bad luck with his mouth,
by which he finds no happiness. (2)

659. "Slight is this bad luck:
the loss of one's wealth at dice,
[the loss] of all including oneself.
It is much worse bad luck
to harbor hate against the holy ones.[170] (3)

660."For a hundred thousand nirabbudas
and thirty-six more, and five abbudas,[171]
the slanderer of noble ones goes to hell,
having set evil speech and mind against them.[172] (4)

661. "The speaker of slander goes to hell,
so too one who, having acted, says: 'I didn't do it.'
Having passed away, both are the same,
men of base actions in the next world. (5)

662. "When one defames an innocent man,
a pure person without blemish,

the evil falls back on the fool himself
like fine dust thrown against the wind."[173] (6)

663. "One intent upon the quality of greed
reviles others by means of speech; [128]
faithless, mean, stingy, miserly,
he is intent upon divisive speech. (7)

664. "Foul-mouthed, liar, ignoble one,
abortionist, evil one, wrongdoer,
base person, unlucky man, low born:
do not speak much here, you who are bound for hell. (8)

665. "You scatter dust to your harm,
when you, evildoer, malign the good.
Having done many bad deeds,
you will go to the abyss for a long time. (9)

666. "For no one's kamma is ever lost;
since it returns, its owner obtains it.
In the other world the dullard,
the evildoer, sees suffering in himself. (10)

667. "He arrives at the place of impalement,
which has iron hooks, sharp blades, and iron stakes. [129]
Then there is the food, which is like a ball
of hot iron, as is appropriate. (11)

668. "When speaking, [the wardens of hell] do not speak sweetly.[174]
They do not hasten; they do not offer shelter.
Those [hell beings] lie on coals spread out;
they enter a blazing mass of fire. (12)

669. "And capturing them in a net,
there [the wardens] strike them with iron hammers;
[the hell beings] come upon blinding gloom,
which is extended like a mist. (13)

670. "Then they enter the Copper Cauldron,
which is a blazing mass of fire;
they are boiled in them for a long time,
rising and sinking in the masses of fire. (14)

671. "Then the evildoer is cooked there
in [copper] mixed with pus and blood. [130]
Whatever region he resorts to,
he is afflicted[175] on making contact there. (15)

672. "There the evildoer is cooked
in water that is the abode of worms.
There is not even a shore to which to go,
for the pots all around are all alike. (16)

673. "Then they enter the Wood of Sword Leaves,
which is so sharp that their bodies are cut to pieces.
Having grabbed the tongue with a hook,
repeatedly slashing it, [the wardens] strike it. (17)

674. "Then they approach the impassable Vetaraṇī,
with its sharp blades, with razor blades.
The dullards fall into it—
those evildoers who have done evil deeds. (18) [131]

675. "While they are weeping there,
brown and spotted dogs devour them,[176]
as do flocks of ravens and very greedy jackals,[177]
while hawks and crows stab at them. (19)

676. "Difficult is this life here,
which the evildoer sees.
Therefore, in the remainder of one's life here,
a person should be dutiful and not be heedless." (20)

677.[178] The wise have counted those loads of sesamum seeds
to which [the life span] in the Paduma hell is compared:
they come to five koṭis of nahutas,
plus another twelve hundred koṭis. (21)

678. As painful as the hells are said to be here,
for just so long one must dwell there;
therefore one should always guard speech and mind
toward those who are pure, virtuous, full of good
qualities. (22)

11 Nālaka (Nālaka Sutta)

Introductory verses

679. The rishi Asita, while passing the day,
saw the Tāvatiṃsa devas, joyful and ecstatic.
Having honored Indra, clad in clean garments,
carrying streamers, they were proclaiming exuberant
praise. (1) [132]

680. Having seen the devas exultant and elated,
having shown them respect, he said this to them:
"For what reason is the group of devas exuberantly
jubilant?
Why do you take streamers and swirl them around? (2)

681. "Even when there was a battle with the asuras,
when the gods were victorious and the asuras defeated,
even then there was no such excitement.
What wonder have the gods seen that they rejoice? (3)

682. "They whistle and sing and play music;
they clap their arms and dance around.
I ask you, dwellers on Mount Meru's peak:
dear sirs, quickly dispel my bafflement." (4)

683. "In Lumbinī, a village in the Sakyan country,
the Bodhisatta—the excellent gem, unequaled—has been
born
into the human world for well-being and happiness;
hence we are so delighted and extremely jubilant. (5)

684. "He is the best of all beings, the foremost person,
the chief bull of men, the best of all creatures. [133]

He will turn the wheel in the grove named for the
rishis,[179]
roaring like a powerful lion, the lord of beasts." (6)

685. Having heard that utterance, he quickly descended,
and then approached the residence of Suddhodana.
Having sat down there, he said to the Sakyans:
"Where is the prince? I too wish to see him." (7)

686. Then the Sakyans showed Asita their son,
who was radiant with splendor and of perfect color;
the prince shone like gold burnished
in the mouth of a furnace by one highly skilled. (8)

687. Having seen the prince blazing like a crested flame,
pure like the moon, lord of stars, moving in the sky,
like the beaming autumn sun freed from clouds,
already delighted, he gained abundant joy. (9)

688. The gods held up a parasol in the sky
with multiple ribs and a thousand circles.
Golden-handled chowries moved up and down,
but none were seen holding the chowries or parasol. (10)
[134]

689. The matted-hair rishi named "Black Glory,"
having seen him like a gold nugget on a red blanket,
with the white parasol being held over his head,
received him, elated and happy. (11)

690. Then, having received the Sakyan bull,
examining him, the master of marks and hymns
was pleased in mind and emitted a cry:
"He is unsurpassed, the best of bipeds." (12)

691. Then, recollecting his own departure,
he became dismayed and shed bitter tears.
Seeing this, the Sakyans asked the weeping rishi:
"Will some misfortune befall the prince?" (13)

692. Seeing the Sakyans dismayed, the rishi said:
"I do not foresee harm for the prince.
There will be no obstacle for him,
not the least, so set your minds at ease. (14)

693. "This prince will reach the foremost enlightenment;
one of supremely purified sight, compassionate for many people,
he will set in motion the wheel of the Dhamma;
his spiritual life will become widespread. (15) [135]

694. "But the remainder of my life here is not long;
my death will occur in the interval.
I will not hear the Dhamma of the one unequaled in fortitude.
Hence I am troubled, distressed, and dejected." (16)

695. Having brought the Sakyans abundant joy,
the holy man left the palace.
Out of compassion for his own nephew,
he enjoined him in the Dhamma
of the one unequaled in fortitude. (17)

696. "When you hear from another the word 'buddha,'
[and] 'one who attained enlightenment
reveals[180] the foremost Dhamma,'
having gone to him, asking about his doctrine,
lead the spiritual life under that Blessed One." (18)

697. Instructed by such a one with benevolent mind,
whose vision of the future was supremely purified,
Nālaka, one with a store of accumulated merit,
expecting the Conqueror, dwelled with guarded faculties. (19)

698. Having heard the word about the Conqueror
setting in motion the excellent wheel [of the Dhamma],
having gone, he saw the chief rishi and was pleased. [136]
Since [the time for] Asita's instruction had arrived,
he asked the excellent muni about supreme munihood. (20)

[The instruction]

699. "This statement of Asita
has been known by me to be true to fact.
Therefore I ask you, O Gotama,
one who has gone beyond all phenomena. (21)

700. "Since I have entered the homeless life,
seeking sustenance on alms round,
being asked, O muni, please explain to me
munihood, the ultimate way." (22)

701. "I will describe munihood to you,"
(the Blessed One said),
"hard to practice and hard to master.
Come, I will tell you about it—
brace yourself and be firm. (23)

702. "One should have the same attitude[181]
whether one is insulted or venerated in the village.
One should guard against anger in the mind;
one should keep calm, without being elated. (24) [137]

703. "Diverse impressions high and low
come forth like flames in a forest.
Women try to seduce a muni—
do not let them seduce you! (25)

704. "Refraining from sexual intercourse,
having given up sensual pleasures fine and coarse;
one should not be hostile or attached
to living beings both frail and firm. (26)

705. "[Reflecting] 'As I am, so are they;
as they are, so am I,'
having taken oneself as the criterion,
one should not kill or cause others to kill. (27)

706. "Having given up desire and greed
for that to which the worldling is attached,

one with vision should practice
so that one may cross this inferno. (28)

707. "Not filling one's belly, moderate in food,
one should be of few desires, without longing.
One is hungerless with respect to desire;
desireless, one is quenched. (29)

708. "Having wandered on alms round,
he should resort to the woods.
Staying at the foot of a tree,
the muni should take his seat. (30)

709. "That steadfast one intent on jhāna
should take delight in the woods.
He should meditate at the foot of a tree,
making himself fully content. (31)

710. "Then, with the passing of the night,
he should approach the village.
He should not welcome invitations
and offerings brought from the village. (32)

711. "When the muni has come to the village,
he should not behave rashly among families.
Having cut off talk aimed at getting food,
he should not utter suggestive words. (33)

712. "'I received something, that is good;
I received nothing, that is fine.'
In both situations remaining impartial,
he returns to the tree itself. (34) [138]

713. "Wandering with bowl in hand,
not dumb though considered dumb,
one should not scorn a small offering
nor should one despise the giver. (35)

714. "High and low is the practice
taught by the Ascetic.

They do not go in two ways to the far shore;
[yet] it is not experienced in a single way. (36)

715. "For one who has no diffusion,
for a bhikkhu who has cut off the stream,
who has abandoned what is to be done and not done,
no fever [of defilements] exists. (37)

716. "I will describe munihood to you,"
(the Blessed One said).
"One should treat it like the blade of a razor.
Having pressed one's palate with the tongue,
exert control over one's belly. (38)

717. "One should not be sluggish in mind,
nor should one ponder much.
Be unpolluted, unattached,
with the spiritual life as one's support. (39)

718. "One should train in a solitary seat
and in the exercise of an ascetic.
It is solitude that is called munihood.
If you will delight alone,[182]
you will light up the ten directions.[183] (40)

719. "Having heard the acclaim of the wise,
of the meditators who have renounced sensual
pleasures,
my follower should develop even more
a sense of moral shame and faith. (41) [139]

720. "Understand this by way of rivers
and in terms of clefts and ravines.
The creeks flow on noisily,
but silently the great rivers flow. (42)

721. "What is empty makes a noise;
what is full is ever quiet.
The fool is like a half-full barrel,
the wise man like a full lake. (43)

722. "When the Ascetic speaks much,[184]
it is meaningful and beneficial.
Knowing, he teaches the Dhamma;
knowing, he speaks much. (44)

723. "But one who, knowing, is self-controlled,
who, knowing, does not speak much:
that muni is worthy of munihood;
that muni has achieved munihood." (45)

12 Contemplation of Dyads (Dvayatānupassanā Sutta)

Thus have I heard. On one occasion the Blessed One was dwelling in Sāvatthī in the Eastern Park in Migāramātā's mansion. Now on that occasion—the uposatha day of the fifteenth, the full-moon night—the Blessed One was seated in the open surrounded by the Sangha of bhikkhus. [140] Then, having surveyed the completely silent Sangha of bhikkhus, he addressed them thus:

"Bhikkhus, if others ask you, 'What is your aim in listening to those teachings that are wholesome, noble, emancipating, leading to enlightenment?' you should answer them thus: 'For the accurate knowledge of things arranged in dyads.' And what would one call a dyad?

[1. The four noble truths][185]

"'This is suffering, this is the origin of suffering'—this is one contemplation. 'This is the cessation of suffering, this is the way leading to the cessation of suffering'—this is a second contemplation. When a bhikkhu dwells thus correctly contemplating a dyad—heedful, ardent, and resolute—one of two fruits is to be expected of him: either final knowledge in this very life or, if there is a residue remaining, the state of non-returning."

This is what the Blessed One said. Having said this, the Fortunate One, the Teacher, further said this:

724. "Those who do not understand suffering,
or the origin of suffering;
who do not know where suffering

completely ceases without remainder;
and who do not know the path
that leads to the allaying of suffering: (1)

725. "they are destitute of liberation of mind
and also of liberation by wisdom.
Incapable of making an end,
they fare on to birth and old age. (2)

726. "But those who understand suffering,
and the origin of suffering;
[who know as well] where suffering
completely ceases without remainder; [141]
and who understand the path
that leads to the allaying of suffering: (3)

727. "they are possessed of mind's liberation
and also liberation by wisdom.
Capable of making an end,
they fare no more to birth and old age. (4)

[2. Acquisition]
"If, bhikkhus, there are those who ask, 'Could there be correct contemplation of dyads in some other way?' you should answer them thus: 'There could be.' And how could there be? 'Whatever suffering originates is all conditioned by acquisition'—this is one contemplation. 'With the remainderless fading away and cessation of acquisitions, there is no origination of suffering'—this is a second contemplation. When a bhikkhu dwells thus . . ." the Teacher further said this:

728. "Sufferings in their many forms in the world
originate based on acquisition.
The ignorant dullard who creates acquisition[186]
encounters suffering again and again.
Therefore, understanding, one should not create
acquisition,
contemplating it as the genesis and origin of suffering. (5)

[3. Ignorance]

"If, bhikkhus, there are those who ask, 'Could there be correct contemplation of dyads in some other way?' you should answer them thus: 'There could be.' And how could there be? 'Whatever suffering originates is all conditioned by ignorance'—this is one contemplation. 'With the remainderless fading away and cessation of ignorance, there is no origination of suffering'—this is a second contemplation. When a bhikkhu dwells thus . . ." the Teacher further said this: [142]

729. "Those who travel again and again
in the saṃsāra of birth and death,
with its becoming thus, becoming otherwise:
that journey is due to ignorance. (6)

730. "It is because of ignorance, this great delusion,
that one has wandered on for so long.
But those beings who have gained clear knowledge
do not come back to renewed existence.[187] (7)

[4. Volitional activities]

"If, bhikkhus, there are those who ask, 'Could there be correct contemplation of dyads in some other way?' you should answer them thus: 'There could be.' And how could there be? 'Whatever suffering originates is all conditioned by volitional activities'—this is one contemplation. 'With the remainderless fading away and cessation of volitional activities, there is no origination of suffering'—this is a second contemplation. When a bhikkhu dwells thus . . ." the Teacher further said this:

731. "Whatever suffering originates
is all conditioned by volitional activities.
With the cessation of volitional activities,
there is no origination of suffering. (8)

732. "When one has known this danger,
'Suffering is conditioned by volitional activities,'
by the stilling of all volitional activities,
by the stopping of perceptions,

the destruction of suffering occurs
when one has known this as it really is. (9)

733. "Seeing rightly, the masters of knowledge,
the wise ones, having correctly known this,
overcome the yoke of Māra
and do not come back to renewed existence. (10) [143]

[5. Consciousness]

"If, bhikkhus, there are those who ask, 'Could there be correct contemplation of dyads in some other way?' you should answer them thus: 'There could be.' And how could there be? 'Whatever suffering originates is all conditioned by consciousness'—this is one contemplation. 'With the remainderless fading away and cessation of consciousness, there is no origination of suffering'—this is a second contemplation. When a bhikkhu dwells thus . . ." the Teacher further said this:

734. "Whatever suffering originates
is all conditioned by consciousness.
With the cessation of consciousness,
there is no origination of suffering. (11)

735. "Having understood this danger,
'Suffering is conditioned by consciousness,'
by the stilling of consciousness, a bhikkhu,
hungerless, has attained nibbāna. (12)

[6. Contact]

"If, bhikkhus, there are those who ask, 'Could there be correct contemplation of dyads in some other way?' you should answer them thus: 'There could be.' And how could there be? 'Whatever suffering originates is all conditioned by contact'—this is one contemplation. 'With the remainderless fading away and cessation of contact, there is no origination of suffering'—this is a second contemplation. When a bhikkhu dwells thus . . ." the Teacher further said this:

736. "Those afflicted by contact,
flowing along with the stream of existence,

have entered upon a deviant path:
the destruction of the fetters is far from them. (13)

737. "But those who have fully understood contact,
who, having known it, delight in peace,
by breaking through contact,
hungerless, are fully quenched. (14)

[7. Feeling]

"If, bhikkhus, there are those who ask, 'Could there be correct contemplation of dyads in some other way?' you should answer them thus: 'There could be.' And how could there be? 'Whatever suffering originates is all conditioned by feeling'—this is one contemplation. 'With the remainderless fading away and cessation of feeling, there is no origination of suffering'—this is a second contemplation. When a bhikkhu dwells thus . . ." the Teacher further said this: [144]

738. "Whether it is pleasant or painful
or neither-painful-nor-pleasant,
whatever there is that is felt
internally and externally, (15)

739. "having known, 'This is suffering,
of a false nature, disintegrating,'
having touched and touched them,
seeing their vanishing, one understands them thus.[188]
Through the destruction of feelings, a bhikkhu,
hungerless, is fully quenched. (16)

[8. Craving]

"If, bhikkhus, there are those who ask, 'Could there be correct contemplation of dyads in some other way?' you should answer them thus: 'There could be.' And how could there be? 'Whatever suffering originates is all conditioned by craving'—this is one contemplation. 'With the remainderless fading away and cessation of craving, there is no origination of suffering'—this is a second contemplation. When a bhikkhu dwells thus . . ." the Teacher further said this:

740. "With craving as partner, a person,
wandering on this long journey,
does not transcend saṃsāra,
with its becoming thus, becoming otherwise. (17)

741. "Having known this danger,
'Craving is the origin of suffering,'
a bhikkhu should wander mindfully,
free of craving, without grasping. (18)

[9. Clinging]

"If, bhikkhus, there are those who ask, 'Could there be correct contemplation of dyads in some other way?' you should answer them thus: 'There could be.' And how could there be? 'Whatever suffering originates is all conditioned by clinging'—this is one contemplation. 'With the remainderless fading away and cessation of clinging, there is no origination of suffering'—this is a second contemplation. When a bhikkhu dwells thus . . ." the Teacher further said this:

742. "Existence is conditioned by clinging;
an existent being undergoes suffering.
For one who is born there is death;
this is the origin of suffering. (19)

743. "Therefore, having correctly understood,
having directly known the destruction of birth,
through the destruction of clinging the wise
do not come back to renewed existence. (20) [145]

[10. Instigation]

"If, bhikkhus, there are those who ask, 'Could there be correct contemplation of dyads in some other way?' you should answer them thus: 'There could be.' And how could there be? 'Whatever suffering originates is all conditioned by instigation'—this is one contemplation. 'With the remainderless fading away and cessation of instigation, there is no origination of suffering'—this is a second contemplation. When a bhikkhu dwells thus . . ." the Teacher further said this:

744. "Whatever suffering originates
is all conditioned by instigation.
With the cessation of instigation,
there is no origination of suffering. (21)

745. "Having known this danger,
'Suffering is conditioned by instigation,'
having relinquished all instigation,
one is liberated in non-instigation. (22)

746. "A bhikkhu with a peaceful mind,
who has cut off the craving for existence,
has finished with the wandering on in births;[189]
for him there is no renewed existence. (23)

[11. Nutriment]

"If, bhikkhus, there are those who ask, 'Could there be correct contemplation of dyads in some other way?' you should answer them thus: 'There could be.' And how could there be? 'Whatever suffering originates is all conditioned by nutriment'—this is one contemplation. 'With the remainderless fading away and cessation of nutriment, there is no origination of suffering'—this is a second contemplation. When a bhikkhu dwells thus . . ." the Teacher further said this:

747. "Whatever suffering originates
is all conditioned by nutriment.
With the cessation of nutriment,
there is no origination of suffering. (24)

748. "Having known this danger,
'Suffering is conditioned by nutriment,'
having fully understood all nutriment,
one is not attached to any nutriment. (25) [146]

749. "Having correctly understood the state of health
through the utter destruction of the influxes,
using with reflection, firm in the Dhamma,
a master of knowledge cannot be designated. (26)

[12. Agitation]

"If, bhikkhus, there are those who ask, 'Could there be correct contemplation of dyads in some other way?' you should answer them thus: 'There could be.' And how could there be? 'Whatever suffering originates is all conditioned by agitation'—this is one contemplation. 'With the remainderless fading away and cessation of agitation, there is no origination of suffering'—this is a second contemplation. When a bhikkhu dwells thus . . ." the Teacher further said this:

750. "Whatever suffering originates
is all conditioned by agitation.
With the cessation of agitation,
there is no origination of suffering. (27)

751. "Having known this danger,
'Suffering is conditioned by agitation,'
therefore having given up impulse,
having put a stop to volitional activities,
without impulse, without clinging,
a bhikkhu should wander mindfully. (28)

[13. Dependency]

"If, bhikkhus, there are those who ask, 'Could there be correct contemplation of dyads in some other way?' you should answer them thus: 'There could be.' And how could there be? 'For one who is dependent there is quaking'—this is one contemplation. 'One who is independent does not quake'—this is a second contemplation. When a bhikkhu dwells thus . . ." the Teacher further said this:

752. "One who is independent does not quake,
but one who is dependent, clinging [to things],
does not transcend saṃsāra,
with its becoming thus, becoming otherwise. (29)

753. "Having known this danger,
'There is great peril in dependencies,'
independent, without clinging,
a bhikkhu should wander mindfully. (30)

[14. Form and formless states]

"If, bhikkhus, there are those who ask, 'Could there be correct contemplation of dyads in some other way?' you should answer them thus: 'There could be.' And how could there be? 'Formless states are more peaceful than states of form'—this is one contemplation. [147] 'Cessation is more peaceful than formless states'—this is a second contemplation. When a bhikkhu dwells thus . . ." the Teacher further said this:

754. "Those beings who fare on to form
and those who dwell in the formless,
not understanding cessation,
come back to renewed existence. (31)

755. "But those who have fully understood forms,
without settling down in formless states,[190]
who are liberated in cessation:
those people have abandoned death. (32)

[15. Truth and falsity]

"If, bhikkhus, there are those who ask, 'Could there be correct contemplation of dyads in some other way?' you should answer them thus: 'There could be.' And how could there be? 'In this world, bhikkhus, with its devas, Māra, and Brahmā,[191] among this population with its ascetics and brahmins, its devas and humans, that which is regarded as "This is true," the noble ones have seen it well with correct wisdom thus: "This is false" '—this is one contemplation. 'In this world . . . with its devas and humans, that which is regarded as "This is false," the noble ones have seen it well with correct wisdom thus: "This is true"'—this is a second contemplation. When a bhikkhu dwells thus . . ." the Teacher further said this:

756. "Behold the world together with its devas
conceiving a self in what is non-self.
Settled upon name-and-form,
they conceive: 'This is true.' (33)

757. "In whatever way they conceive it,
it turns out otherwise.

That indeed is its falsity,
for the transient is of a false nature. (34) [148]

758. "Nibbāna is of a non-false nature:
that the noble ones know as truth.
Through the breakthrough to truth,
hungerless, they are fully quenched. (35)

[16. Happiness and suffering]

"If, bhikkhus, there are those who ask, 'Could there be correct contemplation of dyads in some other way?' you should answer them thus: 'There could be.' And how could there be? 'In this world, bhikkhus, with its devas, Māra, and Brahmā, among this population with its ascetics and brahmins, its devas and humans, that which is regarded as "This is happiness," the noble ones have seen well with correct wisdom thus: "This is suffering"'—this is one contemplation. 'In this world . . . with its devas and humans, that which is regarded as "This is suffering," the noble ones have seen well with correct wisdom thus, "This is happiness"'—this is a second contemplation. When a bhikkhu dwells thus correctly contemplating a dyad—heedful, ardent, and resolute—one of two fruits is to be expected of him: either final knowledge in this very life, or, if there is a residue of clinging, the state of non-returning."

This is what the Blessed One said. Having said this, the Fortunate One, the Teacher, further said this:

759. "Forms, sounds, tastes, odors,
textures, and objects of mind—
all are desirable, lovely, agreeable,
so long as it is said: 'They are.' (36)

760. "These are considered as happiness
in the world with its devas;
but where these cease,
that they consider suffering. (37)

761. "The noble ones have seen as happiness
the ceasing of the personal entity.

Running counter to the entire world
is this [insight] of those who see. (38) [149]

762. "What others speak of as happiness,
that the noble ones speak of as suffering.
What others speak of as suffering,
that the noble ones have known as happiness.
Behold this Dhamma hard to comprehend:
here the foolish are bewildered.[192] (39)

763. "There is gloom for those who are blocked,
darkness for those who do not see,
but for the good it is opened up
like light for those who see.
The brutes unskilled in the Dhamma[193]
do not understand it even when close. (40)

764. "This Dhamma is not easily understood
by those afflicted by lust for existence,
by those flowing in the stream of existence,
deeply mired in Māra's realm. (41)

765. "Who else apart from the noble ones
are able to understand this state?
When they have correctly known that state,
those without influxes attain nibbāna." (42)

This is what the Blessed One said. Elated, those bhikkhus delighted in the Blessed One's statement. And while this discourse was being spoken, the minds of sixty bhikkhus were liberated from the influxes by non-clinging.

IV The Chapter of Octads
Aṭṭhakavagga

1 Sensual Pleasures (Kāma Sutta)

766. [151] When a mortal desires sensual pleasure,
if that succeeds for him,
surely he is elated in mind,
having gained what he desires. (1)

767. But when, full of sensual desire,
a person is aroused by desire,
if those sensual pleasures decline,
he is afflicted as if pierced by a dart. (2)

768. One who avoids sensual pleasures
like a serpent's head with the foot,
being mindful, overcomes
this attachment to the world. (3)

769. Fields, land, or bullion,
cattle and horses, slaves and servants,
women, relatives—when a person greedily
longs for various sensual pleasures, (4)

770. even the weak overpower him;
obstacles crush him.
Then suffering enters him
as water does a broken boat. (5)

771. Therefore, ever mindful, a person
should avoid sensual pleasures.

Having abandoned them, one can cross the flood,
as by bailing out the boat one can reach the far shore. (6)

2 The Octad on the Cave (Guhaṭṭhaka Sutta)

772. Stuck in the cave, densely covered over,
dwelling immersed in bewilderment, [152]
a person such as this is far from seclusion,
for in the world sensual pleasures
are not easily abandoned. (1)

773. Based upon desire, bound to enjoyment of existence,
they let go with difficulty, for there is no release through others.
Concerned, too, with the future or the past,
they hanker for these sensual pleasures or earlier ones. (2)

774. Those greedy for sensual pleasures, intent on them,
are confused, stingy, settled in the unrighteous.
When they come upon suffering they lament:
"What will we be after we pass away here?" (3)

775. Therefore a person should train right here:
whatever in the world one might know as unrighteous,
one should not on its account act unrighteously,
for the wise say this life is short. (4)

776. I see in the world this population trembling all over,
addicted to craving for states of existence;
inferior people prattle in the mouth of death,
not devoid of craving for various states of existence. (5)

777. See them trembling over things taken as "mine"
like fish in a depleted stream with little water.
Having seen this too, one should take nothing as "mine,"
not forming attachment to states of existence. (6)

778. Having removed desire for both ends,
having fully understood contact, without greed,

not doing anything for which one might blame
oneself,
the wise person is not tainted by things seen or heard.
(7) [153]

779. Having fully understood perception,
one can cross the flood.
The muni, untainted by possessions,
with the dart extracted, living heedfully,
does not desire this world or another. (8)

3 The Octad on the Hostile (Duṭṭhaṭṭhaka Sutta)

780. Some speak with hostile minds,
while some speak with minds bent on truth.
The muni does not become involved in an arisen
dispute;
therefore the muni has no barrenness anywhere. (1)

781. How could one transcend one's own view
if, drawn by desire, one is entrenched in a preference?
Taking one's own [view] to be perfect,
one would speak as one understands. (2)

782. When a person, without being asked, proclaims
to others his own good behavior and observances,
the skilled say he is one of ignoble nature,
since on his own accord he proclaims himself. (3)

783. But when a peaceful bhikkhu, one inwardly
quenched,
does not boast of his good behavior by saying, "I am
thus,"
the skilled say he is one of noble nature
who has no swellings anywhere in the world. (4) [154]

784. One who has formulated impure teachings,
put them together and advanced them,
becomes attached to the benefit he sees for himself,
to that peace dependent on the unstable. (5)

785. Attachments to views are not easily overcome;
having decided among teachings, one tightly grasps [a view].
Therefore, among those bases of attachment,
a person rejects and takes up a teaching. (6)

786. One who is cleansed formulates no view
anywhere in the world about various states of existence.
Having abandoned hypocrisy and conceit, through what
would the cleansed one go [astray][194] when he is uninvolved? (7)

787. One involved is embroiled in disputes about teachings;
but how, about what, could one dispute with one uninvolved?
Nothing is taken up or rejected by him;
he has shaken off all views right here. (8)

4 The Octad on the Pure (Suddhaṭṭhaka Sutta)

788. "I see the pure, the supreme health;
a person achieves full purity through what is seen."
Directly knowing thus,[195] having known "[It is] supreme,"
"I contemplate the pure," one falls back on knowledge. (1) [155]

789. If a person gains purity by the seen,
or if one abandons suffering by knowledge,
then one with acquisitions is purified by another;
the view proclaims him as one who asserts thus. (2)

790. A brahmin does not speak of purity by another,
by the seen and the heard,
by good behavior and observances, by the sensed.
Untainted by merit and by evil, he has discarded
what was taken up without creating anything here. (3)

791. Having abandoned the former, attached to another,
carried along by impulse, they do not cross the tie.

They grab hold and let go, like a monkey
grasping and letting go of a branch. (4)

792. Having undertaken observances by himself,
a person goes up and down, attached to perception.
But having realized the Dhamma with knowledge,[196]
the wise one, broad in wisdom, does not go up and
down. (5)

793. One who is remote from all phenomena,
from whatever is seen, heard, or sensed—
how could anyone here in the world categorize him,
that seer behaving openly? (6)

794. They do not construct, they have no preferences,
they do not assert: "[This is] ultimate purity." [156]
Having loosened the knot of grasping that had been tied,
they do not form desires for anything in the world. (7)

795. For a brahmin who has transcended the boundary,
who has known and seen, nothing is tightly grasped.
Not excited by lust or attached to dispassion,
he does not grasp anything here as supreme. (8)

5 The Octad on the Supreme (Paramaṭṭhaka Sutta)

796. Settling [on his own] as supreme among views,
whatever a person esteems as best in the world,
[in comparison] he says all others are "inferior":
therefore he has not transcended disputes. (1)

797. Whatever benefit one sees for oneself
in the seen, the heard, the sensed,
or in good behavior and observances,
having grasped hold of that alone,
one regards all else as inferior. (2)

798. The skilled speak of that as a knot
when one is attached and regards others as inferior.
Therefore a bhikkhu should not be attached to the seen,

to the heard or sensed, or to good behavior and observances. (3) [157]

799. Nor should one construct any view in the world
by means of knowledge or good behavior and observances.
One should not take oneself as "equal"
or think of oneself as "inferior" or "superior." (4)

800. Having abandoned what is taken up, not clinging,
one does not create a dependency even on knowledge.
Not taking sides among those who are divided,
one does not fall back on any view at all. (5)

801. For one who has no wish here for either end,
for various states of existence here or beyond,
there are no places of residence at all
grasped after deciding among teachings. (6)

802. Not even a subtle notion is formulated by him
about what is seen, heard, or sensed here.
How could anyone here in the world categorize him,
that brahmin who does not cling to any view? (7)

803. They do not construct, they have no preferences;
even the teachings are not embraced by them. [158]
A brahmin cannot be led by good behavior and observances;
the impartial one, gone beyond, does not fall back. (8)

6 Old Age (Jarā Sutta)

804. Short, alas, is this life;
one even dies before a hundred years.
Even if one lives longer,
one still dies because of old age. (1)

805. People sorrow over things taken as "mine,"
for there are no permanent possessions.
Having seen that there is separation,
one should not live the home life. (2)

806. Whatever a person conceives thus, "This is mine,"
that too is abandoned at death.
Having understood this, a wise one, my follower,
should not incline to take things as "mine." (3)

807. Just as, on awakening, a person does not see
whatever was encountered in a dream, [159]
so too one does not see a beloved person
who has died and passed away. (4)

808. Although those people were seen and heard,
and were known by such and such a name,
when a person has passed away,
the name alone remains to be uttered. (5)

809. Those who are greedy for personal assets
do not escape sorrow, lamentation, and miserliness.
Therefore the munis, seers of security,
wandered having abandoned possessions. (6)

810. When a bhikkhu lives withdrawn,
resorting to a secluded seat,
they say it is appropriate for him
not to show himself in a fixed dwelling. (7)

811. The muni is not dependent on anything;
he takes nothing as pleasing, nothing as displeasing.
Lamentation and miserliness do not stick to him
as water does not stick to a leaf. (8)

812. Just as a water drop does not stick to a lotus leaf,
or water to the lotus flower,
so the muni does not cling to anything
among the seen, heard, or sensed. (9) [160]

813. One cleansed does not thereby conceive
things seen, heard, or sensed.
He does not wish for purification by another,
for he becomes neither passionate nor dispassionate. (10)

7 Tissa Metteyya (Tissametteyya Sutta)

814. "For one who indulges in sexual intercourse,"
(said the Venerable Tissa Metteyya),
"tell me, dear sir, of the distress.
Having heard your teaching,
we will train in seclusion." (1)

815. "When one indulges in sexual intercourse,
(Metteyya," the Blessed One said),
"even the teaching itself is forgotten,
and he practices wrongly:
this is ignoble in him. (2)

816. "One who previously lived alone
but then resorts to sexual intercourse
is like a vehicle that has gone astray:
in the world they call him a low worldling. (3)

817. "Whatever fame and acclaim he previously enjoyed,
these fall away from him.
Having seen this, one should train
to abandon sexual intercourse. (4)

818. "Oppressed by his thoughts,
he broods like a poor wretch.
Having heard the reprimand of others,
one such as this is humiliated. (5)

819. "Then he prepares weapons [of defense]
when reproached by the words of others.
This is a great thicket for him,
that he sinks into false speech. (6)

820. "He was known as a wise man
when resolved on living alone,
but when he engaged in sexual intercourse,
like a dullard he is afflicted. (7) [161]

821. "Having known this danger
here in the before and after,

a muni should resolutely live alone;
he should not resort to sexual intercourse. (8)

822. "One should train just in seclusion;
this is supreme among the noble ones.
One should not conceive oneself best because of this:
then one is indeed close to nibbāna. (9)

823. "When the muni lives void,
indifferent to sensual pleasures,
people tied to sensual pleasures envy him
as one who has crossed the flood." (10)

8 Pasūra (Pasūra Sutta)

824. "'Here alone is purity,' they declare;
they say there is no purification in other teachings.
Declaring whatever they depend on to be excellent,
many are entrenched in separate truths. (1)

825. "Desiring debate, having plunged into the assembly,
in pairs they accuse one another of being a fool.
Those of different convictions assert their argument,
desiring praise, claiming to be skilled. (2)

826. "Keen on speaking in the midst of the assembly,
wishing for praise, he becomes anxious.
If his assertion is rejected, he feels humiliated.
Upset by blame, he seeks a flaw [in his opponent]. (3)
[162]

827. "If they say his assertion is defective,
and the judges consider it rejected,
the loser laments and sorrows,
he moans: 'He surpassed me.' (4)

828. "These disputes have arisen among ascetics;
in relation to them, one becomes elated and dejected.
Having seen this, too, one should desist from arguments,
for there is no other benefit than praise and gain. (5)

829. "If, however, he is praised there,
having declared his doctrine in the midst of the assembly,
he is thrilled by this and swells with pride,
having obtained the benefit that accords with his wish. (6)

830. "Though his pride is the ground of distress,
he yet speaks from conceit and arrogance.
Having seen this, too, one should not dispute;
for the skilled say this does not bring purity. (7)

831. "Just as a hero, nourished on the king's food,
comes thundering, desiring an opponent,
rush off in his direction, Sūra;[197]
already in the past, there was no scope for a fight. (8)

832. "When they grasp a view and argue,
and assert, 'This alone is true,' [163]
tell them: 'When a debate has arisen
there is no opponent for you here.' (9)

833. "But among those who live remote,
who do not oppose a view with other views,
what will you obtain, Pasūra, from those
who grasp nothing here as supreme? (10)

834. "But now you have come brooding,
devising speculative views in your mind.
You have confronted one who is cleansed:
indeed, you won't be able to succeed." (11)

9 Māgandiya (Māgandiya Sutta)

835. "Having seen Taṇhā, Aratī, and Ragā,
I did not have any desire for sexual intercourse,
so why [should I desire] this, full of urine and feces?
I would not wish to touch her even with my foot." (1)
[164]

836. "If you do not wish a gem such as this,
a woman desired by many rulers of men,

what kind of view, behavior, observances, lifestyle,
existence, and rebirth do you assert?" (2)

837. "Having decided among teachings,
(Māgandiya," said the Blessed One),
"it does not occur to one, 'I assert this,'
[about a view] tightly grasped.
But seeing into views, not grasping any of them,
investigating, I saw the peace within." (3)

838. "Indeed, muni, you speak without grasping
those judgments that have been formulated,"
(said Māgandiya).
"As to that matter called 'the peace within,'
how is it proclaimed by the wise?" (4)

839. "Not by view, nor by learning, nor by knowledge,
(Māgandiya," said the Blessed One),
"nor do I speak of purity through good behavior and observances;
but neither without view, without learning, without knowledge,
without good behavior, without observances—not in that way.
But having relinquished these, not grasping any of them,
peaceful, not dependent, one should not hanker for existence." (5)

840. "If indeed it is not by view, by learning, nor by knowledge," (said Māgandiya),
"nor by good behavior and observances, that one speaks of purity; [165]
nor without view, without learning, without knowledge,
without good behavior and observances—not in that way,
I think this is an utterly confused teaching;
some fall back on purity by means of view." (6)

841. "Asking repeatedly while dependent on a view,
(Māgandiya," said the Blessed One),

"you have become baffled over things tightly grasped.
But from this you have not gained even an inkling;
hence you consider it utterly confused. (7)

842. "One who thinks himself equal, superior, or inferior
might engage in disputes because of this.
Not shaking among these three discriminations,
he does not think 'equal, superior.' (8)

843. "Why would that brahmin assert, 'It's true,'
or with whom would he dispute, 'It's false'?
When for him there is no 'equal' and 'unequal,'
with whom would he engage in debate? (9)

844. "Having left home to roam without abode,
in the village the muni is intimate with none.
Void of sensual pleasures, without preferences,
he would not engage in contentious talk with people. (10)

845. "When he wanders detached from things in the world,
the nāga would not grasp and assert them. [166]
As a thorny-stalked lotus, born in the water,[198]
is untainted by water and mud,
just so the muni, a proponent of peace, free of greed,
is untainted by sensual pleasures and the world. (11)

846. "Because of a view[199] or an opinion
a Veda-master does not become conceited,
for he does not identify with them.
Not led by kamma or by what is heard,
he is not drawn to any abodes. (12)

847. "For one detached from perception there are no knots;
for one liberated by wisdom there are no delusions.
But those who have grasped perceptions and views
wander in the world creating friction." (13)

10 Before the Breakup (Purābheda Sutta)

848. "How does he see, how does he behave,
the one who is said to be 'peaceful'?
When asked by me, O Gotama,
describe the supreme person." (1)

849. "Devoid of craving before the breakup,"
(said the Blessed One),
"not dependent on the past,
not to be reckoned in the middle,
for him there are no preferences. (2) [167]

850. "He is without anger, unafraid,
not boastful, not regretful,
of speaking with reflection, not restless:
he is truly a muni controlled in speech. (3)

851. "He is without attachment to the future;
he does not sorrow over the past.
As a seer of seclusion in the midst of contacts,
he is not led astray among views. (4)

852. "Withdrawn, not a schemer,
without longing, not miserly,
courteous, not [morally] repulsive,
not intent on slander. (5)

853. "Not swept up by enjoyments,
and not swollen with arrogance;
gentle, gifted with ingenuity,
not credulous, not growing dispassionate. (6)

854. "He does not train from a desire for gain,
nor is he irritated over lack of gain.
Not hostile, because of craving
he does not hanker after tastes. (7)

855. "Equanimous, ever mindful,
in the world he does not conceive himself

to be equal, or superior, or inferior:
for him there are no swellings. (8)

856. "He has no dependencies—
having known the Dhamma, he is independent.
No craving is found in him
for existence or nonexistence. (9)

857. "I call him 'peaceful'
who is indifferent to sensual pleasures.
In him no knots are found;
he has crossed over attachment. (10)

858. "He has no sons or cattle,
nor does he possess fields or land. [168]
In him there is nothing to be found
as either taken up or rejected. (11)

859. "That by which they might speak of him—
worldlings as well as ascetics and brahmins—
is not esteemed by him;
therefore he is not stirred up by words. (12)

860. "Devoid of greed, without miserliness,
the muni does not speak [of himself]
as among superiors, or equals, or inferiors.
Not given to mental construction,
he does not enter upon mental constructs. (13)

861. "One who takes nothing in the world as his own,
and who does not sorrow over what is absent,
who does not enter upon things:
he is truly said to be 'peaceful.'" (14)

11 Quarrels and Disputes (Kalahavivāda Sutta)

862. "From where do quarrels and disputes arise,
lamentation, sorrow, and miserliness?
From where do conceit and arrogance arise
along with slander? Please tell me this." (1)

863. "Quarrels and disputes arise from what is pleasing,
as do lamentation, sorrow, and miserliness,
conceit and arrogance along with slander.
Quarrels and disputes are connected with miserliness,
and slanders occur when disputes arise."[200] (2) [169]

864. "From what do pleasing things in the world originate,
and those states of greed that spread through the world?
From what do longing and fulfillment originate,
which a person has about the future?" (3)

865. "Pleasing things in the world originate from desire,
as do those states of greed that spread through the world.
From this originate the longing and fulfillment
that a person has about the future." (4)

866. "From what in the world does desire originate?
And from what do judgments too arise,
and anger, false speech, and perplexity,
and those [other] things the Ascetic has mentioned?" (5)

867. "Desire originates based on what they say
is 'pleasant' or 'unpleasant' in the world.
Having seen the vanishing and coming-to-be of forms,
a person forms a judgment in the world. (6)

868. "Anger, false speech, and perplexity:
these things, too, arise when that dyad exists.
One perplexed should train on the path of knowledge;
having known, the Ascetic stated these things." (7)

869. "From what do the pleasant and unpleasant originate?
When what does not exist do these not come to be?
As to this matter of vanishing and coming-to-be,
tell me from what it originates." (8)

870. "The pleasant and unpleasant originate from contact;
when contact does not exist, these do not come to be. [170]
As to this matter of vanishing and coming-to-be,
I tell you that it originates from this." (9)

871. "From what in the world does contact originate?
From what do possessions too arise?
When what does not exist is there no taking as 'mine'?
When what has vanished do contacts not touch one?" (10)

872. "Contacts[201] are dependent upon name and form;
possessions are based on desire.
When desire does not exist,[202] there is no taking as 'mine.'
When form has vanished, contacts do not touch one." (11)

873. "How must one attain for form to vanish?
How do pleasure and pain also vanish?
Please tell me this, how they vanish.
We would like to know that—such is my thought." (12)

874. "Not percipient through perception,
not percipient through disturbed perception,
not altogether without perception,
not percipient of what has vanished:
form vanishes for one who has so attained,
for concepts due to proliferation are based on perception." (13)

875. "You explained to us whatever we asked you.
Let us now ask something else: please tell me this. [171]
Do some wise men here say that at this point
this is the foremost purity of the spirit,
or do they speak of it as different from this?"[203] (14)

876. "Some wise men here say that at this point
this is the foremost purity of the spirit.

But[204] some among them, claiming to be skilled,
speak of an attainment without residue remaining. (15)

877. "Having known these to be 'dependent,'
and having known the dependencies, the muni, the investigator,
having known, liberated, does not enter disputes;
the wise one does not come upon various states of existence." (16)

12 The Smaller Discourse on Deployment (Cūḷaviyūha Sutta)

878. "Settled each in his own view,
contending, the skilled make diverse assertions:
'One who knows this has understood the Dhamma;
rejecting this, one is not consummate.' (1)

879. "Having contended thus, they dispute
and say: 'The opponent is a fool, unskilled.'
Which assertion among these is truthful,
for they all claim to be skilled?" (2) [172]

880. "If one who does not affirm the opponent's doctrine
is thereby a fool, a brute,[205] deficient in wisdom,
all indeed are fools, utterly deficient in wisdom:
for all these are settled in their views. (3)

881. "But if by their own view they are cleansed,[206]
pure in wisdom, skilled, intelligent,
there is none among them defective in wisdom,
for their views are similarly taken up. (4)

882. "I do not say, 'This is correct,'
as the fools in pairs say to one another.
They all take their own view to be true;
therefore they consider the opponent a fool." (5)

883. "That which some say is 'true, correct,'
others say is 'hollow, false.'
Having contended thus, they dispute.
Why don't ascetics speak in unison?" (6)

884. "Truth, indeed, is one—there is no second;
a person who understands this would not dispute.[207]
These proclaim their own diverse truths;
therefore ascetics do not speak in unison." (7) [173]

885. "But why do they assert diverse truths,
those proponents who claim to be skilled?
Are those truths actually many and diverse,
or do they follow a line of reasoning?" (8)

886. "Truths surely are not many and diverse,
except by [mistakenly] perceiving permanent things in the world.
But having formulated reasoning about views,
they assert the dyad 'true' and 'false.' (9)

887. "The seen, heard, good behavior and observances,
the sensed—dependent on these, he shows disdain.
Based on a judgment, derisive,
he says: 'The opponent is a fool, unskilled.' (10)

888. "As he considers the opponent a fool,
on the same ground he describes himself as 'skilled.'
Of his own accord, claiming himself skilled,
he disdains the other, yet speaks in the same way.[208] (11)

889. "Inflated by that extremist view,
intoxicated with conceit, thinking himself perfect,
on his own accord he has mentally anointed himself,
for that view of his is taken up in such a manner. (12)

890. "If one is deficient because of the opponent's word,
the opponent himself is similarly deficient in wisdom.
But if he is himself a master of knowledge, a wise man,
then there is no fool among ascetics. (13) [174]

891. "Those who assert a teaching
different from this to be defective
have failed to reach purity:
thus the sectarians speak in separate ways,
for they are attached to their own views. (14)

892. "'Here only is purity' they assert;
they say there is no purification in other teachings.
Thus, too, the sectarians, separately entrenched,
firmly assert their own way there. (15)

893. "Asserting firmly his own way,
what opponent here could one consider a fool?
He himself would just provoke strife
by calling his opponent a fool of impure character. (16)

894. "Based on a judgment, taking himself as the measure,
he enters upon further disputes in the world.
Having abandoned all judgments,
a person does not create strife in the world." (17)

13 The Greater Discourse on Deployment (Mahāviyūha Sutta)

895. "Those who are settled in views,
who dispute, saying, 'This alone is truth':
do all of them receive only blame,
or do some there also win praise?" (1) [175]

896. "This [praise] is slight, not sufficient for peace;
I say there are two fruits of disputes.
Having seen this too, one should not dispute,
seeing as security the stage of non-dispute. (2)

897. "Whatever commonplace opinions there are,
a wise person does not get involved in them.
Why would one uninvolved become involved
when he does not acquiesce in what is seen and heard? (3)

898. "Those who take good behavior as supreme
speak of purity through self-control.
Having taken up an observance, they settle on it,
thinking: 'Let's train right here, then there would be
purity.'[209]
Claiming to be skilled, they are led back into existence. (4)

899. "If he has fallen away from good behavior and
observances,
he trembles because he has failed in his action.
He longs and yearns for purity here,
like one on a journey who has lost his caravan. (5)

900. "But having abandoned all good behavior and
observances,
and these deeds, blameworthy and blameless, [176]
not yearning for either purity or impurity,
one should live detached, not grasping peace. (6)

901. "Dependent on austerity or scrupulousness,[210]
or on what is seen, heard, or sensed,
running onward, they declare purity,
not rid of craving for various states of existence. (7)

902. "For one who yearns there are longings
and trembling too over things mentally formulated;
but for one here who has no passing away or rebirth,
why would he tremble and for what would he long?" (8)

903. "The teaching that some here say is supreme,
others say that the same is inferior.
Which assertion of theirs could be true
when they all claim to be skilled?" (9)

904. "They say their own teaching is complete,
but they say the other's teaching is inferior.
Having quarreled thus, they go on disputing,
as they each say their own opinion is true. (10)

905. "If one is inferior when disparaged by an opponent,
no one would be distinguished among teachings.

For they each say the other's teaching is inferior,
while firmly advocating their own. (11) [177]

906. "And their veneration of their own teaching[211]
is done just as they praise their own ways.
All their assertions would be truthful,
since for them purity is exclusively their own. (12)

907. "For a brahmin there is no being led by others,
no selecting among teachings and grasping tightly.
Therefore he has overcome disputes,
since he does not regard another teaching as supreme.
(13)

908. "Saying, 'I know, I see, it is just like this,'
some here fall back on purity through a view.
If one has seen, what good is this to himself?
Having gone too far, they assert purity by another. (14)

909. "Seeing, a person will see name-and-form;
having seen, it is just these that he will know.
Granted, let him see much or little,
the skillful say purity is not won in that way. (15)

910. "A dogmatist is not easily disciplined,[212]
one preferring a formulated view.
Claiming that the good is found in what he depends on,
as a proponent of purity, he saw things that way there.
(16)

911. "Having comprehended,[213] a brahmin
does not take up mental constructs;
he is not a pursuer of views nor a kinsman of knowledge.
[178]
Having known the commonplace opinions,
he maintains equanimity while others grasp. (17)

912. "Having loosened the knots here in the world,
the muni does not take sides in arisen disputes.
He is peaceful among the restless, equanimous,
without grasping while others grasp. (18)

913. "Having abandoned past influxes, not creating new ones,
he does not go along with desire, nor is he a dogmatist.
Released from speculative views, the wise person,
free of self-reproach, is not tainted by the world. (19)

914. "He is remote from all phenomena,
from whatever is seen, heard, or sensed.
With his burden dropped, released,[214]
the muni, not given to mental construction,
does not desist, does not yearn"—
so said the Blessed One. (20) [179]

14 Quickly (Tuvaṭaka Sutta)

915. "I ask you, Kinsman of the Sun, great rishi,
about seclusion and the state of peace.
How having seen does a bhikkhu attain nibbāna,
not clinging to anything in the world?" (1)

916. "By reflection, he should stop [the conceit] 'I am,'
the entire root of concepts due to proliferation,"
[the Blessed One said].
"Whatever cravings there may be internally,
he should always train mindfully for their removal. (2)

917. "Whatever one might know,
whether internally or externally,
one should not be obstinate on that account,
for that is not called quenching by the good. (3)

918. "Because of this one should not think oneself better,
nor should one consider oneself inferior or equal.
Being affected in various ways,
one should not persist in positioning oneself. (4)

919. "It is internally that he should achieve peace;
a bhikkhu should not seek peace through another.
For one who is at peace within himself,
there is nothing taken up, much less rejected. (5) [180]

920. "Just as in the middle of the ocean
no wave arises, but the ocean remains steady,
so too he should be steady, without impulse;
a bhikkhu should not cause a swelling anywhere." (6)

921. "The one with opened eyes declared
the Dhamma he witnessed, the removal of obstacles.
Speak about the practice, venerable one,
the Pātimokkha and also concentration." (7)

922. "One should not be restless with the eyes,
one should block the ears against village gossip.
One should not be greedy for tastes,
and one should not take anything in the world as
'mine.' (8)

923. "When he is touched by a contact,
a bhikkhu should not lament anywhere.
He should not long for any state of existence,
nor should he tremble amid fearful conditions. (9)

924. "Having obtained food and drink,
things to eat or clothes to wear,
he should not hoard them,
nor be agitated if he does not obtain them. (10)

925. "He should be a meditator, not one with restless
feet;
he should refrain from regret; he should not be heedless.
A bhikkhu should dwell amid seats and beds
[in lodgings] where there is little noise. (11) [181]

926. "He should not overindulge in sleep;
he should be devoted to wakefulness, ardent.
He should abandon indolence, hypocrisy, laughing,
and playfulness,
sexual intercourse, and personal ornamentation. (12)

927. "He should not employ Atharva spells,
or interpret dreams, signs, or constellations.

My follower would not decipher animal cries,
or practice healing or making women fertile. (13)

928. "A bhikkhu should not be shaken by blame,
nor should he be elated when praised.
He should dispel greed and miserliness,
as well as anger and slanderous speech. (14)

929. "A bhikkhu should not engage in buying and selling;
he should not do anything that incurs criticism.
He should not form intimacy in the village;
he should not address people from a desire for gain. (15)

930. "A bhikkhu should not be boastful,
and he should not utter insinuating speech.
He should not train himself in impudence;
he should not utter contentious talk. (16)

931. "He should not be led into false speech,
nor should he deliberately do anything deceptive. [182]
Because of his way of life, his wisdom,
or his good behavior and observances,
he should not despise another. (17)

932. "When provoked, having heard many words
from ascetics who speak profusely,
he should not respond to them harshly,
for the good do not retaliate. (18)

933. "Having understood this Dhamma, investigating,
a bhikkhu should always train mindfully.
Having known quenching as peace,
he should not be heedless in Gotama's teaching. (19)

934. "For he is a conqueror who is himself unconquered;
he saw the Dhamma as a witness, not by hearsay.[215]
Therefore, heedful in that Blessed One's teaching,
always honoring it, one should train in accordance with
it." (20)

15 One Who Has Taken Up the Rod (Attadaṇḍa Sutta)

935. "Fear has arisen from one who has taken up the rod:
see the people engaged in strife.
I will tell you of my sense of urgency,
how I was stirred by a sense of urgency. (1) [183]

936. "Having seen the population trembling
like fish in a pool with little water,
having seen them hostile to one another,
fear came upon me. (2)

937. "The world was insubstantial all around;
all the directions were in turmoil.
Desiring an abode for myself,
I did not see [any place] unoccupied. (3)

938. "Having seen those hostile at the end,
discontent came upon me.
Then I saw the dart here,
hard to see, nestled in the heart. (4)

939. "When one is struck by that dart
one runs astray in all directions.
But having drawn out that dart,
one does not run, does not sink."[216] (5)

940. There the trainings are recited:[217]
"Whatever bonds[218] there are in the world,
one should not be intent on them.
Having entirely pierced through sensual pleasures,
one should train for one's own nibbāna. (6)

941. "One should be truthful, not impudent,
without hypocrisy, devoid of divisive speech.
Without anger, a muni should cross over
the evil of greed and miserliness. (7)

942. "One should vanquish sleepiness, torpor, and dullness;
one should not keep company with heedlessness.
A person whose mind is set on nibbāna
should not persist in arrogance. (8) [184]

943. "One should not be led into false speech;
one should not engender affection for form.
One should fully understand conceit,
and one should refrain from rashness. (9)

944. "One should not delight in the old;
one should not form a liking for the new.
One should not sorrow over what is diminishing;
one should not be attached to an attraction. (10)

945. "I call greed the great flood,
I call longing the rapids,
the basis, compulsion,[219]
the swamp of sensuality hard to overcome. (11)

946. "Not deviating from truth, a muni,
a brahmin, stands on high ground.
Having relinquished all,
he is indeed called peaceful. (12)

947. "One who truly is a knower, a Veda-master,
having known the Dhamma, is independent.
Living rightly in the world,
he does not long for anything here. (13)

948. "One here who has crossed over sensual pleasures,
the tie so hard to overcome in the world,
who has cut off the stream, without bonds,
does not sorrow, does not hope. (14)

949. "Dry up what pertains to the past;
let there be nothing afterward.
If you do not grasp in the middle,
you will live in peace. (15)

950. "One who does not claim as 'mine'
anything at all here in name-and-form,
who does not sorrow over what is nonexistent,
truly does not lose out in the world. (16)

951. "One for whom nothing is taken
as 'this is mine' or '[this belongs] to others,'
not finding anything to be taken as 'mine,'
does not sorrow, thinking: 'It is not mine.' (17) [185]

952. "Not bitter, not greedy,
without impulse, everywhere the same—
when asked about one who is unshakable,
I call that the benefit. (18)

953. "For one without impulse, who understands,
there is no activation at all.[220]
Abstaining from instigation,
he sees security everywhere. (19)

954. "The muni does not speak of himself
as among equals, inferiors, or superiors.
Peaceful, without miserliness,
he does not take, does not reject"—
so said the Blessed One. (20)

16 Sāriputta (Sāriputta Sutta)

955. "I have never before seen,"
(said the Venerable Sāriputta),
"nor have I ever heard it from anyone—
a teacher of such lovely speech,
leader of a group, who has come from Tusita, (1)

956. "as the One with Vision is seen
in the world together with its devas.
Having dispelled all darkness,
alone, he achieved delight. (2) [186]

957. "To the Buddha, unattached, impartial,
not a schemer, one who has come as leader of a group,
I have come in need with a question
on behalf of the many here who are bound. (3)

958. "When a bhikkhu is repulsed
and resorts to a solitary seat,
to the foot of a tree or a charnel ground,
or [to a seat] in mountain caves, (4)

959. "to various sorts of lodgings,
how many fearful things are there
because of which a bhikkhu should not tremble
in a lodging with little noise? (5)

960. "How many obstacles in the world
confront one going to the untraveled region,[221]
[obstacles] that a bhikkhu must overcome
when living in a remote lodging? (6)

961. "What ways of speech should he adopt?
On what resorts here should he rely?
What should be the good behavior and observances
of a bhikkhu who is resolute? (7)

962. "Having taken up what training,
dwelling unified, judicious, mindful,
should he blow away his own stains
as a smith [removes the flaws] of silver?" (8)

963. "As one who understands I will tell you
in accordance with the Dhamma,
(Sāriputta," said the Blessed One),
"what is comfortable for one who is repulsed,
if, wishing for enlightenment,
he resorts to a solitary lodging. (9)

964. "A wise one, a mindful bhikkhu of bounded
conduct,
should not be afraid of five perils:

gadflies and other flies, creeping serpents,
encounters with people, four-footed animals, (10) [187]

965. "nor should he fear followers of other teachings,
even when he sees the many fears they pose.
One seeking the good should conquer
any other obstacles [he encounters]. (11)

966. "Afflicted by illness and hunger,
he should endure cold and excessive heat.
The homeless one, affected by these in many ways,
should remain firm, exerting energy. (12)

967. "He should not commit theft or speak falsely;
he should suffuse the frail and firm with loving-kindness.
If he should recognize any blemish of the mind,
he should dispel it as 'a faction of the Dark One.' (13)

968. "He should not come under the control of anger and arrogance,
but should dig them up by their root too.
Then, withstanding the pleasing and displeasing,
he should conquer them as well. (14)

969. "Giving precedence to wisdom, rejoicing in the good,
he should suppress those obstacles.
He should vanquish discontent with remote lodgings;
he should vanquish the four factors of lamentation. (15)

970. "'What will I eat? Where will I eat?
Alas, I slept badly! Where will I sleep?':
one in training, wandering without abode,
should remove these thoughts of lamentation. (16) [188]

971. "Having obtained a meal and clothing in time,
he should know moderation for the sake of contentment here.
Guarded in these things,[222] wandering restrained in the village,

even when provoked, he should not utter harsh
speech. (17)

972. "His eyes should be downcast;
he should not have restless feet;
intent on jhāna, he should be wakeful.
Inwardly concentrated, based on equanimity,
he should cut off regret and inclination to thought. (18)

973. "If reproached with words, a mindful one should
welcome them;
he should break through a barren heart toward fellow
monastics.
He should utter wholesome speech, but not to excess;
he should not intend [speech] that people might blame.
(19)

974. "Further, there are five kinds of dust in the world,
for the removal of which a mindful one should train.
One should vanquish lust for forms and sounds,
for tastes, odors, and tactile objects. (20)

975. "A bhikkhu who is mindful, well liberated in mind,
should remove desire for these things. [189]
At the proper time rightly investigating the Dhamma,
unified, he should destroy darkness"—
so said the Blessed One. (21)

V The Chapter on the Way to the Beyond

Pārāyanavagga

[190] Introductory Verses[223]

976. Desiring the state of nothingness,
a brahmin master of the hymns
went from the delightful city of the Kosalans
to a region in the south. (1)

977. In the domain of Assaka,
in the neighborhood of Aḷaka,
he lived on the bank of the Godhāvarī River
by means of gleaning and fruit. (2)

978. Situated nearby
there was a large village.
With the revenue that arose from it,
he held a grand sacrifice. (3)

979. Having completed the grand sacrifice,
he again entered the hermitage.
When he had re-entered,
another brahmin arrived. (4)

980. He had calloused feet, he was thirsty;
he had dirty teeth and a dusty head.
Having approached [his host],
[the visitor] asked for five hundred [coins]. (5)

981. Having beheld him,
Bāvari[224] invited him to a seat.
He asked about his happiness and health,
and spoke this statement: (6)

982. "Whatever wealth I had to give away,
I have disposed of it all.
Believe me, brahmin:
I do not have five hundred [coins]." (7) [191]

983. "When I am making this request,
if you do not present it to me,
on the seventh day from now
may your head split into seven parts." (8)

984. Having put on a performance,
that charlatan uttered a fearsome curse.
Having heard his statement,
Bāvari was despondent. (9)

985. Not eating, he became emaciated,
stricken by the dart of sorrow.
Then, in such a state of mind,
he did not delight in meditation. (10)

986. Having seen him terrified and despondent,
a deity who desired his good
approached Bāvari
and uttered this statement: (11)

987. "That charlatan who desires wealth
does not understand the head.
He has no knowledge at all
about the head or head-splitting." (12)

988. "If you know, worthy one,
please inform me when you are asked
about the head and head-splitting:
let us hear that word of yours." (13)

989. "I too do not know this matter;
I have no knowledge at all of this.
For the head and head-splitting:
this is what the conquerors have seen." (14)

990. "Then, on this circle of the earth,
who knows about the head
and head-splitting?
Tell me this, O deity!" (15) [192]

991. "Earlier already the world-leader,
a descendent of King Okkāka,
a Sakyan son, the maker of light, (16)
went forth from Kapilavatthu.

992. "He, brahmin, is the Enlightened One
who has gone beyond all phenomena,
who has attained all superknowledge and power,
the one with vision into all phenomena.
Having attained the destruction of all kamma,[225]
he is liberated in the extinction of acquisitions. (17)

993. "The Buddha, the Blessed One in the world,
the One with Vision, teaches the Dhamma.
Go to him and ask him your question:
he will explain that matter to you." (18)

994. Having heard the word
"Enlightened One," Bāvari was elated.
His sorrow diminished,
and he gained abundant rapture. (19)

995. Delighted, elated, exhilarated,
Bāvari asked that deity:
"In what village or town, or in what country,
does the World Protector dwell,
where we might go and pay homage[226]
to the Enlightened One, the best of bipeds?" (20)

996. "The conqueror is in Sāvatthī, in the realm of Kosala;
[there dwells] the one of abundant wisdom, of excellent
vast intelligence.
That Sakyan son, unrivaled, free of influxes, bull of men,
is one who understands head-splitting." (21)

997. He then addressed his pupils,
brahmins who had mastered the hymns:
"Come, brahmin students, I will speak.
Listen to this word of mine. (22) [193]

998. "Now there has arisen in the world
one famed as 'the Enlightened One,'
one whose manifestation in the world
is rarely encountered.
Go quickly to Sāvatthī
and see the best of bipeds." (23)

999. "When we see him, brahmin,
how might we know that he is the Buddha?
Since we do not know, tell us
how we might recognize him." (24)

1000. "The characteristics of a great man
have come down in the hymns.
Thirty-two such marks are explained
complete in their sequence. (25)

1001. "For one whose body has these
characteristics of a great man,
there are only two destinations;
for a third does not exist. (26)

1002. "If he dwells at home,
having conquered this earth
without violence, without a weapon,
he rules over it righteously. (27)

1003. "But if he should go forth
from home to homelessness,

he becomes a buddha with coverings removed,
an unsurpassed arahant. (28)

1004. "Ask him solely with your mind
about [my] birth, clan, characteristics,
hymns, and pupils, and ask further
about the head and head-splitting. (29)

1005. "If he is a buddha,
one of unobstructed vision,
he will reply verbally
to the questions asked by the mind." (30)

1006. Having heard the word of Bāvari,
his sixteen brahmin pupils—
Ajita, Tissa Metteyya,
Puṇṇaka, and Mettagū, (31) [194]

1007. Dhotaka and Upasīva,
Nanda and Hemaka,
the pair Todeyya and Kappa,
and the wise Jatukaṇṇī, (32)

1008. Bhadrāvudha and Udaya,
and the brahmin Posāla,
the intelligent Mogharāja,
and the great rishi Piṅgiya— (33)

1009. all leaders of their own groups,
famed throughout the whole world,
meditators who delighted in the jhānas,
who had formed past habitual formations, (34)

1010. paid homage to Bāvari,
and having circumambulated him,
all with matted locks, wearing hides,
they set out toward the north— (35)

1011. to Patiṭṭhāna of Aḷaka,
then to the former Māhissatī,

to Ujjenī and Gonaddhā,
Vedisā, and Vanasa, (36)

1012. to Kosambī and Sāketa,
the supreme city Sāvatthī,
Setavya and Kapilavatthu,
and the city Kusinārā, (37)

1013. on to Pāvā and Bhoga city,
to Vesālī, to the Māgadhan city [Rājagaha],
and to the Pāsāṇaka Cetiya,
delightful and charming. (38) [195]

1014. As a thirsty person [seeks] cool water,
as a merchant [seeks] great profit,
or one oppressed by heat [seeks] shade,
they hastily climbed the mountain. (39)

1015. On that occasion the Blessed One
in front of the Sangha of bhikkhus
was teaching the Dhamma to the bhikkhus
like a lion that roars in the woods. (40)

1016. Ajita saw the Buddha,
like the glorious sun with a hundred rays,[227]
like the moon on the fifteenth [of the fortnight]
when it has arrived at fullness. (41)

1017. Then, having seen his body
and his features complete,
he stood to one side, thrilled,
and asked the questions mentally: (42)

1018. "Speak with reference to his birth;
tell his clan and characteristics;
tell his perfection in the hymns.
How many pupils does the brahmin teach?" (43)

1019. "His age is a hundred and twenty years,
and by clan he is a Bāvari;

there are three characteristics on his body;
he is a master of the Three Vedas, (44)

1020. "of the characteristics and histories,
along with the lexicon and rules of ritual.
He teaches five hundred pupils;
he has reached perfection in his own teaching." (45) [196]

1021. "O supreme man, reveal in detail
the characteristics of Bāvari.
O you who have cut off craving,
do not let doubt remain in us!" (46)

1022. "He can cover his face with his tongue;
he has a tuft of hair between his eyebrows;
his male organ is enclosed in a sheath:
know thus, brahmin student." (47)

1023. Having heard the questions answered
without having heard anything being asked,
exhilarated, making salutations,
all the people wondered: (48)

1024. "Was it a deva or Brahmā,
or even Indra, the husband of Sujā,
who asked those questions with the mind?
To whom did he reply?" (49)

1025. "Bāvari asks about the head
and the splitting of the head.
Explain this, Blessed One!
Remove our doubt, O rishi!" (50)

1026. "Know ignorance to be 'the head';
clear knowledge is 'head-splitting'
when conjoined with faith, mindfulness,
concentration, desire, and energy." (51)

1027. Thereupon the brahmin student,
uplifted by great exhilaration,

arranged his cloak over one shoulder
and fell with his head at the Buddha's feet. (52)

1028. "The brahmin Bāvari, dear sir,
together with his pupils,
exultant in mind, joyful,
worships your feet, One with Vision." (53) [197]

1029. "May the brahmin Bāvari be happy,
together with his pupils.
May you too be happy!
May you live long, brahmin student! (54)

1030. "Whatever doubt Bāvari has,
and you, or all the others—
you are given permission, so ask
whatever you wish in your mind." (55)

1031. Given permission by the Buddha,
Ajita sat down, and making salutation,
he there asked the Tathāgata
the very first question. (56)

1 The Questions of Ajita (Ajitamāṇavapucchā)[228]

1032. "By what is the world shrouded?"
(said the Venerable Ajita).
"Why does it not shine?
What do you say is its adhesive?
What is its great peril?" (1)

1033. "The world is shrouded by ignorance,
(Ajita," said the Blessed One).
"It does not shine because of avarice and heedlessness.
I say that hankering is its adhesive.
Suffering is its great peril." (2) [198]

1034. "Everywhere the streams are flowing,"
(said the Venerable Ajita).
"What is the barrier against the streams?

Speak of the restraint of the streams:
by what are the streams closed off?" (3)

1035. "Whatever streams there are in the world,
(Ajita," said the Blessed One),
"mindfulness is the barrier against them.
I speak of this as restraint of the streams.
They are closed off by wisdom." (4)

1036. "Wisdom and mindfulness,"
(said the Venerable Ajita),
"and name-and-form, dear sir—
when asked by me please declare:
where does this come to an end?" (5)

1037. "As to this question that you ask,
I will tell you, Ajita,
where name and also form
come to an end without remainder:
it is by the cessation of consciousness
that this here comes to an end." (6)

1038. "Those who have comprehended the Dhamma,
and the diverse trainees here:
when asked by me about their conduct,
let the judicious one declare it, dear sir." (7)

1039. "One should not be greedy for sensual pleasures;
one should be untarnished in mind.
Skillful in regard to all phenomena,
a bhikkhu should wander mindfully." (8) [199]

2 The Questions of Tissa Metteyya (Tissametteyyamāṇavapucchā)

1040. "Who here is contented in the world?"
(said the Venerable Tissa Metteyya).
"For whom is there no agitation?
Who, having directly known both ends,
by reflection does not get stuck in the middle?

Whom do you call a great man?
Who here has transcended the seamstress?" (1)

1041. "One leading the spiritual life among sensual pleasures, (Metteyya," said the Blessed One),
"one without craving, always mindful,
a bhikkhu who is quenched, having comprehended:
for him there is no agitation. (2)

1042. "Having directly known both ends,
by reflection one does not get stuck in the middle.
I call him a great man:
he has here transcended the seamstress." (3)

3 The Questions of Puṇṇaka (Puṇṇakamāṇavapucchā)

1043. "To the one without impulse, seer of the root," (said the Venerable Puṇṇaka),
"I have come in need with a question: [200]
On what ground have many rishis, men, khattiyas, and brahmins
here in the world performed sacrifice to the deities?[229]
I ask you, Blessed One: please declare this to me." (1)

1044. "These many rishis, men, khattiyas, and brahmins, (Puṇṇaka," said the Blessed One),
"who here in the world have performed sacrifice to the deities,
did so, Puṇṇaka, yearning for a state of being.
Bound to old age, they performed sacrifices." (2)

1045. "These many rishis, men, khattiyas, and brahmins," (said the Venerable Puṇṇaka),
"who here in the world, heedful on the path of sacrifice,
performed sacrifices to the deities:
did they cross over birth and old age, dear sir?
I ask you, Blessed One: please declare this to me." (3)

1046. "They yearn, extol, hanker, offer up,
(Puṇṇaka," said the Blessed One).
"They hanker for sensual pleasures because of gain.
Intent on sacrifice, excited by lust for existence,
they did not cross over birth and old age, I say."
(4) [201]

1047. "If, dear sir, those intent on sacrifice,"
(said the Venerable Puṇṇaka),
"by their sacrifices did not cross over birth and old age,
then who here in the world of devas and humans
has crossed over birth and old age, dear sir?
I ask you, Blessed One: please declare this for me." (5)

1048. "Having comprehended the far and near in the
world, (Puṇṇaka," said the Blessed One),
"one without agitation anywhere in the world,
peaceful, fumeless, untroubled, wishless,
has crossed over birth and old age, I say." (6)

4 The Questions of Mettagū (Mettagūmāṇavapucchā)

1049. "I ask you a question, Blessed One, please tell me
this," (said the Venerable Mettagū).
"I consider you a Veda-master, one inwardly developed.
From where have these sufferings arisen
in their many forms in the world?" (1) [202]

1050. "You have asked me about the origin of suffering,
(Mettagū," said the Blessed One).
"As one who understands, I will tell you this.
Sufferings in their many forms in the world
originate based on acquisition.[230] (2)

1051. "The ignorant dullard who creates acquisition
encounters suffering again and again.

Therefore, understanding,[231] one should not create
acquisition,
contemplating it as the genesis and origin of suffering."
(3)

1052. "You have told us what we asked.
Let me ask you another—please speak on this.
How do the wise cross over the flood,
over birth and old age, sorrow and lamenting?
Explain this to me clearly, muni,
for this Dhamma has been understood by you." (4)

1053. "I will proclaim this Dhamma to you,
(Mettagū," said the Blessed One),
"seen in this very life, no matter of hearsay,
having understood which, living mindfully,
one can cross over attachment to the world." (5)

1054. "And I delight, great rishi,
in that supreme Dhamma,
having understood which, living mindfully,
one can cross over attachment to the world." (6)

1055. "Whatever you comprehend,
(Mettagū," said the Blessed One),
"above, below, and across in the middle, [203]
having dispelled delight and attachment to these,
consciousness would not persist in existence. (7)

1056. "A bhikkhu so dwelling, mindful, heedful,
having given up taking things as 'mine,'
right here such a wise one might abandon suffering:
birth and old age, sorrow and lamenting." (8)

1057. "I delight in this word of the great rishi;
well procaimed, Gotama, is the state without
acquisitions.
Certainly the Blessed One has abandoned suffering,
for this Dhamma has been understood by you. (9)

1058. "Surely they too can abandon suffering
whom you, muni, would constantly exhort.
Therefore, having met you, O nāga, I pay homage:
perhaps the Blessed One would constantly exhort me."
(10)

1059. "Whatever brahmin you may know to be a
Veda-master,
owning nothing, unattached to sensual pleasures and
existence,
he has certainly crossed this flood,
and crossed to the beyond, he is unbarren, rid of
doubt. (11)

1060. "And the wise man here, the Veda-master,
having loosened this tie to various states of existence,
[204]
rid of craving, untroubled, wishless,
has crossed over birth and old age, I say." (12)

5 The Questions of Dhotaka (Dhotakamāṇavapucchā)

1061. "I ask you, Blessed One, speak to me of this,"
(said the Venerable Dhotaka).
"I long for your speech, great rishi:
having heard your utterance,
I shall train for my own nibbāna." (1)

1062. "In that case, apply ardor,
(Dhotaka," said the Blessed One).
"Be judicious and mindful right here.
Having heard the utterance from me,
you should train for your own nibbāna." (2)

1063. "I see in the world of devas and human beings,
a brahmin owning nothing, traveling about.
Hence I pay homage to you, O universal eye!
Free me, Sakya, from perplexity." (3)

1064. "I will not be able to free anyone in the world,[232]
Dhotaka, who is still afflicted by perplexity.
But understanding the supreme Dhamma,
you will thereby cross this flood." (4)

1065. "Taking compassion, instruct me, Brahmā,
in the state of seclusion that I can understand. [205]
Just as space is totally unobstructed,
right here I would live, peaceful and unattached." (5)

1066. "I will describe that peace for you,
(Dhotaka," said the Blessed One),
"[seen] in this very life, no matter of hearsay,
having understood which, living mindfully,
one can cross over attachment to the world." (6)

1067. "And I delight, great rishi,
in that supreme peace,
having understood which, living mindfully,
one can cross over attachment to the world." (7)

1068. "Whatever you comprehend
(Dhotaka," said the Blessed One),
"above, below, and across in the middle,
having understood this as 'a tie' in the world,
do not create craving for various states of existence." (8)

6 The Questions of Upasīva (Upasīvamāṇavapucchā)

1069. "Alone, Sakya, unsupported,"
(said the Venerable Upasīva),
"I am not able to cross over the great flood.
Declare to me a basis, O universal eye,
supported by which I might cross over this flood."[233] (1)

1070. "Contemplating nothingness, mindful,
(Upasīva," said the Blessed One),
"supported by 'there is not,' cross over the flood. [206]

Having abandoned sensual pleasures, refraining from perplexity,
night and day see into the destruction of craving." (2)

1071. "One devoid of lust for all sensual pleasures,"
(said the Venerable Upasīva),
"supported by nothingness, having discarded all else,
liberated in the supreme emancipation of perception:[234]
would he stay there without departing?" (3)

1072. "One devoid of lust for all sensual pleasures,
(Upasīva," said the Blessed One),
"supported by nothingness, having discarded all else,
liberated in the supreme emancipation of perception,
would stay there without departing." (4)

1073. "If he would stay there without departing
even for a multitude of years, O universal eye,
would he become cool, liberated right there—
[or] would the consciousness of such a one pass away?"[235] (5)

1074. "As a flame, thrown by a gust of wind,
(Upasīva," said the Blessed One),
"goes out and cannot be designated, [207]
so the muni, liberated from the mental body,
goes out and cannot be designated." (6)

1075. "But does one who has gone out not exist,
or else is he intact through eternity?
Explain this matter clearly to me, O muni,
for this Dhamma has been understood by you." (7)

1076. "There is no measure of one who has gone out,
(Upasīva," said the Blessed One).
"There is no means by which they might speak of him.
When all phenomena have been uprooted,
all pathways of speech are also uprooted." (8)

7 The Questions of Nanda (Nandamāṇavapucchā)

1077. "There are munis in the world,"
(said the Venerable Nanda),
"so people say, but how is this so?
Do they declare one who has knowledge a muni
or one following a particular way of life?" (1)

1078. "Not by view, nor by learning, nor by knowledge,
Nanda, do the skilled here speak of a muni. [208]
They are munis, I say, who live remote,
untroubled, without wishes." (2)

1079. "Those ascetics and brahmins,"
(said the Venerable Nanda),
"who say that purity [is gained] through the seen and heard,
that purity [is gained], too, by good behavior and observances,
who say purity [is gained] through numerous methods—
living restrained[236] there, Blessed One, have they
crossed over birth and old age, dear sir?
I ask you, Blessed One. Please answer me." (3)

1080. "Those ascetics and brahmins,
(Nanda," said the Blessed One),
"who say that purity [is gained] through the seen and heard,
that purity [is gained], too, by good behavior and observances,
who say purity [is gained] through numerous methods—
though they live restrained there, I say
they have not crossed over birth and old age." (4)

1081. "Those ascetics and brahmins,"
(said the Venerable Nanda),
"who say that purity [is gained] through the seen and heard,
that purity [is gained], too, by good behavior and observances,

who say purity [is gained] through numerous
methods—
if, O muni, you say they have not crossed the flood,[237] [209]
then who in the world of devas and humans
has crossed over birth and old age, dear sir?
I ask you, Blessed One. Please answer me." (5)

1082. "I do not say of all ascetics and brahmins,
(Nanda," said the Blessed One),
"that they are shrouded by birth and old age.
Those here who have abandoned the seen, the heard and
sensed,
and all good behavior and observances,
who have abandoned, too, everything of numerous
kinds,
who, having fully understood craving, are without
influxes:
those, I say, are 'persons who have crossed the flood.'" (6)

1083. "I delight in this word of the great rishi.
Well procaimed, O Gotama, is the state without
acquisitions.
Those here who have abandoned the seen, heard, and
sensed,
as well as all good behavior and observances,
who have abandoned, too, everything of numerous
kinds,
who, having fully understood craving, are without
influxes:
I too say: 'They have crossed the flood.'" (7)

8 The Questions of Hemaka (Hemakamāṇavapucchā)

1084. "Those who in the past explained things to me,"
(said the Venerable Hemaka), [210]
"before [my meeting with] Gotama's teaching,
saying, 'Such it was, such it will be,'
all that was hearsay,
all was an increase of thought;
I did not delight in it.[238] (1)

1085. "Declare to me the Dhamma,
O muni, the destruction of craving,
having understood which, living mindfully,
one can cross over attachment to the world." (2)

1086. "The dispelling of desire and lust, Hemaka,
for things here seen, heard, sensed, and cognized—
for whatever has a pleasing nature—
is the state of nibbāna, the imperishable. (3)

1087. "Having understood this, those mindful ones
are quenched in this very life.
And always peaceful, they have crossed over
attachment to the world." (4)

9 The Questions of Todeyya (Todeyyamāṇavapucchā)

1088. "For one in whom sensual desires do not dwell,"
(said the Venerable Todeyya),
"in whom craving is not found
and who has crossed over perplexity,
of what sort is his emancipation?" (1) [211]

1089. "For one in whom sensual desires do not dwell,
(Todeyya," said the Blessed One),
"in whom craving is not found
and who has crossed over perplexity:
there is no further emancipation for him." (2)

1090. "Is he without desire[239] or does he have desire?
Does he possess wisdom or just a wise manner?
So that I can understand, O Sakka,
explain the muni to me, O universal eye." (3)

1091. "He is without desire; he does not have desire.
He possesses wisdom, not just a wise manner.
Understand the muni thus, Todeyya,
as one owning nothing, unattached
to sensual pleasures and existence." (4)

10 The Questions of Kappa (Kappamāṇavapucchā)

1092. "For those standing in the midst of the stream,"
(said the Venerable Kappa),
"when a perilous flood has arisen,
for those oppressed by old age and death,
declare an island, dear sir.
Explain to me the island
so this might occur no more." (1) [212]

1093. "For those standing in the midst of the stream,
(Kappa," said the Blessed One),
"when a perilous flood has arisen,
for those oppressed by old age and death,
let me declare an island to you. (2)

1094. "Owning nothing, taking nothing:
this is the island with nothing further.
I call this 'nibbāna,'
the extinction of old age and death. (3)

1095. "Having understood this, those mindful ones
are quenched in this very life.
They do not come under Māra's control,
nor are they Māra's footmen." (4)

11 The Questions of Jatukaṇṇī (Jatukaṇṇīmāṇavapucchā)

1096. "Having heard of the hero who has no desire for
sensual pleasures," (said the Venerable Jatukaṇṇī),
"I have come to ask the desireless one who has escaped
the flood.
Speak about the state of peace, you of innate vision.
Tell me about it, Blessed One, as it actually is. (1)

1097. "For the Blessed One has overcome sensual desires,
as the splendid sun overcomes the earth with its
splendor.

Since I am one of limited wisdom, teach me the
Dhamma,
you of broad wisdom, so that I might understand
the abandoning here of birth and old age." (2) [213]

1098. "Remove greed for sensual pleasures,
(Jatukaṇṇī," said the Blessed One),
"having seen renunciation as security.
Do not take up or reject anything:
let neither of these exist for you. (3)

1099. "Dry up what pertains to the past,
do not take up anything to come later.
If you will not grasp in the middle,
you will live at peace. (4)

1100. "For one, brahmin, entirely
devoid of greed for name-and-form,
the influxes do not exist by which
one might come under death's control." (5)

12 The Questions of Bhadrāvudha (Bhadrāvudhamāṇavapucchā)

1101. "I entreat the home-leaver,"
(said the Venerable Bhadrāvudha),
"the cutter off of craving, one without impulse,
who has abandoned delight, crossed the flood, won
liberation,
abandoned mental constructs—one extremely wise:
having heard this from the nāga,
they will depart from here.[240] (1)

1102. "Various peoples from [various] countries
have gathered desiring your word, O hero.
Explain matters well to them,
for this Dhamma has been understood by you." (2)

1103. "One should remove all acquisitive craving,
(Bhadrāvudha," said the Blessed One),

"above, below, and across in the middle. [214]
Whatever they cling to in the world,
by this itself Māra pursues a person. (3)

1104. "Therefore understanding this, a mindful bhikkhu
should not cling to anything in the entire world.
Observing, 'They are stuck on taking up,' [he knows]
this population is attached to the realm of death." (4)

13 The Questions of Udaya (Udayamāṇavapucchā)

1105. "I have come in need with a question,"
(said the Venerable Udaya),
"to the seated meditator, dust-free,
who has completed the task, without influxes,
who has gone beyond all phenomena.
Speak of emancipation by final knowledge,
the breaking up of ignorance." (1)

1106. "The abandoning of both,
(Udaya," said the Blessed One),
"sensual desires and dejection;
the dispelling of mental dullness,
the warding off of regrets: (2)

1107. "purified by equanimity and mindfulness,
preceded by thought on the Dhamma—
I call this emancipation by final knowledge,
the breaking up of ignorance." (3) [215]

1108. "By what is the world fettered?
What is its means of traveling about?
By the abandoning of what
is 'nibbāna' spoken of?" (4)

1109. "The world is fettered by delight;
thought is its means of traveling about.
It is by the abandoning of craving
that 'nibbāna' is spoken of." (5)

1110. "How does one live mindfully
for consciousness to cease?
Having come to ask the Blessed One,
let us hear that word of yours." (6)

1111. "For one not seeking delight in feeling
internally and externally,
for one living mindfully thus,
consciousness ceases." (7)

14 The Questions of Posāla (Posālamāṇavapucchā)

1112. "I have come in need with a question,"
(said the Venerable Posāla),
"to the one who points out the past,
who is without impulse, who has cut off doubt,
who has gone beyond all phenomena. (1)

1113. "I ask, Sakya, about the knowledge
of one for whom perception of form has vanished,
who has entirely abandoned the body,
who sees 'there is nothing'
internally and externally:
how is such a one to be led?" (2) [216]

1114. "Directly knowing all stations of consciousness,
(Posāla," said the Blessed One),
"the Tathāgata knows this one
remaining, who is liberated,
who has that as support. (3)

1115. "Having known the origin of nothingness
thus, 'delight is the fetter,'
having directly known it in such a way,[241]
one then sees into it with insight.
This is the real knowledge of the brahmin,
one who has lived the spiritual life." (4)

15 The Questions of Mogharāja (Mogharājamāṇavapucchā)

1116. "I have asked the Sakyan twice,"
(said the Venerable Mogharāja),
"but the One with Vision did not answer me.
Yet I have heard that the divine rishi
answers upon the third request. (1)

1117. "As to this world, the other world,
the brahma world together with the devas,
I do not know your view,
[the view] of the famous Gotama. (2) [217]

1118. "Thus I have come in need with a question
to the one of excellent vision.
How does one look upon the world,
so that the King of Death does not see one?" (3)

1119. "Look upon the world as empty,
Mogharāja, being ever mindful.
Having uprooted the view of self,
one may thus cross over death.
The King of Death does not see
one who looks upon the world thus." (4)

16 The Questions of Piṅgiya (Piṅgiyamāṇavapucchā)

1120. "I am old, weak, my color gone,"
(said the Venerable Piṅgiya),
"my eyesight is not clear, my hearing is faint.
Do not let me perish confused along the way.
Declare the Dhamma that I might understand
the abandoning here of birth and old age." (1)

1121. "Having seen those stricken by forms,
(Piṅgiya," said the Blessed One),
"people who are heedless, afflicted by forms,
therefore, Piṅgiya, being heedful,
abandon form for an end to renewed existence." (2)

1122. "In the four directions, the four intermediate
directions,
above, below: in these ten directions, [218]
there is nothing that you have not seen, heard, and
sensed,
and nothing in the world uncognized by you.
Declare the Dhamma that I might understand
the abandoning here of birth and old age." (3)

1123. "Observing people fallen into craving,
(Piṅgiya," said the Blessed One),
"tormented, crushed by old age,
therefore, Piṅgiya, being heedful,
abandon craving for an end to renewed existence." (4)

Epilogue

Verses Extolling the Way to the Beyond[242]

This is what the Blessed One said while dwelling among the Magadhans at the Pāsāṇaka Cetiya. When entreated by the sixteen attendant brahmins and questioned by each, he answered their questions. If one understands the meaning and the teaching in each of these [sections of] questions, and practices in accordance with the Dhamma, one would go beyond old age and death. Since these teachings lead beyond, this exposition of the Dhamma is designated the Pārāyana, "The Way to the Beyond."

1124. Ajita, Tissa Metteyya, Puṇṇaka, and Mettagū,
Dhotaka and Upasīva, Nanda and also Hemaka; (1) [219]

1125. Todeyya and Kappa, and the wise Jatukaṇṇī,
Bhadrāvudho and Udaya, and the brahmin Posāla,
the intelligent Mogharājā, and the great rishi Piṅgiya: (2)

1126. they approached the Buddha,
the rishi of excellent conduct;
asking subtle questions,
they came to the supreme Buddha. (3)

1127. When asked questions by them,
the Buddha answered in accordance with truth.
With his answers to their questions,
the muni satisfied the brahmins. (4)

1128. Satisfied by the One with Vision,
by the Buddha, Kinsman of the Sun,
they lived the spiritual life
under the one with excellent wisdom. (5)

1129. If one would practice in the way
they were taught by the Buddha
in response to each of their questions,
one would go from the near shore to the beyond. (6)

1130. Developing the supreme path,
one would go from the near shore to the beyond.
That path is for going to the beyond;
therefore it is called "the Way to the Beyond." (7)

Verses Recited about the Way to the Beyond[243]

1131. "I will recite the Way to the Beyond,"
(said the Venerable Piṅgiya).
"As he saw it, just so he expounded it,
the stainless one, the one of broad intelligence.
For what reason would the nāga,[244]
desireless, disentangled, speak falsely? (8) [220]

1132. "Come now, let me explain
the beautiful utterance of the one
who has abandoned stains and delusion,
who has abandoned conceit and denigration. (9)

1133. "The dispeller of darkness, the Buddha, the universal eye,
who has gone to the world's end, transcended all existences,
the one without influxes, who has abandoned all suffering,

who is truly named, O brahmin, he is served by
me. (10)

1134. "As a bird that has left behind a small woods
might settle upon a forest abounding in fruit,
just so, having left those of little vision,
I am like a goose that has arrived at a great lake. (11)

1135. "Those who in the past explained things to me,
before [my meeting with] Gotama's teaching,
saying, 'Such it was, such it will be,'
all that was hearsay,
all was an increase of thought.[245] (12)

1136. "The dispeller of darkness seated alone,
the brilliant one,[246] the maker of light,
Gotama of broad wisdom,
Gotama of broad intelligence— (13) [221]

1137. "he is the one who taught me the Dhamma,
directly visible, immediate,
the destruction of craving, without adversity,
for which there is no simile anywhere." (14)

1138. "Why do you dwell apart from him
even for a moment, O Piṅgiya,
from Gotama of broad wisdom,
from Gotama of broad intelligence, (15)

1139. "the one who taught you the Dhamma,
directly visible, immediate,
the destruction of craving, without adversity,
for which there is no simile anywhere?" (16)

1140. "I do not dwell apart from him
even for a moment, O brahmin,
from Gotama of broad wisdom,
from Gotama of broad intelligence, (17)

1141. "the one who taught me the Dhamma,
directly visible, immediate,
the destruction of craving, without adversity,
for which there is no simile anywhere. (18)

1142. "Heedful, O brahmin, night and day,
I see him with my mind as if with my eyes.
I pass the night paying homage to him;
hence I do not think I am apart from him. (19)

1143. "My faith and rapture, mind and mindfulness,
do not depart from Gotama's teaching.
To whatever direction the one of broad wisdom goes,
I pay homage to him in that same direction. (20) [222]

1144. "Since I am old and feeble,
my body does not travel there,
but I go constantly on a journey of thought,
for my mind, brahmin, is united with him. (21)

1145. "As I lay trembling in the mud,
I floated from island to island.
Then I saw the Enlightened One,
influx-free, who had crossed the flood." (22)

[The Buddha]

1146. "As Vakkali had sent forth faith,
and Bhadrāvudha and Āḷavi Gotama,
just so you too must send forth faith:
then, Piṅgiya, you will go
beyond the realm of death." (23)

[Piṅgiya]

1147. "I am pleased even more,
having heard the word of the muni.
The Enlightened One, with coverings removed,
is not barren, gifted with ingenuity. (24)

1148. "Having directly known about the devas,
he understood everything, high and low.
The Teacher is the end-maker of questions
for those in doubt who acknowledge this. (25) [223]

1149. "The immovable, the unshakable,
has no simile anywhere.
Surely I will go there; I have no doubt about this.
Thus remember me as one with mind resolved." (26)

The Suttanipāta is completed.

Elucidator of the Supreme Meaning (Paramatthajotikā II)

The Commentary to the Suttanipāta

Homage to the Blessed One,
the Worthy One,
the Perfectly Enlightened One

The Purpose of This Work

[1] Having venerated the Triple Gem,
supreme among things worthy of veneration,
I will compose an explanation of the meaning
of the Suttanipāta, [a compilation of suttas]

that is found in the Minor Collection,
and was taught by the World's Protector,
who abandoned all minor types of conduct
and sought the escape from the world.[247]

The question may be asked:
"When it is strewn with hundreds of *gāthās*,
and marked with *geyyas* and *vyākaraṇas*,
why is it designated Suttanipāta?"[248]

[It is said:] Because the word "sutta" is spoken
on account of being well stated and indicating,
because of thoroughly protecting benefits,
and because of producing and putting in order—[249]

therefore, because this was recited[250]
by compiling from here and there
suttas that have such a nature,
it goes under such a designation.

And further, all the suttas stem from
the Impartial One as their source;[251]
this is a compilation of their words,
[hence it is called the "Suttanipāta"].

Because there is no other quality
as a basis for designating them,
it goes under just such a name
as the designation "Suttanipāta."

This work, which has acquired such a designation, has five chapters: the Chapter on the Serpent, the Minor Chapter, the Great Chapter, the Chapter of Octads, and the Chapter on the Way to the Beyond. Of these, the Chapter on the Serpent is the first. By way of suttas, there are seventy suttas: in the Chapter on the Serpent, twelve suttas; in the Minor Chapter, fourteen; in the Great Chapter, twelve; in the Chapter of Octads, sixteen; and in the Chapter on the Way to the Beyond, sixteen.[252] Of these, the Discourse on the Serpent is first. By way of divisions of learning, [2] there are eight recitation sections.

I The Chapter on the Serpent
(*Uragavagga*)

1 The Serpent
(*Uraga Sutta*)

1. Thus, in regard to chapter, sutta, and divisions of learning, the first verse is this one:

> One who removes the anger that has arisen
> as one removes with herbs a snake's spreading venom:
> that bhikkhu gives up the here and the beyond
> as a serpent sheds its old worn-out skin.

Therefore, from this point on, in providing an explanation of the meaning, this is said:

> Having first clarified this procedure—
> by whom, where, when, and why
> this verse was spoken—we will then
> provide an explanation of its meaning.

By whom was this verse spoken, where, when, and why? It is said: Having received the prediction [of future buddhahood] from twenty-four buddhas, the Blessed One fulfilled the pāramīs up to his past life as Vessantara and was then reborn in the Tusita heaven. Having passed away from there, he took birth in a royal family of the Sakyans. In sequence, he made the great renunciation, awakened to the perfect enlightenment at the foot of the bodhi tree, set in motion the wheel of the Dhamma, and taught the Dhamma for the welfare of devas and human beings. [This verse] was spoken by that Blessed One, who as one self-accomplished, without a teacher, had become a perfectly enlightened buddha. And it was spoken at Āḷavī, in order to teach the Dhamma to those who had approached him there when the training rule against the destruction of plant life (Pācittiya 11) was laid down. This here is a brief answer.

But in detail it should be understood by way of the distant background, the intermediate background, and the immediate background. Of these, the "distant background" is the story [of the Buddha's career] from the time of Dīpaṅkara until the present occasion.[253] The "intermediate background" is the story from his time in the Tusita heaven until the present occasion. And the "immediate background" relates the story from his time at the site of enlightenment until the present occasion.

Since the intermediate background and immediate background are already included within the distant background, the detailed explanation should be understood here by way of the distant background. However, this is related in the commentary to the Jātakas, so it is not elaborated upon here; therefore it should be understood in accordance with the detailed method given there. But there is this difference: the story behind the first verse there [in the Jātakas] occurred at Sāvatthī, while here it was at Āḷavī. As it is said: [3]

> On that occasion the Blessed One, the Buddha, was dwelling at Āḷavī at the Aggāḷava Cetiya. Now on that occasion the bhikkhus of Āḷavī, while doing some construction work, cut down trees and ordered trees to be cut down. A certain bhikkhu of Āḷavī cut down a tree. The deity dwelling in that tree said to that bhikkhu: "Bhante, don't cut down my home in order to make a home for yourself." Not heeding her request, the bhikkhu cut the tree down and struck the arm of that deity's child. Then it occurred to that deity: "Let me take this bhikkhu's life right on the spot." But that deity considered: "It isn't suitable for me to take this bhikkhu's life right on the spot. Let me report this matter to the Blessed One." Then that deity approached the Blessed One and reported this matter to him. [The Blessed One said:] "Good, good, deity! It is good that you did not take that bhikkhu's life. For if today you had taken that bhikkhu's life, you would have generated much demerit. Go, deity, in such and

such an area there is an abandoned tree. You should
go there."[254]

Having said this, the Blessed One spoke the following verse for the sake of dispelling the anger arisen in that deity:

One should control the anger that has arisen
just as one does a rolling chariot. (Dhp 222)

Then people complained: "How can the ascetics who are followers of the Sakyan son cut down trees and have them cut down? The ascetics who are followers of the Sakyan son injure life that has one faculty!" When the bhikkhus heard this and reported it to the Blessed One, he laid down this training rule—"There is a Pācittiya offense in destroying plant life"—and spoke the following verse to teach the Dhamma to those who had approached him:[255]

One who removes the anger that has arisen
as one removes with herbs a snake's spreading venom . . .

Thus this [4] one incident is included in three places: the Vinaya, the Dhammapada, and the Suttanipāta. And at this point the outline that was set up has been shown both briefly and in detail, having put aside an explanation of the meaning, namely:

Having first clarified this procedure:
by whom, where, when, and why
this verse was spoken, we will then
provide an explanation of its meaning.

This now is the *explanation of the meaning*. **One who**: anyone who has gone forth, whether from a khattiya family or from a brahmin family, whether junior, of middle standing, or an elder. **Arisen**: the meaning is "sprung up, come up, occurred." What is meant is arisen.[256] And that which is said to have "arisen" is of many kinds, for instance: (1) what is actually occurring, (2) what has occurred and vanished, (3) what has made an opportunity, and (4) what has gained ground.[257]

Among these, (1) all conditioned things that possess arising, [persistence, and dissolution][258] are called *arisen as actually occurring*, with reference to which it is said: "Arisen phenomena, unarisen phenomena, phenomena capable of arising" (Dhs 3, §17).

(2) Wholesome and unwholesome mental qualities that have experienced the taste of their object and ceased—designated "that which has experienced and vanished"—and the remaining conditioned things that have ceased after reaching the three phases of arising, [persistence, and dissolution]—designated "having occurred and vanished"—are together called *arisen as what has occurred and vanished*. This can be seen in such sutta passages as "such a bad view had arisen" (DN I 224,10, MN I 130,4) and "the fulfillment by development of the arisen enlightenment factor of mindfulness" (DN II 303,26, MN I 62,3, SN V 333,4).

(3) Kamma described in such a way as "Those kammas that were done in the past"[259] and so forth are called *arisen as what has made an opportunity* because, though past, they persist in the sense that they prevent the result of another kamma and have made an opportunity for their own result; so too, the result for which an opportunity has been made, though unarisen, [is also called thus] because, once the opportunity has been made, its arising is certain.

(4) An unwholesome state that has not been uprooted in regard to various planes (grounds) is called *arisen as what has gained ground*.

And here the difference between the ground and what has gained ground should be understood. What is called *the ground* is the five aggregates pertaining to the three planes of existence that serve as objects of insight. That which has *gained ground* [5] is the set of defilements capable of arising in those aggregates.[260] And that is not by way of object, for defilements arise in relation to all aggregates by taking them as object; [they even arise in relation to the aggregates] of arahants, which have been fully understood in their divisions such as past, present, and future, and so forth, as for example in the case of the financier's son Soreyya [who was enamored of the arahant-bhikkhu] Mahākaccāna and the youth Nanda [who raped the arahant-bhikkhunī] Uppalavaṇṇā, and so forth.[261] And if [the aggregates taken as object] were "what has gained ground," no one would abandon the root of existence, for these cannot be abandoned.

But "what has gained ground" should be understood in relation to the base.[262] For wherever the aggregates not fully understood by insight arise, from the time of their arising there the defilements that are the root of the round lie latent in them. These should be understood to be "arisen as what has gained ground" in the sense that they have not been abandoned. The base of those defilements is the set of aggregates of one whose defilements are unabandoned, which defilements lie latent in those aggregates; it is not the aggregates of others.[263] And for one whose defilements were unabandoned and remained latent in past aggregates, only past aggregates were the base, not others. The same method in regard to the future and so forth. Similarly, for one whose defilements are unabandoned and lie latent in desire-sphere aggregates, only desire-sphere aggregates are the base, not others. The same method applies to the form and formless spheres.

When these or those defilements, which are the root of the round, have been abandoned by this or that path in the aggregates of any noble person among stream-enterers and so forth, those aggregates can no longer be called "a ground" for them, since they are no longer a base for those abandoned defilements that are the root of the round. But in the case of a worldling, because the defilements that are the root of the round have not been abandoned at all, any kamma that this person does is either wholesome or unwholesome; thus for such a person the round turns with kamma and defilements as its condition.[264] It should not be said of such a person that this is a root of the round only in the aggregate of form but not in the aggregates of feeling and so forth . . . or only in the aggregate of consciousness but not in the aggregate of form and so forth. Why? Because those defilements lie latent in the five aggregates without distinction.

How? Like the soil nutrients and so forth in relation to a tree. For when a large tree is growing on the ground, [6] its roots, trunk, branches, twigs, shoots, foliage, flowers, and fruits grow in dependence on soil nutrients and moisture, with these as conditions. Having filled the sky, the tree, through the succession of seeds, maintains the lineage of trees until the eon's end.

It cannot be said that the soil nutrients and so forth are found only in the roots and not in the trunk and other parts, or that they are only in the fruit and not in the roots and other parts. Why? Because they permeate all the parts, the roots and everything else, without distinction.

Suppose now that a man, unhappy with that tree's flowers and fruit, were to apply the poisonous *maṇḍūka* thorn to the tree on its four sides. In that case the tree would be infected by the poison, so that its soil nutrients and moisture would be depleted; then that tree would turn barren and would no longer be able to maintain the continuity. Just so, when a person is disenchanted with the continuation of the aggregates, he develops the four paths in his own mind; this is like the man's applying the poison to the tree on its four sides. Then, because the defilements that are the root of the round would be completely depleted by that "poisonous application" of the four paths, all the types of kamma, such as bodily kamma and so forth, would have reached a state of mere functionality;[265] his continuum of aggregates would no longer be able to prolong the continuum into another existence by means of its inherent capacity to generate future renewed existence.[266] As a fire devoid of fuel [goes out], so too, with the cessation of the final act of consciousness, this person, free of clinging, would definitely attain final nibbāna.

It is in this way that the difference between the ground and what has gained ground should be understood.

Further, there is another fourfold classification of "arisen": (1) as happening, (2) because an object has been apprehended, (3) as unsuppressed, and (4) as not uprooted.[267]

(1) Among these, *arisen as happening* is the same as "arisen as actually occurring."[268]

(2) *Arisen because an object has been apprehended* refers to the case when an object has come into range of the eye or the other sense doors, and though the defilements do not arise [on the occasion when the object is perceived], because the object has been apprehended their arising at a later time is unavoidable.[269] [7] And here the example given is that of the Elder Mahātissa, whose defilements arose after he had seen the form of a woman while wandering for alms in Kalyāṇigāma.[270] The effort involved here should be understood through the pas-

sage "[One does not tolerate] an arisen sensual thought" and so forth (MN I 11,11, AN II 16,20).

(3) *Arisen as unsuppressed* refers to defilements that have not been suppressed by either serenity or insight. Though they may not have actually arisen in one's mental continuity, [they are called *arisen as unsuppressed*] because there is no cause to prevent their arising. [The appropriate effort involved here] should be understood through the passage "Bhikkhus, this concentration by mindfulness of breathing, when developed and cultivated, is peaceful and sublime, an ambrosial pleasant dwelling that eliminates right on the spot any bad unwholesome qualities that have arisen" (SN V 321,21).

(4) *Arisen as not uprooted* refers to defilements that may have been suppressed by means of serenity or insight but which are still capable of arising because they have not been uprooted by the noble path. The example given here is that of the elder who had attained the eight meditative attainments and was traveling through the sky [by psychic power]. When he heard the sweet voice of a woman singing while she gathered flowers in a grove of blossoming trees, his defilements arose. The effort involved here should be understood through the passage "When one develops and cultivates the noble eightfold path, one eliminates in advance any bad unwholesome qualities that may have arisen" (SN V 51,2).

But these three kinds of "arisen"—because an object has been apprehended, as unsuppressed, and as not uprooted—should be understood to be included by "that which has gained ground."

Thus, of the types of "arisen" distinguished by the aforesaid analysis, the anger arisen [according to the verse] should be understood by way of arisen as "that which has gained ground," "arisen because an object has been apprehended," "arisen as unsuppressed," and "arisen as not uprooted." Why? Because those are the kinds that are to be removed. For it is possible to remove what has arisen in such ways by a particular method of removal, but effort is futile and even impossible in regard to that which has arisen in the sense of "actually occurring," "as what has occurred and vanished," "as what has made an opportunity," and "as happening." For effort is futile in regard to what has occurred and vanished, because it has ceased even before the effort can be applied. And so too in regard to what has made an opportunity. But effort is impossible in regard to what has arisen as actually occurring and as happening, because there is no simultaneous arising of defilements and the cleansing of them.[271] [8]

But as to the word "removes" here:

> Removal is twofold,
> and each one in turn is fivefold.
> By eight kinds of these,
> "removes" is said.

For this removal is twofold: removal by restraint and removal by abandoning. And in this twofold removal, each type of removal is fivefold. For *removal by restraint* is fivefold: restraint by good behavior, restraint by mindfulness, restraint by knowledge, restraint by patience, and restraint by energy.[272] *Removal by abandoning* is also fivefold: abandoning in a particular respect, abandoning by suppression, abandoning by eradication, abandoning by subsiding, and abandoning by escape.[273]

Of these, *restraint by good behavior* is seen here: "He is restrained, fully restrained by the Pātimokkha," etc. (Vibh 246, §511). *Restraint by mindfulness* is seen here: "He guards the eye faculty, he acquires restraint over the eye faculty," etc. (DN I 70,8, MN I 180,31). *Restraint by knowledge* is seen here:

> "Whatever streams there are in the world,
> (Ajita," said the Blessed One),
> "mindfulness is the blocking of them.
> I speak of this as restraint of the streams.
> They are closed off by wisdom," etc. (**1035**).

Restraint by patience is seen here: "He patiently endures cold and heat," etc. (MN I 10,25, AN II 117,32). *Restraint by energy* should be understood in this way: "He does not tolerate an arisen sensual thought but abandons it, dispels it," etc. (MN I 11,11, AN II 16,21). All this restraint is called "restraint" because it restrains bodily and verbal misconduct that is to be restrained, and it is called "removal" because it removes [bodily and verbal misconduct] that is to be removed. Thus it should be understood how removal by restraint is divided into five types.

So too, *abandoning in a particular respect* is the abandoning of the continuous occurrence of this or that source of harm. [It takes place] through this or that kind of knowledge among the factors of insight, such as the delimitation of name-and-form and so forth, as long as [there is] the occurrence [of that knowledge] by way of its non-diminishment in oneself.[274] Thus the view of the personal entity is abandoned by the delineation of name-and-form; [9] the abandoning of both the view of non-causality and the view of erroneous causality, and also of the state of perplexity, by discernment of conditions; the abandoning of apprehension of "I" and "mine" by means of exploration by groups; the abandoning of perception of the path in what is not the path by means of the delineation of what is the path and what is not the path; the abandoning of the annihilation view by the seeing of arising; the abandoning of the eternity view by the seeing of vanishing; the abandoning of the perception of non-peril in what is perilous by seeing appearance as perilous; the abandoning of the perception of gratification by seeing danger; the abandoning of the perception of delight by contemplation of disenchantment; the abandoning of no desire for liberation by desire for liberation; the abandoning of non-reflection by means of reflection; the abandoning of partiality by knowledge of equanimity; the abandoning of opposition to the nature of phenomena and to nibbāna by means of conformity; the abandoning of the grasping of the mark of conditioned things by change-of-lineage.[275]

Abandoning by suppression is the abandoning that consists in the non-arising of the hindrances and, in sequence, the successive opposing qualities such as thought and so forth, as long as there is the occurrence with non-diminishment of either access or absorption concentration.[276]

Abandoning by eradication is the abandoning that consists in the eradication, through their ultimate non-occurrence in one's own mind, of the thicket of defilements[277] pertaining to the origin [of suffering, as accomplished] by one who, through the development of the four noble paths, has become possessed of this or that path, stated in sequence [by the passage] "for the abandoning of views" and so forth (Dhs 80, §277; Dhs 93–97, §§343–60).

Abandoning by subsiding is the abandoning of defilements that is their subsidence at the moment of the fruit.[278]

Abandoning by escape is nibbāna, the abandonment of everything conditioned, because it is the escape from everything conditioned.

All these kinds of abandoning are *abandoning* in the sense of relinquishing and *removal* in the sense of removing; therefore "removal by abandoning" is said. Or because this or that kind of removal occurs in one who possesses this or that kind of abandoning, "removal by abandoning" is said. Thus it should be understood how removal by abandoning, too, is analyzed as fivefold. And because each one is analyzed as fivefold,[279] there are these ten kinds of removal.

Of these, putting aside removal by subsidence and removal by escape,[280] [10] when it is said [in the first verse] "one removes," this means that one removes in one way or another with the remaining eight kinds of removal. How? One removing bodily and verbal misconduct with "restraint by good behavior" removes the anger associated with that misconduct. One removing covetousness and dejection with "restraint by mindfulness" and "restraint by wisdom" removes the anger associated with dejection. One patiently enduring cold and other adverse conditions with "restraint by patience" removes the anger arisen toward one or another cause of resentment.[281] One removing thoughts of ill will with "restraint by energy" removes the anger associated with those thoughts. As one is abandoning the various [unwholesome] qualities by generating in oneself those [wholesome] qualities through which there is abandoning in a particular respect, by suppression, and by eradication, one also removes the anger coexisting with that which is to be abandoned in a particular respect,[282] and that which is to be suppressed and to be eradicated.

And granted, in this case [that is, in the verse under discussion], removal does not occur through removal by abandoning, but when one is removing [a defilement] by means of those qualities through which its abandoning takes place, it is said in a manner of speaking that "one removes it through removal by abandoning."[283] But at the time of abandoning by subsidence there is nothing to be removed, and in the case of the abandoning by escape there is nothing to be produced; thus it is said that one does not remove anything by these.[284] Thus it was said: "Of these, putting aside removal by subsidence and removal by escape, when it is said [in the first verse] 'one removes,' this means that one removes in one way or another with the remaining eight kinds of removal."

Five methods of removing resentment have been stated in this way:

> "Bhikkhus, there are these five ways of removing resentment by which a bhikkhu should entirely remove resentment when it has arisen toward anyone. What five? (1) One should develop loving-kindness for the person one resents . . . (2) One should develop compassion . . . (3) One should develop equanimity . . . (4) One should disregard him and pay no attention to him . . . (5) One should apply the idea of the ownership of kamma to the person one resents, thus: 'This venerable one is the owner of his kamma.' . . . These are the five ways." (AN III 185–86)

And five other methods of removing resentment have been stated in this way:

> "Friends, there are these five ways of removing resentment by which a bhikkhu should entirely remove resentment when it has arisen toward anyone. What five? Here, a person's bodily behavior is impure, but his verbal behavior is pure; [11] one should remove resentment toward such a person."[285] (AN III 186–87)

If one removes resentment by any such method it is said: "He removes it."

Further, anger is also removed when one reflects upon the danger in it, according to the method stated in this exhortation of the Teacher:

> "Bhikkhus, even if bandits were to sever you savagely limb by limb with a two-handled saw, one who gave rise to a mind of hate toward them would not be carrying out my teaching." (MN I 129,15)

One who repays an angry person with anger
thereby makes things worse for himself.
Not repaying an angry person with anger,
one wins a battle hard to win.
One practices for the welfare of both,
one's own and the other's,
when, knowing that one's foe is angry,
one mindfully maintains one's peace. (SN I 162,29–33)

"Bhikkhus, there are these seven things that are gratifying and advantageous to an enemy that come upon an angry man or woman. What seven? (1) Here, an enemy wishes for an enemy: 'May he be ugly!' For what reason? An enemy does not delight in the beauty of an enemy. When an angry person is overcome and oppressed by anger, though he may be well bathed, well anointed, with trimmed hair and beard, dressed in white clothes, still, he is ugly. This is the first thing gratifying and advantageous to an enemy that comes upon an angry man or woman. (2) Again, an enemy wishes for an enemy: 'May he sleep badly!' . . . (3) . . . 'May he not succeed!' . . . (4) . . . 'May he not be wealthy!' . . . (5) . . . 'May he not be famous!' . . . (6) . . . 'May he have no friends!' . . . (7) . . . 'With the breakup of the body, after death, may he be reborn in the plane of misery, in a bad destination, in the lower world, in hell!' . . . When an angry person is overcome and oppressed by anger, having committed misconduct by body, speech, and mind, [12] with the breakup of the body, he is reborn . . . in hell." (AN IV 94–96)

The angry person doesn't know the good;
the angry person doesn't see the Dhamma. (AN IV 96,22)

Carried away by anger,
beings go to a bad destination.
But having understood it correctly,
those with insight abandon that anger. (It 2,29–32)

One should discard anger, give up conceit,
one should overcome all the fetters. (Dhp 221)

> Anger is a cause of harm; anger stirs up mental turmoil. (AN IV 96,14)
>
> O one of broad wisdom, endure wrongdoing;
> the wise are not strong because of anger. (Ja IV 313,29–30)

Therefore, if one removes anger by reflecting in such a way, it is said: "One removes it."

Anger (*kodha*) is the same as resentment (*āghāta*), which originates through any of the nineteen "grounds of resentment." These are the nine stated in the suttas in this way, "Thinking, 'He acted for my harm,' one harbors resentment," and so forth, and their nine converse cases, formulated thus: "Thinking, 'He did not act for my benefit,'" and so forth, making eighteen (Vibh 457, §962; see too AN IV 408–9),[286] along with anger arisen groundlessly,[287] such as on account of tree stumps and thorns and so forth.

As one removes with herbs a snake's spreading venom: Just as, when someone has been bitten by a snake and his entire body is suffused with venom, a physician might put together various medicines from roots, stems, bark, leaves, flowers, and so forth and quickly remove it with the prepared herbs, so too when anger has sprung up in the way stated above and pervades one's mind, one does not tolerate it but removes it by any of the means of removal explained above; one abandons it, dispels it, and terminates it.

That bhikkhu gives up the here and the beyond (*so bhikkhu jahāti orapāraṃ*): Since anger is completely abandoned by the third path, [13] it should be understood that a bhikkhu removing anger in such a way gives up the five lower fetters, which are designated "the here and the beyond." For without distinction, "the beyond" is the name of a shore; therefore when "the here and the beyond" is said, this means "those [fetters] are 'here' ['near'] and become 'the [far] shore' of the ocean of saṃsāra."[288] Or alternatively, "One who removes the anger that has arisen as one removes with herbs a snake's spreading venom": this means that the bhikkhu, established in the fruit of a non-returner by removing anger with the third path, then abandons the here and the beyond. In this expression, "the here" is one's own personhood, "the beyond" the personhood of others. Or "the here" is the six internal sense bases, "the beyond" the external sense bases. So too, "the here" is the human world, "the beyond" the world of the devas. "The here" is the desire realm, "the beyond" the form and formless realms. "The here" is the desire and form realms, "the beyond" the formless realm. "The here" is personhood, "the beyond" is a person's comforts and conveniences. Thus on these interpretations of "the here and the beyond," one abandoning desire and lust by the fourth path is said to "give up the here and the beyond." And here, although the non-returner, by abandoning sensual lust, has no more desire or lust for personhood only here [in the desire realm], still, for the purpose of speaking praise of him as well as of the third path and so forth, all the divisions of "the here and the beyond" are collected together, and "giving up the here and the beyond" is said to take place through the abandoning of desire and lust for them.[289]

Now, to illustrate this meaning, he gives a simile: **as a serpent sheds its old worn-out skin**. Serpents, or snakes, are of two kinds: those that can assume any form at will and those that cannot assume any form at will.[290] Those that can assume any form at will are also twofold: those born in water and those born on land. Those born in water assume form at will only in water, not on land, like the nāga king Saṅkhapāla in the Saṅkhapāla Jātaka (Ja no. 524, V 161 foll.). Those born on land do so only on land, not in water.

When it sheds its old skin, a snake does so in four ways: following the law of its own species, feeling disgust, with a support, and with all its strength. Its "own species" is the class of snakes, those long-bodied creatures. For snakes do not transgress the law of their own species in five matters: in rebirth, in death, in hibernation, in mating only with those of their own species, and in discarding their worn-out skin. For when a snake sheds its skin, it always does so following the law of its own species. And following the law of its own species, [14] it discards the skin while feeling disgust for it. "Feeling disgust" means that when it is half-freed, and hangs down half unfreed, it discards the old skin with a feeling of revulsion. Feeling such disgust, it discards the skin with the support of a stick, a root, or a rock. And relying on a support, it arouses its strength and makes an endeavor. Looking on while bending its tail, it forms a hood and vigorously discards the worn-out skin. Having done so, it then departs wherever it wishes.

In just such a way this bhikkhu, wishing to give up the here and the beyond, also does so in four ways: following the law of his own species, feeling disgust, with a support, and with all his strength. "The law of his own species," for a bhikkhu, is good behavior, as it is said: "He is born with a noble birth" (MN II 103,20). Hence the Buddha says: "A wise man established in good behavior" (SN I 13,20). Thus following the law of his own species, the bhikkhu, by seeing various dangers in them, feels disgust with the here and the beyond, which are classified as one's own personhood and so forth; since they produce suffering, they are like an old worn-out skin. Then, depending on good friends, like the snake he arouses his strength, exceptional right effort. Having divided the night and day into six sessions, he strives and endeavors following the method stated thus: "During the day, while walking back and forth and sitting, he purifies his mind of obstructive qualities" (MN I 355,29, AN I 114,11). As the snake bends its tail while looking on, he bends his legs crosswise, striving with unremitting exertion. And as the snake spreads its hood and discards its skin, he spreads out his knowledge and gives up the here and the beyond. Then, as the snake, having discarded the old skin, departs wherever it wishes, so the bhikkhu, his burden dropped, departs in the direction of the nibbāna element without residue remaining. Hence the Blessed One said:

"One who removes the anger that has arisen
as one removes with herbs a snake's spreading venom:
that bhikkhu gives up the here and the beyond
as a serpent sheds its old worn-out skin." [15]

Thus the Blessed One taught this first verse with its culmination in arahantship.

2. Now the order of explaining the meaning of the second verse should be followed. In this case, too, the outline is:

Having first clarified this procedure—
by whom, where, when, and why

this verse was spoken—we will then
provide an explanation of its meaning.

This will apply to all the verses that follow. But to avoid excessive detail, from now on, without setting up the outline, I will provide the explanation of the meaning, showing the meaning of each verse simply by showing its origin. Thus this second verse begins: "One who has entirely cut off lust."

This is its origin:[291] On one occasion the Blessed One was dwelling at Sāvatthī in Jeta's Grove, Anāthapiṇḍika's Park. Now on that occasion the Venerable Sāriputta's attendant monk was the son of a goldsmith who had gone forth under the elder. Thinking that meditation on the unattractive nature of the body is suitable for young people, Sāriputta assigned him the meditation on unattractiveness for the purpose of destroying lust.[292] His mind, however, did not find any interest in the subject. He informed the elder: "This isn't helpful to me." But the elder, thinking, "It is suitable for young people," explained it to him again. In this way four months passed by, yet the young bhikkhu did not attain even the least distinction.

Then the elder brought the young bhikkhu to the Blessed One, who said: "It is beyond your domain, Sāriputta, to know what is suitable for him. He is one to be guided by a buddha." The Blessed One then created by spiritual power a luminous lotus flower and placed it in his hand, saying: "Come, bhikkhu, set this up in a sandy spot in the shade of your dwelling. Then sit crosslegged facing it and adverting to it as 'red, red.'" It is said that in five hundred past lives this bhikkhu had been a goldsmith. Thus the Blessed One, knowing that a red object would be suitable for him, assigned him a red meditation object. Having done as he was told, instantly [16] the bhikkhu achieved the four jhānas in sequence and began to play with the jhānas by going through them in direct and reverse order.

The Blessed One then resolved: "Let the lotus flower wilt." When the bhikkhu emerged from the jhāna and saw that the flower had wilted and become discolored, he gained the perception of impermanence: "The luminous form has been crushed by decay." Then he applied that perception to himself. Realizing, "Whatever is impermanent is suffering; what is suffering is non-self," he saw the three realms of existence as blazing. While he was seeing this, in a lotus pond not far off young boys were diving in, breaking off lotuses, and heaping them up. The lotuses in the water appeared to him like a blazing fire in a forest of reeds; the petals falling off appeared as if they had dropped down a precipice; the wilted tops of the lotuses placed on dry land appeared as if they were burnt by fire. Then, as he continued to contemplate all phenomena in line with this insight, the three realms of existence appeared even more starkly to be like a blazing house, offering no refuge.

Then the Blessed One, sitting in his Fragrant Cottage, projected an image of his body above the bhikkhu, which spread out before his face. Wondering, "What is this?" he saw that the Blessed One had come and stood in front of him. He rose from his seat and saluted the Blessed One. Then, having considered what was suitable for him, the Blessed One taught him the Dhamma and recited this luminous verse:[293] "One who has entirely cut off lust . . ."

Here the word **lust** is a designation for lust for the five strands of sensual pleasures, which occurs by way of excitation. **Has cut off** means cuts off, demolishes, destroys. The grammarians recognize a present tense meaning for past tense verbs, which are used on account of the meter.[294] **Entirely**: along with the latent tendency.[295] Just as the boys dived into the pond and broke off the lotuses, so a bhikkhu, having entered this abode of the world with its three realms, reflects on the dangers in lust according to the method described thus:

> There is no fire equal to lust. (Dhp 202) [17]

> "I am burning with sensual lust, my mind is consumed
> by fever." (SN I 188,15)

> Those inflamed by lust fall into the stream
> like a spider trapped in its self-made web. (Dhp 347)

> "Friend, inflamed and overcome by lust, with mind
> obsessed by it, one destroys life."[296]

Then, by the kinds of restraint explained above, such as restraint by good behavior, and by the perception of unattractiveness in both sentient and insentient objects, one little by little partly eradicates lust by the path of the non-returner, and thereafter entirely cuts it off by the path of arahantship. In the way explained previously, that bhikkhu gives up the here and the beyond just as a serpent sheds its old worn-out skin. Thus the Blessed One taught this verse with its culmination in arahantship, and at the conclusion of the teaching that bhikkhu was established in arahantship.

3. One who has entirely cut off craving: What is the origin? When the Blessed One was dwelling at Sāvatthī, a certain bhikkhu, dwelling on the bank of the Gaggarā Lotus Pond, pondered unwholesome thoughts driven by craving. Having understood his inclination, the Blessed One spoke this luminous verse.

Here, **craving** is thirst that does not find satisfaction in its objects. It is a designation for craving for sensual pleasures, existence, and nonexistence. **A stream**: Having gone, occurred, it remains inundating everything even up to the peak of existence.[297] **Fast-flowing**: Without reckoning on the dangers pertaining to the present life and future lives, it is able, even in a moment, to arrive at other world spheres and the peak of existence.[298] One reflects on the dangers in all kinds of craving, this fast-flowing stream, thus:

> Expanding upward, hard to fulfill
> desire goes along spreading out.
> Those who are greedy for it
> are those who bear the wheel.[299] (Ja III 207,17–18; Ja IV 4,25–26)

> With craving as partner, a person,
> wandering on this long journey,
> does not transcend saṃsāra,
> with its becoming thus, becoming otherwise. (**740**; It 9,1–4)

> [18] "The world is deficient, insatiable, a slave to craving, great king." (MN II 68,29)

Then, **having dried [it] up** little by little by restraint through good behavior and so forth in the ways explained above, one entirely cuts it off by the path of arahantship. At that very moment that bhikkhu gives up the here and the beyond in all their modes. At the conclusion of the teaching that bhikkhu was established in arahantship.

4. One who has entirely swept up conceit: What is the origin? While the Blessed One was dwelling at Sāvatthī, a certain bhikkhu, on the bank of the Ganges, saw a bridge of reeds, built during the hot season when the stream was thin, being swept away by a great flood. He stood there agitated by the fact that conditioned things are impermanent. Understanding his inclination, the Blessed One spoke this luminous verse.

Here, **conceit** is mental self-importance based on one's social class and other factors. Conceit is threefold: "I am superior," "I am equal," and "I am inferior." Again it becomes ninefold thus: the superior person's conceit of being superior, equal, or inferior; the equal person's conceit of being superior, equal, or inferior; and the inferior person's conceit of being superior, equal, or inferior. One reflects on the dangers in all those kinds of conceit thus:

> Because they are intoxicated by conceit,
> beings go to a bad destination. (It 3,20–21)

Then, destroying it little by little in the ways explained above by restraint by good behavior and other methods, one **has entirely swept up conceit** by the path of arahantship, which is like a great flood because of the extraordinary strength of the world-transcending states; conceit, in contrast, is like a bridge of reeds because of the fragility and weakness of the defilements. What is meant is that one destroys it, cutting it off by abandoning it without remainder.[300] At that very moment that bhikkhu gave up the here and the beyond in all their modes. At the conclusion of the teaching that bhikkhu was established in arahantship.

5. One who finds no core: What is the origin?[301] This verse and the twelve that follow have a single origin. Once the Blessed One was dwelling at Sāvatthī. On that occasion, [19] at the time of his daughter's wedding, a certain brahmin considered: "I will send the girl to her husband's family adorned in flowers that have never before been worn by anyone." Searching Sāvatthī inside and out, he did not see even a wild flower that had not been worn before. He then saw a group of brahmin boys. Thinking that one of them must know, he went up to them and asked. Playfully, they told him: "The flowers of the udumbara tree, brahmin, have never before been worn by anyone in the world.[302] You can adorn your daughter with them." The next day he got up early, distributed food, and went to an udumbara grove on the bank of the Aciravatī River. He examined each tree, one by one, but did not see even a mere stalk. Then, after midday, he crossed to the other bank. There a bhikkhu was sitting and meditating at the foot of a pleasant tree. The brahmin went by without noticing him. He sat, squatted, stood still, and while examining the branches, canopy, and leaves of the tree, he became fatigued. The bhikkhu asked him: "What are you looking for, brahmin?" – "An udumbara flower, sir." – "But there is no such thing as an udumbara flower, brahmin. That was a false statement. Don't weary yourself."

Then the Blessed One, having understood that bhikkhu's inclination, sent forth light, and when the bhikkhu's interest and esteem had arisen, he spoke these luminous verses to him: "One who finds no core in any realms of existence." Here, **in states of existence** means in desire-realm, form-realm, and formless-realm existence; in percipient, nonpercipient, and neither-percipient-nor-nonpercipient existence; in one-constituent, four-constituent, and five-constituent existence.[303] **A core** is permanence or selfhood. **Seeking** is searching with wisdom. **As one seeking flowers in udumbara trees**: Just as [20] the brahmin, though seeking flowers in the udumbara trees, did not find any, so a meditator, examining them with wisdom, does not find any core among all the realms of existence. Seeing with insight those phenomena as impermanent and non-self because of their coreless nature, he gradually attains the world-transcending states and gives up the here and the beyond just as a serpent gives up its worn-out old skin.

This is the meaning and the construal. In the remaining verses, without stating the construal, we will explain merely the distinctive meaning.

6. "One who has no irritations inwardly, having transcended such and such states of existence."[304] Here, firstly, the word *antara* occurs in the texts with many meanings, such as an affair, in the middle, and mind. Here it means mind. **One who has no irritations inwardly**: One in whose mind there are no irritations because they have been uprooted by the third path. [Having transcended such and such states of existence (*itibhavābhavatañca vītivatto*):] Now *bhava* means success and *vibhava* failure; *bhava* means growth and *vibhava* decline; *bhava* means eternalism and *vibhava* annihilationism; and *bhava* means merit and *vibhava* evil.[305] Since *vibhava* and *abhava* are one in meaning, **having transcended such and such states of existence** is spoken of here in many ways: by way of success and failure, growth and decline, eternalism and annihilationism, and merit and evil. The meaning should be understood in whatever way fits the case thus: By the four paths he has transcended "such and such states of existence." [21]

7. One whose thoughts have been burned out: There are these nine kinds of [unwholesome] thoughts: the triad of sensual thoughts, malevolent thoughts, and aggressive thoughts; the triad of thoughts about one's relatives, one's country, and the immortals; and the triad of thoughts connected with solicitude for others, thoughts of gain, honor, and praise, and thoughts of not being looked down upon.[306] A bhikkhu reflects upon the danger in these thoughts as explained in the Samantabhadraka,[307] and by determining upon their antidotes, he "burns them out," scorches them, and incinerates them by the three lower paths, according to each path's specific ability to abandon them. Having thus burned them out, they are **entirely well excised internally**—entirely cut off—by the path of arahantship, so that they never occur again in one's own internal continuum of aggregates and in one's mind, the most interior of all. Thus the meaning should be seen here.

8. One who has neither run too far nor run back:[308] What is meant? One runs too far by excessive energy, falling into restlessness; one runs back by excessive laxity, falling into laziness. So too, one runs too far by tormenting oneself through craving for existence; one runs back by indulging in sensual pleasure through craving for sensual pleasure. One runs too far through an eternalist view; one runs back through an annihilationist view. One who sorrows over the past runs too far; one with high hopes for the future runs back.[309] One runs too far through a view about the past; one runs back through a view about the future. Therefore, by practicing the middle path that avoids both these extremes, one does not run too far or run back. **Who has transcended all this proliferation**: Through the middle path, which culminates in the path of arahantship, one has transcended, surpassed, surmounted, all this threefold proliferation consisting in craving, conceit, and views, which originate from feeling, perception, and thought.[310]

9. In the immediately following verse, the only difference is the line "Having known about the world: 'All this is unreal.'" The word **all** means without omission, everything, [22] with nothing missing. Nevertheless, what is intended here are only the conditioned things that come into the range of insight, classified as the mundane aggregates, sense bases, and elements. **Unreal** means devoid of a real nature. All this is unreal because it lacks a real nature in the way conceived by foolish people on account of the defilements, namely, as permanent or pleasurable or attractive or self. **This**: He says this indicating everything in terms of its directly cognizable nature. **Having known**: having known it with the wisdom of the path, and that is by way of non-delusion, not by way of objective domain.[311] **About the world**: Having known all the phenomena in the cosmos, classified as aggregates and so forth, thus "This is unreal." The connection is: "Having known all this—the things such as the aggregates and so forth—as unreal."

10–13. Now in the following four verses, the distinction consists respectively in "devoid of greed," "devoid of lust," "devoid of hatred," and "devoid of delusion." Here, **greed** is an all-inclusive designation for the first unwholesome root, or it is unrighteous greed, which is spoken of in the passage "Sometimes states of greed arise in relation to those in the position of a mother, in the position of a sister, and in the position of a daughter" (SN IV 111,7–9). **Lust** is a designation for the lust for the five strands of sensual pleasure. **Hatred** is a designation for anger, spoken of earlier. **Delusion** is a designation for lack of knowledge about the four noble truths. In this context, because this bhikkhu, being disgusted with greed, began to practice insight with the wish "May I remove greed and dwell devoid of greed!" the Buddha recited this verse to him, showing perception of the unreal nature of all conditioned things as the means of abandoning greed, and the abandoning of the here and the beyond as the benefit of abandoning greed. This method applies to the following verses as well. But some say that each of the verses here was spoken individually to different bhikkhus who, in the way just explained, had become disgusted with these states [greed, etc.] and had begun to practice insight. [23] One may accept whatever explanation one prefers.

14. This method of explanation applies to the following four verses, but this here is the commentary on the meaning. **Latent tendencies** refers to those things that lie latent in one's mindstream in the sense that they have not been abandoned; this is a designation for sensual lust, aversion, conceit, views, doubt, lust for existence, and ignorance.[312] **Roots** are spoken of in the sense that they impart their own quality to the associated states; **unwholesome** has the sense of insecurity. *Roots* also serve to establish those [associated states]; *unwholesome* has the sense of blameworthy and yielding painful results. Both are a designation for greed, hatred, and delusion; for they have been described thus: "Greed, bhikkhus, is unwholesome and an unwholesome root."[313] Thus **one has no latent tendencies at all** because they have been abandoned by this and that path,[314] and similarly these **unwholesome roots have been uprooted**.

But in this connection, although such a bhikkhu is an arahant, and an arahant "does not take, does not abandon, but lives having abandoned" (SN III 90,18–21), still, it is said "he gives up the here and the beyond," a present tense description [being used to indicate] proximity to the present. Or alternatively, "he gives up the here and the beyond" can be understood to refer to his own internal and external sense bases, which are given up when he attains nibbāna by the nibbāna element without residue remaining.

In this connection, the absence of the latent tendencies can be understood in two ways: through the sequence of the defilements and through the sequence of the paths. *Through the sequence of the defilements*, the latent tendencies to sensual lust and aversion are absent because of the third path; the latent tendency to conceit because of the fourth path; the latent tendencies to views and doubt because of the first path; and the latent tendencies to lust for existence and ignorance because of the fourth path. [24] But *through the sequence of the paths*, the first path is responsible for the absence of the latent tendencies to views and doubt; the second path for the weakening of the latent tendencies to sensual lust and aversion; the third path for their complete absence; and the fourth path for the absence of the latent tendencies to conceit, lust for existence, and ignorance.

Not all the latent tendencies are unwholesome roots; for only the latent tendencies to sensual lust and lust for existence are included by greed as an unwholesome root; and the latent tendencies to aversion and ignorance are, respectively, included by hatred and delusion as unwholesome roots. But the latent tendencies to views, conceit, and doubt are not equivalent to any unwholesome root. Therefore the Blessed One said: "One who has no latent tendencies whatever, whose unwholesome roots have been uprooted." Or else he said this to expound the abandoning of defilements by way of both the absence of the latent tendencies and the uprooting of the unwholesome roots.

15. States born from distress: Here, it is the defilements when first arisen that are called "distress," in the sense of feverish burning. Those mental states that arise in succession afterward, because they are born from such distress, are called "states born from distress." **The near shore**: the personal entity, as it is said: "'The near shore,' bhikkhus, is a designation for the personal entity."[315] **Return** is arising. What is meant? "States born of distress" is a synonym for those defilements that function as a condition for acquiring the aggregates subject to clinging. A bhikkhu who does not have any such defilements because they have been abandoned by the noble path, in the way explained earlier, "gives up the here and the beyond."

16. States born from desire: Here, "states born from desire" should be understood similarly to "states born from distress." The word *vana* is a designation for craving;[316] for that is called "desire" in the sense of longing for its objective domains and resorting to them. *Vanatha* is said with reference to that which extends desire through obsession by it; this is a designation for the latent tendency to craving. *Vanathajā* ("states born from desire") are states born from *vanatha*. But some say that all defilements are also called *vanatha* in the sense of a thicket, and those that arise afterward in succession are called *vanathajā*. [25] And the former is the sense intended here in the Discourse on the Serpent, while the latter is intended in the verse of the Dhammapada.[317] **Causes for bondage to existence**: for the bondage of existence, or alternatively, for future arising by the binding of the mind to the objective spheres.

17. Hindrances: The hindrances are so called because they hinder the mind, or because they hinder beneficial practice. The meaning is that they conceal. These are the five hindrances, sensual desire and so forth. A bhikkhu who has seen the danger in these hindrances, both in general and specifically, according to the method explained in the Samantabhadraka (Vibh 441, §941), abandons them by this and that path.[318] Because they have been abandoned, he is **untroubled** through the absence of the trouble consisting in the defilements and suffering; he has **crossed over perplexity** because he has crossed the perplexity that occurs thus: "Did I exist in the past?" (MN I 8,4, SN II 26,28); and he is **free of darts** because of the removal of the five darts stated thus: "What are the five darts? The dart of lust, the dart of hatred, the dart of delusion, the dart of conceit, the dart of views" (Vibh 440, §940). That bhikkhu gives up the here and the beyond in the way explained earlier.

And here, too, the abandoning of the hindrances can be understood in two ways, through the sequence of the defilements and through the sequence of the paths. Through *the sequence of the defilements*, the abandoning of the hindrances of sensual desire and ill will occurs through the third path, the abandoning of the hindrances of dullness and drowsiness and of restlessness occurs through the fourth path. The abandoning of the hindrances of doubt and the regret "I did not do what is wholesome" [26] occurs by the first path. Through *the sequence of the paths*, the abandoning of the hindrances of regret and doubt occurs by the first path; the weakening of the hindrances of sensual desire and ill will by the second path; their complete abandoning by the third path; and the abandoning of dullness and drowsiness and of restlessness occurs by the fourth path.

Thus the Blessed One brought this teaching to its culmination in arahantship with the words:

> Having abandoned the five hindrances,
> one who is untroubled, crossed over perplexity, free of
> darts:
> that bhikkhu gives up the here and the beyond,
> just as a serpent sheds its worn-out skin.

At the conclusion of the teaching that bhikkhu was established in arahantship. Some say: "In whatever way those verses were taught to those bhikkhus, in just that way, at the conclusion of the verses, those bhikkhus were established in arahantship."[319]

2 Dhaniya
(*Dhaniya Sutta*)

What is the origin? The Blessed One was dwelling at Sāvatthī. On that occasion the herdsman Dhaniya was living on the bank of the Mahī River. This is his past exertion:[320] When the teaching of the Blessed One Kassapa was flourishing,[321] he gave twenty ticket meals to the Sangha day after day for 20,000 years.[322] When he passed away there, he was reborn among the devas. Having passed one period between buddhas in the deva world, in the time of our Blessed One he was reborn as the son of a financier in the city Dhammakoṇḍa, which was located in the mountain region in the middle of the country of Videha. He lived by raising a herd of cattle. He had 30,000 cows, of which 27,000 cows gave milk. Now herdsmen do not dwell in a fixed place. For four months of the year they live on the plateau, and during the remaining eight months they live wherever grass and water are abundant, which is either by the bank of a river or by the bank of a natural lake.

At the time of the rains, he left the village where he lived, [27] seeking a place for his cattle to dwell in comfort. Now at a certain point the Mahāmahī divides in two—into one tributary called the Black Mahī and the other the Mahāmahī—which both flow on until they again converge near the ocean. He entered the island formed by these two branches and there built a shed for the calves and a dwelling place for himself, where he took up residence. He had seven sons, seven daughters, seven daughters-in-law, and many workers.

Now herdsmen know the foresigns of rain. When birds build their nests in the tree tops, and crabs close their entrance holes near the water and stay by entrance holes near high ground, they understand there will be abundant rain. But when birds build their nests in a low place at the edge of the water, and crabs close their entrance holes near high ground and stay by entrance holes near the water, they understand there will be shortage of rain.

Dhaniya had observed the foresigns of abundant rain, so at the time of the rains he left his islet between the two branches of the river and made a dwelling place for himself on the other shore of the Mahāmahī, in an area that would not be inundated with water during the seven weeks that the rains would fall. He enclosed the area on all sides, built sheds for the calves, and settled down there. When he had collected firewood, grass, and other supplies, and food of various kinds had been prepared for his children and all his slaves,[323] workers, and servants of similar class, circles of rain clouds gathered in the four directions. He had his cows milked, the calves tied down in their sheds, and the sheds smoked out in the four directions for the cows. He had his entire household fed, and after all the other tasks were completed, he had lamps lit here and there and ate his own meal together with milk. Then he lay down in his large bed, rejoicing in his own prosperity. When he heard the sound of thunder in the distance, while lying down he uttered this joyful utterance: "I've boiled my rice, I've milked the cows."

18. Here, this is the explanation of the meaning.[324] [28] **The herdsman Dhaniya** was the combined name of this son of a financier. He was called Dhaniya because he possessed the wealth (*dhana*) of cattle, which is distinguished from other kinds of wealth in the saying "There is no wealth equal to cattle" (SN I 6,17), with reference to their helpfulness in providing the world with the five kinds of dairy products.[325] Because he maintained cattle, he was called "herdsman." For one who maintains his own cattle is called a herdsman, while one who works for wages is called a cowhand. He had his own cattle, so he was called a herdsman. [29]

Now when the herdsman Dhaniya, while lying on his large bed in his bedroom, having heard the sound of thunder, said, **I've boiled my rice**, he shows that he has secured for himself the means of allaying bodily suffering and the cause of bodily happiness. When he says, **I've milked the cows**, he shows the means of allaying mental suffering and the cause of mental happiness. **Near the bank of the Mahī** shows his success in acquiring a dwelling place, and **I dwell with my family** shows the absence of sorrow caused by separation from those who are dear. **My hut is thatched**: the dispelling and warding off of bodily suffering. **The fire is kindled**: Since cowherds make three fires by way of encircling the home, producing smoke, and providing warmth, and in his house all those had been made, when he says, "The fire is kindled," with reference to the fire encircling his home in all directions, he shows how he prevents wild animals from coming; with reference to the smoke-producing fire among the cows, made from cow dung and other fuels, he shows how he spares the cows from being troubled by flies, mosquitoes, and other pests; and with reference to the warmth-providing fire in his bedroom, he shows how cowherds ward off the affliction of cold. Showing all this, filled with rapture and joy because he himself, his cattle, and his household were in no way troubled because of the rain, he said: **So if you wish, pour down, O sky god!**

19. While Dhaniya was reciting this verse, the Blessed One, dwelling in his Fragrant Cottage in the large monastery in Jeta's Grove, heard it with the divine ear, purified and surpassing the human. He then surveyed the world with the buddha eye and saw Dhaniya and his wife.[326] He then thought: "Both possess causes.[327] If I go to them and teach them the Dhamma, both will go forth and attain arahantship. But if I do not go, tomorrow both will perish in a flood." In a moment he went through space the seven hundred yojanas to Dhaniya's dwelling place and stood above his hut. Dhaniya kept on repeating that verse again and again and did not stop. He uttered it even when the Blessed One had gone there. Having heard it, to show, "It is not in that way that one is content and secure but in this way," the Blessed One spoke this rejoinder, [30] which is similar in phrasing but not in meaning. For the words "My rice is boiled" and "I don't boil with anger" are as different in meaning as the near shore and far shore of the great ocean, but the phrasing corresponds in some respects, and thus there is similarity in the phrasing.

The meaning of the words that are similar to those in the first verse should be understood in the way stated there. Here follows an explanation of the different terms used by way of both phrasing and meaning. **I don't boil with anger**: I am by nature without anger. For whatever degree of anger may originate from any of the grounds of resentment explained earlier—the very mild kind that arises, burns the heart, and then subsides; and the kind that arises more strongly, because of which one grimaces; and the still stronger kind that makes one move one's jaws, desiring to speak harshly; and the still stronger kind because of which one actually speaks harshly; and the still stronger kind because of which one looks all around for a rod or weapon; and the still stronger kind because of which one reaches for a rod or weapon; and the still stronger kind because of which one grabs hold of a rod or weapon and pursues someone; and the still stronger kind because of which one gives someone one or two blows; and the still stronger kind because of which one kills a relative or family member; and the still stronger kind because of which one later feels regret and takes one's own life, like the minister living in Kālagāma in Sri Lanka, at which point anger has reached its maximum intensity—the Blessed One had completely abandoned all such anger at the site of enlightenment, cut it off at the root, made it like a palm stump. Therefore the Blessed One said: "I don't boil with anger."

I'm rid of barrenness: Five kinds of mental barrenness are spoken of with reference to the stiffening of the mind, because of which the mind becomes barren.[328] Just as crops do not grow in a barren plot of land even though rain falls for four months, so in such a mind wholesome qualities do not grow even though the rain of wholesome causes, such as listening to the good Dhamma, has been falling. Those kinds of mental barrenness were completely abandoned by the Blessed One at the site of enlightenment; therefore the Blessed One said: "I'm rid of barrenness."

I dwell one night near the bank of the Mahī. [31] The Blessed One is not like Dhaniya, who has taken up continuous residence there for the four months of the rains. For the Blessed One has taken up residence there just for that night, having come from a desire for Dhaniya's good. Therefore he says: "I dwell one night."

My hut is open. "Open" means that the covering has been removed. "Hut" here means the body (*attabhāva*). For the body is spoken of in various ways depending on the purpose, such as body, cave, mass, substance, ship, chariot, wound,[329] banner, anthill, hut, and shack. But here it is spoken of as a "hut." For just as the word "house" is used with reference to timber and other materials, similarly the word "body" is used as a designation with reference to a collection of bones and other parts. As it is said:

> "Just as, friends, the space enclosed by timber, vines, clay, and grass is designated 'house,' in the same way, the space enclosed by bones, sinews, muscles, and skin is designated 'bodily form.'" (MN I 190,15)

Or it is a hut because the monkey of the mind resides there. As it is said:

> This hut made of a skeleton
> is the dwelling place of a monkey.
> The monkey goes out from the hut,
> which is endowed with five doors.
> He circles around by a door,
> striking again and again.[330]

That hut, being covered for beings by the roof of craving, conceit, and views, leaks with the rain of lust and the other defilements. As it is said:

> What is covered over leaks;
> what is opened up does not leak.
> Therefore one should open what is covered;
> thus it will not leak [into one's mind].

This verse is stated in two places, in the Khandhakas and the Theragāthā.[331] For in the Khandhakas it is stated with this meaning: "If one conceals an offense, again and again defilements and offenses leak into him. But when one does not conceal them, they do not leak into him." In the Theragāthā it is said [with this intention]: "For one who conceals lust and other defilements, rain leaks through his roof by way of the repeated arising of lust and so forth in regard to desirable objects and so forth. [32] Or for one who tolerates arisen defilements, the hut of his body, covered with the roof of the tolerated defilements, repeatedly leaks with the rain of defilements. But when one's hut has been opened up by destroying the roof of defilements with the wind—that is, with the knowledge of the path of arahantship—the rain does not leak into him." It is this meaning that is intended here. For the roof was destroyed by the Blessed One in the way stated earlier; therefore he says: "My hut is open."

Extinguished: peaceful. **Fire**: the elevenfold fire with which everything is blazing; as it is said, "It is blazing with the fire of lust," and so on in detail.[332] The Blessed One had already extinguished that fire at the foot of the bodhi tree by dousing it with the water of the noble path; therefore he says: "My fire is extinguished."

Speaking in this way, he indirectly censures, exhorts, and instructs Dhaniya for rejoicing over a condition that gives no ground for joy. How? Saying, "I don't boil with anger," he indicates: "Dhaniya, you rejoice, thinking, 'I have boiled my rice,' but you boil rice all your life by exhausting your wealth, and the exhaustion of wealth is a basis for the suffering of earning, guarding [against loss], and so forth; such being the case, you rejoice over what is actually suffering. But I rejoice, thinking, 'I don't boil with anger,' and thus I rejoice over the absence of suffering whether directly visible or pertaining to future lives."

When he says, "I'm rid of barrenness," he indicates: "You rejoice, thinking, 'I have milked the cows,' and so, though you have not done your task, you rejoice thinking that you have done it. But when I rejoice, thinking, 'I'm rid of barrenness,' I rejoice as one who has truly done his task."

When he says, "I dwell one night near the bank of the Mahī," he indicates: "You rejoice, thinking, 'I dwell in company near the bank of the Mahī,' and so you rejoice in a fixed dwelling for four months. Now a fixed dwelling means one is tied to an abode, and that is suffering; in such a case, you rejoice over what is actually suffering. But when I rejoice, thinking, 'I dwell one night near the bank of the Mahī,' I rejoice without a fixed abode, and being without a fixed abode means one is not tied to an abode. Now being without ties is pleasant, and so I rejoice over what is actually pleasant." [33]

When he says, "My hut is open," he indicates: "You rejoice, thinking, 'My hut is thatched,' and so you rejoice because you have a thatched house. But when your house is thatched, the rain of defilements leaks into the hut of your body, because of which you might be swept away by the four floods that arise and thereby you will incur misery and disaster; in such a case, you rejoice over a condition that should give no ground for joy. But when I rejoice, thinking, 'My hut is open,' I rejoice at the absence of defilements covering the hut of the body. Therefore the rain of defilements does not leak into my open hut, and so I won't be swept away by the four floods that might have arisen and brought misery and disaster; in such a case, I rejoice over a condition that should actually give ground for joy."

When he says, "My fire is extinguished," he indicates: "You rejoice, thinking, 'The fire is kindled,' and so, though you have not warded off calamity, you rejoice thinking that you have warded off calamity. But when I rejoice, thinking, 'My fire is extinguished,' I rejoice at the absence of the eleven kinds of fires and fevers, and thus I have actually warded off calamity."

When he says, "So if you wish, pour down, O sky god!" he indicates: "This statement is appropriate for those like us, who have gotten rid of suffering, achieved happiness, and done all our tasks. But it is not appropriate for you, since your prosperity or decline depends on whether or not there is rain. Why then do you say: 'So if you wish, pour down, O sky god!'?"

Therefore it was properly said: "Speaking in this way, he indirectly censures, exhorts, and instructs Dhaniya for rejoicing over a condition that gives no ground for joy."

20. When the herdsman Dhaniya heard this verse spoken by the Blessed One, he did not ask: "Who has spoken a verse?" Rather, fully rejoicing in that good statement, wishing to hear another one like it, he spoke another verse: "No gadflies or mosquitoes." [34] Here he indicates that his cows are secure because there are no gadflies and mosquitoes that assemble, drink their blood, and in an instant bring misery and disaster to cattle—the kind of flies and mosquitoes that cowherds kill with mud and branches as soon as it starts to rain. By mentioning that the cows roam in the meadow where the grass has grown, he indicates they have none of the weariness that comes from going on journeys and are not even troubled by hunger.

He also indicates: "My cattle are not like the cattle of others, which are afflicted by contact with gadflies and mosquitoes, fatigued by going on journeys, and weakened by hunger, and thus cannot endure even a single rainfall. Because the aforementioned problems are absent, my cattle can endure even two or three rains."

21. Since Dhaniya had seen the danger in dwelling on the islet, he had made a raft, crossed the Mahāmahī, and reached the meadow, where he spoke thus, thinking: "I have reached safety, I am staying in a secure place." However, the place where he stood was still dangerous. Therefore the Blessed One, praising the place where he had come as more excellent and sublime than the place where Dhaniya had come, recited this verse, "I made a raft," in which there is similarity in meaning but not in phrasing.[333]

Here, the word *bhisī* is a bound raft that has been stretched out and widened. But in the Dhamma and discipline of the noble one, this is a designation for the noble path. For the noble path is:

> Described here and there as
> a path, a walkway, a road, a pathway,
> a street, an avenue for traveling.
> a boat, a bridge that goes across,
> a raft, a float, a plank for crossing,
> a journey and origination.

With this verse, too, the Blessed One, exhorting him in accordance with the previous method, conveys this meaning: "Dhaniya, you have built a raft, crossed the Mahī, and reached this place. [35] But you will have to build a raft again and cross the river, and this place is not secure. But I have built a raft that combines the factors of the path into a single occasion of mind, bound together by knowledge. And that raft has been **well constructed** because it is complete in the thirty-seven aids to enlightenment, because it possesses development with a single taste in which [its constituents] do not exceed one another,[334] because there is no need to build this raft again, and because it is impossible for anyone, whether a deva or human being, to untie it. By means of it **I have crossed**, gone to the region desired earlier. And going there, I have not gone partially, like a stream-enterer and so forth. Rather, I have **gone beyond**, gone to nibbāna, the destruction of all influxes, the far shore of all phenomena, the supreme security." Or "crossed" means attained omniscience, "gone beyond" means attained arahantship. What did he remove to have gone beyond? **Escaped the flood**: having crossed and passed over the fourfold flood—the flood of sensuality and so forth—he has gone beyond. And now, because there is no further need to cross again, [he says]: **I have no more need for a raft**. "Therefore, it is proper just for me to say: **So if you wish, pour down, O sky god!**"

22. Having heard this, in the previous way, Dhaniya spoke the next verse. **Obedient**: she does what I tell her and complies in all tasks. **Not wanton**: Women have five kinds of wantonness: regarding food, adornments, other men, wealth, and feet. As to their *wantonness regarding food*—divided into meals, cakes, and liquor—a woman even eats stale meals; she even eats food that burns her hand;[335] and she drinks liquor she would buy at double the price. As to *wantonness regarding adornments*, if she does not get any other adornment,[336] she smooths her hair and rubs her face with a mixture of water and oil. As to *wantonness regarding other men*, [36] being called to a congenial place by her own son, she first thinks of engaging in [sexual] misconduct. As to *wantonness regarding wealth*, even if she has obtained the royal goose,[337] her gold diminishes. As to *wantonness regarding feet*, being in the habit of going to parks and so forth, she wastes all the wealth.[338] Showing "My wife does not indulge in any kind of wantonness," Dhaniya says: "not wanton."

Living together with me long: "Living together for a long time, we have grown together from the time she was a virgin." By this he shows that she does not have any interest in other men. **Agreeable**: "Not having any interest in other men, she follows me." **I do not hear any evil about her**: "I do not hear that she has spoken or conversed with such and such a man." He shows that she does not misbehave.

23. Then after Dhaniya had rejoiced in his wife because of her excellent qualities, the Blessed One spoke the next verse, exhorting him in the way stated. In this case there is similarity of both meaning and phrasing. This is the purport: "Dhaniya, you rejoice, thinking, 'My wife is obedient.' But whether or not she is obedient to you, it is hard to know the minds of others, especially of women. For [pregnant women] carrying around a female in the womb cannot guard them. So hard it is for them to guard their minds that those like you cannot know of a woman whether she is really uncorrupted, faithful, or agreeable, or has done nothing evil. But **my mind is obedient**, it accepts my exhortation, and has come under my control. I do not come under its control. And its obedience was evident to everyone on the occasion of the twin miracle, when streams of fire and water of six colors emanated from my body.[339] To emit fire, one must attain the fire kasiṇa and to emit water, the water kasiṇa. To emit blue rays and rays of the other colors, one must attain the blue kasiṇa and the other color kasiṇas. Even for buddhas two states of mind do not occur simultaneously, but there was such mastery over my one mind because of its obedience. [37]

And that mind is **liberated** by the removal of all the bondage of defilements; and because it is liberated, it is this mind, not your wife, that is not wanton. And because it has been **long nurtured** with giving, good behavior, and other qualities from the time of the Buddha Dīpaṅkara, it is this mind that is faithful, not your wife. This is **well tamed**, because it has been tamed by the unsurpassed taming. Because it is well tamed, it does not go astray at the six sense doors but occurs solely in accordance with my own intention, and therefore it is **agreeable**, not your wife."

No evil is found in me: With this, the Blessed One shows the absence of anything evil in his own mind, as Dhaniya claimed for his wife. And the absence of evil in the Blessed One, it should be understood, was not only true at the time he was a perfectly enlightened buddha, but it was also the case during the twenty-nine years he lived at home, when he was subject to lust and other defilements. For then, too, there never arose in him any kind of worldly bodily, verbal, or mental misconduct that would have been rejected by the wise. Thereafter for seven years—six years prior to his enlightenment and a year afterward—Māra followed the Tathāgata, thinking: "Perhaps I will see some evil conduct on his part, even as much as a fraction of a hair." Not seeing any, disillusioned, he recited this verse:

"For seven years I followed the Blessed One,
[trailing him] step by step,
but I have not found an opening
in the Enlightened One, who is mindful." (**446**)

Also, after his enlightenment, the brahmin youth Uttara followed him for seven months, wishing to observe his conduct (MN II 137–40). Not finding any fault, he concluded: "The Blessed One is of purified conduct." For the Tathāgata has four things that he does not need to hide. As it is said:

> "Bhikkhus, there are these four things that the Tathāgata does not need to hide. What four? The Tathāgata is one whose bodily behavior is purified; there is no bodily misconduct on his part that he might need to hide, thinking: 'Let others not find this out about me.' The Tathāgata is one whose verbal behavior is purified . . . whose mental behavior is purified . . . whose livelihood is purified. There is no wrong livelihood on his part [38] that he might need to hide, thinking: 'Let others not find this out about me.'" (AN IV 82)

Thus, since there was no evil in the Tathāgata's mind, not only at the time he was a perfectly enlightened buddha, but also prior to that, he says: "No evil is found in me." The purport of this is: "It is only of my mind, not of your wife, that it is impossible to hear of any evil. Therefore, if anyone can rejoice in these excellent qualities and say, 'So if you wish, pour down, O sky god!' I am the one who can say this."

24. Having heard this, Dhaniya, wishing to drink even more deeply the elixir of excellent sayings, said, "I am employed by myself," showing his own independence. Here, **employed by myself** means that he earns his food and clothing solely through his own work. He shows that he lives solely by doing his own work, not by working for another and receiving wages.

Children: here the word *puttā* (usually meaning "sons") comprises all one's children, both daughters and sons. **I do not hear any evil about them**: "I do not hear any evil about them, that they are thieves or adulterers or immoral."

25. When this was said, the Blessed One spoke the next verse, exhorting Dhaniya in the previous way. This is the purport: "You rejoice, thinking, 'I am independent,' but though you live by doing your own work, in the ultimate sense you are just a slave, since you are the slave of craving, and so you are not free from being called an employee. For this is said: 'The world is lacking, insatiable, a slave of craving' (MN II 68,29). But in the supreme sense, I am not an employee of anyone, for I am not in the employment of anyone, whether another or myself. For what reason? Because **I wander in all the world by what I've earned**.[340] For from the time of Dīpaṅkara until my enlightenment, I was an employee of the knowledge of omniscience. But when I attained omniscience, I got what I earned, like a retired employee of the king. Hence I live by what I've earned, by the state of omniscience and the bliss of world-transcending concentration. [39] Because now there is nothing further to be done by me and no need to increase what has been done, **I have no need at all for wages**, like those to be acquired by people who have not abandoned conception (rebirth). Therefore, if anyone can rejoice in his independence and say, 'So if you wish, pour down, O sky god!' I am the one who can say this."[341]

26. Having heard this, still insatiable in his desire for the nectar of excellent sayings, Dhaniya says, **There are cows**, showing that he possesses the fivefold herd of cattle. These are: *vasā*, mature calves that have not been tamed;[342] *dhenupā*, young calves that drink from cows, or milch cows;[343] *godharaṇiyo*, pregnant cows; *paveṇiyo*, breeding cows, mature cows wishing to mate; and **a bull, chief of cattle** (*usabhopi gavampati*). Early in the morning the cowhands bathe him, feed him, apply the five-finger mark,[344] tie a garland around him, and send him off, saying: "Go, dear, lead the cows to the pasture, guard them, and bring them back." The bull, sent off in such a way, ensures that the cows avoid straying outside the pasture. He makes them roam within it, protects them from such dangers as lions and tigers, and brings them back. Dhaniya shows: "I also have such a bull, chief of cattle, here in my herd of cattle."

27. When he had spoken, the Blessed One, exhorting Dhaniya in a similar way, spoke a verse in rejoinder: "There are no cows." This is the purport here: "Here in our teaching, there are no obsessions (*pariyuṭṭhānā*), designated 'cows,' in the sense of things that are mature and untamed. There are no latent tendencies (*anusayā*), designated 'sucklings,' with reference to young calves in the sense of being the source of cows (that is, the obsessions) or with reference to milch cows in the sense of flowing out. There are no meritorious, demeritorious, or imperturbable volitional activities, designated 'cows in calf' in the sense of sustaining the embryo that has undergone conception. There is no longing or craving, designated 'breeding cows' in the sense of longing for intercourse. And there is no volitionally active consciousness, designated 'a bull, the chief of cattle,' in the sense of predominance, being the forerunner, and being the best.[345] I rejoice in their nonexistence, which is security from all bonds. But you rejoice in their existence, which is the basis of sorrow and grief. Therefore, since I rejoice in security from all bonds, [40] it is proper for me alone to say: 'So if you wish, pour down, O sky god!'"

28. Having heard this, wishing even more to acquire the jeweled substance of excellent sayings,[346] Dhaniya said, "The stakes are planted," showing that he has bound his own herd of cattle to stakes. Here, **stakes** are posts for binding the cattle. They are planted by hammering the smaller ones into the ground, while the larger ones are planted in holes dug in the ground. **Halters** are a special kind of rope, joined to straps, which serve the purpose of binding the calves. **Not even the sucklings can break them**: It is not possible even for the young calves to break them.

29. When he had spoken, the Blessed One, having known the time for the maturation of Dhaniya's faculties, exhorting him in the previous way, recited this verse illustrating the four truths: **Like a bull I have cut through the bonds**. [41] Here, a bull (*usabha*) is the father of cattle, the leader of cattle, the lord of the herd, an ox.[347] **Bonds**: bonds of rope and bonds of defilements.

Rotten creeper: Just as even a gold-colored body is called a putrid body, and as a dog a century old is called a little dog, and as a jackal born today is called an old jackal, so even a fresh creeper is called a rotten creeper in the sense that it lacks heartwood. **I have sundered**: have cut through. **The bed of the womb** (*gabbhaseyyaṃ*) should be resolved into womb and bed. Here, by mentioning "womb," the mode of origin involving birth from the womb is indicated; by mentioning "bed," the others are indicated.[348] Or all these are indicated under the heading of "bed of the womb."

This is the purport here: "Dhaniya, you rejoice in bondage, but like a great bull possessing strength and energy, repelled by bondage, I have cut through the bonds of the five higher fetters with the strength and energy of the fourth noble path; like a giant elephant, I have sundered the bonds of the five lower fetters with the strength and energy of the lower three paths. Or alternatively, I am like a bull that has cut through the bonds—that is, the latent tendencies—and I have sundered, cut off, the obsessions as a giant elephant does a rotten creeper. Therefore **I will never again come to the bed of the womb**. Freed from all kinds of suffering based upon the suffering of birth, it is proper for me to say: 'So if you wish, pour down, O sky god!' Therefore, if you too wish to speak as I do, cut off those bonds."

And here, the bonds are *the truth of the origin*; the bed of the womb is *the truth of suffering*; "I will never again come back," which here means not approaching, and "having cut off, having sundered," which here mean cutting and sundering, signify *the truth of cessation*, respectively without residue remaining and with residue remaining;[349] and that by which one cuts them off and sunders them is *the truth of the path*.

Having heard this verse illustrating the four truths, at the end of the verse Dhaniya, his wife, and two of his daughters—four persons in all—were established in the fruit of stream-entry. Then, through his unshakable confidence and faith, now rooted and settled in the Tathāgata, Dhaniya saw with the eye of wisdom the Dhamma body of the Blessed One, and with a heart stirred by the nature of the Dhamma, he thought: "With the Avīci hell as the lower boundary up to the peak of existence, there is no one else but the Blessed One who could roar such a lion's roar as this: 'I have cut through the bonds. For me there is no bed of the womb.' Is this the Teacher that has come to me?" Then the Blessed One, as if to say, "See now at your pleasure," emitted his bodily aura in Dhaniya's residence: a variegated net of six-colored rays, which was like an outpouring of fine gold. [42]

30. Having seen his residence look as if the sun and moon had entered within, as if it were everywhere illuminated with the light of a thousand brilliant lamps, Dhaniya realized: "The Blessed One has come." At that very moment, too, a cloud poured down rain. Hence the compilers said: "Filling the lowland and highland." **At once**: Rain poured down at the very moment the Blessed One emitted his bodily aura, and Dhaniya, aware, "The Teacher has come to me," released the aura of his mind consisting in faith. But some explain: "The sunrise, too, occurred at that very moment."

31–32. Thus, at that moment when faith arose in him, and the Tathāgata sent forth his radiance, and the sun arose, Dhaniya heard the sound of rain falling. Full of rapture and joy, he spoke about this matter in the next two verses, saying: "It is indeed no small gain for us." Here, since Dhaniya, and his wife and children, had seen the Blessed One's Dhamma body with the world-transcending eye [of wisdom] by penetrating it with the noble path, and had seen his form body with the mundane eye,[350] they acquired faith. Therefore he said: **It is no small gain for us, that we have seen the Blessed One**.

We approach you as a refuge: Although the going for refuge had already been accomplished by penetrating the noble path, and he had thereby gone for refuge in a definitive way, he now verbally undertakes the going for refuge by self-surrender.[351] Or alternatively: by way of the path, he had attained the unshakable refuge, the refuge by self-surrender, but now he goes for refuge by prostration, making this clear to others verbally. **One with Vision**: The Blessed One is the "One with Vision" because he possesses the five eyes: the ordinary eye, the divine eye, the eye of wisdom, the universal eye, and the buddha eye.[352] Addressing him in this way he said: "We approach you as a refuge, One with Vision."

Be our teacher, great muni: He makes this statement next to fulfill the going for refuge by also entering upon the state of a pupil. **My wife and I, obedient,** [43] **would lead the spiritual life under the Fortunate One**: This is by way of undertaking. Here, **spiritual life** (*brahmacariya*, or "pure conduct") is a designation for abstinence from sexual intercourse, the path, the ascetic's duty, the Teaching, and marital fidelity. For in such passages as "one who leads the spiritual life" (MN I 42,9), it is abstinence from sexual intercourse that is called the spiritual life. In such passages as "But this spiritual life of mine, Pañcasikha, is for complete disenchantment" (DN II 251,15–17), it is the path. In such passages as "I recollect, Sāriputta, living a spiritual life possessing four factors" (MN I 77,23), it is the ascetic's duty.[353] In such passages as "This spiritual life is successful and flourishing" (DN II 219,10), it is the Teaching. And in such passages as the following it means marital fidelity:

> We do not transgress against our wives,
> and our wives do not transgress against us.
> Except for them, we live the spiritual life.
> Therefore our young ones do not die. (Ja IV 53,20–22)

But here what is intended is the spiritual life of the higher paths, which is preceded by the spiritual life as the ascetic's duty.

Under the Fortunate One: under the Blessed One; for the Blessed One is called "the Fortunate One" (*sugata*) because he has gone well by avoiding the two extremes, and because he has gone beautifully along the noble path, and because he has gone to the good place, namely, nibbāna.[354]

Having thus asked the Blessed One for the going forth, referred to as "leading the spiritual life," he now says: **Gone beyond birth and death, we would make an end of suffering**, showing the purpose in going forth. What is called **beyond birth and death**[355] is nibbāna. [44] We would go there by the path of arahantship. **Would make an end of suffering**: We would nullify the suffering of the round. Having spoken thus, it is said, they both paid homage to the Blessed One again and requested the going forth, saying: "May the Blessed One let us go forth."

33. Then Māra the Evil One, having seen them both paying homage and requesting the going forth, thought to himself: "They wish to escape my domain. Let me create an obstacle to them." He went to them and recited this verse, showing the excellence of the household life: **One who has sons delights because of sons.**[356] Here "sons" means both sons and daughters. The meaning is that one delights along with one's children or one delights because of one's children. Māra is a certain rebellious deity in the plane of "the devas who exercise control over the creations of others."[357] He is called "Māra" because he kills (*māreti*) anyone he can who wishes to escape his own realm, and he also wishes for the death (*maraṇaṃ icchati*) of anyone that he cannot kill. **The Evil One**: a low person, or one of evil behavior. This is a statement by the compilers, and similar ones are in all verses.[358] As one with sons delights because of his sons, so one with cattle delights along with his cattle or because of his cattle.

Having spoken thus [about sons and cattle being a cause of delight], he now gives the reason proving this point, saying: **For acquisitions are a man's delight.** Here, as to acquisitions, there are four kinds of acquisitions: acquisitions as sensual pleasures, acquisitions as the aggregates, acquisitions as defilements, and acquisitions as volitional activities.[359] For sensual pleasures are called "acquisitions" (*upadhi*) in the sense that pleasure is acquired (*upadhīyati*) in them, because they are the basis for the pleasure spoken about thus: "Whatever pleasure and joy arise dependent on the five strands of sensual pleasure are called the gratification in sensual pleasures" (MN I 85,28). The aggregates, too, are the basis for the suffering rooted in the aggregates; the defilements, the basis for the suffering in the plane of misery; and volitional activities, [45] the basis for the suffering of existence. But here (in this passage) "acquisitions as sensual pleasures" is intended.

That is twofold, by way of beings and conditioned things.[360] Having said, "in sons, in cattle," showing that the chief of these is that bound up with beings, he states the reason thus: "For acquisitions are a man's delight." The meaning is: "Because these acquisitions consisting in sensual pleasures are the delight of a man—since they delight a man by bringing him rapture and joy—therefore it should be understood that one who has sons delights because of sons; so too, one who has cattle delights because of cattle. And you have sons and cattle. Therefore, delight in them; don't wish for the going forth. A monk does not have these acquisitions, and in such a case, though you wish for the end of suffering, you will be miserable."

He now gives another reason proving this point, saying: **without acquisitions one does not delight**. This is its meaning: "One who does not have these acquisitions, being separated from his dear relatives or destitute of enjoyments and commodities, does not delight. Therefore, if you give up these acquisitions, as a monk you will be miserable."

34. Then the Blessed One, having understood, "This is Māra the Evil One, who has come to obstruct them," just as if he were dropping one fruit on top of another fruit, turned the verse around, refuting Māra's assertion with the same simile brought forth by Māra. Showing, "Acquisitions are the basis of suffering," he said: "One who has sons sorrows because of sons." The meaning of the words here is clear; this is is the purport: "Evil One, do not say: 'One who has sons delights because of sons.' For it is an inviolable law that there must be parting and separation from everything dear and beloved, and when people are separated from those who are dear and beloved—from children and wife, from cattle, horses, mares, bullion, gold, and so forth—their hearts are pierced by the dart of grief and they become deranged and even go mad. They experience death and deadly suffering. Therefore grasp this: **One who has sons sorrows because of sons**. And as one with sons sorrows because of sons, **one with cattle likewise sorrows because of cattle**. For what reason? **For acquisitions are a man's sorrow.** And since acquisitions are a man's sorrow, it therefore follows that **without acquisitions one does not sorrow**. One without acquisitions, who has abandoned the tie of acquisitions, is content with a robe to cover his body and almsfood to fill his stomach. Wherever he goes, he goes having taken these along. Just like a bird . . . [46] . . . he understands: 'There is no more coming back to any state of being.'[361] With the destruction of all sorrow in this way, 'one without acquisitions does not sorrow.'" Thus the Blessed One concluded the teaching with its culmination in arahantship.

Or alternatively: "One without acquisitions, [that is,] one without defilements, does not sorrow. For as long as there are defilements, all acquisitions are the roots of sorrow.[362] But with the abandoning of defilements, there is no sorrow." In this way, too, he concluded the teaching with its culmination in arahantship. At the conclusion of the teaching both Dhaniya and his wife went forth. The Blessed One returned to Jeta's Grove through the sky. Having gone forth, they realized arahantship. In the place where they had lived, their cowhands built a monastery, and even today it is known as "the Cowherd Family's Monastery."[363]

3 The Rhinoceros Horn
(*Khaggavisāṇa Sutta*)

[General origination]

What is the origin? All suttas have a fourfold origin: through personal inclination; through the inclination of others; on account of a particular incident; and in response to a question.[364] The origin of the Contemplation of Dyads (III,12) and so forth was through personal inclination. The origin of the Discourse on Loving-Kindness (I,8) and so forth was through the inclination of others. The origin of the Discourse on the Serpent (I,1) and so forth was on account of a particular incident. And the origin of the Discourse to Dhammika (II,14) and so forth was in response to a question.

The general origin of the Discourse on the Rhinoceros Horn was in response to a question; but in specific cases some verses here were spoken when this or that paccekabuddha was asked a question, and some were spoken without a question being asked, but instead were uttered by a paccekabuddha as a joyful utterance in accordance with his own breakthrough.[365] Therefore some verses originated in response to a question, while others originated through personal inclination. [47]

Of these, the general origination in response to a question should be understood from the beginning as follows.[366] On one occasion the Blessed One was dwelling at Sāvatthī. While the Venerable Ānanda was alone in seclusion, the following line of thought arose in him: "The aspiration and undertaking of buddhas has been shown; so too those of disciples.[367] But those of paccekabuddhas have not been shown. I will now go to the Blessed One and inquire about this." So he emerged from seclusion, went to the Blessed One, and in due course asked about this matter. The Blessed One then gave him a discourse about past exertion:[368]

> "Ānanda, there are these five benefits in past exertion. (1) One attains final knowledge early in this present life. (2) If one does not attain final knowledge early in this present life, one attains final knowledge at the time of death. (3) If one does not attain final knowledge at the time of death, one attains final knowledge after being reborn as a deity. (4) Or else one is of quick direct knowledge in the presence of the buddhas. (5) Or in the last time one becomes a paccekabuddha."

Having said this, he further said:

> "Ānanda, paccekabuddhas are equipped with an undertaking and they have practiced past exertion. Therefore an aspiration and undertaking should be recognized for all: buddhas, paccekabuddhas, and disciples."

Ānanda asked: "Bhante, how long does it take for the aspiration of buddhas to be achieved?" [The Buddha replied:] "For buddhas, Ānanda, it takes at minimum four incalculables and 100,000 eons; at the middling level, eight incalculables and 100,000 eons; at the maximum, sixteen incalculables and 100,000 eons. And these divisions should be understood respectively in the case of those for whom wisdom is predominant, those for whom faith is predominant, and those for whom energy is predominant. In those for whom wisdom is predominant, faith is weak and wisdom is sharp (and energy middling). In those for whom faith is predominant, wisdom is middling (and faith is strong).[369] In those for whom energy is predominant, faith and wisdom are weak and energy is strong.[370] But without having completed four incalculables and 100,000 eons, there is no possibility that one could become a buddha earlier, even if one were to give gifts day after day like those of Vessantara [48] and to accumulate all the other pāramīs, such as good behavior, to a corresponding degree.[371] Why not? Because one's knowledge would not have commenced, nor expanded, nor reached maturity. It is just as when grain is growing that needs three, four, or five months to ripen: it is impossible that without having completed that time, the grain might ripen earlier—in a fortnight or a month—even though one fondles it and waters it a thousand times daily. Why not? Because the grain would not have commenced, nor expanded, nor reached maturity. So too, without having completed four incalculables and 100,000 eons, there is no possibility that one could become a buddha. Therefore the fulfilling of the pāramīs must be pursued over the aforementioned time for the maturation of knowledge."

And for one aspiring for buddhahood over such a period of time, eight prerequisites must be met for making the undertaking.

> Human status, achievement of the gender,
> the cause, seeing the Teacher;
> the going forth, possession of excellent qualities,
> service, and strong desire:
> through the assemblage of these eight qualities
> the undertaking reaches success. (Bv 2.58)

The *undertaking* (*abhinīhāra*) is a designation for the fundamental resolution.

(1) Here, *human status* means a human birth. For the resolution does not succeed for one dwelling in other realms of birth apart from human birth, even for one born as a deva. However, one dwelling here who aspires for buddhahood, after having done meritorious deeds such as giving, should aspire for human status. After one has come to dwell there, the resolution should be made.[372] In this way it succeeds.

(2) The *achievement of the gender* (*liṅgasampatti*) is the state of a male. For the resolution does not succeed for women, those of indeterminate gender, and hermaphrodites even when they have achieved a human birth. However, one dwelling there who aspires for buddhahood, after having done meritorious deeds such as giving, should aspire for the state of a male. Having come to dwell there, the resolution should be made. In this way it succeeds.

(3) The *cause* (*hetu*) is the achievement of the supporting conditions for arahantship. [49] For the resolution succeeds for one striving in that existence who is capable of attaining arahantship; it does not succeed for others. Such was the case with the wise Sumedha; for having gone forth at the feet of the Buddha Dīpaṅkara, he was capable of attaining arahantship in that same existence.[373]

(4) The *sight of the Teacher*: personally seeing the buddhas. In such a case it succeeds, not otherwise. This was so for the wise Sumedha, who made his resolution after personally seeing Dīpaṅkara.

(5) The *going forth*: the homeless state. For the resolution succeeds for one who has gone forth either in the Teaching or in a sect of hermits or wanderers who affirm kamma and the efficacy of action. Again, the example is the wise Sumedha; for Sumedha was a hermit when he made his resolution.

(6) *Possession of excellent qualities*: the attainment of such excellent qualities as the jhānas. For the resolution succeeds only for one gone forth who possesses excellent qualities, not for others. Again, the example is the wise Sumedha; for he had already acquired the five kinds of superknowledge and the eight meditative attainments when he made the resolution.

(7) *Service* (*adhikāra*): an exceptional deed, meaning relinquishment. For it succeeds only for one who has made the resolution after showing his willingness to relinquish his life and other achievements, not for others. Again, the example is the wise Sumedha; for he made the resolution after showing his willingness to relinquish his life thus:

> "Let the Buddha along with his pupils
> proceed by stepping upon me.
> Do not tread upon the mud:
> that will bring me well-being."[374] (Bv 2.52)

(8) *Desire*: desire to act. For the resolution succeeds for one who has strong desire. And the strength of that desire should be understood in this way.[375] If he were to hear: "Who desires buddhahood after being tortured in hell for four incalculables and 100,000 eons?" he would be willing to say: "I do." So too having heard it said: "Who desires buddhahood after walking

across a whole world sphere filled with flameless hot coals? Who desires buddhahood after walking across a whole world sphere that has become a solid mass of sharp-pointed stakes? Who desires buddhahood after crossing a whole world sphere filled with water up to the brim? Who desires buddhahood after trampling upon a whole world sphere covered with bamboo thickets, with no space in between?" he would be willing to say, "I do." The wise Sumedha possessed such desire when he made the resolution. [50]

When his undertaking succeeds in such a way, a bodhisatta does not incur these eighteen cases of incapacitation. He is never born blind or deaf; he does not become insane; he is not dumb; he is not crippled; he does not take birth among uncivilized peoples; he is not born to a slave woman; he does not hold a wrong view with fixed consequences;[376] he does not undergo gender change; he does not commit any of the five deeds with immediate retribution;[377] he is not a leper; he does not become an animal smaller than a quail or larger than an elephant; he does not arise among the spirits afflicted with insatiable hunger and thirst, nor among the *kālakañjaka* asuras, nor in Avīci hell, nor in the intersteller regions, nor does he become Māra in the desire realm; nor does he arise in the nonpercipient plane in the form realm, in the pure abodes, or in the formless states of existence; nor does he migrate to another world sphere.

He possesses the four buddha grounds: enthusiasm, astuteness, firmness, and beneficent conduct. These should be understood thus:

By *enthusiasm* energy is meant;
wisdom is called *astuteness*;
firmness is determination,
and *beneficent conduct*, development of loving-kindness.

Also, there are these six inclinations that lead to maturation for enlightenment: the inclination to renunciation, the inclination to solitude, the inclination to non-greed, the inclination to non-hatred, the inclination to non-delusion, and the inclination to escape. Because they possess these, bodhisattas incline to renunciation, seeing the faults in sensual pleasure. They incline to solitude, seeing the faults in company. They incline to non-greed, seeing the faults in greed. They incline to non-hatred, seeing the faults in hatred. They incline to non-delusion, seeing the faults in delusion. They incline to escape, seeing the faults in all states of existence.

But how long does it take for the aspiration of paccekabuddhas to be fulfilled? For paccekabuddhas, two incalculables and 100,000 eons are required. It is not possible in less time than this. The reason should be understood in the way stated earlier [in the case of buddhas]. [51] For one aspiring to become a paccekabuddha in this amount of time, five prerequisites are recognized in making the undertaking:

The human state, the achievement of the gender,
the sight of one devoid of influxes,
service, and desire: these are the causes
for the undertaking [to reach success].

Here, *the sight of one devoid of influxes* means the sight of a buddha, a paccekabuddha, or an arahant disciple. The rest should be understood in the way already stated.

But how much time does it take for the aspiration of disciples to be achieved? For the two chief disciples, one incalculable and 100,000 eons; for the eighty great disciples, 100,000 eons. So too, for the mother, father, attendant, and son of a buddha. It is not possible in less time than this; the reason for this should be understood in the way already stated. The undertaking for all these possesses only two factors: service and desire.

When buddhas arise in the world after having fulfilled the pāramīs through this aspiration and this undertaking in the aforesaid amounts of time, they arise in either a khattiya family or a brahmin family. Paccekabuddhas arise in a family of khattiyas, brahmins, or householders. But the chief disciples, like the buddhas, arise only in families of khattiyas or brahmins. Buddhas never arise when the eon is dissolving, but they arise when the eon is evolving.[378] Without encountering buddhas, paccekabuddhas arise only at a time when buddhas arise.[379] Buddhas attain enlightenment themselves and enlighten others. Paccekabuddhas attain enlightenment themselves but do not enlighten others. They penetrate the taste of the goal only but not the taste of the Dhamma. For they are not able to apply conceptual description to the world-transcending Dhamma and thereby teach it. Their breakthrough to the Dhamma is like a dumb person trying to describe the things he has seen in a dream or like a country-dweller trying to describe the dishes he tasted in the city.

They achieve all the psychic powers, meditative attainments, and analytical knowledges. Their excellent qualities are inferior to those of the buddhas but superior to those of disciples. They give others the going forth and train them in proper behavior.[380] They observe the uposatha with this advice: "One should practice effacement of the mind and should not come to a stop," [52] or else they merely say: "Today is the uposatha." When observing the uposatha, they do so after they have assembled on the Jewel Terrace at the foot of the Mañjūsaka tree on Mount Gandhamādana.

In this way the Blessed One explained to the Venerable Ānanda, fully in all aspects, the aspiration and undertaking of paccekabuddhas. Now, to discuss those paccekabuddhas who had arisen through this aspiration and undertaking, he spoke this Discourse on the Rhinoceros Horn, beginning with the words "Having put down the rod toward all beings." This, firstly, is the general origination of the Discourse on the Rhinoceros Horn in response to a question. Now the specific origination should be explained.

Chapter 1[381]

The first verse

35. Here the origination of this verse should be understood as follows. It is said that this paccekabuddha, when entering the stage of a paccekabodhisatta, fulfilled the pāramīs for two incalculables and 100,000 eons, and then, having gone forth in the teaching of the Blessed One Kassapa, he became a forest dweller and performed the ascetic's duty by fulfilling the observance of going and returning. It is said that there is no one who attains pacceka enlightenment without having fulfilled this observance.

But what is this *observance of going and returning*? Taking and bringing back. We will explain so that it becomes clear.[382]

(1) Here, one bhikkhu takes it but does not bring it back. (2) One brings it back but does not take it. (3) One neither takes it nor brings it back. (4) And one takes it and brings it back.

[1. The bhikkhu who takes it but does not bring it back]
Among these, one bhikkhu, having risen early, does the duties connected with the cetiya terrace and the bodhi tree terrace, waters the bodhi tree, fills the pot for drinking water, and puts it on its stand. He then does all the duties toward his teacher and preceptor, and the eighty-two duties of the Khandhakas and the fourteen major duties.[383]

Having taken care of his physical needs, he enters his lodging and passes his time sitting in meditation until the time comes to walk for alms. When he knows the time has arrived, he puts on his lower robe, fastens the waistband, puts on the upper robe, and places the outer robe over his shoulder. He ties the bowl in its bag, [53] and while attending to the meditation subject, he sets out. When he reaches the cetiya terrace, he venerates the cetiya and the bodhi tree, and on the outskirts of the village, he fully covers himself with the upper robe, and taking the bowl, he enters the village for alms.

When he has entered in this way, a meritorious bhikkhu who gains offerings, who is honored and respected by lay followers, returns to a family of lay supporters or the rest hall, where he is asked various questions by the lay followers. By the time he departs, because he had been answering questions and was distracted by teaching the Dhamma, he has discarded the attention to his meditation subject. When he has arrived back at the monastery, too, he answers questions posed by the bhikkhus, preaches the Dhamma, and becomes engaged in various tasks. In the afternoon, the first watch of the night, and the middle watch, he is detained by the bhikkhus in the same way. In the last watch, overcome by physical inertia, he goes to sleep and does not attend to his meditation subject. This is called *one who takes it but does not bring it back.*

[2. One who brings it back but does not take it]
But one who is often ill has not digested his meal even by the end of the night. Having risen early in the morning, he is not able to perform the aforementioned duties or attend to his meditation subject. Wishing for nothing else but porridge

or medicine, as soon as it is time he takes his bowl and robe and enters the village. Having obtained porridge, medicine, or rice, having completed his meal,[384] he sits down in a prepared seat and attends to his meditation subject. Whether or not he attains distinction, when he returns to the monastery, he continues with the same kind of attention. This is called *one who brings it back but does not take it*. Such bhikkhus in the Buddha's Teaching who, after drinking porridge, have undertaken insight and attained arahantship are beyond counting. In the island of Sri Lanka, in the sitting halls in its villages, there is not a seat where a bhikkhu has not attained arahantship after drinking porridge.

[3. One who neither takes it nor brings it back]

But one who dwells heedlessly and negligently, who violates all the duties, whose mind is constantly overcome by the five kinds of mental barrenness and bondage,[385] who is not intent on attending to a meditation subject, enters the village for alms. He is detained by talking with laypeople and leaves empty. This is called *one who neither takes it nor brings it back*.

[4. One who both takes it and brings it back]

But there is one who [54] rises early, fulfills all his duties in the aforesaid way, sits down crosslegged, and attends to his meditation subject until it is time to walk for alms.

A meditation subject is of two kinds: the generally useful and the personalized.[386] Those generally useful are loving-kindness and recollection of death. Loving-kindness is recognized as generally useful when directed toward the monastic abodes and so forth. For a bhikkhu who dwells with loving-kindness toward the monastic abodes is dear to his fellow monks and thereby lives in comfort, without friction.[387] One who dwells with loving-kindness toward the deities lives happily, protected and guarded by them. One who dwells with loving-kindness toward the king and his chief ministers lives happily, cherished by them. One who dwells with loving-kindness toward the villages and towns and other regions lives happily, honored and respected everywhere by the people when walking for alms and so forth. By developing the recollection of death, one abandons attachment to life and lives heedfully.

But the "personalized" subject is one taken up in accordance with one's temperament and which is to be always maintained. It is called *pārihāriya* because it is to be always maintained, protected, and developed. It may be one of the ten unattractive objects, the kasiṇas, or the recollections, or the delineation of the four elements. It is also called one's root meditation subject. Having first attended to the meditation subjects that are generally useful, afterward one attends to the personalized meditation subject, which we will explain by way of the delineation of the four elements.[388]

One reflects upon this body, in whatever way it is situated or disposed, by way of the elements thus: "In this body, whatever is hard and rough in the twenty solid parts is the earth element. Whatever is moist and has the function of cohesion in the twelve liquid parts is the water element. That which is warmth and has the function of maturation in four ways is the fire element. And that which is gaseous and has the function of distension in six ways is the air element. But any hole or opening not occupied by the four primary elements is the space element. The mind that cognizes them is the consciousness element.[389] Beyond these, there is no other being or individual. This is just [55] a heap of bare conditioned things."

Having attended to the meditation subject by way of its beginning, middle, and end, when one knows it is time, one rises from one's seat, dresses, and goes to the village for alms in the way explained earlier. And when going, one is not deluded in regard to going forward and the other activities, like blind foolish worldlings who think: "A self goes forward, the going forward is caused by a self," or "I go forward, the going forward is caused by me." Rather, one understands: "When the thought 'Let me go forward' is arising, along with that thought the mind-originated air element arises, keeping the body upright. This is diffused throughout this collection of bones considered to be a body, the residence of the earth element and the other elements. Then, because of the diffusion of the air element arisen from mental activity, this collection of bones considered a body goes forward. When it is going forward, in each act of lifting the foot, the fire element accompanied by the air element is dominant; the others are weak. In bringing the foot forward and in shifting it away, the air element accompanied by the fire element is dominant; the others are weak. In dropping the foot, the water element accompanied by the earth element is dominant; the others are weak. In putting the foot on the ground and pressing it against the ground, the earth element accompanied by the water element is dominant; the others are weak. Together with each thought giving rise to them, these elements break up right on the spot: 'Who in this is the one that goes forward, or for whom is there going forward?' In this way, the elements arisen in each phase among the phases in each step—the lifting of the foot and so forth—along with the remaining phenomena inseparable from them, are the phenomena of form; the mind that produces these activities together with the remaining mental phenomena associated with it are the mental phenomena. Together these are the material and mental phenomena. Following that phase of lifting, they do not reach any other phase, such as bringing the foot forward and so forth, but they break up right there. Therefore they are impermanent. Whatever is impermanent is suffering. What is suffering is non-self." Thus he walks along attending only to his meditation subject complete in all aspects.

[For young men who desire their good, having gone forth in the teaching, living together as a group of ten, twenty, thirty, forty, fifty, sixty, seventy, or a hundred, make a pact: "Friends, you have not gone forth because you were oppressed by debt, or oppressed by fear, or to earn a living; but you have gone forth because you wish to be liberated from suffering. Therefore, if a defilement has arisen when you are walking, suppress it even while you are walking; likewise if a defilement has arisen when you are standing, sitting, or lying down, suppress it even while you are lying down." Having made such a pact, while walking for alms, they walk along just attending to their meditation subject, noting the distance by the marker stones at intervals along the road to the alms resort. If a defilement arises in anyone while he is walking, he suppresses it right there. If he is unable to do so, he stands still; then the one coming behind him also stands still. The former reproves himself: "This bhikkhu behind you knows that such a thought has arisen in you; that isn't suitable for you." Then, having developed insight, he enters the plane of the noble ones right there. If he is unable to do so, he sits down; then the one coming behind him also sits down; the same method applies. If he is unable to enter the plane of the noble ones, having suppressed that defilement, he continues on his way, just attending to the meditation subject.][390]

He does not lift a foot with a mind dissociated from the meditation subject. If he lifts it, having turned back, he goes to the former place, like the Elder Mahāphussadeva the Verandah Dweller in Sīhaḷadīpa (Sri Lanka). [56] It is said that he fulfilled the observance of going and returning for nineteen years. People who were plowing, sowing, threshing, and doing other tasks along the road, having seen the elder going along in such a way, would speak about him: "This elder turns back again and again. Has he lost his way or forgotten something?" Unconcerned about this, doing the ascetic's duty with a mind yoked to his meditation subject, he attained arahantship within his twentieth rains retreat. And on the very day he attained arahantship, a deity dwelling at the end of his walkway stood there radiating light from his fingers. The four divine kings, too, and Sakka the ruler of the devas, and Brahmā Sahampati came to attend on him. And having seen that radiance, the forest dwelling Elder Mahātissa asked him the next day: "During the night there was a radiance near your place. What was that radiance?" The Elder Mahāphussa, diverting the conversation, said, "Radiance is the radiance of a lamp, the radiance of jewels," and so forth. Pressed, "Are you concealing something?" he admitted it and reported his attainment.

And like the Elder Mahānāga who resided at the Black Creeper Pavilion. He, too, it is said, while fulfilling the observance of going and returning, decided, "I will first honor the Blessed One's great exertion," and resolved to maintain only the postures of standing and walking for seven years. Having again fulfilled the observance of going and returning for sixteen years, he attained arahantship.

While lifting his foot with a mind yoked to his meditation subject, if he lifted a foot with a mind dissociated from the subject, he would turn around, go back to the vicinity of the village, and stand in an area that would make people wonder: "Is that a cow or a monk?" Having put on his outer robe and taken his bowl, on reaching the gate of the village he would take water from his water bottle, fill his mouth with water, and enter the village, thinking: "When people approach to give almsfood or venerate me, let me not be distracted from the meditation subject even by merely having to say: 'May you live long.'" But if they asked him about the date, "Is today, Bhante, the seventh or the eighth?" he would swallow the water and answer. If no one asked about the date, [57] at the time of leaving, he would spit out the water near the village gate and go.

And like the fifty bhikkhus who entered the rains retreat at the Galambatittha[391] Vihāra in Sri Lanka. It is said that on the day of the uposatha, before entering upon the rains retreat, they made a pact: "As long as we haven't attained arahantship, we will not converse with one another." And when entering the village for alms, they first filled their mouths with water at the village gate. If they were asked about the date or other matters, they swallowed the water and answered; but if no one asked, they would spit out the water by the village gate and go back to the monastery. When people saw the spots where they had spit out the water, they knew: "Today one has come, today two." And they thought: "Are we the only ones with whom they do not speak or do they also not speak with one another? If they do not even speak with one another, surely they must have had a dispute. Come, let us make them pardon each other." They all went to the monastery. Of the fifty bhikkhus there who had entered upon the rains, they did not see even two in one place. Then one astute man among them said: "Sirs, the dwelling place of those who are quarreling is not like this. The cetiya terrace and the bodhi tree terrace are well swept, the brooms neatly stored, drinking water and washing water neatly set up." They then returned home. Within the three months of the rains retreat, those bhikkhus had undertaken insight, attained arahantship, and held the Pavāraṇā ceremony of purity at the great Pavāraṇā.[392]

One thus walks along with a mind yoked to the meditation subject, like the Elder Mahānāga who dwelt at the Black Creeper Pavilion and the bhikkhus who entered the rains retreat at the Galambatittha Vihāra. Having reached the vicinity of the village, one fills the mouth with water, checks out the streets, and enters a street where there are no quarrelsome drunkards or derelicts and no wild elephants or horses and so forth. Walking for alms there, one does not go quickly as if in a hurry. For the ascetic practice of going on alms round is not to be done quickly. [58] But one goes steadily, like a water cart that has reached uneven ground.

And when one has entered among the houses one waits for an appropriate time to determine whether or not the person wishes to give. Having obtained almsfood, one sits down in a suitable place, and while attending to the meditation subject, one establishes the perception of the repulsiveness in nutriment and eats, reflecting on the food by way of the similes of grease on an axle, ointment on a wound, and son's flesh.[393] One eats the food after considering it by way of eight factors, as "neither for amusement nor for intoxication," and so forth.[394] And after one has eaten and washed up, one takes a short rest to remove fatigue after the meal. Then, as in the forenoon, one attends to the meditation subject in the afternoon, the first watch of the night, and the last watch.[395] This is called *one who takes it and brings it back.* It is in this way that one fulfills this observance of going and returning, which is explained as taking and bringing back.

Now one fulfilling this practice, if he has supporting conditions, attains arahantship in the prime of life. If he does not attain it in the prime of life, then he attains it in middle age. If he does not attain it in middle age, then he attains it at the time of death. If he does not attain it at the time of death, then he attains it [in the next life] after becoming a deity. If one does not attain it as a deity, then one attains final nibbāna as a paccekabuddha. If one does not attain final nibbāna as a paccekabuddha, then one attains it in the presence of the buddhas, as one of quick understanding like the Elder Bāhiya or as one with great wisdom like the Elder Sāriputta.

But this paccekabodhisatta[396] went forth in the teaching of the Blessed One Kassapa, became a forest dweller, and fulfilled the observance of going and returning for 20,000 years. Having passed away, he arose in a desire-sphere deva world. Having passed away from there, he was reborn in the womb of the chief queen of the king of Bārāṇasī. Now she was one of those clever women who know the very day they conceive, so she informed the king that she was pregnant. It is in the nature of things that when a meritorious being has been conceived in the womb, [59] the woman obtains special protection of the fetus. Therefore the king gave her special protection for her fetus. From then on, she did not get to swallow anything too hot or too cold, too sour or too salty, too pungent or too bitter. For if the mother swallows something too hot, the fetus feels as if it is in the abode of the Copper Cauldron;[397] if it is too cold, it is like the abode of intersteller space; if the food she has eaten is too sour, salty, pungent, or bitter, the limbs of the fetus experience sharp pains, as if they were cut open with a knife and sprinkled with sour substances and so forth.

The guardians prevent the woman from excessive walking, standing, sitting, and lying down, telling her: "Don't upset the child in your womb by moving around." She is allowed merely to walk back and forth on ground that has been spread over with a soft carpet, and she gets to eat delicious and nutritious food and drink beverages with a good color, fragrance, and flavor. Encircling her, they help her walk back and forth, sit down, and get up.

Being protected in such a way, when the time for her delivery came, she entered the delivery chamber and, just before dawn, gave birth to a son who possessed meritorious characteristics and looked like a ball of red arsenic mixed with champaka oil.[398] On the fifth day they had him adorned and presented him to the king. The king, rejoicing, assigned sixty-six nurses to attend on him. Growing up with all endowments, before long he reached maturity. As soon as he was sixteen years of age, the king consecrated him to kingship and had the three kinds of dancers attend on him.[399] When the prince was consecrated, under the name Brahmadatta he ruled over the entire Jambudīpa with its 20,000 cities. For in the past, there were 84,000 cities in Jambudīpa. Those diminished until there were 60,000; then they diminished still further to 40,000; and in the last period of diminution, there were 20,000. And this Brahmadatta arose during the last period of diminution, so he had 20,000 cities, 20,000 palaces, and 20,000 each of elephants, horses, chariots, [60] infantrymen, and women—consorts and dancing girls—and 20,000 ministers.

While ruling over the great kingdom, he did the preparatory work on a kasiṇa and attained the five superknowledges and the eight meditative attainments. Now since a consecrated king must preside over legal cases, one day, after an early breakfast, he sat in the judgment hall. There they were making an uproar. Thinking, "This noise is an obstacle to meditative attainment," he went up to the terrace of his palace and sat down, thinking to enter a meditative attainment. However, he could not attain it, for he had been distracted by the duties of kingship. He reflected: "What is better, kingship or the ascetic's duty?" He then knew: "The happiness of kingship is limited and fraught with many dangers, but the happiness of the ascetic's duty is vast and rich in many benefits; it is the resort of supreme persons." He instructed one of his ministers: "You administer this kingdom righteously and justly. Do not do anything unrighteous." Having handed over everything, he went up to the top of his palace and dwelled in the bliss of the meditative attainments. He did not permit anyone to approach him except those who gave him toothwood for cleaning his mouth and those who brought his meals.

When he had passed half a month in this way, his chief queen asked: "The king is not seen anywhere, whether going to the park or to see the army or among the dancers. Where has he gone?" They informed her about the matter. She sent for the minister and said to him: "When you accepted the kingdom, you also accepted me. Come, make love to me." He closed both ears and rejected her, saying: "This should not even be heard." But she sent for him a second and a third time, and threatened him if he refused: "If you do not do as I say, I will get you deposed and even have you executed." He was afraid, for "women are firm in their decisions and she may someday have this done." So one day, he went to her in private and made love to her in her bedroom. She was splendid and pleasant to the touch, and he was excited by the lust that arose through contact with her. He often went to her very fearfully, [61] but in time he began to enter her room confidently, as if he were her husband.

Then the king's men reported this news to the king. He did not believe them. They reported this to him a second and a third time. Then, while hidden, he saw this for himself. He assembled all his ministers and informed them. They said, "This adulterer against the king deserves to have his hands cut off; he deserves to have his feet cut off," and thus, starting with impalement on a stake, they described to him all kinds of punishment. But the king said: "If I were to have him executed, imprisoned, or whipped, that would be violence on my part. If I were to take his life, that would be the destruction of life. If I were to confiscate his wealth, that would be stealing. Enough with such deeds! Expel him from my kingdom." The ministers expelled him.

The minister took his wealth and valuables, as well as his wife and children, and went to another realm. The king there, having heard about him, asked him: "Why have you come?" – "Lord, I wish to attend on you." The king accepted him. After a number of days, the minister won his trust and told the king: "Great king, I see honey without flies, and no one is eating it." The king did not heed him, thinking: "Is he saying this because he wishes to ridicule me?" Having found the king's weak spot,[400] having again praised him even more highly, the minister reported the matter to the king, who asked: "What is it?" – "The kingdom of Bārаṇasī, lord." The king said: "Do you want to lead me there and have me killed?" The minister replied: "Do not speak like that, lord. If you don't believe me, send your men." The king sent his men. They went, dug beneath the town gate, and stood in the king's bedroom.

Having seen them, the king asked: "Why have you come here?"

"We are thieves, great king."

The king gave them money, told them not to repeat this behavior, and dismissed them. They went and reported to their own king. He investigated in the same way a second and a third time, until he was convinced: "King [Brahmadatta] is virtuous but not astute." Then he marshaled a four-division army and approached a city across the border, where he sent a message to the minister: "Give me the city or fight!" He reported the matter to Brahmadatta, asking: "Command me, lord. Should I fight or surrender the city?" The king sent him a message: "Do not fight. Surrender the city and come here." He did so. The enemy king, having taken the city, repeated the process with the remaining cities. [62] Each of the ministers there reported the matter to Brahmadatta and received the same reply: "Do not fight, but come back here." And so they returned to Bārāṇasī.

Then the ministers told Brahmadatta: "Great king, let us fight him." But he prohibited them, saying: "That would require me to destroy life."

The ministers said: "Great king, we will take him alive and bring him here." Thus, with various methods, they convinced the king, and began to leave, saying: "Come, great king."

The king said: "If you do not kill, strike, or plunder any beings, I will go."

The ministers replied: "We won't do that, lord. We'll frighten them and chase them away." Then they marshaled a four-division army and, having put lamps into pots, they went at night. That day the enemy king had captured a city near Bārāṇasī. At night, thinking that there was now nothing to worry about, he took off his armor and, being heedless, he and his troops fell asleep. Just then the ministers, having brought along the king of Bārāṇasī, went to the campsite of the enemy king. Taking the lamps out from all the pots, with the army appearing to be a single mass of light, they made a noise. When the minister of the enemy king saw the large army, he was frightened. He went to his own king and shouted: "Get up! Eat the honey without flies!" A second and a third minister did the same. The enemy king, awakened by the noise, was frightened and terrified. Shouts by the hundreds arose. All night long he blabbered, saying: "I believed that minister's word and have now fallen into the hands of my foe."

The next day he considered: "The king is righteous and won't do any harm. Let me go to him and apologize." He then went to Brahmadatta, got down on his knees, and said: "Forgive me, great king. It was my fault." King Brahmadatta exhorted him and said: "Get up, I forgive you." As soon as the king said this, the enemy king felt utterly relieved. He obtained from the king of Bārāṇasi rulership over a neighboring country and the two became fast friends.

Then when Brahmadatta saw the two armies standing as one, welcoming each other, he thought: "Because I could protect the mind of one person—my own—this great mass of people has not shed a drop of blood even small enough for a tiny fly to lick. [63] How wonderful! How excellent! May all beings be happy, without enmity, free from affliction!" In this way, he attained the jhāna of loving-kindness, and taking it as a basis, he explored conditioned things, realized the knowledge of pacceka enlightenment, and attained the state of a self-accomplished one.[401]

While he was sitting on the back of his elephant absorbed in the bliss of the path and fruit, his ministers prostrated to him and said: "It is time to go, great king. The victorious troops are to be honored and the gift of a meal is to be given to the defeated troops."

He replied: "I'm not a king, men. I'm a paccekabuddha."

"What are you saying, lord? Paccekabuddhas don't look like this."

"Then what do paccekabuddhas look like?"

"Paccekebuddhas have hair and whiskers two-inches in length and possess the eight requisites."[402]

He then touched his head with his right hand and at once the marks of a layman vanished and he appeared in the garb of a monk, with hair and whiskers two inches in length and with the eight requisites, looking just like an elder of a hundred years. He then entered the fourth jhāna, rose up from the back of his elephant into the air, and sat on a lotus flower. The ministers venerated him and asked: "Bhante, what is your meditation subject? How did you achieve this?" Since he had used the jhāna of loving-kindness as his meditation subject and had achieved realization by practicing insight on it, showing this matter, he pronounced this verse as both a joyful utterance and an explanation: "Having put down the rod toward all beings."

Here, **all**: without exception. **Having put down**: having laid down. **Beings** (*bhūtāni*): sentient beings; this is a brief account, but we will explain the word in detail in the commentary on the Discourse on Gems (see p. 679). **The rod** is the bodily, verbal, and mental rod; this is a designation for bodily, verbal, and mental misconduct. For bodily misconduct is a rod because it strikes, oppresses; it inflicts misery and disaster. And so too verbal and mental misconduct. Or the rod is simply giving blows.

One should not desire a son: One should not desire any kind of son among these four kinds of sons: a biological son, a territorial son, an adopted son, and a pupil.[403] [64] **How then a companion?**: How is it that one might desire a companion?

Alone: alone consisting in the going forth; alone in the sense of being companionless; alone through the abandoning of craving; alone by being entirely rid of defilements; and alone by having awakened to pacceka enlightenment. For even if one is staying in the midst of a thousand ascetics, by the severing of the fetter of lay life one is alone: such is *alone consisting in the going forth*. Alone in the sense of *being companionless* means that one stands alone, walks alone, sits alone, and sleeps alone; one moves alone and acts alone. Alone in the sense of *the abandoning of craving* is seen here:

> With craving as partner, a person,
> wandering on this long journey,
> does not transcend saṃsāra,
> with its becoming thus, becoming otherwise.
>
> Having known this danger,
> "Craving is the origin of suffering,"
> a bhikkhu should wander mindfully,
> free of craving, without grasping. **(740–41)**

Alone by being *entirely rid of defilements* is expressed thus: "All his defilements have been abandoned, cut off at the root, made like a palm stump, abolished, so they are incapable of arising in the future."

Alone by *having awakened to pacceka enlightenment* is stated thus: "Without a teacher, self-accomplished, by himself he has awakened to pacceka enlightenment."

Nidd II 210–12. Alone: The paccekasambuddha is alone in the way designated the going forth; alone in the sense of being without a companion; alone in the sense of the abandoning of craving; alone as utterly devoid of lust, hatred, and delusion, as utterly without defilements; alone by having gone to the one-way path; alone by having awakened to the unsurpassed pacceka enlightenment.

How is a paccekasambuddha alone *in the way designated the going forth*? The paccekabuddha cuts off the impediment of the household life, the impediment of wife and children, the impediment of relatives, the impediment of possessions; he shaves off his hair and beard, puts on ochre robes, goes forth from the household life into homelessness, approaches the state of ownerlessness, and lives alone, dwells, carries on, and maintains himself alone. How is he alone in the sense of being *without a companion*? When he goes forth, alone he resorts to forest groves, remote lodgings with little sound, little noise, unpopulated, uninhabited, suitable for seclusion. There he lives alone, travels alone, stands alone, sits alone, sleeps alone. How is a paccekasambuddha alone in the sense of *abandoning craving*? Being thus alone, without a partner, dwelling heedful, ardent, and resolute, he undertakes the great striving, disperses Māra together with his army, abandons the net of craving, extensive and adhesive; he dispels it, terminates it, and eliminates it. How is a paccekasambuddha alone as *utterly devoid of lust*? He is alone, utterly devoid of lust through the abandoning of lust; alone, utterly devoid of hatred through the abandoning of hatred; alone, utterly devoid of delusion through the abandoning of delusion; alone, utterly devoid of defilements through the abandoning of defilements. How is a paccekasambuddha alone by *having gone to the one-way path*? The one-way path is the four establishments of mindfulness, the four right kinds of striving, the four bases for spiritual potency, the five faculties, the five powers, the seven enlightenment factors, the noble eightfold path.[404]

How is a paccekasambuddha alone by *having awakened to the unsurpassed pacceka enlightenment*? "Enlightenment" is the knowledge in the four paths, the faculty of wisdom, the power of wisdom, the enlightenment factor of discrimination of qualities, investigation, insight, right view. By that knowledge of enlightenment, a paccekasambuddha awakens to the truth that "all conditioned things are impermanent, all conditioned things are suffering, all phenomena are non-self." He awakens to: "With ignorance as condition, volitional activities [come to be] . . . with the cessation of birth, there is cessation of old age and death." He awakens to: "This is suffering, this is its origin, this is its cessation, this is the way leading to the cessation of suffering. These are the influxes, this is their origin, this is their cessation, this is the way leading to their cessation." He awakens to: "These things should be directly known, these should be fully understood, these should be abandoned, these should be developed, these should be realized." He awakens to the origin and passing away, the gratification, danger, and escape in regard to the six bases for contact, the five aggregates subject to clinging, and the four great elements. He awakens to: "Whatever is subject to origination is all subject to cessation."[405]

One should live:[406] There are these eight kinds of living,[407] namely: for those who possess resolve, living by a posture among the four postures; for those who guard the doors of the sense faculties, living in the sense bases among the internal sense bases; for those who dwell heedfully, living with mindfulness in the four establishments of mindfulness; for those intent on the higher mind, living by concentration upon the four jhānas; for those who possess intelligence, living by knowledge of the four noble truths; for those practicing rightly, living on a path among the four noble paths; for those who have achieved the fruit, living in the attainment of the four fruits of the ascetic life; for the three kinds of buddhas, living among all beings for the good of the world, partly in the case of paccekabuddhas and disciples. As it is said: "*One should live*: There are eight kinds of living, namely, living by a posture," and so forth in detail. [65] One should live in these ways. Or alternatively, another eight kinds of living are stated thus: "One with conviction lives by means of faith . . . (see Nidd II 212–13 just below) . . . and so one lives by living in distinction." One should also live in these ways.

Nidd II 212–13. One should live: There are *eight kinds of living*: living among the postures . . . [as above] . . . living for the good of the world pertains to tathāgatas, arahants, perfectly enlightened ones, and partly in the case of paccekabuddhas, partly in the case of disciples.

There are *another eight kinds of living*: One with conviction lives by means of faith; making an exertion, one lives by means of energy; establishing, one lives by means of mindfulness; being undistracted, one lives by means of concentration; understanding, one lives by means of wisdom; cognizing, one lives by means of consciousness; as one is practicing thus, wholesome qualities are a base (*āyatana*), and so one lives by living among the sense bases; practicing thus one achieves distinction.

There are *still another eight kinds of living*: Through right view, there is living by seeing; through right intention, there is living by application [of the mind]; through right speech, there is living by embracing; through right action, there is living by originating; through right livelihood, there is living by cleansing; through right effort, there is living by exertion; through right mindfulness, there is living by establishment; through right concentration, there is living by non-distraction. These are eight kinds of living. ▮⁝

Like a rhinoceros horn: It is the horn of the rhinoceros animal that is called *khaggavisāṇa*.[408] We will explain the word *kappa* (in *khaggavisāṇakappo*) in the commentary on the Discourse on Blessings (see p. 740). But here it should be understood to mean a counterpart (*paṭibhāga*), as in the statement "We were indeed speaking with the disciple who is like the teacher" (MN I 150,27). What is meant by "like a rhinoceros horn" is "similar to the horn of a rhinoceros."[409]

⁝▮ **Nidd II 213. Like a rhinoceros horn**: As the horn of the rhinoceros is one, without a second, just so the paccekabuddha is like that, similar to that, a counterpart of that. Just as something too salty is said to be like salt, as something too bitter is said to be like bitterness, as something too sweet is said to be like sugar, as something too hot is said to be like fire, as something too cold is said to be like snow, or as a great mass of water is said to be like the ocean, or as a disciple who has attained the power of the superknowledges is said to be like the Teacher, so the paccekabuddha is said to be like that, similar to that, the counterpart of that. He lives rightly in the world alone, without a companion, freed from bondage, and thus he dwells, carries on, behaves, looks after himself, maintains himself, conducts himself. ▮⁝

At this point the commentary on the meaning has been given through the terms. As to the purport and sequence, the verse may be understood thus: "The 'rod,' in the sense explained above, is inflicted on beings when it has not been put down. That rod has been put down toward all beings because it is no longer being inflicted on them and because I am now promoting their well-being through loving-kindness, its opposite. And because the rod has been put down, unlike those people who have not put down the rod, who harm beings with a rod, a knife, a fist, or a clod of earth, I am not harming a single one among them. Based on the loving-kindness meditation subject, I have contemplated with insight whatever is included in [the aggregates of] feeling, perception, volitional activities, and consciousness, as well as any other conditioned things that occur in accordance with it. Thereby I have achieved this pacceka enlightenment." This, firstly, is the purport.

This is the sequence: When he had spoken thus, the ministers asked: "Where will you go now, Bhante?" He then reflected: "Where did the previous paccekabuddhas live?" [66] Having known, he replied: "To Gandhamādana Mountain." Again, they said: "Are you now abandoning us, Bhante? Don't you desire us?" The paccekabuddha then said everything beginning with: "One should not desire a son." This is the purport: "Now I don't even wish for any kind of son among [the four kinds], the biological son and so forth. So how can I wish for a companion like you? Therefore if any among you wish to go with me or to be like me, he should live alone like a rhinoceros horn."

Or alternatively, when the ministers said, "Are you now abandoning us, Bhante? Don't you desire us?" that paccekabuddha answered: "One should not desire a son, how then a companion?" Having seen for himself the excellence of solitary living in the sense stated above, rejoicing, full of rapture and joy, he uttered the joyful utterance: "One should live alone like a rhinoceros horn." Having spoken thus, while the multitude looked on, he rose up into space and went to Gandhamādana.

Now Gandhamādana is situated in the Himalayas[410] beyond seven other mountains: Small Black Mountain, Great Black Mountain, Enveloped by Nāgas, Womb of the Moon, Womb of the Sun, Golden Slope, and Snow Mountain. A slope there called Nandamūlaka is the dwelling place of paccekabuddhas. It has three caves: Golden Cave, Jeweled Cave, and Silver Cave. By the entrance of the Jeweled Cave there is a tree named Mañjūsaka, a yojana high and a yojana wide. All its flowers—whether in the water or on land—especially blossom on the day a paccekabuddha arrives. Surrounding it[411] there is an all-jewel pavilion, where a sweeping wind blows away rubbish; an equalizing wind smoothes out the sand, which consists of gems; a sprinkling wind brings water from Lake Anotatta and sprinkles it; a fragrance-bearing wind brings the fragrances from all the fragrant trees of the Himalayas; a scattering wind scatters flowers and deposits them; [67] and a spreading wind spreads them everywhere. Here there are always prepared seats on which all the paccekabuddhas sit when they assemble on the day a paccekabuddha arrives and on the day of the uposatha. Then a newly arrived[412] paccekabuddha goes there and sits down in a prepared seat. If other paccekabuddhas are present at the time, they immediately assemble and sit in the prepared seats. They then enter a meditative attainment and emerge from it. Then, so that all might congratulate him, the Sangha elder[413] asks the newly arrived paccekabuddha about his meditation subject: "How did you achieve this?" He then answers with a verse that serves as a joyful utterance and an explanation.[414]

When the Blessed One was asked by the Venerable Ānanda, he again recited that same verse, and Ānanda recited it at the council. In this way each verse was recited four times: at the place where the paccekabuddha awakened to enlightenment, at the Mañjūsaka pavilion, at the time Ānanda asked about it, and at the council.

The verse on forming bonds

36. What is the origin? This paccekabodhisatta, too, did the ascetic's duty for 20,000 years in the teaching of the Blessed One Kassapa, in the way stated earlier. Having done the preliminary work on the kasiṇa,[415] he attained the first jhāna, determined the nature of name-and-form, and explored the characteristics. However, since he did not reach the noble path, he was reborn in the brahma world. Having passed away from there, he arose in the womb of the chief queen of the king of Bārāṇasī. Growing up in the aforesaid way, from the time he could distinguish, "This is a woman, that is a man," he was not happy in the hands of his nurses and could not even endure being massaged, bathed, ornamented, and so forth. Only men fed him, and at the time to breastfeed him, his nurses [68] bound him in a bodice and breastfed him while wearing the attire of men. When he smelled the odor of women or heard their voices, he cried, and even when he reached maturity, he did not want to see women. Because of this, they named him Anitthigandha ("Non-Odor of Women").

When the prince turned sixteen, the king thought, "I will establish the family lineage," and he brought suitable girls from various families for him. He ordered a minister: "Make them please the prince." The minister, wishing by some means to get them to please the prince, had an area not far from him encircled by a cloth screen and sent dancers there. The prince, hearing the sounds of singing and musical instruments, asked: "Who is making this sound?" The minister said: "That is the sound of your dancers, lord. Those with merit have such dancers. Rejoice, lord, you are one of great merit." The prince had the minister beaten with a rod and expelled him. The minister reported this to the king. The king, along with the prince's mother, went and apologized to the prince and again sent the minister away.

The prince, feeling extremely troubled by all this, gave fine gold to goldsmiths and commanded them: "Make a statue of a beautiful woman." They made the statue of a woman decked out with all adornments, like one created by the divine craftsman Vissakamma. They showed it to the prince. When the prince saw it, he shook his head with astonishment and sent for his parents. He told them: "If I get a woman like this, I will take her." His parents thought: "Our son has great merit. Surely, there must be some girl in the world who did meritorious deeds with him in past lives." They had the golden statue mounted on a chariot and sent the ministers off, instructing them: "Go, search for a girl like this."

Taking the statue, they traveled through the sixteen major countries, going to each village. They looked over each place, and wherever they saw a crowd of people assembled, at the fords and so forth, they set up the golden statue as if it were a deity, worshiped it with various flowers, fabrics, and adornments, set up a canopy over it, and stood to one side, thinking: "If anyone has seen such a girl, he will start a conversation about it." In such a way, they traveled to all the countries except the realm of Madda, [69] thinking it was just a small country. And so without going there, they turned back.

Then it occurred to them. "Let's go to Madda, too, or else the king will send us out again after we have returned to Bārāṇasī." So they went to the city of Sāgala in the Madda country. Now the king in the city of Sāgala, who was named Maddava, had a daughter sixteen years of age who was very beautiful. Her slave girls had gone to the ford in order to fetch water for her bath. When they saw in the distance the golden statue set up by the ministers, they said: "The princess sent us to get water, yet she has come herself." However, when they got close, they said: "This isn't our mistress. Our mistress is even more beautiful than this." The ministers, on hearing this, approached the king and in a suitable way requested his daughter. He gave her. They then sent a message to the king of Bārāṇasī: "The girl has been found. Will you come yourself or should we bring her?" The king sent back a message: "If I were to come, there would be trouble for the country. Bring her yourselves."

Having taken the girl, the ministers left the city and sent a message to the prince: "We have found a girl similar to the golden statue." When the prince heard this, he was overcome by lust and lost the first jhāna.[416] He sent a series of messengers, urging them: "Bring her quickly, bring her quickly." Everywhere along the way they spent only one night, and when they reached Bārāṇasī, staying outside the city, they sent a message to the king: "Should we enter today or not?" The king commanded them: "A girl brought from an eminent family should be led in with great honor after we have performed auspicious rites. Take her first to the park." They did so. However, being extremely delicate, she was shaken up by the jolting of the vehicle and fatigued by the journey. Thus she contracted a wind sickness,wilted like a flower, and passed away that very night.

The ministers wept, saying: "We have missed out on our honors." The king and citizens wept, saying: "Our family lineage has perished." There was great mayhem in the city. As soon as the prince heard the news, he was stricken with grief. Then the prince set about digging up the root of sorrow. He reflected: "This sorrow does not occur in one who has not been born but only in one who has been born. Therefore, sorrow is conditioned by birth. [70] But by what is birth conditioned?" He then saw: "Birth is conditioned by existence." Attending carefully in such a way, through the spiritual might of his past development, he saw dependent origination in direct and reverse order, and then, even while sitting there exploring conditioned things, he realized pacceka enlightenment.

The ministers, having seen him sitting with peaceful faculties and peaceful mind enjoying the bliss of the path and fruit, prostrated to him and said: "Do not sorrow, lord.

Jambudīpa is large. We will bring a girl even more beautiful than her." He replied: "I am not sorrowing. I am a sorrowless paccekabuddha."

From this point on, we will comment on the verse, omitting whatever is similar to what was said about the first verse. But in the commentary on the verse, it is said, **For one who has formed bonds**. Here, there are five kinds of bonding: by way of sight, hearing, the body, conversation, and shared enjoyment.[417]

Bonding through sight is the lust arisen when they see one another by way of an eye-consciousness process. In this connection, in Sri Lanka, a landowner's daughter saw a young bhikkhu, a reciter of the Dīgha Nikāya residing in the Kalyāṇa Vihāra, walking on alms round in Kāḷadīghagāma. She fell in love with him. Since she could not win him over, she died. When he saw a piece of her sarong, thinking, "I did not get to live together with the girl who wore this cloth," he became heartbroken and died. That youth is an example.[418]

Bonding through hearing is the lust arisen when, by way of an ear-consciousness process, one hears a woman endowed with beauty being described by others or one has personally heard the sound of her laughing, talking, or singing. An example is the youth Tissa, residing at the Pañcaggaḷa Grotto. The daughter of the resident smith of Girigāma, along with five other girls, had gone to a lotus pond, where they bathed and decorated themselves with garlands. While he was traveling through the sky, he heard the girl singing with a loud voice. When he heard her voice he was overcome by sensual lust, lost his distinction, and came to misery and disaster.

Bonding through the body is the lust arisen by caressing one another's bodies. [71] And here the example is a young bhikkhu who preached the Dhamma. It is said that a young bhikkhu at the Mahāvihāra was preaching the Dhamma. When a crowd had come, the king together with his harem arrived. Then the king's daughter was overcome by strong lust based on his form and voice, and he felt the same for her. Having seen this, the king took note of it and erected a screen around her. But they caressed one another and embraced. Having removed the screen, when people looked, they saw that the two had died.

Bonding through conversation is the lust arisen by addressing and conversing with one another. *Bonding through shared enjoyment* is the lust arisen when bhikkhus and bhikkhunīs use things in common. An example is that of the bhikkhu and bhikkhunī who in these two ways fell into a Pārājika.[419] It is said that at the festival of the Maricavaṭṭi Mahāvihāra, King Duṭṭhagāmiṇi the Fearless prepared a great alms offering, which he presented to both Sanghas.[420] When hot porridge was offered, since the youngest sāmaṇera did not have a stand to receive it, the youngest sāmaṇerī gave him her ivory bracelet.[421] The two conversed. Later, after both had received full ordination and had spent sixty years as monastics, they met in India. As they spoke, they remembered their past conversation. At once affection arose in them and they transgressed the training rule, falling into a Pārājika.

When one has formed bonds in any of these ways, **there is affection**,[422] that is, strong lust arises conditioned by the earlier lust. Then, **following on affection, this suffering arises**: Following upon that affection, various kinds of suffering pertaining to the present life and future lives, such as sorrow and lamentation, arise, are produced, come to be, are born. But others say "bonding" is the fixing of the mind on the object. From this comes affection, and from affection comes this suffering. [72]

⁞▮ Nidd II 213–14. Bonding: There are two kinds of bonding: bonding through sight and bonding through hearing. What is *bonding through sight*? Here, someone sees a woman or a girl who is beautiful, lovely, graceful, possessing an extremely beautiful complexion. Having seen her, he grasps the sign through her features: the beauty of her hair, face, eyes, ears, nose, lips, teeth, mouth, and other features. Having seen this, he delights in her, welcomes her, yearns for her, longs for her, and becomes bound by lust. What is *bonding through hearing*? Here, someone hears: "In such and such a village or town there is a woman or girl who is beautiful, lovely, graceful, possessing an extremely beautiful complexion." Having heard this, he delights in her, welcomes her, yearns for her, longs for her, and becomes bound by lust.

Nidd II 214. Affection: There are two kinds of affection, affection through craving and affection through views. What is *affection through craving*? Setting a boundary through craving, setting a limit, one takes possession and claims it as one's own: "This is mine, that is mine; this much is mine, that extent is mine." One claims ownership over forms, sounds, odors, tastes, tactile objects; over bedsheets, coverings, male and female slaves . . . realms and countries and even over the great earth, as far as the 108 streams of craving. What is *affection through views*? The twentyfold view of the personal entity, the tenfold wrong view, the tenfold extreme view, any such view . . . as far as the sixty-two views.[423]

Having spoken this half-verse with the meaning as analyzed, the paccekabuddha said: "Since the suffering of sorrow and so forth arises following on this affection, digging up the root of that suffering, I achieved pacceka enlightenment." When he had spoken the ministers said to him: "Then what are we to do now, Bhante?" He replied: "Whoever wishes to be free from this suffering—whether yourselves or anyone else—**discerning the danger born of affection, one should live alone like a rhinoceros horn**." And here it should be understood that "discerning the danger born of affection" is said with reference to the statement "following on affection, this suffering arises." Or alternatively, [what is meant is that] "I achieved this while discerning as it really is this danger born of affection, that 'for one who has formed bonds' by the aforementioned kinds of bonding 'there is affection' [and] 'following on affection, this suffering arises.'" Having connected the lines together in such a way, the fourth line should be understood to have been stated as a joyful utterance, in the way explained earlier. Everything following this is similar to what was explained in relation to the previous verse.

The verse on friends dear to one's heart

37. What is the origin? This paccekabodhisatta, having arisen in the way explained in connection with the previous verse, was exercising kingship in Bārāṇasī. Having attained the first jhāna, he investigated: "Which is better, the ascetic's duty or kingship?" He then handed his kingdom over to four of his ministers and did the ascetic's duty. Though he had told the ministers to rule righteously and justly, they took bribes and ruled unrighteously. Having taken a bribe while prosecuting the owners, one day they banished a favorite of the king. He entered along with the king's meal stewards and reported everything. The next day the king himself went to the judgment hall. A great crowd of people was making a commotion as if there were a big fight, crying out: "The ministers are taking from the owners what is rightfully theirs." Then the king, having emerged from the judgment hall, went to the top of his palace and sat down, intending to enter a meditative attainment. However, because his mind was distracted by the noise, [73] he could not attain it. Thinking, "What good is kingship when the ascetic's duty is better?" he abandoned his zeal for kingship[424] and again reached a meditative attainment. Practicing insight in the way explained earlier, he realized pacceka enlightenment, and when asked about his meditation subject, he recited this verse.

In this verse, **friends** are such by way of befriending; **those dear to one's heart** are such by winning one's heart. For some people are just friends, because they wish exclusively for one's welfare, but they are not dear to one's heart. Some are just dear to one's heart, because they bring happiness to one's heart when coming, going, standing, sitting, and conversing, but they are not friends. And some are both dear to one's heart and also friends, for both those reasons.[425]

These are twofold: householders and homeless ones. Householder friends are of three kinds: the helper, the one who shares one's happiness and suffering, and the one who is sympathetic. Homeless ones are especially those who point out what is good.[426] These each possess four factors. As it is said:[427]

> "In four cases, householder's son, a helpful friend can be understood. He protects you when you are heedless; he looks after your property when you are heedless; he is a refuge when you are frightened; and when some need arises, he gives you twice the wealth required."

So too:

> "In four cases a friend who shares one's happiness and suffering can be understood. He reveals his secrets to

> you; he guards your own secrets; he does not abandon you when you are in trouble; and he would even sacrifice his life for your sake."

So too:

> "In four cases a sympathetic friend can be understood. He does not rejoice in your misfortune; he rejoices in your good fortune; he stops those who speak dispraise of you; and he commends those who speak praise of you."

So too:

> "In four cases a friend who points out what is good can be understood. He restrains you from evil; he enjoins you in the good; he informs you of what you have not heard; and he points out to you the path to heaven."

Of those, it is householders that are intended here. But in regard to the meaning, it applies to all.

⁝▮ **Nidd II 218. Friends**: There are two kinds of friends, householder friends and homeless friends. What is *a householder friend*? Here, someone gives what is hard to give, relinquishes what is hard to relinquish, does what is hard to do, endures what is hard to endure. He reveals his secrets to you; he conceals your secrets; he does not abandon you when you are in trouble; he would even sacrifice his life for your sake; he does not despise you when you are poor.

What is *a homeless friend*? Here, a bhikkhu is dear and agreeable, respected and esteemed, a speaker and one who endures speech, who gives deep talks; he does not enjoin you in what is wrong but encourages you in the higher good behavior, in developing the four establishments of mindfulness . . . the four right strivings . . . the four bases for spiritual power . . . the five faculties . . . the five powers . . . the seven enlightenment factors . . . the noble eightfold path. ▮⁝

Sympathizing with those friends dear to one's heart, one wishes to promote their happiness [74] and to remove their suffering. **One forsakes the good**: one forsakes, destroys, the good that is threefold by way of this present life, future lives, and the supreme good; and again threefold by way of one's own good, the good of others, and the good of both. One forsakes, destroys, the good in two ways: by destroying that which has been obtained and by failing to produce that which has not been obtained. **With mind attached**: One is attached in mind when one puts oneself in a low position, thinking: "I cannot live without him; he is my resort; he is my support." One is also attached in mind when one puts oneself in a high position, thinking: "They cannot live without me; I am their resort; I am their support." But here it is one attached in mind in such a way [by putting oneself in a high position] that is intended.

This peril: this peril of forsaking the good, which he said with reference to the loss of his own meditative attainment. **In intimacy**: Intimacy is threefold, by way of intimacy with craving, views, and friends. "Intimacy with craving" is craving in its 108 divisions (see AN II 212–13). "Intimacy with views" is views in their sixty-two divisions.[428] "Intimacy with friends" is sympathy with friends because one's mind is attached to them. It is the latter that is intended here, for it was because of this that his attainment was lost. Hence he said: "Seeing this peril in intimacy, I achieved [this state]." The rest should be understood as similar to what was already explained.

The verse on the bamboo shoot

38. What is the origin? In the past, it is said, three paccekabodhisattas had gone forth in the teaching of the Blessed One Kassapa. Having fulfilled the observance of going and coming for 20,000 years, they arose in the deva world. Having passed away from there, the eldest was reborn in the family of the king of Bārāṇasī, the others in families of provincial kings. These two learned a meditation subject, abandoned their kingdoms, and went forth into homelessness, and eventually they became paccekabuddhas. While living on the Nandamūlaka Slope, one day, after emerging from a meditative attainment, they asked themselves: "What was the kamma by reason of which we have attained this world-transcending bliss?" Reflecting, they saw their own practice in the time of the Buddha Kassapa. Then they asked themselves, "Where is the third?" [75] and they saw that he was ruling over Bārāṇasī. They remembered his excellent qualities thus: "He was naturally possessed of excellent qualities such as fewness of desires and so forth. He used to exhort us, speak to us, endure our words, and censure evil. Let us now show him an object and release him." Seeking an opportunity, one day they saw him going to the park decked out with all adornments. Coming through the sky, they stood at the foot of a cluster of bamboos by the entrance to the park. The multitude looked at the king, insatiable with the sight of him. Just then the king thought: "Is there anyone not interested in seeing me?" Looking around, he saw the paccekabuddhas. As soon as he caught sight of them, he felt affection for them.

He descended from the back of his elephant, approached them with a peaceful demeanor, and asked: "Bhante, what are you?" They said: "Great king, we are called 'not getting stuck'." – "What is the meaning of 'not getting stuck'?" – "Not held fast, great king."

Then, pointing to the cluster of bamboos, they said: "Great king, just as this cluster of bamboos stands with its roots, trunks, limbs, and branches completely woven together, such that a man with a knife in his hand would not be able to cut the roots, pull on them, and draw them out, so you yourself have become entangled inside and out, stuck and entwined, and held fast there. But just as this bamboo shoot, though arisen in their midst, is not held fast by anything because it has not sent forth branches, and it is possible to cut it at the top or at the root and draw it out, so, not getting stuck anywhere, we go freely in all directions."

Immediately they attained the fourth jhāna, and while the king looked on, they returned to the Nandamūlaka Slope through the sky. The king then reflected: "When will I, too, be one who does not get stuck?" Having sat down right there, he developed insight and realized pacceka enlightenment. When asked about his meditation subject, in the way explained earlier, he recited this verse. [76]

In this verse, **entwined**: fastened, entangled, woven together.[429] **For wives and sons**: for wives, sons, and daughters.[430] **Concern**: craving and affection. What is meant? "Just as widespread bamboo becomes entwined, so concern for wives and sons entangles one with those objects and one thus becomes entwined with them. In this way, because of that concern, I was entwined just like the widespread bamboo. Having seen such danger in concern, cutting off that concern with the knowledge of the path, like this bamboo shoot, without getting stuck in forms and so forth, or in things seen and so forth, or in greed and so forth, or in regard to desire-realm existence and so forth because of craving, conceit, and views, I achieved pacceka enlightenment." The rest should be understood in the way explained earlier.

The verse on the deer in the forest

39. What is the origin? It is said that in the teaching of the Blessed One Kassapa a meditating bhikkhu passed away and arose in a rich, wealthy, affluent family of a financier in Bārāṇasī. He was well off. Then he committed adultery, and when he died he was born in hell. Having experienced torment there, through the residual result, he took rebirth as a female in the womb of a financier's wife. Now the bodies of those who come from hell are still hot, and thus the financier's wife carried the embryo in her womb with trouble and difficulty, as if the womb were burning. In time she gave birth to a girl. From the day she was born, she was despised by her parents and the other relatives and family members. When she reached maturity, her husband and in-laws in the family into which she married also despised her and considered her unpleasant and disagreeable.

When the Constellation Festival was announced,[431] her husband did not want to celebrate with her; instead, he brought along a prostitute. Having heard of this from her slave women, she went to her husband and, having mollified him in various ways, she said: "Husband, even if a woman is the youngest daughter of ten kings, or the daughter of a wheel-turning monarch, she is still the servant of her husband. When her husband does not speak to her, she feels as much pain as she would if she had been impaled on a stake. [77] If I deserve to be cared for, I should be cared for. If not, then I should be dismissed, and I will return to my own family."

Her husband replied: "Let it be, dear. Do not sorrow. Get prepared to celebrate. We will celebrate the Constellation

Festival." Elated merely by being spoken to just this much, thinking, "Tomorrow I will get to celebrate the Constellation Festival," she prepared many dishes and snacks. On the following day her husband went to the festival grounds without informing her. She kept on looking down the path, thinking, "Now he will send for me, now he will send for me," but seeing that it was already afternoon, she sent people to find him. They returned and informed her: "Your husband has gone." She took all the food she had prepared, mounted a vehicle, and set out for the park.

Just then a paccekabuddha on Nandamūlaka Slope, having emerged from cessation[432] on the seventh day, washed his face in Lake Anotatta, chewed on a toothwood of the nāga creeper, and pondered: "Where shall I walk for alms today?" Having seen that financier's daughter, he knew: "When she shows me honor, that kamma will be exhausted." Having stood on the Red Arsenic Terrace, which extends for sixty yojanas in proximity to the slope, he robed himself, and taking his bowl and extra robe, he entered the jhāna that is the basis for superknowledge. Having come through the sky, he descended on the path opposite her, facing in the direction of Bārāṇasī. The slave women saw him and reported this to the financier's daughter. She descended from her vehicle, paid homage to him, took his bowl, and filled it with flavorful foods of various kinds. She covered it with a lotus flower, placed a lotus flower beneath it, and taking a bouquet of flowers in her hand, she returned to the paccekabuddha. She gave him the bowl, paid homage to him, and then, holding the bouquet of flowers, she made the wish: "Bhante, like these flowers, may I be dear and agreeable to the multitude wherever I arise." Having made such a wish, she made a second wish: "Bhante, dwelling in the womb is painful. May I avoid such a fate and be reborn in a lotus flower." She then made a third wish: "Bhante, womanhood is repulsive. Even the daughter of a wheel-turning monarch must come under the control of another. Therefore, having abandoned womanhood, may I become a man." [78] She also made a fourth wish: "Bhante, having overcome this suffering of saṃsāra, in the end may I attain the deathless which you have attained."

Having made these four wishes, she gave the bouquet of

lotus flowers to the paccekabuddha, prostrated herself fully before him,[433] and made this fifth wish: "May my scent and color be similar to those of a flower." Then the paccekabuddha, having taken the bowl and the bouquet of flowers, stood in the sky and said:

"Whatever you wish for and desire,
may it quickly reach success.
May all your aspirations be fulfilled
like the moon on the fifteenth."[434]

Having blessed the financier's daughter with this verse, he resolved: "Let the financier's daughter see me as I am going." He then returned to Nandamūlaka Slope. When the financier's daughter saw him, she was filled with great rapture. The unwholesome kamma she had done in an earlier existence, failing to find an opportunity to ripen, was exhausted, and she became as pure as a copper pot washed with tamarind. At once, everyone in her husband's family and her own family appreciated her, and ashamed of their behavior, they sent her presents accompanied by endearing words.

Her husband sent his men, telling them: "Quickly, quickly, bring my wife. I forgot about her when I came to the park." From then on, he cherished her as if she were sandalwood applied on the breast, a string of pearls, and a garland of flowers. She enjoyed the pleasure of authority and wealth for the rest of her life, and after death she arose as a male in a lotus flower in the deva world. When that young deva went anywhere, he went in the cup of a lotus flower; and so too when standing, sitting, and lying down, he lay down in the cup of a lotus flower. They named him "the young deva Great Lotus." Through the might of his psychic power, he wandered through the six deva worlds in direct and reverse order. [79]

The king of Bārāṇasī at that time had 20,000 women, but he did not obtain a son from even one. The ministers informed the king: "Lord, a son is needed to continue the family lineage. If you don't have a biological son, then a territorial one will maintain the family lineage." The king replied: "Except for the chief queen, make the remaining dancing girls engage in righteous prostitution for seven days."[435] He sent them outside to carry on in any way they wished, but even then he did not gain a son. Again the ministers said to him: "Great king, your chief queen is foremost among all the women in merit and wisdom. Perhaps our lord may obtain a son from her." The king reported this matter to the chief queen. She said: "Great king, a woman who is virtuous and truthful in speech may obtain a son. How can a son come to one devoid of moral shame and moral dread?" She then ascended the palace, undertook the five precepts, and pondered them again and again.

While the virtuous queen was pondering the five precepts, as soon as the wish for a son arose in her, Sakka's seat became hot. Seeking the reason for this, Sakka understood the situation and decided: "I will grant the virtuous queen the boon of a son." He arrived through space, stood before the queen, and asked her: "What boon will you choose, O queen?" – "A son, great king." – "I will grant you a son, O queen. Do not be morose." He returned to the deva world and considered: "Is there anyone here whose life span is at an end?" He then knew: "Great Lotus is about to pass away from here and arise in a higher deva world." So he went to his palace and made a request: "Dear Great Lotus, go to the human world." Great Lotus replied: "Do not speak in such a way, great king. The human world is repulsive." – "Dear, it was because you had done merit in the human world that you have been reborn here. While living there, you should fulfill the pāramīs. So go, dear." – "Staying in the womb is painful, great king. I can't endure it." – "Why should you have to stay in the womb, dear? For you have created such kamma that you will be reborn in the cup of a lotus flower. Go, dear!" Being asked again and again, he consented.

Then, having passed away from the deva world, Great Lotus [80] was reborn in the cup of a lotus flower in the Stone Slab Pond in the park of the king of Bārāṇasī. And that night, just before dawn, the chief queen saw in a dream that she had gone to the park accompanied by her retinue of 20,000 women and seemed to obtain a son in the Stone Slab Pond, a lake of lotuses. When it became light, observing the precepts, she went there just as in the dream and saw a single lotus flower, which was neither by the bank nor in deep water. As soon as she saw it, affection toward a son arose in her. She entered the pond herself and grabbed the flower. As soon as she took hold of the flower it blossomed. There she saw a boy looking like a golden statue seated on a platter.[436] At the sight of him she cried out: "I've gained a son." The multitude congratulated her a thousand times and sent a message to the king. When the king heard the news, he asked: "Where did she get him?" When he heard what happened, he said: "The park, the pond, and the lotus are surely ours. Therefore, because he has been born in our territory, he's a territorial son." Having brought him into the city, he had 20,000 women nurse him. Whatever woman understood the boy's preference and gave him the kind of food he wished for received a thousand coins as a reward. All of Bārāṇasī was astir with excitement, and all the people sent thousands of presents to the prince.

Having had various foods brought to him, and being told, "Eat this, have a bite of that," the prince felt harassed and disgusted with the food, so he went to the palace entrance and played with a red ball. At the time a certain paccekabuddha was living in Isipatana and depended on Bārāṇasī for alms. Having risen early, he completed all his tasks—the duties connected with his lodging, the needs of the body, and so forth—emerged from seclusion, and considered: "Where will I receive alms today?" Having seen the prosperity of the prince, he investigated: "What kamma did he do in the past?" He understood: "He gave almsfood to one like me and made four wishes. Three of these have been fulfilled, but one remains.[437] By some means I will show him an object." [81]

While walking for alms he went by near the prince. When the prince saw him, he said: "Ascetic! Ascetic! Do not come here; for these people will trouble you, too: 'Eat this, have a bite of that.'" With just this one statement, the paccekabuddha turned back and entered his lodging. The prince said to his retinue: "This ascetic turned back as soon as I spoke to him. Is he angry with me?" Even though they told him, "Those who have gone forth, lord, do not get angry but maintain themselves on whatever the faithful give them," he informed his parents: "That ascetic is really vexed with me. I will apologize to him." Then he mounted an elephant and with the full pomp of royalty he proceeded to Isipatana. There he saw a herd of deer and asked: "What are these?" They told him: "These, master, are called deer." – "Do people pamper them, saying: 'Eat this, have a bite of that, taste this'?" – "No, master. They live wherever they can easily obtain grass and water." The prince took this as his object of thought, reflecting: "When can I live in such a way as they do, living wherever they wish without being guarded by others?"

The paccekabuddha, knowing that the prince was coming, swept his walkway and the path to his lodging, making them smooth,[438] and then he walked back and forth one or two times, leaving visible footprints. Then he swept the areas around his daytime dwelling place and his leaf hut, making them smooth, and then he left visible footprints of his entering but did not leave footprints of his departure. Then he went elsewhere.

When the prince arrived there, he saw that the area had been swept and made smooth. He heard it said by the people in his retinue: "It seems that the paccekabuddha lives here." He said: "Just this morning that ascetic was vexed. Now, if he were to see the area where he lives trampled upon by elephants and horses, he would be even more vexed. You stay here." He descended from his elephant and entered the lodging all alone. When he saw the footprints in the area that had been made thoroughly smooth as though in fulfillment of a duty, [82] he thought: "This ascetic who had been walking back and forth here did not think of working at business and so forth. Surely, he must have thought only of his own welfare."[439] Still investigating, he went to his daytime dwelling place. There he saw his footprints and reflected in the same way. He again followed the footprints [to the hut], opened the door, and entered. He looked around without seeing the paccekabuddha, but he saw the stone slab that the paccekabuddha used as his seat. He again reflected: "The ascetic who had been sitting here did not think of working at business and so forth. Surely, he must have thought only of the ascetic's duty for the sake of his own welfare." He sat down and, reflecting carefully, fulfilled in sequence serenity and insight and realized pacceka enlightenment. Enjoying the world-transcending bliss, he did not come out.

The ministers said: "The king's command is serious. He might even punish us, saying: 'You took my son and delayed long in the forest.' Let's take the prince and go." When they entered the hut, they did not see the paccekabuddha but only the prince sitting in such a way. They discussed the situation: "Since he did not see the paccekabuddha, he is just sitting and reflecting." They said to him: "Lord, the paccekabuddha surely lives here; he has not gone anywhere. Tomorrow we will come back and apologize to him. Don't think: 'I did not see the paccekabuddha.' Come, let's go." The prince said: "I am not thinking. I am beyond thought." – "What did you do, master?" – "I have become a paccekabuddha." When asked about his meditation subject, in the way explained earlier, he recited this verse: "As a deer unbound in the forest."

In this verse, **a deer** (*miga*): there are two kinds of deer, the antelope and the spotted deer.[440] Further, *miga* is a designation for all four-footed animals that dwell in the forest, but here the spotted deer is intended. **In the forest**: [83] apart from a village and the vicinity of a village, the rest is considered forest (see Vin III 46,30); but here a park is intended. Therefore, what is meant is "in a park." **Unbound**: not bound by anything such as a rope and so forth; by this he shows living freely. **Goes off to graze wherever it wants**: It goes to graze in whatever region it wants. It goes as far as it wants. And it eats whatever it wants. For this was said by the Blessed One:

> "Suppose, bhikkhus, a forest deer is wandering in the forest wilds: it walks confidently, stands confidently, sits confidently, lies down confidently. Why is that? Because it is out of the hunter's range. So too, quite secluded from sensual pleasures . . . a bhikkhu enters upon and dwells in the first jhāna. This bhikkhu is said to have blindfolded Māra, to have deprived Māra's eye of its opportunity, to have become invisible to the Evil One," and so on in detail. (MN I 174–75)

A wise person: an intelligent person. **Freedom** is acting in accordance with one's own will, without being subject to others. **Looking out for** means looking upon with the eye of wisdom. Or alternatively, it means with an eye for free qualities and free persons. For the world-transcending qualities—and the persons who possess them—are free because they do not come under the control of the defilements. Freedom is a description of their state. One looks out for that.

Nidd II 223. Free: Two kinds of free: a quality that is free and a person that is free. What *quality is free*? The four establishments of mindfulness, the four right kinds of striving, the four bases for spiritual potency, the five faculties, the five powers, the seven factors of enlightenment, the noble eightfold path. What *person is free*? One possessing this free quality is called a person who is free. **A wise person, looking out for freedom**: A wise person looking out for the state of freedom, seeing it, surveying it, meditating upon it, examining it—"a wise person, looking out for freedom, should live alone like a rhinoceros horn."

What is meant [by the verse]? "I was thinking: 'When can I move about like a deer unbound in the forest, which goes off to graze wherever it wants?' While you were surrounding me on all sides, I was bound and could not go wherever I want. [84] Because I could not go wherever I want, I saw the benefit in being able to go wherever one wants. When my serenity and insight gradually reached fulfillment, I then realized pacceka enlightenment. Therefore any other wise man, looking out for his freedom, should live alone like a rhinoceros horn." The rest should be understood in the way stated.

The verse on being addressed

40. What is the origin? In the past, it is said, there was a king named Ekavajjika ("Spoken-to-Alone") Brahmadatta, who was of a gentle nature. When his ministers wished to consult with him about whether something was right or wrong, they each led him off separately to one side. Then one day, while he was taking his siesta, a certain man asked him to go off to one side, saying: "Lord, I have something you must hear." He got up and went. Again, one asked him while he was sitting in the great assembly hall; one while he was on the back of his elephant; one while he was on horseback; one when he was in a golden chariot; one when he was sitting in a palanquin on the way to the park. The king descended and went off to one side. Another asked him while he was making a tour of the country, and to hear what he had to say, he descended from his elephant and went off to one side.

In this way, having become known as "Spoken-to-Alone," he

became disenchanted and went forth.[441] The ministers increased in power. One of them went to the king and said: "Great king, give me such and such a country." The king replied: "But so and so governs it." He did not accept the king's word, but thinking, "I will take it and govern it," he went there and provoked a quarrel. Both ministers came to the king and reported each other's faults. Having realized, "There is no way to satisfy them," seeing the danger in their greed, the king developed insight and realized pacceka enlightenment. In the way explained earlier, he recited this verse as a joyful utterance. [85]

This is its meaning: "While staying **in the midst of companions**, when **resting** at one's siesta, and **standing** in the great assembly hall, and **going** to the park, and **traveling** on a tour of the country, **one is addressed** in various ways: 'Listen to me about this, give me this,' and so forth. Therefore, having become disenchanted with this, I chose the going forth, which is resorted to by noble people, has numerous benefits, is extremely blissful, and yet is not coveted, not desired, by vile persons who are overcome by greed and other defilements. **Looking out for the freedom that is not coveted**—[free] by way of qualities and persons, and [free] because it does not come under the control of others—I undertook insight and gradually achieved pacceka enlightenment." The rest by the method explained.

The verse on play and delight

41. What is the origin? In Bārāṇasī there was a king named Ekaputtaka ("One-Son") Brahmadatta. He had one son, who was as dear and agreeable to him as his own life. He would take his son along whenever he engaged in any of his activities. One day, when he went to the park, he left his son behind. That same day, the prince fell ill and died. The ministers cremated the body without informing the king, afraid that because of his affection for his son, the news would break the king's heart. In the park, the king got drunk and did not even think of his son. So too the next day when bathing and eating. Then, as he was sitting after his meal, he remembered his son and said: "Bring me my son." In a suitable manner, they reported the news to him.

Then, while overcome by sorrow, the king attended carefully: "When this exists, that comes to be. With the arising of this, that arises." In this way, he gradually explored dependent origination in direct and reverse order [86] and realized pacceka enlightenment. The rest, except for the commentary on the verse, is similar to what was said in connection with the verse on bonding (see pp. 427–28).

But in the commentary on the meaning, **play** is twofold: bodily and verbal. Bodily play is playing with elephants, horses, bows, and swords, and so forth. Verbal play is singing, reciting stanzas, playing the mouth harp, and so forth.[442] **Delight** means delight in the five strands of sensual pleasure. [Affection for a son] is **vast** in that it penetrates one's whole being, right down to the bone marrow.[443] The rest is clear. The sequence, and everything that follows, should be understood in the way explained in relation to the verse on bonding.

The verse on at home in the four directions

42. What is the origin? In the past, it is said, five paccekabodhisattas had gone forth in the teaching of the Blessed One Kassapa. Having fulfilled the observance of going and coming for 20,000 years, they arose in the deva world. Having passed away from there, the eldest became the king of Bārāṇasī, and the others became provincial kings. The four provincial kings learned a meditation subject, abandoned their kingship, and gradually became paccekabuddhas. While living on the Nandamūlaka Slope, one day, having emerged from meditative attainment, they directed their attention to their own kamma and their friend, in the way explained in connection with the verse on the bamboo shoot (see pp. 433–34). Having known, they sought in some way to show an object to the king of Bārāṇasī.

Three times during the night the king woke up frightened, and in his fear he cried out and ran to the rooftop. His chaplain, having risen early, asked him whether he had slept well. "How could I sleep well, teacher?" he replied and told him all the news. The chaplain thought: "It isn't possible to remove this illness by any medical treatment such as an emetic. [87] But I need a means to earn my keep." He then said to the king, frightening him even more: "Great king, this is a portent that you will lose your kingdom, face an obstacle to your life, or undergo some other calamity." Then, to pacify him, the chaplain instructed the king to perform a sacrifice: "You should perform a sacrifice and make an offering of so many elephants, horses, chariots, and so forth, and so much bullion and gold."

Then the paccekabuddhas, having seen many thousands of animals being amassed for the sacrifice, realized: "If this deed is done, it will be hard for him to become enlightened. Let's go there quickly and see him." So they came in the way explained in connection with the verse on the bamboo shoot, and while walking for alms, went in file into the king's court. The king, while standing at his window looking down at the courtyard, saw them down below, and as soon as he spotted them affection arose in him. He summoned them, invited them to seats prepared on the upper terrace, and respectfully fed them. When the meal was finished, he asked: "Who are you?" – "We are called 'those at home in the four directions,' great king." – "What does this mean, Bhante, 'at home in the four directions'?" – "We have no fear or anxiety anywhere in the four directions, great king." – "How is it, Bhante, that you have no fear?" – "Great king, we develop loving-kindness, compassion, altruistic joy, and equanimity. Hence we have no fear." Having said this, they got up from their seats and returned to their own dwelling place.

The king then reflected: "These ascetics say that they have no fear because they develop loving-kindness and the other virtues, but the brahmins commend the slaughter of many thousands of animals. Whose statement is true?" It then occurred to him: "The ascetics wash off what is impure with what is pure, but the brahmins wash off what is impure with what is impure. It isn't possible to wash off what is impure with what is impure, so the statement of the monks must be true." He developed the four divine abodes, beginning with loving-kindness, according to the method, "May all beings be happy!" and so forth. Then, with a mind pervaded by benevolence, [88] he ordered his ministers: "Release all the animals. Let them drink cool water and eat green grass. Let a cool breeze blow upon them."[444] They did so.

Then, while sitting right there, the king reflected: "Because of the advice of my good friends, I am free from an evil deed." Having developed insight, he realized pacceka enlightenment. At his meal time, his ministers told him, "It is time to eat, great king," but he replied, "I am not a king," all in the way explained earlier. Then he recited this verse as a joyful utterance and explanation.

In this verse, **at home in the four directions**: dwelling at ease in the four directions. One "at home in the four directions" [can be understood] also as one for whom the four directions have been pervaded by the development of the divine abodes, according to the method, "He dwells pervading one direction," and so forth.[445] **Unrepelled**: not repelled by beings or conditioned things anywhere in those directions because of fear. **Contented**: contented by way of the twelve kinds of contentment.[446] **With anything whatsoever**: with a superior or inferior requisite. **Obstacles**: This is a designation for bodily and mental disasters, both external ones such as lions and tigers and so forth, and internal ones such as sensual desire and so forth. **Enduring obstacles**: One endures those obstacles by patient acceptance and by such qualities as energy and so forth. **Fearless** through the absence of paralyzing fear.

What is meant? "Like those four ascetics, 'being content with any kind of requisite,' one is established in contentment, the foundation of the practice. One is 'at home in the four directions' through the development of loving-kindness and so forth toward the four directions, and 'unrepelled' through the absence of fear that causes repulsion toward beings and conditioned things.[447] Because one is at home in the four directions, one can endure any obstacles of the kind stated above, and because one is unrepelled one is fearless. Having seen these excellent qualities of the practice, having practiced carefully, I have achieved pacceka enlightenment." Or alternatively: [89] "Having known, 'By being contented with anything like those ascetics, one is at home in the four directions in the way explained,' desiring to be at home in the four directions, I practiced carefully and have achieved it. Therefore, anyone else who desires such a state, enduring obstacles by being at home in the four directions, and being fearless through the absence of repulsion, should wander alone like the horn of a rhinoceros." The rest in the way already explained.

Nidd II 225–26. **At home in the four directions:** The paccekabuddha dwells pervading one quarter with a mind imbued with loving-kindness, likewise the second quarter, the third quarter, and the fourth quarter. Thus above, below, across, and everywhere and with all his heart, he dwells pervading the entire world with a mind imbued with loving-kindness, vast, exalted, measureless, without enmity, without ill will. He dwells pervading one quarter with a mind imbued with compassion . . . with a mind imbued with altruistic joy . . . with a mind imbued with equanimity . . . vast, exalted, measureless, without enmity, without ill will.

Unrepelled: Because he has developed loving-kindness, beings in the eastern quarter are not repulsive to him . . . beings below are not repulsive to him, beings above are not repulsive to him. Because he has developed compassion . . . altruistic joy . . . equanimity, beings in the eastern quarter are not repulsive to him . . . beings below are not repulsive to him, beings above are not repulsive to him.

Contented with anything whatsoever: The paccekabuddha is content with any kind of robe, and he speaks in praise of contentment with any kind of robe, and he does not engage in a wrong search, in what is improper, for the sake of a robe. If he does not get a robe he is not agitated, and if he gets one he uses it without being tied to it, uninfatuated with it, not blindly absorbed in it, seeing the danger in it, understanding the escape. Yet because of this he does not extol himself or disparage others. One who is skillful in this, diligent, clearly comprehending and ever mindful, is said to be a paccekabuddha who stands in an ancient, primal noble lineage. He is content with any kind of almsfood . . . with any kind of lodging . . . with any kind of medicinal requisites . . . He is said to be a paccekabuddha who stands in an ancient, primal noble lineage.[448]

Nidd II 226–27. **Obstacles**. There are two kinds of obstacles: obvious obstacles and hidden obstacles. What are obvious obstacles? Lions, tigers, leopards, bears, hyenas, wolves, thieves, hoodlums, various diseases,[449] cold, heat, hunger, thirst, defecation, urination, gadflies, mosquitoes, wind, a burning sun, and contact with serpents. What are hidden obstacles? Bodily, verbal, and mental misconduct; the hindrances of sensual desire, ill will, dullness and drowsiness, restlessness and regret, and doubt; lust, hatred, delusion, anger, hostility, denigration, insolence, envy, miserliness, hypocrisy, deceitfulness, obstinacy, rivalry, conceit, arrogance, vanity, and heedlessness;[450] all defilements, all misconduct, all distress, all fevers, all torments, all unwholesome volitional activities.

Obstacles. In what sense are these obstacles? They are obstacles because they overwhelm, because they lead to decline, and because their repository is right there (*tatrāsayāti parissayā*). How are they obstacles *because they overwhelm*? Those obstacles subdue that person, overcome him, overwhelm him, obsess him, crush him. How are they obstacles *because they lead to decline*? Those obstacles lead to the decline of wholesome qualities. What wholesome qualities? The right practice, the practice in conformity, the practice that does not go contrary, the practice that accords with the good, the practice that accords with the Dhamma; the fulfillment of good behavior, guarding the doors of the sense faculties, moderation in eating, devotion to wakefulness, mindfulness and clear comprehension; the dedicated development of the four establishments of mindfulness, the four right kinds of striving, the four bases for spiritual potency, the five faculties, the five powers, the seven factors of enlightenment, the noble eightfold path. How are they obstacles because "their repository is right there"? These bad unwholesome qualities that arise are based upon one's own person. Just as beings that dwell in caves sleep in a cave, as beings that live in water sleep in water, as beings that live in the woods sleep in the woods, as beings that live in a tree sleep in a tree, so these bad unwholesome qualities that arise are based upon one's own person.

Nidd II 229. **Fearless**: That paccekabuddha is courageous, fearless, intrepid, bold, one who dwells with fear and terror abandoned, rid of trepidation. ■

The verse on those hard to please

43. What is the origin? It is said that the chief queen of the king of Bārāṇasī had died. When his days of grieving had passed, one day his ministers requested him: "A chief queen is needed in such and such duties of kings. It would be good if our lord would take another queen." The king replied: "In that case, men, find one." While they were searching, the king in the neighboring kingdom died. His queen ruled the kingdom, and she was pregnant. The ministers, knowing she would be suitable for the king, asked her to come. She replied: "A pregnant woman is disagreeable to people. If you can wait until I give birth, so be it. If not, seek another queen."

They reported this matter to the king. The king said: "It does not matter that she is pregnant. Bring her anyway." They brought her. The king made her chief queen and gave her all the accessories of a queen, and he treated her entourage to various presents. In time she gave birth to a son. The king regarded him like his own son, cuddling him on his breast and lap even while engaged in all his activities.

The women of the queen's entourage thought: "The king is treating the prince extremely well. The hearts of kings are not trustworthy.[451] Let us divide him."

They told the prince: "You, dear, are the son of our king, not of this king. Do not trust him." Then, even when the prince was being addressed as "son" by the king, and even when the king took his hand and drew him close, he did not cling to the king as he did in the past. The king wondered: "What is this all about?" Having found out, he thought: "Ah! Even when I treated them well, [90] they have become hostile." Disenchanted, he abandoned the kingdom and went forth. Many of the ministers and members of his entourage, seeing that the king had gone forth, also went forth. People, thinking, "The king and his entourage have gone forth," offered them excellent requisites. The king had the excellent requisites distributed according to seniority. Those who received things of fine quality were content, but the others complained: "Even though we do all the tasks such as sweeping the cells, we obtain poor food and old clothes." When the king learned of this, he thought: "Ah! They complain even when the items are being given according to seniority. Truly, this community is hard to please." Having taken his bowl and robe, he entered the forest alone, undertook insight, and realized pacceka enlightenment. When those who came asked him about his meditation subject, he recited this verse.

The meaning is clear, but this is the construal: "**Even some monastics are hard to please**; those overcome by discontent are like this, and **so, too, householders living at home**. Being disgusted with the difficulty of pleasing them, I undertook insight and achieved pacceka enlightenment." The rest should be understood by the previous method.

The verse on the koviḷāra tree

44. What is the origin? In Bārāṇasī, it is said, the king named Cātumāsika ("Four-Month") Brahmadatta went to the park in the first month of the summer. There he saw a koviḷāra tree[452] covered with thick green leaves in a delightful area. He ordered his bedding to be prepared at the foot of the tree. After he had played in the park, in the evening he lay down there. He went again to the park in the middle month of the summer, when the koviḷāra tree was blossoming, and did the same. He went again in the last month of the summer, when the koviḷāra tree had shed its leaves and appeared like a dried-out tree. He did not notice the tree, but in accordance with his habit he ordered his bedding to be prepared in the same place. Though the ministers knew the situation, from fear of the king's order they prepared his bedding there.

When he finished playing in the park, [91] lying down there in the evening, the king noticed the tree and reflected: "Ah! In the past when this tree was covered with leaves it was beautiful, as if made of jewels. Thereafter, when it had flowers like coral sprouts placed on jewel-colored branches, it was glorious to behold. The area below was strewn with sand as if with pearls; when covered with flowers that had dropped from their stems, it seemed to have been draped in a red blanket. But today it is like a dried-out tree with only its branches left. Alas, the koviḷāra tree is stricken with old age!" He then gained the perception of impermanence: "When even what is insentient is stricken by old age, how much more is the sentient!" Following upon this, he contemplated with insight all conditioned things as suffering and non-self, wishing: "Oh, just as this koviḷāra tree has shed its leaves, so may I discard the marks of a layman!" In stages, even while he was lying on his right side there in his resting area, he realized pacceka enlightenment.

When it was time to go, his ministers said to him, "It's time to go, great king," but he replied, "I am not a king," and so forth, and in the way explained earlier, he recited this verse.

Here, **having discarded**: having removed; **the marks of a layman**: hair, beard, white clothes, ornaments, garlands, scents, ointments, women, children, male and female slaves, and so forth. For these mark the state of a layman; therefore they are called "the marks of a layman." **Whose leaves are shed**: whose leaves have dropped off.[453] **Having cut off**: having cut off with the knowledge of the path. **The hero**: one possessing the energy of the path. **A layman's bonds**: the bonds of sensual pleasures; for sensual pleasures are the bonds of laymen. This, firstly, is the meaning of the terms. But this is the purport: "Thinking, 'Oh, may I discard the marks of a layman, like the koviḷāra tree whose leaves are shed!' I undertook insight and achieved pacceka enlightenment." The rest should be understood by the previous method. [92]

Chapter 2

The verses on a companion

45–46. What is the origin? In the past, it is said, two pacceka-bodhisattas went forth in the teaching of the Blessed One Kassapa. Having fulfilled the observance of going and coming for 20,000 years, they arose in the deva world. When they passed away from there, the elder became the son of the king of Bārāṇasī, the younger the son of his chaplain. The two were conceived on the same day and came out from their mothers' wombs on the same day, and they became childhood friends. The chaplain's son was wise. He said to the king's son: "Friend, after your father passes away, you will gain the kingdom and I will gain the position of chaplain, and it is possible[454] for one who has been well trained to administer a kingdom easily. Come, let's learn a craft." Then, having been invested with the sacred thread around their necks,[455] the two walked for alms among the villages and towns until they reached a village in the frontier region.

Paccekabuddhas had entered that village at the time to walk for alms. People, having seen the paccekabuddhas, were enthusiastic. They prepared seats for them, offered them excellent food of various kinds, and esteemed and venerated them. It then occurred to the two youths: "They are not from high families like us, yet these people may give us alms or not, depending on their wishes, but they show such honor to these monks. Surely, they must know some craft. Let's learn a craft from them."

After the people had left, when they gained an opportunity, they asked the paccekabuddhas: "Bhante, teach us the craft that you know." The paccekabuddhas replied: "It isn't possible to train one who has not gone forth." The two youths asked for the going forth and obtained it. Then the paccekabuddhas taught them the principles of proper behavior, such as how to wear the lower robe and how to cover themselves with the upper robe. They gave them each a separate leaf hut and told them: "Success in this craft depends on delighting in solitude. Therefore you should sit alone, walk back and forth alone, stand alone, and sleep alone." They each entered their own leaf hut and sat down. [93] From the time he sat down, the chaplain's son gained concentration of mind and attained jhāna. But after a short while the king's son became discontent and went to his friend. The other asked: "What's the matter, friend?" He replied: "I'm discontent." The other said: "Then sit here."

Having sat down there, after a short while he said: "It's said, friend, that success in this craft depends on delighting in solitude."

"So it is, friend. Therefore, go to your own sitting place, and we will acquire success in this craft."

The other went back, but after a short while he again became discontent and went to see his friend. This happened, as above, three times.

Having enjoined the king's son in this way, when he had left the chaplain's son thought: "He neglects his own work and repeatedly comes over to me." So he left his hut and entered the forest. The king's son, while sitting in his own hut, again became discontent after a while and went to his friend's hut. He searched for him here and there but did not see him. Then he reflected: "When we were laymen, he would come to me bringing presents, but still he would not get to see me. But now, when I come, not wishing to give me a chance to see him, he has departed. Ah! You mind, you have no shame, since you led me here four times. Now I will no longer come under your control, but rather I will bring you under my control."

Having entered his own lodging, he undertook insight and realized pacceka enlightenment. He then went through the sky to Nandamūlaka Slope. Meanwhile, after the chaplain's son had entered the forest, he undertook insight, realized pacceka enlightenment, and went to the same place. As they sat on the Red Arsenic Terrace, both separately recited these joyful utterances.

In these verses, **judicious**: one with natural astuteness, wise, skilled in the preparation of the kasiṇa and so forth.[456] **Of good behavior** (*sādhuvihāriṃ*): dwelling in absorption (*appanā-vihārena*) or access concentration.[457] **Resolute**: endowed with resoluteness.[458] Endowment with resoluteness is indicated there [in the first line] by judiciousness, but here the meaning is simply one endowed with resoluteness. Resoluteness (*dhiti*) is unrelenting exertion, a designation for the energy that occurs thus: "Willingly, [94] let my skin and sinews remain" and so forth (MN I 481,1; AN I 50,9).[459] There is also an explanation of *dhīra* as one who has reproached evil.[460]

Like a king who has abandoned a conquered realm: As a hostile king, having known "The realm that one has conquered leads to harm," would abandon the kingdom and live alone, so, having abandoned a foolish companion, one should live alone. Or else: **Like a king . . . the realm**: As King Sutasoma, having abandoned the realm that he conquered, lived alone, and as King Mahājanaka did, so one should live alone. This, too, is its meaning.[461] The rest can be understood in accordance with what was already explained, so it is not elaborated.

⁝▯ Nidd II 233. Like a king who has abandoned a conquered realm: A head-anointed khattiya king who is victorious in battle, who has slain his enemies, achieved his purpose, and filled his treasury and storerooms, having relinquished the realm and country, the treasury and storerooms, and the city abounding in bullion and gold, shaves off hair and beard, puts on ochre robes, goes forth from the household life into homelessness, approaches the state of ownerlessness, and lives alone, dwells, carries on, and maintains himself alone; so too the paccekabuddha cuts off the impediment of the household life, the impediment of wife and children, the impediment of relatives, the impediment of friends and companions, shaves off his hair and beard, puts on ochre robes, goes forth from the household life into homelessness, approaches the state of ownerlessness, and lives alone, dwells, carries on, and maintains himself alone.

The verse on eating blamelessly

47. The origin of this verse is similar to that of the verse on the four directions (see pp. 444–45) up to the point where the paccekabuddhas have been seated in seats prepared on the upper terrace. But there is this difference: Unlike the king in that story, this one did not wake up in fear three times during the night, nor did he prepare a sacrifice. After inviting the paccekabuddhas to sit down in the seats prepared on the upper terrace, he asked them: "Who are you?"

They replied: "Great king, we are called 'those who eat blamelessly.'" – "What, Bhante, is the meaning of 'those who eat blamelessly'?" – "Whether we obtain what is good or what is bad, we remain unruffled, great king."

When the king heard this, he thought: "Let me examine them to find out whether or not this is so." That day, he served them broken rice with sour gruel as a side dish. The paccekabuddhas ate it unruffled, as if they were eating ambrosia. The king thought: "That they aren't ruffled this one day is because of their claim. I'll find out tomorrow." He invited them for the next day's meal. On the second day he did the same, and they ate it in the same way. Then the king thought, "Now I'll investigate after I have given them good food," and he again invited them. Over the next two days he showed them great honor and served them with various kinds of delicious food. Again, they ate it in the same way, unruffled, and after reciting a blessing for the king, they left. Soon after they departed, the king reflected: "These ascetics indeed eat blamelessly! Oh, that I too [95] might be one who eats blamelessly!"

Then, having abandoned his large kingdom, he went forth, undertook insight, and became a paccekabuddha. In the midst of the paccekabuddhas at the foot of the Mañjūsaka tree, elucidating his own object, he recited this verse.

The verse is clear with regard to the meaning of its terms, but only the expression **the excellence of companionship** should be understood to mean the excellence of companionship with companions who possess the aggregate of good behavior and other virtues of those beyond training. This is the construal here: "**Surely we praise the excellence of companionship**: We definitely extol this excellence of companionship as stated. How? **One should resort to companions one's equal or better**. Why? When one resorts to those who are better than oneself in regard to good behavior and other virtues, one's own good behavior and other virtues, if unarisen, will arise, and if arisen will come to growth, increase, and maturity. When one resorts to those who are one's equal, by supporting one another and dispelling remorse, one will not fall away from what one has obtained. **Not obtaining these**: If one does not gain companions who are better than oneself or equal to oneself, one should avoid wrong livelihood by scheming and so forth, and eat food that has been acquired justly and righteously.[462] **One who eats blamelessly**: Not arousing aversion or attachment in regard to food, a clansman desiring the good should live alone like the horn of a rhinoceros. For I too, living in such a way, have achieved this attainment."

⁝▮ **Nidd II 234–35. Not obtaining these, as one who eats blamelessly**. There is a person who eats blamefully and a person who eats blamelessly. Who is *the person that eats blamefully*? Here, someone earns his living by scheming, talking, hinting, belittling, pursuing gain with gain; with a gift of wood, a gift of bamboo, a gift of leaves, a gift of flowers, a gift of fruit[463] . . . by going on errands, by delivering messages, by undertaking commissions on foot, by medical service, by construction service, by providing a gift of almsfood; he has gained [his means of living] contrary to Dhamma, unrighteously. Who is *the person that eats blamelessly*? Here, someone does not earn his living by scheming, talking, hinting, belittling, pursuing gain with gain; nor with a gift of wood, a gift of bamboo, a gift of leaves, a gift of flowers, a gift of fruit . . . nor by going on errands, by delivering messages, by undertaking commissions on foot, by medical service, by construction service; nor by providing a gift of almsfood; he has gained [his means of living] in accordance with Dhamma, righteously. ▮⁝

The verse on bracelets of gold

48. What is the origin? A certain king of Bārāṇasī had gone for his siesta during the summertime. Nearby one of his concubines was grinding *gosīsa* sandalwood. On one of her arms she wore a single golden bracelet, on the other two bracelets. These clashed together, while the single one did not make a noise. Having seen this, looking at the concubine again and again, the king reflected: "Just so, there are clashes when one lives in a group, but no clashes when one lives alone." Now on that occasion the queen, decked in all her ornaments, was fanning him. She thought: "It seems the king has fallen in love with that concubine." She then dismissed the concubine and started to grind the sandalwood herself. There were many golden bracelets on both her arms, and as they clashed together they made a loud noise.

The king, even more disenchanted, even while he was lying on his right side [96] undertook insight and realized pacceka enlightenment. As he was lying there enjoying the unsurpassed bliss, the queen approached him with sandalwood in her hands and said: "Let me anoint you, great king." The king said: "Go away. Don't anoint me." She asked: "Why is this, great king?" He answered: "I am not a king." The ministers, having overheard their conversation, approached. When they also addressed him as "great king," he said: "I am not a king." The rest is similar to the explanation given in relation to the first verse.

In the commentary on the verse, "bracelets" (*valayāni*) should be added to "of gold," for the reading is incomplete. This is the construal: "Having seen bracelets of gold on the arm,[464] reflecting thus: 'There are clashes when living in a group, but no clashes when living alone,' I undertook insight and achieved pacceka enlightenment." The rest by the method already explained.

The verse on future peril

49. What is the origin? A certain king of Bārāṇasī, wishing to go forth even while young, ordered his ministers: "Having taken the queen, maintain the kingdom. I will go forth." But the ministers appealed to him: "It is not possible for us, great king, to protect a kingless kingdom. The neighboring states will come and plunder the land. Please wait until you beget a son." The king, being flexible, agreed.

Then the queen became pregnant. The king again ordered

his men: "The queen is pregnant. Having anointed the boy to kingship, maintain the kingdom. I will go forth." The ministers again appealed to him: "It's hard to know, great king, whether the queen will give birth to a son or a daughter. Please wait until she gives birth."

She gave birth to a son. The king then ordered his ministers as before, and with many reasons they again appealed to the king: "Wait, great king, until he is capable." When the prince was capable, [97] the king assembled the ministers and said: "He is now capable. Anoint him to kingship and carry on." And without giving the ministers a chance to reply, he had all the requisites—ochre cloth and so forth—brought from the market. He went forth right in the inner quarters and departed like Mahājanaka (Ja VI 52). His entire entourage, weeping and wailing, followed the king.

The king went to the boundary of his own kingdom. There he made a line with his staff and said: "You should not cross this line." The people lay down on the ground with their heads on the line, weeping, but they made the prince cross the line, telling him: "Now, dear, the command of the king is yours. What can he do?" The prince, crying, "Father, father," ran after the king and caught up with him. Having seen the prince, the king thought to himself: "I ruled the kingdom, taking care of this multitude. Why shouldn't I now be able to take care of one child?" So he took the prince and entered the forest.

There, having seen a leaf hut that had been used by former paccekabuddhas, he dwelled in it together with his son. From then on the prince, who was accustomed to sleeping on luxurious beds, cried because he had to sleep on a straw mat or a bed of ropes. When cold winds blew on him, and he faced other adversities, he cried: "Its cold, father. It's hot, father. Flies are biting me. I'm hungry, I'm thirsty." The king would pass the whole night trying to reason with him. During the day, too, the king would bring him food that he had gathered by walking for alms. The food was a mixture with a lot of millet, black beans, mung beans, and other things. Though the prince was repelled by it, he ate it to satisfy his appetite, and after a few days he wilted like a lotus flower exposed to heat. But by his power of reflection the paccekabodhisatta ate it unruffled.

Then, trying to reason with the prince, he said: "Delicious

food can be obtained in the city, dear. Let's go there." The prince said: "Yes, father." Then, putting him in front, the king returned along the path on which he had come. The queen, the prince's mother, had reflected: "Having taken the prince, now the king won't live long in the forest. After a few days he will return." [98] She had a lookout post[465] built at the place where the king had made a line with his staff and set up her dwelling there. Then the king, standing not far from her dwelling place, told his son: "Your mother, dear, is sitting here. Go to her." And he sent the boy. He stood there looking on until the boy reached that spot, concerned that someone might harm him. The boy ran toward his mother. The guards, having seen him, informed the queen. Accompanied by her retinue of 20,000 dancing girls, she went out and received him and asked for news about the king. When she heard that the king was coming behind, she sent the people forth. But the king immediately went back to his own dwelling, and the people, not seeing him, turned back. Having lost hope, the queen took her son, returned to the city, and anointed him to the kingship. But the former king, having reached his own dwelling, sat down, developed insight, and realized pacceka enlightenment. Later, in the midst of the paccekabuddhas at the foot of the Mañjūsaka tree, he recited this verse as a joyful utterance.

The verse is clear with regard to the meaning of its terms, but this is the purport here: "When I tried reasoning with this partner—the prince—as he complained about the cold and heat and so forth, that was my addressing with words; and clinging[466] arose on account of affection for him: **Thus if I had a partner, I would incur [fond] words of address or verbal friction**. If I did not relinquish this, then in the future, just as now, both would be obstacles to the achievement of distinction. So **looking out for this peril in the future**, I discarded them, practiced carefully, and achieved pacceka enlightenment." The rest in the way already explained.

The verse on sensual pleasures

50. What is the origin? In Bārāṇasī, it is said, the son of a financier, even while young, obtained the post of financier. He had three mansions for each of the three seasons. There he enjoyed himself with all enjoyments, just like a celestial youth. But though he was young, he told his parents: "I will go forth." They prohibited him. He insisted, but again they prohibited him in various ways: "Dear, you are delicate, and the going forth is as hard as walking on the edge of a razor blade." He insisted as before. They considered: [99] "If he goes forth, we will be upset; but if we prohibit him, he will be upset. Let us be upset, but not him." And so they gave him permission.

While his retinue were lamenting, he traveled to Isipatana and went forth under the paccekabuddhas. He did not obtain a fine dwelling but slept on a straw mat spread out on a bed. Since he was accustomed to a fine bed, he was extremely uncomfortable the whole night. In the morning, after attending to his bodily needs, he took his bowl and robe and entered the town for alms along with the paccekabuddhas. There, the elders received the best seat and the best almsfood, while the youngsters were given any old seat and coarse food. He was also extremely miserable because of the coarse food. After a few days, he became thin and pale and grew disenchanted, since the ascetic's duty had not yet reached maturity for him. He then sent a message to his parents and disrobed. But after a few days, he regained his strength and again wished to go forth. In this way, he again went forth and again disrobed. But after going forth the third time, practicing properly, he realized pacceka enlightenment. Having recited this verse as a joyful utterance, in the midst of the paccekabuddhas he again recited this same verse as an explanation.

In this verse, **sensual pleasures** are of two kinds: sensual objects and sensual defilements. Sensual objects are things like agreeable forms and so forth. Sensual defilements are all types of lust, such as desire and so forth.[467] But here sensual objects are intended. They are **colorful** because of the diversity of forms and so forth, **sweet** because they are relished by the world, and **delightful** because they delight the minds of foolish worldlings. **In their diversity**: What is meant is in their manifold nature through the diverse kinds of forms. For those are colorful by way of forms and other sense objects, and forms, too, show diversity by way of blue and other colors. Having thus shown the gratification in them by way of their diversity, he says **they agitate the mind** because they do not allow one to rejoice in the going forth. The rest is clear. Having connected the conclusion with two or three lines, it should be understood in the way explained in relation to the earlier verses.[468] [100]

The verse on adversity

51. What is the origin? It is said that the king of Bārāṇasī had gotten a boil and was experiencing severe pain. Physicians told him: "There won't be relief without surgery." The king promised them safety[469] and had the surgery performed. They split open the boil, removed pus and blood, soothed the pain, and covered the wound with a bandage. Then they gave him proper advice regarding food and behavior. The king became thin because of the coarse food, but his boil vanished. When he thought he was well, he ate rich food, and with his health restored he indulged in the objects he enjoyed. His boil returned to its former condition. In this way, he had the physicians perform surgery on him three times. Shunned by the physicians, he became disenchanted, abandoned the large kingdom, and went forth. Entering the forest, he undertook insight and after seven years realized pacceka enlightenment. Having recited this verse as a joyful utterance, he went to the Nandamūlaka Slope.

In this verse, **adversity** is a designation for adventitious causes of ruin that pertain to the unwholesome. Therefore the strands of sensual pleasures, too, are adversity in the sense that they bring many kinds of ruin and in the sense that they are densely packed. A boil oozes impurity, becomes swollen and putrid, and then bursts open. Therefore these sensual pleasures are **a boil** because they ooze with the impurity of defilements, and because they become swollen, putrid, and burst by way of arising, decay, and dissolution.

Disaster is what overcomes and spreads out by producing what is harmful. This is a designation for such things as punishment by kings and so forth. Therefore these sensual pleasures are a disaster because they bring terrible unpredictable harm;[470] and because they are the basis for all kinds of disasters. Since they plunder one's natural state of health, producing the affliction of defilements, and cause greediness, attacking one's health that consists in good behavior, they are **illness** in this sense of plundering one's health. They are **a dart** in the sense of entering deeply inside, in the sense of piercing within, and in the sense of being hard to remove. [101] They are **peril** because they bring peril in this present life and in future lives. The rest is clear. The conclusion should be understood in the way explained earlier.

The verse on sensitive to cold

52. What is the origin? It is said that in Bārāṇasī there was a king named Sītāluka ("Sensitive-to-Cold") Brahmadatta. Having gone forth, he lived in a forest hut. Because that region was exposed, when the weather was cold it was really cold and when it was hot it was really hot. In the nearby village he did not obtain as much almsfood as he needed. Potable water, too, was hard to obtain, and the wind, the sun's heat, flies, and snakes also bothered him. It occurred to him: "Merely half a yojana from here there is a prosperous region where none of these obstacles exist. I should go there. I can live comfortably and achieve distinction." But he then considered: "Monks are not servants to the requisites. They exercise control over the mind; they do not come under the control of the mind. I will not go." Having reflected thus, he did not go. He thought of leaving three times, but each time he reflected and returned. Then, having lived there for seven years, practicing rightly, he realized pacceka enlightenment. Having recited this verse as a joyful utterance, he went to Nandamūlaka Slope.

In this verse, **cold** is twofold: due to a disturbance of the internal elements [in the body] and due to a disturbance of the external elements. So too for **heat**. **Gadflies** are brownish flies. **Serpents** are long creatures that creep along. The rest is clear. The conclusion, too, should be understood in the way explained earlier.

The verse on the elephant

53. What is the origin? It is said that in Bārāṇasī there was a certain king who died after ruling for twenty years. He was then tormented in hell for twenty years, after which he was reborn as an elephant on a slope in the Himalayas. [102] He was a huge bull elephant, eminent, the chief of the herd, with a massive back,[471] and his whole body was the color of a lotus flower. The baby elephants ate his bundle of bent and twisted branches, and in the pool, too, the female elephants splashed him with mud—all just as in the case of the Pārileyyaka bull elephant (Ud 41–42). Disgusted with the herd, he departed, but the herd followed his tracks. Even up to a third time, whenever he departed, they would follow him.

Then he thought: "Now my grandson is ruling in Bārāṇasī. Let me go to the park that was mine in my former birth. He will protect me there." Then at night, when the herd was asleep, he abandoned the herd and entered the park. The park guard, having seen him, informed the king. The king surrounded him with his army, thinking: "I will capture the elephant." The elephant went straight toward the king. Thinking, "He's coming straight at me," the king drew an arrow. The elephant, afraid of being shot, spoke to the king with a human voice: "Brahmadatta, don't shoot me. I am your grandfather." The king said, "What are you saying?" and asked about everything, and the elephant told him all the news: about the kingdom, his rebirth in hell, and his birth as an elephant. The king said to him: "Do not be afraid, and do not frighten anyone." And he established an estate, guards, and provisions for the elephant.

Then one day, while the king was mounted on the elephant, he reflected: "He exercised kingship for twenty years, was tormented in hell, and as the residue of the result, he was reborn in the animal realm. Even there, unable to endure the friction of living in a group, he has come here. Oh, living in a group is miserable! But solitude is indeed blissful!" Then right there he undertook insight and realized pacceka enlightenment. While he was absorbed in the world-transcending bliss, his ministers approached him, prostrated before him, and said: "It is time to go, great king." He replied, "I am not a king," and then, in the way explained earlier, he recited this verse. [103]

The verse is clear with regard to the meaning of the terms. This is how to construe the purport, and this is by way of reasoning, not by oral tradition: "Reflecting in this way, I undertook insight and achieved pacceka enlightenment: 'As this elephant is a **nāga** because, tamed in the ways of good behavior loved by people, he does not go to the plane of the untamed, or because of the great size of his body, just so, when will I, too, become a nāga because, tamed in the ways of good behavior loved by the noble ones, I do not go to the plane of the untamed, and do not commit any crime, and do not come back again to this state of being, or because of the great size of the body (collection) of my excellent qualities?'"[472]

⁞▮ **Nidd II 242. Nāga**: A large elephant is called a nāga, and a paccekabuddha is also called a nāga. In what way is a paccekabuddha a nāga? He is a nāga because he does not commit crime; a nāga because he does not go; a nāga because he does not come.[473]

How is the paccekabuddha a nāga because *he does not commit crime*? "Crime" refers to bad unwholesome qualities that are defiling, lead to renewed exisence, that are troublesome, result in suffering, and conduce to future birth, old age, and death.

> One who does not commit any crime in the world,
> having discarded all yokes and bondages,
> who is not tied down anywhere, liberated:
> such a one is truthfully called a nāga. **(522)**

How is the paccekabuddha a nāga in the sense that *he does not go*? The paccekabuddha does not go under the influence of desire, under the influence of hatred, under the influence of delusion, under the influence of fear; he does not go under the influence of conceit, views, restlessness, or doubt; he does not go on account of the latent tendencies; he is not moved, led on, swept away, driven by divisive ideas.

How is the paccekabuddha a nāga in the sense that *he does not come*? He does not return to those defilements that have been abandoned by the path of stream-entry, by the path of the once-returner, by the path of the non-returner, by the path of arahantship. ▮⁞

"Just as he, being one who **has abandoned the herd**, **may live in the forest as he pleases**, enjoying the bliss of solitude, and wander alone like a rhinoceros horn, when will I, too, having abandoned my group, live in the forest as I please, exclusively enjoying the bliss of solitude and the bliss of jhāna, and wander alone like a rhinoceros horn, dwelling in the forest in whatever way I wish and for as long as I wish? Just as he has

a massive back, because of his well-shaped hump, when will I, too, have a massive hump, because of the great size of my back [which consists in] the aggregate of good behavior of one beyond training?[474] Just as he is **lotus-like** because his body is similar to a lotus flower or because he has arisen in the lotus family,[475] when will I too be lotus-like because of the greatness of the enlightenment factors, which are similar to lotuses, or because I will have arisen in a lotus through a noble birth? Just as he is **eminent**, endowed with strength, power, and speed, when will I too be eminent, because of my purified bodily conduct and so forth or because of good behavior, concentration, and penetrative wisdom, and so forth?"

Nidd II 243. Just as a bull elephant has a massive back (*sañjātakkhandha*), seven or eight ratanas high, a paccekabuddha too has a massive back consisting in the aggregate (*khandha*) of good behavior, concentration, wisdom, liberation, and knowledge and vision of liberation of one beyond training. Just as a bull elephant is lotus-like, a paccekabuddha too is lotus-like through the flowers of the seven factors of enlightenment. Just as a bull elephant is eminent because of his strength, power, speed, and courage, a paccekabuddha too is eminent on account of his good behavior, concentration, wisdom, liberation, and knowledge and vision of liberation. Just as the bull elephant dwells in the forest as he pleases, so a paccekabuddha dwells in the forest as he pleases: that is, in the forest of the four jhānas; in the liberation of mind by loving-kindness, compassion, altruistic joy, and equanimity; in the base of the boundlessness of space . . . the base of neither-perception-nor-nonperception; in the attainment of cessation, in the attainment of the fruit.

The verse on the impossible

54. What is the origin? It is said that the son of the king of Bārāṇasī, even while young, wanted to go forth. He asked his parents for permission, but they prohibited him. He insisted: "I will go forth." What follows is all similar to the story of the financier's son, already described (see pp. 458–59). [104] Finally they gave him permission, but they made him promise that after going forth he would live in their own park. He did so. In the morning, his mother would go to the park, accompanied by 20,000 dancing girls, and after giving her son porridge and snacks, she would chat with him until midday, when she would enter the city. Then his father would come at midday, feed him, and eat his own meal, after which he would chat with him until evening. Then he set up watchmen and entered the city. In this way the young man passed his days and nights, never alone.

Now on that occasion a paccekabuddha named Ādiccabandhu ("Kinsman of the Sun") dwelled on the Nandamūlaka Slope.[476] Directing his attention he saw the young man and thought: "This youth was able to go forth, but he cannot cut his entanglement." Then he pondered: "Will he become disenchanted on his own or not?" Having known, "It will be too long before he becomes disenchanted on his own," he decided: "Let me show him an object." Having come from the Red Arsenic Terrace, in the way explained earlier, he stood in the park. The king's man saw him and informed the king: "A paccekabuddha has come, great king." The king, delighted at the thought, "Now my son will live contentedly in the company of the paccekabuddha," respectfully attended on the paccekabuddha and requested him to live there. He built everything to accommodate him—a leaf hut, a daytime dwelling, a walkway, and so forth—and made him settle there.

While living there, one day the paccekabuddha found an opportunity to ask the youth: "Who are you?" He replied: "I am a monk." – "But monks aren't like this." – "But, Bhante, what are they like? What is unsuitable for me?"

"You don't recognize what is unsuitable for yourself? Doesn't your mother come in the morning with 20,000 women and ruin your seclusion? And doesn't your father come in the evening with a large mass of troops? And don't watchmen remain here all night long? Real monks are not like you. They are like this." Then, even while he was standing there, by means of spiritual power he showed him a certain dwelling in the Himalayas. The prince saw paccekabuddhas there [105] leaning against a banister,[477] and some walking back and forth, and some engaged in such tasks as dyeing and mending their robes. Having seen this, the prince said: "You do not come here. Is the going forth permitted by you?"

"Yes, the going forth is permitted. From the time they have gone forth, ascetics can go to whatever region they wish in order to work out their own release. Just this much is proper."

Having said this, the paccekabuddha stood in the sky and spoke this half-verse:

> "It is impossible that one who delights in company
> might attain even temporary liberation."

Then, while the youth was watching, he went bodily to the Nandamūlaka Slope. When the paccekabuddha had gone, the prince entered his own hut and laid down. The guard thought: "The prince is asleep, so where can he go now?" and he too fell asleep. Knowing that the guard was not paying attention, the prince took his bowl and robe and entered the forest. There, in seclusion, he undertook insight and realized pacceka enlightenment, and then went to the place of the paccekabuddhas. And there, when he was asked, "How did you achieve this?" he spoke the verse, completing the half-verse spoken by Ādiccabandhu.

This is its meaning: **Temporary liberation** is a mundane meditative attainment. It is called "temporary liberation" because one is liberated from the opposing states only on the occasion when one is actually absorbed in it. [So he said:] "**Having attended to this word of** the paccekabuddha **Kinsman of the Sun (Ādiccabandhu)**—'It is impossible, there is no case where one who delights in company might, with this as the cause, attain this temporary liberation'—I abandoned delight in company, practiced carefully, and achieved this." The rest in the way stated. [106]

Chapter 3

The verse on the contortions of views

55. What is the origin? It is said that in Bārāṇasī a certain king reflected in private: "Just as heat and so forth are the opposites of cold and so forth, is there or isn't there an ending of the round of existence, a state opposed to the round?"[478] He asked his ministers: "Do you know of an ending of the round?" They answered: "We know, great king." – "What is it?" They answered by explaining the eternalist and annihilationist views, such as "The world is finite," and so forth (DN I 22–24).

But the king realized that their answers were deviant and incorrect and concluded: "They do not know but have just taken up views." Having considered, "There is an ending of the round opposed to the round, and I must seek it," he abandoned his kingdom, went forth, and by developing insight, realized pacceka enlightenment. He recited this verse as a joyful utterance and as a verse of explanation in the midst of the paccekabuddhas.

This is its meaning: The **contortions of views**: the sixty-two views; for those are "contortions" in the sense that they contradict,[479] pierce, and run contrary to the right view of the path. Thus they are "contortions of view"; or the views themselves are contortions—hence "contortion-views." **Transcended**: overcome by the path of seeing.[480] **Reached the fixed course**: achieved the definitive state because of being incapable of [taking rebirth in] the lower world and being bound for enlightenment; or [this signifies] the first path, called the fixed course of rightness.[481] At this point what is being referred to is the accomplishment of the function of the first path and his attainment of it.

Now, by the expression **obtained the path**, he shows his attainment of the remaining paths. **I have aroused knowledge**: I have aroused the knowledge of pacceka enlightenment. By this he shows the fruit. **Not to be led by others**: He is not to be guided by others thus, "This is true, that is true." By this he shows he is self-accomplished, or he shows his autonomy, because he has no need to be guided in the knowledge of pacceka enlightenment, which he has already attained. Or alternatively: He has "transcended the contortions of views" by insight[482] and "reached the fixed course" by the first path. [107] He is "one who has obtained the path" through the remaining paths; by the knowledge of the fruit he is "one who has aroused knowledge"; and he is "not to be led by others" because he has achieved all that by himself. The rest should be understood in the way already explained.

The verse on without greed

56. What is the origin? It is said that the chef of the king of Bārāṇasī had prepared a snack and offered it to the king—a snack that was delicious and agreeable to look at—hoping that the king would give him a reward. Just by its smell, the dish whetted the king's appetite and made his mouth water. As soon as he put the first bite into his mouth, his 7,000 taste buds were stimulated as if by nectar. The chef kept on thinking: "Now he will give me something." The king, too, thought, "The chef deserves to be rewarded," but then he considered: "If I reward him because of the taste of this food, I might acquire a bad reputation as a king who is greedy, obsessed with tastes." Thus he did not say anything. Right up until the end of the meal the chef kept on hoping for a reward, but the king still did not say anything from fear of criticism.

Then the chef, thinking, "This king does not have a sense of taste," the next day offered him tasteless food. While eating, the king thought, "Today the chef needs to be punished," but having reflected as on the previous day, he did not say anything from fear of criticism. The chef considered, "The king does not know what is good and what is bad," and having taken all his wages, he cooked something at random and gave it to the king. The king then became disenchanted, thinking: "Oh, the greed for wealth! I rule over 20,000 cities, but because of his greed, I do not even get a simple meal!" Having abandoned his kingdom, he went forth and, developing insight, realized pacceka enlightenment. In the way stated earlier, he recited this verse.

In this verse, **without greed**: greedless. One who is overcome by craving for tastes, who longs for them intensely, longs for them repeatedly, is on that account said to be greedy. Therefore, rejecting this, he says: "without greed." **Without scheming**: One who is without the three kinds of scheming is said to be "without scheming."[483] But in this verse, the purport is: "One is without scheming by not becoming astonished over agreeable food and so forth." [108] **Without thirst**: Thirst is a wish to drink, so its absence is stated as "without a desire to drink." But here it means that one is devoid of a desire to eat from greed for delicious tastes. **Not denigrating**: The characteristic of "denigration" is disparaging the excellent qualities of others. With its absence, one is "not denigrating." This is said with reference to his own denigration of the chef's excellent qualities[484] at the time he [the king] was a layman.

With stains and delusion blown away: Here six qualities should be understood as "stains": the three of greed, [hatred, and delusion], and the three of bodily, [verbal, and mental] misconduct. These are called stains in the sense of lack of clarity according to the situation, in the sense that they obscure one's own nature and ascribe a different nature, and in the sense that they are tarnished. As it is said:

> Here, what are the three stains? The stain of lust, the stain of hatred, and the stain of delusion. These are the three stains. What are another three stains here? The bodily stain, the verbal stain, and the mental stain. (Vibh 427, §924,22–23)

It is said, "With stains and delusion blown away," because one has blown away the other five stains along with delusion, which is the root of all stains. Or else "With stains and delusion blown away" [is said] because one has blown away delusion and just the three stains—the bodily, verbal, and mental stains. Of the others, the blowing away of the stain of lust is indicated by being without greed and so forth, the blowing away of the stain of hatred by the absence of denigration. **Without wishes**: without craving; **for anything in all the world**: in regard to the entire world. The meaning is that one is devoid of craving for existence and nonexistence in regard to the three realms or the twelve sense bases. The rest should be understood in the way stated earlier. Or alternatively, after stating the first three lines, the connection [of the last line to the others] can be posited thus: **eko care** means "one is able to live alone."[485]

The verse on the evil companion

57. What is the origin? In Bārāṇasī, it is said, a certain king was making a tour of the city with the full pomp of royalty when he saw people removing old grain from the granary. He asked his ministers: "What is this, men?"

"Now, great king, fresh grain has been harvested. To make room for it, these people are discarding the old grain."

"How is it, men? Are the grounds of the women's quarters and the troops and so forth full?" [109]

"Yes, great king, they are full."

"Then, men, have an alms hall built. I will give alms. Don't let this grain go to waste without being of benefit."

Then a certain minister of wrong view prevented him, saying, "Great king, there is no giving," and so on up to: "Fools and the wise, having roamed and wandered in the round of rebirths, will make an end of suffering."[486] Having seen a granary being emptied for a second and a third time, the king gave the same command. For a third time the minister prevented him, saying: "Great king, giving is a doctrine of fools."

He became disenchanted, thinking, "Ah! I don't even get to give away my own belongings. What good to me are these evil companions?" Having abandoned the kingdom, he went forth, developed insight, and realized pacceka enlightenment. Then, censuring that evil companion, he recited this verse as a joyful utterance.

This is its concise meaning: A clansman who desires the good **should avoid an evil companion, who shows what is harmful, one settled in unrighteousness**—one who is "evil because he holds to the tenfold evil view";[487] who "shows what is harmful" because he shows what is harmful to others, too;[488] who is "settled in unrighteousness," in bodily misconduct and so forth. **One should not freely associate**: One should not associate with him of one's own will, but if one is subject to another's control, what can one do? **Intent**: stuck here and there by way of view.[489] **Heedless**: one whose mind indulges in the strands of sensual pleasure or who is devoid of wholesome development. One should not associate with one like this, should not resort to him, should not attend upon him, but rather one should live alone like a rhinoceros horn.

Nidd II 250. Intent: One who seeks sensual pleasures, who searches for them, who is disposed to them, who frequents them, reveres them, leans, bends, and inclines toward them, who is resolved on them and dominated by them is intent upon sensual pleasures. One who, on account of craving, seeks forms, sounds, odors, tastes, and tactile objects, who is disposed to them, frequents them, reveres them . . . is also intent upon sensual pleasures. One who, on account of craving, obtains forms . . . who enjoys forms . . . who is dominated by them is intent upon sensual pleasures.

The verse on the learned

58. What is the origin? In the past, it is said, eight paccekabodhisattas had gone forth in the teaching of the Blessed One Kassapa. Having fulfilled the observance of going and coming for 20,000 years, they arose in the deva world—all is similar to what was said about the verse on eating blamelessly (see p. 454), but there is this difference: After inviting the paccekabuddhas to sit down in the seats prepared on the upper terrace, the king asked them: "Who are you?"

"Great king, we are called the learned ones." [110]

The king was delighted, thinking: "I am named the Learned Brahmadatta, yet I am never satisfied with learning. Come, let me hear from them a variegated teaching on the good Dhamma." So, having given the water offering, having served them, at the conclusion of the meal he took the Sangha elder's bowl, paid homage to him, sat down in front of him, and said: "Bhante, please give a Dhamma talk."

The elder said, "May you be happy, great king. Let there be the destruction of lust," then he got up. The king thought: "He isn't learned. The second one must be learned. Tomorrow I will hear a variegated discourse on the Dhamma from him." He invited them for the next day's meal. In this way, he invited them until all had the chance to speak. Each one spoke only one statement, just as the first one had, and then they got up. The only difference is that they said in order: "Let there be the destruction of hatred, the destruction of delusion, the destruction of rebirth, the destruction of the round, the destruction of acquisitions, the destruction of craving."

Then the king thought: "They say, 'We are learned,' yet they do not give a variegated talk. What did they mean?" He began to examine the meaning of their statements. As he examined the statement "Let there be the destruction of lust," he understood: "When lust is destroyed, hatred, delusion, and all other defilements are also destroyed." He was pleased and reflected: "These ascetics are learned in the direct sense. Just as a person who points out the great earth or space with his finger does not point out a region merely the size of his finger but points out the entire earth and the whole of space, so too, when they pointed out one principle, unlimited principles were pointed out." Then he thought: "When will I too become learned in such a way?" Desiring such a state of learning, he abandoned his kingdom, went forth, and developing insight, he realized pacceka enlightenment. He then recited this verse as a joyful utterance.

This is the concise meaning here: **Learned**: learned in a twofold way: completely *learned in the scriptures*, by knowing the three Piṭakas by way of their meaning, and *learned in penetration*, by having penetrated the paths, the fruits, the clear knowledges, and the superknowledges. The same for **a bearer of Dhamma**.[490] **Eminent**: one endowed with eminent bodily, verbal, and mental action. [111] **Gifted with ingenuity**: one whose ingenuity is incisive, whose ingenuity is fluent, and whose ingenuity is both incisive and fluent (see AN II 135,5). Or else the three kinds of "gifted with ingenuity" should be understood by way of learning, inquiry, and achievement. One who understands the scriptures is gifted with ingenuity by way of learning. One who knows how to answer inquiries about the meaning, knowledge, the characteristic, and matters possible and impossible is one endowed with ingenuity in inquiry. One who has penetrated the paths and so forth is one endowed with ingenuity in achievement. One such as this is **learned, a bearer of Dhamma, an eminent friend gifted with ingenuity**.

⁝⁞ **Nidd II 251–52. Gifted with ingenuity**: There are three gifted with ingenuity: one with ingenuity in learning, in interrogation, and in achievement. What is ingenuity *in learning*? Here, someone is naturally learned in the discourses, mixed prose and verse, expositions, verses, inspired utterances, quotations, birth stories, amazing accounts, and questions-and-answers, and displays ingenuity based on this learning. What is ingenuity *in interrogation*? Here, someone displays ingenuity when interrogated about the meaning, the method, characteristics, causes, and matters possible and impossible. What is ingenuity *in achievement*? Here, someone has achieved the four establishments of mindfulness . . . the noble eightfold path, the four noble paths, the four fruits of the ascetic life, the four analytical knowledges, the six superknowledges. He knows the meaning, the doctrine, linguistic expression, and he is ingenious in regard to the meaning known, the doctrine known, and the linguistic expression known. The knowledge regarding the previous three knowledges is the analytical knowledge of ingenuity. He is endowed with this analytical knowledge of ingenuity; hence he is said to be gifted with ingenuity. That paccekabuddha possesses that analytical knowledge of ingenuity; therefore he is "endowed with ingenuity." ⁘

Having known the benefits: Through one's spiritual might, [one knows] the numerous benefits distinguished as one's own benefit, the benefit of others, and the benefit of both, or the benefit pertaining to the present life, pertaining to the future life, and the supreme benefit. **Having removed doubt**: having removed and destroyed doubt about the grounds of doubt, such as "Did I exist in the past?" and so forth (MN I 8,4, SN II 26,28). Being one accomplished in all such tasks, **one should live alone like a rhinoceros horn**.

The verse on ornaments

59. What is the origin? In Bārāṇasī there was a king named Vibhūsaka ("Ornamenter") Brahmadatta. In the morning, after eating porridge or rice, he would get himself adorned with various ornaments. Having inspected his entire body in a large mirror, if he did not like anything, he would remove it and have it replaced with another ornament. One day, while he was so engaged, the time for his midday meal arrived. Without having adorned himself, he wrapped a turban around his head, ate, and went for his siesta. Having arisen again, he continued in the same way until sunset. This happened on the second day and the third day. Then, while he was adorning himself, he got a backache. He thought: "Ah, while I have been busy adorning myself, discontent with ornaments of this kind, I gave rise to greed. But this greed, it is said, leads to the plane of misery. Come, now, let me suppress greed." Having abandoned the kingdom and gone forth, developing insight, he realized pacceka enlightenment and recited this verse as a joyful utterance. [112]

In this verse, play and delight have already been explained. "Sensual pleasure" is the pleasure of sensual objects.[491] For sensual objects, too, are called "pleasure" because they are the objective domain of pleasure; as it is said: "Form is pleasant, immersed in pleasure" (SN III 69,16). Thus **having found no satisfaction in this** physical **world** with this **play, delight, and sensual pleasures**, one does not grasp upon them thus: "This is gratifying" or "This is essential."[492] **Not taking any interest in them**: because one finds no satisfaction,[493] one behaves without interest, without yearning, without craving.

Refraining from ornaments, a speaker of truth, one should live alone. Here, there are two kinds of ornaments: the ornaments of a householder and the ornaments of a homeless one. The ornaments of a householder are clothing, turban, garlands, perfumes, and so forth; the ornaments of a homeless one are decorations of the alms bowl and other requisites. Therefore, the meaning should be understood thus: **one refrains** from ornaments by means of the three kinds of abstinence;[494] one is **a speaker of truth** by not uttering deceptive statements.

Nidd II 252. Sensual pleasure: This is said by the Blessed One: "There are, bhikkhus, these five strands of sensual pleasure. What five? Forms cognizable by the eye that are desirable, lovely, agreeable, pleasing, sensually enticing, tantalizing. Sounds cognizable by the ear . . . Odors cognizable by the nose . . . Tastes cognizable by the tongue . . . Tactile objects cognizable by the body that are desirable, lovely, agreeable, pleasing, sensually enticing, tantalizing. These are the five strands of sensual pleasure. Now the pleasure and joy that arise dependent on these five strands of sensual pleasure are the gratification in sensual pleasures." **Having found no satisfaction . . . not taking any interest in them**: having abandoned, dispelled, eliminated, and terminated amusement, delight, and sensual pleasures in the world.

Nidd II 252–53. Ornaments: There are two kinds of ornaments, those of householders and those of homeless ones. What are *the ornaments of householders*? Hair and beard, garlands and fragrances, ointments, necklaces, earrings, clothing, headwraps, rubbing, massages, bathing, bodywork, mirrors, collyrium, garlands, fragrances, and ointments, facial powder, lipstick, gloves, ribbons, staff, rod, sword, parasol, decorative sandals, turban, jewelry, fans, white clothes, and long nails. What are *the ornaments of homeless ones*? Decoration of the robes, decoration of the alms bowl, decoration of the lodging, decoration and ornamentation of this putrid body or of external requisites.

Nidd II 253. A speaker of truth: The paccekabuddha is a speaker of truth, one bound to truth, trustworthy and reliable, no deceiver of the world.

The verse on sons and wife

60. What is the origin? The son of the king of Bārāṇasī, even in his youth, was appointed to rule the kingdom. As with the paccekabodhisatta spoken of in relation to the first verse, one day, while enjoying the splendor of royalty, he reflected: "While exercising kingship, I create suffering for many. What use do I have for this evil, all for the sake of a single meal? Come now, let me produce happiness." Having abandoned the kingdom and gone forth, developing insight, he realized pacceka enlightenment and recited this verse as a joyful utterance.

In this verse, **wealth** is precious substances such as pearls, jewels, crystal, conch stone, coral, silver, gold, and so forth. **Grain** is of seven kinds: hill rice, paddy, barley, wheat, millet, *varaka*, and *kudrūsaka*.[495] **Relatives** are of four kinds: close relatives, clan members, friends, and colleagues. [113] **According to the limit**: by way of one's own respective limits.[496] The rest in the way stated.

Nidd II 254. To the limit. The defilements abandoned by the path of stream-entry do not recur, do not come back, do not return. The defilements abandoned by the path of the once-returner . . . The defilements abandoned by the path of the non-returner . . . The defilements abandoned by the path of arahantship do not recur, do not come back, do not return.

The verse on a tie

61. What is the origin? In Bārāṇasī, it is said, there was a king named Pādalola ("Footloose") Brahmadatta. In the morning, after eating porridge or rice, he would visit the three companies of dancers in his three palaces. The three companies of dancers were those who came from previous kings, those who came from his immediate predecessor, and those procured in his own time. One morning, he went to the palace of the young dancers. Wishing to please the king, the dancers, who were like the nymphs of Sakka, ruler of the devas, applied themselves to extremely enchanting dance, song, and instrumental music. The king, however, was discontent with them, thinking: "This is nothing special for young ones." So he went to the palace of the middle dancers. Those dancers performed in the same way. There, too, the king was discontent and went to the palace of the eldest dancers. Those dancers too performed in the same way. Because of their age—since they had passed through the reigns of two or three kings—he regarded their dancing as like a play of bones and found their singing disagreeable. Thus he strolled back to the palace of the young dancers, and then to the palace of the middle dancers, without finding contentment anywhere.

He reflected: "These dancers, who are like the nymphs of Sakka, apply themselves with all their might to dancing, song, and instrumental music because they wish to please me. However, I'm discontented everywhere and I just become more greedy. Now this greed, it is said, leads to the plane of misery. Come, now, let me suppress greed." Having abandoned the kingdom and gone forth, developing insight, he realized pacceka enlightenment and recited this verse as a joyful utterance.

This is its meaning: **This is a tie**: he describes his own object of enjoyment. For that is a tie because living beings become attached to it, just like an elephant stuck in the mud. **The happiness here is slight**: At the time that he was enjoying the five strands of sensual pleasure, the happiness there was *slight* in the sense of being base, because it is to be aroused through an inverted perception or because it is included among desire-sphere phenomena. It is transient, like the pleasure that comes from watching a dance illuminated by a flash of lightning; [114] what is meant is that it is temporary. **Giving little gratification, the suffering here is more**: In this connection it is said: "The pleasure and joy, bhikkhus, that arise in dependence on these five strands of sensual pleasure: this is the gratification in sensual pleasures." The suffering in this connection is explained in this way: "And what, bhikkhus, is the danger in sensual pleasures? Here, whatever be the craft by which a clansman earns his living, whether by computation, by accounting," and so forth (MN I 85,28). Comparing them, [the gratification is] slight, a mere drop of water, but the suffering is much more, like the water in the four oceans. Hence it is said: "giving little gratification, the suffering here is more." **This is a hook**: The five strands of sensual pleasure are like a fisherman's hook because they drag one along with a promise of gratification. **Having known thus, a thoughtful person**: having known this in such a way, a wise and intelligent person should abandon all this and live alone like a rhinoceros horn.

The verse on sundering

62. What is the origin? In Bārāṇasī, it is said, there was a king named Anivatta ("Not-Retreating") Brahmadatta. They called him thus because, when he entered a battle he did not retreat until he was victorious, or if he had undertaken any other task, he did not retreat until he had completed it. One day he went to the park. Now on that occasion a forest fire arose. The fire spread, burning up the dry pastures and the grass, without turning back. Having seen this, the king gave rise to the corresponding counterpart sign[497] and reflected: "Like this forest fire, the elevenfold fire[498] spreads without retreating, burning up all beings, and it produces great suffering. For the sake of turning back this suffering, when will I proceed without retreating, like this fire, burning up the defilements with the fire of the knowledge of the noble path?"

Having gone a little further, he saw fishermen catching fish in a river. [115] Among the fish that had entered the net, one large fish broke the net and escaped. The fishermen shouted: "A fish has broken the net and gone!" Having heard their cry, the king gave rise to the corresponding counterpart sign and reflected: "When will I, too, having broken through the net of craving and views with the knowledge of the noble path, escape without getting stuck?" Having abandoned the kingdom and gone forth, having undertaken insight, he realized pacceka enlightenment and recited this verse as a joyful utterance.

In the second line, **a net** is made of cord. **Ambucārī** is a fish, so called because it lives (*carati*) in water (*ambu*). What is meant is: "Like a fish that has broken the net in the water of the river." In the third line, **what has been burnt** means the place that has been burnt. As a fire does not retreat to a burnt place, never comes back there, just so one does not retreat to the strands of sensual pleasure that have been burnt by the fire of path knowledge. What is meant is that one does not return to them. The rest in the way explained earlier.

⁝▮ **Nidd II 256. Like a fire not returning to what has been burnt**: As a fire spreads without turning back, burning up its fuel—grass and wood—just so the defilements abandoned by the paccekabuddha with the path of stream-entry . . . with the path of the once-returner . . . with the path of the non-returner . . . with the path of arahantship do not recur, do not come back, do not return. ▮⁝

The verse on the downcast gaze

63. What is the origin? In Bārāṇasī, it is said, there was a king named Cakkhulola ("Roaming-Eyes") Brahmadatta. Like Footloose Brahmadatta, he was always intent on seeing his dancers, with this difference: When he was discontent, he went here and there, and on seeing this or that dancer, he was extremely delighted, again and again, so that, by looking at his circle of dancers, his craving ever increased. It is said that he saw a landowner's wife who had come to see the dancers and he was smitten by lust for her. He then acquired a sense of urgency, thinking: "Ah,[499] if my craving increases, I will fill up the hells. Come now, let me suppress it."

Having abandoned the kingdom and gone forth, developing insight, he realized pacceka enlightenment and, censuring his own former conduct, he recited this verse as a joyful utterance that illustrates the excellent qualities directly opposed to it. [116]

In this verse, **with downcast gaze**: with eyes cast down. What is meant is: "Having set in order the seven vertebrae of the neck, looking a mere yoke's distance ahead in order to see whatever should be abandoned by avoidance."[500] But one does not let the jawbone strike the chest, for such a way of keeping the eyes downcast is not suitable for an ascetic. **Not footloose**: One's feet do not itch from a desire to join a group, that is, to pair up with a single person or to make a pair a threesome; or one refrains from long journeys and unsettled travel.[501] **With**

guarded faculties: Of the six sense faculties, one guards the faculties other than the one that is mentioned separately (the mind faculty). **With protected mind**: One protects the mind so that it is not plundered by defilements; thus one has a protected mind. **Unpolluted**: By this practice[502] one is not inundated by defilements [arisen] in relation to various objects. **Not feverish with passion**: Since one is not inundated, one does not become feverish with the fires of defilements. Or alternatively, "unpolluted" refers to the external, "not feverish" to the internal. The rest in the way stated earlier.

The verse on the pāricchattaka tree

64. What is the origin? In Bārāṇasī, it is said, there was another king named Cātumāsika ("Four-Months") Brahmadatta, who used to go play in his garden every four months. One day in the middle month of the summer, while entering the park, he saw a pāricchattaka koviḷāra tree covered with leaves and a canopy adorned with flowers. He picked a flower and entered the park. Then one of his ministers, thinking, "The king has picked the best flower," stood on the back of an elephant and picked a flower. In just this way, all the troops picked flowers. Those who did not get to enjoy flowers [117] picked the leaves. Thus the tree was stripped of leaves and flowers, and only the trunk was left. As he was leaving the park in the evening the king saw this and thought: "What has happened to this tree? When I arrived it was adorned with coral-like flowers among its jewel-colored branches, but now it has been stripped of its leaves and flowers."

Not far away he saw another tree that was flowerless and covered with foliage. It occurred to him: "Because its branches were decked with flowers, the pāricchattaka tree was an object of greed for many people, and hence in an instant it has gone to ruin. But that other tree, which is not an object of greed, stands just as it was. This kingdom, too, like the flowering tree, is an object of greed. But the state of a bhikkhu, like the flowerless tree, is no object of greed. Therefore this kingdom is similar to the pāricchattaka tree, which, like the flowerless tree, was covered with leaves until it was plundered. Thus, like the pāricchattaka tree, having covered myself in the ochre robe, I should go forth." Having abandoned the kingdom and gone forth, developing insight, he realized pacceka enlightenment and recited this verse as a joyful utterance.[503]

In this verse, the meaning of the line **clothed in ochre robes, having renounced** (*kāsāyavattho abhinikkhamitvā*) should be understood thus: "Having renounced the home life, having become clothed in ochre robes."[504] The rest can be understood in the way stated, so it is not elaborated.

Nidd II 261–62. Like a päricchattaka tree covered with leaves: As that pāricchattaka koviḷāra tree had dense foliage and cast a thick shade, just so the paccekabuddha bears his complete set of robes and alms bowl.[505] **Clothed in ochre robes, having renounced**: Having cut off the impediment of dwelling in a house, having cut off the impediment of wife and children, having cut off the impediment of relatives, having cut off the impediment of friends and companions, having cut off the impediment of property, having shaved off hair and beard, having put on ochre robes, having gone forth from the household life into homelessness, having reached the state of ownerlessness, the paccekabuddha lives, dwells, conducts himself alone.

Chapter 4

The verse on greed for tastes

65. What is the origin? A certain king of Bārāṇasī, it is said, accompanied by his ministers' sons, was playing in the stone slab lotus pond in the park. His chef offered him a snack, which was like ambrosia, extremely well prepared, imbued with the taste of all kinds of meats. The king became greedy for it and ate it all by himself, without sharing it with anyone else. When he came out from his water sports very late in the day, he ate it quickly, without considering any of those with whom he had shared food in the past. Then he later reflected: "Oh, I have done something evil. I was so overcome by craving for tastes that I forgot about the others [118] and ate everything myself. Come, now, let me suppress craving for tastes." Having abandoned the kingdom and gone forth, developing insight, he realized pacceka enlightenment and recited this verse as a joyful utterance, criticizing his former behavior and showing the opposite virtues.

In this verse, **tastes** are flavors distinguished as sour, sweet, pungent, bitter, salty, alkaline, astringent, and so forth. **Not arousing greed**: not giving rise to craving. **Not hankering for them**: not being agitated by various tastes, such as "I will taste this, I will taste that." **Not nourishing others**: without anyone who has to be nourished, such as a pupil and so forth; what is meant is that one is content simply with maintaining the body.

Or alternatively, he shows: "Unlike formerly in the park, when I did not nourish another because I was greedy and hankered for tastes, I won't be thus, but having abandoned the craving because of which one hankers for tastes, I will 'not nourish another' by not producing another individual existence in the future, an existence rooted in craving." Or alternatively, the defilements are called "other" in the sense that they are damaging to one's good. By not nourishing them, "one does not nourish another." This, too, is the meaning here.

Walking for alms without skipping houses: One walks without deviating; one walks in sequence. This means that when one enters [a village] for alms, one goes without departing from the order of the houses; one goes to rich families and poor families without skipping any.[506] **With a mind unbound to this or that family**: One's mind is not attached anywhere, to families of khattiyas and so forth, because of the defilements, but one is similar to the moon, always like a newcomer. The rest in the way already stated.

The verse on obstructions

66. What is the origin? A certain king of Bārāṇasī, it is said, was an obtainer of the first jhāna. In order to maintain the jhāna, he abandoned the kingdom and went forth. Developing insight, he realized pacceka enlightenment and recited this verse as a joyful utterance.

In this verse, the obstructions are simply the hindrances. The meaning of these has already been explained in relation to the Discourse on the Serpent (see pp. 379–80). [119] Because they obstruct the mind as clouds obstruct the sun and moon, they are called **obstructions of mind**. **Having abandoned** them by access concentration or absorption. **Mental defilements**: the unwholesome qualities that encroach on the mind and oppress it, or such qualities as covetousness and so forth spoken of in the Simile of the Cloth (MN 7) and elsewhere. **Having dispelled**: having scattered, having destroyed; the meaning is, "having abandoned by the path of insight." **All**: without remainder. One equipped with serenity and insight is **independent** because of the abandoning of dependence on views by means of the first path. **Having cut off**, by the remaining paths, **affection and hatred** (the fault of affection) pertaining to the three realms. What is meant is craving and lust.[507] For affection itself is called "the fault of affection" because it is the opposite of excellent qualities. The rest in the way already stated.

Nidd II 265. Independent, having cut off affection and hatred. Independent: There are two dependencies: dependency on craving and dependency on views. **Affection**: There are two kinds of affection: affection on account of craving and affection on account of views. **Hatred**: mental resentment, repugnance, aversion, irritation, hatred, antipathy, anger, ill will, resistance, animosity, ferocity, displeasure, dissatisfaction of the mind. **Independent, having cut off affection and hatred**: The paccekabuddha, having cut off, eradicated, abandoned, dispelled, terminated, and eliminated affection on account of craving, affection on account of views, and hatred, is not dependent on the eye, ear . . . not dependent on things seen, heard, sensed, and cognized; he dwells independent, unattached, freed, detached, with a mind rid of barriers.

The verse on leaving behind

67. What is the origin? A certain king of Bārāṇasī, it is said, was an obtainer of the fourth jhāna. In order to maintain the jhāna, he abandoned the kingdom and went forth. Developing insight, he realized pacceka enlightenment and, indicating the success of his practice, he recited this verse as a joyful utterance.

In this verse, **having left behind**: having put at one's back; the meaning is "having discarded, having cast off." **Pleasure and pain**: bodily comfort and discomfort. **Joy and dejection**: mental comfort and discomfort. **Purified**: purified because freed from nine contrary qualities, namely, the five hindrances, thought, examination, rapture, and pleasure; rid of defilements like refined gold. **Equanimity**: the equanimity of the fourth jhāna. **Serenity**: the serenity of the fourth jhāna.

This is the construal: "Having left behind pleasure and pain": The purport is that pain has been put away earlier on the plane of access to the first jhāna and pleasure on the plane of access to the third jhāna. Having taken the word "and" stated at the beginning [and inserted it] again afterward, [the sense becomes]: "And having left behind joy [120] and dejection." "Earlier" is a governing word (*adhikāra*). Hence he shows: Joy is put away at the access to the fourth jhāna and dejection already at the access to the second jhāna. For these places of abandoning are stated in an expository sense.[508] But in the direct sense, the place for the abandoning of pain is the first jhāna; for the abandoning of dejection, the second jhāna; for the abandoning of pleasure, the third jhāna; and for the abandoning of joy, the fourth jhāna. As it is said: "When one enters and dwells in the first jhāna, here the arisen pain faculty ceases without remainder," and so forth (SN V 207–16). All this is explained in the Atthasālinī, the commentary to the Dhammasaṅgaha (As 176–77). Since previously, in the first jhāna and [in the second and third jhānas], one has already left behind pain, dejection, and pleasure [respectively], in that case, having left behind joy in the fourth jhāna and having gained purified equanimity and serenity by this practice, one should live alone. The rest is clear.

⁘ **Nidd II 266. Having left behind pleasure and pain and previously [discarded] joy and dejection**: Here, with the abandoning of pleasure and pain, and with the previous passing away of joy and dejection, the paccekabuddha enters and dwells in the fourth jhāna, neither painful nor pleasant, which has purification of mindfulness by equanimity. **Having gained purified equanimity and serenity**: In the fourth jhāna equanimity and serenity are purified, cleansed, spotless, without defilement, malleable, wieldy, firm, and imperturbable. Having gained the equanimity and serenity pertaining to the fourth jhāna, one should live alone like a rhinoceros horn. ⁘

The verse on energy aroused

68. What is the origin? A certain frontier king, it is said, whose army consisted of a thousand warriors, had a small realm but great wisdom. One day he reflected, "Although I am of minor stature, because I am wise I can capture the whole of Jambudīpa." He then sent a messenger to a neighboring king, telling him: "You must surrender your kingdom to me within seven days or fight." He then gathered his own ministers and said to them: "Without asking for your permission, I acted rashly and sent this message to such and such a king. What's to be done?" They said: "Is it possible, great king, to call back the messenger?" – "It's not possible. He must have already gone." – "If so, you have destroyed us. It's painful to die by another's sword. Come, let's die by each other's sword, let's stab ourselves, let's hang ourselves, let's take poison." In this way, each of them spoke in praise of death. Then the king said: "What use are these to me? I have my warriors, men."

Then the thousand warriors rose up, each saying: "I'm a warrior, great king! I'm a warrior, great king!" The king thought to himself: "I'll investigate them." [121] He then had a funeral pyre prepared and said: "I acted rashly, men. My ministers have rejected what I did. I myself will enter the funeral pyre. Who will enter along with me? Who will surrender his life to me?" When he had spoken, five hundred warriors rose up and said: "Let us enter, great king." Then the king said to the other five hundred: "What will you do now, dear ones?"

They said: "That is not the act of a man, great king. That's womanly conduct. Since the king has sent a messenger to the opponent king, we will die fighting alongside the king." The king replied: "You are the ones who have surrendered your lives to me." Then he equipped his fourfold army, went out accompanied by the thousand warriors, and settled at the boundary of his realm. When the opponent king heard the news, he became angry and thought: "Ah! That little king couldn't even be my slave!" Then he took all his troops and departed for battle. When the minor king saw them arrayed, he said to his troops: "Dear ones, there are not many of you. You should all mass together, take your swords and shields, and quickly advance straight toward the other king." They did so. Then the opposing army split in two, allowing them to pass in between. They captured the opponent king alive, while the enemy warriors fled. The minor king ran in front, saying: "I'm going to kill you." But the opponent king pleaded for mercy. The minor king granted him mercy, made him take an oath, and made him his own man. Then, together with him, he proceeded against another king, and while stationed at the boundary of the kingdom, he sent a message: "Give me your kingdom or fight!" He surrendered the kingdom, thinking: "I am not capable even of fighting one." Having captured all the kings in this way, in the end he even captured the king of Bārāṇasī.

While ruling over the whole of Jambudīpa accompanied by a hundred kings, he reflected: "In the past I was a minor king, but now, through my own ingenuity, I have become the ruler of all Jambudīpa. [122] But that ingenuity of mine, accompanied by mundane energy, does not lead to disenchantment or dispassion. It would indeed be good for me to use this ingenuity to seek the world-transcending Dhamma." He then gave the kingdom to the king of Bārāṇasī, sent his wife and children back to his own country, and went forth. Having undertaken insight, he realized pacceka enlightenment and then, indicating the success of his own endeavor, he recited this verse as a joyful utterance.

In this verse, by **with energy aroused** he shows his own arousing of energy, initial energy. The supreme goal is nibbāna; **to attain the supreme goal**: for its attainment. By this he shows the fruit to be attained by arousing energy. **With unsluggish mind**: by this he shows the unsluggishness of the mind and mental factors fortified by powerful energy. **Robust conduct**: by this he shows the absence of bodily indolence when standing, sitting, walking back and forth, and so on.

Firmly persistent: by this he shows the energy of striving that occurs thus: "Willingly, let only my skin and sinews remain" (AN I 50,9–13), which is referred to when it is said, in relation to one striving in the gradual training, "he realizes the supreme truth with the body and sees it by piercing it with wisdom" (MN I 480,9). Or alternatively, by this he shows the energy associated with the path. For that is firm, since it has reached fulfillment by development, and it is persistence, because it has entirely departed from opposition. Therefore the person endowed with that, whose persistence is firm, is called "one firmly persistent."

Equipped with strength and power: equipped with bodily strength and the power of knowledge at the moment of the path. Or alternatively: "equipped with strength and power" means equipped with power *that consists in* strength. What is meant is "equipped with the power of sturdy knowledge." By this expression, indicating that his energy is accompanied by insight knowledge, he demonstrates careful striving. The three lines should also be construed by way of preliminary, intermediate, and superior energy. The rest in the way already explained.

The verse on seclusion

69. What is the origin? The origin of this verse is similar to that of the verse on obstructions; there is no difference. But in the commentary on its meaning, **seclusion** [123] is separation by turning away from these and those beings and conditioned things—resorting to aloneness, solitude;[509] the meaning is bodily seclusion. **Jhāna**: It is mental seclusion that is called jhāna, because of burning up the contrary states and because of closely contemplating the object and the characteristics.[510] Here, the eight meditative attainments are called jhāna because of burning up the contrary states such as the hindrances and because of closely contemplating the object; insight, the paths, and the fruits are called jhāna because of burning up the contrary states such as the perception of a being, and because of closely contemplating the characteristics.[511] But here it is the close contemplation of the object that is intended. Thus **not neglecting** this seclusion and jhāna, not ignoring them.[512]

⁝▯ Nidd II 269. Not neglecting seclusion and jhāna. Seclusion: The paccekabuddha is one who delights in seclusion, who is delighted with seclusion, who is intent upon internal serenity of mind, who does not neglect jhāna, who possesses insight, who frequents empty houses, a meditator who is delighted with jhāna, intent upon solitude, who esteems his own good. **Not neglecting jhāna**: The paccekabuddha does not neglect jhāna in two ways: he is intent upon arousing the first jhāna that he has not yet attained . . . the fourth jhāna that he has not yet attained; in this way he does not neglect jhāna. And he pursues, develops, and cultivates the first jhāna that he has already attained . . . the fourth jhāna that he has already attained; in this way too he does not neglect jhāna. ▯⁝

Always acting in accordance with the teachings: in regard to the phenomena such as the five aggregates that come into the range of insight.[513] **Always**: constantly, continuously, without interruption. **Acting in accordance with**: practicing the teaching of insight that accords with conduct[514] in regard to those teachings. Or alternatively, **the teachings** here means the nine world-transcending states,[515] and "in accordance with" is the teaching that is in harmony with those states. This is a designation for insight.

⁞▮ **Nidd II 269. Always acting in accordance with the teachings**: The teachings (*dhammā*) are the four establishments of mindfulness . . . the noble eightfold path. What is in accordance with the teachings (*anudhamma*)? The right practice, the practice in conformity, the unopposed practice, the practice in accordance with the goal, the practice in accordance with the Dhamma, the fulfillment of good behavior, guarding the doors of the sense faculties, moderation in eating, devotion to wakefulness, mindfulness and clear comprehension. Always acting in accordance with the teachings, constantly, consistently, continuously, without interruption, repetitively, like waves on water, in unbroken continuity, in the morning and the afternoon, in the first, middle, and last watches of the night, in the dark fortnight and the bright fortnight, in the rainy season, the cold season, and the hot season, in the first, middle, and final stages of life, one lives, dwells, behaves, conducts oneself accordingly. ▮⁞

Having explored the danger in states of existence: This means contemplating with that insight—which is designated "conduct in accordance with"—the fault in the three states of existence, consisting in their impermanence and so forth.[516] The construal should be understood thus: "Not neglecting this bodily seclusion and mental seclusion, one can be said to have achieved this [pacceka enlightenment] by the practice consisting in insight that has reached its peak; he should live alone like a rhinoceros horn."

⁞▮ **Nidd II 269. Having explored the danger in states of existence**: One who explores the danger in states of existence thus, "All conditioned things are impermanent" . . . [see pp. 1060–61, Nidd I 67–68] . . . "Whatever is subject to origination is all subject to cessation," should live alone like a rhinoceros horn. ▮⁞

The verse on the destruction of craving

70. What is the origin? A certain king of Bārāṇasī, it is said, made a tour of the city with the full pomp of royalty. Because of his physical splendor, those people walking in front, their hearts drawn, turned around and looked up at him alone. So too those walking behind him and those walking on both sides. For it is just natural that people in the world are never satiated in looking at a buddha and in looking at the full moon, the ocean, and a king. Then the wife of a certain landowner, who had gone to the upper story of her mansion, opened the window and stood there looking down. As soon as the king saw her, he was smitten with her and ordered his minister: "Find out, man, whether or not that woman is married." He [124] found out and reported: "She is married."

Then the king reflected: "These 20,000 dancing girls, who are like heavenly nymphs, try to please me alone. But now I have passed over them and crave another man's wife. This craving is dragging me to the plane of misery." Having seen the danger in craving, he decided: "Let me suppress it." Having abandoned the kingdom and gone forth, developing insight, he realized pacceka enlightenment and recited this verse as a joyful utterance.

Here, **craving's destruction** is nibbāna, the non-occurrence of that craving whose danger has been seen. **Heedful**: acting constantly and carefully; **intelligent**:[517] wise, competent; **learned**: one who has the learning that promotes well-being and happiness. What is meant is one endowed with the heritage of learning; **mindful**: able to recollect what was done [and said] long ago. **Comprehended the Dhamma**: one who, by investigation of the Dhamma, has fully understood the Dhamma. **Fixed in destiny**: attained the fixed course through the noble path.[518] **Vigorous in striving**: possessed of right striving and energy.

Nidd II 270. Comprehended the Dhamma: The paccekabuddha has comprehended the Dhamma, known the Dhamma, assessed the Dhamma, scrutinized the Dhamma, recognized the Dhamma, clarified the Dhamma thus: "All conditioned things are impermanent" . . . "Whatever is subject to origination is all subject to cessation." Or alternatively, for the paccekabuddha the aggregates have been compressed, the elements have been compressed, the sense bases have been compressed, the destinations have been compressed, rebirth has been compressed, conception has been compressed, existence has been compressed, saṃsāra has been compressed, the round has been compressed.[519] Or alternatively, the paccekabuddha abides at the limit of the aggregates, at the limit of the elements . . . at the limit of the round, at the limit of conditioned things; he abides in his final existence, in his final body; he maintains his final body.

This is his last existence;
this is his final body.
For him there is no more renewed existence,
no wandering on in birth and death.

Fixed in destiny: It is the four noble paths that are called the fixed course (*niyāma*). One possessing the four noble paths is fixed in destiny (*niyata*). He has attained, achieved, experienced, realized the fixed course. ▯⁝

This line should be construed out of sequence.[520] Thus, one who possesses those qualities such as heedfulness is *vigorous in the striving* conducive to the fixed course. By means of that striving he becomes *fixed in destiny* on attaining the fixed course. Then, with the attainment of arahantship, he becomes one who has *comprehended the Dhamma*. For the arahant is called "one who has comprehended the Dhamma" because he has nothing that needs to be comprehended again. As it is said: "Those who have comprehended the Dhamma, and the diverse trainees here" (**1038**). The rest in the way already explained.

The verse on being unalarmed by sounds

71. What is the origin? A certain king of Bārāṇasī, it is said, owned a park some distance away. One day he rose early and was going to the park when along the way he got down from his vehicle and went to a pond [125] to wash his face. In that place a lioness had given birth to a cub and had gone off to search for prey. The king's man saw it and reported to the king: "There is a lion cub, lord." The king thought: "It is said that a lion is not afraid of anyone." Wishing to investigate this, he ordered the drums to be beaten. The lion cub heard the sound but just continued to lie there. The king repeated this three times. On the third occasion the cub raised its head and looked over the entire retinue but just continued to lie there. Then the king said: "Let's go before the mother returns." As he was traveling he reflected: "The lion cub has just been born this day yet it is not alarmed or frightened. When will I too, having conquered[521] the agitation of craving and views, not be alarmed or frightened?"

Having taken that as an object, he continued on. Next he saw that fishermen had caught fish and had hung the net on branches. He noticed that the wind passed through the net without getting stuck. He took this, too, as an object and thought: "When will I, too, split the net of craving and views or the net of delusion and go along without getting stuck?"

Having come to the park, while sitting on the bank of the Stone-Slab lotus pond he saw lotuses being blown on by the wind. The lotuses bent down and touched the water, but when the wind subsided they again stood up in their original places, untainted by the water. He took that, too, as an object and thought: "When will I, too, though born in the world, stand untainted by the world, just as these lotuses, though born in the water, stand untainted by the water?" Having reflected again and again, "Like a lion, the wind, and the lotuses, respectively, I should be unalarmed, unattached, and untainted," he abandoned the kingdom and went forth. Developing insight, he realized pacceka enlightenment and recited this verse as a joyful utterance.

Here, as to **a lion**, there are four kinds of lions: the savannah lion, the yellow lion, the black lion, and the maned lion. Of these, the maned lion is declared to be foremost, and that is the kind intended here. **Wind** is manifold, such as the eastern wind and so forth. The **lotus** may be red, white, and so forth. Any kind of wind and any kind of lotus among these is appropriate. Here, terror exists because of self-love, and self-love is the stain of craving; that [stain of craving] exists because of greed—whether associated with views or dissociated from views—and it is itself also craving. But attachment exists because of the delusion of one who lacks investigation into this, [126] and delusion is ignorance. Here, the abandoning of craving occurs by means of serenity and the abandoning of ignorance by means of insight. Therefore, having abandoned self-love by means of serenity, [one is not alarmed] by impermanence, suffering, and so forth, **like a lion unalarmed among sounds**. Having abandoned delusion by means of insight, one is unattached to the aggregates and sense bases **like the wind not caught in a net**. And having abandoned greed and views associated with greed by means of serenity alone, one is untainted by greed for wealth and all states of existence, **untainted like a lotus by water**.

And in this case, good behavior is the basis for serenity; serenity is concentration; and insight is wisdom. Thus, when those two qualities (serenity and insight) are accomplished, the three aggregates are achieved.[522] Among these, through the aggregate of good behavior one becomes gentle. Like a lion among sounds, one is not alarmed because of a desire to lash out in anger at those who provoke resentment. Like the wind in the net, one who has penetrated their real nature by means of the aggregate of wisdom is not attached to phenomena classified into the aggregates and so forth. Like the lotus untainted by water, one free of lust by means of the aggregate of concentration is not tainted by lust. In this way, it should be understood, one is unalarmed, unattached, and untainted through the abandoning of ignorance and craving and the three unwholesome roots by means of serenity and insight and the aggregates of good behavior, concentration, and wisdom, respectively. The rest in the way stated earlier.

The verse on one whose strength is in its fangs

72. What is the origin? It is said that a certain king of Bārāṇasī, in order to suppress a frontier rebellion, set forth with a large army, avoiding village and town paths and taking instead a path straight through a forest. Now on that occasion a lion was lying down at the foot of a mountain warming himself in the morning sun. Having seen him, the king's man reported this to the king. The king thought, "It is said that a lion is not alarmed by sound," and he ordered a noise to be made by the drums, trumpets, hand drums, and other instruments. The lion just continued to lie there. The king repeated this three times.

On the third occasion the lion thought, "An opponent of mine is here," and he steadied himself with his four paws on the ground and roared his lion's roar.

As soon as they heard this, the elephant riders descended from their elephants [127] and rushed into the bushes. The hosts of elephants and horses fled in various directions. The king's elephant, too, took the king and fled, crashing through the jungle. Unable to control him, the king caught the branch of a tree and dropped to the ground. Going along a narrow footpath, he arrived at the dwelling place of paccekabuddhas. There he asked the paccekabuddhas: "Bhante, did you hear the sound?" – "Yes, great king." – "The sound of what, Bhante?" – "First the sound of drums and trumpets, and so forth; afterward, the sound of a lion." – "Weren't you afraid, Bhante?" – "No, great king, we aren't afraid of any sound." – "Is it possible, Bhante, for me to be so fearless?" – "It is possible, great king, if you go forth." – "Then let me go forth, Bhante."

Then the paccekabuddhas gave him the going forth and trained him in proper behavior, in the way explained earlier. And in the way explained earlier, he developed insight, realized pacceka enlightenment, and recited this verse as a joyful utterance.

In this verse, **the lion** is so called because it conquers and kills, and because of its speed.[523] It is the maned lion that is intended here. [**By attacking and overpowering**]: The word "lives" should be construed with both "attacking" and "overpowering," yielding "lives attacking" and "lives overpowering." Here, "lives attacking" is said because it lives having attacked, having suppressed, having carried away.[524] "Lives overpowering" is said because it overpowers, terrifies, and subjugates. It *attacks* through its bodily strength, it *overpowers* through its splendor. If anyone should ask, "What does it attack and overpower?" by taking the genitive "of beasts" in an accusative sense,[525] one should answer: "It attacks and overpowers beasts." **Remote** means far away, and **lodgings** are dwelling places. The rest can be understood in the way stated earlier so it is not elaborated.

Nidd II 272. As the lion, king of beasts, who has fangs as its strength, lives by attacking and overpowering: As the lion, the king of beasts, who has fangs as its strength, fangs as its weapon, lives having overpowered, overwhelmed, exhausted, and crushed all other animals, the paccekabuddha, too, who has wisdom as his strength, wisdom as his weapon, lives having overpowered, overwhelmed, exhausted, and crushed all other persons by means of wisdom.

The verse on the immeasurables[526]

73. What is the origin? A certain king, it is said, was an obtainer of jhāna through loving-kindness. Thinking, "Kingship is an obstacle to the bliss of jhāna," [128] in order to maintain the jhāna, he abandoned the kingdom and went forth. Developing insight, he realized pacceka enlightenment and recited this verse as a joyful utterance.

Here, **loving-kindness** is the wish to bring well-being and happiness in the way stated thus: "May all beings be happy!" and so forth. **Compassion** is the wish to remove harm and suffering in the way stated thus: "Oh, may all beings be free from this suffering!" and so forth. **Altruistic joy** is the wish that they not be separated from well-being and happiness in the way stated thus: "They rejoice! How good and excellent it is that beings rejoice!" and so forth. **Equanimity** is looking on impartially at happiness and suffering, thinking: "They will be known through their own kamma." For ease in composing the verse,[527] equanimity has been stated out of sequence, just after loving-kindness, while altruistic joy is stated last. **Liberation**: the four are also liberations because they are liberated from their own contrary qualities. Hence it is said: "At the right time pursuing liberation by loving-kindness, equanimity, compassion, and altruistic joy."[528]

Here, **pursuing** means developing the first three by way of three or four jhānas,[529] and equanimity by way of the fourth jhāna. **At the right time**: When it is said "pursuing at the right time," this means that having pursued loving-kindness and emerged from it, one pursues compassion; then, having emerged from it, one pursues altruistic joy; then, having emerged from the others or from the jhāna without rapture, one pursues equanimity. Or it means at a time when it is convenient to pursue them. **Not antagonized by the whole world**: without animosity toward all the world of beings in the ten directions. For through the development of loving-kindness and so forth, beings are unrepulsive. And aversion, which is opposition to beings, subsides. Hence it is said: "not antagonized by the whole world." This here is a brief account. A detailed discussion of loving-kindness and so forth is given in the Atthasālinī (As 192–97), the commentary to the Dhammasaṅgaha. The rest is similar to what has already been stated.

The verse on the extinction of life

74. What is the origin? It is said that there was a paccekabuddha named Mātaṅga who lived in dependence on Rājagaha; [129] he was the very last of paccekabuddhas. When our bodhisatta had arisen, the deities coming to worship the bodhisatta saw him and said: "Dear sir, dear sir! A buddha has arisen in the world." While emerging from the attainment of cessation, he heard that sound. Having seen that the time for the extinction of his own life had come, he traveled through the sky to the mountain in the Himalayas called "the Great Precipice," the place where paccekabuddhas attain final nibbāna. He threw into the precipice the skeleton of a paccekabuddha who had attained final nibbāna earlier, sat down on a stone slab, and recited this verse as a joyful utterance.[530]

In this verse, **lust, hatred, and delusion** were explained in commenting on the Discourse on the Serpent. **The fetters**: the ten fetters. And **having sundered** them by this and that path. **Not terrified at the extinction of life**: It is passing away, the dissolution of the mind, that is called the extinction of life. Because he had abandoned attachment to life, he was not terrified over the extinction of life. Having shown at this point his own attainment of the nibbāna element with residue remaining, at the conclusion of the verse he attained final nibbāna through the nibbāna element without residue remaining.

The verse on ulterior motive

75. What is the origin? A certain king of Bārāṇasī, it is said, ruled over a prosperous kingdom of the kind described in relation to the first verse (p. 415). He contracted a severe illness and painful feelings arose in him. Twenty thousand women surrounded him and massaged his hands and feet. The ministers reflected: "Now this king won't live. Let us look out for ourselves." So they went to another king and offered to serve him. Though they served him, they didn't get any reward. Meanwhile, the first king recovered and asked: "Where is this one, where is that one?" When he heard the news, he shook his head and fell silent.

Since they did not get anything from the second king, the ministers sank into extreme poverty, so when they heard that the first king had recovered, they returned to him, paid homage to him, and stood to one side. [130] When the king asked them: "Where did you go, dear ones?" they replied: "When we saw that the king had become weak, from fear for our livelihoods, we went to such and such a country." The king shook his head and reflected: "Let me investigate to find out whether or not they would do such a thing again."

He pretended that he had contracted an oppressive illness[531] as before and acted as if he were experiencing severe pain. The women surrounded him and treated him as before. The ministers, too, departed as before, taking even more people with them. In this way, even up to the third time, the king acted in the same way, and each time the ministers departed. Then, when he saw that they had returned the fourth time, he reflected: "Oh, they have acted badly, in that they abandoned me when I was sick and left me without concern!" Disenchanted, he abandoned the kingdom and went forth. Developing insight, he realized pacceka enlightenment and recited this verse as a joyful utterance.

Here, **they resort to you**: They adhere bodily and attend on you. **They serve you**: They perform services, with reverential salutation and a display of deference. **For a motive**: for their own benefit as the reason. They have no other reason for resorting to you and serving you but their own benefit. What is meant is that they serve you for their own sake. **Friends without motive are today very rare**: Those without motive are those who are not motivated by some benefit, [who do not serve one thinking]: "I will get something from him." Such friends who possess the quality of noble friendship are today very rare. They are described thus:

There is the friend who is a helper,
the friend in happiness and suffering,
the friend who points out the good,
and the friend who is sympathetic. (DN III 188,1–4)

Since their wisdom is set up in regard to themselves, they look out only for themselves, not others.[532] Thus it is said: **Wise about their own good**. It is said there is also this ancient reading: **Wise about the visible good**. [131] What is meant is that they have wisdom in regard to the present, visible good; they do not look out for the future.[533] **Impure**: They are possessed of impure, ignoble action of body, speech, and mind. The rest should be understood in the way already stated.

Conclusion

Thus the Discourse on the Rhinoceros Horn, which consists of forty-one verses, should be understood in terms of sequence and meaning, having construed all the verses in the appropriate way, using the method of construal that was stated only in some cases. We did not construe them in every case from fear of too much elaboration.

4 Kasibhāradvāja
(*Kasibhāradvāja Sutta*)

What is the origin? There are the two periods of activity for a buddha: the period of forenoon activities and the period of activities after midday. One day, while dwelling among the Magadhans at Dakkhiṇāgiri, near the brahmin village Ekanālā, after he had completed his forenoon activities, at the conclusion of his activities after midday,[534] the Blessed One surveyed the world with the buddha eye and saw that the brahmin Kasibhāradvāja had the supporting conditions for arahantship. He foresaw: "When I have gone there, we will have a conversation, and at the end of the conversation, when he has heard my teaching of the Dhamma, this brahmin will go forth and attain arahantship." Thus he went there, started a conversation, and spoke this discourse.

In this connection, it might be asked: "What are the activities of a buddha in the forenoon, and what are his activities after midday?"[535] It is said that the Blessed One, the Buddha, would rise early in the morning and take care of his physical needs, such as washing his face and so forth, doing so to benefit his attendant and for the sake of his physical health. Then he would pass the time sitting in seclusion until the time arrived for the alms round. [132] When it was time for the alms round, he would put on his lower robe, fasten the waistband, cover himself with the upper robe, take his bowl, and enter the village or town for alms. Sometimes he would go alone, sometimes accompanied by the Sangha of bhikkhus. Sometimes he would enter in a natural manner, sometimes with many wonders occurring.

Thus when the Buddha would enter for alms, gentle winds

would precede him and clear the ground. Clouds sprinkling drops of water would cause the dust along the path to settle and form a canopy overhead. Other winds would waft flowers and strew them along the road. The elevated areas of the ground would fall and the depressed areas rise up, so that the ground was always level at the time he would step on it. Sometimes soft lotus flowers would receive his feet. As soon as he placed his right foot within the gate post,[536] six-colored rays would be emitted from his body and spread out in all directions, making the mansions, peaked houses, and other buildings appear as if they were enveloped in the sheen of exquisite gold. Elephants, horses, birds, and other animals, each standing in their own places, would break out into melodious sounds; so too would musical instruments such as drums and lutes, as also the ornaments worn by the people.

By that signal people would know: "Today the Blessed One has come for alms." Then, well dressed and well groomed, bringing fragrances, flowers, and other offerings, they would come out from their houses, walk down the road, and respectfully present their offerings to the Blessed One. Having paid homage to him, they would say: "Bhante, give us ten bhikkhus for alms, give us twenty, give us a hundred." Having taken the Blessed One's bowl, they would prepare a seat and respectfully serve him with almsfood. When he had finished his meal, the Blessed One would survey the minds of the people present and teach them the Dhamma in such a way that some would go for refuge, some take the five precepts, some attain the fruits of stream-entry, a once-returner, or a non-returner. Some, having gone forth, would attain arahantship, the foremost fruit. After benefiting the multitude in various ways, he would rise from his seat and return to the monastery.

Upon his return he would sit down in the pavilion, in the excellent seat prepared just for him, waiting until the bhikkhus finished their meal. When they were finished, [133] the attendant would inform the Blessed One and he would then enter the Fragrant Cottage.

These were his *activities in the forenoon*. And what has not been stated here should be understood in the way stated in the Brahmāyu Sutta (MN II 137–40).

With the morning activities completed, the Blessed One

would sit down in the vestibule of the Fragrant Cottage and wash his feet. Then, standing on a footstool, he would exhort the bhikkhus: "Bhikkhus, achieve success by heedfulness. Rare is the arising of a buddha in the world; rare is the gain of the human state; rare is the gain of the opportunity;[537] rare is the going forth into homelessness; rare is it to hear the good Dhamma in the world." Then the bhikkhus would pay homage to the Blessed One and ask for a meditation subject, and the Blessed One would assign them subjects in accordance with their temperament. Having learned those meditation subjects, they would pay homage to the Blessed One and go to their individual living quarters: some to the forest, some to the foot of a tree, some to the mountains or elsewhere, some to the heaven of the four divine kings . . . some to the heaven of the devas who control what is created by others.

The Blessed One would then enter the Fragrant Cottage. If he so wished, he would lie down for a while on his right side, in the lion posture, mindful and clearly comprehending. When his body was refreshed, he would rise and pass the second part of the afternoon surveying the world. In the third part, the people of the village or town where he was dwelling, who had given alms in the morning, would assemble in the monastery, well dressed and well groomed, bringing fragrances, flowers, and other offerings. The Blessed One would go there, displaying whatever wonders were appropriate for the assembly present. Then, having sat down in his excellent seat in the Dhamma hall, he would teach the Dhamma in a way fitting the time and the capacity of the people. When he knew it was time, he would dismiss the assembly.

Then, if he wanted to bathe, he would rise from his seat and go to a place where water was prepared. He would take a bathing cloth from his attendant and enter the bathing room. Meanwhile, his attendant would bring the seat and prepare it in a cell in the Fragrant Cottage. Having refreshed his body, the Blessed One would put on a well-dyed double-layer lower robe, [134] fasten the waistband, arrange his upper robe, and return to his cell, where he would sit alone in seclusion for a while. Then the bhikkhus would arrive from here and there to attend upon the Blessed One. Some would ask questions, some would ask for a meditation subject, some would ask to hear the

Dhamma. The Blessed One would pass the first watch of the night fulfilling their wishes.

In the middle watch of the night the deities of the entire ten-thousandfold world system would get their chance. Having approached the Blessed One, they would ask whatever questions they had in mind, even one only four syllables in length. The Blessed One would pass the middle watch of the night answering their questions.

He divided the last watch of the night into four parts. He would spend one part walking back and forth. In the second part, he would enter the Fragrant Cottage and lie down on his right side, in the lion posture, mindful and clearly comprehending. He would pass the third part in the meditative attainment of fruition. In the fourth part, he would enter the meditative attainment of great compassion and survey the world with the buddha eye in order to see which beings had little dust in their eyes and which had much dust in their eyes, and so forth. These were *his activities after midday*.

Thus at the end of the fourth part of his activities after midday, which consists in surveying the world, the Blessed One was surveying the world to see which beings had performed services in the past to the Buddha, Dhamma, and Sangha and which had not performed such services—such deeds as giving alms, undertaking the precepts, and observing the uposatha—and to see which ones possessed supporting conditions and which did not. While doing so, he saw that the brahmin Kasibhāradvāja had the supporting conditions for arahantship and he knew: "When I have gone there, a conversation will take place, and then, at the end of our conversation, when he hears the Dhamma, this brahmin will go forth and attain arahantship." Thus he spoke this discourse after he had gone there and started a conversation.

Here, the words beginning "Thus have I heard" were spoken by the Venerable Ānanda when he recited the Dhamma at the time of the first great council. They were addressed to the five hundred arahants when he was questioned by the Venerable Elder Mahākassapa. The words "I plow and sow, ascetic" were spoken by Kasibhāradvāja. The words "I too, brahmin, [135] plow and sow" and so forth were spoken by the Blessed One. Having collected all this, it is called the Discourse with Kasibhāradvāja.

Here, as to **thus**, the word "thus" (*evaṃ*) has the meanings of aspect, indication, and emphasis. In its meaning of *aspect*, it conveys the meaning: "Who is capable of understanding in all modes the word of the Blessed One, which is subtle in its various methods; which originates [in response to beings of] numerous inclinations; which is consummate in meaning and phrasing; which applies diverse counteractive measures;[538] which is deep in doctrine, meaning, teaching, and penetration;[539] which conforms to the individual languages of all beings; and has a distinguished nature? Rather, 'thus have I heard' means that even I heard it in a single aspect."

In the meaning of *indication*, by "thus have I heard" he exonerates himself, [as if to say]: "I am not self-accomplished;[540] this was not realized by me," and then he indicates: "This entire discourse now to be spoken was heard by me in this way."

In the aspect of *emphasis*, he awakens in beings a desire to listen, showing his own power of retentiveness in accordance with the praise spoken of him by the Blessed One: "This, bhikkhus, is the foremost of my bhikkhu disciples among those who are learned, namely, Ānanda. This is the foremost of those with a quick grasp, of those with a good memory, of those who are resolute, of personal attendants, namely, Ānanda" (AN I 24–25). [So he is saying:] "Thus have I heard, and it is neither deficient nor excessive with respect to meaning and with respect to phrasing; it should be seen as just so and not otherwise."

Have I heard: By "I" he refers to himself; "heard" signifies what has been cognized through the ear door. Therefore "thus have I heard" means: "Thus I have learned through a cognitive process preceded by ear-consciousness."[541]

On one occasion: at one time. **The Blessed One** (*bhagavā*): What is meant is the one possessed of fortune, the one who has abolished, the one who partakes of.[542] **Among the Magadhans**: The Magadhans are the princes living in that country; also the one country in which they reside, by a convention of speech, is spoken of as "the Magadhans." He was living in that country among the Magadhans. But some expand on it in many ways, for example, they say [the country is called Magadha] because when King Cetiya had spoken falsely and was entering the ground, he was told: "Do not enter the hole" (*mā gadhaṃ pavisa*); others say that when people were searching for the king and were digging up the ground, they were told: "Do not make a hole" (*mā gadhaṃ karotha*).[543] [136] One may accept whatever explanation one prefers.

The word **dwells** (*viharati*) [is derived thus]: Having cut off (*vicchinditvā*) oppression by one posture by adopting another posture, one takes (*harati*) the body to it without falling over.[544] What is meant is that one sets moving (*pavatteti*). Or else "dwells" means that he takes (*harati*) various kinds (*vividhaṃ*) of welfare to beings through the celestial, divine, and noble dwellings.[545] What is meant by "takes" is "brings, applies, generates, arouses." Thus when beings are misbehaving in regard to sensual pleasures, the Blessed One, it is said, dwells in the celestial dwelling in order to arouse in them the wholesome root of non-greed, thinking: "Perhaps when they see this proper behavior, they may arouse a liking for it and become dispassionate toward sensual pleasures!" When he sees beings misbehaving for the sake of authority, he dwells in the divine dwelling in order to arouse in them the wholesome root of non-hatred, thinking: "Perhaps when they see this proper behavior, they may arouse a liking for it and allay their hatred by means of non-hatred!" And when he sees monastics disputing over the Dhamma, he dwells in the noble dwelling in order to arouse in them the wholesome root of non-delusion, thinking: "Perhaps when they see this proper behavior, they may allay their delusion by means of non-delusion!" But there is never a time when one does not dwell in some posture, for there is no maintaining the body without one. This is a brief explanation; we will explain this in detail in the commentary on the Discourse on Blessings.

At Dakkhiṇāgiri: The province on the southern side of the mountain range surrounding Rājagaha is called Dakkhiṇāgiri. So what is meant is "in that province." This is also the name of a monastery there. **Near the brahmin village Ekanālā**: "Ekanālā" was the name of that village, and it is referred to as a brahmin village because a number of brahmins lived there or because it was a grant to brahmins.

Now on that occasion: On an occasion after the Blessed One, with his legs crossed in the invincible posture, had awakened to the unsurpassed perfect enlightenment, had set in motion the excellent wheel of the Dhamma, and was dwelling at the large monastery in Dakkhiṇāgiri in the realm of Magadha, depending on the brahmin village of Ekanālā, [137] waiting for the faculties of the brahmin to ripen; what is meant is, "on that occasion."

The brahmin Kasibhāradvāja: This brahmin lived by plowing (*kasiyā jīvati*) and his clan name was Bhāradvāja, therefore he was called thus. **Five hundred**: five hundred plows, neither more nor fewer. **Had been yoked**: They were fitted with yokes that were placed on the shoulders of the oxen. **At the time of sowing**: at the time of depositing seeds. Now there are two kinds of sowing: the sowing in mud and the sowing in soil; here the sowing in soil is intended, and this was a ceremonial sowing on the first day.

Here, this is the excellence of the instruments: Three thousand oxen were present, all with their horns capped with gold and their hooves with silver. All were adorned with white garlands, five inches thick, richly fragrant with all kinds of fragrances. Their bodies and limbs were perfect and they possessed all the marks of excellence. Some were black, the color of *añjanā*;[546] some were white, the color of clouds; some were red, the color of coral; some were spotted, like cat's eye. Five hundred plowmen—all wearing fresh white clothes, adorned with garlands, with a wreath of flowers over their right shoulders, and their bodies beautifully streaked with yellow orpiment and red arsenic—had arranged themselves in groups with ten men for each plow. The heads of the plows, the yokes, and the goads were covered in gold. Eight oxen were yoked to the first plow, and four to each of the remaining ones. The others had been brought to take turns with those that became tired. In each group there was a cart of seeds; each one plowed and each one sowed.

The brahmin had early trimmed his beard, took a bath, anointed himself with richly fragrant scents, [138] put on a sarong worth five hundred and a shawl worth a thousand. He put two rings on each finger—for a total of twenty rings—fastened lion rings on his ears, tied a turban around his head, put a golden garland around his neck, and entered the workplace accompanied by a group of brahmins. His wife had milk rice cooked in many hundreds of pots and had them loaded on large carts. Then, having bathed in fragrant water, she fully adorned herself and went to the workplace accompanied by a group of brahmin women.

His home, too, was anointed with all kinds of fragrant substances; the offering to the spirits was well prepared with flowers; and in various places across the field, flags had been raised. The assembly that arrived at the workplace, including his retinue and workers, were 2,500 in number. All wore fresh clothes and milk rice had been prepared for all.

Then, at his own meal place, the brahmin had a golden dish washed, had it filled with milk rice, flavored it with ghee, honey, molasses, and other condiments, and made an offering to the plow. His wife took five hundred bowls made of gold, silver, bronze, and copper, took a golden spoon, and went around serving milk rice to the five hundred seated plowmen. But the brahmin, after completing the offering, put on golden sandals, took a golden staff, and moved around giving orders: "Give milk rice here, give ghee there, give sugar here."

Seated in the Fragrant Cottage, the Blessed One knew that the brahmin's food distribution was taking place, and he thought: "This is the time to tame[547] the brahmin." He put on his lower robe, fastened the waistband, covered himself with his outer robe, took his bowl, and set out from the Fragrant Cottage in the manner of an unsurpassed trainer of persons to be tamed. Hence the Venerable Ānanda said: "Then, in the morning, the Blessed One dressed . . ." [139]

In the morning: in the earlier part of the day. The meaning is: "the occasion was the earlier part of the day." Or "in the morning" means *on an occasion in* the morning; what is meant is at a particular moment in the morning. This is an accusative used in connection with the passage of time.[548] **Dressed**: robed himself. This means that he changed out of the lower robe that he wore at the monastery; for it is not the case that prior to this the Blessed One was undressed. **Took his bowl and robe**: He took his bowl with his hands and wore his robe on his body. For it is said that when the Blessed One wishes to enter a village for alms, his sapphire-colored stone bowl comes between his two hands just as a bee settles between two blooming lotus flowers. Therefore the meaning of this should be understood thus: "He received in his hands the bowl that had come in such a way and wore the robe on his body so that it covered both shoulders." Or it is said "he took," meaning that he took them in this or that way, as when it is said: "having taken them along, he departs" (DN I 71,6). Then he approached the place where the brahmin Kasibhāradvāja was working, going along the path that leads there.

But why didn't any bhikkhus follow the Blessed One? It is said that when the Blessed One wants to go somewhere alone, at the time for the alms round he enters the Fragrant Cottage and shuts the door. Then the bhikkhus understand: "Today the Blessed One wishes to enter the village alone. Surely, he has seen some person to be guided." They then take their own bowls and robes, circumambulate the Fragrant Cottage, and go on alms round. Since the Blessed One had done this, the bhikkhus did not follow him. [140]

Now on that occasion, on the occasion when the Blessed One approached the workplace, **the brahmin Kasibhāradvāja's food distribution was taking place**. This refers to what we said above: "His wife took five hundred bowls made of gold, silver, bronze, and copper, took a golden spoon, and went around serving the milk rice to the five hundred seated plowmen." **The Blessed One then approached the food distribution**: For what reason? To benefit the brahmin. For the Blessed One is not like a pauper who approaches a food distribution from a desire to eat. The Blessed One's relatives, the 82,000 royal members of the Sakyan and Koliyan clans, each tried to give him a constant meal from their own individual wealth, but the Blessed One did not go forth for the sake of meals. Rather, he made the five great relinquishments[549] over many incalculable periods of time, and having fulfilled the pāramīs, he went forth with the thought: "Freed, I will free. Tamed . . . Consoled . . . Having attained nibbāna, I will lead others to nibbāna." Therefore, because he himself had been freed and had attained nibbāna, he wandered in the world freeing others and leading them to nibbāna. Thus it should be understood that he approached the food distribution for the purpose of benefiting the brahmin.

And stood to one side: Having approached in such a way, he stood in an elevated place within range of sight and hearing so that the brahmin could see him and hear him speak. Having stood there, he emitted a bodily radiance with the sheen of exquisite gold, surpassing[550] the light of a thousand moons and suns. The entire area, to an extent of forty meters, was covered by the light; the work place, the hall, the walls, the trees, the lumps of plowed soil, and so forth all seemed as if made of gold. Then the men who had been eating milk rice saw the perfectly enlightened Buddha standing to one side, his body stamped with the thirty-two marks of physical excellence and endowed with the eighty minor features, embellished by a fathom-wide aura that enveloped him an arm's span on either side, more resplendent to sight than if it had been ablaze with flags and garlands; [141] he was like a shimmering lake of lotus flowers, like the sky with its multitude of stars scintillating with webs of light rays, shining with glory like the flaming peak of a golden mountain. Then, having washed their hands and feet, the people surrounded him, extending their joined hands in reverential salutation.

The brahmin Kasibhāradvāja saw the Blessed One standing for alms—surrounded by those people—**and said to him: "I plow and sow, ascetic, and having plowed and sown, I eat."** But why did he say this? Was it because he lacked confidence in the Blessed One, who was graceful in every way, who inspired confidence, and who had arrived at supreme taming and serenity? Or could it be that after preparing milk rice for 2,500 people, he would now grudge a spoon of almsfood? In both cases, the answer is no. It was rather that he had seen the people drop their work and look insatiably at the Blessed One, and he became displeased, thinking: "He has come to disrupt my work." Therefore he spoke in such a way.

But when he saw that the Blessed One possessed the marks of physical excellence, he thought: "If he would undertake work, he would be like a crest jewel on the head of the people in all of Jambudīpa. What good could he not achieve? But because he is lazy, instead of undertaking work, he eats by wandering for alms at auspicious sowing ceremonies and other events and dwells intent on bodily fitness." Hence he said: "I plow and sow, ascetic, and having plowed and sown, I eat." The purport is: "I do not neglect work, and yet, unlike you, I do not possess such marks of physical excellence."

You too, ascetic, must plow and sow, and having plowed and sown, you can eat: The purport is: "Possessing such marks, what good could you not achieve?" Further, he had heard: "It is said that a prince born into the royal Sakyan family abandoned kingship as a wheel-turning monarch and has gone forth." Therefore, having realized that this was him, he now says, "I plow and sow, ascetic," criticizing him thus: "Having abandoned the kingship of a wheel-turning monarch, you are weary." Further, being one of sharp wisdom, this brahmin did not speak like this in order to disparage the Blessed One. [142] Having seen the Blessed One's bodily splendor, esteeming the splendor of his wisdom, he also spoke thus in order to start a conversation.

Then the Blessed One, as a way of guiding him, said, **I too, brahmin**, showing that in the world together with its devas he was foremost in plowing and sowing. Thereupon the brahmin thought: "This ascetic says, 'I plow and sow,' but I do not see his tangible plowing equipment, such as a plow fitted with a yoke. Is he speaking falsely or not?" He then inspected the Blessed One from the soles of his feet up to the tips of his hairs, and since he had studied the science of physiognomy, he knew the Blessed One possessed the thirty-two marks of physical excellence. Instantly esteem arose in him and he knew: "It is impossible and inconceivable that someone like him could speak falsely." Thus he stopped addressing the Blessed One by the term "ascetic" and instead addressed him by his clan, saying: "**But we do not see Master Gotama's . . . I eat**." Further, having said this, the astute brahmin knew: "He must have said this with reference to some deep meaning." Wishing to understand the meaning, he addressed the Blessed One in verse. Hence the Venerable Ānanda said: **Then the brahmin Kasibhāradvāja addressed the Blessed One in verse**. Here, "in verse" means in a statement with a fixed number of syllables.

76–77. Here, the brahmin speaks of **plowing**, which refers to the collection of plowing instruments, such as a plow fitted with a yoke and so forth, but the Blessed One says: **Faith is the seed**. Since speaking in a way that matches preliminary items with their counterparts is a strength of the buddhas, the Blessed One, displaying the strength of the buddhas, speaks thus matching preliminary items with their counterparts. But, it might be asked, what is the matching preliminary item here?

Isn't it the case that the brahmin asked the Blessed One about plowing instruments, but the Blessed One said, "Faith is the seed," setting up a seed as the counterpart of something that was not mentioned? In such a case, this explanation becomes incoherent.[551]

In reply, it should be said that no explanation by the buddhas is ever incoherent, nor do they speak without having matched[552] preliminary items with their counterparts. [143] The sequence here should be understood as follows: The brahmin asked the Blessed One about his plowing with such plowing instruments as a yoke and plow. But the Blessed One, out of compassion for him, said, "Faith is the seed," showing his plowing by starting with the basis, in order to inform him about plowing along with its basis, accessories, remaining instruments, and fruit;[553] he did not omit something just because it had not been asked about. For seeds are the basis of plowing, since plowing can be done only when there are seeds and cannot be done in their absence, and it must be done in accordance with the quantity of the seeds. For people plow when there are seeds and do not plow in their absence, and skillful plowmen plow their field in accordance with the quantity of the seeds—not less, to avoid a failure of their crops; and not more, to avoid futile effort. And since seeds themselves are the basis, in showing how to plow by starting with the basis, the Blessed One speaks by matching the preliminary item of his own plowing with its counterpart, seed, the preliminary item in the brahmin's plowing. So he says: "Faith is the seed." It is in such a way that the counterpart of the preliminary item should be understood here.

If it is asked, "Why didn't he first answer what he had been asked about and then afterward speak about the other matter?" it is said: Because of its helpfulness to the brahmin, and because of its ability to engender a succession of good qualities. For this brahmin was wise, but because he had been born into a family with wrong views he was devoid of faith, and when a wise person is devoid of faith, he does not step outside his own domain through faith in others and thus does not achieve distinction. Even if one has weak faith, defined as sufficient confidence to remove the murkiness of the defilements, if it proceeds in conjunction with strong wisdom, it does not bring the achievement of one's aim but is then like an ox yoked to an elephant by a single halter.[554] Therefore faith would be helpful to him. Thus, since faith would be helpful to the brahmin, even though this topic should have been discussed later, the Buddha spoke about it earlier in order to establish the brahmin in faith.

This was done through his skillfulness in teaching, just as elsewhere the Buddha says: "Faith secures provisions for a journey" (SN I 44,12); and "Faith is a person's companion" (SN I 25,16); and "Faith here is a person's best treasure" (**182**a); and "By faith one crosses the flood" (**184**a); and "The great nāga has faith as its trunk" (AN III 346,23); and "A noble disciple, bhikkhus, has faith as his pillar" (AN IV 109,12). Since rain is helpful to the seed, it is capable of being spoken about immediately afterward. [144] Thus even though this subject (faith) should have been discussed later because of its ability to generate a succession of good qualities, it is mentioned earlier, and so too for the others like the pole and the yoke-tie.

Here, **faith** has the characteristic of placidity or trust; its function is to enter upon; its manifestation is conviction or non-murkiness; its proximate cause is the factors of stream-entry or an object worthy of faith. It consists in clarity of mind, similar to the clarity of a mirror or the surface of water and so forth. As the water-clearing jewel clarifies water, so faith clarifies the associated mental qualities.

Seeds are of five kinds: root-seeds, stem-seeds, joint-seeds, cutting-seeds, and actual seeds as the fifth.[555] All of these are designated "seeds" in the sense of growing. As it is said: "And this is a seed in the sense of growing."

In the brahmin's plowing, a seed performs two functions: below, it is secured by means of the root; and above, it sends forth a sprout. Similarly, in the Blessed One's plowing, faith, as the basis, is secured below with good behavior as the root; and above, it sends forth the sprout of serenity and insight. And as the plant, by means of the root, takes in the moisture and nutrients of the soil and grows by way of its stalk for the purpose of ripening in grain, so by means of the root of good behavior, faith takes in the moisture of serenity and insight and grows through the stalk of the noble path for the purpose of ripening in the noble fruit, which is its grain. And as that plant, secured in the ground, comes to growth, development, and maturity by producing roots, sprouts, leaves, stalks, and joints, generates sap, and produces a head of rice replete with many grains of rice, just so, having been established in one's mental continuum, faith comes to growth, development, and maturation by means of the purifications of good behavior, mind, view, the overcoming of doubt, knowledge and vision of what is and what is not the path, and knowledge and vision of the practice; it generates the sap of purification by knowledge and vision[556] and produces the fruit of arahantship replete with many kinds of analytical knowledges and superknowledges. Hence the Blessed One said: "Faith is the seed."

It may be asked: "When more than fifty wholesome mental factors arise together, why is faith alone declared to be the seed?" In reply, it is said: Because it exercises the function of a seed. For just as, among these factors, consciousness alone exercises the function of cognizing, so faith performs the function of a seed. And it is the basis of all wholesome qualities, as it is said: "One in whom faith has arisen draws near. Drawing near, he attends. While attending, he lends an ear. [145] Having lent an ear, he hears the Dhamma. Having heard the Dhamma, he retains the Dhamma in mind. He examines the meaning of the teachings that have been retained in mind. As he examines the meaning, the teachings are accepted through meditation on them. When there is acceptance of the teachings through meditation, desire is born. One in whom desire has arisen makes an effort. Having made an effort, he assesses. Having made an assessment, he strives. Resolute in striving, he realizes with the body the supreme truth and, having pierced it with wisdom, he sees" (MN I 480,3).

Austerity (*tapo*) is so called because it burns up (*tapati*) unwholesome qualities and the body. This is a designation for restraint of the senses, energy, the austere practices, and the practice of extreme austerities.[557] But here restraint of the senses is intended. **Rain** is of many kinds, a downpour of rain, a windy rain, and so forth. Here a downpour of rain is intended. For as the brahmin's seeds and their roots, when assisted by a downpour of rain, increase in their yield of grain and do not wither but flourish, so for the Blessed One, faith and such qualities as good behavior rooted in faith, when assisted by restraint of the senses, do not wither but flourish. Hence he says: "Austerity is the rain." And here the word "my" (*me*) stated in the line "Wisdom is my yoke and plow" should also be connected to these phrases thus: "Faith is *my* seed, austerity *my* rain."

What does he show by this? "In your case, brahmin, when you have sown the seed, if there is rain, that is good; but if there is no rain, then you must irrigate the fields. So when I have sown the seeds of faith in the field of someone's mind, with moral shame as the pole, wisdom as the yoke and plow, and the oxen of energy yoked together with the yoke straps of the mind and spurred on with the goad of mindfulness, there is no absence of rain. For me, this rain consists in constant and continuous austerity."

Wisdom is that by which a person understands, or it itself understands. This is of numerous kinds when divided by way of the desire sphere and so forth, but here it is the wisdom of the path together with insight that is intended. **Yoke and plow**: for as the brahmin has a yoke and plow, [146] the Blessed One has the twofold wisdom (of insight and the path). Here, just as the yoke rests on top of the pole, precedes it, is bound to the pole, serves as support for the yoke straps, and controls the uniform advance of the oxen, so wisdom rests on top of those qualities presided over by the sense of shame. As it is said, "All wholesome qualities have wisdom above them" (AN IV 339,7), and "For wisdom is best, the skilled say, like the moon among the stars" (Ja V 148,8–9). And it precedes in the sense that it is the forerunner of wholesome qualities; as it is said: "Good behavior, glory, and the qualities of the good follow one with wisdom" (Ja V 148,10–11). And it is bound to the pole, because it never arises disconnected from moral shame. And it is the support of the yoke straps, because it is the supporting condition for the yoke strap of concentration, which is here designated "mind." It controls the uniform advance of the oxen of energy, preventing both excessive application and excessive laxity. Just as, at the time of plowing, the plow with the plowshare yoked to it breaks up the compact earth and severs the network of roots, so at the time of insight, wisdom yoked with mindfulness breaks up compactness in regard to continuity, mass, function, and object,[558] and severs all the network of roots consisting in the defilements. And that is so only with respect to world-transcending wisdom, but the other—mundane wisdom—may also be included.[559] Hence he says: "Wisdom is my yoke and plow."

Moral shame is that by which a person feels moral shame, or it itself feels moral shame; it becomes disgusted at the occurrence of the unwholesome. By mentioning this, moral dread is also included as its companion.[560] **The pole** is a piece of timber supporting the yoke and plow. In the case of the brahmin, the pole supports the yoke and plow; so for the Blessed One moral shame supports the yoke and plow that consist in mundane and world-transcending wisdom; for there can be no wisdom in the absence of moral shame. As the yoke and plow, bound to the pole, perform their functions without shaking or slackening, so wisdom bound to moral shame performs its function without shaking or slackening, unadulterated by shamelessness. Hence he says: "Moral shame is the pole."

Indian farmer plowing

http://www.4to40.com/images/coloring_book/ploughing.gif

Mind (*mano*) is a designation for *citta*. But here [147] what is intended by "mind" is concentration associated with the mind. A **yoke strap** is the binding rope, which is threefold: that which binds the yoke to the pole, that which binds the oxen to the yoke, and that which binds the oxen to the driver. Just as the brahmin's yoke strap binds the pole, yoke, and oxen, and ensures that each performs its own function, so the Blessed

One's concentration, in its capacity for non-distraction, binds all those qualities—moral shame, wisdom, and energy—to a single object and ensures that each performs its own function. Hence he says: "Mind is the yoke strap."

Mindfulness is that by which a person recollects a matter done long ago, and so forth; or it itself recollects. It has the characteristic of non-forgetfulness. **Plowshare and goad**: As the brahmin has a plowshare and goad, so the Blessed One has mindfulness joined to insight and the path. Here, as the plowshare protects the plow and precedes it, so mindfulness, by seeking the tracks of wholesome qualities or by bringing awareness to objects, protects the plow of wisdom. Thus its role as a guardian is stated as follows: "He dwells with a mind guarded by mindfulness" (DN III 269,28). And it precedes by way of non-forgetfulness. For wisdom understands things that have become familiar through mindfulness and that are not forgotten. And as the goad, threatening the oxen with a beating, does not let them come to a standstill and prevents them from going astray, so mindfulness, by displaying the peril of the plane of misery, does not allow the oxen of energy to come to a standstill due to laziness; and by restraining them from wandering outside their resort into the arena of sensual pleasures, and by enjoining them [to focus on] their meditation subject, mindfulness prevents them from going astray. Hence he says: "Mindfulness is my plowshare and goad."

78. Guarded in body: guarded by way of the threefold good bodily conduct. **Guarded in speech**: guarded by way of the fourfold good verbal conduct. By this much *good behavior through restraint by the Pātimokkha* has been stated. **Controlled in food and belly**: Here, because all the requisites are included under the heading of *food*, [148] what is meant is being controlled, self-controlled, in regard to the four requisites. The meaning is being without defilement. By this *good behavior consisting in purification of livelihood* is meant. "Controlled in belly" means limiting one's food; moderation in eating is meant. By this, *good behavior consisting in use of the requisites* is stated under the heading of moderation in eating.[561]

What does he show by this? "You, brahmin, after sowing

seed, built a fence—an enclosure of thorn bushes or trees—in order to protect the crops. By this means, cattle, buffalo, and deer cannot enter and plunder the crops. So too, having sown the seed of faith, I built a threefold fence that consists of guarding body, speech, and appetite for food, in order to protect the crops of the various wholesome qualities. By this means, cattle, buffalo, and deer—which represent the unwholesome qualities such as lust—are not able to enter and plunder the crops of the wholesome."

I use truth for weeding: Here, truth is non-deceptiveness through two doors (speech and body). "Weeding" is cutting, snipping, uprooting. Here the accusative is used in an instrumental sense, so that the sense is: "I do weeding by truth."[562] What is meant? "As you, after completing your external plowing, do your weeding with your hand or scythe to remove the weeds that might ruin the crops, so, after completing my internal plowing, I do weeding with truth to remove the weeds of deceitful speech that might ruin the crops of the wholesome." Or "truth" here should be understood to mean truthful knowledge, which is spoken of as "knowledge of things as they really are." In that sense the line should be interpreted thus: "With that, I remove the weeds consisting in the perception of a self and other misperceptions."

Or alternatively, "weeding" signifies "one who does the cutting, who does the snipping, who does the uprooting." In such a case, it is proper to take it in the accusative case thus: "As you make your slave or workman do the weeding, ordering him, 'Remove the weeds,' and so you make him do the cutting, snipping, and uprooting, I do the same with truth." Or alternatively, "truth" is truthfulness in view. In this way, too, it is proper to take it in the accusative case: "I do the weeding, the necessary cutting, the necessary snipping, the necessary uprooting."

Gentleness is my release: The "gentleness" stated in the passage "Bodily non-transgression, verbal non-transgression" (Dhs 286, §1349) [149] is good behavior, but that is not what is intended here; for that has already been stated by way of "guarded in body" and so forth. What is intended, rather, is the fruit of arahantship; for that, too, is called gentleness (*soracca*) because it is delighted (*ratabhāvato*) in the good (*sundara*) nibbāna.[563] **Release**: the giving up of exertion. What is meant? "Whereas for you there is no release in the evening or the next day or the following year, because you must exert yourself, this is not the case for me. There was no release for me in the period beginning from the time of the Buddha Dīpaṅkara, bearer of the ten powers, under whom I yoked the oxen of energy to the plow of wisdom and undertook the great plowing for four incalculables and 100,000 eons, up to the time I awakened to perfect enlightenment. But at the end of that time, as I sat in the invincible cross-legged posture at the foot of the bodhi tree, I obtained the fruit of arahantship accompanied by all excellent qualities. Then, with the subsiding of all toil, I was released and now have no further need for exertion." It is with reference to this that the Blessed One says: "Gentleness is my release."

79. Energy is my beast of burden:[564] Here, "energy" is the striving described as "bodily or mental arousing of energy." The "beast of burden" is that bearing the burden; the meaning is that which carries the burden.[565] Just as the brahmin's plow, the burden that is pulled along by the beast of burden, breaks up the compact earth and severs the network of roots, so the Blessed One's plow of wisdom, pulled along by energy, breaks up the aforementioned compactness [in regard to continuity, mass, function, and object] and severs the network of roots consisting in the defilements. Hence he says: "Energy is my beast of burden."

Or alternatively: the compound *dhuradhorayha* is to be resolved into *dhura* and *dhorayha*, where *dhura* carries the former burden and *dhorayha* carries the original burden.[566] Here, as the brahmin's beasts of burden that carry the burden—the four oxen at each plow—accomplish the task of destroying the roots of the weeds whenever they arise and ensuring the success of the crops, so the Blessed One's beasts of burden that carry the burden—the four right kinds of energetic striving—accomplish the task of destroying the unwholesome roots whenever they arise [150] and ensuring the success of the wholesome. Hence he says: "Energy is my beast of burden."

Carrying one toward security from bondage: Here it is nibbāna that is called "security from bondage" because it is secure from the bonds.[567] "Carrying toward" (*adhivāhana*) is said because one is being carried with that as the aim (*taṃ adhikatvā vāhiyati*) or because one is being carried straight ahead (*abhimukhaṃ vāhiyati*). What does he show by this? "As your beast of burden is carried straight toward the east, the west, and so forth, my beast of burden is carried straight toward nibbāna. Being carried forward in such a way, **it goes ahead without turning back**. Unlike your beast of burden, which turns back again when it reaches the end of the field—and thus is described as 'turning back'—mine has gone only forward from the time of Dīpaṅkara. The defilements abandoned by this and that path do not have to be abandoned again and again, unlike the weeds cut by your plow, which on a later occasion will have to be cut again. Therefore, in abandoning the defilements coexistent with views by the first path, the grosser defilements by the second path, residual[568] defilements by the third path, and all [remaining] defilements by the fourth path, this one goes ahead without turning back."

Or alternatively: **it goes ahead without turning back** means "having become devoid of turning back, it goes." It (*taṃ*) signifies that beast of burden.[569] Thus here, too, the elision of a term should be understood. "And going in such a way, unlike your beast of burden, which does not go to that place where, having gone, a plowman becomes sorrowless, rid of sorrow, dust-free, and thus does not sorrow, this one goes to that place **where one does not sorrow**: By repeatedly spurring on the beast of burden—which symbolizes energy—with the goad of mindfulness, this one goes to that place designated nibbāna the deathless, the utter destruction of all the darts of sorrow, where a plowman like me becomes sorrowless, rid of sorrow, and dust-free, and thus does not sorrow."

80. Now, reaching the conclusion, the Blessed One spoke this verse:

> In such a way this plowing is done
> which bears the deathless as its fruit.
> Having plowed with this kind of plowing,
> one is released from all suffering.

This is its concise meaning: "See, brahmin! **This plowing is done** with the seed of faith assisted by the rain of austerity, with the pole of moral shame tied to the yoke and plow consisting in wisdom with the yoke strap consisting in mind. [151] Having hammered the plowshare of mindfulness to the plow of wisdom, having taken up the goad of mindfulness, protecting oneself by guarding one's body and speech and consumption of food, using truth as the weeding, gentleness as release, and energy as the beast of burden, one goes straight ahead, without turning back, toward security from bondage. At the conclusion of the plowing, it brings one to the fourfold fruit of the ascetic life, and so it **bears the deathless as its fruit**; this plowing has the deathless as its fruit. It is nibbāna that is called 'the deathless.' The meaning is that this plowing has nibbāna as its benefit. Moreover, this plowing does not bear the deathless as its fruit for only one person, for me alone. Rather, **anyone** who plows with this kind of plowing—whether a khattiya, a brahmin, a vessa, or a sudda, whether a householder or a monk—**having plowed with this kind of plowing, is released from all suffering**: one is released from all the suffering of the round, from suffering due to pain, from suffering due to conditioned things, and from suffering due to change."[570] In this way the Blessed One concludes the teaching to the brahmin, having brought it to its consummation in nibbāna through its culmination in arahantship.

Then, having heard the deep teaching, the brahmin understood: "When one eats the fruit of my plowing, the very next day one is hungry again, but his plowing bears the deathless as its fruit, so when one eats its fruit one is released from all suffering." Pleased, the brahmin began to give milk rice as an expression of his pleasure. Hence it is said: **Then the brahmin Kasibhāradvāja**. The **bronze dish** was a golden dish, his own golden plate worth a hundred thousand. **Presented it to the Blessed One**: He flavored it with ghee, honey, and palm syrup, covered it with a double thick lid, lifted it up, and respectfully presented it to the Tathāgata. How? [With the words] **Let Master Gotama eat the milk rice! You are a plowman**. He then states the reason demonstrating that the Buddha is a plowman: **Since you plow . . . as its fruit**.

81. Then the Blessed One said: **Food over which verses have been recited**. Here, what is meant is "that which has been obtained after reciting verses."[571] **Is not to be eaten by me**: It is not fit to be eaten by me. **Of those who see**: of those who rightly see purity of livelihood; [152] or of those who see all around. What is meant is, "of the buddhas." **This is not the principle**: This is not the principle, the regular behavior, namely, "food gained by reciting verses may be eaten." Therefore, **the buddhas reject food over which verses have been recited**: they refuse it and do not eat it.

But does the Blessed One say this because he had recited verses for the sake of milk rice? No, the verses were not recited for this purpose. Rather, from the morning on, the Buddha had stood close to the field without obtaining even a spoonful of almsfood. What he would have obtained after revealing all his buddha-qualities would have been like the payment that actors and dancers obtain after dancing and singing. That is what is meant by "food gained by reciting verses." And since such food is not suitable for the buddhas, it is described as "not to be eaten." This is also not in conformity with the principle of fewness of desires; therefore, out of compassion for later generations, he spoke thus. And when there are those who even reject gains that accrue to them after their own virtues have been revealed by others—such as the modest Ghaṭikāra (see MN II 54,12–15)—in that case, how could the Blessed One, who had reached the peak in fewness of desires, accept a gain that accrued to him because he himself had revealed his own virtues? Hence it is proper for the Blessed One to say this.

At this point the Blessed One has shown the purification of his activity of teaching, acquitting himself of such worldly reproach as this: "Though the brahmin lacked confidence and did not wish to give, the ascetic Gotama, by singing verses, aroused in him a wish to give and then accepted the food. His activity of teaching aims at material gain." Now, showing his purification of livelihood, he says: **There being such a principle, brahmin, this is their conduct**. This is its meaning: "Since there is such a principle—since the buddhas have such a principle of behavior as purification of livelihood or the tenfold good conduct—as it continues to be followed unimpaired, **this is their conduct**: The exclusively clean rule of living of the buddhas, brahmin, their way of seeking and searching [for food], is like the stretching out of the hand in space."

When this was said, the brahmin became dejected, thinking:

"He refused my milk rice. This food is said to be unallowable. Indeed, I'm unlucky! I did not get the chance to make a gift." [153] And then he thought: "Perhaps he would accept something else." Having known his thought, the Blessed One considered: "I have come here after determining the time for my alms round thus: 'In this much time I will awaken the confidence of this brahmin,' and the brahmin has become dejected. Now if, because of his dejection, he becomes angry with me, he won't be able to penetrate the excellent Dhamma of the deathless."

82. Hence, in order to generate confidence in the brahmin, fulfilling the latter's wish and desire, he said: **Serve with other food and drink the consummate one**. Here, **consummate one**: one complete in all excellent qualities or one who has severed all bonds.[572] **The great rishi** (*mahesiṃ*), through the seeking (*esanato*) of great (*mahantaṃ*) excellent qualities,[573] such as the aggregate of good behavior and so forth. **With influxes destroyed**: because all influxes are utterly destroyed. **With regret stilled**: because all regret, beginning with fidgeting with hands and feet, has been stilled.[574] **Serve**: attend upon, provide with. Even though the brahmin had already given rise to such a thought, the Buddha speaks in an indirect way, but he does not say: "Give, bring." The rest here is clear.

The brahmin reflected: "Since this milk rice has been offered to the Blessed One, I am unable to give it to anyone on my own initiative." He then asked: **Then should I give this milk rice to someone else**? The Blessed One knew, "Apart from the Tathāgata and the Tathāgata's disciples, there is no one else able to digest it," and therefore said: **I do not see anyone**. Here, by mentioning **with its devas**, inclusion is made of the devas of the [lower] five desire-sphere planes; by mentioning **with Māra**, inclusion is made of the devas of the sixth desire-sphere plane;[575] by mentioning **with Brahmā**, inclusion is made of the brahmās of the form sphere—but those of the formless sphere are not considered because it was said, "who could eat it." By mentioning **with its ascetics and brahmins**, inclusion is made of ascetics and brahmins opposed to the Buddha's Teaching, as well as of those ascetics who have stilled evil and brahmins who have expelled evil.[576] By the word **population**, inclusion is made of the world of beings. By the phrase **with its devas and humans**, inclusion is made of conventional devas and the rest of humankind.[577] It should thus be understood that here the world as cosmos is included by three terms and the world of beings by way of "population" qualified by two terms. This is a concise explanation, [154] but we will explain in detail when commenting on the Discourse to Āḷavaka (pp. 619–20).

But why is it that no one in all the world including the devas could properly digest it? Because the coarse food had been infused with subtle nutritive essence. For as soon as it was said that this milk rice was intended for the Blessed One, deities infused it with nutritive essence, as was done with the milk rice offered by Sujātā (Ja I 68,27–30), with the dish "boar's delight" prepared by Cunda (DN II 127,21), with each lump of food received by the Blessed One at Verañjā (see Vin III,6–7), and with the remaining sugarballs in Kaccāyana's pot of sugarballs in the Chapter on Medicines (Vin I 225,17–21). Since the subtle nutritive essence had been infused into coarse food, the devas could not digest it; for devas have subtle bodies and they cannot properly digest the coarse food of human beings. Humans, too, could not digest it; for human beings have coarse bodies and they cannot properly digest the subtle celestial nutritive essence. But the Tathāgata could digest it and properly assimilate it with his natural digestive power. Some say: "through his bodily power and the might of his power of knowledge." A disciple of the Tathāgata who is an arahant could digest it through the power of concentration and through his moderation. But others, even those with psychic potency, could not digest it. Or the reason for this is inconceivable; this is the domain of the buddhas.

Therefore: What is meant is: "Since I do not see any others, and it is not proper for me, and what is not proper for me is also not proper for my disciple, therefore, brahmin . . ." **Where there is little vegetation**: in a place where there is little grass, where little grass has grown, such as on top of a rock. **In water where there are no living beings**: in a large body of water devoid of living beings that might die because of the dispersion of the milk rice. This is said in order to protect the living beings living in water, and the vegetation and the living beings dependent on the vegetation. **Sizzled and hissed and gave off**

steam and smoke: Why did this occur? Because of the spiritual might of the Blessed One, not on account of the water, the milk rice, or the brahmin, or others such as devas and yakkhas. For the Blessed One had resolved on such an occurrence in order to arouse in the brahmin a sense of urgency for the Dhamma. **Just as a plowshare**: This is stated to show the simile. [155]

Agitated, with hair bristling: It is said that the 99,000 hairs on his body stood up on end like jeweled ivory pegs fastened to a golden wall. He **prostrated himself with his head at the Blessed One's feet**, rejoicing in the Blessed One's teaching of the Dhamma, and **said to the Blessed One: "Excellent, Master Gotama! Excellent, Master Gotama!"** For this word "*abhikkanta*" is used here in the sense of rejoicing. But a detailed explanation (of *abhikkanta*) will be given in the commentary on the Discourse on Blessings (pp. 739–40). But since it is used in the sense of rejoicing, it should be understood that what is meant is: "Good, good, Master Gotama!"

> A wise one should make a repetition
> in fear, anger, and offering praise;
> in hastening, commotion, and amazement;
> in laughter, sorrow, and confidence.

According to this description, the twofold utterance in this case should be understood by way of confidence and praise. Or alternatively, "excellent" is extremely lovable, extremely desirable, extremely agreeable; what is meant is extremely good.[578] Here, by one utterance of "excellent" he praises the teaching, by the other his own confidence. This is the purport here: "Excellent is Master Gotama's teaching of the Dhamma! Excellent is my confidence based on Master Gotama's teaching of the Dhamma!" Or he praises the word of the Blessed One in paired meanings. This should be construed in such a way as this: "Master Gotama's word is excellent because it destroys faults and brings the achievement of excellent qualities; because it generates faith and generates wisdom; because it is endowed with meaning and endowed with phrasing; because its terms are clear and its meaning is deep; because it is pleasant to the ear and touches the heart; because he does not praise himself and does not disparage others; because it is cool with compassion and clean with wisdom; because it is delightful when it enters the range of hearing and can withstand the pressure of examination; because it gives pleasure when heard and brings benefit when investigated," and so forth.

Following this, he praises the teaching itself with four similes. [156] This is how to construe the purport: "Just as someone might turn upright what was overturned, so when I was opposed to the good Dhamma and had fallen into a bad Dhamma, he lifted me up from the bad Dhamma. As someone might reveal what was hidden, he revealed the Teaching, which had been concealed by the jungle of wrong views from the time the Blessed One Kassapa's teaching disappeared. As someone might show the way to one who was lost, so when I was traveling along a bad path, a wrong path, he showed me the path to heaven and liberation. As someone might hold up a lamp in the darkness, so when I was sunk in the darkness of delusion and did not see forms—the jewels of the Buddha, Dhamma, and Sangha—he held up the lamp of his teaching that dispels the darkness of delusion concealing them. Because he has taught it to me in these ways, 'Master Gotama has made the Dhamma clear in many ways.'"

Or alternatively, according to the opinion of some: (1) this Dhamma is similar to *turning upright what was overturned* because it shows suffering and abandons the inversion of taking what is unattractive to be attractive;[579] (2) it is similar to *revealing what was hidden* because it shows the origin and abandons the inversion of taking what is suffering to be happiness; (3) it is similar to *showing the way to one who is lost* because it shows cessation and abandons the inversion of taking what is impermanent to be permanent; and (4) it is similar to *a lamp in the darkness* because it shows the path and abandons the inversion of taking what is non-self to be a self. Therefore it is made clear "as though turning upright what was overturned . . . or holding up a lamp in the darkness so those with good eyesight can see forms."

But the aggregate of good behavior is shown by the mention of faith, austerity, guarding oneself by body, and so forth; the aggregate of wisdom is shown by the mention of wisdom; the aggregate of concentration by the mention of moral shame, mind, and so forth; and cessation by security from bondage.

Thus two noble truths are shown in their own nature: cessation and the noble path with its three aggregates. Of these, the path is opposed to the origin, and cessation is opposed to suffering. In this way the four noble truths are shown. Therefore it should be understood that "it has been made clear in many ways." [157]

I go for refuge: Although, when he prostrated himself at the Blessed One's feet, he had already gone for refuge through prostration, he now undertakes it verbally. Or else, though he had already gone for refuge to the Buddha alone by way of prostration, now, having made this the starting point, he speaks thus to go for refuge to the others, the Dhamma and the Sangha. **Let Master Gotama consider me**, "Let him know me," **as one who from today has gone for refuge**, "by the threefold going for refuge, as one who has no other teacher," **for life**, "for as long as life continues."[580] At this point the procedure has been shown in accordance with what has been heard by him. Or else, having shown the excellence of the Teacher by the words "turning upright what was overturned" and so forth, now, with the words "I go for refuge" and so forth, he shows the excellence of the pupil. Or having shown by the former expressions his obtaining of wisdom, with this he shows his obtaining of faith.

Now, wishing to do what should be done by a wise person who has obtained faith, he asks the Blessed One: **May I receive**. Here, since the Blessed One had inspired confidence in him with displays of psychic potency and so forth, he requests **the going forth** out of faith, thinking: "The Blessed One abandoned the status of a wheel-turning monarch and went forth, so why shouldn't I do so?" Desiring fulfillment in that, from wisdom he requests **full ordination**. The rest is clear.[581]

In the statement "alone, withdrawn," and so forth, one dwells **alone** by bodily seclusion, **withdrawn** by mental seclusion, **heedful** by not neglecting mindfulness of the meditation subject, **ardent** by ardor consisting in bodily and mental energy, and **resolute** by unconcern for one's body and life; **dwelling** means dwelling in a particular posture; **soon** is said in relation to his going forth. **Clansmen**:[582] Clansmen are twofold, by birth and by conduct; but he was a clansman in both ways. The **household life** refers to the work of agriculture, cattle-rearing, and other occupations, owning property, and bringing up children. **Homelessness** is the state where one has no home; it is a designation for the going forth. They **go forth**, draw near, approach. **That unsurpassed consummation of the spiritual life**: the consummation of the spiritual life of the path; [158] what is meant is the fruit of arahantship, for it is for the sake of this that clansmen go forth.

In this very life: in this very existence. **Realized for himself with direct knowledge**: having directly cognized by himself with wisdom, meaning "having known without dependence on others." **Having entered upon it, he dwelled in it**: Having attained it, or having succeeded in it, he dwelled in it. And dwelling in such a way, **he directly knew: "Finished is birth . . . to any state of being."** By this, he shows his plane of reviewing.

But what birth of his was finished? And how did he directly know this? In reply, it is said: It was not his past birth that was finished, for that was already finished in the past; and it was not his future one, because there is no effort in the future;[583] and it is not the present one, for that already exists. Rather, it is *the birth that might have arisen if the path had not been developed*—birth analyzed by way of one, four, or five aggregates, occurring in states of existence with one, four, or five constituents[584]—that through the development of the path is "finished" by being no longer subject to arise. Having reviewed the defilements abandoned by the development of the path, knowing that, in the absence of defilements, even presently existent kamma is incapable of producing future conception, he knows that birth is finished.

The spiritual life has been lived: The spiritual life of the path has been lived, fully lived, done, practiced, meaning "completed." **What had to be done has been done**: The sixteen functions have been completed by the four paths in relation to the four truths respectively by way of full understanding, abandoning, realization, and development.[585] **There is no more coming back to any state of being** (*nāparaṃ itthattāya*): Now, [taking *itthattāya*] as meaning *for such a state of being*, there is no development of the path again *for the state* consisting in the sixteen functions or for the destruction of the defilements. Or alternatively, [taking *itthattāya*] as meaning *from such a state* *of being,* [the sense is] *from this* continuum of aggregates now occurring in such a mode there is no further continuum of aggregates.[586] He directly knew: "These five aggregates, having been fully understood, stand like a tree cut off at the root." **One of the arahants**: The purport here, it is said, is that the Venerable Bhāradvāja was included among the arahants who were great disciples. [159]

5 Cunda
(*Cunda Sutta*)

What is the origin?[587] Briefly, among the four origins of a discourse—personal inclination, the inclination of others, on account of a particular incident, and in response to a question—the origin of this discourse was in response to a question.[588] But in detail, it should be elaborated in the way that has come down in the discourse as follows: "On one occasion the Blessed One was wandering on tour among the Mallas together with a large Sangha of bhikkhus when he arrived at Pāvā. There the Blessed One dwelled at Pāvā in the mango grove of Cunda the smith's son. . . . Then in the morning the Blessed One dressed, took his bowl and robe, and together with the Sangha of bhikkhus, he went to the residence of Cunda the smith's son. Having gone there, he sat down in the seat prepared for him" (Ud 81–82; see too DN II 127,7–8).

When the Blessed One and the Sangha of bhikkhus were seated, Cunda the smith's son, while serving the Sangha of bhikkhus headed by the Buddha, presented the bhikkhus with golden vessels to receive the curries and sauces. Since a training rule had not yet been laid down, some bhikkhus accepted the golden vessels while others did not accept them. But the Blessed One had only one vessel, his stone alms bowl, for the buddhas do not accept a second vessel. A certain evil bhikkhu took the precious golden vessel that he had received for the meal and put it into his own key bag, intent on stealing it.

When Cunda had finished serving the meal and had washed his hands and feet, he bowed down to the Blessed One and looked out upon the Sangha of bhikkhus. He saw that bhikkhu, but out of respect for the Blessed One and the elders, he acted as if he had not seen him and did not say anything. Further, he thought: "May those of wrong view not get a chance to speak."[589] Wishing to know, "Are only those possessed of restraint to be considered ascetics or are those unrestrained like him also to be considered ascetics?" he therefore approached the Blessed One in the evening and said: "I ask the muni . . ."

83. Here, **I ask**: The method has been stated in the Niddesa in the way that begins thus: "There are three kinds of questions: to clear up what has not been seen," [160] and so forth.[590] **The muni**: The method has been stated there in the way that begins thus: "It is knowledge that is called munihood (*monaṃ*): wisdom, understanding . . . right view. One possessing this knowledge, who has attained munihood, is called a muni. There are three kinds of munihood: bodily sagacity, [verbal sagacity, and mental sagacity]."[591]

But this here is a concise explanation: **I ask**: creating the opportunity, he addressed the Blessed One, the muni of munis, as **the muni**. He praises the muni with words of praise that begin "one of abundant wisdom." Here, he is **of abundant wisdom**, vast wisdom, and its vastness should be understood because it extends to the bounds of what can be known. **Said Cunda the smith's son**: This should be understood in the way explained in relation to the Discourse with Dhaniya. From this point on, without discussing even this much, we will pass over all that has already been covered and comment only on what has not been explained.

The Buddha: among the three kinds of buddhas, the perfectly enlightened Buddha.[592] **Lord of the Dhamma**: the one who, because he gives rise to the Dhamma of the path, is lord over the Dhamma as a father is over his son and as a teacher is over the crafts he has devised; the meaning is, "sovereign of the Dhamma, king of the Dhamma, one who exercises mastery over the Dhamma." And this is said: "The Blessed One, brahmin, is the originator of the path unarisen before, the producer of the path unproduced before, the declarer of the path undeclared before. He is the knower of the path, the discoverer of the path, the one skilled in the path. And his disciples now dwell following that path and become possessed of it afterward" (MN III 8,11–15). **Rid of craving**: devoid of sensual craving,

craving for existence, and craving for nonexistence. **Supreme among bipeds**: Although the Blessed One is supreme not only among bipeds but among all beings—"whether without feet . . . up to those that are neither-percipient-nor-nonpercipient" (see AN II 34,13–16)—"supreme among bipeds" alone is said by delimiting the best; for bipeds are the best of all beings, since wheel-turning monarchs, great disciples, paccekabuddhas, and buddhas arise among them. When it is said that he is supreme among these, [161] what is actually meant is that he is supreme among all beings.

The most excellent of trainers: A trainer is "one who makes run."[593] This is a designation for those who tame elephants and other creatures, and the Blessed One is the best among these because of his ability to tame tamable persons by means of the unsurpassed taming. As it is said: "Guided by the elephant tamer, bhikkhus, the elephant to be tamed runs in one direction, east, west, north, or south. Guided by the horse tamer, the horse to be tamed runs in one direction . . . Guided by the ox tamer, the ox to be tamed runs in one direction . . . Guided by the Tathāgata, the Arahant, the Perfectly Enlightened One, the person to be tamed runs in eight directions. Possessed of material form, he sees forms: this is the first direction . . . he enters and dwells in the cessation of perception and feeling: this is the eighth direction" (MN III 222).

How many: a question requesting an analysis of the subject; **in the world**: in the world of beings; **ascetics**: an indication of the subject being inquired about.

84. When this was said, the Blessed One saw that Cunda the smith's son had not asked a question typical of a layman, such as "Bhante, what is wholesome, what is unwholesome?" and so forth, but he asked a question about ascetics. Directing his attention, he knew, "He asks with reference to that evil bhikkhu," and so he said, "**four kinds of ascetics**," showing that this monk was not an ascetic apart from the mere conventional label. Here, **four** is a delimitation of the number. As to **ascetic**, sometimes the Blessed One uses the word "ascetic" in regard to the sectarians, as when he says: "Whatever observances, ceremonies, and auspicious rites there are among ordinary ascetics and brahmins" (MN I 265,25); sometimes in regard to worldlings, as when he says: "People perceive you, bhikkhus, as 'ascetics, ascetics'" (M I 281,5); sometimes in regard to trainees, as when he says: "Just here, bhikkhus, there is an ascetic, here a second ascetic" (MN I 63,29); sometimes in regard to the arahant, as when he says: "With the destruction of the influxes, one is an ascetic" (MN I 284,22); and sometimes with reference to himself, as when he says: "'Ascetic,' bhikkhus, is a designation for the Tathāgata" (AN IV 340,1). But here he says "four kinds of ascetics," having collected under the first three terms all the noble ones and the virtuous worldling, [162] and under the fourth the other who, though not an ascetic, has a shaven head and ochre cloth around his neck, who is called an ascetic only as a mere conventional label. **There is no fifth**: In this Dhamma and discipline there is no fifth ascetic as a mere conventional label, even by a mere claim.

Asked in person: asked in my presence. **Let me explain them to you**: Let me make those four ascetics clear to you. **The conqueror of the path**: the one who has vanquished all defilements by means of the path.[594] **The teacher of the path**: the one who teaches the path to others. **The one who lives on the path**: any trainee among the seven types of trainees who, because they have not concluded their dwelling on the path, live on the world-transcending path; and the virtuous worldling who lives on the mundane path; or the virtuous worldling can be understood as one who lives on the path because of living with the world-transcending path as his objective. **The defiler of the path**: the immoral person of wrong view, who is a defiler of the path because of practicing in a way that runs counter to the path.

85. Since these four kinds of ascetics had been concisely indicated by the Blessed One thus, "There are four kinds of ascetics," Cunda was unable to penetrate them and know: "This one is the conqueror of the path, this one is the teacher of the path, this is the one who lives on the path, this is the defiler of the path." Thus to ask again, he says: **Whom do the buddhas call a conqueror of the path?**

86. Now, describing for him the four ascetics in four verses, the Blessed One says: "One who has crossed over perplexity."

Here, **one who has crossed over perplexity, free of inner darts** should be understood in the way stated in commenting on the Discourse on the Serpent, but with this distinction: Since in this verse it is the "Buddha-ascetic" that is intended as "the conqueror of the path," therefore "one who has crossed over perplexity" should be understood to mean that by omniscient knowledge he has crossed over non-knowledge about all phenomena, [such non-knowledge] resembling perplexity. For although stream-enterers have crossed over perplexity, as explained earlier, in a way they still have not crossed over doubt insofar as their cognition is obstructed[595] by matters that come within the domain of a once-returner and those at higher levels; and for those who have reached consummation as paccekabuddhas, their cognition is obstructed by matters that come within the domain of a buddha. [163] But the Blessed One has crossed over perplexity in all respects.

Delighted with nibbāna: one whose mind always slopes toward nibbāna by way of the attainment of fruition, and the Blessed One is like this. As it is said: "When the talk is finished, Aggivessana, then I steady my mind internally, settle it, unify it, and concentrate it on that same sign of concentration as before" (MN I 249,27). **Without any greed**: not hankering for anything at all through the greed consisting in craving. **The guide of this world together with its devas**: the guide of this world together with its devas, the leader; the one who brings across, the one who conveys to the beyond. For having taught the Dhamma in accordance with their inclinations and latent tendencies, in numerous discourses such as the Way to the Beyond (Sn chap. V) and the Great Gathering (DN 20), he enabled countless devas and humans to penetrate the truths. **The impartial one**: one like that, in the way just described, one not altered by worldly conditions.[596] The rest here is clear.

87. Thus, having described in this verse the Buddha-ascetic called "the conqueror of the path," now describing the arahant-ascetic, the Blessed One says: "the supreme as supreme." Here, **the supreme** is nibbāna, the foremost, the best of all things. **One here who, having known the supreme as supreme**: one here, in the Teaching, who has known the supreme as supreme by means of reviewing knowledge. **Expounds and analyzes**

the Dhamma right here: One who *expounds* the Dhamma of nibbāna; one who, because he has penetrated it himself, makes it clear to others, saying, "This is nibbāna"; and who *analyzes* the Dhamma of the path, saying: "These are the four establishments of mindfulness . . . this is the noble eightfold path." Or one who *points out* both [nibbāna and the path] with a concise teaching to those who understand quickly, and *analyzes* them with a detailed teaching to those who understand through elaboration.[597] Pointing them out and analyzing them in such a way, he *expounds and analyzes*, roaring a lion's roar thus: "This Dhamma is found only here in the Teaching, not outside of here." Hence it is said: "expounds and analyzes the Dhamma right here."

The muni who has cut off doubt, without impulse: One such as this, [164] who has *cut off his own doubt* by penetration of the four truths and *the doubt of others* by teaching; who is a *muni* because he possesses munihood (*moneyya*); and who is *without impulse* (*aneja*) because he is without craving, which is designated "impulse" (*ejā*)—**is the second bhikkhu, whom they call a teacher of the path.**[598]

88. Thus, although he is the unsurpassed teacher of the path, having himself originated the unsurpassed path, he nevertheless describes the arahant-ascetic as "the teacher of the path," just as a messenger and reader of a letter is called the bearer and illuminator of the king's message as if it were his own. Now, describing the trainee-ascetic and the virtuous worldling-ascetic, he says: **The one on the well-taught trail of the Dhamma**. Here, the explanation of the terms is clear, but this is the explanation of the meaning: it is the *trail of the Dhamma* because it is the way to the Dhamma of nibbāna. It is *well taught*, because it is taught by avoiding both extremes[599] and because it is taught in various ways such as the establishments of mindfulness and so forth in accordance with the inclinations [of the listeners]. **Lives on the path**: the one endowed with the path [who lives on it] because he has not completed the function of the path. **Controlled**: with control by good behavior; **mindful**: because his mindfulness is well established on the body and so forth, or because he recollects what was done and said long ago;[600] **resorting,** by development from the knowledge of dissolution on, **to blameless ways of conduct** consisting in the thirty-seven aids to enlightenment, which are blameless because they are devoid of the slightest fault, and which are ways of conduct because they are to be trodden in sections. This is **the third bhikkhu, whom they call one living on the path**.

89. Having thus described in this verse the trainee-ascetic and the virtuous worldling-ascetic as "one living on the path," the Blessed One now says, "having taken on the dress," describing the one with a shaven head and ochre cloth around his neck, who is an ascetic only by the mere conventional label. Here, **having taken on the dress**: the meaning is, "having assumed the form, having taken on the guise, wearing the distinctive sign (the robe)." **Of the disciplined**: buddhas, paccekabuddhas, and disciples; since their observances are good, they are called "disciplined."[601] **Brazen**: audacious, intrusive; for just as grass and leaves serve to conceal feces, so the immoral person takes on the clothing of the disciplined in order to conceal his own immoral behavior. [165] He enters among the bhikkhus, saying: "I too am a bhikkhu." When some gain is to be given away, and they say, "This should be taken by a bhikkhu of so many years' standing," he comes forward to take it, saying: "I have so many years' standing." Hence it is said: "Having taken on the dress of the disciplined, one brazen . . ."

He is **a corrupter of families** because he corrupts the confidence arisen in people from any of the four types of families, khattiyas and so forth.[602] **Impudent**: He displays the eight types of bodily impudence, the four types of verbal impudence, and the numerous types of mental impudence. This is a concise account, but we will explain in detail in commenting on the Discourse on Loving-Kindness.[603] **Hypocritical**: because he displays hypocrisy, characterized as the concealment of [evil] that one has done; **uncontrolled**: because he lacks control by good behavior; **chaff**: because he is similar to chaff. For just as chaff, though lacking an inner kernel, appears just like paddy because of its outer husk, so someone, though lacking inner substance—such excellent qualities as good behavior and so forth—appears as an ascetic by assuming the guise of an ascetic, wearing "the dress of the disciplined"; thus he is called chaff because he is similar to chaff. But in the Discourse on Mindfulness of Breathing, where it is said, "This assembly, bhikkhus, is without chaff, devoid of chaff, pure, established in heartwood" (MN III 80,7–8), the good worldling, too, is called chaff. But here and in the Discourse on Kapila, where it is said, "Then sweep the chaff away, non-ascetics who imagine themselves ascetics!" (**282**), it is one guilty of a Pārājika that is called chaff.

One living as a dissembler is the defiler of the path: Having taken on the dress of the disciplined, he acts in such a way that people think of him thus: "He is a forest dweller, one who lives at the foot of a tree, a rag-robe wearer, one who lives by alms round, with few desires, content." Displaying such dissembling conduct, which appears proper and polished, this person should be understood as "a defiler of the path" because he defiles the world-transcending path for himself and defiles the path to a good destination for others.

90. Having thus described in this verse "the defiler of the path" the immoral person who is an ascetic by mere conventional designation, he now says, "When a householder . . . has penetrated these," showing that these types should not be confused with one another. This is its meaning: **These** are the four types of ascetics, [166] which he has **penetrated**, known, realized, through their characteristics as described. A **householder**: a khattiya, a brahmin, or anyone else. He is **learned** simply by learning about the characteristics of these four types of ascetics. He is **a noble disciple** because he has learned those characteristics in the presence of the noble ones. Merely by wisely understanding those types of ascetics thus, "This one and that one have such characteristics," he is **wise**.

Since he knows, "They are not all like him" . . . on seeing such [a person]: Having seen this evil bhikkhu doing evil, [he does not think] that the others are similar to the last-described defiler of the path. This is the construal: "A householder who is learned, a noble disciple, one with wisdom, who has penetrated these [four types], has known with wisdom: 'They are not all like him.'[604] So **on seeing such, he does not forsake his faith**: Having seen an evil bhikkhu doing such an evil deed, he does not forsake his faith; his faith is not forsaken, is not destroyed."[605]

Having indicated in this verse that they should not be confused with one another, now the Blessed One says, **for how could one equate them?**, praising the noble disciple who, though he has seen such a thing, knows: "They are not all like him." This is the connection: "This is indeed proper, that a learned noble disciple who has seen someone doing such evil knows: 'They are not all like him.' For what reason? **For how could one equate them: the undefiled with the defiled, the pure with the impure?** How indeed could a learned noble disciple, one who is wise, take the other three types of ascetics, who are undefiled, to be like the defiler of the path, who is defiled by his failure in behavior? [How could he take] the other three types of ascetics, who are pure, to be like the last, who is impure through his impure bodily conduct and so forth, an ascetic only by conventional label? How could he consider them similar?"

At the conclusion of this discourse, neither path nor fruit was explained to the lay disciple. It is simply that his perplexity in this matter was abandoned.

6 Downfall
(*Parābhava Sutta*)

What is the origin? It is said that after having heard the Discourse on Blessings (II,4), those devas thought: "In the Discourse on Blessings, by speaking about the progress and safety of beings, the Blessed One has spoken exclusively of success, not failure. Let us now ask him about the downfall of beings as well, about the reason beings fall down and perish." [167] Then, on the day after the Discourse on Blessings was explained, the deities of ten thousand world spheres, wishing to hear the Discourse on Downfall, assembled in this one world sphere. Having created subtle bodies such that ten, twenty, thirty, forty, fifty, sixty, seventy, and even eighty could fit into an area equal to the tip of a single hair, they stood around the Blessed One, who was seated in the excellent seat prepared for him, radiant, surpassing in glory and splendor all the devas, māras, and brahmās.[606] Then a certain young deva, commanded by Sakka, ruler of the devas, asked the Blessed One the question about the downfall. The Blessed One then spoke this discourse as a response to the question.

Here, the words "Thus have I heard" and so forth were spoken by the Venerable Ānanda. Alternating verses, beginning "We ask Gotama a question," were spoken by the young deva, and the verses that respond to them, beginning "One who succeeds is easily known," were spoken by the Blessed One. Having collected all this, it is called the Discourse on Downfall. Here, whatever has to be said about the words "Thus have I heard" and so forth will be explained in the commentary on the Discourse on Blessings (see pp. 738–40).

91. But when it was said, "A person in a downfall" and so forth, **a person in a downfall**: one who is falling down, who is perishing. **A person**: any being or creature.[607] **We ask Gotama a question**: Indicating [by "we"] he himself along with the other devas, creating an opportunity, the young deva addressed the Blessed One by his clan name. **We have come to ask the Blessed One**: The meaning is: "Having come from various world spheres, we will ask the Blessed One."[608] By this he shows respect. **What is the cause of a downfall?**: Since we have come thus, tell us what is the cause[609] for a person to enter a downfall, what is the door, the origin. The meaning is: "What is the means by which we might know that a person is in a downfall?" Hence when it was said "a person who is in a downfall," he asks about the reason for a person's downfall; for when the reason for a downfall is known, by generalizing from the reason it is possible to know which person is in a downfall. [168]

92. Then, having shown opposites in order to clearly convey the meaning to him, the Blessed One said, "One who succeeds is easily known," pointing out the cause of a downfall by way of a teaching based on persons.[610] This is its meaning: "**One who succeeds** is a person who makes progress, who does not fall away; **is easily known**: it is possible to recognize him easily, without trouble or difficulty. One in a downfall is **one who falls down**, who falls away, who perishes. The person in a downfall, whose cause you ask me about, is also **easily known**. How? For **one who loves the Dhamma is successful**: one who loves, yearns for, longs for, listens to, and practices the Dhamma of the ten courses of wholesome kamma. Because he can be known by seeing or hearing about his conduct, he is easily known. As for the other, too, **one who detests the Dhamma falls down**: one who detests that same Dhamma, who does not love it, yearn for it, long for it, listen to it, or practice it. Because he can be known by seeing or hearing about his misconduct, he is easily known." Thus here, showing opposites, in terms of the meaning it should be understood that the Blessed One shows the means of success to be love for the Dhamma and the cause of a downfall to be detesting the Dhamma.

93. Then, delighting in the Blessed One's statement, that deity said: "Thus we understand this." This is its meaning: "We understand this matter, accept it, and remember it just as it was stated by the Blessed One." **That is the first case of a downfall**: What is meant is: "The characteristic of that first case of a downfall is detesting the Dhamma. Among the causes of a downfall that we have come to learn, so far this one cause of a downfall has been stated." The word analysis here is this: "A case of a downfall is that because of which they fall down." And by what do they fall down? By the cause or reason for a downfall. For only the expressions here are different, but actually whether one speaks of "a case of a downfall" or "a cause of a downfall," there is no difference. Thus, having rejoiced, saying, "We understand one cause of a downfall," from a wish to learn of others, he says: "Tell us the second, Blessed One: What is the cause of a downfall?" The meaning of the verses following this, which speak about the third, fourth, and so forth, should be understood in the same way.

94. On the side of the answer, too, [169] since different beings have different causes of downfall—it is not the case that anyone has all of them or that all have only one—to show the different causes of their downfall, he explains them by way of a teaching based on persons, in the way that begins "The bad are dear to him."

This is the concise explanation of the meaning here: "The bad" are the six teachers,[611] or any others whose bodily, verbal, and mental actions are not peaceful.[612] **The bad are dear to him** as the naked ascetic Kora the Khattiya and so forth were to Sunakkhatta and so forth.[613] "The good" are buddhas, paccekabuddhas, and the disciples of a buddha, or any others who possess tranquil bodily, verbal, and mental action. **He does not treat the good as dear**: He does not take them as dear, attractive, desirable, and agreeable to himself.[614]

The "Dhamma of the bad" is the sixty-two speculative views or the ten courses of unwholesome kamma. **He approves of the Dhamma of the bad**: He yearns for it, longs for it, resorts to it.[615] Thus in this verse the causes of a downfall are said to be threefold: taking the bad to be dear, not treating the good as dear, and approving of the Dhamma of the bad. A person who possesses these qualities fails, falls away. He does not achieve progress either here in this world or beyond; therefore it is called a cause of a downfall. But we will explain this in detail in the commentary on the verse "Not associating with fools, associating with the wise."[616]

96. Lethargic:[617] one who is ever lethargic (who just sleeps) when walking, sitting, standing, and lying down; **gregarious**: one intent on company and who delights in talk; **does not make an exertion**: one who is destitute of energy and vigor, who is not inclined to effort; being incited by others, only seldom and occasionally[618] does he undertake work—household work in the case of a householder, [170] the work of a monastic in the case of a monastic. **Indolent**: naturally indolent, absolutely overcome by dullness, so that he remains standing in the place where he stands, sitting in the place where he sits; on his own initiative he does not even change his posture. And an example here is that of those in the past who were so indolent that they did not flee from a forest fire.[619] This is delimitation by the extreme, but one who is indolent to a lesser degree is also understood as indolent. As a banner is displayed by a chariot, as smoke is displayed by a fire, so when anger is displayed by someone, that person is said to be **one who displays anger**. This is a person of hating temperament, who quickly becomes irritated and whose mind is like an open sore (see AN I 124,3). In this verse five causes of a downfall are mentioned: lethargy, gregariousness, not making an exertion, indolence, and displaying anger. For one who possesses this, if a householder, does not achieve progress as a householder; if a monastic, does not achieve progress as a monastic. Rather, such a person just falls away and fails. Therefore this is called a cause of a downfall.

98. His mother or his father: his parents. **Grown old**: because of bodily feebleness; **their youth gone**: past their youth, eighty or ninety years of age, unable to do their own work. **One who is able**, capable, successful, living happily, **does not support** them, does not take care of them. In this verse, only one cause of a downfall is stated: not supporting one's mother and father, not taking care of them, not serving them. One who possesses this quality does not achieve the benefit in supporting one's mother and father stated thus:

Because of that service
to one's mother and father,
the wise praise one in this world
and after death one rejoices in heaven.
(It 111,5–8; AN II 70,31–32)

Rather, he just fails, incurring blame thus: "If he doesn't even support his mother and father, who else will he support?"; he is considered one to be shunned; and he goes to a bad destination in future lives. Therefore this is called a cause of a downfall.

100. A brahmin is so called because of expelling evils, **an ascetic** because of stilling them.[620] Or a brahmin is one who has arisen in a brahmin family and an ascetic is one who has gone forth. [171] **Or some other mendicant**: any supplicant. **One who deceives with false speech**: Having invited him thus, "Say, Bhante, what you need," or having promised to fulfill his request, one later deceives him by not giving what one promised. In this verse, only one cause of a downfall is stated: deceiving a brahmin or others with false speech. One who does this receives blame here in this world and a bad destination in future lives, and also fails in his purpose of achieving a good destination. For this is said: "An immoral person, who fails in behavior, acquires a bad reputation" (DN II 85,18–19). So too: "One possessing four qualities, bhikkhus, is cast into hell as if brought there. What four? One . . . speaks falsely" (AN II 83,25). So too: "Here, Sāriputta, someone approaches an ascetic or a brahmin and invites him to ask for what he needs but he does not give him what was requested. When he passes away from there, if he comes back to this world, whatever business he undertakes ends in failure. Someone else . . . gives it to him but does not fulfill his expectations. When he passes away from there, if he comes back to this world, whatever business he undertakes does not fulfill his expectations" (AN II 81–82). Thus, incurring blame and other undesirable consequences, he fails. Therefore this is called a cause of a downfall.

102. A person with abundant wealth: one with abundant gold, silver, and gems. **With bullion**: with *kahāpaṇas*;[621] **and food**:

food with many curries and sauces; **eats delicacies alone**: He eats delicacies in a concealed place, without giving any even to his own children. In this verse, only one cause of a downfall is stated: miserliness with regard to food because of one's greed for food. One who possesses this incurs blame, is considered a person to be shunned, and goes to a bad destination in future lives. Therefore this is called a cause of a downfall. In accordance with the discourse, all should be construed in the way that has been stated, but to avoid excessive detail we will now explain the meaning alone without showing the method of construal.

104. A person proud because of social class: One who gives rise to conceit, thinking, "I am of a superior social class," becomes stiff with pride[622] because of this, swollen like a full bellows, and does not [172] bend to anyone. This method also applies to pride because of wealth and clan. He **looks down on his own relative** because of his social class, as the Sakyans did to Viḍūḍabha.[623] And because of wealth, one despises another, thinking, "He is a destitute pauper," and does not treat him properly. Those relatives of his wish for him to fail. In this verse, four causes of a downfall are stated by way of base but they are only one in terms of characteristic.[624]

106. A womanizer: one infatuated with women; having given them whatever he can, he wins over one woman after another. So too, **one fond of liquor**: one who discards all his property and becomes inebriated;[625] **addicted to gambling**: one so intent on playing at dice that he would gamble away even his clothing. In these three ways, whatever he gains is dissipated; hence it should be understood that he **dissipates whatever he has gained**. One like this fails; hence in this verse three causes of a downfall are mentioned.

108. One not content with his own wives: one not content with his own wives who is seen **among prostitutes**, and so too **among the wives of others**. Because he gives wealth to prostitutes and goes to the wives of others, he fails when he is punished by the king and meets other kinds of harm. Hence in this verse the causes of a downfall are stated to be twofold.

110. When a man past his youth, one whose youth is spent, eighty or ninety years of age, **marries a girl with *timbaru* breasts**: marries a young girl whose breasts are like the *timbaru* fruit. **He does not sleep from jealousy over her**: Watching over her out of jealousy, he does not sleep, thinking: "Sexual union and living together with an old man are disagreeable to a young girl. May she not long for a young man!" Since one fails when one burns with sensual lust and jealousy and does not undertake work, in this verse only one cause of a downfall is stated: not sleeping because of jealousy.

112. Debauched: a greedy woman who longs for fish, meat, liquor, and so forth; **a spendthrift**: a wastrel who, to obtain such things, dispenses money as if it were dust; **or a man of similar nature**: or a man who is similar; **one places in authority**: having given him the stamp and seal and so forth, one commissions him to engage in service, to work in one's home, [173] or to work at business such as trade. Since he fails when his wealth is exhausted because of his fault, in this verse only one cause of a downfall is stated: appointing one so described to a position of authority.

114. One of little wealth: because he lacks accumulated wealth and a means of income; **strong craving**: one with strong craving for wealth, who is not content with whatever he gets; **is born into a khattiya family**: is born into a family of khattiyas; **he aspires to rulership here**: because of that strong craving, he desires rulership, either as his own birthright but in a wrong way and out of turn or he desires unobtainable rulership that pertains to someone else. Desiring this, he fails if he gives a little payoff to warriors or others but does not obtain rulership. Hence in this verse only one cause of a downfall is stated: desire for rulership.

115. If that deity were subsequently to ask, "Blessed One, tell us the thirteenth . . . tell us the hundred thousandth," the Blessed One would have explained it. But thinking, "Why ask about them, when not even one of them is a cause of progress?" that deity, finding no pleasure in those causes of a downfall, having asked this much, became remorseful and fell silent. Therefore the Blessed One, having understood his inclination, concluded the teaching with this verse: "Having examined these cases."

Here, **a wise person** is one who is investigative; **having examined**: having inspected with the eye of wisdom; **noble**: not through the path or the fruit but noble in the sense that he does not behave in ways that bring misfortune consisting in the causes of a downfall;[626] **endowed with vision**: one endowed with the vision, with the wisdom, to see failure and avoid it; **passes on to an auspicious world**: Such a one goes to the deva world, which is auspicious, secure, supreme, without calamities. At the conclusion of the teaching, the countless deities who heard about the causes of a downfall, striving carefully in accordance with the sense of urgency that had arisen in them, attained the fruits of stream-entry, a once-returner, and a non-returner. As it is said: [174]

At the Discourse on the Great Gathering,
and the Discourse on Blessings,
the Even-Minded and Advice to Rāhula,
on the Dhamma Wheel and Downfall,[627]
the assembly of deities there
was measureless, not trivial;
and the breakthrough to the Dhamma here
cannot be counted by way of number.

7 Aggikabhāradvāja (The Outcast)
(*Aggikabhāradvāja Sutta*)

The Discourse to Aggikabhāradvāja is also called the Discourse on the Outcast (Vasala Sutta).[628] What is its origin? The Blessed One was dwelling at Sāvatthī in Jeta's Grove, Anāthapiṇḍika's Park. In the way stated in relation to the Discourse with Kasibhāradvāja, while surveying the world with his buddha eye as the night was drawing to an end, he saw that the brahmin Aggikabhāradvāja had the supporting conditions for the refuges and training rules. He knew: "When I have gone there, a conversation between us will take place; then, at the end of the conversation, after he has heard a teaching of the Dhamma, this brahmin will go for refuge and undertake the training rules." Thus, having gone there, while the conversation was occurring, the brahmin asked for a teaching of the Dhamma, and the Blessed One spoke this discourse.[629]

We will explain the words "thus have I heard" and what follows in the commentary on the Discourse on Blessings (see pp. 500–501). **Then in the morning, the Blessed One**, and so forth: This should be understood in the way stated in commenting on the Discourse with Kasibhāradvāja (see pp. 504–5). In the statement "Now on that occasion, at the residence of the brahmin Aggikabhāradvāja," we will explain only those terms that have not been previously explained.

That brahmin sacrificed to and tended the fire, so he was known by the name "Aggika" (Fiery) and by his clan name, "Bhāradvāja"; therefore he was called **Aggikabhāradvāja**. **The residence**: the house. It is said that along the path at the entrance to this brahmin's residence there was a hall for the fire offering. Thus, while it should be said "at the entrance to his residence," because the area was included in the residence, it is said "at the residence." Or this is a locative case in the sense of proximity; the meaning is "near his residence." **A fire had been kindled**: A fire in the fireplace had been taken out, provided with a bundle of firewood, and fanned, [175] and thus it had blazed up and become a mass of soaring flames. **An oblation had been prepared**: Having bathed from the head down, with great honor he had prepared such offerings as milk rice, ghee, honey, and molasses. For everything that can be sacrificed to the fire is called "oblation." **Without skipping any houses**:[630] according to the order of the houses. For to benefit everyone and because of his contentment regarding food, the Blessed One walked for alms without passing over any families, whether high or low. Hence it is said: "While walking for alms without skipping any houses."

Now, given that the Blessed One was perfect in all qualities and graceful in all respects, why didn't the brahmin become pleased on seeing him? And why did he attack the Blessed One with harsh speech? In reply, it is said that this brahmin held the view: "Seeing ascetics while one is engaged in auspicious activities is inauspicious." Hence he thought, "Just at the time when I am feeding Mahābrahmā, a dark-eared shaveling, a low ascetic,[631] comes to my residence," and he was not pleased but came under the control of anger.[632] Then, angry and displeased, expressing his displeasure, he said: "Stop right there, you shaveling!" And since the brahmins held the view, "One with a shaved head is impure," disgusted with him, thinking, "He is impure, hence unworthy of the offerings given to devas and brahmins," he called him **shaveling**. [The purport is:] "Because he is a shaveling he is vile; he should not come to this region." Disgusted with his status as an ascetic, thinking, "Though he is an ascetic, he does not praise such bodily defilement,"[633] he calls him **a low ascetic**.[634] He calls him **an outcast** not only because of anger but also from disgust, thinking: "He gives the going forth to outcasts and is pleased to eat with them and use things in common with them, so he must be even worse than an outcast." Or he spoke thus thinking: "It is bad for outcasts to see an oblation and hear the sacred hymns."[635]

Though spoken to in such a way, the Blessed One maintained a clear facial expression, and in a sweet voice, with a mind cooled by compassion for the brahmin, showing his own unique nature not shared by any other beings, he said: **But do you know, brahmin?** When the brahmin [176] recognized the Blessed One's impartiality, as shown by his facial serenity, and heard his sweet words uttered with a mind cooled by compassion, he felt as if his heart had been sprinkled with ambrosia. Pleased, with clear faculties, humbled, as if he were spitting out poison, he abandoned his aggressive manner of speech based on his social class. He then thought: "Why should I believe that one of low birth is an outcast? According to the supreme meaning that is not an outcast, and low birth is not a quality that makes one an outcast." And he said: **I do not know, Master Gotama**. For it is natural that one who possesses the cause [for attainment] may be harsh before gaining a condition but becomes gentle as soon as a condition is obtained.[636]

Please: Here, this word *sādhu* is used in making a request, in receiving, in encouraging, as meaning "good," in strengthening, as well as in other ways.[637] Here (as rendered "please") it is used in making a request. **In that case**: An indication of his intention; what is meant is: "If you wish to know . . ." Or this is a statement of a cause. Its connection with the other terms should be understood thus: "Since you wish to know, brahmin, attend closely. I will speak to you in such a way that you will know." And there, **listen**: he enjoins him to ward off distraction through the ear faculty; **attend closely**: by enjoining him to strengthen his attention, he enjoins him to ward off distraction through the mind faculty. And the former is to prevent a distorted grasp of the words of the teaching; the latter is to prevent a distorted grasp of its meaning. [177] By the former he enjoins listening to the Dhamma; by the latter, retaining in mind the teachings that have been heard, examining their meaning, and so forth. By the former he indicates: "This Dhamma possesses good phrasing; therefore it should be listened to"; by the latter: "It possesses good meaning; therefore it should be attended to." Or having connected the word "closely" (*sādhukaṃ*) with both terms ("listen" and "attend"), he says, "Listen and attend closely," indicating this point: "Since this Dhamma is deep in doctrine and deep in teaching, therefore listen closely. Since it is deep in meaning and deep in penetration, therefore attend closely."[638]

The brahmin then seemed to become despondent at the thought: "How can I get a foothold in its depth?" To encourage him, the Blessed One said: **I will speak**. The purport of this should be understood thus: "I will speak in a clear way, with well-formulated words and phrases, so that you will understand." Then, having become eager to learn, **the brahmin Aggikabhāradvāja replied to the Blessed One: "Yes, sir."** What is meant is that he accepted the Buddha's injunction. Or by practicing as instructed, he listened with his face turned to him. Then **the Blessed One said this** to him. Now, with reference to the subject to be explained, he said: "A man who is angry and hostile" and so forth.

116. Angry: one in the habit of getting angry; **hostile**: disposed to hostility, a stronger form of anger. One who denigrates, who smears, the good qualities of others is a denigrator; he is evil and a denigrator, thus he is **an evil denigrator**. **Deficient in view**: one who has lost right view, or one who has adopted tenfold wrong view,[639] which is deficient or leads to deformity. **A hypocrite**: one disposed to hypocrisy, whose characteristic is concealment of one's own existent faults. **You should know him as an outcast**: Know such a person as an outcast, because of the raining down of those inferior qualities,[640] because of sprinkling by them, because of inundation by them; for even if he were born on the head of Brahmā, he is just an outcast in the supreme sense. Such only suffices for giving him happiness in his own heart, but nothing more.[641] [178]

Thus here with the first line the Blessed One restrains the brahmin's anger, saying in effect, "One subject to anger and the other faults is an inferior person," teaching about such qualities as anger by means of a teaching based on persons. Thus he teaches in one way about the outcast and the qualities that make one an outcast. Teaching in such a way, he does not resort to such words as "you" and "I," disparaging others and extolling himself, but rather in accordance with the Dhamma, evenly and methodically, he sets the brahmin in the place of an outcast and himself in the place of a brahmin.

117. Now refuting the view of the brahmins that "sometimes even though one destroys life, takes what is not given, and commits other evil deeds, one is still a brahmin," the Blessed One speaks the verses that begin "One here who injures a living being" to teach in other ways the outcast and the qualities that make one an outcast. He speaks for the sake of those beings who engage in such unwholesome deeds as harming, who do not see the danger in them and do not abandon those qualities.[642] Showing them the danger there, he indicates: "These inferior qualities are what make one an outcast."

Here, **once-born**: one born by the other modes of origin apart from those born of eggs; for this one is born only once. **Twice-born**: one born of the egg; for this one is born twice, from the mother's belly and from the egg shell.[643] Hence [it is said] "whether once-born or twice-born." **One here who injures a living being**: One here who, by means of an effort instigated by volition through the bodily door or the door of speech, deprives a being of life. There is also the reading "injures living beings."[644] The connection here should be understood thus: "One here who injures living beings distinguished as once-born or twice-born." **Who has no kindness toward living beings**: By this he refers to the absence of compassion in the mind.[645] The rest should be understood in the way already stated. In the following verses, without even saying this much, we will pass over the terms whose meanings are clear and merely comment on the terms that have not yet been explained.

118. Who strikes: who destroys. **Attacks**: who surrounds with troops. **Villages and towns**: cities too should be included, implied by the word "and." **Notorious as an oppressor**: because of striking and ambushing he is known in the world as one who oppresses villages, towns, and cities.

119. Whether in the village or [179] **in the forest**: "Village" here includes a village, a town, a city, together with their vicinities; apart from this, the rest is forest. In that village or forest, **the belongings of others**: the possessions of other beings that have not been relinquished, whether a living being or an inanimate object. **One who takes what has not been given**: With a mind of theft one takes what has not been given by others, what they have not permitted one to take; by any kind of effort and by any act of stealing one completes the act of acquiring it for oneself.

120. Having taken out a loan: One takes out a loan either (1) *on the basis of a deposit*, when one deposits some article of one's own (pawning); (2) or *on the basis of interest*, when one does not deposit anything but one promises, "After so much time I will give you so much in interest"; (3) or *on the basis of a contract*, as when one says, "When profit arises from this, the capital of mine will be yours," or "The profit will be shared by both of us."[646] **Flees when pressed [to pay it back], saying, "I am not indebted to you"**: Being pressed by the creditor, "Pay back the loan," even though one remains at home "one flees" when one says: "I did not take any loan from you. Who is your witness that I took one?"

121. From desire for some item: from a wish for anything,[647] even a trifle; **a person traveling along a road**: anyone going along a road, whether a woman or a man; **strikes and takes away the item**: murders or beats and takes that article.

122. For his own sake: for the sake of his own life; so too **for the sake of others**; **for the sake of wealth**: for the sake of his own wealth or for the wealth of others. Everywhere the word "and" here has a disjunctive meaning (that is, meaning "or"). **When questioned as a witness**: when asked, "Say what you know," **speaks falsely**: knowing, he says, "I don't know," or not knowing, he says, "I know." He deprives the proper owners of ownership.[648]

123. Seen: seen engaged in what is repulsive;[649] the meaning is, "he is seen committing a transgression." **By force**: by using strength against one who resists; **through endearment**: one who is desired by the wives of others and who desires them himself; this means through mutual affection.

124. His mother or his father: thus even with loving-kindness as the basis; **when they are aged, their youth gone**: with compassion [180] as the basis. **If one who is able does not support**: Though he possesses means and goods, he does not maintain them.

125. Who strikes: who hits with his hand or a clod of earth or any other means; **or verbally abuses**: who arouses anger in them by means of harsh speech.

126. When asked about the good: When asked about any kind of good, whether the directly visible good, the good pertaining to future lives, or the supreme good; **instructs others in what is harmful**: explains only what is harmful; **who gives advice in an obscure way**: or, even if he explains what is good, he gives advice with obscure statements, with unclear words and phrases, such that the other does not understand; or having maintained the closed fist of a teacher, having made the other wait for a long time, he gives advice while holding something back.

127. One who, having done a bad deed: This is the evil desire spoken of in the commentary as the predecessor of hypocrisy,[650] which has come down thus: "Here, someone has engaged in misconduct by body, misconduct by speech, and misconduct by mind. In order to conceal it, he forms an evil desire and wishes: 'Let them not find out about me'" (Vibh 413, §894). **A person of concealed action**: one whose actions are concealed, that is, he acts so that others do not find out about him and he does not disclose the things he has done.

128. Another's family: a family of relatives or a circle of friends. **But does not return the favor to his host**: When the one at whose home he has eaten comes to his own house, he does not honor him with food and drink and so forth; he does not give anything or he gives inferior food.

129. This should be understood in the way stated in the commentary on the Discourse on Downfall (p. 541).

130. If, when the meal time has arrived (*bhattakāle upaṭṭhite*): when it is time to eat. There is also the reading, *upaṭṭhitaṃ*, with the meaning "one who has arrived at the time for the meal" (referring to the brahmin or ascetic).[651] **One verbally abuses . . . and does not give**: He does not think, "Desiring my good, he has come to prompt me to do a meritorious deed," but rather one abuses him with harsh speech. He does not even show a pleasant manner,[652] much less does he give him any food.

131. One here who speaks in the manner of the bad (*asataṃ yo'dha pabrūti*): One here who utters the speech of bad people, like one who, when certain signs appear, says: "On such and such a day, this and that will happen to you." There is also the reading *asantaṃ* (not existing, untrue), meaning "false."[653] He is like a dissolute man who deceives another's wife or female slave by saying: "In such and such a village, I have such a property. Come, go there [181] and be my mistress, and I will give you this and that." **Seeking to obtain something for himself**: One who deceives another, gets something from him, and then wants to flee.

132. One who extols himself: who sets himself in a high position on account of social class and so forth; **and despises others**: who despises others on the same grounds, who degrades them. **Inferior because of his own conceit**: who has fallen away from growth in excellent qualities or has become inferior because of his own conceit, which consists in extolling himself and despising others.

133. One who provokes anger: one who makes others angry by bodily and verbal action; **stingy**: an obstinate miser, one who prevents others from giving to others or from doing meritorious deeds; **of evil desires**: one who desires to win esteem for excellent qualities he does not actually possess; **miserly**: through miserliness over abodes and so forth;[654] **deceitful**: one disposed to deceitfulness, displaying excellent qualities they do not actually have; or one who speaks improperly, saying, "Let me do it," even though he has no desire to do it. **One without moral shame or moral dread**: One who does not have moral shame, characterized as disgust with evil, or moral dread, characterized as fear and dread over doing evil.

134. One who reviles the Buddha: who denigrates the Perfectly Enlightened One, saying, "he is not omniscient" and so forth; **or who reviles his disciple**, saying, "he is one of bad conduct" and so forth. Whether **a wanderer or a householder**: This is a distinction among disciples, meaning his disciple who is a monastic or a householder who provides the requisites. The ancients also recognize here the meaning: "One who reviles with nonexistent faults an outside (non-Buddhist) wanderer or any householder."

135. One not actually an arahant who claims to be an arahant: Though not an arahant, he claims: "I am an arahant." He utters such statements that others take him to be an arahant, or disposes his body in such a way, or has such a wish and tolerates it. **A thief in this world along with Brahmā**: [With the mention of Brahmā] he speaks by way of the superior grade; what is meant is "the entire world." [182] For in the world those who plunder the wealth of others in various ways—by breaking into houses, pillaging, stealing, banditry, ambushing travelers, and so forth—are called thieves. But in the Buddha's Teaching, it is those plundering the requisites and so forth through the excellence of the assembly and so forth. As it is said:

> "There are, bhikkhus, these five kinds of great thieves existing in the world. . . . In this world, bhikkhus, along with its devas . . . this is the foremost great thief: one who lays claim to a superhuman state that is nonexistent, that he does not actually possess."[655]

Here, worldly thieves steal only worldly wealth and grain. The first among the thieves spoken of in the Teaching steals merely such requisites as robes and so forth; the second, the Dhamma of learning; the third, the spiritual life of another; the fourth, valuable goods belonging to the Sangha; and the fifth steals the wealth of excellent qualities, both mundane and world-transcending, such as the jhānas, concentrations, attainments, paths, and fruits, as well as worldly requisites such as robes. As he says: "The country's almsfood, bhikkhus, is eaten by you through theft." Here, it is with reference to the fifth great thief that the Blessed One speaks of "a thief in this world along with Brahmā." For "in this world along with its devas this is the foremost great thief . . . one who lays claim to a superhuman state that is nonexistent, that he does not actually possess." Thus the foremost great thief is stated by way of stealing mundane and world-transcending wealth; therefore here too, with the phrase "in this world along with Brahmā," he shows him by delimiting the superior grade.

This is the lowest outcast: He emphasizes: "He is the lowest of all outcasts." Why? Because of the raining down of the quality of theft in regard to an excellent object. As long as one does not give up that claim, one is not rid of the qualities that make one an outcast.

These outcasts: Now thirty-three or thirty-four kinds of outcasts have been stated. In the *first verse*, [183] there are the five beginning with the angry person, distinguished by way of the defect in their inclinations; or, by dividing the "evil denigrator" into two,[656] there are six. In the *second verse* there is one, the one who injures living beings, determined by the defect in his effort. In the *third*, there is one, the oppressor of villages and towns, determined by the defect in his effort. In the *fourth*, there is one, taking things by way of theft; in the *fifth*, one, cheating on one's debts; in the *sixth*, one, highway robbery by forceful stealing; in the *seventh*, one, bearing false witness; in the *eighth*, one, the betrayal of friends; in the *ninth*, one, lack of gratitude; in the *tenth*, one, injuring and harassing one's benefactors; in the *eleventh*, one, deceiving the heart; in the *twelfth*, two, concealed action and a defect;[657] in the *thirteenth*, one, lack of gratitude; in the *fourteenth*, one, deception; in the *fifteenth*, one, harassing; in the *sixteenth*, one, deception; in the *seventeenth*, two, extolling oneself and disparaging others; in the *eighteenth*, seven, provoking anger and so forth, by way of defects in effort and inclination; in the *nineteenth*, two, by reviling [the Buddha and his disciples]; in the *twentieth*, one, the foremost great thief.

Describing these, he says: **I have explained to you these outcasts that are spoken of**. This is its meaning: "Those kinds of outcast that I previously spoke of concisely, when I asked, 'But do you know, brahmin, what an outcast is or the qualities that make one an outcast?' have now been explained to you in detail. Or alternatively, those that I spoke of by way of persons have been explained by way of qualities as well. Or these that are spoken of by the noble ones by way of action, not by way of social class, I have explained to you in the way that begins 'A man who is angry and hostile.'"

136. Thus, having shown the outcast, because this brahmin was strongly attached to his own view (that personal status is determined by birth), to reject that view the Blessed One now says: "One is not an outcast by birth." This is its meaning: "In the supreme sense, **one is not an outcast by birth, nor by birth is one a brahmin**, but rather **by action one becomes an outcast, by action one becomes a brahmin**: One becomes an outcast by raining down impure action, and one becomes a brahmin by expelling impure action with purified action.[658] Or since you consider an outcast to be inferior and a brahmin to be superior, [184] it is by inferior action that one becomes an outcast and by superior action that one becomes a brahmin." He speaks thus conveying such a meaning.

137–39. Now, to demonstrate that point by means of an example, he spoke the three verses that begin "Understand in this way, too."[659] Among them, two verses have four lines, and one has six lines. This is their meaning: "When I said, 'One is not an outcast by birth,' **understand that in this way, too, according to this example of mine**: Understand that in this way, through the general principle for which this example is stated." What is the example? "The caṇḍāla son, Sopāka . . . from rebirth in the brahma world."

The caṇḍāla son: the son of a caṇḍāla. **Sopāka**: one who collects dead dogs and cooks them in order to eat them.[660] **Famed [under the name] Mātaṅga**: Thus he was known both by the name of his inferior social class and by his livelihood.

Mātaṅga attained supreme fame: He attained marvelous, supreme, most distinguished fame, acclaim, and praise; **so very hard to obtain**: hard to obtain even by those born into eminent families, and very hard to obtain by one born into an inferior family. Thus when he obtained fame **many khattiyas and brahmins came to perform service for him**: In order to serve Mātaṅga, khattiyas, brahmins, and many other people of Jambudīpa—vessas, suddas, and so forth—came to perform service for him.

Being thus served in such a way, **he**, Mātaṅga, **ascended the deva road** of the eight meditative attainments, known as "the road to the deva world,"[661] because of its ability to convey one to the deva world, a designation for the brahma world; **the great path** is called thus because it has been traveled by the great ones, by the buddhas and others. It is **dustless** because it is devoid of the dust of defilements. **Having expunged sensual lust** by that practice, with the breakup of the body, **he passed on to the brahma world**. Even though it was so low, **his social class did not prevent him from rebirth in the brahma world**.

This matter should be understood thus. In the past, it is said, when the Great Man was promoting the welfare of beings in various ways,[662] he arose in a caṇḍāla family that was a Sopāka ("dog-cooker") by livelihood. Named Mātaṅga [185], he was ugly and lived in a leather hut outside the city. He earned his living by wandering for alms within the city. One day, when a festival in the city had been announced, the party-goers were amusing themselves with their own retinues. Now a certain daughter of an affluent brahmin family, fifteen or sixteen years of age, as beautiful and graceful as a deva maiden, decided: "I will play in a way appropriate for my own family lineage." Taking abundant provisions such as various kinds of food on carts, she mounted a vehicle drawn by all white mares and went to the garden grounds accompanied by a large retinue. Her name was Diṭṭhamaṅgalikā ("One Who Has Seen the Auspicious"). It is said that she acquired this name because she did not wish to see any ill-shaped, inauspicious form.

At the time, Mātaṅga got up early, dressed himself in rags, fastened a bronze gong on his arm, and entered the city to collect food,[663] striking the gong when he saw people from a distance. Then Diṭṭhamaṅgalikā set out, with her servants saying, "Get out of the way, get out of the way," pushing away low-born people in front. When Diṭṭhamaṅgalikā saw Mātaṅga in the middle of the city gate, she asked: "Who is this?" He replied: "I am the caṇḍāla Mātaṅga." She said, "When I have seen someone like this, what good could there be for us in going there?" and she had the vehicle turn back. Her people were angry, thinking: "If we had gone to the garden, we would have obtained various kinds of food, but Mātaṅga has created an obstacle for us." Then they said, "Grab the caṇḍāla!" and they beat him with clods of earth. Thinking he was dead, they took him by the feet, threw him aside, covered him with trash, and left.

When he regained consciousness he got up and asked people: "Sirs, was the city gate built for everyone to use or was it built only for the brahmins?" They said: "It is for all to use." "In such a case, when I entered through a gate that is for all to use and maintain myself by begging, Diṭṭhamaṅgalikā's men inflicted misery and disaster upon me." Having wandered from street to street, he informed people of his intention, and then he lay down at the entrance to the brahmin's house, saying: "If I don't win Diṭṭhamaṅgalikā I will not get up." When the brahmin heard that Mātaṅga was lying down at the entrance to his house, he said: "Give him a *kākaṇikā*.[664] Let him go get a body massage with oil." He did not agree to this, [186] but just said: "If I don't win Diṭṭhamaṅgalikā I will not get up." Then the brahmin said: "Give him two *kākaṇikās*. Let him go eat a cake with one *kākaṇikā* and get a body massage with the other." He still did not agree to this but just said the same thing as before. The brahmin said, "Give him a *māsaka*, a *pāda*, half a *kahāpaṇa*, a *kahāpaṇa*, two, three, up to a hundred," but he still did not agree but just said the same thing as before. They were still begging him in this way when the sun set. Then the brahmin's wife, having come down from the mansion, had a tent built around him. She then approached him and begged him: "Dear Mātaṅga, forgive Diṭṭhamaṅgalikā for her wrongdoing. Take 1,000 *kahāpaṇas*, 2,000, 3,000 . . . up to 100,000 *kahāpaṇas*." But he just lay there silently.

Although in such a way they kept on offering him many presents over four or five days, [they could not get him to budge].[665] Meanwhile, khattiya youths and others who had failed to win Diṭṭhamaṅgalikā whispered into Mātaṅga's ears: "It is said that men who strive for many years eventually achieve their desired objective. Do not be disapppointed. Certainly in two or three days you will win Diṭṭhamaṅgalikā." He just lay there silently. Then on the seventh day the neighbors came together and said: "Make Mātaṅga get up or give him the girl, but do not destroy us all." It is said they believed that if someone dies lying down at the entrance to one's house, the residents of his own house along with the residents of seven houses all around become caṇḍāḷas.

Then they dressed Diṭṭhamaṅgalikā in blue rags, gave her a ladle and a pot, led the weeping girl to him, and gave her to him, saying: "Take the girl.[666] Get up and go!" She stood beside him and said, "Get up," but he said: "Lift me up by my hand." She lifted him. Having sat down, he said: "We won't get to live within the city. Come, lead me to my leather hut outside the city." She took him by the hand and led him there. But the Jātaka reciters say that she carried him on her back (Ja IV 376,24–25). [187] Having massaged his body with oil and bathed him in hot water, she prepared rice porridge and gave it to him.

He did not violate the rule against caste contamination, thinking: "This brahmin girl must not be ruined."[667] Half a month later, after he regained his strength, he told her: "I am going to the forest. Do not be disappointed, thinking that I'm away too long." He ordered the people of his household to look after her and then he left the house. He went forth as a hermit, did the preliminary work on a kasiṇa, and after a few days attained the eight meditative attainments and the five superknowledges. Then, thinking, "I will now be agreeable to Diṭṭhamaṅgalikā," he came through the sky, descended at the city gate, and sent for Diṭṭhamaṅgalikā.

When she got the message, she thought: "It seems some acquaintance of mine, a monk, has learned of my misery and has come to see me." She went to him, and when she recognized him, she fell at his feet and said: "Why did you abandon me?" The Great Man said: "Do not be sad, Diṭṭhamaṅgalikā. I will see that you are honored by all the residents of Jambudīpa." He then said: "Go, make the announcement: 'My husband is Mahābrahmā, not Mātaṅga. Having split the mansion of the moon, on the seventh day he will come to me.'"

She replied: "Bhante, I am the daughter of an affluent brahmin, but because of my own bad kamma I have been reduced to destitution.[668] I cannot speak thus." The Great Man said, "You do not know the spiritual might of Mātaṅga," and he displayed numerous wonders so that she would believe him. Having ordered her again in the same way, he went to his own abode. She did as she was told.

People complained: "Having been reduced to the state of a caṇḍāla because of her own bad kamma, how could she gain Mahābrahmā?" Sure of herself, day after day she wandered through the city announcing: "On the sixth day from today . . . on the fifth . . . the fourth . . . the third . . . tomorrow . . . today he will come." [188] Having recognized her confidence,[669] people said, "Sometimes it may happen thus," and they built a pavilion at the doors of their own houses, prepared a canvas screen, adorned some adolescent girls,[670] and said: "When Mahābrahmā arrives, we will give him these girls as a gift." They then sat down looking up at the sky.

On the full-moon night, when the moon had risen in the sky, the Great Man split the mansion of the moon and then, while the people were watching, he emerged in the form of Mahābrahmā. The people thought: "The moon has been doubled!" Seeing him gradually arrive, they drew the conclusion: "Diṭṭhamaṅgalikā spoke truthfully! In order to tame Diṭṭhamaṅgalikā, Mahābrahmā himself had previously come in the guise of Mātaṅga." Thus, while he was being observed by the multitude, he descended into Diṭṭhamaṅgalikā's abode, and she was then in season. He stroked her belly with his thumb, and with the contact she became pregnant. He then said to her: "You have become pregnant. When your son is born, live in dependence on him." While the multitude was watching, he again entered the mansion of the moon.

The brahmins said: "As the wife of Mahābrahmā, Diṭṭhamaṅgalikā has become our mother." They came from all over wishing to honor her, until the gates of the city were packed with visitors. They placed Diṭṭhamaṅgalikā on a pile of gold coins, bathed and adorned her, put her on a chariot, and with great honor led her around the city. They set up a pavilion in the middle of the city, placed Diṭṭhamaṅgalikā on the altar as "the wife of Mahābrahmā," and made her stay there, saying: "Until we build a suitable dwelling place for her, let her stay right here." She gave birth to a son inside the pavilion. On the purification day they bathed her and her son from the head down. Because the boy had been born inside a pavilion, they gave him the name Maṇḍavyakumāra, "Prince of the Pavilion." From then on, the brahmins went around accompanying him, calling him the son of Mahābrahmā. Then many hundreds of thousands of presents of various kinds arrived. The brahmins [189] provided protection for the prince. Those who came did not easily get to see him.

When in time the prince reached maturity, he began to give alms. He did not give to paupers and travelers who arrived out of desire[671] but only to brahmins. Meanwhile the Great Man directed his attention to him, wondering: "Does my son give alms or not?" Seeing that he was giving alms only to brahmins, he decided: "I will make him give alms to everyone." He put on his robes, took his bowl, came through the sky, and stood at the gate of his son's house. When the prince saw him, he thought, "Where has this ugly outcast come from?" and angrily spoke this verse:

"From where have you come, wearing filthy clothes,
a vile creature, like a goblin from the swamp?
On your neck you wear a scarf from a rubbish heap:
who are you, vile one, unworthy of offerings?"

The brahmins shouted, "Grab him, grab him!" and they grabbed hold of Mātaṅga, beat him, and inflicted misery and disaster on him. He went through the sky and settled outside the city. The deities, enraged, grabbed the prince by the throat, turned him upside down, with his feet up in the air and his head down, his eyes bulging, saliva flowing out from his mouth, gasping for breath, beset by pain. When Diṭṭhamaṅgalikā heard this, she asked: "Did anyone come?" They replied: "Yes, a monk came." – "Where did he go?" – "He went that way." She went there, prostrated herself at his feet, and begged him: "Bhante, please pardon your own slave."

Now the Great Man had wandered for alms and obtained some porridge, and on that occasion he was sitting there drinking it. He gave Diṭṭhamaṅgalikā a little porridge and told her: "Go, mix this porridge in a jug of water. Sprinkle it over the eyes, mouth, ears, and nostrils of those who have been deformed by a spirit, and rub it on their body, and they will again become normal." She did as she was told. [190] When the prince's body had returned to normal, she told him: "Go, dear, and apologize to the wise man." Thus she made her son and the brahmins lower themselves at his feet, bow to him, and apologize. He exhorted them: "You should give alms to everyone." Having given them a Dhamma talk, he went back to his own dwelling place and reflected: "Among women, Diṭṭhamaṅgalikā stands out as one who has been tamed, and Maṇḍavyakumāra stands out among men. Now who else is to be tamed?"

He then saw the hermit Jātimanta dwelling on the bank of

the Bandhumatī River, supported by the city of Bandhumatī. The hermit lived at the upper portion of the river, thinking: "Since I am of superior social class, I must not use water used by others." The Great Man set up residence in a higher region. At the time the hermit was to use water, the Great Man brushed his teeth with toothwood and threw the wood into the water. When the hermit saw it being carried down by the water, he wondered: "Who has discarded this?" He went upstream, saw the Great Man, and asked him: "Who are you?" He replied: "The caṇḍāla Mātaṅga, teacher." – "Get lost, caṇḍāla! Don't stay at the upper portion of the river."

The Great Man said, "Yes, teacher," and he settled at the lower portion of the river. Despite this, his toothwood and other things flowed upstream and reached the hermit. Again, the hermit went to him and said: "Get lost, caṇḍāla! Do not live at the lower portion of the river. Live at the upper portion."

The Great Man said, "Yes, teacher," and he did so, and again the same thing happened. The hermit was furious and cursed the Great Man: "At sunrise, your head will split into seven pieces."

The Great Man said, "Yes, teacher, but I won't let the sun come up," and he prevented the sun from rising. Then the residents of Bandhumatī were frightened, thinking: "The night isn't ending and darkness prevails." They went to the hermit and asked him: "Is there, teacher, any safety for us?" For they were under the impression that he was an arahant. He informed them of everything. They then went to the Great Man [191] and begged him: "Bhante, please release the sun." The Great Man replied: "If your arahant comes and apologizes to me, I will release it." The people went to the hermit and said: "Come, Bhante, apologize to the wise Mātaṅga. Do not let us perish because of your quarrel." He replied: "I won't apologize to a caṇḍāla." The people said, "You are destroying us," and they took him by the hands and feet and brought him to the Great Man.

The Great Man said: "I will pardon him if he apologizes to me while lying on his belly at my feet." The people said: "Do so." The hermit said: "I won't venerate a caṇḍāla." Saying, "So you won't venerate him voluntarily," they grabbed him by the hands, feet, beard, and neck and forced him to lie down at the

Great Man's feet. [The Great Man said:] "I pardon him, but out of compassion for him I won't release the sun; for as soon as the sun has risen, his head will split into seven pieces." The people asked: "Then what is to be done, Bhante?" The Great Man replied: "Put him in water up to his neck and cover his head with a lump of clay. When the rays of the sun fall on the lump of clay, it will split into seven pieces. After it has split, let him go elsewhere."

They took the hermit by the hands and feet and did as they were told. When the lump of clay split and fell into the water, the hermit was terrified and fled. Seeing this, people said: "See the spiritual might of the ascetic!" They then related the entire story, starting from his throwing away the toothwood, and they gained confidence in him, saying: "There is no other ascetic like this one."

From then on khattiyas, brahmins, and others throughout all of Jambudīpa, both householders and monks, came to perform service for the wise Mātaṅga. Having lived on until the end of his life span, with the breakup of the body, he was reborn in the brahma world. Hence the Blessed One said: "Understand that in this way, too . . . from rebirth in the brahma world."

140–41. Thus, having demonstrated, "One is not an outcast by birth . . . by action one becomes an outcast," [192] now, to demonstrate, "By birth one is not a brahmin . . . by action one becomes a brahmin," the Blessed One spoke the verses: "Those born into a family of reciters . . . from a bad destination or reproach." Here, **a family of reciters**: a brahmin family that recites the sacred hymns.[672] **Those who specialize in the sacred hymns**: those for whom the Vedas are kinsmen; what is meant is those who take refuge in the Vedas. **They are often seen involved in actions that are bad**: Though born in such a family and having the sacred hymns as kinsmen, they are again and again seen involved in such bad deeds as destroying life.

They are reprehensible in this present life and have a bad destination in a future life: Being seen involved in such actions, in this present life they are reprehensible. They are reproached even by their parents, who say: "They are not our children, these are bad-natured charcoals of the family.[673] Throw them out." And they are reproached by brahmins thus: "They are householders, not brahmins. Do not let them enter the memorial sacrifice, the barley offering, and so forth. Do not converse with them." And other people, too, say: "These are evildoers, not brahmins." Thus they are reprehensible. And in a future life they have a bad destination, such as hell and so forth; the meaning is that they have a bad destination in the other world. There is also the reading: "or in a future life" (instead of "and in a future life"). A bad destination means one in which their destination is suffering, one in which there is the encounter with suffering. **Their social class does not prevent them from a bad destination or reproach**: Thus their superior social class, which you fall back on as essential, does not prevent those brahmins who are seen involved in evil deeds from a bad destination, spoken of here as "a bad destination in a future life," or from reproach, spoken of here as being "reprehensible in this present life."

Thus, by showing that even brahmins born into a family of reciters can fall away in this present life by becoming reprehensible and so forth, and by showing that if they go to a bad destination they lose the status of their brahmin birth in a future life, the Blessed One has demonstrated this point as well: "By birth one is not a brahmin . . . by action one becomes a brahmin." Now concluding the two points, he addresses the brahmin and says:

> "One is not an outcast by birth,
> nor by birth is one a brahmin.
> By action one becomes an outcast,
> by action one becomes a brahmin." [193]

The rest should be understood in the way explained in relation to the Discourse with Kasibhāradvāja (pp. 521–22). Here, the difference is that the passage beginning "as though he were turning upright what had been overturned" should be construed thus: "Just as someone might turn upright what had been overturned, so when I had turned away from action [as the criterion] and had fallen into the doctrine of birth, Master Gotama helped me emerge from the view that one's status as a brahmin or an outcast is determined by birth. Just as one might reveal what was hidden, so he has revealed to me the doctrine of action, which was hidden by the doctrine of birth. As one might show the road to one who was lost, so he showed me the straight, undivided road about status as a brahmin and an outcast. And as one might hold up a lamp in the darkness, so he has held up a lamp with the example of Mātaṅga. In these ways Master Gotama has made the Dhamma clear to me in many ways."

8 Loving-Kindness (*Metta Sutta*)

What is the origin? It is said that bhikkhus, harassed by deities on a slope of the Himalayas, went to the Blessed One at Sāvatthī, and the Blessed One spoke this discourse to them for protection and as a meditation subject. That is a brief account. But the following is a detailed account.

[232][674] On one occasion the Blessed One was dwelling at Sāvatthī as the time for the rains retreat was approaching. At the time several bhikkhus from different provinces who had learned a meditation subject from the Blessed One approached him with a wish to enter the rains retreat elsewhere. The Blessed One explained meditation subjects suitable for the 84,000 different kinds of temperament in this way: To those of a lustful temperament, he taught the eleven meditation subjects on the unattractive nature of the body by way of both the sentient (living) and insentient (dead) bodies.[675] To those of a hating temperament, he taught the four meditation subjects, loving-kindness and so forth.[676] To those of a deluded temperament, he taught such meditation subjects as mindfulness of death. To those of a discursive temperament, he taught such meditation subjects as mindfulness of breathing and the earth kasiṇa. To those of a faith temperament, he taught such meditation subjects as recollection of the Buddha. And to those of an intellectual temperament he taught such meditation subjects as the delineation of the four elements.

Then five hundred bhikkhus who had learned a meditation subject from the Blessed One went out seeking suitable lodgings and a village as an alms resort. They traveled by stages until they saw, on the frontier, a mountain in the Himalayas that was made of stone slabs the color of blue-green crystal. It had cool, thick shade, and it was adorned with blue-green jungle groves. The ground was strewn with sand like silver foil inlaid with nets of pearls, and it was surrounded by pools of pure, sweet, cool water. The bhikkhus passed one night there, and in the early morning, after attending to their bodily needs, they entered a nearby village for alms. The village consisted of a thousand families who lived in dwellings close together, and the people [233] there were faithful and confident. Since monks were a rare sight in the frontier region, as soon as they saw the bhikkhus the people were filled with rapture and joy. They fed the bhikkhus and begged them: "Stay right here, Bhante, for the three months of the rains retreat." They built five hundred meditation huts, which they provided with all the necessary implements: beds, chairs, jugs for drinking water and washing water, and so forth.

The next day the bhikkhus entered another village for alms, and there too the people served them in the same way and begged them to stay for the rains retreat. Noting that there was no obstacle, the bhikkhus consented. They entered the jungle grove and meditated energetically all day and night; when the time gong was struck, they carried on practicing careful attention and sat at the feet of the trees. The splendor of those virtuous bhikkhus surpassed the splendor of the tree deities, who came down from their own palaces, and taking their children, roamed about here and there. This was similar to the situation when kings or royal ministers have gone to a village and occupy the space amid the houses of the villagers, and the people in the houses come out and stay elsewhere, looking on from a distance, wondering, "When will they leave?" Just so, the deities abandoned their own palaces, and roaming about here and there, they looked on from a distance, wondering: "When will the venerable ones leave?" Then they considered: "The bhikkhus have entered the first rains retreat and will have to stay here for three months. But we will have to withdraw, taking our children, and it will be a long time before we are able to live here again. Come now, let's show the bhikkhus frightening objects."

That night, as the bhikkhus were meditating, the deities created the forms of terrifying yakkhas standing before each one, and they also made frightening sounds. When the bhikkhus saw those forms and heard those sounds, their hearts trembled, [234] and they became pale and sallow. Because of this, they could not focus their minds, and with their minds scattered, repeatedly agitated by fear, they lost their mindfulness. Then, when they lost their mindfulness, the deities created foul odors. It seemed as if their brains were being crushed by the foul odors and they experienced severe headaches, yet they did not inform one another of what was happening.

One day, when they had all assembled to attend on the Sangha elder, the elder asked them: "Friends, when you entered this jungle grove, for several days your complexion was pure and bright and your faculties were serene. But now you have become thin, pale, and sallow. Is something here unsuitable for you?" Then one bhikkhu said: "Bhante, at night I see frightening forms and hear frightening sounds, and smell a foul odor, such that my mind does not become concentrated." In the same way, all reported what was happening. The Sangha elder said: "The Blessed One has laid down two observances of the rains retreat,[677] and this lodging is unsuitable for us. Come, friends, let's go back to the Blessed One and ask him about another lodging more suitable for us."

"Excellent, Bhante," the other bhikkhus replied. Then they cleared their lodgings, took their bowls and robes, and, since they were unattached to families, they all departed for Sāvatthī without taking leave of anyone. Traveling in stages, they reached Sāvatthī and went to the Blessed One. Seeing those bhikkhus, the Blessed One said: "Bhikkhus, I have laid down a training rule: 'One should not walk on tour during the rains retreat' (Vin I 138,19–22). Then why [235] are you walking on tour?" They told the Blessed One everything. The Blessed One mentally inspected all Jambudīpa but he did not see another suitable lodging for them, not even a place the size of a four-legged chair. He then told them: "Bhikkhus, there is no other suitable lodging for you. Dwelling there, you can attain the destruction of the influxes. Go back, bhikkhus, and stay in that same lodging. If you wish to be secure from the deities, learn this protective discourse. This will be your protection and a meditation subject." He then spoke this discourse.

But others say that after the Blessed One said, "Go back,

bhikkhus, and stay in that same lodging," he said: "Further, a forest dweller should know how to carry on. That is, in the evening and the morning, there should be two rounds of practice of loving-kindness, two recitations of the protective discourses, two rounds of meditation on the body's unattractive nature, two rounds of mindfulness of death and attention to the eight great bases of urgency. The eight great bases of urgency are: birth, old age, illness, death, and the suffering in the four planes of misery. Or alternatively, the first four are birth, old age, illness, and death; the fifth is the suffering in the plane of misery, followed by the suffering rooted in the round in the past, the suffering rooted in the round in the future, and the suffering rooted in the search for food in the present." Thus, having told them how to carry on, the Blessed One spoke this discourse to those bhikkhus for the sake of practicing loving-kindness, for the sake of protection, and for the sake of reaching jhāna as a basis for insight.[678] [236]

143. This, firstly, is the commentary on the terms in the first verse: **What should be done**: what is to be done; what ought to be done. **The good**: the practice, or anything beneficial to oneself, is called "good" (*attha*) because it is to be taken up (*araṇīyato*);[679] "because it is to be taken up" means "because it is to be approached." **By one skilled in the good**: by one expert in the good. **Yaṃ** ("which") is a relative nominative; **taṃ** ("that") is a demonstrative accusative. Or **yaṃ taṃ** are both nominatives.[680] **Peaceful state**: an accusative. It is peaceful through its characteristic, and a state (*padaṃ*) because it should be attained (*pattabbato*). This is a designation for nibbāna. **Having made the breakthrough**: having arrived at. **Able**: capable; competent. **Upright**: possessed of integrity. **Very upright**: exceptionally upright. **Amenable to advice**: one for whom a word of advice is pleasant. **Gentle**: possessed of gentleness. **Without arrogance**: not arrogant.

This is the commentary on the meaning: "This is what should be done by one who is skilled in the good, having made the breakthrough to that peaceful state." Here, firstly, there is what should be done and what should not be done. Briefly, *what should be done* here is the threefold training. *What should not be done* are such things as defective behavior, defective view, defective conduct, defective livelihood, and so forth.

So too, there is one skilled in the good and one skilled in what is not good. *One skilled in what is not good* is one who, having gone forth in this teaching, does not exert himself properly: one with flawed behavior, who earns his living by any of the twenty-one improper means, that is, by gifts of bamboos, gifts of leaves, gifts of flowers, gifts of fruits, gifts of toothwood, gifts of mouthwash, gifts of bathing implements, gifts of bath powder, gifts of clay; by flattery, bean-soupery, and fondling;[681] by conveying messages by foot; by the work of a physician, by the work of a messenger, by going on errands; [237] by presenting a portion of his almsfood as a gift; by geomancy, astrology, or palmistry.[682] He moves about in the six kinds of wrong resort, that is, among prostitutes, widows, old maids, eunuchs, bhikkhunīs, and taverns. He forms bonds with kings, royal ministers, sectarians and their disciples, in the inappropriate way that laypeople form bonds. He associates with, resorts to, and visits families that are without faith and confidence, that are miserly, abusive, and contemptuous, that wish for loss, harm, discomfort, and trouble for bhikkhus . . . for female lay followers.

One skilled in the good is one who, having gone forth in this Teaching, exerts himself properly: who abandons wrong means of earning his living, who wishes to become established in the fourfold purification of good behavior; who fulfills restraint by the Pātimokkha under the heading of faith, restraint of the sense faculties under the heading of mindfulness, purification of livelihood under the heading of energy, and use of the requisites under the heading of wisdom.

One skilled in the good is also one who purifies restraint by the Pātimokkha by purifying the seven classes of offenses; who purifies restraint of the sense faculties by not giving rise to covetousness and other unwholesome qualities when objects strike against the six sense doors; who purifies his livelihood by avoiding wrong ways of seeking and obtains the requisites in ways praised by the wise and extolled by the buddhas and their disciples; who purifies use of the requisites by way of the aforementioned reflection; and who purifies clear comprehension by reflection upon the purpose and so forth in changing his posture.

Just as one cleans a soiled cloth by means of saline water, or a mirror by means of ash, or as one refines gold in a crucible, so one cleans good behavior by means of knowledge. Having understood this, one cleans good behavior by washing it with the water of knowledge. And just as a hen protects her egg, a yak its tail, a woman her one dear son, and a one-eyed man his one eye, so, being extremely heedful, one protects one's aggregate of good behavior. [238] One who, reflecting in the evening and the morning, does not see even the slightest fault is also one skilled in the good. Or one who, based on the good behavior that gives freedom from remorse, exerts himself in the practice of suppressing the defilements, then does the preparatory work on a kasiṇa, and then obtains the meditative attainments is also one skilled in the good. One who, having emerged from an attainment, explores conditioned things and attains arahantship is the foremost of those skilled in the good.

Among these, those praised as skilled in the good by grounding themselves in the good behavior that gives freedom from remorse, or by exerting themselves in the practice of suppressing the defilements, or by means of the paths and fruits are the ones intended as "skilled in the good" in this sense. And those bhikkhus [in the origin story] were like this. Hence, with reference to those bhikkhus, the Blessed One said, "This is what should be done by one skilled in the good," giving a teaching based on a single person.

(1) Then,[683] as they were wondering, "What should be done?" he said: "having made the breakthrough to that peaceful state." This is the purport: "*This is what* (*yaṃ*) *should be done* by one who wishes to dwell *having made the breakthrough*, by way of penetration, *to that* (*taṃ*) *peaceful* nibbāna-*state* extolled by the buddhas and those enlightened after them." And here "what" (*yaṃ*), stated at the beginning of this [second] line in the verse, accords with the governing expression "should be done" (*karaṇīyaṃ*). But since the phrase "having made the breakthrough to *that* peaceful state" is one whose meaning requires completion, it should be understood that "by one who wishes to dwell" is meant.[684]

(2) Or alternatively, when it is said, "having made the break-

through to the peaceful state," the purport here can be understood thus: "When one has known with mundane wisdom, by way of oral tradition and so forth, the nibbāna-state as 'peaceful,' that which should be done by one who wishes to achieve it is *what should be done by one skilled in the good*, which accords with the governing expression, ['who has made the breakthrough to the peaceful state']."[685]

(3) Or alternatively, when it was said "what should be done by one skilled in the good," as they were wondering, "What?" he said, "having made the breakthrough to that which is the peaceful state . . ." The purport of this should be understood thus: "When one has made the breakthrough to the peaceful state by means of mundane wisdom, *what* (*yaṃ*) *should be done* is this (*taṃ*). . . ." What must be done is what should be done, meaning "what is surely worth doing."[686] But what is that? [239] What else could it be but [practicing] the means to its achievement? And admittedly, this is stated by the first term (namely, "what should be done"), which signifies the threefold training that is worth doing. Thus, in the commentary on the meaning of this, we said: "There is what should be done, and there is what should not be done."

Among these, what should be done is, in brief, the three trainings. But because of its extreme brevity, while some of those bhikkhus understood it, others did not understand. Therefore, in order to clarify the matter for those who did not understand, the Blessed One first spoke this [second] half-verse, "He should be able, upright, very upright, amenable to advice and gentle, without arrogance," elaborating on what is to be done by a bhikkhu, especially a forest dweller.

What is meant? A forest-dwelling bhikkhu who wishes to dwell having made the breakthrough to the peaceful state—or one who has made the breakthrough to that state by means of mundane wisdom and is practicing for its achievement—by possessing the second and fourth factors of striving,[687] without concern for his body and life, *should be able* to practice for the penetration of the truths. Thus in the preparation of the kasiṇa, in the undertaking of his duties, in repairing his own bowl and robes and so forth, in the various tasks to be done for his fellow monks, and in other similar matters, he **should be able**, adroit, diligent, capable. Being able, by possessing the third factor of striving, he should be **upright**. Though he is upright, he should not be satisfied with being upright only once, but as long as he lives, again and again, without laxity, he should be exceptionally [or **very**] **upright**. Or he is upright through lack of deceitfulness, and very upright through lack of hypocrisy; or he is upright by abandoning bodily and verbal crookedness, and very upright by abandoning mental crookedness; or he is upright by not making a display of nonexistent virtues, and very upright by not consenting to gains that might accrue to him because of nonexistent virtues. In this way, he should be upright and very upright by close meditation on the object and on the characteristic, accomplished respectively by the first two trainings and the third training, and by the purification of his endeavor and his disposition.

Not only should he be upright and very upright, but **he should be amenable to advice**. For if, when told, "This should not be done," a person says, "What have you seen? What have you heard? Who are you to speak to me? Are you my preceptor, my teacher, my friend, my companion?" or if he troubles the other by keeping silent, or accepts his word but does not act on it, he is far from achieving distinction. But if, when admonished, one says, "Good, Bhante, that was well stated. One's own faults [240] are hard to see. If you see me doing such a deed again, you should speak to me out of compassion. It has been a long time since I have been admonished by you," and then acts in accordance with the instructions, that person is not far from achieving distinction. Therefore, one should also be amenable to advice, accepting the advice of others and acting upon it.

And just as he is amenable to advice, he should be **gentle**. If householders ask him to convey messages and go on errands, and so forth, he should not be gentle about this but should remain firm. But he should be gentle in the practice of the duties and in the entire spiritual life, capable of application to various tasks like well-worked gold. Or else "gentle" means he should have an open expression on his face, without a frown, pleasant to converse with, hospitable, pleasantly receptive like a good ford. And not only should he be gentle, but he should also be **without arrogance**. He should not despise others because of such things as social class, clan, and other causes of arrogance;

rather, like the Elder Sāriputta, he should maintain a mind like that of a caṇḍāla boy.[688]

144. In this way the Blessed One has described some of the things to be done by a bhikkhu—especially a forest dweller—who wishes to dwell having made the breakthrough to the peaceful state or by one practicing for its achievement. Now, wishing to explain further, he spoke the second verse, "[one should be] content."

Here, one is **content** through the twelve kinds of contentment, which are analyzed in relation to the line "contentment and gratitude" (see pp. 762–64). Or alternatively, "content" means that one is satisfied—satisfied with what is one's own, satisfied with what is present, and equally satisfied.[689] Here, "what is one's own" consists of the four requisites described in the ordination arena and accepted by oneself thus, "[The going forth] depends on food obtained as alms offerings."[690] What is called "satisfied with what is one's own" means one sustains oneself with what is given, whether good or bad, presented respectfully or carelessly, without showing any vexation at the time of receiving it and at the time of using it. "What is present" is what has been gained and exists for oneself. [241] What is called "satisfied with what is present" means that one is satisfied simply with what is present, not desiring anything else, abandoning excessive greed. "Equally" means abandoning fondness and aversion, respectively, toward what is desirable and undesirable. What is called "equally satisfied" means being equally satisfied with all objects.

Easily supported: one supported with ease, easily maintained. A bhikkhu difficult to support shows himself downcast and displeased even when his bowl has been filled with hill rice, meat, boiled rice, and other fine foods, or who denigrates the almsfood in the presence of the donors, saying, "What have you given?" and then gives it to novices or laypeople. When they see him, people avoid him from a distance, thinking: "It isn't possible to maintain a bhikkhu who is difficult to support." But one who is easily supported shows a tranquil expression and is pleased with whatever he receives—whether coarse or fine, little or much—and thereby sustains himself. When they see him, people are extremely trusting, thinking:

"Our venerable is easily supported, satisfied even with a little." Having promised to support him, they do so. It is such a one that is intended here by "easily supported."

Of few duties: one who has few duties, who is not engaged in numerous duties because of delight in work, delight in talking, delight in company, and so forth. Or else what is meant is one who, in the whole monastery, has no duties with respect to building work, Sangha property, the administration of novices and monastery workers, and so forth. He simply shaves his head, clips his nails, prepares his bowl and robes, and does other personal tasks, but otherwise takes the ascetic's duty as his primary task.

A frugal way of living: one whose way of living is frugal. When a bhikkhu who has many goods sets out on a journey, he departs along with many people carrying loads on their heads and hips—bowls, robes, bedsheets, oil, sugarballs, and so forth. In contrast, when one with few requisites who maintains only the eight requisites of an ascetic—bowl, robes, and so forth—sets out on a journey, he departs like a bird, taking everything along with him. [242] Such a one is intended here by "one of a frugal way of living."

Of peaceful faculties: one whose faculties are peaceful, one whose sense faculties are not agitated because of lust and so forth in the encounter with desirable objects and so forth. **Judicious**: intelligent, bright, wise. The purport is one who is wise in maintaining good behavior, wise in seeking robes and so forth, and wise regarding the seven kinds of suitability, that is, regarding abodes and so forth.[691]

Courteous:[692] the meaning is one devoid of the eight cases of bodily impudence, the four cases of verbal impudence, and the numerous cases of mental impudence. The **eight cases of bodily impudence** are modes of improper bodily behavior in regard to the Sangha, a group, an individual, in the refectory, in the sauna, at a ford for bathing, on the path to the alms round, and when entering among the houses. That is, someone here sits down lolling in the midst of the Sangha or he sits crossing his feet and so forth; similarily, in the midst of a group—in the fourfold assembly—and so too in the presence of an individual elder. In the refectory he does not offer a seat to elders, and he bars younger monks from a seat. So too in the sauna. And here he makes a fire and does other things without obtaining permission from elders. In relation to a bathing ford it is said: "Bathing should be done in the order of arrival, without making seniority the criterion." But without taking notice of this, one who comes late enters the water and thereby troubles both the elders and younger monks already present. On the path to the alms round, in order to obtain the best seat, the best water, and the best almsfood, one goes in front of elders, even elbowing one's way; and when entering among the houses, one enters before elders and does such things as play with children.

The **four cases of verbal impudence** are improper verbal utterances in regard to the Sangha, a group, an individual, and among the houses. That is, someone here speaks on the Dhamma in the midst of the Sangha without obtaining permission; so too in a group, as explained earlier, [243] and in the presence of an individual elder. When people ask one a question, one answers without obtaining permission from one's elders. When among the houses, one speaks thus: "What is this? Is there porridge or anything to eat? What will you give me? What is there to eat today? What is there to drink?" and so forth.

The numerous cases of mental impudence are the various kinds of improper thoughts, such as sensual thoughts and so forth, pondered by the mind without falling into any kind of misconduct by way of body or speech.

Without greed when among families: When one approaches families, one is without greed because of craving for the requisites or by forming inappropriate bonds with laypeople. He does not sorrow with them, or rejoice with them, or become happy when they are happy and sad when they are sad, and he does not exert himself to undertake their tasks and duties.

When it was said, "he should be amenable to advice,"[693] the word "should be" (*assa*) here is to be conjoined with all the terms in this verse in this way: "One should be content, one should be easily supported," and so forth.

145. In this way the Blessed One has explained *what should be done further* by a bhikkhu—especially a forest dweller—who wishes to dwell having made the breakthrough to the peaceful state or who wishes to practice for its achievement. Now, wishing to explain *what should not be done*, he spoke this half-verse: "He should not do anything, however slight, because of which other wise people might criticize him." This is its meaning: One who is doing what should be done **should not do anything, however slight**, that is, bodily, verbal, and mental misconduct described as slight or petty. He should not only avoid gross misconduct but should not do anything wrong, even what is trifling and minute.

Then, with the words **because of which other wise people might criticize him**, he shows the directly visible danger in that misconduct. And here others who are unwise are not the standard; for they do what is blameless and blameworthy, what is slightly blameworthy and very blameworthy. The wise alone are the standard; for after investigating and examining a matter, [244] they speak dispraise of one who deserves dispraise and praise of one who deserves praise. Therefore it is said "others who are wise."

In this way, with the opening two and a half verses, the Blessed One has spoken especially for the sake of the forest dweller who wishes to dwell having made the breakthrough to the peaceful state or who wishes to practice for its achievement; but under the heading of the forest dweller, he has also spoken for the sake of all who have learned a meditation subject and wish to dwell thus. He has discussed the approach to the meditation subject, divided into what should be done and what should not be done. Now, with the words "May all beings be happy and secure," he begins to discuss loving-kindness both as a protective device for dispelling the peril from those deities and as a meditation subject for attaining a jhāna to be used as the basis for insight.

Here, **happy**: endowed with happiness; **secure**: without peril, free from disaster; **all**: without omission; **beings** (*sattā*): living beings; **inwardly happy**: happy in mind. And here, "happy" is through physical happiness, "inwardly happy" is through mental happiness, "secure" is through the disappearance of all perils and disasters of both kinds. But why is this said? For the purpose of showing the aspects of developing loving-kindness. For loving-kindness can be developed on the basis of the wish "May all beings be happy," or "May they be secure," or "May they be inwardly happy."

146–47. Having thus shown the development of loving-kindness in brief, from access concentration to the peak of absorption, he spoke the next two verses, beginning "Whatever living beings there are," to show this in detail. Or alternatively, since the mind accustomed to a plurality of objects does not immediately settle into unity, but after having explored an analysis of its objects it becomes settled in stages, he spoke the next two verses, "Whatever living beings there are," for the purpose of settling the mind after it has explored the analysis of the objects into pairs and triads, starting with the frail and firm. Or alternatively, since one's mind easily becomes steady when it focuses on a clear object, [245] the Buddha spoke these two verses, "Whatever living beings there are," indicating the analysis of the objects into pairs and triads beginning with the frail and firm, because he wanted to help each of these bhikkhus settle his mind on whatever object became clear to him.

Here there are four pairs: the frail and firm, the seen and unseen, the far and near, and those that have come to be and those that will come to be. In the case of the six terms beginning with "those that are long," the term "middling" fits into three triads, and the term "fine" into two triads. Thus the passage indicates three triads: the long, short, and middling; the large, fine (small), and middling; and the gross, fine, and middling. **Whatever** is a word meaning "without omission." **Living beings** (*pāṇā*) are existent beings that are living. Or else "living beings" means "those that breathe."[694] By this, he includes beings with five constituents that are dependent on in-and-out breathing. **Beings** (*bhūtā*) are those that have being; by this, he includes beings with one constituent and four constituents.[695] **There are**: that exist.

In this way, with the expression "whatever living beings there are" having shown all beings collectively, classified into pairs and triads, now, with the expression "whether frail or firm, without omission," he shows all these classified by way of this pair. Here, **the frail** are "those that tremble (or thirst)"; this is a designation for those with craving and with fear.[696] **The firm** are those that stand firm; this is a designation for arahants, who have abandoned craving and fear.[697] **Without omission**: with nothing omitted; what is meant is "all." The phrase at the end of the second verse (**147**) should be connected to all the pairs and triads, so that we read: "Whatever living beings there are, whether frail or firm, without omission, may all these beings, too, be inwardly happy," and so on up to "whether they have come to be or will come to be, may all these beings, too, be inwardly happy."

Now of the six terms indicating the three triads, beginning with the long, short, and middling, the **long** are those with long bodies, such as nāgas, fish, and lizards. For the bodies of the nāgas in the ocean measure many hundreds of fathoms, while the bodies of fish and lizards, and so forth, measure many yojanas.[698] The **large** are those with large bodies, such as fish and tortoises in water,[699] [246] and elephants and nāgas on land, and the *dānava*[700] and so forth among spirits. As the Blessed One said: "Rāhu is foremost of those with bodies" (AN II 17,21); for his body is 4,000 yojanas in height and 800 yojanas [wide]; his arm span is 1,200 yojanas, his eyebrows fifty yojanas, and so his fingers, and his palms are 200 yojanas. **Middling**: the bodies of horses, cattle, buffalo, pigs, and so forth. **Short**: beings that are smaller than the tall and middling, such as the dwarfs in the various classes. **Fine** (**small**): those outside the range of the physical eyes; beings with very subtle bodies, such as those born in water, which are perceptible by the divine eye, or lice and so forth. Moreover, those beings in the various classes that are smaller in size than the large and middling and the gross and middling should be understood as fine (small). **Gross**: those beings with round bodies, such as fish, turtles, and oysters and other shellfish, and so forth.

147. Having thus shown beings exhaustively in three triads, now, with the words "whether they are seen or unseen" and so forth, he shows them classified into three pairs. Here, the **seen** are those that have been previously seen when they came into range of one's own vision; the **unseen** are those existing across the ocean, on the other side of mountains, in other world spheres, and so forth. **Whether they dwell far or near**: With this pair, he shows beings dwelling far and near in relation to one's own body. These should be understood relatively. For those beings dwelling within one's own body are near, those outside the body are far. Similarly, those dwelling in one's vicinity are near, those beyond one's vicinity are far. Those dwelling in one's own monastery, village, country, continent, world sphere are said to be near; those dwelling in other world spheres are said to dwell far away.

Those who **have come to be**: those that have been born, generated. This is a designation for arahants, who are reckoned thus: "They have come to be but will not come to be again." Those who **will come to be**: those seeking existence.[701] [247] This is a designation for trainees and worldlings who, because they have not abandoned the fetters of existence, are seeking future existence. Or alternatively, among the four modes of generation, of those beings born from eggs and from the womb it is said "they will come to be" so long as they have not broken out from the egg shell or the cawl. But when they have broken out from the egg shell or the cawl and have emerged, they are said to "have come to be." Of those beings born from moisture and those spontaneously born it is said "they will come to be" at the first mind-moment. From the second mind-moment on, it is said they "have come to be." Or else, when they are born in a particular posture, so long as they have not adopted another posture, it is said "they will come to be." But following this, it is said "they have come to be."

148. In this way, with the two and a half verses beginning "May all beings be happy," the Blessed One in various ways has shown those bhikkhus the development of loving-kindness toward beings by way of wishing for them to come upon welfare and happiness. Now he says, **No one should deceive another**, showing the development of loving-kindness again by way of wishing for them to avoid harm and suffering.[702]

Here, **one . . . another**: one person and another person. **One should not deceive**: one should not cheat. **One should not despise**: one should not scorn. **Anywhere**: in any place, whether in the village or town,[703] in the field, among one's relatives, or in the guild. **Anyone**: anyone whether a khattiya, a brahmin, a householder, a renunciant, one who is fortunate or one who is unfortunate, and so forth. **Because of anger and thoughts of aversion**:[704] because of anger expressed by bodily and verbal vexation, and because of thoughts of aversion accompanied by mental vexation, **no one should wish suffering for another**. [248] What is meant? One should not only develop loving-kindness by attending thus, "May they be happy and secure," but one should also develop it in this way: "No person should deceive another fraudulently, such as by cheating them. No one should despise another in any region anywhere because of the nine cases of conceit[705] on account of social class and so forth. Because of anger or thoughts of aversion no one should wish suffering for another."

149. Having thus shown the development of loving-kindness according to its meaning, as the wish for beings to avoid harm and suffering, he now says, "Just as a mother," showing the practice by means of a simile. This is its meaning: **Just as a mother would protect her son**—as she would protect a bosom son born from within herself—**her only son, with her own life,** by sacrificing her own life in order to ward off suffering from coming upon him, **so one should develop toward all beings a state of mind**, [that is,] loving-kindness, **without boundaries**.[706] One should generate it and extend it again and again, and one should develop it without boundaries by taking unbounded beings as its object or by the exhaustive pervasion of one being.[707]

150. Having thus shown the development of loving-kindness in all aspects, now showing its extension, he says: "And toward the whole world." Here, **loving-kindness** is derived from "friend" (*mitta*), because it is fattened and it protects; that is, it is moistened through a wish to promote well-being and it safeguards from the arrival of harm.[708] Loving-kindness (friendliness) is the state of a friend.[709] **Toward the whole world**: toward the world of beings without omission. **A state of mind**: existing in the mind; such is said because it (loving-kindness) is associated with the mind.[710] **One should develop**: one should extend. **Without boundaries**: without boundaries because it takes measureless beings as its object.[711] **Above**: by this he includes formless-realm existence; **below**: by this he includes desire-realm existence; **across**: by this he includes form-realm existence. **Unconfined**: devoid of confinement; what is meant is the breaking of the barrier. The hostile person is called the barrier; the meaning is that it proceeds toward that person as well. **Without enmity**: devoid of enmity, [249] without the manifestation of the volition of enmity even at intervals; **with-**

out adversaries: the absence of hostile persons; for a person who dwells in loving-kindness is dear to humans, dear to non-humans, and there is no one hostile to him. Hence, because of the absence of hostile persons, that mind is said to be "without adversaries." For "hostile person" and "adversary" are synonyms. This is the commentary on the meaning by way of individual terms.

But this is the commentary on the intended meaning here. It was said, "one should develop toward all beings a mind without boundaries." One should develop this unbounded mind of loving-kindness toward the whole world; one should extend it and bring it to growth, increase, and vastness. How? "Above, below, and across": above as far as the peak of existence; below as far as the Avīci hell; and across to the remaining directions.[712] Or above up to the formless realm, below to the desire realm, and across to the form realm, pervading them without omission. Developing it in such a way, so that it is "unconfined, without enmity, without adversaries," one should also develop it with the absence of confinement, enmity, and adversaries. When success in development is attained, it will be *unconfined* by gaining room everywhere; *without enmity* by the removal of one's own resentment toward others; and *without adversaries* by the removal of the resentment of others toward oneself. So one develops and extends that mind of unbounded loving-kindness—unconfined, without enmity, without adversaries—toward the whole world demarcated as threefold: above, below, and across.

151. Having thus shown the extension of the development of loving-kindness, now showing that there is no fixed posture for one intent on its development, he says: "Whether standing, walking . . . on this mindfulness." This is its meaning: One developing this mind of loving-kindness in such a way [250] need not adopt a fixed posture as is prescribed for other meditation subjects thus, "He sits down, having folded his legs crosswise, straightening his body," and so forth. Dispelling discomfort by adopting any posture as one pleases, **whether standing, walking, sitting, or lying down, as long as one is not drowsy, one should resolve on this mindfulness** of the jhāna of loving-kindness.

Or alternatively, having thus shown the extension of the

development of loving-kindness, now showing mastery over it, he says: "Whether standing, walking." For one who has achieved mastery wishes to resolve on this mindfuiness of the jhāna of loving-kindness as long as the posture lasts, whether standing, walking, sitting, or lying down. Or else by "standing or walking" he indicates that standing [and walking] are not obstacles to it. Moreover, for as long as one wishes to resolve on this mindfulness of the jhāna of loving-kindness, for just so long one resolves on it without becoming drowsy; there is no sluggishness in regard to it. Hence he says: "Whether standing, walking, or sitting, or lying down, as long as one is not drowsy, one should resolve on this mindfulness."

This is the purport: "As to what was said, 'And toward the whole world one should develop an unbounded mind of loving-kindness,' one should develop it in such a way that, whatever posture one adopts, such as standing, etc., as long as the posture lasts, taking no notice[713] that one is standing, etc., as long as one wishes to remain resolved on the mindfulness of the jhāna of loving-kindness, for just so long one can resolve on that mindfulness."[714]

While showing what mastery in the development of loving-kindness entails, after enjoining one to dwell in loving-kindness with the words "one should resolve on this mindfulness," the Blessed One now praises that dwelling with the words "They call this a divine dwelling here." This is its meaning: **They call this** dwelling in loving-kindness—as described by the passage that extends from the words "May all beings be happy and secure" down to "one should resolve on this mindfulness"—**a divine dwelling**, the best dwelling **here**, in the noble Dhamma and discipline. It is *best* because it is devoid of faults and because it brings benefits to oneself and others, and *a dwelling* among the four dwellings: the celestial, divine, and noble [dwellings], and the postures.[715] [251] Hence constantly and continuously, without interruption, one should resolve on this mindfulness whether standing, walking, sitting, or lying down, as long as one is not drowsy.

152. Having thus shown those bhikkhus the development of loving-kindness in its various aspects, he now says: "Not taking up any views." Because loving-kindness has beings as its object, it is close to a view of self. Hence, by way of rejecting the adoption of views, he says this to show those bhikkhus the attainment of the plane of the noble ones reached by using that same jhāna of loving-kindness as a basis.[716] With this verse, he concludes the teaching.

This is its meaning: Having emerged from this dwelling in the jhāna of loving-kindness described thus, "They call this a divine dwelling here," one comprehends the [mental] phenomena there such as thought and examination, and delineates the physical phenomena that go along with them.[717] **Not taking up any views** by the demarcation of these [phenomena] as "name and form," [and by understanding], "This is a heap of bare conditioned things; no being is found here" (SN I 135,19), in stages one becomes **of good behavior**, by way of world-transcending good behavior, and **endowed with vision**, the right view of the path of stream-entry associated with world-transcending good behavior. Following this, greed for sensual objects, the defilement of sensuality, is still not abandoned. But **having removed greed for sensual pleasures** by first weakening it by the path of the once-returner and then abandoning it without remainder by the path of the non-returner—having thus removed it and subdued it—**one never again comes back to the bed of a womb**. One absolutely will not come back again to the bed of a womb. Having been reborn in the pure abodes, one reaches arahantship and attains final nibbāna right there.

Having concluded the teaching in this way, the Blessed One said to those bhikkhus: "Go, bhikkhus, dwell in that same jungle grove. And on the eight days of the month for hearing the Dhamma, having struck the gong,[718] recite this discourse, give a Dhamma talk, hold discussion, rejoice, and pursue, develop, and cultivate this meditation subject. [252] Then those spirits will not show frightening images to you but instead will wish for your good and welfare."

Having replied, "Excellent!" they rose from their seats, paid homage to the Blessed One, circumambulated him, went back, and acted accordingly. The deities were filled with rapture and joy, thinking, "The venerable ones wish for our good and welfare," and they themselves swept the lodgings, prepared hot water, massaged their backs and feet, and set up a guard.

Having developed loving-kindness as they were taught, those bhikkhus took it as a basis, aroused insight, and within that three-month period all attained arahantship, the foremost fruit. They then held the great Pāvaraṇā ceremony in purity.

> In this way those skilled in the good,
> in the Dhamma of one who is skilled,[719]
> accomplished the good that should be done
> as explained by the Lord of the Dhamma.
> Having done this, complete in wisdom,
> they made the breakthrough to the peaceful state
> experiencing supreme peace of heart.
>
> Therefore an intelligent person who wishes to dwell
> having made the breakthrough to that peaceful state—
> the deathless, marvelous state dear to the noble ones—
> should constantly do the good that should be done,
> analyzed into stainless virtue, concentration, and
> wisdom.

9 Hemavata
(*Hemavata Sutta*)

What is the origin?[720] The origin was in response to a question. For when repeatedly questioned by Hemavata the Blessed One said, "In six has the world arisen," and so forth. Here, "Today is the fifteenth" and so forth were spoken by Sātāgira; "thus said the yakkha Sātāgira" and so forth by the compilers; "Is the mind of the impartial one" and so forth by Hemavata; and "In six has the world" and so forth by the Blessed One. Having collected all this, [194] it is called the Discourse to Hemavata; but some call it the Discourse to Sātāgira.[721]

As to the verse that begins "Today is the fifteenth," its origin is as follows. In this present auspicious eon,[722] the Blessed One Kassapa, a perfectly enlightened buddha, arose at a time when human beings had a life span of 20,000 years and he attained final nibbāna after having lived for 16,000 years. People then honored his bodily remains with great veneration. His relics were not dispersed but remained as a single mass like a block of gold; for this is the natural law when buddhas have a long life span. But when the buddhas are short lived, since they attain final nibbāna before the majority of people have had a chance to see them, they resolve: "Let the relics be dispersed." They do so with the compassionate thought: "People in different places will venerate the relics and generate merit." Hence their relics are dispersed like gold dust, as was the case with our Blessed One.

In the case of the Blessed One Kassapa, people made a single relic chamber and built a cetiya one yojana in height and circumference. It had four gates at intervals of a gāvuta.[723] The king, Kikī, took one gate; his son Paṭhavindhara took one; the ministers headed by the general took one; and the citizens headed by the chief financier took one. Its body consisted of red gold, and the bricks, each worth a hundred thousand, were made of various gems, contrasting with the golden color of the cetiya. They built the cetiya using yellow orpiment and red arsenic in place of clay and fragrant oil in place of water.

When the cetiya had been built, two young men who were friends renounced and went forth under elder monks who had been personal disciples [of the Buddha Kassapa]. For under long-lived buddhas only their personal disciples give the going forth, full ordination, and guidance; others do not get this privilege. Then the two young monks asked the elders: "Bhante, how many vocations are there in the Teaching?" The elders said, "Two vocations," and explained to them the vocation of practice and the vocation of scriptural learning: "Here, under *the vocation of practice*, a monk spends five years under his teacher or preceptor, fulfills the various duties, and gains proficiency in the Pātimokkha and in the suttas of two or three recitation sections. [195] He then learns a meditation subject, and without attachment to family or group, he enters the forest, where he strives and struggles for the realization of arahantship. But under *the vocation of scriptural learning*, after mastering one Nikāya—or two or five Nikāyas according to one's ability—one applies oneself to learning the crystal-clear Teaching through the texts and their meaning."

Then the young monks thought: "Of the two vocations, the vocation of practice is indeed superior." But they then thought, "We are still young. We'll fulfill the vocation of practice when we're old, so for now let's fulfill the vocation of scriptural learning," and thus they took up scriptural learning. Being naturally wise, in no long time they came to know the entire Word of the Buddha and were especially skilled in making judgments pertaining to the Vinaya. Based on their learning, they acquired a retinue, and based on their retinue, they acquired gain. Each one had a retinue of five hundred bhikkhus. They illuminated the Teacher's Teaching, and it seemed as if the time of the Buddha had returned.

At the time, two bhikkhus were living in a village dwelling. One was an advocate of the Dhamma, and the other was an advocate of non-Dhamma. The advocate of non-Dhamma was fierce, rough, and loose-tongued. His misconduct became known to the other, who reproached him: "Your deed, friend, is not in accordance with the Teaching." The other turned the talk aside, saying: "What did you see? What did you hear?" The first said: "The Vinaya experts will understand." The advocate of non-Dhamma realized: "If the Vinaya experts judge this case, I will surely be left without a foothold in the Teaching." Thus, wishing to create his own faction, at once he took some requisites and approached the two elders. He presented them with the requisites and offered to live under their guidance, acting as if he wished to serve them and respectfully fulfill all the duties toward them.

Then one day, having gone to serve them, he paid homage to them and stood there even though they dismissed him. The elders asked him: "Do you have something to say?" He said: "Bhante, one bhikkhu has picked a quarrel with me over some misconduct. If he comes here and informs you about that case, do not judge it as it should be judged." The elders [196] replied: "When a case is brought up, it is not proper not to judge it as it should be judged." He persisted: "If such is done, Bhante, I won't have a foothold in the Teaching. Let this evil be mine, but do not pass judgment." Being implored by him, they yielded.

Having received their promise, he returned to his dwelling, thinking: "Everything has been settled in the presence of the Vinaya experts." Despising the advocate of Dhamma even more, he assailed him with harsh speech. The advocate of Dhamma, thinking, "He's become insolent," immediately departed, approached the elders' retinue of a thousand bhikkhus, and said: "Isn't it true, friends, that when a case has been brought up, it should be judged in accordance with the Dhamma, or if it is not brought up for judgment, harmony should be established by having the monks involved confess their transgressions to each other? But these elders neither judged the case nor established harmony. What is this all about?" On hearing this, they too were silent, thinking: "Surely, something is known by the teachers." Then the one who advocated non-Dhamma, having gotten his chance, pressed the speaker of Dhamma thus: "You previously said that the Vinaya experts will understand. Now these are Vinaya experts. Report the case." Then he departed, saying: "From today you're defeated. Don't return to that dwelling."

The advocate of Dhamma then approached those elders and wept loudly, saying: "Without any concern for the Teaching, you instead favored a [dishonest] person, thinking: 'He served and satisfied us.' Without protecting the Teaching, you protected a [dishonest] person. From today on it is not proper for you to judge cases. Today the Blessed One Kassapa has attained final nibbāna!"[724] He departed, lamenting: "The Teacher's Teaching has perished!" Then those bhikkhus, agitated, experienced regret: "While protecting a [dishonest] person, we threw the precious Teaching into a pit." [197]

Because of their regret, they passed away heartbroken.[725] Being unable to take rebirth in heaven, the elder of the two was reborn on Mount Hemavata in the Himalayas as a yakkha named "Hemavata," while the other teacher was reborn on Mount Sāta in the middle region with the name "Sātāgira." The bhikkhus of their retinues who had followed them, also unable to take rebirth in heaven, were reborn as the yakkhas making up their retinues. But their lay supporters, who provided them with their requisites, were reborn in the deva world.

Hemavata and Sātāgira were mighty yakkha kings among the twenty-eight commanders of the yakkhas; and this is the natural law for commanders of the yakkhas, that on eight days each month an assembly of deities takes place on Mount Bhagalavati,[726] on the Red Arsenic Terrace in the Himalayas, for the purpose of making legal judgments, and they must assemble there. At that meeting, as soon as they saw one another, Sātāgira and Hemavata recognized each other, and after each had inquired about the other's place of rebirth, they became remorseful: "We went astray, friend. We practiced the ascetic's duty for 20,000 years, yet because of one evil companion we have been reborn in the yakkha realm, while our lay supporters have been reborn in the desire-sphere deva worlds."

Then Sātāgira said: "Dear sir, the Himalayas are considered wondrous and astounding. If you see or hear of anything wondrous, you should inform me." Hemavata also said: "Dear sir, the middle region is considered to be wondrous and astounding. If you see or hear of anything wondrous, you should inform me." Thus the two companions made a pact with one another, and as they lived on through that rebirth, one era between buddhas passed, until the great earth swelled up one yojana and three gāvutas. [198]

Meanwhile, from the time he made the resolve at the feet of Dīpaṅkara until the Vessantara Jātaka, our bodhisatta fulfilled the pāramīs, after which he was reborn in the Tusita heaven. Having remained there for the length of the life span, when requested by the deities, he made the five great investigations,[727] informed the devas [that he would pass away], and while thirty-two auspicious signs were occurring,[728] he took rebirth here, causing the ten-thousandfold world system to shake. Having seen these wonders, even these yakkhas did not know what had caused them; some say that they did not even see them because they were absorbed in play. The same happened at his birth, his renunciation, and his enlightenment. But at the setting in motion of the wheel of the Dhamma, when the Blessed One addressed the group of five monks and set in motion the excellent wheel of the Dhamma with its three turnings and twelve modes, Sātāgira alone among the yakkhas saw the auspicious signs such as the quaking of the great earth and the other wonders. Having known the cause for their occurrence, he approached the Blessed One along with his retinue and heard his teaching of the Dhamma, but he did not achieve any distinction. Why not? Because, while listening to the Dhamma, he recalled Hemavata and looked out over the assembly, wondering: "Has my friend come or not?" Not seeing him, he was distracted by the thought: "My friend has been cheated, since he is not listening to such a variegated and inspired teaching of the Blessed One." And even though the sun had set, the Blessed One did not conclude his teaching. Then Sātāgira thought: "I will get my friend and return, and then along with him I will listen to the teaching of the Dhamma." So, having created elephant vehicles, horse vehicles, and garuda vehicles, accompanied by the five hundred yakkhas, he set out toward the Himalayas.

Now at the conception, birth, renunciation, enlightenment, and final nibbāna [of a buddha] the thirty-two auspicious signs occur and vanish but do not endure long, while at the setting in motion of the wheel of the Dhamma they are more prominent and last longer before they cease. Therefore Hemavata, too, saw that wondrous display in the Himalayas and thought: "Since I was born, never before has this mountain been so delightful. Now I will get my friend and return, and then along with him I will enjoy the glory of these flowers." Thus he set out toward the middle region.

The two crossed paths above Rājagaha [199] and asked each other about the reason for their journey. Hemavata said: "Dear sir, since I was born, never before has this mountain been so delightful, with the trees flowering out of season. Therefore I have come thinking to enjoy the glory of these flowers together with you." Sātāgira replied: "Do you know, dear sir, the reason for this wonder, why the trees are flowering out of season?" – "I don't." – "This wonder, sir, has occurred not only in the Himalayas but throughout the ten-thousandfold world system. A perfectly enlightened buddha has arisen in the world, and today he has set in motion the wheel of the Dhamma. That's the reason." In this way Sātāgira, having informed Hemavata about the arising of the Buddha, spoke this verse from a desire to lead him to the Blessed One. But some say he spoke thus when the Blessed One was dwelling at the Gotamaka Cetiya.

153. Today is the fifteenth: this night and day is the fifteenth by counting the fortnight. **The uposatha**: so called because it is to be observed (*upavasitabbato*). Or, among the three kinds of uposathas, today is the uposatha of the fifteenth, not the uposatha of the fourteenth or the uposatha of harmony. The word "uposatha" occurs in several senses: as the recital of the Pātimokkha, the eight factors, a mode of dwelling, a prescription, a day, and so forth. In such passages as "Come, friend Kappina, let us go to the uposatha" (see Vin I 105), "uposatha" refers to the recital of the Pātimokkha. In such passages as "It is in such a way, Visākhā, that the uposatha is observed complete in eight factors" (AN IV 256,11–13), it refers to the eight factors, abstaining from the destruction of life and so forth. In such passages as "For the pure one it is always the uposatha" (MN I 39,19), it refers to a mode of living. In such passages as "The uposatha, O king of nāgas" (DN II 174,14), it refers to a prescription. And in such passages as "When he had washed his head on the uposatha day of the fifteenth" (DN II 172,8), it refers to a day. Therefore, rejecting the others, determining it only as the full-moon day in the month of Āsāḷha,[729] he says: "Today is the fifteenth, the uposatha." The meaning is that today is the fifteenth day counting thus: "The first of the fortnight, the second . . ."

On that day celestial entities were present, hence it is said **celestial**. What were they? Forms. [200] For on that night the whole of Jambudīpa was adorned by the radiance of the bodies, clothes, ornaments, and palaces of the devas that had assembled from the ten-thousandfold world system, and by the radiance of the moon shining in a cloudless sky, and it was especially adorned by the bodily radiance of the Blessed One, the supreme deva by purification.[730] Hence it is said: **A celestial night has arrived**. Having generated confidence in his friend by praising the excellent qualities of the night, and having informed him that a buddha had arisen, he next said: **Come, let us see Gotama, the teacher of perfect name**. Here, he is called "one of perfect name" because he is named after his excellent qualities, which are perfect, lofty, complete in all aspects. Thus he is named "Enlightened One" (*buddha*) because "he awakened to the truths, because he awakens this population," and so forth (see pp. 1208–9, Nidd I 344–45). And he is named "Blessed One" (*bhagavā*) "because he has demolished (*bhagga*) lust, demolished hatred," and so forth (see pp. 1086–87, Nidd I 104). This same method in regard to "arahant, perfectly enlightened one, endowed with true knowledge and conduct," and so forth.[731]

Teacher (*satthā*): because he instructs (*anusāsati*) devas and human beings in the good, such as the good pertaining to the present life, and so forth, saying: "Abandon this, undertake that." And further, he is "teacher" in the way stated in the Niddesa: "The Blessed One is a teacher, a caravan leader (*satthavāha*): just as a caravan leader leads a caravan across the desert," and so forth (see pp. 1205–6, Nidd I 334–35). **Come, let us see Gotama**: one from the Gotama clan. What is meant? "Do not be indecisive, wondering whether or not he is the Teacher. Having become fully certain, come, let us see Gotama."

154. When this was said, Hemavata considered: "Speaking of him as 'the teacher of perfect name,' Sātāgira reveals his omniscience. But omniscient ones are rare in the world, and the world has already been inundated by those claiming to be omniscient, such as Pūraṇa Kassapa. If he is omniscient, he must surely have attained the characteristic of impartiality. In that case, I will accept him as such." Then, asking about the characteristic of impartiality, he says: **Is the mind . . . well disposed**? Here, **well disposed** means well established, immovable, unwavering. **Of the impartial one . . . toward all beings?**: [201] [the mind] of one who has attained the characteristic of an impartial one. Or this is itself a question: "Is that teacher of yours impartial (*tādī*) toward all beings or not (*no*)?"[732]

"**Has he mastered**—brought under control—**his intentions**—his thoughts—**toward the desirable and undesirable**, toward such kinds of objects?" What is meant? "As to that teacher of whom you speak, is his mind well disposed toward all beings because he has attained the characteristic of impartiality, or does he appear well disposed only so long as he does not meet a condition for excitement? Is your teacher impartial toward all beings because he has an equal mind or not? And when intentions arise because of lust and hatred toward desirable and undesirable objects, has he brought them under control or does he sometimes come under their control?"

155. Then Sītāgira, because of his certainty regarding the Blessed One's omniscience, affirming all the excellent qualities of the omniscient one, said, "The mind of the impartial one is well disposed," and so forth. Here, "well disposed" means well placed, in the sense of being *without hostility* like the earth; *well established and immovable* like Mount Sineru; and *unshakable* like a pillar by the four kinds of māras and by opposing sects. And it is not astonishing that now, when he is established in omniscience through his completeness in all respects, the mind of the Blessed One should be well disposed and immovable. But even in past lives, at the time he was an animal still subject to lust, he was immovable. For example, when he arose in a family of six-tusked bull elephants, he remained unmoved when he was shot by a poisoned arrow and he did not feel hatred even toward the hunter, but on the contrary he cut off his own tusk and gave it to him. Similarly, when he was a chief monkey and was struck on the head by a huge rock, he showed the path to his assailant. And when he was the wise Vidhura, when a yakkha grabbed him by the feet and threw him down the precipice of Black Mountain, sixty yojanas deep, he taught the Dhamma for the sake of that yakkha.[733] Therefore Sātāgira rightly said: "The mind . . . is well disposed."

The mind of the impartial one is well disposed toward all beings: His mind is well disposed toward all beings because he has attained the characteristic of impartiality, not only so long as he does not meet provocation. [202] For the Blessed One's characteristic of impartiality should be understood as fivefold. As it is said: "The Blessed One is impartial in five ways: impartial toward the desirable and undesirable, impartial because he has renounced, impartial because he is freed, impartial because he has crossed over, and impartial as a descriptive term.[734] How is the Blessed One impartial toward the desirable and undesirable? In the case of gain, the Blessed One is impartial," and so forth; all should be accepted in the way stated in the Niddesa (see pp. 1073–74, Nidd I 82–83), and gain and so forth should be understood in the way elaborated in the Great Commentary.[735] Or this is itself [the answer to] the question: "Is that teacher of yours an impartial one toward all beings or not?" On this alternative, the meaning is: "Our teacher is an impartial one because he has an equal mind toward all beings." For because of his desire to promote their happiness and to remove their suffering, this Blessed One has an equal mind toward all beings: he is the same toward others as to himself; the same toward the young woman Ciñcā as toward [his mother] Mahāmāyā; the same toward Suppabuddha as toward his father Suddhodana; the same toward the murderers Devadatta, Dhanapālaka, and Aṅgulimāla as toward his son Rāhula;[736] he is impartial as well toward the world together with its devas. Therefore Sātāgira rightly said: "The mind of the impartial one is well disposed toward all beings."

Toward the desirable and undesirable: Here, the meaning should be understood thus: Whatever intentions may arise by way of lust and hatred toward desirable and undesirable objects, with the abandoning of lust and so forth by the unsurpassed path he has brought them under control. He never comes under their control, for the Blessed One has unsullied intentions; he is well liberated in mind and well liberated by wisdom.

And here, it should be understood that by "well disposed

in mind," the absence of careless attention is indicated; by "toward all beings, the desirable, and the undesirable," what is indicated is anything that may be present anywhere among the two kinds of objects, distinguished as beings and conditioned things;[737] by "mastery over intentions" what is indicated is the abandoning of defilements through the absence of careless attention in regard to that object. And by "well disposed in mind," purity of mental behavior is indicated; by "impartiality toward all beings," purity of bodily behavior; by "mastery over intentions," purity of verbal behavior, for speech is rooted in one's thoughts. Similarly, by "well disposed in mind," the absence of all such faults as greed and other defilements is indicated; [203] by "impartiality toward all beings," the presence of such excellent qualities as loving-kindness and other virtues; and by "mastery over intentions," the spiritual potency of the nobles one, which consists in perceiving unrepulsiveness in the repulsive and so forth.[738] And in that way his omniscience is indicated.

156. Does he avoid taking what has not been given? Thus, having first asked about impartiality only by way of the mind door, and having heard Sātāgira affirm that, in order to strengthen his conviction he now asks by way of the three doors of action. Or else, having previously asked concisely about purity through the doors of body, speech, and mind, and having heard Sātāgira affirm that, in order to strengthen his conviction he now asks in detail. Here, for ease of composition, he asks first about abstinence from taking what is not given. **Does he keep far from heedlessness?** (*kacci ārā pamādamhā*): He asks whether the Buddha abstains from sexual activity by preventing his mind from drifting among the five strands of sensual pleasure. There is also the reading *kacci ārā pamadamhā*; what is meant is, "Does he keep far from women?"[739] **Is he not devoid of jhāna?**: By this he asks about the strength of his threefold bodily abstinence; for the abstinence of one possessed of jhāna is powerful.[740]

157. Now since it is not only at present that the Blessed One had refrained from taking what is not given and so forth, but he had done so for a long time in the past as well; and since through the spiritual might of this abstinence he had acquired various marks of a great man; and since the world with its devas speaks praise of him thus, "The ascetic Gotama refrains from taking what is not given," Sātāgira, roaring a lion's roar with well-enunciated words, said: **He does not take what has not been given**. The meaning of this is already clear. In the third line of this verse, too, there are two readings: *pamādamhā* and *pamadamhā*. And in the fourth line, the meaning of **not devoid of jhāna** should be understood thus: "He does not neglect jhāna, does not reject it, does not disregard it."

158. Having thus heard about his purity in the door of the body, now asking about his purity in the door of speech, [204] he says: **Does he avoid speaking falsely? Is his way of speaking not rough?**: What is meant is, "Is he one whose speech is not harsh?"[741] [**Does he not say anything destructive?**:] This is a designation for divisive speech, which causes destruction by dividing beings from one another.[742] The rest is already clear.

159. Since it is not only at present that the Blessed One has refrained from false speech and the other verbal transgressions, but he had done so for a long time in the past as well; and since through the spiritual might of this abstinence he has acquired various marks of a great man; and since the world with its devas speaks praise of him thus, "The ascetic Gotama refrains from false speech," Sātāgira, roaring a lion's roar with well-enunciated words, said: **He does not speak falsely**. Here, **falsely**: this is speech that deceives others, misrepresenting what has been seen and so forth.[743] He does not speak that. In the second line, the meaning can be understood either in the first way stated above, as "not one whose way of speaking is rough," or in the second way, as "not one whose way of speaking is not exhausted." In the fourth line, it is wisdom that is called *mantā*.[744] Since the Blessed One delimits his speech by means of this, he speaks only what is meaningful. Not deviating from the meaning, his speech is not idle. For the buddhas there is no meaningless speech as there is for those led on by ignorance. Therefore he says: **With reflection, he speaks what is meaningful**. The rest here is clear.

160. Having thus heard about his purity in the door of speech, now asking about his purity in the mind door, [205] Hemavata asks: **Does he have no lust for sensual pleasures?** Here, **sensual pleasures** means sensual objects.[745] In asking, "Does he have no lust for them through sensual defilement?" he inquires whether he is without covetousness. In asking, **Is his mind unsullied?**, he asks, with reference to being sullied by ill will, whether he is without ill will. In asking, **Has he overcome delusion?**, since one led astray by delusion grasps hold of a wrong view, he asks whether, by overcoming that delusion, he possesses right view. In asking, **Does he have the vision of phenomena?**, he asks about omniscience by way of the unobstructed eye of knowledge that sees into all phenomena, or by way of the five eyes in relation to their five respective objective domains.[746] For he thought: "One is not omniscient merely by purification in the three doors."

161. The Blessed One, even before he reached arahantship, had already abandoned sensual lust and ill will by the path of the non-returner; thus he did not have lust for sensual pleasures and his mind was unsullied by ill will. And by the path of stream-entry he had already abandoned the delusion concealing the truths, which is a condition for wrong view, and thus he had overcome delusion. And having awakened by himself to the truths, he obtained the aforementioned eyes and the name "Buddha" pertaining to the end of emancipation. Therefore, declaring his purity in the mind door and his omniscience, Sātāgira said: **He has no lust for sensual pleasures.**

162. Having thus heard about the Blessed One's purity in the three doors and about his omniscience, Hemavata was thrilled and elated. Through the wisdom clarified by learning that he had acquired in his past birth, he did not stumble for words, but wishing to hear about the wondrous and astounding excellent qualities of an omniscient one, he asked: "Is he endowed with clear knowledge?" Here, **Is he endowed with clear knowledge?**: By this, he asks about his excellence of vision. **Is he pure in conduct?**: By this, he asks about his excellence of behavior. **Have the influxes been destroyed by him?**: By this, he asks about the attainment of the first nibbāna element, here designated the destruction of the influxes, which is to be attained by this excellence of vision and comportment. **Is there for him no renewed existence?**: By this, he asks about his ability to attain the second nibbāna element, or about his condition after he has known supreme solace by means of reviewing knowledge.[747] [206]

163. Now the Blessed One was endowed with all kinds of clear knowledge complete in all respects: the three kinds spoken of in the Discourse on Fear and Dread and elsewhere, which begins thus: "I recollected my numerous past abodes" (MN I 22–23), and the eight kinds spoken of in the Discourse to Ambaṭṭha and elsewhere, which begins thus: "When his mind is thus concentrated . . . attained to imperturbability, he directs it to knowledge and vision" (DN I 100; see DN I 76–85). And through the abandoning of all defilements, his conduct was extremely purified; that is, he possessed the fifteen qualities constituting good conduct, which are stated succinctly in the Discourse on the Trainee thus: "Here, Mahānāma, a noble disciple is endowed with good behavior, guards the doors of the sense faculties, is moderate in eating, and devoted to wakefulness; he possesses the seven good qualities; and he gains at will, without trouble or difficulty, the four jhānas that constitute the higher mind and provide a pleasant dwelling in this very life." These are elaborated thus: "And how, Mahānāma, is a noble disciple endowed with good behavior?" and so forth (MN I 354–55). And these four influxes as well—the influx of sensual desire and so forth—together with their retinues and subtle habitual formations[748]—had all been destroyed by the Blessed One. Since the Blessed One had destroyed the influxes through this achievement of clear knowledge and conduct and thereafter saw by reviewing knowledge, "There is now no renewal of existence," Sātāgira, exhilarated by his certainty about the Blessed One's omniscience, affirming all his excellent qualities, said: **He is endowed with clear knowledge**.

163A.[749] Then, no longer doubting that the Blessed One was the Perfectly Enlightened One and the Blessed One, Hemavata stood in the sky and said, "The muni's mind is accomplished," praising the Blessed One and agreeing with Sātāgira. This is its meaning: **The muni's mind is accomplished**: accomplished,[750] indicated here by the statement "The mind of the impartial one is well disposed"; and again accomplished in bodily **action**, indicated here by the statement "He does not take what has not been given"; and in mental **action**, indicated here by the statement "He does not lust for sensual pleasures"; and in his way of speaking, as indicated here by the statement "He does not speak falsely." [207] Thus because the Buddha is accomplished in mind and endowed with the unsurpassed achievement of clear knowledge and conduct, **in accordance with the Dhamma you [Sātāgira] praise him** through these excellent qualities—in the way that begins "the mind of the impartial one is well disposed"—as **one accomplished in clear knowledge and conduct**. He shows: "You praise him through his actual nature, truthfully, accurately, not solely through mere faith."

163B. Then Sātāgira, agreeing with him, says, "The muni's mind is accomplished. . . . In accordance with the Dhamma you rejoice over him," the purport being: "So it is, dear sir, you have understood and rejoiced over him well."

164. Having spoken thus, again urging him to see the Blessed One, Sātāgira said: **The muni's mind is accomplished. . . . Come, let's go see Gotama**."

165. Then, through the power of the learning he acquired in previous births, praising the Blessed One in terms of the qualities pleasing to himself, Hemavata said to Sātāgira: **Come, let's go see Gotama . . . eating little, greedless**. This is the meaning: He has **antelope calves** because his calves are like those of an antelope. For the calves of the buddhas, like those of an antelope, are gradually rounded; they are not fleshless in front and swollen behind like the belly of a crocodile. The buddhas are **slender**, because their body and limbs are long, short, even, and rounded in the appropriate places; they are not fat like stout people. Or "slender" is said because they have cut away defilements through wisdom. They are **heroes**, because they disperse their internal and external foes. They are [described as] **eating little** because they eat one meal a day and because they limit their food, not in the sense that they eat just two or three morsels. As it is said: "But, Udāyī, I sometimes eat the full contents of my alms bowl or even more. So if my disciples honored me . . . with the thought: 'The recluse Gotama eats little and commends eating little,' then those disciples of mine who live on a cupful of food, a bilva fruit's or half a bilva fruit's quantity of food, should not honor . . . me for this quality, nor should they live in dependence on me" (MN II 7,1–9). They are **greedless** because they do not have desire and lust for food; [208] they eat food that possesses eight factors.[751] They are **munis** because they possess munihood.[752] And they are [described as] **meditating in the woods**, because of their homelessness and their minds incline to seclusion. Hence the yakkha Hemavata said: **Come, let's go see Gotama**.

166. Having spoken thus, again from his wish to hear the Dhamma in the presence of the Blessed One, he spoke this verse: "Having approached the nāga." This is its meaning: **Like a lion**: similar to a maned lion in the sense that he is hard to attack, patient, and fearless. **Wandering alone**, since he is without the craving of which it is said "a person with craving as partner" (**740**). He is also described as "wandering alone" because there is no arising of two buddhas in one world system (AN I 27,38). And the meaning here should also be understood in the way stated in relation to the Discourse on the Rhinoceros Horn. **Nāga**: He is a nāga because he does not go (*n'eva gantāraṃ*) to renewed existence, or because he does not commit crime (*āguṃ na karoti*).[753] He is also a nāga because he is powerful. **Indifferent to sensual pleasures**: indifferent because he is without desire and lust for the two kinds of sensual pleasures.[754]

Having approached . . . let's ask about release from the snare of death: Having approached such a great rishi, let's ask him about nibbāna, the ending of the round, release from the snare of death, from the round with its three planes. Or, "let's ask about release from the snare of death," about the means by which (*yena upāyena*) they are released from the snare of death, a designation for the origin of suffering. Hemavata spoke this verse addressed to Sātāgira, Sātāgira's retinue, and his own retinue.

Just then the Āsāḷha Festival had been announced in Rājagaha. While Rājagaha was everywhere adorned and decorated, as if emulating the splendor of the city of the devas, the female lay follower Kāḷī of Kuraraghara had gone up to the top of her mansion and opened the window. [209] While dispelling the summer fatigue, as she stood in the breeze refreshing herself, she heard from beginning to end the conversation of those yakkha commanders concerning the excellent qualities of the Buddha. Having heard it, thinking, "Buddhas are possessed of such diverse excellent qualities,"[755] she aroused rapture based on the Buddha. Having thereby suppressed the hindrances, while standing right there, she became established in the fruit of stream-entry. Hence the Blessed One appointed her to the position of a foremost disciple thus: "This is the foremost, bhikkhus, of my female lay followers who gain confidence by hearing from another, namely, the female lay follower Kāḷī of Kuraraghara" (AN I 26,27).

167. The two yakkha commanders with their retinue of a thousand yakkhas reached Isipatana in the middle watch of the night. They approached the Blessed One, who was still sitting in the same position in which he had been sitting when he set in motion the wheel of the Dhamma. Having paid homage to him, they extolled the Blessed One and requested permission with this verse: **Let us ask Gotama, the expounder, the instructor**. This is its meaning: He is *the expounder* through a talk delineating the truths in the way that begins "This, bhikkhus, is the noble truth of suffering," [which applies to] the phenomena of the three planes except for craving.[756] He is *the instructor* because he instructs in the knowledge of the task to be done and in the knowledge that the task has been done regarding these four truths, which begin thus: "That noble truth of suffering, bhikkhus, should be fully understood."[757] Or else he is *the expounder* because he explains things using expressions that correspond to the way they should be expressed; *the instructor* because he instructs in those same things in ways appropriate for beings. Or he is *the expounder* of a teaching for those who understand quickly and for those who understand through elaboration; *the instructor* for those who are to be guided through a course of practice.[758] Or he is *the expounder* through a concise teaching, *the instructor* through an analysis using words that bring out different aspects. Or he is *the expounder* through a talk on the specific characteristics of the aids to enlightenment, *the instruc-*

tor by introducing them into the minds of beings. [210] Or he is *the expounder* because he discusses the truths concisely by means of the three turnings,[759] *an instructor* [by explaining them] in detail—an instructor because he set in motion the wheel of Dhamma in detail in the way stated in the Paṭisambhidāmagga thus: "The faith faculty is a *dhamma*, he set that *dhamma* in motion, thus the wheel of the Dhamma," and so forth (Paṭis II 160,16).

One gone beyond all phenomena: He has "gone beyond" all phenomena of the four planes in six ways: by direct knowledge, by full understanding, by abandoning, by development, by realization, and by attainment. Thus, since the Blessed One has gone by directly knowing all phenomena, he has gone beyond by direct knowledge. Since he has gone by fully understanding the five aggregates subject to clinging, he has gone beyond by full understanding. Since he has gone by abandoning all defilements, he has gone beyond by abandoning. Since he has gone by developing the four paths, he has gone beyond by development. Since he has gone by realizing cessation,[760] he has gone beyond by realization. Since he has gone by attaining the meditative attainments,[761] he has gone beyond by attainment. Thus he has gone beyond all phenomena.

The Buddha who has overcome enmity and peril: He is "the Buddha" because he has awakened (*paṭibuddhattā*) from the sleep of unknowing; or "Buddha" should be understood in the entire way explained in the commentary on the refuges (Pj I 13–22). He has *overcome enmity and peril* because he has overcome the five kinds of enmity and peril.[762] While extolling the Blessed One in such a way, with the words "Let us ask Gotama," they request permission.

168. Among those yakkhas, Hemavata was foremost in splendor and wisdom, so he spoke the verse **In what has the world arisen** (*kismiṃ loko samuppanno*)**?**, asking about the subject he intended to ask about. In the first line, **In what** (*kismiṃ*) is a locative in the sense of an absolute construction.[763] The purport is: "When what has arisen, has the world arisen?" He asks with reference to the world of beings and the world of conditioned things.[764] **In what does it form intimacy?**: "In regard to what does it form intimacy through craving and views, [which take things] as 'I' or 'mine'?"; [here *kismiṃ* is] a locative in the sense of location. **Having clung to what is the world** (*kissa loko upādāya*): [*kissa*] is a genitive in the sense of an accusative. This is the purport here: "In dependence on what is it reckoned as 'the world'?"[765] **Afflicted in regard to what?**: *Kismiṃ* is a locative in the sense of an absolute construction and in the sense of a cause. [211] This is the purport here: "When what exists, through what cause, is the world *afflicted*, oppressed, burdened?"[766]

169. Now it is when the six internal and external sense bases have arisen that the world of beings has arisen, and the world of conditioned things by way of wealth, grain, and so forth.[767] And here the world of beings forms the twofold intimacy in those same six internal and external sense bases; for when grasping anything as "I" and "mine," it grasps the eye base or one of the others. As it is said: "If one were to say, 'The eye is self,' that would not be tenable" (MN III 282,14), and so forth. And it is in dependence on these same six sense bases that the twofold world [of beings and conditioned things] is reckoned [as "the world"]. And it is when those same six sense bases exist that the world of beings is afflicted by the manifestation of suffering. As it is said: "When, bhikkhus, there are hands, there is taking up and putting down. When there are feet, there is going forward and returning. When there are joints, there is bending and stretching of the limbs. When there is the belly, there is hunger and thirst. So too, when there is the eye, in dependence on eye-contact, pleasure and pain arise within" (SN IV 171,18 foll.). Similarly, the world of conditioned things is afflicted when impinged upon in these sense bases functioning as receptacles. As it is said, "[Form] impinges on the eye, which is invisible and subject to impingement" (Dhs 170, §597), and "The eye, bhikkhus, is impinged upon by agreeable and disagreeable forms" (see SN IV 175,6). Similarly, the twofold world is afflicted by those same sense bases functioning as causes. As it is said, "The eye is afflicted by agreeable and disagreeable forms" (SN IV 175,6), and "The eye, bhikkhus, is ablaze, forms are ablaze. Ablaze with what? With the fire of lust" (SN IV 20,3; Vin I 34,21). Therefore, answering the question by way of the six internal and external sense bases, the Blessed One said: **In six the world has arisen.**[768]

170. The yakkha on his own had posed the question by way of the round, and the Blessed One answered concisely by way of the twelve sense bases. [212] The yakkha, however, did not clearly grasp the point, and so, wishing to understand the subject and its antidote, he asked concisely about the round and the ending of the round, saying: **What is that clinging**: here, *clinging* has the sense of that which can be clung to (*upādātabbaṭṭhena upādānaṃ*); this is a designation for the truth of suffering.[769] **In which the world is afflicted?**: "When the Blessed One said, 'The world is afflicted in regard to six,' indicating that it is in the six [objects of] clinging that the world is afflicted, *what* is that clinging?" Thus with a half-verse he explicitly asks about the truth of suffering, but the truth of the origin is included as its cause.

When asked about the outlet (*niyyānaṃ*): With this half-verse he asks about the truth of the path; for it is by the truth of the path that a noble disciple fully understands the truth of suffering, abandons its origin, realizes its cessation, and develops the path, and thereby goes out (*niyyāti*) from the world; therefore it is called the outlet. **How is one released from suffering?**: "By what means does one attain release from the suffering of the round, which is spoken of as 'clinging'?" Thus here he explicitly asks about the truth of the path, but the truth of cessation is included as its objective domain.

171. Thus, when the yakkha asked him questions by way of the four truths, having showed these truths both explicitly and implicitly,[770] the Blessed One, answering in the same way, said: **Five strands of sensual pleasure**. Here, by mentioning their objective range, namely, the "five strands of sensual pleasure," the five internal bases that take these as their objective range are included (namely, the eye and so forth). **With mind as sixth**: with mind as the sixth of them. Here, by mentioning the mind base, which is the sixth among the internal bases, the base of mental phenomena, its objective domain, is included. Thus, in answering this question, "What is that clinging?" the Buddha again shows the truth of suffering just by way of the twelve sense bases.[771]

Or else he shows the truth of suffering by way of the twelve sense bases in this way too: by mentioning "mind," the seven consciousness elements are included,[772] and thus by including the first five consciousness elements, their material bases (*vatthūni*), namely, the five sense bases (*āyatanāni*) beginning with the eye are included; and by including the mind element and mind-consciousness element, the mental phenomena base—which can be distinguished into material basis and objective range—is included.[773] But one section of the mind base and mental phenomena base—that which is world-transcending—[213] is not included here, because the description is given with reference to the phrase "in which the world is afflicted."[774]

Having expunged desire for these: The meaning is this: "Here, one delineates those sense bases in various ways—in terms of the aggregates, elements, and name-and-form—and then one ascribes the three characteristics to them and contemplates them with insight. When insight culminates in the path of arahantship, one has completely **expunged**, removed, dissipated, **desire**, namely, craving, **for these**, for the truth of suffering divided into the twelve sense bases."

One is thereby released from suffering: "By this means one is released from the suffering of the round." In this way, he has answered the question posed by this half-verse (**170**cd), "When asked about the outlet, tell: how is one released from suffering?" and he has shown the truth of the path. But the truths of the origin and cessation should be understood to have been already shown, because they are included here in the way stated earlier. Or else, by the first half-verse (**171**ab), the truth of suffering is shown; by *desire*, the truth of the origin is shown; by *having expunged* (*virājetvā*), the truth of cessation is shown through dispassion (*virāgena*)—or the truth of the path is shown on the basis of the statement "through dispassion one is liberated." **Thereby**: by indication of the method,[775] the truth of the path is shown; or, on the basis of the expression "the cessation of suffering," the phrase "one is released from suffering" shows the truth of cessation through release from suffering. In this way, it should be understood, the four truths have been shown here.

172. Having thus shown the outlet through its characteristic in a verse containing the four truths, he says, **This outlet from the world**, concluding with a verbal expression that states it again in its own right. Here, **this** is a reference to what was previously said; **from the world**, from the world with its three realms, **[has been expounded to you] just as it is**: without distortion. **This is what I declare to you**: The purport is: "If you were to ask me a thousand times, this—and nothing else—is what I would declare to you. Why? Because **one is thereby released from suffering**, not otherwise."

Or alternatively: "Even if you had gone out through this outlet one, two, or three times, I would still declare this to you." The meaning is: "I would declare this same thing to you for the sake of achieving a higher distinction."[776] Why? "Because **one is thereby released from suffering** without residue or remainder." He thereby concludes the teaching with its culmination in arahantship. At the conclusion of the teaching the two yakkha commanders together with the thousand yakkhas were established in the fruit of stream-entry.

173. Although Hemavata was one who naturally revered the Dhamma, now that he had been established on the stage of the noble ones [214] he was even more eager to hear a variegated and inspired teaching. Thus he spoke the verse "Who here crosses the flood?" asking about the stages of the trainee and the one beyond training (that is, the arahant). Here, with the line **Who here crosses the flood?**—who crosses the fourfold flood—he asks about the stage of the trainee without distinctions.[777] The word **sea** describes a body of water that is not merely wide and not merely deep but both wide and even deeper; the vast flood of saṃsāra is similar, for this is wide because it has no boundaries on any side and deep because it provides no foothold below or support from above. Therefore, by asking, **Who here crosses the sea?** and **Who does not sink in the deep** sea, **which is without foothold, without support?** he asks about the stage of one beyond training.

174. The bhikkhu **always accomplished in good behavior** is one who does not commit a transgression even at the cost of life. He is **endowed with wisdom**, with mundane and world-transcending wisdom; **well concentrated**, through access and absorption concentration and through the postures and lower paths and fruits;[778] **inwardly reflective** in regard to [the five aggregates] pertaining to himself, because of ascribing the three characters to them and practicing insight on them; and **mindful**, being heedful in the sense of constancy in practice. Since it is by the fourth path that one completely **crosses the flood so hard to cross**, the Blessed One, explaining the stage of the trainee, speaks this verse containing the three trainings: "One always accomplished in good behavior." For here, by achievement in good behavior *the training in the higher good behavior* is shown; by mindfulness and concentration, *the training in the higher mind*; and by inward reflection and wisdom, *the training in the higher wisdom*. Thus the three trainings are shown along with their aids and benefits. For mundane wisdom and mindfulness are the aids to the trainings, and the fruits of the ascetic life are their benefits.

175. Having shown the stage of the trainee by the first verse, he speaks the second verse, showing the stage of the one beyond training. This is its meaning: **One who has abstained from sensual perception**: entirely abstained (*virato*) from any sensual perception whatever by means of the eradication-abstinence associated with the fourth path.[779] There is also the reading "dispassionate" (*viratto*). In that case "sensual perception" (*kāmasaññāya*) is the locative case.[780] But in the Book with Verses, there is also the reading "in regard to sensual perceptions."[781]

Because he has passed beyond the ten fetters by means of the four paths, he is one **who has overcome all fetters**, or he "has overcome all fetters" because he has overcome all the higher fetters just by the fourth path.[782] [215] Because he has utterly destroyed delight, a designation for the craving that seeks delight here and there, and also destroyed the three kinds of existence, he is one **who has utterly destroyed delight and existence**.[783] **He**—such a bhikkhu whose influxes have been destroyed—**does not sink in the deep**, in the vast sea of saṃsāra. With the utter destruction of delight, by reaching the supreme solace, he attains the high ground of the nibbāna element with residue, and by the utter destruction of existence, the high ground of the nibbāna element without residue.[784]

176. Then, having looked over his friend and the assembly of yakkhas, filled with rapture and joy, Hemavata extolled the

Blessed One with the verses that begin "Behold him of deep wisdom." Together with his friend and the entire assembly, he paid homage to the Blessed One, circumambulated him, and returned to his own dwelling place.

This is the commentary on the meaning of those verses.[785] **Of deep wisdom**: one who possesses deep wisdom. "Deep wisdom" should be understood in the way explained in the Paṭisambhidā; for there it is said, "*Deep wisdom*: knowledge that occurs about the deep aggregates," and so forth (Paṭis II 192–93). **The one who sees the subtle meaning**: one who sees the meaning of the questions prepared by astute and learned khattiyas and so forth. Or he is "one who sees the subtle meaning" because he sees the subtle causes of the meanings (effects), causes that are hard for others to penetrate. **Owning nothing**: because of the absence of any "something" such as lust and so forth.[786] **Unattached to sensual pleasures and existence**: because he is unattached to the two kinds of sensual pleasures and the three kinds of existence.[787] **Everywhere released**: through the absence of the bondage of desire and lust for any objects classified into the aggregates and so forth. **Treading the divine path**: treading by attaining the divine path consisting in the eight meditative attainments. Although on that occasion the Blessed One was not treading the divine path, this is said with reference to his previous treading of it, because he had the ability to tread it or because he had achieved mastery over it. Or alternatively, this is said because of treading in the peaceful dwellings,[788] which are the path of the arahants, the devas by purification.[789] **The great rishi**: because of seeking great qualities.[790]

177. In the second verse the praise is expressed in another way. Again, he describes him by mentioning the one who sees the subtle meaning.[791] Or else the meaning is "one who shows subtle meanings."[792] [216] He is **the giver of wisdom** because he explains the practice that leads to the acquisition of wisdom. **Unattached to the lair of sensual pleasures**: unattached to the lair (*ālayo*), which is twofold, by way of craving and views in regard to sensual pleasures. **All-knowing**: one who knows all phenomena; what is meant is "omniscient." **Very wise**: one possessing intelligence, which is a designation for the supreme wisdom that serves as the path to that omniscient state. **The noble path**: the eightfold path or the attainment of fruition. **Treading**: being immersed in it by means of wisdom. This is said because, having known the characteristic of the path, he enters upon it by teaching it; or because he attains the attainment of fruition moment after moment. He has tread it in the past, or at present he has the ability to tread it, which consists in the development of the fourfold path.

178. Today indeed we have had a good sight: "Today it has been well seen *by us*, or today it has been a good sight *for us*." The meaning is the act of seeing. **A good morning, a good arising**: "Today has dawned well for us, or it was a beautiful dawn, and today we have had a good arising, a rising up from sleep in the morning."[793] For what reason? **Since we have seen the Enlightened One**. He conveys his joy based on his excellent fortune in seeing the Buddha.

179. Possessing psychic potency: possessing psychic potency produced by the ripening of kamma. **And fame**: possessing the foremost gain and the foremost retinue. **Go to you for refuge**: Although they had already gone for refuge by means of the path, they nevertheless break out in speech in order to convey their stature as stream-enterers and to express their confidence.

180. From village to village: from celestial village to celestial village; **from mountain to mountain**: from celestial mountain to celestial mountain. **We will wander . . . paying homage to the Enlightened One and to the excellence of the Dhamma**: "We will wander paying homage, with the voice of Dhamma extolling over and over the excellence of the Buddha's enlightenment and the excellent nature of the Dhamma thus: 'The Blessed One is indeed perfectly enlightened; the Dhamma is indeed well expounded by the Blessed One,' and so forth, and also extolling the good practice of the Sangha thus: 'The Blessed One's community of disciples is indeed practicing well.'" The rest is clear. [217]

10 Āḷavaka
(*Āḷavaka Sutta*)

What is the origin?[794] Its origin will become clear through a commentary on the meaning. In the commentary on the meaning, the meaning of the phrase **Thus have I heard. On one occasion the Blessed One . . .** has already been explained. **Was dwelling at Āḷavī, in the abode of the yakkha Āḷavaka**: Here, what is Āḷavī and why was the Blessed One dwelling at the abode of that yakkha? As to this, it is said: That country and city are called Āḷavī; either might be referred to here, for it is said that he was dwelling in Āḷavī near the city of Āḷavī. That abode was not far from the city, about a gāvuta away. It is also said that he dwelled in Āḷavī while dwelling in the country of Āḷavī, for this abode was in the country of Āḷavī.

Every seventh day the king of Āḷavī would leave off the enjoyment of his various dancers, and for the purpose of expelling bandits, repelling hostile kings, and getting exercise, he would go on a deer hunt. One day he made a pact with his troops: "The one on whose side a deer flees is responsible for it." A deer then fled on his own side. The fleet-footed king took a bow and pursued the deer on foot for three yojanas. Now *eṇimiga*[795] are fast for only three yojanas, so when the deer grew fatigued, it entered the water, and as it stood there the king shot it and split it in two. Though he had no need for the meat, in order to avoid the criticism that he was unable to catch the deer, he took it on a pole and set out to return. Not far from the city he saw a large banyan tree with dense foliage, which he approached in order to dispel his fatigue.

Now the yakkha Āḷavaka had obtained a boon from the great king[796] near that banyan tree and at noon he dwelled there eating the living beings that entered the area covered by the tree's shade. [218] When the yakkha saw the king, he approached to eat him. But the king made a pact with him: "Release me, and every day I'll send you a human being and a ceremonial dish of food."[797] The yakkha answered: "When you are heedlessly indulging in your royal enjoyment, you will forget. But I'm not allowed to eat anyone who has not entered my abode or who has not given consent. So if I were to release you, how would I live?"[798] Thus he did not release the king. The king promised: "On the day I do not send you anything, you can take me and eat me." In this way he was set free and headed back toward the city.

Meanwhile, the troops had set up camp along the road. When they saw the king, they went forth to meet him, took his things, and said to him: "Great king, why did you exhaust yourself merely to avoid losing face?" The king did not report the news to them but went back to the city. After his breakfast, he called for the city magistrate and informed him of the matter. The magistrate asked: "Did you limit the time, lord?" – "I didn't." – "You made a mistake, lord, for with evil spirits, it's possible to limit the time. If there is no time limit, the country will face a calamity. But let it be, lord. Even though you did so, be at ease and enjoy the bliss of rulership. I'll take care of the matter."

The magistrate got up early, went to the prison, and said to those due to be executed: "Whoever wants to live must leave." He led the one who emerged first to his home, had him bathed and fed, and then sent him off with the instruction: "Take this dish of food as an offering to the yakkha." As soon as the man entered the area near the foot of the tree, the yakkha ate him as if he were a radish.[799] [219] It is said that on account of the yakkha's spiritual might, the entire body of a human being from the head-hairs down becomes like a lump of butter.

When the men who had brought him to deliver the yakkha's meal saw this, they were terrified and reported the matter to their friends. From then on people refrained from committing crimes, aware that when the king arrests criminals, he gives them to the yakkha. Shortly thereafter, because no new criminals appeared and the old ones were gone, the prisons were empty.

The magistrate reported this to the king. The king then had his own wealth cast along the avenues, thinking: "Perhaps someone may take this out of greed." But no one would even touch it with their foot. Since he did not obtain any criminals, he informed his ministers. The ministers said: "Let's send one old person from each family in turn. An old person is already close to death." But the king prohibited them, saying: "The people will resent us, thinking: 'He sent our father, our grandfather.' Don't set your mind on this."

"In that case, lord, let's send an infant. For they don't feel affection for such a child as they do for their mother or father." The king consented, and they did so. The mothers in the city took their children and fled; pregnant women also fled. They brought their children to other countries and nurtured them there.

In this way, twelve years passed. Then one day, though the men searched the entire city, they could not find even a single child. They informed the king: "Lord, there is no child in the city except your son, the Āḷavaka prince, in the palace." The king said: "As my son is dear to me, so it is for all the world. But there is no one dearer than oneself. Go, give him too, but protect my life." At the time the prince's mother had finished having her son bathed and dressed. She prepared a soft pillow and put the boy to sleep on her lap. The king's men went there on the king's command, and while the nurse was chatting with the 16,000 consorts, they took the boy and left, saying: "Tomorrow he will be the yakkha's meal."

That day, just before dawn, the Blessed One rose [220] and entered the meditative attainment of great compassion in the great Fragrant Cottage in the great monastery in Jeta's Grove. He again surveyed the world with the buddha eye and saw that the prince of Āḷavī had the supporting condition for attaining the fruit of a non-returner; the yakkha the supporting condition for stream-entry; and 84,000 living beings the supporting condition for obtaining the Dhamma eye at the conclusion of the teaching. When it became light, the Blessed One did his forenoon activities, and with the afternoon activities still unfinished—just as the sun set that day, on the uposatha of the dark fortnight—he took his bowl and robe and alone, without a companion, walked along the footpath thirty yojanas from

Sāvatthī. He then entered the abode of that yakkha. Hence it is said: **in the abode of the yakkha Āḷavaka.**[800]

But did the Blessed One dwell at the foot of the banyan tree where Āḷavaka's abode was located or in the abode itself? It is said: "In the abode itself." For just as yakkhas perceive their own abode, so too do the buddhas. Having gone there, he stood at the entrance to the abode.

At the time, Āḷavaka had gone to the Himalayas to attend a gathering of yakkhas. Āḷavaka's door-keeper, named Gadrabha, approached the Blessed One, paid homage to him, and asked: "Bhante, has the Blessed One come at an improper time?"

"Yes, Gadrabha, I have come. If it would not be burdensome for you, I would spend one night at Āḷavaka's abode."

"It will not be burdensome for me, Bhante. But that yakkha is rough and harsh. He does not even pay homage to his mother and father. Do not think about staying here."

"I know his rough character, Gadrabha, but that won't be an obstacle for me. If it would not be burdensome for you, [221] I would spend one night here."

A second time the yakkha Gadrabha said to the Blessed One: "Bhante, Āḷavaka is like a hot frying pan. He does not have regard for his mother and father, for ascetics and brahmins, or for the Dhamma. When others come here, he drives them insane or splits their heart or grabs them by the feet and hurls them across the ocean or across the world sphere."

A second time the Blessed One said: "I know, Gadrabha, but if it would not be burdensome for you, I would spend one night here."

"It will not be burdensome for me, Bhante. But if I allow you without informing him, that yakkha may take my life. Let me inform him, Bhante."

"Inform him as you please, Gadrabha."

"In that case, Bhante, find out for yourself."

Gadrabha then paid homage to the Blessed One and left for the Himalayas. The door to the abode opened for the Blessed One. The Blessed One entered and sat down on the couch of celestial gems where Āḷavaka sat on auspicious days enjoying his splendor. The Blessed One then released a golden light. The yakkha's women, having seen it, drew near, paid homage to the Blessed One, and sat surrounding him. The Blessed One gave them a miscellaneous Dhamma talk: "In the past you gave alms, undertook precepts, and made offerings, and thus you have achieved this fortune. Now you should do the same. Do not be overcome by envy or miserliness toward one another." Having heard the Blessed One's sweet voice, they applauded him a thousand times and continued to sit there surrounding him.

Meanwhile Gadrabha had gone to the Himalayas and informed Āḷavaka: "You should know, dear sir, that the Blessed One is sitting in your mansion." He gave a signal to Gadrabha: "Be quiet! I will go and do whatever is necessary." It is said that his masculine pride caused him to feel ashamed and he therefore checked Gadrabha, telling him: "Don't let anyone in the assembly hear this."

Just then Sātāgira and Hemavata together with their retinues were traveling in the sky on different vehicles, thinking to pay homage to the Blessed One in Jeta's Grove and then go to the gathering of the yakkhas. The route for yakkhas is not everywhere in the sky [222] but only along certain defined tracks that avoid their palaces situated in the sky. But Āḷavaka's palace was situated on the ground, well guarded, surrounded by ramparts, with a well constructed door, watchtower, and gate, and covered above by a bronze net, similar to a casket, and it was three yojanas in height; above it there was a path. Having come to that region, they (Sātāgira and Hemavata) were unable to go further, for even up to the peak of existence no one can travel above an area where a buddha is sitting. Wondering, "What is the reason for this?" they saw the Blessed One. Having descended from the sky as if they were clods of earth, they paid homage to the Blessed One, listened to the Dhamma, circumambulated him, and told him: "We are going to a gathering of yakkhas, Blessed One." Then, praising the Three Jewels, they left for the gathering.

When Āḷavaka saw them, he stepped back and offered them seats. They informed Āḷavaka: "How fortunate you are, Āḷavaka, that the Blessed One is dwelling in your abode. Go, friend, and attend upon the Blessed One." Thus the Blessed One was dwelling in the abode itself, not at the foot of the banyan tree where Āḷavaka's abode was located. Hence it is said: "On one occasion the Blessed One was dwelling at Āḷavī, in the abode of the yakkha Āḷavaka."

Then the yakkha Āḷavaka approached the Blessed One

and said to him: "Get out, ascetic!": But why did he say this? Because he wished to scold him. Here, the connection should be understood from the beginning as follows: Just as a talk on faith is wrongly addressed to one without faith, and a talk on good behavior is wrongly addressed to one of bad behavior, so when Āḷavaka heard praise of the Blessed One from those yakkhas, his heart sputtered with anger just like salt and sugar thrown into a fire. He said: "Who is that Blessed One that he should enter my abode?" They replied: "Don't you know, friend, the Blessed One, our teacher, who, while dwelling in the Tusita heaven, made the five great investigations?" Then they told him everything, up to the setting in motion of the wheel of the Dhamma. They spoke about the thirty-two auspicious signs that occurred at his conception and so forth, and reproached him: [223] "Didn't you see these wonders, friend?" Though he had seen them, because of his anger he said: "I did not see them."

"Friend Āḷavaka, whether or not you have seen them, what good would it do you? What will you do to our teacher, for compared to him you are like a newborn calf in the presence of a great bull with trembling hump;[801] like a baby elephant in the presence of an immense elephant in rut; like an old jackal in the presence of a lion whose shoulders are graced by a resplendent flowing mane; like a fledgling crow with broken wings in the presence of a royal supaṇṇa bird with a body 150 yojanas in girth. Go, do whatever should be done!"

When this was said, Āḷavaka became furious. He got up, stood with his left foot on the Red Arsenic Terrace, and saying, "See now who is mightier, your teacher or I," with his right foot he stepped on the peak of Mount Kelāsa, sixty yojanas long. It gave off sparks, like a hot lump of iron struck by an iron hammer. Standing there, he proclaimed: "I am Āḷavaka!" and the sound spread through all of Jambudīpa.

There are four sounds, it is said, that are heard all over Jambudīpa: (1) that made by Puṇṇaka, commander of the yakkhas, when he beat Dhanañjaya, the Koravya king, at dice, clapped his hands, and proclaimed: "I've won" (Ja VI 282,11–14); (2) that made at the time the teaching of the Blessed One Kassapa was declining, when Sakka, ruler of the devas, turned the young deva Vissakamma into a dog and had him proclaim: "I will devour the evil bhikkhus, and the evil bhikkhunīs, male lay followers, and female lay followers, and all who teach non-Dhamma" (untraced); (3) that made by the Great Man, as told in the Kusa Jātaka, when the city was besieged by seven kings on account of Pabhāvatī, and he put Pabhāvatī on the back of an elephant together with himself, left the city, and proclaimed: "I am Sīhassara, the great king of the Kusas" (see Ja V 310,7); and that made by Āḷavaka when he stood on top of Mount Kelāsa, for then it seemed as if he had made that proclamation at each door throughout Jambudīpa. [224] The Himalayas shook over an area 3,000 yojanas wide through the yakkha's spiritual might.

He created *a whirlwind*, thinking: "With this, I'll drive the ascetic away." The eastern winds and other winds rose up and split mountain peaks measuring a half-yojana, a full yojana, two yojanas, and three yojanas; they uprooted the woods, shrubs, and trees, and so forth, and as they left the city of Āḷavaka, they pulverized the old elephant stalls and whirled the roof tiles in the sky. The Blessed One resolved: "Let no one be injured." When the winds reached the Buddha, they could not even stir the hem of his robe.

Then Āḷavaka created *a downpour of rain*, thinking: "I'll inundate the ascetic with water and kill him." Through his spiritual power rain clouds a hundred and a thousand layers thick rose up and poured down rain. Under the impact of the rainfall the earth was cracked. A great rain cloud came and hovered above the woods and trees, but it could not even wet the Buddha's robe to the extent of a dew drop.

Āḷavaka then aroused *a storm of stones*. Giant mountain peaks, smoking and blazing, came through the sky, but when they reached the Buddha they turned into celestial wreaths. He then aroused *a storm of blows*. Single-edge swords, double-edge swords, knives, spears, arrows, and other weapons, smoking and blazing, came through the sky, but when they reached the Buddha they became celestial flowers. He then aroused *a storm of coals*. Coals the color of the kiṃsuka flower[802] came through the sky, but they turned into celestial flowers strewn at the Buddha's feet. He then aroused *a storm of ashes*. Burning hot ashes came through the sky, but they turned into sandalwood powder that fell at the Buddha's feet. He then aroused *a sandstorm*. Extremely fine sand, smoking and blazing, came through the sky, but the sand grains turned into celestial flowers and fell at the Buddha's feet. He then aroused *a mud storm*. The mud, smoking and blazing, came through the sky, turned into celestial incense, and fell at the Buddha's feet. He then aroused *darkness*, thinking: "I'll frighten the ascetic and drive him away." It was similar to darkness possessing four factors, but when it reached the Buddha the darkness vanished as if dispelled by the light of the sun.

In this way, unable to drive the Blessed One away even with nine kinds of storms [225]—of wind, rain, stones, blows, coals, ashes, sand, mud, and darkness—the yakkha himself approached the Blessed One along with a four-factored army, mixed with various groups of fierce spirits of numerous forms, with their hands [raised as if] to give blows. These groups of fierce spirits made many intimidating gestures and seemed to be coming above the Blessed One, shouting: "Grab him! Kill him!" But like flies on a purified copper ball, they could not get a hold on the Blessed One.

Though such was the case, unlike Māra, who retreated when he came to the site of enlightenment, they did not retreat but created mayhem through half the night. Since he could not cause the Blessed One to stir even with a display of many frightening sights[803] for half the night, Āḷavaka thought: "Let me release my invincible cloth weapon."

It is said that there are four supreme weapons in the world: Sakka's thunderbolt weapon, Vessavaṇa's club weapon, Yama's eye weapon, and Āḷavaka's cloth weapon. If Sakka is angry and strikes his thunderbolt weapon on the top of Mount Sineru, it would split an area over 168,000 yojanas and go up from below. When Vessavaṇa, while still a worldling, discharged his club, it would strike many thousands of yakkhas on the head and again return to him within arm's reach. When Yama is angry, he merely casts a glance with his eye weapon and many thousands of kumbhaṇḍas perish, quivering like sesame seeds on a hot pan.[804] And when Āḷavaka is angry, if he releases his cloth weapon in the sky, it may not rain for twelve years; if he releases it on the ground, all the trees, grass, and other kinds of vegetation dry up and may not grow again for twelve years; if he releases it in the ocean, all the water would dry up like a drop on a hot pan; if he releases it on a mountain, even one like Sineru, the mountain would scatter in pieces.

He thus opened his upper garment[805] and grabbed hold of his mighty cloth weapon. [226] The deities from ten thousand world systems for the most part hurriedly assembled, thinking: "Today the Blessed One will tame Āḷavaka. We will hear the Dhamma there." Wishing to see a fight, the deities assembled, and thus the whole sky was filled with deities. Having walked around higher and higher near the Blessed One, Āḷavaka released his cloth weapon. Making a frightful sound in the sky like a thunderbolt, it smoked and blazed, but in order to crush the yakkha's conceit, when it reached the Blessed One, it turned into a foot-wiping cloth and fell at his feet. Seeing this, Āḷavaka was like a bull whose horns have been cut off, like a serpent whose fangs have been removed. Disgraced and humbled, with his banner of conceit dropped, he reflected: "Even my cloth weapon did not vanquish the ascetic. What is the reason?" [Then he understood:] "The reason is that the ascetic dwells in loving-kindness. Come, let me make him angry and deprive him of his loving-kindness!" It is in this context that it was said: "Then the yakkha Āḷavaka approached the Blessed One . . . and said: 'Get out, ascetic.'" The purport here is this: "Why, without my permission, have you entered my abode and sit in the midst of my harem like the lord of the manor? Isn't it unsuitable for an ascetic to be making use of things that have not been given to him and to be associating with women? Therefore, if you are firm in the duty of an ascetic, get out, ascetic!" But some say he said this after having spoken these and other harsh words.

Then the Blessed One reflected: "It is not possible to train a stubborn person by means of stubbornness. If one breaks bile over a fierce dog's nose, it becomes even more ferocious; similarly, if one remains stubborn, the other will become even more stubborn. But it is possible for one who is gentle to train him." Knowing this, he complied with Āḷavaka's order. Speaking pleasantly, he said, "All right, friend," [227] and went out. Hence it is said: **"All right, friend," the Blessed One said, and he went out.**

Then Āḷavaka's mind softened and he thought: "Indeed, this ascetic is compliant. With just a single order he went out.

I engaged the ascetic in a fight for the whole night yet without a reason I easily make him go out." He again reflected: "Even now I do not know whether he went out because he is compliant or from anger. Let me test him!" He then said: **Come in, ascetic**. Now that Āḷavaka's mind had softened, in order to reinforce the impression that he is compliant, again speaking pleasantly, **the Blessed One said, "All right, friend," and he went in**. Testing his compliancy again and again, **a second time . . . a third time** Āḷavaka said, "Get out, come in," and the Blessed One did so.

If he had not done so, the yakkha's mind, stubborn by nature, would have become even more stubborn, and then he would not have been a fit receptacle for a talk on the Dhamma. Therefore, just as a mother pacifies her weeping son by giving him whatever he wants or by doing whatever he wants, so, to pacify the yakkha, who was "weeping" with defilements, the Blessed One complied with whatever the yakkha said. And just as, when a child will not drink from her breast, a wet nurse will get the child to drink by giving him something or coaxing him, so, to get the yakkha to drink the milk of the world-transcending Dhamma, the Blessed One "coaxed" him by complying with whatever the yakkha wanted. And as a man who wishes to fill a gourd with the four sweets first cleans out its insides, so, wishing to fill the yakkha's mind with the world-transcending four sweets, the Blessed One went out and came in up to the third time in order to clean out the stain of anger within him.

Then Āḷavaka thought: "This ascetic is compliant. When I say, 'Get out!' he goes out, and when I say, 'Come in!' he comes in. Let me exhaust this ascetic by doing so all night long, and then I will grab him by the feet and hurl him across the Ganges." Having given rise to this evil thought, he said for a fourth time: "Get out, ascetic!" Having known his intention, the Blessed One said: **I won't go out**. He also knew: "When I say this, seeking something further to do, he will think he should ask a question, and that will be my chance to give a talk on the Dhamma." [228] And so he said: "I won't go out." The meaning should be regarded in this way: "Since you think thus, I will not go out, friend. Do whatever you want."

Now in the past, when ascetics or wanderers with psychic powers were traveling through the sky, they would come to

Āḷavaka's palace, wondering: "Is this a golden palace, or one made of silver and jewels? Come, let's see it." When they arrived, Āḷavaka would ask them a question, and if they were unable to answer it, he would harass them by driving them insane and in other ways. How? Spirits drive someone insane in two ways: by displaying a frightening form or by crushing the heart base. But Āḷavaka knew that those with psychic powers are not terrified by a frightening form, and so, by means of his own psychic power, he would create a subtle body, enter into them, and crush their heart base. Then their mind would not remain stable, and because of its instability they would become deranged and go insane. When he had driven them insane, he would also split their breast, grab them by the feet, and hurl them across the Ganges, saying: "Those of this sort must never again come to my abode." Therefore, having remembered those questions, Āḷavaka considered: "Let me now harass this ascetic in such a way." He then said, **I'll ask you a question, ascetic**, and so forth.

But where did he get those questions? His mother and father, it is said, while attending on the Blessed One Kassapa, learned eight questions together with their answers. They taught them to Āḷavaka in his youth, but with the passage of time he forgot the answers. Then, thinking, "Let me not lose the questions too," he had them inscribed on a sheet of gold with vermilion and deposited them in his palace. Thus these were buddha-questions that are the domain only of the buddhas.[806]

Now in the case of the buddhas it is not possible for anyone to create an obstruction to gifts relinquished to them, or an obstruction to their life, or an impediment to their omniscient knowledge and fathom-wide aura.[807] Therefore, when he heard that boast of Āḷavaka, showing that the spiritual power of a buddha is not shared in common by anyone in the world, the Blessed One said: [229] **I do not see anyone in this world, friend, with its devas**.

A brief account has already been given by showing the mere meaning of these terms in the way that begins thus: "by the phrase *with its devas*, inclusion is made of the devas of the [lower] five desire-sphere planes" (see pp. 519–20), but a detailed orderly account construing the sequence of terms has not yet been offered. That is stated as follows: By mentioning

with its devas, delimiting those who are superior, all devas are included. But in the multitude of devas that had assembled there, some wondered: "Māra is mighty, the lord of the six desire spheres, who exercises mastery, a contrarian,[808] an enemy of the Dhamma, cruel in his deeds. Can't he drive the Buddha insane?" In order to dispel their uncertainty he said: **with Māra**. Then some thought: "Brahmā is mighty. With a single finger, he creates light in a thousand world spheres; with two fingers . . . with ten fingers in ten thousand world spheres, and he experiences the unsurpassed bliss of the jhāna attainments. Can't he do so?" In order to dispel their uncertainty he said: **with Brahmā**. Then others thought: "There are many ascetics and brahmins opposed to the Teaching, antagonistic toward it, who possess the power of sacred hymns and other powers. Can't they do so?" In order to dispel their uncertainty he said: **in this population with its ascetics and brahmins**. Having thus shown that there is no one in superior positions [who could drive him insane], now, with the phrase **its devas and humans**, referring to conventional devas (kings and royalty) and the rest of humankind, by mentioning those in superior states he showed that there is no one else in the world of beings who could do so. It is in this way that an orderly account construing the sequence of terms should be understood.

Thus the Blessed One, having rebuffed Āḷavaka's threat of harming him, said, **But ask whatever you want, friend**, thereby encouraging Āḷavaka to ask questions. This is the meaning: "Ask, if you want to. It won't be burdensome for me to answer your questions." Or alternatively: "Ask whatever you want. I will answer everything for you." He thus extends to him "the invitation of an omniscient one," which is not shared in common with paccekabuddhas, chief disciples, or great disciples. Whereas the latter say, "Ask, friend, and having heard, we will know," the buddhas say, "Ask, friend, whatever you want"; or "Ask me in your mind, Vāsava, any question you wish" (DN II 275,21); or: [230]

> "Whatever doubt Bāvari has,
> and you, or all the others—
> you are given permission, so ask
> whatever you wish in your mind." (**1030**)

In such a way they extend to devas and human beings the invitation of an omniscient one. And it is not astounding that the Blessed One extended this invitation after he had reached the stage of buddhahood, but he did so too even when he was on the stage of a bodhisatta, still abiding in partial knowledge. Thus at the time he was Sarabhaṅga, he was entreated by the rishis thus:

> "Koṇḍañña, answer the questions;
> the virtuous rishis entreat you.
> Koṇḍañña, this is the rule among men,
> that the burden falls on the eldest."

> [He replied:]

> "You have gained the opportunity, let the good men ask
> any questions you wish to with your mind.
> I will answer each question of yours,
> since I myself have known this world and the next." (Ja V 140,17–29)

And in the Sambhava Jātaka, the brahmin Sucirata wandered all over Jambudīpa three times without meeting anyone who could answer his questions. He finally met Sambhava, a seven-year-old boy playing in the dirt along a road. When the boy was asked, he invited the brahmin with the invitation of an omniscient one, saying:

> "Certainly, I will explain this to you
> as one who is skilled would do,
> so that the king understands it,
> whether or not he acts upon it." (Ja V 65,24–25)

181. When the Blessed One had thus extended to Āḷavaka the invitation of an omniscient one, **the yakkha Āḷavaka then addressed the Blessed One in verse: "What here is a person's best treasure?"**

Here, **what** is an interrogative; **su** is an indeclinable, a mere line filler;[809] **here**: in this world; **treasure:** what brings delight or satisfaction—a designation for wealth. **Well practiced**: well done; [231] **happiness**: bodily and mental comfort; **brings**: yields, provides. **Really** is an emphatic indeclinable; **sweetest** (*sādutaraṃ*) means "extremely sweet"; there is also the reading **most excellent** (*sādhutaraṃ*); **of tastes**: of things designated tastes. **How**: in what way? **How lives the one whose life**: how living is one's life. There is also the reading: **How living of those who live**, meaning "Of those who live, how living."[810] The rest here is clear.

Thus with this verse he asks these four questions: "What here is a person's best treasure? What well practiced brings happiness? What is really the sweetest of tastes? How lives the one whose life they say is best?"

182. Then, answering him in the same way that the Buddha Kassapa had answered, the Blessed One spoke this verse: **Faith is here a person's best treasure**. Here, just as such treasure as bullion and gold brings the happiness of enjoyment and use, dispels such suffering as hunger and thirst, alleviates poverty, is the means for obtaining such precious gems as pearls, and brings the deference of the world,[811] so mundane and world-transcending faith, in corresponding ways, brings mundane and world-transcending resultant happiness; dispels the suffering of birth, old age, and so forth for those practicing with faith as their conveyance; alleviates paucity of excellent qualities; and serves as the cause for obtaining the precious gems such as the enlightenment factors. And according to the following statement, it brings the deference of the world:

> A person of faith and good behavior,
> possessing fame and wealth,
> is honored everywhere,
> in whatever region he resorts to. (Dhp 303)

Thus faith is called a treasure. This treasure of faith follows one along; it is unmatched by anything else; it is a cause for all excellence; and it is also a source of mundane treasure such as bullion and gold and so forth.[812] For it is a person of faith who does meritorious deeds and acquires treasure, while one without faith uses treasure only for harmful purposes; therefore it is said to be **best**. **A person's (a man's)**:[813] the teaching is set forth by way of what is superior, [232] but it should be understood that the treasure of faith is best not only for a man but for a woman and others as well.

The Dhamma: the *dhamma* of the ten courses of wholesome kamma, or the *dhamma* of giving, good behavior, and meditative development. **Well practiced**: well done, well conducted. **Brings happiness**: It brings human happiness, such as that of Soṇa the financier's son, Raṭṭhapāla, and others; celestial happiness, such as that of Sakka and others; and in the end the happiness of nibbāna, such as in the case of Mahāpaduma and others.[814]

Truth: This word "truth" is found with many meanings, for instance, in the statement "One should speak truth, one should not become angry" (Dhp 224), it occurs as truthful speech; in the statement "Ascetics and brahmins standing in truth," it means abstinence; in the statement "Why do they assert diverse truths, those proponents who claim to be skilled?" (**885**), it means views; in the statement "There are, bhikkhus, these four brahmin truths" (AN II 176,26), it means brahmin truths; in the statement "Truth indeed is one—there is no second" (**884**), it means the supreme truth; and in the statement "Of the four truths, how many are wholesome" (Vibh 128, §216), it means noble truths. But here, truthful speech is intended—including nibbāna as supreme truth and truth as abstinence—through the spiritual might of which one exercises control over water and other things and crosses beyond birth, old age, and death. As it is said:

> By an utterance of truth one runs on water,
> by truth the wise even destroy poison,
> by truth the sky thunders and rains,
> firm in truth, they aspire for nibbāna.[815]
>
> Whatever tastes there are on earth,
> truth is the sweetest of those tastes;
> firm in truth, ascetics and brahmins
> cross to the beyond of birth and death. (Ja V 491,6–9)

The sweetest of tastes: the most delectable, the most delicious. The things called tastes may be substances, conduct, sauces, edibles, the remaining condiments, and so forth. Thus in the statement "Taste of roots, taste of stems" (Dhs 180, §628), and so forth, it is things that can be tasted. [Other instances of the word *rasa* are:] "I allow you, bhikkhus, the taste of all [233] fruit juices" (Vin I 246,17), "Master Gotama is tasteless" (Vin III 2,14), "the taste of forms, the taste of sounds" (Vin III 2,16), "no offense in mere tastes," "this Dhamma and discipline has a single taste, the taste of liberation" (AN IV 203,7), "the Blessed One partakes of the taste of the meaning, the taste of the Dhamma," (see p. 1087, Nidd I 104); and so forth. Of these tastes, **truth is the sweetest**, the sweetest or the most excellent, the best, supreme; for such tastes as those of roots nourish the body and bring defiled pleasure; but the taste of truth—truth as abstinence and truthful speech—nourishes the mind with serenity and insight and brings undefiled pleasure; the taste of liberation is sweet because it is permeated by the taste of supreme truth; and the taste of the meaning and taste of the Dhamma are sweet because they occur in dependence on the meaning and the Dhamma that are the means for achieving that [taste of liberation].

Living by wisdom, they say, one's life is best: But here, among those who are blind, one-eyed, and two-eyed,[816] this is the two-eyed householder who lives by undertaking with wisdom the householder's practice—pursuing an occupation, going for refuge, giving and sharing, undertaking the precepts, observing the uposatha, and so forth; and it is the monastic person who takes up with wisdom the practice of a monastic—good behavior that brings freedom from remorse and the higher practices such as purification of mind and so forth. They say that the life of this one living by wisdom—or, among those who live, the one living by wisdom[817]—is best. It is in such a way that the meaning should be seen.

183. Having heard the Blessed One answer his four questions in this way, the yakkha was satisfied and, asking the remaining four questions, he spoke the verse **How does one cross the flood?**[818]

184. Then the Blessed One, answering him just as before, spoke this verse: **By faith one crosses the flood**. [234] Here, although one who crosses the fourfold flood also crosses the vast sea of saṃsāra, overcomes the suffering of the round, and purifies the stains of defilements, nevertheless, because one without faith, lacking faith, does not set out to cross the flood; and because one who is heedless, who sends his mind out among the five strands of sensual pleasure, becomes attached to them and stuck on them, and does not cross the vast sea of saṃsāra; and because one who is lazy lives miserably, tainted by unwholesome qualities; and because one who is unwise, not knowing the path to purification, is not purified—therefore the Blessed One spoke this verse showing the opposite in each case. And in the verse stated in such a way, since the faculty of faith is the foundation for the path of stream-entry, by the line **by faith one crosses the flood** he shows the crossing of the flood of views, the path of stream-entry, and the stream-enterer. Since the stream-enterer possesses heedfulness, a designation for constancy of practice in the development of wholesome qualities, when he achieves the second path, he crosses the remainder of the vast sea of saṃsāra—except for merely one more return to this world—represented by the flood of existence that has not been crossed by the stream-enterer. Therefore, by this line, **by heedfulness, one crosses the sea**, he shows the crossing of the flood of existence, the path of the once-returner, and the once-returner. Since the once-returner achieves the third path by means of energy, and thereby overcomes the suffering of sensual desire, designated the flood of sensual desire and represented by the flood of sensual desire not overcome by the path of the once-returner, by the line **by energy one overcomes suffering** he shows the crossing of the flood of sensual desire, the path of the non-returner, and the non-returner. And since the non-returner achieves the entirely purified wisdom of the fourth path by means of fully purified wisdom free from the muck of sensual desire, and thereby abandons the supreme stain not abandoned by the path of the non-returner, namely, ignorance, by the line **by wisdom one is fully purified** he shows the crossing of the flood of ignorance, the path of arahantship, and the arahant. At the conclusion of this verse, spoken with its culmination in arahantship, the yakkha was established in the fruit of stream-entry.

185. Now, having picked up the word "wisdom" stated in the line "by wisdom one is fully purified," asking a question that combines the mundane and the world-transcendent, Āḷavaka spoke this six-line verse through his own ingenuity: "How does one gain wisdom?" [235] Here, in all cases these questions beginning with "how" are about the means for achieving a benefit.[819] For having known wisdom and so forth to be the benefit, he asks about the means to it: **How**—by what means, through what cause—**does one gain wisdom?**

186. Then the Blessed One, showing how wisdom is gained through four causes, said: "Placing faith." This is the meaning: **Placing faith in the Dhamma of the arahants for the attainment of nibbāna one gains** both mundane and world-transcending **wisdom**. ["Dhamma" here refers to] the Dhamma through which arahants—buddhas, paccekabuddhas, and a buddha's disciples—have attained nibbāna. In the preliminary portion of practice this consists in bodily good conduct and so forth, and in the subsequent portion in the thirty-seven aids to enlightenment. However, that is not attained merely by faith. But since[820] "one who has given rise to faith [in a teacher] visits him; when he visits him, he serves him; when he serves him, he lends an ear; one who lends an ear hears the Dhamma" (MN II 480,1–5)—therefore, from the time of visiting until one hears the Dhamma, one gains **a desire to learn**.[821] What is meant? Having placed faith in that Dhamma, one personally visits teachers and preceptors, whom one serves by doing the duties toward them. When they are satisfied with one's service and wish to say something, because one has not lost one's desire to learn, one lends an ear, and by listening, one gains wisdom. But even when there is a desire to learn, only one who is **heedful**, by constant presence of mindfulness, and **astute**, by being able to distinguish what has been well expressed and badly expressed, gains it, not others. Hence he says: **If one is heedful and astute**.

Thus it is through *faith* that one practices the way that leads to obtaining wisdom; through *a desire to learn* that one carefully listens to the method for achieving wisdom; through *heedfulness* that one does not forget what one has grasped; and through *astuteness* that one grasps it without deficiency or excess, without distortion, and then expands upon it. Or through *a desire to learn* one lends an ear and hears the Dhamma that is the cause for obtaining wisdom; having heard it through *heedfulness*, one retains the Dhamma in mind; [236] through *astuteness*, one examines the meaning of the teachings one has retained in mind and then gradually realizes the supreme truth. Therefore, when asked by him, "How does one gain wisdom?" the Blessed One spoke this verse, "Placing faith . . . astute," showing these four causes.

187. Now, answering the other three questions, the Blessed One spoke this verse that begins with "Doing what is proper." Here, **doing what is proper**: Without overlooking place, time, and other circumstances, one employs the proper means for achieving world-transcendent or mundane wealth. **Dutiful**: By means of mental energy one does not discard one's duty. **One with initiative**: one possessing initiative by way of bodily energy, not relaxing his exertion, in the way stated thus: "One does not think more of cold and heat than of grass" (DN III 185,15–16; Th 232). **Finds wealth**: One obtains mundane wealth like Little Apprentice who, with one mouse, soon earned 200,000, and one obtains world-transcending wealth like the Elder Mahallaka Mahātissa,[822] who made the vow: "I will dwell in three postures." When dullness and drowsiness came upon him, he expelled them by wetting a coil of straw and putting it on his head and by entering water up to his throat. After twelve years, he attained arahantship.

By truthfulness—by truthful speech as "one who speaks truth, who speaks fact," and also by supreme truth—**one wins acclaim** thus: "a buddha, a paccekabuddha, a noble disciple." **By giving**, by giving whatever they wish for and desire, **one binds friends**. Or one binds them by giving what is hard to give, or, under the heading of giving, the four means of attracting and sustaining a retinue are included.[823] What is meant is that one makes friends in these ways.

188. Thus, having answered four questions in a way that is common to householders and monastics and combines mundane and world-transcending aspects, answering this fifth question, "When passing on, how does one not sorrow?" the Blessed One spoke of these four qualities: "The faithful seeker of the household life who possesses these four qualities." This is the meaning: **Faithful**, because he possesses the faith that gives rise to all good qualities, as stated here: "Placing faith in the Dhamma of the arahants"; **seeker of the household life** [237] because he is a householder enjoying sensual pleasures who seeks a home or seeks the five strands of sensual pleasure. An aspect of **truth** was stated here: "By truthfulness one wins acclaim." In the line "One gains wisdom consisting in a desire to learn," **dhamma**[824] was stated by the expression "wisdom desiring to learn."[825] In the line "dutiful, one with initiative," **steadfastness** (*dhiti*) was stated by the expressions "doing what is dutiful" and "one with initiative." An aspect of **generosity** was stated here: "by giving, one binds friends." Thus one in whom **these four qualities** exist **does not sorrow when he passes on**: does not sorrow when he goes from the present world to the next world.

189. Thus the Blessed One, having also answered the fifth question, exhorting the yakkha, said: "Come now." Here, **come now** (*iṅgha*) is an indeclinable in the sense of exhorting. **Others too**: other teachings too. **Ask the many ascetics and brahmins**: or ask the many other ascetics and brahmins who claim to be omniscient, such as Pūraṇa, whether there exists a **better** method for winning acclaim **than truth**,[826] in the way stated by us here, "by truthfulness one wins acclaim"; or whether there is a better method for gaining mundane and world-transcending wisdom **than self-control**, stated here by the section of wisdom desiring to learn:[827] "One gains wisdom from a desire to learn";[828] or whether there is a better method for binding friends **than generosity**, in the way stated here: "by giving, one binds friends"; or whether there is a better method for finding mundane and world-transcending wealth **than patience**, a designation for enthusiastic energy in enduring the great burden. It is spoken of as "dutifulness" and "initiative" undertaken for the sake of this or that benefit, as stated here: "dutiful, one with initiative." [Ask them] **whether**, when passing on from this world to the next world, **there exists here** any better method for not sorrowing than these four qualities stated thus: "truth, *dhamma*, steadfastness, generosity."[829]

This here is a commentary on the meaning together with a brief construing [of the sequence]. But in detail it should be understood by analyzing each individual term according to the methods of commenting on the term by extraction of meanings and extraction of terms.[830]

190. When the Buddha finished speaking, the yakkha abandoned whatever doubt might have motivated him to ask others, and accordingly he said: **Why now should I ask the many ascetics and brahmins?** Informing those who do not know his reason for not asking them, he said: "Today I have understood the good pertaining [238] to future lives." Here, **today** means "starting today." **I have understood**—I have known in the aforesaid way—**the good** (*attho*): By this much he shows the good pertaining to the present life, stated in this way: "One gains wisdom consisting in a desire to learn."[831] **Pertaining to future lives** (*samparāyiko*): By this he refers to "these four qualities" that, when one passes on, cause absence of sorrow in future lives.[832] And **attha** ("good") is a designation for a cause.

For this word *attha* occurs in the sense of the meaning of a passage, as in "with *attha* and with phrasing" (DN I 62,31); in the sense of purpose,[833] as in "I have an *attha*, householder, with bullion and gold" (D II 176,17); in the sense of progress, as in "There is *attha* for those of good behavior" (Ja I 144,19); in the sense of wealth, as in "many people associate for the sake of *attha*"; in the sense of benefit, as in "one practices for the *attha* of both" (SN I 162,31); and in the sense of cause, as in "when an *attha* has arisen, [they desire] a wise man" (Ja I 387,4).

But here it occurs in the sense of cause. Therefore the meaning here should be briefly understood thus: "Today I have understood for myself, in the way explained by the Blessed One, the present-life cause for obtaining wisdom and other benefits, and the future-lives cause for not sorrowing when one passes on. So why now should I ask the many ascetics and brahmins?"

191. Thus, having said, "I have understood the good pertaining to future lives," the yakkha next says, "Indeed, it was for my sake that the Buddha came to stay at Āḷavī," showing that his knowledge is rooted in the Blessed One. Here, **for my sake** (*atthāya*): for my welfare or for my progress. **I have understood where what is given bears great fruit**: "I have understood that the Buddha is foremost of those worthy of offerings; he is the one to whom what is given with the generosity stated among 'these four qualities' bears great fruit." But some say that he said this with reference to the Sangha.

192. Thus, having shown with this verse his achievement of his own welfare, now, showing his practice for the welfare of others, he says: "Now I will travel about." The meaning of this should be understood in the way stated in relation to the Discourse with Hemavata (p. 608). [239]

The conclusion of this verse, the approach of dawn, the sound of applause,[834] and the bringing of the Āḷavaka prince to the yakkha's abode all occurred simultaneously. The king's men, having heard the sound of applause, wondered: "Such applause does not resound for anyone other than the buddhas. Could it be that the Blessed One has come?" They then saw the Blessed One's bodily aura. Unlike in the past, they did not stand outside but entered without fear and saw the Blessed One sitting in the yakkha's abode with the yakkha standing there reverently saluting him. Having seen this, they said to the yakkha: "Great yakkha, this is the prince, brought to you as an offering. Come now, eat him or do with him as you wish."

Since the yakkha was now a stream-enterer he felt ashamed, especially as this was being said in the presence of the Blessed One. Then he took the prince with both hands and presented him to the Blessed One, saying: "Bhante, this prince was sent for me, but I give him to the Blessed One. The buddhas are compassionate, so let the Blessed One accept this boy for his welfare and happiness." Then he recited this verse:

> "This prince has a hundred marks of merit,[835]
> his limbs are complete, his features are full.
> Elated in mind and joyful, I give him to you:
> let the One with Vision accept him for the world's
> welfare."

The Blessed One accepted the prince. While accepting him, as a blessing for the yakkha and the prince, he spoke a verse with one line missing. The yakkha then filled in the fourth line three times, causing the prince to go for refuge, as follows:

"May this prince have a long life,
and, O yakkha, may you be happy.
Dwell without affliction for the welfare of the world.
This prince goes for refuge to the Buddha
. . . to the Dhamma . . . to the Sangha."

The Blessed One then gave the prince back to the king's men, instructing them: "Bring him up and then give him to me again." In this way, the prince passed from the hands of the king's men into the yakkha's hands (*hatthato . . . hatthaṃ*), and from the yakkha's hands [240] into the Blessed One's hands, and from the Blessed One's hands again into the hands of the king's men. For this reason, he came to be called "Hatthaka Āḷavaka"[836]—"Āḷavaka of the Hands."

When the farmers, woodsmen, and other citizens saw that the king's men had returned with the boy, they were frightened and asked: "Could it be that the yakkha did not want the prince because he is too young?" The king's men replied, "Do not be afraid. The Blessed One has ensured our security," and they informed them of everything. Then the entire city of Āḷavī was in an uproar, exclaiming in the direction of the yakkha: "Excellent, excellent!" When the time for the Blessed One to walk for alms arrived, the yakkha took his bowl and robe, accompanied him half way, and then returned.

When the Blessed One had wandered for alms in the city and completed his meal, he sat down in the excellent seat that he prepared for himself at the foot of a secluded tree by the city gate. Thereupon the king and citizens, together with a multitude of people, assembled and approached the Blessed One. Having paid homage to him, they sat down around him and asked: "Bhante, how did you tame such a terrible yakkha?" The Blessed One then related to them the Discourse to Āḷavaka, beginning with the battle: "He sent these nine kinds of storms against me. He created such and such frightful apparitions. He asked me such and such questions, and I answered him in such a way." At the conclusion of the talk, 84,000 people made the breakthrough to the Dhamma.

Thereupon the king and the citizens made an abode for the yakkha near the abode of the great king Vessavaṇa and initiated a perennial offering accompanied by such tributes as flowers and incense. And when the prince reached maturity, they sent him to the Blessed One, telling him: "You owe your life to the Blessed One. Go attend upon the Blessed One and the Sangha of bhikkhus." As he was attending on the Blessed One and the Sangha of bhikkhus, in no long time he was established in the fruit of a non-returner. He learned the entire Word of the Buddha and acquired a retinue of five hundred lay followers. The Blessed One named him one of the foremost disciples: "This, bhikkhus, is the foremost among my male lay disciples who sustain a retinue with the four means of attracting and sustaining a retinue, namely, Hatthaka of Āḷavī" (AN I 26,9). [241]

11 Victory
(*Vijaya Sutta*)

The Discourse on Victory is also called the Discourse on Removing Desire for the Body.[837] What is its origin? It is said that this discourse was spoken under two circumstances; therefore it has a dual origin.

(I) Here, when the Blessed One eventually arrived at Kapilavatthu, he disciplined the Sakyans, gave the going forth to Nanda and others, and allowed women to go forth. Three women named Nandā went forth: Nandā, the sister of the Elder Nanda; Abhirūpanandā, the daughter of King Khemaka the Sakyan; and Janapadakalyāṇinandā.[838]

On that occasion the Blessed One was dwelling at Sāvatthī. Abhirūpanandā was beautiful (*abhirūpa*), lovely, and graceful; hence they gave her the name "Abhirūpanandā." Janapadakalyāṇinandā, too, was peerless in beauty. Because of their infatuation with their own beauty, neither went to attend upon the Blessed One. They did not even want to see him, for they thought: "The Blessed One speaks dispraise of form, criticizes it, and in many ways shows the danger in form."[839] If they were displeased with him, why did they go forth? Because they had no alternative. For on her wedding day, Abhirūpanandā's husband, a Sakyan youth, died; then her mother and father made her go forth against her will. When the Venerable Nanda attained arahantship, Janapadakalyāṇinandā lost hope and thought: "My husband and mother and Mahāpajāpatī, as well as other relatives, have gone forth. Without these relatives the household life is suffering." Thus she went forth, not from faith, but because she did not find any enjoyment in the household life.

When the Blessed One knew that their capacity for knowledge had reached maturity, he instructed Mahāpajāpatī: "Let all the bhikkhunīs come in sequence for an exhortation." [242] When their turn arrived, they sent a proxy. Then the Blessed One said: "When one's turn arrives, one should come oneself; one should not send a proxy." One day when Abhirūpanandā came, the Blessed One aroused a sense of urgency in her by means of a mind-created form, reciting the verse of the Dhammapada (150): "A city built of bones . . ." In sequence he established her in arahantship with these verses from the Therīgāthā (19–20):

"Behold, Nandā, this assemblage
afflicted, impure, putrid,
flowing and oozing,
delighted in by fools.[840]

"Develop the markless state,
discard the latent tendency to conceit.
Then, by breaking through conceit,
you will live at peace."[841]

One day the residents of Sāvatthī gave alms in the forenoon, undertook the uposatha observance, and well dressed and well groomed, bringing incense, flowers, and other items, went to Jeta's Grove to listen to the Dhamma. When the teaching was over, they paid homage to the Blessed One and entered the city. The Sangha of bhikkhunīs, too, heard the Dhamma talk and returned to the bhikkhunī quarters. The people and the bhikkhunīs on that occasion were speaking praise of the Blessed One.

For in the whole world, where people rely on four criteria,[842] there is no one who sees the Perfectly Enlightened One without gaining confidence in him. Persons who *rely upon form* as their criterion gain confidence in the Blessed One when they see his bodily form arisen in the world as if it were an adornment, his form marked with the characteristics of physical excellence, graced with the minor features, endowed with a fathom-wide aura, blazing as if with flags and garlands.[843] Those who *rely upon the voice* as their criterion gain confidence when they hear of his acclaim related in many hundreds of Jātakas and when they hear his voice with its brahma-like sound, endowed with eight factors, its utterances as sweet as the song of the karavīka bird. Those who *rely upon stringency* as their criterion gain confidence when they see his plain alms bowl and the stringent austerities he underwent. Those who *rely upon the Dhamma* as their criterion gain confidence when they investigate the collections of his qualities (*dhammakkhandha*), such as his good behavior and so forth. Therefore they speak praise of the Blessed One in all such cases.

When Janapadakalyāṇinandā reached the bhikkhuni quarters and heard the others speaking praise in many ways of the Blessed One, [243] she told the bhikkhunīs that she wished to see the Blessed One. The bhikkhunīs took her and approached the Blessed One. The Blessed One knew in advance that she would be coming, and so, like a man wishing to remove one thorn with another or one spike with another, he set out to remove her infatuation with beauty by means of beauty itself. Using his own psychic power, he created an extremely beautiful woman, fifteen or sixteen years of age, standing by his side fanning him. When Nandā arrived along with the other bhikkhunīs, she paid homage to the Blessed One, sat down among the bhikkhunīs, and saw the excellence of the Blessed One's form, which extended even up to the tips of his hairs. Then, when she saw the mind-created form standing at his side, she lost her infatuation with her own beauty and became enthralled with the other woman's beauty. She thought: "Oh, this woman is truly beautiful!"

Then the Blessed One displayed that woman as having reached the age of twenty; for women excel in beauty when they are sixteen years of age but not beyond that. When Nandā saw the woman's beauty decline, her fascination with her form diminished.[844] The Blessed One then displayed the woman as one who had never given birth, as one who had given birth once, as a middle-aged woman, and as an old woman. He then showed her getting older until she was a hundred years old, bent over, leaning on a walking stick, with pock-marked limbs. While Nandā was still looking on, he showed the woman die and her body bloated and in various stages of decay, surrounded by crows and other scavengers, being devoured, foul-smelling, disgusting, and repulsive. Having seen that sequence of decay,[845] Nandā thought: "This sequence is common to all, to me as well as to others." The perception of impermanence sprang up in her, and in conformity with it, the perceptions of suffering and non-self arose. The three kinds of existence then appeared to her as like a blazing house, not offering any refuge.

Then, knowing that Nandā's mind had settled on a meditation subject, the Blessed One recited these verses on account of their suitability for her: [244]

"Behold, Nandā, this assemblage
afflicted, impure, putrid,
flowing and oozing,
delighted in by fools.

"As this, so that; as that, so this.
By way of elements[846] see it as empty;
do not come back to the world again.
Having expunged desire for existence,
you will live at peace." (Dhp-a III 117)

At the conclusion of the verses, Nandā was established in the fruit of stream-entry. Then, to lead her to the achievement of the higher paths, the Blessed One spoke this discourse, explaining a meditation subject for insight accompanied by emptiness. This, firstly, is one origin of the discourse.

(II) The second incident occurred while the Blessed One was dwelling at Rājagaha with regard to Sirimā, the younger sister of Jīvaka.[847] Sirimā was the daughter of the courtesan Sālavatī, whose origin story is related in detail in the Chapter on Robes (Vin I 268–69). After her mother passed away, Sirimā assumed her position as chief courtesan. According to the background story to the verse "Conquer anger with non-anger,"[848] she disparaged the daughter of the financier Puṇṇaka, apologized to the Blessed One, listened to his teaching of the Dhamma, and became a stream-enterer. She then provided eight constant meals.[849]

As explained in the background story to another Dhammapada verse,[850] a certain bhikkhu who had received a meal from Sirimā fell so passionately in love with her that he was unable to eat but just lay down on his bed fasting. While he was lying there, Sirimā passed away and was reborn as a queen of Suyāma in the Yāma heaven.[851] The Blessed One prevented her body from being cremated and had the king deposit it in the charnel ground so that others could see it. Accompanied by the Sangha of bhikkhus, the Blessed One went there, bringing that bhikkhu along; the citizens and king also went.[852] People there said: "Previously it was hard to get sight of her even for 1,008 coins, [245] but now there is no one who would want to see her even for a penny." The deva maiden Sirimā arrived, accompanied by five hundred chariots. The Blessed One then spoke this discourse in order to teach the Dhamma to the assembled multitude, and as an exhortation to that bhikkhu he spoke the verse from the Dhammapada (147): "Behold this painted image." This is its second origin.

193. Here, **when one is walking**: when one is going forward by bringing the entire physical body forward toward one's destination; **or standing**: standing by raising the body; **sitting or lying down**: sitting by bending the lower part of the body while holding the upper part erect, lying down by stretching it horizontally; **when one bends and stretches**: bends and stretches the limbs; **this is the motion of the body**: All this is just the motion, the movement, the activity of this sentient body. There is no one else here moving or stretching. Further, when the thought "Let me go forward" is arising, the air element originated by it pervades the body, and because of this there is a bringing forward of the body toward one's destination; there is the manifestation of different forms in different locations.[853] Hence it is said "walking."

Similarly, when the thought "Let me stand" is arising, the air element originated by the thought pervades the body and there is the raising of the body, the manifestion of form in higher and higher positions. Hence it is said "standing." So too, when the thought "Let me sit down" is arising, the air element originated by the thought pervades the body and there is the bending of the lower part of the body and the holding upright of the upper part of the body, the manifestion of form in such a position. Hence it is said "sitting." Similarly, when the thought "Let me lie down" is arising, the air element originated by the thought pervades the body and there is the stretching out of the body horizontally, the manifestion of form in such a position. Hence it is said "lying down."

Thus when it is said that this person named so and so—whether walking, standing, sitting, or lying down [246]—bends and stretches by way of bending and stretching any of the limbs in any posture here or there, this occurs in the way stated through the arising of the thought of bending or stretching. Therefore this is the motion of the body. There is nothing else here; this is empty of any being or person walking or stretching. The supreme meaning here is simply this:

> On account of the difference in the mind,
> there is a difference in the air element.
> Because of the difference in the air element,
> there is difference in the body's motion.

Now when the body is held for a long time in a single posture there is bodily oppression, and a change in postures takes place for the purpose of dispelling that oppression. Therefore, by this verse, with the words "whether one is walking" and so forth, the Blessed One shows *the characteristic of suffering*, which is concealed by the postures. So too, because there is no standing still or any of the other postures at the time one is walking, in speaking of all these postures such as walking as "this is the motion of the body," he shows *the characteristic of impermanence*, which is concealed by continuity. When he says, "This is the motion of the body," which takes place when the combination of factors is occurring, by rejection of a self [as the agent of these activities], he shows *the characteristic of non-self*, which is concealed by the compactness of the perception of a self.[854]

194. Thus, having explained the meditation subject of emptiness by showing the three characteristics, to show once again the unattractive nature of the body, whether sentient or insentient,[855] he begins by saying: "Bound together by bones and sinews." This is its meaning: That to which this motion pertains is this body, which is **bound together by bones and sinews** because it is bound together by 360 bones and 900 sinews. In the explanation of the meditation on the thirty-two aspects in the *Visuddhimagga*, these have been shown by analysis of their color, shape, region, location, and delimitation, and by the method of non-concern.[856] [247] **Plastered with skin and flesh**: Because it has been plastered with *skin*, which extends upward from the tips of the toes, and with *flesh*, which is analyzed into nine hundred pieces, as shown in the *Visuddhimagga*, the body should be understood to be extremely foul-smelling, disgusting, and repulsive. And why should this be understood here? The epidermis[857] that covers the body is as thin as the wings of a fly and, if it were collected from the entire body of a middle-sized person, it would be the size of a jujube-fruit kernel. If the body were not covered by the epidermis in the way the wall of a house is covered by a layer of paint, whether blue or another color, [its repulsive nature would be apparent].[858] However, **covered by the epidermis, the body is not seen as it really is** by foolish worldlings who lack the eye of wisdom. For even the skin (*taca*), which entices those who are lustful for the epidermis,[859] is a designation for the extremely disgusting and repulsive hide (*camma*). And as for that which is enveloped by the skin, when subjected to analysis:

> [It consists of] nine hundred pieces of flesh
> plastered over the carcass,
> which is filled with various families of worms
> and as putrid as a cesspit.

Thus it is also said to have nine hundred pieces of flesh. And as to that which is plastered by flesh:

> There are nine hundred sinews
> in this fathom-tall carcass.
> They bind a collection of bones
> as creepers do a house.

Those [sinews] too, and the 360 putrid, foul-smelling bones that stand in order, overspread by the sinews,[860] are not seen as they really are.

195–96. Because they are enveloped by the skin, which entices those lustful for the epidermis, the various internal kinds of filth,[861] which are extremely impure, foul-smelling, disgusting, and repulsive, are not apparent to worldly people. Without paying attention[862] to the epidermis, which is as thin as the wings of a fly, one should penetrate those parts with the eye of wisdom and see the body thus: "as filled with intestines . . . with bile and grease."[863] [248] All these should be understood by way of their color, shape, region, location, and delimitation, and by the method of non-concern, as explained in the *Visuddhimagga* (249 foll., Ppn 8.83–138).

197–98. Thus, having shown the internal kinds of filth, pointing out that "there is not one thing hidden here similar to pearls and gems, but only this body full of impurity," he now makes plain the repulsive nature of the internal kinds of filth by means of the filthy nature of its secretions. Thus, having brought together what has been stated previously, he next speaks the two verses that begin "Further, from its nine openings."

Here, **further** (*atha*) is an indication of an alternative way. What is meant is: "See the impurity of the body in still another way." **From its nine openings**: from this body's two eye openings, two ear openings, two nostrils, mouth, anus, and urethra. **Impurity flows**: The extremely disgusting and foul-smelling diverse impurity, plain to all the world, flows, runs out, oozes out; there are no such fragrances as *agaru* and sandal, or no such precious substances as jewels and pearls. **Constantly**: And that occurs all the time, both night and day, both morning and evening, when one is standing still and when one is walking. If it is asked, "What is that impurity?" he says: "eye-filth from the eyes" and so forth. **Eye-filth** similar to skin and flesh is exuded through the two eye-openings; **ear-filth** similar to dust and dirt comes out from the ear-openings; **snot** similar to pus flows from the nostrils. **And from the mouth one sometimes vomits**. What does one vomit? **Bile**: when the unfixed bile is agitated, one vomits it; **and vomits phlegm**: not only does one vomit bile, but one sometimes also vomits phlegm, a bowlful measure of which is situated on the stomach lining. That should be understood by way of its color and other qualities in the way explained in the *Visuddhimagga* (261, Ppn 8.128). And besides phlegm, one vomits other similar impure substances, such as stomach matter, blood, and other things.

Having thus shown the vomiting of impurities through seven doors, the Blessed One, who knows the time and knows persons, [249] does not specifically mention the other two doors; but showing the flow of impurities from the entire body in still another way, he says: **sweat and dirt flow from the body**: sweat and dirt, the latter analyzed into the salty layer and grime. This phrase should be connected with the earlier phrase "flows constantly."

199. Just as, when rice is being boiled, the grime from the rice grains and water rise up along with the foam, smear the lid of the pot, and drip out, so when the food that has been eaten and drunk is being digested by the kamma-born fire element, the grime of the food and drink rise up and emerge in the way analyzed, "muck from the eyes," and so forth, and having smeared the eyes and other openings, they then drip out. Now, having shown the impurity of this body in this way, the Blessed One next speaks the verse "Its hollow head is filled with the brain," showing the impure nature of the head through its corelessness and impurity. He does this because in the world the head is considered the supreme part of the body, such that those who take themselves to be extremely eminent do not pay homage [by bowing their heads] even to those who are worthy of homage.

Here, **the hollow**, open, **head is filled with the brain**: packed with the brain, like a white gourd packed with curd. The brain should be understood in the way explained in the *Visuddhimagga* (260, Ppn 8.126). **The fool conceives it as beautiful**: Although the body is filled with various kinds of filth, the fool, misled by wrong thinking, conceives it as beautiful. He conceives it through the three conceivings—of craving, views, and conceit—as "beautiful, pure, attractive, desirable, agreeable." Why? Because he is **led on by ignorance**: because he is led on, impelled, driven by the delusion that conceals the four truths. The purport is that he is compelled thus: "Take it in such a way, adhere to it in such a way, conceive it in such a way." See how this ignorance is a cause of harm!

200. Thus, having shown unattractiveness by way of a sentient (living) body, now, to show it by way of an insentient (dead) body, the Blessed One speaks the verse "And when it is lying dead." He does so since even the body of a wheel-turning king is packed with the aforesaid kinds of filth, [250] so having shown its unattractive nature when he is at the height of his glory, he now shows the same in the state of loss.

This is its meaning: **When it is lying dead**: When such a body is dead because it is bereft of vitality, warmth, and consciousness; **bloated** like a bellows full of air; **discolored** through the disappearance of its color; **cast off in a charnel ground**: discarded like a useless block of wood (see Dhp 41). Then, thinking, "Now he will never rise again," **the relatives are** absolutely **unconcerned with it**. Here, by the word **dead** he shows impermanence; by **lying**, the absence of activity; and by both he enjoins one to abandon intoxication with life and strength. By **bloated**, he shows the loss of shape; by **discolored** the defect in lust for the skin; and by both he enjoins one to abandon intoxication with form and to abandon conceit based on beauty of complexion. **Cast off**: He shows the absence of anything to be grasped; **in a charnel ground**: he shows its disgusting nature, that there is nothing within worth accepting; by both he enjoins one to abandon the perception of beauty and obsession with the idea of "mine." **The relatives are unconcerned with it**: by this he shows the absence of any reversal and enjoins one to abandon intoxication with one's retinue.

201. Thus by the previous verse he has shown unattractiveness by way of an insentient (dead) body that is still intact. Now he speaks the verse **Dogs then devour it**, to show the same by way of a dismembered body. Here, **whatever other beings there are**: Other beings that eat cadavers—crows, hawks, and so forth—also eat it. The rest is clear.

202. Thus, with the words "whether one is walking" and so forth, he shows the body by way of the meditation subject of emptiness; with the words "bound together by bones and sinews" and so forth, he shows the unattractive nature of a sentient (living) body; and by the words "and when it is lying dead" and so forth, he shows the unattractive nature of an insentient (dead) body. By the words "led on by ignorance, the fool conceives it as beautiful," he exposes the attitude of the fool in regard to the utterly unattractive body, which is empty of permanence, pleasure, and selfhood. Under the heading of "ignorance," he also shows the round of saṃsāra. Now, with the words "Having heard the word of the Buddha" and so forth, he sets out to show the attitude of the wise person, and also to show the ending of the round under the heading of full understanding.

Here, **having heard**: having listened to carefully; **the Word of the Buddha**: the Word of the Buddha on removing desire for the body; [251] **a bhikkhu**: a trainee or a worldling;[864] **possessing wisdom**: the wisdom of insight, which occurs in relation to impermanence and so forth; **here**: in the Teaching; **fully understands it**: fully understands the body through the three kinds of full understanding.

How? In the way a skilled merchant looks over his goods, thinking, "There is this and that," and then estimates: "When they are sold for such and such a price, there will be such and such a profit." Having done so, getting back the capital outlay together with the profit, he disposes of those goods. In the same way, the bhikkhu examines the body with the eye of knowledge thus: "There are these bones, sinews, and so forth, these head hairs and body hairs, and so forth." In this way, he fully understands it with *the full understanding of the known*. Scrutinizing it thus, "These things are impermanent, suffering, and non-self," he fully understands it with *the full understanding by scrutinization*. Having scrutinized it thus, on reaching the noble path, with the abandoning of desire and lust for it, he fully understands it by *the full understanding of abandoning*. Or else, when seeing the body—whether sentient or insentient—by way of its unattractive nature, he fully understands it by *the full understanding of the known*; seeing it as impermanent and so forth, he fully understands it by *the full understanding by scrutinization*; and when he abandons it by the path of arahantship, having expelled desire and lust for it, he fully understands it by *the full understanding of abandoning*.[865]

Why does he fully understand it in such a way? **Because he sees it as it really is**. When the subject is established as "one possessing wisdom," [the point is made that] one comes to be possessed of wisdom by hearing the Word of the Buddha. Although the body is evident to everybody, without having heard the Word of the Buddha it is not possible to fully understand it. Therefore, to show the cause of his knowledge and to show as well that it is impossible for those outside here to see it in such a way, he says: "Having heard the Word of the Buddha." He uses the word "bhikkhu" because the presentation of the teaching took place with reference to the bhikkhunī Nandā and the bhikkhu whose mind had been toppled [by passion for Sirimā], and because they are the foremost assembly, and to show the status of a bhikkhu among those who undertake that practice. [252]

203. Now, as to the phrase "because he sees it as it really is," to show *how* one who sees it as it really is *actually sees it*, he says: "As this, so that; as that, so this." This is its meaning: **As this** unattractive sentient body walks, stands, sits, and lies down so long as vitality, warmth, and consciousness have not departed, **so that** insentient body now lying in the charnel ground previously did the same before those things departed. And **as that** body that is now dead does not walk, stand, sit, or lie down after those things have departed, **so this** sentient body will also become like that when those things depart. And **as this** sentient body does not now lie dead in a charnel ground and has not become bloated and deformed in other ways, **so that** body which is now dead was also like that. And **as that** unattractive insentient dead body now lies in a charnel ground, bloated and deformed in other ways, **so this** sentient body will also be like that.

Here, establishing the similarity of the dead body[866] with oneself by reflecting, "As this, so that," one abandons aversion toward the external. And establishing the similarity of oneself with the dead body by reflecting, "As that, so this," one abandons lust for the internal. By understanding them in whatever way equalizes the two (the internal and the external),[867] one abandons delusion in regard to both. Having thus succeeded, by seeing the body as it really is, in abandoning the unwholesome roots in the preliminary portion of the practice, a bhikkhu practicing in such a way eventually reaches the path of arahantship and can thereby expunge all desire and lust. Therefore he says: **internally and externally one should expunge desire for the body**. In the text elision is made of the words "a bhikkhu practicing in such a way, eventually."

204. Having thus shown the stage of the trainee, now showing the stage of the one beyond training,[868] he says: "That bhikkhu possessing wisdom here." This is its meaning: **That bhikkhu possessing wisdom here**—one who, by the wisdom of the path of arahantship, has attained the fruit immediately following the path—has entirely abandoned desire and lust, and is thus **one who has expunged desire and lust**. [253] And it is said that he **has attained the state** that is described as **deathless,** because of the absence of death and in the sense of being excellent; as **peace**, because of the allaying of all conditioned things; as **nibbāna**, because of the absence of weaving, a designation for craving;[869] and as **imperishable** because of the absence of perishing. Or alternatively, when that bhikkhu possessing the wisdom of the path of arahantship comes to abide in the fruit that immediately follows the path, he is called "one who has expunged desire and lust," and he has attained the state as described just above.[870] By this he shows: "He has abandoned this, and he has obtained that."[871]

205. Thus, having discussed the meditation subject of the unattractive by way of both the sentient (living) and insentient (dead) body together with its outcome, he next speaks the pair of verses that begin "This two-footed body," using a concise teaching to criticize the heedlessness that prevents one from obtaining such a great benefit. Although footless bodies and others are also certainly impure, here the two-footed body is stated as a heading or by delimitation of the superior. Or else, while other bodies are also impure, they are prepared with such flavorings as salt and lime and presented to people as food, but not so the human body. Therefore, showing that it is even more impure, he says: **This two-footed body**. By this he shows the human body. **Foul-smelling, is cherished**: being foul-smelling, when it is embellished with flowers and fragrances, it is cherished. **Filled with various kinds of filth**: stuffed with many filthy things, such as head hairs and so forth. **Oozing here and there**: Even though one endeavors to conceal it with flowers and fragrances, the effort is futile, for it still oozes saliva, snot, and other secretions through the nine doors and sweat and dirt through the pores of the skin.

206. Now see: **one who, because of such a body, would think to exalt himself**: any foolish man or woman who would think to exalt themselves through the conceivings of craving, views, and conceit, in such ways as "I" or "mine" or "permanent" and so forth; **or who would disparage others** on account of their social class and so forth, putting themselves in a high position. **What is this due to but lack of vision?**: What else is this exaltation of oneself and disparagement of others due to except the lack of seeing the noble truths with the noble path?

At the conclusion of the teaching, the bhikkhunī Nandā acquired a sense of urgency, thinking: "Alas, I have indeed been such a fool, in that I did not go to attend upon the Blessed One, who for my sake has expounded such a variegated teaching of the Dhamma." [254] Thus agitated, having attended closely to that teaching of the Dhamma, within a few days, by means of that same meditation subject, she realized arahantship.

In the second case (that of the infatuated bhikkhu), it is said, at the conclusion of the teaching 84,000 living beings made the breakthrough to the Dhamma, the deva maiden Sirimā was established in the fruit of a non-returner, and the bhikkhu was established in the fruit of stream-entry.

12 The Muni
(*Muni Sutta*)

From intimacy peril has arisen

What is the origin? There is no single origin for the entire discourse, but this here, firstly, is the origin of the initial four verses. It is said that while the Blessed One was dwelling at Sāvatthī, in a village abode a certain poor widowed woman[872] arranged for her son to go forth among the bhikkhus, and she herself went forth among the bhikkhunīs.[873] Both entered upon the rains retreat at Sāvatthī and often wished to see one another. Whenever the mother obtained something good she took it to her son, and the son did likewise for his mother. In this way, meeting both in the evening and the next morning, sharing their gains, enjoying one another's company, inquiring about the other's happiness and suffering, they became emboldened. Because they often saw one another, a bond was formed between them; because of the bond, intimacy arose; through intimacy, lust found an opening. With their minds in the grip of lust, they no longer thought of themselves as renunciants or even as mother and son. Having overstepped the boundary, they engaged in sexual intercourse. Dishonored, they disrobed and lived at home.

Bhikkhus reported this to the Blessed One. Having censured them with the words "Bhikkhus, did that foolish man think: 'A mother does not fall in love with her son or a son with his mother'? I do not [255] see even one other form" and so forth, the Blessed One then aroused a sense of urgency in the bhikkhus with the rest of the discourse: "Therefore, bhikkhus:

Like a dreadful poison, like boiling oil,
like molten copper, should one avoid women."

Having said this, in order to teach the Dhamma to the bhikkhus again, he recited these four personally applicable verses: "From intimacy peril has arisen."

207ab. Here, it was stated earlier that intimacy is of three kinds, distinguished by way of craving, views, and friendship. Here, intimacy through craving and views is intended. With reference to this, the Blessed One said: "See, bhikkhus, how for that foolish man **from intimacy peril has arisen**. For because of his craving—that is, his wish for the frequent sight of his mother and so forth—the peril of strong defilements arose, on account of which he could not stop but transgressed with his mother. Or the great peril was self-reproach and so forth, because of which he discarded the Teaching and disrobed.

From an abode: According to the passage that begins "By diffusion and confinement in the abode consisting in the sign of forms, one is said to roam about in an abode" (SN III 10,21), it is the different kinds of objects that are called an abode. **There arises dust**: The dust of lust, hatred, and delusion arises. What is meant? It is not only that a peril has arisen from intimacy, but also [dust has arisen from] the alluring object called an "abode" because it is the residence of defilements. Now, because one has violated restraint and overstepped the boundary [in regard to that object], **from that abode there arises dust**, because of which one defiled in mind will meet with misery and ruin. Or alternatively, this pair of lines should be construed thus: "See, bhikkhus, how *from intimacy peril has arisen* for that foolish man, and how for all worldlings *from an abode there arises dust*."

207cd. Having censured in all ways the outlook of the worldling with this first half-verse, the Blessed One spoke the second half-verse, "without an abode," praising his own vision. Here, **without an abode** should be understood as a rejection of the aforesaid abode, [256] and **without intimacy** as a rejection of intimacy. Both these terms are designations for nibbāna. **This truly is the muni's vision**: This state without an abode, without intimacy, is what was seen by the Buddha-muni. Here the word "truly" (*ve*) should be understood as an indeclinable in the sense of amazement. This purport is thereby established: "Whereas even a mother and son trangressed because of intimacy in an abode, the muni has seen this state that is without an abode, without intimacy. How amazing!" Or alternatively, "the muni's vision" is the vision of the muni, the word "vision" bearing the sense of opinion or preference, what one accepts and prefers.[874]

208. In the second verse, **One who, having cut off what has arisen**: When a defilement has arisen, come to be, been produced, in relation to any object, one makes an effort to abandon arisen unwholesome qualities; thereby one cuts it off by ensuring that it is not produced again in relation to that object. A future defilement is said to be "arising," with the characteristic of present occurrence, when it is about to be produced with the concurrence of appropriate conditions and is close to present occurrence. **Would not foster what is arising**: By making an effort to prevent the arising of unarisen unwholesome qualities, one prevents it from being produced. And how does one prevent it from being produced? **One would not nurture it**: One would not provide it with a condition that might produce it or let it encounter [such a condition].[875] In this way, by depriving it of its provisions, one does not foster what is arising.

Or alternatively: Through the development of the path, past defilements are cut off because of the nonexistence of their future results; presently occurring defilements are not fostered because of their nonexistence; and future defilements are not allowed to enter the mind because their ability to arise has been destroyed. Therefore, the meaning should be construed in this way: "One who, having cut off what has arisen by the development of the noble path, would not foster what is presently arising and would not nurture that which arises in the future—he is the one they call a solitary wandering muni, and that great rishi has seen the state of peace." He is **alone** (*ekaṃ*, one) because he is entirely without defilements, or alone in the sense of the best. He is one muni, or one among munis.[876] **Living** is living by conduct for the good of the world complete in all respects and by the other types of conduct. [257]

He saw: The subject is the Buddha-muni, spoken of through his ability in not fostering growth and in not nurturing it as "one who, having cut off what has arisen, would not foster what is arising or nurture it." **The state of peace**: a portion of peace. The meaning should be understood in this way: Among the three types of peace—conventional peace, peace in a particular respect, and ultimate peace, correlated respectively with the sixty-two views, insight, and nibbāna—the great rishi saw that which is best, the ultimate peace in a restless world.[877]

209. In the third verse, **having comprehended**: having considered, having demarcated, having investigated, having known as it really is. The meaning is: "having fully understood by the full understanding of suffering." The **grounds**: those things to which this world is so attached, the sites of the defilements analyzed into the aggregates, sense bases, and elements. **Having crushed the seed**:[878] having crushed, having damaged, having smashed the volitionally active consciousness, which is the seed of those grounds.[879] The meaning is: "having abandoned by abandoning through eradication." **He would not nurture it with moisture**: When that seed is moistened with the moisture (affection)[880] of craving and views, it might produce, by way of future conception, the "crops" of the aforesaid bases. He would not nurture it with that moisture (affection). The meaning is: "by the development of the path opposed to it, he would not let that moisture (affection) enter it."

Truly, that muni, a seer of the final end of birth: By the realization of nibbāna, that Buddha-muni has seen nibbāna, the end of birth and death, and is therefore a seer of the final end of birth. **Having abandoned thought, he cannot be reckoned**: By this development of the four truths, having abandoned the nine classes of unwholesome thoughts,[881] having attained the nibbāna element with residue remaining, he goes about acting for the good of the world, until eventually, with the perishing of the final consciousness, he reaches the nibbāna element without residue remaining. Then he cannot be designated as "a deva or a human being." Or else, whereas one who has not attained final nibbāna has not abandoned sensual thoughts and other such thoughts, and is therefore designated thus, "This person[882] is lustful" or "full of hate," one who has abandoned such thoughts cannot be so designated. The meaning here can also be seen in this way. [258]

210. In the fourth verse, **having known**: having known by way of impermanence and so forth; **all**: without omission; **residences**: states of existence, desire-realm existence and so forth, which are called dwelling places because beings dwell in them. **Not desiring any one of them**: not yearning for even one of those dwelling places because he has seen the danger in them. That Buddha-**muni** is **devoid of greed** because of the disappearance of greedy craving by the power of the development of the path, and he is **greedless** simply because he is devoid of greed. He is not like those who, while not actually devoid of greed, claim to be greedless. Thus he **does not endeavor**, he does not create wholesome or unwholesome kamma that could produce one or another of those dwelling places. For what reason? **For he has gone beyond**: because such a one has gone to nibbāna, which is beyond all dwelling places.

Thus, with the first verse he criticizes the worldling's outlook and praises his own vision; with the second verse, he praises his own achievement of the state of peace through the absence of those defilements because of which the worldling is not at peace; with the third verse, he points out that the worldling can be reckoned in this or that way because he has not abandoned thoughts about the various bases, and he praises his own transcendence of reckoning through the abandoning of such thoughts by the development of the four truths; and by the fourth verse, he points out that the worldling, desiring future dwelling places, endeavors through craving for existence, and he praises his own non-endeavoring through the absence of craving for those [future dwelling places]. Thus with four verses culminating in arahantship he concludes the teaching that originated from a single specific incident.

One who has overcome all

211. What is the origin? The Great Man, having made the great renunciation and eventually attained omniscience, was on the way to Bārāṇasī to set in motion the wheel of the Dhamma when, between the site of enlightenment and Gayā, he met the

Ājīvaka Upaka.[883] Questioned by him in the way that begins "Your faculties are clear, friend," he replied with the verse that begins "One who has overcome all." Upaka then said, "It may be, friend," and having shaken his head, he took a side road [259] and departed. Gradually he reached a certain village of deer hunters in the Vaṅga country. The chief of the deer hunters saw him and thought: "Oh, this ascetic is so frugal, he does not even wear a cloth. He must be an arahant in the world." He led him to his home and served him with a dish of tasty meat. When Upaka finished eating, the hunter, along with his wife and children, paid homage to him and invited him to stay there: "Live right here, Bhante. I will provide you with the requisites." He built a dwelling place and offered it to him. Upaka then lived there.

In the hot season, when the deer had gone far off to cooler regions where water was available, the hunter instructed his daughter Chāvā: "Serve our arahant respectfully." He then left with his son and brother. Now his daughter was beautiful and well proportioned. The next day, when Upaka came to the house and saw the girl coming to serve him the food she had prepared, he was overcome with lust. Unable even to eat, he took the food in a container and went back to his dwelling place. He put the food aside and lay down, without eating anything, determined: "If I get Chāvā I will live; if not, I will die."

After a week the deer hunter returned and asked his daughter for news about Upaka. She said: "He came only one day but hasn't returned since then." The hunter said: "I will go at once and ask about him." Immediately he went there and, while massaging Upaka's feet, asked: "Have you been ill, Bhante?" Upaka just rolled around groaning. The hunter pressed him: "Speak up, Bhante! I will do whatever I can for you." Upaka said: "If I get Chāvā I will live; if not, this will be my death bed." – "But do you know any craft, Bhante?" – "I do not." – "It isn't possible to live the household life if one does not know some craft." – "I do not know any craft. But I will carry the meat for you and sell the meat."

The hunter said: "I am satisfied with that." [260] He gave him an upper garment, brought him home, and gave his daughter to him. After they had lived together for some time, a son was born. They gave him the name Subhadda.

Chāvā mocked Upaka with the lullabies she sang to her son.[884] Unable to bear it any longer, Upaka said: "My dear, I will go to the Infinite Conqueror." He set out for the Middle Country. Now at the time the Blessed One was dwelling at Sāvatthī in the great monastery in Jeta's Grove. The Blessed One ordered the bhikkhus in advance: "If anyone comes asking for 'the Infinite Conqueror,' let him meet me." Upaka eventually reached Sāvatthī and stood in the middle of the monastery, asking: "Is my friend the Infinite Conqueror here in this monastery? Where does he live?" The bhikkhus led him to the Blessed One. The Blessed One taught him the Dhamma in a suitable way, and at the conclusion of the teaching he was established in the fruit of a non-returner.[885]

When the bhikkhus heard the background story they started a discussion: "The Blessed One first taught the Dhamma to a wretched naked ascetic." Having known that this conversation had started, the Blessed One came out from the Fragrant Cottage and, with wonders suitable for the occasion, he sat down in his seat and addressed the bhikkhus: "What was the conversation you were having while you were sitting together here?" They told him everything. The Blessed One then said: "Bhikkhus, the Tathāgata does not teach the Dhamma without a cause and condition. The Tathāgata's teaching of the Dhamma is stainless. It is not possible to find any fault with it. With the support of that Dhamma teaching, bhikkhus, Upaka has now become a non-returner." Having said this, he spoke this verse illustrating the stainless nature of his own teaching.

This is its meaning: With the abandoning of desire and lust for all aggregates, sense bases, and elements connected with the influxes, he is not overcome by them, but rather he himself has overcome all phenomena; hence he is **one who has overcome all**. Because he has known all phenomena—these as well as others—in all aspects, he is **all-knowing**. Because he possesses the bright wisdom that enables him to teach about all phenomena, he is **very wise**. He is without the taints of craving and views [261] by which others are tainted by such things as the aggregates, sense bases, and elements connected with the influxes; hence he is **untainted among all things**. Because he has cast off all these things through the absence of desire and lust for them, he is one **who has cast off all**. With a mind that inclines toward seclusion from acquisitions he is exceptionally freed (*visesena muttattā*) in nibbāna, the destruction of craving; hence he is **liberated** (*vimuttaṃ*) **in the destruction of craving**. What is meant is "intent upon."[886]

He is one the wise know as a muni: He, too, wise beings know as a muni. He highlights himself, saying in effect: "See how distinguished indeed is this muni. How could there be any stain in his teaching?" For here the word *vā* has the sense of highlighting.[887] But some explain: "At that time, when Upaka saw the Tathāgata, he did not believe: 'This is the Buddha-muni.'" The bhikkhus then started their conversation in such a way. The Blessed One then spoke this verse, showing: "Whether he believes or not, the wise know him as a muni."

One with the power of wisdom

212. What is the origin? This verse was spoken with reference to the Elder Revata. Here, the story of Revata's going forth, from the beginning, has been stated in relation to this verse: "Whether in a village or in a forest."[888] After he went forth, he stayed in an acacia woods. While living there he achieved distinction, and the visit and departure of the Blessed One should be understood [as told in the commentary to Dhp 98]. When the Blessed One came back, an old bhikkhu who had forgotten his sandals turned back and found them hanging in a tree. When he reached Sāvatthī, the laywoman Visākhā asked him: "Bhante, is the Elder Revata's dwelling place pleasant?" In his reply he disparaged those bhikkhus who praised it: "Laywoman, they speak falsely. That region is not lovely at all. It is just a miserable, rough acacia woods." Having finished the meal Visākhā had prepared for him, in the afternoon he complained to the bhikkhus who had assembled in the pavilion: "Friends, how can you regard Revata's lodging as pleasant?" [262]

Having known about this, the Blessed One came out from the Fragrant Cottage and, with wonders suitable for the occasion, he sat down in his seat and addressed the bhikkhus: "What was the conversation you were having while you were sitting together here?" They told him: "Bhante, a conversation arose about Revata: 'Since he is a builder, when will he do the ascetic's duty?'"

The Blessed One told them: "Bhikkhus, Revata is not a builder. Revata is an arahant, one whose influxes have been destroyed." Then, with reference to this, he spoke this verse in order to teach the Dhamma to those bhikkhus.

This is its meaning: Because he possesses the power of wisdom through which he abandoned the debilitating defilements or because he has such powers as marvelous transformations and determination, he is **one with the power of wisdom**.[889] Because he is equipped with the four kinds of purified good behavior and the observance of the ascetic practices, he is **equipped with good behavior and observances**. Through the concentration of the path, the concentration of the fruit, and concentration in the postures, he is **concentrated**. **Delighting in jhāna**: delighting *with* jhāna divided into access and absorption, or delighting *in* jhāna; **mindful**: because of abundance of mindfulness; **freed from ties**: because freed from the ties of lust and so forth; **not barren, without influxes**: because of the absence of the five kinds of mental barrenness and the four influxes.[890] **He, too, is one the wise know as a muni**: Wise beings know this one, too, as a muni—one who possesses such excellent qualities as wisdom and is detached from such faults as the ties. He highlights the Elder Revata, saying in effect: "See how distinguished indeed is this arahant-muni. How can it be said of him, 'He is a builder'? or 'When will he do the ascetic's duty?' For he has built his dwelling by the power of wisdom, not by doing building work. He has done his task. Now he need not do the ascetic's duty." For here the word *vā* is used in the sense of highlighting.[891]

Living alone

213. What is the origin? After a sequence of events starting from the site of enlightenment, the Buddha eventually reached Kapilavatthu. At the encounter of father and son, when King Suddhodana (his father) was welcoming him, he said: "Bhante, when you were a householder you wore clothes of cloth from Kāsī made fragrant in a scented casket. How can you now wear worn-out rag robes?" In response, guiding the king, the Blessed One said: [263]

> "Why, father, do you speak of woolen clothes
> and clothes of cloth from Kāsī?
> Rag robes are better than those:
> that is what I have desired."

Showing that he himself was unshakable by worldly conditions, he spoke this seven-line verse in order to teach the Dhamma to the king.[892]

This is its meaning: **Living**—by acting in different postures—**alone**, in the way designated the going forth and so on.[893] A **muni** because of possessing the qualities of munihood; **heedful** in all situations through absence of heedlessness; **not swayed by blame and praise**: not disposed to aversion and preference due respectively to **blame**—abuse, criticism, and so forth—and **praise**, acclaim, adulation, and so forth. And here the eight worldly conditions can also be understood under the heading of blame and praise. **Like a lion not alarmed among sounds**: not experiencing a change in his natural condition when encountering the eight worldly conditions, or absence of alarm when living in remote lodgings, like a lion among the sounds of drums and so forth. **Like the wind not caught in a net** made of thread and so forth; through the four paths, he is **not caught** (unattached) in the net of craving and views. Or he is not caught (unattached) by way of aversion and fondness in encounters with the eight worldly conditions. **Like a lotus not tainted by water**: Though born in the world, by having abandoned the taints—the taints of craving and views through which beings are tainted by the world—he is **not tainted** by the world.

Having given rise to the path leading to nibbāna, he is **a leader of others**—of devas and human beings—along that path. **Not by others led**: because he cannot be led by anyone else who might show him the path. **He, too, is one the wise know as a muni**: He highlights himself, saying in effect: "They know the Buddha-muni." The rest in the way stated.

One who is like a pillar at a ford

214. What is the origin? The sectarians could not tolerate the great gain and honor that accrued to the Blessed One after he first attained full enlightenment on account of his 100,000 excellent qualities, such as: the excellent quality of undertaking the complete ten basic pāramīs, the ten intermediary pāramīs, and the ten supreme pāramīs over four incalculables and 100,000 eons; [264] after he fulfilled the pāramīs, the excellent quality of his rebirth in the Tusita heaven; the excellent quality of his dwelling there; the excellent quality of his great survey of the world; his entry into the womb, his dwelling in the womb, his emergence from the womb, taking steps, surveying the directions, and thundering like Brahmā; his great renunciation, great striving, full enlightenment, and setting in motion the wheel of the Dhamma; the fourfold knowledge of the paths and fruits; the knowledge through which he remains unshakable in the eight assemblies; the knowledge of the ten powers, the knowledge demarcating the four modes of generation, the knowledge demarcating the five destinations; the fourteen kinds of buddha-knowledge, including the six knowledges not shared in common with others and the eight kinds of buddha-knowledge shared with disciples; the knowledge demarcating the eighteen excellent qualities of a buddha; the nineteen kinds of reviewing knowledge; the seventy-seven kinds of knowledge; and so forth. Hence they instructed the young woman Ciñcā to defame the Blessed One in the midst of the four assemblies, in the way told in the background story to the verse "One who oversteps one principle."[894]

On this account the bhikkhus started a conversation: "When the Blessed One was being defamed there was no alteration of his mind." Having known about this, the Blessed One came out from the Fragrant Cottage and, with wonders suitable for the occasion, he sat down in his seat and addressed the bhikkhus: "What was the conversation you were having while you were sitting together here?" They told him everything. The Blessed One then said: "Bhikkhus, the buddhas remain impartial amid the eight worldly conditions." He then spoke this verse in order to teach the Dhamma to the bhikkhus. [265]

This is its meaning: Just as a rectangular or octagonal pillar is planted at a ford, at a bathing place for people,[895] so they can rub their bodies against it: when those from high families and those from low families rub their bodies against it, there is no elation or dejection in the pillar; so too, **one who remains steadfast like a pillar at a ford when others speak provocative words about some matter**. What is meant? "When others, sectarians or others, speak extreme words to him about a certain matter—whether lofty words by way of praise or derogatory words by way of dispraise—he does not fall into either fondness or aversion toward them in regard to that matter, but in his impartiality he remains steadfast like a pillar at a ford."

Devoid of lust, with well-concentrated faculties: "devoid of lust" through the absence of lust for a desirable object, and "with well-concentrated faculties" because of the absence of hatred and delusion toward an undesirable object. Or else he is one whose faculties are steady because they have been well collected; what is meant is one whose faculties are not distracted, one without impulsive faculties.[896] **He, too, is one the wise know as a muni**: They know the Buddha-muni. He highlights himself, saying in effect: "How could there be alteration in his mind?" The rest in the way stated.

One inwardly firm

215. What is the origin? It is said that the daughter of a financier in Sāvatthī came down from her lodge and went to the weaving hall below the lodge. Seeing the people working a shuttle, she acquired the counterpart sign based on its straightness. She thought: "Oh, may all beings abandon crookedness of body, speech, and mind and have minds as straight as a shuttle!" Having again ascended the mansion, she sat down, averting again and again to that same sign. As she practiced in such a way, in no long time the characteristic of impermanence became clear to her, and following on this, the characteristics of suffering and non-self became clear. The three states of existence then appeared to her as if blazing. The Blessed One, seated in the Fragrant Cottage, aware that her insight had reached such a stage, sent forth a luminous image of himself. Having seen the luminous image, she turned her attention to it, wondering: "What is that?" Having seen the Blessed One as if he were sitting beside her, [266] she stood up with her palms joined in reverence. Then, having understood what was suitable for her, the Blessed One spoke this verse in order to teach her the Dhamma.

This is the meaning: One is **inwardly firm**[897] when, because of one's one-pointedness of mind and unshakable liberation, there is no more progress and decline; and when, because one has finished wandering on in birth, there is no more approaching another existence. One is **straight as a shuttle** because one has abandoned crookedness of body, speech, and mind, or because one would not take a wrong course of action.[898] Because one possesses a sense of moral shame and moral dread, one is **disgusted with actions that are evil**: One is disgusted with evil actions, ashamed of them, as if they were excrement and urine.[899] **Investigates the uneven and even**: With the wisdom of the path that accomplishes the functions of abandoning and development [respectively in regard to the uneven and even], investigating and examining the uneven as unevenness (non-rectitude) of bodily action and so forth, and the even as evenness (rectitude) of bodily action and so forth, **he**—that arahant—**is one the wise know as a muni**. What is meant? One inwardly firm, investigating the uneven and the even with the wisdom of the path in the way stated, thereby becomes as straight as a shuttle; not falling into any transgression, he is disgusted with actions that are evil. **He, too, is one the wise know as a muni**: Showing the arahant-muni, as "one who is like this," he taught the verse with its culmination in arahantship. At the conclusion of the teaching the financier's daughter was established in the fruit of stream-entry. And here the word *vā* should be seen as indicating a disjunction or a conjunction.[900]

One self-controlled does nothing evil

216. What is the origin? It is said that when the Blessed One was dwelling at Āḷavī, a certain weaver commanded his seven-year-old daughter:[901] "Daughter, yesterday not much thread remained on the shuttle. Having turned the shuttle, you should come quickly to the weaving hall. Do not be late!" – "Yes," she said. Having gone to the hall, she remained there weaving thread.

That day, after emerging from the meditative attainment of

great compassion, the Blessed One surveyed the world and saw that this girl had the supporting condition for the fruit of stream-entry; [267] he also saw that, at the conclusion of the teaching, 84,000 living beings would make the breakthrough to the Dhamma. So, having taken care of his bodily needs early, he took his bowl and robe and entered the city. When people saw the Blessed One, they approached him, thinking: "Surely today there is someone to be benefited, for the Blessed One has entered early." The Blessed One stood along the path by which that girl was to return to her father. The citizens swept that area, sprinkled it with water, made a presentation of flowers, set up a canopy, and prepared a seat. The Blessed One sat down on the seat prepared for him, and the multitude stood around him. When the girl reached that area, she saw the Blessed One surrounded by the multitude and bowed down to pay homage to him. The Blessed One asked her: "Girl, where have you come from?" – "I do not know, Blessed One." – "Where are you going?" – "I do not know, Blessed One." – "You do not know?" – "I know, Blessed One." – "Then you know?" – "I do not know, Blessed One."

When the people heard this, they complained: "See, sirs! Though this girl has come from her own house, when asked by the Blessed One, she said: 'I do not know.' And though she is going to the weaver's hall, when asked, she again said: 'I do not know.' When the Blessed One said, 'You do not know?' she said: 'I know.' When he said, 'Then you know?' she said: 'I do not know.' Everything she says is contradictory."

Wishing to make the meaning clear to the people, the Blessed One asked her: "What did I ask you and what did you say?" She replied: "There is no one, Bhante, who does not know that I am coming from home and going to the weaver's hall. But you asked me, 'Where have you come from?' with reference to rebirth, and 'Where are you going?' with reference to death. I do not know where I have come from, whether from hell or the deva world. Nor do I know where I will go, whether to hell or the deva world. Therefore I said: 'I do not know.' Then the Blessed One asked me, with reference to death, [268] 'You do not know?' and I know: 'Death is certain for all.' Hence I said: 'I know.' When the Blessed One asked me, with reference to the time of death, 'Then you know?' since I do not know when I will die, whether today or tomorrow, I said: 'I do not know.'"

The Blessed One approved of her answers: "Excellent! Excellent!" The multitude also applauded her, saying: "This girl is wise!" Then, having understood what was suitable for the girl, the Blessed One taught her the Dhamma:

"This world is blind,
few here have insight.
Like a bird freed from a net,
few go to heaven." (Dhp 174)

At the conclusion of the verse, she was established in the fruit of stream-entry, and 84,000 living beings made the breakthrough to the Dhamma.

Having paid homage to the Blessed One, she returned to her father. When her father saw her, he said, "You're late," and in his anger he forcefully threw the loom on the strings. Coming out, it pierced the girl's belly, so that she died right on the spot. Seeing this, he thought: "I did not strike my daughter, but this loom came out forcefully and pierced her belly. Is she alive or not?" Investigating, he saw that she was dead and thought: "People will accuse me of killing my own daughter and then the king might impose a harsh punishment. Let me flee before this happens!" Fleeing from fear of punishment, he came to the Blessed One, learned a meditation subject, and arrived at the dwelling place of bhikkhus living in the forest. He approached those bhikkhus, paid homage to them, and asked for the going forth. They gave him the going forth and taught him the meditation subject on the first five parts of the body.[902]

Having learned it, he strived hard and in no long time attained arahantship, as did his teacher and preceptor. Then they all went to the Blessed One for the great Pavāraṇā, thinking: [269] "We will hold the Pavāraṇā ceremony in purity."[903] When the Blessed One had performed the Pavāraṇā and completed the rains retreat, he set out on tour, accompanied by the Sangha of bhikkhus, and eventually he arrived at Āḷavī. The people there invited the Blessed One to a meal offering, and while giving alms they saw that bhikkhu and taunted him thus: "Having killed his daughter, whom has he come to kill now?" The bhikkhus heard this, and when they approached to attend on the Blessed One they reported this matter to him. The Blessed One said: "Bhikkhus, this bhikkhu did not kill his daughter. She died because of her own kamma." He then spoke this verse in order to teach the Dhamma to the bhikkhus, showing how hard it is for people to understand who is an arahant-muni.

This is its meaning: **One self-controlled**[904] through the control exercised by good behavior in the three doors of action; **does nothing evil**, such as harming others by body, speech, or mind. And he never does so **when young**, abiding in the stage of youth, **and when middle-aged**, abiding in the middle stage of life; and in the same way, if he is an elder, one abiding in the last stage of life. Why not? Because **the muni is restrained**: one whose mind refrains from all evil through the unsurpassed abstinence.

Now this is the construing and purport of the terms: "Irreproachable, he does not scold anyone": That arahant-muni is **irreproachable**, he does not deserve to be scolded, provoked, or harassed either by body or speech with such terms as "daughter-killer" or "weaver" and so forth; for **he does not scold anyone**, he does not scold, provoke, or harass anyone by saying: "I did not kill my daughter. You killed her, or one like you killed her." Further, he should be revered in the way stated thus: "Let the nāga be, do not provoke the nāga, pay homage to the nāga" (MN I 143,12). **He, too, is one the wise know as a muni**: Here the division of words should be understood thus: "The wise ones know him, too, as a muni." And the purport here is this: "These foolish people [270] scold him, not knowing that he is irreproachable. But those who are wise—they know him, too, as a muni. They know: 'He is an arahant-muni.'"

Whether from the top

217. What is the origin? In Sāvatthī, it is said, there was a brahmin known as "giver of the five best things" (*pañcaggadāyako*).[905] When the grain was ripening, he gave these five best things: from the best field, from the best heap, from the best granary, from the best pot, and from the best food. After he had the first ripe crops of hill rice, barley, and wheat brought to him, he had porridge, milk rice, rice cakes,[906] and other things prepared, and since he held the view "The intelligent person who is a giver of the best achieves the best," he gave alms to the Sangha of bhikkhus headed by the Buddha. This was his *gift from the best field*. When the mature crops were cut and threshed, he took the best grains and, in the same way, gave alms. This was his *gift from the best heap*. Again, having filled the granaries with the grain, when the first granary was opened, he took the first grain to be brought out and used it to give alms in the same way. This was his *gift from the best granary*. But whatever was prepared in his own house, he did not give it even to his own children unless he had first given the best of this to monks who arrived. This was his *gift from the best pot*. Again, at the time for his own meal, when food was presented to him he did not eat unless he had first given to the Sangha in the forenoon and to beggars in the afternoon, and if none came, even to the dogs. This was his *gift from the best food*. In this way he came to be designated "the giver of the five best things."

One day, just before dawn, the Blessed One surveyed the world with the buddha eye and saw that this brahmin and his wife had the supporting condition for the path of stream-entry. Having taken care of his bodily needs, [271] he entered the Fragrant Cottage early. When bhikkhus see that the door of the Fragrant Cottage has been shut, they know: "Today the Blessed One wishes to enter the village alone." At the time for the alms round, they circumambulated the Fragrant Cottage and then entered the village for alms. At the time for the brahmin's meal, the Blessed One too came out and entered Sāvatthī. Having seen the Blessed One, people knew: "It seems today there is some being to be benefited; therefore the Blessed One has entered alone." Thus they did not approach the Blessed One in order to invite him to a meal. In stages, the Blessed One reached the door of the brahmin's house and stood there. Now on that occasion the brahmin, having taken his food,[907] was seated, while his wife was standing near him holding his fan. Having seen the Blessed One, she thought: "If this brahmin sees him, he will take the Buddha's bowl and give him all his food, and then I will have to cook again." Feeling displeased, miserly, she positioned the fan in such a way that the brahmin did not see the Blessed One. Aware of this, the Blessed

One sent forth his bodily aura. When he saw the golden radiance, the brahmin looked up, thinking, "What is this?" and he saw the Blessed One standing at the door. The brahmin's wife, too, aware that he had seen the Blessed One, immediately put down the fan, approached the Blessed One, and bowed down in homage to him. As she was rising, the Blessed One, knowing what was suitable for her, spoke this verse:

"One who, in regard to name and form,
takes nothing to be 'mine,'
who does not sorrow over what is nonexistent—
he is truly called a bhikkhu." (Dhp 367)

At the conclusion of the verse, she was established in the fruit of stream-entry. [272] The brahmin, too, brought the Blessed One into the house, offered him the best seat, gave him the water of offering, and presented him with the food prepared for himself, saying: "Bhante, among those worthy of offerings in the world with its devas, you are foremost. Please let me put my food in your bowl." To benefit him, the Blessed One accepted it and ate it. When he had finished his meal, having known what was suitable for the brahmin, he spoke this verse.

This is its meaning: Because it is taken first from the pot it is **from the top**.[908] That which comes from the remainder of the [upper] half of the pot, because it is taken from there, is **from the middle**. That which comes from the remainder of the pot, down to merely one or two spoons, because taken from there, is **from the remainder**. **An alms-collector**:[909] a monk; for apart from water and toothwood, whatever else he lives by is given by others, therefore he is called "one who lives on what is given by others." **He does not think to praise it or disparage it**: If he gains something from the top, because he has abandoned fondness, he does not think he should praise himself or the donor. If he gains something from the remainder, because he has abandoned aversion, he does not speak displeasing words that denigrate the donor, such as "Why has he given this?" **He, too, is one the wise know as a muni**: "The wise know one who has abandoned fondness and aversion, too, as a muni." Thus he taught the brahmin the verse with its culmination in arahantship. At the conclusion of the verse the brahmin was established in the fruit of stream-entry.

The muni who lives abstaining from sexual union

218. What is the origin? In Sāvatthī, it is said, the son of a financier was enjoying himself with all kinds of excellence in his three mansions, built to accommodate the seasons,[910] when, though young, he wished to go forth. He asked his mother and father for permission. As explained in relation to the Discourse on the Rhinoceros Horn, in the origin of the verse "Sensual pleasures are colorful" (pp. 458–59), he went forth and disrobed three times, but the fourth time he attained arahantship. On account of his previous behavior, the bhikkhus said to him: "It's time, friend, to disrobe." But he replied: "Friends, I am now incapable of disrobing." Having heard this, the bhikkhus reported it to the Blessed One. The Blessed One said: "So it is, bhikkhus. He is now incapable [273] of disrobing." The Blessed One then spoke this verse, disclosing that the young man was now an arahant-muni.

This is its meaning: He is **a muni** because he is possessed of the qualities of munihood; **living** by dwelling alone or by acting in accordance with any of the types of conduct previously stated. He is **abstinent from sexual union** by the unsurpassed abstinence, not even forming thoughts about sexual activity as in the past. The connection with the second line is this: If it is asked, "What kind of muni is it that lives while abstinent from sexual union?" it is said: **One who even in youth is not bound anywhere**; that is, one who is not bound, as he was earlier, by sexual lust for the form of any woman, even one in the bloom of youth.[911] Or alternatively, **anywhere** means toward youth, either his own or that of another. He is one who is not bound by lust with the thought: "I am young or she is young. Let me then indulge in sensual pleasure." This, too, is the meaning here.

Not only does he abstain from sexual union, but he is also **abstinent from vanity**, from the vanity of birth and so forth, **and heedlessness**, loss of mindfulness in connection with the strands of sensual pleasure. Thus, just because he abstains from vanity and heedlessness, he is **fully released** from all the bonds of the defilements. Or he is not like one who abstains through mundane abstinence, but rather he is **fully released and abstinent**. Because he is fully released from all the bonds of the defilements, he is abstinent through world-transcending abstinence: this, too, is the meaning. **He, too, is one the wise**

know as a muni: He shows: "The wise know him, too, as a muni. But you do not know him; hence you speak in such a way."

Having known the world

219. What is the origin? The Blessed One was dwelling at Kapilavatthu. On that occasion they performed three auspicious ceremonies for Nanda: the ornamentation ceremony, the consecration ceremony, and the wedding ceremony.[912] The Blessed One was also invited, so he went along with five hundred bhikkhus. Having eaten, as he was leaving he gave Nanda his bowl. When Janapadakalyāṇī[913] saw him leaving, she said to him: "Come back quickly, young master." [274] Out of respect for the Blessed One, Nanda was unable to say, "Take the bowl, Blessed One," so he went to the monastery. Standing in the cell of the Fragrant Cottage, the Blessed One said: "Bring the bowl, Nanda." Having taken it, he asked him: "Will you go forth?" Out of respect for the Blessed One, Nanda was unable to refuse, so he said: "Let me go forth, Blessed One." The Blessed One then gave him the going forth.

Recalling again and again the request of Janapadakalyāṇī, Nanda became fed up with the monk's life. The bhikkhus reported this to the Blessed One. Wishing to dispel Nanda's dissatisfaction, the Blessed One asked him: "Have you ever gone to the Tāvatiṃsa heaven, Nanda?" Nanda replied: "I have not, Bhante."

Then, through his own spiritual might, the Blessed One led him to the Tāvatiṃsa heaven and stood at the door of the Vejayanta palace. Sakka, aware that the Blessed One had arrived, came out from the palace accompanied by a multitude of celestial nymphs. Since they had all given oil for foot massage to the disciples of the Blessed One Kassapa, they had dove-like feet. Then the Blessed One addressed Nanda: "Do you see, Nanda, these five hundred nymphs with dove-like feet?" All should be elaborated.

There is no place in the entire Word of the Buddha which says that one should grasp the marks and features of a woman. But here the Blessed One, through his skill in means, is like a physician who wishes to remove toxins from a patient by first softening them. In this case, wishing to remove Nanda's lust by first softening it, as the unsurpassed trainer of persons to be tamed he instructed Nanda to grasp the marks and features of women like good food.[914]

Afterward, having seen that Nanda was delighting in the spiritual life for the sake of celestial nymphs, the Blessed One ordered the bhikkhus: "You should chide Nanda with the word 'hireling.'"[915] Being chided by the bhikkhus, Nanda was ashamed, and attending carefully, he undertook the practice and in no long time realized arahantship. A deity dwelling in a tree at the end of his walkway reported this matter to the Blessed One. Personal knowledge of this also arose in the Blessed One. But the bhikkhus, [275] unaware of this, continued to chide Nanda just as they did earlier. The Blessed One then spoke this verse in order to teach the Dhamma to the bhikkhus, showing that he was now an arahant-muni, [saying in effect]: "Bhikkhus, now Nanda should no longer be chided in such a way."

This is its meaning: **Having known the world** of the aggregates and so forth; having known, having delineated them by *delineation of the truth of suffering*. **A seer of the supreme goal**: by *realization of the truth of cessation*. He has **crossed**, surmounted, the fourfold **flood** by *abandoning of the origin*; and because he has abandoned the origin, he has also **crossed the ocean**—the sense bases of the eye and the other sense bases—by enduring the waves that consist of forms and the other sense objects[916] through *the development of the path*. He is **an impartial one**, by this attainment of the characteristic of impartiality, as it is said: "an impartial one through this description."[917] Or else the heap of defilements such as sensual lust and so forth is called a flood in the sense of sweeping downward,[918] and an ocean in the sense of whipping up, by turning one over to a contemptible destination.[919] The meaning and purport here [in relation to Nanda] should be understood in this way, too: "By abandoning the origin, he has crossed over that flood and ocean. Now that he has crossed the flood, though you speak to him in such a way, he is an impartial one since he does not show any vexation." **Whose knots are cut, unattached, without influxes**: This is a statement extolling him. He is one *whose knots are cut* because, by the development of the four truths, he has cut through the four knots.[920] He is *unattached* because he is not attached to anything through views or craving. And he is *without influxes* through the absence of the four influxes. **He, too, is one the wise know as a muni**: He shows: "The wise know him, too, as an arahant-muni. But you do not know him; hence you speak to him in such a way."

The two are dissimilar

220. What is the origin? A certain bhikkhu was dwelling in a forest where he was supported by a frontier village in the realm of Kosala. A hunter in that village went to the bhikkhu's dwelling place while pursuing deer. When entering the forest he would see the elder wandering for alms in the village, and when coming out from the forest he would see the elder leaving the village. [276] Thus by often seeing him, there arose in him affection for the elder. When he obtained abundant meat, he gave the elder tasty almsfood. People complained: "This bhikkhu informs the hunter, 'Deer are dwelling in such and such a place, wandering around and drinking water.' Then the hunter kills the deer. Thus both scheme to maintain their lives." Then the Blessed One, while walking on tour through the countryside, came to that region. Bhikkhus who entered the village for alms heard this news and reported it to him. The Blessed One then spoke this verse in order to teach the Dhamma to those bhikkhus, indicating that this bhikkhu was an arahant-muni and thereby demonstrating that his way of life was not at all similar to that of the hunter.

This is its meaning: "Bhikkhus, these **two are dissimilar**—the bhikkhu and the hunter. When people say, 'Their way of life is the same,' that is wrong. Why so? Because **their dwelling and conduct [are] far apart**: Their 'dwelling' is their dwelling place: that of the bhikkhu is in the forest; that of the hunter is in the village. Their 'conduct' is their way of life: that of the bhikkhu is walking on alms round in the village without skipping any houses; that of the hunter is killing deer and fowl in the forest. Further, **the layman supporting a wife**: The hunter supports his wife and children by his work; **and the ascetic owning nothing**: the arahant-bhikkhu, an ascetic because of the purity and excellence of his observances,[921] has no ownership over wife and children based on craving and views. Again, **the layman is unrestrained in harming other living beings**: That hunter, a layman, is unrestrained by way of body, speech, and mind with respect to the harming of other living beings, because he cuts off the life faculty of those beings; **while the muni, ever restrained, protects living beings**: But the other, the arahant-muni, being self-controlled, ever restrained by body, speech, and mind, protects living beings. In such a case, how can their way of life be the same?"

Just as the blue-necked peacock

221. What is the origin? While the Blessed One was dwelling at Kapilavatthu, a discussion arose among the Sakyans: "In terms of the Dhamma, one who becomes a stream-enterer first is senior to one who attains stream-entry afterward. Therefore a bhikkhu who becomes a stream-enterer afterward [277] must pay homage and perform other acts of respect to a layman who becomes a stream-enterer before him." A certain bhikkhu, wandering for alms, heard this discussion and reported it to the Blessed One. The Blessed One, with reference to the principle "This type is different; the form is the basis for veneration,"[922] said: "Bhikkhus, even if a layman is a non-returner, he must pay homage and perform other acts of respect even to a novice who has gone forth that same day." Again, he spoke this verse in order to teach the Dhamma to the bhikkhus, showing the great distinction between a bhikkhu who has become a stream-enterer afterward and a householder who became a stream-enterer earlier.

This is its meaning: The **peacock**, flying in the sky, is called a "crested one" (*sikhī*) because of the presence of a crest (*sikhā*) growing on its head, and a "blue-necked one" because its neck is similar in appearance to a jeweled staff. **A goose**: Among the several kinds of geese—the green goose, the copper-colored goose, the milk-colored goose, the black goose, the drinking goose, and the golden goose—it is the golden goose that is meant here. In terms of speed, the peacock does not approach even a sixteenth of the speed of the golden goose. For the golden goose travels a thousand yojanas in just an hour, while the other cannot even cover a yojana. But in terms of appearance, both are beautiful. Thus although **the layman** who becomes a stream-enterer first is beautiful because of his seeing of the path, **he is no match for** the speed of **the bhikkhu** who becomes a stream-enterer afterward, while the latter is equally beautiful because of his seeing of the path.

What kind of speed is involved here? The speed of insight knowledge for the higher paths. For the layman's knowledge is sluggish, since he is entangled with his wife and children, while a bhikkhu's knowledge is sharp, because he is free from such entanglement. This meaning is indicated by the Blessed One with the line **a muni meditating secluded in the woods**. For this bhikkhu who is a trainee-muni is secluded by bodily and mental seclusion, and he constantly meditates in the woods by closely meditating on the characteristics and the object.[923] The purport here is this: "How can a layman obtain such seclusion and meditation?"

II The Minor Chapter
(*Cūḷavagga*)

1 Gems
(*Ratana Sutta*)

[278] What is the origin?[924] In the past, it is said, disasters such as famine arose in Vesālī. In order to quell them, the Licchavis went to Rājagaha, asked the Blessed One to come, and brought him to Vesālī. When he arrived, the Blessed One spoke this discourse in order to quell those disasters. That is a concise account, but the ancients have explained its origin in detail starting from the story of Vesālī. That should be understood as follows. [158][925]

The chief queen of the king of Bārāṇasī, it is said, became pregnant. Aware of this, she informed the king. The king gave her caretakers during her pregnancy. Being properly cared for, when her time of labor arrived, she entered the delivery room. Now in the case of women possessing merit, the baby emerges at the approach of dawn, and the queen was one who had merit. Thus, at the approach of dawn, she gave birth, but to a lump of flesh, which was like a *bandhujīvaka* flower covered with a layer of lac.[926] She thought: "I might be disgraced in the king's eyes by those who say: 'Other queens give birth to sons that are like golden dolls, but the chief queen gave birth to a lump of flesh.'" Therefore, from fear of being disgraced, she put the lump of flesh in a jar, sealed it, had it stamped with the king's seal, and had it cast into the Ganges. However, as soon as the men disposed of it, deities set up watch over it. They inscribed on gold leaf, with natural vermilion, the words "The offspring of the chief queen of the king of Bārāṇasī" and tied it to the jar. The jar was carried off by the stream of the Ganges, undamaged by waves and other dangers.

Now at the time a certain hermit was living on the bank of

the Ganges, supported by a family of cowherds. In the morning, when he entered the Ganges, he saw the jar coming along, and thinking it was a discarded piece of cloth, he caught hold of it. He then saw the gold leaf inscribed with the words and the king's seal stamped on it. He opened it and saw the lump of flesh. [159] Thinking, "This may be a living fetus, for it does not have a foul odor or show signs of decay," he brought it to his hermitage and kept it in a clean place. After half a month, there were two lumps of flesh. When he saw this, the hermit put them in a better place. After another half a month, each lump sent forth five protuberances, which were to form hands, feet, and a head. After still another half-month, one lump of flesh had become a boy who was like a golden doll; the other became a girl. The hermit felt affection for them as if they were his own children, and milk came forth from his thumb; from then on he obtained meals of milk. Having eaten his meal, he sprinkled the milk into the mouths of the infants. Whatever entered their bellies was all visible, as if it had been placed in a crystal jar, so skinless were they. But others say that the skin of one stuck to that of the other as if it had been sewn to it. Thus, because they were skinless, or because they had adhesive skin, they were known as Licchavis.[927]

To nurture the children, the hermit entered the village for alms in the afternoon and returned late in the day. When the cowherds learned he had taken on this chore, they said to him: "Bhante, the nurturing of children is an impediment for monks. Give the children to us. We'll nurture them. You do your own work." The hermit agreed. The next day, the cowherds smoothed the road, scattered flowers, set up flags and banners, and went to the hermitage with much fanfare. The hermit said: "These children have great merit. Bring them up carefully. When they are grown, marry them to one another. Satisfy the king with the five products of a cow, receive a piece of land, and build a city. There you should anoint the prince." He then gave them the children. They [160] agreed with his request, took the children, and nurtured them.

When the children had grown older, while playing, they would get into disputes with the cowherds' children and strike them with their hands and feet. The other children would cry. When their parents asked them, "Why are you crying?" they would say: "These orphans brought up by the hermit struck us violently." Then their parents said: "Those children harass and afflict the other children. They should not be treated well. They should be avoided (*vajjetabbā*)." From then on, it is said, that region, extending for three hundred yojanas all around, was called "Vajjī."[928]

Then the cowherds, having satisfied the king, received that region as a grant. They built a city there, and when the prince was sixteen years of age, they anointed him and made him king. They married him to the girl and made an agreement: "No girl from outside should be brought here as a bride; and no girl from this place should be given to anyone outside." From their first union, twins were born, a daughter and a son, and each time, sixteen times in all, twins were born. As those children grew up, because the city was unable to contain its abundance of parks, gardens, dwelling places, and environs, three times they surrounded it with a wall, each time extending it by an interval of a gāvuta. Because of its repeated extension, it came to be called Vesālī.[929] This is the story of Vesālī.

By the time the Blessed One arose, Vesālī had become large and successful. It had 7,707 royals, and a similar number of princes, generals, treasurers, and so forth.[930] [161] As it is said: "Now on that occasion Vesālī was successful and prosperous, populous, filled with people, and food was plentiful. It had 7,707 mansions, 7,707 houses with a peaked roof, 7,707 parks, and 7,707 lotus ponds" (Vin I 268,4–10).

Some time later a famine struck, with drought and crop failure. First the poor people died, and their bodies were cast outside. Then, drawn by the smell of the corpses, evil spirits entered the city. Then still more people died, and because of the decay a plague broke out. Thus Vesālī was overrun by three perils: famine, evil spirits, and plague. The citizens went to the king and said: "Great king, three kinds of peril have arisen in this city. Such a disaster has never arisen before, even back through seven generations of royalty. This must have occurred now because of some unrighteous deed of yours." The king called everyone to an assembly in the meeting hall and said: "Investigate whether there is any unrighteousness on my part." They investigated his entire lineage but did not see anything.

Since they did not see any fault on the part of the king, they considered: "How can we quell this peril?" Some citizens suggested inviting the six teachers,[931] saying: "As soon as they enter, it will subside." But others said: "The Buddha, it is said, has arisen in the world. The Blessed One, powerful and mighty, teaches the Dhamma for the benefit of beings. As soon as he enters, all the perils will subside." They were pleased with this and said: "But where is the Blessed One now dwelling? If we send for him, [162] would he come?" But others said: "Buddhas are compassionate. Why shouldn't he come? That Blessed One is now living in Rājagaha, and King Bimbisāra serves him. He would never allow him to come."

"Then let us convince the king and bring him."

They gave abundant presents to two Licchavi princes and sent them, accompanied by a large mass of troops, to King Bimbisāra with the mission: "Make our case to Bimbisāra and bring the Blessed One." They went there, gave the presents to the king, and informed him of their plight, saying: "Great king, send the Blessed One to our city." The king did not agree but said: "You yourselves must ask him."

They went to the Blessed One, venerated him, and said: "Bhante, in our city three perils have arisen. If the Blessed One comes, we will be saved." The Blessed One directed his attention to the situation and saw: "When the Discourse on Gems is spoken in Vesālī, its protective power will pervade 100,000 koṭis of world systems and at the conclusion of the discourse 84,000 living beings will make the breakthrough to the Dhamma." Thus he consented.

When King Bimbisāra heard that the Blessed One had consented, he had an announcement made in the city: "The Blessed One has agreed to go to Vesālī." He approached the Blessed One and asked: "Bhante, have you agreed to go to Vesālī?" – "Yes, great king." – "Then wait, Bhante, until we prepare the road."

Then King Bimbisāra had the five yojanas of ground between Rājagaha and the Ganges smoothed out, built a monastery at each yojana along the way, and announced the time for travel to the Blessed One. The Blessed One then set out accompanied by five hundred bhikkhus. The king had the five yojanas of road strewn knee-deep with flowers of five colors, erected flags and banners, full jars,[932] and plantain trees, [163] and provided two white parasols to be held above the Blessed One and one above each bhikkhu. He himself, along with his own retinue, accompanied the Blessed One for five days to the bank of the Ganges, making offerings of flowers, incense, and other items, settling the Blessed One in each monastery along the way, and giving great meal offerings. At the bank of the Ganges, he decorated a boat with all adornments and sent a message to the people of Vesālī: "The Blessed One has come. Prepare the road and let all come forward to receive him." The people of Vesālī decided, "We will double the offerings," and so they smoothed the three yojanas of ground between Vesālī and the Ganges, provided four white parasols for the Blessed One and two for each bhikkhu, and making offerings, they came to the bank of the Ganges and waited there.

Bimbisāra fastened together two boats, made a pavilion, and adorned it with wreaths of flowers and other items. There he set up a seat for the Buddha made entirely of gems. The Blessed One sat down there. The five hundred bhikkhus boarded the boat and sat down in a suitable way. The king entered the water and followed the Blessed One until the water was up to his neck; then he turned back, saying: "Bhante, I will stay here on the bank of the Ganges until the Blessed One returns." The deities above, as far as the Akaniṭṭha heaven, made offerings, as did the nāgas such as Kambala and Assatara living below in the Ganges.[933] In this way, amid great offerings, the Blessed One crossed the Ganges, a distance of a yojana, and entered the Vesālī people's territory.

Thereupon the Licchavi princes, doubling the offerings made by Bimbisāra, went forward in the water up to their necks to receive the Blessed One. At just that moment, at that instant, a great rain cloud arose in the four directions, rumbling, with a spreading peak of darkness punctuated with flashes of lightning. Then, just as the Blessed One [164] put his first foot down on the bank of the Ganges, a portentous shower began to fall.[934] Those who wanted to get wet got wet; but those who did not want to get wet did not get wet. Everywhere the water streamed as high as the ankles, as high as the thighs, as high as the hips, and even up to the neck. All the corpses were swept away by the water into the Ganges, and the region was thereby purified.

The Licchavi royals hosted the Blessed One at intervals of a yojana along the way. They gave abundant meal offerings and led him to Vesālī in three days, making double the offerings of Bimbisāra. When the Blessed One reached Vesālī, Sakka, ruler of the devas, came surrounded by his company of devas, and because of the convergence of powerful devas, most of the evil spirits fled. Standing at the entrance to the city, the Blessed One addressed the Elder Ānanda: "Learn this Discourse on Gems, Ānanda. Then, having taken the items of ritual offering, walk with the Licchavi youths around the three walls of Vesālī and give protection." Then he spoke the Discourse on Gems.

So when it was asked, "By whom was this discourse spoken, when, where, and why?" the answers to these questions were explained in detail by the ancients in this way, starting with the story of Vesālī.

Thus the Blessed One spoke this Discourse on Gems at the entrance to the city of Vesālī on the very day he arrived there, for the purpose of dispelling those disasters. Having learned it, the Venerable Ānanda, reciting it for the sake of protection, took water in the Blessed One's bowl, and walked around the entire city sprinkling the water. As soon as the elder said, "Whatever," those evil spirits that had not already fled—those living off the rubbish heaps, along the walls, and elsewhere—fled through the four gates, so that the gates were crammed. Some, unable to find room at the gates, broke through the walls and fled. As soon as the evil spirits had left, the plague afflicting people's bodies subsided.[935] Coming out, they made offerings to Ānanda with all sorts of incense, flowers, and other items. The multitude [165] perfumed the meeting hall in the middle of the city with all sorts of incense, erected a canopy, decorated it with all adornments, prepared a seat for the Buddha, and led the Blessed One there. The Blessed One entered the hall and sat down in the seat prepared for him. The Sangha of bhikkhus, too, as well as the royals and the people, sat down in the appropriate seats. Sakka, ruler of the devas, drew near together with the assemblies of devas from two deva worlds, and so did other devas. The Elder Ānanda, too, having walked around all of Vesālī and thereby given it protection, came with the residents of Vesālī and sat down to one side. There the Blessed One spoke this Discourse on Gems to everyone. But others assert that the Buddha recited only the first five verses and the rest were recited by Ānanda at the time of invoking the protection.[936] However it may be, why should we be concerned? We will explain this Discourse on Gems in every way.

222. Here, as to the phrase "Whatever beings" in the first verse, **whatever** means whatever they are like, whether ordinary or powerful; **here** is said with reference to the place where they are assembled, in that region at that moment. **Beings** (*bhūtāni*): the word *bhūta* occurs in the sense of existing, as in the statement "If it exists, there is a Pācittiya offense" (Vin IV 25,23); [166] the five aggregates, as in the statement "Do you see, bhikkhus, this has come to be?" (MN I 260,7); the four primary elements beginning with the earth element, as in the passage "The four great elements, bhikkhu, are the cause" (SN III 101,32); an arahant, as in the passage "The being who devours time" (Ja II 260,21); all beings, as in the passage "All beings in the world will lay down the body" (DN II 157,3); plant life such as trees, as in the passage "In the destruction of plant life" (Vin IV 34,34); and the totality of beings from the devas of the four great kings downward, as in the passage "He perceives beings as beings" (MN I 2,1).[937] But here it should be seen as a general term for spirits.

Gathered: assembled. **Of the earth**: born on the earth; **or in the sky**: or those beings born in the sky; the meaning is "all those beings gathered here." And here, "beings in the sky" are those beings arisen anywhere from the Yāma heaven up to the Akaniṭṭha heaven, for they are born in palaces that appear in space. "Beings of the earth" are those below these, from Mount Sineru downward—those beings arisen on the earth and those dwelling in trees, creepers, etc., on the earth; for those are all born on the earth or in trees, creepers, and mountains, etc., connected to the earth.

Thus, having divided all spirit-beings with the two terms, "whether of the earth or in the sky," the Blessed One collects them again under one term and says: "May all beings indeed be happy." **All**: without omission; **indeed**: a word of emphasis that indicates without omitting even one; **beings**: spirits; **be happy** (*sumanā*): May they be happy (*sukhitamanā*), full of rapture and joy. **And then listen carefully to what is said**: [167] "Having attended, having applied their entire mind, let them listen to my teaching, which brings the achievement of celestial excellence and world-transcending happiness."

Thus here the Blessed One first includes beings with an indeterminate expression, "Whatever beings are gathered here." Then he divides them into two with the words "whether of the earth or in the sky." Then he again unites them with the words "may all beings indeed." With the words "be happy in mind," he enjoins them in the achievement of their wish; with the words "listen carefully to what is said," in the achievement of endeavor; and then he concludes the verse by enjoining them in careful attention and hearing the voice of another, in right personal resolve and reliance on good people, and in the causal roots of concentration and wisdom.[938]

223. Therefore, O beings, listen: Here, **therefore**: a word indicating a reason; **O beings**: a vocative; **all of you**: without omission; **listen**: hear. What is meant? "Since you have left your celestial dwellings and your enjoyments there and gathered here in order to listen to the Dhamma, not to see shows and dancing, therefore, O beings, all of you listen." Or alternatively, having seen that they are happy and wish to listen carefully, induced by the statement "May they be happy and listen carefully," he says: "Since, through your happiness, you are equipped with right personal resolution, reliance on good persons, and purity of wish; and since, through your wish to listen carefully, you are equipped with purity of endeavor based on reliance on good persons and hearing the voice of another, therefore, O beings, all of you listen." Or alternatively, since at the end of the previous verse it was said, "to what is said," referring to that as the reason, he says: "Because it is extremely rare to hear me speak on account of the rarity of obtaining the right occasion free from the eight inopportune conditions,[939] and because my speech, proceeding from the excellent qualities of wisdom and compassion, brings numerous benefits, from my wish to speak about them I said to you: 'Listen to what is said.'" That is what is meant by this line of the verse "Therefore, O beings, all of you listen."

Thus, having enjoined the spirits to listen to what he will say by providing this reason, the Blessed One began to speak the words that were to be heard: [168] **Show loving-kindness**

to the human population. This is its meaning: "Establish friendliness, the wish for their welfare, toward the human population that has been afflicted by the three disasters."[940] The purport here is: "I do not speak through my authority as the Buddha, but rather, for your benefit and for the benefit of this human population, I say: 'Show loving-kindness to the human population.'"

And here, through such discourses as the following, and the discourse on the eleven benefits of loving-kindness,[941] it can be understood how loving-kindness is beneficial to those who practice it:

> Those royal rishis who conquered the earth
> with its multitude of beings
> traveled around performing sacrifices:
> the horse sacrifice, the person sacrifice,
> *sammāpāsa, vājapeyya, niraggaḷa*.[942]
> All these are not worth a sixteenth part
> of a well-developed mind of loving-kindness.
>
> One who does not kill or enjoin killing,
> who does not conquer or enjoin conquest,
> who has loving-kindness toward all beings,
> harbors enmity toward none.
>
> If, with a mind free from hate, one arouses
> loving-kindness
> toward just one being, one thereby becomes good.
> Compassionate in mind toward all beings,
> the noble one generates abundant merit. (AN IV 151)

And by way of the following, it can be understood that it is beneficial to those to whom it is practiced:

> A person on whom the deities take compassion
> always sees good fortune. (DN II 89,2)

Thus, having said, "show loving-kindness to the human population," showing that loving-kindness is beneficial to both, now, showing as well the helpfulness [of people to the deities], [169] he says, **who day and night bring you offerings; therefore, being heedful, protect them**. This is its meaning: "Having made pictures, statues, and other images of the deities, having approached shrines, trees, and other sacred places, they make offerings to the deities during the day, and during the dark fortnight and on other occasions they make offerings at night with lamp offerings.[943] Or having given meal tickets, they make offerings during the day by dedicating the merits acquired to the deities, from the protective deities up to the brahmā deities. They arrange all-night preachings of the Dhamma and other events with ornamental parasols, lamps, and garlands, and then make offerings at night by dedicating the merits acquired to the deities. So how could you not protect them? Since by day and at night they make such offerings dedicated to you, **therefore, being heedful, protect them**. Therefore, because of the offerings, protect and guard those people, remove harm from them, promote their benefit; being heedful, arouse gratitude in your hearts, always recollecting them."

224. Having thus shown how human beings are helpful to the deities, in order to quell the disasters and so that devas and human beings might listen to the Dhamma with a proclamation of the excellent qualities of the Buddha, [Dhamma, and Sangha], the Blessed One starts to employ a declaration of truth in the way beginning with the words "Whatever treasure exists." Here, **whatever** exhausts [the subject], as yet undetermined, without omission. A **treasure** is wealth of any kind used anywhere as an instrument of exchange; it is called a treasure because it produces gladness.[944] **Here** designates the human world, **or beyond** other worlds beyond this. Excepting human beings, when it comes to mentioning all worlds, because it is said later, "or . . . in the heavens," excepting both human beings and the heavens, this term ("or beyond") should be understood to include the remaining beings, such as nāgas, supaṇṇas, and so forth. Thus what is described by these two terms ("whatever treasure") is any items used by human beings for exchange and for adornment and enjoyment, such as gold, silver, pearls, *maṇi* jewels, beryl, coral, rubies, and cats-eye, and the treasure of nāgas, supaṇṇas, and so forth, who have arisen in abodes many hundreds of yojanas wide, in palaces made of gems situated on ground strewn with sand consisting of pearls and jewels. [170]

Or in the heavens: in the deva worlds of the sense sphere and the form sphere; for these are called "heavens" because they are moved to, gone to, by means of beautiful kamma, or because they are the very top.[945] **Gem**: whether with an owner or without an owner. A gem is what leads to delight,[946] what brings, produces, and increases delight; this is a designation for whatever is honored and of great value, inestimable, rarely seen, and used by profound beings. As it is said:

> It is honored, of great value,
> peerless, rarely seen,
> used by profound beings:
> hence it is called a gem.

Sublime: highest, supreme, and that with which one cannot be satiated.[947] Thus what is described by this line of the verse is any gem, whether having an owner—such as those in the heavens, in the palaces many yojanas in size and made entirely of gems, the Sudhamma Hall and the Vejayanta Palace, and so forth—and those without an owner, such as those connected to the empty palaces during an era devoid of the arising of a buddha, when beings are filling up the plane of misery, or any others that have no owner, such as those situated in the ground, in the ocean, in the Himalayas, and so forth. **There is none equal to the Tathāgata**. There exists none that compares to the Tathāgata, the Buddha. What is meant? Whatever treasure or gem might be shown, not even one gem here is equal to the Buddha gem.

Take the gem *in the sense of being honored*, for instance, the wheel gem and jewel gem of a wheel-turning monarch. When these have arisen, the multitude does not show honor elsewhere; no one takes flowers and incense and goes to the places of the yakkhas or the spirits. Everyone shows honor and veneration only to the wheel gem and jewel gem, yearns for boons from them, some of which are fulfilled for them. Yet even these are not equal to the Buddha gem. For if something is a gem in the sense of being honored, the Tathāgata alone is a gem. [171] For when a Tathāgata has arisen, powerful devas and human beings do not show honor elsewhere; they do not venerate anyone else. Thus Brahmā Sahampati venerated the Tathāgata with a wreath of gems the size of Mount Sineru, and other devas and human beings such as King Bimbisāra, King Pasenadi of Kosala, and Anāthapiṇḍika did so according to their ability. Emperor Asoka spent ninety-six koṭis of wealth constructing 84,000 monasteries throughout the whole of Jambudīpa dedicated to the Blessed One after he attained final nibbāna, not to speak of honoring others. Further, who else after attaining final nibbāna was given such honor and respect as the Blessed One was at the places of his birth, enlightenment, first sermon, and final nibbāna, or with images and cetiyas and other marks of respect. Thus there is no jewel equal to the Tathāgata in the sense of being honored.

So too with a gem *in the sense of being of great value*. Take, for instance, cloth from Kāsī. As it is said: "Even when it is old, bhikkhus, cloth from Kāsī is beautiful, pleasant to touch, and of great value" (AN I 248,2–4). Yet even that is not equal to the Buddha gem. For if something is a gem in the sense of being of great value, the Tathāgata alone is a gem. For even when the Tathāgata accepts a piece of cast-off cloth, the act is of great fruit and benefit to the donors, as it was in the case of King Asoka. This was of great value to him. And this passage from a discourse, demonstrating the faultlessness of the expression "of great value" in this context, should be known:

> When he accepts a robe, almsfood, lodging, and medicines and provisions for the sick, this deed is of great fruit and benefit for the donors. This, I say, counts as his being of great value. Just as cloth from Kāsī is of great value, so, I say, this person is similar. (AN I 248,16–20)

Thus there is no gem equal to the Tathāgata in the sense of being of great value.

So too with a gem *in the sense of being inestimable*. [172] Take, for instance, *the wheel gem* that arises for a wheel-turning monarch.[948] It has a hub made of sapphire, a thousand spokes made of the seven gems, a rim made of coral, and a linchpin made of dazzling gold; above each group of ten spokes there is a chief spoke[949] the purpose of which is to catch the wind and give off a sound—a sound which, when produced, is like the sound of a highly skilled musical quintet playing in perfect rhythm. On both sides of the hub there are two lion mouths,[950] the inside of which is hollow as with the wheel of a cart. The wheel has no maker or creator but originates naturally with kamma as condition. When the king has fulfilled the tenfold duty of a wheel-turning monarch, on the very day of the uposatha, the full-moon day of the fifteenth, when observing the uposatha with bathed head, he goes to the upper story of his excellent mansion. While he is seated there purifying his precepts, he sees the wheel rising, like the full moon or the sun. Its sound is heard twelve yojanas away and its form is seen a yojana away. When the multitude see it, they become extremely excited, declaring: "It seems a second moon or sun has appeared." Having come above the city, it stops as if with broken axle at the eastern side of the king's inner palace, not too high and not too low, in a place suitable for the multitude to venerate it with offerings of incense, flowers, and other items.

Following this, *the elephant gem* arises, all white, with red feet, with sevenfold stance, with supernormal power, flying through the air, coming from the uposatha family or the six-tusked family.[951] The one coming from the uposatha family is superior; the one coming from the six-tusked family is the lowest of all. Well trained and tame, having taken a retinue twelve yojanas in extent, he travels over all of Jambudīpa [in the morning] and returns to his own capital city before breakfast.

Following this, *the horse gem* arises, all white, with red feet, with raven-black head, with mane like muñja grass, coming from the royal family of the thundercloud. The rest is similar to the explanation of the elephant gem.

Following this, [173] *the jewel gem* arises. The jewel is fine beryl of the finest type, eight-faceted, and well cut, similar in breadth to the hub of a wheel. It comes from Mount Vepulla. Even in fourfold darkness,[952] it illuminates an area a yojana in extent from the top of the king's standard. Thinking it is day, people begin their work by its light and they even see things as small as ants and termites.

Following this, *the woman gem* arises. She is either his original chief queen or she arrives from Uttarakuru or from the Madda royal family. She is free from the six faults, being neither too tall [nor too short, neither too slim nor too stout, neither too dark nor too fair], surpassing human beauty without reaching divine beauty. When it is cool, for the king her limbs are warm; when it is warm, her limbs are cool. Her touch is like a tuft of cotton-wool split open a hundredfold. From her body the scent of sandalwood comes forth, and from her mouth the scent of the waterlily. She possesses numerous excellent qualities, such as rising before [the king and retiring after him].

Following this, *the steward gem* arises, the king's original treasurer. As soon as the wheel gem has arisen, the divine eye is manifested in him whereby for a yojana in extent he sees hidden stores of treasure, both with owners and ownerless. He approaches the king and proposes: "Lord, you dwell at ease. I shall take care of your financial affairs."

Following this, *the governor gem* arises, the king's original eldest son. As soon as the wheel gem has arisen, he acquires extraordinary shrewdness. Having understood with his own mind the minds of people twelve yojanas in extent, he is capable of suppressing and promoting [those who deserve such treatment]. He approaches the king and proposes: "Lord, you dwell at ease. I shall govern the kingdom for you."

Whatever other gem there may be, in the sense of being inestimable, the worth of which cannot be estimated and appraised as worth a hundred or a thousand or a koṭi, among them there is not even a single gem equal to the Buddha gem. [174] For if a gem has the sense of being inestimable, then the Tathāgata alone is a gem, since it is not possible for anyone to estimate and appraise the Tathāgata by way of good behavior, concentration, wisdom, or any other quality, and then determine: "He has just so many excellent qualities or there is someone equal to him or a counterpart to him." There is no gem equal to the Tathāgata in the sense of being inestimable.

So too with a gem *in the sense of being rarely seen*. For instance, even a wheel-turning monarch, who rarely appears, and his gems, such as the wheel gem, are not equal to the Buddha gem. For if a gem has the sense of being rarely seen, the Tathāgata alone is a gem. How can the wheel-turning monarch and other things be considered gems when many of them arise in a single eon? But since the world is devoid of tathāgatas for incalculable eons, a tathāgata is rarely seen, because they arise seldom and infrequently. And this was said by the Blessed One on the occasion of his final nibbāna:

> "The deities, Ānanda, are complaining: 'We have come from far away to see the Tathāgata. Tathāgatas, arahants, perfectly enlightened buddhas arise in the world seldom and infrequently, and today itself, in the last watch of the night, the final nibbāna of the Tathāgata will take place. Yet this powerful bhikkhu is standing in front of the Blessed One blocking our view, so that we do not get a chance to see the Tathāgata in his final hours.'" (DN II 139,19–26)

Thus there is no gem equal to the Tathāgata in the sense of being rarely seen.

So too with a gem *in the sense of being for use by superior beings*. Take, for instance, the wheel gem and other accessories of a wheel-turning monarch. For inferior persons of low-class families, such as caṇḍālas, bamboo workers, hunters, cart makers, or flower scavengers, even if their wealth amounts to hundreds and thousands of koṭis and they live in an excellent seven-story mansion, [175] these do not become manifest for their use even in a dream. Because they become manifest only for use by a khattiya king well born on both sides who has fulfilled the tenfold duty of a wheel-turning monarch, they are items for use by superior beings. Yet even they are not equal to the Tathāgata. For if something is a gem in the sense of being for use by superior beings, the Tathāgata alone is a gem. For the Tathāgata is not for use, even in a dream, by those without supporting conditions who have inverted views, even if they are considered to be superior beings, like the six [non-Buddhist] teachers—Pūraṇa Kassapa and the others—as well as others of a similar nature. But he is of use for those who have supporting conditions, for the great disciples such as Bāhiya Dāruciriya and others born into eminent families, who have penetrative knowledge and vision and are capable of achieving arahantship even at the conclusion of a four-line verse. For these, while accomplishing the unsurpassed sight, the unsurpassed hearing, the unsurpassed service, and so forth (AN III 325–29), make use of him in various ways. Thus there is no gem equal to the Tathāgata in the sense of being for use by superior beings.

As for a gem *in the sense of producing delight*, take for instance the wheel gem of a wheel-turning monarch. When the wheel-turning monarch sees it, he is pleased, and thus it produces delight for the king. Further, the wheel-turning monarch takes a golden water vessel in his left hand and sprinkles the wheel gem with his right hand, saying: "Roll on, good wheel gem! Conquer, good wheel gem!" (DN III 62,6–7, MN III 172,26). Then the wheel gem goes through space toward the east, emitting a sweet sound like a musical quintet, [176] followed by the wheel-turning monarch with his four-division army spread out over twelve yojanas. By the spiritual might of the wheel, he travels not too high and not too low—below the tall trees but higher than the low trees—receiving presents from the hands of those who have come bringing the flowers, fruits, and sprouts on the trees. When opposing kings come to him in supreme humility, greeting him with such words as "Come, great king!" he instructs them thus, "Do not destroy life," and then he leaves. Wherever the king wishes to eat or take a siesta, there the wheel gem descends from the sky and, as if with broken axle, it stops on even ground that is able to provide all such facilities as water and other things. Again, when the king thinks of continuing his journey, it goes on making a sound in the way described earlier, hearing which his twelve-yojana retinue also continues on. In stages, the wheel gem enters the eastern ocean, and as it is entering, the water recedes to the measure of a yojana and remains as if it had become a wall. The people then take the seven gems [from the ocean] as they wish. The king again takes the golden water vessel and sprinkles the area with water, declaring: "From this point on is my kingdom." Then he returns. His army goes in front, the wheel gem comes up behind, and the king is in the middle. Water fills up the places from which the wheel gem has drawn back. In exactly the same way he goes to the southern, western, and northern oceans.

Having thus traveled over the four directions, the wheel gem rises up in space to a height of three yojanas. Standing there, the king surveys, as if it were a grove of lotuses in full bloom, one world sphere adorned with its four great continents and

2,000 islands, which he conquered by the spiritual might of the wheel gem: the continent of Pubbavideha 7,000 yojanas in circumference, adorned with five hundred islands; and so too, the continent of Uttarakuru, 8,000 yojanas in circumference, [177] and the continent of Aparagoyāna, 7,000 yojanas in circumference, and the continent of Jambudīpa, 10,000 yojanas in circumference.[953] While he is surveying it in such a way, abundant delight arises in him. But while that wheel gem produces such delight for the king, it is not equal to the Buddha gem. For if a gem has the sense of producing delight, then the Tathāgata alone is a gem.

What can this wheel gem do? The delight of a wheel-turning monarch produced by all those gems, the wheel gem and the others, does not amount even to a fraction, a sixteenth part, a portion of a sixteenth part, of celestial delight. Yet for the countless devas and human beings who follow his advice, the other kinds of delight that the Tathāgata produces are more excellent and sublime than that celestial delight: the delight of the first jhāna, and the delight of the second, third, fourth, and fifth jhānas; the delight of the base of the boundlessness of space, the base of the boundlessness of consciousness, the base of nothingness, and the base of neither-perception-nor-nonperception; the delight of the path of stream-entry, and the delight of the fruit of stream-entry; the delight of the path and fruit of the once-returner, the non-returner, and the arahant. Thus there is no gem equal to the Tathāgata in the sense of producing delight.

Further, gems are of two kinds, sentient and insentient. The insentient includes the wheel gem and the jewel gem or anything else devoid of sense faculties, such as gold and silver. The sentient extends from the elephant gem to the governor gem, or anything else equipped with sense faculties. And here, between these two kinds of gems, the sentient gem is declared superior. Why? Because insentient gems—such as gold, silver, jewels, and pearls—are used to adorn the sentient, such as the elephant gem.

Sentient gems, too, are of two kinds: animal gems and human gems. Between these, human gems are declared superior. Why? Because the animal gems are used as conveyances for human gems. [178] Human gems, too, are of two kinds: female gems and male gems. Between these, male gems are declared superior. Why? Because female gems provide service to male gems. Male gems, too, are of two kinds: home-dwelling gems and homeless gems. Between these, homeless gems are declared superior. Why? Because even the wheel-turning monarch, the foremost of home-dwelling gems, pays homage by prostration to homeless gems endowed with such excellent qualities as good behavior; they serve them, attend on them, and thereby achieve celestial and human excellence, and in the end attain the excellence of nibbāna.

Homeless gems, too, are of two kinds: noble ones and worldlings. The gem of the noble ones, too, is of two kinds: trainees and arahants. The gem of arahants, too, is of two kinds: dry-insight arahants and those who use serenity as their vehicle. Those who use serenity as their vehicle, too, are of two kinds: those who have reached the perfection of a disciple and those who have not reached it. Between them, those who have reached the perfection of a disciple are declared superior. Why? Because of the greatness of their excellent qualities. The gem of a paccekabuddha is declared superior to one who has reached the perfection of a disciple. Why? Because of the greatness of his excellent qualities. For many hundreds of disciples like Sāriputta and Moggallāna do not approach even a hundredth portion of the excellent qualities of a single paccekabuddha.

The gem of a perfectly enlightened buddha is declared superior to a paccekabuddha. Why? Because of the greatness of his excellent qualities. For if paccekabuddhas sitting cross-legged next to one another were to fill all of Jambudīpa, they would not amount to a sixteenth part or a portion of a sixteenth part of the excellent qualities of a single fully enlightened buddha. And this was said by the Blessed One: "Bhikkhus, to whatever extent there are beings, whether footless or with two feet . . . the Tathāgata is declared the foremost among them" (AN II 34,13–16). In this way, too, there is no gem equal to the Tathāgata. Hence the Blessed One says: "There is none equal [179] to the Tathāgata."

Thus, having stated that other gems are not equal to the Buddha gem, now, with the words "This too is the sublime gem in the Buddha: by this truth, may there be safety," the Blessed One makes a declaration of truth in order to quell the disasters that have arisen for those beings; and this is based not on social class, nor on clan, family status, beauty, or anything else, but on the uniqueness of the Buddha gem through his excellent qualities, such as good behavior, concentration, and so forth, [which are peerless] in the world from the Avīci hell below up to the peak of existence.

This is its meaning: "Whatever treasure or jewel exists here or beyond or in the heavens, because they are not equal to him with respect to excellent qualities, **This too is the sublime gem in the Buddha**. If this is true, then **by this truth, may there be safety** for these living beings—may there be the existence of what is beautiful,[954] namely, health and absence of disaster." And through this verse, as soon as it was recited by the Blessed One, safety came to the royal community and the peril subsided. The command issued by this verse was accepted by the spirits in 100,000 koṭis of world spheres.[955] [180]

225. Having thus declared truth based on the excellence[956] of the Buddha, now, with the words "Destruction, dispassion," he begins to speak about the excellence of the nibbāna-dhamma. Here, because with the realization of nibbāna, lust and the other defilements are destroyed, utterly destroyed; and nibbāna is their mere destruction, their cessation with no further arising; and nibbāna is disconnected from lust and the other defilements both by way of association and by way of object; and when nibbāna is realized, lust and the other defilements fade away, vanish, and disperse; therefore it is called **destruction** and **dispassion**. Since no arising is discerned for it, no vanishing and no change while it persists, therefore it is called **the deathless** in the sense that it is not born, does not grow old, and does not die. It is **sublime** in the sense of being highest and in the sense that one cannot be satiated by it.[957] **Which . . . [he] attained**: which he found, obtained, realized through his own power of knowledge. **Sakyamuni**: He was a Sakyan because he had been born in a Sakyan family, and a muni because he possessed the qualities of munihood; thus he is called Sakyamuni because he was a muni who was a Sakyan.[958] **Concentrated**: with a mind concentrated by the concentration of the noble path. **There is nothing equal to that Dhamma**: There is no type of dhamma equal to that Dhamma called "destruction" and so on attained by Sakyamuni. Therefore, in another sutta, too, it is said: "To whatever extent there are dhammas conditioned or unconditioned, dispassion is declared the foremost among them" (AN II 34,23–26, It 88,3–6).

Thus, having stated that other dhammas are not equal to the nibbāna-dhamma, now, with the words **This too is the sublime gem in the Dhamma**: **by this truth, may there be safety**, the Blessed One makes a declaration of truth in order to quell the disasters that had arisen for those beings; and this is based on the uniqueness of the gem of the nibbāna-dhamma through its excellent qualities as destruction, dispassion, deathless, and sublime. Its meaning should be understood in the way explained in relation to the previous verse. The command issued by this verse, too, was accepted by the spirits in 100,000 koṭis of world spheres.

226. Having thus declared truth with reference to the excellent nature of the nibbāna-dhamma, now, with the words "The purity that the supreme Buddha praised," he begins to speak about the excellent nature of the path-dhamma. Here, "Buddha" means "one who has awakened to the truths" and so forth, [181] and "supreme" means "highest" and "praiseworthy"; so he is "the supreme Buddha" in that he is a buddha and supreme. Or he is "the supreme Buddha" in that he is supreme among buddhas consisting of those awakened after him and paccekabuddhas.[959]

The purity that the supreme Buddha praised: He praised it, revealed it, here and there in such ways as this: "Of paths, the eightfold, the secure way to the attainment of nibbāna" (MN I 508,31), and "I will teach you, bhikkhus, right concentration with its supports and its equipment" (MN III 71,12). **Purity** is the ultimate cleansing by the eradication of the stain of defilements. **Which they call concentration without interval**: They call it "concentration without interval"[960] because it necessarily yields its fruit immediately after its own occurrence. For when the concentration of the path has arisen, there is no obstacle that can prevent the arising of the fruit. As he says:

> This person may be practicing for realization of the fruit of stream-entry, and it may be time for the eon to burn up, but the eon cannot burn up so long as

> this person has not realized the fruit of stream-entry. This is called a person who persists through the eon. All those endowed with the path, too, are those who persist through the eon. (Pp 13, §17)

The equal of that concentration does not exist: The equal of that concentration without interval, the purity praised by the supreme Buddha, does not exist, whether it be form-sphere concentration or formless-sphere concentration. Why? Because by developing these, one arises here or there in the brahma world, but one may again arise in hell or in other realms; but by developing this concentration of arahantship, the noble person reaches the destruction of all arising [in future states of existence]. Therefore in a sutta it is said: "Whatever conditioned dhammas there are, bhikkhus, [182] the noble eightfold path is declared foremost among them" (AN II 34,19–20).

Thus, having stated that other types of concentration are not equal to the concentration without interval, now, with the words **This too is the sublime gem in the Dhamma**: **by this truth**, the Blessed One makes a declaration of truth based on the uniqueness of the gem of the path-dhamma as stated earlier. Its meaning should be understood in the way explained above. The command issued by this verse, too, was accepted by the spirits in 100,000 koṭis of world spheres.

227. Having declared truth with reference to the excellence of the path-dhamma, now, with the words "The eight persons," he begins to speak about the excellence of the Sangha. Here, **persons** are beings; **eight** is their number. The eight are the four practicing the path and the four standing in the fruit. **Praised by the good**: praised by good persons, by buddhas, paccekabuddhas, disciples, and other devas and human beings. Why? Because they possess such excellent qualities as innately good behavior and so forth. For just as such flowers as the campaka and vakula are innately colorful and fragrant, so these persons have such excellent qualities as innately good behavior and so forth. Hence, like those flowers endowed with color and fragrance, they are dear, agreeable, and praiseworthy among good devas and human beings. Hence it is said: "The eight persons praised by the good."

Or alternatively, **persons** are beings; and **aṭṭhasataṃ (108)** is their number.[961] For there are three stream-enterers: the one-seed attainer, the family-to-family attainer, and the seven-times-at-most attainer. And there are three once-returners: those who attain the fruit in desire-sphere existence, in form-sphere existence, and in formless-sphere existence. All these become twenty-four by [taking each of the six] in correlation with the four modes of practice. There are five [non-returners] in the Aviha pure abode: the attainer of nibbāna in the interval, the attainer of nibbāna upon landing, the attainer of nibbāna without exertion, the attainer of nibbāna through exertion, and the one bound upstream, heading toward the Akaniṭṭha realm. And so too in the Atappa, Sudassa, [183] and Sudassī pure abodes. But there are four in the Akaniṭṭha, excluding the one bound upstream; thus there are twenty-four non-returners. Arahants are of two kinds, the dry-insight arahant and the one who uses serenity as a vehicle. There are four standing on the path, thus fifty-four. All these are twofold by way of those whose progress is governed by faith and those whose progress is governed by wisdom; thus they come to 108.[962] The rest in the way stated earlier.

Constitute these four pairs: All these persons, described in detail as eight or 108, can be concisely grouped into four pairs: one pair consisting of the one standing on the path of stream-entry and the one standing in the fruit, and so on up to the pair consisting of the one standing on the path of arahantship and the one standing in the fruit. **Worthy of offerings**: The persons who were spoken of in detail as eight or 108, and concisely as forming four pairs, are all worthy of offerings, that is, they deserve offerings. "Offerings" are gifts given out of faith in kamma and its fruit, without such considerations as: "He will give me medical service or run messages for me." Persons endowed with such excellent qualities as good behavior deserve those offerings, and these are such; hence they are called "worthy of offerings."

The Fortunate One's disciples: The Blessed One is the Fortunate One because he is endowed with a beautiful manner of going, and because he has gone to the beautiful state, and because he has gone well, and because of enunciating well.[963] All these listen to the word of that Fortunate One; hence they are his disciples.[964] Admittedly, others too listen, but having listened, they do not take up the task to be done. But these, having listened, take up what is to be done, the practice that accords with the Dhamma, and they have attained the paths and the fruits; hence they are called disciples. **Gifts given to them yield abundant fruit**: Even small gifts given to these disciples of the Fortunate One, because of the purification of the offerings through the recipient, are of great fruit.[965] Therefore in another sutta it is said: "To whatever extent, bhikkhus, [184] there are sanghas or groups, the Sangha of the Tathāgata's disciples is declared the foremost among them, that is, the four pairs of persons, the eight types of individuals—this Sangha of the Blessed One's disciples . . . the result is foremost" (AN II 34,29–33).

Thus, having spoken of the excellence of the Sangha gem by way of all those who stand on the path or in the fruit, now, with the words **This too is the sublime gem in the Sangha**, the Blessed One makes a declaration of truth based on that excellence. Its meaning should be understood in the way explained above. The command issued by this verse, too, was accepted by the spirits in 100,000 koṭis of world spheres.

228. Having thus declared truth with reference to the excellence of the Sangha by way of those standing on the path and in the fruit, now, with the words "Those who strived well," he begins to speak about the excellent nature of only those arahants who are enjoying the bliss of the attainment of fruition. Here, **strived well**: those who, having abandoned the numerous kinds of improper search, based on a pure way of life, have undertaken to strive well by applying themselves to insight. Or alternatively, **strived well**: endowed with purified bodily and verbal endeavor; by this he shows their aggregate of good behavior. **With a firm mind**: with a mind endowed with stable concentration; by this he shows their aggregate of concentration. **Who are desireless**: those who, unconcerned with body and life, have departed from all defilements through energy governed by wisdom;[966] by this, he shows their aggregate of wisdom accompanied by energy. **In Gotama's teaching**: In the teaching of the Tathāgata himself, who is a Gotama by way of clan. By this he shows that there is no departure from defilements for those outside here[967] who undertake the diverse kinds of austerity aimed at immortality,[968] since they lack such excellent qualities as proper striving and so forth.

Have reached attainment: Here, "attainment" is what is to be attained. "What is to be attained" is what is worth attaining—that which, having attained, they are ultimately secure from bondage; [185] this is a designation for the fruit of arahantship. They have reached that attainment. **The deathless** is nibbāna. **Having plunged**: having plunged into it by taking it as object; **free of charge**: without expense,[969] without having to pay even a penny. **Perfect peace**: the attainment of fruition, in which defilements and disturbances have subsided. **Enjoying**: experiencing. What is meant? "Those said to have reached attainment are those endowed with good behavior who have strived well in Gotama's teaching, who are firm in mind because they are endowed with concentration, and who are desireless because they are endowed with wisdom. Having plunged into the deathless through this right practice, they are enjoying 'perfect peace,' a designation for the attainment of fruition, which they have obtained free of charge."

Thus, having spoken of the excellence of the Sangha gem by way only of arahants who are enjoying the bliss of the attainment of fruition, now, with the words **This too is the sublime gem in the Sangha**, the Blessed One makes a declaration of truth based on that excellence. Its meaning should be understood in the way explained above. The command issued by this verse, too, was accepted by the spirits in 100,000 koṭis of world spheres.

229. Having thus declared truth with the Sangha as a basis with reference to the excellence of arahants, now, with the words "As a gate post," he begins to speak about the excellence of the stream-enterer alone, which is directly perceptible to the multitude.[970] Here, **a gate post** (*indakhīla*) is a term for a post made of heartwood planted four or five meters in the ground within the threshold of a city for the purpose of holding in place the city gate. **Planted in the ground**: driven into the ground and supported there. **By the four winds**: by the winds coming from the four directions. **Would be unshakable**: it cannot be made to shake or quake. **Similarly I speak of the good person who, having experienced them, sees the noble**

truths: who sees the four noble truths by plunging into them with wisdom. Here, the noble truths should be understood in the way explained in the *Visuddhimagga* (chap. 16).

This here is the concise meaning: "As [186] a gate post planted in the ground, on account of its deep base, cannot be shaken by the four winds, so I speak of this good person as similar, one who, having experienced them, sees the noble truths. Why? Because, just as that gate post cannot be shaken by the four winds, this person cannot be shaken by all the 'winds' of the followers of other sects. Through his vision he cannot be made to shake or quake." Therefore it is said in another sutta:

> "Suppose, bhikkhus, there was an iron pillar or a gate post with a deep base, securely planted, immobile, unshakable. Even if a forceful blast of wind comes—whether from the east, the west, the north, or the south—that pillar would not shake, quiver, or tremble. For what reason? Because the pillar has a deep base and is securely planted. So too, those ascetics or brahmins who understand as it really is: 'This is suffering' . . . 'This is the way leading to the cessation of suffering'—they do not look up at the face of another ascetic or brahmin, thinking: 'He is surely one who really knows, who really sees.' For what reason? Because they have clearly seen the four noble truths." (SN V 444,17–32)

Thus, having spoken of the excellence of the Sangha gem by way of the stream-enterer alone, who is directly perceptible to the multitude, now, with the words **This too is the sublime gem in the Sangha**, the Blessed One makes a declaration of truth based on that excellence. Its meaning should be understood in the way explained above. The command issued by this verse, too, was accepted by the spirits in 100,000 koṭis of world spheres.

230. Having thus declared truth with the Sangha as a basis with reference to the excellence of the stream-enterer in general, now, with the words **Those who have cognized the noble truths**, he begins to speak about the excellence of the lowest grade of stream-enterers, the seven-times-at-most attainer. For there are three kinds of stream-enterers: the one-seed attainer, the family-to-family attainer, and the seven-times-at-most attainer. As it is said:

> Here, a person, with the utter destruction of three fetters, is a stream-enterer. . . . One who, after generating only one more existence, makes an end of suffering is *a one-seed attainer*. One who, after roaming and wandering on among good families two or three times, [187] makes an end of suffering is *a family-to-family attainer*. One who, after roaming and wandering on among devas and humans seven times, makes an end of suffering is *a seven-times-at-most attainer*.[971]

Who have cognized: who, with the radiance of wisdom, have dispelled the darkness of defilements concealing the truths and thereby made them clear and evident to themselves. **The noble truths**: This should be understood in the way stated. **Well taught**: taught well in various ways, conjointly, separately, totally, partly, and so forth; **by the one of deep wisdom**: by the one whose wisdom, because immeasurable, offers no foothold to the knowledge of worldly beings including the devas; what is meant is, "by the Omniscient One." **Even if they are extremely heedless**: Even if those persons who have discerned the truths are extremely heedless because they occupy susceptible positions, such as king of the devas or a wheel-turning monarch, nevertheless, because they have the knowledge of the path of stream-entry,[972] when the name and form that might arise in seven more existences in beginningless saṃsāra have ceased and passed away, following the cessation of the volitionally active consciousness they **do not take an eighth existence**:[973] in the seventh existence itself they undertake insight and attain arahantship.

Thus, having spoken of the excellence of the Sangha gem by way of the seven-times-at-most attainer, now, with the words **This too is the sublime gem in the Sangha**, the Blessed One makes a declaration of truth based on that excellence. Its meaning should be understood in the way explained above. The command issued by this verse, too, was accepted by the spirits in 100,000 koṭis of world spheres.

231. Having thus declared truth with the Sangha as a basis with reference to the seven-times-at-most attainer's excellence, the fact that he does not take an eighth existence, now the Blessed One begins to speak about the excellence of one who, though taking seven more existences, is still distinguished from other persons who have not abandoned the taking up of existence. He says: "Together with one's achievement of vision." [188] Here, **one's** means one of whom it is said, "they do not take an eighth existence." **Achievement of vision**: attainment of the path of stream-entry. For the path of stream-entry is called "vision" because it is the very first seeing of nibbāna that accomplishes the task to be done upon seeing nibbāna.[974] The manifestation of this in oneself is "the achievement of vision." Together with that achievement of vision, **three things are discarded**. The meaning here is: "together with one's achievement of vision, three things are discarded, are abandoned."[975]

Now, to show the things that are abandoned, he says: "the view of the personal entity and doubt, and whatever good behavior and observances there are." Here, **the view of the personal entity** is the twentyfold view occurring in regard to *the existing entity* (body), the actually occurring entity (body), a designation for the five aggregates subject to clinging.[976] Or "the view of the personal entity" is also *the existing view* in regard to the entity, the view that exists in regard to the kind of entity described just above (that is, the five aggregates). Or "the view of the personal entity" is also the view simply in regard to the existing entity, meaning that when the kind of entity described just above exists, it is the view that occurs thus, "the self consists in form," and so forth. And with the abandoning of that, all speculative views are also abandoned, for that is their root.

Wisdom is called "a cure" (*cikicchita*) because it quells all the illness of the defilements. The cure by wisdom has departed from this, or that has departed from this cure by wisdom, thus it is called **doubt**.[977] This is a designation for the uncertainty in eight cases described in the way that begins "He doubts the Teacher."[978] With the abandoning of this, all doubts are abandoned, for that is their root.

Such behavior as the cow behavior and dog behavior, and such observances as the cow observance and dog observance,[979] are what is called **good behavior and observances**; this has come down thus: "The assertion of ascetics and brahmins outside here, [189] that 'purity is achieved through good behavior, purity is achieved by observances'" (Dhs 265, §1222). With the abandoning of this, all austerities aimed at immortality,[980] such as going naked, shaving the head, and so forth, are abandoned, for that is their root. Hence it is said at the end **whatever good behavior and observances there are**. And here it should be understood that the personal-entity view is abandoned with the seeing of suffering; doubt is abandoned with the seeing of its origin; and [attachment to] good behavior and observances is abandoned with the seeing of the path and the seeing of nibbāna.

Having thus shown the abandoning of the round of defilements, now, since the round of results must occur when the round of defilements exists,[981] he says, **One is also freed from the four planes of misery**,[982] showing the abandoning of that [round of results] too as a consequence of the abandoning of that [round of defilements]. Here, the four planes of misery are hell, the animal realm, the sphere of afflicted spirits, and the company of asuras; though taking seven more existences, one is freed from these.

Having thus shown the abandoning of the round of results, now, since the round of kamma is the root of this round of results, showing the abandoning of that as well he says: **and [one] is incapable of doing six deeds**. Here, the deeds referred to are gross misdeeds, and he is incapable of doing these six. These should be understood to be matricide, patricide, killing an arahant, drawing the blood [of the Buddha], creating a schism in the Sangha, and acknowledging someone other [than the Buddha] as one's teacher, as stated in the Group of Ones: "It is impossible and inconceivable, bhikkhus, that a person possessing right view could deprive his mother of life," and so forth (AN I 27,13 foll.).

Although a noble disciple possessing right view would not even deprive an ant or termite of life, nevertheless, these are stated to show how reprehensible the state of a worldling is. Because he does not possess right view, the worldling might even commit these highly blameworthy deeds, while one with vision is incapable of doing them. And the impossibility is stated here to show that he would not do this even in another existence. For in another existence, although he may not recognize his status as a noble disciple, by his very nature he would not do these six things, nor would he violate the five kinds of enmity—the ordinary [190] taking of life and so forth—which, together with acknowledging someone other [than the Buddha] as one's teacher, constitute six things. With reference to this, some read the line as "six and six deeds."[983] The example here is that of the collecting of dead fish, and so forth, by village children who were noble disciples.[984]

Thus, having spoken of the excellence of the Sangha gem by way of the excellence of one who, though taking seven more existences, is still distinguished from other persons who have not abandoned the taking up of existence, now, with the words **This too is the sublime gem in the Sangha**, the Blessed One makes a declaration of truth based on that excellence. Its meaning should be understood in the way explained above. The command issued by this verse, too, was accepted by the spirits in 100,000 koṭis of world spheres.

232. Having thus declared truth with the Sangha as a basis with reference to the excellence of one who, though taking seven more existences, is still distinguished from other persons who have not abandoned the taking up of existence, the Blessed One now shows: "One possessing vision is not only incapable of doing the six deeds but is also incapable of concealing even a trifling bad deed that he may have done." Thus, with the words "Although one does a bad deed," he begins to speak about the excellence of one possessing vision who, even though dwelling heedlessly, does not conceal what he has done.

This is its meaning: It was said by the Blessed One, with reference to the intentional transgression considered a fault by the world: "When a training rule has been laid down by me for disciples, my disciples do not transgress it even for the sake of life" (AN IV 201,10; Ud 55,3–4; Vin II 238,35–36). Apart from this, "although a person possessing vision, due to heedless living caused by lack of mindfulness, does **a bad deed by body**, a transgression that is a conventional fault of the kind prohibited by the Buddha, such as building a hut contrary to regulations or sleeping together with one not fully ordained;[985] or a bad deed **by speech**, such as making a person not fully ordained recite the Dhamma word for word, teaching the Dhamma to a woman in more than five or six sentences, or engaging in idle chatter or speaking harshly;[986] [191] or a bad deed **by mind**, such as giving rise to greed or hatred on any occasion or consenting to gold and silver, or neglecting to reflect on the use of the robes and other requisites, **one is incapable of concealing it**." When he realizes, "This is unallowable and should not be done," he does not conceal it even for a moment but immediately discloses it to the Teacher or to wise fellow monks, makes amends in accordance with the Dhamma, or restrains himself in regard to matters that call for restraint, resolving not to act in such a way again.

Why? Because **such inability is stated for one who has seen the state**: It is stated that a person possessing vision who has seen the nibbāna-state is unable to conceal any bad deed that he has done. How? "Bhikkhus, just as a young, tender infant lying prone at once draws back when he puts his hand or foot on a live coal, so too, this is the character of a person who possesses right view: although he may commit some kind of offense for which a means of rehabilitation has been laid down, still he at once confesses, reveals, and discloses it to the Teacher or wise fellow monks, and then enters upon restraint for the future" (MN I 324,13–16).

Thus, having spoken of the excellence of the Sangha gem by way of the excellence of one possessing vision who, even though dwelling heedlessly, does not conceal a wrong deed, now, with the words **This too is the sublime gem in the Sangha**, the Blessed One makes a declaration of truth based on that excellence. Its meaning should be understood in the way explained above. The command issued by this verse, too, was accepted by the spirits in 100,000 koṭis of world spheres.

233. Having thus declared truth with the Sangha as a basis with reference to the various excellent qualities of the persons included in the Sangha, now the Blessed One, pointing out the excellence of the Triple Gem, again begins to declare truth with the Buddha as a basis, referring to the Dhamma of scriptures taught concisely here and in detail elsewhere. He says: "Like a woodland thicket with flowering crests." Here, a woodland (*vana*) is a multitude of trees marked off by their proximity of location. [192] A thicket (*pagumba*) is a cluster of trees mature in roots, heartwood, softwood, bark, branches, and foliage. A **woodland thicket** (*vanappagumba*) is a thicket in a woodland.[987] **With flowering crests**: with crests that are flowering; with flowers blossoming on all its branches and twigs.[988] In the way explained earlier, that is what is meant by "with flowering crests."

In a summer month, in the first of the summer: in one month of the four months of the summer. In what month? **The first of the summer**: in the month of Citra. For that is called "the first of the summer" or "the youthful spring."[989] From this point on the meaning of the terms is clear. This here is the concise meaning: "In the youthful spring, called 'the first of the summer,' in a woodland grove dense with various kinds of trees, a thicket whose branches have full flowering crests is exceptionally glorious. Just so, by indicating the path leading to nibbāna, he taught the excellent scriptural Dhamma leading to nibbāna—the Dhamma that is exceptionally glorious with its various flowers, analyzed into such things as the aggregates and sense bases, or the establishments of mindfulness and the right strivings, or the groups of virtuous behavior and concentration and so forth. He taught it **for the supreme welfare** of beings, solely because his heart was stirred by great compassion, not for the sake of such things as gain or honor. He taught it for the supreme welfare, nibbāna."[990]

Thus, having spoken of the excellence of the scriptural Dhamma, which is similar to a woodland thicket with full flowering crests, now, with the words **This too is the sublime gem in the Buddha**, the Blessed One makes a declaration of truth founded on the Buddha that is based on that [quality of the Dhamma]. Its meaning should be understood in the way explained above, except that this sublime gem in the Buddha should be construed as the scriptural Dhamma in the aspect stated. [193] The command issued by this verse, too, was accepted by the spirits in 100,000 koṭis of world spheres.

234. Having thus declared truth founded on the Buddha and based on the scriptural Dhamma, now the Blessed One begins to speak about the world-transcending Dhamma with the words "The excellent one, knower of the excellent."[991] Here, **excellent**: What is excellent is what is wished for by those intent on the sublime when they exclaim, "Oh, indeed, may we too be like this!"[992] Or "excellent" means possessed of choice qualities, what is highest or best. **Knower of the excellent**: knower of nibbāna. For nibbāna is excellent in the sense that it is the highest of all things, and he knew this when he himself penetrated it at the foot of the bodhi tree. **Giver of the excellent**: He was a giver of the excellent Dhamma, which partakes of penetration and partakes of habituation,[993] to the group of five, the fortunate group, the matted-hair fire ascetics, and others, both devas and human beings.[994] **Bringer of the excellent**: Because he brought the excellent path, he is called "bringer of the excellent." For while fulfilling the thirty pāramīs starting from the time of Dīpaṅkara,[995] he brought along the excellent ancient path that had been followed by the perfectly enlightened buddhas of the past; hence he is called "bringer of the excellent."

Further, he is "the excellent one" because he obtained the knowledge of omniscience; "knower of the excellent" through the realization of nibbāna; "giver of the excellent" by giving the bliss of liberation to beings; and "bringer of the excellent" by bringing the highest practice. Because no one surpasses him in regard to these world-transcending qualities, he is **unsurpassed**.

Another method: He is "the excellent one" by fulfillment of the foundation of peace; "knower of the excellent" by fulfillment of the foundation of wisdom; "giver of the excellent" by fulfillment of the foundation of relinquishment; and "bringer of the excellent" by fulfillment of the foundation of truth, since he brought the excellent truth of the path.[996] So too, he is "the excellent one" through his accumulation of merit; "knower of the excellent" through his accumulation of wisdom; "giver of the excellent" by imparting the means for attaining buddhahood to those who desire it; "bringer of the excellent" by bringing the means for attaining paccekabuddhahood to those who desire it; and "unsurpassed" because he is without equal in diverse matters, or because he was the teacher of others while he himself was without a teacher. He **taught the excellent Dhamma**, because for their sake he taught those who desire discipleship the excellent Dhamma, which is endowed with such qualities as being well expounded. The rest in the way explained.

Thus, having spoken of his own excellence with reference to the ninefold world-transcending Dhamma,[997] now, [194] with the words **This too is the sublime gem in the Buddha**, the Blessed One makes a declaration of truth founded on the Buddha based on that same quality. Its meaning should be understood in the way explained above, except that this sublime gem in the Buddha should be construed through the excellent ninefold world-transcending Dhamma that he knew, gave, brought, and taught. The command issued by this verse, too, was accepted by the spirits in 100,000 koṭis of world spheres.

235. Having thus declared truth founded upon the Buddha based on the scriptural Dhamma and the world-transcending Dhamma, now, with the words "The old is destroyed," the Blessed One again declares truth founded upon the Sangha based on the excellence of the attainment of nibbāna without residue by those who have listened to the scriptural Dhamma, practiced in accordance with what they have heard, and achieved the ninefold world-transcending Dhamma. Here, **the old is destroyed**: that pertaining to the past is eradicated; **there is no new origination**: manifestation of what is not currently existing; **their minds are dispassionate**: their minds are devoid of lust; **toward future existence**: toward renewed existence at a future time. **With seeds destroyed**: with their seeds cut off; **with no desire for growth**: devoid of desire for growth; **those wise ones**: those bhikkhus with influxes destroyed, who are possessed of resolution,[998] for whom the old is destroyed and there is no new origination, and whose minds are dispassionate toward future existence; **are extinguished like this lamp**: they go out just like this lamp.

What is meant? In the case of ordinary beings the old kamma pertaining to past time has arisen and ceased, but because the moisture of craving has not been abandoned, such kamma has not been destroyed, for it still has the capacity to bring about rebirth. But when their moisture of craving has been dried up by the path of arahantship, that old kamma is destroyed, because, like a seed burnt by fire, it is incapable of yielding results. The kamma that occurs for them now, by venerating the Buddha and other such deeds, is called "new." With the abandoning of craving, that kamma is incapable of yielding fruits in the future, like the flowers of a tree cut down at the root, and so for them there is no origination. In the case of those bhikkhus with influxes destroyed, for whom, by the abandoning of craving, the mind is dispassionate toward future existence, [195] the rebirth-consciousness described thus, "Kamma is the field, consciousness the seed" (AN I 223,22), is itself destroyed with the destruction of kamma; hence they are "with seeds destroyed."

Previously there was desire for "growth," a designation for renewed existence, but when that is also abandoned through the abandoning of its origin, at the time of death, unlike in the past, there is no further origination; thus they are "with no desire for growth." With the cessation of the final occasion of consciousness, those wise ones, so called because they possess intelligence, are extinguished just as this lamp was extinguished. Again, they transcend the range of description as either "possessing form" or "formless" and so forth.

It is said that at that very moment, while lamps were being lit as offerings to the city deities, one lamp went out. Indicating this, he said, "like this lamp."

Thus, having spoken of the excellence of the attainment of nibbāna without residue by those who have listened to the scriptural Dhamma, practiced in accordance with what they have heard, and achieved the ninefold world-transcending Dhamma, as described in the previous two verses, now, with the words **This too is the sublime gem in the Sangha**, the Blessed One concludes the teaching by making a declaration of truth founded upon the Sangha based on that same quality. Its meaning should be understood in the way explained above, except that this sublime gem in the Sangha should be construed through the nibbāna of the bhikkhus with influxes destroyed in the way explained. The command issued by this verse, too, was accepted by the spirits in 100,000 koṭis of world spheres.

At the conclusion of the teaching, safety came to the royal clan, all disasters were quelled, and 84,000 living beings made the breakthrough to the Dhamma.

236–38. Then Sakka, ruler of the devas, reflected: "By making a declaration of truth based on the excellent qualities of the

Triple Gem, the Blessed One has brought safety to the city. For the sake of the city's safety I too should say something based on the excellent qualities of the Triple Gem." Thereupon at the end, he spoke the three verses, "Whatever beings are gathered here." Here, because the Buddha has come thus, in the way those zealous for the welfare of the world should come; [196] and because he has gone thus, in the way they should go; and because he has understood in the way they should understand; and because he has known in the way they should know; and because his utterances are exactly so, he is called "thus gone" (*tathāgata*).[999] And because he is highly venerated by devas and human beings with such external accessories as flowers and incense, and inwardly by practice in accordance with the Dhamma, Sakka, speaking for himself and on behalf of his entire retinue of devas, said: **We pay homage to the thus-gone Buddha, venerated by devas and humans: may there be safety!**

Now in regard to the Dhamma, one eradicating the faction of defilements must go along the path-dhamma through the conjoined power of serenity and insight. And the nibbāna-dhamma is to be "gone to"—penetrated by wisdom—in such a way that one attains the destruction of all suffering, realized in the same way as was done by the buddhas and others;[1000] therefore it too is called "thus gone." And because the Sangha has gone along each path in the way that those practicing for their own welfare must go, it too is called "thus gone." Therefore in the remaining two verses it is also said: **We pay homage to the thus-gone Dhamma . . . may there be safety! We pay homage to the thus-gone Sangha . . . may there be safety!** The rest is clear.

When Sakka had recited these three verses, he circumambulated the Blessed One and then, accompanied by his retinue, returned to the city of the devas. The Blessed One, however, taught the same Discourse on Gems the next day too, on which occasion again 84,000 living beings made the breakthrough to the Dhamma. In such a way, he taught for seven days, and on each day the breakthrough to the Dhamma occurred in the same way.

After staying in Vesālī for half a month, the Blessed One announced to the princes, "I will go." Thereupon the princes doubled their honors [197] and again over three days led the Blessed One to the bank of the Ganges. The nāga kings native to the Ganges reflected: "Human beings honor the Tathāgata. Why don't we?" They then created boats made of gold, silver, and jewels, prepared a divan made all of gold, silver, and jewels, and had the water covered with lotus flowers of five colors. They then approached the Blessed One and said: "Please be so gracious as to accept our offering." The Blessed One consented and embarked on the boat made of gems, while the five hundred bhikkhus each got into their own boat. The nāga kings then led the Blessed One together with the company of bhikkhus to the abode of the nāgas. There, throughout the entire night, the Blessed One taught the Dhamma to the assembly of nāgas. The next day they gave a great alms offering of various kinds of celestial food. The Blessed One spoke words of appreciation and then left the abode of the nāgas.

The earth deities reflected: "Human beings and nāgas honor the Tathāgata. Why don't we?" In the woodland thickets, trees, and mountains, they raised aloft row upon row of parasols, and in this way an extremely great display of honor took place that reached right up to the abode of the Akaniṭṭha brahmās. King Bimbisāra, too, doubled the honors he had shown at the time he came along with the Licchavis, and as explained earlier, he brought the Blessed One back to Rājagaha over a five-day journey.

After the Blessed One arrived back in Rājagaha, one afternoon, when the bhikkhus had assembled in the pavilion, this casual conversation arose: "Oh, the spiritual might of the Blessed One, the Buddha! It was on account of him that in the region extending eight yojanas on either side of the Ganges they made the low land and high land even, spread sand over it, and covered it with flowers. And for a yojana the waters of the Ganges were covered with variously colored lotus flowers, and row upon row of parasols were raised aloft right up to the Akaniṭṭha heaven."

Having known about this event, the Blessed One came out from the Fragrant Cottage and, with wonders suitable for the occasion, sat down in the excellent seat prepared for him in the pavilion. [198] He then addressed the bhikkhus: "What was the conversation you were having while you were sitting together here?" They told him everything.

The Blessed One said: "This distinguished offering, bhikkhus, was not produced for me by my spiritual might as a buddha, nor by the spiritual might of the nāgas, devas, and brahmās. Rather, it was produced by the spiritual power of a slight act of generosity in the past."

The bhikkhus said: "Bhante, we do not know about that slight act of generosity. Please tell us about it."

The Blessed One spoke: "Once upon a time, bhikkhus, there was a brahmin at Takkasilā named Saṅkha.[1001] He had a son, a young man named Susīma, sixteen years of age, who one day approached his father, paid homage to him, and stood to one side. His father said to him: 'What is it, dear Susīma?' He replied: 'I wish, father, to go to Bārāṇasī to learn a craft.'[1002] – 'In that case, Susīma, the brahmin so and so is my friend. Go and study under him.' He then gave him a thousand *kahāpaṇas*. The young man took the money, paid homage to his parents, and eventually reached Bārāṇasī. He approached the teacher in a respectful manner, paid homage to him, and announced himself. The teacher received the youth as his friend's son and showed him every hospitality. When he had dispelled his fatigue from the journey, the youth placed the thousand *kahāpaṇas* at the teacher's feet and asked for the opportunity to learn a craft. The teacher consented and taught him.

"The boy learned quickly and learned much, and whatever he learned he retained in mind without losing it, as if it were lion oil placed in a golden vessel. After just a few months he completed the study of the craft that [normally] takes twelve years to learn. While making a recitation, he saw only the beginning and middle but did not see the end. He then approached the teacher and said to him: [199] 'I see only the beginning and middle of this craft but I do not see its end.' The teacher replied: 'I too, dear, am in the same position.' – 'In that case, teacher, who knows the end of this craft?' – 'In Isipatana, dear, there are rishis. They may know.' – 'Let me approach them and ask, teacher.' – 'Ask, dear, as you wish.'

"The boy went to Isipatana, approached some paccekabuddhas, and asked them: 'Do you know the beginning, middle, and end?' – 'Yes, friend, we know.' – 'Teach me that, too.' – 'In that case, friend, go forth. It isn't possible for a layperson to learn this.' – 'Please, Bhante, let me go forth, or do whatever you wish so that you can teach me the end.' They then gave him the going forth, but since they were unable to instruct him in a meditation subject, they taught him the principles of proper conduct, such as how to wear the lower robe and the upper robe. As he trained with them, since he possessed supporting conditions, in no long time he realized pacceka enlightenment. In all Bārāṇasī he became known as 'the paccekabuddha Susīma.' He reached the peak of gain and fame and acquired a retinue. However, because in the past he had done kamma leading to a short life span, before long he attained final nibbāna. The other paccekabuddhas and the multitude of people cremated the body, took his relics, and built a stūpa at the entrance to the city.

"Then the brahmin Saṅkha thought: 'My son has been gone a long time, and I have not heard any news about him.' Wishing to see his son, he left Takkasilā and eventually reached Bārāṇasī. Seeing a multitude of people who had assembled there, he considered: 'Surely, someone in this crowd has some news about my son.' So he approached and asked: 'A young man named Susīma has come here. Do you have any news about him?' They replied: 'Yes, brahmin, we know about him. He mastered the Three Vedas under a brahmin in this city, went forth under the paccekabuddhas, [200] and having become a paccekabuddha, he attained final nibbāna through the nibbāna element without residue remaining. This stūpa has been built for him.'

"The brahmin struck the earth with his hand, wept and lamented, went to the terrace of the cetiya, plucked out the weeds, brought sand in his upper garment, and scattered it over the terrace of the paccekabuddha's cetiya. He sprinkled the ground all around with water from his waterpot, made an offering of woodland flowers, set up a banner made from cloth, and tied his own parasol above the stūpa. Thereupon he left."

Having related this birth story about the past, the Blessed One gave the bhikkhus a Dhamma talk connecting it with the present thus: "It may be, bhikkhus, that you think he who at that time was the brahmin Saṅkha was someone else. But you should not look at the matter in such a way. At that time, I was the brahmin Saṅkha. I plucked out the weeds on the terrace of the paccekabuddha Susīma's cetiya. As a consequence of that kamma of mine they removed the stumps and thorns along the eight-yojana journey and made the ground smooth and clean.

I scattered sand there; as a consequence, they scattered sand over the eight-yojana journey. I made an offering of woodland flowers; as a consequence, over the nine-yojana journey including land and water, they made a carpet with various flowers. I moistened the ground with water from my pot; as a consequence, a lotus-leaf rain fell on Vesālī. I set up a banner at that cetiya and tied a parasol there; as a consequence, banners were set up and row upon row of parasols were raised aloft right up to the Akaniṭṭha heaven.

"Thus, bhikkhus, this distinguished offering was not produced for me by my spiritual might as a buddha, [201] nor by the spiritual might of the nāgas, devas, and brahmās. Rather, it was produced by the spiritual power of a slight act of generosity in the past."

At the conclusion of the Dhamma talk, he recited this verse:

> "If by renouncing a slight happiness
> one sees a greater happiness ahead,
> the wise person should give up the slight happiness,
> seeing a greater happiness ahead." (Dhp 290)

2 Carrion
(*Āmagandha Sutta*)

[278][1003] What is the origin? Before the Blessed One arose, a brahmin named Āmagandha[1004] went forth in the manner of a hermit together with five hundred young brahmins. Having entered the Himalayas, he had a hermitage built among the mountains and dwelled there subsisting on roots and fruits from the woods. He never ate fish or meat. Then, because those hermits did not obtain salt, lime, and other supplements, they fell ill with jaundice. They decided to go to a populated area in order to obtain salt, lime, and other supplements, and went to a frontier village. The people there were pleased with them,[1005] invited them to a meal, and fed them. When they finished their meal, the people presented them with beds, chairs, water vessels, foot oil, and other requisites, showed them a dwelling place, and said: "Stay here, Bhante. Do not get fed up." They then departed. The next day, too, they offered them a meal, and on each of the following days as well they offered them meals in rotation.

The hermits lived there for four months, during which time they regained their health by partaking of salt, lime, and other supplements. They then informed the people: "We are going, friends." [279] The people gave them oil, rice grains, and other provisions, which they took along and returned to their own hermitage. Annually, they went to that village in the same way, and when the people knew they were coming, they set aside rice grains for meal offerings, and when the hermits arrived they honored them in the same way.

Then, after the Blessed One arose in the world and set in motion the wheel of the Dhamma, he eventually went to

Sāvatthī. While dwelling there he saw that those hermits had excellent supporting conditions, and so, having left Sāvatthī, walking on tour accompanied by the Sangha of bhikkhus, he eventually reached that village. When they saw the Blessed One, the people made a great meal offering and the Blessed One taught them the Dhamma. As a result, some people became stream-enterers, some once-returners, and some non-returners, and some went forth and attained arahantship. Thereafter the Blessed One again returned to Sāvatthī.

The hermits then went to the village. When the people saw them they did not make a commotion as they did previously. The hermits asked them: "Why, friends, don't you treat us as before? Has the king imposed a penalty on this village, or has there been a famine, or has some other monk come to this village whose virtues surpass ours?" The people said: "The king hasn't imposed a penalty, nor has there been a famine, but a buddha has arisen in the world. Teaching the Dhamma for the welfare of many people, that Blessed One came here."

When he heard this, the hermit Āmagandha said: "Did you say 'buddha,' householders?" – "We said 'buddha,' Bhante." This exchange went on three times, after which the hermit said: "Even that word 'buddha' is rare in the world." Being pleased, having expressed his pleasure, he then asked: "Does the Buddha eat carrion or not?" – "What is carrion, Bhante?" – "Carrion, householders, is a name for fish and meat." – "The Blessed One, Bhante, partook of fish and meat."

Having heard this, the hermit was troubled in mind and thought: "Then he cannot be a buddha." [280] But then he reconsidered: "The appearance of the buddhas is said to be rare. Let me go ask him, and then I will find out for myself." He then set off in the direction of the Blessed One. Having asked people about the way, he traveled quickly like a cow longing for her calf,[1006] spending only one night everywhere along the way until he reached Sāvatthī. He then entered Jeta's Grove along with his own retinue.

At the time the Blessed One was sitting in his seat in order to teach the Dhamma. The hermits came up to the Blessed One and, without paying respects, silently sat down to one side. The Blessed One welcomed them with polite talk: "I hope you rishis are getting along well." They replied: "We are getting along well, Master Gotama." Then Āmagandha asked the Blessed One: "Do you eat carrion or not, Master Gotama?" – "What is it that you call carrion, brahmin?" – "Fish and meat, Master Gotama."

The Blessed One said: "Brahmin, fish and meat are not carrion. Rather, carrion means all defilements and bad unwholesome qualities." Then he added: "It is not only you who ask about carrion now. In the past, too, there was a brahmin named Tissa who asked the Blessed One Kassapa about this. He asked him in just this way, and the Blessed One answered him in just this way." Having brought up the verses spoken between the brahmin Tissa and the Blessed One Kassapa, making his case to the brahmin by means of those verses, [the Blessed One Gotama] said: "Wild millet, grains from grasses, highland pulses." This, firstly, is the origin of the present discourse.

In the past, it is said, after having fulfilled the pāramīs over eight inconceivable periods and 100,000 eons, the bodhisatta Kassapa was reborn in the womb of a brahmin woman named Dhanavatī, wife of the brahmin Brahmadatta. That same day his chief disciple also passed away from the deva world and was reborn in the womb of the wife of the brahmin who served as assistant chaplain. Thus the two were conceived on the same day and emerged from the womb on the same day, and on the same day [281] their elders gave the name Kassapa to one and the name Tissa to the other.

The two were friends from the time they played together as infants and as they gradually reached maturity. Tissa's father instructed his son: "Dear, this Kassapa will renounce the lay life, go forth, and become a buddha. You, too, should go forth under him and find release from the cycle of existence." The boy replied, "Excellent," went to the Bodhisatta, and said: "We will both go forth, friend." The Bodhisatta said: "Excellent." Then, when they reached maturity, Tissa said to the Bodhisatta: "Come, friend, let's go forth." But the Bodhisatta did not renounce the lay life. Tissa considered, "His knowledge has not yet reached maturity," so he renounced on his own, went forth in the manner of the rishis,[1007] and lived at a hermitage that he had built at the foot of a mountain.

Some time later the Bodhisatta, while living at home, developed mindfulness of breathing, attained the four jhānas and the modes of direct knowledge, and having gone by his mansion to the site of enlightenment, he resolved: "Let the mansion settle in the appropriate place." It settled in its own place. Since he knew, "It isn't possible for one who has not gone forth to reach the site of enlightenment," he went forth, reached the site of enlightenment, sat down, and strived for seven days, after which he attained perfect enlightenment.

Then 20,000 monks settled at Isipatana. The Blessed One Kassapa addressed them, set in motion the wheel of the Dhamma, and at the conclusion of his discourse, all became arahants. The Blessed One then lived right there at Isipatana with his retinue of 20,000 bhikkhus. Kikī, the king of Kāsi, provided them with the four requisites.

Then one day a citizen of Bārāṇasī, searching for sandalwood in the mountains, arrived at the hermitage of the hermit Tissa. Having paid homage to him, he stood to one side. The hermit saw him [282] and asked: "From where have you come?" – "From Bārāṇasī." – "What is happening there?" – "Bhante, a perfectly enlightened buddha has arisen there."

Having heard that rare expression, the hermit was filled with rapture and joy and asked him: "Does he eat carrion or not?" – "What is carrion, Bhante?" – "Fish and meat, friend." – "The Blessed One eats fish and meat, Bhante."

When he heard this, the hermit was troubled in mind and thought: "Then he cannot be a buddha." But then he reconsidered: "Let me go and ask him. If he says, 'I eat carrion,' then I will reproach him by saying, 'Bhante, this is inappropriate for one of your birth, family, and clan,' and I will then go forth under him and obtain release from the cycle of existence.' Having taken his light gear, he set out, spending only one night everywhere along the way. He reached Bārāṇasī in the evening and entered Isipatana.

At the time the Blessed One was sitting in his seat in order to teach the Dhamma. The hermit came up to the Blessed One and, without paying respects, silently stood to one side. Having seen him, the Blessed One welcomed him with polite talk in the way stated earlier. He replied: "I am getting along well, Master Kassapa." He then sat down to one side and asked the Blessed One: "Do you eat carrion or not, Master Kassapa?" – "I do not eat carrion, brahmin." – "Excellent, excellent, Master

Kassapa! It is good that you do not consume the corpses of other beings. That is proper for one of your birth, family, and clan."

Then the Blessed One thought: "I said, 'I do not eat carrion' with reference to the defilements, but the brahmin interprets this as fish and meat. Tomorrow, I won't go on alms round in the village but will eat the almsfood that is brought from the home of King Kikī. In this way, a conversation will take place about carrion. I will then make my case to the brahmin with a teaching of the Dhamma."

The next day, having risen early and attended to his bodily needs, he entered the Fragrant Cottage. Seeing that the door of the Fragrant Cottage was shut, the bhikkhus knew, [283] "Today the Blessed One does not wish to enter the village together with the bhikkhus," so they circumambulated the Fragrant Cottage and entered the village for alms.

The Blessed One came out from the Fragrant Cottage and sat down in the prepared seat. The hermit too, having cooked potherbs and eaten, sat down near the Blessed One. Kikī, the king of Bārāṇasī, having seen the bhikkhus walking for alms, asked them: "Where is the Blessed One, Bhante?" When he heard that the Blessed One was in the monastery, he sent him various curries and a dish prepared with differently flavored meats. The ministers brought it to the monastery, informed the Blessed One, gave the water of offering, and then served the meal. They first gave him porridge prepared with various meats. When the hermit saw this, he stood there thinking: "Is he eating it or not?" While he was looking on, the Blessed One, drinking the porridge, put a piece of meat in his mouth. When the hermit saw this he was angry. Again, when he finished drinking the porridge, they gave him food with variously flavored curries. When the hermit saw him accept it and eat it, he was infuriated, thinking: "Even though he eats fish and meat, he said, 'I do not eat them.'" When the Blessed One had finished his meal and washed his hands and feet, while he was still sitting there, the hermit went up to him and said: "Master Kassapa, you spoke falsely. This is improper for a wise man, for false speech is condemned by the buddhas. Even those rishis who live at the foot of a mountain and subsist on woodland tubers and fruits do not speak falsely." He then said, "Wild millet, grains from grasses, highland pulses," again praising in verse the excellent qualities of the rishis.[1008] [284]

239. Righteously obtained: Having abandoned such types of wrong livelihood as serving as a messenger and going on errands [for laypeople], they are obtained by gleaning them in the woodlands. **The good**: the noble ones; **do not speak lies, desiring sensual pleasures**: "Thus the rishis, who are without greed and possessiveness, who eat such fare as wild millet, are not like you. Whereas you, desiring such sensual pleasures as tasty food, eat carrion and speak lies, saying, 'I do not eat carrion, brahmin,' they do not speak lies, desiring sensual pleasures." In this way, by praising the rishis, he levels blame at the Blessed One.

240. Having thus indirectly blamed the Blessed One by his praise of the rishis, he now says, **But eating food**, showing first the basis for the blame he intended and then explicitly blaming the Blessed One. This is the meaning: "Any kind of meat such as rabbit or pheasant that has been prepared beforehand by washing, slicing, and so forth, is **well prepared**. It is **well flavored** in the later stage of preparation, by cooking and flavoring. **Given by others**: given not by one's mother or father but by pious people who consider you worthy of offerings. **Presented with respect**: by showing honor. Consuming **delicious food**: delicious and garnished, with the best flavor, nourishing, and capable of maintaining one's strength and power. Not only enjoying any kind of meat, but also **enjoying a dish of fine rice**—this too, boiled hill rice from which the dark grains have been removed—**you eat carrion, O Kassapa!** Eating any kind of meat, and enjoying this dish made of fine rice, O Kassapa, you eat carrion!" He addresses the Blessed One by his clan name. [285]

241. Having blamed the Blessed One on account of his food, he now says, "You say . . . well prepared with the flesh of fowl," blaming him by accusing him of false speech. This is its meaning: "When questioned by me earlier, **you said, O kinsman of Brahmā, 'Carrion is not proper for me,'** you said this definitively, O kinsman of Brahmā." He speaks disparagingly, [with the intention]: "You are a brahmin merely by birth but devoid of the excellent qualities of a brahmin." **Yet you are enjoying**—eating—**a dish of fine rice, well prepared with the flesh of fowl**: He then pointed to a dish of fowl that had been brought for the Blessed One.

While he was speaking in such a way, he kept on looking upon the Blessed One's body from the soles of his feet up to the tips of his hairs and he observed that he possessed the thirty-two marks of physical excellence and eighty minor features and was enveloped by a fathom-wide aura. He reflected: "One with such a body, adorned with a great man's marks of physical excellence and other features, is incapable of speaking falsely. For this tuft of hair growing between his eyebrows, white and soft like cotton-wool, and the body hairs growing singly in each hair socket, are the outcome of speaking truth in previous existences. So how could he speak falsely now? Surely, he must have a different concept of carrion, with reference to which he said: 'I do not eat carrion, brahmin.' Let me question him about this." Then, with esteem, addressing him simply by his clan, he spoke the rest of this verse: **I ask you about this matter, Kassapa: what do you take to be carrion?**

242. Then, explaining carrion to him, the Blessed One said, "Destruction of life," and so forth. Here, **destruction of life**: the killing of living beings. **Beating, mutilating, binding**: Here, beating beings with rods and other things, cutting off their hands and feet and so forth, and binding them by tying them up with ropes. **Fraudulence**: One says, "I will give this, I will do that," [286] but having aroused an expectation, one does not fulfill it. **Cheating**: One deceives others with counterfeit gold and so forth. **Studying useless subjects**: the study of many unbeneficial works. **Resorting to the wives of others**: committing misconduct with the spouses of others.

This is carrion, but not the eating of meat: This unwholesome conduct, such as the destruction of life, is carrion, a stench, the stink of corpses. For what reason? Because it is disagreeable, because it is mixed up with defilements and impurity, because good people are disgusted by it, and because it leads to being extremely foul-smelling. For beings who are swollen with defilements become very foul-smelling because of them, but even the dead bodies of those without defilements are not foul-smelling. Therefore this is carrion. But the eating of meat is blameless when one has not seen, heard, or suspected [that the animal was killed expressly for oneself].[1009] Therefore the eating of meat is not carrion.

243. Having explained carrion in one way with a teaching that has qualities as its basis, now, since carrion is different for different beings—since it is not the case that one being has all of them, or that everyone has just one—therefore, to elucidate the various types of carrion that beings have, with the words "People here uncontrolled in sensual pleasures," the Blessed One next spoke two verses explaining carrion by means of a teaching that has persons as its basis.[1010]

People here uncontrolled in sensual pleasures: those worldlings here in the world who are uncontrolled because they are devoid of restraint in regard to sensual pleasures—a designation for indulging in sexual pleasure[1011]—since they overstep the boundaries even with their mother, maternal aunts, and so forth. **Greedy for tastes**: greedy for tastes cognizable by the tongue, they enjoy tastes while being tied to them, infatuated with them, and blindly absorbed in them, not seeing the danger and understanding the escape. **Mixed up with impurity**: mixed up with impurity, a designation for the various kinds of wrong livelihood in which they engage because of their greed for tastes, in order to obtain those tastes. **Who hold the nihilist view**: those who have adopted wrong view with its ten cases, "There is nothing given," and so forth.[1012] [287] **Warped**: endowed with warped bodily action and so forth. **Stubborn**:[1013] hard to communicate with; having grasped hold of their own views, they hold to them tightly and relinquish them with difficulty. **This is carrion**: As described in this verse with persons as the basis, six other kinds of carrion should be understood, in the same sense as explained earlier: lack of control in regard to sensual pleasures, greed for tastes, failure in livelihood, moral nihilism, warped bodily misconduct and so forth, and stubbornness. **But not the eating of meat**: The eating of meat is not carrion in the sense stated.

244. In the second verse, too, **those who are rough**: those without enjoyment; the meaning is, "those devoted to self-mortification." **Violent**: rough, difficult to advise. **Backbiters**: those who speak sweetly to one's face but dispraise behind one's back; these are called "backbiters" because they are not able to look at one directly, but when one turns around, they act as if they were eating the flesh off one's back. **Betrayers of friends**: when their friends entrust them with their wives, wealth, and lives, they misbehave with them. **Cruel-hearted**: devoid of compassion, desiring harm for beings. **Arrogant**: possessing the arrogance explained thus: "Here, someone on a certain ground such as birth and so forth despises others; such conceit, self-exaltation of the mind" (Vibh 409, §879; somewhat different in text). **Miserly** (*adānasīlā*): those without a generous nature, not inclined to give, who do not delight in sharing. **Who do not give to anyone** (*na ca denti kassaci*): Because of their miserliness, even when asked, they do not give anything to anyone.[1014] Like the people in a family that has never before given, they are heading for [rebirth among] the afflicted spirits consumed by craving.[1015] But some read *ādānasīlā* ("habitual takers"), those in the habit of only taking things but do not give anything to anyone. **This is carrion, but not the eating of meat**: As described in this verse with persons as the basis, [288] there are eight other things that should be understood as carrion in the sense explained earlier: stringency, violence, backbiting, betrayal of friends, cruel-heartedness, arrogance, miserliness, and not giving. But not the eating of meat.

245. Having thus spoken two verses by a teaching that has persons as its basis, again, having understood what was in conformity with the inclination of the hermit Tissa, the Blessed One spoke one verse by means of a teaching that has qualities as its basis. Here, **anger** should be understood in the way explained in relation to the Discourse on the Serpent (see pp. 365–67). **Vanity**: the swollenness of the mind analyzed in the way explained in the Vibhaṅga thus: "Vanity because of social class, vanity because of clan, vanity because of health," and so forth (Vibh 395, §832). **Obstinacy**: rigidity; **recalcitrance**: contrariness, opposition to what is explained methodically in accordance with the Dhanma; **hypocrisy**: concealment of the evil that one has done in the way analyzed in the Vibhaṅga thus: "Here, someone, having committed misconduct with the body" and so forth (Vibh 413, §894). **Envy**: envy of the gains, honor, and achievements of others; **boastfulness**: swollen speech, extolling oneself; **haughtiness**: analyzed in the Vibhaṅga thus: "Here, someone who previously considered himself on an equal level with others, afterward, on a certain ground such as social class, considers himself superior and others as inferior; such conceit . . . self-exaltation of the mind" (Vibh 409, §880). **Intimacy with the bad**: intimacy with bad people. **This is carrion, but not the eating of meat**: This ninefold heap of the unwholesome—anger and so forth—should be understood as carrion, in the same sense as explained earlier, but not the eating of meat.

246. Having thus shown carrion as ninefold by a teaching that has qualities as its basis, again, in the way explained earlier, the Blessed One spoke three verses explaining carrion by means of a teaching that has persons as its basis. Here, **those ill behaved**: those who, because of their misbehavior, [289] are known in the world as "ill behaved"; **debt-evaders, slanderers**: debt-evaders are those who take a loan but do not pay it back, in the way explained in the Discourse on the Outcast (see pp. 549–50); slanderers are those who speak divisive words. **Crooked in their dealings, dissemblers here**: Those crooked in their dealings, when presiding over a legal case, deal with it crookedly, accepting a bribe and judging against the owners; dissemblers are those who dissemble in legal cases. Or **here** means in the Teaching. **Dissemblers**: those who are immoral; because they imitate the virtuous in their deportment and in other ways, this is dissembling, and that makes them dissemblers. **Vile men who here commit wicked deeds**: Those vile men here in the world who commit wicked deeds, a designation for misconduct toward one's parents, the buddhas and paccekabuddhas, and other worthy ones. These six things described by this verse, which has persons as its basis—bad behavior, evasion of debt, slander, crookedness in dealings, dissembling, and committing wicked deeds—should also be understood as carrion, in the sense explained earlier, but not the eating of meat.

247. Those people here uncontrolled toward living beings: those people here in the world who, acting as they wish, kill even a hundred or a thousand beings, and who are uncontrolled because they do not act with even the least bit of kindness. **Who steal from others, intent on inflicting harm**: those who take the belongings of others, their wealth or their life, and then, when others beg them for mercy or try to prevent them from doing so, are intent on inflicting harm on them with fists, clods of soil, or rods. Or **having captured other** beings,[1016] having taken them up thus, "Ten today, twenty today," they are intent on harming them by killing them, imprisoning them, and so forth. **Immoral, cruel**: immoral because of their misconduct, and cruel because of their vicious and bloody-handed deeds; what is intended here are those who kill fish, trap animals, hunt for fowl, and so forth. **Harsh**: harsh in speech. **Disrespectful**: those devoid of such respect as expressed thus, "Now we will not do such and such, we will refrain from such and such." [290] **This is carrion, but not the eating of meat**: These six things described by this verse, which has persons as its basis—lack of control toward living beings, both in the ways stated earlier as "destruction of life, beating, mutilating, binding" and in other ways, along with the harming of others, immorality, cruelty, harshness, and disrespect—should also be understood as carrion, but not the eating of meat. For some things stated earlier are repeated because the audience wishes to hear them, for emphasis, and to reinforce them. Hence later it will be said: "Thus the Blessed One *repeatedly explained* this matter; the master of the sacred hymns understood it."

248. Those who are greedy toward these, hostile, transgressors: Those who are greedy toward these beings on account of greed, hostile on account of hatred, and, not seeing the danger because of their delusion, transgress by repeatedly committing misconduct. Or they are greedy, hostile, and transgressors through lust, hatred, and delusion, designated respectively greed, hostility, and transgression in committing the evil deeds described in such ways as "destruction of life, beating, mutilating, binding." **Ever intent**: ever intent on doing what is unwholesome, never abstaining through reflection.

Are heading for darkness after death: having gone from this world elsewhere; **beings who fall head first into hell**: those who are heading toward darkness, a designation for interstellar darkness[1017] or birth into low families and so forth; and those who fall head first into hell, Avīci and so forth. **This is carrion**: Carrion in the sense stated is here threefold as greed, hostility, and transgression, which are the roots of all carrion and the causes for heading toward darkness and falling into hell. **But not the eating of meat**: Meat-eating is not carrion.

249. Thus the Blessed One has explained carrion in the ultimate sense and shown it as the path to a bad destination. Now, since the hermit perceives the eating of fish and meat to be carrion and the path to a bad destination, [291] and he does not eat them because he wishes to achieve purity by abstaining from them, the Blessed One speaks this six-line verse, "Neither [avoiding] fish and meat," showing that it is impossible to purify oneself in this way or in any way similar to this. Here, all the terms should be construed in connection with the last line thus: "[Avoiding] fish and meat does not purify a mortal who has not overcome doubt . . . sacrifices, and seasonal penances do not purify a mortal who has not overcome doubt." And here, as to **neither [avoiding] fish and meat**, the ancients explain this thus: "Not eating fish and meat does not purify one, and so for fasting." But it would be better if the line were to be construed thus: "Neither the non-eating of fish and meat," that is, "The non-eating of fish and meat does not . . . purify a mortal."[1018] In such a case, it might be asked, wouldn't fasting be omitted? That is not the case, for it is included elsewhere by austerity.[1019] For all the remaining kinds of self-mortification are included here by the phrase "the many austerities aimed at immortality."

Many austerities aimed at immortality: Bodily afflictions undertaken from a desire for the immortal state.[1020] They are *many* through such types of striving as perpetual squatting and so forth. **Austerities**: bodily torments; **sacred hymns**: the Vedas; **oblations**: performance of the fire offering; **sacrifices and seasonal penances**: sacrifices such as the horse sacrifice and seasonal penances.[1021] Seasonal penances include the practice of standing out in the sun's heat during the hot season, dwelling at the foot of a tree during the rainy season, and entering the water during the cold season.

Neither . . . purify a mortal who has not overcome doubt: They do not purify a mortal who has not overcome doubt either by purifying defilements or by purifying existence. Thus "there is no purification when there is the stain of doubt, and you are still in doubt." And here the purport of this phrase "one who has not overcome doubt" is not that hearing the Blessed One's statement [292] "Neither [avoiding] fish and meat" made the hermit doubt that avoiding fish and meat is the path of purification. Rather, this was said with reference to his doubt about the Buddha when he heard that he eats fish and meat.

250. Having shown that the non-eating of fish and meat is unable to purify one, he now spoke a verse, "One guarded over the sense doors," showing things able to purify one. Here, **the sense doors** are the six sense faculties. **One guarded**: one possessed of restraint over the sense faculties. At this point he has shown good behavior accompanied by restraint of the sense faculties. **Should live with sense faculties understood**: He should live—meaning, he should dwell—having understood the six sense faculties by means of the full understanding of the known; having become clear about them. At this point he has shown the demarcation of name-and-form by one whose behavior has been purified.

Firm in Dhamma: firm in the Dhamma of the four truths, which are to be realized by the noble path; by this, he shows the stage of stream-entry. **Delighting in honesty and mildness**: By this he shows the stage of the once-returner; for a once-returner delights in honesty and mildness through the reduction of lust and hatred, which are the causes of bodily crookedness and so forth as well as of mental rigidity. **A wise one who has overcome the ties**: who has overcome the ties of lust and hatred; by this he shows the stage of the non-returner. **Who has abandoned all suffering**: who has abandoned all suffering by abandoning the cause of all the suffering of the round; **is not tainted by things seen and heard**: Having in this way attained arahantship in stages, the wise one—[called thus] because he is endowed with intelligence—is not tainted by any taint[1022] among things seen and heard. Not only is he not tainted by things seen and heard but also by things sensed and cognized; for he has certainly attained the supreme purification. Thus the Blessed One concludes the discourse with its culmination in arahantship.

251–52. The two verses following this, "Thus the Blessed One," were spoken by the compilers. **Thus the Blessed One** Kassapa **repeatedly explained this matter**: With many verses, through a teaching that has both qualities and persons as its basis, [293] he discussed and elaborated on this matter until the hermit understood it. **The master of the sacred hymns understood it**: The brahmin Tissa, a master of the sacred hymns—a master of the Vedas—understood that matter. By what means? Because **the muni . . . elucidated it with variegated verses.** What was the muni like? **Free of carrion, unattached, hard to lead**: "free of carrion" through the absence of the carrion of defilements; "unattached" through the absence of dependence on craving and views; and "hard to lead" because it was impossible for anyone to lead him by means of an externalist view: "This is better, this is excellent."

Thus, **having heard the Buddha's well-spoken word** as he revealed it, the well-expounded Dhamma teaching, **which was free of carrion**, without defilement, **dispelling all suffering**, dispelling all the suffering of the round, **humble in mind [Tissa] venerated the Tathāgata**: The brahmin Tissa venerated him, prostrating himself at the Tathāgata's feet. **And right there declared he would go forth**: While the Blessed One Kassapa was sitting right there in his seat, the hermit Tissa declared he would go forth, meaning that he requested it.

The Blessed One then said to him: "Come, bhikkhu." Instantly it was as if an elder of a hundred rains, equipped with the eight requisites, had arrived through the sky.[1023] He venerated the Blessed One, and after a few days penetrated the knowledge of a disciple's perfection.[1024] He became the chief disciple named Tissa; the second chief disciple was named Bhāradvāja. Thus the chief disciples of that Blessed One [Kassapa] were named Tissa and Bhāradvāja.

Our Blessed One [Gotama] explained carrion to the five hundred hermits headed by their teacher by bringing up and completing the Discourse on Carrion, which consisted of these fourteen verses: the three initial verses spoken by the brahmin Tissa, the nine middle verses spoken by the Blessed One Kassapa, and the two at the end spoken by the compilers. Having heard this, that brahmin also [294] became humble in mind, venerated the Blessed One's feet, and along with his retinue requested the going forth. The Blessed One said: "Come, bhikkhus!" They also achieved ordination by the "Come, bhikkhu!" utterance, came through the sky,[1025] venerated the Blessed One, and after a few days all were established in arahantship, the foremost fruit.

completing the [illegible] recitation. The [illegible] of these fourteen verses [illegible] initial verse is spoken [illegible] the [illegible] [illegible] that the [illegible] verses [illegible] by [illegible] One Kas[illegible] [illegible] and this that [illegible] [illegible] became [illegible] [illegible] [illegible] One [illegible] and all [illegible] [illegible] going [illegible] One [illegible] [illegible] The [illegible] [illegible] [illegible] [illegible] [illegible] [illegible] [illegible] [illegible] [illegible] [illegible] One and [illegible] [illegible] all [illegible] [illegible] [illegible] [illegible]

3 Moral Shame
(Hiri Sutta)

What is the origin? Before the Blessed One arose, there lived in Sāvatthī a rich brahmin with eighty koṭis of wealth. He had one son, who was dear and beloved to him. He brought the boy up with all sorts of enjoyments and luxuries, as if he were a young deity, but he and his wife died before giving him his inheritance. After the boy's parents passed away, the treasurer opened the treasury, gave him his inheritance, and said: "This, master, is the property of your parents, this comes from your grandfather and great grandfather, this has come down through seven generations." The young man looked at the wealth and thought: "This wealth remains, but those who accumulated it have vanished. All have fallen into the hands of death, and they departed without taking any of it. One must abandon one's wealth and pass on to the next world, and it isn't possible to take anything but one's good conduct. Let me now relinquish this wealth and take the wealth of good conduct, which it is possible to take along when one goes."

Each day he gave away 100,000 coins and then reflected again: "This wealth is abundant. Why give away so little? Let me give a great alms offering." He informed the king: "Great king, there is so much wealth in my home. I wish to give a great alms offering. Please, great king, make an announcement in the city." The king did as requested. The young man filled the receptacles of everyone who came and in seven days gave away all his wealth. [295] He then reflected: "Having made such a great relinquishment, it isn't fitting for me to live at home. Let me go forth." He then informed his retinue about this matter. They pleaded with him in various ways, saying: "Master, don't think that your wealth is exhausted. In a short time, by various means, we will collect wealth." However, without acceding to their request, he went forth in the manner of a hermit.

Hermits are of eight kinds:[1026] (1) those with a wife and children; (2) those who subsist by gleaning; (3) those who subsist when the time arrives; (4) the raw-food eaters; (5) the stone fisters;[1027] (6) the cutters with teeth;[1028] (7) the eaters of growing fruit; and (8) the eaters of things freed from the stems.

Of these, (1) those *with a wife and children* go forth together with their wife and children, earning a living by agriculture, trade, and other means, like the jaṭila Keṇiya (see pp. 249–51). (2) Those who *subsist by gleaning* have a hermitage built near the entrance to the city, and there they train young khattiyas, brahmins, and others in various crafts. Rejecting bullion and gold, they accept allowable goods such as sesamum seeds, rice grains, and other foodstuffs. These are superior to those with a wife and children. (3) Those who *subsist when the time arrives* maintain themselves by accepting food at the time for the meal. These are superior to those who live by gleaning. (4) The *raw-food eaters* maintain themselves by eating leaves and fruits that have not been cooked. These are superior to those who subsist when the time arrives. (5) The *stone fisters* wander around with a fist-sized stone or other implement like an axe or a knife, and when they become hungry they take the bark from the trees they chance upon,[1029] undertake the factors of the uposatha, and develop the four divine abodes. These are superior to the raw-food eaters. (6) The *cutters with teeth* wander around without taking a fist-sized stone or any other implement; when they become hungry they use their teeth to tear the bark off any tree they chance upon, eat it, and then undertake the factors of the uposatha and develop the four divine abodes. These are superior to the stone fisters. (7) The *eaters of growing fruit* live near a natural lake [296] or a woodland thicket. They eat only lotus roots in the lake or, when the thicket bears flowers, they eat flowers and fruits when it bears fruits. If there are no flowers and fruits, they live even by eating the shoots of the trees, but they do not go elsewhere for the sake of food and they undertake the factors of the uposatha and develop the four divine abodes. These are superior to the cutters with teeth. (8) The *eaters of things freed from their stems* eat only leaves freed from their stems and fallen to the ground, but they are otherwise similar to the rest. These are the best of all.

This brahmin youth decided, "Among the different ways that hermits go forth, I will go forth in the foremost manner," and so he went forth as one who eats only things freed from their stems. He traveled across two or three mountains in the Himalayas, built a hermitage, and settled down there.

When the Blessed One arose in the world and had set in motion the wheel of the Dhamma, in stages he went to Sāvatthī, where he lived at Jeta's Grove, Anāthapiṇḍika's Park. At the time a citizen of Sāvatthī, searching for sandalwood, etc., in the mountains, arrived at the hermit's hermitage. Having paid homage to him, he stood to one side. The hermit looked at him and asked: "From where have you come?" – "From Sāvatthī, Bhante." – "What is happening there?" – "People there are heedful and do meritorious deeds such as giving." – "Whose exhortations do they heed?" – "That of the Blessed One, the Buddha." Hearing the word "buddha," the hermit was astonished and asked: "Good man, did you say 'buddha'?"

He asked three times, in the way explained in relation to the Discourse on Carrion (p. 714), and then was pleased, thinking: "Even this utterance 'buddha' is rare in the world." He wanted to visit the Blessed One but then reflected: "It would not be fitting for me to call on the Buddha empty-handed. What should I bring along?" He again reflected: "The buddhas do not value material things. Let me bring a gift of Dhamma." He then formulated four questions: [297] "What kind of friend should one not associate with? What kind of friend should one associate with? To what kind of exertion should one apply oneself? What is the foremost of tastes?" Taking these questions, he set off in the direction of the middle region. He eventually reached Sāvatthī and entered Jeta's Grove.

At the time the Blessed One was sitting in his seat preparing to teach the Dhamma. When he saw the Blessed One, without paying respects, he stood to one side. The Blessed One welcomed him, "Is the rishi getting along well?" and he replied: "I am getting along well, Master Gotama." He then considered, "If he is a buddha, I will ask the questions with my mind and he will answer them verbally," and so he asked the Blessed One those questions only with his mind. In reply the Blessed

One then spoke two and a half verses, beginning "One flouting moral shame," to answer the first question.[1030]

253. Their meaning is as follows: **One flouting moral shame**: one transgressing moral shame, one who is shameless, brazen. **Despising it**: looking upon it as foul; for a shameless person despises moral shame and regards it as foul. Hence he does not resort to it or adhere to it, for which reason it is said: "despising it." **Who says, "I am your friend"**: speaking such words as this: "My dear, I am your friend, desiring your welfare and happiness. For your sake I would even give up my life." **But does not do what can be done**: Having spoken in this way, he does not do what can be done; he does not undertake deeds possible for him to do.[1031] Or alternatively, without arousing even the least bit of respect in his mind in regard to such matters, whenever certain tasks arise, he shows one only [the way that leads to] ruin. **One should know of him: "He is not my [friend]"**: A wise person should know of a friend like this: "He is a bogus friend; he isn't my friend."

254. Who utters endearing speech to his friends: Displaying cordiality with terms referring to the past and the future,[1032] sustaining the relationship in an unbeneficial way, [298] he addresses his friends with speech that is only superficially endearing.[1033] **Without following it up [with deeds]**: He utters words to the effect, "I will give, I will do," but does not follow through on them. **The wise understand this one . . . as one who speaks without acting**: The wise understand one such as this, who does not do what he proposes but only utters words, as "one who is just a talker, a non-friend, a bogus friend."

255. He is not a friend who is always alert in suspecting dissension, observing only one's faults:[1034] One should not associate with that type of friend who, suspecting dissension, with nothing better to do,[1035] always dwells close by, alert, looking only for one's fault[1036] so that, if one has done something wrong through carelessness or inattention, or failed to do something through ignorance, [he can bring it up thus]: "When he criticizes me, I will reproach him with this."

Thus, having answered the first question, "What kind of

friend should one not associate with?" the Blessed One next spoke this half-verse, "But he on whom one relies," to answer the second question. This is its meaning: **But he on whom one relies**: One friend, who enters the heart of a friend and relies on him, is **like a son on** his father's **breast**, who rests there assured, not apprehensive that "there might be pain or displeasure for him while I am resting on his breast." In just this way, entrusting even one's wife, wealth, and life to the care of one's friend, one rests assured in one's friendship. One **who cannot be divided by others**, even if they present a hundred or a thousand reasons [for breaking off the friendship], **is truly a friend** with whom one should associate.

256. Thus, having answered the second question, "What kind of friend should one associate with?" the Blessed One next spoke a verse, "One develops a state productive of joy," to answer the third question.[1037] This is its meaning: **A state productive of joy** is what makes for joy. But what is that? Energy, which is said to be productive of joy because it gives rise to rapture, joy, and happiness connected with the Dhamma. As it is said: "Bhikkhus, one who is energetic in a well-expounded Dhamma and discipline lives happily" (AN I 34,23–24). It **brings praise** because it leads to praise. [299] With reference to its fruit, it is called **happiness** because initially it produces celestial and human happiness and finally the happiness of nibbāna. Expecting its fruit, one is **[expectant of] its fruit and benefit**. **Carrying out one's personal duty**: Having taken up a task suitable for a person,[1038] one develops "this state," a designation for the energy of right striving. Such an exertion should be cultivated.

257. Having thus answered the third question,[1039] the Blessed One spoke a verse, "the taste of solitude," to answer the fourth question. Here, it is the supreme fruit [of arahantship] that is called **solitude** because it has arisen through seclusion from defilements. Its **taste** is the associated pleasure, so called in the sense of enjoyment. That same [arahantship] is called **tranquil peace** because it is born from the allaying of defilements or because its object is peace, a designation for nibbāna. That same [arahantship] is called **the taste of rapture in the Dhamma**, because it is the taste of the rapture that never departs from the noble Dhamma and that has arisen in relation to the Dhamma consisting in nibbāna. Having drunk that taste of solitude and that taste of peace, **drinking the taste of rapture in the Dhamma, one is without distress, without evil.**[1040] Having drunk this, one is "without distress" through the absence of the fever of defilements, and drinking it one is also "without evil" because one has abandoned evil. Therefore this is the foremost of tastes.

But some interpret these three things—the taste of solitude, [tranquil peace, and rapture in the Dhamma]—by way of jhāna, nibbāna, and reviewing knowledge, and by way of bodily seclusion, mental seclusion, and seclusion from acquisitions. The previous explanation alone is good. Thus, in answering the fourth question, the Blessed One concluded the teaching with its culmination in arahantship. At the conclusion of the teaching the brahmin went forth under the Blessed One and in just a few days became an arahant possessed of the analytical knowledges.

4 Blessings
(*Mahāmaṅgala Sutta*)

[118][1041] What is the origin? It is said that in Jambudīpa, at the city gates, in the council halls, and in assembly rooms, multitudes assembled and paid minstrels to relate various entertaining tales such as the story of the abduction of Sītā.[1042] Each talk would conclude after four months. One day a discussion about blessings arose: "What now is a blessing? Is what is seen a blessing? Is what is heard a blessing? Is what is sensed a blessing? Who knows what a blessing is?"[1043]

Then one man named "Seen Blessing"[1044] said: "I know what is a blessing. What is seen is a blessing in the world. The 'seen' is a form considered auspicious. For instance, someone here rises early and sees a talking bird,[1045] or a *beḷuva* creeper, or a pregnant woman, or children dressed up and adorned, or a full pot, or a fresh redfish, or a thoroughbred horse, or a chariot of thoroughbreds, or a bull, or a cow, or a *kapila* cow, or any other form considered auspicious. This is called a seen blessing." Some accepted his statement, some did not accept it. Those who did not accept it quarreled with him.

Then a man named "Heard Blessing" said: "The eye, sir, sees what is pure and impure, what is good and bad, what is agreeable and disagreeable. If what is seen by it were a blessing, then everything would be a blessing; therefore the seen is not a blessing. [119] Rather, what is heard is a blessing. The 'heard' is a sound considered auspicious. For instance, someone here, having risen early, hears 'Vaḍḍhā' or 'Vaḍḍhamānā' or 'Puṇṇā' or 'Phussā' or 'Sumanā' or 'Sirī' or 'Sirivaḍḍhā,'[1046] or 'today the stars are good, it's a good occasion, a good day, good luck,' or any other such sound considered auspicious. This is called a heard blessing." Some accepted his statement, some did not accept it. Those who did not accept it quarreled with him.

Then a man named "Sensed Blessing" said: "The ear, sir, hears what is good and bad, what is agreeable and disagreeable. If what is heard by it were a blessing, then everything would be a blessing; therefore the heard is not a blessing. Rather, what is sensed is a blessing. The 'sensed' is an odor, taste, or tactile object considered auspicious. For instance, someone here, having risen early, smells the fragrance of a flower such as a lotus flower, or chews on lucky toothwood, or touches the ground, wet cowdung, a turtle shell, a load of sesamum seeds, or some flower or fruit, or he anoints himself with lucky clay, or puts on a lucky garment, or wears a lucky turban, or he smells, tastes, or touches any other such odor, taste, or tactile object considered auspicious. This is called a sensed blessing." Some accepted his statement, some did not accept it.

The one who took the seen to be a blessing could not convince those who took the heard and sensed to be a blessing. And so for the other two. But those people who accepted the statement of the one who took the seen to be a blessing went around saying: "Only what is seen is a blessing." And those who accepted the statements of those who took the heard and sensed to be a blessing went around saying: "Only what is heard is a blessing, only what is sensed is a blessing." In this way this discussion of blessings spread all over Jambudīpa.

Then the people throughout Jambudīpa, [120] gathering in groups, reflected on blessings thus: "What is a blessing?" Their protective deities heard their discussion and also reflected on blessings. Their friends among the earth deities heard about it from them, and the earth deities, too, reflected on blessings. Their friends among the sky deities heard about it from them . . . and the deities ruled by the four divine kings from them, and in this way it continued up until the deities of the Akaniṭṭha realm heard about it from the Sudassi deities, and they too, gathering in groups, reflected on blessings. Thus reflection on blessings occurred everywhere throughout ten thousand world spheres. And once it had started, it went on for twelve years, and though it was being determined 'This is a blessing, that is a blessing,' they did not reach a final decision.

All human beings, devas, and brahmās—exception made of the noble disciples—were divided into three factions according to whether they sided with the seen, the heard, or the sensed. Not even one person could come to a definitive conclusion, "Just this is a blessing," and so a commotion about blessings arose in the world.

Commotions are of five kinds: commotion about the eon, commotion about a wheel-turning monarch, commotion about a buddha, commotion about blessings, and commotion about munihood.[1047]

(1) Here, when the desire-sphere devas, with loose head bands,[1048] scattered hair, and tearful faces, wiping their tears with their hands, wearing dyed clothes and with disshelved garments, wandering along the path of humans, announce, "After 100,000 years, the end of the eon will occur. This world will perish, the great ocean will dry up, and this great earth along with Sineru, [121] king of mountains, will burn up and perish, and world destruction will occur up to the brahma world. Develop loving-kindness, dear sirs, develop compassion, altruistic joy, and equanimity. Attend on your mother and father, respect the elders in the family. Be vigilant! Do not be heedless!"—this is called *the commotion about the eon*.

(2) When those same desire-sphere devas, wandering along the path of humans, announce, "After 100,000 years, a wheel-turning monarch will arise in the world," this is called *the commotion about a wheel-turning monarch*.

(3) When the devas of the pure abodes adorn themselves with the ornaments of brahmā, put a turban of brahmā on their heads, and—filled with rapture and joy, proclaiming the excellent qualities of a buddha, wandering along the path of humans—announce, "After 100,000 years, a buddha will arise in the world," this is called *the commotion about a buddha*.

(4) When those devas of the pure abodes, having understood the minds of human beings, wandering along the path of humans, announce, "After twelve years, a perfectly enlightened buddha will explain blessings," this is called *the commotion about blessings*.

(5) When those same devas of the pure abodes, wandering along the path of humans, announce, "After seven years, a certain bhikkhu will encounter the Blessed One and ask about

the practice of munihood," this is called *the commotion about munihood.*[1049]

Among these five kinds of commotion, when devas and human beings are divided into three factions according to whether they hold the seen, the heard, or the sensed to be blessings, this commotion about blessings has arisen in the world.

When twelve years had passed during which devas and human beings had repeatedly investigated this matter without reaching agreement, the Tāvatiṃsa deities came together and considered: "Dear sirs, the house master is foremost among the residents of a house; a village headman [122] is foremost among the inhabitants of a village; a king is foremost among all people; and in the same way, Sakka is foremost and chief among us in regard to splendor of merit, authority, and wisdom, and he is the overlord of two deva worlds. Let us ask Sakka about this matter." So they went to Sakka, whose glorious body was dressed and ornamented in ways suitable for the occasion, and who was seated on his throne of yellow marble at the foot of the pāricchattaka tree, accompanied by a retinue of two and a half koṭis of nymphs. They paid homage to Sakka, stood to one side, and said: "You should know, dear sir, that a question about blessings has arisen. Some say that the seen is a blessing, some that the heard is a blessing, and some that what is sensed is a blessing. None of us have come to a conclusion about this. Please explain this as it is."

Being naturally wise, the ruler of the devas asked: "Where did this discussion about blessings first originate?" They replied: "We heard about it, lord, from the deities ruled by the four divine kings. They say they heard about it from the sky deities, who heard about it from the earth deities, who heard about it from the protective deities of human beings; and these say it originated in the human world."

Then the ruler of the devas asked: "Where is the Perfectly Enlightened One living?" – "In the human world, lord." – "Did anyone ask the Blessed One?" – "No, lord." – "Dear sirs, do you discard a fire and try to get light from a firefly? Thinking that I should be asked about this matter, you have passed over the Blessed One, who can point out the nature of blessings without omission! Go, ask the Blessed One. Surely, we will get a glorious answer to this question." He then commanded one young deva: "You ask the Blessed One." [123] That young deva, having adorned himself in ways suitable to the occasion, radiant as a flash of lightning, accompanied by a group of devas, then went to the great monastery in Jeta's Grove. He paid homage to the Blessed One, stood to one side, and in a verse asked the question about blessings. The Blessed One then spoke this discourse to answer the question.

[300][1050] Here, **thus have I heard**: The meaning of this has already been stated concisely in relation to the Discourse to Kasibhāradvāja, but those who wish for a detailed explanation should understand it in the way stated in the *Papañcasūdanī,* the Majjhima Nikāya Commentary. And where it was said in the Discourse to Kasibhāradvāja, "was dwelling among the Magadhans at Dakkhiṇāgiri near the brahmin village Ekanālā," here it is said, "was dwelling at Sāvatthī in Jeta's Grove, Anāthapiṇḍika's Park." Therefore, starting with the word "Sāvatthī," we will here explain terms not previously encountered.

At Sāvatthī: in the city with such a name. It is said that this was the place of residence of a rishi named Savattha. Therefore, just as Kosambī was the residence of Kusamba and Kākandī of Kākanda, so, by using the feminine gender, this place was called Sāvatthī. But the ancients explain it thus: "Whenever there was an encounter of caravans in that place, when the question was asked, 'What goods are available there?' they would say, 'There is everything'; therefore, with reference to this expression, it was called Sāvatthī."[1051] When it is said "at Sāvatthī," what is indicated is his alms resort. Jeta was the name of a prince; the grove that belonged to this Jeta, because it had been planted and cultivated by him, was called Jeta's Grove. [The Blessed One was dwelling] there **in Jeta's Grove**. Anāthapiṇḍika was [so called] because he gave almsfood to the poor.[1052] In **Anāthapiṇḍika's Park**: in the park constructed by the householder Anāthapiṇḍika by spending fifty-four koṭis of money for it.[1053] This indicates that it was a place of residence suitable for monastic persons.

Then a certain deity: This is said without specification because his name and clan are not known. A deity (*devatā*) is just a deva; this is a word common to both females and males. But here this young deva was a male, but he is called "a deity" by use of the common term.[1054] **When the night had advanced**

(*abhikkantāya rattiyā*): Here the word *abhikkanta* is seen in the senses of passage (of time), good, beautiful, appreciation, and so forth. Here it indicates the passage of time. Hence what is meant is that the night had passed, the night had gone by. **Of stunning beauty**: Here *abhikkanta* occurs in the sense of beautiful. The word *vaṇṇa* is seen in the senses of complexion, praise, family, section, cause, shape, measurement, the sense base of visible form, and so forth. Here what is meant is that he had a stunning complexion, a beautiful complexion.

Entire (*kevalakappaṃ*): The word *kevala* has many meanings, such as without omission, for the most part, unadulterated, moderately, firmly, and detachment. Here the meaning intended is "without omission." The word *kappa* has many meanings, such as faith, an expression, time, a description, cutting, an alternative, an elision, and everywhere. Here the meaning intended is "everywhere." Hence when it is said, **the entire Jeta's Grove**, the meaning should be seen in this way: "everywhere in the entire Jeta's Grove."

Having illuminated: having pervaded with light. Like the moon and sun, he made it completely radiant, completely bright.

Approached the Blessed One: He approached the place where the Blessed One was staying, or he approached for the reason that the Blessed One is to be approached by devas and human beings. And for what reason is the Blessed One to be approached? With the intention of achieving various kinds of excellent qualities, just as a large tree constantly bearing fruit is to be approached by flocks of birds with the intention of enjoying its sweet fruits.

Stood to one side: When he stood to one side, how did he stand?

> Not behind, not in front, not too close or too far;
> not in a ditch or against the wind, neither below nor above.
> Having avoided these faults, he stood to one side.

But why did he just stand and not sit down? Because of a wish to return quickly. For when deities come to the human world for a particular reason, they do so like a clean person coming to a latrine. They are naturally repelled by the human world, which is foul-smelling to them even from a hundred yojanas; they do not enjoy it. Hence he did not sit down because he wished to return as soon as he finished the task for which he came. Also, people sit down to dispel their fatigue from walking, but the devas do not have such fatigue; for this reason, too, he did not sit down. Also, he esteemed the great disciples who were standing around the Blessed One; for this reason, too, he did not sit down. Further, he did not sit down simply out of respect for the Blessed One. For when deities wish to sit down, a seat is produced; since he did not wish for one, he did not even think of sitting but stood to one side.

Stood to one side and addressed the Blessed One in verse: Thus that deity, standing to one side for these reasons, spoke in verse to the Blessed One, with a statement that was knit together by metrical syllables and words.

258. [123][1055] **Many**: an indeterminate number. What is meant is many hundreds, many thousands, many hundreds of thousands. **Devas** are so called because they shine; the meaning is that they play with the five strands of sensual pleasures or they shine with their own splendor.[1056] Devas are threefold, by way of convention, rebirth, and purification. As it is said: "As to devas, there are three kinds of devas: conventional devas, devas by rebirth, and devas by purification. Here, 'conventional devas' are kings, queens, and princes. 'Devas by rebirth' are those devas from the realm of the four divine kings upward. Arahants are called 'devas by purification.'"[1057] Of these, devas by rebirth are intended here. **Human beings** are the offspring of Manu. But the ancients say human beings are so called because of the prominence of their mind.[1058] These are fourfold: the inhabitants of Jambudīpa, Aparagoyāna, Uttarakuru, and Pubbavideha.[1059] Here the inhabitants of Jambudīpa are intended. Beings are blessed by these, hence they are **blessings**: the meaning is that they thereby achieve success and progress. **Longing for safety**: wishing for, desiring, yearning for safety, for the existence of all beautiful, excellent, good things pertaining both to the present life and future lives. **Declare**: teach, reveal, point out, disclose, [124] analyze, elucidate **the blessing**—the cause of success, the cause of progress, the cause of all excellence—**that is highest**, most distinguished, most excellent, which brings well-being and happiness to all the world. That is the sequential commentary on the terms in the verse.

This is a summary of the meaning: With a desire to hear the question about blessings, the deities in ten thousand world spheres had assembled in this one world sphere, having created subtle bodies such that ten, twenty, thirty, forty, fifty, sixty, seventy, and even eighty could occupy the space of a mere hair's tip. When that young deva saw them standing there surrounding the Blessed One, who sat in the excellent seat prepared for him, shining with a glory and splendor that surpassed all devas, māras, and brahmās, the young deva discerned with his own mind the minds of human beings throughout all of Jambudīpa, both on that occasion and those of the future. Then, in order to remove the dart of doubt from the minds of all the devas and human beings, he said: "Longing for safety, desiring a state of safety for themselves, many devas and human beings have reflected on blessings, so declare the highest blessing. I ask you with the consent of those devas and to benefit human beings, so, out of compassion for us, O Blessed One, declare the blessing that is highest because it brings exclusively well-being and happiness to all of us."

Not associating with fools

259. Thus, having heard this statement of the young deva, the Blessed One spoke the verse, **not associating with fools**. Here, **not associating with**: not following after, not serving. **Fools**: they live, they breathe, thus they are fools; the purport is that they live merely by breathing in and out but do not live by wisdom.[1060] **The wise**: they advance, thus they are wise;[1061] the purport is that by the movement of knowledge, they enter the good pertaining to the present life and future lives. [125] **Associating with**: following after, serving. **Venerating**: showing honor, respect, esteem, and homage. **Those worthy of veneration**: those who deserve veneration. **This is the highest blessing**: Combining all these—not associating with fools, associating with the wise, and venerating those worthy of veneration—he says that this is the highest blessing. What is meant is: "When you asked, 'State the highest blessing,' accept this as the highest blessing."

That is the commentary on the terms of this verse. The commentary on the meaning should be understood as follows: Having heard the statement of the young deva, the Blessed One spoke this verse. Here, there are four kinds of talk: a talk given when one is asked a question, a talk given without a question being asked, a coherent talk, and an incoherent talk. A talk given when one is asked a question is one given when asked such questions as "I ask you, Gotama, one of broad wisdom: How should one act to become a good disciple?" (**376**ab) and "How, dear sir, did you cross the flood?" (SN I 1,14). A talk given without a question being asked is one given on his own initiative, without being asked a question, such as "What others speak of as happiness, that the noble ones speak of as suffering" (**762**ab). Because of the statement "I teach the Dhamma, bhikkhus, with a basis" (AN I 276,15), all the talks of the buddhas are coherent. In the Teaching there are no incoherent talks. Of the four, this is a talk given when one is asked a question, since it was spoken by the Blessed One when questioned by the young deva.

And as a clever man skilled in the right path and the wrong path, when asked about the path, would first state which path one should avoid and then which path one should take—"In such a place there is a fork in the road; there one should avoid the left path and take the one to the right"—so when asked about things to be cultivated and things not to be cultivated, one first states what should not be cultivated and then what should be cultivated. [126] And the Blessed One is like a man skilled in the path. As it is said: "The man skilled in the path, Tissa, is a designation for the Tathāgata, the Arahant, the Perfectly Enlightened One" (SN III 108,31). For he is "skilled in this world, skilled in the next world, skilled in the realm of death, skilled in what is beyond the realm of death, skilled in Māra's realm, skilled in what is beyond Māra's realm" (MN I 227,1–3). Therefore, having first indicated what should not be cultivated, and then indicating what should be cultivated, he said: "Not associating with fools, associating with the wise." For firstly, one should not associate with or serve fools, who are like the path to be avoided, and then one should associate with and serve the wise, who are like the path to be taken.

But why, when speaking about blessings, does the Blessed One first speak of not associating with fools and associating with the wise? In reply it is said that by associating with fools devas and human beings adopt the view that blessings are to be found among things seen, heard, and sensed, things that are not blessings; therefore the Blessed One first speaks to them of not associating with fools and associating with the wise, criticizing affiliation with those who are not good friends, which is detrimental to one's good pertaining both to this world and the world beyond; instead he praises friendship with good friends, which promotes one's good in both worlds.

Here, **fools** are those beings who enter upon the ways of unwholesome kamma, such as the destruction of life and so forth. They can be identified through three qualities. As it is said: "Bhikkhus, there are these three characteristics that mark a fool" (AN I 102,16). Moreover, the six teachers such as Pūraṇa Kassapa, and such people as Devadatta, Kokālika, Kaṭamorakatissa, Khaṇḍadeviyāputta, Samuddadatta, the young woman Ciñcā, and so forth, as well as the brother of Dīghavida[1062]—these [127] as well as other such beings may be understood as fools. As if taking hold of a blazing coal, by their own wrong understanding they destroy themselves and those who follow their advice, like Dīghavida's brother, who, for the duration of four buddhas, was tortured in hell, with his body sixty yojanas in size rising up and falling down; and like the five hundred families that approved of his view, who were reborn in hell along with him.[1063] As it is said:

> "Bhikkhus, just as a fire that starts in a house made of reeds or grass burns down even a house with a peaked roof, plastered inside and out, draft-free, with bolts fastened and shutters closed; so too, whatever perils arise . . . whatever disasters arise . . . whatever calamities arise, all arise on account of the fool, not on account of the wise person. Thus the fool brings peril, the wise person brings no peril; the fool brings disaster, the wise person brings no disaster; the fool brings calamity, the wise person brings no calamity." (AN I 101,9–18)

Further, a fool is like rotten fish, and one who associates with a fool is like a leaf used to wrap rotten fish; intelligent people find them vile and repulsive. And this is said:

One who ties up putrid fish
with blades of kusa grass
makes the kusa grass smell foul:
so it is in following fools. (It 68,9–12, Ja IV 435,28–29, Ja VI 236,4–5)

And the wise Akitti, when offered a boon by Sakka, ruler of the devas, said this:

"May I never see or listen to a fool,
and may I not dwell with a fool.
May I not converse with a fool
and may I not approve of one."

"What has the fool done to you?
State the reason, Kassapa!
For what reason, Kassapa,
do you not wish to see a fool?"

"The deluded fellow leads one to ruin;
he enjoins one in reckless ways.
He is hard to guide to the good;
spoken to rightly, he gets upset.
He does not know discipline;
it is good not to see such a one."[1064] [128]

Thus, criticizing association with fools from every angle, having said, "not associating with fools is a blessing," the Blessed One, praising association with the wise, now says: **associating with the wise** is a blessing. Here, **the wise** are those beings who enter upon the ways of wholesome kamma, abstinence from the destruction of life and so forth. They can be identified through three qualities. As it is said: "Bhikkhus, there are these three characteristics that mark a wise person" (AN I 102,27). Moreover, buddhas, paccekabuddhas, the eighty great disciples, and other disciples of the Tathāgata, and such people as Sunetta, Mahāgovinda, Vidhura, Sarabhaṅga, Mahosadha,

Sutasoma, and King Nimi—these as well as the youth Ayoghara, the wise Akitti, and others may be understood as wise people.[1065]

These are like guards in time of danger, like a lamp in darkness, like obtaining food and drink when overcome by the suffering of hunger and thirst. They are able to dispel all the perils, disasters, and calamities of those who follow their advice. Thus, by relying on the Tathāgata, countless devas and human beings attained the destruction of the influxes, were established in the brahma world and the deva world, and were reborn in a good destination. Eighty thousand families that placed confidence in the Elder Sāriputta and provided him with the four requisites were reborn in heaven. Similarly in the case of all the great disciples, beginning with Mahāmoggallāna and Mahākassapa. Among the disciples of the teacher Sunetta, some were reborn in the brahma world, some among the devas who control the creations of others . . . and some were reborn in affluent families of householders (see AN IV 104,7–17). And this is said: "Bhikkhus, there is no peril from a wise person, no disaster from a wise person, no calamity from a wise person" (AN I 101,18).

Further, a wise person is like a sweet fragrance, such as tagara or a flower garland, and one who associates with a wise person is like a leaf used to wrap such sweet fragrances; intelligent people find them delightful and worthy of esteem. And this is said: [129]

> One who ties up tagara
> with leaves [fallen from a tree]
> makes the leaves sweetly fragrant:
> so it is in following the wise. (It 68,13–16, Ja IV 436,1–2, Ja VI 236,6–7)

And the wise Akitti, when offered a boon by Sakka, ruler of the devas, said this:

> "May I see and listen to a wise person,
> and may I dwell together with the wise.
> May I converse with a wise one
> and may I approve of him."

"What has the wise person done to you?
State the reason, Kassapa!
What is the reason, Kassapa,
that you wish to see a wise person?"

"The wise person follows what is right;
he does not enjoin one in reckless ways.
He is easy to guide to the good;
spoken to rightly, he is not upset.
He understands discipline;
it is good to encounter him." (Ja IV 241,8–14)

Thus, praising in every way associating with the wise, having said, "associating with the wise is a blessing," the Blessed One now says, **venerating those worthy of veneration, this is the highest blessing,** praising the veneration of those who, by not associating with fools and by associating with the wise, have gradually become worthy of veneration. Here, **those worthy of veneration** are the exalted buddhas, who are devoid of all faults and possessed of all excellent qualities, and after them, paccekabuddhas and noble disciples. For an act of veneration toward them, even a slight one, leads to well-being and happiness for a long time, as seen in the examples of Sumana the garland-maker, Mallikā, and others. Here, we will give merely one example.[1066]

One day, it is said, the Blessed One dressed in the morning, took his bowl and robe, and entered Rājagaha for alms. The garland-maker Sumana had taken some flowers for the king of Magadha[1067] and was going in that direction when he saw the Blessed One, who had arrived at the entrance to the city. He was graceful, pleasing,[1068] blazing with the glory of a buddha. [130] Having seen him, he thought: "When the king receives these flowers, he may pay me a hundred or a thousand coins and that will lead to my happiness merely in this present world. But an offering to the Blessed One bears immeasurable and incalculable fruit and brings well-being and happiness for a long time. Let me offer these flowers to the Blessed One."

Then, with a mind of confidence, he took a handful of flowers and threw them toward the Blessed One. The flowers went through space and remained suspended above the Blessed

One as a garland canopy. Having seen this display of spiritual might, the garland-maker became even more confident in the Blessed One and threw another handful of flowers. These went and formed a garland curtain. In this way, he threw eight handfuls, which went and formed a cottage of flowers. The Blessed One was within the cottage. A multitude of people gathered. The Blessed One looked at the garland-maker and displayed a smile. Thinking, "Buddhas do not display a smile without some reason," Ānanda asked about the reason for his smile. The Blessed One said: "Ānanda, by the spiritual might of this offering, this garland-maker, having wandered in saṃsāra for 100,000 eons among devas and human beings, will finally become a paccekabuddha named Sumanissara." At the conclusion of his statement, in order to teach the Dhamma, he spoke this verse:

"Good is it to do that deed
which one does not regret having done,
the result of which one experiences
pleased, with a happy mind." (Dhp 68)

At the conclusion of the verse, 84,000 living beings made the breakthrough to the Dhamma. In this way it can be understood that even a slight act of veneration toward them leads to well-being and happiness for a long time.

And if that is the case with veneration by material things, what can be said about veneration through practice? Who will praise the fruit of the veneration offered by those people who venerate the Blessed One with their own excellent qualities, such as going for refuge, accepting the training rules, undertaking the factors of the uposatha, the fourfold purification of good behavior, and other practices? For it is said that they venerate the Tathāgata with the supreme veneration. As he said: "Ānanda, the bhikkhu, bhikkhunī, male lay follower, or female lay follower who dwells practicing the Dhamma in accordance with the Dhamma, practicing properly, acting in accordance with the Dhamma, honors, reveres, [131] esteems, and venerates the Tathāgata with the supreme veneration" (DN II 138,17–21). Accordingly, it can be understood that the veneration of paccekabuddhas and noble disciples, too, leads to well-being and happiness.

Further, among householders, an elder brother and sister should be venerated by a younger one; the mother and father by their children; and the husband and parents-in-law by a wife. In this way, too, those worthy of veneration should be understood. For the veneration of them is a blessing because it is a wholesome quality and a cause for growth in such things as longevity. For this is said: "They will esteem their mothers and fathers; they will esteem ascetics and brahmins; they will respect the elders in the family; they will undertake and practice this wholesome quality. Because they undertake these wholesome qualities, they will grow in longevity, they will grow in beauty," and so forth (DN III 74,17–20).

Thus three blessings have been stated by this verse: not associating with fools, associating with the wise, and venerating those worthy of veneration. Here, not associating with fools is a blessing because it protects one from the perils conditioned by associating with fools;[1069] associating with the wise is a blessing because it is a cause for well-being in both this world and the next; and venerating those worthy of veneration is a blessing because it is a cause for a good rebirth and nibbāna in the way stated in the commentary on the manifestation of their fruits.[1070]

From now on, without showing the outline, we will delineate the blessing where it is mentioned and elucidate its nature as a blessing.

The commentary on the meaning of this verse, "Not associating with fools," is finished.

Residing in a suitable place

260. Thus, while with the words "declare the highest blessing" the Blessed One was asked to state only one blessing, like a generous person who, when asked for a little, gives much, [132] he spoke of three blessings in one verse. But because the deities wished to hear still more, and because there exist such additional blessings, and because the Blessed One wished to enjoin different beings in different kinds of blessings in ways appropriate for them, he again started to speak of numerous blessings with the verses that begin "Residing in a suitable place."

Here, in the first verse, **suitable**: fitting; **place**: any place where beings reside—a village, a town, a city, and a country;

residing: residence there. **In the past**: earlier in past births; **merit done**: accumulated wholesomeness. **Oneself**: The mind, or the entire person, is called self; **directing rightly**: right direction, resolution, application of that self. The rest in the way already stated.

That is the commentary on the terms. The commentary on the meaning should be understood as follows: **A suitable place** is a place where the four assemblies dwell, where they practice the bases of meritorious deeds such as giving, and where the Teacher's ninefold teaching shines.[1071] Because residence there is a condition for beings to perform meritorious deeds, it is called a blessing. And an example here is that of the fishermen, etc., who entered Sīhaḷadīpa (Sri Lanka).

Another method of explanation: A suitable place is the region where the site of the Blessed One's enlightenment is located; the region where he set in motion the wheel of the Dhamma; the region at the foot of Gaṇḍa's mango tree where, in the midst of an assembly extending for twelve yojanas, he refuted the opinions of all the sectarian teachers and performed the twin wonder;[1072] the place where he descended from the deva world;[1073] and any other region where the Buddha and other noble ones dwelled, such as Sāvatthī and Rājagaha. Residence there is a blessing because it is a condition for beings to obtain the six unsurpassed things.[1074]

Another method: To the east there is a market town named Kajaṅgala, and past it is Mahāsālā, beyond which are the border districts; on this side is the middle region. In the southeast there is a river named Salalavatī, beyond which are the border districts; on this side is the middle region. In the south [133] there is a market town named Setakaṇṇika, beyond which are the border districts; on this side is the middle region. To the west is a brahmin village named Thūna, beyond which are the border districts; on this side is the middle region. To the north is the mountain named Usīraddhaja, beyond which are the border districts; on this side is the middle region. This middle region, 300 yojanas in length, 250 in width, and 900 in circumference, is called a suitable place.

And it is here that wheel-turning monarchs arise, exercising sovereignty over the four continents and their 2,000 islands; and it is here that great disciples such as Sāriputta and Mahāmoggallāna arise after having fulfilled the pāramīs for one incalculable and 100,000 eons; and it is here that paccekabuddhas arise after having fulfilled the pāramīs for two incalculables and 100,000 eons; and it is here that perfectly enlightened buddhas arise after having fulfilled the pāramīs for four, eight, or sixteen incalculables and 100,000 eons. It is there that beings receive the exhortation from a wheel-turning monarch, become established in the five precepts, and become destined for heaven; and so too when they are established in the exhortation of paccekabuddhas. But when they are established in the exhortation of a fully enlightened buddha and his disciples, they become destined for heaven and nibbāna. Therefore residing there, which is the condition for these types of excellence, is called a blessing.

Merit done in the past is a term for wholesomeness accumulated in a past birth on account of buddhas, paccekabuddhas, and arahants. That too is a blessing. Why? Having come into the presence of buddhas and paccekabuddhas or heard a four-line verse in person from the buddhas or a buddha's disciples, one attains arahantship at the conclusion of the verse. And a human being who has established a foundation in the past and abounds in wholesome roots may, by reason of that same wholesome root, generate insight and attain the destruction of the influxes, like King Mahākappina and his chief queen.[1075] Hence it is said, "merit done in the past is a blessing." [134]

Directing oneself rightly: Here, someone who has been immoral establishes himself in virtuous behavior; one who has lacked faith establishes himself in faith; one who has been miserly establishes himself in generosity. This is called "directing oneself rightly." And this is a blessing. Why? Because it is a cause for abandoning the enmity pertaining to the present life and future lives and for achieving various benefits.

Thus three blessings have been stated by this verse, too: residing in a suitable place, merit done in the past, and directing oneself rightly. The way in which they are blessings has already been elucidated for each.

The commentary on the meaning of this verse, "Residing in a suitable place," is finished.

Much learning

261. Here, **much learning** is erudition; **a craft** is any kind of dexterity; **discipline** is the disciplining of body, speech, and mind; **well trained** is thoroughly trained; **well-spoken speech** is excellent speech. The rest in the way stated earlier.

That is the commentary on the terms. The commentary on the meaning should be understood as follows: **Much learning** is explained as retention of the Teacher's Teaching in the way stated thus, "He retains what he has learned, accumulates what he has learned" (AN II 23,1), and, "Here, a person has learned much—the discourses, mixed prose and verse, expositions" (AN II 7,2–3), and so forth. This is called a blessing because it is a cause for abandoning the unwholesome and achieving the wholesome, and because it is a cause for eventually realizing the supreme truth. For this was said by the Blessed One: "Bhikkhus, a learned noble disciple abandons the unwholesome, develops the wholesome, abandons what is blameworthy, develops what is blameless, and maintains himself in purity" (AN IV 110,12). This too is said:

> "He examines the meaning of the teachings he has retained in mind; when he examines their meaning, he gains a reflective acceptance of those teachings; when he has gained a reflective acceptance of those teachings, desire is born; when desire is born, he makes an exertion; making an exertion, he weighs matters; having weighed matters, he strives; striving, he realizes with the body the supreme truth and [135] he sees it by penetrating it with wisdom." (MN I 480,5–10)

Further, secular learning,[1076] too, when blameless, should be understood as a blessing, for it leads to well-being and happiness in both worlds.

A craft could be the crafts of a layperson or the crafts of a homeless one. The crafts of a layperson are any trades that do not cause harm to others and are devoid of the unwholesome, such as the work of a jeweler, a goldsmith, and so forth; this is a blessing because it leads to good in the present world. The crafts of a homeless one are such things as designing and sewing robes and repairing an ascetic's requisites. These have been praised here and there, as in the passage "Here, a bhikkhu is diligent in undertaking various tasks for his fellow monks," which has been called a protective quality (AN V 24,10–13). This should be understood to be a blessing because it leads to well-being and happiness in both worlds for both oneself and others.

Discipline is the discipline of a layperson and the discipline of a homeless one.[1077] Here, the discipline of a layperson is abstaining from the ten courses of unwholesome kamma. Being well trained in this is a blessing because, by not falling into defilement and delineating the excellent qualities of refined conduct, it leads to well-being and happiness in both worlds. The discipline of a homeless one is not committing any of the seven classes of offenses; one is well trained in this in the way already stated. Or the discipline of a homeless one is the fourfold purification of good behavior.[1078] Since one attains arahantship on the basis of this, being well trained by such a training should be understood as a blessing because it is a cause for achieving mundane and world-transcending happiness.

Well-spoken speech is speech devoid of such faults as false speech and so forth. As he said: "Bhikkhus, when speech possesses four factors, it is well spoken" (see p. 229). Or speech devoid of idle chatter is well spoken. As he said:

"What is well spoken is best, the good say;
speak Dhamma, not non-Dhamma—that is second.
Speak what is pleasant, not unpleasant—that is third;
speak the truth, not lies—that is fourth." (**450**) [136]

This, too, should be understood as a blessing because it leads to well-being and happiness in both worlds. But since this is already comprised within discipline, discipline here should be understood not to include this. Or why trouble with this? Well-spoken speech here should be understood as teaching the Dhamma to others. For like residing in a suitable place, this is called a blessing because it is a condition for beings to achieve well-being and happiness in both worlds as well as nibbāna. And he says:

"The speech that the Buddha utters
for the attainment of nibbāna, the secure,
for making an end to suffering,
is indeed the supreme speech." (**454**)

Thus four blessings have been stated by this verse: much learning, skill in a craft, discipline in which one is well trained, and well-spoken speech. The ways in which they are blessings have already been elucidated for each.

The commentary on the meaning of this verse, "Much learning," is finished.

Attending upon mother and father

262. The commentary on the meaning should be understood as follows:[1079] It is a parent that is called **mother**, and so too **father**. **Serving** means helping them by washing their feet, giving them a massage, rubbing them, bathing them, and providing them with the four requisites. Mother and father are very helpful to their children, desire their good, and take compassion on them. When the children come back after playing outside with their bodies smeared with mud, the parents wipe off the mud, affectionately stroke their head, kiss them, and treat them with affection. Even if the children were to carry their parents around on their head for a hundred years, they would still be unable to repay their parents' kindness. And since the parents raise them, nurture them, and show them this world, they are considered to be "Brahmā" and "first teachers." Therefore [137] attending upon them brings praise here in this world and after death it brings happiness in heaven. Hence it is called a blessing. For this was said by the Blessed One:

Mother and father are called "Brahmā,"
and also "first teachers."
They are worthy of gifts from their children,
for they have compassion for their offspring.

Therefore a wise person should revere them,
and show them due honor,
serve them with food and drink,
with clothes and bedding,

by rubbing and bathing them,
and by washing their feet.

Because of this service
to mother and father,
the wise praise one in this world
and after death one rejoices in heaven. (AN I 132, It 110–11, Ja V 331)

According to another method, attending upon them is fivefold: supporting them, doing their duties, keeping up the family tradition, and so forth. This should be understood as a blessing because it is a cause for the five kinds of well-being in this present life, being restrained from evil and so forth. For this was said by the Blessed One:

> "There are five ways, householder's son, in which a son should attend upon his mother and father as the eastern direction. [He should think:] 'Having been supported by them, I will support them. I will perform their duties for them. I will keep up the family tradition. I will be worthy of my heritage. After their death I will distribute gifts on their behalf.' And there are five ways in which the parents, so served by their son as the eastern direction, show compassion for their son: they restrain him from evil, support him in doing good, have him trained in a craft, find him a suitable wife, and, in due time, hand over his inheritance to him." (DN III 189,5–13)

And further, one who attends upon his mother and father in three [138] ways—by arousing their confidence, by enjoining them in good behavior, or by going forth—is the foremost of those who attend upon mother and father. Attending upon mother and father, which is a way of repaying the help given to one by one's parents, is a blessing for one who acts thus because it is a basis for many benefits both in the present life and future lives.

A wife and children: Here, both the sons and daughters begotten by oneself are designated children.[1080] A wife is any among the twenty kinds of wives.[1081] **Maintaining**: helping them by honoring them and so forth. This should be understood as a blessing because it is a cause for such well-being in the present life as having the work properly organized and so forth. And this was said by the Blessed One:

> "The west should be understood as wife and children.[1082] There are five ways, householder's son, in which a husband should attend upon his wife as the western direction: by honoring her, by not disparaging her, by not being unfaithful to her, by giving her authority, and by providing her with adornments. And there are five ways in which the wife, so supported by her husband as the western direction, has compassion for him: by organizing her work well, by being kind to the servants, by not being unfaithful, by guarding his earnings, and by being skillful and diligent in attending to all the domestic chores." (DN III 190,4–12)

According to another method, "maintaining" is sustaining the relationship by righteous giving, pleasant speech, and beneficent conduct;[1083] for example, covering their expenses on the uposatha days, bringing them to the festivities on the festival days, performing the blessing ceremonies on auspicious days, and exhorting and instructing them in the benefits pertaining to the present life and future lives. That should be understood as a blessing in the way stated, because it is a cause of well-being in the present life and future lives [139] and because it is a cause for being given homage even by the deities. As Sakka, ruler of the devas, said:

> "I pay homage to them, O Mātali,
> those householders who do merits,
> those lay followers of good behavior
> who righteously maintain a wife." (SN I 234,28–29)

An honest occupation: work such as agriculture, cattle-rearing, business, and so forth, which, because carried out in a timely manner, in a suitable manner, with diligence, with vigor and energy, and harmlessly, is devoid of such entangling faults as untimeliness, doing what is unsuitable, inertia, slackness, and so forth. When these tasks are undertaken in such a way, through one's own competence, or that of one's wife and children, or that of one's slaves and workers, it is called a blessing, for it is a cause for obtaining and growing in money and grain. And this was said by the Blessed One:

"Doing what is proper, dutiful,
one with initiative finds wealth." (**187**ab)

"One in the habit of sleeping during the day,
who keeps awake through the night,
dissolute, always intoxicated,
cannot keep a decent house.

"He complains, 'It's too cold, too hot!
Now it is too late!' he says.
The benefits pass such men by,
who in this way neglect their work.

"But one here who thinks no more
of cold and heat than he would of grass,
fulfilling his personal work,
does not depart from happiness." (DN III 185,7–18)

"For one who gathers wealth
like a bee moving around,[1084]
wealth is accumulated
just as an anthill is built up." (DN III 188,11–14) [140]

Thus four blessings have been stated by this verse, too: attending upon one's mother, attending upon one's father, maintaining children and wife, and a decent occupation. Or else by dividing "maintaining children and wife" there can be five blessings, or three [by leaving "maintaining children and wife" undivided and] by joining into one "attending upon mother and father." The way in which they are blessings has already been elucidated for each.

The commentary on the meaning of this verse, "Attending upon one's mother and father," is finished.

Giving and righteous conduct

263. Giving is the volition of relinquishing to another any of the ten objects of giving—food and so forth[1085]—preceded by a clear cognition,[1086] or it is the non-greed associated with that volition. For it is through non-greed that one presents that object to another. Hence it is said: "It is 'giving' because it is through this that [a gift] is given." This is called a blessing because it is the cause for achieving a variety of fruits pertaining to the present life and future lives, such as being dear and agreeable to many people and so forth. And here such discourses as this should be recollected: "A donor, Sīha, a munificent giver, is dear and agreeable to many people" (AN III 39,6).

By another method, giving is said to be of two kinds: the gift of material things and the gift of the Dhamma. Here, the gift of material things should be understood in the way already stated. The gift of the Dhamma is the teaching of the Dhamma made known by the Perfectly Enlightened One from a wish for the well-being of others, one that brings happiness and the destruction of suffering here in this world and in the next world. [141] Of these two kinds of giving, this one is superior. As he says:

> The gift of the Dhamma surpasses all gifts;
> the taste of the Dhamma surpasses all tastes;
> delight in the Dhamma surpasses all delights;
> the destruction of craving surpasses all suffering.
> (Dhp 354)

How the gift of material things is a blessing has already been stated. But the gift of the Dhamma is called a blessing because it is the basis of such excellent qualities as inspiration in the meaning and so forth. For this has been said by the Blessed One: "In whatever way a bhikkhu teaches the Dhamma to others in detail as he has heard it and learned it, in just that way he experiences inspiration in the meaning and inspiration in the Dhamma in relation to that Dhamma" (AN III 21,29–22,3).

Righteous conduct (*dhammacariyā*) is said to be conduct following the ten ways of wholesome kamma. As he said: "Householders, there are three kinds of righteous and balanced bodily conduct" and so forth (MN I 287,23). This righteous conduct should be understood to be a blessing because it is a cause for rebirth in the heavenly world. For this was said by the Blessed One: "So, householders, it is by reason of such righteous and balanced conduct that some beings here, on the breakup of the body, after death, are reborn in a happy destination, in the heavenly world" (MN I 289,34–37).

Relatives are one's maternal or paternal relations back through seven generations. When they suffer loss of wealth or illness and come to one for help, assisting them with food, clothing, money, grain, and so forth is called a blessing because it is a cause for the achievement of distinction pertaining to the present life, such as praise, and that pertaining to future lives, such as going to a good destination.

Blameless deeds are deeds that exemplify good conduct of body, speech, and mind,[1087] such as undertaking the factors of the uposatha, service to others, setting up parks and groves, building bridges, and so forth. These are called a blessing because they are a cause for achieving various kinds of well-being and happiness. [142] And here, such discourses as this should be recollected: "It is possible, Visākhā, that a woman or man who observes the uposatha complete in eight factors may, with the breakup of the body, after death, be reborn in companionship with the devas ruled by the four great kings" (AN I 213,12–15).

Thus four blessings have been stated by this verse: giving, righteous conduct, assistance to relatives, and blameless deeds. The way in which they are blessings has already been elucidated for each.

The commentary on the meaning of this verse, "Giving and righteous conduct," is finished.

Desisting and abstaining from evil

264. Desisting [from evil] is not delighting in evil with the mind when one has seen the danger in it; **abstaining** [from evil] is abstaining from it by way of the doors of action, by body and speech. And this abstinence is threefold: abstinence in an encounter, abstinence by undertaking precepts, and abstinence by eradication.[1088] Here, (1) *abstinence in an encounter* means abstinence from a situation encountered when, for example, one reflects on one's own social class, family, or clan, and considers, "It is not suitable for me to kill this living being or take what is not given," and so for other types of misconduct. (2) *Abstinence by undertaking precepts* occurs by undertaking the training rules; from the time this occurs, one does not commit the destruction of life or other transgressions. (3) *Abstinence by eradication* is associated with the noble path; from the time this occurs, the five perils and enmities have subsided for the noble disciple.[1089]

Evil is the fourfold unwholesomeness, designated "the defilement of action" and elaborated thus: "The destruction of life is a defilement of action. Taking what is not given . . . Sexual misconduct . . . False speech . . ." (DN III 181,26–28). It is summed up in the verse thus: [143]

> "Destruction of life, taking what is not given,
> the uttering of false speech,
> and going to the wives of others:
> the wise do not praise such deeds as these." (DN III 182,1–2)

Desisting and abstaining from all evil is called a blessing because it is a cause for the achievement of various kinds of distinction, such as the abandoning of peril and enmity pertaining to the present life and future lives. And here such discourses should be recollected as this: "A noble disciple refrains from the destruction of life" (see AN II 66,28).

Refraining from intoxicating drink: This is a designation for abstaining from liquor, wines, and intoxicants, which are the basis for heedlessness, as explained earlier (see Pj I 26–27). One who drinks intoxicants does not know the good, does not know the Dhamma, creates trouble for his mother, father, buddhas, paccekabuddhas, and disciples of a tathāgata. He is censured in this present life, goes to a bad destination in a future life, and becomes mad in subsequent lives. But one who refrains from intoxicating drinks puts a stop to those faults and acquires the excellent qualities opposed to them. Therefore refraining from intoxicating drinks should be understood to be a blessing.

Heedfulness in good qualities is the antidote to heedlessness, which is described here: "Not working carefully, not working consistently, not working persistently, for the development of wholesome qualities; shirking one's duty, relinquishing desire, relinquishing the task, non-pursuit, non-development, non-cultivation, non-resolution, non-intentness, heedlessness: any such heedlessness, being heedless, state of being heedless, is called heedlessness" (Vibh 401, §846). By way of its meaning, it should be understood as the non-relinquishing of mindfulness in regard to wholesome qualities. This is called a blessing because it is a cause for the achievement of various kinds of wholesome qualities and because it is a cause for the achievement of the deathless. [144] Here, such teachings of the Teacher should be recollected as these: "One is heedful, ardent" and "heedfulness is the path to the deathless" (Dhp 21).

Thus three blessings have been stated by this verse: abstinence from evil, refraining from intoxicating drinks, and heedfulness in wholesome qualities. The way in which they are blessings has already been elucidated for each.

The commentary on the meaning of this verse, "Desisting and abstaining from evil," is finished.

Reverence and humility

265. Reverence is showing reverence, revering, being reverential in the appropriate way toward those who ought to be revered, such as buddhas, paccekabuddhas, a tathāgata's disciples, one's teacher and preceptor, mother and father, elder brothers and sisters, as well as others. Reverence is a cause for going to a good destination and so forth. As it is said:

> "One honors, respects, reveres, and venerates those who should be honored, respected, revered, and venerated. Through that kamma, performed and undertaken in such a way, with the breakup of the body, after death, one is reborn in a good destination, in a heavenly world. But if instead one comes back to the human state, then wherever one is reborn one is of high birth." (MN III 205,26)

And it is also said, "There are, bhikkhus, these seven qualities of non-decline. What seven? Reverence for the Teacher," and so forth (AN IV 27–31). Therefore reverence is called a blessing.

Humility is meekness and humble behavior, possessing which a person is without conceit, without vanity, like a foot-wiping cloth, like a bull with cut-off horns, like a defanged viper—docile, tender, soft-spoken. This is humility. [145] It is called a blessing because it is a cause for obtaining such excellent qualities as fame. As he said, "One of humble behavior, not stiff with pride, gains fame," and so forth (DN III 192,9–10).

Contentment is contentment with requisites of any kind. It is twelvefold, that is, in regard to the robe there are three types of contentment: contentment according to one's gains, contentment according to one's ability, and contentment according to suitability. The same applies to almsfood and the rest.

This is an analytical explanation. (1) Here, a bhikkhu gains *a robe,* which may be good or bad. He maintains himself with it and does not wish for another one, and even if he gets one, he does not accept it. This is his *contentment according to one's gains* in regard to a robe. But one who is ill feels oppressed or tired when wearing a heavy robe. Thus he exchanges robes with a congenial bhikkhu and is content with a light robe. This is his *contentment according to one's ability* in regard to a robe. Another bhikkhu gains excellent requisites. Having received a costly robe of valuable material, he thinks, "This is fitting for elders long gone forth and for those highly learned," and gives it to them. He himself collects patches of cloth from a refuse heap or elsewhere, stitches them together into a robe, and is content wearing it. This is his *contentment according to suitability* in regard to a robe.

(2) A bhikkhu here gains *almsfood,* coarse or excellent. He maintains himself with it and does not wish for anything else, and even if he gets it, he does not accept it. This is his *contentment according to one's gains* in regard to almsfood. But one who is ill gets worse if he eats coarse almsfood. Thus he gives it to a congenial bhikkhu, eats ghee, honey, milk, and so forth received from him, and is content doing the duty of an ascetic. This is his [146] *contentment according to one's ability* in regard to almfood. Another bhikkhu gains excellent almsfood. Thinking, "This is fitting for elders long gone forth and other monks who

need excellent almsfood," he gives it to them, and he himself is content walking for alms and eating mixed foods. This is his *contentment according to suitability* in regard to almsfood.

(3) A bhikkhu here gains *a lodging*. He is content with it, and even if he gets one that is superior, he does not accept it. This is his *contentment according to one's gains* in regard to a lodging. But one who is ill, if he lives in a cramped lodging, becomes severely ill with jaundice or some other illness. Thus he gives it to a congenial bhikkhu, lives in a cool balmy lodging that accrues to him, and is content doing the duty of an ascetic. This is his *contentment according to one's ability* in regard to lodging. Another bhikkhu does not accept even an excellent lodging that accrues to him. He reflects: "An excellent dwelling is a basis for heedlessness. While staying there, one becomes drowsy and dozes off, and when one awakens sensual thoughts assail one." Thus he refuses it and is content living anywhere—in the open air, at the foot of a tree, or in a leaf hut. This is his *contentment according to suitability* in regard to lodging.

(4) A bhikkhu here gains such *medicine* as gall nuts.[1090] He maintains himself with them and does not wish for anything else, such as ghee, honey, palm syrup, and so forth. Even if he gets these, he does not accept them. This is his *contentment according to one's gains* in regard to medicinal requisites. But one who is ill[1091] and in need of oil gains palm syrup. He gives it to a congenial bhikkhu and, having received oil from him, prepares medicine from it, and is content doing the duty of an ascetic. This is his *contentment according to one's ability* in regard to medicinal requisites. In the case of another bhikkhu, [147] if they were to put gall nuts and cow's urine in one bottle and a blend of the four sweets in another, and say to him, "Bhante, take whichever you want"—supposing both were capable of curing his illness—he would reflect: "Medicine of gall nuts and cow's urine is praised by the buddhas, and it is said: 'The homeless life is based on medicine of cow's urine—you should be keen on this all your life'" (Vin I 58,20). He would refuse the medicine made of the four sweets and be supremely content using gall nuts and cow's urine as medicine. This is his *contentment according to suitability* in regard to medicinal requisites.

All these forms of contentment, thus analyzed, are called contentment. This should be understood to be a blessing because it is a cause for abandoning such bad qualities as excessive desires, great desires, evil desires, and so forth; because it is a cause for a good destination; and, as a provision for the noble path, because it is a cause for the state of being "at home in the four directions." As he said:

> "At home in the four directions, unrepelled,
> contented with anything whatsoever" (**42**ab).

Gratitude is recognizing, and repeatedly recollecting, the help given by anyone, whether little or much. Further, merits are helpful to living beings by protecting them from the suffering of the hells and so forth. Hence gratitude should also be understood as recollection of the helpfulness of merits. This is called a blessing because it is a cause for such excellent achievements as being considered praiseworthy by good people. As he said: "These two persons, bhikkhus, are rare in the world. What two? One who takes the initiative in helping others and one who is grateful and thankful" (AN I 87,1).

Timely listening to the Dhamma: On an occasion when the mind is restless, or overcome by sensual thoughts and other obstacles, listening to the Dhamma is beneficial in dispelling them. Others say that "timely listening to the Dhamma" means listening to the Dhamma every five days. [148] As the Venerable Anuruddha said: "Every five days, Bhante, we sit together all night for a Dhamma talk" (MN I 207,24; Vin I 352,17).

Further, "timely listening to the Dhamma" may also be understood to mean listening to the Dhamma when one is able to approach good friends to hear a teaching that dispels one's doubt. As he said: "From time to time, having approached them, he inquires and asks questions" (DN III 285,5). This "timely listening to the Dhamma" should be understood to be a blessing because it is a cause for achieving various kinds of distinction, such as the abandoning of the hindrances, the four benefits, and the destruction of the influxes. For this is said:

> "When, bhikkhus, a noble disciple listens to the Dhamma with eager ears, attending to it as a matter of vital concern, directing his whole mind to it, on

that occasion the five hindrances are not present in him." (SN V 95,19)

"When, bhikkhus, the teachings have been followed by the ear . . . and are well penetrated by view, four benefits are to be expected." (AN II 185,5–7)

"These four things, rightly developed and coordinated at the proper time, gradually culminate in the destruction of the taints. What four? Timely listening to the Dhamma," and so forth. (AN II 140,9–12; slightly different in original)

Thus five blessings have been stated by this verse: reverence, humility, contentment, gratitude, and timely listening to the Dhamma. The way in which they are blessings has already been elucidated for each.

The commentary on the meaning of this verse, "Reverence, humility," is finished.

Patience, being amenable to advice

266. [149] **Patience** is forbearance, possessing which a bhikkhu remains unaffected when other people insult him with the ten bases of insult[1092] or harm him by injury, imprisonment, and so forth; he acts as if he does not hear or see them, like the preacher of patience (*khantivādī*). As he said:

"In times past I was an ascetic,
one who expounded patience.
Even when the king of Kāsi cut him up
he remained firm in patience." (Ja III 43,1–2)

Or like the Venerable Puṇṇa, he considers his abusers good because they do not inflict more serious harm. As he said: "Bhante, if the people of Sunāparanta abuse me and revile me, I shall think, 'These people of Sunāparanta are good, very good, since they do not give me blows with their fists,'" and so forth (MN III 268,14–18).

And possessing this, one is worthy of praise by the rishis. As the rishi Sarabhaṅga said:

> "Having slain anger, one never sorrows;
> the rishis praise the abandoning of contempt.
> One should endure harsh words from everyone;
> the good call this the highest patience." (Ja V 141,20–21)

One is also worthy of praise by the deities. As Sakka, ruler of the devas, said:

> "When a person endowed with strength
> patiently endures a weakling,
> they call that the supreme patience;
> the weakling must always be patient." (SN I 222,8–9)

One is also worthy of praise by the buddhas. As the Blessed One said:

> "One who, without hatred,
> endures abuse, attacks, and bondage;
> whose power is patience, a powerful troop:
> he is the one I call a brahmin." (**625**) [150]

Patience should be understood to be a blessing because it is a cause for the achievement of the excellent qualities praised here as well as others.

Being amenable to advice means that when one is being spoken to judiciously, one does not respond evasively or fall silent or think of one's own excellent qualities and the faults of others, but after first showing deep respect, reverence, and humility, one expresses appreciation. This is called a blessing because it is a cause for receiving exhortations and instructions from one's fellow monastics and for abandoning one's faults and achieving excellent qualities.

The seeing of ascetics is approaching, serving, recollecting, hearing about, and seeing monastics, those who have stilled their defilements, developed body, good behavior, mind, and wisdom,[1093] and possess the highest taming and serenity. All these acts, preliminary to a teaching, are called "seeing." This should be understood as a blessing. Why? Because of its helpfulness. As the Blessed One said: "Bhikkhus, even seeing those bhikkhus, I say, is helpful" and so forth (SN V 67,15, It 107,4).

When a person desiring well-being sees that virtuous bhikkhus have arrived at his door, if he has something to give, according to his ability he should honor them with a gift. If he has nothing to give, he should bow down and venerate them. If this is not possible, he should salute them. If even this is not possible, he should look upon them with a trusting mind and eyes of affection. For by the merit generated even by seeing them, one does not incur an eye ailment, burning, swelling, or boil for many thousands of births; one has beautiful eyes, clear and of five colors, like the opened jeweled door panels of a mansion made of precious substances; and for 100,000 eons one obtains excellence among devas and human beings.

It is not astonishing that a wise human being should experience such excellent results through the merit properly created by seeing ascetics, but even in the case of animals they praise the excellent results that come simply by looking at ascetics with faith in them: [151]

> "This most fortunate owl,
> dwelling for long on Vedisaka,
> is happy at the time he sees
> the excellent Buddha has arisen.
>
> "Having acquired confidence in me
> and in the unsurpassed Bhikkhu Sangha,
> he will not go to a bad destination
> for a hundred thousand eons.
>
> "Having passed away from the world of the devas,
> impelled by wholesome kamma,
> he will be one of boundless knowledge,
> known by the name 'Somanassa.'"[1094]

Timely discussion on the Dhamma: In the evening or before dawn, two bhikkhus specializing in the suttas discuss a sutta with one another; experts on the Vinaya discuss the Vinaya, Abhidhamma experts discuss the Abhidhamma, the reciters of the Jātakas discuss a Jātaka, the commentators discuss a commentary. Or they hold a discussion at any time for the purpose of purifying the mind when it is in the grip of sluggishness, restlessness, or doubt. This is timely discussion on the Dhamma. This is called a blessing because it is a cause for such excellent qualities as competence in the heritage of the teaching and so forth.

Thus four blessings have been stated by this verse: patience, being amenable to advice, the seeing of ascetics, and timely discussion on the Dhamma. The way in which they are blessings has already been elucidated for each.

The commentary on the meaning of this verse, "Patience," is finished.

Austerity and the spiritual life

267. Austerity (*tapo*) is a term for restraint of the sense faculties, so called because of burning up (*tapanato*) such states as longing and dejection; [152] or it is energy, because it burns up laziness.[1095] A person possessing this is called ardent (*ātāpī*). This should be understood to be a blessing because it is a cause for abandoning longing and other obstacles and for obtaining the jhānas and other attainments.

The **spiritual life** is a designation for abstinence from sexual activity, the duty of an ascetic, the Teaching, and the path. Thus in such passages as this, "Having abandoned the non-spiritual life (sexual activity), he is one who lives the spiritual life (who is celibate)," abstinence from sexual activity is called the spiritual life. In such passages as this, "Do you, friend, live the spiritual life under our Blessed One?" (MN I 147,16), it is the duty of an ascetic. In such passages as this, "I will not attain final nibbāna, Evil One, until this spiritual life of mine is successful, abundant, widespread, and popular" (DN II 106,7–10), it is the Teaching. In such passages as this, "This noble eightfold path, bhikkhu, is the spiritual life, that is, right view," and so forth (SN V 7,29–30), it is the path. But here, because the path will be included later by the seeing of the noble truths, all the remaining meanings are relevant. And this should be understood to be a blessing because it is a cause for achieving the various successively higher stages of distinction.

Seeing of the noble truths is the seeing of the four noble truths by the path, which occurs by way of the breakthrough; their meanings are explained in the *Visuddhimagga*.[1096] This is a blessing because it is a cause for overcoming the suffering of saṃsāra.

Realization of nibbāna: Here it is the fruit of arahantship that is intended by nibbāna; for that is called nibbāna because it has emerged from craving, which is designated "the jungle of the five destinations."[1097] Its attainment, or the reviewing of it, is called "realization." Already with the seeing of the noble truths, the realization of the other nibbāna (that is, nibbāna as the unconditioned, the third noble truth) is accomplished; hence that is not intended here. Thus this realization of nibbāna [153] should be understood as a blessing because it is a cause for dwelling happily in this present life and so forth.[1098]

Thus four blessings have been stated by this verse, too: austerity, the spiritual life, seeing of the noble truths, and the realization of nibbāna. The way in which they are blessings has already been elucidated for each.

The commentary on the meaning of this verse, "Austerity," is finished.

One whose mind does not shake

268. When one's mind does not shake, waver, or tremble when touched and overrun by the eight worldly conditions—by gain and non-gain and the other pairs[1099]—one's mind should be understood to be a blessing because it brings the world-transcending state that is unshakable by anything. But whose mind does not shake when touched by these conditions? It is none other than that of the arahant, one whose influxes are destroyed. And this is said:

As a stone mountain, one solid mass,
is not stirred by the wind,
so no forms and tastes, sounds,
odors, and tactile objects,
and things desirable or undesirable,
stir the mind of the impartial one.
His mind is steady and freed,

and he observes its vanishing. (AN III 379,1–4,
Vin I 185,5–8) [154]

Sorrowless: the mind only of an arahant. For it is sorrowless because it has no "sorrow, sorrowing, sorrowfulness, inner sorrow, inner grief, mental distress" and so forth (Vibh 156, §237). Some say this ("sorrowless") refers to nibbāna, but that does not agree with the earlier term ("one whose mind"). And as it is sorrowless, so the mind of the arahant alone is dust-free and secure. It is **dust-free** because it is devoid of the dust of lust, hatred, and delusion, and **secure**, because it is secure from the four bonds. Although threefold when described in a specific way at any given moment, it should be understood as a blessing because it brings the state foremost in the world, namely, the aggregates of one beyond training,[1100] and because it brings the state of being worthy of gifts and so forth.

Thus four blessings have been stated by this verse: the mind unshaken by the eight worldly conditions, the sorrowless mind, the dust-free mind, and the secure mind. The way in which they are blessings has already been elucidated for each.

The commentary on the meaning of this verse, "One whose mind does not shake when touched by worldly conditions," is finished.

Those who have done these things

269. Having thus spoken of thirty-eight blessings in the ten verses beginning with "not associating with fools," the Blessed One next spoke the concluding verse, "Those who have done these things," extolling these same blessings stated by himself.

This is the commentary on the meaning: **Those who have done these things**: those who have done these things stated by me, beginning with not associating with fools. **Are victorious everywhere**:[1101] They are not defeated anywhere [155] by even one among the four antagonists—the māras of the aggregates, defilements, volitional activities, and Māra the young deva—but they themselves defeat these four māras.

Everywhere they go safely:[1102] Having done these blessings, being undefeated by the four māras, they go safely everywhere, in the present world and the next world, whether standing or walking, and so forth. They go safely because of the absence of the influxes, distress, and fevers that might have arisen by associating with fools and other causes. They go without disaster, without calamity, secure and free from fear.

Theirs is that highest blessing: With this line of the verse, the Blessed One concludes the teaching. How? "In this way, young deva, understand that since those who do such things go safely everywhere, those who undertake these thirty-eight blessings, beginning with not associating with fools, obtain the highest, best, and most excellent blessing."

At the end of the teaching concluded by the Blessed One in such a way, 100,000 koṭis of deities attained arahantship, while the number of those who attained the fruits of stream-entry, once-returner, and non-returner was incalculable. On the next day the Blessed One addressed the Elder Ānanda: "Last night, Ānanda, a certain deity approached me and asked a question about blessings. I spoke to him about thirty-eight blessings. Learn this exposition on blessings, Ānanda, and having learned it, teach it to the bhikkhus." The elder learned it and taught it to the bhikkhus. It has come down right to the present day through the succession of teachers, and thereby this spiritual life has become successful, abundant, widespread, popular, [156] prevalent, and well revealed among devas and human beings. So it should be understood.

Now, in order to facilitate familiarity with these blessings, they are construed here starting from the beginning: These beings, desiring happiness in this present world and the next world and world-transcending bliss, begin by not associating with foolish people, relying upon the wise, and venerating those worthy of veneration. By residing in a suitable place and having done merit in the past, being motivated to engage in the wholesome, they direct themselves rightly. They adorn themselves with much learning, a craft, and discipline, and speak well-spoken words that accord with their discipline. As long as they remain in the lay life, they clear up their past debts by attending upon mother and father, discharge their new debt by maintaining wife and children, and acquire affluence through an honest occupation. By giving, they make proper use of wealth, and by righteous conduct, they make proper use of life. By assisting their relatives, they promote the well-being of their own people, and by blameless deeds, they promote the well-being of other people. By abstaining from evil, they avoid harming others, and by refraining from intoxicating drinks, they avoid harming themselves. By heedfulness in good qualities, they increase their stock of the wholesome, and because their stock of the wholesome has increased, they discard the markings of a layperson, take up the monastic life, and with reverence and humility fulfill their duties toward the Buddha, his disciples, their preceptor, teacher, and others. By contentment they abandon greed for the requisites; by gratitude they stand on the plane of good people; by listening to the Dhamma they abandon mental sluggishness; by patience they overcome all obstacles; by being amenable to advice they protect themselves; by the seeing of ascetics they see application to the practice; and by discussion of the Dhamma they dispel perplexity about things that cause perplexity. By the austerity of sense restraint they purify good behavior; by the spiritual life consisting in the duty of an ascetic, they purify the mind and accomplish the four purifications following it; [157] and by this practice they purify knowledge and vision, represented by "seeing of the noble truths." Thereby they realize nibbāna, which is here a designation for the fruit of arahantship. When they have realized this, their minds are unshaken by the eight worldly conditions just as Mount Sineru is unshaken by blasts of wind, and they are sorrowless, dust-free, and secure. Those who are secure are everywhere undefeated by anyone, and they go safely everywhere. Hence the Blessed One said:

"Those who have done these things
are victorious everywhere;
everywhere they go safely:
theirs is that highest blessing."

5 Sūciloma
(*Sūciloma Sutta*)

[301][1103] What is the origin? Its origin will become clear through the commentary on the meaning. And in the commentary on the meaning, the meaning of the words **thus have I heard** and so forth has already been explained. **[The Blessed One] was dwelling at Gayā at the Ṭaṃkita Bed, the abode of the yakkha Sūciloma**: In this connection, if it is asked, "What is Gayā? What is the Ṭaṃkita Bed? And why was the Blessed One dwelling at the abode of the yakkha Sūciloma?" it is said:

"Gayā" refers to both a village and a ford; both are applicable here. For he was dwelling in an area not far from the village of Gayā, so it is said he was dwelling at Gayā, and the Ṭaṃkita Bed was located in the vicinity of that village, not far away, near the gate. And he was dwelling at the Gayā ford, so it is said that he was dwelling at Gayā. The Ṭaṃkita Bed was a stone bed made of a wide slab of stone mounted horizontally on top of four other stones. The abode of the yakkha was based on this, like the abode of Āḷavaka.

That day, just before dawn, the Blessed One emerged from the meditative attainment of great compassion, surveyed the world with the buddha eye, and saw that two yakkhas, Sūciloma and Khara, both had a supporting condition for the fruit of stream-entry. Therefore, though the site was soiled by spittle, snot, and various other impure excretions of people who assembled there from various quarters, the Blessed One took his bowl and robe, and while it was still dawn, went to the area around the ford and sat down on the Ṭaṃkita Bed, the abode of the yakkha Sūciloma. Hence it is said: "On one occasion the Blessed One was dwelling at Gayā at the Ṭaṃkita Bed, the abode of the yakkha Sūciloma."

Now on that occasion—the occasion when the Blessed One was dwelling there—**the yakkha Khara and the yakkha Sūciloma passed by not far from the Blessed One**: Who were those yakkhas and why were they passing by? It is said that in the past, one of them took oil belonging to the Sangha without permission and anointed his own body with it. Because of that kamma he was tormented in hell and thereafter was reborn in the yakkha realm on the bank of the Gayā Lotus Pond.[1104] As a residual result of that kamma, his body and limbs were deformed [302] and his skin had a rough texture, like a tiled roof. It is said that when he wanted to frighten others, he would do so by raising the scales of his skin, which were like roof tiles. In this way, because the texture of his skin was rough, he acquired the name "the yakkha Khara" (*khara* meaning "rough").

The other, in the time of the Blessed One Kassapa, had been a lay follower who went to the monastery and listened to the Dhamma eight days a month. One day, when a preaching of the Dhamma was announced, he heard the announcement while he was playing in his own field near the entrance to the Sangha's residence hall. Thinking, "If I bathe, I'll be late," he entered the uposatha hall, and with a dirty body lay down disrespectfully on a valuable carpet and fell asleep. But the Saṃyutta reciters say he was a bhikkhu, not a lay follower. Because of that kamma and some other kamma he was tormented in hell and thereafter was reborn in the yakkha realm on the bank of the Gayā Lotus Pond. As a residual result of that kamma, he was hideous and his body hairs were like needles on his body. To frighten beings, he would act as if he were about to stab them with the needles. In this way, because his body hairs were like needles, he acquired the name "the yakkha Sūciloma" ("one with needle-like body hairs").

They had left their abode in order to seek food. Having been gone for a while, as they were returning along the path by which they had gone, they went off to another region and passed by not far from the Blessed One.

Then the yakkha Khara: Why did he speak thus? Khara spoke thus because he saw the attire of an ascetic. But Sūciloma held the belief: "One who gets frightened is not an ascetic; because he has only the outward form of an ascetic, he is a sham ascetic."[1105] Therefore, thinking the Blessed One was like that, he said suddenly: **He is not an ascetic; he is a sham ascetic.** But then, again wishing to investigate, he said: **I'll soon find out whether he is an ascetic or a sham ascetic.** From the words "Then the yakkha Sūciloma" up to "It is just that your touch is bad" the meaning is already clear. The words "he leaned toward the Blessed One" indicate: "He bent his own body toward the Blessed One."

Having seen that the Blessed One did not become afraid, [303] he said: **I'll ask you a question, ascetic.** For what reason? Because he thought: "This human ascetic is not afraid even of the rough touch of a non-human being. Let me now ask him a question that falls within the domain of a buddha. Surely, he won't be able to answer it, and then I will harass him in such a way." Having heard this, the Blessed One said: **I do not see anyone**, and so forth. This should all be understood in the way explained in relation to the Discourse with Āḷavaka (pp. 619–20). **The yakkha Sūciloma then addressed the Blessed One in verse.**

270. What is the source of lust and hatred?: Lust and hatred should be understood in the way already explained. "What is the source?": What is the cause? Or alternatively, by source is meant "born, arisen," so what is meant is "from what source, from what are they born, from what have they arisen?" **Where are born discontent, delight, and hair-raising terror?** *Discontent* is analyzed thus: "Discontent, discontentedness, dissatisfaction, being dissatisfied, aversion, agitation over remote lodgings and superior wholesome qualities" (Vibh 403, §856); *delight* occurs in relation to the five strands of sensual pleasure; and terror of mind is said to be *hair-raising* because it causes the body hairs to rise up. He asks: "Where are these three states born?" **Having originated from what . . . ?**: having arisen from what . . . ? **The mind** (*mano*): the wholesome mind (*kusalacittaṃ*). **Thoughts**: the nine kinds of thoughts, sensual thoughts and so forth, as explained in the commentary on the Discourse on the Serpent.[1106] **Toss one around as boys toss a crow**: He asks: "As village boys, when playing, tie a crow by its feet with a string and toss it up, throw it up,[1107] just so having originated from what do unwholesome thoughts toss up the wholesome mind?"[1108]

271. Then, answering those questions of his, the Blessed One spoke the second verse, "Lust and hatred."[1109] In this passage, **here** is said with reference to the individual; for lust and hatred have the individual as their source.[1110] And discontent, delight, and terror are born from the individual, and unwholesome thoughts such as sensual thoughts and so forth, having originated just from the individual, [304] toss up the wholesome mind. Hence, rejecting any other cause such as primordial nature and so forth,[1111] he says: "have their source here, are born from this, originate from this." The word usage here should be understood in accordance with the method explained in relation to the previous verse.

272ab. Having answered those questions thus, now demonstrating the meaning intended by the words "have their source in the individual, are born from the individual, originate from the individual," he says: **Born from affection, arisen from oneself**. For all these things such as lust and so forth, culminating in thoughts, are born from affection consisting in craving; and being produced in such a way, they have "arisen from oneself," a synonym for the individual consisting of the five aggregates subject to clinging. Hence he said: "Born from affection, arisen from oneself."

Now giving a simile to illustate this point, he says: **like the trunk-born shoots of the banyan tree**. Here, "trunk-born" means born among the trunks; this is a designation for the prop roots. What is meant? Just as the prop roots of a banyan tree, which are said to be born from the trunk, arise when there is the moisture of water, and as they arise, they originate among the various branches of that same banyan tree, in the same way lust and the other defilements arise when there is the internal moisture (affection) of craving, and as they arise, they originate among the various doors, objects, and bases such as the eye in one's own individuality. Therefore it should be understood that these "have their source in the individual, are born from the individual, originate from the individual."

Banyan tree with "trunk-born shoots"
From the *Illustrated London News* and *The Graphic*, via Wikimedia Commons.

272cd–273. This is a comprehensive explanation of the remaining one and a half verses. These things that have arisen in oneself are **manifold, attached to sensual pleasures**. For all these defilements are in every way manifold, of numerous kinds: lust by way of the five strands of sensual pleasure, hatred by way of the [ten] grounds for resentment, and discontent and so forth by way of their respective divisions. This being the case, they become attached, stuck to various sensual objects by way of the bases, doors, objects, and so forth, and they remain woven around them. In what way? **Like a māluvā creeper stretched across the woods**. As a māluvā creeper, stretched across the woods, becomes attached, stuck to the limbs and branches of a tree, and remains woven around them, just so the multitude of defilements remains attached to the manifold sensual objects.

Those who understand their source, they dispel it—listen, O yakkha! [305] What does he indicate by this? "Those beings who understand the source from which the multitude of defilements arise know: 'They arise in one's individuality moistened by the moisture of craving.' Drying up the moisture of craving with the fire of knowledge, [which is kindled by] developing the contemplation of danger, *they dispel it*, abandon it, terminate it. *Listen, O yakkha*, to this well-expressed statement of ours." Thus here, by knowledge of the individual, he indicates the full understanding of suffering; and by the dispelling of the multitude of defilements, such as craving, affection, lust, and so forth, he indicates the abandoning of its origin.

Those who dispel it **cross this flood so hard to cross, uncrossed before, for no renewed existence**. By this he indicates the development of the path and the realization of cessation. For those who dispel the multitude of defilements necessarily develop the path, since there is no dispelling of defilements without development of the path. And those who develop the path cross this fourfold flood—the flood of sensual desire and so forth—which is hard to cross by ordinary knowledge. For the development of the path is the crossing of the flood. **Uncrossed before**: not previously overcome in this long journey [through saṃsāra], not even in a dream; **for no renewed existence**: for nibbāna.

Listening to this verse that explains the four truths, the two companion yakkhas progressed through wisdom in its sequential stages[1112] described thus: "Having listened, they retain the Dhamma in mind; they examine the meaning of the teachings they have retained in mind," (MN I 480,5) and so forth. At the conclusion of the verse, they were established in the fruit of stream-entry, and they became pleasing, of golden complexion, adorned with celestial ornaments.

6 Kapila (Righteous Conduct)[1113]
(Kapila Sutta)

What is the origin? In the way explained in relation to the Hemavata Sutta, after the Blessed One Kassapa had attained final nibbāna, two clansmen who were brothers went forth under his disciples. The elder was named Sodhana, the younger Kapila. Their mother was named Sādhanī and their younger sister Tāpanā. They [306] went forth under the bhikkhunīs.

Then, in the way explained in relation to the Hemavata Sutta, the two brothers asked: "How many vocations are there in the Teaching?" (see p. 586). Having heard the answer, the elder decided: "I will fulfill the vocation of practice." He spent five years under his teacher and preceptor, and on completing his fifth year he learned how to develop a meditation subject and then entered the forest, where he strived hard and attained arahantship. But thinking, "I am still young, so I'll fulfill the vocation of practice when I'm old," Kapila undertook the vocation of scriptural study and became an expert in the Tipiṭaka. Based on his scriptural mastery, he acquired a retinue, and based on his retinue, he acquired gain. He became intoxicated with his learning, considered himself wise, and thought he had understood what he did not actually understand. When others said something is allowable, he said it is not allowable; when they said something is not allowable, he said it is allowable; when they said something is blameworthy, he said it is blameless; when they said it is blameless, he said it is blameworthy. Admonished by the well-behaved bhikkhus not to speak in such a way, he would belittle and denigrate them by saying: "What do you know? You are like an empty fist."

The bhikkhus reported this matter to his brother, the Elder

Sodhana. He too approached his younger brother and said: "Friend Kapila, for those like you the life of the Teaching is proper practice. Friend Kapila, do not say that what is allowable is not allowable . . . and what is blameless is blameworthy." But Kapila did not accept his advice. Sodhana spoke to him two and three times, and then turned away from him [following the maxim]:

> Out of compassion, one should speak
> one time or two times.
> One should not speak more than that,
> like a slave in the presence of his master.[1114]

Having warned him, "You, friend, will be known through your own action," he departed. From then on the well-behaved bhikkhus shunned him.

Being badly behaved himself, he dwelled with a retinue of those who were badly behaved. Then one day, thinking, "I will gather them for the uposatha," he ascended the lion seat, took the decorative fan, sat down, and said three times: "Does any bhikkhu here, friends, recite the Pātimokkha?" Not even one bhikkhu [307] said, "I recite the Pātimokkha," and neither he nor the others recited the Pātimokkha. Then he thought, "The Vinaya does not depend on whether or not the Pātimokkha is heard," and he rose from his seat. In this way he initiated the decline and destruction of the Blessed One Kassapa's Teaching.

That very day the Elder Sodhana attained final nibbāna. Kapila, having initiated the decline of the Teaching, died and was reborn in the great hell Avīci. His mother and sister, following his example, also abused and reviled the well-behaved bhikkhus, so when they died they too were reborn in hell.

Now at that time there were five hundred men who lived by banditry, raiding villages, and so forth. When they fled, pursued by the people of the region, they entered the forest. They did not see any thicket or other place of refuge, but they saw a forest bhikkhu living under a rock ledge not far away. They venerated him and said to him: "Bhante, be our refuge." The elder said: "For you there is no refuge like good behavior. All of you must take the five precepts." They all agreed and undertook the precepts. The elder said: "You are holders of the precepts. Now you should not bear hatred even toward those who destroy your own lives." They all agreed.

Then the people of the region arrived and searching here and there, they saw the bandits and killed them. After their death, they were reborn among the desire-sphere devas. The senior bandit became the senior deva and the others formed his retinue. They spent the interval between two buddhas in the deva world, faring upward and downward. At the time of our Blessed One the senior deva passed away from the deva world and was reborn in the womb of the senior fisherman's wife in a clan of five hundred fishermen that lived in a fishing village near the entrance to Sāvatthī. The others were reborn in the wombs of the wives of the other fishermen. In this way they were all conceived on the same day and all emerged from the womb on the same day.

Thereupon the senior fisherman inquired: "Have any other children been born in this village today?" When he saw those other children, [308] he said, "They will be my son's companions," and he gave all an allowance for their sustenance. All these friends played together from the time they were infants until they reached maturity. Yasoja was their leader.[1115]

Just then, as a residue of his torment in hell, Kapila was reborn as a fish in the Aciravatī River, with a golden color but with a foul odor coming from its mouth. One day all the fishermen's children took nets and went to the river, thinking to catch fish. They cast their nets into the river and that fish entered one of their nets. Seeing this, the entire fishing village shouted and applauded, saying: "Our sons have caught their first fish, and it's a golden fish. The children will be prosperous. Now our king will give us abundant wealth."

Then the five hundred friends put the fish in a boat and went to the king. When the king saw them he asked, "What is this?" and they replied: "It's a fish, lord." When the king saw the golden fish, he said, "The Blessed One must know the reason for its color," and he took the fish to the Blessed One. When the fish opened its mouth, it filled Jeta's Grove with an extremely foul odor.

The king asked the Blessed One: "Why, Bhante, does this fish have a golden color, and why does it emit such a foul odor from its mouth?" [The Blessed One replied:] "Great king, during the time of the Blessed One Kassapa, this fish was a bhikkhu named Kapila who was learned, one who had received the heritage of the Teaching, but he abused and reviled bhikkhus who would not accept his own word and he brought about the destruction of that Blessed One's Teaching. Since he did so, on account of that kamma he was reborn in the great hell Avīci, and as a residual result of that kamma he has now become a fish. Since for a long time he taught the word of the Buddha and spoke praise of the Buddha, as a consequence he has such a color.[1116] But since he abused and reviled the bhikkhus, he emits a foul odor from his mouth. Shall I make him speak up, great king?"

"Yes, Blessed One." [309]

Then the Blessed One addressed the fish: "Are you Kapila?" – "Yes, Blessed One, I am Kapila." – "From where have you come?" – "From the great hell Avīci, Blessed One." – "Where has Sodhana gone?" – "He attained final nibbāna, Blessed One." – "Where has Sādhanī gone?" – "She was reborn in hell, Blessed One."[1117] – "Where has Tāpanā gone?" – "She was reborn in the great hell, Blessed One." – "Where will you go now?" – "To the great hell, Blessed One."

Immediately he was overcome by remorse, struck the boat with his head, died, and was reborn in the great hell. The multitude were stirred by a sense of urgency, and their hair stood up in terror. Then the Blessed One spoke this discourse, teaching the Dhamma in a way suitable for the occasion to the assembly of laypeople and monastics present there.

274. Here, **righteous conduct**: righteous conduct through bodily good conduct and so forth. **The spiritual life**: the spiritual life of the path (see p. 768). **They call this the supreme treasure**: Because good conduct brings attainment of the bliss of heaven and liberation, the noble ones call both mundane and world-transcending good conduct the supreme treasure. The supreme treasure is the supreme gem. The purport is that it accompanies one, depends on oneself, and is not shared in common with kings or others.

At this point, having shown "Whether for a layperson or a monastic, proper practice is the refuge," he now says, "But if one has gone forth," criticizing Kapila and others like him by showing the worthlessness of the going forth devoid of practice. Here is an explanation of the meaning: "Whoever has discarded the features of a layperson and **gone forth**, in the sense explained, **from home to homelessness**, merely by adopting the shaved head, the ochre robes, and so forth.

275. "... **of scurrilous character**, one who uses harsh speech; **who delights in harassing others**, because one delights in harassing others in various ways; **a brute**, because one is like a brute in lacking a sense of moral shame and moral dread, **one's way of life is worse**: the life of such a one is extremely bad, extremely low. Why? Because by this wrong practice **one stirs up dust for oneself**, the numerous kinds [of dust] such as lust and other defilements."

276. Not only is his life worse for this reason, but **a bhikkhu who delights in quarrels** because of his scurrilous nature, [310] **cloaked by the state of delusion** because of his confused understanding of the meaning of what is well stated, **does not know what has been declared** by the well-behaved bhikkhus when they say: "Do not speak thus, friend Kapila. Understand it in this way too." **The Dhamma taught by the Buddha**: He also does not understand the Dhamma taught by the Buddha, even when it is being spoken to him in various ways. Thus, too, his way of life is worse.[1118]

277. Because one like this delights in harassing others, **harassing one who is self-developed**: harassing the self-developed arahant bhikkhus, such as the Elder Sodhana, saying: "You monks who have renounced in old age do not understand the Vinaya, the Suttas, or the Abhidhamma." For this [word *bhāvitattānaṃ*] is a genitive occurring in an accusative sense. Or alternatively, the word "doing" (*karonto*) should be understood in relation to "harassment of those who are self-developed," in the way already stated; in this case [*bhāvitattānaṃ*] directly functions as a genitive.[1119] **Led on by ignorance**: being led on, driven by, motivated by ignorance,[1120] which conceals perception of the danger in harassing those who are self-developed, **one does not know** this activity of harassing those who are self-developed[1121] [to be] **defilement**, because of bringing mental affliction in this very life, [and] **the path leading to hell**, because it causes a fall into hell in the future.[1122]

278. And not knowing this, when through that path he has **entered the lower world**—the fourfold plane of misery—there in the lower world he goes **from womb to womb, from darkness to darkness**. In each group of beings he goes from mother's womb to mother's womb a hundred times, even a thousand times, and from darkness to the darkness in the asura realm, which cannot be dispersed even by the moon and sun. **Such a bhikkhu meets suffering** in its various forms like the fish Kapila **after death**, having gone from here to the next world.

279. For what reason? **As there might be a cesspit, full to the brim, many years old**: As the cesspit of a latrine many years old, being filled to the brim over many years with excrement, would become full, and [311] even if it were washed with a hundred or a thousand buckets of water, there would be no way to remove its foul odor and ugly appearance, and so it would be hard to purify; in the same way, **such a one would be similar**, this person **who is blemished,**[1123] whose actions have been defiled for a long time, who is full of evil like a cesspit with excrement, **is hard to purify**. He is not purified even after experiencing the result of that blemish for a long time. Therefore "a bhikkhu indeed like this, having passed away, undergoes suffering" over a length of time that cannot even be measured by counting the years.

Or alternatively, the connection of this verse [with the previous one] is as follows: When it was said, "A bhikkhu indeed like this, having passed away, undergoes suffering," it might occur to you: "Is it possible for him to do something so that, having passed away, he would not undergo suffering?" It is not possible. Why not? Because "as there might be a cesspit . . . one who is blemished is hard to purify."

280. When in advance **you know one like this, bhikkhus, one attached to the home life**—when you know one like this to be attached to the five strands of sensual pleasure; to be **of evil desires**, because he is possessed by an evil desire to be admired for nonexistent excellent qualities;[1124] of **evil inten-**

tions, because he is possessed by sensual thoughts and other unwholesome thoughts; of **evil conduct**, because he is disposed to evil conduct—to bodily transgression and so forth and to such deeds as offering gifts of bamboo and so forth;[1125] and of **evil resort**, because he resorts to prostitutes and so forth.[1126]

281. . . . having come together in harmony, all of you should shun him: You should avoid him; you should not resort to him. And do not be satisfied by merely shunning him, but even more, **Cast out the trash! Expel the depraved fellow!**[1127] Without concern, cast out that rubbish-like individual just as if he were rubbish. Expel the dregs of a man as if he were an outcast leper with oozing sores that has entered into the midst of khattiyas and so forth. Grab him by the hand or head and drag him out. He shows: "Just as [312] the Venerable Mahāmoggallāna grabbed a person of evil character by the arm, evicted him through the outer gatehouse, and bolted the door, so you should expel this one."[1128] For what reason? Because the residence of the Sangha was built for those who are virtuous, not for those who are immoral.

282. Since this is the case, **then sweep the chaff away, non-ascetics who imagine themselves ascetics**. For as chaff, though inwardly devoid of grain, appears like rice on account of the outer husk, so evil bhikkhus, though inwardly devoid of virtuous behavior and so forth, appear like bhikkhus because of their external accessories such as the ochre robes. Therefore they are called chaff. Sweep away that chaff, scatter it, disperse those who are non-ascetics in the supreme sense but imagine themselves to be ascetics merely because of their attire. Thus **having blown away . . . with the pure.**

283. Ever mindful: respectful and deferential toward one another. **Then, harmonious and judicious, you will make an end of suffering**: Then, as you who are pure make your dwelling with the pure, harmonious by sharing the same views and good behavior, as your wisdom ripens, eventually you prudent ones will make an end of all this suffering of the round. Thus he concluded the teaching with its culmination in arahantship.

At the conclusion of the teaching, those five hundred

fishermens' sons acquired a sense of urgency, and desiring to make an end of suffering, they went forth under the Blessed One. In no long time, having made an end of suffering, they enjoyed with the Blessed One the meditative attainment of imperturbable dwelling. Their enjoyment of that attainment together with the Blessed One should be understood as explained in the Udāna, in the Discourse to Yasoja.[1129]

7 The Tradition of the Brahmins
(*Brāhmaṇadhammika Sutta*)

What is the origin? This is stated in the introduction in this way: "Then some affluent brahmins . . ." [313] **Affluent brahmins**: They were brahmins by birth who were affluent because they had abundant resources. It is said that those who own eighty koṭis of wealth, deposited in storage, are called "affluent brahmins." And these were such; hence it is said "affluent brahmins."[1130] [314]

The brahmanical tradition of the ancient brahmins:[1131] the brahmanical tradition without regard to traditions determined by place, time, and so forth.[1132] **In that case, brahmins**: "Since you ask me, therefore, brahmins, **listen,** lend an ear, **and attend closely,** pay careful attention." So too, *listen* by purity of exertion, *and attend closely* by purity of inclination. *Listen* without distraction, *and attend closely* with mental application. In this way, the purport of these terms, not previously explained, should be understood.

Then, accepting the word uttered by the Blessed One, **those affluent brahmins replied**: **"Yes, sir."** When the Blessed One said, "Listen and attend closely," they consented to do so from a desire to act upon that matter. Then, when they had replied in such a way, **the Blessed One said this** to them. What is that? "The rishis of the past" and so forth.

284. Controlled themselves: controlled in mind by control through good behavior; **were austere**: possessed of austerity through restraint over the sense faculties; **they practiced for their own good**: They acted for their own good by the study of the sacred hymns, the development of the divine abodes, and so forth.

285. The brahmins did not own cattle: The ancient brahmins did not own cattle; they did not take possession of cattle. **Nor did they keep bullion and grain**: [315] As to bullion, the brahmins did not have even a coin;[1133] so too, they did not have the various kinds of grain and cereals, such as paddy, rice, barley, and wheat. For without storing up deposits of gold and silver, **they had study as their wealth and grain**: they possessed wealth and grain that consisted only in study of the sacred hymns. **They guarded a divine treasure**: This abiding in loving-kindness and so forth (*mettādivihāra*) is called a divine treasure (*brahmanidhi*) because it is the best and because it follows one along; they guarded it by being always intent on developing it.

286. As they dwelled in such a way, **whatever was prepared for them, such food was placed at their doors**: Whatever was prepared for the sake of those brahmins, such food was placed at the doors of their own home by the many donors who prepared it with the intention: "We will give this to the brahmins." **People thought**: Their donors thought that the food prepared and placed at their doors should be given to these brahmins who sought gifts of faith, but not more than that. For they did not need anything else; they were content simply with food and clothing as their maximum requirements.

287. With such accessories as **cloths dyed various colors, with bedding**, with decorative spreads and bed sheets, **and with dwellings**, with excellent single-story and double-story mansions; **prosperous provinces and realms paid homage to those brahmins**: Each province and entire realms, saying, "Homage to the brahmins," paid homage to the brahmins in the evening and the morning as if they were devas.

288. Being venerated in such a way, **the brahmins were inviolable** by the people of the world. Not only were they inviolable, but they were also **unconquerable** because no one could overcome them in order to harm them. For what reason? Because they were **protected by Dhamma**: For they maintained the five excellent precepts; the purport is that, since "the Dhamma indeed protects one who practices the Dhamma" (Ja IV 54,30), being protected by Dhamma, they were inviolable and unconquerable. [316] **No one at all obstructed them**: Since they were considered dear and observed the excellent precepts, people fully trusted them just like their own parents; therefore, no one obstructed those brahmins at the doors of their homes, in any way, outside and inside, saying: "You should not enter this place."

289. Thus protected by Dhamma, moving about unobstructed at the doors of homes, **for forty-eight years they observed the spiritual life of virginal celibacy**, observing it from their boyhood on. Even the caṇḍāla-brahmins did so; how much more then the one like Brahmā.[1134] Living the spiritual life in such a way, **the brahmins in the past pursued the quest for knowledge and conduct** by not forsaking the celibate life. Here, the "quest for knowledge" is the study of the sacred hymns. For this is said: "He lives the spiritual life of virginal celibacy for forty-eight years, studying the sacred hymns" (AN III 225,20). "The quest for conduct" is observance of the precepts.[1135]

290. Having lived the spiritual life of celibacy for the stated length of time, thereafter, settling into the householder life, **the brahmins did not marry outside**: those "who were like devas" and those "who remained within the boundary" did not marry a khattiya woman or one from any other social class such as the vessas. **Nor did they purchase a wife** by giving a hundred or a thousand, as some now purchase one. For these sought a wife righteously (*dhammena*). How? Having lived the spiritual life of celibacy for forty-eight years, they wandered seeking a girl as an offering at the door of a brahmin[1136] thus: "I have lived the spiritual life of celibacy for forty-eight years. If there is a girl who has reached maturity, give her to me." Then whoever had a girl who had reached maturity would adorn her, lead her out, sprinkle water over the hand of the brahmin while he is standing at the door, and give the girl to him, saying: "I give her to you as a wife, brahmin, for you to support." [317]

But after having lived the spiritual life of celibacy for so long, why did they seek a wife rather than remain celibate for their entire life span? Because of their wrong view. For they held such a view: "One who does not beget a son cuts off the family lineage and as a result is tormented in hell." It is said that these four are afraid of things that one should not fear: an earthworm, a female bluejay, a *kontanī* bird, and a brahmin. Earthworms, it is said, eat in moderation from fear that they will destroy the earth; they do not eat much soil. The female bluejay lies supine on top of its egg from fear that the sky will fall. The *kontanī* bird does not tread at ease on the ground from fear of an earthquake. Brahmins seek a wife from fear of cutting off the family lineage. And he said in this connection:

> The earthworm, the female bluejay,
> the *kontanī* bird, and a righteous brahmin,
> these four deluded beings are afraid
> when there is no ground for fear.

Thus, having sought a wife righteously, **having united through affection, they agreed to dwell together**: united in body and mind, joined together, bound solely by affection for one another, they agreed to dwell together; not without affection or by compulsion.

291. Even when agreeing[1137] to dwell together out of affection, **apart from that occasion**—that occasion of fertility (*utusamayo*) when a brahmin woman should be approached by a brahmin—**after her fertile season was over, the brahmins never went**[1138] **to her for sexual intercourse during the interval**; they waited until the next occasion arrived.[1139] The purport of **the brahmins** here is those who were like devas and those who remained within the boundary.

292. But without exception they all "praised the spiritual life of celibacy . . . and patience." Here, **the spiritual life of celibacy** is abstinence from sexual intercourse. **Good behavior** is the remaining four training rules. **Rectitude**: uprightness, non-deceitfulness and non-hypocrisy. [318] **Mildness**: non-obstinacy and non-arrogance. **Austerity**: restraint of the sense faculties. **Gentleness**: pleasant behavior, non-repulsive conduct. **Harmlessness**: not being disposed to cause injury with the fists and so forth; a compassionate nature. **Patience**: forbearance. Thus they praised these excellent qualities. Even those who could not entirely fulfill them in practice still regarded them as valuable and praised them by speech.

293. Among those who spoke such praise, **he who was supreme among them, the brahmin**—the highest brahmin, the one like Brahmā—**firm in his exertion** because he possessed firm exertion, **did not engage in sex,** in sexual intercourse, **even in a dream**, even within a dream.

294. "Training in accordance with his practice . . . praised": By this verse, describing from beginning to end the excellent qualities stated in the ninth verse (**292**), he shows the brahmins who were like devas. For these **of intelligent disposition**, being wise, **trained in accordance with the practice** of the brahmin who was like Brahmā, by going forth and developing the jhānas, and they praised by way of practice such qualities as the spiritual life of celibacy and so forth. All these brahmins should be understood in the way explained in the Discourse with Doṇa in the Book of Fives (AN 5:192).

295. Now, showing the brahmins who remained within the boundary, he says: "Having requested rice." This is its meaning: If those brahmins who remained within the boundary wished to perform a sacrifice, then, since they refrained from accepting raw grain, they **righteously requested rice** of various kinds; **bedding,** beds and chairs and so forth; **clothes** of linen and so forth; and **ghee and oil**, ghee from cows and oil from sesamum seeds. They would ask for it righteously, which means standing and indicating what one needs, in the way stated thus:

> The noble ones indicate by standing;
> this is the way the noble ones make a request.[1140]

Having **collected** the items that were offered, such as rice and other items, **they then performed sacrifice.** [319]

But at the sacrifice that was arranged, they did not slaughter cattle: They did not kill cows, and here, under the heading of cattle, all living beings are included. Why didn't they slaughter them? Because they possessed such excellent qualities as the spiritual life and so forth.

296–97. Further, distinctively, "like a mother . . . they did not slaughter cattle." Here, **medicines are produced in them**: In them the five products of a cow are produced,[1141] which serve as medicines for bile conditions and other illnesses. **They give food**: When people eat the five cow products, their hunger subsides, their strength increases, their complexion becomes more beautiful, and bodily and mental happiness arises. Therefore it should be understood that **they give food, strength, beauty, and happiness**.

298. Thus, since they did not slaughter cattle at the sacrifices, their bodies, sustained by the power of their merits, were "delicate . . . this population happily flourished." Here, **delicate**, because their hands and feet and so forth were soft and tender; **with large bodies**, because they were tall and broad; **handsome**, because of their golden complexion and impressive figure; **glorious**, because they acquired gain and retinues; **were keen on what was to be done and avoided**: keen about "this should be done" and "this should not be done"; **according to their own traditions** (*sehi dhammehi*): according to their own customs. **As long as these continued in the world**: Thus as long as those ancient brahmins, who were handsome, graceful, supremely worthy of offerings by the world, continued in this practice, **this population**—this world of beings—**happily flourished**; free from misfortune, peril, and disaster, this population achieved the various kinds of happiness, or it flourished happily, happily achieved prosperity.[1142]

299–300. But as time went by, for those who wished to enter upon the stage of "those who cross the boundary,"[1143] **an inversion took place in them**. Here, "inversion" (*vipallāsa*) is an inverted perception (*viparītasaññā*). **The slight as slight**: having regarded the slight happiness of sensual pleasures as slight—in the sense of being coarse, limited, and unsatisfying—as not approaching even a fraction of the happiness of the jhānas, immeasurable states, and nibbāna;[1144] or having seen the slight, trifling happiness of sensual pleasures as trifling compared to the happiness of the mundane meditative attainments they themselves obtained, which itself is slight compared to world-transcending happiness. [320] What is meant? Those brahmins had previously seen the slight as slight—the happiness of sensual pleasures, the splendor of the king, the adorned women, and the chariots, residences, and dwellings as described—but now there occurred in them an inverted perception—an inversion in the previous perception of renunciation—whereby they saw as "happiness" those sensual objects that were actually suffering.

Well made: well fashioned in woodwork and bronze work. **With colorful coverings**: adorned with lion skins and so forth. **Abodes**: the sites of houses; **residences**: the houses built on them; **designed**: designed by way of length and width; **measured in proportion**: with each section properly measured—courtyard, gate, mansion, roof peak, and so forth.

301. Having acquired such an inverted perception, **the brahmins then coveted . . . and groups of resplendent women**. "Coveted" (*abhijjhāyiṃsu*) means that they nurtured craving for them and contemplated them desiring: "Oh, that this might belong to us!"[1145]

302. Coveting these things in such a way, they considered: "These people are well bathed and well anointed, with their hair and beards trimmed, wearing jewelry and adornments, enjoying the five strands of sensual pleasure. But though they venerate us, we are most pitiable, with bodies soiled by sweat and dirt, with long hair and fingernails, destitute of wealth. And they go around on the backs of elephants, on horseback, in palanquins, and in golden chariots, while we go around on foot. They live in two-storied mansions, while we live in the forest, beneath trees, and so forth. They sleep on excellent beds covered with woolen coverings, while we spread out straw mats or leather pads and sleep on the ground. They eat food of various flavors, while we support ourselves on gleanings. How can we be like them?" They then concluded: "Wealth is desirable. It isn't possible to achieve this success without wealth." Then, having broken into the Vedas, they removed the ancient sacred hymns connected with Dhamma and composed sham hymns connected with non-Dhamma. Desirous of wealth, they then approached King Okkāka and, pleading for safety, told him: "Great king, there are ancient hymns that have come down in the lineage of brahmins. We have kept them wrapped up in a teacher's fist [321] and haven't recited them to anyone, but you, great king, ought to hear them." They then praised the horse sacrifice and other sacrifices. Having praised them, exhorting the king, they said: "Sacrifice, great king. You have abundant wealth and grain. You do not lack the provisions for a sacrifice. If you hold such a sacrifice, for seven generations your family will arise in heaven."

Hence, showing this stratagem of theirs, the Blessed One said: "Having composed hymns to that end . . . you have much wealth." Here, **to that end** means "on account of the wealth that they coveted." For this locative term has the meaning of a cause.[1146] **You have abundant wealth and grain**: The purport is: "You will have abundant wealth and grain in a future life." For the experts in grammar recognize the present tense as also referring to the future by way of anticipation.[1147] **Treasure**: precious substances such as gold and so forth [called treasure (*vittaṃ*)] in the sense that they are a cause of satisfaction (*vitti-kāraṇato*); this refers to wealth as a basis for prosperity. Or alternatively, treasure is assets such as ornaments, which are a cause of delight. **Wealth**: bullion, gold, and so forth. What is meant? Those brahmins, having composed hymns, then approached Okkāka. How? "Great king, you have much treasure and wealth. Sacrifice, then in the future too you will have abundant wealth and grain."

303. Having given the reason, they made their case to the king, "And then . . . the king . . . gave wealth to the brahmins." **Convinced**: persuaded. **The lord of charioteers**: one who is similar to a bull in the sense of being unshakable among the khattiyas who are great charioteers.[1148] As for the horse sacrifice and so forth:[1149] **The horse sacrifice** is so called because they sacrifice a horse here.[1150] This is a designation for a sacrifice involving twenty-one sacrificial posts in which the objects of offering consist of all the items that remain after exception is made for land and men; it is to be performed along with two secondary sacrifices.[1151] **The man sacrifice** is so called because they sacrifice a man here.[1152] This is a designation for a sacrifice in which the objects of offering consist of the wealth mentioned in the case of the horse sacrifice together with land; it is to be performed along with four secondary sacrifices. The ***sammāpāsa*** is so called because they throw a sacrificial peg here.[1153] This is a designation for the *satra* sacrifice,[1154] which is to be performed by one who, having thrown a sacrificial peg each day, and having built an altar in the area where it has fallen, goes in reverse direction along with movable sacrificial posts, starting from the place where he was submerged alongside the Sarasvatī River.[1155] [322] The ***vājapeyya*** is so called because they drink *vāja* here.[1156] This is a designation for a sacrifice involving a sacrificial post of *beḷuva* wood, to be performed with seventeen cattle in which the objects of offering consist of multiples of seventeen;[1157] it is to be performed along with one secondary sacrifice. The ***niraggaḷa*** is so called because there is no bolt here.[1158] This is a designation for an alternative to the horse sacrifice, a term for the sacrifice of everything, in which the objects of offering consist of the items described under the horse sacrifice [but] including land and men; it is to be performed along with nine secondary sacrifices. The rest is clear.

304–5. Now, since it is said, "He then gave wealth to the brahmins," to show what was given he spoke the next two verses, beginning with the words "cattle and bedding." For the king thought, "For a long time they have been troubled by eating coarse food—so let them enjoy the five products of a cow," and he thus gave them herds of cattle together with bulls. So too, he thought, "For a long time, they have been troubled by sleeping on the ground, wearing rough garments, sleeping alone, traveling on foot, and dwelling at the foot of a tree and so forth—let them experience pleasure in using excellent bedding spread with woolen covers made of fleece and so forth," and so he gave them valuable bedding and other items. Thus he gave them these various items and other kinds of wealth, such as bullion and gold and so forth. Hence the Blessed One said: **cattle and bedding and clothes . . . he gave this wealth to the brahmins**.

306. Thus "having obtained wealth there," from that king, ". . . they again approached." What is meant? Those brahmins, having **obtained wealth** from the king through those sacrifices, having sought their food and clothing each day, day after day, over a long time, **agreed to store up** the various objects of sensual pleasure. Then, **as they fell under the control of desire**, as their minds were invaded by craving for taste by enjoying the five products of the cow—milk and so forth—they thought: "Since the milk and other products of cows are delicious, surely their meat must be even more delicious." Thus, on account of meat, **their craving increased still more**. They then considered: "If we get them killed and eat them, we will be criticized. Let's compose hymns." Once again, having broken into the Vedas, they **composed hymns for this purpose** in accordance with their aim—those brahmins [323] composed sham hymns for their purpose—and then they again approached King Okkāka.

307. Speaking about this matter, they said: "Like water . . . you have much wealth." What is meant? "Great king, this has come down in our hymns. **Like water**, which is used by living beings in all such tasks as washing the hands and so forth, and there is no evil for them on that account. Why not? **For that is an implement of beings** arisen for the purpose of being utilized. And like this great **earth**, which is utilized in all such tasks as walking and standing and so forth; and like **bullion**, consisting in *kahāpaṇas*, and **wealth**, gold and silver and so forth, and **grain**, barley and wheat and so forth, which are utilized in business transactions and so forth. **Just so cattle [are useful] to people**: They have arisen for the purpose of being utilized in all tasks. Therefore, having slain them, perform various sacrifices: **Sacrifice, you have much treasure; sacrifice, you have much wealth**."

308–9. Thus, in the way explained earlier, **and then the king . . . slaughtered in sacrifice** cows that previously had not harmed anyone in any way, **not with their feet . . . the king slew them with a knife.** Then, it is said, the brahmins filled a sacrificial pit with cattle, tied up an auspicious bull, led the root to the king, and told him: "Great king, perform the cattle sacrifice. In this way you will clear the path to the brahma world." After the king performed the blessing ceremony, he took a sword and killed many hundreds of thousands of cows together with a bull. The brahmins took pieces of flesh that had been cut up in the sacrificial pit and ate them, and having covered themselves in yellow, white, and red blankets they killed them. Because of that, it is said, whenever cows see people covered up, they become agitated. Hence the Blessed One said: "They did not harm anyone . . . slew them with a knife."

310. When the king began to slaughter the cattle, immediately upon seeing the slaughter of the cattle **the devas** ruled by the four great kings and so forth, **and the fathers**, the brahmās, who are so designated among the brahmins; Sakka, **Indra** the ruler of the devas; and the dānava yakkhas dwelling at the base of mountains, called **the asuras and rakkhasas**, uttered the exclamation, **How unrighteous! How unrighteous!**, and **cried out**, saying: "What a shame, people! What a shame, people!" Thus the cry rose up from the earth and in a moment reached as far as the brahma world, so that the world was filled with the single shout: "What a shame!" For what reason? **Because the knife struck a cow.**

311. Not only did the devas and other beings cry out, but other kinds of harm also arose in the world. [324] **Formerly there were three illnesses**: **desire, hunger, and old age**: craving for trifling things, hunger, and natural old age. **But because of the slaughter of cattle, there came to be ninety-eight**: Those multiplied until they became ninety-eight, including diseases of the eye and so forth.

312. Now, blaming the slaughter of cattle, the Blessed One said: "This unrighteousness." This is its meaning: **This**: a designation for the slaughter of cattle; **unrighteousness** consisting in violence, which is referred to in this way because it departs from righteousness; **by violence** of three kinds, bodily violence and so forth (the other two being violence by speech and mind). The unrighteousness **has come down**, has occurred, **as an ancient custom**, because it has occurred from that time on. From the time it has come down, **they kill the harmless creatures**, the cattle, who do not injure anyone in any way with their feet and so forth. Slaughtering them, **the sacrificers fall**—drop away, decline—**from righteousness**.

313. In such a way this mean practice: In such a way this low practice, this inferior practice; what is meant is "unrighteousness." Or else, since the practice of giving here was also slight, he said "mean practice" with reference to that. **Ancient**: ancient because it has been occurring over this long time. **Is censured by the wise.** And because it is censured by the wise, **wherever they see such a thing, people censure the sacrificer**. How? By saying such things as this: "The brahmins have given rise to a disaster that did not exist before, since they kill cattle and eat their flesh." This is the oral tradition about this.

314. When the Dhamma had thus been lost: when the ancient Dhamma of the brahmins had thus been lost;[1159] **suddas and vessas were divided**: suddas and vessas previously living in harmony were now divided. **Numerous khattiyas were divided**: Many khattiyas too were divided from one another.[1160] **The wife despised her husband**:[1161] And the wife, placed in the position of authority over household matters, equipped with the power of sons and other powers,[1162] despised her husband, reviled him, looked down upon him, and did not serve him respectfully.

315. Being thus divided from one another, **khattiyas and Brahmā's kinsmen . . . have come under the control of sensual pleasures**. Khattiyas and brahmins **and others**, vessas and suddas, **protected by their clan**, because they each had been protected by their own clan in such a way that they did not become miscegenous, all these, **disregarding the doctrine of birth**, having discarded all such claims as "I am a khattiya" and "I am a brahmin," [325] have come under the control of sensual pleasures—a designation for the five strands of sensual pleasures—they have fallen into attachment to them. Because of sensual desire there is nothing forbidden that they do not do.

Thus at this point the Blessed One concluded the teaching, having spoken praise of the ancient brahmins with the nine verses beginning "The rishis of the past" (**284–92**); having shown *the one like Brahmā* with the verse beginning "The supreme brahmin among them" (**293**); *the one like the devas* with the verse beginning "Training in accordance with his practice" (**294**); *the* *one who remains within the boundary* with the four verses beginning "Having requested rice, bedding" (**295–98**); and, with the seventeen verses beginning "But then an inversion took place in them" (**299–315**), he has shown the crying out of the devas and so forth because of the misconduct of *one who has crossed the boundary*. But *the caṇḍāla of a brahmin* (AN III 228–29) has not been spoken of here. Why not? Because there is no instance of his failure. For there are instances of the one like Brahmā, the one like the devas, and the one who remains within the boundary by their excellence [in upholding] the Dhamma of the brahmins; and there is the instance of the one who crosses the boundary by his failure in this respect. But there is no instance of the caṇḍāla brahmin described in the Discourse with Doṇa through his failure to uphold the Dhamma of the brahmins. Why not? Because they only arise after the Dhamma has deteriorated. Therefore, without showing this type, the Blessed One concluded the teaching.[1163]

But now even that caṇḍāla brahmin is rare. It is to this extent that the tradition of the brahmins has been lost. Hence the brahmin Doṇa said: "Such being the case, Master Gotama, we do not even measure up to the level of a caṇḍāla brahmin" (AN III 230,4).

8 On Dhamma (The Boat)
(Dhamma Sutta)

This Discourse on the Dhamma is also called "The Discourse on the Boat."[1164] What is the origin? This discourse was spoken with reference to the Venerable Elder Sāriputta. This is a brief account of the matter, but the detailed account should be understood beginning with the arising of the two chief disciples. That is, [326] it is said that before the Blessed One arose the two chief disciples, having fulfilled the pāramīs for one incalculable period and 100,000 eons, were reborn in the deva world. Not far from Rājagaha there was a tributary village of brahmins named Upatissagāma. The village chief there, a brahmin worth 560 koṭis of wealth, had a wife named Rūpasārī. The first [of the two chief disciples] to pass away was reborn in her womb. Not far away from this village there was another tributary village of brahmins named Kolitagāma. The village chief, a brahmin of similar wealth, had a wife named Moggallānī. The second [of the disciples] to pass away was reborn in her womb on the very same day. Thus the two were conceived on the same day and were born on the same day, and on the same day they gave the name Upatissa to one because he had been born in Upatissagāma, and they gave the name Kolita to the other because he had been born in Kolitagāma.

The two were friends from the days they played together as infants and remained such when they eventually reached maturity. Each had a retinue of five hundred youths. When they went to the park or the riverbank, they always went with their retinues, one group traveling in five hundred golden palanquins, the other in five hundred carriages drawn by thoroughbreds.

At the time a seasonal "hilltop festival" took place in Rājagaha, held in the evening in the middle of the city. The eminent khattiya youths and others residing throughout Aṅga and Magadha would gather here, and while sitting in their well-prepared couches and chairs would watch the festivities. The two friends went along with their retinues and sat down in the seats prepared for them. Thereupon Upatissa, while watching the festivities, looked out at the large crowd that had assembled and reflected: "Before a hundred years have gone by, everyone in this crowd will be dead." It seemed as if death had come to him and was standing on his forehead. The same happened to Kolita. Their minds no longer inclined even to looking at the many kinds of dancers as they were performing; instead, a sense of urgency arose in them.

When the festival was over and the crowd had dispersed, as the two friends were departing with their own retinues, Kolita asked Upatissa: "Why is it, friend, that you did not seem to enjoy watching the dancers and the other performers?" [327] Upatissa revealed his thoughts to Kolita and asked the same question. Kolita too revealed his own thoughts. He then said: "Come, friend. Having gone forth, we will seek the deathless." Upatissa agreed, saying: "Excellent, friend."

Then the two men discarded their wealth and arrived back in Rājagaha. Now at the time a wanderer named Sañjaya had settled at Rājagaha. Together with their respective retinues of five hundred youths, the two friends went forth under him, and within days they had learned the Three Vedas and the entire philosophy of the wanderers. Investigating the beginning, middle, and end of those treatises, they did not see the end and so they asked their teacher: "The beginning and middle of these treatises are seen but the end is not seen, [that of which it could be said]: 'This is what one may attain through these treatises, beyond which there is nothing further to be attained.'" He replied: "I too have not seen their end." They said: "In that case, let us seek out their end." The teacher replied: "Seek as you please."

Having obtained his permission, they then wandered about seeking the deathless and became famous throughout Jambudīpa. When questioned by wise khattiyas and others, they did not founder in replying to them. But so famous had they become that whenever the names Upatissa and Kolita were mentioned, no one said, "Who are they? We don't know of them."

Meanwhile, as they were wandering about in quest of the deathless, our Blessed One arose in the world, set in motion the wheel of the Dhamma, and eventually arrived at Rājagaha. But those wanderers, having traveled through the whole extent of Jambudīpa, did not even find the answer to their question about the goal, let alone did they find the deathless; and so they again returned to Rājagaha.

The sequel should all be understood in detail in the way it has come down in the Chapter on the Going Forth [in the passage beginning] "Then, in the morning, the Venerable Assaji dressed" as far as their going forth (Vin I 39–43). When the two friends had gone forth in such a way, the Venerable Sāriputta [328] realized the knowledge of a disciple's perfection[1165] after half a month. Whenever he lived in the same monastery as the Elder Assaji, after first attending upon the Blessed One, immediately afterward he would go to attend upon the Elder Assaji, thinking with reverence: "This venerable one was my first teacher, with whose support I came to understand the Blessed One's teaching." But whenever he did not live in the same monastery as the Elder Assaji, he would look out in the direction in which the elder was living, prostrate toward him, and pay homage to him with his hands joined in reverential salutation.

Having seen him doing so, some bhikkhus started to talk: "Though Sāriputta has become the chief disciple, he still worships the directions. Even today, it seems, he has not abandoned his brahmin view." Then, with the divine ear element, the Blessed One heard their conversation. Showing himself as still sitting in his excellent seat, he addressed those bhikkhus: "Bhikkhus, in what conversation were you engaged as you sat together here?" They informed him. The Blessed One then said: "Bhikkhus, Sāriputta is not worshipping the directions. He honors, worships, and esteems his own teacher, with whose support he came to understand the teaching. Bhikkhus, Sāriputta is one who venerates his teacher." Having said this, he spoke this discourse in order to teach the Dhamma to those who had assembled there.

316. A person should venerate the one from whom he would learn the Dhamma: the person from whom one would learn—know, understand—*the scriptural Dhamma* consisting in the three Piṭakas, or *the Dhamma of penetration*, consisting in the nine world-transcending states that are to be achieved after hearing the scriptures. **Just as the deities venerate Indra**: Just as the deities in two deva worlds venerate Sakka, the ruler (*inda*) of the devas, so too the pupil should rise early and venerate, honor, and revere the teacher by doing all the reciprocal duties, such as unfastening his sandals and so forth. For what reason? **Being venerated . . . reveals the Dhamma**: That teacher, venerated in such a way, a **learned one** by way of both scriptural learning and penetration, **pleased with him,** with the pupil, reveals the scriptural Dhamma by way of a discourse and the Dhamma of penetration to be achieved by practicing as instructed after one has heard the discourse. [329] Or through a discourse he reveals the scriptural Dhamma and by way of similes he reveals the Dhamma of penetration he himself has achieved.

317. Having attended and listened to it: having attended and listened to the Dhamma revealed by the teacher when he is pleased; **practicing in accordance with the Dhamma**: developing insight, which is "in accordance with the Dhamma" because it moves in conformity with the world-transcending Dhamma; **a wise [pupil]**: a person who is wise through his capacity in upholding;[1166] **who heedfully follows such [a teacher]**: who is heedful, motivated by confidence in him, and follows such a learned [teacher] of the kind previously described; **[that pupil] becomes intelligent, incisive, and astute**: He becomes *intelligent* by the achievement of wisdom, which is designated intelligence; *incisive*, because, after he has understood it, he is capable of instructing others and making it clear to them; and *astute*, because he has penetrated the extremely subtle meaning.[1167]

318. Thus, having praised service to a wise teacher, the Buddha next spoke this verse, "But if one resorts to a petty fool," to criticize association with a foolish teacher. Here, he is **petty** because he engages in petty bodily action and so forth, and **a**

fool because he lacks wisdom. He **has not reached the goal**, has not achieved the goal of scriptural learning and penetration; and he is **full of envy**, unable to tolerate his pupil's progress because of his envious nature. The rest here is clear as far as the terms are concerned. But as to the purport, the teacher is a petty fool because he possesses such petty qualities as this: though he obtains many robes and other requisites, he cannot give such things to his pupils, nor can he give them the gift of the Dhamma, not even by merely uttering the words "impermanence, suffering, non-self." One resorting to such a teacher, who has not reached the goal and who is full of envy, becomes a fool himself, in the way stated thus: "One who ties up putrid fish with blades of kusa grass" (see above p. 745). Therefore, **not having discerned the Dhamma**—the scriptural Dhamma or the Dhamma of penetration—**right here** in the Teaching, and not having understood it even to a slight extent, **one meets death** without having overcome one's doubt about the teachings. It is in such a way that the meaning should be understood.

319–20. Now he spoke the next pair of verses, "It is like a man," for the purpose of illustrating this meaning. [330] As to the purport, as **a man might enter a river** of the kind described; **being swept away** by that river, **flowing with the stream**, going along[1168] with the stream itself, **how could he help others to cross**, how could he lead to the far shore others who wish to get across?[1169] Just so, **without having discerned** by one's own wisdom the twofold **Dhamma** (of scripture and penetration), and **without attending to the meaning under the learned ones**, **not understanding it oneself** because one has not discerned it, and **immersed in doubt** because one has not attended to it, **how can one get others to perceive it**, to recognize it?[1170] It is in such a way that its meaning should be understood. And here one should recollect the sutta passage that begins "Cunda, it is impossible that one who is himself sinking in the mud."[1171]

321. Thus, having stated a simile to show that the fool, because he serves a fool, cannot get others to perceive the Dhamma, the Blessed One spoke the next pair of verses, "But as one who has embarked on a strong boat," to show that a wise person—described here as "one who heedfully follows such [a teacher]"—is able to get others to perceive it. **Knowing the method there**: one who knows the method of steering it along its route, by knowing how to bring the boat in and how to send it out. **Skillful** because he has been trained and because of his dexterity; **thoughtful** because of his ability to deal with any disaster that may have arisen.

322. A knowledge-master (*vedagū*): one who has proceeded by way of the knowledges of the four paths, which are designated "knowledge";[1172] **self-developed** (*bhāvitatto*), with mind developed through that same development of the path; **learned**, in the way already explained; **of unwavering character**: who is not to be moved by the eight worldly conditions. [331] **Those equipped with attentive ears as a supporting condition**: those equipped with attentive ears and with a supporting condition for the paths and fruits.[1173]

323. Thus, having used a simile to illustrate the ability of the wise person to get others to perceive the Dhamma, the Blessed One spoke the last verse, "Therefore one should follow the good person," ordering them to associate with a wise person. This is its concise meaning: "Since those endowed with supporting conditions attain distinction by associating with a wise teacher, **therefore one should follow the good person**. What kind of good person? **One who is intelligent and learned**: *intelligent* because of his excellence of wisdom, and *learned* in the twofold learning explained above. Following such a one, **having known the meaning** of the Dhamma spoken by him, having known it thus, and **practicing along** as instructed, **one who** through that practice **has understood the Dhamma** by way of penetration **can obtain bliss**; he can achieve the world-transcending bliss of the paths, fruits, and nibbāna." Thus the Blessed One concluded the discourse with its culmination in arahantship.

9 What Good Behavior?
(*Kiṃsīla Sutta*)

What is the origin? The Venerable Sāriputta had a friend from lay life, the son of a brahmin who was a friend of the elder's father, the brahmin Vaṅganta. Having relinquished 560 koṭis of wealth, he went forth under the Venerable Sāriputta and learned the entire Word of the Buddha. The elder exhorted him in many ways and assigned him a meditation subject, but he did not thereby attain distinction. Therefore, having known, "He is one to be guided by the Buddha," Sāriputta brought him to the Blessed One, and without specifying a person, he asked, "Having what good behavior?" The Blessed One then spoke what follows.

324. Having what good behavior: What kind of restrained behavior should he possess, or of what temperament should he be? **Having what sort of conduct**: What kind of positive conduct should he possess?[1174] [332] **Fostering what kind of actions**: Developing what actions of body and so forth, **can a person be properly settled**, can a person who is delighted be properly established in the Teaching, **and attain the highest goal**, and attain arahantship, the highest of all goals?

325. Then the Blessed One directed his attention to this matter and reflected: "Half a month after he was ordained, Sāriputta attained the perfection of a disciple, so why does he ask a question appropriate for a worldling who is a beginner in the practice?" He then understood, "He is asking for the sake of his pupil," and without elucidating positive virtue, teaching the Dhamma in a way suitable for him, he said: **One should be**

respectful toward elders. Here, there are four kinds of elders: the elder in wisdom, the elder in excellent qualities, the elder by way of social class, and the elder in age. For even though a learned bhikkhu may be young in age, he may be more mature in the wisdom of learning than elderly bhikkhus with little learning, and thus he is *an elder in wisdom*; even elderly bhikkhus may learn the Word of the Buddha under him and expect him to give them exhortations, to make judgments, and answer questions. Similarly, even a young bhikkhu who has reached achievement in realization is called *an elder in excellent qualities*; based on his exhortation, even elderly bhikkhus initiate insight and attain the fruit of arahantship. Similarly, a head-anointed khattiya king or a brahmin, even though young, is said to be *an elder by way of social class*, because he deserves veneration from the rest of the people. But whoever is born first is said to be *an elder in age*.

Among these, the Blessed One excepted, there was no one equal to the Elder Sāriputta in wisdom; so too in excellent qualities, since after half a month he penetrated the entire knowledge of a disciple's perfection. By way of social class, too, he was born into an affluent brahmin family. Therefore, although he was the same age as that bhikkhu (his pupil), he was his elder in these three ways. But in this passage, when the Blessed One said, "respectful toward elders," he was referring to those who are elders in wisdom and excellent qualities. Therefore, one should be respectful toward elders by acting respectfully toward such elders; and by removing envy over their gains and the other benefits that accrue to them, one should be **without envy**. This is the meaning of the first line.

One should know the proper time: Here, one knows the proper time for going to see one's teachers for the purpose of dispelling arisen lust; one knows the proper time for going to see one's teachers for the purpose of dispelling arisen hatred . . . delusion . . . laziness. Hence in such a way "one should know the proper time for seeing one's teachers."[1175] [333] **A Dhamma talk**: one concerned with serenity and insight. **One who knows the occasion**: One who knows the occasion for that talk, or who knows: "It is rare to get this opportunity to listen to such a talk"; **should listen carefully**: should listen carefully to that talk, and not only to that one, but one should also listen carefully to other **well-spoken words**, such as those connected with the virtues of the Buddha and other matters.

326. In the way stated here [with the phrase],"One should know the proper time for seeing one's teachers," one knows that the time [to see teachers] is for dispelling lust and other defilements arisen in oneself. When going into the presence of one's teachers, **one should go to teachers at the proper time**. Thinking, "I'm a meditator, I observe the austere practices," one should not approach one's teacher to question him wherever one may see him, for instance when he is venerating the cetiya, or on the terrace of the bodhi tree, or on his alms round, or in the very middle of the day. Rather, when he is in his own lodging, sitting in his own seat, and one notices that he won't be troubled, one should approach him to ask about the meditation method or some other topic. And when approaching him in such a way, **having dropped one's pride, with a humble manner**, that is, having dispelled conceit, which causes rigidity,[1176] one should approach in a meek manner, as if one were a foot-wiping cloth, a bull with horns cut off, or a snake with fangs removed. Then **one should recollect and practice the meaning** and so forth stated by the teacher. **The meaning**: the meaning of his statements; **the Dhamma**: the textual teaching; **self-control**: good behavior; **the spiritual life**: the other aspects of the spiritual life pertinent to the Teaching. **One should recollect and practice**: One should recollect the meaning on the occasion when it is explained; one should recollect the Dhamma, self-control, and the spiritual life on the occasions when they are explained. One should not be satisfied merely with recollecting them but should practice all of them; having undertaken them, one should put them into practice. One should undertake their development,[1177] keen about their implementation within oneself. For one doing so is one who does his duty.

327. Thereafter, "delighting in the Dhamma, delighted with the Dhamma, firm in the Dhamma, knowing how to evaluate the Dhamma." In all the expressions here, **Dhamma** is serenity and insight. "Delighting in" and "delighted with" are identical in meaning, or "delighted with the Dhamma" [334] means that one does not wish for anything else. **Firm in the Dhamma**: one proceeds having attained the Dhamma.[1178] **Knowing how to judge the Dhamma**: One knows how to make judgments about the Dhamma, such as "This is the knowledge of arising, that is the knowledge of vanishing." One should be like that.

Now, for a meditator with tender insight, pointless talk such as talk about kings and other irrelevant subjects damages that Dhamma of serenity and insight by arousing delight in external forms and so forth. Therefore this is called speech detrimental to the Dhamma. **One should not engage in talk that corrupts the Dhamma**, but instead, resorting to suitable dwellings, alms resorts, and other conditions, one **should be guided by genuine well-spoken words**. One should be guided by such well-spoken words, which in this context are "genuine" in that they are connected with serenity and insight.[1179] The meaning is that one should pass the time [in such a way].

328. Now because the expression used here, "talk that corrupts the Dhamma," is very concise, he spoke the verse "Laughter, chatter," to make clear the defilement [of wrong speech] together with other defilements for a bhikkhu engaged in serenity and insight. For a bhikkhu practicing insight should simply smile over a humorous matter, should not utter useless **chatter**, should not fall into **lamenting** over loss of relatives and other misfortunes, and should not give rise to **annoyance** over stumps, thorns, and other impediments. It is hypocrisy that is meant by **hypocritical deeds**. **Scheming** is threefold;[1180] **greed** is for requisites; **conceit** is on account of social class and so forth; **stubbornness** is a designation for contrariness; **crudeness** is characterized by harsh speech; **blemishes** are lust and so forth;[1181] and **infatuation** is characterized as excessive craving. These defects should be abandoned like a charcoal pit by one desiring pleasure, like a cesspit by one desiring cleanliness, and like vipers by one desiring to live. Having abandoned these, being **free from vanity** through the vanishing of vanity based on health and so forth, one should wander **inwardly firm**, through the absence of mental distraction. Practicing in such a way, in no long time, through development purified of all defilements, one attains arahantship. Hence the Blessed One said: "having abandoned laughter . . . inwardly firm."

329. Now, a bhikkhu who possesses the defilements spoken of as "laughter, chatter," and so forth, is **impetuous**, one who does not investigate matters but comes under the control of lust [335] and under the control of hatred; and who is **heedless**, who does not constantly work at the development of wholesome qualities. Exhorting one like this with such advice as "One should listen carefully to well-spoken words" would be useless. Therefore the Blessed One spoke the verse "What is understood is the core of well-spoken words," showing, through a teaching with the person as its basis,[1182] how this defilement is opposed to the growth of learning and other virtuous qualities.

This is its meaning: **Well-spoken words** are those connected with serenity and insight; their core is understanding. If they are understood, that is good; but nothing is achieved if the mere sound is perceived. The knowledge produced by learning, by which these words are understood, is indicated by **what has been learned**. And for this knowledge produced by learning, **concentration is the core of what has been understood.** The practice is for the sake of concentration or non-distraction of mind upon the things that have been understood; this is their core.[1183] For no good is accomplished merely by understanding.

But **a person who is impetuous** because he behaves under the control of lust and so forth, and **heedless** because he does not constantly work at the development of wholesome qualities, is one who takes in the mere sound. Hence, because he lacks understanding of the meaning, his **wisdom**, that is, his understanding of well-spoken words, **does not grow**, and his **learning**, because he does not practice for such a purpose, **does not grow**.

330. Having thus shown the deterioration of wisdom and of learning in heedless beings, now showing that those who are heedful achieve both kinds of core, the Blessed One said, "Those who delight in the Dhamma . . . have reached the core of learning and wisdom." Here, **the Dhamma taught by the noble ones** is the Dhamma of serenity and insight; for there is not even one buddha who has attained final nibbāna without having taught the Dhamma of serenity and insight. Therefore **those who delight in the Dhamma taught by the noble ones**, who rejoice in it, who are heedful, who apply themselves constantly to it, **are unsurpassed in speech, mind, and action**. Because they are possessed of the fourfold good conduct by speech, the threefold good conduct by mind, and the threefold good conduct by body, they are unsurpassed by other beings with respect to speech, mind, and action; they are unequaled, foremost, distinguished. At this point he has shown the good behavior associated with the noble path along with the good behavior of the preliminary practice.

Those who in this way have purified their behavior, "being settled in peace,[1184] gentleness, and concentration, have reached the core of learning and wisdom." Those who delight in the Dhamma taught by the noble ones are not only unsurpassed in speech, mind, and action, but being settled in the gentleness of peace and in concentration,[1185] [336] they have reached the core of learning and wisdom. This is a past tense stated by way of anticipation.[1186] Here, **peace** is nibbāna. **Gentleness**, because it delights in the good, is the wisdom that penetrates things as they really are. "Gentleness of peace"[1187] is a designation for the wisdom of the path, which takes nibbāna as its object. **Concentration** is the concentration of the path, which is associated with it. **Settled in**: established in both of these. **The core of learning and wisdom** is the liberation of the fruit of arahantship; for this spiritual life has liberation as its core.

Thus here, by the word "Dhamma," the Blessed One shows the preliminary practice; by the phrase "unsurpassed in speech, mind, and action," he shows the aggregate of good behavior; by the expression "gentleness of peace and concentration," he shows the aggregate of wisdom and the aggregate of concentration. Having shown by these three aggregates the subsequent practice, by the phrase "the core of learning and wisdom" he shows unshakable liberation. Thus he concludes the discourse with its culmination in arahantship. At the conclusion of the discourse, that bhikkhu attained the fruit of stream-entry, and not long after he was established in arahantship, the foremost fruit.

10 Arouse Yourselves!
(*Uṭṭhāna Sutta*)

What is the origin? On one occasion the Blessed One, while dwelling at Sāvatthī, spent the night at Jeta's Grove monastery. In the forenoon, accompanied by the Sangha of bhikkhus, he wandered for alms in Sāvatthī, left the city through the eastern gate, and went to Migāramātā's mansion to pass the day. Now it is said that it was the Blessed One's custom, when he spent the night at Jeta's Grove monastery, to go to Migāramātā's mansion to pass the day; and when he spent the night at Migāramātā's mansion, to go to Jeta's Grove to pass the day. Why? To assist those two families and to exemplify the virtuous quality of great relinquishment. The lower level of Migāramātā's mansion had five hundred chambers with peaked rooftops in which five hundred bhikkhus lived. When the Blessed One stayed in the lower level of the mansion, out of respect for the Blessed One the bhikkhus did not go to the upper level.[1188]

On that day, however, the Blessed One entered a chamber on the upper level; hence the five hundred bhikkhus entered the five hundred chambers on the lower level. They were all junior monks who had recently [337] come to this Dhamma and discipline, and so they were restless, puffed up, with loose sense faculties. Having entered, they slept during the day, got up in the evening, and assembled on the large terrace, where they made a racket and an uproar, engaging in various kinds of worldly conversation such as this: "What did you get in the refectory today? Where did you go?" – "I went to the home of the king of Kosala, friend. I went to Anāthapiṇḍika's home. There such and such foods were served."

Having heard the noise, the Blessed One thought:[1189] "Though living with me, they are heedless. How they act improperly!" He then wished that the Elder Mahāmoggallāna would come. Immediately the Venerable Mahāmoggallāna, having known the Blessed One's thought, arrived by psychic power and paid homage at the Blessed One's feet. The Blessed One then addressed him: "Your fellow monks, Moggallāna, are heedless. It would be good if you would inspire a sense of urgency in them."

"Yes, Bhante," Mahāmoggallāna replied. He immediately entered meditation on the water kasiṇa and then touched the mansion with his toe, so that, while it stood on solid ground,[1190] it shook along with the earth on which it was built, like a ship shaken by a strong wind. Then those bhikkhus, frightened, made a commotion and ran out through the four doors, leaving behind their robes and other possessions. The Blessed One then showed himself to them as if he were entering his Fragrant Cottage through another door. When they saw the Blessed One, they paid homage to him and stood there. The Blessed One asked them: "Why are you frightened, bhikkhus?" They said: "Bhante, Migāramātā's mansion trembled and shook." – "Do you know why, bhikkhus?" – "We don't know, Bhante." The Blessed One explained: "Because you have been dwelling heedlessly, unmindfully, without clear comprehension, it was shaken by Moggallāna in order to arouse in you a sense of urgency." He then spoke this discourse in order to teach the Dhamma to those bhikkhus.

331. Here, **arouse yourselves**: Rise up from indolence, strive, make an effort, do not be lazy. **Sit up**: Having folded your legs crosswise, sit up in order to apply yourselves to your meditation subject. **What good to you is sleeping?**: When you have gone forth to attain final nibbāna through non-clinging, [338] what good to you is sleeping? For it isn't possible to attain any goal by sleeping. **For what sleep can there be for the afflicted, for those injured, pierced by the dart?**: When people are afflicted with a disease that attacks even a small part of their body, such as an eye disease, they do not sleep; and so too when they have been injured by a dart that has entered a mere inch or two, whether the dart is made of iron, bone, ivory, horn, or wood. So how can you sleep when you are afflicted with the diseases of various defilements, which have arisen and damaged your entire bodily and mental organism, when you have been **injured, pierced by the dart**, pierced by the five darts—the dart of lust and so forth—which have entered into your hearts?

332. Having spoken thus, to incite and inspire those bhikkhus even more, the Blessed One said: "Arouse yourselves . . . come under his control." Here, this is the explanation of the meaning together with the construal of the purport: "Thus, bhikkhus, as you have been pierced by the dart of the defilements, it is time for you to awaken. For what reason? This spiritual life, bhikkhus, is cream-of-ghee; the Teacher is present before you. Previously, you have slept for a long time—slept on mountains, on smooth ground, in rough places, even in the tops of trees—because you did not see the noble truths. Therefore, arouse yourselves in order to make an end of sleeping. Sit up and train vigorously for the state of peace."

The meaning of the first line is as explained. In the second line, the word **peace** might refer to three kinds of peace: ultimate peace, peace in a particular respect, and conventional peace.[1191] These are respectively designations for nibbāna, insight, and [the peace conceived] by the adherents of views. But here it is ultimate peace, nibbāna, that is intended. Therefore, **train vigorously** for the sake of nibbāna, train without relaxing your exertion. For what reason? **Do not let the King of Death, having caught you heedless, delude you who have come under his control**: What is meant is this: "Do not let Māra, who also goes by the name 'King of Death,' know, 'They are heedless,' and then delude you so that you come under his control. Do not let him delude you and bring you under his control."

333. Rather than come under his control, **cross over**, overcome, **this attachment**, this craving for the enjoyment of existence, [called attachment] because it is diffused, spread out, and extended among the different objective domains,[1192] **by which devas and humans beings, full of need**, needy for forms, sounds, odors, tastes, and tactile objects, **are held fast** to forms and so forth, dependent on them and attached to them. [339] **Do not let the opportunity pass you by**: Do not let this opportunity of practicing the ascetic's duty pass you by. **Those who have missed the opportunity**—those whom such an opportunity has passed by and who have passed by this opportunity—**sorrow when they arrive in hell**: When established in the fourfold plane of misery, called "hell" because it is devoid of enjoyment, they sorrow in the way stated thus: "Alas, we failed to do good!"

334. Thus, having encouraged and inspired those bhikkhus, the Blessed One now spoke this verse, "Heedlessness is dust," criticizing their heedless manner and ordering them all to dwell in heedfulness. Here, **heedlessness**, in brief, is separation from mindfulness; it is **dust** in the sense of staining the mind. That **follows upon heedlessness**: because it follows upon [prior] heedlessness, the heedlessness that has arisen on successive occasions is also dust. For there is never any heedlessness that is free of dust.

What does he show by this? "Do not become overly confident, thinking: 'We are now young, we'll understand later.' For in youth heedlessness is dust; and in middle age and old age, too, because it follows upon heedlessness, it becomes a large dust heap of rubbish. This is similar to how, in a house, after one or two days there is mere dust, but if it accumulates over several years it becomes a heap of rubbish. Though such is the case, if one learns the Word of the Buddha in the prime of life and does the ascetic's duty in the other stages of life—or having learned the teaching in the prime of life and listened in middle age, if one does the duty of an ascetic in the last stage—a bhikkhu does not dwell in heedlessness, for he is practicing the path that is in conformity with heedfulness. But if one dwells heedlessly in all stages of life, sleeping during the day and indulging in worldly talk as you do, then one gathers the dust of heedlessness in the prime of life and, in the other stages, the great heedlessness that follows upon [that earlier] heedlessness becomes a great mass of dust."

Having thus criticized them for dwelling in heedlessness and ordering them to dwell in heedfulness, the Blessed One said: "By heedfulness, by clear knowledge, draw out the dart from oneself." This is its meaning: "Since in such a way this heedlessness is always dust, therefore, **by heedfulness**, a designation for non-separation from mindfulness, and **by clear knowledge**, a designation for the knowledge of the destruction of the influxes, a wise practitioner should remove **the dart**—the five darts of lust and so forth—**from himself**, lodged within his heart."

Thus the Blessed One concluded the teaching with its culmination in arahantship. At the conclusion of the teaching, those five hundred bhikkhus acquired a sense of urgency and attended to that same teaching of the Dhamma. Reflecting upon it, they undertook insight and became established in arahantship. [340]

11 Rāhula
(*Rāhula Sutta*)

What is the origin? After the Blessed One attained perfect enlightenment, he eventually traveled from the site of enlightenment to Kapilavatthu. There, when the boy Rāhula asked him for his inheritance, saying, "Give me my inheritance, ascetic," the Blessed One ordered the Elder Sāriputta: "Give the boy Rāhula the going forth." The whole account should be understood in the way it is related in the commentary to the Khandhakas.[1193] After the boy Rāhula had gone forth, when he came of age, the Elder Sāriputta gave him full ordination. The Elder Mahāmoggallāna was his ordination teacher.

The Blessed One thought: "This boy comes from a high social class and so forth. He should not give rise to conceit or pride[1194] on account of his social class, clan, family, color, beauty, or other qualities." Thus from his childhood on, until he reached the stage of the noble ones, the Blessed One often exhorted him with this discourse. Therefore at the conclusion of the discourse it is said: "In such a way the Blessed One often exhorted the Venerable Rāhula with these verses."

335. Here, this is the concise meaning of the first verse: "**Do you**, Rāhula, because of constantly living with him, not look down on **the wise man** because of your social class or some other quality? **Is the torchbearer of humankind**—so called because of bearing the lamp of knowledge and the lamp of the Dhamma teaching—**always respected by you?** Is he always venerated by you?" The Blessed One said this with reference to the Venerable Sāriputta.[1195]

336. When this was said, the Venerable Rāhula spoke the verse in reply, "I do not despise the wise man," indicating: "Unlike a vile person, Blessed One, I do not give rise to conceit or pride because of living together." The meaning of this is clear.

337. Then, exhorting him further, the Blessed One spoke the remaining verses, beginning "Having given up the five strands of sensual pleasure." Here, the five strands of sensual pleasure are pleasing to beings, extremely desired and yearned for by beings, [341] and they delight their minds. The Venerable Rāhula had given them up, renouncing the home life out of faith, not because he was compelled to do so by kings or by bandits or on account of debt or on account of fear or to earn a livelihood. Therefore the Blessed One inspired him by saying, **Having given up the five strands of sensual pleasure, so pleasing and delightful to the mind, having renounced the home life out of faith**. Then, instructing him to pursue the practice that corresponds to this renunciation, he said: **be one who makes an end to suffering**.

It might be asked: "Wasn't Rāhula forcibly made to go forth when all he wanted was his inheritance? In that case, why did the Blessed One say, 'having renounced the home life out of faith'?" In reply it is said: "Because he was disposed to renunciation."[1196] For the Venerable Rāhula had been disposed to renunciation for a long time. [In a previous life], having seen the novice Uparevata, the son of the Buddha Padumuttara, when he became a king of the nāgas named Saṅkha he gave alms for seven days and made an aspiration for such a status. From then on, endowed with the aspiration, endowed with the undertaking, he fulfilled the pāramīs for 100,000 eons until he was reborn into his last existence. Thus the Blessed One knew that he had the disposition to renunciation; for this knowledge is one of the Tathāgata's powers. Therefore he said: "having renounced the home life out of faith." Or alternatively, the purport here is this: "for a long time having renounced the home life out of faith, now be one who makes an end to suffering."

338. Now, to show him the practice for making an end to the suffering of the round, starting from the beginning, the Blessed One said "associate with good friends" and so forth. Here, "good friends" are those who excel in good behavior and other qualities. Those associating with them grow in good behavior and other virtues, just as large sāl trees, supported by the Himalayas, grow in their roots and other parts. Hence he said: **Associate with good friends, and resort to a remote lodging, secluded, a place with little noise**: Since a lodging that is remote, distant, secluded, undisturbed, with little noise, with the sounds of deer, boars, and other creatures, is a place where the perception of forest arises, one should resort to such a lodging. **Be moderate in eating**: Know the right measure; know the amount to accept and the amount to consume. Here, when there is only a little of the item to be given and the donor wants to give little, one who knows the amount to accept should take just a little. When there is only a little of the item to be given, though the donor wants to give a lot, one should take just a little. When the item to be given [342] is more ample but the donor wants to give a little, one should take just a little. When the item to be given is more ample and the donor wants to give a lot, one should take after ascertaining one's own capacity, thinking: "Moderation is praised by the Blessed One." One who knows the amount to consume should consume food after reflecting carefully upon it as like son's flesh and like the grease for an axle.

339. Thus, by the above verse, the Blessed One instructed Rāhula to associate with good friends, which is helpful to the spiritual life, and under the heading of lodging and food he encouraged him to undertake good behavior in the use of the requisites. Now, since wrong livelihood is adopted out of craving for robes and so forth, the Blessed One spoke this verse, "Do not give rise to craving for robe and almsfood," prohibiting him from this and enjoining him to undertake good behavior through purification of livelihood. Here, **requisites** refers to requisites in time of illness.[1197] **For these**: for these four grounds for craving to arise in bhikkhus, namely, robes and so forth. **Do not give rise to craving**: "Do not generate craving, dwell without giving rise to it, seeing the danger in the way stated thus: 'These four requisites, which are just for the purpose of concealing the private parts and so forth, are like antidotes for persons who are constantly ill and reinforcements for this very feeble body, which is like a dilapidated house.'" For what reason? **Do not come back to the world again**: "Since one who gives rise to craving for these things is dragged along by craving and comes back to this world again, do not give rise to craving for them. In such a way you will not come back to this world again."

When such was said, the Venerable Rāhula thought, "The Blessed One told me, 'Do not give rise to craving for a robe,'" and he undertook two austere practices connected with robes, namely, using a robe made of rags and using only three robes.[1198] He thought: "The Blessed One told me, 'Do not give rise to craving for almsfood,'" and he undertook five ascetic practices connected with almsfood, namely, going on alms round, eating one meal a day, walking on alms round without skipping houses along the route, eating only from the alms bowl, and refusing food brought after the meal has started. He thought: "The Blessed One told me, 'Do not give rise to craving for a lodging,'" and he undertook six ascetic practices connected with the lodging, namely, dwelling in the forest, dwelling out in the open, dwelling at the foot of a tree, accepting any bedding for use, dwelling in a charnel ground, and the sitter's practice. He thought: "The Blessed One told me, 'Do not give rise to craving for requisites in time of illness,'" and with respect to all requisites he became content through the three types of contentment, namely, contentment according to one's gains, contentment according to one's ability, and contentment according to suitability, [343] in the way an amenable clansman respectfully accepts instruction.[1199]

340. Thus, having enjoined the Venerable Rāhula to undertake good behavior through purification of livelihood, the Blessed One now spoke the verse that begins **Be restrained by the Pātimokkha**, to enjoin him to undertake the remaining kinds of good behavior as well as serenity and insight.[1200] Here, by the first two lines, he enjoins him to undertake good behavior through restraint by the Pātimokkha and good behavior through restraint of the sense faculties. And though **five sense faculties** are stated here because they are evident, it should be understood that the sixth (the mind faculty) is also stated through the characteristic (because it belongs to the same class). **Let your mindfulness be directed to the body**: When you are established in the fourfold purification of good behavior, let your mindfulness be directed to the body by developing it through the delineation of the four elements, the fourfold clear comprehension, mindfulness of breathing, perception of the repulsiveness of nutriment, and so forth. What is meant is "Develop it." **Be full of disenchantment [toward the world]**: The meaning is: "Be dissatisfied with the round of saṃsāra. See that there is no delight in the entire world."[1201]

341. Having at this point shown the stage of access concentration partaking of penetration, now showing the stage of absorption, he spoke the verse beginning "Avoid the mark [of sensual objects]" and so forth. **Avoid**: relinquish by not paying attention to it. **The mark**: the mark of the beautiful, which is the basis for lust. Hence, specifying this, he said: **which is beautiful and connected with lust**. **Develop your mind on the unattractive**: Develop your mind in such a way that meditation on the unattractive nature of the body, whether sentient or insentient, flourishes.[1202] **One-pointed, well concentrated**: "One-pointed" by means of access concentration; "well concentrated" by way of absorption concentration. The meaning is: "Develop your mind in such a way that it becomes like this."

342. Thus, having shown him the stage of absorption, now to show him insight he spoke the verse that begins "And develop the markless state." Here, **develop the markless state**: What is meant is: "When your mind is concentrated by the concentration that partakes of penetration, develop insight." For insight acquires the designation "the markless state" on the basis of such statements as "knowledge of contemplation of impermanence is liberated from the mark of permanence" and "the markless liberation," or [it is called thus] because it does not seize upon the mark of lust and so forth. As it is said: "Friends, by non-attention to all marks, I entered and dwelled in the markless mental concentration. [344] While I was dwelling in such a state, my consciousness ran after marks" (SN IV 269,4).

Discard the latent tendency to conceit: Having obtained the perception of impermanence through this development of the markless state, in stages discard, abandon, relinquish the latent tendency to conceit in accordance with such statements as this: "For one who perceives impermanence, Meghiya, the perception of non-self becomes stabilized. One who perceives non-self attains the eradication of the conceit 'I am'" (AN IV 358,18, Ud 37,19–21).

Then, by breaking through conceit, you will live in tranquil peace: Then, by breaking through conceit, with its destruction, vanishing, abandoning, and relinquishment by the noble path, you will be at peace, quenched, cool, devoid of all distress and fever. Until you attain final nibbāna through the nibbāna element without residue remaining, you will "live" by dwelling in this or that fruition attainment, whether that of emptiness, the markless, or the desireless. Thus he concludes the discourse with its culmination in arahantship.

Following this, the compilers of the texts added the statement that begins "In such a way the Blessed One." After being exhorted in such a way, when his qualities maturing in liberation had ripened, at the conclusion of the "Shorter Discourse of an Exhortation to Rāhula" the Venerable Rāhula, along with many thousands of deities, attained arahantship.[1203]

12 Nigrodhakappa (Vaṅgīsa)
(*Nigrodhakappa Sutta*)

This is also called the Discourse with Vaṅgīsa.[1204] What is the origin? This is stated in the introduction to the discourse. **At the Aggāḷava Cetiya**: At the chief cetiya at Āḷavī.[1205] For before the Blessed One had arisen, there were many cetiyas, such as the Aggāḷava, the Gotamaka, and so forth, that served as abodes of yakkhas, nāgas, and other beings. After the Blessed One arose, people razed them and built monasteries in their place but they called them by the same name. [345] Thus what is meant here is that he was dwelling at the monastery named the Aggāḷava Cetiya. **The Venerable Vaṅgīsa**: Here, "Venerable" is a term of affection, "Vaṅgīsa" was this elder's name. His story, starting from his birth, should be understood as follows.

It is said that he was the son of a wanderer, born from the womb of a female wanderer.[1206] He learned a certain art by the power of which, by knocking on the skull of a corpse, he could determine the rebirth destination of the deceased being. People would bring him the skulls of their own departed relatives from the charnel ground and ask him about their destination. He would say: "He was reborn in this or that hell; he was reborn here or there in the human world." Impressed by this, they gave him much wealth. In this way he became famous throughout Jambudīpa. He had fulfilled the pāramīs for 100,000 eons and was endowed with the resolve.[1207] Accompanied by five hundred men, he traveled among the villages, towns, and capital cities, until he eventually arrived at Sāvatthī.

Now at that time the Blessed One was dwelling at Sāvatthī. The residents of Sāvatthī gave alms in the morning, and in the afternoon, well dressed and attired, taking along flowers, incense, and other offerings, they went to Jeta's Grove to listen to the Dhamma. Vaṅgīsa saw them and asked: "Where is this crowd going?" They told him: "A buddha has arisen in the world. He teaches the Dhamma for the welfare of many people. Let's go there." Accompanied by his retinue, he went along with them. He exchanged greetings with the Blessed One and sat down to one side. Then the Blessed One addressed him, saying: "Is it the case, Vaṅgīsa, that you know an art by which you knock on the skulls of corpses and declare the rebirth destination of beings?" – "Yes, Master Gotama, I know."

The Blessed One then had the skull of one who had been reborn in hell brought and showed it to Vaṅgīsa. Vaṅgīsa tapped it with his fingernail and said: "This is the skull of one reborn in hell, Master Gotama." In this way, the Blessed One showed him the skulls of those who had been reborn in all the destinations of rebirth, and in each case Vaṅgīsa found out where they had been reborn and announced their destination. Then the Blessed One showed him the skull of an arahant. Vaṅgīsa knocked on it again and again, but he could find out nothing. The Blessed One then said: "This is not your domain, Vaṅgīsa. [346] This is my domain alone. That is the skull of an arahant, one whose influxes have been destroyed." He then recited this verse:

"The woods are the destination of deer;
the sky is the destination of birds;
non-being is the destination of existent things;
nibbāna is the destination of arahants." (Vin V 149,22–23)

When he heard this verse, Vaṅgīsa said: "Teach me this art, Master Gotama." The Blessed One said: "This art does not work unless one goes forth." – "In that case, Master Gotama, give me the going forth. I will do whatever you wish, and then you must teach me this art." At the time, the Elder Nigrodhakappa was near the Blessed One. The Blessed One instructed him: "Nigrodhakappa, give him the going forth." Having given him the going forth, Nigrodhakappa taught him meditation on the first five parts of the body.[1208] Eventually Vaṅgīsa became an arahant with the analytical knowledges, and he was designated by the Blessed One as one of the foremost disciples:

"Bhikkhus, the foremost of my bhikkhu disciples among those who possess inspired ingenuity is Vaṅgīsa" (AN I 24,21).

The Venerable Vaṅgīsa's preceptor, the Elder Nigrodhakappa: He gets to be called thus ("preceptor") in the sense that he "makes one consider" what is blameworthy and what is blameless.[1209] Kappa was the elder's name, but because he attained arahantship at the foot of a nigrodha tree, the Blessed One called him "Nigrodhakappa." Thereafter the bhikkhus also called him thus. An "elder" is one who has attained stability in the Teaching.[1210] **Alone** by way of the body; **in seclusion** by way of the mind. One is in seclusion because one has turned away from the multiple sense domains. **The following reflection arose in his mind**: Why did it arise? Because he was not present and because of what he had previously seen. For he was not present at the time his preceptor attained final nibbāna, and he had previously seen [in his preceptor] some old habits such as restless movements of the hands and so forth. And such behavior occurs in non-arahants and also in arahants because of previous habituation.[1211] Thus in the afternoon Piṇḍolabhāradvāja used to go to the park of King Udena to pass the day, [347] because in a past life, when he was a king, he enjoyed himself there; this occurred because of previous habituation. The Elder Gavampati would go to an empty celestial mansion in the Tāvatiṃsa heaven, because in a past life, when he was a young deva, he enjoyed himself there; this occurred because of previous habituation. Pilindavaccha used to address the bhikkhus as "outcast," because in five hundred past births, without a break, he had been a brahmin and spoke in such a way; this occurred because of previous habituation. Therefore, in the case of Vaṅgīsa, because he was not present and because of the habits he had seen, the following reflection arose in his mind: **Did my preceptor attain final nibbāna or not?**[1212] The meaning of the words that follow this are clear. **He arranged his upper robe over one shoulder**: This is stated in such a way here to show the manner of readjustment.[1213] "One shoulder" means that he stood there having covered his left shoulder; he arranged the robe so that it covered his left shoulder.

343. Of perfect wisdom (*anomapaññā*): *Oma* means "limited, deficient." One whose wisdom is not defective is one of perfect wisdom, one of great wisdom.[1214] **In this very life**: this visible state, in this very existence. **Of doubts**: of such thoughts [about the fate of Nigrodhakappa]. **Well known**: eminent; **famous**: endowed with gains and retinue; **inwardly quenched**: one of guarded mind, or one whose mind was not feverish.[1215]

344. His name, which you, Blessed One, gave: "You called him 'Nigrodhakappa' because he used to sit at the foot of a nigrodha tree." He refers to him as he himself understood it; however, the Blessed One did not address him in such a way merely because he used to sit at the foot of a nigrodha tree but because he attained arahantship there. **To the brahmin**: He speaks with reference to his social class; for it is said that he went forth from an affluent brahmin family. **Intent on release**: being intent on release, a designation for nibbāna; what is meant is, "aspiring for nibbāna." **The one who shows the durable**: He addresses the Blessed One. What is "durable" is nibbāna, so called because it is indestructible. And the Blessed One shows that, therefore he says "the one who shows the durable."[1216]

345. O Sakya: He addresses the Blessed One by his family name. **We too all**: He says this, indicating himself along with the rest of the assembly. **O universal eye**: He addresses the Blessed One as the knowledge of omniscience. **Fully attentive**, properly attentive and directed, [348] **our ears**, ear faculties, **are ready to hear**: to hear the answer to this question. **You are our teacher; you are unsurpassed**: This is merely a statement of praise.

346. Cut off our doubt!: He is not actually afflicted by the unwholesome kind of doubt, but he says this referring to his thought [about his teacher's fate], which occurs in the form of doubt. **Tell me this**: I asked you about him when I said: "O Sakya, we too all wish to know about that disciple." **Announce he attained nibbāna, you of broad wisdom. Speak up in our midst**: Having understood that the brahmin attained nibbāna,[1217] Blessed One of great wisdom, in our midst speak to all of us in such a way that we all can understand. **Like thousand-**

eyed Sakka among the devas: This is just a statement of praise. This is its purport: "As thousand-eyed Sakka, in the midst of the devas, speaks words that are respectfully accepted by them, so in our midst, speak words that will be respectfully accepted by us."

347. Praising the Blessed One, he speaks this verse too, **Whatever knots are here**, in order to arouse in him a desire to speak. The knots are covetousness and so forth,[1218] which are called **paths of delusion**, because as long as these are not abandoned there is no abandoning of delusion and doubt; they are also called **factions of ignorance** and **bases of doubt**. All these, **on reaching the Tathāgata, no longer exist**: They are dispersed by the power of the Tathāgata's teaching and perish. For what reason? **For he is the supreme eye for humans**: Because the Tathāgata generates the eye of wisdom that disperses all knots, he is called "the supreme eye for humans."

348. If no man: He speaks this too as a verse of praise in order to arouse in him a desire to speak. **Man** is said with reference to the Blessed One. **Brilliant men** are those like Sāriputta who possess the light of wisdom. This is meant: "If the Blessed One did not dispel the defilements with the force of his teaching, in the way that a wind, coming from the east or elsewhere, dispels a mass of clouds, [349] in such a case, just as the world, enveloped in a mass of clouds, would be utter darkness, a single mass of darkness, so too the world, enveloped by ignorance, would be utter darkness. Under such circumstances, even those who now appear as brilliant men, such as Sāriputta, **would not shine**."

349. He speaks this verse, too, in the same way as the previous one.[1219] This is its meaning: "**But wise men are makers of light**: they ignite the light of wisdom. Therefore **I consider you, O hero**—O Blessed One, endowed with the energy of striving—**to be such a one**: I think of you as a wise man and a maker of light. [**Knowing, we come to one endowed with insight**]: Just knowing, we come to the Blessed One, who is endowed with insight, who sees all phenomena as they really are.[1220] Therefore,

in the assemblies, disclose to us [the fate of] Kappa: point out . . . reveal [the fate of] Nigrodhakappa."

350. He speaks this verse, too, in the same way as the previous ones. This is its meaning: "**Quickly send forth your lovely voice**: Swiftly, without delay, speak the word that is **lovely**, delightful, O Blessed One. As a golden goose that has left its feeding ground, on seeing a woodland grove with a natural lake, would **stretch out**, raising its neck, and would gently send forth a lovely honk with its red beak, in the same way, **gently honk with your rounded voice, well-modulated**, with this well-modulated, measured voice, one of the characteristics of a great man.[1221] **We are all upright: let us hear you!**: Let us all, with our minds undistracted, hear your honking!"

351. He has abandoned birth and death: He speaks this verse, too, in the same way as the previous ones. **Entirely**: with no remainder. Unlike stream-enterers and others, he has abandoned birth and death without any remainder. **Having pressed**, having urged, having insisted, **the pure one**, one who has shaken off all evil,[1222] **I will make him speak**, will make him explain, **the Dhamma. For worldlings cannot act on their wishes**: For worldlings have no ability to act on their wishes; they cannot know or say whatever they wish. **But for the tathāgatas, action is based on comprehension**: But tathāgatas act through investigation; their activities are preceded by wisdom.[1223] The purport is that they can know or say whatever they wish.

352. Now, showing that he acts with comprehension, [350] he spoke the verse "This excellent declaration of yours." This is its meaning: "In that case, Blessed One, as coming **from one of upright wisdom, this excellent declaration of yours**, stated and set forth, **has been accepted** on this and that occasion. [When he predicted], 'The chief minister Santati will rise up to the height of seven palm trees and attain final nibbāna; Suppabuddha the Sakyan, after seven days, will be swallowed up by the earth,'[1224] these declarations as well as others were seen to come true." Therefore, raising his hands even higher in reverential salutation, he said: **This last reverential salutation is**

offered. Knowing, knowing Kappa's destiny, **do not delude us**: do not delude us by not speaking.[1225] He addresses the Blessed One: **you of perfect wisdom**.

353. He spoke this verse entreating the Blessed One in still another way not to delude them. Here, **having understood**, having penetrated, **the noble Dhamma**, the Dhamma of the four truths, **from top to bottom**: by way of the world-transcending and the mundane, the good and the bad, or the distant and the proximate. **Knowing**: knowing everything that can be known. **As one afflicted by heat in summer**—as a weary and thirsty person—**longs for water**, so **I long for your word. Pour down the sound**: "Pour down, stream down, release, send down the sound base, which is designated 'what is heard.'"[1226]

354. Now, showing the kind of word for which he longs, he spoke this verse: **Was it a beneficial spiritual life?** Here, by **Kappāyana** he speaks with veneration of Kappa. **Let us hear just how he was liberated**: He asks: "Was it by the nibbāna element without residue remaining, like those beyond training, or by that with a residue remaining, like the trainees?"[1227]

355. Entreated in this way with twelve verses, the Blessed One, answering him, said, "He cut off craving," and so forth. This is the meaning of the first term: "The craving for this name-and-form—divided into craving for sensual pleasures and so forth[1228]—had long lay dormant in the sense that it had not been abandoned. It is spoken of as 'the stream of Māra,' who is named 'the Dark One.' Kappāyana **cut off that craving here for name-and-form**, which is **the stream of the Dark One that had long lay dormant**." [351] **Said the Blessed One**: This statement was added here by the compilers.

He crossed over birth and death entirely: Having cut off that craving, he entirely crossed over birth and death. He shows: "He attained final nibbāna without residue remaining." **Thus spoke the Blessed One, chief of the five**: Asked by Vaṅgīsa, the Blessed One spoke in such a way. He is called the chief of the bhikkhus of the group of five, his first five pupils, and he is the chief with respect to the five faculties beginning with faith or the five aggregates of Dhamma beginning with good behavior and with respect to his very special eyes.[1229] This statement was added by the compilers.

356. When this was said, Vaṅgīsa, delighting in the Blessed One's statement, spoke the verses beginning with the words "Having heard your word." Here, **best of rishis** (*isisattama*): The Blessed One was a rishi and was best in the sense of supreme. Also, [*isisattama* can be understood as] the seventh rishi, since he was seventh together with the six rishis, Vipassī, Sikhī, Vessabhū, Kakusandha, Konāgamana, and Kassapa.[1230] Vaṅgīsa addressed him thus. **Did not deceive me**: Since he did attain final nibbāna, therefore he did not deceive me in my wish for him to attain final nibbāna. He did not mislead me.

357. Since he lived "intent on release," it is said with reference to him: **The Buddha's disciple was one who acted in accordance with what he said**. **The extended net of Death**: Māra's net of craving extended over the round with its three planes of existence. **The Deceiver**: one of much deception.[1231] [Besides the reading *tataṃ māyāvino*] there is also a reading *tathā māyāvino*, "one of such deceit." The purport is that since Māra approached the Blessed One many times with many kinds of deceit, he is "one of such deceit."

358. The origin, the cause, **of clinging**: of the round; for the round [of rebirths] is here called "clinging" in the sense of that which can be clung to.[1232] He says this with the purport: "It is proper to say, Blessed One, that Kappa saw the origin of that clinging, the cause consisting in ignorance, craving, and so forth." He, **indeed, overcame**—transcended—**the domain of Death**, a designation for the round with its three planes of existence. Full of inspirational joy (*vedajāto*) he said: "He indeed overcame the domain of Death **so hard to cross**." The rest is already clear. [352]

13 Proper Wandering
(*Sammāparibbājanīya Sutta*)

This discourse is also called the Discourse on the Great Gathering[1233] because it was expounded on the day of the Great Gathering. What is the origin? Its origin was in response to a question. For the Blessed One spoke this discourse when questioned by a mind-created buddha.[1234] Together with the questions, it is called the Discourse on Proper Wandering. This is a brief account of the matter, but the detailed account is explained by the ancients beginning with the origin of the Sakyans and the Koḷiyans.

Here, this is the synopsis. It is said that Mahāsammata, the king at the beginning of the eon,[1235] had a son named Roja. Roja's son was named Vararoja, his son was Kalyāṇa, his Varakalyāṇa, and in succession Mandhātā, Varamandhātā, Uposatha, Cara, Upacara, Maghādeva, and following Maghādeva there were 24,000 khattiyas. Following them, there were three Okkāka lineages. The third Okkāka had five chief queens: Hatthā, Cittā, Jantu, Jālinī, and Visākhā. Each of these had a retinue of five hundred women. The eldest had four sons: Okkāmukha, Karakaṇḍu, Hatthinika, and Sinipūra. She also had five daughters: Piyā, Suppiyā, Ānandā, Vijitā, and Vijitasenā. Thus, having had nine children, she passed away. The king then married another beautiful young princess and appointed her to the position of chief queen.

She too gave birth to one son. On the fifth day following his birth, they adorned the newborn child and showed him to the king. The king was delighted and granted a boon to the queen. After consulting with her relatives, she asked the king to give the kingdom to her son. The king refused, saying: "Get out of here, wretch! You want to create an obstacle to my sons." She [353] coaxed the king again and again when they were alone, and then asked him for the boon, arguing: "It isn't proper, great king, to speak falsely." The king then addressed his sons: "Dears, when I saw your youngest brother, Jantukumāra, I rashly granted a boon to his mother. She wants me to turn the kingdom over to her son. After I pass away, you should come back and rule the kingdom." He then dismissed them along with eight ministers.

They took their sisters and left the city, accompanied by a four-division army. Many people followed them, thinking: "When their father passes away, the princes will come back and rule the kingdom. Let's go and serve them." On the first day, their army was a yojana long; on the second day, two yojanas; and on the third day, three yojanas. The princes reflected: "These troops are large. If we were to move against a neighboring king, we could take his country, and he would not be able to stand up against us. But why should we gain rulership by oppressing others? Jambudīpa is large. We will build a city in the forest." They then headed toward the Himalayas.

Searching for a place there to build a city, they went to the dwelling place of a hermit named Kapila, a practitioner of gruesome austerities,[1236] who lived in the Himalayas on the bank of a lotus pond in a large grove of teak trees. On meeting them, he questioned them, and when he heard their report he had compassion for them. It is said that he knew a mystical art called "the terrestrial net," by which he could see virtues and defects forty meters upward in space and below ground. He had applied it in such a way that in a particular region the boars and deers frightened the lions, tigers, and other beasts and made them flee, and mice and frogs frightened serpents. Having seen this, thinking, "This area is an excellent piece of land," he had built a hermitage in that area.

Then he said to the princes: "If you would name the city after me, I give you this place." They agreed to this. The hermit said, "Standing in this place, even the son of a caṇḍāla would be more powerful than a wheel-turning monarch," and he gave them the place, instructing them: "When you build the city, erect the king's house at the hermitage." He himself then made a hermitage at the foot of a nearby mountain and lived there. [354]

The princes built the city, and since it was established in the place where Kapila had lived, they named it Kapilavatthu and made their residence there. The ministers then considered: "These princes have now reached maturity. If their father were around, he would arrange their marriages. But now that is our responsibility." They consulted with the princes, who said: "We don't see any khattiya girls of our own status, or any khattiya youths of similar status for our sisters. Let us not crossbreed."[1237] From fear of crossbreeding, they appointed their eldest sister to the position of mother and coupled with their other sisters. When their father heard this news, he uttered a joyful exclamation: "The princes are Sakyans, indeed, sirs!"[1238] This, firstly, was the origin of the Sakyans. And this was said by the Blessed One:

> "Then, Ambaṭṭha, King Okkāka addressed his ministers and assemblymen: 'Where now, sirs, have the princes settled?' – 'There is, your majesty, a large grove of teak trees (*mahāsākasaṇḍo*) along the bank of a lotus pond on a slope in the Himalayas. The princes now have settled there. From fear of crossbreeding, they have coupled with their own (*sakāhi*) sisters.' Then, Ambaṭṭha, King Okkāka uttered the joyful exclamation: 'The princes are Sakyans, indeed, sirs! The princes are supreme Sakyans, indeed, sirs!' Since then they have been known as Sakyans, and he was the progenitor of the Sakyans." (DN I 92–93)

Then their eldest sister contracted a skin disease and her body became like coral flowers. The princes considered: "If we interact with her, this disease will spread." So they put her in a vehicle as if they were going to play in the park. Having entered the forest, [355] they had a pit dug up and deposited her there along with various kinds of food. They covered it with a roof, plastered the roof, and left.

Now at the time King Rāma had contracted a skin disease, and his harem ladies and dancing girls found him repulsive. Agitated by this, he handed over the kingdom to his eldest son, entered the forest, and sustained himself there on leaves, roots, and fruits. Before long, he recovered his health and his body regained its golden complexion. As he roamed about here and there, he saw a large perforated tree. He hollowed out a space eight meters in extent, constructed a door and a window panel, fitted it with a ladder, and made it his dwelling. He lit a fire in a firepan, and as he lay down at night he heard cries and growls. He noted, "A lion is making a noise in such and such a place, a tiger in such and such place," so when day came he went there, took the remains of their kill, cooked it, and ate it.

Then one day, at the approach of dawn, he lit a fire and sat down. At just that time a tiger had picked up the scent of the princess and had dug into the area, making an opening in the roofboards. When the princess saw the tiger through the opening, she was terrified and cried out in distress. The king heard her cry and realized: "That's the sound of a woman." In the morning he went there and asked: "Who is here?" – "A woman, lord." – "Come out!" – "I won't come out." – "Why not?" – "I am a khattiya woman." Thus, even though she was buried in a pit, she preserved her pride. He questioned her about everything and informed her of his own social class, saying: "I too am a khattiya." He told her: "Come, now, we're like ghee placed in milk." She replied: "I have a skin disease, lord, I cannot come out." He told her: "I am experienced in this and can cure you." He gave her the ladder, lifted her out from the pit, and brought her to his own dwelling place. He gave her the medicines that he himself had used and before long she recovered and regained her golden complexion.

He coupled with her, and as a result of their first union she became pregnant and gave birth to twin sons. The next time she again gave birth to twin sons, and so she give birth sixteen times; thus there were thirty-two brothers. When they eventually reached maturity, their father trained them in all crafts. [356]

Then one day a resident of King Rāma's city, searching for gems in the mountain, came to that region. When he saw the king he recognized him and said: "I know you, lord." When the king asked him where he had come from, he replied: "From the city, lord." The king asked him all the news. While they were conversing in this way the boys arrived. On seeing them, the man asked: "Who are they, lord?" – "These are my sons." – "What will you do now in the forest, lord, surrounded by thirty-two princes? Come and rule the kingdom." – "Enough, man! I'm happy here." Thinking, "Now I've got some news to report," the man returned to the city and informed the king's son.

The king's son, thinking, "I will bring my father back," went to him with a four-division army and in various ways begged his father to return. Again, the king replied, "Enough, dear boy, I'm happy here," and he did not agree. Then the prince considered: "Now my father doesn't wish to return. Let me build a city for him right here." Thus he uprooted the koḷa tree, made a house, and had a city built. Because it was built in the place where they had removed a koḷa tree, he called it Koḷanagara, and because it was built along the pathway of tigers, he called it Byagghapajja ("Tiger's Footpath"). Having thus given it two names, he departed.

When the princes reached maturity, their mother instructed them: "Dears, the Sakyans living at Kapilavatthu are your uncles. Take their daughters." On the day the khattiya girls went to play in the river, the princes went there, blocked off the ford, announced their names, and carried off whichever girl they desired. When the Sakyan royalty heard about this, they said, "Let it be, man, they're our relatives," and kept silent. This was the origin of the Koḷiyans.

Thus it should be understood in detail how the lineage of the Sakyans and Koḷiyans down to King Sīhahānu descended from their intermarriages. But King Sīhahānu had five sons: [357] Suddhodana, Amitodana, Dhotodana, Sakkodana, and Sukkodana.[1239] While Suddhodana was reigning, the Great Man (the future Buddha), having fulfilled the pāramīs, passed away from the Tusita heaven, in the way told in the introduction to the Jātakas, and was reborn in the womb of the king's wife, Queen Mahāmāyā. Eventually the Great Man made the great renunciation, attained perfect enlightenment, and set in motion the wheel of the Dhamma. Having traveled in stages to Kapilavatthu, he established King Suddhodana and the other Sakyans in the noble fruit, and then departed to tour the countryside. Again on a later occasion he returned along with 1,500 bhikkhus and dwelled at Kapilavatthu in the Nigrodha Park.

While the Blessed One was dwelling there, a quarrel broke out between the Sakyans and the Koḷiyans on account of water. How? It is said that the river Rohinī flowed between Kapilavatthu and the Koḷiyan city. Sometimes the river had little water, sometimes much water. When it had little water, the Sakyans and the Koḷiyans both built irrigation channels to conduct the water for the purpose of watering their own crops. One day, while building the channels, their men argued with one another and insulted one another with reference to social class, saying such things as "Your royal ancestors coupled with their own sisters, like animals, like chickens, dogs, and jackals." – "But your royal ancestors lived in the hollow of a tree like little goblins."[1240] Each reported the dispute to their own kings. Furious, they prepared for battle and arrived at the banks of the river Rohinī, their armies as vast as the sea.

Then the Blessed One turned his attention to them and realized: "My relatives have quarreled. I must stop them!" He arrived through the sky and stood between the two armies. But some say that he came from Sāvatthī (Ja V 413,18). Standing [358] there, he spoke the Discourse on One Who Has Taken Up the Rod.[1241] When they heard this, they were all moved by a sense of urgency and discarded their weapons. They paid homage to the Blessed One and prepared a lofty seat for him. The Blessed One descended and sat down. He then related the Phandana Jātaka, the Laṭukika Jātaka, and the Vaṭṭaka Jātaka,[1242] and then related this great chronicle of their lineage, again showing that they had been relatives for a long time. All were exceedingly pleased, thinking: "It seems in the past we were relatives." Then 250 Sakyan youths and 250 Koḷiyan youths offered to accompany the Blessed One. The Blessed One, having seen they had past causes,[1243] said: "Come, bhikkhus!" They all became equipped with the eight requisites produced by psychic power, rose up into the sky, came together, and remained there venerating the Blessed One. The Blessed One took them and went to the Great Wood.

Their wives sent messengers. Enticed by them in various ways, the new monks grew discontented with the celibate life. Realizing that they were discontented, the Blessed One showed them the Himalayas, and wishing to dispel their dissatisfaction by relating the Kuṇāla Jātaka, he said to them: "Have you ever before seen the Himalayas, bhikkhus?" – "No, Blessed One." – "Come, bhikkhus, see them." He led them through the sky by his own psychic power and showed them the various mountains: "This is Golden Mountain, this is Silver Mountain, this is Jewel Mountain." Then he stood on the Red Arsenic Terrace alongside Lake Kuṇāla. He made the resolution: "Let all the animals in the Himalayas come—the four-footed, the many-footed, and so forth—with the kuṇāla bird the last of all." As they were arriving, he pointed them out, announcing the names of their species thus: "These, bhikkhus, are geese, these [359] herons, these cakra birds, karavīkas, hatthisoṇḍakas, and pokkharasātakas."[1244]

Observing them with amazement, they saw that the kuṇāla bird that had arrived last of all, surrounded by a retinue of a thousand female birds, sat in the midst of twigs that had been gathered by two female birds with their beaks. Struck with wonder and astonishment, they asked the Blessed One: "Is it possible, Bhante, that the Blessed One too had once been a king of the kuṇāla birds here in the past?" – "Yes, bhikkhus, I was the one who started this lineage of kuṇālas. For in the past four of us lived here: the rishi Nārada Devala, Ānanda the king of the vultures, Puṇṇamukha the spotted cuckoo, and I the kuṇāla bird." He then proceeded to relate the entire Mahākuṇāla Jātaka.[1245] When they heard this, the bhikkhus lost their longing for their former wives.

Then the Blessed One gave them a talk on the truths, at the end of which the least of them became a stream-enterer, while the others reached higher stages up to non-returner, so that there was not even a single worldling among them, nor did any become an arahant. Then the Blessed One took them, and again they descended in the Great Wood. And when returning, those bhikkhus came by their own psychic power.

To lead them to the higher paths, the Blessed One again taught them the Dhamma. The five hundred bhikkhus undertook insight and became established in arahantship. The one who attained first came first, thinking to inform the Blessed One. Having arrived, he said, "I am enjoying it, Blessed One, I am not dissatisfied," and then he venerated the Blessed One and sat down to one side. In this way, they all came in sequence and sat down around the Blessed One. This was in the evening on the uposatha day in the month of Jeṭṭha (May–June).

As the Blessed One sat in his excellent seat accompanied by the five hundred arahants, the deities from the entire ten-thousandfold world sphere—except the nonpercipient beings and the formless brahmās—created subtle bodies, in the way stated in the commentary on the Maṅgala Sutta (p. 739), and surrounded them, thinking: "We will get to hear a variegated and inspired Dhamma teaching." Four arahant brahmās who had emerged from their meditative attainments [360] did not see their group of brahmās. Having pondered, "Where have they gone?" they found out about the event and arrived late. Unable to find room, they stood at the top of the world sphere and each recited an individual verse. As it is said:

> Then the thought occurred to four deities of the Pure Abodes: "This Blessed One is dwelling among the Sakyans at Kapilavatthu in the Great Wood together with a great Saṅgha of bhikkhus, with five hundred bhikkhus all of whom are arahants. And the deities from ten world systems have for the most part assembled in order to see the Blessed One and the Bhikkhu Saṅgha. Let us also approach the Blessed One and, in his presence, each speak our own verse."

All here should be understood in the way stated in the Sagāthāvagga.[1246]

Having gone, one brahmā found room at the top of the eastern world sphere, where he stood and recited this verse:

> "A great gathering takes place in the woods . . .
> to see the invincible Saṅgha."

As he recited this verse, one standing on the mountain of the western world sphere heard his voice. The second brahmā found room at the top of the western world sphere, where he stood and recited this verse:

> "The bhikkhus there are concentrated . . .
> the wise ones guard their faculties."

The third found room at the top of the southern world sphere, where he stood and recited this verse:

> "Having cut through barrenness, cut the cross-bar . . .
> young nāgas."

The fourth found room at the top of the northern world sphere, where he stood and recited this verse:

> "Those who have gone to the Buddha for refuge . . .
> will fill up the hosts of devas."

The one standing on the mountain of the southern world sphere heard his voice. In this way, these four brahmās stood there praising the assembly, while Mahābrahmā stood having covered one world sphere.

Then the Blessed One, having looked up at the assembly of devas, announced to the bhikkhus: [361] "Bhikkhus, the deities that assembled before the Blessed Ones of the past, those who were arahants and perfectly enlightened buddhas, were at most like those now present before me. The deities that will assemble before the Blessed Ones of the future, those who will be arahants and perfectly enlightened buddhas, will be at most like those now present before me." He then divided that assembly of devas into two types according to whether or not they were capable: "These are capable, those are incapable." He knew of them: "The assembly of the incapable would not understand the Dhamma even if a hundred buddhas were teaching it, while the assembly of the capable is able to understand it." Again, he divided the capable persons into six types by way of temperament: "This many have a lustful temperament; this many have temperaments governed by hatred, delusion, thought, faith, and intelligence." Having comprehended them by way of temperament, he considered what kind of Dhamma teaching to give thus: "What kind of Dhamma teaching would be suitable for this assembly?" Again, he considered the assembly thus: "Would they understand a teaching given according to my own inclination, or through the inclination of others, or because of a special incident, or in response to a question?"[1247] He then realized: "They would understand a teaching given in response to a question."

He next turned his attention to the entire assembly, asking himself: "Is there anyone able to ask a question?" Having known that there was no one who could do so, he then considered: "It would not be suitable for this assembly if I were both to pose the question and answer it myself. Let me then create a mind-created buddha."[1248] He then entered and emerged from the basic jhāna, and having resolved by means of the psychic power of the mind-made body, he created a mind-created buddha.[1249] It appeared together with his mental determination: "Let it be complete in its body and limbs, possessed of the characteristics, equipped with an alms bowl and robe, able to look up and look aside, and so forth." It came from the eastern world system and sat down in a seat that was on an even level with that of the Blessed One.

At this gathering the Blessed One spoke six discourses, one for each of the [six] temperaments: Before the Breakup (IV,10), Quarrels and Disputes (IV,11), The Smaller Discourse on Deployment (IV,12), The Greater Discourse on Deployment (IV,13), Quickly (IV,14), and this Discourse on Proper Wandering. This discourse was to be expounded as suitable for the deities of lustful temperament.

359. Asking a question in order to begin the discourse, he spoke this verse: "I ask the muni of abundant wisdom." [362] Here, **abundant wisdom**: great wisdom; **crossed over**: crossed over the four floods; **gone beyond**: reached nibbāna; **attained nibbāna**: by way of nibbāna with residue remaining: **inwardly firm**: one whose mind cannot be shaken by worldly conditions. **Having renounced the home life and discarded sensual pleasures**: Having discarded sensual objects and renounced the household life; **how would that bhikkhu properly wander in the world?**: how would that bhikkhu properly wander, dwell in the world untainted by the world? How would he transcend the world?

360. Now, since no one wanders properly in the world without having attained the destruction of the influxes, after he had comprehended the entire multitude by way of their temperaments, such as the lustful type and so forth, the Blessed One spoke the fifteen verses beginning "When he has uprooted [concern with] blessings," so that different groups of deities that shared the same defect could abandon their habitual defect. He spoke these verses thereby showing the arahant's practice up to its culmination in arahantship.

Here, in the first verse, **blessings** is a designation for such things as the "seen blessing" and so forth spoken of in relation to the Discourse on Blessings (pp. 735–36). **Uprooted**: well rooted out, eradicated with the sword of wisdom. **Portents**: interpretations of portents that occur thus: "Shooting stars, auroras, and so forth will bring such and such results." **Dreams**: interpretations of dreams that occur thus: "If one has a dream in the morning, this happens; if at noon and so forth, that happens. If one has a dream while lying on one's left side, this happens; if while lying on one's right side, that happens. If one sees the moon in a dream, this happens; if one sees the sun, that happens, and so forth." **Lucky signs**: interpretations of signs that occur when one reads lucky signs on a stick or a piece of cloth and says: "Because of this, that happens." All these should be understood in the way stated in the Brahmajāla Sutta (DN I 9). **When he has abandoned the defects of blessings**: Except for the thirty-eight great blessings [enumerated in the Discourse on Blessings], the rest are called "defects of blessings." [363] One for whom these blessings have been uprooted is "one who has abandoned the defects of blessings." Or alternatively, it is because he has abandoned blessings and such defects as concern with portents that he is "one who has abandoned the defects of blessings."[1250] Because he has achieved the noble path, he does not rely on the belief that purity is to be attained by blessings and so forth. Therefore he **would properly wander in the world**: That arahant would properly wander in the world, untainted by the world.

361. In the second verse, **a bhikkhu should remove lust for sensual pleasures, for pleasures both human and celestial**: By the path of the non-returner he should remove lust for human and celestial strands of sensual pleasure so that it can never arise again. **Having transcended existence, having penetrated the Dhamma**: After one has removed lust in such a way, by the path of arahantship one "penetrates the Dhamma" consisting in the four truths, completing the "breakthrough of full understanding" and so forth;[1251] and by this practice one "transcends existence" of three kinds.[1252] **He would properly**: That bhikkhu would properly wander in the world.

362. In the third verse, **when he has abandoned attraction and repulsion**: when he has abandoned lust and hatred in regard to all objects. The rest should be understood in ways already explained, and the phrase "that bhikkhu would properly wander in the world" should be connected to all verses. From here on, without stating the construal, we will comment only when the method has not been previously explained.

363. In the fourth verse, **what is pleasing and displeasing** should be understood as twofold, by way of beings and conditioned things (inanimate objects). **Having abandoned**: by the abandoning of desire-and-lust and aversion [respectively] in regard to them. **Without clinging**: not grasping anything by means of the four kinds of clinging. **Not depending on anything**: not depending on anything such as form and so forth, or on any kind of existence, by the dependency of craving with its 108 divisions or by the dependency of views with its sixty-two divisions.[1253] **Utterly released from things that fetter**: The "things that fetter" are all phenomena of the three planes of existence, which are the objective domain of the ten fetters; one is "utterly released" from them by fully understanding them in all ways through the development of the path.[1254] And here, by the first line, the abandoning of lust and hatred is stated; by the second, the absence of clinging and dependency; and by the third, release from all other unwholesome states and unwholesome bases. Or else, by the first line, the abandoning of lust and hatred should be understood; by the second, the means leading to this; and by the third, because these have been abandoned, release from things that fetter.

364. In the fifth verse, **in acquisitions**: in the aggregates as acquisitions.[1255] These (aggregates) are also called **things taken up** [364] in the sense that they can be taken up. **Not to be led by others**: Because one has clearly seen impermanence and so forth, one cannot be led by anyone else who might say: "This is better." The meaning of the remaining terms is clear. This is meant: Having completely removed desire and lust for things taken up by the fourth path, one "has removed desire and lust." One **does not find a core in** those **acquisitions**, for one sees that all acquisitions are coreless. Hence one is **not dependent** upon them by either of the two types of dependency (craving and views), nor can one be led by anyone who might say: "This is better." Such an arahant bhikkhu would properly wander in the world.

365. In the sixth verse, **not hostile**: because he has abandoned these three kinds of misconduct (bodily, verbal, and mental), he is not hostile toward those of good conduct. **Having rightly understood the Dhamma**, the Dhamma of the four truths by means of the path. **Aspiring for the state of nibbāna**: aspiring for the state of the extinction of the aggregates without residue remaining.[1256]

366. In the seventh verse, **insulted** means reviled by any of the ten bases of insult.[1257] **He should not nurture resentment**: should not harbor resentment, should not be irritated.[1258] **He should not be intoxicated over food gained from others**: When he gains gifts given out of faith by others, he is not intoxicated, thinking: "I am renowned, famous, one who gains offerings."

367. In the eighth verse, **greed**: unrighteous greed; **existence**: existence divided into desire-realm existence and so forth. Thus these two terms signify craving for existence and for wealth. Or else, by the first term all kinds of craving are indicated, by the second term karmically active existence.[1259] **Refraining from wounding and binding**: Because he has abandoned these defilements and kamma, he refrains from wounding and binding other beings.

368. In the ninth verse, **having understood what is suitable for himself**: having abandoned improper search and other actions inappropriate[1260] for his own status as a bhikkhu, he has understood purity of livelihood by proper search and so forth, and proper practice by being established in it; for nothing is achieved by mere knowledge. **As it is**: as it actually is, as it really is. **Dhamma**: [365] having understood things classified as aggregates, sense bases, and so forth with the knowledge of things as they really are; or having understood the Dhamma of the four truths with the path.[1261]

369. In the tenth verse, "who is wishless, without expectations," **one who has no latent tendencies at all**, because they have been destroyed by the noble path, and **whose unwholesome roots have been uprooted**—he is wishless, without craving, and therefore, because of the absence of any wish, he does not expect anything such as form and so forth. Hence he said **wishless, without expectations**.

370. In the eleventh verse, **one with influxes destroyed**: one for whom the four influxes are destroyed. **With conceit abandoned**: one who has abandoned the ninefold conceit. **The pathway of lust**: the phenomena of the three planes that serve as the objective domain of lust. **Transcended**: overcome by full understanding and abandoning. **Tamed**: having discarded all mischief through the doors,[1262] he has reached the stage of the tamed by means of a noble taming. **Quenched**: become cool by the subsiding of the fires of defilements.[1263]

371. In the twelfth verse, **endowed with faith**: Since he is not dependent upon others in regard to his convictions about the excellent qualities of the Buddha and so forth, he possesses unwavering confidence complete in all respects, and he has not arrived at this ascertainment through faith in another.[1264] As it is said: "I do not go by faith in the Blessed One concerning this, Bhante." **Learned**: possessed of the supreme learning, because he has consummated the function of learning. **A seer of the fixed course**: In the world, which is deluded in the wilderness of saṃsāra, he is a seer of the path, which is the fixed course of rightness that leads to the city of the deathless; what is meant is "one who has seen the path."[1265] **Who, among partisans, does not take sides**: The partisans are the adherents of the sixty-two views, who are mutually opposed; thus among beings who are partisans, who have adopted views, he does not take sides, because he does not adopt such views as "This will be annihilated; this will exist just as it is."[1266] **Aversion**: causing aversion; what is meant is "causing mental distress." This is just an attribute of hatred.[1267]

372. In the thirteenth verse, **a purified conqueror**: one who has vanquished the defilements by the purified path of arahantship.[1268] **Whose coverings are removed**: whose coverings of lust, hatred, and delusion have been removed.[1269] **A master**

of things: attained to mastery over the "things" (*dhammesu*) of the four truths. [366] For it is not possible for anyone to present those things otherwise than in the way in which they have been known;[1270] hence the arahant is called "a master of things." **Gone beyond**: It is nibbāna that is called "the beyond" (or "the far shore"); he is one who has gone there. What is meant is one who has achieved it with a residue remaining. **Without impulse**: free from the quivering of craving. **Skilled in the knowledge of the cessation of conditioned things**: It is nibbāna that is called "the cessation of conditioned things." The wisdom of the noble path is the knowledge of it. He is skilled in it, adroit because he has developed it four times.[1271]

373. In the fourteenth verse, **things past**: the five aggregates that have already occurred and are now gone; **things future**: the five aggregates that have not yet occurred; **overcome mental constructs**: one who has overcome mental constructs of "I" and "mine," or who has overcome mental constructs due to craving and views. **Having overcome them, wise about purity**: One with exceeding wisdom of purity, or one who, having overcome, is wise about purity.[1272] What has he overcome? The three periods of time. For the arahant has overcome the past, which consists in ignorance and volitional activities; he has overcome the future, which consists in birth, old age, and death; and he has overcome the present, the factors from consciousness to existence.[1273] Having transcended all this, having crossed over doubt, he abides with wisdom that has attained supreme purity. Hence it is said: "one with surpassing wisdom of purity." **Released from all the sense bases**: released from the twelve sense bases. For the arahant has gone beyond formulations. Because he has gone beyond formulations and because of his wisdom of purity, he does not approach any sense bases in the future. Hence he said: "released from all the sense bases."

374. In the fifteenth verse, **having known the state**: having known each state (*pada*) among the four noble truths with the wisdom delineating the truths in the preliminary portion of the path; for it is said: "of truths the four states" (Dhp 273b). **Having penetrated the Dhamma**: thereafter, having penetrated the Dhamma of the four truths with the four noble paths. **Having seen clearly the abandoning of the influxes**: Having clearly, plainly, unobstructedly seen nibbāna—designated "the destruction of the influxes"—by means of reviewing knowledge. **With the utter destruction of all acquisitions**: with the utter destruction of all acquisitions—analyzed into the aggregates, strands of sensual pleasure, defilements, and volitional activities—not attached to any of them, that bhikkhu **would properly wander in the world**; he would dwell, go about in the world without attachment. Thus he concludes the teaching. [367]

375. Then the created buddha, praising the teaching of the Dhamma, spoke this verse: "Surely, Blessed One." Here, **one who dwells thus**: one who, having uprooted [concern with] blessings and so forth, dwells with the defects of blessings abandoned; who has also removed lust for sensual pleasures, both celestial and human, who has transcended existence, and dwells having penetrated the Dhamma. Thus [by the words "one who dwells thus"] he shows the bhikkhu described in each of those verses. The rest is clear.

This is the construal: "Surely, Blessed One, it is just so. It is just as you said, beginning with the words 'When he has uprooted [concern with] blessings,' and stating at the end of each verse, 'he would properly wander in the world.' For what reason? A bhikkhu who dwells thus has been tamed by the best taming and has transcended all ten fetters and four bonds. Therefore he would properly wander in the world. I have no doubt about this." Thus, having stated a verse praising the teaching, he concludes the teaching with its culmination in arahantship. At the conclusion of the discourse, 100,000 koṭis of deities attained the foremost fruit, while those who attained the fruits of stream-entry, once-returner, and non-returner were incalculable.

14 Dhammika
(*Dhammika Sutta*)

What is the origin? It is said that while the Blessed One, the world's protector, was living, there was a lay follower named Dhammika ("Righteous One"), who was righteous both by name and by conduct. It is said that he had gone for refuge, was of good behavior, learned, an expert in the three Piṭakas, a non-returner, a gainer of the superknowledges, and could travel through the sky. He had a retinue of five hundred lay followers who were just like himself. One day, when he was alone in seclusion, observing the uposatha, the following reflection arose in his mind at the end of the middle watch of the night: "Let me ask about the practice of a layperson and a homeless one." Accompanied by the five hundred lay followers, he approached the Blessed One and inquired about this matter, and the Blessed One answered him. [368]

Here, whatever is similar to what has already been commented on should be understood in accordance with the previous method of explanation. We will comment only on what has not been previously explained.

376. Here, in the first verse, firstly, **how act**: how practice; **a good disciple**: excellent, blameless, one who achieves the good. The rest is clear by way of the meaning, but this is the construal: "Whether one who has gone from home to homelessness," one who has gone forth, "or those lay followers who live at home": among these two types of disciples, "how does a good disciple act?"

377. Now, he speaks the next two verses, beginning with the words "For you know," showing that the Blessed One is capable of answering this matter. Here, **the course** (*gatiṃ*) is the course of their inclination; **the destination** (*parāyanaṃ*) is the outcome. Or alternatively, **the course** is the realm of rebirth with its fivefold division into the hells and so forth; **the destination** is going beyond the realms of rebirth—final nibbāna, release from the realms.[1274] **There is none equal to you:** there is none similar to you.

378. Having directly experienced all knowledge, you reveal the Dhamma, taking compassion on beings: Having experienced whatever can be known without omission, having penetrated it, taking compassion on beings, you reveal all knowledge and the Dhamma.[1275] You have clearly shown and taught whatever is beneficial to each; you do not have a teacher's closed fist.[1276] **Stainless, you shine radiantly**: Like the moon not obscured by smoke and dust, in the absence of the stains of lust and other defilements you shine radiantly, a stainless one.

379. Now, praising the Blessed One by extolling the young devas to whom the Blessed One taught the Dhamma, he spoke the next two verses, beginning **Erāvaṇa, the nāga king**. This Erāvaṇa, it is said, was the name of a young deva who could assume whatever form he wished;[1277] he lived in a celestial mansion. When Sakka goes to play in the park, Erāvaṇa becomes an elephant, having created a body 150 yojanas in length and with thirty-three frontal globes. On each of his globes there are two tusks, on each tusk seven [369] lotus ponds, in each lotus pond seven lotus plants, on each lotus plant seven lotus flowers, on each flower seven petals, and on each petal seven nymphs are dancing. These are Sakka's dancing girls, known as "the lotus nymphs," who are also mentioned in the Vimānavatthu as "the girls who move around, trained on lotuses."[1278] In the middle of those thirty-three globes is the Sudassana (beautiful) globe, thirty yojanas in size, on which there is a jeweled couch a yojana long spread out in a floral pavilion three yojanas wide. There Sakka, ruler of the devas, surrounded by a company of nymphs, enjoys his celestial splendor. But when Sakka has returned from playing in the park, Erāvaṇa withdraws that form and again becomes a young deva. It is with reference to this that he said: "Erāvaṇa, the nāga king, came into your presence."

When he heard you are "the Conqueror": Having heard, "This Blessed One defeated those of evil nature,"[1279] **having consulted with you,** having asked a question, **he departed [saying] "Excellent," delighted to have heard [your words]**:[1280] Having heard the answer to that question, having rejoiced by saying, "Excellent, Bhante!" he left delighted.

380. King Vessavaṇa Kuvera: Here, that yakkha is a king in the sense of enjoying pleasure.[1281] He is known as Vessavaṇa because he exercises rulership in the royal capital Visāṇā; "Kuvera" was his former name. It is said that he had been an affluent brahmin named Kuvera who did such meritorious deeds as giving alms and so forth, and was reborn as the overlord of the royal capital Visāṇā. Therefore he is called "Kuvera." And this is said in the Āṭānāṭiya Sutta: "The great king Kuvera, dear sir, has a royal capital named Visāṇā; therefore the great king Kuvera is called 'Vessavaṇa'" (DN III 201,6–10).

It may be asked: "Why did Erāvaṇa, who lives farther away in the Tāvatiṃsa heaven, come first, and Vessavaṇa afterward, [370] and this lay follower, living in the same city, come last of all? And how did he know about their coming, on the basis of which he speaks thus?" In reply it is said that at the time Vessavaṇa had mounted his Nārivāhana vehicle, twelve yojanas long, with a couch made of many thousand pieces of coral. Having raised up the coral kunta bird, accompanied by 10,000 koṭis of yakkhas, he had decided: "I will ask the Blessed One a question." Taking the skyway via the path that encircles the spatial celestial mansions, he arrived at a place above the laywoman Nandamātā's residence in the city of Veḷukaṇḍa. This laywoman had this spiritual might: she was of purified behavior; she always refrained from eating outside the prescribed time; she was an expert in the three Piṭakas; and she was established in the fruit of a non-returner. On that occasion she had opened the window panel, and as she stood in a breezy area in order to refresh herself, she recited the Chapter of the Eights and the Chapter of the Way to the Beyond in a sweet voice, with well-enunciated words and phrases.[1282] Vessavaṇa stopped the vehicle right there and listened to the whole recitation until the laywoman spoke the concluding words: "This is what the Blessed One said while dwelling among the Magadhans at the Pāsāṇaka Cetiya. When entreated by the sixteen attendant brahmins . . ." (see p. 344). At the end of the chapter he stretched forth his large neck,[1283] which was like a golden *muraja* drum, and applauded her with the words "Excellent, excellent, sister!" She asked: "Who's here?" – "I am Vessavaṇa, sister!" It is said that the laywoman had become a stream-enterer first, and Vessavaṇa afterward, so he addressed the laywoman as "sister," referring to her as his sibling in the Dhamma.

The laywoman told him: "It's late,[1284] brother. You may come, my dear, at your own convenience." – "I am pleased with you, sister. Let me give you a gift to express my pleasure." – "In that case, my dear, since the workers are not able to bring the ripened rice from my field, order your retinue to bring it." – "So be it, sister." He then ordered the yakkhas to do so. They filled 1,250 granaries. From then on, [371] in common parlance a granary filled to the brim is said to be "like Nandamātā's granary." Having had the granaries filled, Vessavaṇa approached the Blessed One, who said: "You have come late." He replied, "Yes, Bhante," and reported everything.

For this reason, although Vessavaṇa was living in the heaven of the Four Divine Kings, which was closer [to the human realm], he arrived later, while Erāvaṇa did not have any business to attend to along the way, so he arrived first. But even though this lay follower was a non-returner who habitually ate only once a day, nevertheless, having determined that it was an uposatha day, he undertook the factors of the uposatha and in the evening, well dressed and well attired, he went to Jeta's Grove, accompanied by the five hundred lay followers. Having listened to the teaching of the Dhamma, he returned to his own home, explained a lay follower's duties to those lay followers—going for refuge, undertaking the precepts, the benefits of the uposatha, and so forth—and enjoined them in these practices. In his house, five hundred allowable beds with feet measuring a *muṭṭhihattha* had been prepared, each in a private room.[1285] Having entered their own private rooms, they all sat down and entered a meditative attainment, and the lay follower Dhammika, too, did the same.

Now at that time 5,700,000 families lived in the city of Sāvatthī, and the people numbered eighteen koṭis.[1286] Hence, in the first watch of the night, because of the sounds of elephants, horses, people, drums, and so forth, the city of Sāvatthī was one mass of sound like the great ocean. In the middle watch of the night, the sound subsided. At that time, the lay follower emerged from his meditative attainment, turned his attention to his own excellent qualities, and thought: "I dwell blissfully in the bliss of the path and the bliss of the fruit. In dependence upon whom have I obtained this bliss?" He then realized: "In dependence on the Blessed One." Having generated a mind of confidence in the Blessed One, he then asked himself: "In what way does the Blessed One now dwell?" With the divine eye he saw Erāvaṇa and Vessavaṇa, and with the divine ear he heard the teaching of the Dhamma, and with his knowledge encompassing the minds of others he knew that they had minds of confidence. [372] He then reflected: "Let me now ask the Blessed One about the practice leading to both kinds of well-being." Therefore, though living in the same city, he came last of all, and thus he knew about their prior arrival. Hence he said: "Erāvaṇa, the nāga king, came into your presence . . . and he too was delighted to have heard [your words]."

381. He now spoke the next two verses praising the Blessed One by way of his superiority over ascetics and brahmins outside here,[1287] those who are esteemed by the world. Here, **adherents of other sects**:[1288] those who have entered upon the sects of views created by the three founders of sects, the initiators Nanda, Vaccha, and Saṅkicca; the six teachers, Pūraṇa Kassapa and so forth, who have gone forth in their teachings.[1289] Here, Nātaputta was a Nigaṇṭha, the rest were Ājīvikas.[1290] Showing all of them together, he said: "Adherents of other sects." **Given to debate**: Accustomed to instigating debates by claiming, "We are practicing rightly, you are practicing wrongly," they wander around stabbing people with verbal daggers. **Whether Ājīvikas**: Having briefly referred to them collectively (as "adherents of other sects"), he shows them by distinguishing their views.[1291] **All**: He says this to include the disciples of those adhering to still other sects. **As one standing cannot overtake one walking swiftly**: Just as one standing, devoid of motion, cannot overtake a person walking quickly, so standing still, because they lack the motion of wisdom, unable to understand the classification of things, they do not overtake the Blessed One, whose wisdom is extremely rapid.

382. These brahmins given to debate, elders (*brāhmaṇā vādasīlā vuddhā ca*): By this much he indicates those like Caṅkī, Tārukkha, Pokkharasāti, and Jāṇussoṇi.[1292] **And also some who are brahmins:** By this, he merely indicates that there are some middle-aged and young brahmins, such as Assalāyana, Vāsiṭṭha, Ambaṭṭha, and Uttaramānavaka. **Are all dependent on you for the meaning**: They are dependent on you for the meaning thus: "He may answer this question, he may cut off this doubt." **As are others**: [373] He shows: "Others who go about thinking, 'We're debaters'—countless learned khattiyas, brahmins, brahmās, devas, yakkhas, and so forth—are all dependent on you for the meaning."

383. Having praised the Blessed One in various ways, he now speaks the pair of verses beginning "For this Dhamma," first praising him through the Dhamma itself, and then requesting a Dhamma talk. Here, **for this Dhamma**: He says this referring to the thirty-seven aids to enlightenment. **Subtle**: abstruse, hard to penetrate; **blissful**: being penetrated, it brings world-transcending bliss. Therefore, because it brings bliss, it is called blissful. **Well proclaimed**: well taught. **Declare it to us**: Declare that Dhamma to us.[1293]

384. All these bhikkhus: It is said that at that moment five hundred bhikkhus were sitting there. He makes his request indicating them. **And the lay followers**: He indicates his own retinue as well as others.

385. Then the Blessed One said, **Listen to me, bhikkhus**, and so forth, having addressed the bhikkhus first to show the practice of a homeless one. Here, **the cleansing Dhamma; all retain it in mind**: "cleansing" (*dhuta*) because it shakes off (*dhunāti*) defilements. "**I will proclaim to you** such a Dhamma of practice that cleanses defilements. All of you, retain in mind[1294] [and] practice what is proclaimed by me. Do not be heedless."

Deportment is fourfold—walking, [standing still, sitting, and lying down]; **proper for a monk**: accompanied by mindfulness and clear comprehension. But others say this means proceeding by way of the practice of a meditation subject in the forest. **A thoughtful person, seeing the good**: an intelligent person who contemplates what is beneficial; **should adopt that**: should take up that deportment.

386. At the wrong time: Adopting the deportment proper for a monk, a bhikkhu should not wander at the wrong time, which is said with reference to the time beyond midday. A bhikkhu **should walk for alms in the village** only **at the proper time**. For what reason? **For ties stick to one given to untimely wandering**: because many ties—the ties of lust and other defilements—stick to a person who wanders at the wrong time; they envelop him, encompass him, and adhere to him. **Hence** [374] **the buddhas don't wander at the wrong time**: Therefore noble persons who have awakened to the four truths do not wander for alms at the wrong time. At this time, it is said, the training rule that prohibits eating at the wrong time had not yet been laid down.[1295] Therefore, by means of a teaching of the Dhamma [rather than with reference to a rule], he spoke this verse, pointing out to worldlings the danger in such conduct; but noble ones refrain from this untimely wandering from the time they obtain the path, for doing so comes naturally to them.

387. Having thus prohibited wandering at the wrong time, he next says, **Forms and sounds**, showing: "Even when one wanders at the proper time, this is how one should wander." This is its meaning: **Having removed desire**, in the way stated in the Discourse on the Purification of Almsfood (MN 151), etc., for **forms** and other objects that **drive beings mad**, that in various ways cause beings to become mad, **at the** proper **time** only **one should enter for the morning meal**. This is a term for almsfood. The place where almsfood is obtained, by association with it, is also called "the morning meal." The meaning is that one should go to the place where one obtains almsfood.

388. When one has entered in such a way, "having obtained alms . . . keep oneself collected." Here, **alms** is a mixture of various foods received as alms; it is called "alms" (literally "a lump" or "a mass") in the sense that it is amassed by collecting it from here and there. **On the occasion**: within the time period ending at midday. **Having returned alone**: resorting to bodily seclusion, having returned without a companion. **Reflecting inwardly**: reflecting on the continuum of the aggregates, having ascribed the three characteristics to them; **one should not let one's mind wander outside**: one should not direct the mind outside, toward forms and so forth, by way of lust and other defilements. **Keep oneself collected**: keeping the mind thoroughly under control.[1296]

389. While dwelling thus, "If he should converse . . . criticize others." What is meant? **If he**—the meditator—**should converse with a disciple** who has approached from a desire to hear something, **or with anyone else**, whether an adherent of another sect or a householder, **or with a bhikkhu**, one who has gone forth right here [under the Buddha]; then [375] **he should speak about the sublime Dhamma**, about this Dhamma connected with the paths and fruits and so forth, or with any of the ten subjects of discussion, the Dhamma that is "sublime" in that one can never be satiated by it.[1297] One should not utter anything else, not even the least divisive speech or criticism of others.

390. Now showing the defect in criticism of others, he says: "For some contend in debate." This is its meaning: Some foolish people here **contend in debate**, in various kinds of contentious talk designated "blaming others," that is, they become hostile. Wishing to fight, they act as if they were moving in opposition to an army.[1298] **We do not praise those of slight wisdom**: Why not? **Ties from here and there stick to them**: because the ties of disputes, originating from various courses of speech, stick to such persons, adhere to them. Why do they stick to them? **For they send their minds far away**: because, when they contend in debate, they send their minds to places that are far from serenity and insight.

391–92. Having shown how people of slight wisdom behave, now showing how those of great wisdom behave, he says:

"Alms, a dwelling . . . should use these reflectively." Here, **having heard the Dhamma taught by the Fortunate One**: having heard the Dhamma taught by the Blessed One in the Discourse on All Influxes and other discourses, which teach, "Having reflected carefully, he uses the robe to ward off cold," and so forth,[1299] **a disciple of excellent wisdom should use these reflectively**. Here, almsfood is stated by **alms**, and a lodging by **a dwelling with bed and seat**; medicinal requisites are shown under the heading of **water**; and robes are shown by the **cloak**. One should use these four requisites by reflecting that they are "only for the sustenance of this body" and so forth. **A disciple of the one of excellent wisdom** is a disciple of the Tathāgata, the one of excellent wisdom. This may be a trainee or a worldling, or, in the direct sense, an arahant.[1300] For it is said that he has four supports: "Here, having reflected, [376] he uses some things, patiently endures other things, avoids still other things, and dispels still other things" (DN III 270,1–4; AN V 30,27–29). And since a disciple of the one of excellent wisdom would use these things after reflecting on them, he should be understood thus: **in regard to almsfood . . . as a water drop to a lotus leaf**.

393. By showing the conduct of the arahant, he concludes the practice of the homeless one with its culmination in arahantship. Now, to show the practice of the layperson, he says: **Now let me tell you the householder's duty** and so forth. Here, in the first stanza, a **disciple** is a layperson. The rest is clear, but this is the construal: "The **entire**—undiluted, whole, complete—**duty of a bhikkhu** that was explained earlier **cannot be carried out by one with possessions**, by one who possesses such things as fields and land."

394. Having thus rejected the duty of a bhikkhu as appropriate for him, now showing the householder's duty, he says: **one should not kill living beings**. Here, the first couplet speaks of abstaining from the destruction of life as purified in three respects, and the second couplet shows beneficial conduct toward beings.[1301] The third line here ["having put down the rod"] has been explained in all respects in relation to the Rhinoceros Horn; the fourth line, with its distinction between the firm and frail, was explained in relation to the Discourse on

Loving-Kindness.[1302] The rest is clear, but the construal is made by inversion [of the two couplets] thus: "Having put down the rod toward beings frail and firm, one should not kill, or cause to kill, or approve of killing." Or following the words "having put down the rod," we should add the word "one should act [thus toward those in the world both frail and firm]." For otherwise there would be no cohesion between the earlier and later lines.[1303]

395. Having thus shown the first training rule, now showing the second training rule, he says: **Next, a disciple**. Here, **anything** little or much; **anywhere** in the village or the forest. **A disciple**: a lay disciple. **Knowingly**: knowing, "This belongs to another." **Should entirely avoid taking anything not given**: He shows: "One practicing thus should avoid taking anything not given, and never act otherwise."

396. Having thus shown the second training rule purified in three respects, showing the third beginning with its upper limit, he says: **should avoid impure conduct.**[1304]

397. Now showing the fourth training rule, [377] he says: **one who has entered a council or an assembly**. Here, **entered a council**: entered a meeting hall; **entered an assembly**: in the midst of one's guild.

398. Having thus shown the fourth training rule purified in three respects, showing the fifth he says: **intoxicating drink**. This is the meaning: One **should not indulge** in intoxicating drink; **this Dhamma**: the *dhamma* of abstinence from intoxicating drinks. **This ends in madness**: The lightest result of drinking intoxicants is that it leads a human being to madness.

399. Having thus shown the fifth training rule purified in three respects, and having shown the drinking of intoxicants to be a cause of defilement and a cause of divisions, enjoining them even more sternly in abstinence from intoxicants, he says: **Because of intoxication, [they] do evil deeds. Do evil deeds**: do all unwholesome deeds such as the destruction of life. **Causing madness and delusion**: causing madness in the next world and delusion in this world.

400. At this point having shown the constant good behavior of a lay disciple, he now speaks the next two verses, "One should not kill living beings," showing the factors of the uposatha observance. Here, **impure conduct** is inferior conduct; **sex** is indulgence in sexual activity. **One should not eat at night [and] outside the prescribed time**: One should not eat during the night, and during the day one should not eat food that has exceeded the time limit.

401. Perfumes: Here, by the mention of perfumes, other cosmetics such as lotions and powders are included. **A bed**: an allowable bed; **a mat**: a mat made of straw and so forth with allowable spreads; **on the ground**: a spread of long goat hairs, etc., is also allowed. **Eightfold**: not destitute of any factor, like music played by a five-factored ensemble. **Who has reached the end of suffering**: who has reached the end of the suffering of the round. They say that this last couplet was added by the compilers.

402. Having thus shown the factors of the uposatha, now showing the time for the uposatha, he says: "Of the fortnight."[1305] [378] The verse should be construed as follows. **On the fourteenth, fifteenth, and eighth of the fortnight**: having observed the uposatha with its eight factors on these three days; **and during special periods**.[1306] These five months are called the special periods: the month of Āsāḷha, which precedes entry upon the rains retreat, the three months of the rains retreat, and the month of Kattika (following the rains retreat).[1307] But others say it is just these three months, Āsāḷha, Kattika, and Phagguna. Still others say they are four additional days in each fortnight, the days preceding and following the actual uposatha days of the fortnight, that is, the thirteenth, the first day of the new fortnight, the seventh, and the ninth. One may accept whichever interpretation one wants. One should not miss out on merit.[1308] **Confident in mind, having observed the uposatha complete with its eight factors**, in full, not omitting even one day.

403. Having thus shown the time for the uposatha observance, he now says, "in the morning," showing what is to be done by one who has observed the uposatha at these times. **In the morning**, in the earlier part of the following day, one **who has observed the uposatha, rejoicing**, uninterruptedly experiencing joy, **should distribute**, should serve, **food**, porridge, rice, and so forth, and **drink**, any of the eight kinds of drinks,[1309] **in a fitting way**: in a way that befits himself, according to his strength and ability.

404. Having thus shown the task of one who has observed the uposatha, explaining the solemn duty to be observed all one's life and purification of livelihood, and finally showing the state to be achieved by this practice, he now says: **One should righteously support mother and father**. Here, "righteously" means with wealth righteously obtained. [379] **One should engage in a righteous business**: Having avoided these five kinds of unrighteous business—dealing in weapons, beings, meat, liquor, and poisons[1310]—the remaining kinds of business are righteous. And here, under the heading of business, other types of righteous livelihood are included, such as farming and livestock rearing.

This is the construal: "The noble disciple who is endowed with such qualities as constant good behavior, observance of the uposatha precepts, and giving, should engage in a righteous business. Then, with the righteous wealth (*dhammena bhogena*) obtained thereby—[called 'righteous'] because it is acquired without departing from righteousness (*dhammato anapetattā*), one should support one's mother and father. That **layperson**, thus **heedful**, observing this practice explained from the beginning, with the breakup of the body **reaches the devas called self-luminous**; he is reborn in the state of rebirth of the six classes of desire-sphere devas, who are called 'self-luminous' because they dispel darkness with their own radiance and create light."

III The Great Chapter
(*Mahāvagga*)

1 The Going Forth
(*Pabbajjā Sutta*)

[381] What is the origin?[1311] It is said that while the Blessed One was dwelling at Sāvatthī, the Venerable Ānanda reflected as follows: "The stories of the going forth of the great disciples such as Sāriputta have been told, and the bhikkhus and lay followers know them, but the story of the Blessed One's going forth has not been told. Let me tell it." Having sat down in his seat in Jeta's Grove Monastery, he took a decorative fan and spoke this discourse, relating the story of the Blessed One's going forth.

405. Here, one telling of the going forth should tell *how* he went forth, and one relating how he went forth should tell *how, while investigating, he approved of* the going forth. Therefore, having said, "I will tell of the going forth," at the beginning he states how he went forth. **The One with Vision**: the one endowed with the five eyes.[1312]

406. Now, showing the meaning of the words "how, while investigating," he says: "This home life is confinement." Here, **confinement**: since one is weighed down by wife and children and weighed down by defilements, one does not find an opportunity to do what is wholesome. **A basis for dust**: As Kamboja, etc., is a place for the arising of horses, etc., so this is a place for the arising of the dust of lust and so forth.[1313] **An open space**: It is open like (*viya*)[1314] space, the opposite of the confinement just mentioned. **Having seen this, he went forth**: With his heart stirred even more strongly by reflection on illness, old age, and death, he investigated the danger and benefit respectively in the home life and in going forth, and consequently made the great renunciation. [382] On the bank of the Anomā River he cut off his hair with a sword until his hair and beard were at the two finger-lengths appropriate for an ascetic. He next accepted the eight requisites presented by the brahmā Ghaṭīkāra,[1315] and without being instructed by anyone as to how to wear the lower robe and upper robe—since he had been trained in the practice of going forth during many thousands of past births—he put on one ochre lower robe, made one upper robe, put a robe over his shoulder, slung a clay bowl over one shoulder, and determined this as his monastic apparel.

407. Having thus told of the Blessed One's going forth, Ānanda spoke all the rest, beginning with the words "Having gone forth," to show what happened afterward, [that is,] his monastic practice and his going off to strive after leaving the bank of the Anomā River. Here, **he avoided evil deeds with his body**: He avoided the three kinds of bodily misconduct. **He abandoned verbal misconduct**: the four kinds of verbal misconduct. **He purified his livelihood**: Having abandoned wrong livelihood, he practiced only right livelihood.[1316]

408. Having thus purified his behavior with livelihood as the eighth,[1317] from the bank of the Anomā River **the Buddha went to Rājagaha**, covering the distance of thirty yojanas in a week.[1318] Here, although he went to Rājagaha before he had become a buddha, it is permissible to speak of him in such a way because he had undertaken the previous conduct of a buddha. This is similar to the way it is said by worldly convention: "The king was born here; he acquired the kingship here." **Of the Magadhans**: the city in the country of the Magadhans. **Giribbaja**: This is a name for Rājagaha, which is called Giribbaja because it is situated like an enclosure (*vaja*) in the middle of five mountains (*giri*): Paṇḍava, Gijjhakūṭa,[1319] Vebhāra, Isigili, and Vepulla.

He walked for alms: He walked in the city for the purpose of obtaining almsfood. It is said that he stood at the city gate and thought: "If I were to announce my arrival to King Bimbisāra, saying, 'Prince Siddhattha, the son of Suddhodana, has come,' he would present me with many requisites. But it would not be suitable for me, as one who has gone forth, to announce myself and receive the requisites. Let me instead walk for alms." Thus he put on the rag robes offered by the deva, took his clay bowl, entered the city through the eastern gate, [383] and walked for alms from house to house. Hence the Venerable Ānanda said: "He walked for alms [in the city]." **Adorned with the excellent marks**: He had the excellent marks on his body as if they had been strewn there, or he had vast excellent marks. For what is vast (*vipula*) is also spoken of as strewn (*ākiṇṇa*). As it is said, "When a person is vastly fierce (*ākiṇṇaluddo puriso*), badly soiled like a nursing cloth" (SN I 205,1, Ja III 309,8, Ja III 539,9), meaning "extremely fierce."[1320]

409. Bimbisāra caught sight of him: It is said that over the previous seven days a festival had been held in the city, but that day the drum was struck to announce: "The festival is over; now you must resume work." A crowd had assembled in the royal courtyard, and the king opened the window panel, thinking: "I will assign work." While he was looking out upon his troops, he caught sight of the Great Being walking for alms. Hence Ānanda said: "While standing in his palace, Bimbisāra caught sight of him." **He uttered this statement**: He uttered this statement to the ministers.[1321]

410. Now showing his purpose in speaking to those ministers, he said: **Sirs, look at him**. Here, he addressed the ministers and pointed out the Bodhisatta to them. **Handsome**: lovely in body and limbs; **stately**: tall and broad; **pure**: of pure complexion; **endowed with good conduct**: with deportment.

411. It seems he is not from a low family: It seems he has not gone forth from a low family. **[Find out] where the bhikkhu will go**: He speaks with this purpose: "Go quickly to find out where this bhikkhu will go, where he will stay today, for we wish to see him."[1322]

413. His sense doors guarded: because his eyes are downcast; **well restrained** by mindfulness. Or his sense doors are guarded by mindfulness, and he is well restrained because of his graceful manner of wearing his robes. **He quickly filled**

up his bowl: Because he clearly comprehended and was ever mindful, he did not accept anything in excess but quickly filled up his bowl, filling it with the intention: "This much is enough."

414. The muni: Though he had not yet attained munihood, he is called a muni because he was practicing for the sake of munihood or he was called thus in compliance with worldly convention; for people in the world call a monk a muni even though he has not attained munihood.[1323] **He ascended Mount Paṇḍava**: He climbed that mountain. It is said that he had asked people: "In this city, where do monks dwell?" [384] They then informed him: "On the eastern slope at the top of Paṇḍava." Therefore he ascended Mount Paṇḍava. They considered thus: **"His dwelling place must be here!"**[1324]

416. In a mountain cavern like a tiger, a bull, or a lion: He uses this simile because these three animal chiefs sit in a mountain cave devoid of fear and terror.

417. A fine vehicle: the best kind of vehicle, an elephant or horse chariot, a palanquin, and so forth.

418. Having gone along the ground for vehicles: He went as far as it was possible for a vehicle drawn by elephants, horses, and so forth to go along the ground. Then having arrived, he went up to him and sat down.

421. I will give you wealth: "I will give you as much wealth as you desire in Aṅga and Magadha." The syntax should be understood thus: "Enjoy that wealth while you are shining at the head of an army, accompanied by a troop of bull elephants."

422. There is, O king, a country straight ahead: When he was told, "I will give you wealth, enjoy it. Being asked, tell me your birth," the Great Man reflected: "If I wanted rulership, even the four divine kings, etc., would invite me to exercise rulership over their respective realms. Or staying at home, I could have exercised rulership as a wheel-turning monarch. Not knowing this, this king speaks thus. Let me inform him." Then, having extended his arm to indicate the region from which he had come, he spoke thus: "There is, O king, a country straight ahead." Here, saying, **on the slope of the Himalayas**, he shows that there is no lack of excellent crops; for based on the Himalayas even great sāl trees arisen between the rocks grow by five kinds of growth,[1325] [385] how much more then crops sown in a field. **Abounding in wealth and energy**: Saying this, he shows him that there is no lack of the seven kinds of precious substances and that it is administered by heroic men in ways other kings could never imagine.

[Ruled] by one native to the Kosalans:[1326] Saying this, he rejects its rule by a subordinate ruler; for a subordinate ruler is not said to be native. But one for whom a particular country has been his place of residence by way of succession from early times is said to be native to it, and Suddhodana was such a king. By this, he shows, too, that it excels in wealth that has come down in succession.

423. At this point, having shown his own excellence of wealth, by the statement **I am by clan an Ādicca, by birth I am a Sakyan**, he indicates his excellence of birth.[1327] Then, rejecting the king's offer to give him wealth, he says: **I have gone forth from that family, O king, not longing for sensual pleasures**. The purport here, it seems, is this: "If I longed for sensual pleasures, I would not have gone forth, leaving behind such a family possessing wealth and energy and comprised of 82,000 heroic men."

424. Having thus rejected the king's offer, showing next his own reason for going forth, he says: **Having seen the danger in sensual pleasures, having seen[1328] renunciation as security**. This should be connected to the statement (in the previous verse): "I have gone forth." As to the remainder, whatever has not been examined in the commentary to the previous verses is already clear, so it is not examined. Having thus stated his own reason for going forth, wishing to go off for the sake of striving, he addresses the king: **I will go for the purpose of striving: it is here that my mind delights**. This is its meaning: "Since, great king, I have gone forth after I saw renunciation as security, therefore, longing for that supreme renunciation, nibbāna the deathless, which is chief in the sense that it is the

foremost of all things, I will go for the purpose of striving.[1329]
My mind delights here in striving, not in sensual pleasures."

When this was said, the king said to the Bodhisatta: "Previously, Bhante, I heard that Siddhattha, the son of King Suddhodana, [386] had seen the four signs[1330] and had gone forth seeking to become a buddha. Having seen your resolution, Bhante, I am confident that you will attain buddhahood. Bhante, having attained buddhahood, enter my realm first."[1331]

2 Striving
(*Padhāna Sutta*)

425. What is the origin? The Venerable Ānanda concluded the Discourse on the Going Forth with the words "I will go for the purpose of striving: it is here that my mind delights." While seated in the Fragrant Cottage, the Blessed One reflected: "While I was desiring to strive, for six years I undertook the difficult practice of austerities. Today I will describe them to the bhikkhus." Then, having come out from the Fragrant Cottage, sitting in his own seat, he spoke this discourse, beginning with the words "While I was resolved upon striving."[1332]

Here, **resolved upon striving**: with his mind directed toward nibbāna or with his whole being devoted to nibbāna. **To the Nerañjarā River**: He describes the destination. For the river Nerañjarā was the destination of his resoluteness on striving. Hence the accusative case is used here.[1333] But the meaning is: "On the bank of the Nerañjarā." **Very strenuously**: have made an extreme exertion. **Meditating**: engaged in the non-breathing meditation.[1334] **To attain security from bondage**: for the sake of achieving nibbāna, which is security from the four bonds.

426. Namucī: Māra. He does not free (*na muñcati*) devas and human beings who wish to depart from his own realm, but instead creates obstacles for them; hence he is called "Namucī." **Compassionate**: conjoined with sympathy. **Approached me, speaking**: This is clear, but why did he approach? It is said that one day the Great Man reflected: "One concerned about life is always seeking food, but one concerned about life cannot achieve the deathless." [387] From then on he practiced fasting; hence he became thin and pale. Then Māra thought:

"Not knowing whether or not this is the path to enlightenment, he practices extremely fierce austerity. At some time he might transcend my domain." Thus frightened, he approached, thinking: "Having said various things, I will prevent him." Hence he said: **You are thin, pale; you're on the verge of death**.

427. Then, having spoken thus, demonstrating[1335] to him that he was close to death, he said: **A thousand parts belong to death, one fraction of your life remains**. This is its meaning: "This non-breathing meditation and so forth is a thousandfold condition for your death, but your life has only one portion left; thus you are on the verge of death." Thus, having demonstrated that he was close to death, encouraging him to live, he said: **Live, sir, life is better!** If it is asked, "How is it better?" [he replies]: **While living, make merits!**

428. Then, showing what he himself considers merits, he said: "While you are living the spiritual life." Here, **spiritual life** is said referring to occasional abstinence from sexual intercourse, which the hermits practice.

429. Hard to travel is the path: He speaks this half-verse to discourage him from striving. Here, "it is **hard to travel** because one must proceed painfully by undertaking the non-breathing meditation and similar practices; **hard to practice**, because it must be done with an afflicted body and mind; and **hard to achieve**, because it is impossible to reach even by one like you, on the verge of death." It is thus that the meaning should be understood. The half-verse following this, **Speaking these verses, Māra stood in the presence of the Buddha**, was spoken by the compilers. Some even say the whole verse [was spoken by the compilers]. But our opinion is that everything of such a nature here was stated by the Blessed One himself, describing himself as if speaking of someone else.[1336]

430. With a purpose: The purport here is this: "Evil One, you have come with your own purpose, which is to create obstacles for others." [388]

431. Even for the slightest merit: He spoke this verse rejecting this statement: "While living, make merits!" Here, he speaks of **merit** with reference to the merit spoken of by Māra, which leads back to the round of birth and death.

432. Now, reproaching Māra with reference to this statement, "One fraction of your life remains," he spoke this verse: **I have faith**. This is the purport: "Māra, if one does not have faith in the unsurpassed state of excellent peace; or if one has faith but is lazy; or if one has faith and energy but lacks wisdom, you might prevail when asking him to live. But I have trusting **faith** in the unsurpassed state of excellent peace. So too I have **energy**, unrelenting bodily and mental exertion. And diamond-like **wisdom exists in me**. **When I am so resolute**, with dedicated aspiration,[1337] **why do you ask me to live**? Why do you ask me about life?" And here, by the statement "Wisdom exists in me," mindfulness and concentration are implied. "In such a case, since I am so resolute and not devoid of even one among the five faculties through which they attain nibbāna, why do you ask me to live? Isn't it 'better to live a single day with energy firmly aroused, meditative and possessed of wisdom, while seeing arising and passing away'?"[1338]

433. Having thus reproached Māra, he recites the next three verses showing the condition of his own body and mind. The meaning of the terms is clear. But this is an explanation of the purport: "**This wind** that moves through my body, aroused by the force of energy applied to the non-breathing meditation, **might dry up even the streams of the rivers** in the world, such as the Ganges and Yamuna, **so why, when I am resolute, should it not dry up my blood?**, a mere four *nāḷis*?"[1339]

434. "Not only would my blood dry up, but while the blood is drying up [389] the bile spread throughout my body, both the fixed and unfixed kinds, the four *nāḷis* of phlegm that cover food eaten and drunk, and the similar amounts of urine and nutritive essence, would dry up. And while they are drying up, my muscles would waste away. And while in stages **my muscles are wasting away, my mind becomes even more serene**; it definitely does not founder because of that. You do not understand such a state of mind, but having seen the mere body you say: 'You are thin, pale, you're on the verge of death.' And not only does my mind become serene, but **my mindfulness**

and wisdom and concentration become more firm. There is not even the least bit of heedlessness or delusion or mental distraction."

435. "While I am dwelling in such a way, I have experienced extreme pain—the utmost of those feelings due to striving that ascetics and brahmins experience, whether in the past, present, or future—**yet my mind does not turn to sensual pleasures**, not even to one among the five strands of sensual pleasure, unlike those whose minds seek pleasure when afflicted by pain; who seek coolness when afflicted by heat; who seek food when afflicted by hunger; and who seek water when afflicted by thirst. Not even one thought of this kind has arisen: 'Oh, may I eat delicious food and lie down on a comfortable bed!' You, Māra, **behold the purity of the being**!"

436–38. Having in this way shown his own purity, the Blessed One next spoke the following six verses, beginning "Sensual pleasures are your first army." In these verses, having first described Māra's army for the purpose of demolishing his wish to obstruct him—the reason Māra came there—he then shows that he is invincible by that army. Here, it should be understood that **sensual pleasures are your first army**, because at the beginning sensual defilements in regard to sensual objects delude beings leading the household life. Having overcome these and entered upon homelessness, **discontent** arises in regard to remote lodgings or other extremely wholesome qualities. And this has been said: "For one who has gone forth, friend, contentment is hard to accomplish" (SN IV 260,22). Thereafter, because their life is dependent upon others, **hunger and thirst** afflict them. Being afflicted by hunger and thirst, the **craving** of search fatigues their minds.[1340] Then, [390] since their minds are fatigued, **dullness and drowsiness** enter them. Because of this, they are unable to achieve distinction, and so **cowardice**—a designation for terror—arises while they are dwelling in forest lodgings that are hard to endure. Since they are full of worry and apprehension, and pass a long time without enjoying the flavor of seclusion, **doubt** about the practice assails them thus: "Could it be that this is not the path?" Having dispelled that doubt, when they achieve some trifling distinction, conceit, **denigration, and pride** arise. Having dispelled these too, on account of some superior achievement of distinction, **gain, honor, and praise** arise. Infatuated with gain and so forth, teaching a counterfeit of the Dhamma, they achieve **wrongly obtained fame**. Established upon that, on account of their social class and so forth, they **extol themselves and look down at others**.

439. Having thus summarized this tenfold army, describing it as "your army," he said: "**This is your army, Namucī, the squadron of the Dark One**." [It is Māra's army] because it assists Namucī, called "the Dark One" because he possesses dark qualities. Here, a **squadron** is that which delivers blows to ascetics and brahmins, that which creates obstacles for them. **A weakling does not conquer it, but having conquered, one gains bliss**: "A weak person concerned with his body and life does not conquer such an army of yours, but a hero conquers, and having conquered, he achieves the bliss of the path and the bliss of the fruit."[1341]

440. And since one gains bliss, desiring that bliss **I wear muñja grass**. Warriors in battle, determined not to retreat, tie muñja grass to their head, standard, or weapon in order to show that they will not retreat. He too says [in effect]: "Consider me as one who wears it. If I were to be defeated by your army, **wretched would life be to me**. Therefore consider me thus: **It's better that I die in battle than live on defeated**." The meaning is: "It's better that I die in battle against you, the creator of obstacles for those practicing rightly, than that I live on defeated."[1342]

441. If it is asked, "Why is death better?" the answer is: "Some ascetics . . . the disciplined ones travel." **Engulfed here**, submerged, swallowed up by your army, which begins with sensual pleasures and ends with self-exaltation and disparagement of others. **Some ascetics and brahmins** [391] **are no longer seen**: They do not shine with such excellent qualities as good behavior and so forth; it is as if they have entered darkness. Being submerged, even if, once in a while, they rise up to the surface saying "good is faith," like a submerged person who rises to the surface, still, because they have been overwhelmed by that army, **they do not know the path**—the secure path leading to nibbāna—**by which the disciplined ones**, all buddhas, paccekabuddhas, and so forth, **travel**.[1343]

442. When he heard this verse, Māra departed without saying anything. After he had left, the Great Being, unable to achieve any distinction by that difficult practice of austerities, eventually reflected: "Could there be another path to enlightenment?" and so forth.[1344] Thereafter, having eaten substantial food and regained his strength, early on the full-moon day in the month Visākhā he consumed the milk-rice offered by Sujātā, sat down for his daytime dwelling in the excellent forest grove, and there passed the day attaining the eight meditative attainments.

In the evening he went toward the site of the great bodhi tree, received eight handfuls of straw from Sotthiya, scattered them at the foot of the bodhi tree, and while he was being honored and revered by the deities of the ten-thousandfold world system, he made the fourfold resolve of energy thus:

> "Willingly let only my skin and sinews
> and my bones be left behind;
> let the flesh and blood of my body
> all dry up without residue."

He then sat down in the invincible cross-legged posture, having made the vow: "So long as I have not attained buddhahood, I will not break this posture." Having known this, Māra the Evil One considered: "Today Siddhattha has sat down after making a vow. Today itself that vow of his must be impeded." He then assembled his army throughout this world sphere, which extended twelve yojanas in breadth and nine yojanas in height, and mounted his royal elephant Girimekhala, 150 yojanas in size.[1345] Having created a thousand arms, he took up various weapons, and shouting, "Capture him, destroy him, attack him," he created rains of the kind described in the commentary on the Discourse with Āḷavaka (see p. 615). When those rains reached the Great Man, they were transformed in the way described there. He then struck the elephant on its earlobe with his diamond goad, led him to the Great Man, and said: "Get up from your seat, Siddhattha!" The Great Man replied: "I will not get up, [392] Māra." Then, surveying his army with its banners surrounding him, he recited these verses: "Having seen the bannered army all around."

Here, **with his vehicle ready**, together with the royal elephant Girimekhala prepared, **I will go out to meet him in battle**: I will go out facing him, and that is just by spiritual force, not by body.[1346] Why? **May he not dislodge me from my place**: What is meant is: "May Māra not make me stir from this place, from this invincible posture!"

443. Cannot overcome: It is unable to endure, or it does not overcome. **A fresh clay bowl**: a pot made of fresh clay. The rest here is clear.

444. He now says, "Having gained mastery," showing: "Having destroyed your army, Māra, victorious in battle, consecrated as a king of the Dhamma, I will do this." Here, **having gained mastery over my intention**: having abandoned all wrong intention by the development of the path, having mastered intention through the occurrence solely of right intention. **And with mindfulness well established**: Having made my own mindfulness well established upon the four bases, the body and so forth. Thus, with my intention mastered and mindfulness well established, **I will wander from realm to realm, guiding many disciples** among devas and human beings.

445. Then, being guided by me, **heedful and resolute . . . to the state where one does not sorrow**: the purport is, to nibbāna the deathless.

Having heard these verses, Māra then said: "Having seen such a spirit,[1347] aren't you afraid, bhikkhu?" – "No, Māra, I am not afraid." – "Why aren't you afraid?" – "Because I have fulfilled the merits of the pāramīs such as giving and the rest." – "Who knows that you have done such deeds as giving and the rest?" – "What need is there for a witness here, Evil One? Even in a single existence, when I was Vessantara,[1348] because of the spiritual might of the acts of giving I performed, this great earth itself bore witness by quaking seven times in six ways."

When this was said, the great earth, as far as its boundaries of water, trembled and let loose a frightful noise. Having heard this, Māra was as frightened as if he had been struck by lightning, lowered his banner, and fled along with his retinue.

Then, during the three watches of the night, the Great Man realized the three clear knowledges, and with the arrival of dawn he uttered this joyful utterance: "This saṃsāra with its many births . . . [393] . . . attained the destruction of all cravings."[1349]

446–48. When he heard the sound of this utterance, Māra came back, thinking: "He claims to be a buddha. Let me follow him and observe his conduct. If there is any flaw in his conduct of body or speech, I will harass him." Thus, having already followed him for six years when he was in the stage of a bodhisatta, he followed him for another year after he had attained buddhahood. Since he did not see any fault on the part of the Blessed One, he spoke these verses of disappointment: "For seven years."[1350]

This is the construal: "For seven years I followed the Blessed One step by step, seeking an opening, not abandoning him anywhere, but though I followed him I did not find an opening. I am like a crow that perceived as fat a stone that looked like fat. Having pierced it on one side with his beak, he did not find anything tasty, so he circled it and pierced it on all sides, thinking: 'Perhaps we'll find something tender here, perhaps I may obtain something tasty.' But when he did not find anything tasty anywhere, he realized it was just a stone and so he departed disappointed. In the same way, I have circled the Blessed One on all sides, piercing his bodily actions and so forth with the beak of my slight wisdom, thinking: 'Perhaps somewhere we'll find something tender—some impure bodily conduct and so forth—where there may be something tasty.' But now, not finding anything tasty, **just like the crow that attacked the stone, we leave Gotama disappointed**."

449. As he spoke in such a way, it is said, heavy sorrow arose in Māra on account of his futile effort for seven years. While his body and limbs were slumping because of this, his lute, called "the Yellow Beḷuva Fruit," fell from his armpit. [394] This was the lute which, when played upon once with the fingers,[1351] gives off a sweet sound for four months. Sakka took it and gave it to Pañcasikha. He did not even realize it was falling. Hence the Blessed One said:

> "So much was he stricken with sorrow
> that his lute fell from his armpit.
> Thereupon that saddened spirit
> disappeared right on the spot."[1352]

Some say the compilers spoke this, but we do not agree with that opinion.

3 Well Spoken
(*Subhāsita Sutta*)

This discourse originated through his own inclination.[1353] For the Blessed One was fond of well-spoken words, so he spoke this discourse to prohibit the badly spoken utterances of beings by showing his own well-spoken utterances. Here, **thus have I heard**, etc., are the words of the compilers. "There the Blessed One . . .": This is new; the rest should be understood in the way already explained. Therefore this is stated for the purpose of explaining only what is new.

There: an indication of the place and time; for this indicates on *what occasion* he was dwelling there and *in which monastery* he was dwelling. Or it indicates *the place and time* suitable for what was to be spoken; for the Blessed One does not speak on the Dhamma at an unsuitable place or time. And the proof of this was his statement: "This is not the time, Bāhiya" (Ud 7,31). **The Blessed One**: an indication of the one revered by the world.[1354] **The bhikkhus**: an indication of the suitable persons to listen to the talk. **Addressed**: called, spoke to, summoned.

Bhikkhus: an indication of the way of addressing them. And that is said to affirm that they are endowed with such qualities as the habitual practice of mendicancy. Showing by this that their practice is resorted to by both inferior and superior people, [395] he restrains elation and dejection.[1355] And by this address "bhikkhus," preceded by a glance of the eyes and a heart softened by compassion, he makes them turn their faces toward himself. And indicating by that same expression that he wishes to speak, he arouses in them a wish to listen. And by that same expression, the purpose of which is to enlighten them, he enjoins them to listen and attend closely. For the excellence of the teaching is dependent on listening and attending closely.

If it is asked, "When others are present, devas and human beings, why does he address only the bhikkhus?" [it is said in reply] because they are the eldest, the best, close by, and always present. For this teaching of the Dhamma is given in common to all assemblies, without singling out particular persons. But the bhikkhus are *the eldest* in the assembly because they have arisen first; they are *the best*, because by giving primacy to the homeless state, they emulate the conduct of the Teacher and because they are recipients of the entire teaching. They are *close up*, because they sit near the Teacher, and they are *always present* because they dwell near the Teacher. Hence, when teaching the Dhamma in common to all assemblies, the Blessed One addresses only the bhikkhus. Further, he addresses only them because they are a receptacle for this talk and because they are to practice as instructed.

Venerable sir (*bhadante*): this is a term of reverence. **Those bhikkhus**: Those bhikkhus whom the Blessed One addressed, responding to the Blessed One, reply to him.

Four factors: through four causes or with [four] components. The *four causes* of well-spoken speech are abstaining from false speech and so forth. The *four components* are truthful speech and so forth. But when the word "factor" occurs in the sense of cause, "four" (*catūhi*) is the ablative case ("through four"); when it occurs in the sense of component, it is the instrumental case ("with four"). **Possesses**: is conjoined with. **Speech** is uttered speech, which has come down in such passages as "speech, discourse, assertion" (Dhs 182, §636) and "smooth, pleasant to hear" (DN I 4,25, MN I 179,36) and so forth. But speech that has come down as intimation (*viññatti*), as in the passage "If[1356] a kamma is created by speech" (untraced); and as abstinence (*virati*), as in the passage "Refraining and abstaining from the four kinds of verbal misconduct . . . is called right speech" (Dhs 84, §299); [396] and as volition (*cetanā*), as in the passage "Harsh speech, bhikkhus, resorted to, developed, and cultivated leads to hell" (AN IV 248,1)—that is not intended here.[1357] Why not? Because they are not utterances. **Well spoken**: By this he shows that it leads to benefit. **Not badly spoken**: By this he shows that it does not lead to harm. **Blameless**: devoid of such faults as lust and so forth, which are considered blameworthy. By this he indicates the purity of the motive and the absence of faults in the speaker. **Irreproachable**: free of reproach; by this he indicates its excellence in all aspects. **By the wise**: By this he indicates that foolish persons are not a criterion in matters of blame and praise.

What four?: This is a question asked from a desire to speak. **Here**: in this teaching. **Bhikkhus**: an address to those to whom he wishes to speak. **A bhikkhu**: an example of the person uttering speech of the kind described. **Speaks only what is well spoken**: In a teaching that takes a person as its basis, this is a descriptive term[1358] for one factor among the four factors. **Not what is badly spoken**: a negation of speech that is the opposite of that particular factor of speech. Hence he rejects the view: "Even false speech and so forth may sometimes be spoken." "Not what is badly spoken"; by this[1359] he indicates the abandoning of wrong speech; "what is well spoken": by this he shows the characteristic of the speech that may be spoken by a good person who has abandoned wrong speech. This is similar to the non-doing of evil and the acquisition of the wholesome.[1360] But in order to indicate the factors he states what should be spoken without first stating what should not be spoken. This method applies to the phrases "speaks only on the Dhamma" and the rest as well.

And here, **speaks only what is well spoken, not what is badly spoken**: by this, speech devoid of the fault of divisiveness and conducive to harmony is indicated. **Speaks only Dhamma, not non-Dhamma**: by this, thoughtful speech that does not depart from the Dhamma and is devoid of the fault of idle chatter is indicated.[1361] By the other two, pleasant and truthful speech are indicated, respectively devoid of harshness and lies. **Possesses these four factors**: He concludes that statement, explicitly showing those factors.

And particularly here, by asserting, [397] "When speech possesses these four factors, it is well spoken," he rejects, from the perspective of the Dhamma, those who consider speech to be "well spoken" when it simply possesses such components as a proposition and so forth, and has terms such as nouns and so forth, and when it is perfect with respect to gender, number, case, tense, and so forth.[1362] For speech that may be complete with respect to its components and so forth, if it is divisive, etc., is still badly spoken, for it leads to harm for oneself and others. On the other hand, speech that possesses these four factors, even if it is included in the languages of foreigners or in a song sung by a servant girl, is still well spoken, for it brings mundane and world-transcending well-being and happiness.

The example is given of a Sinhalese servant girl in Sīhaḷadīpa (Sri Lanka) who, while guarding the crops alongside the road, was singing a song in the Sinhala language about birth, old age, and death. Sixty bhikkhus who practiced insight meditation, traveling along the road, heard her while she was singing and attained arahantship right there. Similarly, a bhikkhu named Tissa, who had undertaken insight meditation, was traveling close to a lotus lake while a servant girl was plucking lotus flowers in the lake and singing this song:

> "In the morning the red lotus, in full bloom,
> is withered by the light of the sun.
> Just so beings who have attained the human state
> are crushed by the force of old age."

When he heard her singing this song, he attained arahantship. In the period between buddhas, a certain man together with his seven sons had come out from a woods while a woman was threshing rice grains with a pestle and singing this song:

> "This is fully crushed by old age;
> this is enveloped by wilted skin and hide.
> This is broken apart by death,
> food to be devoured by death.
>
> "This is an abode of worms,
> full of various corpses.
> This is a vessel of impurity;
> this is like a plaintain trunk." [398]

Having heard this song, he and his sons attained enlightenment as paccekabuddhas. Examples are mentioned of others who, in similar ways, attained the plane of the noble ones.

Now it isn't astonishing that each time the Blessed One, who is skilled in knowing the inclinations and latent tendencies of beings, spoke such verses as "all conditioned things are impermanent," five hundred bhikkhus who heard those verses attained arahantship, or that many other devas and human beings who heard his talks about the aggregates, sense bases, and other topics did so.

Thus speech that possesses these four factors, even if it is included in the language of the barbarians or in a song sung by a servant girl, still should be understood as well spoken. It is just because it is well spoken that it is blameless and irreproachable by the wise, that is, by those who desire the good and who rely upon the meaning, not upon the expression.

This is what the Blessed One said: The Blessed One stated this characteristic of what is well stated. **Having said this, the Fortunate One, the Teacher, further said this**: And having stated this characteristic, the Teacher then said something else. The compilers added all this showing the verse to be stated. Here, the word "further" (*aparaṃ*) is said with reference to the verse composition. And that [verse composition] is twofold: (1) an illustration of that same point [that is, the point of the prose portion] for an assembly that has come later, or as confirmation and reinforcement, etc., of good information that has not been heard; and (2) an illustration of a different point by illustrating a point that, for some reason, had been omitted previously [in the prose portion], as in the case of the verse "When a person has taken birth, an axe is born inside his mouth" and so forth (**657**ab). But here it is an illustration of the same point [as the prose portion].[1363]

450. The good: the buddhas and so forth; for they praise **well-spoken speech** as **best**, as supreme. But this is said in the beginning with reference to the order that has been described, [so it also means "first" followed by] second, third, and fourth.[1364]

At the conclusion of the verse, the Elder Vaṅgīsa was pleased with the Blessed One's well-spoken statement. To show that he expressed his pleasure with the statement that the Blessed One uttered, the compilers added the words "Then the Venerable Vaṅgīsa."[1365]

An inspiration has come to me: "My share [399] shines." **Then express your inspiration**: "Then let your share shine."[1366]

451. One does not torment: does not torment by causing remorse. **Nor cause injury**: does not hurt by dividing people from one another. **That speech truly**: That speech is definitely well spoken. With this he extols the Blessed One by means of non-divisive speech.

452. Gladly welcomed: [Speech] that is delighted in, that brings endearment, that goes directly to a gladdened heart. **Words that bring nothing bad**: Not uttering harsh words, which have a bad, disagreeable, repugnant impact on others, one should speak only words that are pleasing, sweet in meaning and expression; what is meant is that one should utter only pleasant speech. With this verse he extols the Blessed One by means of pleasant speech.

453. Deathless: similar to the deathless through its sweetness.[1367] And this is said: "Truth is the sweetest of tastes" (**182**c); or it is deathless because it is a condition for nibbāna the deathless. **This is an ancient principle**: This truthful speech is an ancient prnciple, a tradition of conduct. For just this was practiced by the ancients; they did not speak lies. Hence he says: **The good and the Dhamma, good people say, are established upon truth**. Here, this should be understood thus: "Because they were established upon truth, they were established upon their own good and that of others; and precisely because they were established upon the good, they were established upon the Dhamma."[1368] Or the other two (good and Dhamma) should be understood simply as qualifying truth. They were established upon truth. What is it like? **The good and the Dhamma**: [Truthful speech] is good because it does not depart from the good of others; it creates no hindrance. And since it creates no hindrance, [such speech] is Dhamma because it does not depart from the Dhamma; it accomplishes only the good that is in conformity with the Dhamma (*dhammikam eva atthaṃ*). With this verse he extols the Blessed One by means of truthful words.

454. Secure: without peril, without disaster. If it is asked, "For what reason," it is said, because it is **for the attainment of nibbāna, for making an end to suffering**: because it brings the extinction of defilements and leads to making an end to the suffering of the round. Or alternatively, the meaning here can be understood thus: Since the speech that the Buddha utters is secure because it reveals the secure path for the sake of the two nibbāna elements—for making an end to suffering by the attainment of nibbāna—**that indeed is supreme speech**, [400] that speech is the best of all speech.[1369] By this verse, extolling the Blessed One because of his thoughtful speech, he concludes the teaching with its culmination in arahantship. This here is the explanation of terms not previously encountered. The rest should be understood in the way already explained.

4 The Sacrificial Cake (Sundarikabhāradvāja)[1370] (*Pūraḷāsa Sutta*)

What is the origin? As the night was drawing to an end, the Blessed One surveyed the world with his buddha eye and saw that the brahmin Sundarikabhāradvāja had the supporting conditions for arahantship. He knew: "If I go there, a discussion will take place and then, at the end of the discussion, when he has heard a teaching on the Dhamma, this brahmin will go forth and attain arahantship." Thus he went there, started a discussion, and spoke this discourse.

Here, the passage beginning "Thus have I heard" is the words of the compilers; the passage beginning "What is the worthy one's social class?" is the words of the brahmin; and the passage beginning "I am not a brahmin" is the words of the Blessed One. Having been assembled, all this is called the Discourse on the Sacrificial Cake. Here, whatever is similar to what has already been explained should be understood in the way previously stated. We will comment only on what has not been previously explained, passing over terms that are already clear.

Among the Kosalans: The Kosalans were the princes who dwelled in the country. "Kosalans" is said as a conventional name of the particular country in which they lived. [So he was dwelling] in that country among the Kosalans. But some explain the word thus: In the past the king heard that the prince Mahāpanāda, when watching actors and other entertainers, did not even flash a smile. The king issued an edict: "I will adorn with all ornaments whoever makes my son laugh." Then, having left their plows behind, a large crowd assembled, and the people displayed various amusements for more than seven years, but they still could not make the prince laugh. Thereupon Sakka sent a celestial actor, who performed a celestial play [401] and made him laugh. The people then departed for their own homes. When they saw their friends and dear ones on the road, they showed them hospitality, saying: "I hope you are well, sir! I hope you are well, sir!" (*kacci bho kusalaṃ, kacci bho kusalaṃ*). Therefore, based on the word *kusala*, that region was called Kosala.

Now on that occasion: on the occasion when the Blessed One, wishing to guide that brahmin, had gone to him and was dwelling with his head covered, passing the time in the sitting posture at the foot of a tree on the bank of that river. **Sundarikabhāradvāja**: the brahmin who was staying on the bank of that river and was offering a fire sacrifice. He was of the Bhāradvāja clan; therefore he was called thus.[1371] **Was offering a fire sacrifice**: He was kindling the fire by feeding it the oblation. **Performing the fire oblation**: He was tending the fire place by sweeping it, oiling it, making offerings, and so forth. **Who now might eat the remains of the offering?**: It is said that when the brahmin saw the milk-rice remaining from the offering, he thought: "The milk-rice cast into the fire has been eaten by Mahābrahmā, but there is this remainder. If I give it to a brahmin, one born from the mouth of Brahmā, my son and my father will be satisfied and the path leading to the brahma world will be well cleared. Let me search for a brahmin." He then **rose from his seat and surveyed the four directions** in order to look for a brahmin, thinking: "Who might eat the remains of the offering?"

At the foot of a certain tree: at the foot of the best tree in that grove. **With his head covered**: with his body covered including his head. But why did the Blessed One do this? With his superhuman strength,[1372] couldn't he ward off a snowfall and a cold wind? There is this reason, too, for it is not that the buddhas do not take care of the body in all ways,[1373] but the Blessed One knew: "When the brahmin comes, I will uncover my head. Having seen it, the brahmin will start a discussion, and then, in the course of our discussion, I will teach him the Dhamma." Thus he did this for the purpose of starting a discussion. **Having seen him . . . [402] . . . approached the Blessed One**: It is said that when the brahmin saw the Blessed One, he perceived him as a brahmin and approached with the thought: "He has been engaged in striving all night with his head covered. Having first given him the water of offering, I will give him these sacrificial remains." **This worthy one is shaven-headed, this worthy one is a shaveling**: Having seen the tips of his hair as soon as the Blessed One uncovered his head, he said, "shaven-headed," but looking more closely, not seeing even a slight tuft,[1374] heckling him, he said: "A shaveling." Such was the view of those brahmins. **To turn back**: from the place he was standing when he saw him. **Are also shaven-headed**: for some reason they have shaven heads.

455. I am not a brahmin:[1375] He shows: "I am surely not a brahmin." **Nor am I a prince**: I am not a khattiya. **I am not a vessa or anything else**: I am not anything else, a sudda or a caṇḍāla. Thus he emphatically rejects being addressed in terms of social class.[1376] Why? Because just as the rivers, on reaching the great ocean, [give up their separate waters], so clansmen who have gone forth discard their former names and clans. And the proof of this is the Discourse to Pahārāda (AN IV 202,7–14). Thus, having rejected being addressed in terms of social class, revealing himself as he really is, he says: **Having fully understood the clans of worldlings, owning nothing, with reflection I live in the world**. If it is asked, "How did he fully understand clan?" it should be replied that the Blessed One fully understood the five aggregates by way of the three kinds of full understanding, and when those were fully understood, clan was also fully understood.[1377] He is one **owning nothing** through the absence of the "somethings" of lust and so forth. **With reflection**, having known, he lives by bodily action and so forth accompanied by knowledge.[1378] Hence he says: "Having fully understood . . . in the world." It is wisdom that is called reflection, and he lives by means of that. Hence he says: "with reflection, I live in the world."

456. Having thus revealed himself, criticizing the brahmin thus, "Even when you now see such an obvious sign, you do not know what should be asked and what should not be asked," he says: "Clad in my cloak . . . to ask me about my clan." Here, the three robes are intended by the word "cloak," in the sense that they are stitched together from cut pieces of cloth. He wears these, has put them on, [403] hence **clad in my cloak**. **Homeless**: without a home; the purport is: "without craving." But the Blessed One has dwelling places of various kinds, such as the large Fragrant Cottage in Jeta's Grove, the Karerimaṇḍalamāḷa, the cottage at Kosambī, the Sandalwood Māḷa, and so forth; so it is not correct to take it with reference to these.

With head shaved: with his head hairs gone, with hair and beard shaved off. **Fully quenched within**: with a mind in which the fever [of defilements] has been fully allayed, or with a guarded mind. **Since I am unattached to people here**: "Because, having abandoned affection for implements, I am unattached to people, not bonding with them, utterly secluded. When I am thus clad in my cloak . . . unattached to people here, **it is unfitting, brahmin, to ask me about my clan**: Since I am one who has already gone forth, it is unsuitable, brahmin, to ask me about my original name and clan."

457. When this was said, the brahmin, exonerating himself from criticism, said: **Brahmins, sir, ask other brahmins: "Is the worthy one a brahmin?"** This is what is meant: "I, sir, did not ask anything unfitting. For in our brahmin system, when brahmins encounter other brahmins, they ask about their social class and clan thus: 'Is the worthy one a brahmin? Is the worthy one a Bhāradvāja?'" When this was said, to soften the brahmin's mind, the Blessed One showed his own acquaintance with the Vedic hymns, saying: "But if you say you are a brahmin . . . twenty-four syllables." This is its meaning: "If you say, 'I am a brahmin,' and you say I am not a brahmin, in that case **let me ask you about the Sāvittī, with its three phrases and twenty-four syllables**.[1379] Tell it to me."

And here the Blessed One asks with reference to this noble Sāvittī—[that is,] "I go for refuge to the Buddha, I go for refuge to the Dhamma, I go for refuge to the Sangha"—which is the beginning of the three Piṭakas, the Vedas in the ultimate sense. It is excellent in meaning and excellent in expression, revealed by all the buddhas, who are brahmins in the ultimate sense. For if the brahmin were to say something else, surely the Blessed One would say to him: "This, brahmin, is not called Sāvittī in the discipline of the noble one." Then, having shown him the worthless nature [of his statement], he would have established him right here [in his own teaching]. But having heard, "Let me ask you about Sāvittī, with its three phrases [404] and twenty-four syllables"—which is recognized by his own system, uttered with a brahma-like voice, referring to the characteristics and expression of Sāvittī—the brahmin drew the conclusion: "Surely, this ascetic has reached consummation in the system of the brahmins, yet in my ignorance I reviled him by thinking he is not a brahmin. He is indeed a proper brahmin who has mastered the Vedic hymns." He then thought: "Come now, let me ask him about the method of the sacrifice and the method of determining those who are worthy of offerings."

458. Asking him about this matter, he then spoke a pair of irregular verses:[1380] "On what ground have rishis, men, khattiyas, and brahmins here in the world performed many sacrifices to the deities?" This is its meaning: **On what ground**: for what purpose, desiring what. Have **rishis,** and **khattiyas,** and **brahmins** and other **men, performed**— arranged, done—**sacrifices to the deities.**[1381] **Many**: of many kinds, of numerous kinds distinguished as gifts of food, drink, and so forth. Or the question is: "On what ground have **many** rishis, men, khattiyas, and brahmins performed sacrifices?"[1382] He asks with the purport: "How does that deed of theirs succeed?"

Then, showing him the meaning, the Blessed One spoke the remaining couplet, stating: "If an accomplished one . . . it succeeds for him, I say." Here, **an accomplished one**[1383] is one who has reached the end of the round through the three types of full understanding. One is **a Veda-master** (*vedagū*) because one has gone by having pierced the defilements with the *vedas* [consisting in] the four kinds of path knowledge.[1384] **From anyone**—from one who may be a rishi, a man, a khattiya, or a brahmin—**at the time of sacrifice**, when any kind of food is available, even forest leaves, roots, fruits, and so forth, then **gains an offering**, should get any item that may be given by him, **it succeeds for the donor**: that act of sacrifice flourishes; it may be of great fruit, **I say**.

459. Then, having heard this deep teaching of the Blessed One about the supreme sacrifice,[1385] [spoken] in an extremely sweet voice with a steady tone, the brahmin, [405] full of rapture and joy, esteeming the excellence and purity of the Buddha's body and all his excellent qualities, spoke the verse: "Surely, indeed." Here, the words **thus said the brahmin** were added by the compilers; the rest were spoken by the brahmin. This is its meaning: "**Surely, this offering of his must succeed**: This gift of mine given today will succeed, will flourish, will be of great fruit. **Since we have seen such a Veda-master**: since we have seen one like you, sir, a master of the Vedas. You alone are a master of the Vedas, not the other kind. **It is because** prior to this occasion **we have not seen those like you**—those who are masters of the Vedas and who are accomplished—**that other people eat the sacrificial cake**, the oblation and cake prepared by us at the sacrifice."

460. Then, when the Blessed One knew that the brahmin was pleased with him and was ready to accept his word, wishing to reveal to him in various ways those who are worthy of offerings, [doing so] in a manner that would be fully clear to him, the Blessed One spoke the verse "Therefore, O brahmin." This is its meaning: "Since you are pleased with me, **therefore, brahmin, approach me here and ask your question.**"[1386] He says this indicating himself. Now the line that occurred earlier, "as you seek the good," should be connected with the later line.[1387] Thus the construal should be understood thus: "In accord with the seeking of the good, **as you seek the good . . . perhaps you may find here**—while standing right here, or here in the Teaching—you will definitely gain, will acquire, an arahant worthy of offerings who is **at peace** through the allaying of the fire of defilements; **smokeless** through the vanishing of the smoke of anger; **untroubled** through the absence of suffering; **desireless** through the absence of many desires; and **very wise** through the best kind of wisdom." Or alternatively, the construal here should be understood thus: "Since you are pleased with me, therefore, brahmin, you who are seeking some benefit, approach and ask one who is peaceful, smokeless, untroubled, desireless"—he says this indicating himself—"asking thus, perhaps you may find here one very wise, an arahant worthy of offerings."

461. Then the brahmin, acting as instructed, said to the Blessed One: "**Master Gotama, since I delight in sacrifice . . . an offering succeeds**." Here, sacrifice, offering, and giving are one in meaning. [406] Therefore, the meaning should be construed thus: "I delight in giving, and because of that delight in giving I wish to give a gift. However, I do not know how. Since I do not know how, instruct me, and instructing me in an utterly clear way, please tell me where an offering succeeds." There is also the reading "how an offering [succeeds]."[1388]

Then, wishing to speak, the Blessed One said: "In that case, brahmin, lend an ear. I will teach you the Dhamma."

462. As the brahmin was lending an ear, the Blessed One spoke this verse "Ask not of social class" in order to instruct him. Here, **ask not of social class**: If you desire the success of your offering, great fruitness from your gift, do not ask about social class (or birth); for social class is not a criterion when seeking one who is worthy of offerings. **But ask of conduct**: But rather ask about conduct, about such excellent qualities as good behavior and so forth; for this is the criterion when determining who is worthy of offerings.

Now he gives an example to illustrate the meaning of this: **fire is indeed produced from any wood**. This is its purport: "Here, fire is produced from wood, but it does not exercise the function of fire only when produced from [such fine kinds of wood] as sāl wood, but not when produced from [such inferior kinds of wood] as a dog's drinking trough; rather, it exercises this function because it possesses such qualities as a flame. So too, it is not the case that only one born into a family of brahmins or other high families is worthy of offerings but not one born into a family of caṇḍālas and other low families; rather, **though from a low family**, as also from a high family, **a steadfast muni**—an arahant-muni—**is a thoroughbred restrained by moral shame**. One of pedigree stock, by possessing excellent qualities headed by steadfastness and moral shame, is supremely worthy of offerings; for he maintains excellent qualities through steadfastness and restrains faults through a sense of moral shame. And this has been said: 'For out of a sense of moral shame, the good do no evil' (SN I 21,29, Ja III 472). Hence I say: 'Ask not of social class: fire is indeed produced from any wood. Ask of conduct: Though from a low family, a steadfast muni is a thoroughbred restrained by moral shame.'" This is a brief account. A detailed explanation should be understood in accordance with the Assalāyana Sutta.[1389] [407]

463. Having thus instructed him in purification for the four classes, the Blessed One next spoke the verse that begins "One tamed by truth," in order to show where an offering succeeds and how an offering succeeds. Here, "by truth" means by the supreme truth, for one who has attained this is tamed. Hence he says: **One tamed by truth, endowed with taming**: one who has tamed the sense faculties. **Who has reached the end of the Vedas** (*vedantagū*): who has reached the end of defilements through the Vedas, or who has reached the end of the Vedas, which is the knowledge of the fourth path.[1390] **One who has lived the spiritual life**: one who has lived the spiritual life of the path, which [because the goal has been won] need not be lived again. **One should make a timely oblation to him**: Having taken note when there is an object of one's own to be given and a recipient is present, *at that time* one should present the gift to such a one who is worthy of offerings.

464. Sensual pleasures: sensual objects and sensual defilements.

465. With well-concentrated faculties: with undistracted faculties. **Freed like the moon from the grip of Rāhu**: As the moon is freed from the grip of Rāhu, just so, freed from the grip of defilements, they shine and glow brightly.[1391]

466. Mindful: possessed of mindfulness. **Things taken as "mine"**: things taken as "mine" on account of craving and views.

467. With the words "having renounced sensual pleasures," from this point on he speaks with reference to himself. Here, **having renounced sensual pleasures**: having abandoned sensual defilements. **Faring triumphant**: because he has abandoned those [sensual defilements], he fares triumphant over sensual objects. It is nibbāna that is called **the end of birth and death**, and he **has known** that through his own power of wisdom. **Cool**

as a lake: These seven great lakes in the Himalayas—Anotatta, Kaṇṇamuṇḍa, Rathakāra, Chaddanta, Kuṇāla, Mandākinī, and Sīhappapātaka—are always cool, for they are not touched by fire or the heat of the sun. Because he has extinguished the fever of the defilements, he is cool like those lakes.

468. Equal: the same as. **To equals**: to the buddhas such as Vipassī and so forth.[1392] For they are called "equals" because they are equal with respect to penetration; there is no difference among them with respect to the excellent qualities to be acquired by penetration or with respect to the faults to be abandoned. There are, however, differences between them with respect to their time of preparation, life span, family, height, renunciation, striving, bodhi tree, and aura. The difference between them *with respect to their time of preparation* is that between the minimum, [408] whereby some fulfill the pāramīs for four incalculables and 100,000 eons, and the maximum, whereby they do so for sixteen incalculables and 100,000 eons. The difference *with respect to life span* is that between the minimum, for those who arise at a time when the life span is a hundred years, and the maximum, when the life span is 100,000 years. The difference *with respect to family* is that some arise in a khattiya family and others in a brahmin family. The difference *with respect to height* is that some are tall, eighty-eight cubits in height, while some are short, fifteen or eighteen cubits in height. The difference *with respect to renunciation* is that some depart by way of elephant, horse-drawn chariot, or palanquin, or through the air. Thus Vipassī and Kakusandha departed by a horse-drawn chariot; Sikhī and Koṇāgamana, on the back of an elephant; Vessabhū, by palanquin; and Kassapa, through the air; while Sakyamuni went by horseback. The difference *with respect to striving* is that some engage in striving for a week, some for half a month, a month, two months, three months, six months, a year, or two, three, four, five, or six years. The difference *with respect to their bodhi trees* is that some [attain enlightenment] beneath an assattha tree, some beneath another kind of tree such as a nigrodha tree. The difference *with respect to their aura* is that they are furnished with a radiance that may extend a fathom wide, eighty fathoms wide, or boundlessly.[1393] Here, the radiance that is a fathom wide or eighty fathoms wide is the same for all, but the boundless radiance travels far, near, one gāvuta, two gāvutas, a yojana, many yojanas, even to the boundaries of a world sphere. The bodily radiance of the Buddha Maṅgala extended over the ten-thousandfold world sphere. Though such is the case, for all buddhas it occurs subject to their mind; it travels as far as each wishes it to go.

Apart from these eight differences, there is no distinction among them with respect to the remaining excellent qualities to be acquired by penetration or with respect to the faults to be abandoned. Therefore they are called "equal," and thus they are "equal to the equal."

Far from unequals: Those who are not their equal are unequal; this signifies all other beings, such as paccekabuddhas and so forth. They are far from those who are unequal [to themselves] because of their dissimilarity. Even if paccekabuddhas sitting knee to knee were to fill up all Jambudīpa, their excellent qualities would not amount to even a sixteenth portion of those of one perfectly enlightened buddha. [409] What then should be said of disciples and others? Hence it is said: "far from unequals." The word "far" should be construed in connection with the two words, **Tathāgata is** (in pāda b).

One of boundless wisdom: of unlimited wisdom. For compared to the wisdom of worldly people, the wisdom of the eighth is superior.[1394] Compared to the latter's wisdom, that of a stream-enterer is superior, and so on as far as the wisdom of a paccekabuddha, which is superior to the wisdom of an arahant. But compared to the wisdom of a paccekabuddha, the wisdom of the Tathāgata should not be called "superior" but should rather be called "boundless." Hence he said: "one of boundless wisdom." **Untainted**: untainted by the taints of craving and views. **Here or beyond**: either here in this world or in the other world. Here the construal is as follows: "The Tathāgata is equal to equals and far from unequals. Why? Because he is of boundless wisdom and untainted here or beyond; hence the Tathāgata is worthy of the sacrificial cake."

469. He in whom there is no hypocrisy: This verse and others that are similar, it should be understood, are stated for the purpose of removing the idea that the brahmins, who possess such faults as hypocrisy and so forth, are worthy of offerings. Here, **with no sense of "mine"** signifies the abandonment of the idea "This is mine" in relation to beings and conditioned things.

470. Residence: the residence of craving and views;[1395] for it is because of this that the mind resides (*nivisati*) in the three realms of existence. Hence that is said to be the residence **of the mind**. Or else it resides right there, because it is unable to relinquish this and depart; for this reason, too, it is called a residence. **Possessions**: craving and views themselves, or the things possessed because of them; **at all**: even the most trivial. **Clinging to nothing**: because of the absence of that residence and those possessions, not clinging to any phenomenon.

471. Concentrated with the concentration of the path. **And has known the Dhamma**, who has known all knowable phenomena,[1396] **with the supreme view**: with omniscient knowledge.

472. Influxes of existence: craving for existence, attachment to jhāna, and lust associated with the eternalist view. **Caustic speech**: speech that is grating and harsh. **No longer exist**: because they have been burnt up and have vanished. But both [participles, burnt up and vanished] may be conjoined with both [influxes and caustic speech]. **In every way**: in relation to all the aggregates, sense bases, and so forth.

473. Among those held by conceit: among those stuck because of conceit. **Who has fully understood suffering**: who has fully understood the suffering of the round by means of the three kinds of full understanding.[1397] **With its field and ground**: along with its causes and conditions; what is meant is, "together with kamma and defilements."

474. Not dependent on desire: not reliant on craving. [410] **A seer of seclusion**: a seer of nibbāna. **Who has overcome the view**: who has transcended the sixty-two varieties of wrong view; **made known by others**: conveyed by others.[1398] **Bases** (*ārammaṇā*): conditions; this means the causes of renewed existence.

475. Far and near: good and bad. Or else "far" means external and "near" means internal. **Penetrated**: penetrated with knowledge. **Phenomena**: phenomena such as the aggregates, sense bases, and so forth. **Liberated in the destruction of clinging**: liberated in nibbāna by taking nibbāna as object; one who has gained liberation with nibbāna as object.[1399]

476. He who has seen the destruction and end of the fetters and of birth: one who has seen the destruction and end of the fetters and who has seen the destruction and end of birth. And here, by "he who has seen the destruction and end of the fetters," the nibbāna element with residue remaining is meant, and by "he who has seen the destruction and end of birth," the nibbāna element without residue remaining is meant. For this expression "destruction and end" is a designation for the ultimate destruction, the abandoning by eradication.[1400]

The pathway of lust: the object of lust, or lust itself; for lust, too, because it is a pathway to the bad destinations, is called "the pathway of lust," as with "the pathway of kamma."

Pure, faultless, stainless, flawless: He is *pure* because of his purified bodily behavior and so forth; *faultless* because of the absence of those faults because of which it is said: "This population has the fault of lust, the fault of hatred, and the fault of delusion"; *stainless* because of the disappearance of the eight stains of persons;[1401] *flawless* because of the absence of defilements, for one who is defiled is called "flawed" because of defilement. Or because he is pure, he is faultless; because he is faultless, he is stainless; because of the absence of external stains, he is flawless, for one who is stained is called "flawed." Or because he is stainless, he commits no crime, and hence he is flawless; for it is the committing of crime, by inflicting injury, that is called "a flaw."

477. He who, by himself, does not perceive a self:[1402] Seeing by insight (*vipassanto*) with a mind associated with knowledge, he does not see in his own aggregates any other self; he sees just mere aggregates.[1403] Because of the absence of the view that arises as true and certain—namely, "with self I perceive self" (MN I 8,19)—not perceiving a self by himself, he instead [411] sees aggregates with wisdom. **Concentrated**: with the concentration of the path; **upright**: because of the absence of bodily crookedness and so forth; **inwardly firm**: because he cannot be shaken by worldly conditions. Since impulse—a designation for craving—and the five kinds of mental barrenness and eight cases of doubt are all absent, he is **without impulse, not barren, free from doubt**.

478. Delusions within: [things with] delusion as cause, with delusion as condition; this is a designation for all defilements.[1404] **And whose knowledge sees into all phenomena**: one who has realized the knowledge of omniscience. For that knowledge extends to all phenomena, and the Blessed One sees that; he dwells having realized: "It has been achieved by me." Hence it is said: "And whose knowledge sees into all phenomena." **Enlightenment**: arahantship. **Unsurpassed**: not shared by paccekabuddhas and disciples. **Auspicious**: secure, without disaster, or glorious. **Of the spirit**: of a person.[1405] **Purity**: cleansing. For here, by the absence of delusions within, the absence of all faults is indicated; because of this, he has eradicated the causes of saṃsāra and is one **who bears his final body**; by knowledge and vision, all his excellent qualities have originated. With this, there is attainment of unsurpassed enlightenment, and following this there is nothing further to be abandoned or achieved. Hence he said: "to this extent there is purity of the spirit."

479. When such was said, the brahmin became even more pleased with the Blessed One and, giving expression to his pleasure, he said: "Let my offering." This is its meaning: "When, previously, I sacrificed to the fire as representing Brahmā, I did not know whether that offering of mine was truthful or a lie. But today **let my offering be a truthful offering**." He speaks pleading: "Let it be just a truthful offering." **Since I have found such a Veda-master**: since, while standing right here, I have found a Veda-master in you. **Brahmā himself has been made manifest**: you are Brahmā himself seen directly.[1406] **Let the Blessed One receive it from me; let the Blessed One enjoy my sacrificial cake**: He said this while presenting the remainder of the offering.

480–81. The Blessed One then spoke the next two verses in the way stated in the Discourse to Kasibhāradvāja (see pp. 517–18).

482. Then the brahmin thought: "He himself does not want it. Who else was he referring to when he said: 'Serve with other food and drink the consummate one, the great rishi with influxes destroyed, with regret stilled'?" Not understanding the meaning of that verse, [412] desiring to know it, he said: "Please [tell me], Blessed One." **Seeking someone** worthy of offerings **at the time of sacrifice**: the reading should be completed with "[to whom] I should present it." This is what is meant: "Since I have come upon your exhortation, please, Blessed One, tell me so that I might understand who that consummate one might be." The purport is: "Tell me who might eat my offering, one I might seek out at the time of sacrifice and to whom I might present it. If you do not eat it, show me such a one worthy of offerings."

483. Then the Blessed One spoke three verses, "One in whom aggression has disappeared," showing in a clear way who is worthy of offerings.

484. Here, **one who has removed [the ends of] the boundaries:**[1407] A boundary is a border, the conduct of good people. Taking its end, its conclusion, as the region beyond [the boundary], it is the defilements that are called "the ends of the boundaries." He is the one who removes them. Some also say: "The 'ends of the boundaries' are trainees and worldlings to be guided by a buddha; he is their guide."[1408]

Who is skilled in birth and death: who is skilled in knowing: "Such is birth, such is death." **Possessed of munihood**: possessed of wisdom, or possessed of bodily sagacity and so forth.[1409]

485. Having removed the frown: Some stupid people, on seeing a mendicant, make a frown. The meaning is: "Remove that. Show a pleasing expression." **With reverential salutation**: with joined palms extended in salutation.

486. Then the brahmin spoke a verse extolling the Blessed One. **The receptacle of sacrifice**: that to which a sacrifice should be made, or "having come from here and there, a sacrifice should be made here." What is meant is one who is a basis for gifts.

As to the rest here, whatever has not been explained in the preceding verses was passed over because the meaning is clear and can be understood even without explanation. What follows should be understood in the way stated in the commentary on the Discourse to Kasibhāradvāja. [413]

5 Māgha
(*Māgha Sutta*)

What is the origin? This is already stated in the introduction to the discourse. For this brahmin student Māgha was a donor, a lord of giving. It occurred to him: "Is a gift given to beggars and vagrants who arrive of great fruit or not? I will ask the ascetic Gotama about this matter. It is said that the ascetic Gotama knows the past, future, and present." Having approached the Blessed One, he asked, and the Blessed One answered in accordance with his questions. Having assembled the statements of the compilers, the brahmin, and the Blessed One, they call it "The Discourse to Māgha."

Here, **Rājagaha** is the city with such a name. Because it was possessed by [such ancient kings as] Mandhātu, Mahāgovinda, and others, it was called Rājagaha. They explain the name in other ways as well,[1410] but what does it matter? This is just the name of the city. This city comes to be in the time of a buddha and in the time of a wheel-turning monarch; at other times it is empty, possessed by yakkhas, and it serves as their springtime woods.[1411] Thus having shown his alms resort, next showing his place of residence, it is said **on Mount Vulture Peak**. This was called "Vulture Peak" because vultures lived on its peaks, or because the peaks looked like vultures.

"Then the brahmin student Māgha . . . said to the Blessed One": Here, **Māgha** was the name of this brahmin. He is called "brahmin student" because he had not passed beyond the stage of a pupil, though he was actually an adult. Some say that he was called thus because of his past practice, like the brahmin student Piṅgiya; for though the latter was 120 years of age, he was known as "the brahmin student Piṅgiya" because of his past practice. The rest should be understood in the way stated.

"Master Gotama . . . do I generate much merit?": Here, **a donor, a lord of giving**: a donor and a lord of giving. For one who gives what belongs to another at the other's behest is a donor, but because he does not exercise ownership over the gift, he is not a lord of giving. But Māgha gives only what belongs to himself; hence he says: "Master Gotama, [414] I am a donor, a lord of giving." For this is the meaning here, but elsewhere it is possible to explain the terms in this way: "One who is intermittently overcome by miserliness is a donor, but one who is not so overcome is a lord of giving."

Bountiful: "I know the word of supplicants.[1412] As soon as it is said, 'This one deserves this, that one deserves that,' [I know it] by ascertaining the distinction among persons or by taking account of helpfulness." **Devoted to charity**: one fit to be asked for things.[1413] He indicates: "One who is not devoted to charity, on seeing supplicants, frowns and speaks harsh words to them, etc. I am not like that." **Righteously**: having avoided stealing, cheating, and deception, by walking for alms, that is, by begging. For begging is the principle by which brahmins seek wealth. And as they go begging, what is given to them by others who wish to assist them is said to be **wealth righteously gained, righteously acquired**. He is one who has obtained it in such a way. Hence he says: "I seek wealth righteously . . . righteously acquired." **I give to even more people**: I give to even more people than that. He shows: "There is no limit. I give the wealth I have gained here without any limits."

Surely: an adverb in the sense of definitely. For giving—even a gift given to animals—is definitely praised by all buddhas, paccekabuddhas, and disciples. And this is said: "Everywhere giving is praised, nowhere is giving criticized" (untraced). Therefore the Blessed One, too, praising giving, said: "Surely, student . . . you generate much merit."

Thus when the Blessed One said "one generates much merit," the brahmin questioned the Blessed One further, wishing to learn about the purification of offerings through a recipient worthy of offerings.[1414] Hence the compilers said: **Then the brahmin student Māgha addressed the Blessed One in a**

verse. The explanation of the meaning has already been stated. [415]

487. In the verses beginning "I ask," **bountiful**: one who understands the words; what is meant is, "one who knows in all ways the purport of the words spoken by beings."[1415] **Purified**: become pure, of great fruit, by way of those worthy of offerings. But the construal here is as follows: "**When a householder devoted to charity, a lord of giving, wanting merit, sacrifices . . . by giving food and drink to others here**—not merely by placing offerings in the fire—**intent on merit**, not intent on receiving favors, a good reputation, and so forth, **in sacrificing, how is his offering purified?**"

488. Such a one succeeds through those worthy of offerings: The one devoted to charity can succeed, can reach success, can purify the gift, can make the offering very fruitful, through those who are worthy of offerings, not otherwise. With this, the Blessed One has answered his question: "In sacrificing, how is his offering purified?"

489. The construal should be understood thus: "When a householder devoted to charity sacrifices by giving to others, **describe, Blessed One, those worthy of offerings**."

490. Showing him in various ways those who are worthy of offerings, the Blessed One then spoke the verses beginning "Those who wander unattached." Here, **unattached**: not stuck fast by the ties of lust and so forth; **consummate**: with their tasks completed; **self-controlled**: with guarded minds.

491–92. Tamed with the unsurpassed taming; **liberated** through liberation by wisdom and of mind; **untroubled** through the absence of any future suffering of the round; **desireless** through the absence of present defilements. The following verse should be understood to show the spiritual might of development. And this discourse is cited here as proof: "When, bhikkhus, a bhikkhu is intent on development, even though he does not form the wish 'May my mind be liberated from the influxes by non-clinging!' yet his mind is liberated from the influxes by non-clinging" (SN III 153,4–6; AN IV 126,16–18).

493–95. Those who have abandoned lust . . . Those in whom there is no hypocrisy . . . Those who have not fallen prey to cravings: those who are not sunk in[1416] cravings for sensual pleasures and so forth.[1417]

496. Craving: [416] the sixfold craving, for visible forms, etc. **For any state of existence**: for eternal existence or annihilation. Or alternatively *bhavābhavāya* means for the nonexistence of existence; what is meant is for the non-production of renewed existence.[1418] **Here or beyond**: This is a term of elaboration for this: "for anything in the world."

498–99. Those devoid of lust . . . Those who are at peace: those who have allayed the defilements. And because they are at peace, they are **devoid of lust, not irritated . . . having abandoned them here**: Having discarded the aggregates occurring here in the world, thereafter they do not go elsewhere. Following this, some add this verse:

> "Those homeless ones who have abandoned sensual
> pleasures,
> who are well self-restrained, straight as a shuttle."[1419]

501. As islands in themselves: The arahants are spoken of as wandering about taking their own excellent qualities as their own island.

502. Those here in the continuum of the aggregates, sense bases, and so forth; **who know this**: who know the aggregates, sense bases, and so forth; **just as it is**: knowing it by way of impermanence and so forth, they know it according to its actual nature.[1420] **This is the last life, there is no renewed existence**: those who know thus: "This is our last birth, now there is no renewed existence."

503. A Veda-master: Now the Blessed One spoke this verse with reference to himself. Here, **mindful**: possessed of mindfulness of the six constant dwellings.[1421] **Attained to enlightenment**: attained to omniscience; **the refuge of many**: who for many devas and human beings is a refuge by destroying their peril.[1422]

504. Having thus learned about those who are worthy of offerings, the brahmin was pleased and said: "Surely my questions were not asked in vain." Here, **you know this matter just as it is**: For here in the world you know all that is knowable just as it is, you know it according to its actual nature; what is meant is that you know it exactly as it is. [417] **For this Dhamma has been thus understood by you**: The purport is: "For this element of Dhamma (*dhammadhātu*) has been well penetrated by you in such a way that you know whatever it is you wish to know."

505. Thus, having praised the Blessed One, having understood the excellence of the sacrifice to occur through the excellence of those [recipients who are] worthy of offerings, the brahmin also wishes to learn of the excellence of the sacrifice complete in six factors through the excellence of the donor, and thus he asks a further question: "When one devoted to charity." Here, this is the construal: "When one devoted to charity gives and sacrifices to others, declare to me, Blessed One, the excellence of the sacrifice."

506. Then the Blessed One explained this to him in two verses. Here, this is the construal of the meaning: "Undertake sacrifice, Māgha, and when sacrificing make the mind placid in every way," make the mind placid in the three periods of time. The excellence of the sacrifice is as stated thus:

> Prior to giving, one is joyful; while giving, one makes
> the mind placid;
> after giving, one is elated: this is the excellence of the
> sacrifice. (AN III 337,12, Ja III 300,17)

The sacrifice will excel in that way. In this connection if one should ask, "How is the mind to be made placid?" [the answer is] by abandoning faults. How does one abandon faults? By taking the sacrifice as the basis: **For one sacrificing, the sacrifice**

is the basis: established upon this, one discards faults. The sacrifice, consisting in the thing to be given, is the basis for one sacrificing with a mind preceded by loving-kindness toward beings, a mind in which the darkness of delusion has been dispelled by the lamp of right view. Established here upon the sacrifice, taking [the thing to be given] as the basis, one discards the three faults thus: one discards greed for the thing to be given, anger toward the recipient of the gift, and delusion based on both of these.

507. Being **devoid of lust** for wealth, **having removed hatred** toward beings, when these have been abandoned, one with the five hindrances abandoned, **developing a measureless mind of loving-kindness** by pervasion of unlimited beings or by total pervasion of one being, thereby attains in sequence access and absorption concentration. Then, for the purpose of again expanding one's development, **constantly heedful day and night** in all postures, one **pervades all directions measurelessly** with [the mind of] jhāna based on loving-kindness.

508. Then, not knowing that loving-kindness is the path to the brahma world, having heard [from the Buddha] about the development of loving-kindness [in a way] that was entirely beyond his own domain, the brahmin [418] felt even more esteem for the Blessed One as an omniscient one. Since he himself was intent on the brahma world, imagining rebirth in the brahma world to be purity and freedom, he spoke the verse "Who is purified?" asking about the path to the brahma world.

Here, referring to one who makes merit leading to the brahma world, he asks: **Who is purified, freed?** And with reference to one who does not make [such merit], he asks: **And who is bound? By what means does one go to the brahma world?**: through what cause?[1423] **Brahmā made manifest, seen by me today**: Brahmā today has been made manifest, is seen; **for in truth you are like Brahmā to us**: with deep respect he makes an oath referring to the Blessed One's similarity to Brahmā. **How is one reborn?**: Still with deep respect, he asks again. **O luminous one**: He addresses the Blessed One.

509. If a bhikkhu attains three or four jhānas through loving-kindness and then, taking this as the basis, develops insight and attains arahantship, he is purified and freed; such a one does not go to the brahma world.[1424] But if one attains three or four jhānas through loving-kindness and then relishes it, thinking, "This attainment is peaceful," one is bound. But as long as one has not lost the jhāna, through that same jhāna one goes to the brahma world. Therefore, although the Blessed One does not admit that one who is purified and freed goes to the brahma world, without mentioning this, he spoke this verse, "One who sacrifices," showing, in a way suitable for the brahmin, how the one that is bound goes to the brahma world through that jhāna.

Here, **threefold** is said with reference to placidity of mind during the three periods of time (see p. 907); with this he shows the three factors by way of the donor. **Such a one should accomplish it with those worthy of offerings**: Such a person performing that sacrifice possessing the threefold excellence should perform and complete that sacrifice endowed with the threefold excellence by taking [as recipients] those worthy of offerings, the arahants; with this he shows the three factors by way of the recipients.

Having sacrificed thus, one rightly devoted to charity: One devoted to charity who in this way, on the foundation of the jhāna of loving-kindness, rightly performs the sacrifice endowed with six factors, **is reborn** [419] **in the brahma world, I say**, by means of that jhāna of loving-kindness serving as decisive support for the six-factored sacrifice. Encouraging the brahmin thus, he concludes the teaching. The rest is clear in all verses as to the meaning, and the concluding passage should be understood in the way previously stated.

6 Sabhiya
(*Sabhiya Sutta*)

What is the origin? This is already stated in the introduction to the discourse. In the sequential explanation of the meaning, too, whatever is similar to what has been previously encountered should be understood in the way previously stated. We will explain what has not been previously encountered, avoiding those terms whose meanings are sufficiently clear.

In the Bamboo Grove, the squirrels' feeding ground: "Bamboo Grove" is the name of a park. It is said to have been surrounded by bamboos and by a rampart eighteen cubits high. Fitted with a watchtower above its entranceway, it was a delightful lush green in color. Hence it was called the Bamboo Grove. People also fed squirrels here, so it was called the squirrels' feeding ground.

In the past, it is said, a certain king came to the park in order to amuse himself. He got drunk and fell asleep. His entourage, thinking, "The king is asleep," enticed by the flowers and fruits and so forth, left in various directions. Then a black snake, attracted by the scent of liquor, came out from a certain tree hollow and headed toward the king. A tree deity saw this and, thinking, "I will save the king's life," came in the guise of a squirrel and made a sound in the king's ear. The king awakened and the snake retreated. When the king saw this, he thought, "This squirrel saved my life," and he established a feeding ground for squirrels there and declared it a sanctuary. [420] Therefore, from that time on, the place came to be known as "the squirrels' feeding ground."

The wanderer Sabhiya: Sabhiya was his name, and he was called "wanderer" with reference to his going forth as an outsider.[1425] **A deity who had formerly been a blood relation**: This was neither his mother nor father but a young deva spoken of as "a deity who had formerly been a blood relation" because he was favorably disposed to Sabhiya, just like a mother and father.

It is said that when the Blessed One Kassapa attained final nibbāna, three young men went forth under his personal disciples at the golden cetiya built for him (see pp. 585–86). They learned meditation subjects suitable for their temperaments, went to a border region, and did the ascetic's duty in a forest abode. At intervals they went to the city to venerate the cetiya and listen to the Dhamma. On a later occasion, not wishing to be separated from the forest even temporarily, they dwelled heedfully right there, but while dwelling in such a way they did not achieve any distinction. It then occurred to them: "When we go on alms round, we are anxious about our lives, and it isn't possible for one anxious about his life to achieve a world-transcending state. It would be miserable to die as worldlings. Let's build a ladder, climb up a mountain, and do the ascetic's duty unconcerned about body and life." They did so.

Then that same day the most senior of them, who possessed suitable supporting conditions, realized arahantship along with the six superknowledges. He went to the Himalayas by means of psychic potency, washed his face in Lake Anotatta, and walked for alms among the people of Uttarakuru. When he finished his meal, he again went to another region, filled his alms bowl, took water from Lake Anotatta and toothwood from a nāga creeper, and returned to his companions. He told them: "Behold, friends, my spiritual might! This almsfood is from Uttarakuru. This water and toothwood have been brought from the Himalayas. Eat this food and do the ascetic's duty. I will constantly serve you in such a way."

Having listened to him, they said: "You have done *your* task, Bhante. Even merely conversing with you is delaying us. Now don't [421] come back to us again." Since he could not convince them to accept his offer, he departed.

Then, after two or three days, another one of the group became a non-returner possessed of the five superknowledges. He too did the same. When the other rejected his offer, he too left. The last one, after rejecting the offer, continued to strive, but on the seventh day after they had climbed the mountain, failing to achieve any distinction, he died and was reborn in the deva world. On that very same day the elder who had become an arahant attained final nibbāna and the non-returner arose in the pure abodes. The young deva (that is, the former third bhikkhu) enjoyed celestial bliss while rising and descending among the six desire-sphere deva worlds, and in the time of our own Blessed One, he passed away from the deva world and was conceived in the womb of a certain female wanderer.

It is said that she was the daughter of a khattiya. Her parents offered her to a wanderer with the intention that their daughter would learn the diverse philosophical systems. She had sexual relations with a male wanderer student and became pregnant. When the other female wanderers saw that she was pregnant, they expelled her. While traveling elsewhere, she gave birth in a council hall along the way. Hence she gave her son the name "Sabhiya."[1426]

When Sabhiya grew up, he too went forth among the wanderers. He learned various treatises and became a prominent debater. He traveled all over Jambudīpa for the purpose of refuting other doctrines, but he did not see any debater equal to himself. Thus he built a hermitage by the entrance to the city and settled there, where he taught his art to young khattiyas and others.

Meanwhile the Blessed One had set in motion the excellent wheel of the Dhamma, and eventually he came to Rājagaha and stayed at the Bamboo Grove, the squirrels' feeding ground. Sabhiya, however, did not know that the Buddha had arisen.[1427] But that brahmā in the pure abodes (his former fellow meditator) emerged from a meditative attainment and asked himself: "Through whose spiritual might have I attained this distinction?" He then recalled that he had done the ascetic's duty at the time of the Blessed One Kassapa, and he also recollected his former companions. He reflected: "One of them has attained final nibbāna. Where now is the other?" He then realized: "Having passed away from the deva world, he has arisen in Jambudīpa but he does not even know that a buddha has arisen. Let me now instruct him to follow the Buddha." He then formulated twenty questions, and during the night he came to Sabhiya's hermitage, [422] stood in the sky, and called out: "Sabhiya, Sabhiya!" While sleeping, Sabhiya heard the sound three times. He came out, saw the radiance, and stood with his palms joined in reverence. The brahmā then said to him: "For your sake, Sabhiya, I have brought twenty questions. Learn them, and you should lead the spiritual life under any ascetic or brahmin who answers these questions for you." It is with reference to this young deva that it was said: "A deity who had formerly been his blood relation had briefly recited a number of questions." **Briefly recited**: as a mere outline, not as an analysis.[1428]

When this was said, Sabhiya learned the questions in sequence with just a single recitation. The brahmā, however, deliberately did not inform him that the Buddha had arisen. Thus he said, "You should lead the spiritual life under him," with the intention: "Seeking the meaning, the wanderer will know the Teacher on his own and realize that the ascetics and brahmins outside here are worthless." But when commenting on the Apadāna of the Elder Sabhiya among the verses of the elder monks in the Group of Fours, they say: "His mother, having reflected on her own misconduct, was disgusted by it, developed jhāna, and was reborn in the brahma world. The questions were recited by that brahmā deity" (untraced).

Those: Now the overview and identification of the terms to be explained.[1429] **Ascetics and brahmins**: ascetics and brahmins by worldly convention because they have gone forth. **Leaders of sanghas**: those who have groups [of followers].[1430] **Leaders of groups**: teachers who make the claim: "We are omniscient." **Teachers of groups**: teachers of a group of monks and householders by way of recitation, interrogation, and so forth. **Well known**: renowned and prominent. **Famous**: possessing gains.[1431] **Ford-makers**: builders of fords of views, which are to be entered and relied upon by those who follow their example. **Considered holy by many people**: considered by many people thus: "These holy men are saintly men, good men."[1432]

Pūraṇa was his name, **Kassapa** his clan. It is said that he was a slave by birth; [423] he was born filling a [group of] a hundred slaves, so they gave him the name Pūraṇa.[1433] Having fled and gone forth among the naked ascetics, he described himself by his clan, saying, "I am a Kassapa," and claimed to be omniscient.[1434]

Makkhali was his name, and because he was born in a cowshed, he was called **Gosāla** ("one of the cowshed"). He too, it is said, was just a slave by birth. Having fled, he went forth and claimed to be omniscient. **Ajita** was his name; because he wore a blanket of hair to show his fewness of desires, he was called **Kesakambali** ("one of the hair blanket"); he too claimed to be omniscient. **Pakudha** was his name, **Kaccāyana** his clan. Because of his fewness of desires, and because he believed there is a soul in water, he refused to bathe, rinse the mouth, and so forth; he too claimed to be omniscient. **Sañjaya** was his name, but his father was named Belaṭṭha, so he was called **Belaṭṭhaputta**. **Nigaṇṭha** was his name because of his going forth, and he was called **Nātaputta** because of his father's name.[1435] It is said that his father's name was Nāta, and so his son was called Nātaputta; he too claimed to be omniscient. All of them had retinues of five hundred pupils.

He asked them those questions, but they did not reply: He asked those six teachers the twenty questions, but they could not reply. **Irritation**: disturbance of mind and mental factors; **hatred**: a hostile state of mind. Both are simply designations for anger, distinguished respectively as mild and sharp. **Displeasure**: being displeased; dejection is meant.[1436] **They displayed**: they showed through bodily and verbal expressions; they made plain.

To the lower life: to the state of a householder. For in comparison to monastic life, the state of a householder is said to be lower, since it is inferior in such excellent qualities as good behavior and so forth, or because it allows for the inferior indulgence in sensual pleasures; in contrast, monastic life is said to be higher. **Revert**: regress. **Enjoy sensual pleasures**: indulge in sensual pleasures. It is said that it was in such a way that he came to recognize the worthlessness of those renunciants who claimed to be omniscient. And having come to this conclusion by means of the thought that had arisen, as he continued to investigate, **it occurred to the wanderer Sabhiya: "Now this ascetic Gotama, too. . . ."** Yet **those worthy ascetics and brahmins [did not reply]**; however **an ascetic should not be belittled or disparaged just because he is young**, and so forth. **Elders** (*therā*): who have reached firmness (*thirabhāvappattā*) in their own ascetic state. **Of long-standing**: [424] knowers of gems, because of their own claim, "We know the gem of nibbāna," and they are also considered thus by the world; or they are knowers of many nights.[1437] **Should not be belittled**: should not be despised; should not be thought of as lowly. **Disparaged**: What is meant is that one thinks he should not be accepted, asking: "Why is he known?"[1438]

510. Perplexed and full of doubt: While Sabhiya was exchanging greetings with the Blessed One, esteeming him as an omniscient one as shown by his excellence of form and his tamed and peaceful demeanor, his restlessness vanished and he said: "Perplexed and full of doubt." Here, wondering, "Will I get an answer to these?" he was *perplexed* with regard to whether his questions would be answered; and he was *full of doubt* because he had the doubt: "What is the meaning of this and that question?" Or he was *perplexed* because of weak doubt, being perplexed about the meaning of those questions; and he was *full of doubt* because of strong doubt, being troubled while investigating them and unable to settle them.[1439] **Being asked questions by me in sequence**, according to the order of the questions, **answer me in accordance with the Dhamma**: answer me by setting up the text in a way that accords with the meaning.

511. It is said that, wandering in this and that direction, he had come "from afar," along a route of seven hundred yojanas.[1440] Hence the Blessed One said: **You have come from afar**. Or else he said this with the intention: "You have come from afar because you have come from the teaching of the Blessed One Kassapa."

512. Ask me: With this verse, he extends to him the invitation of an omniscient one.[1441] **You wish in your mind**: you wish with the mind.[1442]

Pleased: with a mind suffused with rapture, jubilation, and joy. **Elated**: uplifted in body and mind; [425] but this term is not in all readings. Now showing the qualities through which he is pleased, it is said: **jubilant, full of rapture and joy**.[1443]

513. Gentle (*soratam̥*): well allayed (*suvūpasantam̥*).[1444] There is also the reading *sūratam̥*, meaning "one who has thoroughly refrained" (*suṭṭhu uparataṃ*). **Enlightened** (*buddho*): one who is wide awake, or one to be enlightened by the Buddha.[1445] Thus asking four questions with each verse, Sabhiya asks a total of twenty questions. But the Blessed One devotes a single verse to each question and thus he answers with twenty verses each culminating in arahantship.

514. Here, a bhikkhu in the supreme sense is one who has broken up the defilements and attained nibbāna;[1446] therefore, in answering Sabhiya's question, "What must one attain to be called a bhikkhu?" the Blessed One said: "When by the path" and so forth. This is its meaning: By the path developed **by oneself, one has attained nibbāna**, one has attained the full extinction of defilements,[1447] and because one has attained nibbāna, one has **crossed over doubt**. **Abandoned nonexistence and existence**, distinguished respectively as failure and success, decline and growth, annihilationism and eternalism, and demerit and merit,[1448] one has **lived [the spiritual life]** of the path and is **finished with renewed existence**. One worthy of such words of praise is **a bhikkhu**.

515. Now since it is by fully refraining from wrong practice and by the allaying of the manifold defilements that one is gentle, showing this meaning, the Blessed One spoke the answer to the second question in the way that begins "Equanimous toward everything." This is its meaning: **Toward everything**: toward objects such as forms and so forth. He is **equanimous** through the six-factored equanimity that occurs thus: "Having seen a form with the eye, he is neither happy nor unhappy" (AN II 298,25, AN III 279,14–16); and he is **mindful** through abundance of mindfulness. **He does not injure anyone**: He does not harm any being, whether firm or frail and so forth, **in all the world**, in the entire world. **An ascetic** because of calming down evil;[1449] **who has crossed over** by crossing the flood; **unsullied** through the abandoning of sullied intentions; **for whom there are no swellings**: for whom these seven swellings—lust, hatred, delusion, conceit, views, defilements, and misconduct—whether gross or subtle do not exist.[1450] By this dwelling in equanimity, abundance of mindfulness, and non-harming, and by fully refraining from wrong practice and

[426] by the allaying of the various defilements such as the floods and so forth, **he is gentle**.

516. Now since one whose faculties have been developed, who is fearless and unalterable, is tamed, showing this meaning, the Blessed One answered the third question with the verse "One whose faculties." This is its meaning: **One whose** six **faculties**, the eye and so forth, **have been developed** by *the development of their objective resorts* after having ascribed to them the three characteristics, impermanence and so forth; and by *the development by habituation* by causing them to acquire the fragrance of mindfulness and clear comprehension.[1451] And as **internally** by the development of their objective resorts, so **externally in all the world**. Wherever there is some defect in the faculties or the possibility of some defect, there, because of covetousness and so forth, they have not been developed. Thus, **having pierced through**, having known, penetrated,[1452] **this world and the next**, the world of one's own continuum of aggregates and the world of others' aggregates, as one who wants to die an unsluggish death he **awaits the time**: he waits for, expects, the time of life's destruction, yet does not fear death. As the Elder [Sāriputta] said:

> For me there is no fear of death,
> nor is there attachment to life.
> I have no desire for death,
> nor do I have desire for life.
> I just await the time
> as a servant does his wages. (Th 606)

One developed . . . is tamed: One whose faculties have been developed in such a way is tamed.

517. "Enlightened" is a name for one who is endowed with understanding and who has awakened from the sleep of defilements.[1453] Therefore, showing that meaning, he answers the fourth question with the verse "Having examined all *kappa*" (*kappāni viceyya kevalāni*). Here, *kappa* are craving and views; these latter are called "mental constructs" because they categorize things in this way or that way.[1454] **Having examined**:

having explored by way of impermanence and so forth.[1455] **Saṃsāra**: And this saṃsāra is a designation for the sequence of the aggregates and other groups, as stated:

> The sequence of the aggregates,
> the elements and sense bases,
> occurring uninterruptedly:
> this is what is called saṃsāra.

And when he speaks of examining that saṃsāra in its entirety, he refers to insight into the three rounds, that is, into the aggregates and into the kamma and defilements that are the roots of the aggregates. **Both passing away and rebirth**: having examined both of these, the passing away and rebirth of beings; [427] "having known" is the meaning. By this he refers to the knowledge of passing away and rebirth.

Rid of dust, unblemished, purified: through the disappearance of the dust of lust and so forth, through the absence of blemishes, and through the disappearance of the stains, he is "rid of dust, unblemished, purified." **One who has attained the destruction of birth**: one who has attained nibbāna. **They call him enlightened**: They call one enlightened who, by possessing this understanding (*buddhi*) distinguished into world-transcending insight and the knowledge of passing away and rebirth, and by awakening from the sleep of defilements,[1456] has attained the destruction of birth through this practice that is rid of dust, etc.

Or alternatively, when it is said, "Having examined all *kappa*," this can mean: "Having examined many eons of world-dissolution and world-evolution in the way stated, 'There I was,' and so forth"; by this he refers to the first clear knowledge.[1457] When it is said, "Saṃsāra, both passing away and rebirth," this can mean: "Having examined this saṃsāra and both the passing away and rebirth of beings in the way stated, 'These beings' and so forth"; by this he refers to the second clear knowledge. By the rest he refers to the third clear knowledge. By the knowledge of the destruction of the influxes there is removal of dust and so forth and the attainment of nibbāna. "They call him enlightened": Thus they call him enlightened who possesses cognition divided by way of the threefold clear knowledge.

519. Thus, having answered the questions posed by the first verse, [he next answers] the questions posed by the second verse. Since a brahmin in the supreme sense, one who has attained brahmahood, the supreme state, is one who has expelled all evil,[1458] showing this, he answers the first question with the verse that begins "Having expelled." This is its meaning: One who, **having expelled all types of evil** by means of the fourth path, is **inwardly firm**—simply "firm" is meant—such a one, just by having expelled all types of evil, **is stainless**, one who has attained stainlessness, brahmahood, the supreme state. Through the concentration of the supreme fruit, in which the stain of defilements that are distractions from concentration have subsided, he is **well concentrated**. **Having gone beyond saṃsāra** by overcoming the cause of saṃsāra; **consummate** because his task has been completed; **unattached** because he is not dependent because of craving and views. And he **is called such a one** [an impartial one] because he is unalterable by worldly conditions.[1459] One worthy of such praise is **brahmā**, he is a brahmin.[1460]

520. Since one is called an ascetic because one has calmed down evil, [428] and is ritually bathed because one has washed off evil, and a nāga because one does not commit crimes, showing this, he answers the three questions with the following three verses.

Here, **one who is peaceful**: one who abides having calmed down defilements by means of the noble path. **Such a one is truthfully called an ascetic:** one of such a nature is called an ascetic.[1461] At this point the question has been answered, but the remaining words of praise have the purpose of arousing esteem in Sabhiya. Since one who is calmed does not take conception on account of merit or evil, he is called one **having abandoned merit and evil**. By the disappearance of dust, he is **dustless**.[1462] **Having understood this world and the next** by way of impermanence and so forth, **such a one has transcended birth and death**.

521. "Having washed away . . . one who has ritually bathed":[1463] Here the meaning should be understood thus: Having **washed away**, having washed off with the knowledge of the path, **all**

types of evil capable of arising because of internal and external objects **in all the world** of the sense bases, a designation for the internal and external sense bases. Because he has washed away evil, **among devas and humans given to mental construction he does not enter upon mental constructs**, upon mental constructs due to craving and views.[1464] They call him **one who has ritually bathed**.

522. In the fourth verse too, **one who does not commit any crime in the world**, one who does not commit even the slightest crime, a designation for evil, **is truthfully called a nāga**.[1465] At this point the question has been answered, but the remaining words of praise [have the same purpose] as stated above. For one who does not commit any crime because he has abandoned criminality by means of the path, **having discarded all yokes**, the yoke of sensuality and so forth, and all **bondages**, the ten fetters, **is not tied down anywhere**, by any tie, to the aggregates and so forth, and he is **liberated truthfully** by the two kinds of liberation.[1466]

524. Thus, having answered the questions posed by the second verse, [he next answers] the questions posed by the third verse. It is the sense bases that are called **the fields**, since it is said: "This eye, this eye base . . . this field, this basis" (Dhs 170, §597). **Having conquered** them, having defeated them, having vanquished them, or **having examined them**, having examined and investigated them by way of impermanence and so forth,[1467] [one does so with respect to] **all** without omission, particularly **the celestial, the human, and the brahma field**, which are the cause of the ties. [429] The celestial is divided into the twelve sense bases, and so too the human, but the brahma field is divided into six sense bases—the eye base and so forth—among the twelve bases.[1468] Having conquered or examined all those, one is then **freed from the bondage that is the root of all fields**, from that ignorance, craving for existence, and so forth that are the root and bondage to all fields. Thus, because one has conquered or examined these fields, one is called **a field-knower**.[1469]

Here, on the basis of the statement "Kamma is the field, consciousness the seed, and craving the moisture" (AN I 223–24), some say that the fields are kamma. They explain "the celestial, the human, and the brahma field" here thus: "The celestial is kamma that leads to the devas; the human is kamma that leads to the human state; and the brahma field is the kamma that leads to the brahmās."

525. Now kammas are called "stores," since they are similar to stores in the sense that they are one's own, and it is by cutting them off, by eradicating them, that one is skillful.[1470] Therefore, showing that meaning, the Blessed One answered the second question with the verse "Having examined all stores." This is its meaning: **Having examined all stores,**[1471] this being a designation for wholesome and unwholesome kammas; having examined them with mundane and world-transcending insight by way of their objective domains and functions as impermanent and so forth. Specifically, as to those that are the cause of the ties, **the celestial** and **the human** are divided into the eight desire-sphere wholesome volitions, **and the brahma store** into the nine exalted wholesome volitions.[1472] Thereafter, by the development of the path, one is **freed from the bondage that is the root of all stores**, [the bondage] consisting in ignorance, craving for existence, and so forth. Thus, through the cutting off of these stores, **such a one is truthfully said to be skillful**. Or alternatively, the three kinds of existence and the twelve sense bases should be understood as "sheaths,"[1473] similar to the sheaths of a snake, in the sense that they are dwellings of beings and phenomena. From this point, the construal should be undertaken by way of these as well.

526. Now one is not called a pundit merely because one ponders,[1474] but one is also called a pundit because one has approached the translucencies (*paṇḍarāni*), settled upon them with investigative wisdom. Therefore, showing this meaning, he answered the third question with the verse "Having examined both kinds of." [430] This is its meaning: It is the sense bases that are called **translucencies**; for these are customarily spoken of in such a way because of their natural purity. **Having examined both, internal and external**, by way of impermanence and so forth, when the stains have been blown away by means of this practice, one **wise about purity . . . is truthfully**

said to be a pundit, since the transparencies have been understood with wisdom. The rest is a statement of praise; for **such a one has transcended the dark and bright**, a designation for evil and merit. Therefore he is extolled thus.

527. Now it is said: "It is knowledge that is called munihood, that which is wisdom, understanding . . . right view. One possessing this knowledge is called a muni" (see p. 1036). Therefore, showing this meaning, he answered the fourth question with the verse "Having known." This is its meaning: **Having known the nature of the bad and good**:[1475] the nature of the bad and the good consists in the unwholesome and the wholesome. Since he has known this with investigative knowledge, **internally and externally, in all the world**, he has **escaped the tie**, the seven ties divided into lust and so forth, **and the net**, the twofold net of craving and views; hence **he is a muni**, for he possesses investigative wisdom, which is designated munihood. **Worthy of veneration by devas and humans**: This is a statement of praise; for one who is a muni with influxes destroyed is worthy of veneration by devas and humans. Therefore he is extolled in such a way.

529. Thus, having answered the questions posed by the third verse, [he next answers] the questions posed by the fourth verse. Now one called **a Veda-master** in the supreme sense is one who has completely destroyed the defilements by the "four Vedas," which consist in the knowledge of the [four] paths.[1476] And **having examined all the Vedas**, the treatises of all **ascetics and brahmins**, by way of impermanence and so forth through the function of that same development of the path, with the abandoning of desire and lust for them one has **transcended all Vedas**. And whatever feelings arise, whether conditioned by the Vedas or otherwise, [431] **one [is] rid of lust for all feelings**. Therefore, showing that meaning, without saying, "One who has attained this," he answered the first question with the verse "Having examined all the Vedas."

530. In the second question, it is one who has understood (*anubuddho*) that is said to be **cognizant** (*anuvidito*). **Having known proliferation [and] name-and-form**:[1477] having understood, through the contemplation of impermanence and so forth, proliferation—consisting in craving, views, and conceit—and the name-and-form conditioned by them, **internally**, in one's own continuum; and not only internally but **externally, as the root of illness**: having known that ignorance, craving for existence, and so forth, or that proliferation itself, as the root of this illness consisting in name-and-form in the continuum of others.[1478] By that development one is **freed from bondage, the root of all illnesses**, or **freed from all bondage, the root of illnesses**;[1479] [one is freed] from ignorance, craving for existence, and so forth, or from that proliferation itself. Therefore, showing this, he answered the second question with the verse "Having known."

531. Here, it was asked: "How is one heroic?" **One who**, by means of the noble path, **has abstained from all evils**, and because of abstaining from such things does not take on future conception, abides **having transcended the suffering of hell**.[1480] He is **an abode of energy**, a dwelling of energy.[1481] That arahant is worthy of being called **heroic**. Therefore, showing this, he said: "One who has abstained." **Keen in striving, such a one is truthfully said to be a hero**:[1482] these are statements of praise. For he is "keen in striving" by having strived for the path and the jhānas (or for the jhānas of the path); "a hero," because of his ability to shatter the defilements, which are the enemies; and he is "such a one" because he remains unalterable. Therefore he is extolled in such a way. The rest should be construed and explained accordingly.

532. Here, it was asked: "How does one get to be called 'thoroughbred'?" [432] Now in the world a horse or elephant that has abandoned all wiles and faults and knows the tasks to be done is called a thoroughbred. Yet even he has not entirely abandoned faults. But the arahant has abandoned them, and therefore in the supreme sense it is the arahant who should be called "thoroughbred." Showing this, he answered the fourth question with the verse "One whose bonds." This is its meaning: **One whose bonds have been cut off, internally and externally**: one whose "bonds," a designation for the internal and external fetters, have been cut off, severed, with the knife of wisdom. These bonds are **the root of ties**: the root of the ties to various objects since their adhesiveness has not been overcome. Or alternatively, when one's bonds that are the root of ties internally and externally—[the bonds consisting in] lust and so forth—have been cut off, one is then **freed from bondage, the root of all ties**, freed from *all* bondage that is the root of the ties, or [freed] from bondage that is the root of *all* ties. **Such a one is truthfully called a thoroughbred.**[1483]

534. Thus, having answered the questions posed by the fourth verse, [he next answers] the questions posed by the fifth verse. Now those whom the grammarians praise as a learned scholar merely because of his ability to recite metrical compositions is a learned scholar merely in a conventional sense. A noble one, however, from whom evil has been washed off by learning, is a learned scholar in the supreme sense.[1484] Therefore, showing this meaning, without saying, "Having attained this," the Blessed One answered the first question with the verse "Having learned." This is its meaning: "One in this world who has learned by way of the function of the wisdom born of learning—or who has learned by way of the task to be accomplished—directly knows all phenomena that come within range of insight, whatever there is, whether blameworthy or blameless, by way of impermanence and so forth, and by this practice he conquers the defilements and phenomena that are the basis for defilements. Thus he is designated a conqueror." Since he has **learned and directly known all phenomena in the world, whatever there is, both blameworthy and blameless,** they call **the conqueror**, because of his learning, **a learned scholar**. And he is rid of perplexity, liberated from the bondage of defilements, untroubled by lust and so forth everywhere among the aggregates and sense bases and so forth; therefore, because his evil has been washed off, they also call him a learned scholar who is **rid of perplexity, liberated, untroubled everywhere**.

535. Now [433] a noble one is one who should be approached—meaning "should be resorted to"—by people who desire their well-being.[1485] Therefore, showing the excellent qualities because of which one should be approached, he answered the second question with the verse "Having cut off." This is its meaning: **Having cut off** the four **influxes** and the two **attachments** with the knife of wisdom,[1486] **that wise one**—an intelligent, bright person who has acquired the knowledge of the four paths—**does not return to the bed of the womb** by way of renewed existence; he does not go to any womb. **Having dispelled the threefold perception**, sensual perception and so forth,[1487] **[and] the mire**, a designation for the strands of sensual pleasure, **he does not enter upon mental constructs**, any mental constructs due to craving and views. **They call him "a noble one"** who possesses such excellent qualities as the cutting off of influxes and so forth.

Or a noble one is spoken of on account of remoteness from bad qualities and on account of not carrying on in ways that lead to loss;[1488] therefore, showing those meanings too, he answered the second question with this verse. For bad qualities such as the influxes are considered types of loss, and these have been cut off and dispelled by him and he is not motivated by them. Thus they are remote from him, and he does not carry on in them. Therefore they also call him a noble one in the sense that "bad qualities are remote from him," and in the sense that "he does not carry on in them." Thus the construal here may be understood in this way as well. With this alternative [interpretation of] the meaning, the line "that wise one does not return to the bed of the womb" is just a statement of praise.

536. Now it was asked, "How is one well conducted?" Here, it is one who has attained the goal of good conduct that deserves to be called "well conducted." Therefore, showing this, he answered the third question with the verse "One here." Here, **one here**: one in this teaching. **In good types of conduct**: in the fifteen qualities, good behavior and so forth, stated in relation to the Discourse with Hemavata (see p. 597).[1489] **Accomplished**: who has attained what is to be attained—one who, based on good conduct, because of good conduct, with good conduct as the condition, has attained the state to be attained, namely, arahantship. He is **well conducted**: By accomplishing the means of good conduct one is well conducted. At this point the question has been answered; the rest is a statement praising him. For one accomplished in good conduct is **skillful**, clever, and always understands the nibbāna-dhamma [434] because his mind is constantly inclined toward nibbāna.[1490] **One not tied down anywhere** among the aggregates and so forth; **liberated** by the two liberations; **for whom there are no aversions**.

537. Now one is a wanderer through the banishing of kamma and so forth. Therefore, showing this meaning, he answered the fourth question with the verse "Whatever kamma there is that ripens in suffering." **That ripens in suffering**: whose result is suffering. All kamma of the three realms is spoken of, because it produces suffering in the course of existence. **Above**: in the past; **below**: in the future; **or across in the middle**: at present. For what is across is neither above nor below but in between the two; hence it is called "in the middle." **Having banished**: having driven away, having blown away.[1491] **A practitioner of full understanding**: one who practices by delimiting with wisdom. This has been an explanation of new terms.

Now this is how to construe the purport: Whatever kamma there is included in the three periods of time, productive of suffering, one has banished [that kamma] by drying up the moisture of craving and ignorance by means of the noble path, preventing it from generating conception (rebirth). Because one has banished it in such a way, by practicing through the full understanding of that same kamma, one is "a practitioner of full understanding." Not only does one terminate kamma itself, but through the "full understanding of abandoning" with respect to these qualities—hypocrisy, conceit, greed, and anger—a practitioner of full understanding terminates name-and-form, that is, he banishes them. Through the banishing of these things—kamma and so forth—they call him a wanderer. This expression "accomplished one" is a statement praising him.

538. Delighted with the Buddha's answers to his questions, Sabhiya spoke verses extolling him, which begin "There are sixty-three approaches." In these verses, "approaches" are bathing places, fords; the meaning is views.[1492] He says: **There are sixty-three approaches . . . the dark flood**: These amount to *sixty-three* (line 1) by including the sixty-two speculative views of the Brahmajāla Sutta together with personal-entity view.[1493]

By way of subject matter rather than origin, these are **based on** treatises that are **proclamations of ascetics** who belong to other sects (line 2). But *by way of origin*, these are based both on [435] **labels**, conventional names such as "woman, man,"[1494] and on the inverted **perception** of fools who, due to wrong reflection, oral tradition, and so forth, conclude: "A self like this must exist"; they arise in these ways—based on both of these (conventional names and inverted perception) but not by personal direct cognition (line 3). Having removed these, the Blessed One **went over the dark flood** (line 4). [Taking the reading] *oghatam' agā*, the meaning is "he overcame the darkness of the flood." Or taking the reading *oghantam agā*, the meaning is "he went to the end of the flood."

539. Following this, he said: **You have reached the end, gone beyond suffering**. He said this with reference to nibbāna, which is the end of the suffering of the round and its beyond.[1495] [This is said] because with its attainment there is absence of suffering and because it is the opposite [of suffering]. Or else, the Blessed One is one who has gone beyond because he has gone to nibbāna. Addressing him, he said: "You, one gone beyond, have reached the end of suffering." This is the connection here.

Perfectly enlightened: completely enlightened and enlightened by himself. **I think you are one**: From deep respect he says: "I think you yourself, not another." **Luminous**: complete in luminosity since he dispels darkness for others too; **intelligent**: possessing wisdom, intelligence capable of knowing whatever is to be known without dependence on anyone else; **abounding in wisdom**: one of infinite wisdom; here the omniscient knowledge is intended. Addressing him as **end-maker of suffering**, he said, **You led me across**: you led me across my doubt.

540. He speaks the half-verse, "When you understood my perplexity," as an act of homage. Here, he says **perplexity** with reference to the twenty questions; for he had been perplexed about them. **The ways of munihood**: the ways of knowledge.

542. Cleared away: made devoid of reeds; what is meant is "cut off."

543. O nāga, you, the nāga (*nāga nāgassa*): One *nāga* is a vocative, the other is used in connection with "are speaking . . . rejoice."[1496] The expression "in your teaching of the Dhamma" is needed to complete the reading. **All the devas**: both those dwelling in the sky and those dwelling on earth. **Nārada and Pabbata**: It is said that these were two groups of wise devas; they too rejoiced in it. He spoke all this out of confidence and on the basis of reasoning.[1497] [436]

544. Having heard the Buddha's excellent answers, which were worth rejoicing in, Sabhiya joined his palms in reverence and said: "Homage to you." **Thoroughbred of men**: one possessed of high quality among men. **Counterpart**: one who is a match.

545. You are the Buddha, because of penetrating the four truths; **the Teacher**, because of your instruction and because of leading the caravan.[1498] **The muni, the conqueror of Māra**: the Buddha-muni by conquering the four māras.[1499]

546. The acquisitions: the four consisting in the aggregates, the defilements, the strands of sensual pleasure, and volitional activities.

547. By merit: You are **not tainted** by the world, because of not doing them, or also because there is no future enjoyment of the fruits of [merits] done in the past. Or [you are not tainted] by the taint of craving and views that are their cause. **Pays homage to the Teacher**: As he said this, having embraced the Blessed One's ankles, he prostrated himself.

But individual differences are recognized by me: I recognize a difference among persons who formerly belonged to another sect with respect to the probationary period; not all must live on probation. Who need not live on probation? The jāṭilas who attend the fire, one who is a Sakyan by birth, and one who has discarded the trait when he arrives,[1500] and one who, even if he has not discarded the trait when he arrives, possesses supporting causes for attaining the paths and fruits. And the wanderer Sabhiya was such a one. Therefore, permitting him to go forth, the Blessed One said to him, "But individual differences are recognized by me," the purport being: "There is no need for you, Sabhiya, to live on probation in order to fulfill the duty of a sectarian. I have understood that you desire good and have supporting causes for attaining the paths and fruits." But showing his own respect, Sabhiya said: "If, Bhante . . ."

All that and anything else of a similar nature that has not been explained here [has been passed over] either because the meaning is already clear or because the way to understand it has been stated previously. Hence it should be understood in accordance with what was previously explained. [437]

7 Sela
(*Sela Sutta*)

What is the origin? This is already stated in the introduction [to the discourse]. In the sequential explanation of the meaning, terms similar to those already encountered should be understood in the way previously stated. We will explain new terms, passing over those terms whose meanings are already clear.[1501]

Among the Aṅguttarāpans: Aṅga itself was a country. Because it was not far from the waters to the north of the Ganges,[1502] it was also called Uttarāpā ("northern waters"). The waters to the north of which Ganges? The Mahāmahī Ganges. In order to make it clear which river that is, the explanation is given starting from the beginning.

It is said that Jambudīpa measures 10,000 yojanas in extent. There a region measuring 4,000 yojanas, inundated with water, is designated "ocean." People live in an area of 3,000 yojanas. The Himalayas are situated in an area of 3,000 yojanas; 500 yojanas in height, they are adorned with 84,000 peaks and embellished with 500 rivers flowing all around. That is where the seven great lakes are situated—Lake Anotatta and the others spoken of in the commentary to the Discourse on the Sacrificial Cake—each fifty yojanas in length, width, and depth, and with a circumference of 150 yojanas. Of these, Anotatta is surrounded by these five mountains: Sudassana Peak, Citra Peak, Kāḷa Peak, Gandhamādana Peak, and Kelāsa Peak. Sudassana Peak is made of gold, 200 yojanas in height, and curves inward in the shape of a crow's beak, so that it conceals the lake. Citra Peak is made of all kinds of precious substances. Kāḷa Peak is made of stibnite. Gandhamādana Peak is made of soil.[1503] Inside, it is the color of mung beans; [438] it is covered with various kinds of medicinal herbs, and on the uposatha day of the dark fortnight it glows like a blazing coal. Kelāsa Peak is made of silver. All are the same height and shape as Sudassana and stand concealing that lake. All are rained upon through the spiritual might of the devas and nāgas, and the rivers flow down from them. All the water enters Anotatta. When the moon and sun move south or north they illuminate the area between the mountains, and when they move straight they do not illuminate it; hence it came to be called Anotatta ("Not Heated"). The bathing places there are well prepared, with charming stepping stones and clear waters similar to quartz, without fish and turtles. The buddhas, paccekabuddhas, arahants, and rishis bathe in them, and devas, yakkhas, and so forth treat them as their playground.

On its four sides there are four mouths, called the lion mouth, the elephant mouth, the horse mouth, and the bull mouth, out of which four rivers flow. On the bank of the river that departs through the lion mouth, lions are more numerous; and so too elephants, horses, and bulls are more numerous [alongside the rivers that depart] through the elephant mouth and so forth. The river that departs from the east encircles Anotatta three times, and, without approaching the other three rivers, travels down the eastern slope of the Himalayas, along a route uninhabited by people, until it enters the ocean. The rivers that depart from the west and the north also encircle it, and travel down the western and northern slopes of the Himalayas, along routes uninhabited by people, until they enter the ocean. But the river that departs from the south, [439] having encircled it three times, travels south in a straight course of sixty yojanas on top of the rocks. Having struck against the mountain and risen up, it forms a stream of water three gāvutas in breadth,[1504] which travels sixty yojanas through the sky and lands on a rock named Tiyaggaḷa ("Triple Bolt"), which has been split by the force of the stream. There a lotus pond measuring fifty yojanas, named Tiyaggaḷa, is formed. Having broken through the bank of the lake and entered the stone, the river travels sixty yojanas. Then, having split the dense earth and traveled sixty yojanas through a tunnel, it strikes the horizontal mountain called Vijjha[1505] and continues on after dividing into five streams like the five fingers of the hand.

In the place where it travels as it encircles Anotatta three times, it is called Āvaṭṭagaṅgā ("Whirling Ganges"). In the place where it travels straight for sixty yojanas on top of the rock, it is called Kaṇhagaṅgā ("Black Ganges"). In the place where it travels sixty yojanas through the sky, it is called Ākāsagaṅgā ("Sky Ganges"). In the area of fifty yojanas on the Tiyaggaḷa Rock it is called the Tiyaggaḷa Lotus Pond. In the place where, after breaking through the bank and entering the rock, it travels sixty yojanas, it is called Bahalagaṅgā ("Thick Ganges"). In the place where it travels by tunnel for sixty yojanas after splitting the earth, it is called Ummaggagaṅgā ("Tunnel Ganges"). And in the places where, after striking against the horizontal mountain called Vijjha, it continues on after dividing into five streams, it is given five names: the Ganges, the Yamunā, the Aciravatī, the Sarabhū, and the Mahī. Thus these five great rivers originate in the Himalayas. This fifth among them, named the Mahī, is what is intended here as "the Mahāmahī Ganges."

The country not far from the waters to the north of that Ganges is what should be understood as Aṅguttarāpa. "Among the Aṅguttarāpans" means in that country. **Traveling on tour**: making a long journey. [440] Here, the Blessed One's tours are of two kinds: a quick tour and a leisurely tour.[1506] The *quick tour* is a sudden trip he makes when he sees capable persons even at a distance.[1507] This is illustrated by his going out to meet Mahākassapa; for going out to meet him, the Blessed One traveled three gāvutas in a moment. So too when he made journeys of thirty yojanas to tame Āḷavaka (I,10), and likewise for the sake of Aṅgulimāla (MN II 97–98). And when he went forty-five yojanas for Pukkusāti (Ps V 46–47), twenty yojanas for Mahākappina (Mp I 322), and seven yojanas for the sake of Dhaniya (I,2), these too were quick tours. But *the leisurely tour* occurs when he travels through villages, towns, and cities in sequence, benefiting the world by walking on alms round and other activities. The latter is intended here; he was traveling on tour in this way.

With a great Sangha of bhikkhus: a group of monks that was large in number and great in excellent qualities. **He arrived at a town of the Aṅguttarāpans named Āpaṇa**: That town was named Āpaṇa because of the abundance of markets (*āpaṇabahulatāya*); it is said that there were 20,000 distinct shop entrances there.

The jaṭila Keṇiya: His name was "Keṇiya," and he was a jaṭila, a hermit. It is said that he had been an affluent brahmin, but for the sake of safeguarding his wealth, he went forth as a hermit, gave a present to the king, received a plot of land, and built a hermitage there, where he lived as the support of a thousand families. They say that in his hermitage, too, there was a palm tree that brought forth one golden fruit each day. During the day he wore ochre robes and matted his hair, but at night he indulged himself fully furnished with the five objects of sensual pleasure.

The son of the Sakyans: an indication that he came from a high-class family. **Who went forth from a Sakyan family**: an indication that he had gone forth out of faith. What is meant is that he was not overcome by any misfortune, [441] but having left his family while it was still thriving, he had gone forth out of faith. **A good report**: "good" in that it possesses good qualities; what is meant is excellent. "Report" is words of praise. **Thus that Blessed One**: This is the construal: "That Blessed One thus is an arahant, thus is perfectly enlightened . . . thus is the Blessed One." What is meant is "for this and that reason."[1508]

Here, the Blessed One should be understood to be **an arahant** for the following reasons: (1) because of being far away; (2) because of destroying the foes (3) and destroying the spokes; (4) because he is worthy of the requisites and other gifts; and (5) because he did not engage in secret evil-doing.[1509]

(1) He is an arahant because of *being far away*, for he is far away from all defilements which, along with the habitual formations, he destroyed by the path. (2) He is also an arahant because of *destroying the foes*, since he has destroyed his foes, that is, the defilements, by the path. (3) He is also an arahant because of *destroying the spokes*, for at the site of enlightenment, settled firmly on the ground of good behavior with his feet of energy, with his hand of faith he took up the axe of knowledge that destroys kamma and destroyed all the spokes of the wheel of saṃsāra that had been revolving since beginningless time—with its hub made of ignorance and craving for existence; its spokes made of meritorious, [demeritorious, and imperturbable] volitional activities; its rim made of old age and death,

pierced with the axle consisting in the origin of the influxes, and joined to the chariot of the threefold existence. (4) He is also an arahant because of his *worthiness to receive the requisites* and other gifts, since as one worthy of offerings, he is worthy of the requisites such as robes as well as honor and reverence. (5) And he is an arahant because of *the absence of secret evil-doing*; for he never acts like those fools in the world who consider themselves wise yet do evil secretly from fear of dishonor. And in this connection it is said:

> Because he is far away, and because
> he has destroyed the foe—defilements,
> and destroyed the spokes of saṃsāra's wheel,
> and because he is worthy of requisites,
> and does no evil deeds in secret,
> the muni is therefore called an arahant.

He is **perfectly enlightened**, for he was enlightened to the truths perfectly and by himself; **accomplished in true knowledge and conduct** because he possesses extremely purified knowledge and conduct of awesome tread; [442] and **fortunate** ("well gone") because of his beautiful manner of going and because he has gone to the good place, because he has gone well, and because of his perfect enunciation.

He is a **knower of the world** because he has understood the world in all ways. For he has understood in all ways *the world of conditioned things* consisting in the aggregates, sense bases, and so forth, by way of their specific nature, origin, cessation, and the means to their cessation. He has thoroughly understood the world of conditioned things thus: "One world: all beings subsist through nutriment. Two worlds: name and form. Three worlds: the three feelings. Four worlds: the four kinds of nutriment. Five worlds: the five aggregates subject to clinging. Six worlds: the six internal sense bases. Seven worlds: the seven stations for consciousness. Eight worlds: the eight worldly conditions. Nine worlds: the nine abodes of beings. Ten worlds: the ten bases. Twelve worlds: the twelve sense bases. Eighteen worlds: the eighteen elements."[1510]

He has understood in all ways *the world of beings* thus: "He knows the inclination of beings; he knows their latent tendences; he knows their temperament; he knows their disposition; he knows beings with little dust in their eyes and much dust in their eyes, with sharp faculties and tender faculties, with good manners and bad manners, who are easy to instruct and hard to instruct, who are capable and incapable of realization."[1511]

[As for the *world as cosmos*] one world sphere is 1,203,450 yojanas in length and width. In circumference it is 3,610,350.[1512] There:

> Two hundred thousand [yojanas]
> and four times ten thousand (= 240,000):[1513]
> this earth, stored with treasures,
> is said to have that much thickness.
>
> Four hundred thousand [yojanas]
> and eight times ten thousand (= 480,000):
> the water resting on the air
> is said to have that much thickness.
>
> The wind that goes up in the sky
> nine hundred thousand [yojanas],
> and another sixty thousand (= 960,000):
> this is the extent of the world.

Such is its extent. And here:

> Immersed 84,000 yojanas
> deep down in the sea, [443]
> Sineru, the tallest mountain,
> rises up the same in height.
>
> Seven concentric mountain ranges
> ring Sineru in such a way
> that each in depth and height
> is half its predecessor's size.
>
> Celestial, gleaming with various gems,
> these great mountains are called
> Yugandhara, Īsadhara, Karavīka, Sudassana,

Nemindhara, Vinataka, and Assakaṇṇa:
abodes of the great heavenly kings,
resorted to by devas and yakkhas.

Adorned with 84,000 peaks,
the Himalaya mountains rise up
five hundred yojanas in height,
three thousand in length and width.

The Jambu tree called *naga*,
after whose glory Jambudīpa is named,
has a trunk fifteen yojanas in girth—
a trunk fifty yojanas in height—
with branches all round of equal length,
thus a hundred yojanas wide and tall.

The world sphere's mountain range
sinks down 82,000 yojanas into the sea.
It rises up an equal height,
surrounding the whole world sphere.

Here, the moon's disk is forty-nine yojanas [across] and the sun's disk is fifty yojanas. The Tāvatiṃsa abode is 10,000 yojanas, and so too the abode of the asuras, the great Avīci hell, and Jambudīpa. Aparagoyāna is 7,000 yojanas, and so too Pubbavideha. Uttarakuru is 8,000 yojanas. And here each great continent is surrounded by five hundred islands. All this constitutes a single world sphere. Between adjacent world spheres are the interstellar hells.

Thus, with the boundless buddha knowledge, he has understood in all ways the world as cosmos; he has known boundless world spheres, boundless world systems. Thus, because he has understood the world in all ways, the Blessed One is a "knower of the world."

Because there is no one superior to himself in excellent qualities, he is **unsurpassed**. He is the **trainer of persons to be tamed** because he trains persons who can be tamed with diverse methods of discipline. Because he instructs and liberates in the appropriate way through teachings conducive to the good pertaining to this present life, the good pertaining to future lives, and the supreme good, [444] he is **the teacher**. Mention is made expressly of devas and humans to delimit them by way of those who are superior and to include those persons capable of realization. But he also instructs nāgas and others in the mundane good. Because he has awakened to everything that can be known by way of the knowledge pertaining to the end of emancipation, he is **the Enlightened One.**[1514]

Further:

> Since he partakes of fortune, possesses abolition,
> is endowed with blessings, and is one who analyzes,
> is one who has resorted, and has rejected migration
> in the realms of existence, he is **the Blessed One.**[1515]

This is a concise account. These terms are explained in detail in the *Visuddhimagga*.[1516]

This world with its devas: These terms should be understood in the ways explained in relation to the Discourse with Kasi Bhāradvāja (see pp. 519–20) and the Discourse with Āḷavaka (see pp. 619–20). **Having directly known and realized** by direct cognition **on his own**, by himself, without being guided by others; **he makes it known**: enlightens, communicates, reveals. Out of compassion for beings, having abandoned the unsurpassed bliss of seclusion, the Blessed One **teaches a Dhamma**. And whether he teaches little or much of it, what he teaches is good in the beginning and so forth. How so? If there is just a single verse, because of the overall excellence of the Dhamma, with its first line it is **good in the beginning**; with its second and third lines it is **good in the middle**; and with its last line it is **good in the end**. A discourse of one section is *good in the beginning* through the introduction, *good in the end* through its conclusion, and *good in the middle* through the rest. A discourse of several sections is *good in the beginning* through the first section; *good in the end* through the last section; and good in the middle through the rest.

The Dhamma as the entire Teaching, too, is *good in the beginning* through good behavior, which is beneficial to oneself;[1517] *good in the middle* through serenity, insight, the path, and the fruit; and *good in the end* through nibbāna. Or it is *good in the beginning* through good behavior and concentration; *good in the middle* through insight and the path; and *good in the end* through the fruit and nibbāna. Or it is *good in the beginning* because the Buddha was well enlightened; *good in the middle* because of the excellent nature of the Dhamma; and *good in the end* because of the excellent practice of the Sangha. [445] Or it is *good in the beginning* through the complete enlightenment to be achieved by one who, having heard it, practices for such a purpose;[1518] *good in the middle* through a paccekabuddha's enlightenment; and *good in the end* through a disciple's enlightenment. Being heard, it leads to good because it is possible to suppress the hindrances and so forth just by listening to it; hence it is *good in the beginning*. Being practiced, it leads to good because by practice it leads to the bliss of serenity and insight; hence it is *good in the middle*. And when it has been practiced in such a way, it leads to good because, when the fruit of practice is concluded, it leads to the state of impartiality;[1519] hence it is *good in the end*. And it is *good in the beginning* because of the purity of its origin, since it originates from the Protector (the Buddha); it is *good in the middle* through the purity of its meaning; and it is *good in the end* through the purity of its function.[1520] Hence whether he teaches little or much of it, what he teaches has the quality of being good in the beginning and so forth.

With meaning and phrasing: When teaching this Dhamma, he reveals the spiritual life of the Teaching and the spiritual life of the path—he indicates it in various ways—and in accordance with circumstances it has *meaning* because of the excellence of its meaning, and it has *phrasing* because of the excellence of its phrasing. It has *meaning* because of the agreement of its terms with their meanings in manifesting, revealing, disclosing, analyzing, elucidating, and proclaiming; it has *phrasing* because of the excellence of its syllables, terms, phrases, language, and descriptions. It has *meaning* because of the depth of meaning and the depth of penetration; it has *phrasing* because of the depth of the doctrine and the depth of teaching.[1521] It has *meaning* because it is the domain of the analytical knowledges of the meaning and ingenuity; it has *phrasing* because it is the domain of the analytical knowledges of doctrines and language.[1522] It has *meaning* because it is pleasing to inquisitive people, since it is to be realized by the wise; it has *phrasing* because it is pleasing to worldly people since it merits faith. It has *meaning* because its purport is deep; it has *phrasing* because its phrasing is clear.

A spiritual life that is perfectly complete and pure: It is *perfectly complete*, entirely complete, since there is nothing to be added to it; and it is *pure* because it is faultless, since there is nothing to be removed from it. Since it comprises the three trainings, it is a spiritual life (*brahmacariyaṃ*) because it is to be lived (*caritabbato*) by those who have become Brahmā,[1523] by those who are best, and because it is their way of life (*cariya-bhāvato*). Therefore it is said: "He teaches a Dhamma . . . reveals a spiritual life that is perfectly complete and pure."

Further, since he teaches with a cause, with an origin, he teaches what is *good in the beginning*. Since [he teaches] in a way appropriate for the people to be guided, without inversion of the meaning, and because it is furnished with the citation of reasons, it is *good in the middle*. [446] And because it ends with a conclusion and with the obtaining of faith by the listeners, it is *good in the end*. Teaching it in such a way, he reveals a spiritual life, and because there is the manifestation of achievement through practice it is with *meaning*; and because there is the manifestation of the heritage [of scriptures] through learning it is *with phrasing*. Because it is possessed of the five groups of qualities—good behavior and so forth—it is *perfectly complete*; and because it is without defilement, set forth for the purpose of ferrying beings across, and taught without concern for worldly gain, it is *pure*. It is called "the spiritual life" because it is the way of life of buddhas, paccekabuddhas, and disciples, who have become Brahmā in the sense of being the best. Therefore it is said: "He teaches a Dhamma . . . reveals a spiritual life that is perfectly complete and pure."

Now it is good: now it is excellent; what is meant is that it leads to good and happiness. **With a talk on the Dhamma**: a talk concerning the benefits of offering drinks; for Keṇiya had heard about the Blessed One's arrival in the evening, and he would have been ashamed of going to see the Blessed One with empty hands. Having considered, "Although they refrain from eating outside the proper time, drinks are allowable for them," he went there bringing well-prepared jujube juice on five hundred poles. All should be understood as described in the Chapter on Medicines that begins thus: "Then it occurred to the jaṭila

Keṇiya: 'What should I take to the ascetic Gotama?'"[1524] Then, just as the Blessed One gave a talk on the benefits of building a resthouse to the Sakyans in the Discourse on the Trainee (MN 53); and just as he gave a talk on harmonious living to the three young monks in the Gosiṅga Sāl Woods (MN 31); and just as he gave a talk on the ten subjects of discussion to the bhikkhus from his native land in the Discourse on the Relay of Chariots (MN 24), so in this case he **instructed** him with an appropriate talk on the benefits of offering drinks; **encouraged** him by enjoining him to do such deeds of merit again; **inspired** him by generating enthusiasm; and **gladdened** him by praising him with an account of the excellent fruits pertaining to the present life and future lives.

Being even more pleased with the Blessed One, Keṇiya invited him to the next day's meal, but the Blessed One accepted only after refusing three times. Hence it is said: **Then the jaṭila Keṇiya . . .** [447] **. . . The Blessed One consented in silence**. But why did the Blessed One refuse? [Because he knew]: "By repeatedly asking me, his store of merit will increase and he will prepare even more. Thereby what is prepared for 1,250 bhikkhus will suffice for 1,550." If it is asked, "From where will the other three hundred come?" it is said: "The Blessed One spoke thus because he had foreseen: 'When the food is prepared, the brahmin Sela together with his three hundred students will go forth.'"

My friends and companions: my friends and workers. **Relatives and family members**: my blood relations of common ancestry and my remaining relatives such as sons and daughters. **The preparatory work**: the duties to be done physically. **The jaṭila Keṇiya himself set up a pavilion**: made a pavilion covered by a canopy.[1525]

Of the Three Vedas: of the Ṛgveda, the Yajurveda, and the Sāmaveda.[1526] **With their lexicon and rules of ritual**:[1527] A "lexicon" is a lexicon of nouns, a science (or treatise, *sattha*) showing the synonyms for such things as trees and so forth. The "rules of ritual" is the division of the procedures for the acts, a science helpful to poets.[1528] **With their phonology and etymology**: "Phonology and etymology" are *sikkhā* and *nirutti*.[1529] **With historical lore as the fifth**: "Historical lore" (*itihāsa*) is a designation for accounts of ancient events, connected with such a statement as "So it was, so it was" (*itiha āsa itiha āsa*). Having taken the Atharva Veda as the fourth, historical lore is the fifth among them; thus it is said "with historical lore as the fifth."[1530] **Skilled in philology and grammar**: He recited and understood their terms and the rest of the grammar.[1531] **Fully versed in natural philosophy and in the marks of a great man**: He had fulfilled, without omisson, natural philosophy—the science of disputation—and the subject of the marks of a great man, the 12,000 treatises on the marks of a great man.[1532] What is meant is that he was not deficient; for one who is deficient is not able to maintain these either by way of meaning or by way of texts. [448]

While walking and wandering around for exercise: He was taking a short walk for the purpose of stretching his legs in order to dispel fatigue caused by sitting for a long time, wandering here and there. **A marriage** (*āvāho*): the taking of a girl. **A giving in marriage** (*vivāho*): the giving of a girl. **A great sacrifice**: a great almsgiving.[1533] **Seniya**: so called because he possessed a large army (*senā*). *Bimbi* means gold, and thus he was called **Bimbisāra** because his complexion was similar to that of high-grade gold.

Then, because he had established a foundation in the past,[1534] when he heard the word "buddha" he felt as if he had been anointed with ambrosia. Expressing his astonishment, he said: **Did you say "Buddha," Keṇiya?** Answering him correctly, Keṇiya said: **I said "Buddha," Sela**. Sela then asked him again in order to confirm the reply, and Keṇiya answered in the same way. Then, showing how rare it is to encounter the word "buddha," even in a thousand eons,[1535] he said: **Even this sound "buddha" is rarely encountered in this world**. Having heard the word "buddha," wishing to investigate whether he was truly a buddha or one merely in name, the brahmin thought or actually said: "Now the thirty-two marks of a great man have been handed down . . . who has removed the coverings in the world." **In our hymns**: in the Vedas.

Before it was announced, "A tathāgata will arise," devas from the pure abodes assumed the guise of brahmins and taught the Vedas, inserting the marks [of a great man] into them, thinking: "Prominent beings will recognize the Tathāgata in accordance with them." Hence previously the marks of a great man came down in the Vedas, but after the Tathāgata attained final nibbāna they gradually disappeared and thus at present they do not exist.[1536] **A great man**: a man who is great through such excellent qualities as resolve, undertaking, knowledge, and compassion. [449] **Only two possible destinies**: only two possible outcomes.[1537] Although the marks of a wheel-turning monarch are not the same as those of a buddha, they are still spoken of as if they were identical because they are of the same kind. Therefore it is said: **who is endowed with them**.

A wheel-turning monarch: He is *a king* (monarch) because he delights the world with his four wondrous qualities and with the four means of attracting and sustaining a retinue.[1538] He is *a wheel-turner* in that he turns the wheel gem; it turns through the four wheels of excellence, and with these he governs others,[1539] and there exists in him the turning of the wheels of the postures for the well-being of others. And here "king" is a general term and "wheel-turner" is its qualifier.[1540] He is **righteous** (*dhammiko*) in that he acts in accordance with the Dhamma; that is, he behaves in the right way, in a balanced way. He is a **king who rules by the Dhamma** (*dhammarājā*) because he has become king after gaining his kingdom righteously (*dhammena*). Or he is **righteous** because he enacts the *dhammas* that promote the well-being of others; he is a **king who rules by the Dhamma** because he enacts the *dhammas* that promote his own well-being. **A ruler of the four quarters**: a ruler over the earth bounded by the four oceans and adorned with the four continents. **Victorious**: because inwardly he has conquered such foes as anger and so forth, and externally he has conquered all other kings. **Who has attained stability in his country**: who has attained stability, firmness, in the country, since he cannot be deposed by anyone; or the country has attained stability under him in that people are peaceful, engaged in their own activities, unshakable, immovable.

That is, [450] **the wheel gem . . . the governor gem as the seventh**: These were explained in the commentary to the Discourse on Gems (see pp. 684–86). By means of the wheel gem this wheel-turning monarch conquers those who have not been conquered. By means of the elephant gem and the horse gem he travels around in his realm at his pleasure. By means of the governor gem he safeguards his realm. With the other three he experiences the pleasure of wealth. And by the first (the wheel gem) his power of exertion is complete; by the elephant gem, horse gem, and steward gem, his power of dominion is complete; by the governor gem, his power of counsel is complete; and by the woman gem and the jewel gem, he experiences the fruit of the threefold power. By the woman gem and the jewel gem, he experiences the pleasure of wealth; by the rest, the pleasure of rulership. The first three arise for him by the spiritual might of the kamma generated through the wholesome root of non-hatred; the middle three by the spiritual might of the kamma generated through the wholesome root of non-greed; and the last through the spiritual might of the kamma generated through the wholesome root of non-delusion.

His sons . . . are brave and heroic: They are not cowardly but have bodies like young devas. It is as if their bodies were made of energy. **Crush the armies of others**: If an opposing army should confront them, they are capable of crushing it. **He rules . . . by means of the Dhamma**: by means of the Dhamma of the five precepts, "A being should not be killed," and so forth.

He becomes an arahant, a perfectly enlightened buddha, whose coverings in the world are removed: Here, in the world darkened by defilements—covered over by the coverings of lust, hatred, delusion, conceit, views, ignorance, and misconduct—he removes that covering and dwells generating light on all sides; thus he is one "whose coverings are removed." There, by the first term his worthiness of offerings is indicated; by the second, the cause of this, since he is perfectly enlightened; by the third, the removal of the coverings on account of his buddhahood. [451] Or alternatively, "whose coverings are removed" should be resolved into "without turning and without coverings"; that is, devoid of the round of existence and devoid of coverings.[1541] Hence he is an arahant through the absence of the round, and a perfectly enlightened buddha through the absence of coverings. In this way, the pair of causes for the former pair of terms is stated.[1542] And here, the first is established by means of the second kind of self-confidence; the second is established by the first kind of self-confidence; and the third is established by the third and fourth kinds of self-confidence.[1543] And the first accomplishes the eye of the Dhamma, the second the eye of a buddha, and the third the universal eye.[1544]

Now, wishing to go to see the Blessed One, he asked: **Where is Master Gotama . . . now living?** When this was said, Keṇiya answered, **By that green line of the grove**: the row of green trees. It is said that the rattan grove was like a row of clouds. Describing the place where the Blessed One was dwelling, he said: "There, by that green line of the grove, Master Sela."

Step by step: He prohibits going in a hurry. **Hard to approach**: He gives the reason. Since they are hard to approach, **come quietly, sirs**. If it is asked, "But for what reason are they hard to approach?" the answer is that they are **like lions that wander alone**.[1545] For as lions, having no need for companions, wander alone, so too do those Blessed Ones because of their love of seclusion. **And when I am speaking**: He instructs those students how to behave when in the Buddha's vicinity.

He was perplexed: He gave rise to perplexity, thinking: "Oh, that I might see them"; **doubtful**: troubled when investigating them from different angles but unable to see them; **he could not decide**: could not settle that doubt; **and make up his mind about them**: he was not sure that the Blessed One had the marks in full. [452] Or *perplexed* indicates weak uncertainty; *doubtful* a middling degree of uncertainty; *being indecisive* strong uncertainty; and *not being able to make up one's mind* is the mental obscurity caused by those three qualities. For the Blessed One's male organ, golden like the calyx of a lotus, was enclosed in a sheath like that of an elephant. Because it was covered by his robe, Sela could not see his male organ, nor could he observe the size of his tongue, which was inside his mouth. Thus he was perplexed and doubtful about those two marks.

Such a feat of psychic potency: Of what kind? Why need we say anything about this? The Elder Nāgasena already spoke about this in his reply to a question asked by King Milinda:

> "Bhante Nāgasena, the Blessed One did something bad."
>
> "What is that, great king?"

"In front of the multitude, Bhante, he displayed his private parts to the brahmin Brahmāyu and his pupil Uttara, and to the sixteen brahmin pupils of Bāvarī, and to the three hundred young brahmins who were pupils of the brahmin Sela."

"Great king, the Blessed One did not display his private parts; rather, he displayed an image. For he performed such a feat of psychic potency, great king, that he showed a mere image of their form while they remained beneath his under-robe, which was fastened by his belt, and covered by his upper robe."

"But, Bhante, when the image was seen, wasn't the organ itself seen?"

"Let this be, great king. If there were a being who would be able to awaken by seeing his heart, the Buddha would take out his heart and show it to him."

"You are clever, Bhante Nāgasena."[1546]

Here, the length of the tongue was shown by touching the ear holes, its thinness by touching the nostrils, and its width by covering the forehead.[1547] [453]

554. When Sela had spoken, the Blessed One, fulfilling Sela's wish [expressed thus], "Those who are arahants, perfectly enlightened ones, reveal themselves as such when their own qualities are spoken of," said: "I am already a king."[1548] This is the purport here: "Sela, when you entreat me, 'You are fit to be a king, a wheel-turner,' be at ease, for **I am already a king**. For whereas another king might rule over a hundred yojanas, or two, three, four, or five hundred yojanas, or a thousand yojanas, and whereas a wheel-turning monarch [454] might rule over the four continents right up to their boundaries, I do not have such a limited domain. For **I am the unsurpassed king of the Dhamma** who rules over immeasurable world systems across, bounded by the peak of existence above and the Avīci hell below. I am the foremost of beings, whether they be without feet, with two feet, or more. For there is no one equal to me with respect to good behavior, [concentration, wisdom, liberation, and] the knowledge and vision of liberation. Thus I am the unsurpassed king of the Dhamma, and **I turn the wheel**

by means of the Dhamma, unsurpassed, a designation for the aids to enlightenment, the four establishments of mindfulness and so forth." It is the wheel of command, "Abandon this, enter and dwell in that"; or it is the wheel of the Dhamma itself, [set in motion] by the Dhamma of learning, thus: "Now this, bhikkhus, is the noble truth of suffering." **The wheel that cannot be turned back**: The wheel that cannot be turned back by any ascetic or brahmin or anyone in the world.

555–56. Having seen the Blessed One reveal himself in such a way, Sela, filled with rapture and joy, spoke the next pair of verses, "You claim to be an enlightened one," for the purpose of confirming this again. Here, **Who is your general?**: He asks: "Who is the Dhamma king's general that helps turn the Dhamma wheel set in motion by him by means of the Dhamma?"

557. On that occasion the Venerable Sāriputta was seated at the Blessed One's right side, shining with splendor like a heap of gold. Pointing him out, the Blessed One spoke the verse "The wheel set in motion by me." Here, **the Tathāgata's offspring**: one who is born because of the Tathāgata, who is born with the Tathāgata as cause.[1549]

558. Thus, having answered the question, "Who is your general?" since Sela had said, "You claim to be a buddha," the Blessed One, wishing to remove his doubt, spoke the next verse, "What should be directly known," to make him understand: "I do not merely put forth a claim, but rather there is a reason I am a buddha." Here, **what should be directly known** is clear knowledge and liberation; **what should be developed** is the truth of the path; and **what should be abandoned** is the truth of the origin. Since the fruits are established when the causes are mentioned, their respective fruits—the truth of cessation and the truth of suffering—are already indicated. Hence this also indicates: "What should be realized has been realized, and what should be fully understood has been fully understood."[1550] [455]

Having thus shown the development of the four truths along with clear knowledge and liberation, which are the fruits of developing the truths, he demonstrates his buddhahood through a cogent reason thus: "Having awakened to that which one should awaken to, I have become a buddha."[1551]

559–61. Having in this way revealed himself directly, now urging the brahmin to overcome doubt about himself, the Blessed One spoke the next three verses: "So remove your doubt about me." **Surgeon**: because of cutting out the seven darts, the darts of lust and so forth.[1552] **I have become Brahmā**: I have become the best. **Peerless**: beyond measure, beyond comparison, incomparable. **One who has crushed Māra's army**: who has crushed Māra's entourage, stated thus: "Sensual pleasures are your first army," and so forth, and "having seen . . . the army equipped with banners all around."[1553] **All my enemies**: all opponents, consisting in the [fivefold] Māra of the aggregates, defilements, volitional activities, death, and the young deity Māra, and so forth. **Having mastered**: having brought under my control. **Without fear from anywhere**: fearless everywhere.

562–64. When this was said, the brahmin Sela immediately gained confidence in the Blessed One, and wishing to go forth, he spoke the next three verses, "Sirs, hear this," as his excellent supporting conditions had reached maturity while he was being properly exhorted. Here, **one of dark birth**: one born into a low family, among caṇḍālas and so forth.

565. Then those students, also wishing to go forth, spoke the verse "If, sir, you now approve"; for these young men had established a foundation together with him.

566. Then Sela, delighted with his students, pointing to them, spoke the verse "There are three hundred brahmins here," requesting the going forth [on their behalf].

567. Now in the past, under the teaching of the Blessed One Padumuttara, Sela had been the leader of a group of three hundred men. Together with them he had constructed a monastic cell, and having done other meritorious deeds such as giving alms, he experienced successive excellence among devas and human beings. Finally, in his last existence, he had become the teacher of those same men. That kamma of theirs, maturing toward liberation, [456] had become a supporting condition for their going forth by the "Come, bhikkhus" method.[1554] Therefore, letting them go forth by the "Come, bhikkhus" method, the Blessed One spoke the verse "The spiritual life is well proclaimed."

Here, **directly visible**: directly cognizable; **immediate**: the fruit is to be attained without an interval of time, since it arises immediately after the path. **As:**[1555] on the basis of which; on the basis of the spiritual life of the path. **The going forth will not be barren for one who trains heedfully**, for one who remains inseparable from mindfulness while training in the three trainings. Hence he said: "The spiritual life is well proclaimed . . . for one who trains heedfully."

And having said this, the Blessed One said: "Come, bhikkhus." All then appeared wearing robes and carrying alms bowls, and having come through the sky, they paid homage to the Blessed One.[1556] Thus the compilers said, with reference to their ordination by the "Come, bhikkhus" method: "Then the brahmin Sela . . . the full ordination."

Had put aside his bowl: with the hand withdrawn from the bowl; what is meant is "with hand removed from the bowl."[1557]

568. "Fire offerings are the best of sacrifices": The Blessed One spoke thus, expressing appreciation to Keṇiya in a way agreeable to his mind. Since among the brahmins there is no sacrifice without the tending of the fire, it is said: **Fire offerings are the best of sacrifices**: fire offerings are foremost, fire offerings are chief. **Sāvittī the best of Vedic hymns**, because it must be read first by those who recite the Vedas. **The best of human beings is a king**, because he is their leader. **The sea the best for flowing rivers**, because it contains them and they flow into it.

569. The moon is the best of celestial bodies, because [the months] are designated by it, as when it is said, "Today is Kattikā, today is Rohiṇī," and because it gives off light, and because of its gentleness. **The sun the best of things that shine**, because it is foremost of shining things. **For those desiring merit, the Sangha is best for those who sacrifice**: This was said especially on that occasion with reference to the Sangha headed by the Buddha because it is the foremost of those worthy of offerings. Hence he shows: "The Sangha is the best source of merit."

570. He spoke this verse, "Since we went to you for refuge," as a declaration of final knowledge. [457] This is its meaning: "**One with Vision**: Blessed One with the five eyes. **This is the eighth day . . . since we went to you for refuge**. Therefore, **in these seven nights . . . we have been tamed in your teaching** with the unsurpassed taming. Oh, the spiritual might of you as refuge!"

Following this, he praises the Blessed One with two verses (**571–72**) and with the third (**573**) he asks to venerate him:

> "Here these three hundred bhikkhus stand
> saluting you with reverence.
> Extend your feet, O hero:
> let these nāgas pay homage to the Teacher."

8 The Dart
(*Salla Sutta*)

What is the origin? The Blessed One, it is said, had a lay supporter whose son had died. Overcome by sorrow for his son, he did not eat for a week. Out of compassion for him, the Blessed One went to his home and spoke this discourse to dispel his sorrow.

574. Here, **without a sign**: devoid of a sign indicating the way something should be done, for instance, by saying: "When I lower my eyes or raise my eyebrows, at that sign steal the goods." This does not happen with life, for it isn't possible to have it this way: "As long as I am doing this or that, you must live and must not die." **Unknown**: Hence it is not possible to know with certainty, "I have just this much time or that much time to live," or by way of the limits of the life span for a particular realm. For whereas the life span of beings in the realm of the four divine kings and other celestial realms is fixed, the life span **of mortals** (human beings) is not; thus it is not known with certainty. **Difficult**: Because its occurrence is dependent on numerous conditions, life is hard, not easily maintained. Thus, for instance, life is dependent on breathing in and out, on the primary elements, on edible food, on warmth, and on consciousness. If one does not breathe in, one does not continue to live; so too if one does not breathe out. Or among the four elements, [458] when there is a disturbance in the earth element, the body becomes as stiff as a block of wood, as if bitten by a viper of the "wooden-mouth" type. As it is said:

The body becomes stiff when bitten
by a snake of the wooden-mouth type;
through a disturbance of the earth element,
it becomes as if caught by a wooden-mouth snake.[1558]

When there is a disturbance in the water element, the body becomes putrid, oozing pus, flesh, and blood, and all that is left behind are bones and skin. As it is said:

The body becomes putrid when bitten
by a snake of the putrid-mouth type;
through a disturbance of the water element,
it becomes as if caught by a putrid-mouth snake.

When there is a disturbance in the fire element, it becomes feverish all over, as if thrown into a pit of coals. As it is said:

The body becomes hot when bitten
by a snake of the fire-mouth type;
through a disturbance of the fire element,
it becomes as if caught by a fire-mouth snake.

When there is a disturbance in the air element, severe pains run through its joints and sinews, as if the body were smashed by rocks and its bones pulverized. As it is said:

The body is severed when bitten
by a snake of the dagger-mouth type;
through a disturbance of the air element,
it becomes as if caught by a dagger-mouth snake.

In this way, when the elements of the body are disturbed, one does not live. But when the elements carry on smoothly, performing their respective functions in regard to one another—[the earth element] serving as a foundation and so forth[1559]—life continues. Thus life is dependent on the primary elements.

During a famine, etc., when the supply of food is cut off, beings are seen to perish; thus life is also dependent on edible food. So too when the food and drink are spoiled, the kamma-produced fire is exhausted and beings undergo loss of life; thus life is dependent upon heat. But when consciousness has ceased, from the time it has ceased,[1560] the life of beings does not continue; this too is clearly seen in the world. Thus life is also dependent upon consciousness. In this way, it should be understood that life is difficult because it occurs in dependence on numerous conditions.

And short: It is short, slight, because compared to the life of the devas, human life is like dew drops on blades of grass, or because it does not endure beyond a mind-moment. For even in the case of a being with a long life span, at the past mind-moment it lived but does not live and will not live; [459] at a future mind-moment it will live but does not live and did not live; and at the present mind-moment it lives but did not live and will not live. And this is said:

> Life and individuality,
> pleasure and pain in their entirety . . .
> even they do not live
> for two consecutive mind-moments.[1561]

And conjoined with suffering: And this life is not only without a sign, unknown, difficult, and short, but it is conjoined with the suffering of cold and heat, contact with flies and mosquitoes, hunger and thirst, and the suffering intrinsic to conditioned things, the suffering of change, and the suffering of pain.[1562] What is meant? "Since such is the life of mortals, until the time of your own death you should intensify your Dhamma practice and do not grieve over your son."

575. Then you might also think: "Even though I protected my son in every way possible, still he died; therefore I sorrow." Even in such a case, do not sorrow, **for there is no way by which those who have been born will not die**: When beings have been born, it is not possible by any means to protect them from death, thinking: "May they not die." Since the father thought, "Death is fitting for those who have reached old age, Bhante, but my son died too young," the Blessed One said: **Death occurs also when one has reached old age: for such is**

the nature of living beings. The point is that death occurs both to those who have reached old age and to those who have not reached old age; there is no fixed determination in this matter.

576. Now using an example to demonstrate this point, he says: "Just as when fruits have ripened." This is its meaning: **When fruits have ripened**: From the time of sunrise, when a tree is being warmed by the heat of the sun, the soil nutrients and moisture proceed from the leaves to the branches, from the branches to the trunk, from the trunk to the roots, and thus in sequence from the roots they enter the earth; but from the time of sunset, they proceed from the earth to the roots, from the roots to the trunk, and thus in sequence they again rise to the branches, leaves, and sprouts. Thus ascending, when the fruits are ripe, they do not enter the stalk. Then, when the stalk is being warmed by the heat of the sun, a fever[1563] arises. With that, the fruits constantly fall, one after another, and with their falling **there is fear of their falling**, fear *because of* their falling.[1564] Just so, **for mortals who have taken birth, there is always fear of death**, [460] for beings are similar to ripened fruit.

577. And what is more: **Just as the clay pots . . . the life of mortals**.

578. Therefore understand this: **Both the young . . . as their destination**.

579. And having understood that, understand this too: **When those overpowered by death . . . nor can one protect one's relatives**.

580. And since "the father cannot protect his son, nor can one protect one's relatives," therefore "even as the relatives are looking on . . . to be slaughtered." This is the construal here: "As the relatives are watching, wailing profusely in many ways, each of the mortals is led away like a cow to be slaughtered. See, lay follower, how the world is without a protector!"

581. The buddhas, paccekabuddhas, and others endowed with intelligence understand: "**Thus the world is stricken by death**

and by old age, and it is not possible for anyone to protect it." **Therefore the wise do not sorrow, having understood the way of the world**. What is meant is: "Having known this nature of the world, they do not sorrow."

582. You, however, "who do not know the path . . . lament without purpose." What is meant? "You who do not know **the path by which he has come** into the mother's womb, or the path by which he **has gone** elsewhere after passing away here, **not perceiving either end, yet lament without purpose**. But the wise, seeing these things, having understood the way of the world, do not sorrow."

583. Now, demonstrating the futility of lamentation stated here with the words "you yet lament without purpose," he says, "If while he is lamenting," and so forth. If such a bewildered person could derive some benefit, a wise person too would indulge in lamentation.

584. It is not by weeping: This is the construal here: "**It is not by weeping or sorrowing that one attains peace of mind**. Rather, as one weeps and sorrows, **one's suffering arises still more and one's body is harmed** by turning pallid and so forth."

585. The departed are not thereby sustained: The dead are not maintained by that lamentation; it is not helpful to them. Therefore **lamentation is useless.**

586. Not only is it useless, but it also leads to harm. Why? Because [461] **without abandoning sorrow . . . one comes under the control of sorrow**.

587. Thus, having shown the futility and harmfulness of sorrow, now exhorting him to remove sorrow, he says: "Behold others, too." Here, **about to depart**: on the verge of leaving for the next world. **Living beings just trembling here**: living beings trembling here with the fear of death.

588. In whatever way they conceive it, "He will have a long life, he will be healthy," **it turns out otherwise**: Though conceived in such a way, he falls ill and dies. **Such is separation**, contrary to the way the matter is conceived. "**See**, lay follower, the nature of the world." The purport here should be construed in this way.

590. Having heard it from the arahant: Having heard this teaching of Dhamma from the arahant; **realize, "It is not possible for me"**:[1565] clearly understanding, "It is not possible for me to bring the departed one back to life," **one should stop lamentation**.

591. And what is more: "If one's shelter were blazing . . . a tuft of cotton wool." Here, **a sensible person**, endowed with sense; **wise**, with natural wisdom; **learned**, through the wisdom of abundant learning; **skilled**, with a reflective nature. Or these can be construed by way of the wisdom formed by reflection, learning, and meditation.

592. Not only sorrow, but "lamentation . . . the dart from oneself." Here, **muttering**: craving;[1566] **dejection**: mental suffering. **The dart**: this [sorrow], which is a terrible dart in the sense of being hard to remove and in the sense of piercing one's insides. Or it is the sevenfold dart stated previously, the dart of lust and so forth.

593. When that dart has been drawn out, **with the dart drawn out . . . one is quenched**.[1567] Thus he concludes the discourse with its culmination in arahantship. Here, **unattached**: unattached because of craving and views. Since the rest here has been explained previously, the meaning is already clear and therefore it is not commented on. [462]

9 Vāseṭṭha
(*Vāseṭṭha Sutta*)

What is the origin? This is already stated in the introduction to the discourse. We will provide an explanation of its meaning, avoiding terms that have been previously explained and those whose meanings are sufficiently clear.[1568]

Icchānaṅgala is the name of a village. **Caṅkī**, **Tārukkha**, **Todeyya** are conventional names of affluent brahmins. **Pokkharasāti**, **Jāṇussoṇi** are names based on attributes.[1569] It is said that the former was born inside a lotus flower in a lotus pond. A certain hermit took that lotus and saw the child lying there. He raised the child and presented him to the king, who gave him the name "Pokkharasāti" because he was found lying in a lotus flower (*pokkhare sayitattā*). The latter indicates one's position. It is said that the position of royal chaplain was named "Jāṇussoṇi," so he was known by such a name.

Why were all these and other very well-known affluent brahmins staying at Icchānaṅgala? To recite and investigate the Vedas. It is said that at the time the brahmins in Kosala who knew the Vedas had assembled in this village to recite the Vedas and examine their meaning. Hence at intervals they would come from their own village estates and stay there.

This chance conversation arose between them: While Vāseṭṭha and Bhāradvāja were walking around engaged in friendly conversation, right in the middle of their discussion, this other topic arose. **Of pure descent** (*saṃsuddhagahaṇiko*): of a pure womb, that is, born in the womb of a brahmin woman. In some passages the word *gahaṇī* refers to digestive power, as when it is said that one has "an even digestion" (*samavepākiniyā gahaṇiyā*), but here it is the mother's womb. **As far back as the seventh generation of ancestors**: This means going backward seven generations through one's mother's mother and one's father's father. And here, one's paternal grandfather and paternal grandmother are one's paternal grandparents, and one's maternal grandfather and maternal grandmother are one's maternal grandparents, and these lines of grandparents [463] are simply called "ancestors." A "generation" refers to the normal life span, though this is a mere expression. But by way of meaning, it is just the line of paternal grandparents that is called a generation of grandparents. **Unassailable**: not disparaged by anyone who could say, with reference to one's birth: "What is he?" **Impeccable**: never insulted in regard to some fault in one's birth. **Proficient in the observances**: proficient in behavior. **Convince**: persuade, sway, win the argument.

594. Acknowledged to possess the knowledge we claim: We are acknowledged by our teachers thus, "You are knowers of the Three Vedas," and we ourselves claim to be such. **I am Pokkharasāti's pupil and he a pupil of Tārukkha**: Showing the excellence of his teacher and his own excellence, he says in effect: "I am the senior student of Pokkharasāti, his foremost pupil, and he is the foremost pupil of Tārukkha."

595. Consummate: reached the conclusion. Now, showing how they are consummate, he says: "skilled in philology . . . like our teachers." Here, **in recitation**: in the Vedas.[1570]

596. By action: by the tenfold action along the path of wholesome action.[1571] For it was with reference to the sevenfold bodily and verbal action that he said previously, "When one is virtuous," and it was with reference to the threefold mental action that he said, "perfect in the observances"; for one endowed with that is perfect in behavior. Now showing this with another expression, he said: **But I say one is such by action**.

599. The eye arisen in the world: In the world submerged in the darkness of ignorance, he dispels that darkness and has arisen as the eye because he instructs the world in the good pertaining to this present life and so forth.[1572]

600. After Vāseṭṭha had praised him thus and made his request, the Blessed One, [464] benefiting the two men, said: **I will explain to you both. In proper sequence**: The purport here should be understood thus: "Put aside for now your reflections on the nature of a brahmin. I will explain the matter to you in proper sequence, starting from the grass, trees, moths, and butterflies." Thus these young men are to be guided by a detailed explanation. **For their kinds differ from one another**: For the classes of those living beings are different from one another; they are of various kinds.[1573]

601. Then, in analyzing the generic divisions among living beings, he begins by first discussing the divisions among those that are non-sentient.[1574] For what purpose? To make it easier to demonstrate [the divisions] among sentient beings. For when the generic division among non-sentient beings is grasped, the divisions among sentient beings become clearer.

Know the grass and trees as well: Here, "grasses" have soft insides and hard exteriors; therefore palm trees and coconut trees are included in grasses. "Trees" have soft exteriors and hard interiors. **They do not even make claims**: They do not claim: "We are grasses; we are trees." **Their distinctive mark is produced by birth**: Even though they make no claims about themselves, their shape—which is similar for rooted grasses and so forth—is produced solely by birth. For what reason? **For their kinds differ from one another**: Because grasses are one kind, trees are another; and among the grasses as well, palm trees are one kind, coconut trees are another; and so it should be elaborated. What does he show by this? That their differences in birth, by which they are understood to be of different kinds, can be recognized even without any claim on their own part or instruction from others. And if one were a brahmin by birth, one would have to be recognized as distinct from khattiyas, vessas, and suddas even without any claim on one's own part or instruction from others. But one is not so recognized; therefore one is not a brahmin by birth. We will explain this point by verbal analysis later, when we come to the verse "While among these many kinds" (**607**).

602. Thus, having shown the divisions by way of birth among non-sentient beings, now showing the same among sentient beings, he says, "Next come the moths," etc.[1575] [465]

607. Now, having shown the division in the kinds of living beings that dwell on dry land, in water, and in the sky, he next speaks a verse, "While among these many kinds," in which he explains the purpose for which he showed this. Its meaning should be understood by way of the explanation of the purport stated briefly above.

608–10. However, when he speaks the verses beginning "Not by the hairs" and so forth, he himself shows whatever should be stated in detail. This is the construal there: "When it was said, 'among humans there are no distinctive marks produced by their particular birth,' it should be understood as follows how there are no such marks." **Not by the hairs**: Unlike with elephants, horses, deer, and other animals, for humans there is no law to the effect: "The hairs of brahmins are like this, the hairs of khattiyas are like that." All the rest should be construed in this way. **Birth does not make a distinctive mark as it does for the other kinds of beings**: This should be understood as the conclusion drawn from what was just stated. This is its construal: "Since in terms of the hairs and so forth 'among humans there are no distinctive marks produced by their particular birth,' therefore it should be understood that 'birth does not make a distinctive mark as it does for the other kinds of beings.'"

611. Now, since there is no such distinction of kinds, to show how this difference between brahmins, khattiyas, and the other classes has arisen, he spoke the verse "Separately." This is its meaning: Unlike in the case of the animals, whose differences in the shape of their hairs and so forth are determined by their mode of origin, [466] among human beings such differences do not exist in the individual bodies of brahmins and the other classes. And since this does not exist, **classifi-**

cation among human beings is spoken of by designation: that "classification"—the way of assigning differences such as "brahmin, khattiya"—is spoken of by mere convention.[1576]

612–19. To this extent the Blessed One has refuted the claim of Bhāradvāja. Now if one were a brahmin by birth, even one deficient in livelihood, virtue, and conduct would be a brahmin. But the ancient brahmins, as well as other wise people in the world, did not recognize such a person as having the status of a brahmin. Therefore, showing that point to promote the claim of Vāseṭṭha, the Blessed One spoke the eight verses beginning "The one among humans."[1577]

620. Since it has been demonstrated that, according to both the creed of the brahmins and worldly convention, one deficient in livelihood, virtue, and conduct does not have the status of a brahmin, it follows that one is not a brahmin by birth but by one's excellent qualities. Therefore, no matter into which family one has been born, one with excellent qualities is a brahmin. This is the principle here. Having already brought up this principle by way of its general import, now enunciating that same principle, he says: "I do not call someone a brahmin." This is its meaning: Whether one is born anywhere among the four modes of genesis[1578] or has originated specifically from one praised as the mother of a brahmin,[1579] [they call] him "one of [a certain] genealogy and maternal origin."[1580] But the genealogy spoken of by the brahmins, when they say "he is well born on both sides" and so forth, is a brahmin's pure ancestral lineage.[1581] And by the expression "of pure descent," what is indicated is the excellence of the mother. Because one has been born and has originated in such a way, one is said to be "of [good] genealogy and maternal origin." But **I do not call someone a brahmin, based on genealogy and maternal origin**, merely because of his genealogy and maternal origin. [467] Why not? Because **he is just a pompous speaker**[1582] **if he is impeded by things**,[1583] because he is distinguished from others who are impeded by things merely by using the word "honored sir." But one who has been born into any family, through the absence of the "somethings" (impediments) of lust and so forth, is "one who owns nothing," and by the relinquishment of all grasping, is "one who takes nothing." [Therefore] **one who owns nothing, taking nothing: he is the one I call a brahmin**. Why? Because he has expelled evil.[1584]

621. And what is more, there are twenty-seven verses beginning with "One who has cut off all fetters." Here, **all fetters**: the tenfold fetter. **Who is not agitated**: who is not frightened because of craving.[1585] **Who has overcome all ties**: because he has overcome the ties of lust and so forth. **Detached**: through the absence of the four bonds as well. **He is the one I call**—I speak of as—**a brahmin**.

622. The strap: anger occurring as a fastening; **thong**: craving occurring as a binding; **the reins and bridle-band**: the reins of the sixty-two views accompanied by the bridle-band of the latent tendencies. Having cut off all this, because he has also lifted the shaft of ignorance, he is one **whose shaft is lifted**. **Enlightened** because of having awakened to the four truths. He is the one I call a brahmin.[1586]

623. One who, without hatred, one who, without getting angry, **endures insults** by the ten bases of insult, and beating by fists and so forth,[1587] and **bondage** by shackles and so forth; **whose power is patience**, because he has the power of patience; **a powerful troop**, because he has the powerful troop of patience, which has become a troop through repeated arising.[1588]

624. Observant: observing the austere practices;[1589] **of good behavior** through the fourfold purification of good behavior;[1590] **without swellings** because he has no swelling of craving; **tamed** by the taming of the six sense faculties; **bearing his final body** because his bodily form has reached its end.

625. One who does not cling: one who does not cling within to the twofold sensual pleasures,[1591] who does not take a stand upon sensual pleasures.

626. Of suffering: the suffering of the aggregates. **Whose bur-**

den is lowered: who has dropped the burden of the aggregates. **Detached**: from the four bonds or from all defilements. [468]

627. One of deep wisdom: possessing wisdom that proceeds among the deep aggregates and so forth; **intelligent**: because of wisdom nourished by the Dhamma;[1592] **skilled in the path and the non-path**: because he is adroit in knowing what is the path and what is not the path thus: "This is the path to a bad destination; that is the path to a good destination. This is the path to nibbāna; that is not the path." **Who has reached the supreme goal**: a designation for arahantship.

628. One who does not form bonds: who does not form bonds by avoidance of seeing, hearing, conversation, shared enjoyment, and body.[1593]

629. Having put down the rod: having laid down, having dropped the rod; **toward all beings frail and firm**: toward those who are frail because of craving and fear, and those who are firm through their steadfastness due to the absence of craving. **Who does not kill or make others kill**: who, having put down the rod because aversion toward all beings has vanished, does not kill anyone of his own accord or cause others to kill.

630. Not hostile, one who, through the absence of resentment, is not hostile even when **among those** worldly masses **who are hostile** because of resentment. **Quenched** (peaceful), who has put down the rod, **among those who take up the rod**, among people given to violence who inflict blows on others, even on those who have a weapon in hand. **Not taking**, through the absence of grasping, **among those who take** because they grasp the five aggregates as "I" and "mine."

631. From the point of an awl: As mustard seeds do not remain on the tip of an awl, so lust and so forth, and denigration—denigration of the excellent qualities of others—do not remain in the mind.

632. Rough: harsh. **Articulate**: conveying the meaning. **Truthful**: factual. **Does not hurt**: does not cause another to adhere to him by causing anger.[1594] The arahant would utter only such kind of speech.

633. One **who does not take anything** in the world belonging to others. **Long or short** clothes, ornaments, and so forth; **subtle or gross** jewels, pearls, and so forth; **fine or plain**: of great value or of little value. [469]

634. Without desire: without craving; **detached**: disconnected from all defilements.

635. Attachments: cravings. **Who, through knowledge, is rid of doubt**: Having understood the eight bases as they really are, he is without doubt, rid of doubt with its eight cases.[1595] **Arrived at firm ground in the deathless**: arrived by having plunged into the deathless nibbāna.[1596]

636. Who has transcended ties: who has overcome the ties, divided into lust and so forth. **Both**: having discarded the two, merit and evil.[1597] **Sorrowless**, without the sorrow rooted in the round; **dustless**, through the absence internally of the dust of lust and so forth; and **pure**, through the absence of defilement.

637. Stainless: devoid of stains due to clouds and so forth;[1598] **pure**: without defilement; **clear**: of placid mind; **limpid**: devoid of the turbidity of defilements. **For whom delight in existence is destroyed**: for whom craving for the three kinds of existence is destroyed.[1599]

638. One—a bhikkhu—**who has passed beyond this swamp** of lust, the **mire** of defilements, the round of **saṃsāra**, and **delusion**, the non-penetrating of the four noble truths; **who has crossed** the four floods, arrived at the **beyond**; **a meditator** by the twofold jhāna;[1600] **without impulse** by the absence of craving; **rid of doubt** through the absence of doubt; **who has attained nibbāna**, by the extinguishing of defilements without clinging, through the absence of clingings.

639. One, a person, **here** in the world who has discarded both kinds of **sensual pleasures**, who wanders **without a home**, with sensual desire destroyed and with existence destroyed.[1601]

640. One here in the world who has discarded craving at the six sense doors, and without need to dwell in a house, wanders having become **without a home, with craving and existence destroyed**: through the utter destruction of craving and existence.[1602]

641. The human bond: the human life span and the five kinds of sensual pleasure. The same method applies to **the celestial bond**. **Transcended**: having discarded the human bond and overcome the celestial one, he is **fully detached** from all four bonds.

642. Delight (*ratiṃ*): delight in the five kinds of sensual pleasure. **Discontent** (*aratiṃ*): dissatisfaction with dwelling in the forest. [470] **Become cool**: quenched;[1603] **without acquisitions**: without defilements. **A hero**: one possessing energy who has overcome the whole world of the aggregates.

643. One who knows: one who clearly knows in all modes the passing away and rebirth of beings; **unstuck** because of not being fastened; **fortunate** (*sugataṃ*) because he has proceeded well in practice; **enlightened** because of his understanding of the four truths.

644. One whose destination these devas and others **do not know; with influxes destroyed** because he has completely destroyed the influxes; **an arahant** because of his remoteness from defilements.

645. Before: in regard to the aggregates of the past; **after**: in regard to those of the future; **and in the middle**: in regard to those of the present. **One for whom there is nothing at all**: one for whom there is no impediment—a designation for the obsession of craving—in regard to these objects.[1604]

646. The chief bull because of his similarity to a chief bull by reason of his fearlessness; **excellent**, in the sense of supreme; **hero** because of his excellence of energy; **great rishi** (*mahesī*) because of his having sought out (*esitattā*) the great aggregates of good behavior and so forth; **whose victory is won** because of his victory over the three kinds of Māra;[1605] **cleansed** because of washing away the defilements; **enlightened** because of awakening to the four truths.

647. One who knows his past abodes, having made them clear; **heaven**: the twenty-six deva worlds; **the plane of misery**, which is fourfold; which he **sees** with the divine eye. **And has reached** arahantship, designated **the destruction of birth**. **He**—such a one—**is the one I call a brahmin**.

648. Having described the brahmin by way of his excellent qualities, the Blessed One spoke the next two verses, "For the name and clan ascribed to one," showing: "Those who adhere to the belief that one is a brahmin by birth do not understand this as a conventional expression; this view of theirs is a bad view." This is its meaning: **For the name and clan ascribed to one**—that is, "brahmin, khattiya, Bhāradvāja, Vāseṭṭha"—**are a designation in the world**, a descriptive term, a mere conventional expression. Why? Because **having originated by convention**, come down by convention, [471] **they are ascribed here and there**: given to one by one's relatives and family members at the time one is born. If they were not assigned in such a way, no one, on seeing someone else, would know: "He is a brahmin" or "a Bhāradvāja."

649. For those who do not know this—that [name and clan] are assigned in such a way—**wrong view has long been their tendency**: for those beings who do not know that name and clan are assigned merely as conventional usage, wrong view has been a latent tendency in their heart for a long time. Because they have tended to that view, **it is just not knowing** name and clan **that they say: "One is a brahmin by birth."** It is just not knowing that they speak in such a way.[1606]

650. Having thus shown, "Those who adhere to the belief that one is a brahmin by birth do not understand this as a conventional expression; but their view is a bad view," now directly rejecting the doctrine of class determination by birth and advancing the doctrine of action,[1607] he said, "One is not a brahmin by birth" and so forth. Here, **by action one becomes a brahmin, by action one becomes a non-brahmin**. When it is said, "One becomes a farmer by action" and so forth, this is set forth for the purpose of elaborating upon the meaning of this half-verse.

651–52. Here, **by action**: by present action, the volition activating the work of farming and so forth.

653. Seers of dependent origination: those who see dependent origination thus: "Through this condition, such comes to be." **Skilled in action and its result**: skilled in action and its result thus: "Birth in a respectable or despised family occurs by way of action (kamma); other kinds of inferiority and superiority, too, occur when inferior and superior actions (kamma) are bringing forth their result."[1608]

654. By kamma the world goes round:[1609] In this verse, the words "world," "population," and "sentient beings" are identical in meaning; the distinction is merely verbal. And here the first line should be understood as a repudiation of the view: "There is Brahmā, Mahābrahmā, the supreme, the creator, the controller, the father of those who have come to be and will come to be." [472] For it is by kamma that the world goes round and by which one arises in the various destinations [of rebirth]. So who can be its creator?

With the second line he shows: "When one has thus arisen because of kamma, in the course of existence [following birth] one still goes round through past and present kamma, one continues experiencing pleasure and pain and achieving inferior and superior status and so forth." With the third line he draws the conclusion. Thus in all respects beings continue on **fastened by kamma**, bound by kamma itself, not otherwise.

With the fourth line, he illustrates the point with a simile: **like the linch pin of a moving chariot**. Just as the linch pin is the fastening of a moving chariot, which does not move if it is not fastened by the pin; so too, as the world arises and continues on thus, kamma is its fastening, and it does not arise and continue on if it is not fastened by kamma.

655. Now, since the world is fastened by kamma, he speaks the pair of verses, "By austerity," showing the best state through the best action.[1610] Here, **by austerity**: by restraint of the senses; **the spiritual life**: by the remaining kinds of best conduct dependent on the training; **by self-control**: by good behavior; **by inner taming**: by wisdom. **By this**—by the best action, which is holy (*brahmabhūtena*) in the sense of the best[1611]—**one becomes a brahmin**. Why? Because **this is supreme brahminhood**: because this action is supreme brahmahood.[1612]

There is also the reading *brahmānam* (instead of *brāhmaṇam*). This is its meaning: *Brahmānaṃ* is what leads to Brahmā; what leads to, brings, brahmahood.

656. Peaceful: one with the defilements stilled. **As Brahmā and Sakka:** One like this is not only a brahmin, but **for those** wise ones **who understand** he is also Brahmā and Sakka. What is meant is: **Know him thus, Vāseṭṭha**. The rest should be understood in the way already stated. [473]

10 Kokālika
(*Kokālika Sutta*)

What is the origin? The origin of this discourse will become clear through the commentary on the meaning. And in the commentary on the meaning, the words "Thus have I heard" should be understood in the way already stated. But when it is said, "Then the bhikkhu Kokālika," [it may be asked:] "Who is this Kokālika and why did he approach?"

In reply it is said: He was the son of the financier Kokāli in the city of Kokāli in the Kokāli country. Having gone forth, he stayed in a monastery built by his father. He was called Cūḷa Kokālika ("Little Kokālika"). He was not Devadatta's pupil, the son of a brahmin known as Mahākokālika ("Great Kokālika").[1613]

It is said that when the Blessed One was dwelling at Sāvatthī, the two chief disciples (Sāriputta and Moggallāna) were wandering on tour of the countryside together with five hundred bhikkhus. As the time for entering the rains approached, wishing to dwell together in seclusion, they dismissed those bhikkhus, took their own bowls and robes, reached that city in that country, and went to the monastery. There they exchanged greetings with Kokālika and said to him: "Friend, we will stay here for the three months [of the rains]. Don't inform anyone." He agreed. When the three months had passed, the next day he entered the city early and announced: "You did not know that the chief disciples had come here and have been living here, so no one has offered them any requisites." The citizens said: "Why didn't you inform us, Bhante?" – "Why should I need to inform you? Didn't you see two bhikkhus living here?" –

"Were those the chief disciples?" Having quickly assembled, they brought ghee, sugar, cloth, and other items and placed them in front of Kokālika. He thought: "The chief disciples are extremely frugal. If they learn that an offering has been obtained by suggestive speech, they will not accept it. Not accepting it, they will surely say: 'Give it to a resident monk.' Let me go and try to make them accept this offering." [474] He did so.

When the elders saw him, they knew the offering had been obtained through suggestive speech. Considering, "These requisites are suitable neither for us nor for Kokālika," they refused them and left, without saying: "Give them to the resident monk." Thereby Kokālika became dejected, thinking: "Since they did not accept these items themselves, why didn't they turn them over to me?"

They went to the Blessed One. Now if, after doing the Pavāraṇā,[1614] the Blessed One does not go on a tour of the countryside himself, he sends the chief disciples, telling them, "Wander on tour, bhikkhus, for the well-being of many people," and so forth. That is the custom of tathāgatas. Now on that occasion the Blessed One did not wish to go himself, so he again sent them: "Go, bhikkhus, wander on tour." Together with five hundred bhikkhus, they wandered on tour and in stages arrived at that same city in that same country. The citizens, having recognized the elders, prepared alms along with the requisites and constructed a pavilion in the middle of the city where they offered alms to the elders and presented them with the requisites. The elders accepted them and gave them to the Sangha of bhikkhus.

When Kokālika saw this, he thought: "Previously they were of few desires, but now they are overcome by greed and have evil desires. Previously, it seems, they only appeared to be frugal, content, and fond of solitude; but they are evil bhikkhus, with evil desires, who make a false display of excellent qualities." He approached the elders and said to them: "Friends, previously you seemed to be frugal, contented, and fond of solitude; but now you have become evil bhikkhus." Having said this, he took his bowl and robe and hurriedly departed that very day, thinking: "I will go and report this to the Blessed One." So he set off in the direction of Sāvatthī and in stages approached the Blessed One. It was for this reason that Kokālika approached.[1615] Hence it is said: **Then the bhikkhu Kokālika approached the Blessed One**.

As soon as the Blessed One saw him coming in a hurry, he turned his attention to him and knew: "He has come to malign the chief disciples." He then considered: "Is it possible to prevent him from doing so?" He saw: "It is not possible. [475] He has come to insult the elders and he will definitely arise in the Paduma hell." Though he had seen this, he still tried to prevent him three times by saying: "Do not say so." He did this to avoid criticism from others who might have said: "Having heard Kokālika slandering Sāriputta and Moggallāna, he did not try to stop him"; he also did this to show the grave blame in slandering the noble ones.

Not long after the bhikkhu Kokālika left: shortly after he left. **His entire body became covered**: His entire body was suffused with boils, without missing an area even as small as the tip of a hair. They split his bones and then rose up [covering his body].[1616] By the spiritual might of the buddhas, such a kamma does not yield its result while one is still in their presence but only when one has left the range of their sight; therefore the boils rose up shortly after he left. Hence it is said: "Not long after the bhikkhu Kokālika left."

If it is asked, "Why didn't he just stay there?" it is said: Through the spiritual might of kamma; for as a kamma that had gained the opportunity, it was bound to bring its results, and thus it did not permit him to stay there. Driven by the spiritual might of the kamma, he rose from his seat and departed.

They burst open: When they broke open his entire body became like a breadfruit. Beset by misery and disaster, overcome by suffering, with his body afflicted, he lay down at the entrance to Jeta's Grove. As people arrived to listen to the Dhamma, they saw him and said: "Shame on Kokālika, shame on Kokālika! He did what was improper, and now he is beset by misery and disaster on account of his own mouth." Having heard this, [476] the protective deities said "For shame!" The sky deities followed the protective deities, and in this way the one cry "For shame!" arose up to the Akaniṭṭha heaven.[1617]

A bhikkhu named Turū, who had been Kokālika's preceptor and had attained the fruit of a non-returner, had been reborn in the pure abodes. When he emerged from his meditative attainment, he too heard the cry "For shame!" and came to exhort Kokālika to be pleased with Sāriputta and Moggallāna. But Kokālika refused his advice, and instead insulted him as well. He then died and was reborn in the Paduma hell. Hence it is said: "Then, because of that illness, the bhikkhu Kokālika died and, as a result of harboring animosity toward Sāriputta and Moggallāna, he was reborn in the Paduma hell."

Then . . . Brahmā Sahampati: Who was this brahmā, and why did he approach the Blessed One and speak to him? During the time of the Blessed One Kassapa, he had been a bhikkhu named Sahaka. He became a non-returner and arose in the pure abodes. There they knew him as "Brahmā Sahampati." He thought: "I will approach the Blessed One and announce [that Kokālika was reborn in] the Paduma hell. Then the Blessed One will inform the bhikkhus, and those bhikkhus who are skilled in the sequence [of the teaching] will ask about the life span there. When explaining, the Blessed One will show the danger in slandering the noble ones." It was for this reason that he approached the Blessed One and spoke to him. A certain bhikkhu also asked, and answering him, the Blessed One said, "Suppose, bhikkhu," and so forth.[1618]

Abbuda hell: There is no separate hell called "Abbuda." Rather, a region of torment in the Avīci hell the duration of which is counted by abbudas is called the Abbuda hell. The same method applies to Nirabbuda hell and so forth. There, too, the calculation of years should be understood thus: [477] As a hundred 100,000s (10 million) make a koṭi, so a hundred 100,000 koṭis make a pakoṭi. A hundred 100,000 pakoṭis make a koṭi-pakoṭi; a hundred 100,000 koṭi-pakoṭis make a nahuta; a hundred 100,000 nahutas make a ninnahuta; a hundred 100,000 ninnahutas make one abbuda; and twenty of these make a nirabbuda. This method everywhere. But some say these obtain their names through the different kinds of lamentation and different kinds of punishments that occur in each, while others say these are just the cold hells.

Further: This is said with reference to the inclusion of verses illustrating specific matters related to the subject. For among the twenty verses stated here by way of the text-reading,[1619] only the one verse (**660**) that begins "For a hundred thousand" illustrates the matter stated [in the prose portion], while the rest illustrate different matters. The pair of verses at the end (**677–78**) are not in the text-reading decided in the Great Commentary;[1620] hence we said "twenty verses."

657. Here, **an axe**: harsh speech, which is like an axe in the sense that it cuts oneself. **Cuts**: slices off one's own root, a designation for one's wholesome roots.

658. Or blames a person deserving praise: One who criticizes a person who deserves praise about the highest matter,[1621] accusing him of having evil desires and so forth. **Collects**: accumulates. **Bad luck**: a crime.[1622]

659. This bad luck: this crime. **At dice**: gambling at the game of dice. **Of all including oneself**: of all one's wealth together with oneself. **To harbor hate**: His hatred is a worse stroke of bad luck; **against the holy ones**: against buddhas, paccekabuddhas, and a buddha's disciples, who are called "holy ones" because they have "gone well" and because they have "gone to a good state."[1623]

660. Why? Because **for a hundred thousand nirabbudas . . . against them**. Because for so many years [478] **the slanderer of noble ones goes to hell, having set evil speech and mind against them**. What is meant is that he is tortured there. This, in brief, is the life span in the Paduma hell.

661. Now, illustrating in another way the meaning of the words "This stroke of bad luck is itself much worse when one harbors hate against the holy ones," he says, "The speaker of slander," and so forth.[1624] Here, **the speaker of slander**: one who falsely slanders the noble. **To hell**: to the Paduma hell. **Having passed away, both are the same**: Having departed from here, both are the same because they are reborn in hell.

662. And what is more: "When one defames an innocent man."[1625] Here, someone is **innocent** through the absence of hatred; **pure** through the absence of the stain of ignorance; **without blemish** by not traveling among evil desires. The meaning can also be construed thus: one is pure because one is innocent, and without blemish because one is pure.

663. Having thus demonstrated that the bad luck of harboring hatred against the holy ones is worse, he now speaks fourteen verses called "verses of hurried cases."[1626] It is said that these were spoken by the Venerable Mahāmoggallāna as an exhortation to Kokālika while he was dying; but some ascribe them to Mahābrahmā. This summary, "One intent upon the quality of greed" and so forth, is stated in order to include them along with this discourse.

Here, in the first verse greed itself is called **the quality of greed** because it has been described as a quality or because it occurs numerous times;[1627] it is a designation for craving. **Stingy**: not understanding a statement, because of not accepting an exhortation even from the buddhas.[1628] **Miserly**: on account of the five kinds of miserliness. **Intent upon divisive speech**: speech uttered with a wish to divide the chief disciples [from the Buddha]. This is what is meant: "Friend Kokālika, one like you, intent upon the quality of greed, reviles others by means of speech; you who are faithless, mean, stingy, miserly, intent upon divisive speech, revile by speech another person who should not be reviled. Hence I speak to you [479] the next three verses that begin 'Foul-mouthed.'"

664. This is the meaning of terms that are not clear:[1629] **abortionist**: a killer of existence, a destroyer of growth.[1630] **Low born**: a low-born son of the Buddha.

665. You scatter dust: You throw the dust of the defilements upon yourself. **The abyss** (*papataṃ*): a deep pit. There is also the reading *papaṭaṃ*, with the same meaning, and the reading *papadaṃ*; the meaning is "the great hell."

666. It returns (*eti ha taṃ*): Here *ha* is an indeclinable. "It" (*taṃ*) is that wholesome or unwholesome kamma. Or alternatively, [we can read *ha taṃ* as] *hataṃ*, [equivalent to] "gone, practiced," meaning "accumulated." **Its owner**: One is the owner because one has created that kamma, for he **obtains it**. What is meant is that one's [kamma] does not perish. And since one obtains it, **the dullard, the evildoer, sees suffering in himself**.

667. Now, showing the suffering that the dullard sees, he says: "He arrives at the place of impalement, which has iron hooks" and so forth.[1631] Here, the meaning of the first couplet is as follows. It was with reference to the place of impalement with its iron hooks that the Blessed One said: "The wardens of hell, bhikkhus, then inflict on him the punishment called the fivefold transfixing."[1632] He arrives there, and when he has arrived, they make him lie down on the blazing copper ground, where he is struck in five places by the wardens of hell; [thus] **he arrives at** [the place], **which has sharp blades and iron stakes**, the latter being a designation for the hot iron spike.[1633] It was with reference to this that the Blessed One said: "They drive a hot iron stake through his hand."

The following couplet is stated with reference to the sequel. After he has been tortured there for many thousands of years, so that he may experience the remainder of the result, in stages he reaches the shore of the River of Caustic Water. When it is said, "They put a hot iron ball in his mouth; they sprinkle hot copper in his mouth," that is said with reference to this. Here, **iron** is copper; **like a ball**: in shape like a *beḷuva* fruit. And here, by mentioning "iron," copper [is meant]; [480] for an iron ball should be understood through the other [as copper].[1634] **As is appropriate**: as suits the kamma that was done.

668. In the following verses, **when speaking**, when saying, "Grab him, hit him," the wardens of hell **do not speak sweetly**, do not speak sweet words. **They do not hasten**: They do not run toward him with a pleasant expression on their faces; rather, they approach him in order to inflict misery and disaster. **They do not offer shelter**: They do not serve as shelter, as a cavern, as a resort; rather, they approach grabbing him and hitting him. **Those [hell beings] lie on coals spread out**: After they have climbed a mountain of coals, for many thousands of years they lie down on spread-out coals. **They enter**: being cast into the great hell, they are submerged in it; **a blazing mass of fire**: a fire blazing on all sides, or a fire blazing equally in all directions.[1635] The great hell is the one described as having four corners;[1636] for those standing a hundred yojanas all around, looking at it, the eyes split.

669. And capturing them in a net: Having wrapped them in an iron net as hunters catch a deer, **[the wardens] strike them**: This punishment is not mentioned in the Devadūta.[1637] **[The hell beings] come upon blinding gloom**: They go to the hell called "Wailing in Smoke" (*dhūmaroruva*), described as gloomy because of the thick darkness, blinding one with the darkness. Or it is said that when they smell the caustic smoke, their eyes split, and because of that they go blind. **Which is extended like a mist**: The meaning is, "And that blinding gloom is extended like a mist." There is also the reading *vikataṃ* ("altered, deformed," instead of *vitataṃ*).[1638] This punishment, too, is not mentioned in the Devadūta.

670. Then they enter the Copper Cauldron: Now this Copper Cauldron, which extends to the ends of the earth, 200,000 yojanas and four nahutas deep, is filled to the brim with molten copper. **They are boiled in them for a long time**: they are boiled in those cauldrons for a long time.[1639] [481] **Rising and sinking in the masses of fire**: Going up and sinking down in turns, they are cooked there in a swirl of foam. This should be understood in the way stated in the Devadūta (MN III 183,17–20, AN I 141,22–27).

671. In [copper] mixed with pus and blood: in the cauldron of copper mixed with pus and blood. **Afflicted**: oppressed; there is also the reading *kilijjati*, meaning "putrifies."[1640] **On making contact there**: on being touched by that pus and blood. This punishment, too, is not mentioned in the Devadūta.

672. In water that is the abode of worms: In the Devadūta this Copper Cauldron is also called "the Hell of Excrement." There needle-mouthed creatures bore through his outer skin right down until they devour his bone marrow. **There is not even a shore to which to go**: for there is no shore to which one can escape; **for the pots all around are all alike**: Since one is turned upside down in the upper portion of the cauldron, the pots everywhere are all completely alike, and therefore there is no shore to which one can escape.

673. The Wood of Sword Leaves should be understood in the way described in the Devadūta. From a distance this appears like a delightful mango grove. Driven by greed, the hell beings enter it. Then the leaves, stirred by the wind, fall down and cut their bodies and limbs. Hence it is said: **their bodies are cut to pieces**. When they enter it, their bodies are completely cut up. **Having grabbed the tongue with a hook, repeatedly slashing it, [the wardens] strike it**: Having run swiftly into the Wood of Sword Leaves, the wardens of hell use a hook to drag the tongues of the liars who have fallen down. Just as men stretch wet leather on the ground and beat it with planks, so they beat their tongues, split them with axes, [482] cut them slice by slice,[1641] and strike them. Each cut-off slice then revives again and again. There is also the reading *āracayāracayā*, meaning "having twirled around."[1642] This punishment, too, is not mentioned in the Devadūta.

674. Vetaraṇī: This river is described in the Devadūta as "a great river of caustic water" (MN III 185,27–30). It is said that it appears full of water, like the Ganges. Then the hell beings jump into it, thinking: "We will bathe, we will drink." **With its sharp blades, with razor blades**: It is said that in the upper and lower sections of that river, as well as on both shores, razors with sharp blades rise up as if set up in sequence. Hence it is said, "with its sharp blades, with razor blades." Wishing for water, **they approach** that river with its sharp blades, with razor blades. Having approached it, driven by their evil kamma, **the dullards fall into it**.

675. Flocks of ravens: flocks of black crows.[1643] **Very greedy** (*paṭigiddhā*):[1644] fully overcome by greed; some say [the word means] large vultures. **Hawks** (*kulala*): hawk birds; some say this is a name for armies. **Crows** (*vāyāsā*): non-black crows. This punishment, too, is not mentioned in the Devadūta. Those mentioned there that are not mentioned here should be understood to be the antecedents and sequels of these.

676. Now, having shown all this infernal life, he speaks the next verse, "Difficult," as an exhortation. This is its meaning: **Difficult is this life here**, in hell, with its various punishments, **which the evildoer sees. Therefore, in the remainder of one's life here**, as one's life continues on here in the world, **a person should be dutiful** by pursuing such wholesome deeds as going for refuge and so forth. And while doing one's task, one should act with persistence and should **not be heedless**, one should not fall into heedlessness even momentarily.

This [483] here is a cumulative explanation, but the remaining words [in the text] are easily understood, either because they have been previously explained or because they are already clear; therefore an explanation of each word has not been given.

11 Nālaka
(*Nālaka Sutta*)

What is the origin? It is said that [in a former life] Nālaka saw a disciple of the Blessed One Padumuttara who had undertaken the practice of munihood, and desiring such a state, from that time on he fulfilled the pāramīs for 100,000 eons, eventually becoming a hermit named Nālaka, a nephew of the rishi Asita. On the seventh day after the Buddha set in motion the wheel of the Dhamma, he asked the Blessed One about the practice of munihood in the two verses that begin "This has been known," and the Blessed One answered him in the way that begins with the words "I will describe munihood to you." But after the Buddha's parinibbāna, the Venerable Mahākassapa, making the compilation, asked the Venerable Ānanda about the practice of munihood, inquiring by whom and when Nālaka was instructed to ask the Blessed One. Wishing to clarify this, Ānanda spoke the twenty verses of the background story that begin "The rishi Asita." All this is called the Discourse with Nālaka.[1645]

679. The rishi Asita: He was a rishi who had gained such a name because his body was of a black color.[1646] **While passing the day**: in the place where he passed the day. **Joyful**: successful, flourishing; **ecstatic**: delighted. Or alternatively, **joyful**: exultant; **ecstatic**: happy.[1647] **Clean garments**: unsoiled garments; for the garments of the devas, produced by the wish-fulfilling tree, do not collect dust or dirt. **Carrying streamers**: having taken up celestial cloths, called "streamers" because they are like streamers in this world.

It is said that Asita had been the chaplain of Suddhodana's

father, the king Sīhahanu. Before Suddhodana was anointed, Asita was a teacher of crafts, but when the former was anointed, he became chaplain. When he came to attend upon the king in the evening and the morning, the king, as in his youth, did not show proper respects but merely saluted him with joined palms. For, it is said, this is the nature [484] of the Sakyan kings when they have been anointed. Disappointed because of this, the chaplain said: "Let me go forth, great king." The king, knowing his decision, entreated him: "In that case, teacher, you should live in my garden, so that I can see you often." Asita consented, and having gone forth as a hermit, he lived in the garden, where he was supported by the king. Having done the preliminary work on the kasiṇas, he attained the eight meditative attainments and the five superknowledges. From then on, after taking his meal in the king's court, he spent the rest of the day dwelling in the Himalayas or in one of the heavens such as that of the four divine kings.

One day, having gone to the Tāvatiṃsa heaven, he entered a jeweled palace and was sitting on a couch of celestial jewels enjoying the bliss of concentration. Having emerged in the evening, standing in the doorway of the palace, looking around here and there, he saw the devas headed by Sakka waving cloths along a road sixty yojanas in length, frolicking and reciting stanzas praising the excellent qualities of the bodhisatta. Therefore the Venerable Ānanda said: "The rishi Asita . . . proclaiming exuberant praise."[1648]

680. Having seen this, he asked: "For what reason . . . swirl them around?"

681. The gods were victorious: In order to elucidate this, this sequential discussion should be understood:[1649] It is said that [in a former life] Sakka had been a young man named Magha, the head of a group of thirty-three men residing in Macalagāma in the Magadha country. Having fulfilled seven vows,[1650] he was reborn in the Tāvatiṃsa heaven along with his retinue. Then the devas previously living there said, "Young devas have arrived on a visit; let's honor them," [485] and they presented them with celestial lotus flowers and offered them half the realm. Sakka, however, was not content with half a realm, so he convinced his own retinue [to rebel]. One day, when the previous devas were drunk, Sakka and his companions grabbed their feet and threw them into the abyss off Mount Sineru. The asura abode then came into being for them. It extended 100,000 yojanas at the bottom tier of Mount Sineru and was adorned with the trumpet-flower tree, a counterpart of the pāricchattaka coral tree.[1651]

Then, having recovered their mindfulness, not seeing the Tāvatiṃsa abode, they thought: "How wretched we are! We perished because we got drunk on liquor. Let us now not drink liquor, let us drink non-liquor. Now we are no longer gods (*surā*) but have become non-gods (*asurā*)." From then on they were known by the designation "asura."[1652] Declaring, "Now let's wage war against the devas," they scaled Sineru from all sides. Then Sakka, having gone out to fight the asuras, again threw them into the ocean, and at the four gates he set up a statue of himself. The asuras thought, "Sakka is indeed heedful; he stands there always keeping watch." They then went back to their city. Announcing their victory, the devas went around waving cloths and held a festival.

Since he could bring to mind forty eons in the past and future,[1653] Asita considered, "When in the past did these devas play in such a way?" Having seen the victory of the devas in their war with the asuras, he said:

> "Even when there was a battle with the asuras,
> when the gods were victorious and the asuras defeated,
> even then there was no such excitement."

At that time there was no such joyful excitement. So **what wonder have the gods seen that they rejoice?** Today, what wonder have the gods seen that they rejoice in such a way?

682. They whistle: They make a whistling sound with the mouth.[1654] They **sing** various songs; **play music** on 68,000 instruments. **I ask you**: Even though he was able to direct his attention to this matter and find out for himself, he asked from a desire to hear their statement. **Dwellers on Mount Meru's peak**: dwellers on the top of Sineru. For the abode of the asuras, extending for 10,000 yojanas, is on the bottom tier of

Mount Sineru. [486] The four great continents, accompanied by their 2,000 islands, are on the middle tier. The Tāvatiṃsa heaven, extending for 10,000 yojanas, is on the upper tier. Thus the devas are called "dwellers on the top of Mount Meru." **Dear sirs**: He addresses the devas. What is meant is "without suffering, without ailment."[1655]

683. In the third verse, spoken by the devas to tell him the reason, **the Bodhisatta** is an awakening being, a being able to reach perfect enlightenment. **Hence we are so delighted**: That is the reason we are delighted. The purport is: "Having attained buddhahood, he will teach the Dhamma in such a way that we and other groups of devas will attain the plane of trainees and of those beyond training.[1656] Human beings, too, who hear his teaching but cannot attain nibbāna will practice giving and other meritorious deeds and fill up the deva world." Now although the pair of terms, "delighted" and "jubilant," are indistinguishable in meaning, they are used to answer the pair of questions: "What wonder have you seen that the gods rejoice?" and "For what reason is the group of devas so jubilant?"[1657]

684. Now in the fourth verse, stated to tell him the reason they are delighted that the Bodhisatta has been born, by mentioning **beings** (*satta*) they include devas and humans, and by mentioning **creatures** (*pajā*) they include those in the remaining destinations. Thus by the two terms he shows the Bodhisatta's supremacy over the five destinations. For animals, too, such as lions, possess such excellent qualities as fearlessness; but he surpasses them in this respect as well. Therefore he is called "the best of creatures." But among devas and human beings there are four kinds of persons, those practicing for their own well-being and so forth;[1658] among these, he is **the foremost person**, one practicing for both kinds of well-being (his own and that of others), and he is **the chief bull of men** because among men he is similar to a chief bull. Hence, speaking praise of him, they utter these two terms.

685. That utterance: the explanation given by the devas.

686. Burnished . . . by one highly skilled: The purport is "burnished by a skilled gold worker, [487] by one who makes it radiant."

687. Lord of stars: The moon, which among the stars is like a chief bull. **Pure**: devoid of such defilements as clouds and so forth. **Already delighted**: filled with joy merely by hearing about him, **he gained abundant joy**—having seen him, he was again filled with joy.

688. This verse is stated to show the honor the devas constantly gave to the Bodhisatta. **A parasol**: a celestial white parasol; **with a thousand circles**: possessing a thousand circles made of bright gold. **Moved up and down**: They rose and fell fanning his body.

689. Named "Black Glory": He is being referred to by the names "Black" and "Glory." It is said that they also called him and addressed him as "Glorious Black One."[1659] Here the word "prince" should be stated as the subject, or one should fill in the reading. In a previous verse (**687**a), "having seen" (*disvā*) is stated with reference to the occasion when [the prince] had not yet come into arm's range [of Asita];[1660] but here [the object is the prince] when he has been brought into arm's range [of Asita] for the sake of receiving him. Therefore, the repetition of "having seen" is not a fault.[1661] Or the former occurrence refers to [Asita's] experience of joy at seeing him, as suggested by the statement at the end of the verse, "he gained abundant joy." This one refers to [Asita's] receiving him, as suggested by the statement at the end, "happy, [he] received him." And in the former case the connection is with the prince, while here the connection is also with the white parasol. [Thus what is intended here is:] *having seen* the prince looking like a gold nugget on a costly Gandhāran red blanket and the white parasol being held over his head—the parasol of the kind spoken of above (**688**) with the words "The gods held up a parasol." But some say this is stated with reference to a human parasol. For like the devas, human beings too approached the Great Man with parasols, chowries, peacock fans, and palm-leaf fans in their hands. In such a case, too, there is nothing [488] exceptional about this statement; therefore it is good just as it has been said. **Received him**: He received him in both hands. It is said that they brought the prince forward to make him venerate the rishi, but the prince's feet turned around and settled on the rishi's head.[1662] Having seen that wonder, too, the rishi received him, elated and happy.

690. The master of marks and hymns: One who had reached mastery in the marks and in the Vedas. **He is unsurpassed**: It is said that when the soles of the Great Being's feet were pointing toward him, Asita saw the wheels on them, and then, looking for the other marks, he saw he possessed them all. He then spoke thus, having known: "Surely he will be a buddha."

691. His own departure: his going to the formless realm by way of rebirth. **He became dismayed and shed bitter tears**: Having recollected his own imminent rebirth in the formless realm, he was upset, thinking: "Now I will not get to hear his teaching of the Dhamma." Dejected, overcome by grief, he wept and shed tears.

[Question:] "But if he inclined his mind toward the form realm, wouldn't he have arisen there? So there was no reason for him to weep." [Reply:] "It is not that he would not have arisen there, but because he lacked the skill, he did not know this method." [Question:] "Though such is the case, isn't it incorrect to say that dejection arose in him, since it would have been suppressed by his achievement of the meditative attainments?" [Reply:] "This is not so, because it was only suppressed. For defilements eradicated by the development of the path do not arise, but in those who gain the meditative attainments they arise through a strong condition." [Question:] "If the defilements arose, he would have lost the jhāna, so how could he be going to the formless realm?" [Reply:] "Because he could easily achieve it again. For when defilements have arisen, those who gain the meditative attainments do not fall into a strong transgression, but as soon as the surge of defilements has subsided, they easily attain distinction [in the meditative attainments] again. It is hard to know of them, 'These have lost their distinction,' and he was one like this." [489]

692. Not the least: Not even to a slight degree. He says with reference to his buddhahood, to be spoken of in the following verse.

693. The foremost enlightenment: omniscient knowledge. For that is called "enlightenment" because it is a complete awakening that occurs through the absence of cognitive inversion, and it is called "foremost" because it is the best among all kinds of knowledge, since it is without obstruction anywhere. **Will reach**: will attain. **One of supremely purified sight**: a seer of nibbāna; for that is "supremely purified" because it is exclusively purified.[1663]

694. In the interval: before his attainment of enlightenment. **Unequaled in fortitude**: unequaled in energy.

695. The holy man . . . enjoined him: Having known that his own remaining life span was short, and having known by his own power that his nephew—the student Nālaka, the son of his younger sister—had accumulated merit, apprehensive that on reaching maturity he might become heedless, **out of compassion for his own nephew** he went to his sister's house and asked: "Where is Nālaka?" She answered: "He's outside playing, Bhante." Having ordered her to bring him, that very moment he gave him the going forth of a hermit and enjoined him, admonished him, and instructed him.

696. How? "When you hear from another the word 'buddha' . . . lead the spiritual life under that Blessed One." *Dhammamaggaṃ* is the path to nibbāna, the supreme state. Or it is the *dhamma* that is *foremost*, that is, nibbāna together with the practice.[1664] **The spiritual life**: the ascetic's duty.

697. By such a one: by one settled in that. The purport is: "By one who, with the suppression of the defilements [490] and the gaining of concentration, on that occasion was one with suppressed defilements and a concentrated mind." **Whose vision of the future was supremely purified**: Because he had seen, "In the future Nālaka will see the supremely purified nibbāna in the presence of the Blessed One," the rishi is spoken of in this way as one whose vision of the future was supremely purified. **One with a store of accumulated merit**: one who had accumulated merit from the time of the Buddha Padumuttara. **Expecting**: awaiting; **dwelled**: having gone forth, lived in the manner of a hermit; **with faculties guarded**: who guarded his ear faculty. It is said that from that time on he did not submerge himself in water, thinking: "If I enter water my ear faculty might be damaged, and then I will be unable to hear the Dhamma."

698. Having heard the word: While Nālaka was dwelling in such a way, in stages the Blessed One attained enlightenment and set in motion the wheel of the Dhamma in Bārāṇasī. Nālaka heard of this from benevolent deities who came to him and reported the word **about the Conqueror setting in motion the excellent wheel** in such a way as this: "The wheel of the Dhamma has been set in motion by the Blessed One. Indeed, the Blessed One, the Perfectly Enlightened One, has arisen." While the deities were making a commotion about munihood for seven days,[1665] on the seventh day Nālaka went to Isipatana and saw the Blessed One, the chief of rishis, who was sitting on his excellent seat with this intention: "Nālaka will come and I will teach him the Dhamma." **He was pleased**: As soon as he saw him, Nālaka was pleased in mind.

Supreme munihood: the supreme knowledge; what is meant is the knowledge of the path. **Since [the time for] Asita's instruction had arrived**: Since the time for the instruction given by the rishi Asita had arrived. Hence this was the time indicated by Asita when he instructed Nālaka: "When he reveals[1666] the foremost Dhamma, go to him, question him, and lead the spiritual life under that Blessed One." The rest is clear. This, firstly, is the explanation of the background verses.

699.[1667] In the pair of verses on the questions, **This has been known**: This has been understood by me.[1668] **True to fact**: without distortion. What is the purport? "Asita, having known, 'This prince will attain the foremost enlightenment,' told me, [491] 'When[1669] you hear from another the word "buddha," [know] that one who attained enlightenment reveals the foremost Dhamma.' Today having seen the Blessed One in person, it is known by me that this statement of Asita is true to fact."[1670] **One who has gone beyond all phenomena**: In six aspects in the way explained in relation to the Discourse with Hemavata.[1671]

700. Entered the homeless life: one who has gone forth. **Seeking sustenance on alms round**: seeking sustenance by walking on undefiled alms round, as practiced by the noble ones. **Munihood** (*moneyya*): that pertaining to the munis. **The ultimate way**: the ultimate practice.[1672]

701. Being asked by him in such a way, the Blessed One explained the practice of munihood in the way that begins "I will describe munihood to you." **Hard to practice and hard to master**: What is meant is: "It is painful to do, and being done, it is painful to master, to endure." This is the purport here: "I would describe munihood to you if it were pleasant to practice and to master. But it is very hard to practice and hard to master. From the time one is a worldling onward, it must be practiced without giving rise to a defiled mind. For it is such that a single disciple of a single buddha practices it and masters it."

Thus, having aroused Nālaka's enthusiasm by showing him the difficulty in practicing and mastering munihood, wishing to say more to him, the Blessed One says: "Come, I will tell you about it. Brace yourself and be firm." **Come** (*handa*) is an indeclinable in the sense of resolve.[1673] **I will tell you about it**: I will tell you about munihood. **Brace yourself**: Fortify yourself with the support of energy, which is capable of doing what is hard to practice. **Be firm**: Be steadfast by not relaxing the exertion capable of withstanding that which is hard to master and endure. What is meant? [492] "Since you have accumulated the provision of merit, I have definitely made up my mind. I will explain that munihood to you, even though it is hard to do and hard to master. So brace yourself and be firm."

702. Thus, wishing to explain the observance of munihood, the supreme effacement,[1674] after instructing Nālaka to brace himself and be firm, the Blessed One first speaks a half-verse, "One should have the same attitude," showing the abandoning of defilements bound up with the village. Here, **the same attitude**: remaining the same, an identical attitude, without difference,[1675] **whether one is insulted or venerated**: in relation to insults and veneration. Now, to show the method by which one maintains the same attitude, he speaks the next half-verse, "guard against anger." This is its meaning: When insulted, **one should guard against anger in the mind**; when venerated, **one should keep calm, without being elated**. Even if one is venerated by the king, one should not become excited, thinking: "He is venerating me."

703. He now speaks a verse, "Diverse impressions high and low," showing the abandoning of defilements bound up with the forest. This is its meaning: **In a forest**, various objects come forth, **high and low** by way of the desirable and undesirable, and enter into range of the eye and so forth. These are like flames in the sense that they burn. Or just as, when a forest is burning, flames come forth "high and low" in their diversity—flames that may be accompanied by smoke and without smoke, blue, yellow, and red, large, small, and middling—so in the forest various objects come forth in their diversity—lions and tigers, humans and non-humans, the cries of various birds, flowers, fruits, shoots, and so forth—some frightening, some enticing, some annoying, some deluding. Hence he says: "Diverse impressions high and low come forth like flames in a forest."

Among the high and low objects coming forth are some women who walk on tour through parks and forests, or those who ordinarily walk in the forest such as firewood collectors and so forth. Having seen him in seclusion, these **women try to seduce a muni** by smiling, talking, weeping, or wearing loose attire. **Do not let them seduce you!**: "Act in such a way that they do not seduce you." [493]

704. Having thus shown him the way to conduct himself in the village and the forest, now, showing restraint by good behavior, the Blessed One speaks a pair of verses: "Refraining from sexual intercourse." **Having given up sensual pleasures fine and coarse**: having given up the remaining five objects of sensual pleasure, good and bad, additional to sexual intercourse; for by abandoning these, one's abstinence from sexual intercourse is well equipped; hence he said: "One should not kill or cause others to kill." This is the purport.

The terms "[one should] not be hostile," and so forth, are stated to show the excellence of abstaining from the destruction of life, which is stated here by the words "one should not kill or cause others to kill." This is a brief explanation: **one should not be hostile** toward living beings on the side of one's opponents, **nor should one be attached** to those on one's own side. This applies to all living beings, **both frail and firm,** that is, to those with craving and those without craving.[1676]

705. [Reflecting] "As I am, so are they" with respect to the desire to live and not to die, and the desire for happiness and aversion to suffering, one removes hostility toward them by understanding their similarity to oneself. In just the same way, one removes attachment toward oneself because of one's similarity to others, "**as they are, so am I**." Having thus discarded attachment and hostility with respect to both sides, **having taken oneself as the criterion** with respect to aversion toward death, **one should not kill** any beings, whether frail or firm, whether by one's own hand or other means, and **one should not cause others to kill** by command and so forth.[1677]

706. Thus, having briefly taught him the *good behavior of restraint by the Pātimokkha* under the heading of abstinence from sexual intercourse and abstinence from the destruction of life, and having shown *restraint of the sense faculties* by the words "having given up sensual pleasures," and so forth, now, by the words "having given up desire" and so forth, he speaks a verse showing *purification of livelihood*.[1678] Its meaning is as follows: It is craving that is called "desire," because it desires objects that have not been obtained; for "if one gets one thing, one wants a second; having gotten two, one wants a third; if one gets 100,000, one wants still more." And that craving is also greed, because it greedily gobbles up an object that has been obtained. **Having given up desire and greed for that to which the worldling is attached**: The worldling is attached, fastened, bound by desire and greed to robes and so forth. Having given up both [desire and greed] for such things, [494] not violating[1679] purification of livelihood for the sake of the requisites, **one with vision**—one with the eyes of knowledge—**should practice** this way of munihood. Practicing in such a way, **one may cross this inferno,** one may cross this craving for the requisites, the cause of wrong livelihood; it is designated "an inferno" in the sense that it is hard to fill. Or what is meant is that one may cross by this practice.

707. Having thus shown purification of livelihood under the heading of abandoning craving for the requisites, he now speaks the verse "He should not fill his belly," showing, under the heading of moderation in eating, good behavior in the use of the requisites and the practice in conformity with it up to the attainment of arahantship.[1680] Its meaning is as follows: Among the requisites, such as any kind of robes righteously acquired in accordance with the Dhamma, firstly, when eating food:

> While room remains for four or five lumps,
> one should instead drink water.
> For a bhikkhu resolute in striving,
> this is sufficient for living in comfort. (Th 983)

In the way stated thus, **not filling one's belly**: One should not have a swollen belly like a bellows filled with air, for because of torpor following a meal one might have to struggle with dullness and drowsiness. Instead of filling one's belly, one should be **moderate in food**, one should know the right amount of food, limiting one's food by reflection on the benefits [of moderation] and the faults [of gluttony] thus, "Neither for amusement," and so forth.[1681] Being moderate in food in this way, **one should be of few desires**, through the four kinds of fewness of desires, that is, in regard to the requisites, the austere practices, learning, and achievement; for a bhikkhu practicing the way of munihood must definitely be of few desires. Among these, (1) *fewness of desires in regard to the requisites* is being content through the three kinds of contentment with respect to each requisite.[1682] (2) *Fewness of desires in regard to the austere practices*—on the part of one who observes the austere practices—is not desiring: "May others know me as one who observes the austere practices!" (3) *Fewness of desires in regard to learning*—on the part of one who is highly learned—is not desiring: "May others know me as learned!" (4) *Fewness of desires in regard to achievement*—on the part of one who has reached achievement—is not desiring: "May others know me as one who has achieved a wholesome state!" like the Elder Majjhantika.[1683] And this should be understood to apply to those below the achievement of arahantship; for this practice is for the sake of arahantship.

One who in this way has few desires [495] should be **without longing**, having given up the longing of craving by the path of arahantship. Thus being without longing, **one is hungerless with respect to desire; desireless, one is quenched**. Beings are hungry with desire, insatiable like those afflicted by hunger and thirst. When one is desireless, and hungerless because of desirelessness, one is unafflicted and has attained supreme satisfaction. Thus because one is hungerless, one is quenched, one whose fevers of defilements have subsided. Thus here the construal should be understood in irregular word order.[1684]

708. Thus, having discussed the practice up to the attainment of arahantship, the Buddha now speaks a pair of verses, "Having wandered on alms round," discussing the practice of a bhikkhu who seeks the attainment of arahantship as his goal. He does so in terms of the austere practices and the duty regarding a dwelling place. And here, by **having wandered on alms round**, the austere practice of eating only food collected on alms round is indicated. But the superior type of almsfood ascetic also undertakes the practices of going on alms round without skipping any houses, eating only one meal a day, eating only from the alms bowl, and refusing food brought later, and also the practice of wearing rag-robes; therefore six factors of austere practice are actually stated by this.[1685] By **he should resort to the woods** the factor of dwelling in the forest is indicated. By **staying at the foot of a tree** the factor of dwelling at the foot of a tree is indicated, and by **should take his seat** the factor of the sitting practice.[1686] But because they are in conformity with this, the factors of dwelling in the open air, accepting any bed, and dwelling in a charnel ground are indicated in the appropriate place. Thus, with this verse, he explains to the Elder Nālaka the thirteen austere practices.

709. That steadfast one intent on jhāna: He is bent on, intent on, the jhānas by attaining a jhāna that has not yet arisen and by adverting to, entering, resolving upon, emerging from, and reviewing the arisen jhāna.[1687] **Steadfast**: possessed of resolution. **Should take delight in the woods**: He should find delight in the woods, that is, he should not delight in a lodging in a village. [496] **He should meditate at the foot of a tree, making himself fully content**: He should be intent not only on mundane jhāna but should meditate right there at the foot of that tree, making himself extremely content by attaining the world-transcending jhāna associated with the path of stream-entry and the higher stages; for the mind is extremely content only with the attainment of supreme consolation, the world-transcending jhāna, not with the other. Hence he says: "making himself fully content." Thus in this verse he discusses delight in a lodging in the woods and arahantship by way of intentness on jhāna.

710. Now, having heard this Dhamma teaching, the Elder Nālaka was extremely keen on fulfilling the practice by entering the woods and even going without food. But by going without food it isn't possible to practice the ascetic's duty; for if one undertakes this, life does not continue. Food must be sought for, but without giving rise to defilements. That is the method here. Therefore the Blessed One spoke the six verses, "Then, with the passing of the night," and so forth, in which he discussed the duty of the alms round, concluding with the attainment of arahantship. He did so to show him: "One should wander for alms even on successive days, but without giving rise to defilements."

Here, **then**—after the alms round and entering the woods referred to just above with the words "Having wandered on alms round, he should resort to the woods"—**with the passing of the night**—when the night has passed, on the next day—**he should approach the village:** Having done the duties that constitute good conduct, one should develop one's practice in seclusion until the time for the alms round; then one should go to the village, attending to the meditation subject in the way explained under "the duties of going and returning."[1688] **He should not welcome invitations**: A bhikkhu fulfilling the practice should not welcome invitations such as "Bhante, you should take your meal in our house," nor should he entertain such thoughts as "Is she giving or not? Is she giving good food or bad food?" He should not accept. But if they take his bowl on their own initiative, fill it, and return it to him, he may eat the food and do the ascetic's duty. The austere practice is not disrupted, but he should not enter the village for that purpose. **And offerings brought from the village**: If, when he has entered the village, they bring food even on a hundred platters, [497] again he should not welcome it. He should not accept even one portion of it but rather should exclusively wander on alms round in the order of the houses.

711. When the muni has come to the village, he should not behave rashly among families: When a muni practicing for the sake of munihood has gone to the village, he should not behave rashly among families, that is, he should not bond with laypeople in unfitting ways, by joining in their sorrows and so forth. **Having cut off talk aimed at getting food, he should not utter suggestive words**:[1689] Acting as if he were observing silence,[1690] one should not speak words aimed at obtaining food, words that involve insinuation, roundabout talk, hinting, or intimation.[1691] When one is ill, if one wishes, one may speak for the purpose of curing one's illness. Except for intimation regarding lodgings, one who is healthy should not say anything that involves insinuation, roundabout talk, or hinting for the sake of the other requisites.

712. This is the meaning of this verse: When one has entered the village for the sake of almsfood, even if one has gained just a little, one should reflect on it thus: "**I received something, that is good**." If one gets nothing, one should reflect: "**I received nothing, that is fine**."[1692] **In both situations**, gain and non-gain, **remaining impartial**, without alteration,[1693] **he returns to the tree itself**.[1694] As a man seeking fruit might approach a tree, and whether or not he gets fruit, he departs in a neutral state of mind, neither elated nor disheartened, in just this way, having approached families, whether or not one gets anything, one departs in a neutral state of mind.

713. Wandering with bowl in hand: The meaning of the verse is clear.

714. High and low: This is the connection of this verse [with the others]: Observing the duties regarding the alms round, one should not become complacent even tentatively but should fulfill the practice. For the essence of the Teaching is practice, and that is "high and low . . . experienced singly." This is the meaning: This practice of the path **taught by the Ascetic**—by the Buddha—is **high and low**, that is, divided into the superior and inferior. For [the path of] pleasant practice and quick superknowledge is high, while that of painful practice and sluggish superknowledge is low. The other two are high with respect to one factor and low with respect to one factor.[1695] Or the first alone is high and the other three are low. And by that practice, high or low, **they do not go in two ways to the far shore**. [498] The meaning is that they do not go to nibbāna twice by a single path. Why not? Because the defilements abandoned by a particular path do not have to be abandoned again. By this he shows [that one who has attained the path] is not subject to falling away. **[Yet] it is not experienced in a single way**: And that far shore is incapable of being experienced only once. Why not? Because there is no abandoning of all the defilements by a single path. By this he shows that there is no [attainment of] arahantship by just one path.[1696]

715. Now, showing the benefit of the practice, he speaks the verse "For one who has no diffusion." This is the meaning: For a bhikkhu practicing in such a way, there is **no diffusion**,[1697] no craving [called diffusion] because it spreads out by way of the 108 currents of craving; for it has been abandoned by that practice. By cutting off the stream of defilements, he **has cut off the stream**. By the abandoning of the wholesome and unwholesome, he **has abandoned what is to be done and not done**. For him **no fever [of defilements] exists**, not even the least, arisen from lust or hatred.

716. Now, having heard these verses, the Elder Nālaka thought: "If munihood consists in just this much, it is easily done, not hard, and it is possible to fulfill it without much trouble." Therefore, showing that munihood is indeed hard to do, the Blessed One said: "I will describe munihood for you." **One should treat it like the blade of a razor**: The blade of a razor is a simile for it. What is the purport? A bhikkhu practicing munihood should make use of the requisites by taking up the simile of a razor blade. As someone licking a razor blade smeared with honey would guard against cutting his tongue, so when making use of righteously acquired requisites, one should guard one's mind against the arising of defilements. For it is not easy to obtain the requisites in a pure manner and to use them blamelessly; thus the Blessed One speaks profusely about reliance on the requisites. **Having pressed one's palate with the tongue, exert control over one's belly**: Having pressed one's palate with the tongue, dispelling craving for tastes, not using the acquired requisites in a defiled way, one should exert control over one's belly.

717. One should not be sluggish in mind: [499] One should never be indolent by coming to a standstill in the development of wholesome qualities. **Nor should one ponder much**: One should not ponder much by thinking about one's relatives, country, the gods, and so forth. **Be unpolluted, unattached, with the spiritual life as one's support**:[1698] Be without defilements, unattached to any state of existence on account of craving or views, taking as one's support the spiritual life, the entire Teaching consisting in the threefold training.

718. In a solitary seat: in a secluded seat. And here, under the heading of a seat, all the postures are meant. What is meant is: "One should train in solitude in all the postures." **And in the exercise of an ascetic**: in pursuit of the development of the thirty-eight meditation objects in which ascetics are to exercise themselves,[1699] or in just a division of the thirty-eight objects that is the exercise of ascetics. This is the dative case; what is meant is "for the purpose of the exercise." And here, by "a solitary seat," what is meant is bodily seclusion, and by "the exercise of an ascetic," mental seclusion. **It is solitude that is called munihood**: This solitude by way of bodily and mental seclusion is what is called munihood. **If you will delight alone**: This line refers to the following verse; the connection is with the line "then you will light up the ten directions."[1700] **You will light up**: you will illuminate, that is, by developing this practice you will be renowned in all directions.

719. This is the meaning of the four lines that begin "Having heard the acclaim of the wise": **Having heard the acclaim of the wise**—the renown by which "you will light up the ten directions"—**of the meditators who have renounced sensual pleasures**, you should not become puffed up because of that but should **develop even more a sense of moral shame and faith**. Feeling moral shame because of that acclaim, you should arouse the faith, "This is the emancipating way," and develop the practice further. **My follower**: in such a case one is my disciple.

720. Understand this by way of rivers: When I say, "Develop even more a sense of moral shame and faith," I meant that one should not become puffed up. Understand this, too, through this example of rivers, and understand the opposite case through clefts and ravines. [500] How? **The creeks flow on noisily, but silently the great rivers flow**. For the creeks—all the small rivers running through clefts, ravines, and so forth—flow noisily, making a sound, as if they were puffed up. But the great rivers—the Ganges and the others—flow silently. Just so, one who becomes puffed up, thinking, "I am fulfilling munihood," is not my follower. My follower, having aroused a sense of moral shame and faith, is always humble.

721–22. And what is more: **What is empty . . . like a full lake**. Here the question may arise: "If the fool is like a half-full barrel because of his verbosity, and the wise man like a full lake because of his calmness, why does the Buddha-ascetic get so busily engaged in teaching the Dhamma and speak so much?" In connection with this, he speaks the verse beginning "When the Ascetic." This is the meaning: **When the Ascetic**—the Buddha—**speaks much, it is meaningful and beneficial**: it is possessed of meaning, possessed of Dhamma, connected with well-being and not with excitement.[1701] Moreover, **knowing, he teaches the Dhamma**:[1702] even if he teaches all day, he does so without mental proliferation, for all his verbal action is accompanied by knowledge.[1703] Teaching thus, **knowing, he speaks much**, saying in diverse ways: "This is good for you; that is good for you." It isn't the case that he just talks a lot.

723. The connection with the final verse is this: Thus the Buddha-ascetic, possessing the knowledge of omniscience, knowingly teaches the Dhamma, knowingly speaks much. **One self-controlled** who knows the Dhamma taught by him by means of the knowledge partaking of penetration, and **who, knowing, does not speak much: that muni is worthy of munihood; that muni has achieved munihood**. This is the meaning: One knowing that Dhamma who is self-controlled, guarded in mind, who knowingly does not speak much—who does not make any statement that does not lead to the welfare and happiness of beings—**that muni**, one who practices for the sake of munihood, **is worthy of munihood**, a designation for the practice of munihood. But not only is he worthy of it, but even more, it should be understood, **that muni has achieved munihood**, a designation for the knowledge of the path of arahantship.[1704] Thus the Buddha concludes the teaching with its culmination in arahantship.

Having heard this, the Elder Nālaka reduced his desires in regard to three things: seeing, hearing, and questioning. For at the conclusion of the teaching, pleased in mind, [501] he paid homage to the Blessed One and entered the forest. Never again did he have the longing: "May I see the Blessed One!" This was his *fewness of desires in regard to seeing*. So too, he never again had the longing: "May I again hear a discourse on the Dhamma!" This was his *fewness of desires with regard to hearing*. And he never again had the longing: "May I again ask about the practice of munihood!" This was his *fewness of desires with regard to questioning*.

Being of few desires, he entered the foothills of the mountains. Thereafter he did not spend two days in the same woodland grove; he did not sit for two days at the foot of the same tree; and he did not enter the same village for alms on two days. Wandering in this way from woods to woods, from tree to tree, and from village to village, following the appropriate practice, he was established in the foremost fruit.

But a bhikkhu who fulfills the practice of munihood to the highest degree lives for only seven more months; one who fulfills it to a middling degree lives for seven more years; and one who fulfills it to a minor degree lives for sixteen more years. Nālaka fulfilled it to the highest degree; therefore, having lived on for seven months, when he knew that his vital formations were coming to an end, he bathed, put on his under-robe, tied his belt, and covered himself with his double-thick outer robe. Then, facing in the direction of the Buddha, he paid homage with a prostration, extended his joined palms in reverence, and while leaning against Hiṅgula Mountain, he attained final nibbāna through the nibbāna element without residue remaining. Having known that he attained final nibbāna, the Blessed One went there with the Sangha of bhikkhus, had the body cremated, had the relics collected, and had a cetiya built, and then he left.[1705]

12 Contemplation of Dyads
(*Dvayatānupassanā Sutta*)

What is the origin? The origin of this discourse was his own inclination. For the Blessed One taught this discourse of his own inclination. This is a brief statement, but the detailed account will be shown in the explanation of its meaning. [502]

Here, **thus have I heard** and so forth should be understood in the way already explained. **In the Eastern Park**: in the park to the east of the city of Sāvatthī. **In Migāramātā's mansion**: Here, the female lay follower Visākhā was called Migāramātā ("Migāra's mother") because she was appointed to the position of a mother by her own father-in-law, the financier Migāra.[1706] Having given away the "great creeper ornament" (*mahālatāpilandhana*),[1707] worth nine koṭis of wealth, Migāramātā built the mansion, a peaked house with a thousand rooms, five hundred upstairs and five hundred downstairs. Thus it was called "Migāramātā's mansion." [He was dwelling] in that mansion of Migāramātā.

Now on that occasion . . . the Blessed One: an occasion when the Blessed One was based at Sāvatthī, dwelling in the Eastern Park in Migāramātā's mansion. **The uposatha day of the fifteenth**: by mentioning the uposatha day, this is a statement denying that it fell on the remaining uposatha days.[1708] **The full-moon night**: It was the fifteenth day by the counting of days; full because of its fullness, since it excelled in the qualities of the night, being devoid of such defilements as clouds and so forth; and a full-moon night because of the fullness of the moon. **Seated in the open**: He was sitting in his excellent seat that had been prepared for him in an open area outside in the courtyard of Migāramātā's jeweled mansion.

Having surveyed the completely silent Sangha of bhikkhus: He surveyed the completely silent Sangha of bhikkhus, which was silent wherever he looked—silent by way of speech and again silent by way of body. He surveyed in each direction the completely silent Sangha of bhikkhus sitting around him, consisting of many thousands of bhikkhus, for the purpose of deciding on a suitable Dhamma teaching thus: "Here there are this many stream-enterers, this many once-returners, this many non-returners, this many good worldlings who have undertaken insight. What kind of Dhamma teaching would be suitable for this Sangha of bhikkhus?" [503]

Bhikkhus, those teachings that are wholesome: the thirty-seven aids to enlightenment,[1709] or the textual teachings that elucidate them, which are wholesome in the sense of being healthy, blameless, having desirable fruits, and originating from wholesomeness.[1710] **Noble, emancipating, leading to enlightenment**: noble in the sense that they should be approached; emancipating in the sense that they emancipate from the world; and leading to enlightenment in the sense that they lead to arahantship, which is designated enlightenment. **What is your aim in listening to those teachings?**: What is your aim, your reason, your purpose in listening to them. What is meant is: "Why do you listen to those teachings?"[1711]

For the accurate knowledge of things arranged in dyads:[1712] Accurate knowledge is undistorted knowledge. What is meant? Accurate knowledge is a designation for insight into things defined as twofold by division into the mundane and the world-transcending, and so forth.[1713] It is just for the purpose of this, not more than this. For this much is achieved by listening. Beyond this is the achievement of distinction by development. **And what would one call a dyad?** The purport is: "If, bhikkhus, you should think, 'And what, Bhante, would you call dyad-ness?'" But the term meaning is: "And what would you call dyad-ship?"[1714]

[1. The four noble truths]

Now the Blessed One, showing a dyad, begins by saying: **This is suffering**, etc. Here, in regard to the teachings of the four truths taken as a dyad, **this is one contemplation** occurs by seeing one segment, the mundane one, or suffering together with its cause, thus: "This is suffering, this is the origin of suffering." The other, the **second contemplation**, occurs by seeing the second segment, the world-transcending one, or cessation together with the means to its attainment. And here, the first occurs by way of the third and fourth purifications, the second by way of the fifth purification.[1715] **Dwells thus correctly contemplating a dyad**: in the way stated, he correctly contemplates things arranged in dyads, **heedful** through non-separation from mindfulness, **ardent** through bodily and mental energy, and **resolute** through unconcern about body and life. [504] **Final knowledge in this very life**: arahantship in this very existence. **Or, if there is a residue remaining, the state of non-returning**: The remainder of the aggregates to be acquired by way of renewed existence is called "the residue remaining."[1716] He shows that if this exists, the state of non-returning is to be expected. Here, although the lower fruits are also obtained by one who contemplates dyads, the Buddha speaks thus to arouse enthusiasm for the higher fruits.

This is what the Blessed One said: a statement by the compilers. [**Having said this**:] The [first] **this** (*idaṃ*) indicates the statement beginning "Those teachings that are wholesome" and so forth. The [second] **this** (*etaṃ*) indicates the auxiliary verses that are to be stated, beginning thus: "Those who do not understand suffering." And these verses, by elucidating the four truths, illustrate the point that was stated [in the prose portion]. Though such is the case, they are stated for the sake of those coming later who prefer verses and for those with distracted minds who, failing to grasp what was stated previously,[1717] would wish [for verses], thinking: "Now it would be good if he would speak them." Or else they convey a different point; that is, having shown those who do not practice insight and those who practice insight, the verses show in each case, respectively, the continuation of the round of saṃsāra and the ending of the round; therefore, the verses are stated for the purpose of conveying a different point.[1718] The same method applies to the statements in the verses that follow.

724. Who do not know where: he shows nibbāna; for **suffering completely ceases** in nibbāna, ceases in all modes, ceases along with its cause, and ceases **without remainder**. **The path**: the eightfold path.

725–27. They are destitute of liberation of mind and also of liberation by wisdom: Here, *liberation of mind* should be understood as the concentration of the fruit of arahantship, obtained with the fading away of lust; *liberation by wisdom* should be understood as the wisdom of the fruit of arahantship, obtained with the fading away of ignorance. Or *liberation of mind* through the fading away of lust is the fruit of arahantship attained by one of craving temperament, who suppresses the defilements through the power of jhāna that has reached absorption; *liberation by wisdom* through the fading away of ignorance is the fruit of arahantship attained by one of speculative temperament who gains mere access to the jhāna and then practices insight. Or *liberation of mind* is the fruit of the non-returner, achieved through the fading away of lust, with specific reference to sensual lust; *liberation by wisdom* is the fruit of arahantship, achieved through the fading away of ignorance in all its modes. **Making an end**: making an end to the suffering of the round. [505] **They fare on to birth and old age**: They have fared on *to* birth and old age or they have fared on *through* birth and old age; it should be understood that they are not freed from birth and old age. The rest here, starting from the beginning, is already clear.

At the end of the verses, sixty bhikkhus, having learned this teaching, developed insight and attained arahantship even while sitting in the same seats. And as here, so with respect to all the other sections.

[2. Acquisition]

Then, to show contemplation of dyads in various ways, the Blessed One said: **Could there be proper contemplation of dyads in some other way? Conditioned by acquisitions**: Conditioned by kamma connected with the influxes, for kamma connected with the influxes is here intended by acquisition.[1719] **With the remainderless fading away and cessation**: With the cessation through remainderless fading away, or[1720] through the cessation that consists in the remainderless fading away.

728. Based on acquisition: conditioned by kamma. **Contemplating it as the genesis and origin of suffering**: contemplating, "Acquisition is the genesis and cause of the suffering of the round."[1721] The rest here is clear. Thus this section, too, having elucidated the four truths, is stated with its culmination in arahantship. And as here, so with all sections.

[3. Ignorance]

Conditioned by ignorance: Conditioned by the ignorance that underlies the accumulation of kamma leading to existence.[1722] But everywhere **suffering** is just the suffering of the round.

729. In the saṃsāra of birth and death: in birth, the production of the aggregates; in death, the breakup of the aggregates; and in saṃsāra, the succession of the aggregates.[1723] **With its becoming thus, becoming otherwise**: the human state and any state of existence other than this.[1724] **Journey**: the state of a condition.[1725]

730. But those beings who have gained clear knowledge: those beings with influxes destroyed who have proceeded by piercing the defilements with the clear knowledge of the path of arahantship.[1726]

[4. Volitional activities]

Conditioned by volitional activities: conditioned by meritorious, demeritorious, and imperturbable volitional activities.[1727]

732. When one has known this danger: When one has known this danger, that **suffering is conditioned by volitional activities. By the stilling of all volitional activities:** by the stilling of all the aforementioned kinds of volitional activities by path knowledge, because of its capacity to yield the fruit when they are destroyed. **By the stopping of perceptions:** by the stopping of sensual perceptions and so forth by the path itself. **When one has known this as it really is:** [506] when one has accurately known this destruction of suffering.

733. Having correctly known this: having known the conditioned to be impermanent and so forth.[1728] **The yoke of Māra**: the round with its three planes. The rest is clear.

[5. Consciousness]

Conditioned by consciousness: Conditioned by volitionally active consciousness coarisen with kamma.[1729]

735. Hungerless: without craving; **has attained nibbāna**: has attained nibbāna by the extinguishing of defilements.

[6. Contact]

Conditioned by contact: conditioned by contact associated with volitionally active consciousness. Thus here contact is stated without mentioning name-and-form and the six sense bases, the next terms to be stated in sequence;[1730] because those are combined with form, they are not associated with kamma,[1731] and this suffering of the round may originate either from kamma or from [mental] phenomena associated with kamma.

736–37. Flowing along with the stream of existence: flowing along with craving. **Fully understood**: having fully understood it by the three kinds of full understanding. **Having known it**: having known it by the wisdom of the path of arahantship. **Delight in peace**: delight in nibbāna by way of fruition attainment. **By breaking through contact**: by cessation of contact.

[7. Feeling]

Conditioned by feeling: conditioned by feeling associated with kamma.

739. Having known, "This is suffering": having known all feeling to be a cause of suffering; or having known it to be suffering by way of the suffering due to change, persistence, and non-knowledge.[1732] **Of a false nature**: subject to perishing;[1733] **disintegrating**: subject to being worn away by old age and death. **Having touched and touched them**: having contacted and contacted them with the knowledge of arising and vanishing.[1734] **Seeing their vanishing**: seeing their dissolution in the end. **One understands them thus**: One understands those feelings thus, or one understands their nature of suffering.[1735] **Through the destruction of feelings**: by the knowledge of the path following this, through the destruction of the feelings associated with kamma.

[8. Craving]

Conditioned by craving: Conditioned by the craving that underlies the accumulation of kamma. [507]

741. Having known this danger, "Craving is the origin of suffering": having known this danger in craving, that it is the origin of suffering.

[9. Clinging]

Conditioned by clinging: conditioned by the clinging that underlies the accumulation of kamma.

742. Existence: resultant-existence, the manifestation of the aggregates. **An existent being undergoes suffering**: a being that has arisen undergoes the suffering of the round. **For one who is born there is death**: Where fools think, "A being undergoes happiness," he says, "For one who is born there is death," showing: "There too there is just suffering."[1736]

743. In the second verse the construal is this: **Having correctly understood** by way of impermanence and so forth, **having directly known the destruction of birth**—nibbāna—**through the destruction of clinging, the wise do not come back to renewed existence.**

[10. Instigation]

Conditioned by instigation: conditioned by energy associated with kamma.[1737]

745. One is liberated in non-instigation: liberated in nibbāna, which is non-instigation.[1738]

[11. Nutriment]

Conditioned by nutriment: conditioned by nutriment associated with kamma. Another method: Beings are fourfold as those who fare on to form, those who fare on to feeling, those who fare on to perception, and those who fare on to volitional activities.[1739] Here, the beings in the eleven planes of the desire realm are "those who fare on to form," for they make use of edible food as their nutriment. The beings in the form realm, except the nonpercipient beings, are "those who fare on to feeling," for they make use of contact as their nutriment. The beings in the three lower planes of the formless realm are "those who fare on to perception," for they make use of the nutriment of mental volition produced by perception. The beings at the peak of existence are "those who fare on to volitional activities," for they make use of the nutriment of consciousness produced by volitional activities. Thus in this way, too, it should be understood: **Whatever suffering originates is all conditioned by nutriment**.

749. The state of health: nibbāna. **Using with reflection**: using the four requisites after reflecting on them. Or, having comprehended the world as five aggregates, twelve sense bases, and eighteen elements, using with the knowledge "impermanent, suffering, non-self." **Firm in the Dhamma**: firm in the Dhamma of the four truths; **cannot be designated**:[1740] He cannot be designated as "a deva" or "a human being" and so forth. [508]

[12. Agitation]

Conditioned by agitation: conditioned by agitation that underlies the accumulation of kamma, of any kind among the types of agitation due to craving, conceit, views, kamma, and defilements.[1741]

751. Having given up impulsion:[1742] having relinquished craving. **Having put a stop to volitional activities**: having brought to cessation kamma and volitional activities associated with kamma.

[13. Dependency]

For one who is dependent there is quaking: for one who is dependent on the aggregates through craving, views, and conceit there is the quaking of fear, as there was for the devas in the Discourse on the Lion.[1743]

[14. Form and formless states]

States of form: the form-sphere planes of existence or the form-sphere meditative attainments. **Formless states**: the formless-sphere planes of existence or the formless meditative attainments. **Cessation**: nibbāna.

755. Have abandoned death: They proceed having abandoned the three kinds of death: death as dying, death as the defilements, and death as the young deva (Māra).

[15. Truth and falsity]

That which is said with reference to name-and-form; for that **is regarded as**—seen as, perceived by the world as—**"This is true"**: as stable, beautiful, happiness, and self. **The noble ones have seen it**[1744] **well with correct wisdom thus: "This is false."** Though this is grasped as stable and so forth, it is false, not as it seems. But the second **that which** is said with reference to nibbāna. For that is regarded by the world thus, "**This is false**": there is nothing here, because of the absence of form, feeling, and so forth. **The noble ones have seen it well with correct wisdom thus: "This is true"**: The noble ones have seen this as true in the supreme sense, because it never departs from its purity, the absence of defilements; nor from happiness, because it is the antidote to suffering; nor from permanence, because it is absolute peace.[1745]

756. Conceiving a self in what is non-self: conceiving a self in name-and-form, which is non-self. **They conceive: "This is**

true": They conceive this name-and-form as "true" by taking it as stable and so forth.

757. In whatever way they conceive it: Whatever form or feeling they conceive as "My form, my feeling," and so forth; **it turns out otherwise**, that name-and-form turns out otherwise than the way it is conceived.[1746] For what reason? **That indeed is its falsity:** Since it is [509] false with respect to the way in which it is conceived, therefore it is otherwise. But why is it false? For the transient is of a false nature: because what is transient, fleeting in its presence, is of a false nature, a perishable nature,[1747] and name-and-form is just like that.

758. The breakthrough to truth: the comprehension of truth.

[16. Happiness and suffering]

That which: this is said with reference to the six desirable objects. For that **is regarded** by the world **as "This is happiness,"** as moths regard a lamp, fish regard bait, monkeys regard paste, and so forth. **The noble ones have seen it well with correct wisdom thus: "This is suffering":** in the way stated thus: "Sensual pleasures are colorful, sweet, delightful, but in their diversity they agitate the mind" (**50**ab). But the second **that which** is said with reference to nibbāna, which is regarded by the world thus, "**This is suffering,**" because of the absence of sensual pleasures. **The noble ones have seen it well with correct wisdom thus: "This is happiness"**: The noble ones [have seen this] as happiness in the supreme sense.

761. The noble ones have seen as happiness the ceasing of the personal entity: The noble ones have seen as happiness the cessation of the five aggregates, that is, nibbāna. **Running counter**: this insight **of those who see**, of the wise, goes against the grain.

762. What others: this is said with reference to sensual objects. The second **what others** refers to nibbāna. **Behold**: He addresses the listener. **Dhamma**: the nibbāna-dhamma. **Here the foolish are bewildered**: For what reason are they bewildered?

763. There is gloom for those who are blocked, [510] **darkness for those who do not see**: For those fools who are blocked, enveloped, by ignorance, there is gloom causing blindness, because of which they are unable to see the nibbāna-dhamma. **But for the good it is opened up like light for those who see**: For the good persons nibbāna is opened with the vision of wisdom, as light is for those who see. **The brutes unskilled in the Dhamma do not understand it even when close**: Nibbāna is close because it can be achieved immediately after delimiting the mere skin pentad in one's own body,[1748] or because it is simply the cessation of one's own aggregates. People who have become brutes—or those who are unskilled in the Dhamma of what is the path and not the path, or in the Dhamma of the truths[1749]—do not understand it even when it exists so close.

764. In every case, **it is not easily understood by those afflicted by lust for existence.** Here, **those deeply mired in Māra's realm:**[1750] those mired in the round with its three planes.

765. This is its meaning: "Apart from the noble ones, who else is able to understand this nibbāna-state? When it is completely known by the fourth noble path, having immediately become free from the influxes, they attain nibbāna through the extinction of the defilements; or, having completely known it, having become free from the influxes, in the end they attain nibbāna through the nibbāna element without residue remaining." Thus he concludes the discourse with its culmination in arahantship.

Thus while these sixteen expositions were being given, each time the minds of sixty bhikkhus were liberated from the influxes through non-clinging, for a total of 960. Each of the sixteen expositions can be subdivided into four, so that sixty-four [aspects of] the truths are taught here in different ways as determined by the people to be guided.

IV The Chapter of Octads
(*Aṭṭhakavagga*)

1 Sensual Pleasures
(*Kāma Sutta*)

[511] What is the origin?[1751] It is said that when the Blessed One was dwelling at Sāvatthī, a certain brahmin, intending to sow barley, was plowing a field between Jeta's Grove at Sāvatthī and the bank of the Aciravatī River. As the Blessed One was entering for alms, accompanied by the Sangha of bhikkhus, he noticed the brahmin and, directing his attention to him, he saw that his barley would perish. Again, directing his attention to the excellence of his supporting conditions, he saw that he had the supporting condition for the fruit of stream-entry. Asking himself, "When might he attain it?" he saw: "After his crops have perished, when he is overcome by sorrow and has heard a teaching on the Dhamma." Then he reflected: "If I approach the brahmin at that time, he will not think of listening to my exhortation. For brahmins have various preferences. From now on, let me benefit him. Thus he will become favorably disposed toward me and will listen to my exhortation."

The Blessed One approached the brahmin and asked him: "What are you doing, brahmin?" The brahmin thought: "The ascetic Gotama, who is from a high family, acts cordially toward me." He was immediately pleased with the Blessed One and replied: "I am plowing my field, Master Gotama, so that I can sow barley."

Then the Elder Sāriputta reflected: "The Blessed One has been cordial toward the brahmin. Now tathāgatas do not act in such a way without a cause or reason. Let me too be cordial toward him." He then approached the brahmin and treated him cordially in the same way. The Elder Mahāmoggallāna and the other eighty great disciples all did the same, and the brahmin was very pleased.

When the crops were thriving, one day, after finishing his meal, on the way back from Sāvatthī to Jeta's Grove, the Blessed One left the road, went up to the brahmin, and said to him: "Your barley field looks good, brahmin." – "It is indeed good, Master Gotama. If it flourishes, I will share a portion with you." [512]

After four months had passed, the barley ripened. Then, while the brahmin was eagerly thinking, "I will cut it down today or tomorrow," a great rain cloud gathered and poured down rain all night. The Aciravatī River overflowed and inundated the barley. The brahmin was distressed throughout the night, and in the morning, when he went to the bank of the river and saw that his crop was destroyed, he was overcome by sorrow, thinking: "I'm ruined. How will I live now?"

As the night was coming to an end, the Blessed One surveyed the world with the buddha eye and knew that the time had come that day for the brahmin to hear a teaching of the Dhamma. Having entered Sāvatthī on alms round, he stood by the door to the brahmin's house. When the brahmin saw the Blessed One he thought: "The ascetic Gotama has come to console me in my sorrow." He prepared a seat, took the Blessed One's bowl, and invited him to sit down.

Though he knew the reason, the Blessed One asked the brahmin: "Brahmin, are you in a bad mood?" – "Yes, Master Gotama. My entire barley field was flooded." The Blessed One said: "One should not become dejected at a time of loss or jubilant at a time of success. For sensual pleasures sometimes succeed and sometimes fail." Having known what was suitable for the brahmin, he spoke this discourse as a Dhamma teaching.

We will explain in brief merely the connection of the terms and meanings.[1752] A detailed account should be understood in the way stated in the Niddesa. And as in this discourse, so in all the discourses to follow.

766. Sensual pleasure: objects of sensual pleasure, a designation for agreeable forms and so forth pertaining to the three planes.[1753] **Desires**: wishes for. **If that succeeds for him**: While that person is desiring it, that object, a designation for sensual pleasure, succeeds for him. What is meant is that he obtains it. **Surely he is elated in mind**: He is definitely content in mind.

Nidd I 1–2. Sensual pleasure: In brief, there are two kinds of sensual pleasures: sensual objects and sensual defilements. What are *sensual objects*? Agreeable forms, sounds, odors, tastes, and tactile objects; bedsheets, coverings, male and female slaves, goats and rams, fowl and pigs, elephants, cattle, horses, and mares; fields, land, bullion, gold, villages, towns, cities, realms, countries, treasuries, storehouses; and any enticing object—these are sensual objects. Further, sensual pleasures may be past, future, or present; internal, external, or both internal and external; inferior, middling, or superior; infernal sensual pleasures, human sensual pleasures, and celestial sensual pleasures; sensual pleasures presently at hand, mentally created sensual pleasures, not mentally created sensual pleasures, sensual pleasures created by others;[1754] possessed sensual pleasures and unpossessed sensual pleasures; owned sensual pleasures and unowned sensual pleasures. Even all phenomena pertaining to the desire sphere, the form sphere, and the formless sphere that are the basis of craving, that are objects of craving, that are sensual pleasures in the sense of being desired, in the sense of being enticing, in the sense of being intoxicating, are called sensual objects.

What are *sensual defilements*? Sensuality as desire, as lust, as desire and lust, as intention, as lustful intention; sensual desire for sensual pleasures, sensual lust, sensual delight, sensual craving, sensual affection, sensual passion, sensual infatuation, sensual attachment, the flood of sensuality, the bond of sensuality, clinging to sensual pleasures, the hindrance of sensual desire: these are called sensual defilements.

If that succeeds for him: **That** refers to sensual objects, agreeable forms, sounds, odors, tastes, and tactile objects. **Succeeds**: prospers, succeeds; he gains them, obtains them, acquires them, finds them. **Elated in mind**: joyful, thrilled, exhilarated, pleased, jubilant, overjoyed with the elation, joy, gladness, glee, happiness, exhilaration of mind connected with the five strands of sensual pleasure.

767. Full of sensual desire: While that person is wishing for sensual pleasures or being carried off by sensual desire; [513]

aroused by desire: aroused by craving. **If those sensual pleasures decline, he is afflicted as if pierced by a dart**: He is pained as if pierced by a dart made of iron or some other substance.

Nidd I 3–4. Full of sensual desire (*kāmayānassa*): Wishing for sensual pleasures, enjoying them, longing for them, yearning for them, hankering for them. Or alternatively, one goes by way of sensual craving (*kāmataṇhāya yāyati*), is led by it, is swept away by it, is carried off by it, as a person goes by way of an elephant vehicle, a horse vehicle, a bullock vehicle, a goat vehicle, a ram vehicle, a camel vehicle, or a donkey vehicle.[1755] **If those sensual pleasures decline**: Either those sensual pleasures decline, or one declines from sensual pleasures. How do *those sensual pleasures decline*? While one is living, kings take one's possessions, or thieves take them, or fire burns them, or a flood sweeps them away, or undear relatives take them, or one loses what one has stored up, or strenuous labors fail, or a wastrel arises in the family who dissipates and squanders those possessions; and impermanence is the eighth.[1756] Thus those sensual pleasures dwindle and decline. And how does *one decline from sensual pleasures*? While those possessions endure, one passes away, dies, perishes. Thus one dwindles and declines, expires and falls, disappears and perishes in relation to those sensual pleasures. **He is afflicted as if pierced by a dart**: As one pierced by an iron dart is afflicted, disturbed, wounded, pained, dejected, so when objects of sensual pleasure change and alter there arise sorrow, lamentation, pain, dejection, and anguish. Pierced by the dart of sensual desire and the dart of sorrow, he is afflicted, disturbed, wounded, pained, dejected.

768. One who avoids sensual pleasures: either by suppressing desire and lust for them or by eradicating them. It is craving that is designated **attachment to the world**, because it persists having spread out over the entire world.[1757] Having become **mindful**, one **overcomes** it.

Nidd I 5–6. One avoids sensual pleasures in two ways, by suppression or eradication.[1758] And how does one avoid them *by suppression*? Seeing, "Sensual pleasures are like a chain of bones, giving little gratification; like a piece of meat, because they are shared in common with many; like a grass torch, because they leave a hot trail; like a charcoal pit, because of scorching badly; like a dream, because of their transience; like borrowed goods, because they are temporary; like fruits on a tree, because of breaking off and damaging; like a butcher's knife and chopping block, because of cutting up; like a sword stake, because of piercing; like a snake's head, because of their danger; like a mass of flame, because of causing torment," one avoids sensual pleasures by suppression.[1759] Developing recollection of the Buddha, recollection of the Dhamma, recollection of the Sangha, recollection of good behavior, recollection of generosity, recollection of the deities, mindfulness of breathing, mindfulness of death, mindfulness directed to the body, the recollection of peace, one avoids sensual pleasures by suppression. Developing the first jhāna . . . the second jhāna . . . the third jhāna . . . the fourth jhāna . . . the base of the boundlessness of space . . . the base of the boundlessness of consciousness . . . the base of nothingness . . . the attainment of the base of neither-perception-nor-nonperception, one avoids sensual pleasures by suppression.[1760]

How does one avoid sensual pleasures *by eradication*? Developing the path of stream-entry, one avoids them by eradicating the sensual pleasures that lead to the realm of misery; developing the path of the once-returner, one avoids them by eradicating coarse sensual pleasures; developing the path of the non-returner, one avoids them by eradicating residual sensual pleasures; developing the path of arahantship, one avoids them by eradicating them entirely and in all respects, without any remainder. Thus one avoids sensual pleasures by eradication.

Nidd I 7. Attachment to the world: It is craving that is called attachment, that is, lust, passion, compliance, attraction, delight, delight and lust, passion of the mind, desire, infatuation, adhesion, greed, greediness, the tie, the mire, impulse, illusion, the maker, the generator, the seamstress, the ensnarer, the torrent, attachment, the thread, the extent, the accumulator, the partner, wish, the conduit to existence, the woods, the jungle, the link, affection, concern, the binder . . . sensual craving, craving for existence, craving for nonexistence; craving for form, craving for the formless, craving for cessation; craving for forms, for sounds, for odors, for tastes, for tactile objects, for mental phenomena; the flood, the yoke, the knot, clinging, obstruction, a hindrance, a covering, a binding, a defilement, a latent tendency, an obsession, a creeper, avarice, the root of suffering, the basis of suffering, the origination of suffering; Māra's snare, Māra's bait, Māra's domain, the river of craving, the net of craving, the leash of craving, the ocean of craving, covetousness, greed as an unwholesome root. **The world**: the world of the plane of misery, the human world, the deva world; the world of the aggregates, the world of the elements, the world of the sense bases. **Being mindful**: One is mindful in four ways: by developing the establishment of mindfulness that consists in contemplation of the body . . . contemplation of feelings . . . contemplation of mind . . . contemplation of phenomena. One is mindful in another four ways: by avoiding unmindfulness, by doing the things that are to be done to gain mindfulness, by destruction of the things that are obstacles to mindfulness, and by not forgetting the things that are a basis for mindfulness. One is mindful in another four ways: by having mindfulness, by mastery over mindfulness, by proficiency in mindfulness, by not declining in mindfulness. One is mindful through recollection of the Buddha, through recollection of the Dhamma, through recollection of the Sangha, through recollection of good behavior, through recollection of generosity, through recollection of the deities, through mindfulness of breathing, through mindfulness of death, through mindfulness directed to the body, through recollection of peace.

One overcomes attachment to this world: Being mindful, one crosses attachment to this world, one crosses over, one crosses beyond, one transcends, one goes beyond it.

770. The defilements, which are designated **the weak, overpower him**—that person—they subdue him, crush him. Or **weak** defilements **overpower him**, that person, who is weak because he lacks the power of faith and the other powers; that is, because of his weakness they overpower him.[1761] Now while the one greedy for sensual pleasures is seeking and safeguarding sensual pleasures, **obstacles**—obvious obstacles such as lions and so forth as well as hidden obstacles such as bodily misconduct and so forth—**crush him**. **Then suffering** of birth and so forth **enters him**, that person overcome by the hidden obstacles, **as water does a broken boat**.

Nidd I 9. Even the weak overpower him: Weak defilements are powerless, of little power and little strength, inferior, low, slight, worthless, insignificant. Those defilements subdue that person, overwhelm him, overcome him, obsess him, crush him; thus the weak overpower him. Or alternatively, it is the person who is weak, powerless, of little power and little strength, inferior, low, slight, worthless, insignificant; one who does not have the powers of faith, energy, mindfulness, concentration, wisdom, moral shame, and moral dread. Those defilements subdue that person, overwhelm him, overcome him, obsess him, crush him: thus too the weak overpower him.

Nidd I 10. Obstacles crush him: There are two kinds of obstacles: obvious obstacles and hidden obstacles . . . [as at pp. 447–48, Nidd II 226–27] . . . so these bad unwholesome qualities that arise are based upon one's own person.

Nidd I 13. Then suffering enters him: The suffering of birth enters him, the suffering of old age, of illness, of death; of sorrow, lamentation, pain, dejection, and anguish; the suffering of hell, of the animal realm, of the realm of afflicted spirits, of the human realm; . . . the suffering of the death of mother, the death of father, brother, sister, son, or daughter; the suffering of loss of relatives, loss of wealth, loss through illness, loss of good behavior, loss of view. All these enter him. **As water does a broken boat**: As from all sides water enters a broken boat that has given way out on the water—it enters from the front, from the back, from below, and from the sides—so suffering enters that person from each of the obstacles: the suffering of birth . . . the suffering of loss of view.

771. Therefore, ever mindful: by the development of mindfulness directed to the body and so forth, **a person should avoid sensual pleasures**: by way of suppression and eradication,[1762] avoiding in all ways the defilement of sensuality in regard to sensual objects such as forms and so forth. **Having abandoned them**—those sensual pleasures, by the path that effects their abandoning—**one may cross the flood**, which is fourfold.

When a boat is weighed down by water, **by bailing out the boat one can reach the far shore** ("can go beyond") easily in that lightened boat. Analogously, having bailed out the heavy water of defilements from the boat of one's personal existence, by means of that lightened personal existence one can go beyond ("reach the far shore"); one can reach nibbāna, the "beyond" of all phenomena. One can proceed by the attainment of arahantship and attain final nibbāna by the nibbāna element without residue remaining.

⁝▮ **Nidd I 14. Having abandoned them, one can cross the flood.** Having fully understood objective sensual pleasures, having abandoned sensual defilements, having dispelled them, terminated them, eliminated them; having abandoned the hindrances of sensual desire, ill will, dullness and drowsiness, restlessness and regret, and doubt, one can cross, cross over, cross beyond, overcome, transcend the flood of sensuality, the flood of existence, the flood of ignorance, and the flood of views.

Nidd I 15. As by bailing out the boat one can reach the far shore: When a heavy boat is weighed down by water, having bailed it out, one can easily reach the far shore ("go beyond"), quickly and smoothly, in a lightened boat. Similarly, having fully understood objective sensual pleasures, having abandoned sensual defilements, having abandoned the hindrances of sensual desire, ill will, dullness and drowsiness, restlessness and regret, and doubt . . . obliterated them, one can easily go beyond, quickly and smoothly. The "beyond" is the deathless nibbāna, the stilling of all volitional activities, the relinquishment of all acquisitions, the destruction of craving, dispassion, cessation, nibbāna.

One can go beyond: One can achieve the beyond, experience the beyond, realize the beyond. One who wishes to go beyond has "gone beyond," one going beyond has "gone beyond," one who has actually gone beyond has "gone beyond."[1763] ▮⁝

Thus the Blessed One concluded the teaching with its culmination in arahantship. [514] At the conclusion of the teaching, the brahmin and his wife were both established in the fruit of stream-entry.

2 The Octad on the Cave
(*Guhaṭṭhaka Sutta*)

What is the origin?[1764] It is said that when the Blessed One was dwelling at Sāvatthī, the Venerable Piṇḍola Bhāradvāja, wishing to spend the day in a cool place, went to King Udena's garden, the Water Woods, on the slope of the Ganges at Kosambī.[1765] At other times too, he went there simply from past habit, as the elder Gavampati did to the Tāvatiṃsa heaven, as explained in the commentary on the Discourse with Vaṅgīsa. Having entered a meditative attainment at the foot of a tree on the bank of the Ganges, he remained sitting there through the day. That same day King Udena also went to amuse himself in the garden. Having amused himself in the garden with dance and song through most of the day, drunk on liquor, he put his head in the lap of one of his women and fell asleep.

Thinking, "The king is asleep," the other women got up and were gathering flowers and fruits in the garden when they saw the elder. They felt a sense of moral shame and moral dread, told each other to keep quiet, and silently approached the elder. After paying homage to him, they sat down around him. When he emerged from his attainment, the elder taught them the Dhamma. Delighted, they said, "Excellent, excellent!" and listened.

The woman who had taken the king's head in her lap thought: "They have left me and gone off to play." Being envious of them, she shook her thigh and woke the king. When the king woke up and did not see the women, he asked: "Where are those wretches?" She said: "Oblivious to you, they have gone off to amuse the ascetic." Furious, he headed toward the elder. When the women saw the king, some got up, but some said, "Great king, we are listening to the Dhamma from the monk," and did not rise. The king became even more [515] furious, and without even venerating the elder, he asked him: "Why have you come here?" – "For seclusion, great king." – "Do those who have come for seclusion sit around like this surrounded by women? Explain your seclusion!"

Though fearless, the elder realized, "He did not ask for a talk on seclusion because he wants to learn," and therefore he remained silent. The king said to him: "If you do not speak, I will have you eaten by red ants." He took a nest of red ants from an asoka tree, scattering them over himself. Having wiped his body, he took another sack and headed toward the elder. The elder thought: "If this king attacks me, he may be heading for the realm of misery." And so, out of compassion for him, he rose up into the sky by psychic power and departed.

Thereupon the women said: "Great king, when other kings see such a monk they worship him with flowers, incense, and other offerings. But you were about to attack him with a sack of red ants. You were prepared to destroy your family heritage."

Recognizing his fault, the king fell silent and asked the garden warden: "Has the elder come here on other days as well?" – "Yes, great king." – "In that case, inform me when next he comes." One day, when the elder came, the garden warden informed him. The king approached the elder, asked him a question, and went for refuge for life.

But on the day when he was threatened with the sack of red ants, the elder traveled through the sky, again sank into the earth, and emerged at the Blessed One's Fragrant Cottage. The Blessed One was lying down on his right side in the lion's pose, mindful and clearly comprehending. When he saw the elder he asked: "Bhāradvāja, why have you come at an untimely hour?" The elder then informed him of everything that had happened. On hearing this, the Blessed One said: "What good is a talk on seclusion for one who is greedy for sensual pleasures?" Then, while still lying on his right side, he spoke this discourse in order to teach the Dhamma to the elder.

772. Stuck: fixed. **In the cave**: in the body. For the body is called a cave because it is the dwelling place of such wild beasts as lust and other defilements. **Densely covered over**:[1766] covered over with the dense net of defilements such as lust; by this, internal bondage is indicated. **Dwelling**: dwelling under the control of lust and so forth; **immersed in bewilderment** (*mohanasmiṃ pagāḷho*): The strands of sensual pleasure are called bewilderment;[1767] for devas and human beings are deluded (*muyhanti*) by them, swallowed up in them; [516] by this, external bondage is indicated. **A person**—a being—**such as this is far from seclusion**: Such a person is far from the three kinds of seclusion, bodily seclusion and so forth. For what reason? **For in the world sensual pleasures are not easily abandoned**.

Nidd I 17. Stuck in the cave. It is the body that is called the cave. An abode, a mass, a boat, a chariot, a banner, an anthill, a city, a nest, a hut, a boil, a pot, a nāga—these are other designations for the body. One is stuck, attached, fixed, fastened to the cave, bound down in it. **Densely covered over:** Covered over by lust, hatred, delusion, anger, hostility, denigration, insolence, envy, miserliness, hypocrisy, deceitfulness, obstinacy, vehemence, conceit, arrogance, vanity, and heedlessness; covered over by all defilements, all misconduct, all disturbances, all fevers, all afflictions, all unwholesome volitional activities.

Nidd I 18. Dwelling: A person dwelling lustful because of lust, full of hate because of hatred, deluded because of delusion, bound down in conceit, seizing wrongly by views, distracted because of restlessness, indecisive because of doubt, tenacious because of the latent tendencies. **Immersed in bewilderment**: It is the five strands of sensual pleasure that are called bewilderment, that is, forms, sounds, odors, tastes, and tactile objects that are desirable, wished for, agreeable, endearing, connected with sensuality, and enticing. Why are they called bewilderment? Because devas and humans, for the most part, are deluded, confused, and bewildered by the five strands of sensual pleasure.

Nidd I 19–20. A person such as this is far from seclusion: There are three kinds of seclusion: bodily seclusion, mental seclusion, and seclusion from the acquisitions. What is *bodily seclusion*? Here, a bhikkhu resorts to a secluded lodging: a forest, the foot of a tree, a mountain, a ravine, a hillside cave, a charnel ground, a woodland grove, the open air, a heap of straw. He dwells bodily secluded. He goes alone, stands alone, sits alone, sleeps alone.

What is *mental seclusion*? The mind of one who has entered the first jhāna is secluded from the hindrances; the mind of one who has entered the second jhāna is secluded from thought and examination; the mind of one who has entered the third jhāna is secluded from rapture; the mind of one who has entered the fourth jhāna is secluded from pleasure and pain; the mind of one who has entered the base of the boundlessness of space is secluded from the perception of form, from perception of impingement, from perception of diversity; the mind of one who has entered the base of the boundlessness of consciousness is secluded from the perception of the base of the boundlessness of space; the mind of one who has entered the base of nothingness is secluded from the perception of the base of the boundlessness of consciousness; the mind of one who has entered the base of neither-perception-nor-nonperception is secluded from the perception of the base of nothingness. The mind of a stream-enterer is secluded from the view of the personal entity, doubt, and seizing upon good behavior and observances, from the latent tendencies to views and doubt, and from the coexistent defilements. The mind of a once-returner is secluded from the coarse fetters of sensual lust and aversion, from the coarse latent tendencies to sensual lust and aversion, and from the coexistent defilements. The mind of a non-returner is secluded from the residual fetters of sensual lust and aversion, from the residual latent tendencies to sensual lust and aversion, and from the coexistent defilements. The mind of an arahant is secluded from [the fetters of] lust for form and the formless, conceit, restlessness, and ignorance; from the latent tendencies to conceit, lust for existence, and ignorance, from the coexistent defilements, and from all external objects.

What is *seclusion from the acquisitions*? The defilements, the aggregates, and volitional activities are called acquisitions. It is the deathless nibbāna that is called seclusion from the acquisitions. It is the stilling of all volitional activities, the relinquishment of all acquisitions, the destruction of craving, dispassion, cessation, nibbāna.

Bodily seclusion is for those who dwell secluded in body, who delight in renunciation. Mental seclusion is for those with purified minds who have attained supreme cleansing. Seclusion from the acquisitions is for those persons without acquisitions, who have reached the end of volitional activities.

Nidd I 20–21. Sensual pleasures are not easily abandoned: There are two kinds of sensual pleasures: sensual objects and sensual defilements . . . [as at p. 1015, Nidd I 1–2] . . . Sensual pleasures are hard to abandon, hard to give up, hard to relinquish, hard to suppress, hard to unravel, hard to disentangle, hard to cross, hard to overcome, hard to dismiss. ⁞⁝

773. Thus, in the first verse, having demonstrated that "a person such as this is far from seclusion," again showing the nature of such beings, he speaks the verse "Based upon desire." Here, **based upon desire**: caused by craving. **Bound to enjoyment of existence**: bound to enjoyment of existence, which enjoyment consists in pleasant feeling and so forth. **They let go with difficulty**: Those things that are the basis for enjoyment of existence [are difficult to let go of]; or those beings bound to them, based upon desire, let go with difficulty.[1768] **For there is no release through others**: They cannot be released by another. Or this is a statement of the reason: "Those beings let go with difficulty. Why? Because they cannot be released by another." The meaning is: "If they are to be released, they must be released by their own strength."

Concerned, too, with the future or the past: Being concerned about future or past sensual pleasures. **They hanker for these sensual pleasures or earlier ones**:[1769] They yearn with strong craving for these present sensual pleasures or earlier ones, even the two kinds, past and future. It should be understood that these two lines are connected with this line: "they let go with difficulty, for there is no release through others." Otherwise it would not be known [of the words] "concerned with" and "they hanker for" what they are doing or what has been done.

⁝⁞ **Nidd I 22. Bound to enjoyment of existence**: One enjoyment of existence—pleasant feeling. Two enjoyments of existence—pleasant feeling and a desirable object. Three enjoyments of existence—youth, health, and life. Four enjoyments of existence: gain, fame, praise, and pleasure. Five enjoyments of existence—agreeable forms, sounds, odors, tastes, and tactile objects. Six enjoyments of existence—endowment with eyes, ears, nose, tongue, body, and mind. Beings are bound to them, bound down in them, bound up with them, fastened to them, fixed upon them, impeded by them; hence "based upon desire, bound to the enjoyment of existence." **They let go with difficulty**: Those bases for enjoyment of existence are difficult to let go of; or beings let go of these with difficulty. How are those bases for enjoyment of existence *difficult to let go of*? Pleasant feeling is difficult to let go of. A desirable object is difficult to let go of . . . endowment with eyes, ears, nose, tongue, body, and mind is difficult to let go of. Those bases for enjoyment of existence are difficult to let go of. How do beings *let go with difficulty*? Beings let go of pleasant feeling with difficulty, let go of a desirable object with difficulty. . . . With difficulty they let go of endowment with eyes, ears, nose, tongue, body, and mind. Thus beings let go with difficulty.

Nidd I 23. For there is no release by others: Those who are themselves stuck in the mud cannot rescue others stuck in the mud. For it was said by the Blessed One: "Cunda, it is impossible that one who is himself sinking in the mud could rescue another who is sinking in the mud; so too it is impossible that one who is himself untamed, undisciplined, unpeaceful, could tame another, discipline him, and lead him to peace" (MN I 45,3–10). Thus there is no release by others.

Or else, there is no one else who can release them. For if they are released, those practicing in accordance with the Dhamma are released by themselves, by their own strength, their own power, their own energy, their own exertion. Thus there is no release by others. Thus too there is no release by others.

And this too was said by the Blessed One:

"I will not be able to free anyone in the world,
Dhotaka, who is still afflicted by perplexity.
But understanding the supreme Dhamma,
you will thereby cross this flood." (**1064**)

Thus too there is no release by others. And this too was said by the Blessed One:

By oneself is evil done; by oneself is one defiled.
By oneself is evil left undone; by oneself is one purified.
Purity and impurity depend upon oneself;
no one can purify another. (Dhp 165)

Thus too there is no release by others. And this too was said by the Blessed One: "So too, brahmin, nibbāna exists and the path leading to nibbāna exists and I am present as the guide.

Yet when my disciples have been advised and instructed by me, some of them attain nibbāna, the ultimate goal, and some do not attain it. What can I do about it? The Tathāgata is one who shows the way" (MN III 6,3–8). The Buddha points out the path. Those practicing it on their own are freed. Thus too there is no release by others.

774. Having demonstrated with the first verse that "one such as this is far from seclusion," and having shown with the second verse the nature of such beings, now showing the evil deeds done by them, he speaks the verse "Those greedy for sensual pleasures." This is its meaning: **"Those** beings **greedy for sensual pleasures,** with the craving to enjoy them, **intent on them** because they are intent in seeking for them and so forth, **are confused** because they have fallen into delusion; **stingy** because they have gone down, because of miserliness, and because they do not accept the word of the buddhas and other munis;[1770] **settled in the unrighteous**: in unrighteousness of body and so forth. **When they come upon the suffering** of death at the end time, **they lament: 'What will we be after we pass away here?'"**

Nidd I 26–27. Stingy (*avadāniyā*): They are *avadāniyā* because they go down, because they are miserly, because they do not accept the word, pronouncement, teaching, instruction of buddhas and disciples. How are they *avadāniyā* because they go down? They go to hell, to the animal realm, to the sphere of afflicted spirits. How are they *avadāniyā* because they are miserly? There are five kinds of miserliness: regarding dwellings, families, gains, praise, and the Dhamma. Those people endowed with this miserliness, stinginess, are negligent. How are they *avadāniyā* because they do not accept the instruction of the buddhas and disciples? They do not take in their instruction, do not want to listen, do not bend their ear, do not incline their minds to understand. **Settled in the unrighteous**: settled in unrighteous bodily action, unrighteous verbal action, unrighteous mental action; settled in such unrighteous deeds as destroying life, taking what is not given, sexual misconduct, false speech, divisive speech, harsh speech, idle chatter, covetousness, ill will, wrong view; settled in unrighteous volitional activities, in the unrighteous five strands of sensual pleasure; in the unrighteous five hindrances, settled deeply in them, established upon them, attached to them, engaged with them, adhering to them, resolved on them, fastened to them, fixed upon them, impeded by them; hence "stingy, settled in the unrighteous."

They lament: "What will we be after we pass away here?": "Will we become hell beings? Will we go to the animal realm? To the sphere of afflicted spirits? Will we become human beings, devas, beings with form, formless beings, percipient beings, nonpercipient beings, beings that are neither percipient nor nonpercipient?" Having entered upon doubt, uncertainty, ambiguity, they prattle, babble, sorrow, languish, lament, weep beating their breast, and fall into confusion: "What will we become on passing away here?"

775. Since this is the case, **Therefore a person should train . . . this life is short**. Here, **should train**: should enter upon the three trainings. [517] **Right here**: in this teaching itself.

Nidd I 28–29. Therefore a person should train right here: There are three trainings: the training in the higher good behavior, the training in the higher mind, and the training in the higher wisdom. What is *the training in the higher good behavior*? Here, a bhikkhu is virtuous; he dwells restrained by the Pātimokkha, possessed of good conduct and resort, seeing danger in minute faults. Having undertaken the training rules, he trains in them. This is the training in the higher good behavior. And what is *the training in the higher mind*? Here, secluded from sensual pleasures, secluded from unwholesome states, a bhikkhu enters and dwells in the first jhāna . . . the fourth jhāna. This is the training in the higher mind. And what is *the training in the higher wisdom*? Here, a bhikkhu possesses the wisdom that discerns arising and passing away, which is noble and penetrative and leads to the complete destruction of suffering. He understands as it really is: "This is suffering" . . . "This is the origin of suffering" . . ."This is the cessation of suffering" . . . "This is the way leading to the cessation of suffering" . . ."These are the influxes" . . ."This is the origin of the influxes" . . ."This is the cessation of the influxes" . . . "This is the way leading to the cessation of the influxes." This is the training in the higher wisdom.

Directing one's attention to these three trainings, one should train; knowing them, one should train; seeing them, one should train; reviewing them, one should train; determining the mind, one should train. One should train by resolving through faith, applying energy, establishing mindfulness, concentrating the mind, and understanding with wisdom. Directly knowing what should be directly known, one should train; fully understanding what should be fully understood, one should train; abandoning what should be abandoned, one should train; developing what should be developed, one should train; realizing what should be realized one should train.[1771] **Right here**: in this view, in this Dhamma, in this discipline, in this teaching, in this spiritual life, in the teaching of this teacher, in this existence, in this human world.

Nidd I 30–32. For the wise say this life is short: Life is short on two grounds: life is short because of its transience or short because of its essential fragility.[1772] How is life short *because of its transience*? At the past mind-moment one lived but does not live and will not live; at the future mind-moment one will live but does not live and did not live; at the present mind-moment one lives but did not live and will not live.[1773]

Life and individuality,
pleasure and pain in their entirety,
are joined in a single mind-moment,
a moment that flies quickly by.

Even those deities that abide
for 84,000 eons—
even they do not live
for two consecutive mind-moments.

Those aggregates that have ceased,
whether of one dying or living here,
are all alike in that once gone
they never again return.

Those that have immediately dissolved,
and those of the future that will dissolve,
and those in between that have ceased,
are not different in nature.

One is not born through a future event;
one lives in the present only;
with the mind's dissolution the world perishes:
this is a description in terms of the supreme meaning.[1774]

They proceed as if flowing down,
undergoing change at will;
they occur in an unbroken stream
conditioned by the six sense bases.

Those [aggregates] dissolved do not go into storage;
there is no accumulation of them in the future.
Those that are produced merely stand
like mustard seeds on a needle's point.

For those phenomena that have been produced,
their dissolution stands in front of them.
They are subject to disintegration;
they are not combined with the old.

Not being seen, those [aggregates] come;
with their dissolution, they depart from sight.
Like a flash of lightning in the sky,
they arise and they vanish.

How is life short *because of its essential fragility*? Life is dependent on inhalation, on exhalation, on the great elements, on food, on warmth, on consciousness. Their root is weak, their past causes are weak, their conditions are weak. Their shared ground is weak, their association is weak, their coexistence is weak, their conjunction is weak. These are mutually weak, mutually unstable; they collapse together. None is able to safeguard the others, nor can any preserve the others. There is no one who produces them.

There is none who disappears because of anyone;
these must break up in their entirety.
These that are produced are due to past causes;
and those which produced them died in the past.
Those of the past and those that come later
never encounter one another.[1775]

Further, compared to the life of the devas in the realm of the four divine kings, human life is short; and so too when human life is compared to the life of the other devas up to those in the company of Brahmā.

Nidd I 32. The wise say life is short: The wise are those possessed of intelligence. It is wisdom that is called intelligence,[1776] that is, wisdom, understanding, discrimination, investigation, discrimination of phenomena, discernment, acuity, sharpness, skillfulness, prudence, perspicacity, insight, clear comprehension, the faculty of wisdom, the power of wisdom, the knife of wisdom, the mansion of wisdom, the light of wisdom, the radiance of wisdom, the lamp of wisdom, the gem of wisdom, non-delusion, discrimination of phenomena, right view. They are wise because they possess that wisdom. The wise say: "The life of humans is short, life is limited, life is slight, life is momentary, life is fleeting, life is transient, life is evanescent, life does not last long."

776. Now showing how those who do not act in such a way come to ruin, he speaks the verse "I see." Here, **I see**: I perceive with the fleshly eye and so forth; **in the world**: in the plane of misery and so forth; **this population**: this mass of beings; **trembling all over**: trembling here and there; **addicted to craving**: overcome by craving, fallen into craving; **for states of existence**: for desire-realm existence and so forth. **Inferior people**: people of inferior actions; **prattle in the mouth of death**: When the end time has arrived, they lament in the mouth of death. **For various states of existence**: for desire-realm existence and so forth. Or alternatively, **for various states of existence**: for existence after existence; what is meant is for repeated existence.

Nidd I 33–34. I see in the world this population trembling all over. I see: I see with the fleshly eye; I see with the divine eye; I see with the wisdom eye; I see with the buddha eye; I see with the universal eye. **Trembling all over**: trembling with craving, trembling with views, trembling with defilements, trembling with exertion, trembling over the results, trembling because of misconduct; trembling when made lustful because of lust, full of hate because of hatred, deluded because of delusion, bound down in conceit, seizing wrongly by views, distracted because of restlessness, indecisive because of doubt, tenacious because of the latent tendencies; trembling because of gain and non-gain, because of fame and dishonor, because of praise and blame, because of pleasure and pain; trembling because of birth, old age, illness, and death, trembling because of sorrow, lamentation, pain, dejection, and anguish; trembling with the suffering of hell, the animal realm, the sphere of afflicted spirits, or the human realm; trembling on account of various diseases; trembling with suffering due to loss of relatives, loss of wealth, loss through illness, loss of good behavior, and loss of [right] view.

Nidd I 34. Addicted to craving for states of existence. Craving for forms, sounds, odors, tastes, tactile objects, and mental phenomena. **For states of existence**: for desire-realm existence, form-realm existence, formless-realm existence. **Not devoid of craving for various states of existence**. **Craving** for forms . . . and mental phenomena; **for various states of existence**: not rid of craving, not devoid of craving, for existence after existence;[1777] for desire-realm existence in kamma existence and in renewed existence; for desire-realm existence in kamma existence, for form-realm existence in renewed existence; for form-realm existence in kamma existence, for formless-realm existence in renewed existence; for formless-realm existence in kamma existence; for ever-repeated existence in renewed existence; for ever-repeated destinations, for ever-repeated rebirth, for ever-repeated conception, for the ever-repeated production of personal being.[1778]

777. Now since those not rid of craving tremble and prattle in such ways, he speaks the verse "See them trembling," enjoining them to remove craving. Here, **see**: he addresses the listeners. **Over things taken as "mine":** over an object grasped as "mine" through the "mineness" of craving and views. **This too**: this danger too.

Nidd I 35. See them trembling over things taken as "mine." There are two ways of taking things as "mine": on account of craving and on account of views. What is taking things as "mine" *on account of craving*? Whatever is possessed and considered to be "mine," bounded, circumscribed, delimited, and designated by craving thus: "This is mine, that is mine; this much is mine, this extent is mine; my forms . . . tactile objects; bed sheets, covers, male and female slaves, goats and rams, fowl and pigs, elephants, cattle, and horses; fields, land, bullion, gold, villages, towns, and royal cities, realms and countries, treasuries and storerooms." One takes even the whole earth as "mine" because of craving. To whatever extent the 108 currents of craving flow, this is taking things as "mine" on account of craving. What is taking things as "mine" *on account of views*? The twenty kinds of view of the personal entity, the tenfold wrong view, the ten extreme views. In whatever way the sixty-two speculative views occur, this is taking things as "mine" on account of views.[1779]

See them trembling over things taken as "mine." They tremble when they are anxious about being deprived of an object taken as "mine"; they tremble when being deprived of it; they tremble after they have been deprived of it. They tremble when they are anxious the object will deteriorate; they tremble when it is deteriorating; they tremble when it has deteriorated. See them trembling, shuddering, quivering, quaking.

Nidd I 36. Like fish in a depleted stream with little water: As fish in a pool with little water, with slight water, where the water has evaporated, tremble, shudder, quiver, and quake when they are attacked, pulled out, and eaten by crows, herons, and cranes, so does this population tremble, shudder, quiver, and quake when anxious about being deprived of an object taken as "mine" . . . when the object has deteriorated.

One should take nothing as "mine": Having abandoned taking things as "mine" on account of craving, having relinquished taking things as "mine" on account of views, one should not take as "mine" the eye, ear, nose, tongue, body, or mind; forms . . . tactile objects, or mental phenomena; family, group, abode, gain, fame, praise, pleasure, robes, almsfood, lodging, or medicinal requisites; any realm of existence or mode of existence—in the desire realm, the form realm, or the formless realm—in the past, future, or present, whatever is seen, heard, sensed, or cognized.

778. Thus having shown the gratification with the first verse, and the danger with the following four verses, he now speaks a pair of verses, "Having removed desire for both ends," to show the escape along with the means and the benefit of the escape;

or having shown with all these verses the danger, degradation, and defilement in sensual pleasures, he now speaks this pair of verses to show the benefit in renunciation. Here, **for both ends**: for the two limits, contact and the origination of contact, and so forth; **having removed desire**: having removed desire and lust; **having fully understood contact**: having fully understood, by the three kinds of full understanding, contact such as eye-contact and so forth, or all name-and-form concurrent with contact, that is, the non-material phenomena associated with that [contact] and the material phenomena that serve as their bases, doors, and objects.[1780] **Without greed**: not greedy for anything included in form and so forth. **Not doing anything for which one might blame oneself, the wise person is not tainted by things seen or heard**: A wise person endowed with such intelligence is not tainted by things seen or heard, not even by one taint of the two kinds of taints. Untainted like space, he has reached the ultimate cleansing.

⁝⁝ Nidd I 37. Having removed desire for both ends. Contact is one end, the origin of contact is the second end; the past is one end, the future is the second end; pleasant feeling is one end, painful feeling is the second end; name is one end, form is the second end; the six internal sense bases are one end, the six external sense bases are the second end; the personal entity is one end, the origin of the personal entity is the second end.[1781] Having removed, having abandoned, having dispelled, having terminated, having obliterated desire for both ends.

Contact: eye-contact, ear-contact, nose-contact, tongue-contact, body-contact, mind-contact; designation contact, impingement contact; contact to be felt as pleasant, contact to be felt as painful, contact to be felt as neither painful nor pleasant; wholesome contact, unwholesome contact, indeterminate contact; contact of the desire sphere, of the form sphere, of the formless sphere; emptiness contact, markless contact, wishless contact; mundane contact, world-transcending contact; past contact, future contact, present contact—any such contact is called contact.

Nidd I 37–38. Having fully understood contact: Having fully understood contact with the three kinds of full understanding: full understanding of the known, full understanding by scrutinization, and full understanding by abandoning.

What is *full understanding of the known*? One knows contact. One knows and sees: "This is eye-contact . . . this is present contact." This is full understanding of the known.

Nidd I 38. What is *full understanding by scrutinization*? Having known contact thus, one scrutinizes it. One scrutinizes it as impermanent, as suffering, as a disease, as a boil, as a dart, as misery, as affliction, as alien, as disintegrating, as adversity, as a calamity, as peril, as a disaster, as shaking, as fragile, as unstable, as not a shelter, as not a cavern, as not a refuge, as hollow, as void, as empty, as non-self, as danger, as subject to change, as coreless, as the root of misery, as a murderer, as extermination, as subject to influxes, as conditioned, as Māra's bait; as subject to birth, old age, illness, and death; as subject to sorrow, lamentation, pain, dejection, and anguish; as subject to defilement; by way of its origin, its passing away, its gratification, its danger, and the escape from it.

What is *full understanding by abandoning*? Having scrutinized contact in such a way, one abandons, dispels, terminates, and eliminates desire and lust in regard to contact.

Nidd I 39. Not doing that for which one might blame oneself: One blames oneself for two reasons: because of what one has done and because of what one has not done. How so? One blames oneself, thinking: "I have done bodily, verbal, and mental misconduct; I have not done bodily, verbal, and mental good conduct. I have violated the ten courses of unwholesome conduct; I have not observed the ten courses of wholesome conduct. I have not fulfilled good behavior, guarding the doors of the sense faculties, moderation in eating, devotion to wakefulness, mindfulness and clear comprehension. I have not developed the four establishments of mindfulness, the four right kinds of striving, the four bases for spiritual potency, the five faculties, the five powers, the seven factors of enlightenment, the noble eightfold path. I have not fully understood suffering, abandoned its origin, developed the path, and realized cessation." ∎

779. Having fully understood perception: This is the concise meaning of this verse: [518] Having fully understood not only contact but perception too by the three kinds of full understanding—perception divided into sensual perception and so forth—or having fully understood all name-and-form concurrent with perception, in the way explained previously, by this practice one **can cross the** fourfold **flood**. Then, as one who has crossed, the arahant-**muni [is] untainted by possessions**: by abandoning the taints of craving and views, [he is untainted] by possessions involving craving and views. **With the dart extracted**, having extracted the darts of lust and so forth, **living heedfully** with abundance of mindfulness—or having lived heedfully in the preparatory stage of practice, having extracted the dart through the practice of heedfulness—**he does not desire this world or another**, divided into one's own personal being and that of others and so forth. Rather, with the cessation of the final occasion of mind, being without the fuel of clinging, he attains final nibbāna like a fire that goes out for lack of fuel.[1782]

Nidd I 40. Having fully understood perception, one can cross the flood. Perception: sensual perception, malevolent perception, aggressive perception; perception of renunciation, benevolent perception, non-aggressive perception; perception of form, sound, odor, taste, tactile objects, and mental phenomena. **Having fully understood perception**: having fully understood perception with the three kinds of full understanding: full understanding of the known, full understanding by scrutinization, and full understanding by abandoning. What is *full understanding of the known*? One knows perception. One knows and sees: "This is sensual perception . . . this is perception of mental phenomena." What is *full understanding by scrutinization*? Having known perception thus, one scrutinizes it. One scrutinizes it as impermanent . . . by way of its origin, its passing away, its gratification, its danger, and the escape from it. What is *full understanding by abandoning*? Having scrutinized perception in such a way, one abandons, dispels, terminates, and eliminates desire and lust in regard to perception. **One can cross the flood:** One can cross the flood of sensuality, the flood of existence, the flood of views, and the flood of ignorance.

Nidd I 41. The muni, untainted by possessions. The muni: It is knowledge that is called munihood (*moneyya*), that which is wisdom, understanding . . . non-delusion, discrimination of phenomena, right view. One possessing this knowledge, who has attained munihood, is called a muni. There are three kinds of munihood: bodily sagacity, verbal sagacity, and mental sagacity.[1783] What is *bodily sagacity*? Bodily sagacity is the abandoning of the three kinds of bodily misconduct and the practice of the three kinds of bodily good conduct; knowledge of a bodily object . . . full understanding of the body . . . the path associated with full understanding . . . the abandoning of desire and lust for the body . . . the cessation of the bodily activity . . . the attainment of the fourth jhāna.[1784] What is *verbal sagacity*? Verbal sagacity is the abandoning of the four kinds of verbal misconduct and the practice of the four kinds of verbal good conduct; knowledge of a verbal object . . . full understanding of speech . . . the path associated with full understanding . . . the abandoning of desire and lust for speech . . . the cessation of the verbal activity . . . the attainment of the second jhāna. What is *mental sagacity*? Mental sagacity is the abandoning of the three kinds of mental misconduct and the practice of the three kinds of mental good conduct; knowledge of a mental object; full understanding of mind . . . the path associated with full understanding . . . the abandoning of desire and lust for mind . . . the cessation of the mental activity . . . the attainment of the cessation of perception and feeling.

Nidd I 42. There are six kinds of munis possessing these three kinds of sagacity: householder munis, homeless munis, trainee munis, munis beyond training, pacceka munis, and munis among munis. Those householders who have seen the state [of nibbāna] and understood the teaching are *householder munis*. Monastics who have seen the state [of nibbāna] and understood the teaching are *homeless munis*. The seven trainees are *trainee munis*. Arahants are *munis beyond training*. Paccekabuddhas are *pacceka munis*. Tathāgatas, arahants, perfectly enlightened ones are called *munis among munis*.

Possessions: There are two kinds of possessions: possessions [acquired through] craving and possessions [acquired through] views.[1785] **Untainted**: There are two kinds of taints: the taint of craving and the taint of views. Having abandoned the taint of craving and relinquished the taint of views, the muni is not tainted by possessions. He dwells untainted, freed, escaped, released, detached, with a mind rid of boundaries.

Nidd I 42. With the dart extracted. The seven darts are the dart of lust, the dart of hatred, the dart of delusion, the dart of conceit, the dart of views, the dart of sorrow, the dart of perplexity. One for whom these darts have been abandoned, eradicated, allayed, quelled, made incapable of arising, burnt up by the fire of knowledge, is said to have extracted the dart. Hungerless, quenched, cooled, experiencing bliss, he dwells having himself become holy.[1786]

Nidd I 43. He does not desire this world or another. He does not desire this world, his own personal being; he does not desire another world, the personal being of another. He does not desire this world, his own five aggregates; he does not desire another world, the five aggregates of others. He does not desire this world, the internal sense bases; he does not desire another world, the external sense bases. He does not desire this world, the human world; he does not desire another world, the deva world. He does not desire this world, the desire realm; he does not desire another world, the form realm and formless realm. He does not desire this world, the desire realm and form realm; he does not desire another world, the formless realm. He does not desire another destination, rebirth, conception, existence, saṃsāra, or the round. ⁞

Thus the Blessed One concluded the teaching with its culmination in arahantship. Thus simply setting up the guideline of the Dhamma, he did not generate any further path or fruit, since the person being taught was already an arahant.

3 The Octad on the Hostile (*Duṭṭhaṭṭhaka Sutta*)

What is the origin? The origin is indicated in the first verse. In the way explained in relation to the Discourse on the Muni,[1787] the sectarians, unable to endure the gain and honor that accrued to the Sangha of bhikkhus, ordered the female wanderer Sundarī [to discredit the Buddha].[1788] It is said that she was an extremely beautiful white-robed wanderer. Having bathed, put on clean clothes, and adorned herself with garlands, perfume, and lotions, when the residents of Sāvatthī were leaving Jeta's Grove after listening to the Blessed One's Dhamma, she left Sāvatthī and headed toward Jeta's Grove. When people asked her where she was going, she said: "I am going to pleasure the ascetic Gotama and his disciples." She would then linger around the gatehouse at the entrance to Jeta's Grove and enter the city when the gatehouse was closed. In the morning, she would again go to Jeta's Grove and walk around as if seeking flowers near the Fragrant Cottage. [519] When people came to serve the Buddha, they would ask her, "Why have you come?" and she would say something at random.[1789]

After half a month had passed in this way, the sectarians killed her, buried her in a pit, and in the morning raised an uproar, saying: "We have not seen Sundarī." They reported this matter to the king and got his permission to enter Jeta's Grove. Wandering around, they exhumed her body, put her on a stretcher, and brought it to the city, where they made a complaint. All should be understood in the way it has come down in the text [of the Udāna].

That day, as the night was coming to an end, the Blessed One surveyed the world with his buddha eye and knew: "Today the sectarians will defame us. I should not let the multitude believe them, set their minds against us, and thereby head toward a rebirth in the realm of misery." He shut the door to the Fragrant Cottage and remained inside. He did not enter the city for alms. When the bhikkhus saw that the door was shut, they entered the city as on previous days. When people saw the bhikkhus, they insulted them in various ways. The Venerable Ānanda reported this event to the Blessed One and said: "Bhante, we have been defamed by the sectarians. We cannot live here. Jambudīpa is large, so let's go elsewhere." – "But if we are also defamed there, Ānanda, where will you go?" – "To still another city, Blessed One." Then the Blessed One said: "Wait, Ānanda! The commotion will persist for only seven days. After seven days have passed, those who have defamed us will regain their senses." In order to teach the Dhamma to the Elder Ānanda, he spoke this verse: "They speak."

780. Here, they **speak**: they blame the Blessed One and the Sangha of bhikkhus. **Some speak with hostile minds, while some speak with minds bent on truth**: The purport is: "Some with hostile minds and some who perceive it as true, the sectarians being those 'with hostile minds' and those who hear their statement and believe them being those 'with minds bent on truth.'"[1790] **An arisen dispute**: the dispute over the insult [520] that has arisen. **The muni does not become involved**: Because he was not the perpetrator and because he is unshakable, the Buddha-muni does not become involved. **Therefore the muni has no barrenness anywhere**: For this reason, it should be understood, this muni is not barren anywhere because of lust and so forth.

⁂ **Nidd I 44. Some speak with hostile minds**: The sectarians, who have hostile minds, antagonistic minds, belligerent minds, blame the Blessed One and the Sangha of bhikkhus on false grounds.[1791] **While some speak with minds bent on truth**: Those who believe the sectarians, who trust them, who are convinced by them, who think they are truthful, who perceive them as truthful, who think they are genuine, who perceive them as genuine, who think of them as honest, who perceive them as honest, blame the Blessed One and the Sangha of bhikkhus on false grounds. **The muni does not become**

involved in an arisen dispute: The dispute that has arisen is the insult and blame directed against the Blessed One and the Sangha of bhikkhus on false grounds. One who becomes involved in a dispute does so for two reasons: the perpetrator becomes involved in a dispute because he is the perpetrator; or being admonished and blamed, one becomes irritated, bears ill will, feels resentment, and displays irritation, hatred, and resentment, thinking: "I am not the perpetrator."[1792] The muni does not become involved in a dispute for two reasons: not being the perpetrator, he does not become involved in a dispute since he is not the perpetrator; or being admonished and blamed, he does not become irritated, bear ill will, feel resentment, and display irritation, hatred, and resentment, thinking: "I am not the perpetrator."

Nidd I 45. Therefore the muni has no barrenness anywhere: He does not have the five kinds of mental barrenness,[1793] nor does he have the three kinds of barrenness: the barrenness of lust, the barrenness of hatred, and the barrenness of delusion. These have been abandoned . . . burnt up by the fire of knowledge. **Anywhere**: anywhere internally, externally, or both internally and externally. ⁘

781. Having spoken this verse, the Blessed One asked Ānanda: "When the bhikkhus are being scolded and disparaged, Ānanda, what do they say?" – "Nothing, Blessed One." – "Ānanda, one should not remain silent under all circumstances, simply thinking, 'I am virtuous.' For in the world:

> When the wise man is in the midst of fools,
> they do not know him if he does not speak.
> (AN II 51,29–30)

"The bhikkhus, Ānanda, should reply to those people as follows," and then in order to teach him the Dhamma he spoke this verse: "The speaker of slander goes to hell."[1794] Having learned this verse, the elder told the bhikkhus: "You should reply to the people with this verse." The bhikkhus did so. Wise people became silent. The king, too, sent his men everywhere, and when he learned that the sectarians had given a bribe to some derelicts to murder Sundarī and that those derelicts had been caught and detained, he reviled the sectarians. People, too, when they saw the sectarians, struck them with clods of earth and scattered dirt over them, saying: "They defamed the Blessed One." Having seen this, the Elder Ānanda informed the Blessed One. The Blessed One then spoke this verse to the elder: "How indeed could one transcend one's own view . . . as one understands."

This is its meaning: "**How could one transcend one's own view**: How could one transcend that view—the view of the sectarians, 'After we have murdered Sundarī and spread dispraise of the Buddhist ascetics, we will enjoy the honor received in that way'—**if, drawn by desire, one is entrenched in a preference** for that view?" Rather, dishonor rebounded on those same sectarians who were unable to transcend that view. Or the statement applies as well to the eternalist and so forth; for in their case, too: "How could one transcend one's own view if, drawn by desire, one is entrenched in a preference for that view?" Rather, **taking one's own [view] to be perfect**, taking those speculative views posited by oneself to be complete, **one would speak as one understands**.

:B Nidd I 45. How could one transcend one's own view: The sectarians who held the view, the opinion, the belief, the intention, "Having killed the female wanderer Sundarī and spread dispraise of the Sakyan ascetics, in such a way we will again receive this gain, fame, honor, esteem," were not able to overcome their own view, their own opinion, their own belief, their own intention. Rather, dishonor came upon them. In such a case, how indeed could one transcend one's own view?[1795] Or alternatively, if one holds the doctrine "The world is eternal: this alone is true, anything else is false" . . . "The world is not eternal" . . . "The world is finite" . . . "The world is infinite" . . . "The soul and the body are the same" . . . "The soul is one thing, the body another" . . . "A tathāgata exists after death" . . . "A tathāgata does not exist after death" . . . "A tathāgata both exists and does not exist after death" . . . "A tathāgata neither exists nor does not exist after death: this alone is true, anything else is false," how could one transcend, go beyond, overcome, pass beyond one's own view? For what reason? Because that view has been accepted and adopted, grasped, seized, adhered to, clung to, and resolved upon. In such a case, how indeed could one transcend one's own view? **Entrenched in a preference**: established in, adhering to, engaged with, clinging to, resolved upon one's own view, one's own preference, one's own belief.

Nidd I 46. Taking one's own [view] to be perfect: One takes one's own [view] as perfect, one takes it as complete, takes it as flawless, takes it as foremost, the best, distinguished, most eminent, supreme, most excellent. One takes as perfect [the view]: "This teacher is omniscient" . . . "This Dhamma is well proclaimed" . . . "This group is practicing well" . . . "This view is excellent" . . . "This practice is well prescribed" . . . "This path is emancipating." **One would speak as one understands**: If one understands, "The world is eternal" . . . "A tathāgata neither exists nor does not exist after death: this alone is true, anything else is false," one would speak, state, declare, elucidate, communicate in such a way.

782. Then, after a week had passed and the king had the corpse removed, [521] one evening the king went to the monastery. After paying homage to the Blessed One, he said to him: "Bhante, when you were being defamed, shouldn't you have reported this matter to me?" The Blessed One replied: "Great king, it is not fitting for the noble ones to declare to others: 'I am virtuous, possessed of excellent qualities.'" He then spoke the remaining verses, "When a person, without being asked," in response to this incident that had arisen. Here, **good behavior and observances**: such good behavior as restraint by the Pātimokkha and so forth, and such ascetic observances as dwelling in a forest and so forth. **The skilled say he is one of ignoble nature, since on his own accord he proclaims himself**: If one speaks of oneself thus on one's own,[1796] the skilled say one's declaration shows: "He is one of ignoble nature."

Nidd I 47. Proclaims to others his own good behavior and observances. There is that which is both good behavior and an observance. There is an observance that is not good behavior. What is both good behavior and an observance? "Here a bhikkhu is of good behavior, restrained by the Pātimokkha, possessed of good conduct and resort, seeing danger in minute faults. Having undertaken the training rules, he trains in them." Here, self-control, restraint, and non-transgression are good behavior; the undertaking of them is observance. Good behavior has the meaning of restraint; observance has the meaning of undertaking. That is what is called good behavior and observance. What is an observance that is not good behavior? Eight austere practices: the forest-dwelling factor, the almsfood factor, the rag-robes factor, the three-robes factor, the alms round without skipping houses factor, the refusal of food brought afterward factor, the sitting factor, the sleeping anywhere factor—these are called observances, not good behavior. The undertaking of energy, too, is called an observance, not good behavior.[1797]

Nidd I 48. Without being asked, proclaims to others: Unasked, not questioned, not invited, not requested, not entreated, he proclaims his own good behavior or observances, saying: "I am of good behavior; I follow certain observances; I have good behavior and observances." Or on the basis of his social class or clan or family, beauty or wealth or study, work or craft or knowledge or ingenuity, or on any other basis [he boasts about this] . . . or he says: "I am one who gains the first jhāna . . . I am one who gains the base of neither-perception-nor-nonperception." He talks about it, speaks about it, indicates it, expresses it.

Nidd I 49. The skilled say he is one of ignoble nature. Those who are skilled in the aggregates, in the elements, in the sense bases, in dependent origination, in the establishments of mindfulness, in the four right kinds of striving, in the bases for spiritual potency, in the faculties, in the powers, in the enlightenment factors, in the path, in the fruits, in nibbāna—those skilled ones say thus: "This is the nature of the ignoble, not the nature of noble ones; this is the nature of fools, not the nature of the wise; this is the nature of bad people, not the nature of good people." **Since on his own accord he proclaims himself.** He proclaims himself thus: "I possess good behavior, or I possess observances, or I possess good behavior and observances. . . . I am one who gains the first jhāna . . . one who gains the attainment of the base of neither-perception-nor-nonperception." **B**ː

783. Peaceful: peaceful through the allaying of the defilements such as lust; so too, **inwardly quenched**. One who **does not**

boast of his good behavior, saying, "I am thus": one who does not boast of his own good behavior in such ways as "I am one of good behavior" and so forth. What is meant is that he does not make statements about himself on the basis of his good behavior. **The skilled say he is one of noble nature**: The buddhas and others who are skilled in the aggregates and so forth say of one who does not boast about himself: "He is one of noble nature." **Who has no swellings anywhere in the world**: The connection is: "The skilled say that one who does not boast about himself—the arahant for whom the seven swellings such as lust do not exist anywhere in the world—is 'one of noble nature.'"

⁞▮ **Nidd I 50. A peaceful bhikkhu**: peaceful through the stilling of lust, the stilling of hatred, the stilling of delusion, the stilling of anger, hostility, denigration, insolence, envy, miserliness, hypocrisy, deceitfulness, obstinacy, vehemence, conceit, arrogance, vanity, and heedlessness; of all defilements, all misconduct, all disturbances, all fevers, all afflictions, all unwholesome volitional activities. **A bhikkhu**: One is a bhikkhu by having broken (*bhinnattā*) seven qualities: the view of the personal entity, doubt, seizing upon good behavior and observances, lust, hatred, delusion, and conceit. **Inwardly quenched**: One is inwardly quenched by having extinguished lust . . . all unwholesome volitional activities.

Nidd I 51. The skilled say he is one of noble nature. Those who are skilled in the aggregates . . . in nibbāna say: "This is the nature of noble ones, not of the ignoble; this is the nature of the wise, not of fools; this is the nature of good people, not of bad people." **Who has no swellings anywhere in the world**. There are seven swellings: the swelling of lust, the swelling of hatred, the swelling of delusion, the swelling of conceit, the swelling of views, the swelling of defilements, and the swelling of kamma. One who does not have these is an arahant, one whose influxes are destroyed. ▮⁞

784. Having shown the conduct of the arahant, now showing the conduct of the sectarian adherents, he says: "One who has formulated impure teachings." Here, **one who**: any theorist. **Formulated**: fabricated; **put together**: composed with reasons; **advanced**: given preference to; **teachings**: views.

Becomes attached to the benefit he sees for himself, to that peace dependent on the unstable:[1798] One who advances these impure speculative views does so because he sees a benefit for himself in that view, such as honor in this present life [522] and an excellent destination in a future life. Therefore, he becomes attached to that benefit and to that view, which is designated "peace dependent on the unstable" because it is unstable, dependently arisen, and conventionally spoken of as peace. Because one is attached to this, one might extol oneself with nonexistent virtues and denigrate others with nonexistent faults.

⁘ **Nidd I 51–52. Formulated, put together**. **Formulated**: two kinds of formulation: formulation due to craving and formulation due to views. **Put together**: put together, composed, posited. Or else, "put together (conditioned)" as in "impermanent, conditioned, dependently arisen, subject to destruction, vanishing, fading away, cessation." **One for whom**: the theorist. **Teachings**: the sixty-two views. **Advanced (preferred)**: There are two kinds of preferences: preferences due to craving and preferences due to views. Because of not abandoning preference due to craving and not relinquishing preference due to views, he lives preferring that craving or that view, he lives accompanied by that craving or that view. **Impure**: not cleansed, not purified, defiled, defiling.

Nidd I 52. The benefit he sees for himself: He sees two kinds of benefit in his own view: the benefit pertaining to the present life and the benefit pertaining to future lives. What is *the benefit pertaining to the present life*? When the teacher holds a certain view his disciples hold that view. The disciples honor, revere, esteem, venerate, and show respect to the teacher holding that view, and on that account he gains such requisites as robes, almsfood, lodging, and medicinal requisites. What is *the benefit pertaining to future lives*? He expects some future fruit from that view thus: "This view can lead to rebirth as a nāga, a supaṇṇa, a yakkha, an asura, a gandhabba, a divine king, as Indra, Brahmā, or a deva. This view leads to purity, to purification, to full purification, to freedom, to liberation, to release. By this view they are purified, fully purified, freed, liberated, released. By this view I will be purified, fully purified, freed, liberated, released." He sees these two benefits in his own view.

Nidd I 52–53. He becomes attached . . . to that peace dependent on the unstable. There are three kinds of peace: ultimate peace, peace in a particular respect, and conventional peace. What is *ultimate peace*? It is the deathless nibbāna that is called ultimate peace, that is, the stilling of all volitional activities, the relinquishment of all acquisitions, the destruction of craving, dispassion, cessation, nibbāna. What is *peace in a particular respect*? For one who has attained the first jhāna, the hindrances have calmed down; for one who has attained the second jhāna, thought and examination have calmed down; for one who has attained the third jhāna, rapture has calmed down; for one who has attained the fourth jhāna, pleasure and pain have calmed down. For one who has attained the base of the boundlessness of space, perception of form, perception of impingement, and perception of diversity have calmed down; for one who has attained the base of the boundlessness of consciousness, perception of the base of the boundlessness of space has calmed down; for one who has attained the base of nothingness, perception of the base of the boundlessness of consciousness has calmed down; for one who has attained the base of neither-perception-nor-nonperception, perception of the base of nothingness has calmed down. This is peace in a particular respect. What is *conventional peace*? The peace based on a view, the sixty-two speculative views. Moreover, it is conventional peace in this sense that is intended here as "peace."

Nidd I 53. Peace dependent on the unstable. He is attached to an unstable peace, a volatile peace, an unsteady peace, a wobbling peace, a peace that is impermanent, dependently arisen, subject to destruction, vanishing, fading away, and cessation. ⁂

785. For one who is so attached, "Attachments to views . . . and takes up a teaching." Here, **attachments to views** is a designation for dogmatic adherence to claims of truth.[1799] They **are not easily overcome**, they cannot be overcome easily. **Having decided among teachings, one tightly grasps [a view]**: Attachments to views are not easily overcome because, after one has decided on a view among the sixty-two speculative views, one tightly grasps and adheres to one. **Therefore, among those bases of attachment, a person rejects and takes up a teaching**: Since they are not easily overcome, a person rejects and adopts this or that teaching among these attachments to views, which are divided [by way of practice] into the goat's behavior, the cow's behavior, the dog's behavior, the fivefold burning, the rocky precipice, the squatter exertion, lying down on thorns, and so forth,[1800] and divided by way of teacher, teaching, and group. One rejects one and takes hold of another, one discards this one and grasps that one, as a forest monkey grabs this or that branch of a tree. Rejecting teachings and taking up other teachings in such a way because of one's fickle mind, one might achieve fame for oneself and defame others through the ascription of nonexistent virtues to oneself and nonexistent faults to others.

Nidd I 53. Having decided among teachings, one tightly grasps [a view]. Among teachings: among the sixty-two speculative views. **Having decided**: having decided, having discriminated, having examined, having assessed, having scrutinized, having recognized, having made clear;[1801] **one tightly grasps [a view]**: Among the bases of attachment, there is the grasping of a section, the grasping of a part, the grasping of one's choice, the grasping of a portion, the grasping of an accumulation, the grasping of a collection. It is grasped, seized upon, adhered to, clung to, resolved upon [with the conviction]: "This is true, genuine, real, factual, actual, undistorted."

Nidd I 54. Therefore among those bases of attachment: for that reason, among those attachments to views; **a person rejects and takes up a teaching**: One rejects for two reasons: one rejects because another dissuades one or one rejects because one is unable to succeed. How does one reject *because another dissuades one*? Another dissuades one thus: "That teacher is not omniscient; his Dhamma is not well expounded; his company is not practicing well; his view is not excellent; his practice is not well prescribed; his path is not emancipating. Here there is no purity, purification, or full purification, no freedom, liberation, or release. Here, none are purified, fully purified, freed, liberated, released. They are inferior, wretched, low, miserable, of inferior disposition, worthless, insignificant." Being dissuaded [by such arguments] one rejects the teacher; one rejects his teaching; one rejects his company of followers; one rejects his view, practice, and path. How does one reject *because one is unable to succeed*? Being unable [to succeed through] good behavior, one rejects good behavior; being unable [to succeed through] an observance, one rejects the observance; being unable [to succeed through] good behavior and observances, one rejects good behavior and observances. **One takes up a teaching**: One accepts a teacher; one accepts a teaching; one accepts a company [of followers]; one accepts a view, a practice, a path; one grasps it, seizes it, adheres to it.

786. One who is cleansed . . . when he is uninvolved? What is meant? He is "cleansed" because he possesses wisdom, which shakes off (cleans off) all speculative views and other such faults. One **who is cleansed**, by possessing the qualities of cleansing, is the arahant, who has shaken off all evil.[1802] Such a one **formulates no view anywhere in the world about various states of existence**. Through the nonexistence of such a view, **through what would the cleansed one go [astray]** along the improper track that the sectarians take, concealing the evil deed they have done because of hypocrisy or conceit? **Having abandoned hypocrisy and conceit, through what would the cleansed one go [astray]** to the faults of lust and so forth? Whether in this life or in future lives, in what way can he be reckoned among particular destinations, the hells and so forth? **When he is uninvolved**: When he is uninvolved through the absence of the two involvements, those of craving and views.

Nidd I 54. One who is cleansed formulates no view. Cleansed: It is wisdom that is called cleansing. Why is wisdom called cleansing? Because it is by wisdom that bodily, verbal, and mental misconduct are shaken off and cleansed; that lust, hatred, delusion, anger . . . [as at p. 1023, Nidd I 17] . . . all unwholesome volitional activities are shaken off. Therefore wisdom is called cleansing.

Nidd I 55. Or it is by right view that wrong view is shaken off and cleansed; by right intention that wrong intention . . . by right speech . . . by right action . . . by right livelihood . . . by right effort . . . by right mindfulness . . . by right concentration . . . by right knowledge . . . by right liberation that wrong liberation is shaken off and cleansed. Or it is by the noble eightfold path that all defilements, all misconduct, all distress, all fevers, all torments, all unwholesome volitional activities are shaken off and cleansed. The arahant is possessed of these cleansing qualities. Therefore the arahant is one who is cleansed. He has shaken off lust, shaken off evil, shaken off defilements, shaken off fevers, hence he is cleansed. **Anywhere**: any place internally, externally, or internally and externally.

Nidd I 56. Formulates: There are two kinds of formulation: formulation due to craving and formulation due to views. **About various states of existence**: about existence after existence; about desire-realm existence in kamma existence and in renewed existence . . . [as at p. 1032, Nidd I 34] . . . about the ever-repeated production of personal being.

Nidd I 56–57. Having abandoned hypocrisy and conceit: It is devious conduct that is called **hypocrisy**. Here, someone engages in bodily misconduct, verbal misconduct, and mental misconduct. In order to conceal it, he forms an evil wish thus, "May no one find out about me"; he thinks, "May no one find out about me"; he says, "May no one find out about me"; he exerts himself bodily, "May no one find out about me." Such hypocritical behavior is called hypocrisy. **Conceit**: Conceit is singlefold as elation of mind. It is twofold as exaltation of oneself and disparagement of others. It is threefold as the conceit: "I am better," or "I am equal," or "I am worse." It is fourfold as conceit based on gain, based on fame, based on praise, based on pleasure. All this conceit, conceitedness, elation, self-exaltation is called conceit. **Having abandoned hypocrisy and conceit**: the cleansed one, having abandoned, dispelled, terminated, and eliminated hypocrisy and conceit.

Nidd I 57. Through what would the cleansed one go [astray] when he is uninvolved: There are two involvements, through craving and through views. He has abandoned involvement through craving and relinquished involvement through views. Since he has abandoned involvement through craving and relinquished involvement through views, on account of what lust would he go, on account of what hatred, what delusion, what conceit, what view, what restlessness, what doubt, what latent tendencies would he go [to be designated] as lustful, or full of hate, or deluded, or bound down [by conceit] or seizing [upon views] or distracted [by restlessness] or undecided [because of doubt] or tenacious [because of the latent tendencies]? Those volitional activities have been abandoned. Since they have been abandoned, through what would he go to any destination [to be designated] a hell being, an animal, an afflicted spirit, a human being, or a deva, etc.? There is no cause, no condition, no reason through which he would go [astray]. ■:

787. [523] As for one who is involved through the presence of those two: "One involved . . . all views right here." Here, **one involved**: one dependent on craving and views; **is embroiled in disputes about teachings**:[1803] is embroiled in disputes about these or those qualities thus, "lustful" or "full of hate." **But how, about what, could one dispute with one uninvolved?**: How, with reference to what lust or hatred, could one say "lustful" or "full of hate" about the arahant, who, with the abandoning of craving and views, is uninvolved? The purport is: "He is thus blameless, so how can he be one who conceals what he has done, as the sectarians do?" **Nothing is taken up or rejected by him**: For him there is no view of self or annihilationist view, or there is no grasping and letting go, called "taken up and rejected."[1804] If it is asked, "For what reason is there none?" it is said: **he has shaken off all views right here**. Because right here in this existence, he has shaken off all speculative views with the wind of knowledge, abandoned them, dispelled them.

:■ **Nidd I 58. But how, about what, could one dispute with one uninvolved?**: There are two involvements, through craving and through views. He has abandoned involvement through craving and relinquished involvement through views. Since he has done so, through what lust can one speak of him as lustful, through what hatred as full of hate, through what delusion as deluded . . . through what latent tendencies as tenacious? Those volitional activities have been abandoned, and because they have been abandoned, through what can one speak of his destination as a hell being . . . or as one neither percipient nor nonpercipient? There is no cause, no condition, no means by which one can speak of him, discuss, explain, indicate, and express him. **Nothing is taken up or rejected by him. Taken up**: there is no view of self. **Rejected**: there is no annihilationist view. **Taken up**: there is nothing grasped. **Rejected**: there is nothing to let go. If one grasps anything, it is to be let go. If there is something to be let go, something has been grasped. The arahant has overcome grasping and letting go, transcended growth and decline. He has lived the spiritual life, completed the practice, finished the journey, reached the goal; for him there is no more renewed existence with its wandering on in birth and death. **He has shaken off all views right here**: For him the sixty-two speculative views have been abandoned, eradicated, allayed, stilled, made incapable of arising, burnt up by the fire of knowledge.

Thus the Blessed One concludes the teaching with its culmination in arahantship. Having heard the teaching, the king was pleased, and having paid homage to the Blessed One, he departed.

4 The Octad on the Pure
(*Suddhaṭṭhaka Sutta*)

What is the origin?[1805] In the past, it is said, in the time of the Blessed One Kassapa, a certain landowner living in Bārāṇasī went to the borderland with five hundred carts in order to acquire merchandise. There he became friendly with a woodsman, gave him a present, and asked him: "Friend, have you seen any sandalwood?" The other said, "Yes, master," and brought him into a sandalwood forest, where he filled all his carts with sandalwood. The landowner said to the woodsman: "When you come to Bārāṇasī, friend, bring some sandalwood along." Then he returned to Bārāṇasī.

At a later time the woodsman took sandalwood and went to visit him. The landowner treated him with perfect hospitality. In the evening, he had the sandalwood ground to a powder, filled a box, and sent him to the bathing ford along with his own man, saying: "Go, friend, bathe and return." [524]

Now on that occasion a festival was taking place in Bārāṇasī. Having offered alms in the morning, in the evening the residents of Bārāṇasī dressed in clean clothes, took garlands, incense, and other offerings, and went to worship the great cetiya of the Blessed One Kassapa. When he saw them, the woodsman asked: "Where is everyone going?" Hearing that they were going to worship the cetiya at the monastery, he went there himself. There he saw people making offerings of various items at the cetiya—yellow orpiment, red arsenic, and so forth. Since he did not know how to paint a picture, he took the sandal and made a disk the size of a bronze tray above the golden bricks at the great cetiya. Then at sunrise the rays of the sun appeared. Having seen this, he was pleased and made a wish: "Wherever I am reborn, may such rays appear on my chest."

After he passed away, he was reborn among the Tāvatiṃsa devas. Rays appeared on his chest and his chest shone like the moon, so they called him "the young deva Candābha (Moonlight)." Because of his success, he passed one interval between buddhas being reborn up and down in the six deva worlds. When our Blessed One arose, he was born into an affluent brahmin family in Sāvatthī. In the same way, the disk of rays similar to the moon appeared on his chest. On the day of name-giving, the brahmins had a blessing ceremony performed for him. When they saw the disk they were surprised, thinking, "This boy has the auspicious marks of merit," and they gave him the name Candābha.

When he reached maturity, the brahmins took him, adorned him, dressed him in a fine jacket, put him in a chariot, and worshipped him as if he were Mahābrahmā. They traveled through the villages, towns, and royal capitals, announcing: "Whoever sees Candābha gains fame and wealth and other achievements, and in the next life goes to heaven." Wherever they went, people [525] came in greater and greater numbers, saying: "He is said to be Candābha. Whoever sees him gains fame, wealth, and heaven." All of Jambudīpa was astir. The brahmins did not show him to those who came with empty hands but only to those who brought a hundred or a thousand coins.

Traveling around in such a way with Candābha, the brahmins eventually reached Sāvatthī. Now on that occasion, after he had set in motion the excellent wheel of the Dhamma, the Teacher eventually came to Sāvatthī and lived there, where he taught the Dhamma in Jeta's Grove for the well-being of many people. When Candābha reached Sāvatthī he was unknown, like a small river that has chanced upon the ocean. No one proclaimed his name.

In the evening he saw a multitude of people heading toward Jeta's Grove, taking garlands, incense, and other offerings. He asked them where they were going and they said: "A buddha has arisen in the world and is teaching the Dhamma for the well-being of many people. We are going to Jeta's Grove to listen to it." He too went there accompanied by the group of brahmins.

Now on that occasion the Blessed One was sitting in his own excellent seat in the Dhamma hall. Candābha approached the Blessed One, greeted him with sweet words, and sat to one side. Immediately his light vanished; for within a range of eighty hatthas[1806] of the Buddha's light, no other light can shine. As he sat down, he realized: "My light has vanished." He got up and started to leave, but a certain man said to him: "Are you leaving, Candābha, because you are afraid of the ascetic Gotama?" He replied: "I'm not going because I'm afraid, but because my light does not compare with his glory." Having again sat down in front of the Buddha, he saw the excellence of his form, light rays, characteristics, and so forth, from the soles of his feet to the tips of his head hairs. He thought: "The ascetic Gotama is very powerful. The light that appeared on my chest is trifling. Having taken me even for just so long, the brahmins wander all over Jambudīpa, but though the ascetic Gotama possesses such excellent characteristics, he has no conceit or pride. Surely, possessing perfect qualities, he must be the teacher of devas and human beings."

Extremely pleased in mind, he paid homage to the Blessed One [526] and requested the going forth. The Blessed One instructed an elder monk to give him the going forth. Having done so, the elder taught him the meditation subject on the first five parts of the body.[1807] He developed insight and in no long time attained arahantship. He became famous as "the Elder Candābha."

With reference to him, the bhikkhus started a discussion: "Is it the case, friends, that those who saw Candābha gained fame or wealth or went to heaven or attained purity just by seeing his form visible through the eye door?" The Blessed One spoke this discourse in response to this case.[1808]

788. Here is the meaning of the first verse: "Bhikkhus, there is no purity through such kind of sight. Further, the foolish theorist who saw the brahmin Candābha or anyone like him saw one who was impure because stained by defilements, and one who was ill because he had not overcome the illness of defilements. Yet he claims that he directly knows: '**I see the pure, the supreme health.**'"[1809] And by that sight—a designation for a view—[he claims] **a person achieves full purity**.

Directly knowing thus, **having known** that sight as **supreme**, **contemplating** that sight as **pure**, he **falls back on** this sight as **knowledge** of the path.

⁞▯ **Nidd I 60. I see the pure, the supreme health**: **I see the pure**: "I inspect, observe, contemplate, examine the pure; **the supreme health**, that which has attained supreme health, attained protection, attained a cavern, attained a refuge, attained the fearless, attained the imperishable, attained the deathless, attained nibbāna. **A person achieves full purity through what is seen**: By seeing a form with eye-consciousness[1810] a person achieves purity, purification, full purification, freedom, liberation, release; a person is purified, fully purified, freed, liberated, released." **Directly knowing thus, having known "[It is] supreme":** Directly knowing thus, understanding, cognizing, recognizing, penetrating. Having known, having understood, having assessed, having scrutinized, having recognized, having made clear: "This is supreme, foremost, the best, distinguished, the most eminent, the highest, the most excellent." **"I contemplate the pure," one falls back on knowledge**: One who sees the pure is one who contemplates the pure. One **falls back on knowledge**, one falls back on the belief that knowledge occurs by seeing forms with eye-consciousness,[1811] one falls back on the belief that this is the path, one falls back on the belief that this is the way, one falls back on the belief that this is emancipation. ▯⁞

789. But that is not knowledge of the path. Hence he spoke the second verse: "If a person gains purity by the seen." This is its meaning: If one holds that **by the seen**—a designation for the sight of forms—**a person gains purity** from defilements, or that **one abandons suffering**—the suffering of birth and so forth—**by knowledge**, in such a case **one is purified by another**, by something other than the noble path, by that which is not the path to purity. The consequence then follows that **one with acquisitions**, one who still has the acquisitions of lust and so forth, is purified. Yet it is not the case that one like this is purified. Therefore **the view proclaims him as one who asserts thus**:[1812] That view itself declares of one asserting, in accordance with his view, "The world is eternal" and so forth: "He is one of wrong view."

Nidd I 61. If a person gains purity by the seen: If by seeing a form with eye-consciousness a person achieves purity, purification, full purification, freedom, liberation, release; **or if one abandons suffering by knowledge**: If by seeing a form with eye-consciousness a person abandons the suffering of birth, old age, illness, and death; the suffering of sorrow, lamentation, pain, dejection, and anguish; **then one with acquisitions is purified by another**: A person **with acquisitions**—one with lust, hatred, delusion, conceit, craving, views, defilements, clinging—is purified, fully purified, freed, liberated, released **by another**, by what is not the path to purity, by a wrong practice, by a way that is not emancipating, by some means *other than* by the establishments of mindfulness, the right kinds of striving, the bases for spiritual potency, the faculties, the powers, the enlightenment factors, the noble eightfold path. **The view proclaims him as one who asserts thus**: The view itself proclaims that person thus: "This person is one of wrong view, one of a distorted perspective"; **as one who asserts thus**: as one who asserts, who declares: "The world is eternal" . . . "A tathāgata neither exists nor does not exist after death: this alone is true, anything else is false."

790. As to the third verse, "A brahmin," this is its meaning: "One who is **a brahmin** because he has expelled evil—the arahant-brahmin who has achieved the destruction of the influxes through the path—**does not speak of purity by another**, by some means other than the knowledge of the noble path, [527] through wrong knowledge arisen in regard to **the seen**, a designation for forms considered auspicious; in regard to **the heard**, a designation for auspicious sounds; in regard to **good behavior**, a designation for non-transgression; in regard to **observances** such as the elephant observance; and in regard to **the sensed**, earth and so forth."[1813] The rest is stated for the purpose of praising this brahmin. For **he is untainted by merit** pertaining to the three realms of existence or by any **evil**. Because he has abandoned the view of self, or because he has abandoned all grasping, he has **discarded what was taken up.**[1814] Because he does not create meritorious volitional activities, it is said: **without creating anything here**. Therefore the Blessed One said this, praising him in such a way. The connection of all this, it should be understood, is with the earlier line ("a brahmin does not speak of purity by another").

Nidd I 62. A brahmin does not speak of purity by another: **A brahmin**: One who has expelled the view of the personal entity, doubt, seizing of good behavior and observances, lust, hatred, delusion, and conceit; one who has expelled bad unwholesome qualities that are defiling, lead to renewed existence, are troublesome, result in suffering, and conduce to future birth, old age, and death. **A brahmin does not speak of purity by another**: He does not speak of purity . . . release by another, by what is not the path to purity, by a wrong practice, by a non-emancipating way, other than by the establishments of mindfulness . . . the noble eightfold path.

Nidd I 62–64. By the seen and the heard, by good behavior and observances, by the sensed: There are some ascetics and brahmins who hold that purity comes through *what is seen*. They believe that seeing certain forms is auspicious, while seeing other forms is inauspicious.[1815] There are some ascetics and brahmins who hold that purity comes through *what is heard*. They believe that hearing certain sounds is auspicious, while hearing other sounds is inauspicious. There are some ascetics and brahmins here who believe that purity . . . release comes by *good behavior*, by mere good behavior, by mere self-control, by mere restraint, by mere non-transgression. There are some ascetics and brahmins here who believe that purity comes *through observances*. They take up the elephant observance, the horse observance, the cow observance, the dog observance. There are some ascetics and brahmins who hold that purity comes *through what is sensed*. They get up early and touch the earth, touch grass, touch cowdung, touch a tortoise, step on a plowshare, touch a heap of sesamum seeds, eat auspicious sesamum seeds, anoint themselves with sesamum oil, brush their teeth with auspicious toothwood, bathe in auspicious mud, dress in auspicious clothes, wear an auspicious turban. A brahmin does not say that purity is attained through the seen, the heard, good behavior, observances, or what is sensed.

Nidd I 64. He is untainted by merit and by evil: It is wholesome volitional activity pertaining to the three realms of existence that is called merit. Everything unwholesome is called demerit. Since meritorious volitional activity, demeritorious volitional activity, and imperturbable volitional activity have been abandoned by him, cut off at the root, made like a palm stump, eliminated so that they are no more subject to future arising, he is untainted by merit and by evil. **He has discarded what was taken up**: discarded the view of a self; discarded grasping; given up, cast away, let go, abandoned, relinquished whatever has been grasped, seized, adhered to, clung to, resolved upon with craving and views; **without creating anything here**: not creating meritorious volitional activity, demeritorious volitional activity, or imperturbable volitional activity. ❚⁝

791. Having said, "He is untainted by merit and evil, having discarded what was taken up, without creating anything here, a brahmin does not speak of purity by another," now, showing the ineffectiveness[1816] of the view of those theorists who say that purity is achieved by another, he states the verse "Having abandoned the former." This is its meaning: Those who assert that purity occurs by another, because they have not abandoned this view, still seize and let go. On that account, **having abandoned the former** teacher and so forth, **attached to another**, **carried along by**, overcome by, **impulse**—a designation for craving—**they do not cross the tie**, consisting in lust and so forth. And since they do not cross the tie, **they grab hold** of this or that teaching and **let go** of another as a monkey does a branch.

⁝❚ **Nidd I 65. Having abandoned the former, attached to another**: Having abandoned a former teacher, they become attached to another teacher; having abandoned a former teaching . . . a former group . . . a former view . . . a former practice . . . a former path, they become attached to another path. **Carried along by impulse**: It is craving that is called impulse. **Carried along by impulse**, swept up by impulse, fallen into impulse, overcome by it, obsessed by it, **they do not cross the tie**: They do not cross the tie of lust, the tie of hatred, the tie of delusion, the tie of conceit, the tie of views, the tie of defilements, the tie of misconduct. **They grab hold and let go**: They grab a teacher, let him go, and grab another teacher; they grab a teaching . . . a group . . . a view . . . a practice . . . a path, let it go, and grab another. ❚⁝

792. The connection with the fifth verse is as follows: One who has "undertaken observances by himself" is the one spoken of above: "the view proclaims him as one making such assertions." The **observances** are the elephant observance and so forth. **Up and down**: to and fro, inferior and superior, or from teacher to teacher. **Attached to perception**: stuck on sensual perception and so forth. **But having realized the Dhamma with knowledge, the wise one**: The arahant, a wise one in the supreme sense, having realized the Dhamma of the four truths with the knowledge of the four paths.[1817] The rest is clear.

Nidd I 66. Observances: the elephant observance, the horse observance, the cow observance, the dog observance, the crow observance, the Vāsudeva observance, the Baladeva observance, the Puṇṇabhadda observance, the Maṇibhadda observance, the fire observance, the nāga observance, the supaṇṇa observance, the yakkha observance, the asura observance . . . or the direction observance.[1818] **A person goes up and down, attached to perception**: He goes from teacher to teacher, from teaching to teaching, from group to group, from view to view, from practice to practice, from path to path. **Attached to perception**: attached to, fixed upon, stuck to sensual perception, malevolent perception, aggressive perception, perception of views. Like goods attached to a hook on a wall or a peg, so one is attached to sensual perception . . . perception of views.

Nidd I 67–68. But having realized the Dhamma: Having realized the Dhamma, having made the breakthrough to: "All conditioned things are impermanent . . . All conditioned things are suffering . . . All phenomena are non-self." Having realized the Dhamma: "With ignorance as condition, volitional activities [come to be] . . . with birth as condition, old age and death [come to be] . . . With the cessation of ignorance, there is cessation of volitional activities . . . With the cessation of birth, there is cessation of old age and death." Having realized the Dhamma: "This is suffering; this is its origin; this is its cessation; this is the way leading to its cessation. These are the influxes; this is their origin; this is their cessation; this is the way leading to their cessation." Having realized the Dhamma: "These things should be directly known; these things should be fully understood; these things should be abandoned; these things should be developed; these things should be realized."[1819] Having realized the Dhamma, having made the breakthrough to the origin and passing away, the gratification, danger, and escape in regard to the six bases for contact, in regard to the five aggregates subject to clinging, in regard to the four great elements. Having realized the Dhamma, having made the breakthrough to: "Whatever is subject to origination is all subject to cessation."

Nidd I 68. The wise one, broad in wisdom, does not go up and down: One broad in wisdom is one of great wisdom, wide wisdom, joyous wisdom, quick wisdom, sharp wisdom, penetrative wisdom, endowed with wisdom vast and extensive like the earth. He does not go from teacher to teacher . . . from path to path.

793. One who is remote from all phenomena, [528] **from whatever is seen, heard, or sensed**: The arahant of broad wisdom is remote from all phenomena, whatever is seen, heard, or sensed, in that, amid all those phenomena, he dwells having destroyed the army of Māra.[1820] **How could anyone here in the world categorize him?**: With what mental construct due to craving or with what mental construct due to views could anyone here in the world categorize him? Or with what lust and so forth, as previously stated, for these have been abandoned? **That seer**: one of such purified vision; **behaving openly**: one whose behavior has been opened up by the removal of the covering of craving and other defilements.

Nidd I 68–69. One who is remote (*visenibhūto*) from all phenomena, from whatever is seen, heard, or sensed: It is Māra's army that is called the army (*senā*). Māra's army is bodily misconduct, verbal misconduct, mental misconduct, lust, hatred, delusion, anger . . . [as at p. 1023, Nidd I 17] . . . all unwholesome volitional activities. When all Māra's army and all the battalions of defilements have been vanquished, defeated, demolished, decimated, and overturned by the four noble paths, one is said to be a destroyer of the army (*visenibhūto*: remote). One is remote from the seen, remote from the heard, remote from the sensed, remote from the cognized.

Nidd I 69. How could anyone here in the world categorize him?: There are two kinds of mental constructs: mental constructs due to craving and mental constructs due to views.

When mental constructs due to craving have been abandoned and mental constructs due to views have been relinquished, by what lust, by what hatred, by what delusion, by what conceit, by what view, by what restlessness, by what doubt, by what latent tendences could anyone think of him as "lustful" or "full of hatred" or "deluded" or "bound down [by conceit]" or "seizing [upon views]" or "distracted [by restlessness]" or "undecided [because of doubt]" or "tenacious [because of the latent tendencies]"?[1821] Those volitional activities have been abandoned by him. When they are abandoned, how could one think of him in terms of destinations, as "a hell being" or "an animal" or "an afflicted spirit" or "a human being" or "a deva"; as "having form" or as "formless"; as "percipient" or "nonpercipient" or "neither-percipient-nor-nonpercipient"? There is no cause, no condition, no ground by which one might think of him, categorize him, and put him in a category.

That seer behaving openly: That seer of the pure, seer of the purified, seer of the fully purified, seer of the cleansed, seer of the fully cleansed; or alternatively, one of pure vision, purified vision, fully purified vision, cleansed vision, fully cleansed vision. **Behaving openly**: The coverings are craving, views, defilements, misconduct, and ignorance. Those coverings have been opened up, dispersed, removed, withdrawn, abandoned, eradicated, allayed, stifled, made incapable of arising, burnt up by the fire of knowledge. **Behaving**: wandering, dwelling, living, acting, carrying on, maintaining oneself. ▮⁝

794. The connection and meaning of the verse "They do not construct" are as follows: "And what is more, those of this sort **do not construct, they have no preferences** by any of the two kinds of mental construction and preferences." Because they have achieved supreme, ultimate purity, **they do not assert: "[This is] ultimate purity,"** they do not assert supreme ultimate purity, saying: "The view of non-doing or eternalism is ultimate purity."[1822] **Having loosened the knot of grasping that had been tied**: Having loosened the fourfold knot of grasping, on account of which one grasps form and so forth, having cut the knot tied in their own minds with the knife of the noble path. The rest is clear.

⁝▮ Nidd I 70. They do not construct, they have no prefer-

ences. **Mental constructs**: There are two kinds of mental constructs: mental constructs due to craving and mental constructs due to views. For them, mental constructs due to craving have been abandoned and mental constructs due to views have been relinquished. Since that is so, they do not construct any mental constructs due to craving or to views; they do not engender, generate, produce, or create such mental constructs. **They have no preferences**: There are two kinds of preferences: preferences due to craving and preferences due to views. For them, preference due to craving has been abandoned and preference due to views has been relinquished. Since that is so, they do not have a preference due to craving or a preference due to views; they do not bear them as their banner and flag, as their authority, nor do they go about accompanied by craving or by views. Hence they do not construct, they have no preferences. **They do not assert: "[This is] ultimate purity"**: They do not assert ultimate purity, purity through saṃsāra, the eternalist doctrine, the view of non-doing.[1823]

Nidd I 70–71. Having loosened the knot of grasping: There are four knots: the bodily knot of longing, the bodily knot of ill will, the bodily knot of seizing upon good behavior and observances, and the bodily knot of dogmatic adherence to claims of truth. Attachment to one's own view is the bodily knot of longing. Resentment, bitterness, ill will toward the doctrines of others is the bodily knot of ill will. Seizing upon one's own good behavior, observances, or good behavior and observances is the bodily knot of seizing upon good behavior and observances. One's own view is the bodily knot of adherence to dogmatic claims of truth. Why is this called "the knot of grasping"? Through these knots one takes up form, feeling, perception, volitional activities, and consciousness; one takes up a destination, a rebirth, conception, existence, the round of saṃsāra; one clings to them, grasps them, seizes upon them, adheres to them. Hence this is called the knot of grasping. **Having loosened** or untied those knots.

795. The verse "For a brahmin who has transcended the boundary" is stated as a teaching based on a single person; but its connection [with what precedes] is similar to the previous ones. It should be understood together with the explanation of the meaning thus: "And what is more, for one of broad wisdom like this, who **has transcended the boundary** by passing beyond the four boundaries of defilements,[1824] and who is **a brahmin** by having expelled evil, **who has known** with the knowledge of others' minds and the knowledge of past abodes, and **seen** with the fleshly eye and the divine eye, **nothing is tightly grasped by him**." What is meant is that one such as this adheres to nothing. **Not excited by lust** through the absence of sensual lust, **or attached to dispassion** through the absence of attachment to form and formless states,[1825] **he does not grasp anything here**, as "This is **more**."[1826]

Nidd I 71. For a brahmin who has transcended the boundary: There are four boundaries. The *first boundary* consists in the view of the personal entity, doubt, seizing upon good behavior and observances, the latent tendency to views, the latent tendency to doubt, and the coexistent defilements. The *second boundary* consists in the coarse fetters of sensual lust and aversion, the coarse latent tendencies to sensual lust and aversion, and the coexistent defilements. The *third boundary* consists in the residual fetters of sensual lust and aversion, the residual latent tendencies to sensual lust and aversion, and the coexistent defilements. The *fourth boundary* consists in lust for form, lust for the formless, conceit, restlessness, ignorance, the latent tendency to conceit, the latent tendency to lust for existence, the latent tendency to ignorance, and the coexistent defilements. One who has passed beyond these four boundaries by the four noble paths is called "one who has transcended the boundary."

Nidd I 72. Not excited by lust or attached to dispassion: Those attached to the five strands of sensual pleasure, greedy for them, bound to them, infatuated with them, cleaving to them, fastened to them, impeded by them, are said to be "excited by lust." Those attached to the form-sphere and formless-sphere meditative attainments . . . impeded by them, are said to be "attached to dispassion." When sensual lust, lust for form, and lust for the formless are abandoned, cut off at the root, made like a palm stump, eliminated so that they are no more subject to future arising, one is "not excited by lust or attached to dispassion."

He does not grasp anything here as supreme: For the arahant, whose influxes have been destroyed, nothing is grasped, seized, adhered to, clung to, and resolved upon thus: "This is supreme, foremost, the best, distinguished, the most eminent, the highest, the most excellent." That [grasping] has been abandoned, eradicated, stifled, allayed, made incapable of arising, burnt up by the fire of knowledge.

Thus he concludes the teaching with its culmination in arahantship. [529]

5 The Octad on the Supreme
(*Paramaṭṭhaka Sutta*)

What is the origin? It is said that when the Blessed One was dwelling at Sāvatthī, various sectarians assembled. They each explained their own view, saying, "This is supreme, that is supreme," and thereby started a quarrel. People reported this to the king. The king gave the order: "Gather several blind men and show them an elephant."[1827] The king's men assembled several blind men, presented them with an elephant, and told them: "Feel it." They each touched a particular part of the elephant. The king then asked them: "What is an elephant like?" The one who touched the trunk said: "Great king, an elephant is like the pole of a plow." Those who touched the tusks and the other parts reviled him, saying, "Do not lie to the king," and they said, "The elephant is like a peg in a wall," and so forth. After hearing them all, the king dismissed the sectarians, saying: "Your systems are just like this."

A certain monk on alms round heard about this and reported it to the Blessed One. Taking this case as the origin, the Blessed One addressed the bhikkhus: "Bhikkhus, just as the blind men, not knowing what an elephant is like, disputed over the part they touched, so the sectarians, not knowing the Dhamma that culminates in emancipation, seize this and that view and dispute over them." He then spoke this discourse to teach the Dhamma.

796. Here, **settling [on his own] as supreme among views**: Each one settling on his own view, holds: "This is supreme." **Whatever a person esteems as best**: whatever teacher and so forth he takes to be best; **he says all others are "inferior"**:

he says of all others apart from his own teacher and so forth: "These are inferior." **Therefore he has not transcended disputes**: For this reason, he has not actually transcended quarrels over views.

⁞ **Nidd I 73. Settling on [his own] as supreme among views**: There are some ascetics and brahmins who are theorists. Having grasped, taken up, seized upon one or another view among the sixty-two speculative views, they live each in their own view, dwell in it, abide in it, settle on it, holding: "This is supreme, foremost, the best, distinguished, the most eminent, the highest, the most excellent." **Whatever a person esteems as best in the world . . .** : Whatever he takes as best, when he takes as best, "This teacher is omniscient"; when he takes as best, "This Dhamma is well expounded" . . . "This company is practicing well" . . . "This view is excellent" . . . "This practice is well prescribed" . . . "This path is emancipating."

Nidd I 74. . . . He says all others are "inferior": apart from his own teacher, teaching, group, view, practice, and path, he rejects, dismisses, disdains all the systems of others. He says: "That teacher is not omniscient; his Dhamma is not well expounded; his group is not practicing well; his view is not excellent; his practice is not well prescribed; his path is not emancipating. Here there is no purification or liberation. Here, none are purified, fully purified, freed, liberated, released. They are inferior, wretched, low, miserable, of inferior disposition, worthless, insignificant." **Therefore he has not transcended disputes**: For this reason he has not overcome quarrels over views, arguments over views, contention over views, disputes over views, strife over views. ⁞

797. When one has not transcended disputes, **whatever benefit** of the kinds stated earlier **one sees for oneself**, in the view arisen in regard to these bases, **in the seen, the heard, the sensed, or in good behavior and observances**, having adhered to that benefit in one's own view as "This is [530] the best," **one regards all else**—other teachers and so forth—**as inferior**.

⁞ **Nidd I 74–75. Whatever benefit one sees for oneself:** The theorist sees two kinds of benefit in his own view: the benefit pertaining to the present life and the benefit pertaining to future lives . . . [as at p. 1046, Nidd I 52] . . . He sees these two benefits in his own view.

Nidd I 75. Having grasped hold of that alone: Having grasped this, taken it up, and seized upon it, they adhere to it thus: "This is supreme, foremost, the best, distinguished, the most eminent, the highest, the most excellent." **One regards all else as inferior**: One regards any other teacher, teaching, group, view, practice, and path as inferior, wretched, low, miserable, of inferior quality, worthless, insignificant. ▫

798. Since one who looks at things in such a way **is attached** to his own teacher and so forth, and **regards others**, the teachers and so forth of others, **as inferior, the skilled speak of that** viewpoint **as a knot**, as bondage. Since this is so, **a bhikkhu should not be attached to the seen, the heard or sensed, or to good behavior and observances**. What is meant is: "He should not adhere to them."

▫ **Nidd I 75. The skilled speak of that as a knot**: Those who are skilled in the aggregates . . . [as at p. 1044, Nidd I 49] . . . in nibbāna—those skilled ones say: "This is a knot, this is a fastening, this is bondage, this is an impediment." ▫

799. Not only should one not be attached to the seen, heard, and so forth, but **one should not construct any view in the world**, creating additional ones that had not previously arisen.[1828] Of what kind? **By means of knowledge or good behavior and observances**: One should not construct a view of the kind constructed by means of knowledge—the knowledge of the meditative attainments and so forth[1829]—or by means of good behavior and observances. And not only should one not construct a view, but further, on account of conceit, **one should not take oneself as "equal" or think of oneself as "inferior" or "superior"** in regard to such matters as social class and so forth.

▫ **Nidd I 76–77. Nor should one construct any view in the world by means of knowledge or good behavior and observances**: Based on knowledge of the eight meditative attainments or the knowledge of the five superknowledges or wrong knowledge, or based on good behavior or observances or good behavior and observances, one should not construct, engender, generate, or create any view. **One should not take oneself as "equal"**: One should not take oneself thus, "I am equal," on one ground or another, whether social class, clan, family, beauty, wealth, skill in recitation, mastery over work or a craft or some branch of knowledge, learning, or ingenuity; **or think of oneself as "inferior" or "superior"**: One should not take oneself thus, "I am inferior" or "I am superior," on one ground or another whether social class . . . or ingenuity.

800. Thus, not constructing any view and not conceiving oneself [by way of conceit], **having abandoned what was taken up, not clinging**: having abandoned what was previously grasped here, not grasping anything else, **one does not create a dependency** of the two types **even on** the aforesaid **knowledge**. Not doing so, not taking a course determined by desire and so forth,[1830] **among those who are divided**, among beings riven by diverse views, **not taking sides, one does not fall back on any view at all**, one does not rely on any view among the sixty-two views.

Nidd I 77–78. Having abandoned what was taken up: Having abandoned the view of self; having abandoned the grasping of self;[1831] having abandoned dispelled, terminated, eliminated whatever has been grasped, seized, adhered to, clung to, resolved upon with craving and views.[1832] **Not clinging**, not clinging, not grasping, not seizing, not adhering by way of the four kinds of clinging, **one does not create a dependency even on knowledge**:[1833] One does not create dependency through craving or dependency through views even by the knowledge of the eight meditative attainments, or the knowledge of the five superknowledges, or wrong knowledge. **Not taking sides among those who are divided**: Among those who are riven by different views, different opinions, different preferences, different beliefs, among those who adopt a course of action motivated by desire, hatred, delusion, or fear, one does not adopt a course of action motivated by desire, hatred, delusion, or fear, or by lust, hatred, delusion, conceit, views, restlessness, doubt, or the latent tendencies.

Nidd I 78. One does not fall back on any view at all: The sixty-two speculative views have been abandoned by him, eradicated, allayed, stilled, made incapable of arising, burnt up by the fire of knowledge. He does not fall back upon any view, does not take recourse to them.

801. Now, beginning with the words "For one who has no wish here for either end," he speaks three verses praising the arahant spoken of in the previous verse. **Either end**: these are classified as contact and so forth, as stated previously. **Wish**: craving; **for various states of existence**: for ever-repeated existence; **here or beyond**: here, classified as one's own personal being and so forth, or beyond, classified as the personal being of others and so forth.

Nidd I 78–79. For one who has no wish here for either end: This is said of an arahant, one whose influxes have been destroyed. **End:** Contact is one end . . . [as at p. 1034, Nidd I 37] . . . the origin of the personal entity is the second end. It is craving that is called **wish**. **For various states of existence**: for existence after existence, for desire-realm existence . . . [as at p. 1032, Nidd I 34] . . . for the ever-repeated production of personal being. **Here or beyond**: his own personal being or the personal being of another; his own five aggregates or the five aggregates of others; the internal sense bases or the external sense bases; the human world or the deva world; the desire realm or the form realm and formless realm; the desire realm and form realm or the formless realm. For one who has no such wish, no such craving, for whom it has been abandoned . . . burnt up by the fire of knowledge.

Nidd I 79. There are no places of residence at all: There are two places of residence, craving and views. For the arahant there are no such places of residence; they have been abandoned . . . burnt up by the fire of knowledge. **Grasped after deciding among teachings**: "teachings" are the sixty-two views. **Having decided** among them, having discriminated them, having examined them, having assessed them, having scrutinized them, having recognized them, having clarified them. **Grasped**: the grasping of a section, the grasping of a part, the grasping as best, the grasping of a portion, the grasping of an accumulation, the grasping of a collection. There is nothing grasped, seized upon, adhered to, clung to, resolved upon [with the conviction]: "This is true, genuine, real, factual, actual, the undistorted truth."

802. About what is seen: about purity through what is seen; this method also in regard to the heard and so forth. **Notion**: a view originated by perception. [531]

⁞⁞ **Nidd I 79–80. Not even a subtle notion is formulated by him about what is seen, heard, or sensed here**: For the arahant, whose influxes are destroyed, there is no view arisen from perception, with perception as forerunner, with perception dominant,[1834] in the shape of perception, [a view] thought up, formulated, composed, put together, established by perception—[a view] about the seen or purity through what is seen, about the heard or purity through what is heard, about the sensed or purity through what is sensed. These do not exist . . . they have been burnt up by the fire of knowledge.

Nidd I 80. How could anyone here in the world categorize him?: There are two kinds of mental constructs: mental constructs due to craving and mental constructs due to views . . . [as at pp. 1061–62, Nidd I 69] . . . There is no cause, no condition, no ground by which one might conceive him, categorize him, and put him in a category. ⁞⁞

803. Even the teachings are not embraced by them: Even the teachings of the sixty-two speculative views are not embraced by them with the conviction: "This alone is true, anything else is false."[1835] **The impartial one, gone beyond, does not fall back**: Gone beyond to nibbāna, one who is impartial in five ways does not come again to the defilements abandoned by this and that path.[1836] The rest is clear.

⁞⁞ **Nidd I 81. They do not construct, they have no preferences. Mental constructs:** There are two kinds of mental constructs, mental constructs due to craving and mental constructs due to views. What are *mental constructs due to craving*? Whatever is possessed and considered to be "mine," bounded, circumscribed, delimited, and designated by craving thus: "This is mine, that is mine; this much is mine, this extent is mine; my forms . . . tactile objects." . . . One takes even the whole earth as "mine" because of craving. To whatever extent the 108 currents of craving flow, these are mental constructs due to craving. What are *mental constructs due to views*? The twenty kinds of view of the personal entity, the tenfold wrong view, the ten extreme views. In whatever way the sixty-two speculative views occur, these are mental constructs due to views.[1837] For arahants, mental constructs due to craving have been abandoned and mental constructs due to views have been relinquished. Since that is so, they do not construct anything because of craving or because of views; they do not engender, generate, produce, or create such mental constructs.

They have no preferences: There are two kinds of preferences: through craving and through views. For them, preference through craving has been abandoned and preference through views has been relinquished. Since that is so, they do not have a preference due to craving or due to views; they do not bear them as their banner and flag, as their authority, nor do they go about accompanied by craving or by views. Hence they do not construct, they have no preferences.

Even the teachings are not embraced by them: It is the sixty-two speculative views that are called teachings. **By them**: by arahants, whose influxes are destroyed. **Not embraced**: The view is not embraced: "The world is eternal" . . . "A tathāgata neither exists nor does not exist after death: this alone is true, anything else is false."

Nidd I 82. The impartial one, gone beyond, does not fall back: It is the deathless nibbāna that is called "the beyond," the stilling of all volitional activities, the relinquishment of all acquisitions, the destruction of craving, dispassion, cessation, nibbāna. He has gone beyond, reached the beyond, gone to the end, reached the end, gone to the pinnacle, reached the pinnacle; for him there is no renewed existence, no wandering on in birth and death. **Does not fall back**: He does not repeat, does not fall back on, does not return to the defilements abandoned by the path of stream-entry; he does not fall back on, does not return to the defilements abandoned by the path of the once-returner; he does not fall back on, does not return to the defilements abandoned by the path of the non-returner; he does not fall back on, does not return to the defilements abandoned by the path of arahantship.

Nidd I 82–83. The impartial one: The arahant is "impartial" (*tādī*) in five ways: impartial toward the desirable and undesirable; impartial because he has renounced; impartial because he has crossed over; impartial because he is freed; and impartial as a descriptive term. How is the arahant impartial *in regard to* *the desirable and undesirable*? The arahant is impartial in regard to gain and non-gain, fame and disrepute, praise and blame, pleasure and pain. He has abandoned fondness and resentment, passed beyond favoring and resisting, overcome compliance and opposition. How is the arahant impartial *in the sense of renounced*? The arahant has renounced lust, hatred, delusion, anger . . . all unwholesome volitional activities. How is the arahant impartial *in the sense of having crossed over*? The arahant has crossed over the flood of sensuality, the flood of existence, the flood of views, the flood of ignorance; he has lived the spiritual life, completed the practice; for him there is no more renewed existence with its wandering on in birth and death. How is the arahant impartial *in the sense of being freed*? The arahant's mind is freed, liberated, well liberated from lust, from hatred, from delusion . . . from all unwholesome volitional activities. How is the arahant impartial *as a descriptive term*? The arahant is impartial through a description as one of good behavior, as possessing faith, as energetic, as mindful, as concentrated, as wise, as one having the three clear knowledges, as one having the six superknowledges.

6 Old Age
(*Jarā Sutta*)

What is the origin?[1838] On one occasion, after spending the rains at Sāvatthī, the Blessed One considered the reasons for making a tour of the countryside: for instance, it is conducive to bodily health, it gives the opportunity for laying down new training rules, one can tame people who are to be guided, and when a suitable case arises, one can relate a Jātaka story and so forth. Having considered thus, he set out on a tour of the countryside. While traveling in stages, one evening he arrived at Sāketa and entered the Añjana Grove.

When the residents of Sāketa heard that the Blessed One had arrived, they knew it was not the time to go see the Blessed One. The next day, when it became light, taking garlands, incense, and other offerings, they went to the Blessed One, made their offerings, paid homage, greeted him, and then stood around him until the time came for the Blessed One to enter the village. Then, accompanied by the Sangha of bhikkhus, the Blessed One entered Sāketa for alms.

A certain affluent brahmin of Sāketa was leaving the city when he saw the Blessed One at the entrance to the city. On seeing him, there arose in him the affection of a father for his son, and he headed toward the Blessed One, lamenting: "It has been such a long time since I have seen you, my son." The Blessed One informed the bhikkhus: "Bhikkhus, let this brahmin do whatever he wishes. Do not hinder him." The brahmin came like a cow attached to its calf [532] and he embraced the Blessed One's body all around, front and back, on the right and on the left, saying: "It has been such a long time since I have seen you, my son. We have been separated so long." If he did not get the chance to do so, he would have died with a broken heart. He then said to the Blessed One: "Blessed One, I am able to give alms to the bhikkhus who have come with you. Please grant me the favor." The Blessed One consented with silence.

The brahmin took the Blessed One's bowl, and going ahead, he informed his wife: "Our son has come. Prepare a seat for him." She did so, and stood awaiting the Blessed One's arrival. When she saw him along the road, there arose in her the affection of a mother for her son, and she grabbed the Blessed One by his feet, weeping: "It has been such a long time since I have seen you, my son." She then led the Blessed One to the house and served him with due honor. When he finished his meal, the brahmin removed his bowl. Having understood what was suitable for them, the Blessed One taught them the Dhamma, and at the conclusion of the teaching, both became stream-enterers.

They then entreated the Blessed One: "Bhante, as long as the Blessed One lives in dependence on this city, he should receive almsfood only at our house." The Blessed One refused, saying: "The buddhas do not go exclusively to a single place." They then said: "In that case, Bhante, having walked for alms together with the Sangha of bhikkhus, always take your meal here. Then, after you have taught the Dhamma, return to your dwelling." To benefit them, the Blessed One did so.

People then started to speak of the brahmin and his wife as "the Buddha's father" and "the Buddha's mother" and his family came to be called "the Buddha's family." The Elder Ānanda asked the Blessed One: "I know the Blessed One's mother and father. But why do they say, 'I am the Buddha's mother, I am the Buddha's father'?" The Blessed One replied: "Ānanda, in five hundred consecutive past births this brahmin and his wife were my father and mother. In five hundred past births they were my elder aunt and uncle, and in five hundred past births they were my junior aunt and uncle. They speak with reference to their past affection." He then spoke this verse: [533]

> "Because of previously dwelling together or a present
> benefit,
> affection arises for someone as a lily is born in water."

Then, having stayed in Sāketa as long as he wished, the Blessed One continued on his journey and returned to Sāvatthī. The brahmin and his wife continued to approach the bhikkhus, heard suitable Dhamma teachings, reached the remaining paths, and attained final nibbāna by the nibbāna element without residue remaining.[1839]

The brahmins in the city assembled and said: "Let us honor our relatives." The lay followers who were stream-enterers, once-returners, and non-returners also assembled and said: "Let us honor our fellows in the Dhamma." They all set their corpses in a bier covered with a woolen cloth and, while offering garlands, incense, and other items, brought them out from the city.

As the night was coming to an end, the Blessed One, while surveying the world with his buddha eye, knew the couple had attained final nibbāna. He realized: "When I have gone there, people will hear my Dhamma teaching and many will make the breakthrough to the Dhamma." So, taking his bowl and outer robe, the Blessed One left Sāvatthī and entered the cremation ground. When people saw him they said: "The Blessed One has come wishing to honor the bodily remains of his mother and father." They venerated him and stood there.

Venerating the bier, having brought it to the cremation ground, the citizens asked the Blessed One: "How should the householder noble disciples be venerated?" The Blessed One said, "They should be venerated in the same way that arahants are venerated," and with that intention, he spoke this verse showing they had become arahant-munis:

"Those munis who are harmless ones,
always restrained by the body,
go to the imperishable state,
where having gone one does not sorrow." (Dhp 225)

Then, having surveyed the assembly, teaching the Dhamma suitable for that occasion, he spoke this sutta.[1840]

804. Here, **short, alas, is this life**: This life of human beings, alas, is short and brief, because of the brevity of its duration and because of its essential brevity. This should be understood in the way stated in the Discourse on the Dart (see p. 953).[1841] **One even dies before a hundred years**: One dies even in the earliest fetal stage, and so forth. **Longer**: beyond a hundred years; **one still dies because of old age.**[1842]

⁝▮ **Nidd I 84–86. Short, alas, is this life**: Life is short on two grounds: life is short because of the brevity of its duration and because of its essential brevity . . . [as at pp. 1029–31, Nidd I 30–32] . . . and so too when human life is compared to the life of the other devas up to those in the company of Brahmā.

Nidd I 86–87. One even dies before a hundred years: One dies in the embryonic stage, in the successive fetal stages, as soon as one is born, in the birth chamber, at the age of half a month, a month . . . a year . . . two years, three years . . . ten years, twenty years, thirty years, forty years, fifty years, sixty years, seventy years, eighty years, ninety years. **Even if one lives longer**: If one lives one year beyond a hundred, or two years . . . ten years . . . twenty years . . . thirty years . . . forty years; **one still dies because of old age**: old, aged, advanced in years, come to the last stage, one dies from old age; there is no escaping death. ▮⁝

805. Over things taken as "mine": over objects they possess. [534] **Seeing that there is separation**: This actual separation, this existing separation. It is not possible to avoid separation.

⁝▮ **Nidd I 88. For there are no permanent possessions:** There are two kinds of possession, possession through craving and possession through views. Possession through craving is impermanent, conditioned, dependently arisen, subject to destruction, vanishing, fading away, cessation, and change. Possession through views is impermanent, conditioned, dependently arisen, subject to destruction, vanishing, fading away, cessation, and change. There are no possessions that are permanent, everlasting, eternal, not subject to change.

Nidd I 89. Having seen that there is separation: Having seen that there is parting, separation, alteration—since they exist, since they are perceived.[1843] For the Blessed One has said (DN II 144,10–15): "Enough, Ānanda, do not weep, do not lament! Haven't I already said that there must be parting and separation from everything dear and agreeable? How is it possible to prevent what is born, arisen, conditioned, subject to disintegration from disintegrating? That is impossible." With the change and alteration of the previous aggregates, elements, and sense bases, subsequent aggregates, elements, and sense bases occur. **One should not live the home life**: Having cut off the entire impediment of dwelling at home, the impediment of children and wife, the impediment of relatives, the impediment of friends and companions, the impediment of things stored up, having shaved off one's hair and beard and put on ochre robes, one should go forth from the household life into homelessness, enter the state of ownerlessness, and dwell alone.

806. My follower:[1844] One who is known as "my lay follower or monk," or one who takes as his or her own the three objects of reverence, the Buddha and so forth.

Nidd I 90. Whatever a person conceives thus, "This is mine": "Whatever" refers to anything pertaining to form, feeling, perception, volitional activities, and consciousness. One conceives it through craving, through views, through conceit, through defilements, through misconduct, through exertion, and through the resultants. **Having understood this**: Having understood this danger; **a wise one, my follower**: one who takes the Buddha as "mine," who takes the Dhamma as "mine," who takes the Sangha as "mine." He takes the Blessed One as "mine," and the Blessed One supports that person. For the Blessed One has said: "Those bhikkhus who are deceivers, stubborn, talkers, imposters, haughty, and unconcentrated are not bhikkhus of mine. . . . But those bhikkhus who are honest, sincere, steadfast, compliant, and well concentrated are bhikkhus of mine. They have not strayed from this Dhamma and discipline, and they achieve growth, progress, and maturity in this Dhamma and discipline" (AN II 26,16–24). **Should not incline to take things as "mine"**: Having abandoned taking things as "mine" through craving, having relinquished taking things as "mine" through views, my follower should not incline, should not bend down, should not be inclined, bent, disposed to that.

808. The name alone remains to be uttered: All things such as form and so forth are abandoned, but the mere name remains to be uttered, to be declared thus: "Buddharakkhita, Dhammarakkhita."

⁝▮ **Nidd I 92. The name alone remains to be uttered**: What pertains to form, feeling, perception, volitional activities, and consciousness is abandoned, discarded, disappears, disintegrates, and the name only remains to be uttered, to be spoken, to be pronounced, to be expressed. ▮⁝

809. The munis: arahant-munis; **seers of security**: seers of nibbāna.

⁝▮ **Nidd I 93. Seers of security**: It is nibbāna the deathless that is called security. Those who see security, who see the shelter, the cave, the refuge; who see the fearless, the imperishable, the deathless; who see nibbāna. Therefore the munis, seers of security, wandered having abandoned possessions. ▮⁝

810. This verse is stated to show the appropriate course of practice in the world stricken by death. **Lives withdrawn**: lives having withdrawn his mind from this and that. **A bhikkhu**: a good worldling or a trainee. **They say it is appropriate for him not to show himself in a fixed dwelling**:[1845] They say it is fitting that one practicing in such a way not show himself in a dwelling classified as the hells and so forth. The purport is that in such a way one may be freed from death.

⁝▮ **Nidd I 95. They say it is appropriate for him not to show himself in a fixed dwelling. Appropriate (concord):** There are three kinds of concord: concord of a group, concord about the teachings, and concord of non-production. What is *concord of a group*? When many bhikkhus dwell in concord, harmoniously, without disputes, blending like milk and water, viewing each other with eyes of affection (see AN I 70,25–27), this is concord of a group. What is *concord about the teachings*? There is no dispute, no disagreement, about these teachings: the four establishments of mindfulness . . . the noble eightfold path. In unison they adopt them, trust them, settle upon them, and resolve on them: this is concord about the teachings. What is *concord of non-production*? Even if many bhikkhus attain final nibbāna in the nibbāna element without residue remaining, no decrease or fullness of the nibbāna element is perceived for them (see AN IV 202–3): this is concord of non-production. **A**

dwelling: Hell is the dwelling of hell beings; the animal realm is the dwelling of animals; the realm of afflicted spirits is the dwelling of afflicted spirits; the human world is the dwelling of human beings; the deva world is the dwelling of devas. **They say it is appropriate for him**: They say it is suitable, fitting, proper, correct that he not show himself in hell, in the animal realm, in the realm of afflicted spirits, in the human world, in the deva world. ▮⁞

811. The next three verses are stated for the purpose of praising the arahant, who was shown by the phrase "not to show himself in a fixed dwelling." **On anything**: on the twelve sense bases.

⁞▮ **Nidd I 96. The muni is not dependent on anything. Anything**: the twelve sense bases, that is, the eye and forms . . . the mind and mental phenomena. **Not dependent**: There are two dependencies: dependency through craving and dependency through views. The dependency through craving has been abandoned by the muni and the dependency through views has been relinquished, thus the muni is not dependent on the eye, ear, nose, tongue, body, or mind, on forms, sounds, odors, tastes, tactile objects, or mental phenomena, on a family . . . a group . . . an abode . . . on gain, fame, praise, and pleasure . . . on a robe, almsfood, lodging, and medicinal requisites . . . on existence in the desire realm, the form realm, or the formless realm . . . on percipient existence, nonpercipient existence, or existence that is neither percipient nor nonpercipient . . . on existence with one constituent, with four constituents, or with five constituents[1846] . . . on the past, the future, or the present . . . on anything seen, heard, sensed, or cognized. ▮⁞

812. Anything among the seen, heard, or sensed: Here the connection should be understood thus: "So the muni does not cling to anything seen and heard, or here among things sensed."[1847]

⁞▮ **Nidd I 98. So the muni does not cling to anything**: There are two kinds of adhesion: adhesion due to craving and adhesion due to views. Having abandoned adhesion due to craving and relinquished adhesion due to views, the muni does not cling to the seen, does not cling to the heard, does not cling to the sensed, does not cling to the cognized. He dwells untainted, freed, escaped, released, detached, with a mind rid of boundaries. ▮⁝

813. One cleansed does not thereby conceive things seen, heard, or sensed: Here too the connection should be understood thus: "He does not conceive in terms of that object that is seen and heard, or he does not conceive in regard to things sensed." **For he becomes neither passionate nor dispassionate**:[1848] He does not become passionate like the foolish worldling, nor does he become dispassionate like the good worldling and the trainee. Rather, because he has already destroyed lust, he is designated "dispassionate." The rest is clear.

⁝▮ **Nidd I 98–99. One who is cleansed does not thereby conceive among the seen, heard, or sensed**: It is wisdom that is called cleansing. Why is wisdom called cleansing? Because it is by wisdom that bodily, verbal, and mental misconduct are shaken off and cleansed; that lust, hatred, delusion, anger . . . [as at p. 1023, Nidd I 17] . . . all unwholesome volitional activities are shaken off. Therefore wisdom is called cleansing. The arahant possesses these cleansing qualities. Therefore the arahant is cleansed. He has shaken off lust, shaken off evil, shaken off defilements, shaken off fevers, hence he is cleansed.

One who is cleansed does not conceive the seen, does not conceive in regard to the seen, does not conceive from the seen, does not conceive: "What is seen is mine." He does not conceive the heard . . . the sensed . . . the cognized, does not conceive in regard to the cognized, does not conceive from the cognized, does not conceive: "What is cognized is mine."[1849] This too was said by the Blessed One: "Bhikkhus, 'I am' is a conceiving; 'I am this' is a conceiving; 'I shall be' is a conceiving; 'I shall not be' is a conceiving; 'I shall consist of form' is a conceiving; 'I shall be formless' is a conceiving; 'I shall be percipient' is a conceiving; 'I shall be nonpercipient' is a conceiving; 'I shall be neither percipient nor nonpercipient' is a conceiving. Conceiving is a disease, conceiving is a tumor, conceiving is a dart. Therefore, bhikkhus, you should train yourselves thus: 'We will dwell with a mind devoid of conceiving'" (SN IV 202,20–27).

Nidd I 99. He does not wish for purification by another: A cleansed one does not wish for purity, purification, full purification, freedom, liberation, release by another, by what is not the path to purity, by a wrong practice, by a course that is not emancipating, other than by the establishments of mindfulness . . . the noble eightfold path. **For he becomes neither passionate nor dispassionate**: All foolish worldlings become passionate; the seven trainees including the good worldling become dispassionate. The arahant becomes neither passionate nor dispassionate. He is already dispassionate because he is rid of lust through the destruction of lust, rid of hatred through the destruction of hatred, rid of delusion through the destruction of delusion. He has lived the spiritual life, completed the practice . . . for him there is no renewed existence with its wandering on in birth, old age, and death.

At the conclusion of the teaching, 84,000 living beings made the breakthrough to the Dhamma. [535]

7 Tissa Metteyya
(*Tissametteyya Sutta*)

What is the origin? It is said that when the Blessed One was dwelling at Sāvatthī, two friends, named Tissa and Metteyya, came to Sāvatthī.[1850] In the evening they saw a multitude of people heading toward Jeta's Grove. When they asked, "Where are you going?" people told them: "A buddha has arisen in the world. He is teaching the Dhamma for the well-being of many people. We are going to Jeta's Grove to listen to it." They also went, thinking: "We too will listen."

Since the Blessed One does not teach without bringing forth fruit, as they sat in the assembly listening to his teaching, they thought: "It isn't possible for one staying at home to fulfill this Dhamma." When the multitude left, they asked the Blessed One for the going forth. The Blessed One instructed a certain bhikkhu: "Give them the going forth." After he gave them the going forth and taught them the meditation subject on the first five parts of the body, that bhikkhu set off for a forest abode. Metteyya said to Tissa: "Friend, our preceptor is going into the forest. Let us also go."

But Tissa said: "Enough, friend! I wish to see the Blessed One and listen to the Dhamma. You go." And he did not go. Metteyya then went with his preceptor, and doing the work of an ascetic in the forest, before long he attained arahantship together with his preceptor and teacher. But Tissa's elder brother had died of an illness. When he heard this, he went to his own village. There his relatives enticed him and he disrobed.

Together with his preceptor and teacher, Metteyya came to Sāvatthī. When the Blessed One had completed the rains residence, walking on tour of the countryside, in stages he arrived at that village. There Metteyya paid homage to the Blessed One and said: "Bhante, my friend from lay life is in this village. Please wait a moment out of compassion for him." He then entered the village and brought his friend to the Blessed One. Standing to one side, for the sake of his friend he asked the Blessed One a question with the first verse. [536] Answering him, the Blessed One then spoke the remaining verses. This is the origin of this discourse.

814. Here, **for one who indulges in sexual intercourse**: for one who engages in the sexual act. **Venerable** (*āyasmā*): this is a term of affection. **Tissa**: the name of that elder; for he went by the name "Tissa." **Metteyya**: the clan; he was known just by way of the clan. Therefore, in the account of the original incident, it was said: "Two friends named Tissa and Metteyya." **We will train in seclusion**: He requests a teaching for the sake of his friend. But he himself had already completed the training.

⁝▯ **Nidd I 101–2. One who indulges in sexual intercourse**: What is called sexual intercourse is a bad practice (*asaddhamma*), a vulgar practice, a vile practice—coarse, ending with an ablution, done in secret, the act of coupling. Why is it called "sexual intercourse"? Because it is an act done by a couple who are lustful, impassioned, defiled, possessed, obsessed in mind, by a couple who are similarly inclined. As a quarrel, an argument, a conversation, a dispute, a legal case, a debate are done by a couple, so it is for sexual intercourse.[1851] **Venerable Tissa Metteyya**: "Venerable" is a term of affection and respect. "Tissa" was that elder's name. "Metteyya" was that elder's clan.

Nidd I 102–3. We will train in seclusion: There are three kinds of seclusion: bodily seclusion, mental seclusion, and seclusion from the acquisitions. What is bodily seclusion? . . . [as at pp. 1023–24, Nidd I 19–20] . . . Seclusion from the acquisitions is for those persons without acquisitions, who have reached the end of volitional activities. ▯⁝

815. Even the teaching itself is forgotten: The twofold teaching, by way of learning and practice, is lost. **This is ignoble in him**: This is ignoble in that person, namely, wrong practice.

⁝▯ **Nidd I 104. The Blessed One**: This is a term of reverence. Further, he is the Blessed One (*bhagavā*) because he has demolished (*bhagga*) lust, demolished hatred, demolished delusion, demolished conceit, demolished views, demolished the thorn,[1852] demolished defilements. He is the Blessed One because he has divided up (*bhaji*), analyzed, classified the gem of the Dhamma; he is the Blessed One because he has made an end to states of existence; he is the Blessed One because he is developed in body, developed in good behavior, developed in mind, and developed in wisdom; or he is the Blessed One because he resorts to (*bhaji*) remote lodgings in forests and woodlands, places with little sound, little noise, far from the crowd, isolated from people, suitable for retreat; or he is the Blessed One because he partakes of (*bhāgī*) robes, almsfood, lodgings, and medicinal requisites; or he is the Blessed One because he partakes of the taste of the meaning, the taste of the Dhamma, the taste of liberation, the higher good behavior, the higher mind, the higher wisdom; or he is the Blessed One because he partakes of the four jhānas, the four measureless states, the four formless meditative attainments; or he is the Blessed One because he partakes of the eight emancipations, the eight bases for overcoming, and the nine attainments of sequential dwelling; or he is the Blessed One because he partakes of the ten developments of perception, the ten kasiṇa attainments, concentration through mindfulness of breathing, and the attainment of unattractiveness; or he is the Blessed One because he partakes of the four establishments of mindfulness, the four right kinds of striving, the four bases for spiritual potency, the five faculties, the five powers, the seven factors of enlightenment, and the noble eightfold path; or he is the Blessed One because he partakes of the ten Tathāgata powers, the four grounds of self-confidence, the four analytical knowledges, the six superknowledges, and the six buddha qualities. "Blessed One" is not a name given by mother, father, brother, sister, friends and companions, family members and other relatives, ascetics and brahmins or deities. "Blessed One" is a name pertaining to the end of emancipation, a designation accruing to the buddhas, the blessed ones, along with realization, with the obtaining of the omniscient knowledge at the foot of the bodhi tree.[1853]

Nidd I 104–5. Even the teaching itself is forgotten: In two ways the teaching is forgotten: the teaching as a body of learning is forgotten, and the teaching as practice is forgotten.[1854] What is *the teaching as a body of learning*? That which has been learned—the discourses, mixed prose and verse, expositions, verses, inspired utterances, quotations, birth stories, marvelous accounts, and questions-and-answers[1855]—this is the teaching as a body of learning. What is the teaching as practice? The right practice, the practice in conformity, the practice that does not go contrary, the practice that accords with the good, the practice that accords with the Dhamma; the fulfillment of good behavior, guarding the doors of the sense faculties, moderation in eating, devotion to wakefulness, mindfulness and clear comprehension; the four establishments of mindfulness . . . the noble eightfold path. That is forgotten, obscured, confused, rejected. **And he practices wrongly**: He destroys life, takes what is not given, breaks into houses, plunders wealth, commits banditry, ambushes highways, goes to the wives of others, and speaks falsely. **This is ignoble in him**: This is an ignoble quality in that person, a foolish quality, a deluded quality, an ignorant quality, an evasive quality, namely, this wrong practice.

816. One who previously lived alone: One who had dwelled alone either by way of the going forth or in the sense of relinquishing a group. He **is like a vehicle that has gone astray. In the world they call him a low worldling**: Just as an elephant vehicle or some other vehicle that is uncontrolled enters an uneven road, injures the rider, and falls off a cliff, so when a person leaves the homeless life, by entering upon unrighteous bodily misconduct and so forth he injures himself[1856] in the hells and so forth and falls off the cliff of birth and so forth; hence they say he is like a vehicle gone astray and a low worldling.

Nidd I 105–6. One who previously lived alone. One previously lived alone in two ways: in the way designated the going forth and by separation from a group. How did one previously live alone *in the way designated the going forth*? Having cut off the impediment of dwelling at home, the impediment of a wife and children, the impediment of relatives, the impediment of friends and companions, the impediment of possessions, having shaved off hair and beard, having put on ochre robes, having gone forth into homelessness, having entered upon the state of ownerlessness, one lives, dwells, carries on, goes on, maintains oneself alone. How did one previously live alone *by separation from a group*? Having thus gone forth, one resorts to remote lodgings in forests and woodlands, places with little sound, little noise, far from the crowd, isolated from people, suitable for retreat. One goes alone, stands alone, sits alone, sleeps alone, enters the village for alms alone, returns alone, sits alone in a private place, resolves on walking back and forth alone.

Nidd I 106. Like a vehicle that has gone astray: An elephant vehicle, a horse vehicle, an ox vehicle, a goat vehicle, and so forth, goes astray, takes a wrong path. As that vehicle that has gone astray takes a wrong path, so the one who leaves the homeless life takes a wrong path: he takes up wrong view . . . wrong concentration. As the vehicle that has gone astray runs into a tree stump or a stone, so the one who leaves the homeless life runs into unrighteous bodily action, unrighteous verbal action, and unrighteous mental action; he runs into such unrighteous deeds as destroying life, taking what is not given, sexual misconduct, false speech, divisive speech, harsh speech, idle chatter, covetousness, ill will, and wrong view; he runs into unrighteous volitional activities, the unrighteous five strands of sensual pleasure, and the unrighteous hindrances. As the vehicle that has gone astray injures the vehicle and the driver, so the one who leaves the homeless life injures himself in hell, in the animal realm, in the realm of afflicted spirits, in the human world, in the deva world. As the vehicle that has gone astray falls off a cliff, so the one who leaves the homeless life falls into the cliff of birth, old age, illness, and death, the cliff of sorrow, lamentation, pain, dejection, and anguish.

Nidd I 107. They call him a low worldling. **Worldlings** (*puthujjanā*): In what sense are they worldlings? They generate many defilements, hence they are worldlings.[1857] They have not destroyed the many views of the personal entity; hence they are worldlings. They look up to many teachers. . . . They have not emerged from the many destinations. . . . They create many diverse volitional activities. . . . They are swept away by many diverse floods. . . . They are tormented by many diverse torments. . . . They are burnt by many diverse fevers. . . . They are attached to the manifold five strands of sensual pleasure. . . .

They are obstructed, enveloped, blocked, covered, concealed, and overturned by the five hindrances; hence they are worldlings. **They call him a low worldling**: They call the worldling low, inferior, wretched, miserable, worthless, insignificant. ▮⁝

817. Whatever fame and acclaim—gain, honor, and praise—**he previously enjoyed**, when he was a monk, **fall away from him**. That fame and acclaim fall away from him when he leaves monastic life. **Having seen this**: having seen the fame and acclaim that came to him in the past and their subsequent loss; **one should train to abandon sexual intercourse**: One should train in the three trainings. Why? In order to abandon sexual intercourse.

818. For one who does not abandon sexual intercourse, [537] **oppressed by his thoughts . . . is humiliated**. **The reprimand of others**: words of blame from his preceptor and others. **Humiliated**: discomfited.

⁝▮ **Nidd I 109–10. Oppressed by his thoughts, he broods like a poor wretch**: Troubled, oppressed, weighed down, pursued, and closed in by sensual thought, malevolent thought, aggressive thought, and thought of views, like a poor wretch, like a dullard, like a stupid person he meditates, premeditates, out-meditates, and mismeditates. Just as an owl on a branch waiting for a mouse meditates, premeditates, out-meditates, and mismeditates, or just as a jackal on a riverbank waiting for fish meditates, premeditates, out-meditates, and mismeditates, or just as a cat waiting for a mouse by an alley or drain or rubbish bin meditates, premeditates, out-meditates, and mismeditates, or just as a donkey unladen, standing by a door-post or a dust-bin or a drain, meditates, premeditates, out-meditates, and mismeditates (see MN I 334,18–34), so the one who leaves the homeless life meditates, premeditates, out-meditates, and mismeditates like a poor wretch, like a dullard, like a stupid person—troubled, oppressed, weighed down, pursued, and closed in by sensual thought, malevolent thought, aggressive thought, and thought of views.

Nidd I 110. Having heard the reprimand of others, one such as this is humiliated: His preceptors, teachers, or their colleagues, or his friends, acquaintances, cohorts, and companions reprimand him thus: "It is a loss for you, friend, it is your misfortune, that after you had gained such an excellent teacher and had gone forth in such a well-expounded Dhamma and discipline, and had met such a group of noble ones, you gave up the Buddha, the Dhamma, the Sangha, and the training, and reverted to the lower life for the sake of inferior sexual intercourse. You did not have faith in cultivating wholesome qualities. You did not have a sense of moral shame in cultivating wholesome qualities. You did not have moral dread in cultivating wholesome qualities. You did not have energy in cultivating wholesome qualities. You did not have wisdom in cultivating wholesome qualities" (see AN III 4,25–29). Having heard their words, he is humiliated, oppressed, hurt, distressed, and dejected. ▮⁞

819. The connection of the following verses [with the preceding] is clear. Among these, **weapons**: bodily misconduct and so forth; for these are called weapons in the sense that they cut oneself and others.[1858] Especially, when he is reproached, he uses the weapons of false speech against them, saying: "For this reason I left the monastic life." Hence he says: **This is a great thicket for him, that he sinks into false speech**. "Great thicket" is great bondage.[1859] What is it? That he sinks into false speech. Thus it should be understood: "This sinking into false speech is a great thicket for him."[1860]

⁞▮ **Nidd I 110–11. He prepares weapons [of defense]**: There are three kinds of weapons: the bodily weapon, the verbal weapon, and the mental weapon. The three kinds of bodily misconduct are *the bodily weapon*; the four kinds of verbal misconduct are *the verbal weapon*; and the three kinds of mental misconduct are *the mental weapon*. **When reproached by the words of others**: When reproached by his preceptors . . . companions, he deliberately speaks falsehood, saying: "I delighted in the monastic life, Bhante, but I had to take care of my mother; therefore I left. I had to take care of my father . . . brother . . . sister . . . son . . . daughter . . . friends . . . colleagues . . . family members . . . relatives; therefore I left." He prepares a verbal weapon, creates it, produces it, makes it, builds it.

Nidd I 111. This is a great thicket for him: This is a great thicket, a great woods, a great wilderness, a great marsh, a great swamp, a great impediment, great bondage, namely, deliberately speaking falsehood. **That he sinks into false speech**: Here, someone speaks falsehood. If he is summoned to a council, to an assembly, to his relatives' presence, to his guild, or to the court, and questioned as a witness thus: "So, good man, tell what you know," then, not knowing, he says, "I know," or knowing, he says, "I do not know"; not seeing, he says, "I see," or seeing, he says, "I do not see." Thus he consciously speaks falsehood for his own ends, or for another's ends, or for some trifling worldly end.[1861]

820. Like a dullard he is afflicted: Killing living beings and so forth, and experiencing the suffering caused by this, and seeking and guarding wealth, he is afflicted like a fool.

Nidd I 112. He was known as a wise man. Here, someone previously, when an ascetic, received acclaim and praise: "He is wise, experienced, intelligent, learned, eloquent, a gifted speaker, an expert in the Suttas, an expert in the Vinaya, an exponent of the Dhamma . . . one who attains the base of neither-perception-nor-nonperception." He was known thus, esteemed thus, honored thus.

Nidd I 112–13. Like a dullard he is afflicted: Like a dullard, like a fool, he is troubled, afflicted, tormented. He destroys living beings, takes what is not given . . . commits adultery, speaks falsehood. Then kings arrest him and subject him to various punishments. They have him flogged with whips, beaten with canes, beaten with clubs; they have his hands cut off, his feet cut off, his hands and feet cut off; his ears cut off, his nose cut off, his ears and nose cut off; they have him subjected to the "porridge pot," to the "polished-shell shave," to "Rāhu"s mouth," to the "fiery wreath," to the "flaming hand," to the "blades of grass," to the "bark dress," to the "antelope," to the "meat hooks," to the "coins," to the "lye pickling," to the "pivoting pin," to the "rolled-up palliasse"; and they have him splashed with boiling oil, devoured by dogs, impaled alive on stakes, and his head cut off with a sword.[1862] Seeking wealth, he does not find it, and on account of his failure he experiences pain and dejection. Seeking wealth, he finds it, and then he experiences the pain and dejection of guarding it. If, while he is guarding it, his wealth is plundered, then he experiences pain and dejection because of his loss. Thus engaging in sexual intercourse, he is afflicted like a dullard.

821. Having known this danger here in the before and after: Having known the danger in leaving the monastic life, in the before and after here in this teaching, before [when he was a monk] and after leaving the monastic state, as expressed in the lines beginning "Whatever fame and acclaim he enjoyed in the past fall away from him."

Nidd I 114–15. A muni should resolutely live alone: One resolutely lives alone in two ways: in the way designated the going forth and by separation from a group . . . [as at pp. 1088–89, Nidd I 105–6] . . . maintains oneself alone. One should be resolute in living alone, one should be steadfast, one should undertake it firmly, one should be persistent in cultivating wholesome qualities.

822. This is supreme among the noble ones: The purport is: "This living in seclusion is supreme among the noble ones such as the buddhas; therefore **one should train just in seclusion**." **One should not conceive oneself best because of this**: Because of that seclusion one should not conceive, "I am best," that is, one should not be proud.

823. Void: secluded, devoid of bodily misconduct and so forth. **People tied to sensual pleasures envy him as one who has crossed the flood**: Beings fastened to sensual objects envy one who has crossed the four floods, as debtors envy one freed from debt.

Nidd I 116–17. When the muni lives void: dwells void, secluded, solitary; unoccupied, secluded, solitary in regard to bodily misconduct, verbal misconduct, and mental misconduct; unoccupied, secluded, solitary in regard to lust, hatred, delusion, anger . . . all unwholesome volitional activities. **Indifferent to sensual pleasures**: There are two kinds of sensual pleasures: sensual objects and sensual defilements. Having fully understood sensual objects, having abandoned sensual defilements, one is indifferent to sensual pleasures—one has given up sensuality, cast away sensuality, let go of sensuality, abandoned sensuality, relinquished sensuality, become dispassionate. One dwells hungerless, quenched, cooled, experiencing bliss, having himself become holy.

People tied to sensual pleasures envy him as one who has crossed the flood: Beings excited by sensual pleasures, greedy for them, infatuated with them, stuck on them, impeded by them, envy one who has crossed the floods of sensuality, existence, views, and ignorance, who has crossed the path of all volitional activities, who has gone beyond, reached the end, attained the deathless, attained nibbāna. As debtors yearn for freedom from debt, as the sick yearn for health, as prisoners yearn for release from prison, as slaves yearn for freedom, as travelers on a journey through the wilderness yearn for safety, so those excited by sensual pleasures envy one who has crossed the flood . . . one who has attained nibbāna.

Thus he concluded the teaching with its culmination in arahantship. At the conclusion of the teaching, Tissa attained the fruit of stream-entry and afterward, having gone forth, realized arahantship. [538]

8 Pasūra
(*Pasūra Sutta*)

What is the origin?[1863] It is said that while the Blessed One was dwelling at Sāvatthī, a wanderer named Pasūra, a great debater, had set up a rose-apple branch, claiming: "In all Jambudīpa I am the foremost in debate. Therefore, as the rose-apple tree is the insignia of Jambudīpa, so it should be mine too." Not encountering any rival in debate in all of Jambudīpa, he eventually came to Sāvatthī, where he made a heap of sand at the city gate and set up the branch, announcing: "Whoever is able to debate with me should break this branch." Then he entered the city.

A multitude of people gathered there. Now on that occasion the Venerable Sāriputta, having finished his meal, was leaving Sāvatthī. When he saw the branch, he asked some village boys: "What is this?" They told him all. He then said: "In that case, pull up the branch, break it with your feet, and declare: 'Whoever wants to debate should come to the monastery.'" Then he departed.

When the wanderer had walked for alms, finished his meal, and returned, he saw that the branch had been pulled up and broken. He asked: "Who did this?" When someone said, "The Buddha's disciple, Sāriputta," he was delighted and declared: "Today let the wise see my victory and the ascetic's defeat." He then entered Sāvatthī to bring judges, and while wandering along the roads, squares, and streets, he announced: "Let those come forth who want to hear my ingenuity as I debate the ascetic Gotama's chief disciple!" Thinking, "We will hear the words of the wise," many people came out, both believers in the Teaching and non-believers. Then Pasūra, accompanied by the multitude, went to the monastery, thinking: "When he says this, I will say that." To avoid an uproar and commotion in the monastery, and to avoid bringing in crowds of people, Sāriputta sat down in a seat prepared for him at the tower by the entrance to Jeta's Grove.

The wanderer approached the elder and asked: "Was it you, monk, who broke my rose-apple banner?" Sāriputta replied: "Yes, wanderer." – "Then let's have some discussion." The elder accepted, saying: "Let's begin."

[Pasūra:] "You ask questions, ascetic, and I will answer." [539] Sāriputta said: "Which is harder, wanderer, to ask questions or to answer them?" – "Answering questions, monk. What could be hard about asking questions? Anyone could ask anything." – "In that case, wanderer, you ask and I will answer."

The wanderer was surprised at this and thought: "That was an appropriate bhikkhu to break my branch in its place." Then he asked the elder: "What is a person's sensuality?" The elder said: "Lustful intention is a person's sensuality" (see SN I 22,26; AN III 411,11). When he heard that, glaring at the elder, wishing to ascribe defeat to him, he said: "Then, monk, you don't say that beautiful and variegated objects are a person's sensuality?" – "I don't, wanderer."

The wanderer got him to confirm his thesis three times and then addressed the judges: "Hear, sirs, the error in the ascetic's assertion." [Then turning to Sāriputta] he said: "Monk, don't your fellow monks live in the forest?" – "Yes, wanderer, they do." – "While they live there, do they entertain sensual thoughts?" – "Yes, wanderer, those who are worldlings spontaneously think such thoughts." – "If that is so, how could they be ascetics? Wouldn't they be laymen who enjoy sensual pleasures?" Having spoken thus, he further said this:

"You say lovely things in the world are not sensual
  pleasures,
but that sensual pleasure is lustful intention.
In that case, even a bhikkhu thinking unwholesome
  thoughts
would be for you [a layman] enjoying sensual pleasures."

Then the elder, exposing the error in the wanderer's assertion, said: "Do you say, wanderer, that lustful intention is not a person's sensuality, but that the beautiful and variegated objects are?" – "Yes, monk." Then the elder addressed the judges: "Hear, sirs, the error in the wanderer's assertion." [Then turning to Pasūra] he said: "Friend Pasūra, do you have a teacher?" – "Yes, monk, I do." – "Does he see visible objects cognizable by the eye, or hear sounds and so forth with the other sense faculties?" [540] – "Yes, monk, he does." – "If that is the case, how could he be a teacher? Wouldn't he be a layman who enjoys sensual pleasures?" Having spoken thus, he further said this:

"You say those lovely things in the world are sensual pleasures,
but that lustful intention is not sensual pleasure.
In that case, it would follow that, seeing agreeable forms,
hearing agreeable sounds, smelling agreeable odors,
tasting agreeable flavors, and touching agreeable textures,
even your teacher would be one who enjoys sensual pleasures."

When this was said, the wanderer was speechless, thinking: "This monk is a great debater. I will go forth under him and learn the art of debate." He then went to Sāvatthī, sought a bowl and robe, and entered Jeta's Grove. There he saw Lāḷudāyī,[1864] endowed with a golden body, graceful in all his bodily movements and gestures, and thought: "This bhikkhu is one of great wisdom, a great debater." Having gone forth under him, he beat him in debate. Then, still clad in the robes, he departed for the center of the sectarians. He again announced, as before, "I will debate the ascetic Gotama," and went to Jeta's Grove accompanied by the multitude, saying: "Thus I will beat the ascetic Gotama." The deity dwelling in the tower at the entrance to Jeta's Grove, thinking, "He is not a vessel,"[1865] bound his mouth shut. Having approached the Blessed One, he sat there as if he were mute. People looked at him, thinking, "Now he will ask a question, now he will ask a question," and they made an uproar and commotion, saying: "Speak up, Pasūra, speak up, Pasūra!" Then the Blessed One said, "What can Pasūra say?" and he spoke this discourse in order to teach the Dhamma to the assembly present.

824. This, firstly, is a concise account of the first verse: These theorists declare with reference to their own views: **Here alone is purity**. But **they say there is no purification in other teachings**. In such a case, [541] **declaring whatever they depend on**—their own teacher and so forth—**to be excellent**, asserting the excellence **there**, "This doctrine is excellent," **many** ascetics and brahmins **are entrenched in separate truths**, such as "The world is eternal" and so forth.

⁝▮ **Nidd I 118–19. Here alone is purity**: They declare: "Here alone is purity, purification, full purification, freedom, liberation, release." They declare as purity . . . release: "The world is eternal" . . . "A tathāgata neither exists nor does not exist after death: this alone is true, anything else is false." **They say there is no purification in other teachings**: Except for their own teacher, teaching, group, view, practice, and path, they reject all other doctrines. They speak thus: "That teacher is not omniscient . . . [as at p. 1048, Nidd I 54] . . . worthless, insignificant."

Nidd I 119. Whatever they depend on: Whatever teacher, teaching, group, view, practice, and path they depend on, **declaring it to be excellent**: speaking of it as excellent, speaking of it as splendid, speaking of it as wise, speaking of it as solid, speaking of the method, of reasons, of characteristics, of causes, of possibilities according to their own belief; **there**: in their own view, opinion, preference, and belief. **Many are entrenched in separate truths**: Many ascetics and brahmins are entrenched in many separate truths: "The world is eternal" . . . "A tathāgata neither exists nor does not exist after death: this alone is true, anything else is false." They are settled upon these, attached to them, involved with them, cling to them, are resolved on them. ▮⁝

825. And being so entrenched, the verse says, "desiring debate." Here, **they accuse one another of being a fool**: Two people accuse one another of being a fool, regard one another as a fool, thus: "This one is a fool, that one is a fool." **Those of different convictions assert their argument**: Those dependent on their different teachers and so forth engage in arguments with one another. **Desiring praise, claiming to be skilled**: Both of them, desiring praise, regard themselves thus: "We are skilled debaters, learned debaters."

⁞▯ **Nidd I 120. Those of different convictions assert their argument**: Those dependent on another teacher, teaching, group, view, practice, path. It is a quarrel, a squabble, contention, dispute, strife that is called argument. Or else **argument**: they assert talk that is unnourishing; they start a quarrel, a squabble, a contention, a dispute, strife.[1866] **Claiming to be skilled**: speaking as wise, speaking as steadfast, speaking of the method, of reasons, of characteristics, of causes, of possibilities according to their own belief. ▯⁞

826. As they make their claims, each one is necessarily "keen on speaking." Here, **keen on speaking** means eager to speak in a debate. **Wishing for praise, he becomes anxious**: Desiring praise for himself, he becomes perplexed and anxious even before the debate, thinking: "How can I beat him?" **If his assertion is rejected**: If his assertion is rejected by the judges, who say: "Your statement misses out on the meaning, your statement misses out on the expression." **Upset by blame**: When his assertion is thus invalidated, he is upset by the blame that has arisen. **He seeks a flaw**: He seeks a flaw in his opponent.

⁞▯ **Nidd I 120–21. He becomes anxious**: Before the conversation, he becomes perplexed and anxious thinking: "Will I be victorious or defeated? How can I beat him? How can I strike back at him? How can I make a distinction? How can I respond to a distinction? How can I entangle him? How can I disentangle myself? How can I take a stab at him? How can I encircle him?" **If his assertion is rejected**: The judges who exercise judgment reject him, saying: "Your statement misses out on the meaning, your statement misses out on the expression, your statement misses out on both the meaning and the expression. You have misinterpreted the meaning, you have misstated the expression, you have misinterpreted the meaning and misstated the expression." **He feels humiliated**: He is oppressed, hurt, afflicted, dejected. ▯⁞

827. Not only is he upset, but the next verse says: "If they say his assertion is defective." Here, **they say his assertion is defective . . . rejected**: They say it is defective and rejected by way of both the meaning and the expression. **The loser laments**: Because of this, he babbles: "I must think of something else." **Sorrows**:

He sorrows thinking: "Victory is his." **He moans: "He surpassed me"**: He babbles even more, saying: "He overcame me in debate."

828. These disputes have arisen among ascetics: Here, it is outside wanderers who are called "ascetics." **In relation to them, one becomes elated and dejected**: In relation to these debates, those experiencing elation and dejection on account of victory or defeat become elated and dejected. **One should desist from arguments**: One should abandon quarrels; **for there is no other benefit than praise and gain.**[1867]

⁝▌ **Nidd I 123. In relation to them, one becomes elated and dejected**: There is victory and defeat, gain and non-gain, fame and dishonor, praise and blame, pleasure and pain, joy and sorrow, the desirable and the undesirable, attraction and repulsion, elation and dejection, compliance and hostility. With victory, the mind is elated; with defeat, the mind is dejected . . . with joy the mind is elated, with sorrow the mind is dejected. **Having seen this**: Having seen this danger in quarrels over views, in squabbles over views, in contention over views, in disputes over views, in strife over views; **one should desist from arguments. For there is no other benefit than praise and gain**: Other than praise and gain, there is no benefit for oneself, no benefit for others, no benefit for both; no benefit pertaining to the present life, no benefit pertaining to future lives; no plain benefit, no deep benefit, no secret benefit, no hidden benefit, no implicit benefit, no explicit benefit, no blameless benefit, no undefiled benefit, no pure benefit, no supreme benefit. ▐⁝

829. But since there is no other benefit than praise and gain, one obtaining the supreme gain, **if he is praised there** on account of his view thus, "He is excellent," [542] **having declared his doctrine in the midst of the assembly, he is thrilled by this** victory. And being thrilled, or laughing with a display of his teeth,[1868] **he swells with pride**. For what reason? Because he has **obtained the benefit** of victory **that accords with his wish**.

⁝▌ **Nidd I 124. He is thrilled by this and swells with pride** (*so hassatī unnamatī ca tena*): Because of that victory he is joyful, thrilled, ecstatic, pleased, with his intention fulfilled. Or else, he laughs with a display of teeth. He is swollen with pride because of that victory, uplifted, vain.

830. He yet speaks from conceit and arrogance: Here, not realizing that his pride is "the ground of distress,"[1869] he just speaks from conceit and arrogance.

Nidd I 125. His pride is the ground of distress: His pride, elation, vanity, haughtiness, the mind's desire to excel: this is the ground of distress, the ground of destruction, the ground of oppression, the ground of hurt, the ground of disaster, the ground of calamity.

831. Having thus shown the fault in debate, he now speaks the verse "Just as a hero," refusing to accept the adversary's assertion. Here, **on the king's food**: on wages in the form of meals. **Comes thundering, desiring an opponent**: He describes the theorist as like one who comes thundering, desiring an opponent. **Rush off in his direction**: Go off in the direction of your opponent. **Already in the past, there was no scope for a fight**: He shows: "The group of defilements that might have led to a fight did not exist even in the past; it was already abandoned at the foot of the bodhi tree."[1870]

Nidd I 126. Rush off in his direction, Sūra: Wherever the theorist is, rush off in that direction, head there, go there, advance there; he is your adversary, opponent, foe, challenger. **Already in the past, there was no scope for a fight**: Already at the foot of the bodhi tree, the battalions of defilements did not exist; they were abandoned, eradicated, stilled, stifled, made incapable of arising, burnt up by the fire of knowledge. There was [no scope] for a fight, for a quarrel, for an argument, for contention, for a dispute, for strife.

832.[1871] **Nidd I 127. Tell them: "When a debate has arisen there is no opponent for you here"**: Tell those theorists who are your adversaries, your opponents, your foes, your challengers in debate, in refutation, in striking back, in making distinctions, in responding to distinctions, in entanglement, in disentanglement, in stabs, in encirclement: "There is no opponent for you here when a debate has arisen." When a debate has arisen, opponents who counter, who argue back, who take the opposite side, who make quarrels, arguments, contention, disputes, and strife do not exist; they have been abandoned . . . burnt up by the fire of knowledge. **▣▪**

833. But among those who live remote: who have destroyed the army of defilements. **What will you obtain?**: What adversary will you gain?

▪▣ Nidd I 127–28. But among those who live remote: It is Māra's army that is called the army (*senā*) . . . [as at p. 1061, Nidd I 68–69] . . . When all Māra's army and all the battalions of defilements have been vanquished, defeated, demolished, decimated, and overturned by the four noble paths, one is said to be remote (a destroyer of the army). These are arahants whose influxes are destroyed. **What will you obtain, Pasūra?**: Among those arahants whose influxes are destroyed, what adversary, opponent, foe, challenger will you obtain? **From those who grasp nothing here as supreme**: For those arahants whose influxes are destroyed, there is nothing grasped, seized, adhered to, clung to, resolved upon thus: "This is supreme, foremost, the best, distinguished, the most eminent, the highest, the most excellent."[1872] **▣▪**

834. Brooding: thinking, "Will I gain victory?" and so forth. **You have confronted one who is cleansed**: You have gotten into a contest with the Buddha, who has shaken off defilements. **Indeed, you won't be able to succeed**: Like jackals with lions, having gotten into a contest with one who is cleansed, you won't be able to advance even one step or succeed in your contest.

▪▣ Nidd I 129–30. You have come brooding: You have come thinking, pondering, considering: "Will I be victorious or defeated? . . . [as at p. 1099, Nidd I 120–21] . . . How can I encircle him?" **You have confronted one who is cleansed: indeed, you won't be able to succeed**: The wanderer Pasūra is not capable of entering into a contest with the Buddha, the Blessed One, not able to grapple with him, to discuss matters with him. Why not? The wanderer Pasūra is inferior, wretched, low, miserable, of inferior disposition, worthless, insignificant; the Blessed One is foremost, the best, distinguished, the most eminent, the highest, the most excellent. Just as a hare cannot enter a contest with an intoxicated elephant; as a jackal cannot enter a contest with a lion, king of beasts; as a calf cannot enter a contest with a bull; as a crow cannot enter a contest with a garuda; as a caṇḍāla cannot enter a contest with a wheel-turning monarch; as a goblin cannot enter a contest with Indra, king of the devas—just so the wanderer Pasūra is not capable of entering into a contest with the Buddha, the Blessed One. Why not? The wanderer Pasūra is one of low wisdom, inferior wisdom, insignificant wisdom, trifling wisdom, while the Blessed One is of great wisdom, wide wisdom, joyous wisdom, quick wisdom, sharp wisdom, penetrating wisdom. The Blessed One is "the originator of the path not arisen before, the creator of the path not created before, the teacher of the path not taught before; he is the knower of the path, the finder of the path, the one skilled in the path. His disciples presently live following the path and acquire it afterward" (MN III 8,11–15, SN III 66,15–19).

Nidd I 130. The Blessed One is one who truly knows, one who truly sees; he is the eye, he is knowledge, he is the Dhamma, he is Brahmā; he is the speaker, the proclaimer, the elucidator of the good, the giver of the deathless, the lord of the Dhamma, the Tathāgata. There is nothing unknown to the Blessed One, nothing unseen, unrecognized, unrealized, untouched by wisdom. Whether past, future, or present, all phenomena in all modes enter the range of the Blessed One's portal of knowledge.[1873] Whatever can be known, whether his own good, the good of others, the good of both, the good pertaining to the present life, the good pertaining to future lives, superficial meaning, profound meaning, hidden meaning, concealed meaning, implicit meaning, explicit meaning, blameless good, undefiled good, cleansed good, ultimate good:[1874] all that is encompassed by the Buddha's knowledge.

Nidd I 131. All the bodily actions, all the verbal actions, all the mental actions of the Buddha, the Blessed One, are accompanied by knowledge. His knowledge extends as far as the knowable; the knowable extends as far as his knowledge. Neither exceeds the other; those two things share common boundaries. The Blessed One's knowledge proceeds in regard to all phenomena. All phenomena [can be known] dependent on the Blessed One's directing his attention to them, dependent on his wish, dependent on his attention, dependent on the bent of his mind.

The Blessed One's knowledge proceeds in regard to all beings. He understands the inclinations of all beings, their latent tendencies, their temperaments, their dispositions, whether they have little dust in their eyes or much dust in their eyes, sharp faculties or dull faculties, good qualities or bad qualities, whether they are easy to teach or hard to teach, whether they are capable or incapable of attainment. The world with Māra and Brahmā, this population with its ascetics and brahmins, its devas and human beings, is encompassed by the Buddha's knowledge.

Just as all fish and tortoises from the whales on down move around in the great ocean, so too the world with Māra and Brahmā, this population with its ascetics and brahmins, its devas and human beings, moves around in the Buddha's knowledge. Just as all birds from the garuda on down move in just a portion of the sky, so all those with wisdom equal to that of Sāriputta move around in just a portion of the Buddha's knowledge. The Buddha's knowledge pervades and surpasses the wisdom of devas and human beings.[1875]

9 Māgandiya
(*Māgandiya Sutta*)

What is the origin?[1876] On one occasion, while dwelling at Sāvatthī, as the night was coming to an end [543] the Blessed One surveyed the world with his buddha eye and saw that the brahmin Māgandiya and his wife, living in the town of Kammāsadamma in the land of the Kurus, had the supporting conditions for arahantship. He immediately traveled there from Sāvatthī, sat down in a forest glade not far from Kammāsadamma, and emitted a golden radiance. At just that moment Māgandiya had gone there to wash his face. Seeing the golden radiance, wondering, "What is this?" he looked around and was pleased when he saw the Blessed One. For his daughter had a golden complexion. Many khattiya princes and other eminent men had courted her without success. The brahmin had decided: "I will give her only to an ascetic with a golden complexion." When he saw the Blessed One, he thought: "He has the same complexion as my daughter, so I will give her to him." Therefore he was pleased when he saw the Blessed One.

He quickly returned home and told his wife: "Dear, dear, I have seen a man whose complexion is the same as our daughter's. Adorn the girl, and we will give her to him." His wife bathed the girl with fragrant water and was adorning her with raiment, flowers, and ornaments when the time for the Blessed One's alms round came. The Blessed One entered Kammāsadamma for alms.

The brahmin couple, meanwhile, took their daughter and went to the place where the Blessed One had been sitting. Though she did not see the Blessed One there, the wife looked around and saw the straw mat that served as the Blessed One's seat. Now, by their power of determination, the place where the buddhas have lived and their footprints remain impeccable. The woman said to her husband: "This, brahmin, must be his straw mat." – "Yes, dear." – "In that case, brahmin, it was pointless for us to come here." – "Why, dear?" – "See, brahmin, how the mat is impeccable. It was used by one who has overcome sensual desire." – "When we are seeking the auspicious, dear, don't say anything inauspicious."

Again, walking around here and there, the woman saw the Blessed One's footprints and said: "See the footprints, brahmin. This being is not bound to sensual pleasures." – "How do you know, dear?" Showing her own power of knowledge, she replied: [544]

"The footprints of one who is lustful are arched;
the footprints of a hating person are dragged along;
those of a deluded person are forcefully pressed down;
but these are footprints of one with coverings
removed."[1877]

But this conversation of theirs was interrupted, for the Blessed One, having finished his meal, returned to the forest glade. When the brahmin woman saw the Blessed One's form, adorned with the excellent marks, enveloped by a fathom-wide aura, she asked her husband: "Is this the one you saw?" – "Yes, dear." – "Then it was pointless for us to come here. It's impossible that one like this would enjoy sensual pleasures."

While they were speaking in this way, the Blessed One sat down on the straw mat. The brahmin took his daughter with his left hand and his water vessel with his right, approached the Blessed One, and said: "Good monk, both you and this girl have a golden complexion. She is suitable for you. I give her to you to maintain as a wife. Accept this girl with a sprinkling of water."[1878] The brahmin went up to the Blessed One and stood there wanting to hand her over. Without addressing the brahmin, speaking as if conversing with another, the Buddha spoke this verse: "Having seen Taṇhā."

835. This is its meaning: "**Having seen Taṇhā, Aratī, and Ragā,** Māra's daughters, when they came to seduce me by creating various forms at the foot of the goatherd's banyan tree,[1879] **I did not have any desire for sexual intercourse, so why [should I desire] this,** the body of this girl, **full of urine and feces? I would not wish** at any time **to touch her even with my foot,** so how could I dwell together with her?"

⁞ **Nidd I 133. So why [should I desire] this, full of urine and feces?**: "So why [should I desire] this body full of urine, feces, phlegm, and blood, an edifice of bones bound together by sinews, plastered with blood and flesh, enveloped by inner skin, covered with outer skin, full of holes and openings, oozing and exuding, inhabited by groups of worms, full of various impure parts? I would not wish to contact it with my foot, how then dwell together with it?" ⁞

836. Then Māgandiya thought: "It is said that monks, having abandoned human sensual pleasures, go forth for the sake of celestial sensual pleasures. Yet he does not wish for celestial sensual pleasures or even this gem of a woman. What might be his view?" He then spoke the second verse to ask. Here, a **gem such as this**: He speaks with reference to the celestial gem of a woman. **A woman**: He refers to his own daughter.[1880] **What kind of view, behavior, observances, lifestyle**: "What kind of view, [545] and behavior, and observances, and lifestyle";[1881] **existence and rebirth do you assert?**: "or what kind of existence and rebirth do you assert for yourself?"[1882]

⁞ **Nidd I 133.** [Māgandiya said:] "It is not astonishing that a human being desiring celestial sensual pleasures would not desire human sensual pleasures, or that one desiring human sensual pleasures would not desire celestial sensual pleasures. But you do not desire either." He asks: "What is your point of view? What view do you hold?"[1883] ⁞

837. The connection of the next two verses, which occur as answer and question, is already clear. The concise meaning of the first verse is this: "**Having decided among teachings**, among the sixty-two speculative views, **it does not occur to one**, to me, Māgandiya, **'I assert this,' [about a view] tightly grasped** thus: 'This alone is truth, anything else is false.' Why not? Because **seeing** the danger **in views, not grasping** any view, **investigating** the truths, **I saw** nibbāna, called **the peace**

within because it is the stilling of internal lust and other defilements.

Nidd I 134–35. Having decided among teachings. Among teachings: among the sixty-two views. **Tightly grasped**: There is nothing grasped, seized upon, adhered to, clung to, resolved upon [with the conviction]: "This is true, genuine, real, factual, actual, the undistorted truth." That has been abandoned . . . burnt up by the fire of knowledge. **But seeing into views, not grasping any of them**: "Seeing the danger in views, I do not grasp, do not seize, do not adhere to views. Or they are not to be grasped, not to be seized, not to be adhered to."[1884]

Or alternatively: "'The world is eternal' . . . 'A tathāgata neither exists nor does not exist after death: this alone is true, anything else is false.' This is the resort to views, the thicket of views, the wilderness of views, the contortion of views, the vacillation of views, the fetter of views. It is accompanied by suffering, by distress, by anguish, and fever. It does not lead to disenchantment, to dispassion, to cessation, to peace, to direct knowledge, to enlightenment, to nibbāna. Seeing this danger in views, I do not grasp views, do not seize upon them, do not adhere to them. Or they are not to be grasped, not to be seized, not to be adhered to."

Or alternatively: "These views, thus grasped and seized upon, have such an outcome, such a future destiny. Seeing this danger in views, I do not grasp views, do not seize upon them, do not adhere to them. Or they are not to be grasped, not to be seized, not to be adhered to."

Or alternatively: "These views lead to hell, to the animal realm, to the sphere of afflicted spirits. Seeing this danger in views, I do not grasp views, do not seize upon them, do not adhere to them. Or they are not to be grasped, not to be seized, not to be adhered to."

Or alternatively: "These views are impermanent, conditioned, dependently arisen; they are subject to destruction, to vanishing, to fading away, to cessation. Seeing this danger in views, I do not grasp views, do not seize upon them, do not adhere to them. Or they are not to be grasped, not to be seized, not to be adhered to."

Nidd I 136. Investigating, I saw the peace within: "Investigating, discriminating, examining, assessing, scrutinizing, elucidating, recognizing, 'All conditioned things are impermanent,' investigating, 'All conditioned things are suffering,' investigating, 'All phenomena are non-self' . . . investigating, 'Whatever is subject to origination is all subject to cessation.' **I saw the peace within**: I saw the stilling of lust, the stilling of hatred, the stilling of delusion, anger . . . the stilling of all unwholesome volitional activities, their calming down, allaying, quenching, subsiding, peace." ▮⁝

838. This is the concise meaning of the next verse: Speculative views are said to be **judgments**, since they are grasped by these and those beings after judging among them, and they are said to be **formulated** in that they are put together with their own reasons.[1885] Without having grasped speculative views, **muni, you speak. As to that matter called "the peace within,"** tell me, **how is it proclaimed by the wise?** How is that state revealed by the wise?

⁝▮ **Nidd I 136. Those judgments that have been formulated**: It is the sixty-two views that are called judgments. They are thought up, formulated, composed, established. Or alternatively, "those judgments that have been formulated" are impermanent, conditioned, dependently arisen, subject to destruction, vanishing, fading away, cessation, and change: hence they are formulated (constructed). ▮⁝

839. Then, showing the way in which the wise describe that state together with its contrary, the Blessed One spoke the verse "Not by view." Here, **not by view**: he rejects views, learning, the knowledge of the eight meditative attainments, and the good behavior and observances of outside ascetics. **Nor do I speak**: By joining the word "say" (*āha*) with "not" (*na*) everywhere, and by making a change of persons, the meaning should be understood thus: "I do not speak of purity by view." And as here, so too for the following terms.[1886] **But neither without view**: I do not speak of it without the tenfold right view; **without learning**: without the ninefold learning;[1887] **without knowledge:** without the knowledge of kamma as one's own and the knowledge in conformity with the truths;[1888] **without good behavior**: without restraint by the Pātimokkha; **without observances**: without the observance of the austere practices. **Not in that way**: I do not speak [of purity] by any single one of these factors, merely by view and so forth. **But having relinquished these, not grasping**: "Having relinquished" the former qualities pertaining to the dark side, view and so forth, by eradicating those things; and "not grasping" the latter factors, those pertaining to the bright side, absence of view and so forth, by non-identification with them. **Peaceful, not dependent, one should not hanker for existence**: [546] By this practice one becomes "peaceful" through the allaying of lust and other defilements. "Not dependent" upon anything such as the eye and so forth, one should not hanker for existence, one should be able not to desire, not to yearn. This is the purport of "the peace within."

Nidd I 137–38. Not by view, nor by learning, nor by knowledge: One does not speak of purity, purification, full purification, freedom, liberation, release through what is seen, through what is heard, through what is seen and heard, nor even by knowledge. **Or by behavior and observances**: One does not speak of purity . . . release by good behavior, by observances, by good behavior and observances. **But neither without view, without learning, without knowledge, without good behavior, without observances—not in that way**: A *view* should be accepted: the tenfold right view: "'There is what is given, sacrificed, and offered; there is fruit and result of good and bad deeds; there is this world and the world beyond; there are mother and father; there are beings who are spontaneously reborn; there are in the world ascetics and brahmins of right attainment and right practice who understand this world and the world beyond and make them known to others" (as at MN I 288, AN V 268). *Learning* (hearing) should be accepted: the voice of another, discourses, mixed prose and verse, expositions, verses, inspired utterances, quotations, birth stories, marvelous accounts, and questions-and-answers. *Knowledge* should be accepted: knowledge of kamma as one's own, knowledge in conformity with the truths, the superknowledges, knowledge of the meditative attainments. *Good behavior* should be accepted: restraint by the Pātimokkha. *Observances* should be accepted: the eight austere practices, namely, the forest-dwelling factor . . . [as at p. 1044, Nidd I 47] . . . the sleeping anywhere factor.

Nidd I 138. But neither without view, without learning, without knowledge, without behavior, without observances—not in that way: not by mere right view, nor by mere learning, nor by mere knowledge, nor by mere good behavior, nor by mere observances does one attain the peace within. Yet without these things one does not attain the peace within. Further, these things are provisions to attain the peace within, to achieve it, experience it, realize it.

Nidd I 139. But having relinquished these, not grasping any of them: Abandoning is recognized by eradicating the qualities pertaining to the dark side; non-identification is recognized in regard to the wholesome qualities of the three realms. When the qualities pertaining to the dark side are abandoned by eradication, cut off at the root, made like a palm stump, eliminated so that they are no more subject to future arising, and when there is non-identification with the wholesome qualities of the three realms, at that point one does not grasp them, does not seize them, does not adhere to them. Or alternatively, they should not be grasped, should not be seized, should not be adhered to.[1889]

Peaceful, not dependent, one should not hanker for existence: **Peaceful** through the stilling of lust, hatred, delusion, anger . . . of all unwholesome volitional activities. **Not dependent** by having abandoned dependency through craving and having relinquished dependency through views. Not dependent on the eye . . . on mind, on forms . . . on mental phenomena . . . on the past, future, and present . . . . on things that are seen, heard, sensed, and cognized. **One should not hanker for existence**: should not hanker for desire-realm existence, should not hanker for form-realm existence, should not hanker for formless-realm existence. ▮⁝

840. When this was said, not comprehending the meaning of the Buddha's words, Māgandiya spoke the verse "If indeed it is not by view." Here, the words "view" and the others should be understood in the way already explained. But while he speaks of both sides, the reference is only to the factors pertaining to the dark side. **Utterly confused**: extremely confused, or confusing. **Fall back on**: know.

⁝▮ **Nidd I 141. I think this is an utterly confused teaching**: I think, I know, I understand, I recognize thus: "This is an utterly confused teaching, a foolish teaching, a deluded teaching, an ignorant teaching, an evasive teaching."[1890]

841. Then, rejecting his question based on that view, the Blessed One spoke the verse "Dependent on a view, asking repeatedly." This is its meaning: "Māgandiya, **asking repeatedly**, again and again, **while dependent on a view, you have become baffled over** those speculative views that you have **tightly grasped**. **But from this** internal peace spoken of by me, from the practice, from the Dhamma teaching,[1891] **you have not gained even an inkling**, a correct perception. For that reason, you regard this Dhamma **as utterly confused**."

Nidd I 141–42. You have become baffled over things tightly grasped: "You are deluded, baffled, confused by that same view that you grasp, seize, adhere to, cling to, resolve on. **But from this you have not gained even an inkling**: From this internal peace, or from this practice, or from this teaching of the Dhamma, you have not obtained a correct perception, an accurate perception, a perception of the characteristics, a perception of causes, a perception of possibilities, how then knowledge? Thus from this you have not gained even an inkling." Or alternatively: "You have not obtained a mere inkling of impermanence or conformity with the perception of impermanence, of suffering or conformity with the perception of suffering, of non-self or conformity with the perception of non-self. **Hence you consider it utterly confused**. For that reason you consider it an utterly confused teaching, a foolish teaching, a deluded teaching, an ignorant teaching, an evasive teaching."

842. Having thus shown Māgandiya's involvement in disputes to be caused by his bafflement over ideas tightly grasped, he now speaks the verse "One who thinks himself equal, superior," showing that he himself, being one who has removed bafflement over those other teachings, does not enter into disputes. This is its meaning: "**One who thinks** in terms of this threefold conceit or a view might get into a dispute **because of this** conceit or that view, or with that person. But **not shaking among these three discriminations, he**—'one like me'—**does not think 'equal, superior.'**" We should add "or inferior" to complete the reading.

843. And what is more, there is the verse: "Why would that brahmin assert, 'It's true'?" This is its meaning: "One like me, who has abandoned conceit and views, is a **brahmin** because he has expelled evil and so forth. **Why would that brahmin assert: 'It's true'?**: What position would he declare, or for what reason would he declare: 'My position is true, yours is false'? Or because of what conceit or view, or with what person, would he dispute? **When for him**, for an arahant like me, **there is no 'equal,'** no occurrence of the thought, 'I am equal,' or 'unequal,' no occurrence of a thought in the other two aspects (superior or inferior), **with whom**, among those who are his equals and so forth,[1892] **would he engage in debate**?"

844. Wouldn't such a person definitely be one described as "having left home"?[1893] [547] Here, **having left home**: having discarded any room for consciousness based upon form and so forth by abandoning desire and lust for it; **to roam without abode**: not running because of craving to such abodes as the sign of forms and so forth. **In the village the muni is intimate with none**: He does not form intimacy with laypeople in the village. **Void of sensual pleasures**: separated from all sensual pleasures because of the absence of desire and lust for sensual pleasures. **Without preferences**: not producing personal existence in the future. **He would not engage in contentious talk with people**: He would not utter any contentious speech with people.

845. Such a one is described in the verse: "When he wanders detached." Those **things in the world** from which he is **detached** are speculative views. **The nāga would not grasp and assert them**: The nāga, so called in the sense that "he does not commit a crime,"[1894] would not grasp and assert those speculative views. **As a thorny-stalked lotus, born in the water, is untainted by water and mud, just so the muni, a proponent of peace, free of greed**—just so the muni, who advocates internal peace and is free of greed through the absence of greed—**is untainted by sensual pleasures and the world**: untainted by the two kinds of sensual pleasures and by the world consisting of the plane of misery and so forth.

⁞⁞ **Nidd I 148. As a thorny-stalked lotus, born in the water** (*elambujaṃ kaṇḍakaṃ vārijaṃ yathā*): *Elaṃ* means water. *Ambujaṃ* (water-born) means a lotus (*padumaṃ*). *Kaṇḍakaṃ* means a thorny stalk. *Vāri* means water. *Vārijaṃ* (water-born) means a lotus. **A proponent of peace**: The muni who is a proponent of peace, of protection, of a cavern, of a refuge, of the fearless, of the imperishable, of the deathless, of nibbāna. ▮⁝

846. And what is more, the verse says: "A Veda-master." Here, **because of a view . . . a Veda-master**: "A master of the Vedas (knowledges) of the four paths like me is not a view-goer,[1895] or one going by a view, or one who falls back on that as the essence." The meaning here is this: A view-goer (*diṭṭhiyāyako*) is one who *goes along with a view*, with *diṭṭhiyā* taken as the instrumental case. Also, a view-goer is one who *goes to a view*, with *diṭṭhiyā* taken as the genitive case in an accusative sense. **Or an opinion . . . does not become conceited**: Neither does he become conceited because of an opinion, thoughts about form and so forth. **For he does not identify with them**: He does not identify with them by way of craving and views; he is not one who takes them as a support; he is not one like that. **Not led by kamma or by what is heard**: He is not one to be led by kamma consisting in meritorious volitional activities and so forth, or by what is heard, by [the tenet of] purification through what is heard and so forth. **He is not drawn to any abodes**: Because he has abandoned the two means of approach, he is not drawn to any of the abodes of craving and views.

⁝▮ **Nidd I 149–50. A Veda-master**: It is the knowledge of the four paths that is called the Vedas. One who, through those Vedas, has gone to the end of birth, old age, and death, who has reached the end, gone to the peak, reached the peak, gone to the limit, reached the limit . . . gone to the deathless, reached the deathless, gone to nibbāna, reached nibbāna; or one who has gone to the end of the Vedas, or gone to the end through the Vedas, is a Veda-master, or one is a Veda-master by having understood (*viditattā*) seven things—the view of the personal entity, doubt, seizing upon good behavior and observances, lust, hatred, delusion, and conceit—or by having understood the bad unwholesome qualities that are defiling, conducive to renewed existence, troublesome, that result in suffering, and lead to future birth, old age, and death.[1896]

Nidd I 150. For he does not identify with them: He does not take them as supreme, take them as a support, by way of craving and by way of views. Since craving, views, and conceit have been abandoned by him, cut off at the root, made like a palm stump, eliminated so that they are no more subject to future arising, he does not identify with them, does not take them as supreme, does not take them as a support.

Not led by kamma or by what is heard: He is not one to be led by kamma consisting in meritorious volitional activities or demeritorious volitional activities or imperturbable volitional activities. Nor is he one to be led by [the tenet of] purification through what is heard or by the voice of another or by the opinion of the multitude.

Nidd I 151. He is not drawn to any abodes: There are two means of engagement: engagement by craving and engagement by views. Because he has abandoned engagement by craving and relinquished engagement by views, he is not drawn to any abodes, not tainted by them, has not approached them, is not attached to them, is not resolved upon them, has departed from them, escaped from them, is freed from them, detached from them, and dwells with a mind rid of boundaries.

847. The verse speaks of such a one as "detached from perception." Here, **detached from perception**: one who has abandoned sensual perception and so forth by meditative development preceded by the perception of renunciation. By this term, "one liberated in both respects" and "one who has made serenity the vehicle" are intended. **For one liberated by wisdom**: one liberated from all defilements through meditative development preceded by insight. [548] By this term, the dry-insight practitioner is intended.[1897] **But those who have grasped perceptions and views wander in the world creating friction**: Those who have grasped perceptions—sensual perception and so forth—are principally householders who create friction with one another on account of sensual pleasures. Those who have grasped views are principally renunciants who create friction with one another on account of teachings.[1898]

Nidd I 151. For one detached from perception there are no knots: When one develops the noble path with serenity as forerunner, at the outset one's knots are suppressed, and when arahantship is attained, the knots, delusions, hindrances, sensual perception, malevolent perception, aggressive perception, and perception of views are abandoned . . . no more subject to future arising. **For one liberated by wisdom there are no delusions**: When one develops the noble path with insight as forerunner, at the outset one's delusions are suppressed, and when arahantship is attained, the delusions, knots, hindrances, sensual perception, malevolent perception, aggressive perception, and perception of views are abandoned . . . no more subject to future arising.

Nidd I 151–52. But those who have grasped perceptions and views wander in the world creating friction: Those who grasp perception—sensual perception, malevolent perception, aggressive perception—create friction because of their perception. Those who grasp views—"The world is eternal" . . . "A tathāgata neither exists nor does not exist after death"—create friction because of their view. They create friction between teacher and teacher, between teaching and teaching, between group and group, between view and view, between practice and practice, and between path and path.

As for the rest here, whatever was not explained should be understood in accordance with what was previously explained. At the conclusion of the teaching, the brahmin and his wife went forth and attained arahantship.

10 Before the Breakup
(*Purābheda Sutta*)

What is its origin?[1899] The origin of this discourse and the next five—Quarrels and Disputes, the Smaller Discourse on Deployment, the Greater Discourse on Deployment, Quickly, and One Who Has Taken Up the Rod—is similar to the origin of the Discourse on Proper Wandering (II,13) and is therefore explained in the same way. But there is a distinction, since at the Great Gathering the Blessed One spoke the Discourse on Proper Wandering by making a mind-created buddha ask him questions in order to teach the Dhamma in a way suitable for the deities of lustful temperament. But at the same Great Gathering, some devas had given rise to the thought: "What should be done before the dissolution of the body?" When the Blessed One knew this, in order to benefit them, he made a mind-created buddha accompanied by 1,250 bhikkhus arrive through the sky, and he made [the mind-created buddha] ask him questions. In such a way he spoke this discourse.

848. Here, in the question, firstly, the mind-created buddha asks about the higher wisdom, **How does he see?**, about the higher good behavior, **How does he behave?**, and about the higher mind: **the one who is said to be "peaceful."**

849. In answering, however, the Blessed One does not answer explicitly about the higher wisdom and so forth. Rather, because one is called "peaceful" (*upasanto*) with the allaying (*upasamā*) of defilements by the power of the higher wisdom and so forth, the Blessed One speaks the verses that begin "devoid of craving," showing the allaying of those defilements in accordance with the inclinations of those various deities. The eight verses (**849–56**) that begin there (with "devoid of craving") should be understood to be connected grammatically with this verse: "I call him 'peaceful'" (**857**a). The verses that follow are connected with the very last line of all: "he is truly said to be 'peaceful'" (**861**d). [549]

As for the sequential explanation of the terms, **devoid of craving before the breakup**: one who has abandoned craving prior to the breakup of the body. **Not dependent on the past**: not dependent on the past, the past period of time and so forth; **not to be reckoned in the middle**: neither to be reckoned as "lustful" and so forth in the present period of time; **for him there are no preferences**: because of the absence of the two kinds of preferences (due to craving and views), the arahant also has no preferences in regard to the future period of time. "I call him peaceful": thus the construal should be understood here. This method applies everywhere, but from this point on, without showing the construal, we will only explain the unclear terms.

Nidd I 154. Devoid of craving before the breakup: Before the body's breakup, before the laying down of the body, before the cutting off of the life faculty, devoid of craving, rid of craving, with craving given up, with craving expelled, free of craving, with craving abandoned, with craving relinquished, with lust abandoned and relinquished, hungerless, quenched, cooled, experiencing bliss, one who dwells having himself become holy.

Nidd I 155. Not dependent on the past: It is the past period of time that is called the past. He has abandoned craving and relinquished views in regard to the past period of time, hence he is not dependent on the past. Or alternatively, he does not bring delight to bear on the past, thinking: "I had such form . . . such consciousness in the past" (MN III 188,9–14). Or else his consciousness is not bound by desire and lust, thinking: "Such was my eye in the past and I experienced such forms" . . . "Such was my mind in the past and I experienced such mental phenomena" (MN III 196,12–23). Or he does not enjoy [memories of] laughing, talking, and playing with women in the past. **Not to be reckoned in the middle**: It is the present period of time that is called the middle. He has abandoned craving and relinquished views in regard to the present period of time, hence he is not reckoned as "lustful, full of hate, deluded, bound down [by conceit], seizing [upon views], distracted [because of restlessness], indecisive [because of doubt], or tenacious [because of the latent tendencies]." Those volitional activities have been abandoned; hence he is not reckoned by way of a destination of rebirth as a hell being . . . a deva, as one with form . . . one neither percipient nor nonpercipient.

Nidd I 155–56. For him there are no preferences: Preference through craving has been abandoned and preference through views has been relinquished. Or alternatively, he does not bring delight to bear on the future, thinking: "May I have such form . . . such consciousness in the future" (MN III 188,21–26). Or else his mind does not wish to obtain that which he has not obtained and he does not delight in that because of the absence of such a wish: "May my eye be thus in the future and may I experience such forms." . . . "May my mind be thus in the future and may I experience such mental phenomena" (MN III 197,5–13). Or else his mind does not wish to obtain that which he has not obtained and he does not delight in that because of the absence of such a wish: "By this good behavior, observance, austerity, or spiritual life I will be a deva or one [in the retinue] of the devas" (MN I 102,10). ■⁞

850. Unafraid: not fearful because of not gaining this or that; **not boastful**: not in the habit of boasting about his good behavior and so forth; **not regretful**: one who does not fidget with his hands and so forth. **Speaking with reflection**: One who utters speech after thoughtful comprehension. **Not restless**: devoid of restlessness. **He is truly a muni controlled in speech**: He is one self-controlled in speech whose speech is devoid of the four faults.[1900]

⁞■ **Nidd I 156–57. Without anger**: Anger arises in ten ways: (1) Thinking, "They acted for my harm," one becomes angry. (2) . . . "They are acting for my harm" . . . (3) . . . "They will act for my harm" . . . (4) . . . "They acted for the harm of one who is pleasing and agreeable to me" . . . (5) . . . "They are acting for the harm of one who is pleasing and agreeable to me" . . . (6) . . . "They will act for the harm of one who is pleasing and agreeable to me" . . . . (7) . . . "They acted for the benefit of one who is displeasing and disagreeable to me" . . . (8) . . . "They are acting for the benefit of one who is displeasing and disagreeable to me" . . . (9) . . . "They will act for the benefit of one who is displeasing and disagreeable to me," one becomes angry. (10) And one becomes angry without a reason (see AN V 150). Any such anger, hatred, ill will, hostility, irritation, annoyance, displeasure of the mind is called anger.

Further, anger should be understood in terms of its degrees as extreme or slight. There is a time when anger is merely murkiness of the mind, but there is no contortion or grimacing of the face. There is a time when anger is merely contortion and grimacing of the face, but not yet clenching of the jaw. There is a time when anger is merely clenching of the jaw, but not yet utterance of harsh speech . . . not yet looking around [for a weapon to injure the other] . . . not yet grasping hold of a rod or knife . . . not yet threatening with a rod or knife . . . not yet giving a blow with the rod or knife . . . not yet cutting and slashing . . . not yet breaking and smashing . . . not yet severing the other's limbs . . . not yet taking the other's life. There is a time when anger is merely the taking of life, but has not yet reached the point of total relinquishment. But when through anger one slays other people and then slays oneself, at that point anger has reached its extreme expression, its extreme manifestation. One for whom this anger is abandoned . . . burnt up by the fire of knowledge is "one without anger."

Nidd I 157–58. Unafraid: Here, someone is afraid, fearful, anxious. He is afraid, fearful, anxious, frightened, and terrified: "I do not gain a family [of supporters], a group, a dwelling, gain, fame, praise, pleasure, a robe, almsfood, a lodging, medicinal requisites, an attendant in time of illness. I am not well known." Here a bhikkhu is unafraid, not fearful, not anxious. He is not afraid, fearful, anxious, frightened, and terrified: "I do not gain a family. . . . I am not well known."

Nidd I 158. Not boastful: Here, someone is a braggart, a boaster. He brags and boasts: "I am of good behavior . . . [as at p. 1044, Nidd I 48] . . . I am one who gains the base of neither-perception-nor-nonperception." Desisting and abstaining from such bragging and boasting, departing and escaping from it, released and detached from it, one lives with a mind rid of boundaries. Such a one is not boastful.

Nidd I 158–59. Not regretful: Regret is fidgeting with the hands, fidgeting with the feet, fidgeting with the hands and feet;[1901] [regret arising because of] the perception of what is not allowable as allowable, the perception of what is allowable as not allowable; the perception of the improper time as the proper time, the perception of the proper time as the improper time; the perception of what is blameless as blameworthy, the perception of what is blameworthy as blameless—any such regret, compunction, mental remorse, uneasiness of mind is called regret. Further, regret arises for two reasons: because of what was done and because of what was not done. How so? Regret arises when one thinks: "I have engaged in bodily misconduct; I have not engaged in bodily good conduct. I have engaged in verbal misconduct; I have not engaged in verbal good conduct. I have engaged in mental misconduct; I have not engaged in mental good conduct." Or else regret arises when one thinks: "I have not fulfilled good behavior, guarding the doors of the sense faculties, moderation in eating, devotion to wakefulness, mindfulness and clear comprehension, the four establishments of mindfulness . . . the noble eightfold path. I have not fully understood suffering, abandoned its origin, developed the path, and realized cessation." One for whom this regret has been abandoned . . . burnt up by the fire of knowledge is said to be not remorseful.

Nidd I 160. Speaking with reflection: It is wisdom that is called reflection. Even when he speaks much, he speaks after having thoughtfully controlled his speech. He does not speak anything badly expressed, badly uttered, badly spoken. **He is truly a muni controlled in speech**: Here, having abandoned false speech, a bhikkhu abstains from false speech; he speaks truth, adheres to truth; he is trustworthy and reliable, no deceiver of the world. Having abandoned divisive speech, he abstains from divisive speech; he does not repeat elsewhere what he has heard here in order to divide [those people] from these, nor does he repeat to these what he has heard elsewhere in order to divide [these people] from those; thus he is one who reunites those who are divided, a promoter of unity, who enjoys concord, rejoices in concord, delights in concord, a speaker of words that promote concord. Having abandoned harsh speech, he abstains from harsh speech; he speaks words that are gentle, pleasing to the ear, lovable, words that go to the heart, courteous words that are desired by many people and agreeable to many people. Having abandoned idle chatter, he abstains from idle chatter; he speaks at a proper time, speaks what is truthful, speaks what is beneficial, speaks on the Dhamma and the discipline; at the proper time he speaks such words as are worth recording, reasonable, succinct, and beneficial. He is possessed of the four kinds of verbal good conduct, he utters speech devoid of the four faults, and he refrains from the thirty-two kinds of pointless talk. ▮⁝

851. Without attachment: without craving. **As a seer of seclusion in the midst of contacts**, one who sees seclusion from selfhood and so forth in present eye-contacts and so forth, **he is not led astray among views**: he is not led by any view among the sixty-two views.

⁝▮ **Nidd I 161–62. A seer of seclusion in the midst of contacts**: As to *contact*, there is eye-contact, ear-contact, nose-contact, tongue-contact, body-contact, mind-contact; designation contact, impingement contact; contact to be felt as pleasant, contact to be felt as painful, contact to be felt as neither painful nor pleasant; wholesome contact, unwholesome contact, indeterminate contact; desire-sphere contact, form-sphere contact, formless-sphere contact; emptiness contact, signless contact, wishless contact; mundane contact, world-transcending contact; past contact, future contact, present contact.

A seer of seclusion in the midst of contacts: He sees eye-contact as secluded from a self or from what belongs to a self, or from anything permanent, everlasting, eternal, not subject to change. So too he sees ear-contact . . . mind-contact; contact to be felt as pleasant, contact to be felt as painful, contact to be felt as neither painful nor pleasant; wholesome contact, unwholesome contact, indeterminate contact; desire-sphere contact, form-sphere contact, formless-sphere contact; he sees mundane contact as secluded from a self or from what belongs to a self, or from anything permanent, everlasting, eternal, not subject to change.

Or alternatively, he sees past contact as secluded from present and future contact; future contact as secluded from past and present contact; and present contact as secluded from past and future contact. Or he sees those contacts that are noble, without influxes, world-transcending, connected with emptiness as secluded from lust, hatred, delusion, anger . . . from all unwholesome volitional activities.

He is not led astray among views: For him, the sixty-two views have been abandoned . . . burnt up by the fire of knowledge. He does not fall back upon or rely on any view as essential.

852. Withdrawn: departed from lust and other defilements by the abandoning of them; **not a schemer**: not a cheater through the three means of scheming; **without longing**: devoid of longing and craving; **not miserly**: devoid of the five kinds of miserliness; **courteous**: devoid of impudence in bodily conduct and so forth; **not [morally] repulsive**: because he possesses good behavior and so forth, he is not repulsive but charming and agreeable. **Not intent on slander**: not intent on creating slander that is to be brought about in two ways.

Nidd I 163–65. Withdrawn: Withdrawn through the abandoning of lust, hatred, delusion, anger . . . all unwholesome volitional activities. **Not a schemer**: There are three means of scheming: that consisting in the use of requisites, that consisting in the postures, and that consisting in insinuating talk.

What is the means of scheming consisting in *the use of the requisites*? Here, householders invite a bhikkhu to receive robes, almsfood, lodgings, and medicinal requisites. Being of evil desires, motivated by desire, eager, he rejects a robe, almsfood, a lodging, and medicinal requisites from a desire for more of them. The householders think: "This ascetic is one of few wishes, content, fond of solitude, detached, energetic, a proponent of the austere practices." Then they invite him to more and more robes and the other requisites. He says: "You have faith, things to be given are present, and I am a recipient. If I do not accept these, you will be deprived of merit. I have no need of them, but let me accept them out of compassion for you." And so he accepts many robes, much almsfood, many lodgings, and many medicinal requisites.

What is the means of scheming consisting in *the postures*? Being of evil desires, motivated by desire, eager, someone thinks, "People will esteem me thus," and he composes his way of walking, his way of standing, his way of sitting, his way of lying down; he walks as if in concentration, stands as if in concentration, sits as if in concentration, lies down as if in concentration, and meditates in public.[1902]

What is the means of scheming consisting in *insinuating talk*? Being of evil desires, motivated by desire, eager, intending to gain esteem, thinking, "People will esteem me thus," someone makes statements relating to the noble Dhamma. He says: "The ascetic who wears such a robe is very powerful. The ascetic who uses such an alms bowl is very powerful." Or else he utters talk that is deep, mysterious, subtle, obscure, world-transcending, connected to emptiness, saying: "This ascetic is one who gains such peaceful dwellings."

One for whom these three means of scheming have been abandoned . . . burnt up by the fire of knowledge is said to be not a schemer.

Nidd I 165. Without longing, not miserly: It is craving that is called longing. One for whom this longing, this craving, has been abandoned . . . burnt up by the fire of knowledge is said to be without longing. As for **not miserly**, there are five kinds of miserliness: miserliness related to dwellings, families, gains, praise, and the Dhamma (Vibh 440, §940.3). One for whom this miserliness has been abandoned . . . burnt up by the fire of knowledge is said to be not miserly.

Nidd I 166–68. Courteous (without impudence): Impudence is of three kinds: bodily impudence, verbal impudence, and mental impudence. What is *bodily impudence*? Here, someone displays bodily impudence when in the midst of the Sangha or a group, in the refectory, in the sauna, at a ford for bathing, when entering among the houses, and when one has entered among the houses.[1903] How does he display bodily impudence in regard to the Sangha? Here, someone is disrespectful when in the midst of the Sangha; he stands encroaching upon elder bhikkhus, sits encroaching upon elder bhikkhus, stands before them, sits before them, sits in a high seat, sits with his head covered, speaks while standing, speaks while waving his arms. And so in the other cases.

What is *verbal impudence*? Here, someone displays verbal impudence when in the midst of the Sangha or a group . . . and when one has entered among the houses. How does he display verbal impudence in the midst of the Sangha? Here, someone is disrespectful in the midst of the Sangha; without permission from elder bhikkhus or without being requested by them, he speaks on the Dhamma to bhikkhus who have come to the monastery, answers a question, recites the Pātimokkha, speaks while standing, speaks while waving his arms. And so in the other cases.

What is *mental impudence*? Here, someone who has not gone forth from a high family mentally places himself on the same level as one who has gone forth from a high family. Someone who has not gone forth from a great family . . . from a rich family . . . from an eminent family mentally places himself on the same level as one who has gone forth from an eminent family. Someone who is not knowledgeable about the Suttas . . . who is not an expert in the Vinaya . . . who is not a speaker on the Dhamma . . . who is not a forest dweller . . . who does not observe sleeping anywhere . . . who is not an obtainer of the first jhāna . . . not an obtainer of the base of neither-perception-nor-nonperception mentally places himself on the same level as one who is an obtainer of the base of neither-perception-nor-nonperception. One for whom these three kinds of impudence have been abandoned . . . burnt up by the fire of knowledge is called courteous.

Nidd I 168–69. Not [morally] repulsive: There is a person who is repulsive and one who is not repulsive. What kind of person is *repulsive*? Here, a person is immoral, of bad character, impure, of suspect behavior, secretive in his actions, not an ascetic though claiming to be one, not a celibate though claiming to be one, inwardly rotten, corrupt, depraved. Or someone is prone to anger and easily exasperated. Even if he is criticized slightly he loses his temper and becomes irritated, hostile, and stubborn; he displays anger, hatred, and bitterness. Or someone is angry, hostile, denigrating, presumptuous, envious, miserly, crafty, hypocritical, stubborn, arrogant, of evil desires, of wrong view, one who seizes upon his own view, holds it and grasps it, and does not relinquish easily. What kind of person is *not repulsive*? Here, a bhikkhu is of good behavior, restrained by the Pātimokkha, possessed of good conduct and resort, seeing danger in minute faults. Having undertaken the training rules, he trains in them. Or he is not prone to anger or often exasperated.

Even if he is criticized a lot he does not lose his temper and become irritated, hostile, and stubborn; he does not display anger, hatred, and bitterness. Or he is not angry . . . not one who seizes upon his own view, who does not hold it and grasp it, but relinquishes easily. All foolish worldlings are repulsive. The good worldling and the eight noble ones are not repulsive.

Nidd I 169. Not intent on slander: As to slander, here someone utters divisive speech. Having heard something here, he repeats it elsewhere in order to divide [those people] from these; or having heard something elsewhere, he repeats it to these people in order to divide [them] from those. Thus he is one who divides those who are united, a creator of divisions, one who enjoys factions, rejoices in factions, delights in factions, a speaker of words that create factions. This is called slander. Or one creates slander for two reasons: from desire for endearment or with the intention of causing a breakup. ■:

853. Not swept up by enjoyments: devoid of intimacy with craving for enjoyable objects, the strands of sensual pleasure. **Gentle**: possessing gentle bodily action and so forth; **gifted with ingenuity**: possessing ingenuity in learning, in interrogation, and in achievement. **Not credulous**: He does not believe anyone about a matter he has attained himself.[1904] **Not growing dispassionate**: He does not now become dispassionate because he is already dispassionate through the destruction of lust.[1905]

:■ **Nidd I 171. Gifted with ingenuity**: There are three gifted with ingenuity: one with ingenuity in learning, in interrogation, and in achievement. What is ingenuity *in learning*? Here, someone is naturally learned in the discourses, mixed prose and verse, expositions, verses, inspired utterances, quotations, birth stories, marvelous accounts, and questions-and-answers, and displays ingenuity based on this learning. What is ingenuity *in interrogation*? Here, someone displays ingenuity when interrogated about the meaning,[1906] the method, characteristics, causes, and what is possible and impossible. What is ingenuity *in achievement*? Here, someone has achieved the four establishments of mindfulness . . . the noble eightfold path, the four noble paths, the four fruits of the ascetic life, the four analytical knowledges, the six superknowledges. He knows the meaning, the doctrine, and the linguistic expression, and he is ingenious in regard to the meaning known, the doctrine known, and the linguistic expression known. The knowledge regarding the previous three knowledges is the analytical knowledge of ingenuity. He is endowed with this analytical knowledge of ingenuity; hence he is said to be gifted with ingenuity.

Nidd I 171–72. Not credulous: He does not place faith in anyone else—in another ascetic or brahmin, in a deva or Māra or Brahmā—regarding the Dhamma that he has directly known for himself and personally cognized: "All conditioned things are impermanent." . . . "Whatever is subject to origination is all subject to cessation." As it is said: "Sāriputta, do you have faith that the faculty of faith . . . the faculty of wisdom, when developed and cultivated, has the deathless as its ground, the deathless as its destination, the deathless as its final goal?" – "Bhante, I do not go by faith in the Blessed One about this. Those by whom this has not been known, seen, understood, realized, and experienced with wisdom—they would have to go by faith in others about this. But those by whom this has been known, seen, understood, realized, and contacted with wisdom—they would be without perplexity or doubt that the faculty of faith . . . the faculty of wisdom, when developed and cultivated, has the deathless as its ground, the deathless as its destination, the deathless as its final goal. I am one who has known, seen, understood, realized, and experienced this with wisdom. I am without perplexity or doubt that the faculty of faith . . . the faculty of wisdom, when developed and cultivated, has the deathless as its ground, the deathless as its destination, the deathless as its final goal" (SN V 220–21).

> The person without faith,
> knower of the Unmade, breaker of links,
> destroyer of opportunities, who has expelled all desires,
> he indeed is the supreme person. (Dhp 97)[1907]

Not growing dispassionate: All foolish worldlings are subject to passion. The good worlding and the seven trainees are growing dispassionate. The arahant is neither subject to passion nor one who grows dispassionate. Through the destruction of lust, hatred, and delusion, he is already dispassionate, rid of lust, rid of hatred, rid of delusion. ❖

854. He does not train from a desire for gain: He does not train in the discourses and so forth from a desire for gain. **Not hostile, because of craving he does not hanker after tastes**: Not hostile through the absence of hostility, [550] he does not, because of craving, enter upon greed for the tastes of roots and other flavors.[1908]

Nidd I 173. He does not train from a desire for gain, nor is he irritated over the lack of gain. How does one train from a desire for gain? Here, bhikkhus,[1909] a bhikkhu sees another bhikkhu who gains robes, almsfood, lodgings, and medicinal requisites. He wonders how this is so. It then occurs to him: "This venerable one is an expert in the Suttas . . . an expert in the Vinaya . . . a speaker on the Dhamma . . . an expert in the Abhidhamma.[1910] Thus he gains robes, almsfood, lodgings, and medicinal requisites." For the sake of gain, on account of gain, by reason of gain, for acquiring gain, seeking gain, he masters the Abhidhamma. Thus he trains from a desire for gain. Or else he sees that the other bhikkhu is a forest-dweller, one who subsists on almsfood, one who wears rag robes, one who uses only three robes, one who goes on alms round without skipping houses, one who refuses food brought afterward, one who undertakes the sitting practice, one who sleeps anywhere. For the sake of gain he undertakes these practices.

And how does he not train for the sake of gain? Here, a bhikkhu learns the Suttas, learns the Vinaya, learns the Abhidhamma, undertakes the austere practices, not for the sake of gain, not on account of gain, not by reason of gain, not for acquiring gain, not seeking gain, but only for the sake of taming himself, for the sake of calming himself, for the sake of attaining nibbāna.

Nidd I 174. Nor is he irritated over lack of gain. How is one irritated over lack of gain? Here, one becomes irritated, thinking: "I do not gain a family [of supporters], a group, a dwelling, gain, fame, praise, pleasure, a robe, almsfood, a lodging, medicinal requisites, or an attendant in time of illness. I am not well known." He bears ill will, feels resentment, and displays irritation, hatred, and resentment. Thus he becomes irritated over lack of gain. How is one not irritated over the lack of gain? Here, someone does not become irritated over such thoughts, and he does not bear ill will, feel resentment, or display irritation, hatred, and resentment. Thus he does not become irritated over lack of gain.

Nidd I 174–75. Not hostile, because of craving he does not hanker after tastes. Not hostile: What is called hostility is resentment, repugnance, aversion, irritation, hatred, antipathy, anger, ill will, resistance, animosity, ferocity, displeasure, dissatisfaction of the mind. One for whom this hostility is abandoned . . . burnt up by the fire of knowledge is said to be not hostile. **Craving**: craving for forms, sounds, odors, tastes, tactile objects, mental phenomena. **Tastes**: tastes of roots, of trunks, of bark, of leaves, of flowers, of fruits; sour, sweet, bitter, tart, salty, pungent, acrid, medicinal, delicious, not delicious, cold, hot. Some ascetics and brahmins are greedy for tastes and seek the tastes they like, seeking ever more. One for whom this craving for tastes has been abandoned . . . burnt up by the fire of knowledge consumes food after reflecting carefully: "I eat neither for amusement nor for intoxication nor for the sake of physical beauty and attractiveness, but only for the support and maintenance of this body, for avoiding harm, and for assisting the spiritual life, considering: 'Thus I shall terminate the old feeling and not arouse a new feeling, and I shall be healthy and blameless and dwell at ease.'" He abandons, dispels, terminates, eliminates craving for tastes. He has desisted from craving for tastes, abstained, refrained, departed, escaped from it, been released and detached from it, and lives with a mind rid of boundaries.

855. Equanimous: possessing the six-factored equanimity; **mindful**: equipped with mindfulness consisting in contemplation of the body and so forth.

Nidd I 176–77. Equanimous: possessing the six-factored equanimity. Having seen a form with the eye, one is neither joyful nor saddened but dwells equanimous, mindful, and clearly comprehending. Having heard a sound with the ear . . . Having smelled an odor with the nose . . . Having experienced a taste with the tongue . . . Having felt a tactile object with the body . . . Having cognized a mental phenomenon with the mind, one is neither joyful nor saddened but dwells equanimous, mindful, and clearly comprehending. Having seen a form with the eye . . . cognized a mental phenomenon with the mind, one does not lust after one that is enticing, does not hate one that is repulsive, is not deluded by one that is deluding, does not become irritated by one that is irritating, does not become intoxicated over one that is intoxicating, is not defiled by one that is defiling. In the seen there is merely what is seen, in the heard merely what is heard, in the sensed merely what is sensed, in the cognized merely what is cognized. One is not tainted by the seen, the heard, the sensed, and the cognized.

Nidd I 178. For him there are no swellings: There are seven swellings: the swelling of lust . . . the swelling of kamma.[1911] For the arahant whose influxes are destroyed these swellings do not exist, are not found, are not apprehended; they have been abandoned . . . burnt up by the fire of knowledge.

856. No dependencies: no dependencies on craving and views. **Having known the Dhamma**: having known the Dhamma in the modes of impermanence and so forth; **he is independent**: independent with respect to those [two] dependencies. He shows: "Without knowledge of the Dhamma, there is no absence of dependencies." **For existence or nonexistence**: for eternal being or for annihilation.

Nidd I 179. Having known the Dhamma: Having known, "All conditioned things are impermanent" . . . "Whatever is subject to origination is all subject to cessation," **he is independent**: having abandoned dependency on craving, having relinquished dependency on views, he is not dependent on the eye . . . the mind; not dependent on forms . . . tactile objects; not dependent on a family, a group, a dwelling . . . on anything seen, heard, sensed, or cognized.

No craving is found in him for existence or nonexistence. No craving: craving for forms, for sounds, for odors, for tastes, for tactile objects, for mental phenomena. **For existence**: for the view of existence; **for nonexistence**: for the view of nonexistence; **for existence**: for the eternalist view; **for nonexistence**: for the annihilationist view; **for existence**: for ever-repeated existence, for ever-repeated destinations, for ever-repeated rebirth, for ever-repeated conception, for the ever-repeated production of personal being. For the arahant whose influxes have been destroyed this craving does not exist, is not found, is not apprehended; it has been abandoned . . . burnt up by the fire of knowledge.

857. I call him "peaceful": I say that the one described in such ways in each of the preceding verses is "peaceful." **He has crossed over attachment**: He has crossed over the great craving, designated "attachment" because of its diffusion and so forth.[1912]

⁞⁞ **Nidd I 180. In him no knots are found**: There are four knots: the bodily knot of longing, the bodily knot of ill will, the bodily knot of seizing upon good behavior and observances, and the bodily knot of dogmatic adherence to claims of truth . . . [as at p. 1063, Nidd I 70–71] . . . For the arahant whose influxes have been destroyed these knots do not exist . . . burnt up by the fire of knowledge. ⁞⁞

858. Now, praising the one who is peaceful, he says, "He has no sons," and so forth. Here, "sons" are of four kinds, biological sons and so forth. And here, it should be understood, sons and other possessions are stated under the name "sons." For those are not found with him, or because of their absence they do not exist.

⁞⁞ **Nidd I 181. He has no sons**: There are four kinds of sons: the biological son, the territorial son, the adopted son, and the apprentice son.[1913] ⁞⁞

859. That by which they might speak of him, that fault—lust and other defilements—by which worldlings, even all devas and humans, and ascetics and brahmins outside here might speak of him as being "lustful" or "full of hate," **is not esteemed by him**: that fault such as lust is not esteemed by that arahant. **Therefore he is not stirred up by words**: for that reason, he is not shaken amid words of blame.

⁞⁞ **Nidd I 181–82. That by which they might speak of him—worldlings as well as ascetics and brahmins. Worldlings**: They generate many defilements, hence they are worldlings . . . [as at pp. 1089–90, Nidd I 107] . . . They are obstructed, enveloped, blocked, covered, concealed, and overturned by the five hindrances; hence they are worldlings. **Ascetics**: wanderers outside here. **Brahmins**: those who are pompous speakers.[1914] The lust, hatred, delusion, conceit, views, restlessness, doubt, latent tendencies by which they might speak of him as lustful, or full of hate, or deluded, or bound down [by conceit], or seizing [upon views], or distracted [by restlessness], or indecisive [because of doubt], or tenacious [because of the latent tendencies]—those volitional activities have been abandoned. Since they are abandoned, there is no cause, no condition, no reason by which they could speak of him as a hell being, an animal, an afflicted spirit, a human being, or a deva, as having form or as formless, as percipient or as nonpercipient or as neither-percipient-nor-nonpercipient.

860. Does not speak [of himself] as among superiors: He does not include himself among those who are distinguished and assert because of arrogance: "I am distinguished." The same method in regard to the other two (equals and inferiors). **Not given to mental construction, he does not enter upon mental constructs**: Such a one does not enter the two kinds of mental constructs. Why not? It is said: "Because he is not given to mental construction but is one who has abandoned mental constructs."

Nidd I 183–84. Not given to mental construction, he does not enter upon mental constructs: There are two kinds of mental constructs: mental constructs due to craving and mental constructs due to views. When mental constructs due to craving have been abandoned and mental constructs due to views have been relinquished, because they have been relinquished, he does not enter upon mental constructs due to craving or mental constructs due to views. **Not given to mental construction**: There are two kinds of mental constructs: mental constructs due to craving and mental constructs due to views. When mental constructs due to craving have been abandoned and mental constructs due to views have been relinquished, because they have been relinquished, he does not construct anything by way of craving or by way of views; he does not engender, generate, produce, or create such mental constructs.

861. As his own: embraced as "mine." **And who does not sorrow over what is absent**: he does not sorrow over what is nonexistent and so forth. **Who does not enter upon things**: who does not enter upon things because of desire and so forth. **He is truly said to be "peaceful"**: Such a supreme person is said to be peaceful.

Nidd I 185. Who does not enter upon things: He does not proceed along the course of desire, hatred, delusion, or fear. He does not proceed because of lust, hatred, delusion, conceit, views, restlessness, doubt, or the latent tendencies. He is not moved, led, swayed, carried off by divisive teachings.

Thus he concluded the teaching with its culmination in arahantship. At the conclusion of the teaching, 100,000 koṭis of deities attained arahantship, and there was no counting of those who became stream-enterers and so forth. [551]

11 Quarrels and Disputes
(*Kalahavivāda Sutta*)

What is the origin? This too originated at the same Great Gathering. When some deities gave rise to the thought, "From where do the eight things—quarrels and so forth—come forth?" to make these matters clear to them, in the way already explained, the Blessed One had a mind-created buddha question him and the discourse was spoken in response.[1915] Here, there is a clear connection between all the verses because they follow a question-and-answer sequence. But the explanation of unclear terms should be understood as follows.

862. From where do quarrels and disputes arise: From where are quarrels and the preliminary disputes born? **Lamentation, sorrow, and miserliness,** from where do they arise?: **From where do conceit and arrogance arise along with slander**—all these eight defilements? **Please tell me this**: I ask you, tell me about this matter.

⁝⁝ **Nidd I 186. Quarrels and disputes**: From one angle, quarrel and dispute are the same. A quarrel is a dispute and a dispute is a quarrel. Or alternatively, from another angle, the preliminary phase of a quarrel is called a dispute. Kings dispute with kings, khattiyas with khattiyas, brahmins with brahmins, householders with householders; mother disputes with son, son with mother, father with son, son with father; brother disputes with brother, brother with sister, sister with brother, friend with friend (MN I 86,18–22). This is a dispute. What is a quarrel? Laypeople intent on violence create a quarrel by body and speech; monastics, committing an offense, create a quarrel by body and speech. This is a quarrel. **From where do they arise?**: From where are they born, from where do they originate, from what are they produced, what is their origin? He asks about the root of quarrels and disputes, about the cause, the basis, the origin, the foundation, the ground, the condition.

Nidd I 187. Lamentation, sorrow, and miserliness. Lamentation: for one affected by loss of relatives, loss of wealth, loss of health, loss of good behavior, loss of view, or who encounters some other misfortune or is affected by some other painful state, the wail and lament, wailing and lamenting, the state of having wailed and lamented, babbling, blabbering, and blathering. **Sorrow**: for one affected by loss of relatives, loss of wealth, loss of health, loss of good behavior, loss of view, or who encounters some other misfortune or is affected by some other painful state, sorrow, sorrowing, sorrowfulness, inward sorrow, inward misery, inward burning, the consumption of the mind, dejection, the dart of sorrow. **Miserliness:** There are five kinds of miserliness: miserliness related to dwellings, families, gains, praise, and the Dhamma. Further, there is the grip of miserliness over the aggregates, over the elements, and over the sense bases.

Conceit and arrogance. Here, *conceit*: someone generates conceit because of social class, clan, family lineage, beauty, wealth, learning, line of work, skill in a craft, sphere of knowledge, learning, ingenuity, or for some other reason. *Arrogance*: someone looks down at others because of social class . . . or for some other reason. **Slander:** Here someone utters divisive speech . . . [as at p. 1126, Nidd I 169] . . . Or one creates slander for two reasons: from desire for endearment or with the intention of causing a breakup.

863. Arise from what is pleasing: they are born from a pleasing object; the application (*yutti*) here is stated in the Niddesa. **Quarrels and disputes are connected with miserliness**: By this he shows that not only a dear object but miserliness too is a condition for quarrels and disputes. And here it should be understood that all those things are stated under the heading of quarrels and disputes. And as miserliness is a condition for them, so disputes, too, are a condition for slanders. Hence he says: **and slanders occur when disputes arise**.

⁞█ **Nidd I 188–89. Quarrels and disputes arise from what is pleasing**: There are two kinds of pleasing things: beings (*sattā*) and inanimate things (*saṅkhārā*). What beings are pleasing? Those who desire one's good, who desire one's well-being, who desire one's comfort, who desire one's security; one's mother, father, brother, sister, son, daughter, friends, companions, relatives, other family members. What inanimate things are pleasing? Agreeable forms, sounds, odors, tastes, and tactile objects. They create a quarrel when anxious about being deprived of a pleasing object, when being deprived of it, when deprived of it. They create a quarrel when anxious about the change of a pleasing object, when it is changing, when it has changed. They dispute when anxious about being deprived of a pleasing object, when being deprived of it, when deprived of it. They dispute when anxious about the change of a pleasing object, when it is changing, when it has changed. They lament . . . they sorrow . . . when it has changed. They protect, guard, embrace a dear object, take it as "mine," and hoard it. **Conceit and arrogance along with slander**: Based on a pleasing object they generate *conceit*, generate *arrogance*. Here someone utters divisive speech . . . [as above] . . . Or one creates slander for two reasons: from desire for endearment or with the intention of causing a breakup. █⁞

864. From what do pleasing things in the world originate, and those states of greed that spread through the world?: It was said that quarrels arise from what is pleasing. [He now asks]: "From what do pleasing things in the world originate?" And not only pleasing things but also the greed of those greedy ones—khattiyas and others—who wander in the world motivated by greed, overcome by greed: from what does that greed originate?[1916] Thus he asks about two matters (pleasing things and states of greed) with a single question. **Longing and fulfillment**: Longing and the success of that longing; **which a person has about the future**: which serve for supporting; what is meant is that they are a support.[1917] This too is just a single question.

865. Originate from desire: Originate from desire, from sensual desire and so forth. **As do those states of greed that spread**

through the world: The greed of those greedy ones—khattiyas and others—who wander about also originates from desire. Thus he answers both matters together. **From this originate**: what is meant is that they originate from desire itself. [552]

Nidd I 191. Pleasing things in the world originate from desire: Desire is sensual desire, sensual lust, sensual delight, sensual craving, the flood of sensuality, the bond of sensuality, clinging to sensual pleasures, the hindrance of sensual desire. Further, there are five kinds of desire: desire in seeking, desire in obtaining, desire in using, desire in storing up, and desire in spending. What is *desire in seeking*? Here, someone who is avid, needy, stirred by desire, seeks forms, sounds, odors, tastes, tactile objects. What is *desire in obtaining*? Here, someone who is avid, needy, stirred by desire, obtains forms . . . tactile objects. What is *desire in using*? Here, someone who is avid, needy, stirred by desire, uses forms . . . tactile objects. What is *desire in storing up*? Here, someone who is avid, needy, stirred by desire, stores up wealth, thinking: "This will be useful in emergencies." What is desire *in spending*? Here, someone who is avid, needy, stirred by desire, spends wealth on elephant troops, cavalry, charioteers, archers, and infantry, thinking: "They will protect me, guard me, and accompany me." **As do those states of greed that spread through the world**: *Those*: khattiyas, brahmins, vessas, and suddas, householders and monastics, devas and humans. *Greed*: that which is greed, being greedy, greediness, passion, covetousness, greed as an unwholesome root.

Nidd I 191–92. From this originate the longing and fulfillment: It is craving that is called longing. As to fulfillment, here someone seeking forms obtains forms; he is fulfilled by forms. Someone seeking sounds . . . tactile objects, a family, a group, an abode, gain, honor, praise, pleasure, a robe, almsfood, a lodging, medicinal requisites, the Suttas, the Vinaya, the Abhidhamma . . . the first jhāna . . . the base of neither-perception-nor-nonperception obtains the base of neither-perception-nor-nonperception; he is fulfilled by the base of neither-perception-nor-nonperception. The success of one's longing is spoken of as fulfillment. **That a person has about the future**: those supports of a person that are islands, protectors, caverns, refuges, goals, supports.

866. Judgments: judgments based on craving and views. **And those [other] things the Ascetic has mentioned**: From what arise those other unwholesome qualities that the Buddha-ascetic has mentioned, those associated with anger and so forth.

⁞▮ **Nidd I 193. And those [other] things the Ascetic has mentioned**: Those things that accompany anger, false speech, and perplexity, which are coarisen with them, concomitant with them, associated with them, having a single arising, a single cessation, a single basis (the same sense organ), and a single object.[1918] ▮⁞

867. Desire originates based on what they say: Desire arises by way of longing for union and separation **based on that** which is **pleasant or unpleasant**, a designation for pleasant and painful feeling and those objects that are their basis. At this point the question "From what in the world does desire originate?" has been answered. **Having seen the vanishing and coming-to-be of forms**, having seen the waning and arising of forms, **a person forms a judgment in the world**: In the world—the plane of misery and so forth—a person forms a judgment based on craving for the purpose of acquiring wealth or a judgment based on views, such as "My self has arisen" and so forth. But the application here has already been stated in the Niddesa. By this much the question "From what do judgments too arise?" has been answered.

⁞▮ **Nidd I 194. Desire originates based on that which they say is "pleasant" or "unpleasant" in the world:** Desire arises based on the pleasant and unpleasant, based on pleasure and pain, based on joy and dejection, based on the desirable and the undesirable, based on attraction and aversion. **Having seen the vanishing and coming-to-be of forms. Forms**: the four great elements and the form dependent on the four great elements. What is the coming-to-be of forms? The coming-to-be of forms is their arising, origination, production, manifestation. What is the vanishing of forms? The ending of forms is their destruction, waning, breakup, dissolution, impermanence, disappearance. **Having seen the vanishing and coming-to-be of forms**: having assessed, having scrutinized, having recognized, having clarified them.

Nidd I 194–95. A person forms a judgment in the world: There are two kinds of judgment, judgment based on craving and judgment based on views. How does one form a *judgment based on craving*? Here, someone does not obtain unarisen wealth and loses arisen wealth. It occurs to him: "Why is it that I do not obtain unarisen wealth and lose arisen wealth?" He thinks: "It is because I am intent on liquor, wine, and intoxicants, the basis for heedlessness, that I do not obtain unarisen wealth and lose arisen wealth. It is because I am intent on roaming the streets at late hours . . . because I am intent on festivals . . . on gambling . . . on evil friends . . . . on laziness that I do not obtain unarisen wealth and lose arisen wealth." Having known this, he does not resort to the six channels for loss of wealth and resorts to the six channels for acquiring wealth.[1919] Or else he undertakes agriculture or business or livestock cultivation or archery or government service or some other craft. Thus one forms a judgment based on craving. How does one form *a judgment based on views*? When the eye has arisen, one thinks: "My self has arisen." When the eye has disappeared, one thinks: "My self has disappeared and gone." When the ear . . . the mind has arisen, one thinks: "My self has arisen." When the mind has disappeared, one thinks: "My self has disappeared and gone." Thus one forms a judgment based on views.

868. These things, too, arise when that dyad exists: These things such as anger and the rest arise when the dyad of the pleasant and unpleasant exists. The way they arise has been stated in the Niddesa. At this point the third question has been answered.

Now, showing one who might be perplexed by the questions answered the method for abandoning perplexity, he says: **One perplexed should train on the path of knowledge**. This means that he should train in the three trainings for knowledge and vision, for the achievement of knowledge. Why? **Having known, the Ascetic stated these things**: because the Buddha-ascetic spoke about these things only after having known them. He does not lack knowledge about these things.[1920] But if one does not know them oneself because of one's lack of knowledge, this is not due to a fault in the teaching. Therefore "one perplexed should train on the path of knowledge; having known, the Ascetic stated these things."

Nidd I 195–96. Anger, false speech, and perplexity: Anger, false speech, and perplexity arise based on a desirable object and based on an undesirable object. How does anger arise based on an undesirable object? Anger naturally arises based on an undesirable object. Anger arises when one thinks: "He harmed me, he is harming me, he will harm me. He harmed, is harming, will harm one pleasing and agreeable to me. He benefited, is benefiting, will benefit one displeasing and disagreeable to me." How does anger arise based on a desirable object? Anger arises when one is anxious about being deprived of a desirable object, when one is being deprived of it, when one has been deprived of it. Anger arises when one is anxious about the change of a desirable object, when it is changing, when it has changed.

How does false speech arise based on an undesirable object? Here, someone bound by chains speaks a deliberate lie in order to get free from bondage. How does false speech arise based on a desirable object? Here, someone speaks a deliberate lie for the sake of agreeable forms . . . tactile objects, for the sake of a robe, almsfood, lodging, or medicinal requisites.

How does perplexity arise based on an undesirable object? One wonders: "Will I recover from illness of the eyes, ears, nose, tongue, body, the head, the earlobes, the mouth, the teeth?" How does perplexity arise based on a desirable object? One wonders: "Will I get desirable forms . . . tactile objects, a family, a group, an abode, gain, fame, praise, pleasure, a robe, almsfood, lodging, or medicinal requisites?"

Nidd I 196–98. When that dyad exists: When the pleasant and unpleasant exist, when pleasure and pain exist, when joy and dejection exist, when the desirable and the undesirable exist, when attraction and aversion exist. **One perplexed should train on the path of knowledge**: One perplexed should train in the higher good behavior, in the higher mind, in the higher wisdom in order to achieve knowledge . . . [as at pp. 1028–29, Nidd I 28–29] . . . This is the training in the higher wisdom. **Having known, the Ascetic stated these things**: Having known, having understood, having assessed, having scrutinized, having clarified, having recognized, he stated, pointed out, taught, proclaimed, established, disclosed, analyzed, elucidated, revealed: "All conditioned things are impermanent" . . . "Whatever is subject to origination is all subject to cessation."

869–70. From what do the pleasant and unpleasant originate?: Here, by "the pleasant and unpleasant," it is only pleasant and unpleasant feeling that are intended.[1921] **As to this matter of vanishing and coming-to-be**: This is what is meant: "As to this matter of the vanishing and coming-to-be of the pleasant and unpleasant, tell me from what it originates."[1922] And here, what should be understood as the denotation of "vanishing and coming-to-be" are the views of nonexistence and existence based on the vanishing and coming-to-be of the pleasant and unpleasant.[1923] [553] Thus in regard to the answer to this question, it is said in the Niddesa: "The view of existence originates from contact, and the view of nonexistence also originates from contact." **Originates from this**: originates from contact.

⁞▯ **Nidd I 199–200. The pleasant and unpleasant originate from contact**: In dependence on a contact to be felt as pleasant, a pleasant feeling arises. With the cessation of that contact to be felt as pleasant, the corresponding feeling that had arisen ceases and becomes still. In dependence on a contact to be felt as painful, a painful feeling arises. With the cessation of that contact to be felt as painful, the corresponding feeling that had arisen ceases and becomes still. In dependence on a contact to be felt as neither painful nor pleasant, a neither-painful-nor-pleasant feeling arises. With the cessation of that contact to be felt as neither painful nor pleasant, the corresponding feeling that had arisen ceases and becomes still. **The pleasant and unpleasant originate from contact**: The pleasant and unpleasant have contact as basis, contact as origin, are born of contact, produced by contact. **When contact does not exist, these do not come to be:** When contact does not exist, the pleasant and unpleasant do not originate, do not arise, are not engendered, are not produced, do not become manifest. **As to this matter of vanishing and coming-to-be, I tell you that it originates from this**: The view of existence originates from contact, and the view of nonexistence also originates from contact. I tell you that they originate from contact, are born of contact, are produced from contact. ▯⁞

871. When what has vanished do contacts not touch one?: When what has been transcended do the five kinds of [sensory] contact—eye-contact and so forth—not touch one?

872. Dependent upon name and form: dependent on the associated "name" (mentality) and the "form" (material form) consisting in the sense base and object.[1924] **When form has vanished, contacts do not touch one**: When form has been transcended, the five kinds of [sensory] contact do not touch one.[1925]

Nidd I 201–2. Contacts are dependent upon name and form: Dependent on the eye and forms, eye-consciousness arises; the meeting of the three is contact. The eye and forms pertain to form (material form); apart from eye-contact, the associated mental phenomena pertain to name (mentality).[1926] Thus contact is dependent upon name and form. So too for the ear and sounds, the nose and odors, the tongue and tastes, and the body and tactile objects. Dependent on the mind and mental phenomena, mind-consciousness arises; the meeting of the three is contact. The base consisting of form pertains to form; mental phenomena that partake of form pertain to form; the associated mental phenomena apart from mind-contact pertain to name (mentality).[1927] Thus contact is dependent on name and form.

Possessions: There are two kinds of possessions: possessions [acquired through] craving and possessions [acquired through] views.[1928] These are based on desire, caused by desire, conditioned by desire, instigated by desire, produced by desire. **When desire does not exist, there is no taking as "mine"**: There are two ways of taking as "mine": taking as "mine" through craving and taking as "mine" through views. When desire does not exist, is not found, is not apprehended,[1929] taking things as "mine" does not exist, is not found, is not apprehended.

Nidd I 202–3. When form has vanished (been recognized): Form has vanished (been recognized) in four ways: by being known, by being scrutinized, by being abandoned, and by passing beyond it.[1930] How does form vanish (how is it recognized) by *being known*? One knows thus: "All form consists of the four great elements and the form dependent on the four great elements." How by *being scrutinized*? Having known it thus, one scrutinizes form as impermanent, suffering, an illness, a boil, a dart, misery, alien, disintegrating, empty, non-self . . . by way of its origin and passing away, its gratification, danger, and the escape from it. How by *being abandoned*? Having scrutinized it thus, one abandons desire and lust in regard to form. As the Blessed One said: "Bhikkhus, abandon desire and lust in regard to form. In such a case, that form will be abandoned, cut off at the root, made baseless like a palm stump, obliterated, not subject to arise in the future" (SN III 27,14–19). How by *passing beyond it*? For one who has obtained the four formless meditative attainments, forms have ended, been overcome, been passed beyond, been transcended. Thus form has ended in these four ways. **When form has vanished, contacts do not touch one**: When form has been recognized, been clearly understood, been overcome, passed beyond, transcended, the five kinds of contact do not touch one: eye-contact, ear-contact, nose-contact, tongue-contact, and body-contact. ▯⁝

873. How must one attain—how must one practice—**for form to vanish?**: so that form does not occur or might not occur? **How do pleasure and pain also vanish?**: He asks only about desirable and undesirable form.

⁝▯ **Nidd I 203. How must one attain for form to vanish? How must one attain**: for one who practices in what way, who behaves in what way, who acts in what way, who continues on in what way, who carries on in what way, who persists in what way;[1931] **for form to vanish**, to disappear, to be overcome, to be surpassed, to be transcended? **How do pleasure and pain also vanish?**: How do pleasure and pain vanish, disappear; how are they overcome, how are they surpassed, how are they transcended? ▯⁝

874. Not percipient through perception: Form ends for one who has attained in such a way that he is not percipient through normal perception; **not percipient through disturbed perception**: not percipient through a disturbed, deformed, perception, as in the case of one who is mad or mentally unhinged; **not altogether without perception**: not one devoid of perception, one who has entered the attainment of cessation or a nonpercipient being; **not one percipient of what has vanished**: not one who has overcome perception in the way described "through the overcoming of all perceptions of form," that is, he is not a gainer of the formless jhānas.[1932] **Form vanishes for one who has attained such a state**: Form vanishes for one who is not percipient through a perception and the other alternatives mentioned, but who has acquired the path to the formless, who has attained in the way described thus: "With his mind thus concentrated . . . he directs his mind for the purpose of attaining the base of the boundlessness of space."[1933] **For concepts due to proliferation are based on perception**: He shows that even for one practicing in such a way, these perceptions and the proliferations due to craving and views that originate from them have not been abandoned.

⁞▮ **Nidd I 204–5. Not percipient through perception, not percipient through disturbed perception**: Those who abide in normal perception are said to be "percipient through perception"; this one being described does not abide in normal perception. Those who are mad and mentally unhinged are said to be "percipient through disturbed perception"; this one is not mad or mentally unhinged. **Not altogether without perception, not percipient of what has vanished**: Those who have entered the attainment of cessation and nonpercipient beings are called "without perception"; but this one has not entered cessation and is not a nonpercipient being. Those who are obtainers of the four formless meditative attainments are called "those who are percipient of what has vanished"; but this one is not an obtainer of the four formless meditative attainments. **Form vanishes for one who has so attained**: "Here, with the abandoning of pleasure . . . a bhikkhu enters and dwells in the fourth jhāna. When his mind is thus concentrated, purified, cleansed, unblemished, rid of defilement, malleable, wieldy, steady, and attained to imperturbability, endowed with the path to the formless states, he directs and inclines his mind for the purpose of attaining the base of the boundlessness of space": for one who has attained thus, for one practicing thus . . . form vanishes. **For concepts due to proliferation are based on perception**: Proliferations themselves are "concepts due to proliferation":[1934] concepts due to proliferation by craving, concepts due to proliferation by views, concepts due to proliferation by conceit are based on perception, arise from perception, are generated by perception, produced by perception. ▮⁞

875. Do some wise men here say that at this point this is the foremost purity of the spirit, or do they speak of it as

different from this?:[1935] He asks: "Is it at this point that wise ascetics and brahmins here speak of foremost purity, or do they speak of it as different from this, as superior to the formless meditative attainments?"

Nidd I 205–6. Do some wise men here say that at this point this is the foremost purity of the spirit?: Some ascetics and brahmins say that these formless meditative attainments are foremost, the best, distinguished, the most eminent, the highest, the most excellent. **Of the spirit**: of a being, of a person, of a human, of an individual, of a soul, of a living entity, of a human being.[1936] **Purity**: purity, purification, full purification, freedom, liberation, release. **Wise men**: Those who claim to be wise, who claim to be steadfast, who speak of methods, causes, characteristics, reasons, possibilities according to their own belief. **Or do they speak of it as different from this?**: Or do some ascetics and brahmins say that there is a purity, purification, full purification, freedom, liberation, release of the spirit that is different from this, superior to the formless meditative attainments, reached by surpassing, overcoming, transcending these formless meditative attainments?

876. Some wise men here say that at this point this is the foremost purity of the spirit: Some ascetics and brahmins who are eternalists, who consider themselves wise, say that the foremost purity is attained at this point. **But some among them speak of an attainment**: Some annihilationists among them speak of annihilation as an attainment.[1937] **Claiming to be skilled in that without residue remaining**: asserting they are skilled in that without residue remaining.[1938]

Nidd I 206–7. Some wise men here say that at this point this is the foremost purity of the spirit: There are some ascetics and brahmins who are eternalists who say that these formless meditative attainments are foremost . . . most excellent. **But some among them claiming to be skilled speak of an attainment without residue remaining**: Some among these ascetics and brahmins who are annihilationists, fearful of existence, delight in nonexistence. They assert the calming down, the stilling, the allaying, the cessation, the subsiding of a being,[1939] saying: "With the breakup of the body, when this self is annihilated, destroyed, and does not exist after death, at that point there is no residue remaining."[1940] **Claiming to be skilled**: Those who claim to be skilled, claim to be wise . . . according to their own belief. ⁞⁞

877. Having known these to be "dependent": having known these theorists [554] to be "dependent on the views of eternalism and annihilation"; **having known the dependencies, the muni, the investigator**: having known their dependencies, the investigator, the wise man, the Buddha-muni; **having known, liberated**: having known phenomena as suffering, impermanent, and so forth. **The wise one does not come upon various states of existence**:[1941] He does not approach repeated rebirth.

⁞⁞ **Nidd I 207–8. Having known these to be "dependent"**: having known these to be dependent on the eternalist view, having known these [others] to be dependent on the annihilationist view, having known these to be dependent on both the eternalist and annihilationist view. **Having known, liberated**: freed, liberated, released, well liberated by the ultimate emancipation without clinging. Having known, "All conditioned things are impermanent" . . . "All conditioned things are suffering" . . . "All phenomena are non-self" . . . "Whatever is subject to origination is all subject to cessation," he is freed . . . well liberated by the ultimate emancipation without clinging. **The wise one does not come upon various states of existence**: He does not approach desire-realm existence in kamma existence and in renewed existence . . . [as at p. 1032, Nidd I 34] . . . ever-repeated conception, the ever-repeated production of personal being. ⁞⁞

Thus he concludes the teaching with its culmination in arahantship. At the conclusion of the teaching, a breakthrough occurred similar to that described in connection with the Discourse on the Breakup.

12 The Smaller Discourse on Deployment
(*Cūḷaviyūha Sutta*)

What is the origin? This too originated at that Great Gathering.[1942] Some deities there gave rise to the thought: "All these theorists say: 'We are outstanding.'[1943] Is it only those settled in their own view who are outstanding or those who accept some other view as well?" To make this matter clear to them, in the way already explained, the Blessed One had a mind-created buddha question him and the discourse was spoken in response.

878–79. Here, the two verses at the beginning pose the questions. Among them, **settled each in his own view**: abiding each in their own view; **contending, the skilled make diverse assertions**: having strongly grasped their view, claiming "We are skilled," they make many different assertions; they do not speak in unison. **One who knows this has understood the Dhamma**: They say this with reference to that view. **Rejecting this, one is not consummate**: They say: "One rejecting this is inferior." **A fool**: defective; **unskilled**: ignorant.

⁝⁝ Nidd I 209. Settled each in his own view: There are some ascetics and brahmins who are theorists. Having grasped one or another view among the sixty-two views, having adopted it, seized it, adhering to it, they dwell in their own view, dwell together with it, abide in it, settle into it. **One who knows this has understood the Dhamma**: One who knows this Dhamma, view, practice, path has understood, discerned, seen, penetrated the Dhamma. **Rejecting this, one is not consummate**:

One who rejects this Dhamma, view, practice, path, is defective, incomplete, imperfect, inferior, deficient. ⁝

880–81. Now there are three verses of reply. These are constructed by deploying the meaning stated in the latter couplet against that stated in the former couplet.[1944] Because of that deployment this sutta is named "The Shorter Deployment"—["shorter"] because it uses fewer deployments than the following discourse. Here, **the opponent's doctrine**: the opponent's view. **All indeed are fools**: For what reason? Because **all these are settled in their views. But if by their own view . . . intelligent**: If by their own view they are not cleansed, are still defiled, [555] **pure in wisdom, skilled, intelligent**: if they are pure in wisdom and skilled and intelligent.[1945] Or there is also the reading: "But if by their own view they are cleansed." This is its meaning: "But if by their own view they are cleansed, pure in wisdom, skilled, intelligent." **There is none among them**—not even one—**defective in wisdom**. For what reason? **For their views are similarly taken up**, just like the others.

882. The concise meaning of the verse "I do not say" is as follows: When those two contestents **in pairs say to one another**, "[You're] a fool," **I do not say, "This is correct,"** accurate. For what reason? Because they **all take their own view** thus: "This alone is truth, anything else is false." And for that reason **they consider the opponent a fool.**[1946]

883. In the question, **that which some say is "true, correct"** refers to a view.

884. Truth, indeed, is one: In the answer, the one truth is cessation or the path. **A person who understands this would not dispute**: A person who understands would not dispute about this truth.[1947]

⁝ **Nidd I 214–15. Truth, indeed, is one**: It is said the cessation of suffering, nibbāna, is called the one truth: the stilling of all volitional activities, the relinquishment of all acquisitions, the destruction of craving, dispassion, cessation, nibbāna. Or alternatively, what is called the one truth is the truth of the path, the truth of emancipation, the way leading to the cessation of suffering, the noble eightfold path, that is, right view . . . right concentration. **A person who understands this would not dispute** (*yasmiṃ pajā no vivade pajānaṃ*). **Person**: a designation for beings (*pajā ti sattādhivacanaṃ*). **Who understands:** understanding this truth, knowing it, recognizing it, penetrating it, persons would not create a quarrel, would not create an argument, would not contend, would not create a dispute, would not create strife.[1948] **These proclaim their own diverse truths**: They proclaim, assert, declare, expound, explain, express [their views]: "The world is eternal" . . . "A tathāgata neither exists nor does not exist after death: this alone is true, anything else is false." **Therefore ascetics do not speak in unison**: Therefore they do not speak as one but speak differently, speak diversely, speak contrary to one another, speak in separate ways.

885. Or do they follow a line of reasoning?: Or do the speakers merely go along with their own line of reasoning.[1949]

Nidd I 216. Or do they follow a line of reasoning?: Or do they go along with reasoning, with thought, are they led, swept along, driven along [by reasoning]. Or do they assert [a doctrine] hammered out by reasoning, following an investigation, based on their own ingenuity?[1950]

886. In the answer, "Truths surely are not many and diverse," **except by [mistakenly] perceiving permanent things**: except because of grasping things as "permanent" through mere perception. **But having formulated reasoning about views**: having merely generated their own wrong thoughts about views. But since they also generate views when they generate thoughts about views, in the Niddesa it is said: "they engender speculative views."

Nidd I 216. Truths surely are not many and diverse, except by [mistakenly] perceiving permanent things in the world: Apart from the grasping of permanence by perception, only one truth is spoken of in the world: the cessation of suffering, nibbāna. Or it is the truth of the path that is spoken of as the one truth—the truth of the emancipating way, the way leading to the cessation of suffering, the noble eightfold path. **But having formulated reasoning about views, they assert the dyad "true" and "false"**: Having reasoned, reflected, pondered various lines of reasoning, thought, and reflection, they engender, generate, produce, and create speculative views, and having done so, they say: "My [view] is true, yours is false."[1951] ⠿

887–88. He now speaks the verses that begin "The seen, heard" and so forth, to show the wrong conduct of the theorists who, though diverse truths are nonexistent, follow a mere line of reasoning. Here, **the seen**: The purport is: "purity through what is seen." The same method applies to the heard and so forth.[1952] **Dependent on these . . . he shows disdain**: Having depended on these speculative views, he also shows disdain, lack of esteem, a designation for lack of purity.[1953] **Based on a judgment, derisive, he says: "The opponent is a fool, unskilled"**: Thus, showing disdain, basing himself on that judgment about views, jubilant and derisive, he says: "The opponent is inferior and ignorant." [556] **Yet speaks in the same way**: He asserts that very same view or that person.

889. The meaning of the verse "Inflated by that extremist view" is as follows: He is **inflated**, filled up, puffed up, **by that extremist view**, which exceeds the actual characteristic of things; and he is **intoxicated with conceit** based on that view, thinking: "I am perfect, consummate." Thus **thinking himself perfect**, on his own, **he has mentally anointed himself**,[1954] he has anointed himself thus: "I am a wise man." For what reason? **For that view of his is taken up in such a manner**.

⠿ **Nidd I 218–19. Inflated by that extremist view**: It is the sixty-two speculative views that are called extremist views. Why are they called extremist views? All these views exceed reasons, exceed the characteristics of things, exceed possibilities; hence they are called extremist views. Also, all views are extremist views. Why are all views called extremist views? Because having surpassed one another, overcome one another, transcended one another, they engender speculative views. **On his own accord he has mentally anointed himself**: On his own, with his mind, he has anointed himself thus: "I am skilled, learned, wise, perceptive, knowledgeable, bright, intelligent." ⠿

890. The connection and meaning of the verse "If one is deficient" are as follows: And what is more, someone, based on a judgment, derisively says: "The opponent is a fool, unskilled." If the latter is **deficient because of the opponent's word**, because he is spoken of by him in such a way, **the opponent himself is similarly deficient in wisdom**: he too is deficient in wisdom for just the same reason. For the other too called him a fool. Then his word is no criterion. **But if he is himself a master of knowledge, a wise man**, in such a case **there is no fool among ascetics**, for they are all wise men in their own opinion.

891. The connection and meaning of this verse, "Those who assert a teaching," are as follows: Though it was said, "But if he is himself a master of knowledge, a wise man, then none among ascetics is a fool," it might occur to someone: "Why is this so?" It is said in reply to this: "Because **'those who assert a teaching different from this to be defective have failed to reach purity': thus the sectarians speak in separate ways.**" That is, because the sectarians speak in separate ways, saying: "Those who assert a teaching different from this have failed to reach the path to purity and are defective."[1955] But why do they speak in such a way? Because **they are attached to their own views.**

⁘▮ **Nidd I 220. Those who assert a teaching different from this to be defective have failed to reach purity**: Those who assert a teaching, a view, a practice, a path different from this one have missed, failed, stumbled, fallen away from the path to purity, the path to purification, the path to full purity, the clean path, the polished path; they have failed to reach final knowledge. They are defective, incomplete, imperfect, inferior, deficient. ▮⁘

892–93. And as they are so attached, the next verse says: "'Here only is purity' they assert." **Their own way**: their own path. Among those who firmly assert their claims, when each sectarian is **asserting firmly his own way, what opponent here could one consider a fool?** Those firmly asserting their own way, saying, "This alone is truth," are, concisely, the eternalists and annihilationists, or in detail, the nihilists, the theists, those who believe in fixed destiny, and so forth. Speaking thus, what opponent could one rightly regard as a fool? [557] In their own opinion, don't they all consider themselves wise and of good practice? In such a case, **he himself would just provoke strife.**

Speaking of the opponent thus, "He is a fool, one of impure character," he would provoke a quarrel with himself. Why? Because in their own opinion, they all consider themselves wise and of good practice.

⁑ **Nidd I 221. "Here only is purity" they assert**: They say there is purity, purification, full purification, freedom, liberation, release here, [in the view]: "The world is eternal" . . . "A tathāgata neither exists nor does not exist after death: this alone is true, anything else is false."

They say there is no purification in other teachings: Except for their own teacher, teaching, group, view, practice, and path, they reject all other doctrines. They speak thus: "That teacher is not omniscient . . . [as at p. 1048, Nidd I 54] . . . worthless, insignificant." **Thus, too, the sectarians separately entrenched**: A sect is a speculative view; the sectarians are the theorists.[1956] The sectarians are entrenched in separate speculative views, established in them, adhering to them, involved with them, cleaving to them, resolved on them. **Firmly assert their own way there**: The teaching is their own way, the view is their own way, the practice is their own way, the path is their own way. They assert their own way firmly, persistently, strongly, steadily. ⁑

894. Thus in all respects, **based on a judgment, taking himself as the measure, he enters upon further disputes in the world**: Based on a view, weighing himself and other teachers, he gets into even more disputes. Having understood such danger in judgments, **having abandoned all judgments** by the noble path, **a person does not create strife in the world**.

⁑ **Nidd I 222–23. Based on a judgment, taking himself as the measure**: It is the sixty-two speculative views that are called judgments. Based upon a view as a judgment, established on it, grasping it, seizing it, adhering to it, based on a judgment, **taking himself as the measure**, having taken himself as the measure, he holds: "This teacher is omniscient; this teaching is well expounded; this group is practicing well; this view is excellent; this practice is well prescribed; this path is emancipating." **He enters upon further disputes in the world**: It is the future that is called "further (above)." Putting his own doctrine above, he himself enters upon a quarrel, enters upon an argument, enters upon contention, enters upon dispute, enters upon strife. Or he creates a quarrel . . . creates strife with still another doctrine. **A person does not create strife in the world**: He does not create a quarrel . . . does not create strife. ⁂

Thus he concluded the teaching with its culmination in arahantship. At the conclusion of the teaching, there was a breakthrough similar to that described in connection with the Discourse on the Breakup.

13 The Greater Discourse on Deployment
(*Mahāviyūha Sutta*)

What is the origin?[1957] This too originated at that same Great Gathering. Some deities there gave rise to the thought: "Do those settled in views receive only blame from the wise or do they also receive praise?" To make this matter clear to them, in the way already explained, the Blessed One had a mind-created buddha repeatedly question him and the discourse was spoken in response.

896. Now, those theorists who assert, "This alone is truth," also win praise sometimes and somewhere. However, this praise, a fruit of their [success] in debate, is slight, unable to allay lust and other defilements; much less can blame, the second fruit of their [performance in] debate, do so. Therefore, showing this point, in the answer he first says: **This [praise] is slight, not sufficient for peace; I say there are two fruits of disputes.**[1958] Here, **I say there are two fruits of disputes**: blame and praise, or their counterparts such as victory and defeat. **Having seen this too**: having seen too the danger in the fruits of disputes, "Blame is simply undesirable, while praise is not sufficient to bring peace," [one should not dispute], **seeing as security the stage of non-dispute**: [558] seeing nibbāna, the stage of non-dispute, as security.

⁝⁝ **Nidd I 225. I say there are two fruits of disputes**: There are two fruits of quarrels about views, arguments about views, contention about views, disputes about views, strife about views: victory and defeat, gain and loss, fame and dishonor, praise and blame, pleasure and pain, joy and dejection, the desirable and undesirable, satisfaction and aversion, elation and misery, attachment and hostility.

897. Thus, not disputing, the verse says: "Whatever common-place opinions there are." Here, **opinions**: views; **common-place**: originated by worldlings. **Why would one uninvolved become involved**: With what should he get involved, what single thing among form and the others, which is an involvement in the sense of a thing to be approached—or for what reason should he become involved—**when he does not acquiesce in what is seen and heard?**: when he has no affection for [the doctrines of] purity through what is seen and heard?

Nidd I 227. When he does not acquiesce in what is seen and heard: when he does not acquiesce in the seen or [in the doctrine of] purification through the seen, in the heard or [in the doctrine of] purification through the heard, in the sensed or [in the doctrine of] purification through the sensed; when he does not arouse desire, does not arouse affection, does not arouse attachment to them.[1959]

898. Speaking of those outside here, the verse says: "Those who regard good behavior as supreme." This is its meaning: **Those who regard good behavior as supreme** are those who conceive good behavior itself to be supreme, who assert that purity is to be achieved merely by self-control. **Having taken up an observance**—such as the elephant observance and so forth—**they settle on it. Right here**: in the view. **They are led back into existence**: They speak while cleaving to existence, while **claiming to be skilled**, asserting: "We are skilled."

Nidd I 227. Those who take good behavior as supreme: There are some ascetics and brahmins who assert that good behavior is supreme. They speak of purity . . . release through mere good behavior, through mere self-control, through mere restraint, through mere non-transgression. An example is Samaṇamuṇḍikāputta, who said: "When a person possesses four qualities, I describe him as complete in the wholesome, supremely wholesome, one attained to the ultimate, an invincible ascetic. What four? He does no evil deed with the body, utters no evil speech, thinks no evil thought, and does not undertake an evil livelihood" (MN II 24,7–9).

899. Among those who regard good behavior as supreme, there may be one practicing in such a way who has fallen away. This is the meaning of the verse: **If he has fallen away from good behavior and observances** because he has been dissuaded by others or is incapable of them, **he trembles because he has failed in his action**, in that action of good behavior and observances or in meritorious volitional activities and so forth. And not only does he tremble, but he **longs and yearns for purity** through good behavior and observances and prattles about it. In what way? **Like one on a journey who has lost his caravan**: as one dwelling far from home who has lost his caravan yearns for his home or his caravan.

Nidd I 228–29. If he has fallen away from good behavior and observances: There are two causes by which one falls away from good behavior and observances: because of dissuasion by others or because of one's inability. How does one fall away because of *dissuasion by others*? Another convinces one: "That teacher is not omniscient; that teaching is not well expounded; that group is not practicing well; that view is not excellent; that practice is not well prescribed; that path is not emancipating. There is no purity . . . release here. " Being dissuaded, one falls away from that teacher . . . one falls away from that path. How does one fall away because of one's inability? Being incapable of good behavior, one falls away from good behavior; being incapable of observances, one falls away from observances; being incapable of good behavior and observances, one falls away from good behavior and observances.

900. This verse speaks of the noble disciple **having abandoned all good behavior and observances**, the cause for those taking good behavior as supreme to tremble. Here, **blameworthy and blameless**: all unwholesome and mundane wholesome. **Not yearning for either purity or impurity**: not yearning for this purity consisting in the five strands of sensual pleasure and so forth, and impurity distinguished into the unwholesome and so forth; **one should live detached**: one should live detached from purity and impurity. **Not grasping peace**: not having grasped a view.

Nidd I 230. Having abandoned all good behavior and observances: Having abandoned all [views of] purity through good behavior, all [views of] purity through observances, all [views of] purity through good behavior and observances. **Not yearning for either purity or impurity**: Those who yearn for impurity yearn for unwholesome qualities, the five strands of sensual pleasure, the sixty-two speculative views, the wholesome qualities pertaining to the three realms of existence. Good worldlings who yearn for purity yearn to enter upon the fixed course.[1960] Trainees yearn for the supreme state, arahantship. Those who have attained arahantship do not yearn for the five strands of sensual pleasure . . . or even the supreme state, arahantship. Arahants have transcended yearning; they do not yearn for either progress or decline. They have lived the spiritual life . . . for them there is no more repeated existence, saṃsāra with birth, old age, and death. **One should live detached**: One should desist from, abstain from, refrain from purity and impurity. **Not grasping peace**: It is the sixty-two speculative views that are called peace; not grasping the peace of views, not seizing them, not adhering to them. ▮⁝

901. Having shown the distress of the outsiders—those who settle on the doctrine of good behavior as supreme and the doctrine of purification by self-control—and having shown the conduct of the arahant who has abandoned good behavior and observances, now, showing in another way the outsiders who hold the doctrine of purification, he speaks the verse "Dependent on austerity or scrupulousness." This is its meaning: There are other ascetics and brahmins, **dependent on austerity or scrupulousness**,[1961] on austerity aimed at immortality,[1962] or on a certain position among the views of purity through what is seen and so forth; or **running onward** through the view of non-doing, **not rid of craving for various states of existence, [559] they declare purity**—they assert it, they expound it.[1963]

⁝▮ **Nidd I 231. Dependent on austerity or scrupulousness**: There are some ascetics and brahmins who assert austerity and scrupulousness, who take austerity and scrupulousness as the essence, who rely on austerity and scrupulousness.[1964] **Running onward, they declare purity**: There are some ascetics and brahmins who assert running onward. Who are these ascetics and brahmins? Those ascetics and brahmins who hold to ultimate purity, the view of purification through saṃsāra, the view of non-doing, eternalism. They assert purity . . . release in saṃsāra.

902. For one who yearns there are longings: This is the purport: Among those declaring purity who are not rid of craving—even one who thinks of himself as having attained purity—because they are not rid of craving for those various states of existence, they have repeated longings for this or that object. For when craving is indulged it just fosters craving. Not only does he have longings, but **trembling too over things mentally formulated**, that is, there is trembling over the objects formulated by him because of craving and views.[1965] But for one rid of craving for various states of existence, since he **has no passing away or rebirth** in the future, **why would he tremble and for what would he long?** This is the connection of this verse. The rest should be understood in the way stated in the Niddesa.

Nidd I 232–33. For one who yearns there are longings: It is craving that is called yearning. **For one who yearns**: for one who desires, one who wishes, one who hankers, one who longs. **Longings**: It is craving that is called longing. **And trembling too over things mentally formulated**: There are two kinds of mental formulation, mental formulation due to craving and mental formulation due to views. They tremble when they are anxious about being deprived of an object taken as "mine"; they tremble when being deprived of it; they tremble after they have been deprived of it. They tremble when they are anxious it will deteriorate; they tremble when it is deteriorating; they tremble when it has deteriorated.

For one here who has no passing away or rebirth: This is the arahant, one whose influxes have been destroyed, for whom there is no going or coming, no going in time, no various states of existence, passing away and rebirth, production and dissolution, birth, old age, and death; for whom these have been abandoned . . . burnt up by the fire of knowledge. **Why would he tremble and for what would he long?**: Through what lust would he tremble, through what hatred, what delusion, what conceit, what view, what restlessness, what doubt, what latent tendencies? Those volitional activities have been abandoned, and because they have been abandoned, on account of what destination would he tremble, when there is no cause or condition through which he might become a hell being . . . one who is neither percipient nor non-pericipient? ◧▪

903. This is the question.

904. Now, since not even one of their assertions here is true, he spoke this answer, "They say their own teaching is complete," showing that they simply assert their positions as mere views. Here, **opinion** means view.

905. Thus, when they say their own teaching is complete and that the teaching of another is inferior, for each one, the verse says, **if one is inferior when disparaged by an opponent**. This is the meaning: "If one were inferior because one is criticized by another, **no one would be distinguished—foremost—among teachings**. For what reason? **For they each say the other's teaching is inferior, while** all **firmly advocate their own**."

906. And what is more, the verse says, "And their veneration of their own teaching."[1966] This is its meaning: And as those sectarians praise their own ways, just so is **their veneration of their own teaching**. For they exceedingly honor their teachers and so forth. If they were the standard in this matter, in such a case **all their assertions would be truthful**. For what reason? **Since for them purity is exclusively their own**: Purity is not achieved elsewhere, nor in the supreme sense; for those whose minds are led in dependence on others have merely grasped a view about the self.

▪◧ **Nidd I 236. And their veneration of their own teaching.** What is veneration of one's own teaching? One honors, reveres, esteems, and venerates one's own teacher thus: "This teacher is omniscient." One honors one's own teaching, group, view, practice, path thus: "This path is emancipating." ◧▪

907. But in the opposite case, that of a brahmin in the sense that he has expelled evil,[1967] the verse states, **for a brahmin there is no being led by others**. This is its meaning: [560] Because he has clearly seen in accordance with the principle "All conditioned things are impermanent" and so forth, there is no knowledge to be brought to a brahmin by others, **no select-**

ing among teachings, among views, **and grasping tightly**, [with the conviction]: "This alone is truth." For this reason he has overcome quarrels about views, and **he does not regard another teaching as supreme**, a teaching apart from the establishments of mindfulness and so forth.

Nidd I 236–37. For a brahmin there is no being led by others: A brahmin is not led by others; he does not attain through others, is not dependent on others, is not bound to others, but knows and sees, unconfused, clearly comprehending, mindful. There is no being led [to see] "All conditioned things are impermanent" . . . "Whatever is subject to origination is all subject to cessation." **Since he does not regard another teaching as supreme**: He does not regard another teacher, teaching, group, view, practice, path as foremost . . . most excellent, apart from the establishments of mindfulness . . . the noble eightfold path.

908. The connection and meaning of the verse "[Saying], 'I know'" is as follows: A brahmin in the supreme sense does not regard another teaching as supreme; but the sectarians, knowing and seeing through the knowledge of others' minds and so forth, and asserting, **"I know, I see, it is just like this," fall back on purity through a view**. Why? Because even **if one** among them **has seen** some matter as it actually is with the knowledge of others' minds and so forth, **what good is this to himself?**:[1968] What is achieved by this seeing? Has he accomplished the full understanding of suffering, or the abandoning of its origin, or anything else? Since in all respects they have bypassed the noble path, those sectarians **assert purity by another**. Or those sectarians, having bypassed the Buddha and so forth, assert purity by another.

Nidd I 238. Saying, "I know, I see, it is just like this": "I know with the knowledge of others' minds, or I know with the knowledge that recollects past abodes. I see with the fleshly eye, or I see with the divine eye. It is just like this, this is true, actual, real, accurate, undistorted." **Some here fall back on purity through a view**: Some ascetics and brahmins fall back on purity . . . release through a view, the view: "The world is eternal" . . . "A tathāgata neither exists nor does not exist after death: this alone is true, anything else is false." **What good is**

this to himself?: There is no full understanding of suffering, no abandoning of its origin, no development of the path, no realization of the fruit, no eradication of lust, hatred, delusion, and other defilements, no ending of the round of saṃsāra. **Having gone too far**: Those sectarians have bypassed, overshot, missed the path to purity, the path to purification, the path to cleansing. **They assert purity by another**: They assert purity . . . release apart from the establishments of mindfulness . . . the noble eightfold path. Or alternatively, the buddhas, their disciples, and paccekabuddhas have bypassed, overcome, transcended the impure path of those sectarians, and they assert purity . . . release by means of the four establishments of mindfulness . . . the noble eightfold path. ⠿

909. The connection and meaning of the verse "Seeing, a person" are as follows: And what is more, when he has seen with the knowledge of others' minds and so forth, **seeing, a person will see name-and-form**, but nothing beyond that. **Having seen, it is just these** names-and-forms **that he will know** as permanent or as happiness, but not otherwise. Seeing thus, **granted, let him see much or little** of name-and-form as permanent and as happiness, **the skillful say purity is not won in that way**, by his seeing in such a way.

⠿ **Nidd I 239. Seeing, a person will see name-and-form**: Seeing with the knowledge of others' minds or with the knowledge that recollects past abodes, or seeing with the fleshly eye or with the human eye, one will see just name-and-form as permanent, happiness, and self; one does not see the origination, passing away, gratification, danger, and escape from those things. ⠿

910. The connection and meaning of the verse "Seeing, a person" are as follows: Although there is no purity by such seeing, **a dogmatist** who asserts, "I know, I see, it is just like this," or a dogmatist who, on the basis of seeing, falls back on purity through a view and says, "This alone is truth," **is not easily disciplined, one preferring a formulated view. Claiming that the good is found in what he depends on**, in a certain teacher and so forth, **as a proponent of purity**, [561] thinking of himself thus, "I am one whose doctrine is purified, whose seeing is purified," **he saw things that way there**:[1969] he saw without distortion right there in his own view. The purport is: "He saw this matter in just the way his view occurs; he does not wish to see otherwise."

⁞▮ **Nidd I 240. A dogmatist is not easily disciplined. A dogmatist** is one who holds: "The world is eternal" . . . "A tathāgata neither exists nor does not exist after death: this alone is true, anything else is false." **Not easily disciplined**: A dogmatist is not easily disciplined, is hard to convince, hard to make reflect, hard to make consider, hard to instill confidence in. **One preferring a formulated view**: He goes about preferring—giving precedence to—a view that has been formulated, composed, and established.[1970] **He saw things that way there**: He saw as true, actual, real, accurate, undistorted through his own view, his own opinion, his own preference, his own belief. ▮⁞

911. Thus, while the sectarians are predisposed to a constructed view, **having comprehended**—having known[1971]—**a brahmin does not take up mental constructs . . . nor a kinsman of knowledge**: he is not bound to craving or views by the knowledge of the meditative attainments. **Commonplace opinions**: views originated by worldlings. **While others grasp**:[1972] that is, while others grasp hold of those opinions.

⁞▮ **Nidd I 241–42. Having comprehended, a brahmin does not take up mental constructs**: Having comprehended, having known, having assessed, having scrutinized, having clarified, having recognized, "All conditioned things are impermanent" . . . "Whatever is subject to origination is all subject to cessation," a brahmin does not enter upon, does not take up, does not grasp, does not seize, does not adhere to mental constructs due either to craving or to views. **He is not a pursuer of views**: For him, the sixty-two views have been abandoned . . . burnt up by the fire of knowledge; hence he does not go by a view nor does he fall back on a speculative view as the essence. **Nor a kinsman of knowledge**: He does not create a bond to craving or a bond to views on account of the knowledge of the eight meditative attainments or the five superknowledges. **The commonplace opinions**: the opinions of views, the sixty-two speculative views. **He maintains equanimity while others grasp**: Others grasp, seize, adhere by way of craving and by way of views. But the arahant maintains equanimity; he does not grasp, does not seize, does not adhere. ▮⁝

912. And what is more, the next verse says, "having loosened the knots." Here, **without grasping**: devoid of grasping; there is no grasping for him, or he does not grasp, hence he is "without grasping."

⁝▮ **Nidd I 242–43. Having loosened the knots:** There are four knots: the bodily knot of longing, the bodily knot of ill will, the bodily knot of seizing upon good behavior and observances, and the bodily knot of dogmatic adherence to claims of truth . . . [as at p. 1063, Nidd I 70–71] . . . **Having loosened** or untied those knots. **The muni does not take sides in arisen disputes**: When disputes have arisen among those motivated by desire, hatred, delusion, or fear, he is not motivated by desire, hatred, delusion, or fear. He does not proceed because of lust, hatred, delusion, conceit, views, restlessness, doubt, or the latent tendencies. He is not moved, led, swayed, carried off by divisive teachings. **He is peaceful**: peaceful through the calming down of lust, hatred, delusion, anger . . . the calming down of all unwholesome volitional activities. These have been stilled, allayed, quenched, banished, silenced; hence he is peaceful, calm, quenched. **Equanimous**: The arahant possesses the six-factored equanimity; having seen a form with the eye, having heard a sound with the ear . . . he is neither joyful nor dejected but dwells in equanimity, mindful and clearly comprehending. **Without grasping while others grasp**: While others are grasping by way of craving and by way of views, the arahant maintains equanimity and does not grasp, does not seize, does not adhere. ▮⁝

913. And what is more, the next verse says, such a one **having abandoned past influxes**: defilements capable of arising with past forms and so forth as objects.[1973] **Not creating new ones**: those capable of arising with present forms and so forth as objects. **Free of self-reproach**: not reproaching himself because of what he has done or failed to do.

⁝▮ **Nidd I 243–44. Having abandoned past influxes**: It is past form, feeling, perception, volitional activities, and consciousness that are called past influxes. Having abandoned defilements that might have arisen in regard to those past conditioned things, [it is said] "having abandoned past influxes." **Not creating new ones**: New ones are present form . . . consciousness. Not creating desire, affection, lust in regard to present conditioned things. **He does not go along with desire**: He is not motivated by desire . . . [as at p. 1166, Nidd I 242–43] . . . carried off by divisive teachings. **Nor is he a dogmatist**: not a dogmatist who holds, "The world is eternal" . . . "A tathāgata neither exists nor does not exist after death: this alone is true, anything else is false."

Nidd I 244–45. Free of self-reproach: One reproaches oneself for two reasons: because of what was done and because of what was not done. How so? One reproaches oneself when one thinks: "I have engaged in bodily misconduct; I have not engaged in bodily good conduct . . . [as for regret at p. 1121, Nidd I 158–59] . . . I have not fully understood suffering, abandoned its origin, developed the path, and realized cessation." Thus one reproaches oneself.

914. And being thus free of self-reproach, the next verse says: "He is remote from all phenomena." Here, **all phenomena** are the teachings of the sixty-two views; **from whatever is seen,** distinguished in such ways.[1974] **Not given to mental construction**: He does not create the two kinds of mental constructs. **Does not desist**: unlike good worldlings and trainees, he does not possess [the factors] of desisting; **does not yearn**: he is without craving. The rest has already been clarified here and there, so it is not explained.

Nidd I 245. He is remote from all phenomena: It is Māra's army that is called the army . . . [as at p. 1061, Nidd I 68–69] . . . all unwholesome volitional activities. When all Māra's army and all the battalions of defilements have been vanquished, defeated, demolished, decimated, and overturned by the four noble paths, one is said to be a destroyer of the army (*visenibhūto*: remote). He is remote from the seen, remote from the heard, remote from the sensed, remote from the cognized.

Nidd I 246. With his burden dropped. There are three burdens: the burden of the aggregates, the burden of the defilements, and the burden of volitional activities. What is *the burden of the aggregates*? The form . . . consciousness that are [picked up] at conception. What is *the burden of the defilements*? Lust, hatred, delusion, anger . . . all unwholesome volitional activities. What is *the burden of volitional activities*? Meritorious volitional activity, demeritorious volitional activity, and imperturbable volitional activity. Since these three burdens have been abandoned, cut off at the root, made like a palm stump, eliminated so they are no more subject to future arising, he is said to have dropped the burden.

Nidd I 248. Not given to mental construction, he does not desist, does not yearn. **Not given to mental construction** since mental construction due to craving has been abandoned and mental construction due to views has been relinquished. **He does not desist**: All foolish worldlings are excited by lust. Good worldlings and the seven trainees desist, abstain, refrain in order to attain what has not yet been attained, achieve what has not yet been achieved, realize what has not yet been realized. The arahant has already desisted, abstained, refrained; now detached, he dwells with a mind rid of boundaries. **He does not yearn**: It is craving that is called yearning, and that has been abandoned . . . burnt up by the fire of knowledge.

Thus he concluded the teaching with its culmination in arahantship. At the conclusion of the teaching, there was a breakthrough similar to that described in connection with the Discourse on the Breakup. [562]

14 Quickly
(*Tuvaṭaka Sutta*)

What is the origin?[1975] This too originated at that same Great Gathering. Some deities there gave rise to the thought: "What is the practice for the attainment of arahantship?" To make this matter clear to them, in the way already explained, the Blessed One had a mind-created buddha question him and the discourse was spoken in response.

915. Here, in the first verse, firstly, **I ask**: Here, questions are analyzed by way of those asked to clear up what has not been seen before and so forth. **How having seen**: Having seen in what manner? How does his seeing occur?

⁝ Nidd I 250–51. I ask you, Kinsman of the Sun. I ask: There are three kinds of questions: a question to clear up what has not been seen; a question to confirm what has been seen; a question to eliminate uncertainty. What is *a question to clear up what has not been seen*? Some matter is ordinarily unknown, unseen, unassessed, unscrutinized, obscure, unrecognized; one asks a question in order to know about it, to see it, to assess it, to scrutinize it, to clarify it, to recognize it. What is *a question to confirm what has been seen*? Some matter is ordinarily known . . . recognized; one asks a question to ensure that one is in agreement with other wise people. What is *a question to eliminate uncertainty*? Somebody who is ordinarily prone to doubt, prone to uncertainty, indecisive, asks a question to eliminate uncertainty, asking: "Is it like this or not, what is it, how is it?"

There are other threefold groups of questions: a question asked by human beings, by nonhumans, by emanations; a question concerning one's own good, the good of others, and the good of both; a question about the good pertaining to the present life, the good pertaining to a future life, and the supreme good; a question about the blameless, non-defilement, and cleansing; a question about the past, the future, and the present; a question about the internal, the external, and both; a question about the wholesome, the unwholesome, and the indeterminate; a question about the aggregates, the elements, and the sense bases; a question about the establishments of mindfulness, right striving, and the bases for spiritual power; a question about the faculties, the powers, and the enlightenment factors; a question about the path, the fruit, and nibbāna.

Nidd I 251. Kinsman of the Sun (*ādiccabandhu*): The sun is a Gotama by clan, and the Blessed One is a Gotama by clan; the Blessed One is by clan a relative and kinsman of the sun. Therefore the Buddha is the Kinsman of the Sun.

About seclusion and the state of peace: There are three kinds of seclusion: bodily seclusion, mental seclusion, and seclusion from the acquisitions. . . . [as at pp. 1023–24, Nidd I 19–20] . . . **Peace**: From one angle, both peace and the state of peace are just nibbāna the deathless. From another angle, the state of peace [path to peace][1976] is the qualities that lead to the achievement, attainment, and realization of peace: the four establishments of mindfulness . . . the noble eightfold path.

Nidd I 252–53. Great rishi (*mahesi*): The Blessed One is a great rishi, for he has sought, searched for, pursued the great aggregate of good behavior, the great aggregate of concentration, the great aggregate of wisdom, the great aggregate of liberation, and the great aggregate of the knowledge and vision of liberation.[1977] He has sought, searched for, pursued the splitting of the great mass of darkness, the breaking up of the great inversions, the removal of the great dart of craving, the unraveling of the great compound of views, the lowering of the great banner of conceit, the allaying of great volitional activity, the crossing of the great flood, the subsiding of the great fever, the raising up of the great banner of the Dhamma. He has sought, searched for, pursued the great establishments of mindfulness, the great right kinds of striving, the great bases of psychic potency, the great faculties, the great powers, the great enlightenment factors, the great noble eightfold path. He has sought, searched for, pursued the great supreme goal, the deathless nibbāna.

Nidd I 253. How having seen does a bhikkhu attain nibbāna: How having seen does he extinguish[1978] his own lust, hatred, delusion, anger . . . all unwholesome volitional activities? **A bhikkhu**: a bhikkhu who is a good worldling or a trainee.

916. Now, one attains nibbāna when one sees in such a way that one stops the defilements. Therefore, conveying that point, the Blessed One spoke the five verses beginning "By reflection," instructing the assembly of devas in various ways to abandon the defilements. Here the concise meaning of the first verse [of the five] is as follows: Because they are designated "proliferations," proliferations themselves are "concepts due to proliferation."[1979] The root of this is the defilements such as ignorance and so forth. **By reflection,**[1980] **he should stop . . . the entire root of concepts due to proliferation** and (*ca*) the conceit occurring in the mode **"I am."**[1981] **Whatever cravings there may be**, that might arise, **internally, he should always train mindfully for their removal**:[1982] he should train with mindfulness established.

Nidd I 254–55. The entire root of concepts due to proliferation: Proliferations themselves are concepts due to proliferation. There are concepts due to proliferation associated with craving; there are concepts due to proliferation associated with views. What is the root of proliferation associated with craving? Ignorance is a root, careless attention is a root, the conceit "I am" is a root, lack of moral shame is a root, lack of moral dread is a root, restlessness is a root. What is the root of proliferation associated with views? Ignorance is a root . . . restlessness is a root. **By reflection, he should stop [the conceit] "I am"**: It is wisdom that is called reflection. **I am**: in regard to form, there is the conceit "I am," the desire "I am," the latent tendency "I am."[1983] In regard to feeling . . . perception . . . volitional activities . . . consciousness, there is the conceit "I am," the desire "I am," the latent tendency "I am." By reflection, one should stop the entire root of concepts due to proliferation and (*ca*) the conceit "I am."

Nidd I 255–56. He should always train mindfully for their removal: One is mindful by developing four causes:

contemplation of the body, contemplation of feelings, contemplation of mind, and contemplation of mental phenomena. One is mindful through another four causes: one is mindful by avoiding lack of mindfulness, by doing those things that are to be done with mindfulness, by eliminating those things contrary to mindfulness, and by not forgetting the bases of mindfulness. **Should train**: There are three trainings . . . this is the training in the higher wisdom. **For their removal**: For the removal of those cravings, for putting them away, for abandoning them, allaying them, relinquishing them,[1984] one should train in the higher good behavior, the higher mind, and the higher wisdom. ⁑

917. Thus, having already given in the first verse a teaching conjoined with the three trainings, culminating in arahantship, he speaks the verse "Whatever one might know" to teach it again by way of the abandoning of conceit. Here, **Whatever one might know, whether internally**—one might know one's own excellent quality, such as coming from a high-class family and so forth—**or externally**, one might know externally the excellent quality of one's teacher and preceptor, **one should not be obstinate on that account**: one should not be obstinate because of that quality.

⁑ **Nidd I 257–58. Whatever one might know, whether internally**: Whatever internal excellent quality one might recognize, whether wholesome or indeterminate. What is one's own excellent quality? One may have gone forth from a high-class family or from a wealthy family, or one may be well known and famous among laypeople and monastics, or one may gain the requisites such as robes, or one might be an expert in the Suttas or the Vinaya, or an exponent of the Dhamma, or a forest dweller or observer of the other austere practices, or a gainer of the first jhāna . . . a gainer of the base of neither-perception-nor-nonperception. **Or externally**: the excellent qualities of one's preceptor or teacher. **One should not be obstinate on that account**: One should not be obstinate because of one's own excellent qualities or those of the others; one should not be stubborn, one should not be conceited, one should not be elated, one should not be uplifted, stiff with pride, stuck up. **For that is not called quenching by the good**: for that is not called quenching by the good persons, by the buddhas, their disciples, and paccekabuddhas. ⠿

918. Now, showing the manner of not doing so, he speaks the verse "Because of this." This is its meaning: **Because of this** conceit, [563] **one should not think**, "I am better," "I am inferior," or "I am similar." **Being affected in various ways**, by such qualities as coming from a high-class family and so forth, **one should not persist in positioning oneself** in such a way as this: "I have gone forth from a high-class family."[1985]

919. Having thus taught by way of the abandoning of conceit, now to teach by way of the allaying of defilements,[1986] he speaks the verse "It is internally." Here, **it is internally that he should achieve peace**: he should allay all the defilements such as lust within himself. **A bhikkhu should not seek peace through another**: he should not put aside the establishments of mindfulness and so forth and seek peace by some other method.

⠿ **Nidd I 259. It is internally that he should achieve peace**: It is internally that he should still lust; internally that he should still hatred, delusion, anger . . . all unwholesome volitional activities. **A bhikkhu should not seek peace through another**: He should not seek peace through another, through an impure path, a wrong practice, a non-emancipating course, apart from the four establishments of mindfulness . . . apart from the noble eightfold path. **For one who is at peace within himself**: one for whom lust is allayed internally . . . for whom all unwholesome volitional activities are allayed internally, extinguished, made to subside; **there is nothing taken up, much less rejected**: **Taken up**: there is no view of self . . . [as at pp. 1051–52, Nidd I 58] . . . for him there is no more renewed existence with its wandering on in birth and death. ⠿

920. Now, having shown the impartiality of the arahant who is at peace within himself, he speaks the verse "Just as in the middle." This is its meaning: **Just as in the middle of the ocean**: in the middle measuring 4,000 yojanas, that is, the center between the upper and lower levels, or in the middle of the ocean situated between the mountains, **no wave arises**, but it **remains steady**, not shaking, **so too** the arahant who is **without impulse**

should be steady, not shaking amid gain and so forth. **A bhikkhu** such as this **should not cause a swelling**—of lust and so forth—**anywhere.**

Nidd I 260–61. Just so he should be steady, without impulse: He does not shake because of gain; he does not shake because of lack of gain; he does not shake because of fame; he does not shake because of dishonor; he does not shake because of praise; he does not shake because of blame; he does not shake because of pleasure; he does not shake because of pain; he does not tremble, does not quake, does not waver, does not shudder—thus he is steady. **Without impulse**: without craving. **A bhikkhu should not cause a swelling anywhere**: There are seven **swellings**: the swelling of lust . . . [as at p. 1045, Nidd I 51] . . . the swelling of kamma.

921. Now, appreciating this Dhamma teaching that has been taught with its culmination in arahantship, the mind-created buddha speaks the verse "The one with opened eyes," asking about the initial practice for arahantship. Here, **the one with opened eyes**: the one possessing the five eyes that have been opened without obstructions; **declared**: explained; **the Dhamma he witnessed**: the Dhamma he himself has known directly, that he has personally cognized; **the removal of obstacles**: the removing of obstacles. **Speak about the practice**: Now speak of the conduct. **Venerable one** (*bhaddante*): He directly addresses the Blessed One [with this word, which means] "May excellence be with you." Or alternatively, what is meant is: "Speak about your excellent practice."[1987] **The Pātimokkha and also concentration**: He asks, dividing the practice [into two segments]. Or with the word "practice" he asks about the path; by the other words, he asks about good behavior and concentration.

Nidd I 261. The one with opened eyes: The Blessed One has opened the five eyes: the fleshly eye, the divine eye, the wisdom eye, the buddha eye, and the universal eye.

How does the Blessed One have opened eyes with respect to *the fleshly eye*? The Blessed One's fleshly eyes are of five colors: blue, yellow, red, black, and white. . . . With his natural fleshly eyes, included in his body, produced by the kamma of his good conduct in previous lives, he sees a yojana all around him both by day and at night. Even in the midst of the fourfold darkness—when the sun has set, and on the uposatha night of the dark fortnight, and in a dense jungle, and when a large dark cloud has arisen—in such fourfold darkness he still sees a yojana all around. There is no wall or door panel or rampart or mountain or thicket or creeper that can obstruct his seeing of forms. If one were to mark a single sesamum seed and place it in a cartload of sesamum seeds, he would be able to pick out that seed. Such is the fully purified natural fleshly eye of the Blessed One.

Nidd I 262. How does the Blessed One have opened eyes with respect to *the divine eye*? With the divine eye, which is purified and surpasses the human, he sees beings passing away and being reborn, inferior and superior, beautiful and ugly, fortunate and unfortunate, and he understands how beings fare in accordance with their kamma thus: "These beings who engaged in misconduct by body, speech, and mind, who reviled the noble ones, held wrong view, and undertook kamma based on wrong view, with the breakup of the body, after death, have been reborn in the plane of misery, in a bad destination, in the lower world, in hell; but these beings who engaged in good conduct by body, speech, and mind, who did not revile the noble ones, who held right view, and undertook kamma based on right view, with the breakup of the body, after death, have been reborn in a good destination, in a heavenly world." Thus with the divine eye, which is purified and surpasses the human, he sees beings passing away and being reborn, inferior and superior, beautiful and ugly, fortunate and unfortunate, and he understands how beings fare in accordance with their kamma (MN I 70–71). And if he wishes, the Blessed One can see one world system, two, three, four, five world systems; ten, twenty, thirty, forty, fifty, a hundred world systems; a thousandfold minor world system, a thousand-to-the-second-power middling world system, a thousand-to-the-third-power great world system (AN I 227–28).

How does the Blessed One have opened eyes with respect to *the wisdom eye*? The Blessed One is of great wisdom, wide wisdom, joyous wisdom, swift wisdom, sharp wisdom, penetrating wisdom; he is skilled in making distinctions with wisdom, one with differentiating knowledge, one who has achieved the analytical knowledges, one who has attained the four kinds of self-confidence, who bears the ten powers, a manly bull, a manly lion, a manly elephant, a manly thoroughbred, a manly draft animal, one of boundless knowledge, boundless splendor, boundless glory. . . . The Blessed One is the originator of the path not arisen before, the creator of the path not created before, the teacher of the path not taught before; he is the knower of the path, the finder of the path, the one skilled in the path. His disciples presently live following the path and acquire it afterward (MN III 8,11–15, SN III 66,15–19).

Nidd I 263. The Blessed One is one who truly knows, one who truly sees . . . [as at pp. 1103–4, Nidd I 130–31] . . . This world with its devas, with Māra, with Brahmā, this population with its ascetics and brahmins, its devas and human beings, is encompassed by the Buddha's knowledge.

Nidd I 264. How does the Blessed One have opened eyes with respect to *the buddha eye*? Surveying the world with the eye of a buddha, the Blessed One sees beings with little dust in their eyes and much dust in their eyes, with sharp faculties and dull faculties, with good qualities and bad qualities, easy to teach and hard to teach, and some who dwell seeing fear in blame and in the other world. Just as in a pond of blue or red or white lotuses, some lotuses that are born and grow in the water thrive immersed in the water without rising out of it, and some other lotuses that are born and grow in the water rest on the water's surface, and some other lotuses that are born and grow in the water rise out of the water and stand clear, unwetted by it; so too, surveying the world with the eye of a buddha, he sees . . . some who dwell seeing fear in blame and in the other world.

The Blessed One knows: "This person is of lustful temperament, this one of hating temperament, this one of deluded temperament, this one of discursive temperament, this one of faithful temperament, this one of intelligent temperament. The Blessed One explains the unattractive [nature of the body] to the person of lustful temperament; the development of loving-kindness to the person of hating temperament; he settles the person of deluded temperament in study, questioning, timely listening to the Dhamma, timely discussion of the Dhamma, and dwelling together with a teacher; he explains mindfulness of breathing to the person of discursive temperament;

to the person of faithful temperament, he explains an object that inspires confidence, such as the good enlightenment of the Buddha, the good nature of the Dhamma, and the good practice of the Sangha; and to the person of intelligent temperament he explains an object of insight, the features of impermanence, suffering, and non-self.

Nidd I 265. How does the Blessed One have opened eyes with respect to *the universal eye*? It is the knowledge of omniscience that is called the universal eye. The Blessed One possesses the knowledge of omniscience:

> There is nothing here unseen by him,
> nothing unknown or uncognized;
> he has directly known whatever can be known;
> hence the Tathāgata is the universal eye.

Nidd I 265–66. The Dhamma he witnessed: The Dhamma directly known by him, directly cognized by him—not through hearsay, not through report, not through a lineage of teachers, not through a collection of scriptures, not through logic, not through deduction, not through reflection on reasons, not through acceptance of a view after pondering it. **The removal of obstacles**: There are two kinds of obstacles: obvious obstacles and hidden obstacles . . . [as at pp. 447–48, Nidd II 226–27] . . . all unwholesome volitional activities. The removal of obstacles, the abandoning of obstacles, the allaying of obstacles, the relinquishing of obstacles, the subsiding of obstacles, the deathless nibbāna. ❚❚

922–23. Since restraint of the sense faculties is the way to protect one's good behavior, [564] or since this teaching, being taught in this sequence, was suitable for those deities, the Blessed One begins "One should not be restless with the eyes," showing the practice beginning with restraint of the sense faculties. Here, **one should not be restless with the eyes**: One should not be restless with the eyes by wishing to see what one has not seen before and so forth. **One should block the ears against village gossip**: One should block the ears against pointless talk. **When he is touched by a contact**: by contact with illness. **He should not long for any state of existence**: For the purpose of dispelling that contact he should not yearn for some state of existence such as desire-realm existence; **nor should he tremble amid fearful conditions**: He should not tremble amid such fearful conditions for that contact, such as lions, tigers, and so forth; or he should not tremble amid the other objective domains, those of the nose faculty and mind faculty. Thus full restraint of the sense faculties is stated. Or else, having shown restraint of the sense faculties by the previous lines, with this line he shows: "One living in the forest who sees or hears something fearful should not tremble."

Nidd I 269–71. One should not be restless with the eyes: How is one restless with the eyes? Here someone has restless eyes. Thinking, "One should see what one has not seen, skip over what one has already seen," he goes from park to park, from garden to garden, from village to village, from town to town, from city to city, from realm to realm, from country to country, engaging in long journeys, in endless journeys in order to see forms. Or else a bhikkhu, whether he has entered among the houses or is traveling along a street, goes unrestrained, looking at an elephant, a horse, a chariot, pedestrians, women and men, boys and girls, shops, the doors of houses; he looks up, looks down, looks in different directions. Or else, having seen a form with the eye, a bhikkhu grasps its sign and features. Since he is unrestrained in the eye faculty, bad unwholesome states of longing and dejection invade him; he does not practice restraint over it, does not guard the eye faculty, does not undertake restraint of the eye faculty. Or else, some ascetics and brahmins, consuming food offered in faith, are intent on unsuitable shows, such as dancing, singing, music . . . a battlefield, a military camp, a battle array, or a regimental review.[1988] Refraining from all this is not being restless with the eyes.[1989] One should abandon restlessness of the eyes, dispel it, terminate it, abolish it; one should desist from it, abstain from it, refrain from it, and dwell with a mind rid of boundaries.

Nidd I 271. One should block the ears against village gossip: It is the thirty-two kinds of pointless talk that are called "village gossip," that is, talk about kings, thieves, and ministers of state; talk about armies, dangers, and wars; talk about food, drink, garments, and beds; talk about garlands and scents; talk about relations, vehicles, villages, towns, cities, and countries;

talk about women and talk about heroes; street talk and talk by the well; talk about those departed in days gone by; rambling chitchat; speculation about the world and about the sea; talk about becoming this or that. One should block the ears from such village gossip, restrain them, guard them, protect them, close them off.

One should not be greedy for tastes: There is the taste of roots, the taste of stems, the taste of bark, the taste of leaves, the taste of flowers, the taste of fruits, sour, sweet, bitter, acrid, salty, caustic. There are ascetics and brahmins who are greedy for tastes, who are excited, greedy, infatuated with tastes. He has abandoned this craving for tastes . . . burnt it up by the fire of knowledge. Reflecting wisely, he consumes food, not for amusement . . . blameless and dwells at ease.[1990]

Nidd I 272. One should not take anything in the world as "mine": There are two ways of taking things as "mine": on account of craving and on account of views. . . . [as at pp. 1032–33, Nidd I 35] . . . Having abandoned taking things as "mine" on account of craving, having relinquished taking things as "mine" on account of views, one should not take as "mine" the eye . . . mind, or forms . . . mental phenomena, or family, group, abode, gain, fame, praise, pleasure, robes, alms-food, lodging, medicinal requisites . . . or the past, future, or present . . . or whatever is seen, heard, sensed, or cognized. **Anything**: anything pertaining to form, feeling, perception, volitional activities, or consciousness.

923. Nidd I 272–73. When he is touched by a contact: contact with illness. He is touched by illness, by illness of the eyes, ears, nose, tongue, body, headache, ear ache, mouth disease, dental disease[1991] . . . by cold, by heat, by hunger, by thirst, by defecation, by urination, by gadflies, mosquitoes, wind, sun, and serpents. **He should not long for any state of existence**: He should not long for desire-realm existence, form-realm existence, or formless-realm existence. **Nor should he tremble amid fearful conditions**: From one angle, fear and a fearful condition are the same, said to be the external object: lions, tigers, leopards, bears, hyenas, wolves, buffaloes, horses, elephants, scorpions, centipedes, bandits, or hoodlums. From another angle, fear is the fear that originates in the mind: fear of birth, old age, illness, and death; fear of kings, bandits, fire, and floods; fear of self-reproach, reproach by others, punishment, and a bad destination (AN II 121,17 foll.); fear of waves, crocodiles, whirlpools, and fierce fish (AN II 123,14 foll.); fear for one's livelihood, fear of dispraise, fear as timidity in an assembly, fear of madness, fear of a bad destination. Having seen or heard about such fearful conditions, one should not tremble, become frightened, anxious, agitated, terrified, but should dwell having abandoned fear and terror, rid of alarm. ▪︎⁚

924. Having obtained . . . he should not hoard them: Having gained by righteous means any of these items such as food, he should not hoard them, thinking: "It is always hard for one living in a forest lodging to gain such things."

925. He should be a meditator, not one with restless feet: He should take delight in meditation and should not have restless feet. **He should refrain from regret**: He should dispel regret and fidgeting with the hands and so forth. And here, through consistency in practice, **he should not be heedless.**

⁚▪︎ **Nidd I 275. He should be a meditator, not one with restless feet. A meditator** (*jhāyī*): One is a meditator through the first jhāna, through the second, third, and fourth jhānas. One is a meditator through jhāna with thought and examination, through jhāna without thought but with mere examination, through jhāna without thought and examination. One is a meditator through jhāna with rapture, through jhāna without rapture, through jhāna accompanied by rapture, through jhāna accompanied by enjoyment, through jhāna accompanied by pleasure, through jhāna accompanied by equanimity. One is a meditator through the emptiness jhāna, through the markless jhāna, through the wishless jhāna. One is a meditator through mundane jhāna, through world-transcending jhāna. One delights in jhāna, is intent on oneness, reveres the supreme good.[1992]

Nidd I 275–76. Not one with restless feet: How does one have restless feet? Here someone has restless feet. He goes from park to park, from garden to garden, from village to village, from town to town, from city to city, from realm to realm, from country to country, engaging in long journeys, in endless journeys. Or else, even within the monastery he has restless feet. Without any benefit, without a cause, restless and agitated, he goes from cell to cell, from dwelling to dwelling . . . from cave to cave . . . from hut to hut . . . from the foot of one tree to the foot of another. He indulges in much idle chatter, such as talk about kings . . . [as at pp. 1178–79, Nidd I 271] . . . talk about becoming this or that. He should abandon restlessness of the feet, dispel it, terminate it, abolish it; one should desist from it, abstain from it, refrain from it. He should delight in seclusion, be delighted with seclusion, be intent on internal serenity of mind, not neglecting meditation, be endowed with insight, one who frequents empty huts, a meditator, one who delights in jhāna, who is intent on oneness, who reveres the supreme good.

Nidd I 276–77. He should refrain from regret: Regret is fidgeting with the hands . . . [as at p. 1121, Nidd I 158–59] . . . One should desist from such regret, abstain from it, refrain from it, depart, escape, be released and detached from it, and live with a mind rid of boundaries. **He should not be heedless**: He should be one who acts with care, who acts consistently, who acts persistently, who does not backslide, who does not discard desire, who does not discard effort, who is heedful in wholesome qualities.

926. Nidd I 278. He should not overindulge in sleep: He should divide the night and day into six portions, should practice in five portions, and lie down in one portion. **He should be devoted to wakefulness**: Here, during the day, while walking back and forth and sitting, a bhikkhu should purify his mind of obstructive qualities. In the first watch of the night, while walking back and forth and sitting, he should purify his mind of obstructive qualities. In the middle watch of the night he should lie down on the right side in the lion's posture, with one foot overlapping the other, mindful and clearly comprehending, after noting in his mind the idea of rising. After rising, in the last watch of the night, while walking back and forth and sitting, he should purify his mind of obstructive qualities.[1993] **Ardent**: It is energy that is called ardor. One who possesses this energy is called ardent.

Nidd I 278–79. He should abandon indolence, hypoc-

risy, laughing, and playfulness. Indolence: torpor, laziness. **Hypocrisy** is devious conduct. Here, someone engages in bodily misconduct, verbal misconduct, and mental misconduct. In order to conceal it, he forms an evil wish thus, "May no one find out about me" . . . [as at p. 1050, Nidd I 56–57] . . . This is called hypocrisy. **Laughter**: One laughs making an excessive display of the teeth. For this has been said by the Blessed One: "Bhikkhus, this is childishness in the discipline of the noble one, namely, laughter with an excessive display of the teeth" (AN I 261,5). **Playfulness**: There are two kinds of playfulness, bodily and verbal. What is bodily playfulness? One plays with elephants, horses, chariots, and bows. One plays at various games—board games, sports, and toys.[1994] What is verbal playfulness? Imitating the sounds of various instruments with the mouth, mimicry, shouting, singing, and joking. **Ornamentation**: There are two kinds of ornaments, those of householders and those of homeless ones . . . [as at p. 474, Nidd II 252–53] . . . decoration and ornamentation of this putrid body or of external requisites. ▮⁝

927–30. Atharva spells: employment of spells taken from the Atharva.[1995] **In buying and selling**: He should not engage [in buying and selling] with the five kinds of co-religionists by way of deception, or out of a desire for profit.[1996] **He should not do anything that incurs criticism**: Not generating the defilements that bring criticism, he should not arouse criticism toward himself from other ascetics and brahmins. **He should not form intimacy in the village**: He should not form intimacy in the village by bonding with laypeople and others. **Insinuating speech**: talk connected with robes and so forth, [565] or talk directed to such a purpose.

⁝▮ **Nidd I 280–81. He should not employ Atharva spells, or interpret dreams, signs, or constellations**. The followers of the Atharva *employ Atharva spells*. When a city is beseiged or a battle is underway, they cause a calamity for the enemies in the opposing army; they cause a disaster, an illness, fever, sharp pains, piercing, dysentery.[1997]

Those who *interpret dreams* say that if one has such a dream in the morning, such will be the result; if one has such a dream at noon . . . in the evening . . . in the first, middle, or last watches of the night . . . when lying on one's right side, left side, back, or when crooked; if one sees the moon, the sun, the ocean, Sineru the king of mountains, an elephant, a horse, a chariot, a foot soldier, an army regiment, a park, a garden, a landscape, or a pond, such will be the result.

Sign-readers *interpret signs*. They read the signs of jewels, walking sticks, clothes, swords, spears, bows, weapons; the signs of women and men, girls and boys, and slaves; the signs of elephants, horses, buffaloes, bulls, oxen, goats, rams, chickens, quails, lizards, lotus pericarps, turtle shells, and deer.

Those who *read the constellations* read the twenty-eight constellations and say: "With this constellation one should enter the house; with this, one should put on a head-dress; with this, one should get married; with this, one should take up a fan; with this, one should go to live together."

One should not practice Atharva spells, or interpret dreams, signs, or constellations. One should not learn them, study them, acquire them, or employ them.

Nidd I 284. A bhikkhu should not engage in buying and selling: The kinds of buying and selling rejected in the Vinaya are not intended in this context. How does one engage in buying and selling? By deception, or desiring a profit, one exchanges bowls or robes or any other requisite with the five [fellow monastics]. One should abandon such buying and selling.

He should not do anything that incurs criticism: What are the defilements that incur criticism? There are some ascetics and brahmins who are powerful, who have the divine eye, who know the minds of others, and there are deities too who are powerful, who have the divine eye, who know the minds of others. They criticize one for coarse defilements, for middling defilements, and for subtle defilements. What are *coarse defilements*? Bodily misconduct, verbal misconduct, and mental misconduct. What are *middling defilements*? Sensual thought, malevolent thought, and aggressive thought. What are *subtle defilements*? Thought about relatives, thought about one's country, thought about the immortals,[1998] thought connected with solicitude for others,[1999] thought connected with gain, honor, and praise, and thought connected with not being despised. One should abandon those defilements that incur criticism so that one will not be criticized because of those coarse, middling, or subtle defilements; one should desist from them, abstain from them, refrain from them, and dwell with a mind rid of boundaries.

Nidd I 285. He should not form intimacy in the village: How does one form intimacy in the village? Here, a bhikkhu bonds with laypeople in the village, enjoying things with them, sorrowing with them, happy when they are happy, sad when they are sad, and he undertakes tasks and duties on their behalf. Or else, having dressed in the morning, taking his bowl and robe, he enters a village or town for alms, with body unguarded, with speech unguarded, without establishing mindfulness with the mind, with sense faculties unrestrained. He attaches himself here and there, grasps here and there, becomes bound here and there, meets misery and disaster here and there. He should not form intimacy in the village, should not grasp, should not be bound, should not be impeded; he should be without greed, devoid of greed, rid of greed; he should dwell having himself become holy.

931–32. When provoked, having heard many words from ascetics who speak profusely: When provoked, when ruffled by others, having heard many undesirable words from those who speak profusely, whether ascetics or others such as khattiyas and so forth; **he should not respond**: he should not speak back. Why not? **For the good do not retaliate.**

Nidd I 293. From ascetics who speak profusely: From ascetics outside here (outside the Buddha's teaching) who have entered upon wandering, who engage in wandering. **Who speak profusely**: Khattiyas, brahmins, vessas, suddas, householders, monastics, devas, and humans who insult one, revile one, scold one, harass one, injure one, trouble one with many undesirable, unlovely, disagreeable words.[2000] **He should not respond to them harshly**: He should not speak back harshly, in a rough way. He should not return insults, should not scold back, should not get into an argument, should not create a quarrel, should not create an argument, should not create contention, should not create a dispute, should not create strife; he should abandon and dispel quarrels, arguments, contention, dispute, and strife. **For the good do not retaliate**: The good is one who is calm through the calming down of lust, hatred, delusion . . . of all unwholesome volitional activities, who is peaceful, very peaceful, quenched, tranquil.[2001] The good do not retaliate, fight back, strike back, counterattack.

933. Having understood this Dhamma: Having known this entire Dhamma as it has been stated. **Having known quenching as peace**: Having known the quenching of lust and so forth as peace.

Nidd I 294. Having understood this Dhamma: Having understood, having known, this Dhamma that has been explained, taught, prescribed, set up, opened up, analyzed, clarified, revealed. Or having understood, having known, qualities (*dhammaṃ*) righteous and unrighteous, even and uneven, blameworthy and blameless, inferior and superior, dark and bright, criticized by the wise and praised by the wise. Or having understood, having known, the right practice, the practice in conformity . . . [as at p. 1088, Nidd I 104–5] . . . the noble eightfold path, nibbāna, and the way leading to nibbāna. **Investigating**: investigating, examining, assessing, scrutinizing, clarifying, recognizing that "all conditioned things are impermanent" . . . "whatever is subject to origination is all subject to cessation." **Always train mindfully**: One is mindful on four grounds: mindful when developing the establishment of mindfulness through contemplation of the body, feelings, mind, and phenomena. **Should train**: There are three trainings: the training in the higher good behavior, the training in the higher mind, and the training in the higher wisdom. Directing one's attention to these three trainings . . . [as at pp. 1028–29, Nidd I 28–29] . . . one should train. **Having known quenching as peace**: Having known the quenching of lust, hatred, and delusion as peace; having known the quenching of anger . . . of all unwholesome volitional activities as peace.

Nidd I 295. He should not be heedless in Gotama's teaching: In Gotama's teaching, in the Buddha's teaching, in the Conqueror's teaching, in the Tathāgata's teaching, in the deva's teaching, in the arahant's teaching, he should be one who acts with care, who acts consistently, who acts persistently, who does not backslide, who does not discard desire, who does not discard effort, who is heedful in wholesome qualities, thinking:

"When will I fulfill the aggregate of good behavior, concentration, wisdom, liberation, and the knowledge and vision of liberation? When will I fully understand suffering, abandon the defilements, develop the path, and realize cessation?"

934. If it is asked, "Why shouldn't he be heedless?" the verse says: "For he is a conqueror." Here, **a conqueror**, because he has overcome forms and so forth. **Unconquered**: unconquered by them. **He saw the Dhamma as a witness, not by hearsay**: He saw the Dhamma by direct cognition, not by hearsay. **Always honoring it, one should train in accordance with it**: Always honoring it, one should train in the three trainings. The rest everywhere is already clear.

Nidd I 295–96. For he is a conqueror who is himself unconquered: A conqueror of forms, a conqueror of sounds, a conqueror of odors, a conqueror of tastes, a conqueror of tactile objects, a conqueror of mental phenomena. Unconquered by any defilements, he conquered those bad unwholesome qualities that are defiling, conducive to renewed existence, troublesome, that result in suffering, that lead to future birth, old age, and death. **Heedful in that Blessed One's teaching**: He should be one who acts with care . . . [as at p. 1181, Nidd I 276–77] . . . who is heedful in wholesome qualities.

But taken as a whole, here by "one should not be restless with the eyes" and so forth (**922–23**), restraint of the sense faculties is indicated; by "when he gains food and drink" and so forth (**924**), good behavior consisting in the use of the requisites is indicated under the rejection of hoarding; by [restraint from] sexual intercourse (**926**), from false speech (**931**), and from slanderous speech (**928**), the good behavior consisting in restraint by the Pātimokkha is indicated; by "he should not employ Atharva spells, or interpret dreams, signs," and so forth (**927**), good behavior consisting in purification of livelihood is indicated. By "he should be a meditator" (**925**), concentration is indicated; by "investigating" (**933**), wisdom is indicated; by "he should always train mindfully" (**933**), again the three trainings are concisely shown; by "he should dwell amid seats and beds [in lodgings] where there is little noise" (**925**) and "he should not overindulge in sleep" (**926**) and so forth, the embracing of the factors that assist cultivation of good behavior, concentration, and wisdom, and removal of their obstructions, are indicated.

Thus, having explained the complete course of practice to the mind-created buddha, the Blessed One concluded the teaching with its culmination in arahantship. At the conclusion of the teaching, there was a breakthrough similar to that described in connection with the Discourse on the Breakup. [566]

15 One Who Has Taken Up the Rod (*Attadaṇḍa Sutta*)

What is the origin? When explaining the origin of the Discourse on Proper Wandering, it was said that a quarrel had broken out between the Sakyans and the Koḷiyans on account of water.[2002] Having known about it, the Blessed One thought: "My relatives have started a quarrel. Let me restrain them." Then, standing between the two armies, he spoke this discourse.

935. Here, the meaning of the first verse is as follows: Whatever fear has arisen in the world, whether pertaining to the present life or to future lives, all that **fear has arisen from one who has taken up the rod**: it has arisen because of one's own misconduct.[2003] Such being the case, **see the people engaged in strife**: "See the Sakyan people and their opponents engaged in strife, harming and oppressing one another." Having censured the people practicing wrongly, hostile to one another, to arouse in them a sense of urgency by showing the right practice, he says: **I will tell you of my sense of urgency, how I was stirred by a sense of urgency**: The purport is "in the past, when I was still a bodhisatta."

⁘ **Nidd I 297–98. Fear has arisen from one who has taken up the rod**: There are three kinds of rod (violence): bodily violence, verbal violence, and mental violence. *Bodily violence* is the threefold bodily misconduct; *verbal violence* is the fourfold verbal misconduct; *mental violence* is the threefold mental misconduct.[2004] There are two kinds of fear: fear pertaining to the present life and fear pertaining to future lives. What is fear *pertaining to the present life*? Here, someone engages in misconduct of body, speech, and mind. He destroys life, takes what is not given, breaks into houses, plunders wealth, commits banditry, ambushes highways, goes to the wives of others, and speaks falsely. They arrest him and present him to the king. The king censures him; being censured, he is frightened and experiences pain and dejection. From where does this fear, pain, and dejection come? It has arisen from his own violence (from one who has taken up the rod).

The king is not satisfied with this, but has him imprisoned and bound up . . . imposes a fine on him . . . inflicts various punishments on him . . . [as at p. 1092, Nidd I 112–13] . . . Because of these punishments, he is frightened and experiences pain and dejection. From where does this fear, pain, and dejection come? It has arisen from his own violence (from one who has taken up the rod). The king is the lord over these four kinds of punishment.

Nidd I 298–300. Because of his own kamma, with the breakup of the body, after death, he is reborn in the plane of misery, in a bad destination, in the lower world, in hell. They drive a hot iron spike through his hands and feet and the middle of his chest. There he experiences painful, severe, sharp feelings, but he does not die as long as his bad kamma is not exhausted.[2005] . . . From where does this fear, pain, and dejection come? It has arisen from his own violence (from one who has taken up the rod).

936. Now, showing the mode in which he was stirred by a sense of urgency, he says: "Having seen the population trembling." Here, **trembling**: shaking on account of craving and so forth. **Having seen them hostile to one another**: having seen various beings belligerent toward one another; **fear came upon me**: fear entered me.

Nidd I 301–2. Having seen the population trembling: Trembling with craving, trembling with views, trembling with defilements, trembling with misconduct, trembling with endeavor, trembling with the results; trembling with lust, hatred, and delusion; trembling with birth, old age, illness, and death; trembling with the suffering of hell, of the animal realm, of the realm of afflicted spirits, of the human realm; trembling because of the suffering due to the death of relatives, the loss of wealth, the loss due to illness, the loss of good behavior, the loss of [right] view. **Like fish in a pool with little water**: As fish in a place with little water, where the water is evaporating, tremble while being attacked, picked up, and eaten by crows, herons, and storks, so this population trembles with the trembling of craving . . . the loss of [right] view.

937. The world was insubstantial all around: Starting [below] from hell, all around the world was insubstantial, destitute of any permanent substance; **all the directions were in turmoil**: all the directions were shaken by impermanence. **Desiring an abode for myself**: desiring shelter for myself; **I did not see [any place] unoccupied**: I did not see any place uninhabited by old age and so forth.

Nidd I 303–4. The world was insubstantial all around: The world of hell, the world of the animal realm, the world of the realm of afflicted spirits, the human world, the deva world, the world of the aggregates, the world of the elements, the world of the sense bases, this world, the world beyond, the brahma world, the deva world: this world is insubstantial, substanceless, devoid of substance, without permanent substance, without substance of happiness, without substance of self; without anything permanent, stable, eternal, or not subject to change. As a reed, a lump of foam, a water bubble, a mirage, a plantain trunk, a magical illusion is insubstantial, substanceless, devoid of substance, so is the world insubstantial . . . without anything permanent, stable, eternal, or not subject to change.

Nidd I 304–5. All the directions were in turmoil: The conditioned things of the east, the west, the north, the south, the intermediate directions, above, and below were in turmoil, in commotion, agitated by impermanence, accompanied by birth, overrun by old age, conquered by illness, stricken with death, established on suffering, without a shelter, without a cavern, without a refuge, not offering refuge. **Desiring an abode for myself**: desiring a shelter, a cavern, a refuge, a destination, a resort; **I did not see [any place] unoccupied**: all youth was occupied by old age, all health was occupied by illness, all life was occupied by death, all gain was occupied by loss, all fame was occupied by dishonor, all praise was occupied by blame, all pleasure was occupied by pain.

938. Having seen those hostile at the end, discontent came upon me: Having seen beings with stricken minds still hostile even at the end of youth and so forth, when old age and so forth, the end-maker, the destroyer, has arrived, discontent came upon me. **Then I saw the dart here:** [567] the dart of lust and so forth in these beings; **nestled in the heart**: settled in the mind.

⁞▮ **Nidd I 305–6. Having seen those hostile at the end**: Old age ends all youth, illness ends all health, death ends all life . . . pain ends all pleasure. **Having seen them hostile**: Beings desiring youth are opposed by old age . . . beings desiring pleasure are opposed by pain. **Then I saw the dart here**: seven darts—the darts of lust, hatred, delusion, conceit, views, sorrow, and perplexity. ▮⁞

939. If it is asked, "How mighty is that dart?" the verse says: "When one is struck by that dart." Here, **one runs astray in all directions**: One runs in all the directions of misconduct and in all the major and intermediate directions, eastward and so forth. **But having drawn out that dart, one does not run, does not sink**: Having extracted that dart, one does not run in those directions and does not sink in the four floods.

⁞▮ **Nidd I 306–7. When one is struck by that dart**. There are seven darts: the darts of lust, hatred, delusion, conceit, views, sorrow, and perplexity.

What is *the dart of lust*? That which is lust, passion, compliance, attraction, delight and lust . . . covetousness, greed as an unwholesome root—this is the dart of lust.

What is *the dart of hatred*? Thinking, "They acted for my harm," resentment arises. . . . "They are acting for my harm" . . . "They will act for my harm" . . . (as at pp. 1119–20, Nidd I 156–57) . . . resentment arises. Any such wrath, irritation, displeasure of the mind—this is the dart of hatred.

What is *the dart of delusion*? Ignorance of suffering . . . ignorance of its origin . . . of its cessation . . . of the way leading to the cessation of suffering; ignorance about the past, the future, the past and future; ignorance about conditionality and dependently arisen phenomena. Any such lack of vision, lack of understanding, delusion, confusion, bewilderment, delusion as an unwholesome root—this is the dart of delusion.

What is *the dart of conceit*? The conceit, "I am superior," "I am equal," "I am inferior." Any such conceit, pride, vanity, sense of self-importance—this is the dart of conceit.

What is *the dart of views*? The twenty views of the personal entity, the tenfold wrong view, the ten extremist views. Any such view, speculative view, thicket of views, desert of views, wriggling of views, vacillation of views . . . even up to the sixty-two speculative views—this is the dart of views.

What is *the dart of sorrow*? The sorrow, sorrowing, and sorrowfulness, the mourning and dejection that arise in one afflicted by loss of relatives, by loss of health, by loss of weath, by loss of good behavior, by loss of view, or by any other misfortune—this is the dart of sorrow.

What is *the dart of perplexity*? Doubt about suffering . . . doubt about conditionality and dependently arisen phenomena. Any such doubt, uncertainty, wavering of the mind, indecision, vacillating, mental hesitancy—this is the dart of perplexity.

Nidd I 307–8. When one is struck by that dart one runs astray in all directions. Struck by *the dart of lust*, one engages in misconduct of body, speech, and mind. One kills living beings, takes what is not given, breaks into houses, plunders wealth, commits banditry, ambushes highways, commits adultery, and speaks falsely. Thus struck by the dart of lust, one runs off, runs astray in all directions, one roams and wanders on. Or else, struck by the dart of lust, seeking wealth, one launches out to cross the ocean by ship. Facing cold and heat, attacked by gadflies, mosquitoes, wind, sun, and serpents, dying of hunger and thirst, one travels to [various regions].[2006] Seeking wealth, if one does not obtain it, one experiences pain and dejection; while if one has obtained wealth, one experiences pain and dejection on account of guarding it against kings, thieves, fire, floods, and unloved heirs. If, while one is guarding and securing it, the wealth is plundered, one experiences pain and dejection because of separation from it. Thus struck by the dart of lust, one runs off, runs astray in all directions, one roams and wanders on.

So too when struck by the dart of hatred . . . by the dart of delusion . . . by the dart of conceit, one kills living beings, takes what is not given, breaks into houses, plunders wealth, commits banditry, ambushes highways, commits adultery, and speaks falsely. Thus struck by the dart of conceit, one runs off, runs astray in all directions, one roams and wanders on.

Nidd I 308–10. Struck by *the dart of views*, one goes naked, rejecting conventions. . . . One is an eater of greens or millet . . . one feeds on fallen fruits. One wears hemp robes, robes of hemp-mixed cloth . . . a covering made of owls' wings. One pulls out hair and beard . . . in such a variety of ways one pursues the practice of tormenting and mortifying the body.[2007] Thus struck by the dart of views, one runs off, runs astray in all directions, one roams and wanders on.

Struck by *the dart of sorrow*, one sorrows, grieves, laments beating one's breast, and becomes distraught.[2008] Thus struck by the dart of sorrow, one runs off, runs astray in all directions, one roams and wanders on.

Nidd I 310–11. Struck by *the dart of perplexity*, one is full of doubt, full of uncertainty, divided, thinking: "Did I exist in the past? Did I not exist in the past? What was I in the past? How was I in the past? Having been what, what did I become in the past?" Or one runs forward into the future, thinking: "Will I exist in the future? Will I not exist in the future? What will I be in the future? How will I be in the future? Having been what, what will I become in the future?' Or one is now inwardly perplexed about the present thus: "Do I exist? Do I not exist? What am I? How am I? This being—where has it come from and where will it go?" (MN I 8,4–15, SN II 26–27). Thus struck by the dart of perplexity, one runs off, runs astray in all directions, one roams and wanders on.

One constructs those darts, and one runs to the east, west, north, and south. One runs to a destination, to hell . . . to the deva world; one runs off, runs astray in all directions, one roams and wanders on from destination to destination, from rebirth to rebirth, from conception to conception, from existence to existence, from saṃsāra to saṃsāra, from round to round.

Nidd I 311. But having drawn out that dart, one does not run: Having extracted that dart of lust . . . dart of perplexity, one does not run to the east, west, north, and south. One does not run to a destination, to hell . . . to the deva world; one does not run off, does not run astray in all directions, does not roam and wander on from destination to destination, from rebirth to rebirth, from conception to conception, from existence to existence, from saṃsāra to saṃsāra, from round to round. **Does not sink**: does not sink in the flood of sensuality, in the flood of existence, in the flood of views, in the flood of ignorance.

940. And among the beings pierced by such a mighty dart, the verse says, "Here the trainings are recited: 'Whatever bonds there are in the world.'" This is its meaning: In the world, the five strands of sensual pleasure are the things that people covet; hence they are called **bonds**; or they are called bonds because they have been pursued over a long time. **There**, on that basis, the numerous **trainings**, such as training with elephants and so forth, are discussed or learned.[2009] See how heedless this world is! Since a wise person **should not be** intent **on those** bonds or on those trainings, having instead **entirely pierced through sensual pleasures** by the seeing of impermanence and so forth, **he should train for his own nibbāna.**

Nidd I 312–13. Here the trainings are recited: Whatever bonds there are in the world: The **trainings**: training with elephants, horses, chariots, bows, spears, and darts; training in bodily cures, training in exorcism, training in pediatrics. **Are recited** (*anugīyanti*): are sung, chanted, expounded, discussed, explained, expressed. Or alternatively, they are grasped, learned, retained, preserved, defined, for the purpose of obtaining bonds. It is the five strands of sensual pleasure that are called **bonds**. For the most part deities and human beings long for the five strands of sensual pleasure; for that reason the five strands of sensual pleasure are called bonds.

Having entirely pierced through sensual pleasures: "Having pierced through" means having penetrated. Having penetrated, "All conditioned things are impermanent," having penetrated, "All conditioned things are suffering," having penetrated, "All phenomena are non-self" . . . having penetrated, "Whatever is subject to origination is all subject to cessation"; **one should train for one's own nibbāna**: one should train in the higher good behavior, in the higher mind, in the higher wisdom, for the extinguishing of one's own lust, hatred, delusion, anger . . . for the stilling, allaying, extinguishing, relinquishment, subsiding of all unwholesome volitional activities.

941. Now, showing how one should train for nibbāna, he says, "One should be truthful," and so forth. Here, **truthful**: One should be truthful in speech, truthful in knowledge, and follow the truth of the path. **Devoid of divisive speech**: one who has abandoned divisive speech.

⁝▯ **Nidd I 313. Without hypocrisy**: Hypocrisy is devious conduct. Here, someone engages in bodily misconduct, verbal misconduct, and mental misconduct. In order to conceal it, he forms an evil wish thus: "May no one find out about me" . . . [as at p. 1050, Nidd I 56–57] . . . Such hypocritical behavior is called hypocrisy. One for whom this hypocrisy is abandoned . . . burnt up by the fire of knowledge is said to be without hypocrisy. ▯⁝

942. One should vanquish sleepiness, torpor, and dullness: One should overcome these three qualities: drowsiness, bodily lethargy, and mental lethargy.

⁝▯ **Nidd I 315–16. A person whose mind is set on nibbāna**: Here, when someone gives gifts, undertakes precepts, observes the uposatha duties, sets up water for drinking and washing, sweeps the cells, venerates a cetiya, offers incense and garlands to a cetiya, circumambulates a cetiya, or does any kind of wholesome volitional activity pertaining to the three realms of existence, it is done not for the sake of a good destination, not for the sake of a rebirth, not for the sake of conception, not for a particular state of existence, not for the sake of saṃsāra, not for the sake of the round. He does all this for the purpose of detachment, leaning toward nibbāna, inclining toward nibbāna, bent upon nibbāna. Or having turned his mind away from all conditioned elements, he directs his mind to the deathless element: "This is the peaceful, this is the sublime: the stilling of all volitional activities, the relinquishment of all acquisitions, the destruction of craving, dispassion, cessation, nibbāna."

> The wise do not give gifts for the bliss of acquisitions,
> nor for the sake of renewed existence.
> Surely, they give gifts for an end to renewed existence,[2010]
> for the destruction of sensuality and acquisitions.

The wise do not develop jhānas for the bliss of
acquisitions,
nor for the sake of renewed existence.
Surely, they develop jhānas for an end to renewed
existence,
for the destruction of sensuality and acquisitions.

Desiring quenching (nibbāna), they give gifts,
with minds so inclined, resolved upon that.
As rivers approach the ocean,
they take nibbāna as their destination. ⁞⁞

943. One should refrain from rashness: from acting rashly through lustful conduct and so forth when excited by lust.

944. One should not delight in the old: One should not delight in the past; **for the new**: for what is present. **What is diminishing**: what is perishing. **One should not be attached to an attraction**: One should not be dependent on craving; for it is craving that is called "attraction" because of attracting one to forms and so forth.[2011]

⁞⁞ **Nidd I 318–19. One should not delight in the old**: Past form, feeling, perception, volitional activities, and consciousness are what is called the old. One should not delight in past conditioned things on account of craving and views; one should not welcome them and cling to them; one should abandon delighting in them, welcoming them, and clinging to them. **One should not form a liking for the new**: Present form, feeling, perception, volitional activities, and consciousness are what is called the new. One should not engender a liking for present conditioned things on account of craving and views; one should not create a desire for them, affection for them, lust for them. **One should not sorrow over what is diminishing**: One should not sorrow over what is declining, vanishing, disappearing; one should not grieve, seize on them, lament, weep beating one's breast, and become distraught. **One should not be attached to an attraction**: It is craving that is called attraction. For what reason is craving called attraction? Because of craving, one is attracted to form . . . to consciousness, drawn toward it, grasps it, seizes upon it, and adheres to it; one is attracted to a destination, to a rebirth, to conception, to existence, to saṃsāra, to the round; one is drawn toward it, grasps it, seizes upon it, and adheres to it. ▮⁝

945. If it is asked, "For what reason should one not be attached to an attraction?" the verse says: "I call greed the great flood." This is its meaning: I speak of craving, designated "attraction," as **greed** because it greedily covets things such as forms and so forth. And what is more, I call it a **flood** in the sense of inundating; a **rapids** in the sense of rushing on; **longing**, in the sense of causing one to mutter, "This is mine, that is mine"; [568] the **basis**, in the sense of being hard to let go of; **compulsion**, in the sense of motivating.[2012] And for the world, it is **the swamp of sensuality hard to overcome** in the sense that it is an impediment and hard to pass beyond. Or else, when it is said, "One should not be attached to an attraction," if it is asked, "What is this attraction?" [it is said:] "I call [it] greed." The connection of this verse can be understood in this way too. Here is the construing of terms: "It is greed that I call 'attraction.' So too, this is called the great flood; I call it that. I call it the rapids, I call it longing, I call it compulsion. I call it the swamp of sensuality hard to overcome in the world together with its devas."

⁝▮ **Nidd I 319–20. I call greed the great flood**: It is craving that is called greed—that which is lust, passion . . . covetousness, greed as an unwholesome root. It is craving that is called the great flood. It is craving that is called the rapids, longing, the basis, compulsion. **The swamp of sensuality hard to overcome**: The mud of sensuality, the defilement of sensuality, the bog of sensuality, the impediment of sensuality is hard to overcome, hard to go beyond, hard to cross, hard to surmount, hard to transcend. ▮⁝

946. Thus when one is not attached to this attraction, or its synonyms such as greed, the verse says, "not deviating from truth." This is its meaning: Not deviating from the three kinds of truth, one called **a muni** because one has attained munihood is **a brahmin who stands on the high ground** of nibbāna.[2013] Such a one, **having relinquished all**—the sense bases—**is indeed called peaceful**.

⁝▮ **Nidd I 320. Not deviating from truth**: not deviating from truthful speech, from right view, from the noble eightfold path. **A brahmin stands on high ground**: It is nibbāna the deathless that is called high ground. One is a brahmin because of expelling seven things.[2014]

Nidd I 321. Having relinquished all: It is the twelve sense bases that are called all: the eye and forms . . . the mind and mental phenomena. When desire and lust for the internal and external sense bases have been abandoned, cut off at the root, made like a palm stump, eliminated so that they are no more subject to future arising, one has given up, discarded, dropped, abandoned, and relinquished all. ▯⁝

947. And what is more, the verse says: "One who is truly a knower." Here, **having known the Dhamma**: having known conditioned things by way of impermanence and so forth.[2015] **Living rightly in the world**: living rightly in the world through the abandoning of the defilements responsible for living improperly.

⁝▯ **Nidd I 321–22. A Veda-master**: It is the knowledge in the four paths that is called the Vedas . . . one devoid of lust for all feelings, who has passed beyond all the Vedas, is a Veda-master.[2016] **Having known the Dhamma**: Having known, "All conditioned things are impermanent" . . . "Whatever is subject to origination is all subject to cessation"; **he is independent**: having abandoned the dependency on craving and relinquished the dependency on views, he is not dependent on the eye, ear, nose . . . not dependent on things seen, heard, sensed, and cognized. ▯⁝

948. And thus, not longing, the verse says: "One here who has crossed over sensual pleasures." Here, **the tie**: and who has crossed the sevenfold tie; **does not hope**: does not long for.[2017]

⁝▯ **Nidd I 323. Does not hope**: does not consider, does not ponder, does not anticipate. Or alternatively, he is not born, does not grow old, does not die, does not pass away, is not reborn. ▯⁝

949. Therefore, if any among you wishes to be like this, the verse says, I tell you: "Dry up what pertains to the past." Here, **the past**: past kamma and the defilements that are subject to arising with respect to past conditioned things; **let there be nothing afterward**: let there be nothing such as lust subject to arise with respect to future conditioned things. **If you do not grasp in the middle**: If you do not grasp any present phenomena such as form, then **you will live in peace**.

Nidd I 324. Dry up what pertains to the past: Dry up those defilements that might arise with reference to past conditioned things; or dry up past karmic volitional activities, those karmic volitional activities that have not yet ripened. **Let there be nothing afterward**: With reference to future conditioned things, do not create anything of lust, anything of hatred, anything of delusion, anything of conceit, anything of views, anything of defilements, anything of misconduct. Do not generate them, do not engender them, do not produce them; abandon, dispel, terminate, eliminate them. **If you do not grasp in the middle**: It is present form, feeling, perception, volitional activities, and consciousness that are called the middle. Do not grasp them on account of craving and views. **You will live in peace**: with the stilling of lust, the stilling of hatred, the stilling of delusion . . . the stilling of all unwholesome volitional activities, with their calming down, allaying, extinguishing, vanishing, subsiding, you will be peaceful, calm, quenched, stilled.

950. Thus, having shown the attainment of arahantship with the expression "you will live in peace," he now speaks the following verses as praise of the arahant. Here, **does not claim as "mine"**: the taking [of things] as "mine" or the object grasped as "This is mine." **Does not sorrow over what is nonexistent**: does not sorrow because of its nonexistence, because of its absence. **Does not lose out**: does not undergo loss.

951–52. And what is more, the verse says, "One for whom nothing." [569] Here, **nothing**: nothing such as form and so forth. And what is more, the next verse says, "Not bitter." Here, **not bitter**: not envious; some read, "not proud."[2018] **Everywhere the same**: the purport is "equanimous." What is meant? When asked about the person who does not tremble—the one who does not sorrow, thinking, "It is not mine"—**I call that the benefit** for that person, which is fourfold: being not bitter, not greedy, not impulsive, everywhere balanced.

⁝▮ **Nidd I 330. Not bitter**: What is bitterness? Here, someone is bitter; he envies others for their gain, honor, respect, esteem, veneration, and offerings. One who has abandoned and eradicated such bitterness . . . burnt it up in the fire of knowledge is said to be not bitter.

Everywhere the same: It is the twelve sense bases that are called all: the eye and forms . . . the mind and mental phenomena.[2019] When desire and lust for the internal and external sense bases have been abandoned, cut off at the root, made like a palm stump, eliminated so that they are no more subject to future arising, one is said to be everywhere the same. ▮⁝

953. And what is more, the verse says, "for one without impulse." Here, **activation** (*nisaṅkhiti*): any volitional activity among the meritorious volitional activities and so forth. For that is called "activation" because it is activated or because it activates.[2020] **Instigation**: instigation consisting in meritorious volitional activity and so forth.[2021] **He sees security everywhere**: He sees no fear everywhere.

⁝▮ **Nidd I 331–32. There is no activation at all**: It is meritorious volitional activity, demeritorious volitional activity, and imperturbable volitional activity that are called activation. Since these have been abandoned, cut off at the root, made like a palm stump, eliminated so that they are no more subject to future arising, there is no activation at all; it has been abandoned . . . burnt up by the fire of knowledge. **Abstaining from instigation**: It is meritorious volitional activity, demeritorious volitional activity, and imperturbable volitional activity that are called instigation. Since these have been abandoned . . . he has desisted, abstained, refrained from instigation. **He sees security everywhere**: Lust, hatred, delusion are makers of fear . . . defilements are makers of fear. When these are abandoned, he sees security everywhere, sees no peril anywhere, sees no hazard anywhere, sees no calamity anywhere, sees no disaster anywhere. ▮⁝

954. Seeing thus, the verse says, "The muni does not speak." Here, **does not speak**: does not speak of himself, because of conceit, as among equals, or among inferiors or superiors. **He does not take, does not reject**: He does not grasp and does not dismiss anything of form and so forth. The rest everywhere is already clear.

Nidd I 332–33. He does not take, does not reject: **He does not take**: He does not take up form, does not cling to it, does not grasp it, does not adhere to it; he does not take up feeling, perception, volitional activities, consciousness, a destination, rebirth, conception, existence, saṃsāra, the round . . . does not adhere to it. **Does not reject**: He does not abandon form, does not dispel it, does not terminate it, does not eliminate it; he does not abandon feeling . . . the round . . . does not eliminate it.

Thus, the Blessed One concluded the teaching with its culmination in arahantship. At the conclusion of the teaching five hundred Sakyan youth and Koḷiyan youths went forth by means of the "Come, bhikkhu" procedure. The Blessed One took them and entered the Great Wood.

16 Sāriputta
(*Sāriputta Sutta*)

This is also called "The Discourse on the Elder's Questions."[2022] What is the origin? The origin of this discourse is stated in the explanation of the verse of the Dhammapada (181):

> Even the devas envy them,
> those enlightened ones who are mindful,
> the wise ones devoted to meditation
> who delight in the peace of renunciation.

The background begins when the financier of Rājagaha [570] obtained a block of sandalwood and had a bowl made from it, which he suspended in space.[2023] The Venerable Piṇḍola Bhāradvāja then used his psychic power to acquire the bowl, for which reason the Buddha prohibited his monastic disciples from disclosing their supernormal powers to laypeople (Vin II 112,13). The sectarians then wanted to enter into a contest of miraculous powers with the Blessed One. To hold the contest, the Blessed One went to Sāvatthī, followed by the sectarians. Then [in sequence there took place] King Pasenadi's approaching the Buddha, the manifestation of Gaṇḍa's mango tree, [the Buddha's] prohibiting the four assemblies from performing a miracle in order to triumph over the sectarians, [the Buddha's] performance of the twin miracle, the Blessed One's journey to the Tāvatiṃsa realm after he performed the miracle, his teaching the Dhamma there for three months, and his descent from the deva world to the city of Saṅkassa at the request of the Elder Anuruddha; at intervals [between these events] he expounded a number of Jātakas. Finally, while being venerated by the deities of ten thousand world spheres, the Blessed One came down to the city of Saṅkassa on the middle jewel staircase.[2024] He stood on the bottom rung of the staircase and stated the verse of the Dhammapada.

While he was standing on the bottom rung of the staircase, the Venerable Sāriputta was the first to pay homage to him, followed by the bhikkhunī Uppalavaṇṇā, and then by the multitude of people. Thereupon the Blessed One reflected: "In this assembly, Moggallāna is known as foremost in psychic potency, Anuruddha in the divine eye, Puṇṇa as a speaker on the Dhamma. But this assembly does not know whether Sāriputta is foremost in any quality. Let me show that Sāriputta is foremost in wisdom." He then asked the elder a question. The elder answered each question that the Blessed One asked him, whether a question about worldlings, a question about trainees, or a question about those beyond training. People then knew of him: "He is foremost in wisdom." [571]

Then the Blessed One said: "It is not only now that Sāriputta is foremost in wisdom, but in the past too when over a thousand rishis, subsisting on forest roots and fruits, were living at the foot of a mountain.[2025] When their teacher fell ill, they attended upon him. The eldest pupil said: 'I will bring suitable medicine. Be heedful in looking after the teacher.' He went to an inhabited area, but the teacher passed away while he was gone. When the pupils knew that the teacher was about to pass away, they asked him whether he had reached any meditative attainment. He replied, with reference to the base of nothingness: 'There is nothing.' The pupils thought: 'The teacher did not have any attainment.' When the eldest pupil returned with the medicine and saw their teacher had died, he asked them: 'Did you ask the teacher anything?' – 'We asked, and he said, "There is nothing," so the teacher did not have any attainment.' – 'When he said, "There is nothing," the teacher declared that he had attained the base of nothingness. The teacher should be honored.'"

> Though over a thousand of them have assembled,
> those without wisdom might weep for a hundred years.
> Even one wise person is better
> who understands the meaning of a statement.

When the Blessed One had concluded the Jātaka, for the sake of his five hundred pupils, Sāriputta recited eight verses, beginning with the verse of praise, "I have never before seen," in order to ask about the lodging, resort, behavior, observances, and so forth that are suitable for bhikkhus. The Blessed One spoke the verses that follow to explain these points.

955. Here, **never before**: before his descent in the city of Saṅkassa. **Of such lovely speech**: of such beautiful speech; **leader of a group, who has come from Tusita**: He is said to have come from Tusita because he entered his mother's womb after passing away from the Tusita realm.[2026] He is the "leader of a group" because he is the teacher of a group, or because he has come leading a group from the deva world called "Tusita" in the sense that they are content; or because he has come as the leader of contented arahants.[2027]

Nidd I 334. I have never before seen: I have never before seen the Blessed One with these eyes, in this body, when, after spending the rains retreat on the yellowstone seat at the foot of the päricchattaka tree in the Tāvatiṃsa heaven, accompanied by a group of devas, he descended to the city of Saṅkassa by the middle jeweled staircase. This sight was never seen by me before. **Nor have I ever heard it from anyone**: from any khattiya or brahmin or vessa or sudda, householder or monastic, deva or human being.

Nidd I 334–35. Of such lovely speech: Of such sweet speech, such endearing speech, speech that goes to the heart, soft speech like the cry of the karavīka bird.[2028] The speech uttered from the Blessed One's mouth has eight qualities: it is smooth, comprehensible, soft, resonant, rounded, not diffuse, deep, and melodious.[2029] The Blessed One communicates to the assembly with the sound of his voice, but his voice does not extend beyond the assembly. The Blessed One has a brahma-like voice, speaking [with a voice like the sound of] the karavīka bird.

A teacher: The Blessed One is a teacher, a caravan leader. As a caravan leader leads beings across a wilderness—a wilderness of bandits, a wilderness with wild beasts, a wilderness short of food, a waterless wilderness—enabling them to reach safe ground, so the Blessed One is a caravan leader who leads beings across the wilderness of birth, old age, illness, and death, the wilderness of lust, hatred, delusion, conceit, views, defilements, and misconduct, enabling them to reach safety, the deathless nibbāna. Thus the Blessed One is a caravan leader.

Nidd I 335–36. Leader of a group, who has come from Tusita: Having passed away from the Tusita realm, mindful and clearly comprehending, the Blessed One entered his mother's womb; thus he has come as the leader of a group. Or else the devas are called "contented." They are contented, pleased, joyful, full of rapture and happiness; he came as the leader of a group from the deva world. Or else arahants are called "contented." They are contented, pleased, with their wishes fulfilled; he came as the leader of the group of arahants.

956. As the One with Vision is seen in the world together with its devas: He is seen among humans *just as* [he is seen] in the world together with its devas; or else, [572] **as . . . is seen**: he is seen truthfully, without distortion.[2030] **The One with Vision**: one with supreme vision. **Alone**: alone in the way designated the going forth and so on. **Delight**: the delight of renunciation and so forth.

Nidd I 336–37. As the One with Vision is seen: As the deities see the Blessed One teaching the Dhamma while sitting on the yellowstone seat at the foot of the pāricchattaka tree in the Tāvatiṃsa heaven, so do human beings see him. As human beings see him, so do the deities see him. As he is seen by the devas, so is he seen by human beings. As he is seen by human beings, so is he seen by the devas. In such a way, too, as the One with Vision is seen. Or else, whereas some ascetics and brahmins who are untamed are seen as tamed, who are unpeaceful are seen as peaceful, who are uncalm are seen as calm, who have not attained nibbāna are seen as having attained nibbāna, not thus is the Blessed One seen. The Blessed One is really, truly, actually, factually, genuinely tamed and is seen as tamed; peaceful and seen as peaceful; calm and seen as calm; he has attained nibbāna and is seen as having attained nibbāna. And the buddhas, the blessed ones, do not posture; they have fulfilled their aspirations.

Nidd I 337–41. The One with Vision: The Blessed One is "the One with Vision" by way of the five eyes: the fleshly eye, the divine eye, the wisdom eye, the buddha eye, and the universal eye . . . [as at pp. 1174–77, Nidd I 261–65] . . . "hence the Tathāgata is the universal eye."

Having dispelled all darkness: Having dispelled, discarded, abandoned, terminated, obliterated all the darkness of lust, the darkness of hatred, the darkness of delusion, the darkness of conceit, the darkness of views, the darkness of defilements, the darkness of misconduct, all of which cause blindness, lack of vision, lack of knowledge, which are obstructive to wisdom, bring distress, and do not lead to nibbāna.

Nidd I 341–44. Alone, he achieved delight. **Alone**: alone in the way designated the going forth; alone in the sense of being without a partner; alone in the sense of the abandoning of craving; alone as utterly devoid of lust, hatred, and delusion, as utterly without defilements; alone by having gone to the one-way path; alone by having awakened to the unsurpassed perfect enlightenment.[2031]

How was the Blessed One alone *in the way designated the going forth*? Even when young, in the prime of life, with his mother and father weeping, the Blessed One abandoned his circle of relatives, cut off the impediment of the household life, the impediment of wife and child, the impediment of relatives, the impediment of possessions, shaved off his hair and beard, put on ochre robes, went forth from the household life into homelessness, approached the state of ownerlessness, and lived alone. How was he alone in the sense of being *without a partner*? When he had gone forth, alone he resorted to forest groves, remote lodgings with little sound, little noise, unpopulated, uninhabited, suitable for seclusion. There he lived alone, traveled alone, stood alone, sat alone, slept alone. How was the Blessed One alone in the sense of *abandoning craving*? Being alone, without a partner, dwelling heedful, ardent, and resolute, he undertook the great striving at the foot of the bodhi tree on the bank of the Nerañjarā River; there, having dispersed Māra together with his army, he abandoned the net of craving, extended and adhesive; he dispelled it, terminated it, and eliminated it. How was the Blessed One alone as *utterly devoid of lust*? He was alone, utterly devoid of lust through the abandoning of lust; alone, utterly devoid of hatred through the abandoning of hatred; alone, utterly devoid of delusion through the abandoning of delusion; alone, utterly devoid of defilements through the abandoning of defilements. How was the Blessed One alone by *having gone to the one-way path*? The one-way path is the four establishments of mindfulness . . . the noble eightfold path.

How was the Blessed One alone by *having awakened to the unsurpassed perfect enlightenment*? "Enlightenment" is the knowledge in the four paths, the faculty of wisdom, the power of wisdom, the enlightenment factor of discrimination of qualities, investigation, insight, right view. By that knowledge of enlightenment, the Blessed One awakened to the truth that "all conditioned things are impermanent, all conditioned things are suffering, all phenomena are non-self." He awakened to: "With ignorance as condition, volitional activities [come to be] . . . with the cessation of birth, there is cessation of old age and death." He awakened to: "This is suffering, this is its origin, this is its cessation, this is the way leading to the cessation of suffering. These are the influxes, this is their origin, this is their cessation, this is the way leading to their cessation." He awakened to: "These things should be directly known; these things should be fully understood, these should be abandoned, these should be developed, these should be realized." He awakened to the origin and passing away, the gratification, danger, and escape in regard to the six bases for contact, the five aggregates subject to clinging, and the four great elements. He awakened to: "Whatever is subject to origination is all subject to cessation."

He achieved delight: He achieved the delight of renunciation, the delight of seclusion, the delight of peace, the delight of enlightenment. ▮⁝

957. I have come in need with a question: I have come needful with a question, or with a question for those who are needful, or there is a coming with a question.[2032] **On behalf of the many here who are bound**: On behalf of the many pupils[2033] here, khattiyas and so forth, for pupils are said to be "bound" because they live in dependence on their teachers.

⁝▮ **Nidd I 344–45. To the Buddha**: The Blessed One who is self-accomplished, who without a teacher awakened by himself to the truths among things not heard before, who attained omniscience in regard to them and mastery over the powers. In what sense was he a buddha? He was a buddha as one who awakened to the truths, as one who awakens this population, as all-knowing, as all-seeing, as not being guided by others, as one who has opened up,[2034] as one whose influxes are destroyed, as one without defilements, as one utterly devoid of lust, hatred, and delusion, as one utterly without defilements, as one who has gone to the one-way path, as one who awakened to the unsurpassed perfect enlightenment. "Buddha" is not a name given by mother, father, brother, sister, friends and companions, family members and other relatives, ascetics and brahmins or deities. "Buddha" is a name pertaining to the end of emancipation, a designation accruing to the buddhas, the blessed ones, along with realization, with the obtaining of the omniscient knowledge at the foot of the bodhi tree.[2035]

Unattached: There are two dependencies: dependency through craving and dependency through views. For the Buddha, the Blessed One, the dependency through craving has been abandoned and the dependency through views has been relinquished; he dwells unattached, independent, detached, with a mind rid of boundaries.

Nidd I 345–46. Impartial: The Blessed One is impartial in five ways: he is impartial in regard to the desirable and undesirable; impartial in the sense of renounced; impartial in the sense of having crossed over; impartial in the sense of being freed; and impartial as a descriptive term . . . [as at pp. 1073–74, Nidd I 82–83] . . . as one having the three clear knowledges, as one having the six superknowledges, as one having the ten powers.

Nidd I 347–49. Not a schemer: There are three means of scheming: that consisting in the use of requisites; that consisting in the postures; and that consisting in insinuating talk . . . [as at pp. 1123–24, Nidd I 163–65] . . . For the Blessed One these three means of scheming have been abandoned . . . burnt up by the fire of knowledge. Therefore the Buddha is not a schemer.

Nidd I 349. As leader of a group: He is "leader of a group" as the teacher of a group, as one who maintains a group, as one who exhorts a group, as one who instructs a group, as one who confidently approaches a group; as one whom a group wishes to listen to, lends an ear to, and applies the mind to understand; as one who lifts a group up from the unwholesome and establishes it in the wholesome; the leader of a group of bhikkhus, of a group of bhikkhunīs, of a group of male lay followers, of a group of female lay followers; the leader of a group of kings, khattiyas, brahmins, vessas, suddas; the leader of a group of brahmās, the leader of a group of devas; the head of the Sangha, leader and teacher of a group.

On behalf of the many here who are bound: On behalf of the many humans and devas who are bound, committed, attendants, pupils.[2036] **I have come in need with a question**: I have come needy with a question, I have come wishing to ask a question, I have come wishing to hear [the answer to] a question. Or else: There is a coming, an arrival, an approach, a visit on behalf of those who need to ask a question, on behalf of those who wish to ask a question, on behalf of those who wish to hear [the answer to] a question. Or else: There is the coming to you with a question; you are capable, you are able, to answer a question asked by me. Take up this burden.

958–62. Repulsed: repelled by birth and so forth; **a solitary seat**: a secluded bed and stool; **various sorts of lodgings**: various, that is, inferior or superior; lodgings, such as monasteries. **How many obstacles?**: how many calamities? **The untraveled region**: nibbāna; for this is untraveled in that it has not been visited before, and a "region" in that that it can be pointed out. Hence it is called the untraveled region.

Nidd I 350. Repulsed: repulsed by birth, by old age, by illness, by death; by sorrow, lamentation, pain, dejection, and anguish; by the suffering due to loss of relatives, loss of wealth, loss of health, loss of good behavior, and loss of view.

963. Thus the Venerable Sāriputta first extols the Blessed One with three verses, and then with five verses, for the sake of his five hundred pupils, he asks about lodgings, resort, good behavior, and observances. Being asked to clarify these matters, the Blessed One begins to answer with the words "As one who understands."[2037] Here, this is the meaning of the first verse: "**As one who understands I will tell you**—I speak as one who understands would speak—**in accordance with the Dhamma**, according to the Dhamma, what is a **comfortable** dwelling, Sāriputta, for a bhikkhu **who is repulsed** by birth and so forth, **if, wishing for enlightenment, he resorts to a solitary lodging.**"

964. Of bounded conduct (*sapariyantacārī*): behaving within the four boundaries, good behavior and so forth. **Encounters with people**: [573] contact with bandits and so forth.

⁝⁞ **Nidd I 364–65. Of bounded conduct**: There are four boundaries: the boundary of restraint by good behavior; the boundary of restraint of the sense faculties; the boundary of moderation in eating; and the boundary of devotion to wakefulness.

What is the boundary of *restraint by good behavior*? Here, a bhikkhu is of good behavior; he dwells restrained by the Pātimokkha, possessed of good conduct and resort, seeing danger in minute faults. Having undertaken the training rules, he trains in them.

What is the boundary of *restraint of the sense faculties*? Here, having seen a form with the eye . . . Having heard a sound with the ear . . . Having smelled an odor with the nose . . . Having tasted a taste with the tongue . . . Having felt a tactile object with the body . . . Having cognized a mental phenomenon with the mind, a bhikkhu does not grasp its marks and features. Since, if he left the mind faculty unrestrained, bad unwholesome states of longing and dejection might invade him, he practices restraint over it; he guards the mind faculty, he undertakes the restraint of the mind faculty.

What is the boundary of *moderation in eating*? Here, reflecting carefully, a bhikkhu consumes food neither for amusement nor for intoxication nor for the sake of physical beauty and attractiveness, but only for the support and maintenance of this body, for avoiding harm, and for assisting the spiritual life, considering: "Thus I shall terminate the old feeling and not arouse a new feeling, and I shall be healthy and blameless and dwell at ease."

What is the boundary of *devotion to wakefulness*? Here, during the day, while walking back and forth and sitting, a bhikkhu purifies his mind of obstructive qualities. In the first watch of the night, while walking back and forth and sitting, he purifies his mind of obstructive qualities. In the middle watch of the night he lies down on the right side in the lion's posture, with one foot overlapping the other, mindful and clearly comprehending, after noting in his mind the idea of rising. After rising, in the last watch of the night, while walking back and forth and sitting, he purifies his mind of obstructive qualities.

Nidd I 366. Encounters with people: There may be bandits or hoodlums, whether or not they have committed a crime. They ask a bhikkhu a question, refute his assertion, or insult him, revile him, scold him, harm him, injure him, harass him. Harm from such people is called "encounters with people." ⁞⁞

965. Followers of other teachings: apart from the seven co-religionists,[2038] all the rest are outsiders.

966. The homeless one: the one who is without an abode for karmically active consciousness and so forth.[2039]

967. Thus, having answered the matters asked about in the three verses that begin "When a bhikkhu is repulsed" (**958–60**), now, beginning with the words "He should not commit theft" and so forth, he answers the matters asked about in the way that begins "What ways of speech should he adopt?" (**961**). **If he should recognize any blemish of the mind**: If he should recognize any blemish of the mind, he should dispel them all as **"a faction of the Dark One."**

⁞⁞ **Nidd I 369. A faction of the Dark One**: The Dark One is Māra, the overlord, the end-maker, Namuci, kinsman of the heedless. The "faction of the Dark One" is Māra's faction, Māra's snare, Māra's bait, Māra's meat, Māra's sphere, Māra's residence, Māra's range, Māra's bondage. One should abandon that, dispel it, terminate it, eliminate it. ⁞⁞

968. But should dig them up by their root too:[2040] He should dwell having dug up ignorance and so forth, the root of anger and arrogance. **Then, withstanding the pleasing and displeasing, he should conquer them as well**:[2041] Thus overcoming the pleasing and displeasing, he should definitely conquer them; the purport is that he should not relax his exertion in regard to them.

⁞⁞ **Nidd I 370. Should dig up their root too**: What is the root of anger? Ignorance is a root, careless attention is a root, the conceit "I am" is a root, lack of moral shame is a root, lack of moral dread is a root, restlessness is a root. What is the root of arrogance? Ignorance is a root . . . restlessness is a root. He should dwell having dug up the root of anger and arrogance, having extracted it, having uprooted it, having abandoned it, dispelled it, terminated it, eliminated it. **Withstanding the pleasing and displeasing**: There are two kinds of pleasing things: beings and inanimate things. What kind of beings are pleasing? Those who desire one's good, who desire one's well-being, who desire one's comfort, who desire one's security: mother, father, brothers, sisters, sons, daughters, friends, companions, relatives, other family members. What inanimate things are pleasing? Agreeable forms, sounds, odors, tastes, and tactile objects. There are two kinds of displeasing things: beings and inanimate things. What kind of beings are displeasing? Those who desire one's misfortune, who desire one's harm, who desire one's discomfort, who desire one's endangerment, who desire to take one's life. What inanimate things are displeasing? Disgreeable forms, sounds, odors, tastes, and tactile objects. **Surely**: a word expressing affirmation, certainty, absence of doubt, lack of ambiguity, definitiveness, decisiveness.[2042] **Withstanding the pleasing and displeasing, he should conquer them as well**: Conquering the pleasing and displeasing, pleasure and pain, joy and dejection, the desirable and undesirable, he should withstand them, or withstanding them, he should conquer them.[2043] Ⅱ:

969. Giving precedence to wisdom: making wisdom the forerunner; **rejoicing in the good**: possessing good rapture. **He should vanquish the four factors of lamentation**: He should vanquish the factors of lamentation to be stated in the following verse.

970. These thoughts: two pertain to almsfood, two to lodgings; hence there are four thoughts. **Wandering without abode**: wandering without impediments, wandering without craving.

971. In time: at the time for almsfood; **having obtained a meal**: a designation for almsfood; **and clothing**: a designation for a robe, at the time for robes; **he should know moderation**: he should know the right amount in acceptance and usage; **for the sake of contentment here**, in the Teaching, or this word ("here") is a mere indeclinable. This means that he should know moderation for this purpose. **Guarded in these things . . . he**: that bhikkhu, guarded with respect to those requisites; **wandering restrained**: [574] dwelling self-controlled, with his postures protected or with the doors of body, speech, and mind protected.

972. Intent on jhāna: intent on jhāna by arousing that which has not been attained and pursuing that which has been attained. **Inwardly concentrated, based on equanimity**: with a concentrated mind, having aroused the equanimity of the fourth jhāna; **he should cut off regret and inclination to thought**: he should cut off regret, fidgeting with the hands and so forth; and he should cut off thought, that is, sensual thought and so forth, and the inclination to thought, that is, sensual perception and so forth.

Nidd I 379. Intent on jhāna: One is intent on jhāna in two ways: If the first jhāna has not arisen, one is intent on arousing it; if the second . . . the third . . . the fourth jhāna has not arisen, one is intent on arousing it. Or else, if the first jhāna . . . the fourth jhāna has arisen, one repeats it, develops it, cultivates it.

Nidd I 379–80. He should cut off regret and inclination to thought. Regret: fidgeting with the hands . . . [as at p. 1121, Nidd I 158–59] . . . mental unease. There are nine [unwholesome] thoughts: sensual thought, malicious thought, aggressive thought, thought about relatives, thought about one's country, thought about the immortals, thought connected with solicitude for others, thought about gain, honor, and praise, and thought about not being despised. Sensual perception is the inclination to sensual thought, malevolent perception is the inclination to malevolent thought, aggressive perception is the inclination to aggressive thought. Or else ignorance . . . careless attention . . . the conceit "I am" . . . lack of moral shame . . . lack of moral dread . . . restlessness is an inclination to thought.

973. If reproached with words, a mindful one should welcome them: Reproached in words by his preceptor and others, being mindful, he should welcome their reproach. **He should utter wholesome speech**: He should utter speech originated by knowledge; **but not to excess**: he should not utter speech that exceeds the boundaries, that goes beyond the boundary of time and the boundary of good behavior. **He should not intend [speech] that people might blame**: He should not arouse the intention to utter talk that might be blamed by people.[2044]

974. Five kinds of dust: The five kinds of dust arc lust for forms and so forth; **for the removal of which a mindful one should train**: Having established mindfulness, he should train in the three trainings in order to remove them. One who has thus trained, not others, **should vanquish lust for forms . . . and tactile objects**.

⁞▮ **Nidd I 383. Five kinds of dust**: The dust of forms, the dust of sounds, the dust of odors, the dust of tastes, the dust of tactile objects.

> It is lust that is dust, not fine particles;
> "dust" is a designation for lust.
> Having abandoned this dust, the wise
> dwell in the teaching of the one devoid of dust.
>
> It is hatred that is dust, not fine particles . . .
> dwell in the teaching of the one devoid of dust.
>
> It is delusion that is dust, not fine particles . . .
> dwell in the teaching of the one devoid of delusion. ▮⁞

975. Then, the verse says, one gradually training for their removal "should remove desire for these things." Here, **for these things**: for forms and so forth. **Rightly investigating the Dhamma at the proper time**: at the time described in this way, "When the mind is restless, this is the time for concentration" (SN V 114,20)—at that time, investigating all conditioned things by way of impermanence and so forth; **unified, he should destroy darkness**: one-pointed in mind, he should destroy all the darkness of delusion and so forth. There is no doubt about this. The rest everywhere is clear.

⁞ **Nidd I 385–86. At the proper time**: When the mind is restless, it is the time for serenity; when the mind is concentrated, it is the time for insight.

At the proper time he exerts the mind;
again, at another he restrains it.
At the proper time he encourages the mind;
at [another] time he concentrates it.
One who, at the proper time, looks on with equanimity
is a meditator skilled in the proper time.

At what time should there be exertion?
At what time is there restraint?
What is the time for encouragement?
What is the time for serenity?
How does one describe to a meditator
the mind's time of equanimity?

When the mind is sluggish, that's the time for exertion;
when it is restless, that's the time for restraint;
when the mind is apathetic,
one should then at once encourage it.

When the mind has been encouraged,
when it is neither sluggish nor restless,
that is the time for serenity:
the mind should delight internally.

When, by this method,
the mind is concentrated,
having known the concentrated mind,
one should look on with equanimity.

A wise one who thus knows the time,
understands the time, skilled in the time,
from time to time should note
the mark of the mind.

Nidd I 386. At the proper time rightly investigating the Dhamma: Investigating the Dhamma rightly thus: "All conditioned things are impermanent" . . . "Whatever is subject to origination is all subject to cessation." **Unified**: with one-pointed mind, undistracted mind, unscattered mind, serenity, the faculty of concentration, the power of concentration, right concentration. **He should destroy darkness**: He should destroy, abandon, dispel, terminate, eliminate the darkness of lust, the darkness of hatred, the darkness of delusion, the darkness of views, the darkness of conceit, the darkness of defilements, the darkness of misconduct, all of which cause blindness, lack of vision, lack of knowledge, which are obstructive to wisdom, bring distress, and do not lead to nibbāna.

The Blessed One: This is a term of reverence. Further, he is the Blessed One because he has demolished lust, demolished hatred, demolished delusion . . . [as at pp. 1086–87, Nidd I 104] . . . "Blessed One" is a name pertaining to the end of emancipation, a designation accruing to the buddhas, the blessed ones, along with realization, with the obtaining of the omniscient knowledge at the foot of the bodhi tree. ⁞⁞

Thus the Blessed One concluded the teaching with its culmination in arahantship. At the conclusion of the teaching, the five hundred bhikkhus attained arahantship, and thirty koṭis of devas and human beings made a breakthrough to the Dhamma.

V The Chapter on the Way to the Beyond
(*Pārāyanavagga*)

Introductory Verses
(*Vatthugāthā*)

[575] The origin of the introductory verses of "The Chapter on the Way to the Beyond" is as follows: In the past, it is said, there was a carpenter, a citizen of Bārāṇasī, who was peerless in the lineage of his own teacher. He had sixteen pupils, each of whom in turn had a thousand students. Thus, including both teachers and students, there were altogether 16,017 men who earned their living in dependence on Bārāṇasī. They would go to a mountainous area, where they would collect trees and prepare them in various shapes for making mansions. Having built a raft, they would bring them to Bārāṇasī. If the king wished, they constructed a one-story mansion . . . or a seven-story mansion and gave it to him. If not, they would sell them to others and thereby support their wives and children. One day their teacher reflected: "It isn't possible to earn a living by carpentry forever. This kind of work is hard when one gets old." He then addressed his students: "Dears, bring some soft-wood trees, such as fig trees and so forth."

They agreed and brought such trees. He made from them a wooden bird, entered it, and started the machine. The wooden bird rose up into the sky like a royal garuda, coasted above the woods, and landed in front of the students. Then the teacher told them: "My dears, by making such wooden vehicles, we can gain a kingdom anywhere in Jambudīpa. You build them, too. Let's win a kingdom. It is hard to live by carpentry."

They did so and told the teacher, who asked them: "Which realm should we acquire?" – "Bārāṇasī, teacher." – "Enough, my dears! Don't think of this. If we were to gain this realm, people would refer to us as 'the carpenter king, the carpenter prince,' and we would always be called 'carpenter.' Jambudīpa is large. Let's go elsewhere."

Having embarked on the wooden vehicles along with their wives and children, [576] with their weapons ready, they headed toward the Himalayas. They entered a certain city in the Himalayas and beseiged the residence of the king. They acquired rulership there and anointed their teacher as ruler. He became known as "King Wooden Vehicle." The city, too, because it had been acquired by him, was named "Wooden Vehicle City," and so too the entire realm. King Wooden Vehicle was righteous, and so too the princes, the sixteen pupils who were appointed to the post of ministers. Being benefited by the king with the four means of attracting and sustaining a retinue,[2045] the realm became extremely successful, prosperous, and secure. The citizens were deeply fond of the king and his retinue, saying: "We have gained an excellent king, an excellent royal retinue."

One day some merchants, bringing merchandise from the middle districts, came to Wooden Vehicle City. They took a present and visited the king, who asked them: "From where have you come?" – "From Bārāṇasī, lord." He asked them about all the news there and said: "Establish a bond of friendship between us and your king." They agreed. He gave them a gratuity, and when the time came for their departure, he again spoke to them kindly and sent them off. When they reached Bārāṇasī, they informed the king. The king declared, "Starting today, I exempt merchants who come from Wooden Vehicle City from customs duties," and he added: "Let King Wooden Vehicle be my friend." In this way, though the two had never met, they became friends.

King Wooden Vehicle, too, announced in his entire city: "Starting from today, I exempt merchants who come from Bārāṇasī from customs duties, and a gratuity should be given to them." Then the king of Bārāṇasī sent a letter to King Wooden Vehicle, saying: "If anything wonderful, worthy of being seen or heard, arises in your country, let us also see it or hear it." The latter sent him a similar letter in reply. [577] As time went by, King Wooden Vehicle obtained extremely valuable and precious blankets, in color like the rays of the newly arisen sun. He thought: "I will send them to my friend." He had the ivory workers carve out eight ivory caskets and put the blankets into them. He had the lac masters make eight balls of lac similar to outside balls of lac, had them placed in a container, wrapped it in a cloth, stamped it with the royal insignia, and sent his ministers with the message: "Give this to the king of Bārāṇasī." And he included a letter that said: "You should inspect this present in the middle of the city, surrounded by your ministers."

They went and gave the present to the king of Bārāṇasī. He read the letter, assembled his ministers, and in the royal courtyard in the middle of the city, he broke the seal, removed the wrapping, and opened the container. When he saw the eight balls of lac, he felt embarrassed, thinking: "My friend has sent me balls of lac as he would to little children who play with balls of lac." He then struck one ball of lac against the seat on which he was sitting. Immediately, the lac fell off and the ivory casket, having obtained an opening, split into two portions. When he saw the blanket inside, he opened the others and the same thing happened. Each blanket was eight meters long and four meters wide. When a blanket was stretched out, it seemed as if the royal courtyard was being illuminated by the light of the sun. On seeing this, the crowd applauded and waved cloths, delighted to know: "King Wooden Vehicle, the unseen friend of our king, has sent him a present suitable for one friend to send to another."

The king called dealers and had each blanket evaluated. They informed him that all the blankets were invaluable. The king then thought: "It is proper for one giving a present afterward to offer a present that surpasses the one given to him. But the present sent by my friend is invaluable. What can I send my friend?" [578] Now at that time the Blessed One Kassapa had arisen and was living at Bārāṇasī. So the king thought: "There is no gem superior to the Triple Gem. Let me inform my friend that the Triple Gem has arisen."

He then had the following verse inscribed with natural vermilion on gold foil:

"The Buddha has arisen in the world,
for the welfare of all living beings.
The Dhamma has arisen in the world,
for the happiness of all living beings.

The Sangha has arisen in the world,
the unsurpassed field of merit."

He also described the practice of a bhikkhu up to the attainment of arahantship. He placed the letter in a box made of the seven gems, this in a box made of maṇi jewels, the box of maṇi jewels in one made of cat's eyes, the box of cat's eyes in one made of rubies, this in a box made of gold, this in a box made of silver, this in a box made of ivory, and this in a box made of heartwood. He had the heartwood box placed in a basket, wrapped the basket with a cloth, had an excellent royal elephant decked with golden flags and golden ornaments and a golden net, and set up a couch on top of it, and had the basket mounted on the couch. Then, with a white parasol held above it, with offerings being made of all sorts of incense, flowers, and other items, with hundreds of hymns of praise being sung, accompanied by all sorts of music, he himself led it along the road to the boundary of his own kingdom, a road that he had ornamented for the occasion. And standing there, he sent the present to the neighboring kings, with the instruction: "You should convey this present with similar honors." When they heard this, those kings in turn came out along the road and brought the present as far as the boundary of the realm of Wooden Vehicle.

When King Wooden Vehicle heard of this, he came out along the road, and venerating the gift in the same way, brought it to the city. He assembled his ministers and citizens, and in the royal court he removed the cloth around the gift, opened the basket, and saw the boxes. In sequence, he opened all the boxes until he saw the letter inscribed on gold foil. [On reading it] he was delighted, thinking: "My friend has sent me a precious present extremely hard to obtain even in 100,000 eons." He then thought: "We have heard indeed what we had not heard before, namely, that the Buddha has arisen in the world. Let me go see the Buddha and hear the Dhamma." He then addressed his ministers: "It is said that the gems of the Buddha, the Dhamma, and the Sangha [579] have arisen in the world. What do you think should be done?" They replied: "You stay here, great king. We will go and find out what is happening."

Then the sixteen ministers, accompanied by their 16,000 followers, paid homage to the king and departed, saying: "If the Buddha has arisen in the world, you will not see us again. If he has not arisen, we will return." The king's nephew, having venerated the king last, said: "I too will go." [The king said:] "Dear, if you learn that the Buddha has arisen, come back and inform me." He agreed and left. As they traveled, passing only one night wherever they stopped, they eventually reached Bārāṇasī. However, before they arrived, the Blessed One attained final nibbāna. They traveled around to all the monasteries, asking, "Who is the Buddha? Where is the Buddha?" and when they met his personal disciples, they inquired from them. The disciples told them that the Buddha had attained final nibbāna. They wept, exclaiming: "Alas, we made such a long journey but we did not even get to see him." But they asked: "Bhante, did the Blessed One give you any exhortation?" – "Yes, lay disciples, he did. He said one should be established in the three refuges, should undertake the five precepts, should observe the eight factors of the uposatha, should give gifts, and should go forth." Having heard this, all the ministers except the nephew went forth. The nephew departed for the realm of Wooden Vehicle, taking along a relic of use.[2046] A "relic of use" includes the bodhi tree, the alms bowl, a robe, and so forth. But he also brought an elder who was a Dhamma practitioner[2047] of the Blessed One, an upholder of the Dhamma, an upholder of the Vinaya. In stages, he reached the city and informed the king: "The Buddha arose in the world, but he has attained final nibbāna." He then told him about the exhortation. The king approached the elder and heard the Dhamma. He built a monastery, constructed a cetiya, and planted a sapling of the bodhi tree. Having taken on himself the three refuges and constant precepts, he also observed the eight factors of the uposatha and gave gifts. He lived out the remainder of his life span and was reborn in the desire-sphere deva world. Those 16,000 pupils who had gone forth died as worldlings and became the retinue of that same king.

Having passed one interval between buddhas in the deva world, [580] before our Blessed One arose, he passed away from the deva world and was reborn as the son of the chaplain under the father of King Pasenadi. He was named Bāvari. He had three characteristics of a great man, was a master of the Three Vedas, and after his father passed away, he ascended to the position of chaplain. The others, the 16,016 students,[2048] were reborn in the same place into brahmin families in Sāvatthī. The sixteen senior students studied under Bāvari; the other 16,000 studied under them. Thus they again all encountered one another.

When King Mahākosala died, they anointed Pasenadi to kingship. Bāvari became his chaplain too. The king gave Bāvari the wealth given by his own father and still more wealth. For when he was young, he studied under him. Thereafter Bāvari informed the king: "Great king, I will go forth." – "Teacher, while you are here it is as if my father is still here. Do not go forth." – "Enough, great king. I will go forth." Since the king could not prevent him, he entreated him: "Then go forth in my royal garden, in a place where I can see you each evening and the next morning." Together with his sixteen pupils and their own retinues totaling 16,000, the teacher went forth in the manner of a hermit and lived in the royal garden. The king provided him with the four requisites and attended upon him in the evening and the next morning.

Then one day the students said to the teacher: "Living near a city is said to be a great impediment. Let's go, teacher, to an uninhabited area. It is said that living in remote lodgings is beneficial for those who have gone forth." The teacher agreed and informed the king. The king tried three times to prevent him, but being unable to stop him, he gave him 200,000 coins and ordered two ministers: "You should get a hermitage built wherever the rishis wish to live and offer it to them." Then the teacher, accompanied by the 16,016 jaṭilas (matted-hair ascetics) and assisted by the ministers, set out from the northern country and headed south. Having referred to this matter, at the time of the council, the Venerable Ānanda, when setting up the introduction to the "Chapter on the Way to the Beyond," recited these verses.

976. Here, **the city of the Kosalans**: from a city in the Kosala country, that is, from Sāvatthī. **The state of nothingness**: seclusion from possessions and commodities.[2049] [581]

977. In the domain of Assaka, in the neighborhood of Aḷaka: That brahmin settled in a realm close by the domains of the two Andhaka kings, Assaka and Aḷaka; the purport is "in the middle of the two realms." **On the bank of the Godhāvarī River**: In the place where the Godhāvarī was divided in two and formed an island three yojanas in size entirely covered by a wood-apple forest, where in the past Sarabhaṅga (Ja V 132,1–8) and others lived. It is said that when he saw that region, he informed the ministers: "This was the past abode of ascetics; it is suitable for those who have gone forth." The ministers, to acquire the land, then gave 100,000 coins to King Assaka and 100,000 to King Aḷaka. The kings gave them the region and another two yojanas, for a total of five yojanas. That region, it is said, was between the boundaries of their realms. There the ministers had a hermitage built. They had more money brought from Sāvatthī, settled people in a village to serve as an alms resort, and left. **By means of gleanings and fruit**: by wandering in order to glean and by forest roots and fruits.

978. Nearby: near the bank of the Godhāvarī or near the brahmin. **With the revenue that arose from it, he held a grand sacrifice**: The revenue that arose in that village through farming and other occupations amounted to 100,000 coins. Having taken it, the landowners went to King Assaka and said: "Let your majesty accept this revenue." He said: "I won't accept it. Bring it to the teacher." The teacher did not accept it for himself but made a grand sacrifice of gifts. In this way he gave gifts year after year.

979. Having completed the grand sacrifice: Performing a grand sacrifice of gifts year after year, one year, after he completed the grand sacrifice, he left the village and **again entered the hermitage**. [582] And when he entered, having entered his leaf hall, he sat down recollecting his gifts, thinking: "It is good that I have given." **When he had re-entered, another brahmin arrived**: The latter's young wife did not want to do housework, and so she sent him saying: "Brahmin, this Bāvari gives away 100,000 coins every year on the bank of the Godhāvarī. Go and ask him for five hundred coins and bring me a slave woman."

980–81. With calloused feet: the soles of his feet were calloused from traveling along the road, or [his legs] were calloused from heel striking against heel, ankle against ankle, knee against knee. **Asked about his happiness and health**: He asked, "Are you happy, brahmin? Are you healthy?"

984. Having put on a performance: Having taken cowdung, wild flowers, kusa grass, and so forth, he quickly went to the gate of Bāvari's hermitage, smeared the ground with the cowdung, scattered the flowers, spread the grass, washed his left foot with the water from his waterpot, took seven steps, and rubbed the soles of his own feet. In this way he put on such a show. **Uttered a fearsome curse**: He recited words that produce fear; the purport is that he spoke this verse: "When I am making this request . . ." **Despondent**: dejected.

985–86. He became emaciated: He withered away, thinking: "That utterance may sometimes become true." **A deity**: a deity dwelling in his hermitage.

991. Earlier: when he was twenty-nine years old.[2050] But the Buddha arose in the world after Bāvari had already been living for eight years on the bank of the Godhāvarī.

992. Who has attained all superknowledge and power: who has attained all the powers *through* superknowledge, or who has attained all superknowledges *and* powers.[2051] **He is liberated**: [583] liberated in mind through the process that takes [nibbāna] as an object.[2052]

996. Of excellent vast intelligence: one of supreme vast wisdom, or one of vast wisdom that is delighted in the real.[2053]

997. Who had mastered the hymns: who had mastered the Vedas.

1004. Ask him solely with your mind: Ask these seven questions solely with the mind.[2054]

1009. Who had formed past habitual formations:[2055] Since they had gone forth in the past, in the teaching of the Blessed One Kassapa, their minds had acquired the meritorious habitual formations of the practice of going and returning.

1011. The former Māhissatī: What is meant is: "the former city named Māhissatī."[2056] **Gonaddhā** is a name for Godhapura. **That named Vanasa**: the city Tumbava; but some read Vanasāvatthī. It is said that when they had gone from Vanasāvatthī to Kosambī, and from Kosambī to Sāketa, the sixteen jaṭilas had acquired a retinue that extended six yojanas.

1012. Then the Blessed One considered: "The jaṭilas of Bāvari are coming, attracting a multitude of people. But their faculties are not yet ripe, and this place is not suitable for them. However, the Pāsāṇaka Cetiya in the Magadha plain is suitable for them. For when I am teaching the Dhamma there, a multitude will make the breakthrough to the Dhamma. And when they come after passing through all the cities, they will come with many people." Thus, accompanied by the Sangha of bhikkhus, he went out from Sāvatthī [584] heading toward Rājagaha.

When they reached Sāvatthī, the jaṭilas entered the monastery and asked: "Who is the Buddha? Where is the Buddha?" Having gone to the Fragrant Cottage, having seen the Blessed One's footprints, in accordance with the verse "The footprints of one who is lustful are arched . . . these are footprints of one with coverings removed" (see p. 1106), they concluded: "He is an omniscient buddha." The Blessed One, meanwhile, passed in stages through the cities of Setavya, Kapilavatthu, and so forth, attracting a multitude of people, and went to the Pāsāṇaka Cetiya. The jaṭilas, too, at once left Sāvatthī, passed through all those cities, and went to the Pāsāṇaka Cetiya. Hence it is said: **to Kosambī and Sāketa . . . and the city Kusinārā**.

1013. The Māgadhan city: Rājagaha. **Pāsāṇaka Cetiya**: In the past there had been a shrine for a deva on top of a large boulder, but when the Blessed One appeared, a dwelling had been built there. Hence it was still called the Pāsāṇaka Cetiya with reference to the former expression.

1014. As a thirsty person [seeks] cool water: Following the Blessed One hurriedly, in the morning those jaṭilas took the path he had taken the previous evening, and in the evening took the path he had taken in the morning. Having heard, "The

Blessed One is here," they became very joyful and climbed the cetiya. Hence it is said: **they hastily climbed the mountain**.

1017. He stood to one side, thrilled: Having seen the Blessed One sitting in the great pavilion built by Sakka at the Pāsāṇaka Cetiya, they exchanged greetings with the Blessed One. The Blessed One said, "I hope the rishis are keeping well," and they said, "We hope Master Gotama is keeping well," and so forth. When these cordial greetings were finished, the senior student, Ajita, stood to one side, thrilled in mind, **and asked the questions mentally.**[2057]

1018–20. With reference to his birth: with reference to his age, he asks: "Tell us the birth (age) of our teacher." **Perfection**: his completion. **Characteristics**: characteristics of a great man. [585] **He teaches five hundred pupils**: He himself teaches five hundred brahmin students who are by nature lazy and unintelligent. **In his own teaching**: in his own brahmanic teaching, the teaching based on the Three Vedas.

1021. Reveal in detail the characteristics: an elaboration of the characteristics. He asks: "What are the three characteristics on his body?"[2058]

1024. To whom did he reply?: To what person among the devas and so forth did the Buddha reply with this answer?[2059]

1025–26. Thus, having heard the answers to five of his questions, asking the remaining two, the brahmin said: "the head and the splitting of the head." Then, answering him, the Blessed One spoke the verse "Know ignorance to be 'the head.'" Here, since ignorance, lack of knowledge of the four truths, is the head of saṃsāra, he said: **Know ignorance to be "the head."** Since the knowledge of the path of arahantship accompanied by coarisen **faith, mindfulness, concentration, desire** to accomplish, **and energy**, all occurring with a single flavor,[2060] splits that head, he therefore says: **clear knowledge is "head-splitting"** and so forth.

1027–30. Uplifted by great exhilaration: Then, having heard these answers to his questions, uplifted by the great rapture that had arisen—free of laxity, elated in body and mind—he bowed down and spoke this verse: "The brahmin Bāvari." Taking compassion on him, the Blessed One spoke the verse "May the brahmin Bāvari be happy" and invited them with the invitation of an omniscient one, saying: "Whatever doubt Bāvari has." Here, **or all the others**: or the remaining 16,000.

1031. He there asked the Tathāgata the very first question: There at the Pāsāṇaka Cetiya, or there in the assembly, or there among the members of his retinue, Ajita asked first. The rest in all the verses is already clear. [586]

1 Ajita
(*Ajita Sutta*[2061])

1032. In this question, **shrouded**: concealed. **What do you say is its adhesive?**: What do you say is the adhesive of this world?[2062]

Nidd II 21. By what is the world shrouded? The world: the world of hell, the world of the animal realm, the world of the sphere of afflicted spirits, the human world, the deva world; the world of the aggregates, the world of the elements, the world of the sense bases; this world, the next world, the brahma world, the deva world—this is called the world. By what is this world obstructed, shrouded, occluded, covered, concealed, enclosed? **What do you say is its adhesive?**: What is the adhesive of the world, its fastening, its bondage, its defilement? By what is the world stuck, defiled, smeared, bonded, fastened, impeded? **What is its great peril?**: What is the world's great peril, oppression, abrasion, disaster, calamity?[2063]

1033. It does not shine because of avarice and heedlessness: It does not shine because of miserliness and heedlessness.[2064] For miserliness does not allow it to shine through such virtuous qualities as giving and so forth, heedlessness through good behavior and so forth. **Hankering is its adhesive**: Craving is the adhesive for the world, just as monkey glue is for a monkey. **Suffering:** the suffering of birth and so forth.

Nidd II 22. The world is shrouded by ignorance. Ignorance: lack of knowledge of suffering, its origin, its cessation, and the way leading to the cessation of suffering; lack of knowledge of the past, the future, the past and the future; lack of knowledge of specific conditionality and dependently arisen phenomena. Such lack of knowledge, lack of vision, non-realization, non-understanding, non-comprehension, delusion as an unwholesome root—this is called ignorance. **The world**: The hell world, the animal world, the world of the sphere of afflicted spirits, the human world, the deva world; the world of the aggregates, the world of the elements, the world of the sense bases; this world, the other world; the brahma world, the deva world: this is called the world. This world is obstructed, shrouded, occluded, covered, concealed, enclosed—the world is shrouded by ignorance.

Nidd II 23. It does not shine because of avarice and heedlessness. It is the five kinds of miserliness that are called **avarice**: that is, miserliness regarding dwellings, families, gains, praise, and the Dhamma—such miserliness, avarice, meanness, stinginess, niggardliness is called miserliness. **Heedlessness** is the straying and laxity of the mind in regard to bodily misconduct, verbal misconduct, mental misconduct, and the five strands of sensual pleasure. It is carelessness, lack of constancy, lack of persistence, regression, lack of determination, lack of devotion to the development of wholesome qualities. Because of this miserliness and this heedlessness, the world does not shine, blaze, burn, radiate, nor is it known and perceived.

Nidd II 23–24. I say that hankering is its adhesive: It is craving that is called hankering, that which is lust, passion . . . [as at pp. 1017–18, Nidd I 7] . . . covetousness, greed as an unwholesome root. **Suffering is its great peril**: The suffering of birth, old age, illness, and death; sorrow, lamentation, pain, dejection, and anguish; the suffering of hell, of the animal realm, of the realm of afflicted spirits, of the human realm; the suffering rooted in entering the womb, abiding in the womb, and emerging from the womb; the suffering of being bound up with birth and the infant's dependence on others; self-inflicted suffering and suffering inflicted by others, the suffering of conditioned things, the suffering due to change; illness of the eyes and other kinds of illness; the suffering of the death of mother, the death of father, brother, sister, son, or daughter; the suffering of loss of relatives, loss of wealth, loss through illness, loss of good behavior, loss of view. Its origination is perceived through the beginning of these things; its cessation is perceived through their passing away. The result is based upon kamma. Kamma is based upon the result. Form is based upon name (mentality). Name is based upon form. The suffering of being accompanied by birth, pursued by old age, overcome by illness, stricken by death, of being established upon suffering, without shelter, without a cavern, without a refuge, refugeless: this is called suffering. This suffering is the world's peril, great peril, oppression, abrasion, disaster, calamity.

1034. Everywhere the streams are flowing: The streams of craving and so forth flow among all the sense bases such as visible forms.[2065] **What is the barrier to the streams?** What is their obstruction? What is the protection against them? **Speak of the restraint**: Speak of the restraint of them—a designation for the barrier to them. By this, he asks about the abandoning with remainder. **By what are the streams closed off?**: By what are these streams closed off, cut off? By this, he asks about the abandoning without remainder.

Nidd II 25. Everywhere: among all the sense bases. **The streams**: the stream of craving, the stream of views, the stream of defilements, the stream of misconduct, the stream of ignorance. **Are flowing**: They flow from the eye toward visible forms, from the ear toward sounds . . . from the mind toward mental phenomena.

1035. Mindfulness is the barrier against them: Mindfulness, conjoined with insight, searching out[2066] the spheres[2067] of wholesome and unwholesome qualities, is the barrier against those streams. **I speak of this as restraint**: The purport is: "I declare mindfulness itself to be restraint of the streams." **They are closed off by wisdom**: These streams are completely closed off by the wisdom of the path, which penetrates impermanence and so forth in regard to visible forms and so forth.

Nidd II 26. Mindfulness is the barrier against them. Mindfulness: mindfulness, recollection, being ever mindful, remembering, bearing in mind, non-floating, non-forgetfulness, mindfulness as a faculty, mindfulness as a power, mindfulness as an enlightenment factor, the one-way path: this is called mindfulness. **A barrier:** an obstruction, a hindrance, restraining, protecting, guarding. **I speak of this as restraint of the streams**: I say, explain, elucidate, reveal that this is an obstruction, a hindrance, restraining, protecting, guarding against the streams.

Nidd II 27–28. They are closed off by wisdom: Wisdom is

understanding . . . [as at p. 1031, Nidd I 32] . . . non-delusion, discrimination of phenomena, right view. When one knows and sees, "All conditioned things are impermanent," the streams are closed off by wisdom. When one knows and sees, "All conditioned things are suffering" . . . "All phenomena are non-self" . . . [as at pp. 1060–61, Nidd I 67–68] . . . When one knows and sees, "Whatever is subject to origination is all subject to cessation," the streams are closed off by wisdom.

1036. Wisdom and mindfulness: In the question, he asks: "Where does all this cease, the wisdom and mindfulness mentioned by you and the remaining **name-and-form**? **When asked this** question **by me, please declare**.

Nidd II 28. Name (mentality): the four formless (mental) aggregates. **Form**: the four great elements and the form dependent on the four great elements.

1037. In the answer, since wisdom and mindfulness are already comprised by "name," they are not mentioned separately. This is the concise meaning here: "As to this question that you ask, Ajita, 'Where does this come to an end?' I will tell you 'where name and also form come to an end without remainder.' [587] They come to an end here together with the cessation of consciousness, neither earlier nor later. They cease right here with the cessation of consciousness; their cessation occurs through the cessation of consciousness." This means that their cessation does not extend beyond the cessation of consciousness.[2068]

Nidd II 29–30. It is by the cessation of consciousness: With the cessation of volitionally active consciousness by the knowledge of the path of stream-entry, except for seven existences, whatever name and form might have arisen in beginningless saṃsāra cease here, abate, disappear, subside. With the cessation of volitionally active consciousness by the knowledge of the path of the once-returner, except for two existences, whatever name and form might have arisen in five existences cease here, abate, disappear, subside. With the cessation of volitionally active consciousness by the knowledge of the path of the non-returner, except for one existence, whatever name and form might have arisen in the form realm or formless realm cease here, abate, disappear, subside. With the cessation of volitionally active consciousness by the knowledge of the path of arahantship, whatever name and form might have arisen cease here, abate, disappear, subside. When the arahant attains final nibbāna by way of the nibbāna element without residue remaining, with the ceasing of the final consciousness, wisdom and mindfulness and name and form cease here, abate, disappear, subside. 🞓

1038. At this point, by the statement "Suffering is its great peril," the truth of suffering is revealed; by the phrase "the streams," the truth of the origin; by the statement "They are closed off by wisdom," the truth of the path; and by the phrase "come to an end without remainder," the truth of cessation. Although in this way he had heard the four truths, Ajita did not achieve the plane of the noble ones. Thus again asking about the practice of the trainee and the one beyond training, he spoke the verse "Those who have comprehended the Dhamma." Here, **those who have comprehended the Dhamma**: those who have thoroughly investigated things by way of impermanence and so forth; this is a designation for arahants. **Trainees**: the remaining noble persons who are training in good behavior and so forth. **Diverse**: many, since there are seven types of persons.[2069] **Let the judicious one declare it, dear sir**: When asked by me, you who are judicious—that is, wise—speak of the practice of trainees and those beyond training.

🞓 **Nidd II 30–31. Those who have comprehended the Dhamma**: This refers to the arahants, those with influxes destroyed. For they have comprehended the Dhamma, known the Dhamma, assessed the Dhamma, scrutinized the Dhamma, clarified the Dhamma, recognized the Dhamma. They have comprehended the Dhamma thus: "All conditioned things are impermanent" . . . [as at pp. 1060–61, Nidd I 67–68] . . . "Whatever is subject to origination is all subject to cessation." Or they have comprehended the aggregates, elements, sense bases . . . saṃsāra, the round. Or they stand at the boundary of the aggregates, the boundary of the elements, the boundary of the sense bases, the boundary of destinations of rebirth, the boundary of rebirth, the boundary of conception, the boundary of existence, the boundary of saṃsāra, the boundary of the round. The arahants, bearing their final body, stand in their final existence, stand in their final body. **Trainees**: In what do they train? They train in the higher good behavior, in the higher mind, in the higher wisdom. What is the training in the higher good behavior? . . . [as at pp. 1028–29, Nidd I 28–29] . . . realizing what should be realized one should train. **Here**: in this view, in this Dhamma, in this discipline, in this teaching, in this spiritual life, in the teaching of this teacher, in this personal existence, in this human world. ⁞

1039. Now, since the trainee must abandon all defilements beginning with the hindrance of sensual desire, the Blessed One shows the practice of the trainee by the first couplet: "One should not be greedy for." This is its meaning: **One should not be greedy for sensual pleasures**, for sensual objects because of the sensual defilement. Abandoning the qualities such as bodily misconduct that tarnish the mind, **one should be untarnished in mind**.

But the one beyond training, having fully assessed all conditioned things by way of impermanence and so forth, is **skillful in regard to all phenomena**, and **mindful** through the mindfulness involved in contemplation of the body and so forth; he is one who has attained the state of **a bhikkhu** by having demolished the view of the personal entity and other defilements.[2070] Therefore, by the second couplet, "Skillful in regard to all phenomena," the Blessed One shows the practice of the one beyond training.

⁞ **Nidd II 32–33. One should not be greedy for sensual pleasures**: In brief, there are two kinds of sensual pleasures: sensual objects and sensual defilements. What are *sensual objects*? Agreeable forms, sounds, odors, tastes, and tactile objects . . . [as at p. 1015, Nidd I 1–2] . . . Even all phenomena pertaining to the desire sphere, the form sphere, and the formless sphere that are the basis of craving, objects of craving, which are sensual pleasures in the sense of being desired, in the sense of being enticing, in the sense of being intoxicating, are called sensual objects. What are *sensual defilements*? Sensuality as desire, as lust, as desire and lust, as intention, as lustful intention; sensual desire for sensual pleasures, sensual lust, sensual delight, sensual craving . . . the hindrance of sensual desire.

Nidd II 33–34. Skillful in regard to all phenomena: Skillful in regard to all phenomena thus: "All conditioned things are impermanent" . . . "Whatever is subject to origination is all subject to cessation." Or alternatively: skillful in all phenomena as impermanent, as suffering, as a disease . . . [as at p. 1035, Nidd I 38] . . . by way of its origin, its passing away, its gratification, its danger, and the escape from it. In this way, too, one is skillful in all phenomena.

Nidd II 34–35. Mindful: One is mindful in four ways: one is mindful by developing the establishment of mindfulness through contemplation of the body in the body; one is mindful by developing the establishment of mindfulness through contemplation of feelings in feelings; one is mindful by developing the establishment of mindfulness through contemplation of mind in mind; one is mindful by developing the establishment of mindfulness through contemplation of phenomena in phenomena. **A bhikkhu**: One is a bhikkhu by having demolished seven things: the view of the personal entity, doubt, seizing upon good behavior and observances, lust, hatred, delusion, and conceit. Demolished are bad unwholesome qualities that are defiling, that lead to renewed existence, that are troublesome, that result in suffering, and that lead to future birth, old age, and death. **A bhikkhu should wander mindfully**: Mindfully he should wander, mindfully go, mindfully stand, mindfully sit, mindfully lie down; be mindful when going forward and returning, when looking up and looking aside, when bending and stretching the limbs, when wearing the robe and carrying the bowl. **B:**

Thus the Blessed One concluded the teaching with its culmination in arahantship. At the conclusion of the teaching Ajita was established in arahantship along with his thousand pupils. The eye of Dhamma arose in many thousands of others. Together with their attainment of arahantship, [588] the antelope hides, matted locks, bark garments,[2071] and so forth disappeared on the Venerable Ajita and his pupils. By being addressed, "Come, bhikkhus," they all became bhikkhus with hair two inches long, wearing robes and carrying bowls produced by psychic power. Honoring the Blessed One with reverential salutation, they then sat down.

2 Tissa Metteyya
(*Tissametteyya Sutta*)

1040. What is the origin? The origin of all the discourses is in response to questions. Because those brahmins had been invited by the Blessed One when he said, "You have been given permission, so ask," they each asked about the points on which they had doubts. And when he was asked by each, he answered each one. Thus it should be understood that these discourses were spoken in response to questions.

When the questions of Ajita were finished, Mogharājā began to ask, "How should one look upon the world so that the King of Death does not see one?" but the Blessed One knew that his spiritual faculties were not yet mature and rejected him, saying: "Wait, Mogharājā! Let someone else ask their question." Then Tissa Metteyya, asking about the points on which he had doubts, spoke the verse "Who here?" Here, **agitation** is trepidation due to craving and views. **By reflection does not get stuck**: through wisdom does not get stuck?[2072]

⁝⁞ **Nidd II 36–37. For whom is there no agitation?**: There is the agitation of craving, the agitation of views, the agitation of conceit, the agitation of defilements, the agitation of sensuality. For whom is there no such agitation, in whom does it not exist, in whom is it not found? For whom has it been abandoned, eradicated, allayed, stilled, made incapable of arising, burnt up by the fire of knowledge? **Who here has transcended the seamstress?**: Who here has overcome, escaped, transcended, surmounted, exceeded the seamstress craving. ⁞⁝

1041–42. Explaining this matter to him, the Blessed spoke the pair of verses "One leading the spiritual life."[2073] Here, **one**

leading the spiritual life among sensual pleasures: One who leads the spiritual life on account of sensual pleasures. What is meant is one who, having seen the danger in sensual pleasures, has undertaken the spiritual life. At this point he has shown who is "contented." **One without craving** and so forth has no agitation. [589] Here, **who is quenched, having comprehended**: one who, having investigated things by way of impermanence and so forth, is quenched by the extinguishing of lust and so forth. The rest is clear in the ways previously explained here and there.

Nidd II 37. One who leads the spiritual life among sensual pleasures: It is desisting from a bad practice, abstinence from it, refraining from it, abstaining from it, not doing it, that is called the spiritual life. Moreover, in the direct sense, it is the noble eightfold path that is called the spiritual life, that is, right view . . . right concentration. One equipped and provided with this noble eightfold path is called "one who leads the spiritual life." **One without craving**: There is craving for forms . . . craving for mental phenomena. One for whom this craving has been abandoned . . . burnt up by the fire of knowledge is called "one without craving."

Nidd II 38. A bhikkhu who is quenched, having comprehended: It is knowledge that is called comprehension, and that is wisdom, understanding . . . [as at p. 1031, Nidd I 32] . . . non-delusion, discrimination of phenomena, right view. Having comprehended, having known, having assessed, having scrutinized, having clarified, having recognized, "All conditioned things are impermanent" . . . "Whatever is subject to origination is all subject to cessation." Or alternatively: having comprehended as impermanent, as suffering . . . and the escape from them. **Quenched**: quenched by the extinguishing of lust, the extinguishing of hatred, the extinguishing of delusion, anger, hostility, denigration, insolence, envy, miserliness, hypocrisy, deceitfulness, obstinacy, vehemence, conceit, arrogance, vanity, and heedlessness; quenched by the extinguishing of all defilements, all misconduct, all distress, all fevers, all torments, all unwholesome volitional activities.

Nidd II 39–40. Having directly known both ends, by reflection one does not get stuck in the middle. Ends: Contact is one end, the origin of contact is the second end, the cessation of contact is the middle.[2074] The past is one end, the future is the second end, the present is the middle. Pleasant feeling is one end, painful feeling is the second end, neither-painful-nor-pleasant feeling is the middle. Name is one end, form is the second end, consciousness is the middle. The six internal sense bases are one end, the six external sense bases are the second end, consciousness is the middle. The personal entity is one end, the origin of the personal entity is the second end, the cessation of the personal entity is the middle. It is wisdom that is called reflection, which is wisdom, understanding . . . non-delusion, discrimination of phenomena, right view.

[**Does not get stuck**.] As to "adhesive," there are two kinds of adhesive: the adhesive of craving and the adhesive of views.[2075] What is *the adhesive of craving*? The craving that takes possession of things and claims them to be one's own: "This is mine, that is mine, this much is mine. This much of forms . . . tactile objects . . . the realm, the country, the treasures, the storage facilities." One even takes the entire great earth to be "mine" because of craving, even up to the 108 currents of craving:[2076] this is the adhesive of craving. What is *the adhesive of views*? The twenty kinds of view of the personal entity, the tenfold wrong view, the ten extremist views; any such views, even up to the sixty-two speculative views: this is the adhesive of views.

Having directly known both ends, by reflection one does not get stuck in the middle. Having directly known both ends and the middle by reflection (*mantāya*), having known, having assessed, having scrutinized, having clarified, having recognized, one does not get stuck; one has departed, escaped, been released, been detached, and dwells with a mind rid of barriers.

He has here transcended the seamstress: It is craving that is called the seamstress. For him that seamstress craving—any lust, passion . . . covetousness, greed as an unwholesome root—has been abandoned . . . burnt up by the fire of knowledge. He has overcome, escaped, transcended, surmounted, surpassed the seamstress craving.

Thus the Blessed One concluded this discourse, too, with its culmination in arahantship. At the conclusion of the teaching this brahmin was also established in arahantship along with his thousand pupils, and for many thousands of others the eye of Dhamma arose. The rest is similar to the previous case.

3 Puṇṇaka
(*Puṇṇaka Sutta*)

This too was spoken after rejecting Mogharājā in the way stated earlier.

1043. Here, **seer of the root**: seer of the unwholesome roots and so forth. **Rishis**: the jaṭilas called "rishis." **Sacrifices**: things to be given. **Performed**: sought after.[2077]

Nidd II 41–43. The one without impulse, seer of the root: It is craving that is called impulse. The Buddha, the Blessed One, has abandoned that impulse of craving, cut it off at the root, made it like a palm stump, eliminated it so that it is no more subject to future arising; therefore the Buddha is without impulse. The Blessed One is not excited by gain, non-gain, fame, obscurity, praise, blame, pleasure, and pain; he is not shaken, not agitated, not provoked—thus he is without impulse. **The seer of the root**: The Blessed One is the seer of the root, seer of the cause, seer of the source, seer of the origination, seer of the nutriment, seer of the basis, seer of the condition, seer of the origin. The Blessed One knows and sees these three unwholesome roots—greed, hatred, and delusion. The Blessed One knows and sees these three wholesome roots—non-greed, non-hatred, and non-delusion. Or else, the Blessed One knows and sees: "Ignorance is the root of volitional activities . . . birth is the root of old age and death." Or else, the Blessed One knows and sees: "The eye is the root of eye-disease . . . the body is the root of bodily disease, the mind is the root of mental disease."

Nidd II 43–44. I have come in need with a question: I have come needy with a question . . . [as at p. 1210, Nidd I 349] . . .

Take up this burden. **Rishis**: Those called rishis who have gone forth in the manner of a rishi: Ājīvakas, Nigaṇṭhas, jaṭilas, and hermits.[2078] **To the deities**: The Ājīvaka deities [are sacrificed to] by the Ājīvaka disciples, the Nigaṇṭha deities by the Nigaṇṭha disciples, the jaṭila deities by the jaṭila disciples, the wanderer deities by the wanderer disciples, and so forth. They each consider their own deities as worthy of offerings. **Many**: These objects of sacrifice are many, or these performers of the sacrifice are many, or those who receive offerings are many.[2079] How are *those objects of sacrifices* many? These sacrifices are of many things: robes, almsfood, lodgings, and medicinal requisites, food, drink, clothes, vehicles, garlands, fragrances, ointments, resthouses, and lamps. How are *those who perform the sacrifice* many? Many are those who perform the sacrifice: khattiyas, brahmins, vessas, suddas, householders, renunciants, devas, and human beings. How are *those who receive offerings* many? Many are those who receive offerings: ascetics and brahmins, beggars, travelers, mendicants, and supplicants. Thus those who receive offerings are many. ▮:

1044. Yearning: longing for forms and so forth. **For a state of being**: They did so wishing for human existence and so forth. **Bound to old age**: dependent on old age; and here all the suffering of the round is spoken of under the heading of old age. Hence he shows: "Because of this, on account of the suffering of the round, they performed sacrifices without being released from it."

:▮ **Nidd II 46–48. These many rishis, men, khattiyas, and brahmins . . . performed sacrifice**, giving away items of offering—robes, almsfood, lodging, medicines, and other items—**yearning for a state of being**: yearning to obtain forms, sounds, odors, tastes, tactile objects; yearning to obtain sons, wives, wealth, fame, authority; yearning for existence in a family of affluent khattiyas, in a family of affluent brahmins, in a family of affluent householders, among the devas in the heaven of the four divine kings, the Tāvatiṃsa devas, the Yāma devas, the Tusita devas, the devas who delight in creation, the devas who control what is created by others, the devas of Brahmā's company. **For a state of being**: yearning to be reborn here, yearning to be reborn into a family of affluent khattiyas . . . yearning to be reborn among the devas of Brahmā's company. **Bound to old age, they performed sacrifice**: dependent on old age, illness, and death; dependent on sorrow, lamentation, pain, dejection, and anguish; dependent on the destinations of rebirth, dependent on rebirth, dependent on conception, dependent on existence, dependent on saṃsāra, dependent on the round. █⁝

1045. Heedful on the path of sacrifice, did they cross over birth and old age, dear sir?: Here, sacrifice itself is "the path of sacrifice." This is meant: "Being heedful in sacrifice, performing sacrifices, did they cross over the suffering of the round?"

1046. They yearn: They long to obtain visible forms and so forth; **extol**: praise their sacrifices by saying such things as "What was offered is pure"; **hanker**: break out into speech in order to obtain forms and so forth; **sacrifice:** give. **They hanker for sensual pleasures because of gain**: Because of obtaining forms and so forth, again and again they hanker only for sensual pleasures. What is meant is that they say, "Oh, may those things be ours!" and intensify craving for them. [590] **Intent on sacrifice**: resolved on sacrifice; **excited by lust for existence**: on account of such yearnings, excited by lust for existence; or, being incited by lust for existence, forming such yearnings; **they did not cross over** the suffering of the round, birth and so forth.

⁝█ **Nidd II 49–51. They yearn**: They yearn to obtain visible forms . . . tactile objects; they yearn to obtain sons, wives, wealth, fame, authority; they yearn for existence in a family of affluent khattiyas . . . the devas of Brahmā's company. **They extol**: They extol *the sacrifice*, saying the offering was pure, agreeable, excellent, timely, allowable, based on investigation, blameless, often given, done with a confident mind. They extol *its fruit*, saying that on this basis they will obtain visible forms . . . existence among the devas of Brahmā's company. They extol *those who receive the offerings*, saying they are of excellent social class, excellent clan, reciters, bearers of the hymns, masters of the Three Vedas with their accessories; that they are devoid of lust, hatred, and delusion, or practicing for the removal of lust, hatred, and delusion; that they have faith, good behavior, concentration, wisdom, liberation, and the knowledge and vision of liberation. **They hanker**: They hanker to obtain visible forms . . . existence among the devas of Brahmā's company. **They offer up**: They give, sacrifice, relinquish robes, almsfood, lodgings, medicinal requisites; food, drink, clothes, vehicles, garlands, fragrances, and ointments; beds, residences, and lamps. **Excited by lust for existence, they did not cross over birth and old age, I say**: Excited by lust for existence, greedy for existence, tied to, infatuated with, and sunk in existence, stuck in and impeded by existence, though intent on sacrifice, they did not cross over birth, old age, and death, did not overcome them, did not transcend them; they continue to revolve in birth, old age, and death; they continue to revolve in the course of saṃsāra. ▮⁝

1047–48. Then who here . . . ?: Now who else has crossed? **Having comprehended**: Having investigated with knowledge; **the far and near**: far things and near things, such as the personal being of others and one's own personal being. **Fumeless**: devoid of the fumes of bodily misconduct and so forth; **untroubled**: devoid of the trouble of lust and so forth; **he has crossed over**: such an arahant has crossed over birth and old age.

⁝▮ **Nidd II 53–55. Having comprehended the far and near in the world**: It is knowledge, wisdom, understanding . . . non-delusion, discrimination of phenomena, right view that is called comprehension. **The far and near**: It is one's own personal being that is called near, another's personal being that is called far. It is one's own form, feeling, perception, volitional activities, and consciousness that are called near; it is the form . . . consciousness of others that are called far. It is the six internal sense bases that are called near, the six external sense bases that are called far. It is the human world that is called near, the deva world that is called far. It is the desire realm that is called near; it is the form and formless realms that are called far. It is the desire and form realms that are called near; it is the formless realm that is called far. **Having comprehended the far and near in the world**: Having comprehended them as impermanent, as suffering, as a disease . . . [as at p. 1035, Nidd I 38] . . . by way of their origin, their passing away, their gratification, their danger, and the escape from them. **One without agitation anywhere in the world**: There is the agitation of craving, the agitation of views, the agitation of conceit, the agitation of defilements, the agitation of sensuality. The arahant, whose influxes are destroyed, is one without this agitation, one for whom it has been abandoned . . . burnt up by the fire of knowledge.

Peaceful: By the stilling of lust, hatred, delusion, anger . . . [as at p. 1023, Nidd I 17] . . . by the stilling of all unwholesome volitional activities, one is peaceful. **Fumeless**: without the fumes of bodily misconduct, verbal misconduct, and mental misconduct; without the fumes of lust, hatred, and delusion . . . without the fumes of all unwholesome volitional activities. Or alternatively, it is anger that is called fumes. One for whom this anger has been abandoned . . . burnt up by the fire of knowledge is called fumeless. Through the abandoning of anger one is fumeless; through the full understanding of the basis of anger one is fumeless; through the full understanding of the cause of anger one is fumeless; by cutting off the cause of anger one is fumeless. **Untroubled**: Lust is trouble, hatred is trouble, delusion is trouble . . . all unwholesome volitional activities are trouble. One for whom these troubles have been abandoned . . . burnt up by the fire of knowledge is called untroubled. **Wishless**: It is craving that is called wish. One for whom this craving has been abandoned . . . burnt up by the fire of knowledge is called wishless. **He has crossed over birth and old age, I say**: He has crossed over, overcome, transcended birth, old age, and death, I say.

Thus the Blessed One concluded this discourse, too, with its culmination in arahantship. At the conclusion of the teaching this brahmin, too, was established in arahantship along with his thousand pupils, and for many thousands of others, the eye of Dhamma arose. The rest is similar to what has already been stated.

4 Mettagū
(Mettagū Sutta)

1049. I consider you a Veda-master, one inwardly developed: I think of you thus: "He is a Veda-master," and "He is one who has developed himself."

⁝⁞ **Nidd II 55–57. I ask you a question.** There are three kinds of questions: a question to clear up what has not been seen; a question to confirm what has been seen; a question to eliminate uncertainty . . . [as at pp. 1169–70, Nidd I 250–51] . . . a question about the path, the fruit, and nibbāna.

Nidd II 57–60. I consider you a Veda-master, one who is inwardly developed. How is the Blessed One *a Veda-master* (*vedagū*).[2080] It is the knowledge of the four paths that is called the Vedas. Through those Vedas, the Blessed One has gone to the end of birth, old age, and death, has reached the end, gone to the peak, reached the peak, gone to the limit, reached the limit . . . gone to the deathless, reached the deathless, gone to nibbāna, reached nibbāna. Or he is a Veda-master as one who has gone to the end of the Vedas, or gone to the end through the Vedas, or because he has understood seven things—the view of the personal entity, doubt, seizing upon good behavior and observances, lust, hatred, delusion, conceit—or because he has understood the bad unwholesome qualities that are defiling, conducive to renewed existence, troublesome, that result in suffering, and lead to future birth, old age, and death.

How is the Blessed One *inwardly developed* (*bhāvitatto*)? The Blessed One is developed in body, developed in good behavior, developed in mind, developed in wisdom, one who has developed the establishments of mindfulness . . . the noble eightfold path, who has abandoned defilements, penetrated the unshakable, and realized cessation. He has fully understood suffering, abandoned its origin, developed the path, and realized cessation. He has directly known what should be directly known, fully understood what should be fully understood, abandoned what should be abandoned, developed what should be developed, and realized what should be realized. He is unlimited, great, deep, measureless, hard to fathom, a source of many gems like the ocean.

Nidd II 60–61. From where have these sufferings arisen: The suffering of birth, old age, illness, and death . . . [as at pp. 1234–35, Nidd II 23–24] . . . The suffering of being accompanied by birth, pursued by old age, overcome by illness, stricken by death, of being established upon suffering, without shelter, without a cavern, without a refuge, refugeless: this is called suffering. From what have these sufferings arisen, how are they engendered and produced? He asks about the root, the cause, the source, the origination, the instigation, the production, the nutriment, the basis, the condition, the origin.

1050. As one who understands, I will tell you this: As one understanding explains, just so I will explain it. **Sufferings . . . originate based on acquisition**: The various sufferings such as birth and so forth originate based on acquisition such as craving and so forth.

Nidd II 63–64. Sufferings originate based on acquisition. There are ten acquisitions: acquisition through craving, acquisition through views, acquisition through defilements, acquisition through kamma, acquisition through misconduct, acquisition through nutriment, acquisition through aversion, acquisition as the four clung-to elements,[2081] acquisition as the six internal sense bases, acquisition as the six classes of consciousness; all suffering is acquisition in the sense of being pained. These are spoken of as the ten kinds of acquisitions.[2082] **Sufferings**: the suffering of birth, old age, illness, and death . . . the suffering of being accompanied by birth, pursued by old age, overcome by illness, stricken by death, of being established upon suffering, without shelter, without a cavern, without a refuge, refugeless. These sufferings originate based on acquisition, caused by acquisition, conditioned by acquisition, produced by acquisition.

1051. When sufferings originate based on acquisitions, the verse says "The ignorant dullard." Here, **understanding**: knowing conditioned things by way of impermanence and so forth. **Contemplating it as the genesis and origin of suffering**: Contemplating, "Acquisition is the genesis and cause of the suffering of the round."[2083]

⁝⁝ **Nidd II 64. Of suffering**: of the suffering of birth, the suffering of old age, the suffering of illness, the suffering of death, the suffering of sorrow, lamentation, pain, dejection, and anguish. **Contemplating the origin**: contemplating the root of suffering, contemplating the cause, the source, the origination, the production, the nutriment, the basis, the condition, the origin. Contemplation is knowledge, wisdom, understanding . . . non-delusion, discrimination of phenomena, right view. One who possesses this contemplative wisdom is said to be contemplating: contemplating the birth and origin of suffering. ⁝⁝

1052. For this Dhamma has been understood by you: This Dhamma has been understood so that, however you convey it, beings understand it.

1053. I will proclaim this Dhamma to you: [591] I will teach you the Dhamma of nibbāna and the Dhamma of the way leading to nibbāna. **In this very life**: when this Dhamma of suffering and so forth is seen, or in this very existence.[2084] **No matter of hearsay**: to be directly cognized by oneself. **Having understood which**: having understood the Dhamma by exploring it thus, "All conditioned things are impermanent," and so forth.

⁝⁝ **Nidd II 67**. *Diṭṭhe dhamme* means: I will expound teachings (*dhamme*) that are seen (*diṭṭhe*), known, assessed, scrutinized, clarified, recognized, namely: "All conditioned things are impermanent" . . . "Whatever is subject to origination is all subject to cessation." Or else, I will expound suffering in regard to suffering that is seen; I will expound the origin in regard to the origin that is seen; I will expound the path in regard to the path that is seen; I will expound cessation in regard to cessation that is seen. Or else *diṭṭhe dhamme* means directly visible, immediate, inviting one to come and see, applicable, to be personally experienced by the wise.[2085] I will expound teachings that are seen in such a way. **No matter of hearsay**: It is not a matter of hearsay, not report, not [something come down] through a lineage of teachers, not a collection of scriptures, not [arrived at] by logical reasoning, by inferential reasoning, by reasoned cogitation, or by the acceptance of a view after pondering it,[2086] but it is to be directly and personally known by oneself, a teaching to be personally cognized. I will expound that.

1054. And I delight: I yearn for your word elucidating that Dhamma in the way stated, and I delight in that supreme Dhamma.[2087]

Nidd II 69. Great rishi: Why is the Blessed One a great rishi? He has sought, searched for, pursued the great aggregate of good behavior, the great aggregate of concentration, the great aggregate of wisdom, the great aggregate of liberation, and the great aggregate of the knowledge and vision of liberation . . . [as at pp. 1170–71, Nidd I 252–53] . . . He has sought, searched for, pursued the great supreme goal, the deathless nibbāna. **That supreme Dhamma** (*dhammamuttamaṃ*): It is the deathless nibbāna that is called the supreme Dhamma—the stilling of all volitional activities, the relinquishment of all acquisitions, the destruction of craving, dispassion, cessation, nibbāna.

1055. Above, below, and across in the middle: Here, it is the future period that is called **above**, the past period that is called **below**, and the present period that is called **across in the middle**.[2088] **Having dispelled delight and attachment to these, consciousness**: In regard to these things that are above and so forth, dispel craving and attachment to views and volitionally active consciousness.[2089] And having dispelled, **[one] would not persist in existence**:[2090] Such being the case, one would not persist even in twofold existence. Such, firstly, is the connection in the case when the word *panujja* is taken to have the meaning *panudehi* ("dispel," a singular second-person imperative). But when it is taken to have the meaning *panuditvā* ("having dispelled," an absolutive), this itself is the connection: "[one] would not persist in existence."

Nidd II 70. Whatever you comprehend: Whatever you understand, know, cognize, recognize, penetrate, whatever you comprehend. **Above, below, and across in the middle**. **Above**: the future; **below**: the past; **across in the middle**: the present. **Above**: the deva world; **below**: the hell world; **across in the middle**: the human world. **Above**: the formless realm: **below**: the desire realm; **across in the middle**: the form realm. **Above**: pleasant feeling: **below**: painful feeling; **across in the middle**: feeling that is neither painful nor pleasant. **Above**: the soles of the feet: **below**: the tips of the hairs; **across in the middle**: in between.

Nidd II 70–71. Having dispelled delight and attachment to these, consciousness would not persist in existence:[2091] **To these**: to those things that have been pointed out, taught, proclaimed, set up, disclosed, analyzed, clarified, revealed. It is craving that is called **delight**. **Attachment**: there are two kinds of attachment, attachment through craving and attachment through views. **Having dispelled consciousness**: consciousness associated with meritorious volitional activity, consciousness associated with demeritorious volitional activity, consciousness associated with imperturbable volitional activity. Having dispersed, having dispelled; disperse, dispel, discard, abandon, dismiss, terminate, eliminate delight, attachment, and volitionally active consciousness.[2092]

Nidd II 71. Would not persist in existence: Two kinds of existence: kammically active existence and renewed existence acquired at conception. What is *kammically active existence*? Meritorious volitional activity, demeritorious volitional activity, imperturbable volitional activity. What is *renewed existence acquired at conception*? The form, feeling, perception, volitional activities, and consciousness acquired at conception. **Would not persist in existence**: Abandoning, dispelling, terminating, eliminating delight, attachment, volitionally active consciousness, kammically active existence, and renewed existence acquired at conception, [it/one] would not persist in kammically active existence, [it/one] would not persist in, continue in, renewed existence acquired at conception.[2093] ⠿

1056. The verse speaks of one **so dwelling**, who, having dispelled these, does not persist in existence. Here, **right here**: in this teaching, or in this existence.

⠿ **Nidd II 71–72. A bhikkhu**: a bhikkhu who is a good worldling or a trainee. **So dwelling**: who dwells abandoning, dispelling, terminating, eliminating delight, attachment, volitionally active consciousness, kammically active existence, and renewed existence acquired at conception. **Having given up taking things as "mine"**: There are two ways of taking things as "mine": through craving and through views. Having abandoned taking things as "mine" through craving and relinquished taking things as "mine" through views, a bhikkhu lives having given up taking things as "mine." ▫

1057. Well procaimed, Gotama, is the state without acquisitions: Here, "the state without acquisitions" is nibbāna. It is with reference to this that, addressing the Blessed One, he said: "Well procaimed, Gotama, is the state without acquisitions."

▫ **Nidd II 73. The state without acquisitions**: It is the defilements, the aggregates, and volitional activities that are called acquisitions. The abandoning, allaying, relinquishment, subsiding of acquisitions is the deathless nibbāna. ▫

1058. It is not only you who have abandoned suffering, but as the verse says: **They too**. Here, **constantly**: carefully or always.[2094]

▫ **Nidd II 74. Would constantly exhort**: would carefully exhort, would frequently exhort, would exhort and instruct again and again. **I pay homage**: I pay homage with the body or with speech or with the mind; I pay homage by practice in accordance with the goal, or I pay homage by practice in accordance with the Dhamma, or I honor, respect, esteem, and venerate. **O nāga**: The Blessed One is a nāga because he does not commit crime; a nāga because he does not go; a nāga because he does not come. How is the Blessed One a nāga because *he does not commit crime?* . . . [as at p. 463, Nidd II 242] . . . He does not return to those defilements that have been abandoned by the path of stream-entry, by the path of the once-returner, by the path of the non-returner, by the path of arahantship. ▫

1059. Now, though this brahmin has understood the Blessed One thus, "Certainly the Blessed One [592] has abandoned suffering," the Blessed One spoke the verse "Whatever brahmin," exhorting him by referring to a person who has abandoned suffering, without applying this to himself. This is its meaning: "Whomever you recognize thus: 'He is **a brahmin** because he has expelled evil; **a Veda-master** because he has gone through the Vedas; **owning nothing** because of the absence of things; and **unattached to sensual pleasures and existence** because he has no attachment to sensual pleasures and to states of existence,' you should know: **He has certainly crossed this flood, and crossed to the beyond, he is unbarren, rid of doubt**."

Nidd II 75–76. Brahmin: One is a brahmin because one has expelled seven things:[2095] the view of the personal entity, doubt, seizing upon good behavior and observances, lust, hatred, delusion, and conceit. Expelled are bad unwholesome qualities that are defiling, that lead to renewed existence, that are troublesome, that result in suffering, and that lead to future birth, old age, and death. **Owning nothing**: Lust is something, hatred is something, delusion is something, conceit is something, views are something, defilements are something, misconduct is something. One for whom these "somethings" have been abandoned . . . burnt up by the fire of knowledge is called "one owning nothing."[2096]

Nidd II 76–77. He has crossed beyond: He has crossed the flood of sensuality, the flood of existence, the flood of views, the flood of ignorance; he has crossed the path of saṃsāra, emerged from it, overcome it, passed beyond it, transcended it. He has lived the spiritual life, completed the practice, finished the journey, reached the goal, reached the peak, maintained the spiritual life, attained the supreme view, developed the path, abandoned defilements, penetrated the unshakable, realized cessation. He has fully understood suffering, abandoned its origin, developed the path, realized cessation, directly known what should be directly known, fully understood what should be fully understood, developed what should be developed, realized what should be realized. . . . He stands at the end of the aggregates, at the end of the elements, at the end of the sense bases, at the end of destinations, at the end of rebirth, at the end of conception, at the end of existence, at the end of saṃsāra, at the end of the round. He stands in his final existence, in his final body. The arahant is one who bears his final body.

> This is his final existence, this is his last body;
> for him there is no renewed existence, no wandering
> in birth and death.

Nidd II 77. Crossed beyond: It is the deathless nibbāna that is called the beyond—the stilling of all volitional activities, the relinquishment of all acquisitions, the destruction of craving, dispassion, cessation, nibbāna. He has gone beyond, reached the beyond, gone to the end, reached the end, gone to the peak, reached the peak, gone to the limit, reached the limit, gone to the conclusion, reached the conclusion, gone to the shelter, reached the shelter, gone to the cavern, reached the cavern, gone to the refuge, reached the refuge, gone to the fearless, reached the fearless, gone to the imperishable, reached the imperishable, gone to the deathless, reached the deathless, gone to nibbāna, reached nibbāna. He has lived the life, completed the practice . . . for him there is no more renewed existence with its wandering on in birth and death.

Unbarren: Lust is barrenness, hatred is barrenness, delusion is barrenness, anger is barrenness . . . [as at p. 1023, Nidd I 17] . . . all unwholesome volitional activities are barrenness. One for whom these kinds of barrenness have been abandoned . . . burnt up by the fire of knowledge is said to be unbarren.

Rid of doubt: Doubt about suffering, about its origin, about its cessation, about the way leading to its cessation; doubt about the past, about the future, about both the past and the future; doubt about specific conditionality and dependently arisen phenomena. One for whom such kinds of doubt have been abandoned . . . burnt up by the fire of knowledge is said to be rid of doubt. ▪▪

1060. And what is more, the verse says, **And the wise man**. Here, **here**: in this teaching, or in this existence. **Having loosened**: having released. The rest everywhere is clear.

▪▪ **Nidd II 78. Various states of existence**: for desire-realm existence in kamma existence and in renewed existence . . . [as at p. 1032, Nidd I 34] . . . for the ever-repeated production of personal being. **Ties**: There are seven ties: lust, hatred, delusion, conceit, views, defilements, and misconduct. Having released or loosened these ties.

Nidd II 79. Rid of craving, untroubled, wishless: There is craving for visible forms . . . craving for mental phenomena. One for whom this craving has been abandoned . . . burnt up by the fire of knowledge is said to be rid of craving. **Untroubled**:

Lust is trouble, hatred is trouble, delusion is trouble . . . all unwholesome volitional activities are trouble. One for whom these troubles have been abandoned . . . is said to be untroubled. **Wishless**: It is craving that is called wish. One for whom that wish has been abandoned . . . is said to be wishless. **Has crossed over birth and old age, I say**: One who is rid of craving, untroubled, wishless, has crossed over birth, old age, and death, emerged from them, overcome them, passed beyond them, transcended them. ⁞

Thus the Blessed One concluded this discourse, too, with its culmination in arahantship. At the conclusion of the teaching, in the way already stated, there was a breakthrough to the Dhamma.

5 Dhotaka
(*Dhotaka Sutta*)

1061. I shall train for my own nibbāna: I shall train in the higher good behavior and so forth for the extinguishing (*nibbānatthāya*) of my own lust and so forth.

⁝▮ **Nidd II 80–81. I shall train for my own nibbāna**. There are three trainings: the training in the higher good behavior, the training in the higher mind, and the training in the higher wisdom . . . [as at pp. 1028–29, Nidd I 28–29] . . . This is the training in the higher wisdom. **For my own nibbāna**: for the extinguishing of my own lust, my own hatred, my own delusion . . . for the extinguishing of all unwholesome volitional activities, for their stilling, allaying, extinguishing, relinquishing, subsiding, one should train in the higher good behavior, in the higher mind, in the higher wisdom. . . . One should train, resolved through faith, applying energy, establishing mindfulness, concentrating the mind, and understanding with wisdom. One should train, directly knowing what should be directly known, fully understanding what should be fully understood, abandoning what should be abandoned, developing what should be developed, and realizing what should be realized. ▮⁝

1063. When the Blessed One had spoken, Dhotaka, being pleased, spoke the next verse, praising the Blessed One and entreating him to free him from his perplexity.

⁝▮ **Nidd II 82. I see in the world of devas and human beings**. There are three kinds of devas: conventional devas, devas by rebirth, and devas by purification. What are *conventional devas*? Kings, princes, and queens are called conventional devas. What are *devas by rebirth*? The devas of [the realm of] the four divine kings, the Tāvatiṃsa devas, the Yāma devas, the Tusita devas, the devas who delight in creating, the devas who exercise control over the creations of others, the devas of Brahmā's company, and devas still higher than these. What are *devas by purification*? The Tathāgata's disciples who are arahants, with influxes destroyed, and paccekabuddhas. But the Blessed One is a deva among those three kinds of devas; he is the supreme deva, the deva above the devas, the lion of lions, the nāga of nāgas, the leader of leaders, the muni of munis, the king of kings. **I see in the world of devas and human beings**: I see in the human world a deva who is the supreme deva, the deva above the devas.

Nidd II 83. A brahmin owning nothing, traveling about. Who owns nothing: Lust is something, hatred is something, delusion is something, conceit is something, views are something, defilements are something, misconduct is something. These "somethings" have been abandoned by the Buddha, the Blessed One, cut off at the root, made like a palm stump, eliminated so that they are no more subject to future arising; therefore the Buddha is one who owns nothing. **A brahmin:** The Blessed One is a brahmin by having expelled seven things . . . [as at p. 1257, Nidd II 75–76] . . . and that lead to future birth, old age, and death.

Nidd II 83–84. Universal eye: It is the omniscient knowledge that is called "the universal eye." The Blessed One is endowed with that. Therefore I pay homage to you, O universal eye. It is doubt that is called **perplexity**. There is doubt about suffering . . . [as at p. 1258, Nidd II 77] . . . doubt about specific conditionality and dependently arisen phenomena. **Free me, Sakya, from perplexity**: Free me, release me, liberate me; draw out and remove from me the dart of perplexity. ⁞▯

1064. Then the Blessed One, under the heading of "crossing the flood," spoke the next verse, showing that release from perplexity is entirely dependent upon oneself. Here, **I will not be able**: What is meant is: "I will not endeavor."[2097]

▯⁞ **Nidd II 84. I will not be able to free**: I am not able to free you, to release you, to liberate you, to set you free, to draw out and remove from you the dart of perplexity. Or else, I do not strive, do not endeavor, do not make an effort to teach the

Dhamma to persons without faith, without desire, who are lazy, indolent, and do not practice. Or else, there is no other liberator. Those who want to be liberated should liberate themselves by their own strength, their own power, their own energy, their own exertion, practicing by themselves the right course of practice, the practice in conformity [with the goal], the non-oppositional practice, the practice in accordance with the goal, the practice in accordance with the Dhamma. Thus I will not be able to release [such a one].[2098]

Nidd II 85. Understanding the supreme Dhamma: It is the deathless nibbāna that is called the supreme Dhamma, the stilling of all volitional activities . . . nibbāna. **You will thereby cross this flood**: You will cross the flood of sensuality, the flood of existence, the flood of views, and the flood of ignorance. ▮⁝

1065. When this was said, Dhotaka, being even more pleased, spoke the next verse, "Instruct me, O Brahmā," extolling the Blessed One and requesting instruction. Here, **Brahmā** is a designation for the best; hence he said this when addressing the Blessed One. [593] **The state of seclusion**: the state of nibbāna, which is seclusion from all conditioned things. **Totally unobstructed**: unhindered in any way. **Right here I would live, peaceful**: being right here.[2099] **Unattached**: independent.

⁝▮ **Nidd II 86–87. The state of seclusion**: It is the deathless nibbāna that is called the state of seclusion, the stilling of all volitional activities, the relinquishment of all acquisitions, the destruction of craving, dispassion, cessation, nibbāna. **Just as space is totally unobstructed:** Just as space does not move, does not grasp, is not bound, is not impeded, so, being unobstructed like space, [you] would not move, would not grasp, would not be bound, would not be impeded. As space is not dyed by red, yellow, blue, or crimson dyes, so, being unobstructed like space, [you] would not be affected by lust, hatred, delusion, or defilements. As space does not become irritated, does not bear ill will, does not feel resentment, does not strike back, so being like space, [you] would not become irritated, bear ill will, feel resentment, or strike back.

Right here I would live, peaceful (being) and unattached. Right here peaceful (being): Being right here, sitting right here, sitting in this very seat, sitting in this assembly. Or alternatively, right here I would be peaceful, calm, tranquil, quenched, still. **Unattached**: There are two dependencies (attachments): dependency through craving and dependency through views. Having abandoned the dependency through craving and relinquished the dependency through views, one is not dependent on the eye . . . the mind . . . [as at p. 1081, Nidd I 96] . . . on anything seen, heard, sensed, or cognized. One is unattached, independent, released and detached, and lives with a mind rid of boundaries.

1066–67. The following two verses should be understood in the way stated in the commentary on the Discourse to Mettagū [pp. 1253–54], the only difference being that there "Dhamma" was referred to, while here he refers to "peace" (*santiṃ*).

1068. In this verse, the way to understand the first couplet has already been stated. In the second couplet, **tie** has the sense of fastening, tying one down. The rest everywhere is clear.

Nidd II 90. Having understood this as "a tie" in the world: having known, having assessed . . . having clarified: "This is a tie, this is a fastening, this is bondage, this is an impediment." **Do not create craving for various states of existence**: Do not create, produce, generate craving for existence after existence; for desire-realm existence in kamma existence and in renewed existence . . . [as at p. 1032, Nidd I 34] . . . for the ever-repeated production of personal being.

Thus the Blessed One concluded this discourse, too, with its culmination in arahantship. At the conclusion of the teaching there was a breakthrough to the Dhamma in the way already stated.

6 Upasīva
(*Upasīva Sutta*)

1069. Unsupported: not reliant on either a person or a teaching. **Supported by which**: a person or a teaching supported by which.

⁝ **Nidd II 91–92. Alone**: I have no person as a partner; I have no teaching (*dhamma*) as a partner. There is no person or teaching depending on which I can cross the great flood of sensuality, the flood of existence, the flood of views, and the flood of ignorance. **Unsupported, I am not able to cross over the great flood:** Unsupported by either a person or a teaching, I am not able to cross over the great flood of sensuality, the flood of existence, the flood of views, and the flood of ignorance. **Declare to me a basis**: Declare, explain, teach, proclaim, establish, disclose, analyze, elucidate, reveal a basis, a support, a foundation. **Universal eye**: It is the omniscient knowledge that is called "the universal eye." The Blessed One is endowed with that. **Supported by which I might cross this flood**: a person or teaching depending on which I can cross the great flood of sensuality, the flood of existence, the flood of views, and the flood of ignorance. ⁝

1070. Now, this brahmin was one who gained the base of nothingness, but he did not know that it, too, was actually a support. Therefore the Blessed One spoke the verse "Contemplating nothingness, mindful," showing him that support and a higher pathway to emancipation. Here, **contemplating nothingness**: having mindfully entered that attainment of the base of nothingness and emerged from it, seeing it by way of impermanence and so forth; **supported by "there is not"**: having taken as a basis the attainment occurring, "there is nothing"; **cross over the flood**: with the insight occurring from that point on, cross over the entire fourfold flood in a suitable way. **Night and day see into the destruction of craving**: Having made it manifest, see nibbāna night and day;[2100] by this, he explains to him the pleasant dwelling in this very life.

⁘ **Nidd II 92. Contemplating nothingness, mindful**: That brahmin was one who naturally gained the attainment of the base of nothingness, but he did not know: "This is my support." The Blessed One showed him that support and a higher pathway to emancipation. Having mindfully entered that attainment of the base of nothingness and emerged from it, contemplating, discerning, inspecting, meditating on, investigating the mind and mental factors produced therein as impermanent, as suffering, as a disease . . . [as at p. 1035, Nidd I 38] . . . by way of their origin, their passing away, their gratification, their danger, and the escape from them.

Nidd II 93. Supported by "there is not," cross over the flood: "There is nothing": the attainment of the base of nothingness. Why so? Having mindfully entered the attainment of the base of the boundlessness of consciousness and emerged from it, one negates that same consciousness, eliminates it, makes it disappear, and sees: "There is nothing." For that reason, supported by the attainment of the base of nothingness, "there is nothing," sustained by it, having taken it as a basis, cross over the flood of sensuality, the flood of existence, the flood of views, and the flood of ignorance.

Having abandoned sensual pleasures, refraining from perplexity: There are two kinds of sensual pleasures: sensual objects and sensual defilements. **Having abandoned sensual pleasures:** Having fully understood sensual objects, and having abandoned, dispelled, terminated, eliminated the sensual defilements. **Refraining from perplexity**: It is doubt that is called perplexity. Refraining from such doubts as doubt about suffering. . . . Or alternatively, desisting from the thirty-two kinds of pointless talk, refraining from them.[2101] **Night and day see into the destruction of craving**: *Nattaṃ* is night (*ratti*); *aho* is day (*divaso*). Night and day see, observe, discern, survey, meditate on, investigate the destruction of craving, the destruction of lust, the destruction of hatred, the destruction of delusion, the destruction of a destination [for rebirth], the destruction of rebirth, the destruction of conception, the destruction of existence, the destruction of saṃsāra, the destruction of the round. ▮⁝

1071–72. Now, when he heard, "Having abandoned sensual pleasures," seeing that he himself had abandoned sensual pleasures by way of suppression, he spoke the next verse. Here, **having discarded all else**: having discarded the other six attainments below [that base of nothingness]. [594] **In the supreme emancipation of perception**: in the base of nothingness, which is highest among the seven emancipations of perception.[2102] **Would he stay there without departing?** He asks: "Would that person stay there in the brahma world of the base of nothingness, without leaving?" Then the Blessed One spoke the third verse to him, acknowledging that one might stay there even for 60,000 eons.

⁝▮ **Nidd II 94–95. Supported by nothingness, having discarded all else**: Having discarded the lower six attainments, overcome them, transcended them, supported by the attainment of the base of nothingness, leaning on it, arrived at it, adhering to it, intent upon it. **Liberated in (intent upon) the supreme emancipation of perception.**[2103] It is the seven meditative attainments [accompanied by] perception that are called "emancipations of perception."[2104] The emancipation through attainment of the base of nothingness is the foremost, the best, the most outstanding, the most eminent, the highest, and the most excellent of those meditative attainments [accompanied by] perception. He is intent by the emancipation of intentness[2105] upon that supreme, foremost state; he is intent on it, practicing for it, attentive to it, esteeming it, leaning toward it, inclined to it, sloping toward it, intent on it by giving precedence to it. **He would stay there without departing**: He would stay there, in the base of nothingness, for 60,000 eons, without departing, without separating from it, without vanishing, without disappearing, without deteriorating. Or else, without lust, without hatred, without delusion, without defilement, he would persist there without departing. ▮⁝

1073. When he heard about his staying there, he spoke the next verse, "If he would stay there," asking about eternal existence or annihilation. **A multitude of years**: a count of many years, meaning an accumulation.[2106] **Would he become cool, liberated right there**: Would that person, liberated from the various sufferings, attain coolness right there in the base of nothingness? The purport is: "Does one who has attained nibbāna persist, having become eternal?" **Would the consciousness of such a one pass away**: He asks about annihilation: "Or else (*udāhu*), would the consciousness of such a one attain final nibbāna without clinging?" Or he asks about conception: "Would it perish for the purpose of taking conception?"[2107]

⁝▯ **Nidd II 96–97. If he would stay there without departing**. If he would stay there, in the base of nothingness, for 60,000 eons, without departing, without separating from it, without vanishing, without disappearing, without deteriorating. Or else, without lust, without hatred, without delusion, without defilement, he would persist there without departing. **Would he become cool, liberated right there—[or] would the consciousness of such a one pass away?**: He asks about the eternal existence or annihilation of one who has attained the base of nothingness: "Having attained the state of coolness right there, would he stay there as permanent, everlasting, eternal, not subject to change, just like eternity itself? Or would his consciousness pass away (*caveyya*), be annihilated, be abolished, be destroyed, no longer exist? Would the consciousness that undergoes conception in renewed existence be generated in the desire realm, the form realm, or the formless realm?" Or alternatively, he asks about the final nibbāna and conception of one who has been reborn in the base of nothingness: "Would it attain final nibbāna right there by way of the nibbāna element without residue remaining? Or would his consciousness pass away and again produce a conception consciousness in the desire realm, the form realm, or the formless realm?" **Of such a one**: Of one like that, of one similar to him, of one who partakes of that, of one reborn in the base of nothingness. ▯⁝

1074. Then the Blessed One, without adopting either annihilation or eternal existence, spoke the verse "As a flame," showing the final nibbāna through non-clinging of a noble disciple who has arisen there. **Cannot be designated**: It cannot be described thus: "It has gone in such and such a direction." **So the muni, liberated from the mental body**: So the trainee-muni who has arisen there, naturally liberated earlier from the form body, generates the fourth path there [in the base of nothingness]; because he has then fully understood the Dhamma body, he is also liberated from the mental body.[2108] Thus, having become an arahant liberated in both respects, when he goes out—a designation for final nibbāna through non-clinging—he can no longer be designated "a khattiya" or "a brahmin" and so forth.[2109] [595]

⁝⁝ **Nidd II 97–98. As a flame, thrown by a gust of wind**: As a flame thrown, flung, tossed, tossed away, suppressed by a gust of wind from the east, west, north, or south, or any other wind; **goes out**: goes out, disappears, ceases, abates, subsides; **cannot be designated**: cannot be indicated, reckoned, described thus: "It has gone to the east, to the west, to the north, to the south, above, below, across, or to an intermediate direction." There is no cause, no condition, no means by which it might be designated.

Nidd II 98. So the muni, liberated from the mental body: the muni, naturally liberated earlier from the form body. Having overcome it (the form body) in a particular respect, it has been abandoned by suppression.[2110] Based on what is presently existent, the four noble paths are obtained by that muni. Because he has obtained the four noble paths, he has fully understood the mental body and the form body. Because he has fully understood the mental body and the form body, he is freed from the mental body and from the form body—liberated, well liberated, by way of ultimate emancipation through non-clinging.

Thus the muni, liberated from the mental body, **goes out**: attains final nibbāna by way of the nibbāna element without residue remaining; **cannot be designated**: because he has attained final nibbāna by way of the nibbāna element without residue remaining, he cannot be indicated, reckoned, or described as "a khattiya" or "a brahmin" or "a vessa" or "a sudda"; as "a householder" or "a monastic"; as "a deva" or "a human being"; as "one having form" or as "one without form"; as "percipient" or "nonpercipient" or "neither-percipient-nor-nonpercipient." There is no cause, no condition, no means by which he might be designated. In this way he goes out and can no longer be designated.

1075. Now, when he heard the expression "goes out," not thoroughly discerning its meaning, he spoke the verse "But does one who has gone out." This is its meaning: "**Does one who has gone out not exist**, or is it that **through eternity,** by an eternal nature, he is **intact (healthy)**, not subject to change? Explain this matter well to me, O muni." For what reason? **For this Dhamma has been understood by you**.

Nidd II 98. But does one who has gone out not exist?: Does one who has gone out not exist, has he ceased, been annihilated, been destroyed? **Or else is he intact (healthy) through eternity?**: Or else would he persist as permanent, everlasting, eternal, not subject to change, just like eternity itself?

1076. Then the Blessed One spoke the verse "There is no measure of one who has gone out," showing that he cannot be described in such ways. Here, **of one who has gone out**: of one who has attained final nibbāna through non-clinging; **there is no measure**: there is no measurement by way of form and the other aggregates. **No means by which they might speak of him**: no means by which they might speak of him in terms of lust and so forth. **When all phenomena have been uprooted**: When all such phenomena as the aggregates have been uprooted. The rest everywhere is clear.

Nidd II 99. There is no measure of one who has gone out: For one who has gone out, who has attained final nibbāna by way of the nibbāna element without residue remaining, there is no measure by way of form, no measure by way of feeling, no measure by way of perception, no measure by way of volitional activities, no measure by way of consciousness. No [such measure] is found or apprehended; it has been abandoned, eradicated, allayed, stilled, made incapable of arising, burnt up by the fire of knowledge.

There is no means by which they might speak of him: Those volitional activities have been abandoned by means of which they might describe him, on account of lust, hatred, delusion, conceit, views, restlessness, doubt, and the latent tendencies [respectively] as "lustful" or "hating" or "deluded" or "bound down [by conceit]" or "seizing [upon views]" or "distracted [by restlessness]" or "undecided [because of doubt]" or "tenacious [because of the latent tendencies]." Because those volitional activities have been abandoned, there is no cause, no condition, no means by which they might speak of him, discuss him, describe him, express him through a destination [of rebirth] as "a hell being" or "an animal" or "an afflicted spirit" or "a human being" or "a deva"; as "one having form" or as "formless"; as "percipient" or "non-percipient" or "neither-percipient-nor-nonpercipient." So there is no means by which they might speak of him.

Nidd II 100. When all phenomena have been uprooted: when all phenomena, all the aggregates, all the sense bases, all the elements, all destinations, all rebirths, all modes of conception, all existences, all states in saṃsāra, all states in the round have been rooted out, uprooted, removed, extricated, fully extricated, abandoned, eradicated, allayed, stilled, made incapable of arising, burnt up by the fire of knowledge. **All pathways of speech are also uprooted**: It is the defilements, aggregates, and volitional activities that are called pathways of speech. For such a one, speech and pathways of speech, designations and pathways of designation, language and pathways of language, description and pathways of description have been rooted out, uprooted . . . burnt up by the fire of knowledge.

Thus the Blessed One concluded this discourse, too, with its culmination in arahantship. At the conclusion of the teaching there was a breakthrough to the Dhamma in the way already stated.

7 Nanda
(Nanda Sutta)

1077. In the world, people, khattiyas and so forth, **say**, with reference to the Ājīvakas, Nigaṇṭhas, and others: "**There are munis.**"[2111] **But how is this so? Do they declare one who has knowledge a muni**, do they speak thus of one who has a particular knowledge, such as the knowledge of the meditative attainments and so forth? **Or one following a particular way of life**, a designation for any of the various stringent ways of life?

Nidd II 101. There are munis in the world. There are: there exist, there are present, there are found. **Munis**: Ājīvakas, Nigaṇṭhas, jaṭilas, and hermits called munis. **Do they declare one who has knowledge a muni?**: Do they declare one a muni because one has knowledge of the eight meditative attainments or knowledge of the five superknowledges? **Or one following a particular way of life?**: Or do they declare one a muni because one is devoted to any of the numerous and diverse kinds of extremely austere and stringent ways of life?

1078. Then the Blessed One spoke the verse **not by view**, first rejecting both of these and then describing the muni for him.[2112]

Nidd II 101. Not by view: not by purity of view. **Nor by learning**: nor by purity of learning. **Nor by knowledge:** nor by knowledge of the eight meditative attainments or the five superknowledges or wrong knowledge. **The skilled**: Those who are skilled in the aggregates, skilled in the elements, skilled in the sense bases, skilled in dependent origination, skilled in the establishments of mindfulness . . . in the path, in the fruits, in nibbāna, do not say one is a muni because one possesses purity of view or purity of learning or the knowledge of the eight meditative attainments or the five superknowledges.

Nidd II 102. They are munis, I say, who live remote, untroubled, without wishes:[2113] It is Māra's army that is called the army. Māra's army is bodily misconduct, verbal misconduct, mental misconduct, lust, hatred, delusion, anger . . . [as at p. 1061, Nidd I 68–69] . . . all unwholesome volitional activities. When all Māra's army and all the antagonistic defilements have been vanquished, defeated, demolished, decimated, and overturned by the four noble paths, one is said to be a destroyer of the army (to be remote). **Untroubled**: Lust is trouble, hatred is trouble, delusion is trouble . . . all unwholesome volitional activities are trouble. Those arahants with influxes destroyed for whom these troubles have been abandoned . . . burnt up by the fire of knowledge are called untroubled. **Without wishes**: It is craving that is called wish. Those arahants with influxes destroyed for whom this craving has been abandoned . . . burnt up by the fire of knowledge are called wishless. Those, I say, are munis.

1079–80. Now, in order to remove his confusion about the doctrine of those who assert that purity comes through view and so forth, he asks: "Those ascetics and brahmins . . . ?" Here, **through numerous methods**, through superstitious belief in auspicious signs.[2114] **Those living restrained there**: those guarded with respect to their own view. The Blessed One then spoke the second verse, indicating that there is no purity in such a way.

Nidd II 106. I say they have not crossed over birth and old age: I say they did not cross over birth, old age, and death; they did not cross beyond them, did not cross out of them, did not overcome them, did not transcend them. They have not departed from birth, old age, and death; they have not escaped from them, have not passed beyond them, have not overcome them, have not transcended them. They revolve around in birth, old age, and death; they revolve in the pathway of saṃsāra; they are accompanied by birth, pursued by old age, oppressed by illness, stricken by death. They are without a shelter, without a cavern, without a refuge, refugeless.

1081–82. Having heard, "they have not crossed," wishing to know who has crossed, he asks: "Those ascetics and brahmins." Then the Blessed One [596] spoke the third verse, showing those who have crossed birth and old age under the heading of those who have crossed the flood. **Shrouded**: occluded, enveloped. **Having fully understood craving**: having fully understood craving by the three kinds of full understanding. The rest is everywhere clear because the method has been stated earlier.

Nidd II 108. I do not say of all ascetics and brahmins, Nanda, that they are shrouded by birth and old age: I do not say, Nanda, that all ascetics and brahmins are obstructed by birth and old age, shrouded by them, occluded by them, covered by them, enveloped by them, enclosed by them. I declare that there are those ascetics and brahmins who have abandoned birth, old age, and death, cut them off at the root, made them like a palm stump, eliminated them so that they are no more subject to future arising. **Those here who have abandoned the seen, the heard and sensed, and all good behavior and observances**: Those who have abandoned all [views about] purity through what is seen; those who have abandoned all [views about] purity through what is heard; those who have abandoned all [views about] purity through what is sensed; those who have abandoned all [views about] purity through what is seen, heard, and sensed; those who have abandoned all [views about] purity through good behavior; those who have abandoned all [views about] purity through observances; those who have abandoned all [views about] purity through good behavior and observances. **Who have abandoned, too, everything of numerous kinds:** who have abandoned [the view of] purity, purification, full purification, freedom, liberation, release through the numerous and diverse kinds of superstitious beliefs in auspicious signs.

Nidd II 109. Who, having fully understood craving, are without influxes: those, I say, are "persons who have crossed the flood." Craving: craving for forms, sounds, odors, tastes, tactile objects, and mental phenomena. **Having fully understood craving**: Having fully understood craving with the three kinds of full understanding: full understanding of the known, full understanding by scrutinization, and full understanding by abandoning. What is *full understanding of the known*? One knows craving. One knows and sees: "This is craving for forms . . . this is craving for mental phenomena." What is *full understanding by scrutinization*? Having known craving in such a way, one scrutinizes it. One scrutinizes it as impermanent, as suffering, as a disease . . . [as at p. 1035, Nidd I 38] . . . by way of its origin, its passing away, its gratification, its danger, and the escape from it. What is *full understanding by abandoning*? Having scrutinized craving in such a way, one abandons it, dispels it, terminates it, and eliminates it. As the Blessed One said: "Bhikkhus, abandon desire and lust for craving. In such a way that craving will be abandoned, cut off at the root, made like a palm stump, eliminated so that it is no more subject to future arising."[2115]

Having fully understood craving: having fully understood craving with these three kinds of full understanding. **Without influxes**: There are four influxes: the influx of sensuality, the influx of existence, the influx of views, the influx of ignorance. Those who have abandoned these influxes, cut them off at the root, made them like a palm stump, eliminated them so that they are no more subject to future arising—those without influxes are the arahants whose influxes have been destroyed. **Those, I say, are "persons who have crossed the flood"**: Those who, having fully understood craving, are without influxes, I say, have crossed the flood of sensuality, the flood of existence, the flood of views, and the flood of ignorance; they have crossed over, crossed beyond, crossed out of, passed beyond, overcome, transcended all the pathways of saṃsāra. ❚⁝

1083. Thus the Blessed One concluded this teaching, too, with its culmination in arahantship. But at the conclusion of the teaching, Nanda, delighting in the Blessed One's statement, spoke the verse **I delight in this word**. In this case, too, in the way already stated, there was a breakthrough to the Dhamma.

8 Hemaka
(Hemaka Sutta)

1084. Those who in the past explained things to me: Those such as Bāvari and others who in the past explained their own beliefs to me. **All was an increase of thought**: All was an increase of sensual thought and so forth.[2116]

⁞⁞ **Nidd II 112–13. Those who in the past explained things to me**: The brahmin Bāvari and his other teachers who explained their own view, their own opinion, their own preference, their own belief, their own outlook, their own position. **All that was hearsay**: All that was hearsay, report, [come down from] a lineage of teachers, a collection of scriptures, logical thought, inferential reasoning, reached by reasoned reflection, by the acceptance of a view after pondering it. They did not explain a teaching that they had directly and personally known for themselves, a teaching personally cognized. **All was an increase of thought**: All was an increase of thought, an increase of sensual thought, malevolent thought, and aggressive thought; an increase of thought about relatives, thought about one's country, thought about the immortals, and thought connected with solicitude for others; an increase in thought connected with gain, honor, and praise; an increase in thought connected with not being despised. **I did not delight in it**: I did not find or obtain satisfaction there. ⁞⁞

1086. Then, explaining that Dhamma to him, the Blessed One spoke the next two verses, beginning "The dispelling."

⁞⁞ **Nidd II 114–15. For things here seen, heard, sensed, and cognized. Seen**: seen with the eye; **heard**: heard with the ear; **sensed**: smelled with the nose, tasted with the tongue, and contacted with the body; **cognized**: cognized with the mind. **For whatever has a pleasing nature**. And what in the world has a pleasing and agreeable nature? The eye in the world has a pleasing and agreeable nature . . . forms . . . eye-consciousness . . . eye-contact . . . feeling born of eye-contact . . . perception of forms . . . volition regarding forms . . . craving for forms . . . thought about forms . . . examination of forms . . . examination of mental phenomena in the world has a pleasing and agreeable nature.[2117]

Nidd II 115. Desire and lust: sensual desire, sensual lust, sensual delight, sensual craving . . . clinging to sensual pleasures, the hindrance of sensual desire. **The dispelling of desire and lust**: the abandoning of desire and lust, the allaying of desire and lust, the relinquishment of desire and lust, the subsiding of desire and lust, the deathless nibbāna. **The state of nibbāna, the imperishable**: the state of nibbāna, the shelter-state, the cavern-state, the refuge-state, the state without perils. **The imperishable**: the permanent, the everlasting, the eternal, that which is not subject to change—the state of nibbāna, the imperishable.[2118]

1087. Having understood this, those mindful ones: Those who, seeing with insight according to the method, "All conditioned things are impermanent," and so forth, eventually understand this state of nibbāna, the imperishable, who are mindful through mindfulness as contemplation of the body and so forth. **Are quenched in this very life**:[2119] Because they have understood the Dhamma, because they have seen the Dhamma, they are quenched with the extinguishing of lust and so forth. The rest everywhere is clear.

Nidd II 115. Having understood this, those mindful ones. Having understood: Having understood "All conditioned things are impermanent . . . All conditioned things are suffering . . . All phenomena are non-self" . . . [all as at pp. 1060–61, Nidd I 67–68] . . . "Whatever is subject to origination is all subject to cessation." **This:** the deathless nibbāna, the stilling of all volitional activities . . . nibbāna. **Those mindful ones**: Those arahants with influxes destroyed, who are mindful on four grounds: they are mindful because they have developed the establishment of mindfulness consisting in contemplation of the body . . . in contemplation of feeling . . . in contemplation of mind . . . in contemplation of phenomena, they are called mindful.

Nidd II 116. Who have seen the Dhamma (in this very life): who have seen the Dhamma, known the Dhamma, assessed the Dhamma, scrutinized the Dhamma, clarified the Dhamma, recognized the Dhamma: "All conditioned things are impermanent" . . . "Whatever is subject to origination is all subject to cessation."

Quenched: quenched through the extinguishing of lust, hatred, delusion . . . of all unwholesome volitional activities; calm, peaceful, tranquil, quenched, stilled through the pacifying, calming down, tranquilization, allaying, extinguishing, disappearance, and subsiding of lust, hatred, delusion . . . of all unwholesome volitional activities. **Always peaceful**: at all times, permanently, forever, constantly and continuously peaceful through the pacifying and extinguishing of lust, hatred, delusion . . . of all unwholesome volitional activities; calm, peaceful, tranquil, quenched, stilled through the pacifying, calming down, tranquilization, allaying, extinguishing, disappearance, and subsiding of these things. **They have crossed over attachment to the world**: It is craving that is called attachment. They have crossed over, crossed beyond, crossed out of, passed beyond, overcome, transcended attachment to the world.

Thus the Blessed One concluded this discourse, too, with its culmination in arahantship. At the conclusion of the teaching, as before, there was a breakthrough to the Dhamma.

9 Todeyya
(Todeyya Sutta)

1088. Of what sort is his emancipation? He asks how his emancipation may be recognized. [597]

1089. In response the Blessed One spoke the second verse, showing him the nonexistence of another emancipation. Here, **there is no further emancipation**: for him another emancipation does not exist.

⁝▮ **Nidd II 118. There is no further emancipation**: When he is liberated by this emancipation, he is liberated. By this emancipation he has done what had to be done. ▮⁝

1090–91. Though it was said, "The destruction of craving itself is emancipation," he did not recognize the meaning, so he again asked: **Is he without desire or does he have desire?**[2120] Here, **just a wise manner**:[2121] On account of knowledge of the meditative attainments and so forth, does he create mental constructs due to craving or mental constructs due to views? Then, explaining that matter to him, the Blessed One spoke the second verse. The rest is clear.

⁝▮ **Nidd II 118–19. Is he without desire or does he have desire?**: Is he without craving or does he have craving? Does he have desire for forms, sounds, odors, tastes, tactile objects; for family, a group, an abode; for gain, fame, praise, and pleasure, for robes, almsfood, a lodging, or medicinal requisites; for the desire realm, the form realm, the formless realm; for desire-realm existence, form-realm existence, formless-realm existence . . . for the past, the future, the present; for things seen, heard, sensed, and cognized? Does he wish for them, relish them, desire them, yearn for them, hanker for them?

Does he possess wisdom or just a wise manner?: Is he wise, reflective, knowledgeable, lucid, intelligent, or on account of knowledge of the eight meditative attainments or the five superknowledges, or on account of wrong knowledge, does he think up, construct, engender, generate, produce, create mental constructs due to craving or mental constructs due to views?

Nidd II 120. He is without desire; he does not have desire: He is without craving. One without craving does not have desire for form . . . for mental phenomena. He does not wish for them, relish them, desire them, yearn for them, hanker for them. **He possesses wisdom, not just a wise manner**: He is wise, reflective, knowledgeable, lucid, intelligent. It is not the case that on account of knowledge of the eight meditative attainments or the five superknowledges, or on account of wrong knowledge, he thinks up, constructs, engenders, generates, produces, creates mental constructs due to craving or mental constructs due to views. **As one owning nothing**: Lust is something . . . [as at p. 1257, Nidd II 75–76] . . . misconduct is something. One for whom these "somethings" have been abandoned . . . burnt up by the fire of knowledge is called "one owning nothing." **Sensual pleasures**: In brief, there are two kinds of sensual pleasures: sensual objects and sensual defilements . . . [as at p. 1015, Nidd I 1–2] . . . these are called sensual pleasures as defilements. **Existence**: Two kinds of existence: kammically active existence and renewed existence acquired at conception . . . [as at p. 1255, Nidd II 71] . . . This is renewed existence acquired at conception. **One owning nothing, unattached to sensual pleasures and existence**: A person who owns nothing and is unattached to sensual pleasures and existence, unstuck, unfastened, unimpeded, who has departed from them, escaped, been released, been detached, and who dwells with a mind rid of barriers. ⁂

Thus the Blessed One concluded this discourse, too, with its culmination in arahantship. At the conclusion of the teaching, as before, there was a breakthrough to the Dhamma.

10 Kappa
(Kappa Sutta)

1092. In the midst of the stream: What is meant is "in saṃsāra," which is "in the midst" because its beginning or end cannot be discerned. **So this might occur no more**: so this suffering would not occur again.[2122]

Nidd II 121–22. In the midst of the stream: It is saṃsāra that is called the stream. A beginning of saṃsāra is not discerned; an end of saṃsāra is not discerned. Beings stand in the middle, in saṃsāra; they are established there, settled, involved, sticking to it, resolved upon it. How is it that *a beginning of saṃsāra is not discerned*? It is not the case that the round has turned for just so many births, years, and eons but not before that . . . for just so many koṭis of births, years, and eons but not before that . . . for just so many hundreds of thousands of koṭis of births, years, and eons but not before that. How is it that *an end of saṃsāra is not discerned*? It is not the case that the round will turn for just so many births, years, and eons but not after that . . . for just so many koṭis of births, years, eons but not after that . . . for just so many hundreds of thousands of koṭis of births, years, and eons but not after that.

Nidd II 123–24. When a perilous flood has arisen: When the flood of sensuality, the flood of existence, the flood of views, and the flood of ignorance have arisen. **Perilous**: the peril of birth, the peril of old age, the peril of illness, and the peril of death. **Declare an island**: Speak about an island, a shelter, a cavern, a refuge, a resort, a support. **So this might occur no more**: so that this suffering might cease right here, might be allayed, might disappear, might subside, so that the suffering of conception in renewed existence might not be produced; so that it might not be produced in the desire realm, the form realm, or the formless realm . . . in existence, or in saṃsāra, or in the round; so that it might cease right here . . . might subside. ⠿

1093–94. Then the Blessed One, explaining that matter to him, spoke the next three verses (**1093–95**). Here, **owning nothing** is the antidote to owning something; **taking nothing** is the antidote to taking. This means the subsiding of owning and taking. **The island with nothing further**: without another island as its equal; this means that it is the best.[2123]

⠿ **Nidd II 125–26. Owning nothing**: Lust is something, hatred is something, delusion is something, conceit is something, views are something, defilements are something, misconduct is something. The abandoning of owning, the allaying of owning, the relinquishment of owning, the subsiding of owning, the deathless nibbāna. **Taking nothing**: It is craving that is called "taking." The abandoning of taking, the allaying of taking, the relinquishment of taking, the subsiding of taking, the deathless nibbāna. **This is the island with nothing further**: There is no island better than that one. Rather, that island is the foremost, the best, the most distinguished, the chief, the highest, the most excellent. **I call this "nibbāna"**: It is craving that is called "the weaving." The abandoning of weaving, the allaying of weaving, the relinquishment of weaving, the subsiding of weaving: the deathless nibbāna.[2124] **The extinction of old age and death**: the abandoning of old age and death, their allaying, relinquishment, subsiding, the deathless nibbāna.

1095. Nor are they Māra's footmen: They are not Māra's minions, attendants, pupils. The rest everywhere is clear.

⠿ **Nidd II 126–27. Having understood this**: Having understood "All conditioned things are impermanent" . . . [as at pp. 1278–79, Nidd II 115–16] . . . and subsiding of lust, hatred, delusion . . . of all unwholesome volitional activities. **They do not come under Māra's control**: They do not come under Māra's control, nor does Māra exercise control over them. They have overcome, vanquished, overwhelmed, exhausted, and crushed Māra, Māra's faction, Māra's trap, Māra's hook,

Māra's bait, Māra's domain, Māra's residence, Māra's range, Māra's bondage. **Nor are they Māra's footmen**: They could not be Māra's footmen, minions, attendants, pupils. They are the footmen, minions, attendants, pupils of the Buddha, the Blessed One.

Thus the Blessed One concluded this discourse, too, with its culmination in arahantship. At the conclusion of the teaching, as before, there was a breakthrough to the Dhamma. [598]

11 Jatukaṇṇī
(Jatukaṇṇī Sutta)

1096. Having heard of the hero who has no desire for sensual pleasures: Having heard of the hero, the Buddha, one "who does not desire sensual pleasures" because of a lack of desire for sensual pleasures, in the way that begins "Thus the Blessed One."[2125] **I have come to ask the desireless one**: I have come to ask the Blessed One, the one without desire. **You of innate vision**: you who have the innate eye of omniscient knowledge.[2126] **Tell me about it**: He makes another request. For one making a request should speak even a thousand times, not to mention twice.

⁂ **Nidd II 128. Who has no desire for sensual pleasures**: In brief, there are two kinds of sensual pleasures: sensual objects and sensual defilements. Because the Buddha, the Blessed One, has fully understood sensual objects and abandoned sensual defilements, he does not desire sensual pleasures. Since the Blessed One does not desire sensual pleasures, the Buddha is desireless, without desire, one who has renounced desire, expelled desire, let go of desire, abandoned desire, relinquished desire; he is rid of lust, devoid of lust . . . he has relinquished lust. Hungerless, quenched, cooled, experiencing bliss, he dwells having himself become holy.[2127]

The state of peace (steps to peace): From one angle, this is the deathless nibbāna, the stilling of all volitional activities, the relinquishment of all acquisitions, the destruction of craving, dispassion, cessation, nibbāna. But from another angle, it is the qualities that lead to the achievement of peace, to the experience of peace, to the realization of peace, namely, the four establishments of mindfulness . . . the noble eightfold path;

these are called states of peace (steps to peace). **You of innate vision**: It is the knowledge of omniscience that is called vision. Vision and the state of a conqueror arose in the Buddha, the Blessed One, simultaneously at the foot of the bodhi tree, neither preceding nor following the other. Therefore the Buddha is called one of innate vision. ⁞

1097. As the splendid sun overcomes the earth with its splendor: as [the sun], which possesses splendor, overcomes [the earth] with its splendor. **So that I might understand the abandoning here of birth and old age**: so that right here I might understand the Dhamma that is the abandoning of birth and old age.[2128]

⁞ **Nidd II 129–30. As the splendid sun overcomes the earth with its splendor**: As the sun, the splendid one endowed with splendor, crosses the sky, spreading over and warming the earth, scattering all gloom and dispelling all darkness throughout space, and displaying its light, so the Blessed One, splendid with knowledge, endowed with the splendor of knowledge, dispels the gloom of defilements and the darkness of ignorance, displays the light of knowledge, has fully understood sensual objects, and has abandoned, overcome, vanquished, overwhelmed, exhausted, and crushed sensual defilements.

Nidd II 130. Since I am one of limited wisdom . . . you of broad wisdom: I am one of limited wisdom, inferior wisdom, slight wisdom, slender wisdom. But you are one of great wisdom, wide wisdom, joyous wisdom, quick wisdom, sharp wisdom, penetrative wisdom, endowed with wisdom vast and extensive like the earth. **Teach me the Dhamma**: the Dhamma that is good in the beginning, good in the middle, and good in the end, with meaning and phrasing, a spiritual life that is perfectly complete and pure; the four establishments of mindfulness . . . nibbāna and the way leading to nibbāna. Teach it, describe it, establish it, disclose it, analyze it, elucidate it, reveal it. **So that I might understand**: so that I might know, understand, recognize, penetrate, achieve, experience, realize. **The abandoning here of birth and old age**: the abandoning of birth, old age, and death right here, their allaying, relinquishment, and subsiding, the deathless nibbāna.[2129] ⁞

1098. Then, explaining the Dhamma to him, the Blessed One spoke the next three verses. Here, **having seen renunciation as security**: having seen nibbāna and the way leading to nibbāna as security.[2130] **Take up**: grasp by way of craving or views. **Or reject**: or dismiss, to let go.[2131] **Anything**: Let there not be the "something" that is lust and so forth.

⁝▯ **Nidd II 131. Having seen renunciation as security**: Having seen, having perceived, having assessed, having scrutinized, having clarified, having recognized the right practice, the practice in conformity, the unopposed practice, the practice in accordance with the goal, the practice in accordance with the Dhamma, the fulfillment of good behavior, guarding the doors of the sense faculties, moderation in eating, devotion to wakefulness, mindfulness and clear comprehension, the four establishments of mindfulness, the four right kinds of striving, the four bases for spiritual potency, the five faculties, the five powers, the seven factors of enlightenment, the noble eightfold path, nibbāna, and the way leading to nibbāna as security, as a shelter, as a cavern, as a refuge, as providing refuge, as without peril, as imperishable, as the deathless, as nibbāna. **Do not take up or reject anything. Take up**: grasp, seize, clutch, clasp, resolve upon. **Reject**: let go, discard, dispel, terminate, eliminate. **Anything**: Lust is something . . . misconduct is something. Let this "something" not be found in you, not occur in you, not exist in you; abandon it, dispel it, terminate it, eliminate it. ▯⁝

1099. What pertains to the past: defilements arisen with reference to past conditioned things. The rest everywhere is clear.

⁝▯ **Nidd II 131–32. Dry up what pertains to the past**: Dry, dry up, wither, wither away any defilements that might arise with reference to past conditioned things. Make them seedless, abandon them, dispel them, terminate them, eliminate them. **Do not take up anything to come later**: It is the lust . . . the misconduct occurring with reference to future conditioned things that is called "to come later." Let this something not occur in you, do not generate it, do not engender it, do not produce it. Abandon it, dispel it, terminate it, eliminate it. **If you will not grasp in the middle**: It is present form, feeling, perception, volitional activities, and consciousness that are called "in the middle." If you will not grasp present conditioned things by way of craving or views, crave for them, seize upon them, delight in them, seek delight in them, cling to them; if you will abandon, dispel, terminate, and eliminate delighting, welcoming, clinging, obsession, seizing, attachment. **You will live at peace**: By the stilling of lust, hatred, delusion, anger . . . by the stilling of all unwholesome volitional activities, you will live at peace, calm, tranquil, quenched, stilled.

1100. Nidd II 132–33. For one, brahmin, entirely devoid of greed for name-and-form. Name (mentality): the four formless (mental) aggregates. **Form**: the four great elements and the form dependent on the four great elements. For one entirely devoid of greed for name-and-form: for one rid of greed, who has renounced greed, expelled greed, freed from greed, abandoned greed, relinquished greed; for one devoid of lust . . . relinquished lust. **The influxes do not exist:** the influx of sensuality, the influx of existence, the influx of views, the influx of ignorance. **By which one might come under death's control**: Those influxes by which one might come under death's control do not exist; they have been abandoned, eradicated, allayed, quelled, made incapable of arising, burnt up by the fire of knowledge.

Thus the Blessed One concluded this discourse, too, with its culmination in arahantship. At the conclusion of the teaching, as before, there was a breakthrough to the Dhamma.

12 Bhadrāvudha
(*Bhadrāvudha Sutta*)

1101. The home-leaver: the leaver of an abode. **The cutter off of craving**: the one who has cut off the six classes of craving. **One without impulse**: unshaken by worldly conditions. **Who has abandoned delight**: who has abandoned longing for future forms and so forth. For craving, though a single state, [599] is spoken of here in various ways in order to praise the Buddha. **Who has abandoned mental constructs**: who has abandoned the two kinds of mental constructs. **Having heard this from the nāga**—having heard your word, Blessed One, for you are the nāga—**they will depart from here**: many people will depart from the Pāsāṇaka Cetiya.

Nidd II 133–34. The home-leaver: Desire, lust, delight, craving, engagement and clinging, mental standpoints, adherences, latent tendencies in relation to the form element have been abandoned by the Buddha, the Blessed One, so that they are no more subject to future arising; therefore the Buddha is a home-leaver. So too in relation to the feeling element, the perception element, the volitional activities element, the consciousness element; therefore the Buddha is a home-leaver.[2132]

Nidd II 134. The cutter off of craving: Craving for forms . . . craving for mental phenomena has been cut off by the Buddha, eradicated, allayed, stilled, made unable to arise, burnt up by the fire of knowledge; therefore the Buddha is a cutter off of craving. **One without impulse**: It is craving that is called impulse. That impulse—craving—has been abandoned by the Buddha, the Blessed One, cut off at the root . . . not subject to future arising. Because he has abandoned impulse, being without impulse, he is not stirred by gain or lack of gain, by fame or dishonor, by praise or blame, by pleasure or pain. Therefore the Buddha is without impulse. **Who has abandoned delight**: It is craving that is called delight. That delight has been abandoned by the Buddha, the Blessed One. **Crossed the flood:** crossed the flood of sensuality . . . the flood of ignorance, crossed all the pathways of saṃsāra, overcome them, transcended them**. Won liberation**: The Blessed One's mind is freed from lust, freed from hatred, freed from delusion . . . freed from all unwholesome volitional activities, liberated from them, well liberated from them. **Who has abandoned mental constructs**: There are two kinds of mental constructs, mental constructs due to craving and mental constructs due to views. For the Buddha, the Blessed One, mental constructs due to craving have been abandoned and mental constructs due to views have been relinquished. Since that is so, the Buddha is one who has abandoned mental constructs. ▮⁝

1102. Various people from [various] countries have gathered: from countries such as Aṅga have gathered here.

⁝▮ **Nidd II 135. Various people**: khattiyas, brahmins, vessas, and suddas; householders and renunciants; devas and humans. **From [various] countries**: from Aṅga, Magadha, Kaliṅga, Kāsī, Kosala, Vajjī, Malla, Cetiya, Vaṃsa, Kuru, Pañcala, Maccha, Surasena, Assaka, Avantī, Yona, and Kamboja.[2133] ▮⁝

1103. Then the Blessed One spoke the next two verses, teaching him the Dhamma in accordance with his inclination. Here, **acquisitive craving**:[2134] the craving and grasping that take up forms and so forth; what is meant is craving and clinging. **Whatever they cling to in the world**: whatever they cling to in these directions, above and so forth. **By this itself Māra pursues a person**: By this itself Māra, as the aggregates obtained at conception, follows that being produced by the kammic volitional activities, which are in turn produced with clinging as condition.[2135]

⁝▮ **Nidd II 136. Acquisitive craving**: It is craving for form . . . that is called acquisitive craving. And why is it called acquisitive craving? Through that craving they acquire form, cling to it, grasp it, seize it, adhere to it; they acquire feeling . . . perception . . . volitional activities . . . consciousness . . . a destination, rebirth, conception, existence, saṃsāra, the round, cling to it, grasp it, seize it, adhere to it. Therefore it is called acquisitive craving.

Nidd II 137. Above, below, and across in the middle: **Above**: the future . . . [as at pp. 1254–55, Nidd II 70] . . . **across in the middle**: in between. **By this itself Māra pursues a person**: By this itself, Māra as the aggregates acquired at conception, Māra as the elements, Māra as the sense bases, Māra as a destination, Māra as rebirth, Māra as conception, Māra as existence, Māra as saṃsāra, Māra as the round, pursues, follows, trails a person, a being, a man or a woman, a human being, a creature. ▮⁞

1104. Therefore, understanding this: Therefore, knowing the danger thus or knowing conditioned things by way of impermanence and so forth. **Observing, "They are stuck on taking up"**: **In the entire world** that is stuck to forms and so forth, forms that are called "taking up" in the sense that they are things that can be taken up, observing this population stuck in the realm of death—or alternatively, observing persons who are stuck on taking up, settled on taking up, and observing this population tied by taking up, attached to the realm of death, unable to transcend it—one should not cling to anything in the entire world. The rest everywhere is clear.

⁞▮ **Nidd II 138. A mindful bhikkhu should not cling to anything in the entire world. A bhikkhu**: a bhikkhu who is a good worldling or a bhikkhu who is a trainee. **Mindful**: mindful in four ways, by developing the establishment of mindfulness consisting in contemplation of the body [and so forth]. **Anything**: anything pertaining to form, feeling, perception, volitional activities, or consciousness. **In the entire world**: in the entire plane of misery, in the entire human world, in the entire deva world, in the entire world of the aggregates, the elements, and the sense bases. **Observing, "They are stuck on taking up"**: Those who take up, cling to, grasp, seize, adhere to form, feeling, perception, volitional activities, consciousness . . . saṃsāra, the round, are said to be "stuck on taking up." **This population**: a designation for beings. It is the defilements, aggregates, and volitional activities that are called **the realm of death**. Just as goods on a wall peg or ivory hook are stuck, tightly stuck, fastened, bound there, so too the population is stuck, tightly stuck, fastened, bound to the realm of death, stuck in Māra's realm.

Thus the Blessed One concluded this discourse, too, with its culmination in arahantship. At the conclusion of the teaching, as before, there was a breakthrough to the Dhamma.

13 Udaya
(*Udaya Sutta*)

1105. Here, **emancipation by final knowledge**: He asks about the emancipation arisen through the might of wisdom.[2136] Now since Udaya was one who gained the fourth jhāna, the Blessed One spoke the next two verses, showing from different angles emancipation by final knowledge through the fourth jhāna that he had obtained. [600]

⁝▯ **Nidd II 139. The meditator**: The Blessed One is a meditator. He meditates through the first jhāna, the second jhāna, the third jhāna, the fourth jhāna. He meditates through jhāna with thought and examination; through jhāna without thought but with examination only; through jhāna without thought and examination. He meditates through jhāna accompanied by rapture, through jhāna without rapture, through jhāna accompanied by ease, through jhāna accompanied by equanimity. He meditates through the jhāna of emptiness, through the jhāna of the markless, through the jhāna of the wishless. He meditates through mundane jhāna and through world-transcending jhāna. He delights in jhāna; he is intent on unity; he esteems his own good. **Dust-free**: Lust is dust, hatred is dust, delusion is dust . . . all unwholesome volitional activities are dust. That dust has been abandoned by the Buddha, the Blessed One, made like a palm stump, eliminated so that it is no more subject to future arising; therefore the Buddha is dustless, dust-free, one rid of dust, who has abandoned dust, who is disconnected from dust, who has transcended dust.

It is lust that is dust, not fine particles;
"dust" is a designation for lust.

Having abandoned this dust, the One with Vision,
the Conqueror, is called one devoid of dust.[2137]

It is hatred that is dust, not fine particles . . .
the Conqueror, is called one devoid of dust.

It is delusion that is dust, not fine particles . . .
the Conqueror, is called one devoid of dust.

Nidd II 140–41. Who has gone beyond all phenomena: The Blessed One has gone beyond all phenomena through direct knowledge, through full understanding, through abandoning, through development, through realization, through attainment. He has gone beyond through direct knowledge of all phenomena; through the full understanding of all suffering; through the abandoning of all defilements; through the development of the four paths; through the realization of cessation; through the attainment of all meditative attainments. He has attained mastery over good behavior, concentration, wisdom, and liberation.

Nidd II 141. Speak of emancipation by final knowledge: It is emancipation by arahantship that is called emancipation by final knowledge. Explain emancipation by arahantship, teach it, describe it, establish it, disclose it, analyze it, elucidate it, reveal it. **The breaking up of ignorance**: the breaking apart of ignorance, its abandoning, allaying, relinquishment, subsiding, the deathless nibbāna.

1106. Here, **the abandoning of sensual desires**: I declare that this abandoning of sensual desires for one who has attained the first jhāna is also emancipation by final knowledge. All the terms should be construed in such a way.

Nidd II 142–43. The abandoning of sensual desires: Sensual desire in regard to sensual pleasures, sensual lust, sensual delight, sensual craving, sensual affection, sensual thirst, sensual fever, sensual infatuation, sensual clutching, the flood of sensuality, the bond of sensuality, clinging to sensual pleasures, the hindrance of sensual desire. **Dejection:** mental unease, mental pain, the uneasy painful feeling born of mind-contact. **The abandoning of both**: The abandoning, allaying, relinquishment, and subsiding of both sensual desire and dejection. **The dispelling of mental dullness**: the dispelling, abandoning, allaying, relinquishment, subsiding of mental lethargy, unwieldiness, listlessness, sluggishness, slothfulness, dullness, tedium of mind. **Regret**: Regret is fidgeting with the hands, fidgeting with the feet, fidgeting with the hands and feet . . . [as at p. 1121, Nidd I 158–59] . . . any such regret, mental remorse, uneasiness of mind that arises. **The warding off of regrets**: The obstructing of regrets, the blocking of them, their abandoning, allaying, relinquishment, subsiding, the deathless nibbāna. ▮⁝

1107. Purified by equanimity and mindfulness: purified by the equanimity and mindfulness of the fourth jhāna. **Preceded by thought on the Dhamma**: By this, he refers to the emancipation of arahantship achieved by one who, based on that emancipation of the fourth jhāna, sees the jhāna factors with insight. For thought on the Dhamma, which is analyzed into right intention and so forth associated with the path, is the forerunner of the emancipation of arahantship. Hence he says: "preceded by thought on the Dhamma." **The breaking up of ignorance**: And I call this emancipation by final knowledge "the breaking up of ignorance," using a figurative description [of the effect by way of] its cause,[2138] because it has arisen on the basis of nibbāna, which is designated the breaking up of ignorance.

⁝▮ **Nidd II 143–44. Purified by equanimity and mindfulness**: These are the equanimity and mindfulness in the fourth jhāna. In the fourth jhāna equanimity and mindfulness are purified, cleansed, fully purified, brightened, made flawless, rid of defilement, malleable, wieldy, firm, and imperturbable. **Preceded by thought on the Dhamma**: It is right intention that is called thought on the Dhamma. That precedes and leads; it is a forerunner of emancipation by final knowledge; hence the latter is preceded by thought on the Dhamma. Or else it is right view that is called thought on the Dhamma. That precedes and leads; it is a forerunner of emancipation by final knowledge; hence the latter is preceded by thought on the Dhamma. Or it is the insight preparatory to the four paths that is called thought on the Dhamma. That precedes and leads; it is a forerunner of emancipation by final knowledge; hence the latter is preceded by thought on the Dhamma. **Emancipation by final knowledge**: It is the emancipation of arahantship that is called emancipation by final knowledge. **The breaking up of ignorance**: The breaking up of ignorance, its abandoning, allaying, relinquishment, subsiding, the deathless nibbāna.

1108. Having heard nibbāna referred to by the expression "the breaking up of ignorance," he spoke the next verse, "By what is the world fettered?" asking: "By the abandoning of what is 'nibbāna' spoken of?"[2139]

1109. Then, explaining the matter to him, the Blessed One spoke the verse "The world is fettered by delight." Here, **thought** is sensual thought and so forth.

Nidd II 145. The world is fettered by delight: It is craving that is called delight. Any lust, passion . . . covetousness, greed as an unwholesome root, this is called delight. The world is yoked by this delight, bound by it, attached to it, conjoined with it, stuck to it, fastened to it, impeded by it, thus the world is fettered by delight. **Thought**: Nine kinds of thoughts: sensual thought . . . [as at p. 1277, Nidd II 112] . . . thought of not being despised. These nine kinds of thought are the world's means of traveling about, of examining, of pondering. By means of these nine kinds of thought, the world travels about, examines, ponders.

1110. Now, asking about the path to nibbāna, he spoke the verse "How does one live mindfully . . . ?" Here, **consciousness** is the volitionally active consciousness.[2140]

1111. Then, explaining the path to him, the Blessed One spoke the verse "For one not seeking delight in feeling." Here, **mindfully thus**: mindfully and with clear comprehension thus. The rest everywhere is clear.

Nidd II 146–47. Not seeking delight in feeling internally and externally: While one dwells contemplating feelings in feelings internally, one does not seek delight in feeling, does not welcome it, does not remain clinging to it. While one dwells contemplating feelings in feelings externally . . . internally and externally, one does not seek delight in feeling, does not welcome it, does not remain clinging to it. While one dwells contemplating the nature of origination . . . the nature of vanishing . . . the nature of origination and vanishing while contemplating feelings in feelings internally, one does not seek delight in feeling, does not welcome it, does not remain clinging to it. While one dwells contemplating the nature of origination . . . the nature of vanishing . . . the nature of origination and vanishing while contemplating feelings in feelings externally, one does not seek delight in feeling, does not welcome it, does not remain clinging to it. While one dwells contemplating the nature of origination . . . the nature of vanishing . . . the nature of origination and vanishing while contemplating feelings in feelings internally and externally, one does not seek delight in feeling, does not welcome it, does not remain clinging to it. One abandons, dispels, terminates, and eliminates delight, welcoming, clinging, obsession, seizing, adherence. In these twelve ways, as one dwells contemplating feelings in feelings, one abandons delight . . . adherence. Or alternatively, seeing feeling as impermanent, as suffering, as a disease . . . [as at p. 1035, Nidd I 38] . . . by way of its origin, its passing away, its gratification, its danger, and the escape from it, one abandons, dispels, terminates, and eliminates delight . . . adherence. In these forty ways, as one dwells contemplating feelings in feelings, one abandons delight . . . adherence.

For one living mindfully thus: For one living thus mindful and clearly comprehending; **consciousness ceases**: Consciousness accompanied by meritorious volitional activity, consciousness accompanied by demeritorious activity, consciousness accompanied by imperturbable volitional activity ceases, abates, disappears, subsides.

Thus the Blessed One concluded this discourse, too, with its culmination in arahantship. At the conclusion of the teaching, as before, there was a breakthrough to the Dhamma.

14 Posāla
(Posāla Sutta)

1112. Points out the past: The Blessed One points out his own past and that of others in the way that begins "[He recollects] one birth" and so forth.

Nidd II 148–49. The one who: the Blessed One, self-accomplished, who without a teacher, among things not heard in the past, on his own awakened to the truths and attained omniscience in regard to them and mastery over the powers. **Points out the past**: The Blessed One points out his own past and that of others, he points out the future, he points out the present. How does the Blessed One point out *his own past*? The Blessed One points out, in his own case, one past birth, two births, three births, four births, five births, ten births, twenty births, thirty births, forty births, fifty births, a hundred births, a thousand births, a hundred thousand births, many eons of world-dissolution, many eons of world-evolution, many eons of world-dissolution and world-evolution thus: "There I was so named, of such a clan, of such a social class, such was my food, such my experience of pleasure and pain, such my life span; passing away from there, I was reborn elsewhere, and there too I was so named, of such a clan, of such a social class, such was my food, such my experience of pleasure and pain, such my life span; passing away from there, I was reborn here." Thus he points out his manifold past abodes with their aspects and details. Thus the Blessed One points out his own past. How does the Blessed One point out *the past of others*? The Blessed One points out, in the case of others, one past birth, two births . . . "he was reborn here." Thus he points out their manifold past abodes with their aspects and details. Thus the Blessed One points out the past of others. When relating five hundred Jātakas, the Blessed One points out *his own past as well as that of others;* so too when relating the Mahāpadāna Sutta, the Mahāsudassana Sutta, the Mahāgovinda Sutta, and the Maghadeva Sutta he points out his own past as well as that of others.

The knowledge of the diversity in faculties is a tathāgata-power of the Tathāgata; the knowledge of the inclinations and latent tendencies of beings . . . the knowledge of the twin miracle . . . the knowledge of the meditative attainment of great compassion . . . the omniscient knowledge . . . the unobstructed knowledge . . . the knowledge that is unstuck, unimpeded, without obstruction anywhere is a tathāgata-power of the Tathāgata. In this way the Blessed One points out the past, the future, and the present of himself and of others.[2141]

Nidd II 149–50. Who is without impulse, who has cut off doubt: It is craving that is called impulse. That impulse of craving has been abandoned by the Buddha, cut off at the root, made like a palm stump, eliminated so that it is no more subject to future arising; therefore the Buddha is without impulse. **Who has cut off doubt**: Doubt about suffering . . . doubt about specific conditionality and dependently arisen phenomena. That doubt has been abandoned by the Buddha . . . burnt up by the fire of knowledge. **Who has gone beyond all phenomena**: The Blessed One has gone beyond all phenomena through direct knowledge . . . [as at p. 1296, Nidd II 140–41] . . . through the attainment of all meditative attainments. ⁂

1113. One for whom perception of form has vanished: one who has overcome perception of form; **who has entirely abandoned the body**: who has entirely abandoned the form body in a particular respect and by way of suppression; the purport is "when one has abandoned conception in form-realm existence." [601] **Who sees "there is nothing"**: by clearly seeing the absence of consciousness one sees "there is nothing"; this refers to one who gains the base of nothingness. **I ask, Sakya, about the knowledge**: I ask about the knowledge of this person; how is it to be recognized? **How is such a one to be led?**: How is he to be led? How is higher knowledge to be aroused in him?

Nidd II 150–51. Of one for whom perception of form has vanished: What is perception of form? The perception of one who has entered a form-sphere meditative attainment, or of one who has been reborn in the form sphere, or of one dwelling happily in this present life: this is perception of form. For one who has obtained the four formless meditative attainments, perception of form has vanished, gone away, been surpassed, been overcome, been transcended: this is one for whom perception of form has vanished. **Who has entirely abandoned the body**: one for whom the entire form body acquired at conception is abandoned; one's form body is abandoned by overcoming it in a particular respect and by abandoning it through suppression.[2142] **Who sees "there is nothing" internally and externally**: the attainment of the base of nothingness. How is the attainment of the base of nothingness [the referent of] "there is nothing"? Having mindfully entered the base of the boundlessness of consciousness and emerged from it, one negates that same consciousness, abolishes it, makes it disappear, while one sees: "There is nothing." In that way, the attainment of the base of nothingness is [the referent of] "there is nothing." **How is such a one to be led?**: How is such a one—the attainer of the base of nothingness—to be led, to be guided, to be directed? How is he to arouse higher knowledge?

1114. Then, having shown him his own unobstructed knowledge in regard to such a person, the Blessed One spoke the next two verses to explain that knowledge. Here, **directly knowing all stations of consciousness, the Tathāgata**: the Tathāgata, directly knowing all the stations of consciousness thus: "Four by way of volitional activities and seven by way of conception." **Knows this one remaining**: knows this person remaining by way of kammic volitional activities thus: "This one will have such a future [rebirth] destination." **One who is liberated**: one resolved on the base of nothingness.[2143] **Who has that as support**: constituted by that.[2144]

Nidd II 151. All the stations of consciousness: The Blessed One knows the four stations of consciousness that occur by way of volitional activity and he knows the seven stations of consciousness that occur by way of conception. How does the Blessed One know the four stations of consciousness that occur *by way of volitional activity*? For this has been said by the Blessed One: "Consciousness, bhikkhus, while standing, might stand engaged with form, based on form, established on form; with a sprinkling of delight, it might come to growth, increase, and expansion. Or consciousness, while standing, might stand engaged with feeling . . . engaged with perception . . . engaged with volitional activities, based on volitional activities, established on volitional activities; with a sprinkling of delight, it might come to growth, increase, and expansion" (SN III 53,10–14). In this way the Blessed One knows the stations of consciousness that occur by way of volitional activities.

Nidd II 151–52. And how does the Blessed One know the stations of consciousness that occur *by way of conception*? This has been said by the Blessed One (AN IV 39–40; see too DN III 253):

> (1) "There are, bhikkhus, beings that are different in body and different in perception, such as humans, some devas, and some in the lower world. This is the first station of consciousness.[2145] (2) There are beings that are different in body but identical in perception, such as the devas of Brahmā's company that are reborn through the first [jhāna]. This is the second station of consciousness.[2146] (3) There are beings that are identical in body but different in perception, such as the devas of streaming radiance. This is the third station of consciousness.[2147] (4) There are beings that are identical in body and identical in perception, such as the devas of refulgent glory. This is the fourth station of consciousness.[2148] (5) There are beings that, with the complete surmounting of perceptions of forms, with the passing away of perceptions of sensory impingement, with non-attention to perceptions of diversity, [perceiving] 'space is boundless,' belong to the base of the boundlessness of space. This is the fifth station of consciousness. (6) There are beings that, by completely surmounting the base of the boundlessness of space, [perceiving] 'consciousness is boundless,' belong to the base of the boundlessness of consciousness. This is the sixth station of consciousness. (7) There are beings that, by completely surmounting

the base of the boundlessness of consciousness, [perceiving] 'there is nothing,' belong to the base of nothingness. This is the seventh station of consciousness."

In this way the Blessed One knows the stations of consciousness by way of conception.

Nidd II 152–53: Directly knowing: understanding, cognizing, penetrating. **The Tathāgata knows this one remaining**: The Blessed One knows the one who remains here by way of kammic volitional activity thus: "With the breakup of the body, after death, this person will be reborn in the plane of misery, in a bad destination, in the lower world, in hell." The Blessed One knows the one who remains here by way of kammic volitional activity thus: "With the breakup of the body, after death, this person will be reborn in the animal realm . . . this person will be reborn in the sphere of afflicted spirits . . . this person will be reborn among human beings . . . this person, who is practicing well, will be reborn in a good destination, in the heavenly world."[2149]

Nidd II 154–55: One who is resolved on (liberated), who has that as support.[2150] **Resolved**: Resolved on the base of nothingness; resolved by emancipation, resolved there, resolved upon it, dominated by it. Or else, the Blessed One knows: "This person is resolved on forms, resolved on sounds, resolved on odors, resolved on tastes, resolved on tactile objects, resolved on families, resolved on a group, resolved on an abode; resolved on gain, fame, praise, and pleasure; resolved on robes, almsfood, a lodging, or medicinal requisites; resolved on the Suttas, the Vinaya, or the Abhidhamma; resolved on dwelling in the forest, resolved on going on alms round, resolved on wearing rag robes, resolved on going on alms round without skipping houses, resolved on refusing food brought afterward, resolved on the sitter's practice, resolved on accepting any assigned lodging;[2151] resolved on the first jhāna . . . resolved on the attainment of the base of neither-perception-nor-nonperception."[2152] **Who has that as support**: who consists of the base of nothingness, who has that as support, who has kamma as support, who has the result as support, who esteems kamma, who esteems conception. Or alternatively, the Blessed One knows: "This person has form as support . . . this one has the attainment of the base of neither-perception-nor-nonperception as support."[2153] ⁂

1115. Having known the origin of nothingness: Having known the kammic volitional activity generating [rebirth into] the base of nothingness, asking: "Just how is that an impediment?" **Thus, "delight is the fetter"**: having known delight, consisting in lust for the formless, as the fetter there. **One then sees into it with insight**: Having emerged from the meditative attainment of the base of nothingness, one contemplates that meditative attainment with insight by way of impermanence and so forth. **This is the real knowledge**: This is the undistorted knowledge of arahantship that has gradually arisen in that person who contemplates with insight in such a way. The rest everywhere is clear.

Nidd II 155. Having known the origin of nothingness: It is the kammic volitional activity leading to the base of nothingness that is called the origin of nothingness. Having known the kammic volitional activity leading to the base of nothingness as "the origin of nothingness," having known it as a fastening, having known it as bondage, having known it as an impediment, having assessed it . . . having recognized it. **Thus, "delight is the fetter"**: It is lust for the formless that is called the fetter of delight. That kamma is stuck, fastened, impeded by that lust for the formless. Having known lust for the formless as "the fetter of delight"; having known it as a fastening, as bondage, as an impediment, having assessed it . . . having recognized it. The word "thus" (*iti*) is just a liaison term, a connective term, a filler, a word to complete the whole, a term assisting smooth diction, a term indicating sequence.[2154]

Nidd II 156. One then sees it with insight: Having attained the base of nothingness and emerged from it, one sees with insight the mind and mental factors arisen there as impermanent, as suffering, as a disease . . . [as at p. 1035, Nidd I 38] . . . by way of their origin, their passing away, their gratification, their danger, and the escape from them.

The real knowledge: This is the real, actual, accurate, undistorted knowledge. **Of the brahmin, one who has lived the spiritual life**: The seven trainees, inclusive of the good worldling, are living [the spiritual life], dwelling in it, abiding in it, following it, for the attainment of the as-yet-unattained, for the achievement of the as-yet-unachieved, for the realization of the as-yet-unrealized. The arahant has lived the spiritual life, done what had to be done, laid down the burden, attained his own good, utterly destroyed the fetters of existence, and is liberated through perfect knowledge. He has lived the life, completed the practice . . . for him there is no more renewed existence.

Thus the Blessed One concluded this discourse, too, with its culmination in arahantship. At the conclusion of the teaching, as before, there was a breakthrough to the Dhamma.

15 Mogharāja
(*Mogharāja Sutta*)

1116. Here, **twice**: two times. Previously—at the end of the Discourse to Ajita and the Discourse to Tissa Metteyya—he had asked the Blessed One a question twice, [602] but the Blessed One, waiting for his faculties to mature, did not answer him. Hence he said: "I have asked the Sakyan twice." **Yet I have heard that the divine rishi answers upon the third request**. I have heard thus: "When asked a reasonable question up to the third time, the Blessed One, the Perfectly Enlightened One—the rishi who has become a deva by purification answers."[2155] It is said that he had heard this already on the bank of the Godhāvarī River. Hence he said: "Yet I have heard that . . . a third request."

⁞▮ **Nidd II 157–61. The One with Vision**: The Blessed One is the One with Vision on account of five kinds of eyes: the fleshly eye, the divine eye, the wisdom eye, the buddha eye, and the universal eye. How is the Blessed One called "One with Vision" on account of the fleshly eye? . . . [as at pp. 1174–77, Nidd I 261–65] . . . Thus the Blessed One is "One with Vision" on account of the universal eye.

Nidd II 161–62. The divine rishi: The Blessed One is a deva and also a rishi; thus he is a divine rishi.[2156] Just as kings who have gone forth are called royal rishis, and as brahmins who have gone forth are called brahmin rishis, so the Blessed One, being a deva and also a rishi, is a divine rishi. Or alternatively: The Blessed One is also a rishi because he was one who went forth. He was a rishi because he sought, searched for, pursued the great aggregate of good behavior . . . [as at pp. 1170–71, Nidd I 252–53] . . . the great supreme goal, the deathless nibbāna. ▮⁞

1117. This world: the human world; **the other world**: the rest apart from that; **together with the devas**: except for the brahma world, the remainder, including devas by rebirth and conventional devas. Or else "the brahma world together with the devas" is a mere example, as when it is said: "In the world together with the devas." Hence the entire world, in the way stated, should be understood.

1118. To the one of excellent vision: the one of foremost vision. He shows: "The one who is capable of seeing the aspirations, dispositions, destinations [of rebirth], destiny, and so forth of the world together with the devas."

1119. Look upon the world as empty: See the world as empty on two grounds: by considering its occurrence as beyond mastery or by contemplating it as consisting of hollow conditioned things.[2157] **Having uprooted the view of self**: having drawn out[2158] the view of the personal entity. The rest everywhere is clear.

Nidd II 164. Look upon the world as empty. **The world**: the hell world . . . [as at p. 1234, Nidd II 22] . . . the brahma world together with the devas—this is called the world. A certain bhikkhu said to the Blessed One: "It is said, Bhante, 'the world, the world.' In what way is it called the world?" – "It is worn away, bhikkhu, therefore it is called the world. And what is worn away? The eye is worn away, forms are worn away, eye-consciousness is worn away, eye-contact is worn away, and whatever feeling arises with eye-contact as condition—whether pleasant, painful, or neither-painful-nor-pleasant—that too is worn away. The ear is worn away . . . and whatever feeling arises with mind-contact as condition . . . that too is worn away. It is worn away, bhikkhu, therefore it is called the world" (SN IV 52,8–15).

Nidd II 164–66. Look upon the world as empty: One looks upon the world as empty on two grounds: by considering its occurrence as beyond mastery or by contemplating it as consisting of hollow conditioned things. How does one look upon the world as empty *by considering its occurrence as beyond mastery*? Mastery over form is not possible; mastery over feeling

. . . over perception . . . over volitional activities . . . over consciousness is not possible. For this has been said by the Blessed One: "Bhikkhus, form is non-self. If this form were a self, this form would not lead to affliction and it would be possible to determine form thus: 'May my form be thus. May my form not be thus.' But since form is non-self, form leads to affliction and it is not possible to determine form thus: 'May my form be thus. May my form not be thus.' Feeling . . . Perception . . . Volitional activities . . . Consciousness is non-self . . . But since consciousness is non-self, consciousness leads to affliction and it is not possible to determine consciousness thus: 'May my consciousness be thus. May my consciousness not be thus'" (SN III 66–67).

For this has been said by the Blessed One: "Bhikkhus, this body is not yours nor does it belong to others. It is old kamma, to be seen as generated by volitional activity and fashioned by volition, as something to be felt. In regard to that, the instructed noble disciple attends carefully and closely to dependent origination thus: 'When this exists, that comes to be; with the arising of this, that arises. When this does not exist, that does not come to be; with the cessation of this, that ceases. That is, with ignorance as condition, volitional activities [come to be]. . . . Such is the origin of this whole mass of suffering. . . . Such is the cessation of this whole mass of suffering'" (SN II 64–65). It is in this way that one looks upon the world as empty by considering its occurrence as beyond mastery.

Nidd II 166. And how does one look upon the world as empty *by contemplating it as consisting of hollow conditioned things*? No core is found in form, in feeling, in perception, in volitional activities, in consciousness. Form is coreless, without a core, devoid of a core—any core of permanence, or core of happiness, or core of selfhood, or anything permanent, everlasting, eternal, or not subject to change. Feeling . . . Perception . . . Volitional activities . . . Consciousness is coreless, without a core, devoid of a core—any core of permanence . . . or anything not subject to change. As a lump of foam, as a water bubble, as a mirage, as the trunk of a plantain tree, as a magical illusion are coreless, without a core, devoid of a core, so too are form . . . consciousness coreless, without a core, devoid of a core—any core of permanence . . . not subject to change (see SN III 140–42). It is in this way that one looks upon the world as empty by contemplating it as consisting of hollow conditioned things. Thus one looks upon the world as empty on these two grounds.

Nidd II 166–67. Further, one looks upon the world as empty in six ways. The eye is empty of self or anything belonging to self or anything permanent, everlasting, eternal, or not subject to change. The ear is empty . . . The nose is empty . . . The tongue is empty . . . The body is empty . . . The mind is empty . . . of anything not subject to change. Forms . . . Mental phenomena are empty . . . Eye consciousness . . . Mind-consciousness is empty . . . Eye-contact is empty . . . Mind-contact is empty . . . Feeling born of eye-contact is empty . . . Feeling born of mind-contact is empty . . . Perception of forms is empty . . . Perception of mental phenomena is empty . . . Volition regarding forms is empty . . . Volition regarding mental phenomena is empty . . . Thought of forms is empty . . . Thought of mental phenomena is empty . . . Examination of forms is empty . . . Examination of mental phenomena is empty of self or anything belonging to self or anything permanent, everlasting, eternal, or not subject to change. It is in this way that one looks upon the world as empty in six ways.

Further, one looks upon the world as empty in ten ways. Form is seen as vacant, as hollow, as empty, as non-self, as coreless, as a murderer, as extermination, as the root of misery, as connected with the influxes, as conditioned. Feeling . . . Perception . . . Volitional activities . . . Consciousness . . . Passing away . . . Rebirth . . . Conception . . . Existence . . . Saṃsāra . . . The round is seen as vacant, as hollow, as empty, as non-self, as coreless, as murderous, as extermination, as the root of misery, as connected with the influxes, as conditioned. It is in this way that one looks upon the world as empty in ten ways.

Further, one looks upon the world as empty in twelve ways. Form is not a being, not a soul, not a person, not a human being, not a woman, not a man, not a self, not belonging to a self, not an "I," not "mine," not a someone, not belonging to anyone. Feeling . . . Perception . . . Volitional activities . . . Consciousness is not a being . . . not belonging to anyone. It is in this way that one looks upon the world as empty in twelve ways.

Nidd II 167–69. For this has been said by the Blessed One:

"Bhikkhus, whatever is not yours, abandon it. When you have abandoned it, that will lead to your welfare and happiness. And what is it, bhikkhus, that is not yours? Form is not yours: abandon it. When you have abandoned it, that will lead to your welfare and happiness. Feeling is not yours . . . Perception is not yours . . . Volitional activities are not yours . . . Consciousness is not yours: abandon it. When you have abandoned it, that will lead to your welfare and happiness.

"Suppose, bhikkhus, people were to carry off the grass, sticks, branches, and foliage in this Jeta's Grove, or to burn them, or to do with them as they wish. Would you think: 'People are carrying us off, or burning us, or doing with us as they wish'?" – "No, Bhante. For what reason? Because it is neither our self nor what belongs to our self." – "So too, bhikkhus, form . . . consciousness is not yours: abandon it. When you have abandoned it, that will lead to your welfare and happiness." (SN III 33–34)

The Venerable Ānanda said to the Blessed One: "Bhante, it is said: 'Empty is the world, empty is the world.' In what way, Bhante, is it said: 'Empty is the world'?" – "Ānanda, it is because the world is empty of self and of what belongs to self that it is said: 'Empty is the world.' And what is empty of self and of what belongs to self? The eye, Ānanda, is empty of self and of what belongs to self. Forms are empty . . . Eye-consciousness is empty . . . Eye-contact is empty . . . Whatever feeling arises with mind-contact as condition—whether pleasant or painful or neither-painful-nor-pleasant—that too is empty of self and of what belongs to self. It is, Ānanda, because it is empty of self and of what belongs to self that it is said: 'Empty is the world.'" (SN IV 54,5–16)

It is in this way, too, that one looks upon the world as empty.

"For one who sees as it really is
a bare origination of phenomena,
a bare continuum of conditioned things,
there is no fear, O chief.

"When one sees with wisdom
the world as like grass and timber,
one does not wish for anything else
other than the end of rebirth."[2159]

It is in this way, too, that one looks upon the world as empty.

> "So too, a bhikkhu investigates form to the extent that there is a range for form, feeling to the extent that there is a range for feeling, perception to the extent that there is a range for perception, volitional activities to the extent that there is a range for volitional activities, and consciousness to the extent that there is a range for consciousness. As he investigates this, whatever notions of 'I' or 'mine' or 'I am' previously occurred to him no longer occur." (SN IV 197–98)

Nidd II 169–70. Look upon the world as empty: Perceive the world as empty, see it, assess it, scrutinize it, recognize it, clarify it. **Being ever mindful**: One is mindful in four ways, by developing the establishment of mindfulness consisting in contemplation of the body [and so forth]. **Having uprooted the view of self**. It is the twentyfold view of the personal entity that is called the view of self. Here the uninstructed worldling, who is not a seer of the noble ones and is unskilled and undisciplined in their Dhamma, who is not a seer of good persons and is unskilled and undisciplined in their Dhamma, regards form as self, or self as possessing form, or form as in self, or self as in form. He regards feeling . . . perception . . . volitional activities . . . consciousness as self, or self as possessing consciousness, or consciousness as in self, or self as in consciousness. Such a view, a speculative view . . . even including the sixty-two speculative views: this is the view of self. **Having uprooted the view of self**: Having uprooted the view of self, having extracted it, drawn it out, fully drawn it out, pulled it up, fully pulled it up, abandoned it, dispelled it, terminated it, eliminated it. **One may thus cross over death**: One may thus cross over mortality, cross over old age, cross over death, cross out of them, cross beyond them, overcome them, transcend them.

Nidd II 170–71. The King of Death does not see one who looks upon the world thus: Mortality is the King of Death, Māra is the King of Death, dying is the King of Death. The King of Death does not see him, does not discern him, does not find him, does not encounter him.

For this was said by the Blessed One:

> "Suppose a forest deer is wandering in the forest wilds: he walks confidently, stands confidently, sits confidently, lies down confidently. Why is that? Because he is out of the hunter's range. So too, quite secluded from sensual pleasures, secluded from unwholesome qualities, a bhikkhu enters and dwells in the first jhāna . . . the cessation of perception and feeling, and his influxes are destroyed by his seeing with wisdom. This bhikkhu is said to have blinded Māra, to have become invisible to the Evil One by depriving Māra's eye of its opportunity. He has crossed beyond attachment to the world. He walks confidently, stands confidently, sits confidently, lies down confidently. Why is that? Because he is out of the Evil One's range (MN I 174–75)." ⁘

Thus the Blessed One concluded this discourse, too, with its culmination in arahantship. At the conclusion of the teaching, as before, there was a breakthrough to the Dhamma.

16 Piṅgiya
(*Piṅgiya Sutta*)

1120. I am old, weak, my color gone: It is said that this brahmin was overcome by old age, 120 years old. And he was so weak that when he intended to take a step here, he would step elsewhere. And his previous skin color had faded. [603] Hence he said: "I am old, weak, my color gone." **Do not let me perish confused along the way**: Do not let me perish without having realized your Dhamma, still ignorant along the way. **The abandoning here of birth and old age**: Right here, at your feet, or at the Pāsāṇaka Cetiya, declare to me the abandoning of birth and old age, the Dhamma of nibbāna, which I might understand.

⁝⁞ **Nidd II 172. Do not let me perish confused along the way. Confused**: immersed in ignorance, without knowledge, not cognizant, with weak wisdom. **Along the way**: May I not pass away along the way, without having understood, achieved, known, obtained, experienced, realized your Dhamma, view, practice, and path. **Declare the Dhamma that I might understand**: Declare, teach, proclaim, establish, disclose, analyze, elucidate, reveal the Dhamma that is good in the beginning, good in the middle, and good in the end, with meaning and with phrasing, the perfectly complete, perfectly pure spiritual life: the four establishments of mindfulness . . . the noble eightfold path, nibbāna and the way leading to nibbāna. **The abandoning here of birth and old age**: the abandoning of birth, old age, and death right here, their allaying, relinquishment, and subsiding, the deathless nibbāna. ⁞⁝

1121. Now, since Piṅgiya spoke the verse "I am old" from concern about his body, the Blessed One spoke the verse "Having seen those stricken by forms" in order to remove his affection for his body. Here, **by forms**: because of forms, with forms as condition.[2160] **Stricken**: tormented on account of punishments and so forth. **Afflicted by forms**: People are afflicted and oppressed by forms on account of illness of the eyes and so forth.

⁞⁞ **Nidd II 173. Having seen those stricken by forms**: When there is form, they inflict various punishments on them. They have them flogged with whips . . . [as at p. 1092, Nidd I 112–13] . . . and they have their head cut off with a sword. Thus, because of forms, with forms as condition, by reason of forms, beings are stricken, attacked, injured, wounded. **People who are heedless, afflicted by forms**: afflicted, disturbed, oppressed, besieged; they become ill and dejected. They are afflicted by illness of the eyes, illness of the ears . . . illness of the body . . . by contact with flies, mosquitoes, wind, the sun's heat, and serpents.

Nidd II 174. Abandon form for an end to renewed existence: Form is the four great elements and the form dependent on the four great elements. Abandon form for an end to renewed existence, so that your form might cease right here and no new existence would be produced, whether in the desire realm or the form realm or the formless realm; whether in desire-realm existence or form-realm existence or formless-realm existence; whether in percipient existence or nonpercipient existence or neither-percipient-nor-nonpercipient existence; whether in one-constituent existence or four-constituent existence or five-constituent existence; so that you do not generate, do not engender, do not produce, do not create another destination or rebirth or conception or existence or saṃsāra or round; so that right here it might cease, be allayed, disappear, subside. ⁞⁞

1122–23. Though he had thus heard the practice explained by the Blessed One up to arahantship, because of his weakness due to old age, Piṅgiya still did not achieve distinction. Thus, extolling the Blessed One with this verse, "In the four directions," he again requested a teaching. The Blessed One then spoke the verse "Observing people fallen into craving," again showing the practice up to arahantship. The rest everywhere is clear.

Nidd II 175–76. Fallen into craving: accompanied by craving, pursued by craving, inundated by craving, overcome by craving. **Tormented, crushed by old age**: tormented by birth, tormented by old age, tormented by illness, tormented by death, tormented by sorrow, lamentation, pain, dejection, and anguish; tormented by the suffering of hell . . . tormented by suffering through loss of [right] view; struck by calamity, by misfortune, by disaster. **Crushed by old age**: accompanied by birth, pursued by old age, overcome by illness, stricken by death; without a shelter, without a cavern, without a refuge, refugeless. **Abandon craving for an end to renewed existence**: Abandon craving for an end to renewed existence so that your craving might cease right here and no new existence would be produced . . . so that right here it might cease, be allayed, disappear, subside.

Thus the Blessed One concluded this discourse, too, with its culmination in arahantship, and at the conclusion of the teaching Piṅgiya was established in the fruit of a non-returner. It is said that at intervals he thought: "It is too bad that my uncle Bāvari did not get to hear such a variegated and inspired teaching." Being distracted by his affection, he could not attain arahantship. But his pupils, a thousand jaṭilas, attained arahantship. By being addressed, "Come, bhikkhus," they all appeared wearing robes and carrying bowls produced by psychic power.

Epilogue

Verses Extolling the Way to the Beyond

Following this, praising the teaching, the compilers said: "This is what the Blessed One said." **This is what the Blessed One said**: He spoke this Way to the Beyond. **The sixteen attendants**: the sixteen together with Piṅgiya, who was Bāvari's attendant, or the sixteen who were attendants of the Buddha, the Blessed One. [604] And they were **brahmins**. But the sixteen assemblies seated there, in front and behind, to the left and to the right, extended six yojanas each way, thus twelve yojanas in diameter. **Entreated**: requested. **Understands the meaning**: understands the meaning of the text. **Understands the Dhamma**: understands the text.[2161]

1124–26. The Way to the Beyond: Having assigned a designation to this exposition of the Dhamma, reciting the names of those brahmins, they said: "Ajita, Tissa Metteyya . . . came to the supreme Buddha." **The rishi of excellent conduct**: The great rishi who possesses the good behavior of the Pātimokkha and so forth, which is the foundation for attaining nibbāna. The rest is already clear.

⁝▮ **Nidd II 180. The rishi of excellent conduct**: Excellent conduct is restraint by good behavior, restraint of the sense faculties, moderation in eating, devotion to wakefulness, the seven good qualities, and the four jhānas (see MN I 358,3–13). ▮⁝

1128. Following this, **they lived the spiritual life**: they lived the spiritual life of the path.

⁝▮ **Nidd II 181. They lived the spiritual life:** It is desisting from engagement in a bad practice . . . [as at p. 1242, Nidd II 37] . . . Or, in the direct sense, it is the noble eightfold path that is called the spiritual life, that is, right view . . . right concentration.

1130. Therefore it is called "The Way to the Beyond": It is called the way to nibbāna, which is the beyond.

Nidd II 182. One would go from the near shore to the beyond: It is the defilements, the aggregates, and volitional activities that are called the near shore. It is the deathless nibbāna that is called the beyond (the far shore).

Verses Recited about the Way to the Beyond

When the Blessed One had taught the Way to the Beyond, the sixteen jaṭilas attained arahantship,[2162] and there was a breakthrough to the Dhamma by the remaining devas and humans, who numbered fourteen koṭis. For this was said by the ancients:

> Then on the delightful Pāsāṇaka,
> at the meeting on the Way to the Beyond,
> the Buddha led fourteen koṭis of beings
> to attain the deathless.

When the teaching of the Dhamma was finished, by the spiritual might of the Blessed One, the people who had come from here and there appeared in their own respective villages and towns. The Blessed One, too, went to Sāvatthī, accompanied by many thousands of bhikkhus, including the sixteen attendants. There Piṅgiya paid homage to the Blessed One and said: "I shall go, Bhante, to report to Bāvari that a buddha has arisen; for I made a promise to him." Then, permitted by the Blessed One, he went to the bank of the Godhāvarī River by a journey of knowledge[2163] and headed toward the hermitage by foot.

While the brahmin Bāvari was seated looking out at the road, he saw Piṅgiya coming in the distance in the manner of a bhikkhu, without his ascetic's bag, matted locks, and other appurtenances, and he inferred: "A buddha [605] has arisen in the world." Still, when Piṅgiya arrived, he asked him: "Has a buddha arisen in the world?" – "Yes, brahmin, he has arisen. Seated at the Pāsāṇaka Cetiya, he taught us the Dhamma. I will teach it to you." Then Bāvari and his retinue, with great honor, venerated him and prepared a seat. Seated there, Piṅgiya said: "I will recite the Way to the Beyond" and so forth.

1131. Here, **I will recite**: I will recite what was recited by the Blessed One. **As he saw it**: As he saw it himself, with his full awakening to the truths and with his knowledge not shared in common with others. **Desireless** (*nikkāmo*): one who has abandoned desire (or sensuality). There is also the reading *nikkamo*, meaning "energetic," or "departed from the unwholesome faction." **Disentangled:**[2164] without the jungle of defilements, or just without craving. **For what reason would he . . . speak falsely?**: He shows: "Those defilements on account of which one might speak falsely have been abandoned by him." With this he arouses the brahmin's eagerness to listen.

1132–34. Beautiful: possessing excellent qualities. **Who is truly named**: who truthfully has the name "Buddha."[2165] **Might settle upon a forest abounding in fruit**: having arrived at a forest bearing many fruits and so forth. **Having left those of little vision**: those with limited wisdom such as Bāvari. **At a great lake**: at a great body of water such as Lake Anotatta and so forth.

1136–37. Of broad wisdom: whose banner is wisdom; **of broad intelligence**: of vast wisdom. **Directly visible, immediate**: whose fruit is to be seen by oneself, and whose fruit is to be attained without an interval of time; **without adversity**: without the adversity of defilements.

⁘ **Nidd II 194–95. He is the one who taught me the Dhamma**: The Blessed One, self-accomplished, who without a teacher, among things not heard before, awakened to the truths and attained omniscience with respect to them and mastery over the powers—he taught me the Dhamma that is good in the beginning . . . [as at p. 1317, Nidd II 172] . . . nibbāna and the way leading to nibbāna. **Directly visible, immediate**: It is directly visible, immediate, inviting one to come and see, applicable, to be personally experienced by the wise—in this way it is directly visible. Or alternatively, one who develops the noble eightfold path in this very life achieves, finds, obtains the fruit immediately after that path, without interval—in this way too it is directly visible.[2166] **Immediate**: Whereas, when people give temporal wealth, they do not obtain [the results] without interval but wait for some time, this Dhamma is not like that. One who develops the noble eightfold path in this very life achieves, finds, obtains the fruit immediately after that path, without interval, not elsewhere, not in the next world—in this way it is immediate. **B:**

1138–43. Then Bāvari spoke to him the two verses: "Why do you dwell apart from him?" Showing that he does not part from the Blessed One, Piṅgiya then said: "I do not dwell apart from him" and so forth. **I see him with my mind as if with my eyes**: I see the Buddha with my mind just as if with my eyes. [606] **I pay homage to him in that same direction**: He shows: "In whatever region the Buddha is, I bend, lean, slope in that direction."

1144. United with him: He shows: "United, applied to, intent on where the Buddha is."

1145. As I lay trembling in the mud: in the mud of sensuality. **I floated from island to island**: I went from teacher to teacher and so forth. **Then I saw the Enlightened One**: Having taken hold of bad views, wandering around, I then saw the Buddha at the Pāsāṇaka Cetiya.

1146. At the conclusion of the previous verse, the Blessed One, while still in Sāvatthī, understood that the faculties of both Piṅgiya and Bāvari had reached maturity. He then emanated a golden radiance. While Piṅgiya was seated, praising the Buddha's excellent qualities to Bāvari, he noticed that radiance. Wondering, "What is this?" he looked up and saw the Blessed One as if he were actually standing in front of him. He then told Bāvari: "The Buddha has come." The brahmin rose from his seat, joined his palms in reverence, and stood there. The Blessed One, extending his radiance, showed himself to the brahmin. Then, having understood what was suitable for both of them, addressing Piṅgiya alone, he spoke this verse: "As Vakkali."

This is its meaning: As the Elder **Vakkali** was one resolved on faith, and with faith as the instrument attained arahantship;

and as **Bhadrāvudha**, one of the sixteen brahmin students, and as **Āḷavi Gotama** had done so, just so you too must send forth faith.[2167] Then, resolving on faith, [607] having undertaken insight in the way stated thus, "All conditioned things are impermanent," and so forth, **you will go** to nibbāna, **beyond the realm of death**. Thus he concluded the teaching with its culmination in arahantship. At the conclusion of the teaching, Piṅgiya was established in arahantship and Bāvari in the fruit of a non-returner. But the brahmin Bāvari's five hundred pupils became stream-enterers.

⁞▮ **Nidd II 203. As Vakkali had sent forth faith, and Bhadrāvudha and Āḷavi Gotama**: As the Elder Vakkali, one with faith, who esteemed faith, who was led by faith, resolved on faith, governed by faith, attained arahantship—and so the other two—as they sent forth faith, **just so you too must send forth faith**: You must release faith, send forth faith, send forth steady faith, resolve, trust.[2168] You must send forth faith . . . trust that "all conditioned things are impermanent" . . . "whatever is subject to origination is all subject to cessation." **Then, Piṅgiya, you will go beyond the realm of death**: It is the defilements, the aggregates, and the volitional activities that are called the realm of death. It is the deathless nibbāna that is said to be beyond the realm of death. You will go beyond, you will achieve the beyond, you will experience the beyond, you will realize the beyond. ▮⁞

1147–48. Now, proclaiming his own confidence, Piṅgiya said: "I am pleased even more" and so forth. Here, **gifted with ingenuity**: possessing the analytical knowledge of ingenuity. **Having directly known about the devas**: Having known the qualities that make the devas;[2169] **high and low**: superior and inferior. What is meant is that he has known all the qualities that make the deva status for himself and others. **Of those in doubt who acknowledge this**: Of those who are actually in doubt but claim: "We are without doubts."[2170]

⁞▮ **Nidd II 204–5. I am pleased even more**: I have even more faith, more trust, more resolve. I have even more faith that "all conditioned things are impermanent" . . . "whatever is subject to origination is all subject to cessation." **The Enlightened One, with coverings removed:**[2171] There are five coverings: the covering of craving, the covering of views, the covering of defilements, the covering of misconduct, and the covering of ignorance. Those coverings have been removed by the Blessed One, the Buddha; they have been destroyed, uprooted, abandoned, eradicated, allayed, quelled, made incapable of arising, burnt up by the fire of knowledge; therefore the Buddha is one with coverings removed.

Nidd II 206–7. The Teacher is the end-maker of questions. The Teacher: The Blessed One is a teacher, a caravan leader. As a caravan leader leads beings across a wilderness . . . [as at pp. 1205–6, Nidd I 334–35] . . . so the Blessed One is a caravan leader who leads beings across the wilderness of birth . . . enabling them to reach safety, the deathless nibbāna. Thus the Blessed One is a caravan leader. **The end-maker of questions**: the end-maker of questions for those on the way to the beyond (*pārāyanikapañhānaṃ*), an end-maker of Sakka's questions, of Suyāma's questions, of the questions of bhikkhus, bhikkhunīs, male lay followers, female lay followers, kings, khattiyas, brahmins, vessas, suddas, devas, and brahmās. **For those in doubt who acknowledge this**: Those who have come in doubt are relieved of their doubt; those who come with qualms are relieved of their qualms; those who come undecided are relieved of their indecision; those who come with lust, hatred, and delusion are freed from lust, hatred, and delusion; those who come with defilements are freed from defilements. ▮⁞

1149. The immovable: immovable by lust and so forth; **the unshakable**: not subject to change. By these two terms he speaks of nibbāna. **Surely I will go there**: I will definitely go to the nibbāna element without residue remaining. **I have no doubt about this**: I have no doubt about nibbāna. **Thus remember me as one with mind resolved**: When Piṅgiya was instructed, "just so you too must send forth faith," in accordance with this exhortation of the Blessed One, he aroused faith within himself and achieved liberation with faith as the instrument. Then, showing that he had resolved on faith, he said to the Blessed One: "Thus remember me as one with mind resolved." This is the purport: "Just as you told me, so remember me as one resolved."

⁞▮ **Nidd II 207–8. The immovable, the unshakable**: It is the deathless nibbāna that is called the immovable. Nibbāna cannot be moved by lust, hatred, delusion . . . by all unwholesome volitional activities. Nibbāna is permanent, everlasting, eternal, not subject to change; thus it is immovable. **Unshakable**: It is the deathless nibbāna that is called unshakable. For nibbāna, no arising is discerned, no vanishing is discerned, no alteration of that which persists is discerned. Nibbāna is permanent, everlasting, eternal, not subject to change. **Thus remember me as one with mind resolved**: Thus remember me as one leaning toward nibbāna, sloping toward nibbāna, inclined to nibbāna, resolved on nibbāna.

Conclusion

[At the beginning of this work] it was said:

> Having venerated the Triple Gem,
> supreme among things worthy of veneration,
> I will compose an explanation of the meaning
> of the Suttanipāta, [a compilation of suttas]
>
> that is found in the Minor Collection,
> and was taught by the World's Protector,
> who abandoned all minor types of conduct
> and sought to ferry the world across.[2172]

At this point, that commentary to the Suttanipāta, with its five chapters beginning with the Chapter on the Serpent, and with its seventy suttas, beginning with the Discourse on the Serpent, [608] has been completed.

Hence, it is said:

> Whatever wholesome kamma has been achieved
> by me
> in composing this commentary to the Suttanipāta,
> it was undertaken from a wish
> that the good Dhamma long endure.
>
> By the spiritual might of that wholesome kamma,
> may people quickly achieve progress.
> May they come to growth and maturity
> in the Dhamma proclaimed by the Noble One.

This commentary on the Suttanipāta named "Elucidator of the Supreme Meaning"[2173] was composed by the elder who is adorned with supreme and pure faith, wisdom and energy, in whom are gathered a collection of excellent qualities, such as honesty, gentleness, and others, due to the practice of good behavior, one who is capable of delving into and fathoming the views of his own and others' systems, who is possessed of keenness of wisdom, who is strong in unerring knowledge of the Teacher's Teaching as divided into the Tipiṭaka and its commentaries, a great expositer, gifted with sweet and noble speech that springs from the ease born of perfection of the vocal instrument, a speaker of what is appropriately said, a superlative speaker, a great poet, an ornament in the lineage of the elders who dwell in the Mahāvihāra—those who are shining lights in the lineage of elders whose intellects are well established in the superhuman states embellished with such special qualities as the six kinds of superknowledge and the analytical knowledges—by one who has abundant purified intelligence and who bears the name Buddhaghosa conferred by his teachers.

May it continue here to show
the way to purity of virtue, etc.,
for clansmen seeking out the means
to ferry them across the world
as long as in this world
shall last the name "Buddha,"
by which is known the great rishi, the Impartial One,
purified in mind, supreme in the world.

Appendix 1
Parallels to Suttas of the Suttanipāta

I. Pāli Canon

I,3 Khaggavisāṇa Sutta	Ap I 8–13 (90–131)
I,4 Kasibhāradvāja Sutta	SN 7:11
I,8 Metta Sutta	Khp 9
I,10 Āḷavaka Sutta	SN 10:12
II,1 Ratana Sutta	Khp 6
II,3 Hiri Sutta	Ja III 196,10–23
II,4 Mahāmaṅgala Sutta	Khp 5
II,5 Sūciloma Sutta	SN 10:3
II,12 Vaṅgīsa Sutta	Th 1263–79 (verses only)
III,3 Subhāsita Sutta	SN 8:5
III,4 Sundarikabhāradvāja Sutta	SN 7:9 (part only)
III,7 Sela Sutta	MN 92; Th 818–41 (verses only)
III,10 Kokālika Sutta	SN 6:10; AN 10:89

II. Other Traditions

I,1 Uraga Sutta
    Gāndhārī: GDhp 81–90
    Prakrit: Patna Dhp 398–414
    Sanskrit: Udv 18.21, 18.21A–F, 32.55–80

I,3 Khaggavisāṇa Sutta
    Gāndhārī: Salomon 2000, 115–201
    Sanskrit: Mvu 357–59

I,4 Kasibhāradvāja Sutta
    Chinese: SĀ 98 (T II 27a10–27b28); SĀ^{2} 264 (T II 466b18–466c11); SĀ^{3} 1 (T II 493a7–493b11)

I,5 Cunda Sutta
Sanskrit: Mahāparinirvāṇa Sūtra §26 (Waldschmidt 1951, 252–64)
Chinese: DĀ 2 (T I no. 1, 18b9–18c6); T I no. 5, 167c6–168a11; T I no. 6, 183b10–183b27; T I no. 7, 196c12–196c23 (part-parallel)
I,7 Vasala Sutta
Chinese: SĀ 102 (T II 28b19–29b20); SĀ² 268 (T II 467b27–468b18)
I,9 Hemavata Sutta
Chinese: SĀ 1329 (T II 365c6–367b4); SĀ² 328 (T II 483c17–485a23); T IV no. 198, 183b17–184b2
I,10 Āḷavaka Sutta
Chinese: SĀ 1326 (T II 364b21–365a23); SĀ² 325 (T II 482c8–483b03)

II,1 Ratana Sutta
Sanskrit: Mvu I 290–95
II,4 Mahāmaṅgala Sutta
Chinese: T IV no. 211, 609a12–609b14
II,5 Sūciloma Sutta
Sanskrit: Śag 11.1–4
Chinese: SĀ 1324 (T II 363b29–364a01); SĀ² 323 (T II 481c15–482a15)
II,7 Brāhmaṇadhammika Sutta
Chinese: MĀ 156 (T I 678a24–679a25)

III,1 Pabbajjā Sutta
Sanskrit: Mvu II 198–200; Saṅghabhedavastu (Gnoli 1977, 1:94–96)
Chinese: T XXII no. 1428, 779c26-780a24
III,2 Padhāna Sutta
Sanskrit: Mvu II 238–40; Lalitavistara 18:1–22
III,3 Subhāsita Sutta
Sanskrit: Śag 20 (**450** only)
Chinese: SĀ 1218 (T II 332a08–332a29); SĀ² 253 (T II 462b19–462b19)
III,6 Sabhiya Sutta
Sanskrit: Mvu III 389–94
Chinese: T III no. 190, 833b8–835b22

III,7 Sela Sutta
Chinese: EĀ 49.6 (T II 798a25–799c16)
III,10 Kokālika Sutta
Chinese: SĀ 1278 (T II 351b12–352a13); SĀ[2] 276 (T II 470a14–470b20); EĀ 21.5 (T II 603b02–603c17)
III,11 Nālaka Sutta
Sanskrit: Mvu III 386–89; Saṅghabhedavastu (Gnoli 1977, 1:52–55, *vatthugāthā* only)

IV,1–16 Aṭṭhakavagga
Chinese: T IV no. 198 (佛說義足經, *Arthapada Sūtra). The correspondence of suttas and verses is as follows.
IV,1 Kāma Sutta, **766–71**
Sanskrit: Śag 40.1–6
Chinese no. 1: T IV 175c17–175c24
IV,2 Guhaṭṭhaka Sutta, **772–79**
Chinese no. 2: T IV 176a24–176b10
IV,3 Duṭṭhaṭṭhaka Sutta, **780–87**
Chinese no. 3: T IV 177b28–177c2, 177c7–177c18
IV,4 Suddhaṭṭhaka Sutta, **788–95**
Chinese no. 4: T IV 178a2–178a17
IV,5 Paramaṭṭhaka Sutta, **796–803**
Chinese no. 5: T IV 178b27–178c13
IV,6 Jarā Sutta, **804–13**
Chinese no. 6: T IV 179a3–179a22
IV,7 Tissametteyya Sutta, **814–23**
Chinese no. 7: T IV 179b11–179c1
IV,8 Pasūra Sutta, **824–34**
Chinese no. 8: T IV 179c18–180a11
IV,9 Māgandiya Sutta, **835–47**
Chinese no. 9: T IV 180b5–180c2
IV,10 Purābheda Sutta, **848–61**
Chinese no. 15: T IV 187c10–188a8
IV,11 Kalahavivāda Sutta, **862–77**
Chinese no. 10: T IV 181b18–181c20
IV,12 Cūḷaviyūha Sutta, **878–94**
Chinese no. 11: T IV 182a27–182c2
IV,13 Mahāviyūha Sutta, **895–914**
Chinese no. 12: T IV 183a4–183b14

IV,14 Tuvaṭaka Sutta, **915–34**
Chinese no. 13: T IV 184b12–184c22
IV,15 Attadaṇḍa Sutta, **935–54**
Chinese no. 16: T IV 189b12–189c22
IV,16 Sāriputta Sutta, **955–75**
Chinese no. 14: T IV 186b14–186c26

V,1 Ajitamāṇavapucchā, **1032–39**
Sanskrit: Śag 39.1–6, 9–10
V,14 Udayamāṇavapucchā, **1110–11**
Sanskrit: Śag 39.7–8

I thank Bhikkhu Anālayo for suggesting parallels from non-Pāli traditions additional to those I had already located.

Appendix 2
Verse Parallels from the Yogācārabhūmi Śarīrārthagāthā

(from Enomoto 1989, 17–35)

To I,9: **173–75**
ka etam oghaṃ tarati rātriṃdivam atandritaḥ /
anālambe 'pratiṣṭhe ca ko gaṃbhīre na sīdati // Śag 10.1
sarvataḥ śīlasaṃpannaḥ prajñāvān susamāhitaḥ /
adhyātmacintī smṛtimāṃs taratīmaṃ sudustaraṃ // Śag 10.2
viraktaḥ kāmasaṃjñābhyo rūpasaṃyojanātigaḥ /
anālambe 'pratiṣṭhe ca sa gaṃbhīre na sīdati // Śag 10.3

To I,10: **183–84**
kena svid oghaṃ tarati kenottarati cārṇavaṃ /
duḥkhaṃ tyajati kena svit kena svit pariśudhyati // Śag 9.1
śraddhayā tarati hy ogham apramādena cārṇavaṃ /
vīryeṇa duḥkhaṃ tyajati prajñayā pariśudhyati // Śag 9.2

To II,5: **270–73**
rāgadveṣau bhagavan kinnidānāv aratiratī romaharṣaḥ kuto 'yam /
kutaḥsamutthāś ca mano vitarkāḥ kumārakā dhātrīm ivāśrayante // Śag 11.1
snehajā ātmasaṃbhūtā nyagrodhaskandhakā yathā /
pṛthagviṣaktāḥ kāmeṣu mālutā vā latā vane // Śag 11.2
rāgaś ca dveṣaś ca itonidānāv aratiratī romaharṣaḥ ito 'yaṃ /
itaḥsamutthāś ca mano vitarkāḥ kumārakā dhātrīm ivāśrayante // Śag 11.3
ye tān prajānanti yatonidānāṃs te tāṃ janā yakṣa vinodayanti /

ta arṇavaṃ saṃpratarantīhaugham atīrṇapūrvam
apunarbhavāya // Śag 11.4

To III,3: **450**
subhāṣitaṃ hy uttamam āhur āryāḥ priyaṃ vaden nāpriyaṃ
tad dvitīyaṃ /
satyaṃ vaden nānṛtaṃ tat tṛtīyaṃ dharmaṃ vaden
nādharmaṃ tat caturtham // Śag 20

To IV,1: **766–71**
kāmān kāmāyamānasya tasya cet tat samṛdhyati /
addhā prītamanā bhavati labdhvā martyo yad īpsitaṃ //
Śag 40.1
tasya cet kāmāyamānasya chandajātasya jaṃtunaḥ /
te kāmāḥ parihīyaṃte śalyaviddha iva rūpyate // Śag 40.2
yaḥ kāmāṃ parivarjayati sarpasyeva śirāt padaṃ /
sa imāṃ viṣaktikāṃ loke smṛtaḥ samativartate // Śag 40.3
kṣetravastuhiraṇyaṃ ca gavāśvamaṇikuṇḍalaṃ /
striyo dāsān pṛthakkāmān yo naro hy abhigṛdhyati //
Śag 40.4
abalaṃ vā balīyāṃso mṛdnaṃty enaṃ parisravāḥ /
tata enaṃ duḥkham anveti bhinnāṃ nāvam ivodakaṃ //
Śag 40.5
yasya tv etat samucchinnaṃ tālamastakavad dhataṃ /
śokās tasya nivartante udabindur iva puṣkarāt // Śag 40.6

To V,1: **1032–39** (Śag 39.7–8 = **1110–11**)
kenāyaṃ nivṛto lokaḥ kenāyaṃ na prakāśate /
kiṃ cābhilepanaṃ brūṣe kiṃ ca tasya mahad bhayam //
Śag 39.1
avidyānivṛto lokaḥ pramādān na prakāśate /
jalpābhilepanaṃ brūmi duḥkhaṃ tasya mahad bhayaṃ //
Śag 39.2
sravanti sarvataḥ srotāḥ srotasāṃ kiṃ nivāraṇaṃ /
srotasāṃ saṃvaraṃ brūhi kena srotaḥ pidhīyate // Śag 39.3
yāni srotāṃsi lokasya smṛtiḥ teṣāṃ nivāraṇaṃ /
srotasāṃ saṃvaraṃ brūmi prajñayā hi pidhīyate // Śag 39.4
prajñāyāś ca smṛteś caiva nāmarūpasya sarvaśaḥ /
ācakṣva pṛṣṭa etan me kutraitad uparudhyate // Śag 39.5
prajñā caiva smṛtiś caiva nāmarūpaṃ ca sarvaśaḥ /

vijñānasya nirodhād dhi atraitad uparudhyate // Śag 39.6
kathaṃ smṛtasya carato vijñānam uparudhyate /
ācakṣva pṛṣṭa etan me yathātatham asaṃśayaḥ // Śag 39.7
adhyātaṃ ca bahirdhā ca vedanāṃ nābhinandataḥ /
evaṃ smṛtasya carato vijñānam uparudhyate // Śag 39.8
ye ca saṃkhyātadharmāṇo ye ca śaikṣāḥ pṛthagvidhāḥ /
teṣāṃ me nipakasyeryāṃ pṛṣṭaḥ prabrūhi mārṣa // Śag 39.9
kāmeṣu nābhigṛdhyeta manasānāvilo bhavet /
kuśalaḥ sarvadharmeṣu smṛto bhikṣuḥ parivrajet //
Śag 39.10

Appendix 3
Numerical Sets Mentioned in the Commentaries

3 barrenness, kinds of (*khila*): the barrenness of lust, of hatred, of delusion
3 clear knowledges (*vijjā*): recollection of past lives, knowledge of the passing away and rebirth of beings, knowledge of the destruction of the influxes
3 conceit, kinds of (*māna*): "I am superior, I am equal, I am inferior"
3 craving, kinds of (*taṇhā*): for sensual pleasures, for existence, and for nonexistence
3 existence, kinds of (*bhava*): desire-realm existence, form-realm existence, formless-realm existence
3 full understanding, kinds of (*pariññā*): full understanding of the known, full understanding by scrutinization, and full understanding by abandoning
3 gems (*ratana*): the Buddha, the Dhamma, and the Sangha
3 realms (*dhātu*): the desire realm, the form realm, and the formless realm
3 refuges (*saraṇa*): the Buddha, the Dhamma, and the Sangha
3 seclusion, kinds of (*viveka*): bodily seclusion, mental seclusion, and seclusion from the acquisitions
3 trainings (*sikkhā*): the higher good behavior, the higher mind, and the higher wisdom
4 acquisitions (*upadhi*): as sensual pleasures, as the aggregates, as defilements, and as volitional activities
4 analytical knowledges (*paṭisambhidā*): in regard to the meaning, the doctrine, linguistic expression, and ingenuity
4 bases for psychic potency (*iddhipāda*): the basis for spiritual power that possesses concentration due to desire, due to

energy, due to mind, and due to investigation, each accompanied by volitional activities of striving

4 bonds (*yoga*): the bonds of sensuality, craving for existence, views, and ignorance

4 clinging, kinds of (*upādāna*): clinging to sensual pleasures, clinging to views, clinging to good behavior and observances, and clinging to a doctrine of self

4 elements (*dhātu*): earth, water, fire, and air

4 establishments of mindfulness (*satipaṭṭhāna*): contemplation of the body, feelings, mind, and phenomena

4 floods (*ogha*): the floods of sensuality, craving for existence, views, and ignorance

4 fruits (*phala*): fruits of stream-entry, of the once-returner, of the non-returner, of arahantship

4 good behavior, kinds of (*sīla*): restraint according to the Pātimokkha, restraint of the sense faculties, purification of livelihood, and reflection on the use of the requisites

4 influxes (*āsava*): the influxes of sensuality, craving for existence, views, and ignorance

4 knots (*gantha*): the bodily knot of longing, the bodily knot of ill will, the bodily knot of seizing upon behavior and observances, and the bodily knot of dogmatic adherence to claims of truth

4 māras: the aggregates, the defilements, death, an evil deity

4 means of attracting and sustaining a retinue (*saṅgahavatthu*): giving, endearing speech, beneficial conduct, and equality of treatment

4 modes of generation (*yoni*): birth from the egg, from the womb, from moisture, and spontaneous birth

4 noble truths (*ariyasacca*): suffering (to be fully understood), its origin (to be abandoned), its cessation (to be realized), the way to its cessation (to be developed)

4 nutriments (*āhāra*): edible food, contact, mental volition, and consciousness

4 origins of a sutta (*uppatti*): through the Buddha's personal inclination, through the inclination of others, on account of a particular incident, and in response to a question

4 paths (*magga*): paths of stream-entry, of the once-returner, of the non-returner, and of arahantship

4 postures (*iriyāpatha*): walking, standing, sitting, and lying down

4 requisites (*paccaya*): robes, almsfood, a lodging, and medicines and other supports for the sick
4 right striving, kinds of (*sammappadhāna*): to prevent the arising of unarisen unwholesome mental qualities, to abandon arisen unwholesome mental qualities, to arouse unarisen wholesome mental qualities, and to develop arisen wholesome mental qualities
5 aggregates (*khandha*): form, feeling, perception, volitional activities, and consciousness
5 aggregates (of an arahant, also *khandha*): good behavior, concentration, wisdom, liberation, and knowledge and vision of liberation
5 bondages of the mind (*cetaso vinibandha*): sensual lust, attachment to the body, lust for form, sloth, and desire to be reborn as a deity
5 commotions (*kolāhala*): about the eon, about a wheel-turning monarch, about a buddha, about blessings, and about munihood
5 darts (*salla*): the darts of lust, hatred, delusion, conceit, and views
5 destinations (*gati*): the hell realm, the animal realm, the sphere of afflicted spirits, the human realm, and the deva world
5 eyes (*cakkhu*): the fleshly eye, the divine eye, the wisdom eye (or Dhamma eye), the buddha eye, and the universal eye
5 faculties (*indriya*): the faculties of faith, energy, mindfulness, concentration, and wisdom
5 mental barrenness, kinds of (*cetokhila*): doubt about the Buddha, doubt about the Dhamma, doubt about the Sangha, doubt about the training, and anger with one's fellow monastics
5 miserliness, kinds of (*macchariya*): regarding dwellings, families, gains, praise, and the Dhamma
5 powers (*bala*): the powers of faith, energy, mindfulness, concentration, and wisdom
5 superknowledges (*abhiññā*): modes of psychic power, the divine ear, knowledge of the minds of others, recollections of one's own past lives, and knowledge of the passing away and rebirth of beings
7 darts (*salla*): the darts of lust, hatred, delusion, conceit, views, sorrow, and perplexity

7 factors of enlightenment (*bojjhaṅga*): mindfulness, discrimination of phenomena, energy, rapture, tranquility, concentration, and equanimity

7 latent tendencies (*anusaya*): the latent tendencies to sensual lust, lust for existence, aversion, conceit, views, doubt, and ignorance

7 stations of consciousness (*viññāṇaṭṭhiti*): seven realms of existence in which consciousness arises. See pp. 1304–5 (Nidd II 151–52).

7 swellings (*ussada*): the swellings of lust, hatred, delusion, conceit, views, defilements, and kamma

8 doubt, cases of (*vicikicchā*): doubt about the Teacher, the Dhamma, the Sangha, and the training; doubt about the past, the future, and the past and future together; and doubt about conditionality and dependently originated phenomena

8-fold noble path (*ariya aṭṭhaṅgika magga*): right view, right intention, right speech, right action, right livelihood, right effort, right mindfulness, and right concentration

8 meditative attainments (*samāpatti*): the four jhānas and the four formless attainments

8 worldly conditions (*lokadhamma*): gain and non-gain, fame and dishonor, praise and blame, pleasure and pain

9 abodes of beings (*sattāvāsa*): the seven stations of consciousness augmented by the realm of nonpercipient beings and the base of neither-perception-nor-nonperception

9 thoughts, kinds of (*vitakka*): sensual thought, malicious thought, aggressive thought, thought about relatives, thought about one's country, thought about the immortals, thought connected with solicitude for others, thought about gain, honor, and praise, and thought about not being despised

9 world-transcending states (*lokuttaradhamma*): the four paths, the four fruits, and nibbāna

10 bases of anger (or resentment) (*āghātavatthu*): (1) Thinking, "They acted for my harm," one becomes angry. (2) . . . "They are acting for my harm" . . . (3) . . . "They will act for my harm" . . . (4) . . . "They acted for the harm of one who is pleasing and agreeable to me" . . . (5) . . . "They are acting for the harm of one who is pleasing and agreeable to me"

. . . (6) . . . "They will act for the harm of one who is pleasing and agreeable to me" . . . . (7) . . . "They acted for the benefit of one who is displeasing and disagreeable to me" . . . (8) . . . "They are acting for the benefit of one who is displeasing and disagreeable to me" . . . (9) . . . "They will act for the benefit of one who is displeasing and disagreeable to me," one becomes angry. (10) And one becomes angry without a reason.

10 bases of insult (*akkosavatthu*): "One insults others thus: 'You are a bandit, a fool, an idiot, a thief; you are a camel, a ram, a bull, an ass, an animal; you are bound for hell.'" (Spk I 229,12–13). A slightly different group of ten is at Spk I 342,14–17 and Dhp-a I 211–12.

10 extremist views (*antaggāhikā diṭṭhi*): "the world is eternal" or "the world is not eternal"; "the world is finite" or "the world is infinite"; "the soul and the body are the same" or "the soul is one thing, the body is another"; "a tathāgata exists after death," "a tathāgata does not exist after death," "a tathāgata both exists and does not exist after death," or "a tathāgata neither exists nor does not exist after death"

10-fold wrong view (*micchādiṭṭhi*): "There is nothing given, nothing sacrificed, nothing offered; there is no fruit or result of good and bad actions; there is no this world, no other world; there is no mother, no father; there are no beings spontaneously reborn; there are in the world no ascetics and brahmins of right conduct and right practice who, having realized this world and the other world for themselves by direct knowledge, make them known to others."

11 fires (*aggi*): the fires of greed, hatred, and delusion; of birth, old age, and death; of sorrow, lamentation, pain, dejection, and anguish

12 sense bases (*āyatana*): eye and forms, ear and sounds, nose and odors, tongue and tastes, body and tactile objects, mind and mental phenomena

18 elements (*dhātu*): eye, forms, and eye-consciousness; ear, sounds, and ear-consciousness; nose, odors, and nose-consciousness; tongue, tastes, and tongue-consciousness; body, tactile objects, and body-consciousness; mind, mental phenomena, and mind-consciousness

20 views of the personal entity (*sakkāyadiṭṭhi*): form as self, self as possessing form, form as in self, self as in form; and so for feeling, perception, volitional activities, and consciousness

62 speculative views (*diṭṭhigata*): various views about the self and the world, referring to the past and the future (see DN I 12–39)

108 currents of craving (*taṇhāvicarita*): 18 internal, 18 external, each occurring with reference to the past, the future, and the present (see AN II 211–13)

Notes

Notes to the Introduction and Guide

1. Pj II 1,12: *Tathārūpāni suttāni, nipātetvā tato tato; saṅgīto ca ayaṃ tasmā, saṅkhamevamupāgato.*
2. Vin I 197,38–198,3: *Sādhu, sādhu, bhikkhu. Suggahitāni kho te, bhikkhu, aṭṭhakavaggikāni, sumanasikatāni sūpadhāritāni.*
3. Ud 59,22–28: *Sādhu sādhu, bhikkhu, suggahitāni te, bhikkhu, soḷasa aṭṭhakavaggikāni sumanasikatāni sūpadhāritāni.*
4. For references to the Aṭṭhakavagga/Arthavargīya in the texts of the various Buddhist schools, see Bapat 1951, 1–2, summarizing a paper by Sylvain Lévi. Jayawickrama also discusses Lévi's findings at PBR 1976, 144–45.
5. This monograph is available online in an electronic file created by scanning installments from the old *Pāli Buddhist Review*, in which it was published serially over a two-year period. Unfortunately the scanning of the articles was poorly done and words with Pāli diacritics are often misrepresented.
6. See note 358.
7. I add this qualification because I have included in the category of "bhikkhus" two suttas that do not mention an interlocutor or auditor. One is II,9, in which an unidentified speaker asks questions related to monastic training and the Buddha answers accordingly. II,10 has no other voice, but it has the tone of a discourse in which the Buddha speaks specifically to monks rather than to laypeople or a mixed audience.
8. The Dhaniya Sutta itself says that they both went forth; the commentary, Pj II 46,9, adds that they attained arahantship. In the case of the Māgandiya Sutta the information about their going forth and attainment of arahantship is in the commentary, at Pj II 548,8.
9. Respectively I,6, I,7, II,2, II,4, and II,14.
10. See Thapar 1997, 251–57.
11. The introductory verses of the Pārāyanavagga depict the

sixteen pupils of Bāvari as brahmins, but even if this is true, they do not approach the Buddha as representatives of the brahmanic tradition but as humble seekers of illumination. Thus I do not count them here.

12. DN I 39–41: *Tesaṃ bhavataṃ samaṇabrāhmaṇānaṃ ajānataṃ apassataṃ vedayitaṃ taṇhāgatānaṃ paritassitavipphanditameva.*
13. In a recent essay Ṭhānissaro (2016) offers an insightful discussion of the role of right view in relation to Sn's critical attitude toward views.
14. On the *asekhā sammādiṭṭhi*, see MN I 446,32 and AN V 221,21.
15. Collins 1982, 117. See his entire discussion of the topic, pp. 116–31.
16. MN I 298,14–16: *Rāgo kho, āvuso, kiñcano, doso kiñcano, moho kiñcano. Te khīṇāsavassa bhikkhuno pahīnā, ucchinnamūlā.*
17. On the sources of the Pāli commentaries, see Endo 2013, 17–45.
18. The title is mentioned in the colophon (see p. 1330).
19. Since both Pj I and Pj II comment on the three suttas they share in common—the Metta, the Ratana, and the Maṅgala—Helmer Smith did not include the commentaries on these in his edition of Pj II. The Burmese and Sri Lankan editions of Pj II do include the commentaries on these suttas, but for consistency I used the PTS edition of Pj I as my source.
20. He twice refers to the Atthasālinī, the commentary to the Dhammasaṅgaṇī (at p. 483 and p. 494). In the commentary to the Maṅgala Sutta (p. 739), he directs the reader to the *Papañcasūdanī*, the Majjhima Nikāya Commentary, for an explanation of *evaṃ me sutaṃ*. He mentions the Jātaka Commentary (p. 356). And when relating the background to the Rāhula Sutta, he says (p. 819) that a full account of Rāhula's going forth "should be understood in the way it is related in the commentary to the Khandhakas," presumably referring to the *Samantappāsādikā*, the Vinaya Commentary.
21. From here on, the numbers in bold refer to the commentarial section rather than to Sn.
22. Pj II 46,16–17: *attajjhāsayato, parajjhāsayato, aṭṭhuppattito, pucchāvasito.*
23. *Bahukāra, bhāvetabba, pariññeyya, pahātabba, hānabhāgiya, visesabhāgiya, duppaṭivijjha, uppādetabba, abhiññeyya, sacchikātabba.*
24. Pj II 503,15–17: *Yadetaṃ lokiyalokuttarādibhedena dvidhā vavatthitānaṃ dhammānaṃ vipassanāsaṅkhātaṃ yathābhūtañāṇaṃ.*
25. In the passages from the Niddesa that I have translated, the Abhidhamma is mentioned at p. 1128, p. 1138, and p. 1305.
26. This list of seventeen occurs in the repetition series at the end of the books of the Aṅguttara Nikāya, for instance at AN I 299, II 256–57, III 277–78, etc.

27. *Pahīnā samucchinnā vūpasantā paṭipassaddhā abhabbuppattikā ñāṇagginā daḍḍhā.*
28. For a discussion of the Buddha's *sabbaññutaññāṇa,* see Endo 1997, 58–79.
29. This is the gist of the explanation offered by Pj II. For the detailed account, see note 288.
30. For consistency I use the Pāli forms of familiar words rather than the forms these words assume in other dialects.
31. Jayawickrama (PBR 1976, 80) notes that the position of a sutta in a vagga provides indirect evidence for the time of its incorporation into the work, such that its placement at the beginning or the end of a chapter can be seen as a sign of lateness.
32. Jayawickrama PBR 1977, 21.
33. http://www.ancient-buddhist-texts.net/Buddhist-Texts/C4-Uraga-Verses/Uraga-Verses.pdf.
34. Jayawickrama regards them as an interpolation and presents reasons for this claim at PBR 1977, 150–51.
35. Norman writes that "the Sanskrit word *khaḍga* 'rhinoceros' is a non-Aryan word as Kuiper and Mayrhofer have explained, and it is to be separated from the Sanskrit word *khaḍga,* 'sword.' The original meaning of *khaḍga* was therefore 'rhinoceros' when it was first borrowed into Indo-Aryan, and it is not an abbreviation of *khaḍgaviṣāṇa* as has been suggested."
36. See p. 423.
37. At Ja V 416,20, V 538,2, VI 497,12, and VI 578,24. At Ja VI 277,27, we find the gloss, *palāsādā ti khaggamigā,* which assumes that the reader was familiar with *khagga* as the name of an animal.
38. Mil 23,20–31: *Milindo rājā khaggaparivārito viya gajo . . . bhīto ubbiggo utrasto saṃviggo lomahaṭṭhajāto vimano dummano bhantacitto vipariṇatamānaso.*
39. See note 408.
40. Ap I 7 (1.88): *Paccekabuddhānaṃ samāgatānaṃ, paramparaṃ byākaraṇāni yāni; ādīnavo yañca virāgavatthuṃ, yathā ca bodhiṃ anupāpuṇiṃsu.*
41. Ap I 7 (1.84–86): *Ye pubbabuddhesu katādhikārā, aladdhamokkhā jinasāsanesu. Ten'eva saṃvegamukhena dhīrā, vināpi buddhehi sutikkhapaññā; ārammaṇenāpi parittakena, paccekabodhiṃ anupāpuṇanti. Sabbamhi lokamhi mamaṃ ṭhapetvā, paccekabuddhehi samo'va natthi.*
42. The verse, Ap I 8 (1.90), differs from **35** (= Ap 1.91) only in pāda c, which reads: *mettena cittena hitānukampī,* "with a mind of loving-kindness, compassionate for their welfare."
43. Pp 14: *Idh'ekacco puggalo pubbe ananussutesu dhammesu sāmaṃ saccāni abhisambujjhati; na ca tattha sabbaññutaṃ pāpuṇāti, na ca balesu vasībhāvaṃ – ayaṃ vuccati puggalo "paccekasambuddho."*

44. For a discussion of the paccekabuddha based on other texts of Early Buddhism, see Anālayo 2010 and Anālayo 2015.
45. A sūtra preserved in Chinese translation, EĀ 12.6 (at T II 570a23–570b19), establishes a close connection between Mahākassapa and the pratyekabuddha ideal. In this sūtra Mahākassapa declares: "If the Tathāgata had not accomplished supreme and right awakening, I would have accomplished Pratyekabuddhahood." For a translation and study of this text, see Anālayo 2015.
46. See Salomon 2000, 14–15.
47. The others are the Āmagandha Sutta (II,2), the Brahmadhammika Sutta (II,7), the Sundarikabhāradvāja Sutta (III,4), and the Vāseṭṭha Sutta (III,9). While other suttas in Sn show the Buddha in dialogue with brahmins, they do not critique the premises and practices of Brahmanism.
48. The word *vasala* is not the technical term used to designate an outcast. According to PED *vasala* literally meant "little man," but it seems that in the Buddha's time the word served as a pejorative implying outcast status.
49. Jayawickrama notes (PBR 1977, 146): "The occurrence of these stanzas in the Saṃyutta, independently of the rest of the respective poems, suggests the existence of a set of riddles dealing with Buddhist topics prior to their being incorporated in longer poems."
50. For other external evidence for the early existence of the Munigāthās, see Jayawickrama PBR 1977, 40.
51. The first three pādas are at SN II 284,3–5 with a different last line. It occurs again, with still other variations, at MN I 171,3–5 (= Dhp 353), where the Buddha declares his status to a wandering ascetic.
52. The second couplet of **221** actually uses the two words in succession as if they were synonyms.
53. At Dhp-a III 436–48. For an English translation, see BL 3:168–76.
54. For a detailed examination of the relationship between the two versions of the sutta, see Ānandajoti, http://www.ancient-buddhist-texts.net/Buddhist-Texts/C1-Ratanasutta/Ratanasutta.pdf.
55. There is a problem, here, however, in relation to the formal declarations of the discourses that the noble disciple is free from *four* bad destinations, which deviates from the usual specification in the Nikāyas of three bad destinations. On this see note 982.
56. The allowance to eat meat "pure in three respects" (*tikoṭiparisuddha*) is at Vin I 238,7–9. See too MN I 369,7–10: "In three

cases, Jīvaka, I say that meat may be eaten: when it has not been seen, heard, or suspected [that the animal was killed for oneself]." (*Tīhi kho ahaṃ, jīvaka, ṭhānehi maṃsaṃ paribhogan ti vadāmi. Adiṭṭhaṃ, asutaṃ, aparisaṅkitaṃ – imehi kho ahaṃ, jīvaka, tīhi ṭhānehi maṃsaṃ paribhogan ti vadāmi.*) While the Buddha's last meal has been a subject of scholarly debate, at AN III 49,19–23 he tells a lay supporter that he will accept a dish of pork (*sūkaramaṃsa*).

57. Jayawickrama discusses the different ways of construing the title at PBR 1976, 143–46. He here argues in favor of *artha* over *aṭṭhaka* as the original sense, but in his translation of Sn he renders the title "Chapter of the Eights."
58. Bapat (1951, 10–12) briefly compares the stories in the two traditions and finds that "no less than seven of the sixteen Chinese stories introducing these sūtras are quite different from those in Pāli." I would say that it is remarkable that nine of the stories show some correspondence, which suggests that they originate from a common source. Bapat also says in connection with the stories: "It is found that the Chinese translator has often misunderstood the original and so his translation is not correct."
59. At **1086**a the four are joined in a compound, *diṭṭhasutamutaviññātesu*.
60. Jayawickrama (PBR 1978, 50) notes twenty occurrences of the group in the Aṭṭhakavagga. They occur in connection with views about the means to purification at **790**b (= **797**b, **887**a), **793**b, **798**c, **802**a, **887**a, **1082**cd (= **1083**cd).
61. MN I 135,23–24: *Kullūpamo mayā dhammo desito nittharaṇatthāya, no gahaṇatthāya.*
62. Jayawickrama (PBR 1976, 150–56) cites both internal and external evidence pointing to the later origins of the *vatthugāthā*. He conjectures that the earliest date for this section is the second century B.C.E.
63. There is indication of this in the Apadāna. In his verses at Ap II 486–87 (vv. 347–49), Mogharāja says that he was born into a khattiya family and ascended to rulership but could find no joy because he was afflicted with a skin disease. He therefore renounced the throne and went forth into homelessness as a pupil of the brahmin Bāvari. Ajita, in his verses at Ap I 337 (vv. 511–13), states that he renounced the home life and went forth under Bāvari. He heard about the Buddha while he was dwelling in the Himalayas (*himavante vasanto'haṃ, assosiṃ lokanāyakaṃ*) and approached him in quest of the supreme goal. This contradicts the report of the *vatthugāthā* that he came up from the south.

Notes to the Suttanipāta

64. On parenthetical lines identifying the speaker, the person being addressed, or both, see pp. 34–35.
65. Reading with Ce and Be *gavampatīdha atthi*, as against Ee *gavampatī ca atthi*. Norman too prefers *gavampatīdha*; see GD 149–50.
66. Be and Ce have the plural here, *bhavanti snehā*, while Ee has the singular *bhavati sneho*. Pj II has the singular in the lemma: Be *bhavati sneho*, Ce and Ee *bhavati sineho*.
67. Be *sajjamāno* must be a typographical error. Nidd II 219 (Be) and Pj II (Be) both read *asajjamāno*.
68. Reading *saṃsīnapatto* with Ce and Ee in both text and Pj II, as against Be *sañchinnapatto*. See note 453.
69. The verse is identical with Dhp 328.
70. Or, on the alternative interpretation suggested by Pj II, "the country he has ruled." See note 461.
71. The first three lines are identical with Dhp 329a–c.
72. For a discussion of my rendering of this line, see note 503.
73. Pj II explains that the four *brahmavihāras* are stated out of sequence for metrical reasons.
74. For the most part I adopt from Norman (at GD 9) the renderings of terms related to plowing.
75. I follow Pj II's explanation of *maggajina*, as against Norman's suggestion that *jina* is derived from *jña*. See note 594.
76. I read with Be and Ce *maggakkhāyī*, as against Ee *maggajjhāyī*. See GD 175.
77. *Dutiyaṃ bhikkhunaṃ*. I take this as an accusative singular. See note 598.
78. I take the correct reading to be *n'etādisā ti* (< *na* + *etādisā*), as in the lemma of Pj II (Ee). See note 604.
79. On the basis of the Skt parallel, I would change the nominative *saddhā* to accusative *saddhaṃ*. See note 605.
80. I read here with Ce and Ee *padissati*, as against Be *padussati*, and in the next line *dissati* as against *dussati*.
81. *Timbaru*: a kind of fruit, probably the size of the breasts of a girl still in puberty.
82. I read *'dha* (= *idha*) with Ce and Ee as against Be *ca*.
83. Pj II calls it the Aggikabhāradvājasutta, after the brahmin.
84. I here follow Be *pānaṃ vihiṃsati*, as against Ce and Ee *pānāni hiṃsati*. Pj II recognizes both readings, which were apparently already found in the manuscripts available to the commentator. See p. 549.
85. Except for the last line, the verse is identical with **98**.
86. Except for the last line, the verse is identical with **100**.

87. I translate on the basis of the alternative reading, *upaṭṭhitaṃ*, in place of *upaṭṭhite*. Pj II recognizes both readings.
88. I translate on the basis of the alternative reading *asantaṃ*, in place of the primary reading *asataṃ*. Pj II recognizes both readings.
89. *Brāhmaṇā mantabandhavā*. Literally "brahmins who are kinsmen of the sacred hymns."
90. According to a note in Ee, these verses were included in only two of the Burmese-script manuscripts available to the editors. However, Pj II comments on them, and Be and Ce take them as authentic and give them separate numbers.
91. Ee punctuates as if **163–67** were all spoken by Sātāgira. Pj II, however, explains that **163**[A] was spoken by Hemavata, **163**[B]**–64** by Sātāgira, **165–66** by Hemavata, and **167** by both yakkhas together. For clarity I have added the speakers' names in brackets, following the ascriptions in Pj II.
92. Reading with Be and Ce *vīro* as against Ee *dhīro*. The gloss in Pj II clearly supports *vīro*.
93. The parallel at SN I 215,2 has a couplet here not in the Sn version: *asmā lokā paraṃ lokaṃ, evaṃ pecca na socati*, "That is how one does not sorrow when passing from this world to the next."
94. Pj II says that this text is also called the Kāyavicchandanika-sutta, "The Discourse on Removing Desire for the Body."
95. Be counts this line as the beginning of a new verse, which it numbers 234. Such a division seems arbitrary, even mistaken. I follow Ce and Ee, which treat this as a single verse of eight lines.
96. I read *bhuñjasi/bhuñjasī* with Be and the lemma in all three editions of Pj II, as against Ce and Ee *bhuñjatī*.
97. Reading *viditindriyo* with Be and Ce and all three editions of Pj II, as against Ee *vijitindriyo*. While *vijitindriyo* makes better sense, the gloss by Pj II, *ñātapariññāya chaḷindriyāni viditvā pākaṭāni katvā careyya*, confirms that the commentator read *viditindriyo*.
98. In pāda b I read *sakhāham* with Ce and Ee, as against Be *tavāham*. On the reading of pāda c, see note 1031. Pāda d needs a word to complete the sense. I adopt "friend" from Pj II.
99. This and the Buddha's reply are also at I,10, p. 185.
100. Most editions of Sn and SN 10:3, as well as their commentaries, read: *kumārakā dhaṅkam iv' ossajanti*. A variant *vaṅkam* is found in several manuscripts. Anderson and Smith chose *vaṅkam* for their edition of Sn, but in his edition of Pj II, Smith replaced it with *dhaṅkaṃ*, which I adopt. Norman discusses the line at GD 211–12.
101. Be numbers both the preceding verse and this one 274. How-

ever, Pj II (Be) numbers the two verses 274 and 275, and thus at this point the numbering of Pj II (Be) outstrips that of Sn (Be) by one.

102. The text calls this the Dhammacariyasutta, but Pj II titles it the Kapilasutta with reference to the commentarial background story.
103. Be includes the last couplet here in the following verse, but I follow Ce and Ee.
104. Reading with Be *tato devā pitaro ca*, also adopted by Norman and apparently supported by Pj II.
105. Reading *patiṃ bhariyā'vamaññatha.*
106. Pj II comments on this sutta under its alternative title, Dhammasutta, "On Dhamma," but mentions its primary title.
107. I prefer Ee *sutañca viññātaṃ samādhisāraṃ* to Be and Ce *sutañca viññātasamādhisāraṃ*. The latter reading is adopted by all three editions of Pj II, but the line makes better sense if *viññātaṃ* is taken as a distinct subject.
108. This pāda, as it has come down in Ee, is missing three syllables. Both Be and Ce duplicate a word, *pamādo rajo pamādo*. In the parallel, Th 404, Ce reads *pamādo rajo sabbadā* (Be *pamādo rajo pamādo*; Ee *pamādo rajo*). Pj II does not cite a lemma, but its comment, *na hi kadāci pamādo nāma arajo atthi*, may have been based on an original that had *sabbadā*. I translate on the assumption *sabbadā* should be added to the line.
109. Pj II comments on this sutta under its alternative title, Nigrodhakappasutta, but mentions its primary title. The verses are also at Th 1263–78.
110. See note 1212.
111. All three editions use the plural *pucchāma*, but Th 1263 has the singular *pucchāmi*.
112. I read with Be *vīra*, as against Ce and Ee *dhīra*. The gloss in Pj II, *padhānaviriyasamannāgata*, indicates that *vīra* was the reading available to the commentator.
113. With Be, I would insert a space, reading *vaggu vagguṃ*, taking *vaggu* as a vocative and *vagguṃ* in apposition to *giraṃ*.
114. I read with Be and Ce *sutaṃ pavassa*, as against Ee *sutassavassa*.
115. Reading *uppātā* with Be and Ce, defined by DOP as "an unusual or startling event, taken as a portent."
116. Reading with Ee and Pj II *sabbūpadhīnaṃ parikkhayā*, as against Be *sabbupadhīnaṃ parikkhayāno* and Ce *sabbupadhinaṃ parikkhayāno*. See Sn (Ee) p. 65, note 9.
117. Norman reads *mantayitvā jagāma*. *Jagāma* is a perfect form of *gacchati*. See note 1280.
118. I read here with Be and Ce *taṃ no vada* as against Ee *tvaṃ no vada*. Pj II recognizes the latter as a variant but gives primacy to the former.

119. Vāsava is another name for Sakka, ruler of the devas.
120. I read here with Ce and Ee *dharātha*, as against Be *carātha*.
121. Ce and Ee have *gāmaṃ* as against Be *gāme*.
122. With Be and Ce I read *va*, as against Ee *ca*. The gloss *viya* in Pj II supports *va*.
123. Reading *tato* with Ce and Ee, as against Be *tayo*, "three (messengers)."
124. I read with Ce and Ee *aṇumattenapi puññena attho*, as against Be *aṇumattopi puññena attho*.
125. I read with Be and Ce, and all three editions of Pj II, *dhiratthu mama jīvitaṃ*. Ee has *idha* for *mama*.
126. I read with Be *bhecchāmi*, corresponding to *bhetsyāmi* at Mvu II 240,11. Ce and Ee have *gacchāmi*.
127. I here follow Be, which reads *paṭibhāti maṃ bhagavā, paṭibhāti maṃ sugatā ti*. Ee omits the utterance addressed to *bhagavā*, while Ce has *bhagavā* in both utterances.
128. On my rendering of this verse, see note 1368 below, and CDB 461–62, note 510.
129. Pj II comments on this discourse under its alternative title, the Pūraḷāsasutta, "The Sacrificial Cake." The sutta has a part-parallel at SN 7:9, with a similar prose opening but with only a few shared verses.
130. Ee prints this sentence as prose but includes it under verse 457 (in its numbering scheme). Be numbers it as if it were a distinct two-line verse and Ce incorporates it as part of the verse that includes the following lines. In several of the following stanzas, too, it is uncertain whether the lines are to be taken as prose or verse. For details, see Norman's comments on each verse in GD.
131. Sāvittī (Skt Sāvitrī) is a verse or prayer addressed to the sun, especially the celebrated verse of the Ṛgveda, III,62,10, also called Gāyatrī.
132. Norman treats this sentence as part of the verse, but with Be and Ee I take it to be a prose interjection. Ce counts this sentence as a separate verse.
133. The text here changes from the singular to the plural.
134. I translate this line in accordance with its evident meaning rather than in compliance with the interpretation proposed by Pj II. See note 1392.
135. I translate on the basis of Ee, which reads *yo attanā attānaṃ nānupassati*. Be has *yo attano attānaṃ nānupassati*, while Ce has *yo attanāttānaṃ nānupassati*, which seems to support Ee.
136. Ee prints the last two lines here as prose, Be and Ce represent them as verse. Norman writes: "I am uncertain about the metre" (GD 250).

137. Reading *kathaṃ* with Be as against Ce and Ee *kattha*, "where?" All three editions of Pj II read *kathaṃ* in the construal.
138. Be reads pādas ab *yesu na māyā vasati na māno, khīṇāsavā vūsitabrahmacariyā*, followed by the refrain. Be then adds another verse in which pādas ab read *ye vītalobhā amamā nirāsā, khīṇāsavā vūsitabrahmacariyā*, followed by the refrain. In Ce and Ee, which I follow, the additional verse is absent. Rather, in **494** the first line of the additional verse in Be becomes pāda b, and there is no line *khīṇāsavā vūsitabrahmacariyā*.
139. In this verse the subject changes from the plural *ye* of the preceding verses (with its attributes also in the plural) to the singular *yo vedagū*, and the recipient of the offering changes, correspondingly, from plural *tesu* to singular *tamhi*.
140. *Ken'attanā gacchati brahmalokaṃ*. I render this line in accordance with the gloss of Pj II: *ken'attanā ti kena kāraṇena*. See note 1423.
141. Ee prints these lines (and the parallel lines in the next verse) as prose, but Norman proposes that they "can be taken as Śloka meter, with resolution of the sixth syllable in pāda d and of the first syllable in pāda e" (GD 255–56). Hence I include them in the verses.
142. Norman suggests taking *sādhu* and *samāhito* separately (GD 258), but since Pj II explains them jointly with a single comment, I take *sādhusamāhito* as a compound.
143. I read with Be *sa brahmā*. Ce omits *sa* and Ee puts it in brackets, but Norman points out that the meter requires it. Pj II identifies *brahmā* here with *brāhmaṇo*, and thus I use "brahmin" to maintain consistency between the question and the answer.
144. All three editions read *suddhipañño*, as does the lemma in Pj II (Be). The lemma in Pj II (Ce and Ee) has *suddhapañño*, "one of pure wisdom."
145. Following the gloss in Pj II, I read the compound *viriyavāso*. Norman and Jayawickrama have both adopted this reading.
146. All three editions of both text and Pj II read *dhīro*, but I accept Norman's proposal (at GD 262) that we read *vīro*, "hero," which matches the question and the theme of the verse.
147. Readings vary here: Ce *ājāni* and Ee *ajāni* are both aorists, while Be *ājānāti* is present indicative. Norman does not have a note on these variants. All three editions of Pj II have *ājānāti*, but an aorist works better.
148. I read with Be *uddhamadho tiriyañvāpi majjhe*. Ce and Ee have *cāpi* for *vāpi*, but all three editions of Pj II read *vāpi* in the lemma.
149. I read with Ee *parivajjayitā*, which corresponds to *parivarjayitvā* at Mvu III 400,13. Both Ce and Be have *paribbājayitvā*, "having banished," the reading adopted by Pj II.

150. *Oghatam*, as Norman points out (GD 264), is a contraction of *oghatamaṃ*.
151. Both Be and Ee print *nāganāgassa*, without hiatus, but I follow Ce, which has *nāga nāgassa*, supported by Pj II; see note 1496.
152. I add this phrase on the authority of Pj II, which says: *dhammadesanan ti pāṭhaseso*.
153. The verse is identical with **545**.
154. The verse is identical with **546**.
155. I accept Norman's suggestion that we read *niccaṃ* for *pāto*. See note 1564.
156. I adopt the variant *paralokito*, divided as *paralok'ito*, following Norman at GD 73.
157. Literally "It is not possible for me." I add the phrase in brackets based on Pj II. See p. 956.
158. Reading *bho* in place of Ee *kho*.
159. I have added the section headings here and below.
160. I render *jāti* variously, according to context, as "birth," "class," and "kind."
161. Reading with Be *paccattañca sarīresu* as against Ce and Ee *paccattaṃ sasarīresu*. MN (Ce) has *paccattaṃ ca sarīresu*.
162. *Yājako*. More literally, one who performs the sacrifice.
163. I read *sace* with Be and Ce and all three editions of Pj II, as against Ee *sa ve*. MN (Ce) has *sace*.
164. Following Norman, I read with Be and Ce *yo 'dha* as against Ee *yo ca*.
165. I read with Ce *nirāsasaṃ* (Be *nirāsāsaṃ*) as against Ee *nirāsayaṃ*.
166. Compare with **136**.
167. In Ee the name appears as Kokāliya, but Be and Ce of Sn, and all three editions of Pj II, have Kokālika. Norman (at GD 148) comments on *ka / ya* alternation in Pāli names.
168. The *āmalaka* (Sinhala, *artalu*), or myrobalan, is a medicinal fruit roughly the size of an olive.
169. The *beḷuva* (Sinhala, *belli*) is a hard-shelled fruit that can grow to the size of a large orange.
170. *Yo sugatesu manaṃ padosaye*. See note 1623 on the wider use of the term *sugata*.
171. On these large units of measurement, see p. 972.
172. The parallels, SN 6:10 and AN 10:89, end here.
173. In adding closing quotation marks, I follow Pj II, which ascribes the next series of verses to Moggallāna or (according to some) Mahābrahmā.
174. In this verse and those that follow, I assign in brackets the subjects of the action based on the ascriptions in Pj II.
175. I read with Be and Ce *kilissati*, as against Ee *kilijjati*, which Pj II recognizes as an alternative. See note 1640.

176. I follow Pj II, which explains that "brown [and] spotted" in pāda b should be connected with "dogs" in pāda c rather than with "ravens" in pāda b (*sāmā sabalā ti etaṃ parato soṇā ti iminā yojetabbaṃ*).
177. Here Ce and Ee have *paṭigijjhā*; so too the Thai edition. Be has *paṭigiddhā*. See note 1644.
178. Pj II 477,13–14 says: "These last two verses are not in the text-reading explicated in the Great Commentary" (*avasāne gāthādvayameva pana mahā-aṭṭhakathāyaṃ vinicchitapāṭhe natthi*). Hence I do not enclose them in quotation marks but treat them as a later addition.
179. *Isivhaye vane*. This alludes to Isipatana, where the Buddha gave his first discourse.
180. Reading *vivarati* with Be as against Ce and Ee *vicarati*.
181. Be and Ce read *samānabhāgaṃ*, as against Ee *samānabhāvaṃ*. The lemma of Pj II in all three editions has *–bhāgaṃ*, as does the Skt parallel at Mvu III 387,6.
182. I read pāda d *eko ce abhiramissasi* with Be and Ee.
183. *Atha bhāsihi* (Be *bhāhisi*) *dasadisā* appears to be an extra line. Pj II suggests it belongs with the next verse, but it makes better sense here, as in Be. Either way we would wind up with an irregular verse of five lines.
184. As Pj II explains, *samaṇo* here refers to the Buddha. See p. 996.
185. Here and below I have added the subheadings to make explicit the topic of the section.
186. The text uses the plural *upadhīnaṃ* in the prose portion but the singular accusative *upadhiṃ* in the verse. On *upadhi* see pp. 61–62.
187. I read with Ce and Ee *nāgacchanti*, as against Be *na te gacchanti*.
188. I read here with Ce and Be *evaṃ tattha vijānāti* as against Ee *evaṃ tattha virajjati*. But see note 1735.
189. I read with Be *vikkhīṇo jātisaṃsāro*, as against Ce and Ee *vitiṇṇo jātisaṃsāro*.
190. I read with Be *arūpesu asaṇṭhitā*, as against Ce and Ee *arūpesu susaṇṭhitā*, "well settled in formless states." See It 62,9 where all editions have *arūpesu asaṇṭhitā*, glossed by It-a II 42,16 *arūpabhavesu appatiṭṭhahantā*.
191. Ee is missing *sabrahmakassa*, present in Be and Ce. Both Norman and Jayawickrama translate on the basis of Ee here.
192. Be and Ce treat the last two pādas of this verse and the first two pādas of the next as a separate verse, thus reading three verses of four pādas each. I follow Ee, which has two verses of six pādas each.
193. It is necessary to read this line with the punctuation as in Ee *magā dhammass' akovidā*. Be *maggā dhammassa kovidā* and Ce *magā dhammassa 'kovidā* should be amended accordingly.

194. *Sa kena gaccheyya anūpayo so*. I add "astray" in brackets to capture the purport of the various explanations offered by Pj II and Niddesa. See p. 1049.
195. I read with Be *evābhijānaṃ* (= *evaṃ abhijānaṃ*), supported by the glosses in Pj II and Niddesa. Ce and Ee have *etābhijānaṃ* (= *etad abhijānaṃ*).
196. The text has *vedehi* (a plural), perhaps to set up a contrast with the Vedas of the brahmins.
197. I take *sūra* here, which means "hero," to be a short form of the adversary's name, Pasūra.
198. Reading with Ce and Ee *elambujaṃ kaṇṭakaṃ vārijaṃ yathā*. Be has *jalambujaṃ*.
199. Reading with Ce and Ee *diṭṭhiyā* as against Be *diṭṭhiyāyako*.
200. In the Pāli itself this is a verse of five pādas.
201. With Ce and Ee, I read the plural *phassā*. Be has the singular *phasso*, as does the citation of the verse in Niddesa.
202. Against Ee *icchā na santyā*, I read with Be and Ce the locative absolute *icchāy'asantyā*. This is the reading of the line as cited in Niddesa, supported by the gloss.
203. This is another five pāda verse.
204. I read *pan'eke* here with Be and Ce, as against Ee *pun'eke*.
205. Reading with Ce and Ee *bālo mago* as against Be *bālomako*.
206. There are both negative and affirmative readings of this line. I follow the affirmative reading of Ee *sandiṭṭhiyā ce pana vīvadātā*, as against the negative readings of Ce *sandiṭṭhiyā c'eva na vevadātā* and Be *sandiṭṭhiyā c'eva na vīvadātā*. Pj II glosses on the basis of the negative reading but admits the affirmative as an alternative.
207. I read the text as in Be and Ce, *yasmiṃ pajā no vivade pajānaṃ*, which is supported by Pj II. Ee has *yasmiṃ pajāno vivade pajānaṃ*.
208. Reading with Ce and Ee *tath'eva* as against Be *tadeva*.
209. I follow Norman in reading *suddhi* here in place of *suddhiṃ*, found in all three editions.
210. With Ee, I read *tapūpanissāya*, followed by Norman. Be and Ce have *tamūpanissāya*. See note 1961.
211. I read with Ce and Ee *sadhammapūjā ca pana tath'eva*. Be's *saddhammapūjā* should be corrected.
212. Reading with Be and Ce *subbinayo* for Ee *suddhināyo*. Pj II (Ee) also has *subbinayo* in the lemma.
213. I follow Be here in reading the absolutive *saṅkhā*, as against Ce and Ee, which have the present participle *saṅkhaṃ*. Pj II and Niddesa both gloss the word as an absolutive. See p. 1165.
214. Reading with Be *vippamutto*, as against Ce and Ee *vippayutto*.
215. Apparently "he" (*so*) here refers to "that Blessed One," the Buddha, in pāda c, not to the monk.

216. Reading with Be and Ce *na sīdati,* as against Ee *nisīdati.*
217. *Tattha sikkhānugīyanti.* This seems to be a remark by the compilers that was absorbed into the sutta. See note 2009.
218. I read with Ce and Ee *gathitāni.*
219. Though all three editions have *pakappanaṃ,* with Pj II (Be) I read *pakampanaṃ* (*kampanaṃ* in Ce and Ee).
220. Reading with Ce *kāci nisaṅkhiti.*
221. I read with Be and Ce *agataṃ disaṃ,* as against Ee *amataṃ disaṃ.* Pj II and Niddesa clearly comment on *agataṃ.*
222. Reading with Be and Ce *so tesu.* Ee *sotesu* should be corrected.
223. Ee numbers the Introductory Verses section as "1" and Ajita's Questions as "2," with the number indicating the speaker in parenthesis after the section title. To maintain correspondence between the section numbers and the brahmin students, I leave the Introductory Verses section unnumbered and begin the section numbering with Ajita's Questions.
224. I follow Ce, which has the name as *Bāvari,* followed too by Norman. Be and Ee have the name as *Bāvarī.*
225. Reading with Be and Ce *sabbakammakkhayaṃ.* Ee *sabbadhammakkhayaṃ* should be corrected accordingly.
226. Reading with Ce and Ee *namassemu* as againt Be *passemu,* "might see."
227. Reading with Ce *sataraṃsiva* (Be *sataraṃsiṃ va*). Norman accepts Ee *vītaraṃsi va,* but *sataraṃsi* occurs elsewhere: *suvaṇṇavaṇṇaṃ sambuddhaṃ, sataraṃsiṃva bhāṇumaṃ* at Ap I 130, I 146, and *suvaṇṇavaṇṇaṃ sambuddhaṃ, sataraṃsiṃva uggataṃ* at Ap I 191.
228. Following Norman and Jayawickrama, I have not translated the word *māṇava,* "brahmin student," in the section titles.
229. This question is also found at **458**, where a discussion about the purpose of sacrifice seems more appropriate.
230. The last two pādas of this stanza, together with the next, constitute **728**, a six-pāda stanza.
231. Be has *pajānaṃ* as against Ce and Ee *hi jānaṃ.* Niddesa has *pajānaṃ,* which is supported by the synonyms that follow. In **728** both Ce and Ee have *pajānaṃ.*
232. I read with Be *sahissāmi* as against Ce and Ee *gamissāmi.* See note 2097.
233. I read the verb as the first person *tareyyaṃ,* with Be and Ce and all three editions of Nidd II, as against Ee *tareyya.*
234. All three editions have *vimutto* here but Ce has *dhimutto* (= *adhimutto*) in the parallel line of the next verse. Pj II does not cite the line, but Niddesa has *dhimutto.* See note 2103.
235. Ee's *bhavetha* should be corrected to *cavetha.* I have added "or" in brackets, following the explanations of Niddesa and Pj II. Norman, however, does not see alternatives here, but trans-

lates: "If he should remain there . . . would consciousness disappear for him in such a state?"

236. Ee *yathā* here and just below in the reply should be corrected to *yatā*, as in Be and Ce.
237. In Ce this line begins a new verse, while in Be and Ee this line and those that follow are included in the same verse as the preceding lines.
238. I follow the verse division of Be and Ce, which is also supported by Nidd II. Ee takes *nāhaṃ tattha abhiramiṃ* as the beginning of the next verse.
239. Here and in the reply I read *nirāsaso* with Be and Ce as against Ee *nirāsayo*.
240. The text has *apanamissanti ito*, without specifying the subject of the plural verb. The subject must be the various peoples (*nānājanā*) mentioned in the next verse.
241. Reading with Be and Ce *evaṃ etaṃ*, as against Ee *evam evaṃ*.
242. In Be and Ce this section is titled Pārāyanatthutigāthā. Ee does not give it a title. Ee numbers this section "18" but I follow Be and Ce, which do not number it.
243. In Be and Ce this section is titled Pārāyanānugītigāthā. Ee does not give it a title.
244. Reading with Be and Ce *nāgo*, as against Ee *nātho*. *Nāgo* is confirmed by the gloss in Niddesa.
245. As at **1084**.
246. Reading with Be and Ce *jutimā*.

Notes to the Suttanipāta Commentary

247. There is a word play here. The Suttanipāta is included in the Khuddaka Nikāya, the "Minor Collection," but it was taught by the Buddha, who had abandoned all minor conduct (*khuddācārappahāyinā*). Be has another verse following this one that is not included in Ce or Ee but is cited in a footnote in Ee. Since the verse simply repeats the author's purpose in composing this commentary, it seems redundant and I do not include it. There is a discrepancy between the last line here (pāda c of the Pāli) and in the same verse at the end of the work, where *lokanittharaṇesinā*, "sought to ferry the world across," replaces *lokanissaraṇesinā*, "sought the escape from the world." See p. 1329.
248. These are three of the nine genres into which the teachings are classified in the Nikāyas; see MN I 133,24–25, AN II 103,9–11, etc. *Gāthā* are verses. *Geyya* are discourses in mixed prose and verse. *Vyākaraṇa* are explanations and expositions. Since *sutta* is the first of these nine types—presumably in the narrow sense of

discourses given in straight prose—the author is posing the question why this work is called "Suttanipāta" when it includes texts from other genres besides suttas in this narrow sense.

249. The answer here is intended to give the word *sutta* a wider meaning. I follow the word order of Ce and Ee. In Be *sūcanato* and *savanā* are reversed. A similar explanation of *sutta* is at As 19,15–16.
250. Reading with Ce and Ee *saṅgīto ca*. Be has *samūhato*.
251. Reading with Ce and Ee *pamāṇattena*, as against Be *pamāṇantena*. On *tādī*—Impartial One—as an epithet of the Buddha, see pp. 59–60.
252. Pj II is here counting each of the *pucchās* or "question sections" of the Pārāyanavagga as a sutta but not the introductory verses (the *vatthugāthā*) or the epilogue.
253. Dīpaṅkara was the twenty-fourth buddha, counting back, under whom the future Buddha Gotama first received the prediction of future buddhahood. See Bv 8–10, Ja I 12–16.
254. According to Sp IV 760, this tree was not in Āḷavī but at the boundary of Jeta's Grove. The deity that had previously resided in that tree had passed away. Therefore it is described as abandoned (*vivitto*).
255. The rule is Pācittiya 11. The incident is recorded at Vin IV 34, commented upon with citation of the verses at Sp IV 760. The verse from the Uraga Sutta is commented on at Sp-ṭ III 16–17.
256. This may sound redundant in English, but Pj II is here glossing the relatively rare word *uppatitaṃ* with the more common *uppannaṃ*, both meaning "arisen."
257. (1) *Vattamāna*, (2) *bhutvāpagata*, (3) *okāsakata*, (4) *bhūmiladdha*.
258. This refers to the three temporal phases of all conditioned things: *uppāda* (arising), *ṭhiti* (duration), and *bhaṅga* (dissolution), based on the canonical statement: "There are, bhikkhus, three defining characteristics of the conditioned. What three? An arising is perceived, a vanishing is perceived, the alteration of that which stands is perceived" (AN I 152,6–9).
259. A parenthetical citation in Pj II (Be) refers this to MN III 164,25–28, which is slightly different: *Yāni'ssa pubbe pāpakāni kammāni katāni kāyena duccaritāni vācāya duccaritāni manasā duccaritāni tāni'ssa tamhi samaye olambanti ajjholambanti abhippalambanti*. See too AN II 172,11–15: *'Yāni kho pana tāni pubbe attanā katāni pāpakāni kammāni saṃkilesikāni ponobhavikāni sadarāni dukkhavipākāni āyatiṃ jātijarāmaraṇikāni, tesaṃ vipāko mā nibbattī' ti natthi koci pāṭibhogo – samaṇo vā brāhmaṇo vā devo vā māro vā brahmā vā koci vā lokasmiṃ*. ("There can be no guarantor, neither an ascetic, nor a brahmin, a deva, Māra, Brahmā, or anyone in the world, that bad kamma—defiled, conducive to renewed existence,

troublesome, ripening in suffering, leading to future birth, old age, and death—will not produce its result.")

260. Be has two sentences here that seem superfluous and are not in Ce or Ee: *Tena hi sā bhūmiladdhā nāma hotī ti. Tasmā bhūmiladdhan ti vuccati.* I exclude them from the translation.

261. The youth Soreyya gave rise to a lustful thought regarding Mahākaccāna and thereupon turned into a woman; the story is at Dhp-a I 325 (BL 2:23). The rape of Uppalavaṇṇā is at Vin III 35,1–7, with more details at Dhp-a II 48–50 (BL 2:27–29). Here the rapist is said to have been a cousin of hers named Nanda. After he raped her, the earth split open beneath him and he fell into the Avīci hell.

262. That is, the base (*vatthu*) of the defilements is the set of aggregates of one in whom the defilements arise, not the aggregates of the person that these defilements take as an object. Thus, when Soreyya felt lust for Mahākaccāna, his own aggregates were the base of those defilements, their ground, that in which those defilements gained ground. The lust itself was "that which has gained ground." As long as these defilements remain, even if only as latent tendencies, they are still considered "arisen in the sense of that which has gained ground." It is only when they have been eradicated that they cannot be considered "arisen" in this sense.

263. I read here with Ce and Ee *na paresaṃ khandhā* as against Be *na itare khandhā*.

264. I follow Ee, which reads *icc'assa kammakilesapaccayā vaṭṭaṃ vaṭṭati*. Be and Ce have *icc'assa kilesappaccayā vaṭṭaṃ vaḍḍhati*. The parallel passage at Vism 688,13–14 has the same reading as Ee here.

265. *Kiriyabhāvamattaṃ*. This expression refers to the Abhidhamma classification of an arahant's actions, including his states of mind, as *kiriya*, deeds, rather than *kamma*; they are so classified because they are incapable of generating *vipāka*, kammic results, whether in this life or in future lives. On the concept of *kiriya* in relation to an arahant's deeds, see CMA 49–51.

266. I read here with Ce *na āyatiṃ punabbhavābhinibbattadhammatamāgamma bhavantarasantānaṃ nibbattetuṃ samattho hoti*, as against Be *āyatiṃ punabbhavābhinibbattadhammatamāgamma bhavantarasantānaṃ nibbattetuṃ samattho na hoti*. Logically, the sense does not differ between the two, but the Ce reading makes it clearer that the negation applies to the entire clause.

267. (1) *Samudācāra*, (2) *ārammaṇādhiggahita*, (3) *avikkhambhita*, (4) *asamūhata*.

268. *Vattamānuppannameva samudācāruppannaṃ*. This is the same as the first of the previous set of four.

269. The idea that the arising of defilements is unavoidable (*avassaṃ*) seems problematic, but Vism-mhṭ II 472 (VRI §837), commenting on a similar passage at Vism II 689,7–10, says: "*Definite arising*: because, when there is a convergence of conditions, their arising is certain on account of the occurrence of careless attention in such a way" (*ekantena uppattito ti paccayasamavāye sati tathā ayonisomanasikārassa tattha nibbattattā niyamena uppajjanato*).

270. Mp I 23,3–9 mentions a young monk who had gone from his own monastery, the Kalyāṇi Mahāvihāra, to another monastery to study. After finishing his recitation, he walked for alms in the village despite warnings from his elders, and his attention became fixated on a woman he saw on alms round. After returning to his own dwelling, he caught sight of the cloth that she had worn that day (collected by another monk from the charnel ground) and realized she had just died. Thinking of her, he was so consumed by the fire of lust that he died.

271. This alludes to the Abhidhamma depiction of the mind as a series of discrete occasions of cognition. Since defiled mental acts and wholesome mental acts cannot occur simultaneously, the effort to dispel defilements must occur either on occasions of mind subsequent to those when the defilements actually arise or in advance, to prevent the arising of defilements on a later occasion. Defilement and the cleansing of a defilement cannot occur at the same mind-moment.

272. *Sīlasaṃvaro, satisaṃvaro, ñāṇasaṃvaro, khantisaṃvaro, viriyasaṃvaro.* Pj II will exemplify each of these types of restraint by citing texts to which they are applicable.

273. *Tadaṅgappahānaṃ, vikkhambhanappahānaṃ, samucchedappahānaṃ, paṭippassaddhippahānaṃ, nissaraṇappahānaṃ.*

274. The Pāli here is far from transparent. Vism 693,34–694,3 offers a clearer definition of this type of abandoning. The passage is translated by Ñāṇamoli (at Ppn 22.112) thus: "But what is called *abandoning by substitution of opposites* [= 'abandoning in a particular respect'] is the abandoning of any given state that ought to be abandoned by means of a particular factor of knowledge which, as a constituent of insight, is opposed to it, like the abandoning of darkness at night by means of a light" (*yaṃ pana rattibhāge samujjalitena padīpena andhakārassa viya tena tena vipassanāya avayavabhūtena ñāṇaṅgena paṭipakkhavaseneva tassa tassa pahātabbadhammassa pahānaṃ, idaṃ tadaṅgappahānaṃ nāma*).

275. Also at Vism 694,3–12, Ppn 22.112. The last here is not in the series at Vism 694.

276. That is, thought and examination (*vitakka-vicāra*) are opposed

states (*paccanīkadhammā*) of the second jhāna, rapture (*pīti*) of the third jhāna, etc. With the attainment of access concentration or the first jhāna, the five hindrances are suppressed; with the second jhāna, thought and examination are suppressed; with the third jhāna, rapture is suppressed, etc.

277. Reading with Be and Ce *kilesagahanassa*, as against Ee *kilesagaṇassa*.

278. I read here with Ce *yaṃ pana phalakkhaṇe paṭippassaddhattaṃ kilesānaṃ, idaṃ paṭippassaddhippahānaṃ*. Be adds *pahānaṃ* after *kilesānaṃ*, but this addition is not found in the definition of the same term in other commentaries—such as Spk, Paṭis-a, It-a—even in the Burmese editions.

279. "Each one" refers to removal by restraint and removal by abandoning.

280. These are not relevant here because subsidence occurs on the occasion of the fruit, and the escape is nibbāna. Neither is a kind of removal that is actually practiced, as is explained just below on p. 364.

281. Ten bases of resentment (*āghātavatthu*) are mentioned at AN 10:79 (V 150), but they are all described in terms of persons who cause resentment rather than natural conditions such as cold and heat.

282. Reading with Ce and Ee *tadaṅgappahātabb'ekaṭṭhaṃ*. Be has *tadaṅgappahātabbaṃ*.

283. *Kāmañc'ettha pahānavinayena vinayo na sambhavati, yehi pana dhammehi pahānaṃ hoti, tehi vinentopi pariyāyato "pahānavinayena vinetī" ti vuccati*. The purport seems to be that there are other methods of removing defilements besides those mentioned under "removal by abandoning," including those referred to in the sutta citations to follow. No matter what methods are used to remove a defilement, one removing it in such ways can be said in a manner of speaking (*pariyāyato*) to be removing it through "removal by abandoning." I am thankful to Petra Kieffer-Pülz for help in interpreting this passage.

284. Abandoning by subsidence occurs in the fruition stage (*phala*), and in this nothing is actually abandoned; the fruit arises through the actual abandoning of defilements by the path. The "abandoning by escape" is nibbāna, and since nibbāna is ever-existent it is not something to be produced by abandoning defilements.

285. The discourse is spoken by Sāriputta. The other four ways of removing resentment occur on the basis of his pure verbal conduct, on the basis of his occasional placidity of mind, on the basis of his complete failure in these three respects, and

on the basis of his success in these three respects (pure bodily conduct, pure verbal conduct, and placidity of mind).

286. Oddly Pj II considers the nine antidotes to resentment to be grounds of resentment.

287. *Aṭṭhāne ca kuppati* is mentioned at AN V 150,22.

288. *Avisesena hi pāran ti tīrassa nāmaṃ, tasmā orāni ca tāni saṃsārasāgarassa pārabhūtāni cā ti katvā orapāran ti vuccati.* This explanation is a strained attempt to solve the problem posed by the refrain, which extols the giving up of the "beyond" or far shore (*pāraṃ*) as well as the "here" or near shore (*oraṃ*). In standard Buddhist diction, *pāra* represents nibbāna, the escape from perilous saṃsāra, which is equated with *orimaṃ tīraṃ*, the near shore (see SN IV 175,14–15), but this cannot be the meaning here. Pj II offers more convincing explanations just below. We find a similar seeming "paradox" at Dhp 385, *yassa pāraṃ apāraṃ vā, pārāpāraṃ na vijjati . . . tamahaṃ brūmi brāhmaṇaṃ*. Here Dhp-a IV 141,9–10 interprets *pāraṃ* as the internal sense bases and *apāraṃ* as the external sense bases—exactly the opposite of the identifications given by Pj II. In a recent paper Dhivan Jones (2016, 85–88) interprets the refrain on the basis of the Simile of the Great Tree-Trunk at SN 35:241 (IV 179–81), where the near shore is identified with the internal sense bases and the far shore with the external sense bases (as in Pj II). It is possible that the refrain was not meant to be unequivocal in sense and that the alternative explanations Pj II offers of *orapāraṃ* are all partly valid. I take the primary meaning to be the giving up of existence in any realm, whether in this world (*oraṃ*) or in some higher world (*pāraṃ*). We find this idea suggested by the refrain often used by one who attains arahantship: "He understands: 'There is no [coming back] to another state of being'" (*nāparaṃ itthattāyā ti pajānāti*). Nyanaponika (2009, 8–9), while recognizing this as the primary meaning, holds that "'the here and the beyond' also applies to all those various discriminations, dichotomies, and pairs of opposites in which our minds habitually move." One thing that we can be sure of is that the antithesis between *oraṃ* and *pāraṃ* was not intended to convey the idea that the liberated bhikkhu transcends the duality of saṃsāra and nibbāna, which would be inconsistent with the basic standpoint of the Nikāyas.

289. The point seems to be that while, strictly speaking, the phrase "he gives up the here and the beyond" refers only to the arahant, who has given up attachment to all the pairs of opposites stated above, the non-returner is so described *in anticipation* of his assured abandoning of desire and lust on attaining arahantship.

290. *Kāmarūpī ca akāmarūpī ca.* I follow DOP here, which defines *kāmarūpī* as "having the ability to assume any form at will." The word occurs in this sense at Ap I 31 (v. 376c). At Mp I 397,18, this ability is ascribed to Māra, who assumed the form of the Buddha (*māro . . . attano kāmarūpitāya dasabalassa sarikkhakaṃ rūpaṃ māpetvā*) and tried to convince a lay follower that the five aggregates are sometimes permanent and eternal. See too the story at Vin I 86–87, about a serpent that assumed the form of a brahmin youth in order to be ordained as a bhikkhu. This led the Buddha to issue a rule that an animal should not be ordained.
291. The story also occurs at Dhp-a III 425–28 (BL 3:161–63).
292. The *asubhakammaṭṭhāna* consists in meditation either on the thirty-one (or thirty-two, with the addition of the brain) impure aspects of the body or on corpses in different stages of decay. On the former, see AN V 109,19–28. The meditation on the decay of a corpse is at Vism chap. 6.
293. *Imaṃ obhāsagāthaṃ abhāsi.* Sp-ṭ III 42 explains this expression to mean that he spoke verses after first sending forth light (*obhāsagāthaṃ abhāsī ti obhāsavissajjanapubbakabhāsitagāthā obhāsagāthā, taṃ abhāsī ti attho*).
294. This is said because Pj II has glossed the aorist *udacchidā* with present-tense verbs *ucchindati, bhañjati, vināseti.*
295. *Asesan ti sānusayaṃ.* Lust for sensual pleasures (*kāmarāgānusaya*) is one of the seven latent tendencies, on which see AN 7:11 (IV 9). In the word analysis (not translated) Pj II glosses *bhisapupphaṃ* with *padumapuppham*, and *saroruhaṃ* with *sare virūḷhaṃ*, taking *bhisapupphaṃ* as the noun—*bhisa* being the thick stalk of the lotus—and *saroruhaṃ* as an adjective describing the flower. Norman, at GD 139–40, takes *saroruhaṃ* as the noun and *bhisapupphaṃ* as an adjective. Pj II glosses *vigayha* with *ogayha pavisitvā*, "having entered," thus taking it as the absolutive of *vigāhati*. To support this, it relates a story of boys entering a lake and gathering lotuses. I follow Norman in taking *vigahya* as an absolutive of *viggaṇhāti* (= Skt *vigṛhya* in the sense of seizing). Brough (1962, 199) writes: "It can hardly be disputed that the sense of 'seizing' or 'plucking' the lotus flower is intended here."
296. There does not seem to be a sutta that reads exactly like this, but see AN I 216,5–8: *Ratto kho, āvuso, rāgena abhibhūto pariyādinnacitto attabyābādhāyapi ceteti, parabyābādhāyapi ceteti, ubhayabyābādhāyapi ceteti, cetasikampi dukkhaṃ domanassaṃ paṭisaṃvedeti.* ("Friend, inflamed and overcome by lust, with mind obsessed by it, one intends for one's own harm, the harm of others, and the harm of both, and one

experiences mental pain and dejection.") AN I 189,19–20 has: *Luddho panāyaṃ, kālāmā, purisapuggalo lobhena abhibhūto pariyādinnacitto pāṇampi hanati.* ("This greedy person, Kālāmas, with a mind overcome and obsessed by greed, destroys life.")

297. *Bhavagga* denotes the sphere of neither-perception-nor-nonperception, the highest plane in the formless realm, the most refined state of existence within saṃsāra.

298. Pj II evidently takes *saritaṃ* as a past participle, glossed *gataṃ pavattaṃ*, and treats *sīghasaraṃ* just below as an adjectival compound, both qualifying *taṇhaṃ*. I prefer to take *saritaṃ* as a noun used metaphorically. On the established reading, this verse would differ from the others in the opening group by the absence of a simile. To make this verse consistent with the others, Norman adopts Brough's suggestion (GD 140; see Brough 1962, 200), that in place of *visosayitvā* we read *va sosayitvā*, with *va* the short form of *iva* = like. However, all editions of Sn have *visosayitvā*. The Patna Dhp parallel, v. 410, has *viśodhayittā*, from a different verb but retaining the prefix *vi-*. Udāna-v *aśoṣayajñaḥ* is too different to be of help.

299. On the last line, *te honti cakkadhārino*, Ja III 207,23 says: "They bear this razor-wheel" (*te etaṃ khuracakkaṃ dhārenti*). *Khuracakka* refers to a wheel in hell used as an instrument of torture.

300. *Anavasesappahānavasena ucchindanto vadhetī ti vuttaṃ hoti.* This derivation shows Pj II takes *udabbadhī* as an aorist of **ubbadheti* (*ud* + *vadheti*). Norman (at GD 140–41) refers to a suggestion by R. Morris that *udabbadhī* should be understood as *udabbahi*, from the root *vṛh*, "to extirpate." In the GDhp version, the accompanying simile is that of plucking a lotus (= 2b of the Pāli version), as suggested by the fragment *bisa . . . vikaśa*. See Brough 1962, 130, 199.

301. In the Patna and Gāndhārī parallels, and also in Uv, verse 5 of the Pāli version stands at the beginning of the series. Ānandajoti comments (2016, 13): "it very much seems that the Pāli verse 5 is misplaced, and should come at the beginning of the sutta, with Pāli verse 1 following it."

302. *Ficus glomerata*. Norman (1993, 245) refers to Emeneau's observation that "the species of the genus *Ficus* possess the peculiarity that the inflorescence is in the form of crowded compact clusters of flowers placed inside a fleshy stalk, and pollination is effected by fig wasps that develop from eggs laid in the gall-flowers, one of the three types of flowers found in the inflorescence." Norman discusses other references to the udumbara flower in the Pāli Canon and Buddhist Skt literature (1993, 246–47).

303. *Ekavokāracatuvokārapañcavokārabhavesu*. The nonpercipient

realm is "one-constituent existence," since the aggregate of form alone exists there. The formless realms are "four-constituent existence," since the aggregate of form is absent there. All other realms, where all five aggregates are found, are "five-constituent existence."

304. The same couplet is at Ud 20,4 with a similar commentarial explanation at Ud-a 164,4 foll.

305. Although Pj II takes *itibhavābhavataṃ* to involve a *sandhi* of *bhava* and *abhava*, it is more likely, as suggested by Norman (GD 142), that the long vowel is simply a rhythmical lengthening, so that the intended meaning is "one state of existence or another," "various states of existence," or with the *iti* here, "such and such a state of existence." The suffix *–taṃ* makes this an abstract noun indicating a general condition. I suspect that what is meant by this term is desire for a particular kind of rebirth, as in the seventh impure way of living the spiritual life (at AN IV 55,21–24), described thus: "One lives the spiritual life aspiring for a particular group of devas, thinking: 'By this good behavior, observance, austerity, or spiritual life, I will become a deva or one among the devas'" (*aññataraṃ devanikāyaṃ paṇidhāya brahmacariyaṃ carati imināhaṃ sīlena vā vatena vā tapena vā brahmacariyena vā devo vā bhavissāmi devaññataro vā*). For more on *bhavābhava*, see note 1418.

306. For definitions of these thoughts, see Vibh 410–12 (§§885–90).

307. This seems to be an alternative name for the Khuddakavatthu (chap. 17) of Vibh.

308. The Pāli has *yo nāccasārī na paccasārī*. Norman suggests reading *yo nâccasarī na p'accasārī*, taking the second verb to be the causative of the first. The rendering he proposes—"who has not transgressed nor even caused [another] to transgress"—has no discernible relationship to the theme of the verses and thus I find it unsatisfactory. Nyanaponika renders the line "who neither goes too far nor lags behind." While this rendering corresponds to Pj II's comments, it is hard to see how "lags behind" can be derived from *paccasārī*. Jayawickrama has "he who has neither overstepped nor moved backwards."

The line is discussed at length by Brough (1962, 202–5), Levman (2014, 336–42), and most recently, with a critical overview of prior interpretations, by Dhivan Jones (2016, 96–103). Jones (p. 101) correlates the two verbs with the Simile of the Great Tree-Trunk (see note 288), taking them to mean that the monk does not approach either the internal sense bases or the external sense bases. He astutely points out that the line echoes the refrain, such that "running too far" would lead one to the "beyond" or the "far shore," and "running back" would lead one to the "here" or the "near shore." The idea of "running too far" and "running back" can also be connected with the attitude of the noble disciple (at SN II 226–27) who, by penetrating dependent origination, does not "run back" into the past or "run forward" into the future, plagued by questions about his personal identity. The verbs used in this passage, *paṭidhāvati* for running back into the past and *upadhāvati* for running ahead into the future, correspond to the verbs of the Uraga text, in their indicative form respectively *paṭisarati* and *atisarati*. Both roots, *dhāv* and *sar*, convey the idea of running.

This interpretation can also appeal for support to the Bhaddekaratta Suttas (MN nos. 131–34), which elaborate on a poem spoken by the Buddha that instructs a monk not to revert to the past or yearn for the future (*atītaṃ nānvāgameyya, nappaṭikaṅkhe anāgataṃ*). One reverts to the past when the mind becomes bound by memories of the past; one yearns for the future by building up hopes and expectations about future outcomes. One also gets shaken in the present when one adopts a view of a real self inherent in the five aggregates.

In pāda b of the verse, *sabbaṃ accagamā imaṃ papañcaṃ*, the verb *accagamā* mirrors the verb *accasārī* in pāda a. *Accagamā* is an aorist of *atigacchati*, just as *accasārī* is an aorist of *atisarati*. But here the idea of "going beyond" has a positive flavor—it signifies transcendence rather than bondage. What the bhikkhu transcends is *papañca*, a word that suggests unchecked proliferation of mental activity as well as the multiplicity and diversity of the world. The proliferation referred to here may be the longings for the past and expectations for the future, as well as the construction of such ideas as "I," "mine," and "my self."

309. It seems that in this pair and the one that follows, the explanation would make better sense if we invert the verbs, so that one "runs back" through attachment to the past and "runs too far" through projections into the future.

310. *Imaṃ vedanāsaññāvitakkappabhavaṃ taṇhāmānadiṭṭhisaṅkhātaṃ tividhaṃ papañcaṃ*. This may be alluding to MN I 111,35–112,13, which explains how *papañca* arises in a cognitive process that proceeds through *vedanā*, *saññā*, and *vitakka*. *Papañca* is said to be the "proliferation" of notions of "I," "mine," and "self" in its various modalities. See SN IV 203,11–15: *Asmī ti, bhikkhave, papañcitam etaṃ, ayam aham asmī ti papañcitam etaṃ, bhavissan ti . . . na bhavissan ti . . . rūpī bhavissan ti . . . arūpī bhavissan ti . . . saññī bhavissan ti . . . asaññī bhavissan ti . . . n'evasaññīnāsaññī bhavissan ti papañcitam etaṃ*. ("Bhikkhus, 'I am' is a proliferation; 'I am this' is a proliferation; 'I

shall be' is a proliferation; 'I shall not be' is a proliferation; 'I shall consist of form'... 'I shall be formless'... 'I shall be percipient'.... 'I shall be nonpercipient'... 'I shall be neither percipient nor nonpercipient' is a proliferation.")

311. *Tañca pana asammohato, na visayato.* This is said because the actual object of the path is nibbāna, but the realization of nibbāna removes delusion, enabling one to know that conditioned realities are all "unreal."
312. See AN IV 9,5–7, Vibh 448 (§949).
313. The text cited is untraceable.
314. This point will be elucidated just below.
315. *Sakkāya*: the composite of the five aggregates subject to clinging. A translation of the word is almost impossible. My past attempts, as "personality" and "identity," are inadequate. *Sakkāya* is a compound of *sat* = "existent" and *kāya* = "body," but what is meant is not solely the physical body but the entire conglomeration of material and mental factors that constitute the empirical person.
316. Pj II here provides an etymological explanation of *vanatha*, which I omit in translation. This is the Pāli: *Vacanatthe pana ayaṃ viseso – vanute, vanotī ti vā vanaṃ yācati sevati bhajatī ti attho. Taṇhāy'etaṃ adhivacanaṃ. Sā hi visayānaṃ patthanato sevanato ca vanan ti vuccati. Taṃ pariyuṭṭhānavasena vanaṃ tharati tanotī ti vanatho, taṇhānusayass'etaṃ adhivacanaṃ.* The explanation is arrived at by conflating two homonyms, on which see PED *vana*[1] and *vana*[2].
317. The reference is to Dhp 283. Dhp-a III 424,8–15 explains: *Mahantamahantā bhavākaḍḍhanakā kilesā vanaṃ nāma, pavattiyaṃ vipākadāyakā vanathā nāma. Pubbappattikā vanaṃ nāma, aparāparuppattikā vanathā nāma. Taṃ ubhayaṃ catutthamaggañāṇena chinditabbaṃ.* ("The very strong defilements that drag one into a new existence are called *vana*; those that yield their results in the course of existence [hence weaker] defilements are called *vanatha*. Those arisen earlier are called *vana*; those arisen later are called *vanatha*. Both are to be cut off by the knowledge of the fourth path.") Pj II is denying here that in relation to **16**, *vanatha* applies to all defilements; it holds, rather, that it signifies only craving.
318. Though Pj II here explains the abandoning of the five hindrances by way of their eradication by the world-transcending paths, the Nikāyas typically assign the abandoning of the five hindrances to the stage preparatory to the attainment of the jhānas. It is thus temporary suppression rather than final eradication. In such a case, the placing of the verse on the hindrances at the end of the poem seems to indicate a lack of systematic order. In the standard Nikāya model, it is the

unwholesome roots and the latent tendencies that are eradicated by the world-transcending attainments, yet here these are placed in stanza **14**. The Gāndhārī parallel matches the Pāli in its arrangement of the verses. The order of the verses in Udāna-v conforms more closely to the standard model, with the hindrances abandoned prior to the unwholesome roots and latent tendencies.

319. I follow Be here: *Ekacce yena yena tesaṃ bhikkhūnaṃ yā yā gāthā desitā, tena tena tassā tassā gāthāya pariyosāne so so bhikkhu arahatte patiṭṭhito 'ti vadanti.*
320. *Pubbayoga.* A technical term signifying the practices in a past life that created the wholesome conditions for attainment in the present life. See p. 402.
321. Reading *dippamāne* with Ce and Ee, as against Be *dibbamāne.*
322. *Salākabhattāni.* These are meals that a lay supporter offers to a fixed number of monks or nuns without specifying the recipients. The ones to receive the meals are determined by lottery or rotation. The Nikāyas say that the life span of humans under previous buddhas was far longer than in the present era when Gotama Buddha's teaching prevails. See DN II 3–4.
323. Reading *dāsa* with Ce and Ee, as against Be *dāra.*
324. I omit several sentences that give simple word glosses and an explanation of the word *iti*, used to indicate the end of a direct quotation.
325. Milk, curd, whey, butter, and ghee (*khīra, dadhi, takka, navanīta, sappi*). See Vin I 244,34.
326. On the buddha eye (*buddhacakkhu*), see pp. 1176–77. This motif, of the Buddha surveying the world to discover capable recipients of his teaching, is not apparent in the Nikāyas. It may have entered the commentaries through the oral narrative tradition about the Buddha. See p. 497 on the Buddha's daily routine.
327. *Hetusampannā.* That is, causes or supporting conditions for achieving some wholesome state, in this case, arahantship.
328. See Appendix 3.
329. *Vaṇo ti pi* is in Be but not in Ce or Ee.
330. The last two lines of the Pāli are also at Th 125 (but with *muhuṃ muhuṃ* instead of *punappunaṃ*). The full verse is at Th-a I 29,11–12. The commentary to Th 125 explains "striking" thus: "As a monkey eating the fruit of a tree, because of his own zeal, lets go of one branch and grabs another, causing the tree to shake many times, so the mind lets go of one object among the objects such as visible forms and grabs another, repeatedly striking without giving it a chance to remain motionless by way of concentrating the mind. It circles around that same object such as visible form and wanders where it wishes."

331. Vin II 240,24–25, Th 447, and also at Ud 56,33–34.
332. The eleven fires, referred to in the Āditta Sutta, are lust, hatred, delusion, birth, old age, death, sorrow, lamentation, pain, dejection, and anguish. See Vin I 34,21, SN IV 20,3–6.
333. *Atthasabhāgaṃ no byañjanasabhāgaṃ*. There actually seems to be no similarity with regard to either meaning or phrasing. On this, Norman remarks (GD 147–48): "Although no one seems to have commented upon the fact, it is clear that **21** is not the expected response to **20**, and we must assume that the true opposite to **20** has been lost. The lost verse presumably gave some punning reference by the Buddha to insects and cattle in lush pastures. It would seem that **21**, as it stands, contains portions of both Dhaniya's statement and the Buddha's reply, since pāda c seems to contradict pāda a."
334. See Paṭis I 29–34, which states that all the factors of enlightenment are developed in such a way that they do not exceed one another (*aññamaññaṃ nātivattanti*) and have a single taste (*ekarasaṭṭhena bhāvanā*).
335. *Hatthotāpakampi khādati*. My rendering is tentative. *Otāpeti* usually means "to warm in the sun, to put (in the sun) to dry." Since Indians traditionally take up their food with the hand, perhaps it means that she takes up food while it is too hot. But it is hard to understand how this relates to wantonness.
336. Here and below the masculine singular present participles in Be should be corrected to feminine present participles as in Ce and Ee. Thus change *alabhamāno* to *alabhamānā*, etc.
337. *Haṃsarājaṃ gahetvāna, suvaṇṇā parihāyatha*. The reference is to a goose with golden feathers. See Ja I 475–76, Vin IV 259.
338. *Pādalolatāya ārāmādigamanasīlo hutvā sabbaṃ dhanaṃ vināseti*. The intention is not clear to me. *Pāda*, feet, is apparently exemplified by her going to parks on foot, but perhaps "wantonness regarding feet" means using her feet as a fetish for purposes of seduction.
339. On the twin miracle (*yamakapāṭihāriya*), see Dhp-a III 213–15, BL 3:45–46.
340. *Nibbiṭṭhena carāmi sabbaloke*. *Nibbiṭṭha* is the past participle of *nibbisati*, "settles, earns, gains."
341. Norman remarks (GD 149): "The fact that the whole of the Buddha's reply in **25** is concerned with Dhaniya's statement in **24**a, and there is no parallel in **25**b to Dhaniya's comment about his sons [children] in **24**bc . . . suggests that once again a verse has disappeared and two verses, dealing with sons and wages, have been telescoped together." I am not sure that I would agree with this. The Buddha may have found it sufficient to elaborate upon his freedom of movement without needing to refer to his freedom from paternal duties. Since

there are no parallels to this sutta, it is hard to draw definitive conclusions about textual corruption.

342. PED defines *vasā* as "a cow (neither in calf nor giving suck)." See too SED *vaśā*.

343. Norman translates *dhenupā* as bullocks, explaining that the lines of **28**, *dāmā muñjamāyā navā susaṇṭhānā, na hi sakkhinti dhenupāpi chettuṃ,* imply that the *dhenupā* are the strongest except for the bull. But DOP, following Pj II, has "a suckling calf (or a milch cow)," and I have followed the latter.

344. *Pañcaṅgulaṃ datvā*. Apparently an identifying mark made with the five fingers dipped in a dye. See Ja I 166,21–23: *tātā, imaṃ eḷakaṃ nadiṃ netvā nhāpetvā kaṇṭhe mālaṃ parikkhipitvā pañcaṅgulikaṃ datvā maṇḍetvā ānetha;* Ja III 304,21–23: *tassa purisassa rattiṃ āgantvā abhiramitvā gacchantassa piṭṭhiyaṃ pañcaṅgulikaṃ datvā pāto va rañño ārocesi.*

345. Norman (at GD 150) suggests that the Buddha's meaning can be interpreted more simply by taking the five types of cattle to represent the five sense faculties. See SN I 114–16.

346. Reading with Ce and Ee *tat'uttarimpi subhāsitaratanasāraṃ adhigantukāmo*. Be has *tatuttaripi subhāsitaṃ amatarasaṃ adhigantukāmo,* "wishing even more to acquire the nectar-like taste of excellent sayings."

347. *Usabho ti gopitā gopariṇāyako goyūthapati balībaddo*. Pj II 40,17–21 cites various opinions about types of bulls, which I do not translate. It dismisses them all as mere verbiage (*sabbe ete papañcā*) and says they all can be understood as having the sense of peerless (*sabbe v'ete appaṭisamaṭṭhena veditabbā*).

348. See MN I 73,3–15 on the four *yonis* or modes of generation: birth from eggs, birth from the womb, birth from moisture, and spontaneous birth (*aṇḍajā yoni, jalābujā yoni, saṃsedajā yoni, opapātikā yoni*).

349. *Anupādisesavasena, saupādisesavasena*. It 38–39 explains that the nibbāna element "with residue remaining" is nibbāna experienced by the living arahant through the eradication of greed, hatred, and delusion; the nibbāna element "without residue remaining" is nibbāna attained when the arahant passes away.

350. I translate in accordance with the punctuation of Ce: *dhammakāyaṃ disvā lokuttaracakkhunā, rūpakāyaṃ disvā lokiyacakkhunā, saddhāpaṭilābhaṃ labhi*. The punctuation in Be, *dhammakāyaṃ disvā, lokuttaracakkhunā rūpakāyaṃ disvā, lokiyacakkhunā saddhāpaṭilābhaṃ labhi,* suggests that he saw the form body with the world-transcending eye and gained faith with the mundane eye. The contrast between the Buddha's *dharmakāya* and *rūpakāya* played a major role in early Mahāyāna Buddhism, before it was replaced by the *trikāya* or three bodies doctrine.

351. On the different modes of going for refuge, see Sv I 231–32. The world-transcendent going for refuge is accomplished with the seeing of the four noble truths at the moment of the path of stream-entry. The mundane kinds of going for refuge are fourfold: by self-surrender, by taking the refuges as support, by entering upon the state of a pupil, and by prostration (*attasanniyyātanena, tapparāyaṇatāya, sissabhāvūpagamanena, paṇipātena*).
352. On the five eyes, see Appendix 3, and for details, pp. 1174–77.
353. *Samaṇadhamma*. Usually this refers to the practice of meditation, but here it is used to signify a course of extreme asceticism such as the Buddha practiced before he discovered the eightfold path.
354. See Pj I 183,19–21; Vism 203,11 foll., Ppn 7.33–34.
355. *Jātimaraṇassa pāraṃ*. This could also be rendered "the far shore of birth and death."
356. The verse and its rejoinder occur as an independent sutta at SN I 6.
357. *Vasavattibhūmiyaṃ*. This refers to the *paranimmitavasavatti bhūmi*, the sixth of the six desire-sphere heavenly worlds.
358. *Saṅgītikārānametaṃ vacanaṃ, sabbagāthāsu ca īdisāni*. This refers to the line *iti māro pāpimā*, "said Māra the Evil One," which in modern editions is enclosed in parentheses. Identifying lines about speakers and auditors in other verses, when enclosed in parentheses, were also added by the compilers.
359. *Cattāro upadhayo kāmūpadhi, khandhūpadhi, kilesūpadhi, abhisaṅkhārūpadhi*.
360. *So sattasaṅkhāravasena duvidho*. The dichotomy of "beings" and "conditioned things" is a commentarial distinction between the potential objects of clinging. "Conditioned things" may refer to the constituent elements of a being (as distinct from the being apprehended as a unitary whole) or to inanimate objects, such as wealth and other material possessions.
361. From *so santuṭṭho hoti kāyaparihārikena cīvarena* to *nāparaṃ itthattāyā ti pajānāti* is an allusion to the "sequential training," which we find in full in such suttas as DN 2, MN 27, MN 51, and AN 4:198.
362. I follow Ce and Ee, which read *sokamūlā honti*. Be has *sokaphalā va honti*: "they have sorrow as their fruits."
363. Ce and Ee have *gokulaṅkavihāro*, Be *gopālakavihāro*.
364. *Attajjhāsayato, parajjhāsayato, aṭṭhuppattito, pucchāvasito*.
365. Reading with Ce and Ee *attano abhisamayānurūpaṃ*. Be has *attanā adhigatamagganayānurūpaṃ*, "in accordance with the way he attained the path." *Abhisamaya* as "breakthrough" here signifies the attainment of full enlightenment.

366. The entire passage below, as far as p. 496, is also at Ap-a I 138–203.
367. The aspiration (*patthanā*) is the vow to attain the final goal in a particular way, either as a buddha, a paccekabuddha, or a disciple. The undertaking (*abhinīhāra*) is the resolution, usually made in the presence of a living buddha. The aspiration and undertaking of the future Buddha Gotama are shown at Bv 2.54–57, elaborated at Bv-a 64 foll. The aspiration and undertaking of specific disciples are described at Mp I 135 foll.
368. *Bhagavā pubbayogāvacarasuttaṃ abhāsi. Pubbayogāvacara,* it seems, refers especially to rigorous meditation practice. This passage occurs only in the commentaries but not in the Nikāyas. Apart from Ap-a I 139,10–15, which is parallel to Pj II, it is also cited at Th-a I 13,8–14. By "in the last time" (*pacchime kāle*) presumably what is meant is the time after a buddha's teaching has vanished.
369. This last clause, in parenthesis, is only in Be.
370. I follow Be here: *viriyādhikānaṃ saddhāpaññā mandā, viriyaṃ balavaṃ.*
371. Vessantara was the past incarnation of the Buddha Gotama in which he fulfilled the perfection of giving (*dānapāramitā*). He is the protagonist of Ja no. 547.
372. The point here seems to be that one aspiring for buddhahood who is presently a deva should do meritorious deeds and then dedicate the merit to achieving human birth. On achieving human status, that being can make the aspiration for buddhahood and, if the other conditions are fulfilled, receive the prediction of success from a buddha. The same holds for those presently female and so forth.
373. Sumedha was the past incarnation of the Buddha Gotama in which he made his vow to attain buddhahood. He did so at the feet of the Buddha Dīpaṅkara and received the prediction of future success. See Bv 2.34–69.
374. Pj II, Ce and Ee, read *sukhāya,* "happiness," but Pj II, Be, and all three editions of Bv have *hitāya.*
375. What follows occurs at Ap-a I 17,7–20, in connection with the aspiration of Sumedha (the future Buddha Gotama), and at Ap-a I 140–41,1–12, in the more exact parallel to the present passage of Pj II, on the general career of an aspirant for buddhahood. It is also at Ja I 14–15, Cp-a 283–84, and elsewhere.
376. *Na niyatamicchādiṭṭhiko hoti.* "Wrong views with fixed consequences" are views that deny kamma and its fruits, the validity of moral distinctions, and causes for defilement and purification (*natthikavāda, akiriyavāda, ahetukavāda*). Such views are said to block the paths to liberation and a higher rebirth. See Vism-mhṭ I 187.

377. Matricide, patricide, murdering an arahant, drawing the blood of the Buddha with a mind of hatred, and causing a schism in the Sangha. While the idea of the *pañcānantariyakammāni* is found in the Nikāyas (for example, at AN 6:87 and AN 6:94), the term itself seems to be commentarial.
378. The parallel passage at Ap-a I 150 (Be) adds here "so too paccekabuddhas" (*tathā paccekabuddhā*).
379. All three editions read here: *paccekebuddhā buddhe appatvā buddhānaṃ uppajjanakāle yeva uppajjanti*. Ap-a I 150 (Be), however, states just the opposite: "But paccekabuddhas do not arise at a time when buddhas arise" (*te pana buddhānaṃ uppajjanakāle na uppajjanti*). I follow the text of Pj II here, but since, in the Nikāyas, the Buddha never speaks of any contemporary paccekabuddhas, Ap-a seems to have the preferred reading.
380. I follow Ce and Ee, which read: *aññe pabbājetvā ābhisamācārikaṃ sikkhāpenti*. Be has the opposite: *na aññe pabbājetvā ābhisamācārikaṃ sikkhāpenti*, "they do not give others the going forth and train them in proper behavior." Since in several of the background stories to follow, paccekabuddhas do give the going forth and basic instructions to their pupils, Ce and Ee must be correct here. The stories show that the common conception of the paccekabuddha as "a silent buddha" and as one who lives in complete solitude is mistaken.
381. This is a chapter *internal* to the commentary to this sutta. The commentary groups the stories to the forty-one verses into four chapters.
382. The discussion to follow is also at Sv I 186 foll., Ps I 255 foll., and Spk III 186 foll.
383. The Khandhakas are the chapters of the Mahāvagga and Cūḷavagga, two parts of the Vinaya Piṭaka dealing with procedures outside the Pātimokkha. The duties toward the preceptor are described at Vin I 44–50; the duties toward the teacher (essentially identical with these) are at Vin I 58–61. The fourteen major duties are mentioned in the Vattakkhandhaka (Cūḷavagga chap. 8); they include duties toward visitors, toward residents, when going on a journey, when reciting the blessing after a meal, and so forth.
384. I read with Be and Ce *bhattakiccaṃ niṭṭhāpetvā*.
385. See Appendix 3. The sources are MN I 101–4, AN III 248–50.
386. The distinction is between *sabbatthaka* and *pārihāriya*. *Sabbatthaka* can be understood as derived from *sabba* + *attha*, "all good," or from *sabbattha* meaning "everywhere." A similar passage is at Vism 97–98, Ppn 3.57–60.
387. I read with Be *asaṅghaṭṭo*, as against Ce and Ee *asaṃsaṭṭho*.
388. *Catudhātuvavatthāna*. Explained in detail at Vism 347 foll., Ppn 11.27 foll.

389. Though initially the commentator referred to the analysis of the *four* elements, he actually explains the six elements, adding the space and consciousness elements.
390. The passage in brackets is in Be but not in Ce or Ee. It is based on the parallels at Sv I 188–89, Ps I 257–58, and Spk III 186.
391. As in Ce and Ee. Be has *Kalambatittha*.
392. The Pavāraṇā is the ceremony held on the last day of the rains retreat, when the bhikkhus invite one another to point out any faults they may have committed during the retreat.
393. The simile of son's flesh is at SN II 98–99.
394. This is the beginning of the canonical reflection on the use of food, as at MN I 10,8–12: "Reflecting wisely, one uses almsfood neither for amusement nor for intoxication nor for the sake of physical beauty and attractiveness, but only for the endurance and continuance of this body, for ending discomfort, and for assisting the holy life, considering: 'Thus I shall terminate old feelings without arousing new feelings and I shall be healthy and blameless and shall live in comfort.'"
395. *Purimayāmaṃ pacchimayāmañca*. Ce and Ee also have *majjhimayāmaṃ*, "the middle watch." Be, which excludes the middle watch, seems in better accord with the canonical instructions on wakefulness, as at MN I 273–74, SN IV 177,13–20, and AN I 114,10–17, etc.
396. The paccekabodhisatta whose story underlies the first verse; he was mentioned before the long digression on the observance of going and returning.
397. *Lohakumbhivāso*. One of the hells; see **670–71**.
398. *Manosilā*: red arsenic or realgar. Be reads *pakkatela* as against *campakatela* in Ce and Ee. The Champaka tree (*Magnolia champaca*) is a tree native to South and Southeast Asia. It bears fragrant white and yellow flowers used for worship and ornamentation.
399. I read with Ce and Ee *tividhanāṭakāni*. Be has *vividhanāṭakāni*, but Pj II explains the three kinds of *nāṭakāni* just below at pp. 475–76.
400. *Antaraṃ labhitvā*. See DOP p. 148a, 2 (iii), where "weakness, weak point" is given as a possible meaning of *antara*.
401. *Sayambhutaṃ pāpuṇi*. *Sayambhū*, which I render "self-accomplished," is a technical term used only in relation to perfectly enlightened buddhas and paccekabuddhas, who attain their realization fully on their own, without depending on instructions from another.
402. *Aṭṭhaparikkhārasamannāgato*. Presumably these are the same as the eight requisites of a bhikkhu: three robes, a waistband, an alms bowl, a razor, a water strainer, and a needle-and-thread.

403. *Atrajo, khettajo, dinnako, antevāsiko.* On *atraja* as an incorrect back-formation from *attaja* (Skt *ātmaja*), see Norman 2006, 96, 127. The terms are explained at Ja I 135,14–17, with the third and fourth inverted: "The biological son is one born on account of oneself; the territorial son is one born on one's back, in one's lap, in one's thigh, and so forth; the apprentice is one who studies a craft under one; an adopted son is one given for the purpose of being brought up by oneself." For an example of a territorial son, see pp. 438–39.

This pāda of the Pāli does not correspond thematically to the previous two pādas and seems misplaced. The Gāndhārī parallel (v. 1) has here a line that corresponds to pāda c of the additional verse of Ap, *mettena cittena hitānukampī*. The Skt parallel at Mvu 358,1 reads: *nikṣiptadaṇḍo trasathāvareṣu*. Both alternatives better fit the theme of the verse.

404. The Niddesa here extends the reference of *ekāyanamaggo* from the four *satipaṭṭhānas* to all thirty-seven *bodhipakkhiyā dhammā*.

405. In the Pāli text, each phrase represents a distinct object of realization, but I have grouped them into the sets to which they belong. The first three point to the three characteristics (*tilakkhaṇa*). Next comes the formula for dependent origination, in the order of both arising and cessation; the text spells out each link in the sequence, but I have translated only the beginning and end of this familiar series (on which see SN chap. 12). This is followed by the four noble truths, which are exemplified first by *dukkha* or suffering and then by the *āsavas* or influxes, as we find in the canonical account of enlightenment (for the Buddha at MN I 23,15–21 and for a disciple at MN I 183,25–32). Next comes a set of five terms related to the four noble truths. All four noble truths are to be directly known, but each truth entails a particular task (*kicca*). Thus at SN 56:29 (V 436) it is said that the truth of suffering should be fully understood, the truth of the origin abandoned, the truth of cessation realized, and the truth of the path developed. At MN III 289–90 it is said that the five aggregates should be fully understood, ignorance and craving for existence abandoned, serenity and insight developed, and clear knowledge and liberation realized. The five terms—origin, passing away, gratification, danger, and escape—constitute a template used for contemplating various groups of phenomena (see CDB pp. 36–39). The last phrase, "whatever is subject to origination is all subject to cessation," is commonly used to describe the arising of the Dhamma eye, the first breakthrough to realization.

406. The verb *carati*, of which *care* is the short optative form, has numerous shades of meaning. DOP has the following: (1)

moves, goes, walks, roams, goes about, grazes; (2) journeys, wanders, travels about; (3) goes about (one's life), goes one's way, lives, behaves, conducts oneself; (4) acts, performs, practices; (5) undergoes, undertakes. Of these, I take the third to be most pertinent to the present passage and to similar occurrences in Sn. It does not necessarily mean "wanders," though in the case of monks and ascetics, wandering is integral to their way of life.

407. This is based on Nidd II 212, slightly elaborated, and thus I abridge the corresponding passage in the excerpt from Nidd II 212–13 just below.

408. *Khaggavisāṇaṃ nāma khaggamigasiṅgaṃ*. This definition makes it clear that the commentator understands *khaggavisāṇa* as the horn of the rhinoceros, and not the rhinoceros itself. Ap-a, however, allows both interpretations. At Ap-a I 133,32 and 153,4–5 it echoes the Niddesa and Pj II, taking the expression to refer to the horn. But at Ap-a I 203,6–7, it proposes the alternative derivation: "*Khaggavisāṇa*: It roams around pulverizing mountains, etc., as if cutting trees, etc., with a sword. . . . 'Sword' means like a sword. The animal whose horn is [like] a sword is a rhinoceros." (*Khaggavisāṇakappo ti khaggena rukkhādayo chindanto viya sakasiṅgena pabbatādayo cuṇṇavicuṇṇaṃ kurumāno vicaratī ti khaggavisāṇo. . . . Khaggaṃ viyā ti khaggaṃ. Khaggaṃ visāṇaṃ yassa migassa so 'yaṃ migo khaggavisāṇo.*) On the ambiguity, see pp. 98–100.

409. *Khaggavisāṇakappo ti khaggavisāṇasadiso ti vuttaṃ hoti*. While my rendering sounds redundant in English, the commentator is saying that the purport is living alone *like the solitary horn of a rhinoceros*, not living alone like a rhinoceros. Nidd II 213, too, interprets the expression in this way, as can be seen from the excerpt. Both Norman and Jayawickrama translate the term in accordance with the commentary.

410. Be and Ce read *Gandhamādano nāma himavati*. Ee is missing *himavati*.

411. Reading with Ce and Ee *parito* as against Be *tassūparito*. The latter would put the pavilion on top of the tree, which seems unlikely.

412. Reading with Ce and Ee *atha sampati*, as against Be *ayaṃ tattha pakati*.

413. *Saṅghathero*. The use of this term shows that the commentary is modeling an assembly of paccekabuddhas on an assembly of bhikkhus.

414. *Udānavyākaraṇagāthaṃ bhāsati*. This indicates the dual function of the verses. Some are said to be uttered as exclamations of joy over the attainment, some to explain to others how the

attainment was reached, and some, like the present one, serve both functions.

415. Following Be and Ce; in Ee *antokasiṇaparikammaṃ*, *anto–* should probably be deleted. A global search through CST4 for *antokasiṇ** turns up no instances of this compound.
416. No previous mention was made in the story of the prince attaining jhāna in his life as a prince, but only in his previous life.
417. Nidd II 213 mentions only two kinds of bonding, by sight and hearing (see just below), but Nidd II-a 96 expands the typology to five. The five are also at Ps II 143–45.
418. See Mp I 23,3–9. The story is a little different there.
419. A transgression entailing expulsion from the Sangha.
420. *Ubhatosaṅgha*. What is meant is both the order of bhikkhus and the order of bhikkhunīs.
421. *Dantavalaya*. See PED sv *danta* and SED sv *valaya*. I follow these dictionaries, but since personal ornamentation is prohibited for monastics, something allowable must have been used.
422. Here Pj II uses the singular, Ce *bhavati sineho*, Be *bhavati sneho*, in contrast to the plural reading in Sn. See note 66.
423. For these classifications of views, see Appendix 3.
424. Reading with Ce and Ee *rajjussukkaṃ*, as against Be *rajjasukhaṃ*, "the bliss of kingship."
425. It is questionable to me that the original intends to make a distinction between *mitta* and *suhajja* (or *suhada*). DN III 187, cited by Pj II just below, uses the expression *mitto suhado* as though the two words were synonyms, perhaps with *suhada* qualifying *mitta*.
426. Nidd II 218 gives a fuller definition just below.
427. The following citations on different kinds of friends are from DN III 187. There, however, the section on the friend who points out what is good precedes that on the friend who is sympathetic.
428. These are the sixty-two speculative views analyzed in the Brahmajāla Sutta, DN 1. For a translation of the sutta and its commentaries, see Bodhi 2007b.
429. Pj II explains *va* in pāda a to be the emphatic *eva* rather than the comparative *iva*: *Vakāro avadhāraṇattho, evakāro vā ayaṃ, sandhivasen'ettha ekāro naṭṭho.*
430. *Puttesu dāresu cā ti puttadhītubhariyāsu*. The plural *dāresu* is in the root text. Though monogamy would have been the rule among ordinary householders, royalty and wealthy merchants often had several wives.
431. *Nakkhatte ghosite*. Apparently a festival held in conjunction with a particular constellation.

432. *Nirodhā vuṭṭhāya*. That is, from the meditative attainment called *nirodhasamāpatti* or *saññāvedayitanirodha*, "the cessation of perception and feeling."
433. *Pañcapatiṭṭhitena vanditvā*. Literally "venerated him with the five supports," that is, having placed the two knees, two hands, and head on the ground.
434. That is, the fifteenth night of the bright fortnight, the night of the full moon.
435. *Avasesā itthiyo sattāhaṃ dhammanāṭakaṃ karotha*. DOP explains *dhammanāṭaka* as "'virtuous' or 'legitimate' prostitution."
436. I read with Ce *āsīnasuvaṇṇapaṭimaṃ* as against Be and Ee *āsittasuvaṇṇapaṭimaṃ*.
437. Strangely, the narrator seems to have forgotten that earlier the prince (as the neglected wife) made *five wishes*, of which four had been fulfilled.
438. Here and below reading with Be and Ce *maṭṭhaṃ katvā*, as against Ee *maṇḍaṃ katvā*.
439. From this point on until the end of the background story, I follow Ce and Ee, which differ considerably from Be.
440. Ce and Ee: *dve migā tiṇamigo pasadamigo*; Be *dve migā eṇīmigo pasadamigo*. Nidd II 221 (Be, so too Ce) reads *eṇimigo*, so I take this to be the definitive reading. Dhammika 59 identifies the *pasadamiga* with the *citraka* or *cittamiga*, which must be the modern chital (*Axis axis*).
441. I follow Ce and Ee, which read: *Evaṃ so ekavajjiko ti pākaṭo hutvā nibbinno pabbaji*. Be has *Evaṃ so tehi nibbinno hutvā pabbaji*.
442. Nidd II 224 mentions even more types of sports, games, and musical expressions, not easy to identify.
443. The phrase echoes the expression used by Suddhodana the Sakyan in his request to the Buddha not to allow monks to give novice ordination to a son without permission from the parents: *Puttapemaṃ, bhante, chaviṃ chindati . . . aṭṭhiṃ chetvā aṭṭhimiñjaṃ āhacca tiṭṭhati. Sādhu, bhante, ayyā ananuññātaṃ mātāpitūhi puttaṃ na pabbājeyyuṃ* (Vin I 82–83).
444. See AN IV 45–46.
445. Nidd II 225, cited below, also explains *cātuddisa* with the formula for the four immeasurables, but see AN II 28,25–30, which says that one who fulfills the four "lineages of the noble ones" (*ariyavaṃsa*) dwells in each of the four directions "conquering discontent, unconquered by discontent" (*catūhi ariyavaṃsehi samannāgato bhikkhu puratthimāya cepi disāya viharati . . . dakkhiṇāya cepi disāya viharati sveva aratiṃ sahati, na taṃ arati sahati*). AN II 27,10–12 states that "one who is content has no distress of mind . . . [and] is not repelled in the directions" (*tuṭṭhassa . . . vighāto hoti cittassa disā nappaṭihaññati*). The verb there corresponds to *appaṭigho* in the present verse.

446. This is probably referring to the three aspects of contentment mentioned in the Niddesa just below: being content oneself, speaking in praise of contentment, and not engaging in a wrong search for the object needed. Applied to each of the four requisites, these total twelve. The mention of contentment further connects this verse to the *ariyavaṃsa*.
447. See note 360.
448. This passage is modeled on AN II 27–28; see too SN II 194–95.
449. The text enumerates some forty kinds of illness.
450. These seventeen defilements are mentioned in the Repetition Series at the end of each of the major numerical sections of AN. Thus, for example, at the end of the Fours, it is said that the four establishments of mindfulness, the four right strivings, and the four bases of spiritual potency are to be developed for direct knowledge, full understanding, destruction, abandoning, etc., of each of these seventeen defilements. They are referred to often in the two Niddesas.
451. I read with Ce and Ee *avissāsaniyāni rājahadayāni*. Be has *ativissāsaniyāni rājahadayāni*, "the hearts of kings are extremely trustworthy," which seems the opposite of what the context requires.
452. Dhammika 50 identifies this as the *Bauhinia variegata*, "an ornamental tree with thick broad leaves, a stocky trunk, and large beautiful mauve and white flowers splashed with purple. The tree drops its leaves before flowering."
453. *Saṃsīnapatto ti patitapatto* (so Ce and Ee; Be has *sañchinnapatto*). The Be and Ce versions of Nidd II mirror this difference in the root text, but Ee of Niddesa has *sañchinnapatto*. Norman writes (GD 158): "It seems clear that we should read *saṃsīna-* as the lectio difficilior, and assume that *sañchinna-* has entered the text from the gloss." See SED *saṃśriṇāti*, passive *saṃśīryate*, which can mean "to be dissipated or routed, fly in different direction." SED also has *śīrṇa*, the past participle of root *śrī*, as meaning, among other things, "withered, faded, shrivelled, shrunk, decayed, rotten." The Gāndhārī version (v. 19) is a hybrid of **44** and **64**. It has *[o]śiṇapatro*, which further supports *saṃsīnapatto*.
454. Ee is missing *sakkā* here.
455. Reading with Ce *yaññopavītakaṇṭhā hutvā*, as against Be *pubbopacitakammā hutvā*, evidently a normalization. SED explains *yajñopavīta*: "the investiture of youths of the three twice-born castes with the sacred thread or (in later times) the thread itself (worn over the left shoulder and hanging down under the right)."
456. This last term is not at Nidd II 232, which merely offers a string of synonyms for wise: *paṇḍitaṃ paññavantaṃ buddhimantaṃ ñāṇiṃ vibhāviṃ medhāviṃ*.

457. Nidd II 232 offers a similar explanation of *sādhuvihārī* as one who attains the four jhānas, the four immeasurables, the four formless attainments, the attainment of cessation, and fruition attainment. It seems to me unlikely that this was the original intent of the expression.
458. Skt *dhīra* is a homonym that can mean either wise or steady. SED defines *dhīra*[1] (from root *dhī*, "to perceive, think, reflect") as "intelligent, wise, skillful, clever," and *dhīra*[2] (related to *dhṛ* or *dhā*) as "steady, constant, firm, resolute, brave, courageous." The same ambivalence attaches to the Pāli word. Pj II evidently takes *dhīra* here in the sense of "steady," since it glosses *dhīraṃ* as *dhitisampannaṃ*, and according to DOP *dhiti* (corresponding to Skt *dhṛti*) means "firmness; constant, steadfast energy; resolution." Nidd II 233, however, takes *dhīra* in the first sense, as indicated by the gloss: *dhīraṃ paṇḍitaṃ paññavantaṃ buddhimantaṃ ñāṇiṃ vibhāviṃ medhāviṃ*. Dhp-a IV 29,5, commenting on the same line at Dhp 329, also favors this interpretation, glossing *dhīran* with *paṇḍitaṃ*.
459. *Dhīran ti dhitisampannaṃ. Tattha nipakattena dhitisampadā vuttā. Idha pana dhitisampannamevā ti attho. Dhiti nāma asithilaparakkamatā, kāmaṃ taco ca nhāru cā ti evaṃ pavattaviriyass'etaṃ adhivacanaṃ.*
460. *Dhikkatapāpo ti pi dhīro*. See DOP sv *dhikkata*.
461. On King Sutasoma, see Ja no. 537 (V 455 foll.); on King Mahājanaka, Ja no. 539 (VI 30 foll.). It seems that Pj II is offering two interpretations of *raṭṭhaṃ vijitaṃ*. On the first, beginning with *yathā paṭirājā*, *vijitaṃ* is taken as the past participle meaning "conquered." On the second, illustrated by the examples of King Sutasoma and King Mahājanaka, who both renounced their own kingdoms—not realms they had conquered—*vijitaṃ* is taken simply as a synonym of *raṭṭhaṃ*. In support of the second alternative, Norman writes (GD 159): "We may assume then that *vijitaṃ* and *raṭṭhaṃ* are in apposition, with *vijitaṃ* simply meaning 'kingdom,' with no idea of conquest." An alternative interpretation, not in the commentary but better suited to the context, is that the king abandons his own country when it has been conquered by others.
462. Nidd II 234–35 gives a long list of types of wrong livelihood and right livelihood (for monks) to illustrate how one eats blamably and blamelessly. Blamable types of livelihood include scheming, talking, hinting, trickery, offering bribes, and so forth.
463. Here Nidd II mentions various other types of livelihood considered inappropriate for a renunciant. I have selected only a few. Some of these terms are explained at Vism 23–30, Ppn 1.61–82.

464. I read with Be and Ce: *disvā bhujasmiṃ suvaṇṇassa valayāni "gaṇavāse sati saṅghaṭṭanā . . ."* Ee is missing *suvaṇṇassa valayāni*, necessary to complete the meaning.
465. Ce and Ee have *guttiṃ*, as against Be *vatiṃ*, "fence."
466. The noun *abhisajjanā* is ambiguous. According to DOP, the verb from which it is derived, *abhisajjati*, can mean either (1) is attached, is occupied, or (2) is offended; and *abhisajjanā* is defined as "offense (or attachment)." Pj II interprets *abhisajjanā* as "attachment" or "clinging," as does Nidd II 236, which merely comments: "There are two kinds of *sajjanā*, due to craving and due to views" (*dve sajjanā taṇhāsajjanā ca diṭṭhisajjanā ca*). The verse's use of the disjunction *vā*, however, suggests that *vācābhilāpo* and *abhisajjanā* are contraries. I thus take *vācābhilāpo* as implying affection and *abhisajjanā* as abusive speech or "verbal friction." Norman translates it "abuse," while Jayawickrama, following Pj II, has "deep attachment." Although I render *abhisajjanā* in the verse in accordance with my own understanding, here, to capture the intent of Pj II, I render it "clinging."
467. Ee is missing *chandādayo*, which is in Be and Ce.
468. Strangely, Pj II does not expand on the line "Having seen danger in the strands of sensual pleasure" (*ādīnavaṃ kāmaguṇesu disvā*), but Nidd II 237–39 quotes at length from MN I 85–88.
469. *Rājā tesaṃ abhayaṃ datvā*. Apparently in ancient India if surgery on a king went wrong, the king would punish the surgeon.
470. Reading with Ce and Ee *aviditatibbānatthāvahahetutāya*.
471. I read with Be *sañjātakkhandho*, which accords with the verse, rather than *sujātakkhandho*, in Ce and Ee.
472. *Evaṃ kudāssu nām'āhampi ariyakantesu sīlesu dantattā* (i) *adantabhūmiṃ nāgamanena*, (ii) *āguṃ akaraṇena*, (iii) *puna itthattaṃ anāgamanena ca, guṇasarīramahantatāya vā nāgo bhaveyyaṃ*. There are three puns here on the word *nāga*: (i) not coming (*na āgamana*) to the plane of the untamed; (ii) not committing a crime (*āguṃ akaraṇena = na āguṃ karoti*); and (iii) not coming back again to this state of being (*itthattaṃ anāgamanena = itthattaṃ na āgacchati*).
473. *Āguṃ na karotī ti nāgo; na gacchatī ti nāgo; na āgacchatī ti nāgo.* These are puns similar to those used by Pj II.
474. Both back (or more literally the trunk of the body) and aggregate render the word *khandha*.
475. Norman translates *padumī* as "spotted" rather than "lotus-like," explaining (at GD 161) that he follows SED, which gives *padmin* as meaning "spotted (as an elephant)," and Edgerton, who says that the name refers to the white spots, called

"lotuses," found on the bodies of elephants. But a broader meaning may be intended. The word *padumi* also occurs at Vv 5 (v. 32), again in relation to an elephant described as *padumi padumapattakkhi padumuppalajutindharo*. See too the gloss on the word at Vv-a 35–36: *Padumī ti padumasamānavaṇṇatāya "paduman" ti laddhanāmena kumbhavaṇṇena samannāgatattā padumī*. ("*Lotus-like* because he is possessed of frontal globes that are called 'lotuses' because their color is similar to that of a lotus.")

476. Ādiccabandhu is often used in the Nikāyas as an epithet for the Buddha (see **540**d, **915**a, **1128**b). See too DPPN sv Ādiccabandhu. It seems that by identifying Ādiccabandhu as the name of a paccekabuddha, Pj II is trying to uphold an old tradition that ascribes all these verses to paccekabuddhas. But the evidence to the contrary is compelling. Nidd II 243–44, while also taking Ādiccabandhu to be the name of a paccekabuddha, quotes a canonical statement (MN III 110,28–32) that exactly fits the context: "Indeed, Ānanda, it is impossible that a bhikkhu who delights in company, takes delight in company, and devotes himself to delight in company . . . will ever enter upon and dwell in either the liberation of mind that is temporary and delectable or in that which is perpetual and unshakable" (*so vat'ānanda, bhikkhu saṅgaṇikārāmo saṅgaṇikarato saṅgaṇikārāmataṃ anuyutto . . . sāmāyikaṃ vā kantaṃ cetovimuttiṃ upasampajja viharissati, asāmāyikaṃ vā akuppanti – n'etaṃ ṭhānaṃ vijjati*). This strongly suggests that the verse refers to the Buddha Gotama himself.

477. *Ālambanabāhaṃ nissāya*. For *ālambanabāhā* DOP has "a handrail, a banister."

478. *Vaṭṭaṃ* and *vivaṭṭaṃ* refer respectively to saṃsāra and nibbāna.

479. Reading with Ce and Ee *viruddhaṭṭhena*, as against Be *visūkaṭṭhena*.

480. *Dassanamaggena atikkanto*. The "path of seeing" is the path of stream-entry, by which one first directly *sees* the four noble truths and nibbāna, the truth of cessation.

481. *Patto niyāman ti avinipātadhammatāya sambodhiparāyaṇatāya ca niyatabhāvaṃ adhigato, sammattaniyāmasaṅkhātaṃ vā paṭhamamaggaṃ*. On entering "the fixed course of rightness" as meaning the attainment of the first path, see SN III 225: "This one is called a faith-follower (and Dhamma-follower) who has entered the fixed course of rightness, entered the plane of good persons, transcended the plane of worldlings, one who is unable to pass away without having realized the fruit of stream-entry" (*ayaṃ vuccati saddhānusārī* [*dhammānusārī*], *okkanto sammattaniyāmaṃ, sappurisabhūmiṃ okkanto, vītivatto puthujjanabhūmiṃ . . . abhabbo ca tāva kālaṃ kātuṃ yāva na*

sotāpattiphalaṃ sacchikaroti). See too AN III 174–76, AN III 441–42.

482. Reading with Ce and Ee *vipassanāya*, as against Be *samathavipassanāya*, "by serenity and insight."

483. On the three kinds of scheming (*tividhaṃ kuhanavatthu* = *tīṇi kuhanavatthūni*), see pp. 1123–24.

484. Reading with Ce and Ee *guṇamakkhanabhāvaṃ*, as against Be *guṇamakkhanābhāvaṃ*.

485. *Eko carituṃ sakkuṇeyya*. This is said because the optative form *care* can be interpreted either as a soft injunction, "one should live," or as an indication of ability, "one can, one is able to live." I prefer to take it in the former sense, consistent with the rendering used in the previous verses.

486. These are lines from the stock formulas for wrong views mentioned in the Nikāyas, as is the following statement by the minister.

487. The tenfold evil view (*dasavatthukā pāpadiṭṭhi*) is the same as the tenfold wrong view. See Appendix 3.

488. Reading with Ce and Ee *paresampi anatthaṃ dasseti*, as against Be *paresampi anatthaṃ passati*. Nidd II 249 (§143) says only that he is possessed of the tenfold wrong view (*dasavatthukāya micchādiṭṭhiyā samannāgato*).

489. The word *pasuta* does not necessarily denote a blameworthy quality but essentially means "intent upon, keen on." However, the verse is clearly using it in a negative sense. While Pj II interprets *pasuto* by way of wrong views, Nidd II 250 explains the expression as one intent on sensual pleasures.

490. Following Ce and Ee, *tathā dhammadharo*. Be has *āgatāgamo dhammadharo*, "a bearer of Dhamma is one who has received the heritage."

491. *Kāmasukhan ti vatthukāmasukhaṃ, vatthukāmāpi hi sukhassa visayādibhāvena sukhan ti vuccanti*. Nidd II 252 quotes the stock sutta definition (as at MN I 85,28–29): "The pleasure and joy that arise in dependence on these five strands of sensual pleasure are called sensual pleasure" (*yaṃ kho, bhikkhave, ime pañca kāmaguṇe paṭicca uppajjati sukhaṃ somanassaṃ, idaṃ vuccati kāmasukhaṃ*).

492. *Alaṅkaroti* typically means "to adorn," but DOP defines the negative form as "finds no satisfaction in," and the negative absolutive *analaṅkaritvā* as "thinking insufficient, not finding satisfaction in." Nidd II 252 does not offer a gloss of the word, but it is clear from the context that this is the meaning intended.

493. I read here with Ce *analaṅkaraṇena* (or Ee *analaṃkaraṇena*) as against Be *alaṅkaraṇena*.

494. Natural abstinence when a situation for transgression arises, abstinence by undertaking precepts, and abstinence by eradicating the defilements responsible for transgression. See Ps I 203,24–27: *yā tasmiṃ samaye pāṇātipātā ārati viratī ti evaṃ vuttā kusalacittasampayuttā virati, sā bhedato tividho hoti sampattavirati samādānavirati samucchedavirati.*
495. *Sālivīhiyavagodhumakaṅkuvarakakudrūsaka.* The exact identity of some of these grains is uncertain. See Ṭhānissaro 2007 1:371 for a discussion. *Kudrūsaka* is probably the dark grain called *kurukkan* in Sri Lanka. It is used to make *kurukkan roti,* a nutritious flat bread similar to chapati.
496. *Yathodhikānī ti sakasakaodhi vasena ṭhitān'eva.* The term *yathodhi* in relation to the elimination of defilements occurs at MN I 37,28: *yathodhi kho pan'assa cattaṃ hoti vantaṃ muttaṃ pahīnaṃ paṭinissaṭṭhaṃ.* As Nidd II 254 (cited just below) explains, each of the four noble paths abandons the defilements appropriate to itself.
497. *Tappaṭibhāganimittaṃ uppādesi.* Usually *paṭibhāganimitta* refers to the mentally created image used as an object of meditation, but here it seems to mean a course of reflection and insight based on an observed event.
498. See Appendix 3.
499. With Ce and Ee, I read here *are,* as against Be *puna.*
500. With Ce and Ee I read *parivajjanāpahātabbadassanatthaṃ,* as against Be *parivajjagahetabbadassanatthaṃ.* Pj II is alluding here to one of the seven methods for abandoning *āsavas,* mentioned at MN I 10,34, that is, avoiding such things as wild elephants, wild horses, wild bulls, ferocious dogs, etc.
501. See AN 5:221–22 (III 257).
502. I read *paṭipattiyā* with Be and Ce, as against Ee *paṭipātiyā.*
503. In pāda b of the verse, Be and Ce have *sañchannapatto,* as against Ee *saṃchinnapatto,* "whose leaves have fallen." Norman, at GD 164–65, accepts *sañchannapatto* but suggests *channa* may be from Skt *śanna* (root *śad*), "fallen, decayed, withered" (SED). Jayawickrama accepts the Ee reading and renders the phrase "with its leaves destroyed." Nidd II 261 has *sañchannapatto,* explained as "covered with foliage, with thick shade" (*bahalapattapalāso sandacchāyo*). Regardless of the reading and the commentarial attempts to construe the sense, the simile, it seems, must convey the idea of shedding leaves to match the way a renouncer sheds his layman's garb in taking on the ochre robes. For the various versions of the two pāricchattaka verses, see the insert below.

The Khaggavisāṇa verses on the koviḷāra and pāricchattaka trees

Sn 44 (v. 10)

Be

Oropayitvā gihibyañjanāni, sañchinnapatto yathā koviḷāro,
chetvāna vīro gihibandhanāni, eko care khaggavisāṇakappo.

Ce

Oropayitvā gihīvyañjanāni, saṃsīnapatto yathā koviḷāro,
chetvāna vīro gihībandhanāni, eko care khaggavisāṇakappo.

Ee

Oropayitvā gihivyañjanāni, saṃsīnapatto yathā koviḷāro,
chetvāna vīro gihibandhanāni, eko care khaggavisāṇakappo.

Ap 99

Be

Oropayitvā gihibyañjanāni, sañchinnapatto yathā koviḷāro;
chetvāna vīro gihibandhanāni, eko care khaggavisāṇakappo.

Ce

Oropayitvā gihibyañajanāni saṃsīnapatto yathā koviḷāro,
chetvāna viro gihibandhanāni eko care khaggavisāṇakappo.

Sn 64 (v. 30)

Be

Ohārayitvā gihibyañjanāni, sañchannapatto yathā pārichatto;
kāsāyavattho abhinikkhamitvā, eko care khaggavisāṇakappo.

Ce

Ohārayitvā gihīvyañjanāni, sañchannapatto yathā pārichatto,
kāsāyavattho abhinikkhamitvā, eko care khaggavisāṇakappo.

Ee

Ohārayitvā gihīvyañjanāni, saṃchinnapatto yathā pārichatto,
kāsāyavattho abhinikkhamitvā, eko care khaggavisāṇakappo.

Ap 119

Be

Ohārayitvā gihibyañjanāni, sañchannapatto yathā pārichatto;
kāsāyavattho abhinikkhamitvā, eko care khaggavisāṇakappo.

Ce

Ohārayitvā gihibyañajanāni, saṃchinnapatto yathā pārichatto,
kāsāyavattho abhinikkhamitvā, eko care khaggavisāṇakappo.

Mvu 4

Otārayitvā gṛhivyañjanāni, saṃśīrṇapatro yathā pāripātro,
kāṣāyavastro abhiniṣkramitvā, eko care khaḍgaviṣāṇakalpo.

Gāndhārī 19 (hybrid of Sn 44 and 64)

Ośaḍaita gīhiviṃjaṇaṇi, [o]śiṇapatro yasa koviraḍo
*kaṣa(*yavastro abhinikkhamitva, eko care khargaviṣaṇagapo).*
(Salomon 2000, 146–48)

504. *Kāsāyavattho abhinikkhamitvā ti imassa pādassa gehā abhinikkhamitvā kāsāyavattho hutvāti evamattho veditabbo.* Apparently this is said merely to confirm that one *first* renounces the home life and *then* takes on the ochre robe, rather than the reverse, as *kāsāyavattho abhinikkhamitvā* in the text might suggest.

505. Evidently Niddesa here takes the simile as describing the ascetic *after* his renunciation. This connects pāda b to pāda c, which seems disjointed. If we are to accept the reading *sañchannapatto*, it makes better sense to interpret this as describing the pāricchattaka tree *before* it has shed its leaves and thus as applying to the subject before he has "cast off the marks of a layman."

506. *Sapadānacārī*. This is one of the thirteen austere practices. See Vism 67–68, Ppn 2.31–34.

507. *Sesamaggehi chetvā tedhātukaṃ sinehadosaṃ, taṇhārāgan ti vuttaṃ hoti.* Pāli *dosa*, in the compound *sinehadosaṃ*, is a homonym representing two distinct Skt words: *dveṣa*, "hatred," and *doṣa*, "defect, fault." I translate the verse and lemma on the supposition that *dosa* represents Skt *dveṣa*; but I render Pj II's gloss following its explanation, which takes *dosa* as Skt *doṣa*. My rendering of the verse follows Nidd II 265, cited just below, which glosses *dosa* with a register of terms for hatred. Affection and hatred correspond to the first two hindrances, sensual desire and ill will.

508. *Pariyāyato*: in an indirect sense, in a way convenient for the purpose of exposition. This is contrasted with *nippariyāyato*, the direct sense, a rigorously precise sense, a sense to be taken literally.

509. *Paṭisallānan ti tehi tehi sattasaṅkhārehi paṭinivattitvā sallāṇaṃ ekattasevitā ekībhāvo.* The sentence explains *paṭisallāṇa* as prefix *paṭi* + base *sallāṇa*. The commentaries often distinguish the objects of attachment as *satta*, living beings taken as conventional entities, and *saṅkhārā*, their constituents along with external objects. Salomon (2000, 167) discusses some of the problems with this verse. Contrary to Salomon, I do not see any problem with supposing that *paṭisallānaṃ* and *jhānaṃ* both function as accusative objects of *ariñcamāno*, with *ca* understood. On the distinction between beings and conditioned things, see note 360.

510. *Jhānan ti paccanīkajhāpanato ārammaṇalakkhaṇūpanijjhānato ca cittaviveko vuccati.* Here, *jhāna* is explained on the basis of the verb *jhāpeti*, "to burn up," and again, more accurately, on the basis of the verb *upanijjhāyati* (*upa* + *ni* + *jhāyati*), "to contemplate closely."
511. All three editions read here *vipassanāmaggaphalāni sattasaññādipaccanīkajhāpanato, lakkhaṇūpanijjhānato yeva c'ettha phalāni.* The parallels, Nidd II-a 125 and Ap-a I 200, instead read: *Vipassanāmaggaphalāni sattasaññādipaccanīkajhāpanato lakkhaṇūpanijjhānato ca jhānan ti vuccati.* I follow the latter. Insight and the path "burn up" the perception of a being (a synonym for the view of a self) because insight sees into the non-self nature of phenomena and the path eradicates *sakkāyadiṭṭhi,* the view of a substantial self. Nidd II 268–69 provides a simpler explanation of the phrase, translated just below.
512. Be has an additional gloss here, *anissajjamāno,* "not relinquishing," not in Ce or Ee.
513. The explanation plays on several meanings of the word *dhamma,* visible in the Pāli but hard to replicate in translation: *Dhammesū ti vipassanūpagesu pañcakkhandhādidhammesu . . . Anudhammacārī ti te dhamme ārabbha pavattanena anugataṃ vipassanādhammaṃ caramāno. Atha vā dhammā ti nava lokuttaradhammā, tesaṃ dhammānaṃ anulomo dhammo ti anudhammo.* Pj II takes *dhammesu* in the verse in the broad sense of "phenomena," particularly the phenomena to be seen with insight. It might be better, however, to understand *dhammesu* here as the teachings and *anudhamma* as the practice that accords with the teachings. The explanation at Nidd II 269, just below, supports my interpretation.
514. Reading with Ce and Ee *pavattanena* as against Be *pavattamānena.*
515. The four paths, four fruits, and nibbāna.
516. Norman remarks (GD 166) that while it is possible to take *sammasitā* as an agent noun in *–tar,* it is more likely an example of an absolutive in *–tā.* Pj II uses the present participle *samanupassanto* in its paraphrase, which does not show how it understands *sammasitā* grammatically.
517. *Aneḷamūgo.* Literally "not dumb." I translate following Nidd II 270: *Aneḷamūgo ti so paccekasambuddho paṇḍito paññavā buddhimā ñāṇī vibhāvī medhāvī.* Pj II too glosses the word with *paṇḍito vyatto.*
518. *Niyato ti ariyamaggena niyāmaṃ patto.* In the Nikāyas, *niyata* is used to describe one who has attained the stage of stream-entry and is therefore "fixed in destiny," bound to reach full

liberation. Just below, Nidd II 270 identifies *niyāma* with the noble paths themselves.

519. *Khandhā saṃkhittā dhātuyo saṃkhittā āyatanāni saṃkhittāni*, etc. I wonder whether *saṃkhitta*, though present in Be and Ce, could be a wrong transcription for *saṅkhātā*.

520. *Uppaṭipāṭiyā esa pādo yojetabbo*. With Ce and Ee I read *pādo* here, as against Be *pāṭho*. On *uppaṭipāṭiyā* DOP says: "in an irregular order, not successively, in an inverted order, the other way round."

521. Reading with Ee *jetvā*, as against Be and Ce *chetvā*, "having cut off."

522. *Tayo khandhā siddhā honti*. This refers to the three "aggregates" of training—good behavior, concentration, and wisdom—as the sequel will make clear.

523. *Sahanā ca hananā ca sīghajavattā ca sīho*. There are puns here that cannot be replicated in translation. The word *sīha* is being derived by combining the syllables *sa* and *ha*, and again from *sīgha*, meaning "speed."

524. I follow Ce and Ee here: *pasayha niggahetvā pavāhetvā caraṇena*. Be is missing *pavāhetvā*.

525. With this suggestion, Pj II seems to be construing the genitive plural *migānaṃ* as the object of *pasayha* and *abhibhuyya*, though it is obvious that *migānaṃ* should be taken with *rājā* as an epithet for the lion—"king of beasts"—with the object of the two absolutives left implicit. It is possible, however, that Pj II is simply offering this as an alternative in order to determine the object of the lion's attack, without proposing that *migānaṃ* be taken literally as an accusative. Nidd II 272 offers the expected explanation, which I translate just below.

526. *Appamaññā*, popularly known as *brahmavihārā*, "the divine abodes." Interestingly, in the Nikāyas, the group name *brahmavihārā* seems to be used for the four states only when they are explained as means to rebirth in the brahma world. On the one occasion when they are given a group name as general meditation practices they are called *catasso appamaññāyo* (at DN III 223,25). By the time of the commentaries, *brahmavihārā* seems to have prevailed.

527. *Gāthābandhasukhatthaṃ*. That is, for metrical reasons.

528. The four immeasurables as they appear in the text are accusatives—*mettaṃ*, *upekkhaṃ*, *karuṇaṃ*, and *muditaṃ*—functioning as adjectives in apposition to *vimuttiṃ*, thus "the loving-kindness liberation," and so forth.

529. It is said that the first three immeasurables are attainable at the level of the three lower jhānas, while equanimity as a jhāna is attainable only at the level of the fourth jhāna. The alternative

given above, "by way of the three or four jhānas" (*tikacatukkajjhānavasena*), is said with reference to the Abhidhamma system, which counts five jhānas by adding a second jhāna without *vitakka* but accompanied by *vicāra* and a third jhāna in which both *vitakka* and *vicāra* are absent (see Dhs 51–54, §§167–75). The third jhāna of the sutta system becomes the fourth jhāna in this scheme, and the fourth jhāna of the sutta system becomes the fifth jhāna in this scheme. A basis for the fivefold scheme of jhānas is found in suttas that distinguish three kinds of *samādhi*, in which there is a *samādhi* without *vitakka* but accompanied by *vicāra*. See, for example, DN III 219,19–20, MN III 162,13–16.

530. It is strange that the Pāli tradition allows a paccekabuddha to still be alive at the time a bodhisatta takes birth into his final existence. In the Mvu it appears that pratyekabuddhas must vanish before the bodhisattva is conceived. See Mvu I 357 (trans. Jones 1949, 1:302–3).
531. Reading with Be *ābādhikarogena*, as against Ce and Ee *svābhāvikarogena*.
532. *Attani ṭhitā etesaṃ paññā, attānaṃyeva olokenti, na aññan ti attaṭṭhapaññā*. This explanation plays upon the contrast between concern only for one's own good and concern for the good of others.
533. *Diṭṭhatthapaññā ti ayampi kira porāṇapāṭho, sampati diṭṭhiyeva atthe etesaṃ paññā, āyatiṃ na pekkhantī ti vuttaṃ hoti*. This explanation plays upon the contrast between concern only for temporal benefit in this present life and concern for one's long-term future benefit.
534. *Purebhattakiccaṃ niṭṭhāpetvā pacchābhattakiccāvasāne*. Since dawn marks the beginning of a day, the forenoon activities begin at dawn, and the "conclusion of his activities after midday" occurs just before the break of dawn on the following day.
535. A parallel description of the Buddha's daily routine is at Sv I 45–48. For an English translation, see Bodhi 2007b: 98–100.
536. *Indakhīla*. DOP (sv *inda*) defines this as "a post or stone planted in the ground at the door of a house or palace or at the city gates against which the door or gate was closed; a threshold."
537. I read with Ce and Ee *khaṇasampatti dullabhā*. Be has *saddhāsampatti dullabhā*. *Khaṇasampatti* probably refers to AN IV 227,8–18, which speaks about the "one unique opportune moment that is the right occasion for living the spiritual life," namely: a buddha has arisen in the world, and he teaches the Dhamma, and a person has been reborn in the central provinces, and he is wise, intelligent, astute.
538. *Vividhapāṭihāriyaṃ*. The word *pāṭihāriya* is often used to desig-

nate a "wonder" or "miracle," as above in the description of the wonders that occur when the Buddha enters the town on alms round (p. 498). But it can also signify the capacity of his teaching to "remove opposition." This follows from the literal meaning of the verb *paṭiharati*, "to take away." The Nikāyas mention three kinds of "wonders": the wonder of psychic powers, the wonder of mind-reading, and the wonder of instruction (*iddhipāṭihāriyaṃ, ādesanāpāṭihāriyaṃ, anusāsanīpāṭihāriyaṃ*); the last is extolled as the supreme wonder (see DN I 212–14).

I translate here the explanation of *vividhapāṭihāriyaṃ* at Sv-ṭ I 46–47; the same explanation is at Ps-ṭ I 24, Spk-ṭ I 21, and Mp-ṭ I 24: "Here, as to the etymology of the term *pāṭihāriya*, they speak of *pāṭihāriya* because of taking away opponents (*paṭipakkhaharaṇato*), [that is] because of removing such defilements as lust. But the Blessed One has no opponents such as lust to be taken away. In the case of worldlings too, the spiritual powers occur when the opponents [of their minds] have been destroyed, that is, when their minds are devoid of defilements and possessed of eight excellent qualities. Therefore it is not possible to speak of *pāṭihāriya* in this case, using the expression in relation to them. But the defilements in those who are to be trained by the Blessed One, the Great Compassionate One, are opponents; so if the word *pāṭihāriya* is used because of the 'taking away of those opponents,' in such a case this is correct usage of the term. Or alternatively: The sectarians are the opponents of the Blessed One's teaching. *Pāṭihāriya* signifies the taking away of them. For they are taken away (*haritā*), removed, by means of psychic powers, mind-reading, and instruction, by taking away their views and by rendering them incapable of expounding their views. . . . Because it is manifold in the Blessed One's teaching, divided by way of psychic powers [and mind-reading and instruction] and by way of various objective domains, he says: 'applies diverse counteractive measures.'" The "eight excellent qualities" mentioned above are those present when the mind is concentrated through the fourth jhāna: purified, cleansed, unblemished, rid of defilement, malleable, wieldy, steady, and attained to imperturbability.

539. *Dhammatthadesanāpaṭivedhagambhīraṃ*. The fourfold depth in relation to dependent origination is explained at Sv II 493–95. For a translation, see Bodhi 1995, 64–67.

540. *Nāhaṃ sayambhū*. On *sayambhū* see note 401.

541. *Evaṃ mayā sotaviññāṇapubbaṅgamāya viññāṇavīthiyā upadhāritan ti*. This alludes to the Abhidhamma mode of explanation

according to which learning occurs when a cognitive process through the ear door is followed by mind-door cognitive processes that understand the meaning conveyed by the sounds.

542. *Bhagavā ti bhāgyavā, bhaggavā, bhattavā*. These are three alternative derivations of the word "*bhagavā*." For a detailed explanation, see pp. 1086–87.
543. The allusion is to Ja No. 422, III 454–61.
544. Pj II here derives *viharati* from the prefix *vi-* in *vicchinditvā* and the verb *harati*.
545. *Divya-brahma-ariyavihārehi vā sattānaṃ vividhaṃ hitaṃ haratī ti viharati*. The three are mentioned at DN III 220,18. Sv III 1006,19–20 explains: "The eight meditative attainments are the celestial abode, the four immeasurables are the divine abode, and the attainment of fruition is the noble abode" (*aṭṭha samāpattiyo dibbo vihāro, catasso appamaññā brahmā vihāro, phalasamāpatti ariyo vihāro*). AN I 182–84 speaks of the three as "high and luxurious beds" (*uccāsayanamahāsayana*).
546. A black substance used by women as a cosmetic for the eyes.
547. Reading with Be and Ce *dametuṃ*, as against Ee *nāmetuṃ*.
548. *Evaṃ accantasaṃyoge upayogavacanaṃ labbhati*.
549. The relinquishment of limbs, body, wealth, wife, and kingdom. See It-a I 118,30–32: *aṅgapariccāgaṃ, attapariccāgaṃ, dhanapariccāgaṃ, dārapariccāgaṃ, rajjapariccāgan ti imāni pañca mahāpariccāgāni pariccajitvā*.
550. Ce and Ee have *atisemānaṃ*; Be has *atibhāsayamānaṃ*. See DOP sv *atiseti, atisayati*.
551. The objection raised here is that the brahmin asked about plowing, but the Buddha spoke about a seed, not plowing. Since the Buddha typically matches his answers with the questions, his present answer seems to miss the brahmin's question. The commentator argues that the Buddha's response was still apt because seeds are essential to plowing.
552. Here I read with Be *anāropetvā* as against Ce and Ee *āropetvā*.
553. *Samūlaṃ saupakāraṃ sasesasambhāraṃ saphalaṃ kasiṃ ñāpetuṃ mūlato paṭṭhāya kasiṃ dassento āha: saddhā bījan ti*.
554. The point is that, just as the wild elephant would lead the ox astray so that plowing could not be done, weak faith would prevent wisdom from accomplishing its proper task, the eradication of defilements.
555. *Mūlabījaṃ, khandhabījaṃ, phalubījaṃ, aggabījaṃ, bījabījaṃ*. For examples of each, see Vin IV 34–35.
556. This alludes to the seven purifications, the framework of Vism.
557. The austere practices (*dhutaṅga*), such as wearing rag robes and living in the forest, were allowed by the Buddha to promote contentment and fewness of desires. In contrast,

extreme austerities (*dukkarakārikā*) veer toward self-mortification and are therefore rejected as deviations from the middle way.

558. *Vipassanākāle dhammānaṃ santatisamūhakiccārammaṇaghanaṃ bhindati*. Spk-ṭ I 237 explains the distinctions here: "This is the distinction between compactness in regard to continuity and the others: *Compactness in regard to continuity* is the occurrence of things as if they constitute a unity because of the immediate succession of preceding and following phenomena. *Compactness in regard to mass* is the occurrence of things that appear as a unity because they are amassed as one. *Compactness in regard to function* is the occurrence of things as if they constitute a unity because of the difficulty of distinguishing their functions. *Compactness in regard to object* is the occurrence of things as if they constitute a unity because they have a single object."
559. I understand this to mean that only world-transcending wisdom—the wisdom of the path—severs the defilements, but the mundane wisdom of insight breaks up the fourfold compactness.
560. In the Nikāyas, the two qualities—*hiri* and *ottappa*—are often mentioned as a pair. *Hiri* is shame at doing evil based on one's own sense of self-respect; *ottappa* is dread of the consequences of doing evil.
561. In this passage, according to Pj II, three of the four kinds of *sīla* recognized by the commentaries are indicated. On the four, see Vism 15–16, Ppn 1.42.
562. *Karaṇatthe c'etaṃ upayogavacanaṃ veditabbaṃ. Ayaṃ hi ettha attho "saccena karomi niddānan" ti.*
563. *Soracca*, from *sorata* (< *su* + *rata*), usually means "gentleness, restraint, meekness" (PED). But Pj II here takes *surata* in the sense of "well delighted," delighted with the good, which is nibbāna.
564. Norman, at GD 169–70, argues for the reading *–dhoreyya*, mentioned at Pj II 149, note 6, as a variant in Sinhala-script editions. This agrees with the Skt form *dhaureya*, on which see SED.
565. Be and Ce: *Dhurāyaṃ dhorayhaṃ dhuradhorayhaṃ, dhuraṃ vahatī ti attho*. Ee is missing *dhuradhorayhaṃ*.
566. *Atha vā purimadhuraṃ vahantā dhurā, mūladhuraṃ vahantā dhorayhā; dhurā ca dhorayhā ca dhuradhorayhā*. As I understand it, this rather dense explanation envisages two pairs of oxen, four animals in all, carrying each plow. The front pair of oxen is a bearer of the burden because it also leads the pair of oxen closer to the plow. The four oxen in the analogy correspond to

the four right kinds of striving; see DN III 221,11–22, SN V 244, AN II 15,13–26.

567. *Yogakkhemādhivāhanan ti ettha yogehi khemattā yogakkheman ti nibbānaṃ vuccati.* This explanation follows from the identification of *yoga* in the compound with the four "bonds" or "yokes" in such sources at AN II 10 and Dhs 255, §1157: the bond of sensuality, the bond of existence, the bond of views, and the bond of ignorance. Norman renders the term "rest from exertion."

568. Although all three editions have *anusahagate,* I suspect this is an error, probably of ancient origins, for *aṇusahagate.* See DOP sv *aṇu.*

569. *Atha vā gacchati anivattan ti nivattanarahitaṃ hutvā gacchatī ti attho. Tan ti taṃ dhuradhorayhaṃ.* Whereas the former explanation takes *anivattantaṃ* as a present participle qualifying *naṅgalaṃ,* the plow (a neuter noun), this alternative resolves *anivattantaṃ* into the masculine present participle *anivattaṃ + taṃ. Nti* in the VRI text of Be should be corrected to *Tan ti.*

570. These are three aspects of *dukkha.* See DN III 216,22. They are analyzed at Vism 499,14–21, Ppn 16.34–35.

571. *Gāthābhigītan ti gāthāhi abhigītaṃ, gāthāyo bhāsitvā laddhan ti vuttaṃ hoti.* The same exchange is recorded at SN I 167, SN I 168, and SN I 173. Although Pj II takes pains to relate this verse to the present context (parallel to SN I 173), it does not seem to belong here. I believe the original setting of this exchange is the one recorded at Sn p. 85 (here p. 235), and at SN I 167 and SN I 168. In each of these cases a brahmin offers the Buddha the oblation used in the sacrificial ritual. This food is truly that "over which verses have been recited," and since they are Vedic verses, the Buddha would have reason to reject the offering. CPD (sv *abhigīta*) suggests the Buddha rejects such food because it has been "spoken over with mantras" by the brahmin while chanting the sacrificial hymns. If this suggestion is tenable, we might suppose that in the process of oral transmission the original passage about the Buddha's refusal of the food was mechanically transposed to the present sutta, where it seems out of place.

572. *Kevalinan ti sabbaguṇaparipuṇṇaṃ, sabbayogavisaṃyuttaṃ vā ti attho.* The definition highlights two implications of the term *kevalī*: perfection and separation. The term plays a more prominent role in Jainism, where a *kevalī* is one who has attained absolute knowledge. Jayawickrama remarks (PBR 1977, 157): "The origin and conception of the idea is definitely pre-Buddhistic, but it need not be through any Jaina influence that its adoption has taken place in Buddhism."

573. There is a word play here that explains *mahesi* on the basis of *mahā* and *esī,* thus "a great seeker" or "a seeker of the great." *Mahesi* is actually the Pāli counterpart of Skt *maharṣi* (*mahā* + *ṛṣi*) meaning "great rishi." See too pp. 1170–71.
574. *Kukkucca* is used in two senses: (1) as regret for past misconduct; and (2) as agitated behavior, exemplified by playing with one's hands and feet. See p. 1121.
575. According to Ps I 33,36–34,3, Māra dwells in a section of the sixth desire-sphere heaven, among the devas who exercise control over the creations of others, "like a rebel prince in a frontier region."
576. These are edifying etymologies. Here *brāhmaṇa* is related to the verbal root *bāh,* "to expel," a pun that would have been apparent in dialects of Middle Indo-Aryan in which *brāhmaṇa* was pronounced *bāhaṇa*. With the Sanskritization of the texts, the pun was obscured. In a similar way, the commentaries relate *samaṇa* to the verbal root *sam* (Skt *śam*), "to calm down, to become still," when it is actually related to the Skt root *śram,* "to strive." In Skt a connection between *śramaṇa* and *śamita* would be less apparent. On these puns, see Norman 2006a, 134.
577. What is meant by "conventional devas" (*sammutideva*) is royalty, since kings were often addressed as "deva." I do not find this explanation of *deva* convincing in this context. I think it here refers to the deities that dwell close to the human plane, distinguished from those that dwell in the heavenly planes.
578. This explanation derives *abhikkanta,* not from the verb *kamati* (Skt *kramati*), "to step," but from its homonym *kamati,* "to desire."
579. On the four "inversions" (*vipallāsa*) see AN 4:49 (II 52).
580. Pj II here comments on expressions that are not in this particular passage of the root text, but which are found in the stock canonical passage on a layperson's going for refuge.
581. The parallel of this sutta, SN 6:11 (I 171–73), ends with the brahmin declaring himself a lay follower, without asking for monastic ordination and becoming an arahant. This indicates that the transmission lines of reciters responsible for the different collections could attach different concluding pericopes to a sutta that was otherwise substantially the same.
582. *Kulaputto* of Ee should be corrected to *kulaputtā,* as in Ce and Be.
583. Here I follow Be, which reads *anāgate vāyāmābhāvato*. Ce and Ee have *pubbe c'etarahi ca anāgatattā eva,* but *anāgate vāyāmābhāvato* is found in Ce of the commentaries to the four major Nikāyas when commenting on the same phrase.
584. See note 303.

585. The truth of suffering is to be fully understood, the truth of its origin to be abandoned, the truth of cessation to be realized, and the truth of the path to be developed. On this see SN V 436, §29. Each of the four noble paths accomplishes these four functions (the first three partly, the fourth without remainder). Thus the four functions occurring on the occasions of the four paths amount to sixteen functions.

586. Here, consistently with other commentaries, Pj II offers two explanations of *nāparaṃ itthattāya*, depending on whether *itthattāya* is taken as a dative or as an ablative. However, since the stem *itthatta* is clearly neuter, the commentarial explanation of *itthattāya* as an ablative seems unacceptable. The inflectional termination *–āya* is clearly a dative, but I take the dative differently from the commentaries. I understand it to mean: "there is no return *to existence* in *any* state of being." In this way, the expression conveys the same sense as the other declaration of liberation, *natthi dāni punabbhavo*, "Now there is no renewed existence" (see SN III 29,30). Elsewhere (for instance, at DN I 17,33, MN II 130–31, and AN I 63–64) *itthatta* signifies the human state (or perhaps the entire desire realm) as contrasted with higher states of being.

587. Chinese parallels are in DĀ 2 (T I 18b3–18c6) and individual translations of the Mahāparinirvāṇa Sūtra. A fragmentary Skt version (reconstructed Skt juxtaposed with Pāli, Tibetan, and translation of Chinese) is in Waldschmidt 1951, 252–64. The Cunda episode is §26 in this edition.

588. See p. 401.

589. *Micchādiṭṭhikānaṃ vacanapatho mā ahosi*. Literally "Let there not be any course of words for those of wrong views." The point, it seems, is that he did not want news of the theft to spread and give those antagonistic to the Buddha's teaching a chance to denigrate the Sangha.

590. The three are a question to clear up what has not been seen, a question to confirm what has been seen, and a question to eliminate doubt. See pp. 1169–70.

591. See pp. 1036–37.

592. I follow Ce and Ee, *tīsu buddhesu sammāsambuddhaṃ*, as against Be *tīsu buddhesu tatiyabuddhaṃ*. Spk I 25,25–29 distinguishes four kinds of buddhas: an all-knowing buddha who has attained perfect enlightenment (*sammāsambodhiṃ patto sabbaññubuddho*), a paccekabuddha, a buddha of the four truths (*catusaccabuddho*, that is, an arahant disciple), and a learned buddha (*sutabuddho*), one with clear understanding based on learning. Dhp-a III 237,22–23 refers to three kinds of

buddhas: buddhas, paccekabuddhas, and those enlightened by following a buddha (*buddhā ca paccekabuddhā ca anubuddhā ca*).

593. *Sāretī ti sārathi. Sārathi* is actually derived from *sa* + *ratha*, "one with a chariot."

594. *Maggena sabbakilese vijitāvī.* Norman (GD 174–75) takes *maggajino* to be from Skt *mārga-jña* and thus to be equivalent to *maggaññū*, with the *svarabhakti* vowel added. However, I find Pj II's explanation cogent enough to accept "conqueror" as the intended sense. In Sn alone, the Buddha is referred to as *jina* at **372**a, **379**b, **697**d, **698**a, and **996**a. *Maggajino* occurs at Th 1230, glossed at Th-a III 191,32 with *maggena vijitakileso*. The Chinese versions of the sutta, at T I 18b16, T I 167c21, and T I 183b10 all render the first ascetic as 道殊勝, which could mean "one victorious over the path," hence corresponding to *maggajino*. The fragmentary Skt version is ambivalent, with *mārgajñaḥ* (= Pāli *maggaññū*) in the initial enumeration of types (= Sn **84**) but *mārgajinaṃ* in the questions about the types (= Sn **85**).

595. Reading with Be and Ce *paṭihatañāṇappabhāvattā*. The point is that all noble ones from the stage of stream-enterer up have abandoned the defiled doubt included among the three lower fetters, but the noble ones of any lower level still cannot understand matters that can be known by noble ones of a higher level.

596. *Tādin ti tādisaṃ yathāvuttappakāralokadhammehi nibbikāraṃ.* On *tādī* as meaning "impartial," see pp. 59–60 and pp. 1073–74. Although I do not think *tādī* always bears this special sense, I believe this nuance of "one not altered by worldly conditions" is sometimes intended (see Jayawickrama, PBR 1977, 32).

597. *Ubhayampi vā ugghaṭitaññūnaṃ saṅkhepadesanāya ācikkhati, vipañcitaññūnaṃ vitthāradesanāya vibhajati.* See AN II 135,11.

598. *Bhikkhunaṃ* can be taken as either genitive plural (= *bhikkhūnaṃ*) or accusative singular. I treat it as accusative singular. Commenting on *dutiyaṃ bhikkhunaṃ*, Norman (at GD 176) says that since *bhikkhunaṃ* "is certainly accusative singular in **513**, it is probably the same here."

599. The extremes of sensual indulgence and self-mortification, and philosophically, the extremes of eternalism and annihilationism.

600. On *sati* as memory, see SN V 197,10–13. The two aspects of *sati* are merged at SN V 198,16–22.

601. *Subbatānan ti buddhapaccekabuddhasāvakānaṃ, tesaṃ hi sundarāni vatāni, tasmā te subbatā ti vuccanti. Subbata* is from *su* + *vata* (= Skt *suvrata*), literally "of good observances," where *vata* indicates modes of ascetic behavior.

602. *Kuladūsaka.* "Corruptor of families" is discussed under the thirteenth Saṅghādisesa offense. See Vin III 179–86. The rule itself is at Vin III 184, with the analysis immediately following.

603. See pp. 574–75.
604. Ee has *ne 'tādisā' ti*, with *ne* an accusative object. Be has *netādisā ti*, which is ambiguous, and Ce *te tādisā ti*, which agrees in sense with Ee. I take the correct reading to be *n'etādisā ti* (< *na* + *etādisā*), as in the lemma of Pj II (Ee). The Skt supports this with its reading *sarve nāpy evaṃvidhā bhavanti*, where *na* is the negation and *evaṃvidhā* corresponds to *etādisā*.
605. *Na hāpeti, na hāyati, na nassati saddhā ti*. This apparently accepts the causal verb *hāpeti* but, to preserve the status of *saddhā* as a nominative subject, treats it as equivalent to passive *hāyati*, glossed with a passive synonym, *nassati*. The Skt fragment reads the line *jñātvaitān + + + ti tasya śraddhām*, and on this basis I suggest amending *saddhā* in the Pāli to *saddhaṃ*.
606. I read with Be *sabbadevamārabrahmāno*. While Ce and Ee here have *–mānusa–* in place of *–māra–*, in the parallel portion of its commentary on the Maṅgala Sutta (II,4), Ce (248,11) has *sabbadevamārabrahmāno*.
607. Reading with Be *jantuṃ*. Ce and Ee *jānituṃ* should be corrected accordingly.
608. Be has *bhavantaṃ* in both the lemma and the paraphrase, but in both places I read *bhagavantaṃ* with Ce and Ee. All three editions of the text have *bhagavantaṃ*.
609. *Mukha*, literally "door, entrance." The words that follow—*dvāra, yoni, kāraṇa*—are glosses on *mukha*.
610. *Puggalādhiṭṭhānāya desanāya*. Here the Buddha is teaching a quality (namely, downfall) on the basis of a person (the one who is in a downfall). On the distinction between teachings based on persons and teachings based on qualities, see p. 72.
611. The six rival teachers of the Buddha. See p. 214 and pp. 914–15.
612. Pj II here is apparently shifting between two meanings of *santa*, as an adjective meaning "good," based on the present participle of *atthi*, "to be," and as an adjective meaning "peaceful," based on the past participle of *sammati*, "to become peaceful." I take the former sense as intended by the text. So too does Norman, who has "bad men" and "good men," and Jayawickrama, who has "the wicked" and "the good."
613. DN III 6–9. Sunakkhatta was a bhikkhu who admired the ascetic Kora the Khattiya and thought he was an arahant. At MN I 68,6–13 it is said that after he left the Buddha's Dhamma and discipline, he repeatedly disparaged the Buddha in the assembly at Vesālī, claiming the Buddha did not possess any superhuman powers.
614. Pj II 169,13–16 has a comment of mainly grammatical interest: "The difference in expressions here should be understood by way of the disciples to be guided. Or alternatively, 'he does not

treat the good' means 'he does not associate with the good,' as the grammarians explain that 'he treats the king as dear' means 'he associates with the king.' The word 'dear' (*piyaṃ*) then means 'rejoicing, contented, exultant' (*piyan ti piyamāno, tussamāno, modamāno ti attho*)." On this explanation "he does not treat the good" is understood to mean "he does not associate with the good," with *piyaṃ* taken as a short form of a present participle, *piyamāno*, "rejoicing." Thus the sense would be: "He does not, while rejoicing, associate with the good."

615. *Sevati* is in Be only.
616. Stanza **259**, in the Maṅgala Sutta. See p. 199.
617. *Niddāsīlī*. Literally "whose habit is sleep." Similarly, *sabhāsīlī* is "one whose habit is the meeting hall."
618. Be is missing *kadāci karahaci*, found in Ce and Ee.
619. Ja III 139–41.
620. *Pāpānaṃ bāhitattā brāhmaṇaṃ, samitattā samaṇaṃ*. See note 576.
621. An ancient Indian coin.
622. *Thaddha*, literally "stiff," here signifies stiffness because of pride.
623. Viḍūḍabha was the son of King Pasenadi and a former slave woman of the Sakyans. When he learned that the Sakyan royalty had treated him with contempt because of his mixed parentage, he became furious and massacred them. The story is at Dhp-a I 345 foll. (BL 2:36 foll.).
624. *Imāya gāthāya vatthuto catubbidhaṃ, lakkhaṇato ekaṃyeva parābhavamukhaṃ vuttaṃ*. The four bases are pride on account of social class, wealth, and clan, and looking down on one's own relatives. The single characteristic is pride.
625. I read with Ce and Ee *surāpānappamatto*. Be has *surāpānapayutto*.
626. *Parābhavasaṅkhāte anaye na iriyatī ti ariyo*. This is a word play that explains *ariya* as = *a* + *iriya*, the negation (*na*) of behavior (*iriyati*) that brings misfortune.
627. Respectively, DN 20, Sn II,4, AN 2:36, MN 147, SN 56:11, and the present sutta.
628. *Aggikabhāradvājasuttaṃ vasalasuttan ti pi vuccati*. In the text it is called the Vasala Sutta.
629. SN I 166–67 records a similar encounter between the Buddha and a brahmin named Aggikabhāradvāja, but there the discussion is not about the meaning of *vasala* but of *tevijja brāhmaṇa*, a "triple-knowledge brahmin."
630. *Sapadānaṃ piṇḍāya caramāno*. See p. 481.
631. Reading with Be and Ce *kāḷakaṇṇī muṇḍakasamaṇako* (Ee *muṇḍasamaṇako*). These are all pejorative expressions. I have added "low" to capture the scornful tone.

632. Here I read with Ce and Ee *rosavasaṃ*, as against Be *dosavasaṃ*, and just below *rosavasen'eva* as against *dosavasen'eva*. The meanings are almost the same.
633. *Īdisaṃ kāyakilesaṃ na vaṇṇetī ti ca samaṇabhāvaṃ jigucchanto samaṇakā ti āha*. I do not understand why this should be a ground for criticism. I suspect the text is corrupted here.
634. *Samaṇaka*. My rendering is intended to convey the pejorative connotation of the suffix *–ka*.
635. Reading with Ce and Ee *āhutidassanamantasavanena pāpaṃ hoti*. Be has *–matta–* for *–manta–*, which seems to be an error.
636. *Laddhamatte paccaye muduko hoti*. Presumably this means a condition for subduing his pride and anger.
637. Pj II 176,10–20 gives citations illustrating each use of *sādhu*. I omit this passage in translation.
638. See note 539.
639. See Appendix 3.
640. *Taṃ evarūpaṃ puggalaṃ etesaṃ hīnadhammānaṃ vassanato siñcanato anvāssavanato vasalo ti jāneyya*. This seems to derive the word *vasala* from *vassana*, which means "raining down," here the raining down of bad qualities. I take it that *siñcana* and *anvāssavana* merely amplify the idea of raining down. PED explains *vasala* as from Vedic *vṛṣala*, the diminutive of *vṛṣan*, meaning "little man."
641. *Evaṃ attano hadayatuṭṭhimattaṃ, na paranti*. The expression is strange. Helmer Smith must also have been perplexed by the phrase, since he has a note "*sic*" here. The rendering I use was suggested by Bhikkhu Anālayo (in a personal note).
642. Reading with Ce and Ee *te dhamme nappajahanti*, as against Be *te dhamme uppādenti*.
643. SED gives two primary meanings for *dvija* (Pāli *dija*): (1) "a man of any one of the first 3 classes, any Āryan, (esp.) a Brahman (re-born through investiture with the sacred thread)"; and (2) "a bird or any oviparous animal (appearing first as an egg)." Under *ekajanman* and *ekjāti*, SED has a *śūdra* (a member of the lowest class).
644. *Pāṇāni hiṃsatī ti pi pāṭho*. Ce and Ee adopt this reading in the text of Sn.
645. Thus, since the harming of living beings occurs through body or speech, and lack of kindness through the mind, all three doors of action (body, speech, and mind) are covered.
646. The three methods are *nikkhepagahaṇa*, *vaḍḍhigahaṇa*, and *āyogagahaṇa*. I could not find a meaning of *āyoga* that fits the context. A note in Ce says that in many manuscripts the third method is *iṇagahaṇa*.

647. The gloss *icchāya* indicates that *kiñcikkhakamyatā* should be taken as a truncated instrumental.
648. I follow Ce and Ee here: *sāmike asāmike karoti*. Be has *sāmike asāmike, asāmike ca sāmike karoti*, "He deprives the proper owners of ownership and transfers ownership to those who are not the proper owners."
649. *Paṭidissatī ti paṭikūlena dissati*. An attempt to explain the rare verb *paṭidissati* by grafting on to the passive verb *dissati* the prefix of *paṭikūla*, "repulsive."
650. Reading with Ee: *Aṭṭhakathāya māyāpubbabhāgā pāpicchatā vuttā*. Ce has a similar reading, but with *mayā pubbabhāgā*. It is not clear which commentary is being referred to. Be has *ettha mayā pubbabhāge pāpicchatā vuttā*.
651. See note 87.
652. Be and Ce have *sammukhabhāvamattampi c'assa na deti*, Ee *sukhumabhāvamattampi c'assa na deti*. Neither reading makes particularly good sense, so I render this as best fits the context.
653. The primary reading is *asataṃ*, a genitive plural, which Pj II 180,29 glosses with *asajjanānaṃ* (a negation of *sat* + *jana*, "good people"). The alternative, *asantaṃ*, accusative singular, is a negation of *santaṃ*, "existent, real." I translate Sn on the basis of the alternative but here follow Pj II.
654. Pj II here alludes to the five kinds of miserliness: over abodes, families, gains, praise, and Dhamma. See AN III 266, Vibh 441 (§940.3).
655. Be and Ce cite the entire passage, which is at Vin III 89–90. Ee, which I follow, cites only the beginning and end. The first great thief is a thief in the usual sense, a robber. The second is one who becomes learned in the Dhamma and Vinaya and then extols himself. The third groundlessly accuses a pure monk of breaking his vow of celibacy. The fourth is a monk who steals valuable goods belonging to the Sangha. And the fifth is the one who makes a false claim to a superhuman state: the jhānas, the paths, and the fruits.
656. That is, by taking *pāpamakkhī* as a *dvanda* compound, with *pāpa* and *makkhī* as separate items.
657. Reading with Ce and Ee *paṭicchannakammavipattivasena*. Be has *paṭicchannakammantavasena*. It is not clear how two qualities are involved here, unless we regard doing a bad deed and concealing it as two separate items rather than as two aspects of a single bad quality.
658. *Aparisuddhaṃ kammaṃ vassanato vasalo hoti, parisuddhena kammunā aparisuddhaṃ bāhanato brāhmaṇo hoti*. Word plays are involved relating *vasala* to *vassana*, "raining down," and *brāhmaṇa* to *bāhana*, "expelling." See note 576. Since the word rendered "action" is *kamma*, the Buddha's reply is ambiguous.

While this could also be taken to mean that one becomes an outcast and a brahmin as the retributive result of one's impure and pure kamma, respectively, this is contrary to the Buddha's intention here. Other suttas, however, speak of how one is reborn in high and low families as a result of one's conduct in past lives. Thus the ambiguity persists.

659. Jayawickrama (PBR 1977, 90) remarks that "stanzas 137–42 appear as a subsequent addition made by a later editor. It is quite probable that the earliest form of this sutta did not include these six stanzas." He sees the story of Mātaṅga as "a separate sutta or as a separate section appended to the sutta at a subsequent date," with the repetition of **136** at the end serving to tie the story to the rest of the sutta.
660. *Attano khādanatthāya mate sunakhe labhitvā pacatī ti sopāko.* Apparently this was a name based on his caste, and Mātaṅga his personal name.
661. *Devalokayānasaññitaṃ aṭṭhasamāpattiyānaṃ abhiruyha.* The juxtaposition of *devayānaṃ* and *mahāpathaṃ* in the text suggests that *yāna* is used here in the sense of a road rather than a vehicle. SED gives as meanings of *yāna* a path, course; a journey, travel; a vehicle of any kind. While *devaloka* usually refers to the desire-sphere heavens, here it is identified with the brahma world.
662. The "Great Man" (*mahāpurisa*) here is the Bodhisatta, the future Buddha Gotama in his past lives. The story here has a parallel in Ja no. 497 (IV 376 foll.) and Cp-a 152 foll.
663. Reading with Ce and Ee *bhojanatthāya*, as against Be *bhājanahattho*, "dish in hand."
664. A coin of low value, perhaps a penny.
665. The sentence as it now stands seems defective both grammatically and in sense.
666. Reading with Be *gaṇha dārikaṃ*, as against Ce and Ee *handa dārikaṃ*.
667. This seems to mean that he did not have sexual relations with her.
668. Reading with Ce and Ee *kapaṇabhāvaṃ*, as against Be *caṇḍālabhāvaṃ*. All three have *caṇḍālabhāvaṃ* just a few lines down.
669. Reading with Ce and Ee *vissatthabhāvaṃ ñatvā* as against Be *vissatthavācaṃ sutvā*.
670. I translate on the basis of Be: *attano attano gharadvāresu maṇḍapaṃ kārāpetvā, sāṇipākāraṃ sajjetvā, vayappattā dārikāyo alaṅkaritvā*.
671. Reading with Ce and Ee *āsāya*, as against Be *sālāya*.
672. Pj II 192,4 states that along with the prevalent reading *ajjhāyakakule jātā*, "born into a family of reciters," there

is another reading—in Ce and Ee *ajjhāyakā kule jātā*, in Be *ajjhāyakākuḷe jātā*—meaning "reciters of the hymns born into an impeccable brahmin family" (*ajjhāyakā anupakuṭṭhe ca brāhmaṇakule jātā*).

673. *Dujjātā ete kulassa aṅgārabhūtā*. Perhaps this was an ancient Indian idiom equivalent to our expression "the black sheep of the family."

674. The PTS edition of Pj II includes only the first few sentences of the commentary on the Metta Sutta, which is also included in Khp. Thus bracketed page numbers in this commentary refer to Pj I 252 foll. (Ee), commenting on the Metta Sutta in Khp.

675. *Saviññāṇakāviññāṇakavasena ekādasavidhaṃ asubhakammaṭṭhānaṃ*.

676. These are the four immeasurables or divine abodes (*brahmavihārā*): loving-kindness, compassion, altruistic joy, and equanimity.

677. The earlier three-month rains retreat begins on the day following the Āsāḷha full moon, usually beginning in July and ending in October; the later rains retreat begins and ends a month later, usually beginning in August and ending in November. See Vin I 137,28–31.

678. I pass over several sentences that are found in Pj I but not in Pj II.

679. There is an "edifying" word play here, impossible to replicate in English, by which *attha* (Skt *artha*) is derived from *araṇīya* meaning "to be approached" or "to be taken up."

680. I understand Pj I to be saying that *yantaṃ* in pāda b can be taken in two ways. On the first interpretation, *yaṃ* as nominative belongs with *karaṇīyaṃ* and *taṃ* as accusative with *santaṃ padaṃ*. On the second, both *yaṃ* and *taṃ* are nominatives belonging with *karaṇīyaṃ*. But the grammatical situation is still more complex, as the commentary will show in what follows.

681. I follow Ñāṇamoli here at Ppn 1.62 and 1.75–76.

682. A fuller enumeration of wrong occupations for an ascetic is at DN I 8–12; see Bodhi 2007b: 58–62.

683. This passage concerns the grammatical referents of the pronouns *yaṃ* and *taṃ*. Readers who find it too technical may go directly to the sentence: "Among these, what should be done is, in brief, the three trainings." I translate in accordance with the reading and punctuation of Pj I (Ee). Be punctuates somewhat differently. For a rendering that differs in some respects from mine, see Ñāṇamoli 1960, 274–75. As I understand this passage, on the first construal, *yaṃ* belongs with *karaṇiyaṃ* and *taṃ* with *santaṃ padaṃ*. On the second, *yantaṃ* belongs with *karaṇiyaṃ* and *santaṃ padaṃ* does not have a pronoun. On the

third *yantaṃ* belongs with *santaṃ padaṃ* and *karaṇiyaṃ* does not have a pronoun.

684. *Ayaṃ pana yasmā sāvasesapāṭho attho, tasmā "viharitukāmenā" ti vuttan ti veditabbaṃ. Sāvasesapāṭho attho* literally means "a reading whose meaning has a remainder." The point is that another phrase is needed to complete the sense, namely, "who wishes to dwell." Pj I interprets the purport thus: "This is what should be done by one *who wishes* to make the breakthrough to that peaceful state." This adjustment to the reading seems contrived. *Abhisamecca* is an absolutive of *abhisameti,* which along with its corresponding noun *abhisamaya* occurs in the Nikāyas in three contexts: (1) the "breakthrough" to the Dhamma achieved by a stream-enterer or those on higher paths (as in the compound *dhammābhisamaya*); (2) the attainment of arahantship (as in *mānābhisamaya,* "the breakthrough of conceit"); and (3) the Buddha's attainment of enlightenment (SN II 5,19: *ahu paññāya abhisamayo*). The initial "breakthrough" is arrived at when insight reaches maturity and culminates in the world-transcending path experience. At each breakthrough, the disciple attains a "glimpse" of nibbāna, the unconditioned element. The seeing of the four noble truths, the distinctive achievement of the stream-enterer, includes the seeing of nibbāna, the truth of cessation. This *does not mean* that the disciple has "attained nibbāna" in the sense of a final achievement. That comes only with the attainment of arahantship. But even with the breakthrough to the first stage, the stream-enterer sees nibbāna, the unconditioned state, in a world-transcending experience that opens up the irreversible path to arahantship. And this, as I understand it, is what the text is saying here. Since a stream-enterer has already seen nibbāna, the sutta seems to be addressed to stream-enterers and once-returners who have "made the breakthrough" by seeing nibbāna, "the peaceful state," with world-transcending wisdom and are now training for the higher stages of the path. Thus the sense of the sentence can be expressed thus: "What should be done by one skilled in the good who has made the breakthrough to that peaceful state [is as follows]."

685. In other words, on this construal the introductory term (*adhikāra*) here is "by one who wishes to make the breakthrough to—or to achieve—the peaceful state," and both pronouns, *yaṃ* and *taṃ* ("that which"), should be connected with "should be done by one skilled in the good." This contrasts with the first construal, which connects *yaṃ* with *karaṇīyaṃ* and *taṃ* with *santaṃ padaṃ.*

686. I follow Ce and Ee *yaṃ karaṇīyaṃ tan ti yaṃ kātabbaṃ, taṃ*

karaṇīyaṃ, karaṇāraham eva tan ti vuttaṃ hoti as against Be *yaṃ karaṇīyaṃ kātabbaṃ, taṃ karaṇīyaṃ, karaṇārahameva tan ti vuttaṃ hoti*. On this construal, as I understand it, *yaṃ* is to be taken in connection with *karaṇīyaṃ* and *taṃ* with everything that follows, starting with *sakko uju ca*, which represents the means for making the breakthrough to the peaceful state, nibbāna.

687. See AN III 65. The five factors are: (1) faith in the Buddha's enlightenment, (2) good health, (3) honesty and openness, (4) energy in cultivation, and (5) the wisdom that discerns arising and passing away.

688. *Caṇḍālakumārakasamena cetasā*. The caṇḍālas were a community of outcasts. Pj I refers here to AN IV 376,11–16, where Sāriputta says: "Just as a caṇḍāla boy or girl, clad in rags and holding a vessel, enters a village or town with a humble mind; so too, I dwell with a mind like a caṇḍāla boy. . . ."

689. *Tussatī ti tussako, sakena tussako, santena tussako, samena tussako ti santussako*. These are attempts to explain the word *santussaka* by breaking it down into the base, *tussaka*, and the prefix *saṃ*, which the commentary derives from *saka*, *santa*, and *sama*, respectively, "one's own, what is present, and equally."

690. This alludes to a passage recited to newly ordained bhikkhus at the time of ordination (Vin I 58,12–22), explaining to them that the going forth depends on the most stringent use of the four requisites: on food gathered on alms round, on robes stitched from cast-off rags, on dwelling at the foot of a tree, and on putrid urine as medicine—but in each case making more lenient allowances, such as meals by invitation, robes made of fine materials, dwelling in monasteries and lodges, and the use of other medicines.

691. See Vism 127–28, Ppn 4.35–41. The seven kinds of suitability apply to abodes, alms resort, speech, companions, food, climate, and posture.

692. *Appagabbho*. Literally "nonimpudent."

693. In my translation, to accord with normal English syntax, I place "should be" before "able." In the text, however, for metrical reasons, the optative verb *assa*, "should be," occurs in the line *suvaco c'assa mudu anatimānī*, where it is understood to apply to the terms in both the preceding line—*sakko ujū ca sūjū ca*—and the terms in the following verse, *santussako, subharo*, and so forth.

694. *Pāṇantī ti pāṇā*. This is said because the word *pāṇa*, meaning life, and by extension living being, originally meant "breath," conceived as vital energy or life force.

695. See note 303. Pj II here divides the compound *pāṇabhūtā* into

two, *pāṇā* and *bhūtā*, assigning to each a distinct referent. It is doubtful that this was the original intention.

696. *Tasantī ti tasā, sataṇhānaṃ sabhayānañ c'etaṃ adhivacanaṃ*. In Pāli two verbs that are distinct in Skt have become conflated: *tṛṣyati*, "to be thirsty, thirst for," and *trasati/trasyati*, "to tremble, quiver, be afraid." Thus Pāli has two homonymous verbs; see DOP *tasati/tassati*[1] and *tasati/tassati*[2]. The former is the basis for such Pāli words as *taṇhā/tasiṇa*, "craving," the latter of such words as *uttāsana* and *santāsa*, "terror, fright." The verb *paritassati* and noun *paritassanā* are probably both derived from *tṛṣyati*, but because of the conflation, they are explained as related to both craving and fear. For the original meaning of *tasathāvara*, as "moving and unmoving," see DOP sv *tasa*.

Norman 2004, 81, takes the expression in its original sense (see SED *trasa* and *sthāvara*), but since, on this interpretation, *thāvara* signifies vegetation or inanimate objects, this would mean that *mettā* would be developed toward non-sentient objects, which is contrary to the intent of the practice. While the commentarial explanation may be forced, I would surmise that even during the Buddha's time *tasathāvara* had lost its original sense and had come to serve as a conventional expression applicable solely to the domain of *sentient* beings.

697. Reading with Be and Ee *pahīnataṇhābhayānaṃ*.

698. *Anekayojanappamāṇāpi macchagodhādīnaṃ attabhāvā honti*. Since a yojana is equivalent to about six miles, this is hardly acceptable by way of modern knowledge.

699. Reading with Be *jale macchakacchapādayo*.

700. DOP defines this as "one of a class of supernatural beings; a demon."

701. The commentaries take *sambhavesī* as a compound of *sambhava* + *esī*, "a seeker of existence," but I follow Norman in taking the word as a future active participle; on this see GD 187 and Geiger 1994, 183: §193A.

702. Pj I 247,15 rejects a variant it considers unsatisfactory: *idāni pana 'paraṃ hī' ti pi paṭhanti, ayaṃ na sobhano*.

703. Reading with Be *gāme vā nigame vā*.

704. Pj I 247,22 explains *vyārosanā* and *paṭighasaññā* as truncated instrumentals, representing *vyārosanāya* and *paṭighasaññāyā*. It offers several other examples of truncated instrumentals. *Paṭighasaññā* is literally "perception of aversion," or "perception [accompanied] by aversion," which do not work well in English. *Paṭighasaññā* here must be distinguished from the same compound in the formula for attainment of the base of the boundlessness of space (*paṭighasaññānaṃ atthaṅgamā*), which is explained as perception that occurs through the

impingement of sense objects on the five physical sense faculties.

705. Reading with Be and Ce *navahi mānavatthūhi*. These are the three basic modes of conceit—taking oneself to be superior, equal, or inferior—each distinguished according to whether one is actually superior, actually equal, or actually inferior. See Vibh 405–9 (§§866–77).

706. *Evampi sabbabhūtesu idaṃ mettākhyaṃ mānasaṃ bhāvaye, punappunaṃ janaye vaḍḍhaye*. With the expression *mettaṃ mānasaṃ*, Pj I 248,15 takes *mānasaṃ* here as a mental factor dependent on *manas* rather than as synonymous with it. The Abhidhamma, however, includes both *manas* and *mānasaṃ* in a list of synonyms for *citta* as for example at Dhs 22, §6: *Yaṃ tasmiṃ samaye cittaṃ mano mānasaṃ hadayaṃ . . . tajjāmanoviññāṇadhātu, idaṃ tasmiṃ samaye cittaṃ hoti*.

707. *Tañca aparimāṇasattārammaṇavasena ekasmiṃ vā satte anavasesapharaṇavasena aparimāṇaṃ bhāvaye ti*. Mp-ṭ III 190 (= It-a I 92,18–21) elaborates on this, using "measureless" (*appamāṇa*) in place of "unbounded" (*aparimāṇa*): "Immeasurable by way of exhaustive pervasion—by way of pervasion without limits—because, unlike with the meditation on unattractiveness [of the body], one does not select a single portion of the object; and [immeasurable] by way of proficient development through the immeasurability of the object" (*asubhabhāvanādayo viya hi ārammaṇe ekadesaggahaṇaṃ akatvā anavasesapharaṇavasena anodhiso pharaṇavasena ca appamāṇārammaṇatāya paguṇabhāvanāvasena appamāṇaṃ*).

708. *Mejjati tāyati cā ti mitto, hitajjhāsayatāya siniyhati, ahitāgamato rakkhati cā ti attho*. There is a word play here relating *mitta*, friend, to *mejjati*, "to become fat or oily" (because it is "moistened" by concern for the well-being of others), and to *tāyati*, to protect, (because it safeguards others from harm). The word *mettā* is derived from *mitta*, "friend," but "friendliness" conveys too casual a meaning and "good will" or "benevolence" may miss the emotional resonances of *mettā*. Apart from the title, this is the only explicit mention of *mettā* in the sutta.

709. *Mittassa bhāvo mettaṃ*.

710. *Manasi bhavan ti mānasaṃ, taṃ hi cittasampayuttattā evaṃ vuttaṃ*. Again, adhering to a strict distinction between mind and mental factors, Pj II takes *mānasaṃ* as derivative upon *manas* rather than as synonymous with it.

711. I read with Be and Ce *appamāṇasattārammaṇatāya*. Ee has *aparimāṇasattārammaṇatāya*.

712. The peak of existence (*bhavagga*) is the highest formless plane of existence, the base of neither-perception-nor-nonperception. Avīci is the lowest of the hell realms.

713. For *anādiyitvā* in this sense, see DOP sv *ādiyati*², "attends to, takes notice of, shows respect to."
714. Be reads *tāvatā vitamiddho hutvā etaṃ satiṃ adhiṭṭheyyā ti*. I follow Ce and Ee, which do not include *vitamiddho hutvā*, "being without drowsiness."
715. *Catūsu divyabrahmaariyairiyāpathavihāresu niddosattā attanopi paresampi atthakarattā ca.* I understand this clause to be an explanation why the development of loving-kindness is called *brahma* in the sense of "best" (*seṭṭha*) and a "dwelling" (*vihāra*).
716. That is, a basis for developing insight and reaching the path.
717. I read with Ce and Ee *tesañca vavatthādianusārena*, as against Be *tesañca vatthādianusārena*.
718. *Gaṇḍiṃ ākoṭetvā*. The gong, or wooden block, is struck to signal to all the monks, spread out over the jungle grove, that it is time to gather for the communal meeting.
719. I read with Ce and Ee *evaṃ hi atthakusalā kusalassa dhamme*, as against Be *evañhi atthakusalena tathāgatena*. Pj I (Ce) has the same reading as Be here.
720. A parallel to the sutta, which includes a background similar to the last part of the commentarial origin story, is included in the *Arthapada Sūtra as no. 13, preserved in Chinese translation at T IV 183b16 foll. The verses start at 183b29. For an English translation, see Bapat 1951, 114–21.
721. The bracketed page numbers are again those of Pj II (Ee).
722. *Imasmiṃyeva bhaddakappe*. The eon is called "auspicious" or "excellent" (*bhadda*) because five buddhas arise within it: three predecessors of Gotama, who is the fourth, and Metteyya, who is to arise in the future.
723. Since there are four gāvutas to a yojana, and the yojana is estimated to be six miles, this makes a gāvuta about 1.5 miles.
724. *Ajja parinibbuto kassapo bhagavā*. This is said in the sense indicated by the next sentence. Even though the Buddha Kassapa had passed away years earlier, he was still considered to be "alive" because his teaching flourished. But once the elder monks became corrupt, favoring dishonest persons over the Dhamma, it was as if he had truly passed away.
725. *Upahatāsayattā kālaṃ katvā*. Literally "they passed away with their aspiration injured."
726. So Ce and Ee. Be has *nāgavatimaṇḍape*.
727. *Pañca mahāvilokanāni viloketvā*. The five great investigations, as explained at Bv-a 273, are: (1) *investigation of the time* (*kāla*), to decide on a time when the life span of human beings is less than 100,000 years and at minimum a hundred years; (2) *investigation of the continent* (*dīpa*), to determine that the rebirth takes place in Jambudīpa; (3) *investigation of the region* (*desa*), to determine that the rebirth takes place in the Middle Region

(*majjhimadesa*); (4) *investigation of the family* (*kula*), to determine that the rebirth takes place in either a brahmin family or a khattiya family; and (5) *investigation of the mother* (*mātā*), to decide upon a mother who is virtuous and has fulfilled the pāramīs for 100,000 eons.

728. The thirty-two signs (*dvattiṃsapubbanimittāni*), enumerated at Ud-a 149–50, It-a I 133–34, etc., include the quaking of the ten-thousandfold world system, the manifestation of great radiance, the blind being able to see, the deaf being able to hear, the mute being able to speak, those with bent bodies becoming erect, cripples being able to walk, and so forth.

729. Roughly extending from June to July in the Western calendar.

730. The texts mention three kinds of devas: by rebirth (celestial beings), by convention (kings, queens, and princes, called "deva" by their subjects), and by purification (arahants). See pp. 1261–62. Here the Buddha is called supreme among the devas by purification.

731. Detailed explanations of the Buddha's epithets are at Vism 198–212, Ppn 7.4–64.

732. The explanation here devolves on two alternative ways of taking *tādino*, either as a genitive singular or as a nominative singular *tādī* (shortened m.c. to *tādi*) followed by *no*, a negative interrogative. On the first alternative, the question is whether "the mind of the impartial one" is well disposed toward beings; on the second alternative, the first couplet of the Pāli would be translated thus: "Is his mind well disposed? Is he or isn't he impartial toward all beings?" On *tādī* in the sense of impartiality, see just below.

733. The references are respectively to Ja V 52–53, Ja V 68, and Ja VI 308.

734. *Bhagavā pañcah'ākārehi tādī, iṭṭhāniṭṭhe tādī, cattāvī ti tādī, muttāvī ti tādī, tiṇṇāvī ti tādī, tanniddesā ti tādī.* Ce and Ee are missing *muttāvī ti tādī*, included in Be and Nidd I 345. The phrase is necessary to complete the five aspects.

735. *Mahā-aṭṭhakathāyaṃ vitthāritanayena veditabbā.* The Mahā-aṭṭhakathā was one of the old Sinhala commentaries.

736. See DPPN for details.

737. See note 360.

738. At AN III 169–70, the Buddha advises the monks to practice these contemplations, but the collective designation *ariyā iddhi* (or *ariyiddhi*), it seems, is first applied to them only at Paṭis II 212–13. At DN III 113,9, they are spoken of as *iddhi anāsavā anupadhikā, ariyā ti vuccati*.

739. See PED, sv *pamadā*, "a young (wanton) woman, a woman." See too SED, sv *pramadā*. In such a case we would expect a feminine ablative ending rather than a masculine-neuter one.

SED also cites *pamada* as a masculine noun meaning "joy, pleasure, delight," apparently with reference to sensual delight.

740. On the threefold abstinence, see p. 760.

741. Pj II 204,1–8 includes an etymology of *na khīṇavyappatho* thus: *Ettha khīṇātī ti khīṇo, hiṃsati vibadhatī ti attho. Vācāya patho vyappatho, khīṇo vyappatho assā ti khīṇavyappatho. Taṃ na-kārena paṭisedhetvā pucchati: "na khīṇavyappatho" ti, na pharusavāco ti vuttaṃ hoti. "Nākhīṇavyappatho" ti pi pāṭho, na akhīṇavacano ti attho. Pharusavacanaṃ hi paresaṃ hadaye akhīyamānaṃ tiṭṭhati. Tādisavacano kacci na so ti vuttaṃ hoti.* I would translate: "Here, *khīṇa* (= rough) is derived from the verb *khīṇāti*, which means 'injures, harms.' *Vyappatho* is a way of speech. *Khīṇavyappatho* is thus one whose way of speaking is rough. With the syllable *na* (= not) he asks rejecting that. Thus what is meant is: 'Is he one whose speech is not harsh?' There is also the reading *nākhīṇavyappatho*, which means 'not one whose way of speaking is not exhausted.' For harsh speech remains in the hearts of others without becoming exhausted. What is meant (by the question) is: 'Is he one whose speech is not like that?'"

742. Again, Pj II 204,8–10 offers a complex etymology of *vebhūtikaṃ*/*vebhūtiyaṃ* thus: *Vibhūtī ti vināso, vibhūtiṃ kāyati* [Be: *kāsati*] *karoti vā ti vibhūtikaṃ, vibhūtikameva vebhūtikaṃ, vebhūtiyan ti pi vuccati, pesuññass'etaṃ adhivacanaṃ*. In short, the alternative readings *vebhūtikaṃ* and *vebhūtiyaṃ* are derived from *vibhūti*, which is explained by the more familiar synonym *vināsa*, "destruction." In relation to speech this is taken to be a designation for divisive speech. Norman, however, translates this term as "untruths," apparently taking the prefix *ve-* in the privative sense relative to *bhūti*, understood as reality or truth. This, however, would seem to repeat the question about abstaining from false speech and thus would not add anything to the inquiry.

743. This seems to be an allusion to AN II 227,12–20: "One says that one has seen what one has not seen, heard what one has not heard, sensed what one has not sensed, cognized what one has not cognized. . . . One says that one has not seen what one has seen, has not heard what one has heard, has not sensed what one has sensed, has not cognized what one has cognized" (*adiṭṭhe diṭṭhavādī hoti, asute sutavādī hoti, amute mutavādī hoti, aviññāte viññātavādī hoti . . . diṭṭhe adiṭṭhavādī hoti, sute asutavādī hoti, mute amutavādī hoti, viññāte aviññātavādī hoti*).

744. *Mantā ti paññā vuccati*. Pj II's explanation, *tayā* [Be: *tāya mantāya*] *paricchinditvā atthameva bhāsati*, apparently takes *mantā* to be the truncated instrumental of a feminine noun. Norman (at GD 190–91) interprets *mantā* as a nominative agent noun. While this is also feasible, I follow Pj II.

745. Since sensual defilement (*kilesakāma*) is indicated by the verb *rajjati*, Pj II takes *kāmesu* here to signify the objects of sensual pleasure (*vatthukāma*). On the distinction between *kilesakāma* and *vatthukāma*, see p. 1015.
746. On the five eyes (*pañcacakkhu*), see pp. 1174–77.
747. The reference here is to the two nibbāna elements, that "with residue remaining" (*saupādisesanibbānadhātu*), the nibbāna experienced by a buddha or arahant during life, and that "without residue remaining" (*anupādisesanibbānadhātu*), the complete cessation of the round of rebirths, attained when a buddha or arahant passes away. Since at this point the Buddha had not actually attained the nibbāna element without residue remaining, the question, according to Pj II, can only pertain to *his ability* to attain it.
748. *Saparivārā savāsanā*. The "retinues" (*parivārā*) presumably refers to the other defilements associated with each of the influxes; the "habitual formations" (*vāsanā*) are subtle habits induced by the defilements, which in the case of other arahants persist even after the defilements have been eliminated. Buddhas alone, it is said, have eliminated the defilements along with the habitual formations.
749. See note 91.
750. I read here with Ee and just below *puna sampannaṃ*, whereas Ce and Be read *puṇṇaṃ sampannaṃ*, "completely accomplished."
751. *Aṭṭhaṅgasamannāgataṃ āhāraṃ āhārenti*: This refers to the eight factors in the reflection on the proper use of food. See note 394.
752. *Moneyyasampattiyā munino*. On *moneyya* as the defining mark of the *muni*, see pp. 1036–37.
753. These are word plays derived from the word *nāga*: the first merges *na* and *ga* (from *gantāraṃ*); the second combines *na* and *āguṃ* (in *āguṃ na karoti*). In the Nikāyas the word *nāga* is used as an epithet for a bull elephant, a cobra, a dragon-like being, an arahant, and the Buddha. See pp. 462–63.
754. Sensual defilements and sensual objects.
755. I read with Be and Ce *evaṃ vividhaguṇasamannāgatā buddhā ti buddhārammaṇaṃ pītiṃ uppādetvā*.
756. Craving is excluded because it is comprised under the second noble truth, the origin of suffering.
757. Each noble truth is to be comprehended by way of three kinds of knowledge: knowledge of the truth itself (*saccañāṇa*), knowledge of the task to be done (*kiccañāṇa*), and knowledge that the task has been done (*katañāṇa*). These are the three turnings of the wheel of the Dhamma (*tiparivaṭṭaṃ*), and as applied to four truths, they yield twelve aspects of the knowledge of the truths (*dvādasākāraṃ*). See SN V 422–23.

758. See AN II 135,11, which distinguishes disciples into four classes based on their capacity for understanding: those who understand quickly (*ugghaṭitaññū*), those who need elaboration (*vipañcitaññū*), those who can be guided (*neyya*), and those who grasp only the words (*padaparama*).

759. Reading with Be *tīhi* as against Ce and Ee *tehi*.

760. Reading with Be and Ce *nirodhaṃ sacchikaronto*.

761. Be has *sabbā samāpattiyo*. Ce and Ee do not include *sabbā*.

762. *Pañcaverabhayānaṃ atītattā verabhayātītaṃ*. The five are transgressions of the five precepts. See SN II 68–69, AN IV 405–6.

763. *Bhāvenabhāvalakkhaṇe bhummavacanaṃ*. The locative absolute is a grammatical construction in which the subject of a subordinate clause and its action (described by either a past participle or a present participle) occur in the locative case, to distinguish them from the subject and verb of the sentence's primary clause. The locative absolute serves a similar purpose as is served in English by clauses that begin with "when" or "while" to introduce a subordinate subject and its action. Thus here Pj II takes *kismiṃ* to be a locative with an implicit past participle, indicated by the gloss *kismiṃ uppanne loko samuppanno hoti*. I do not think it necessary, however, to take *kismiṃ* as part of a locative absolute. It makes perfectly good sense as a simple locative pronoun, and so I render it.

764. Vism 204–5, Ppn 7.37, distinguishes three kinds of world: the world of conditioned things, the world of beings, and the spatial or cosmic world (*tayo lokā saṅkhāraloko sattaloko okāsaloko*).

765. While Pj II takes *kissa* in pāda c to be a genitive used in the sense of an accusative, Norman (at GD 192–93) suggests that *kissa* is a contraction of *kiṃ sa*, where *sa* = Skt *svid*. I take *upādāya* in pāda c to be an absolutive with the literal meaning "having clung," completed by the finite verb *vihaññati* in pāda d, with *loko* in pāda c serving as a mere metrical filler. This seems supported by the absence of a corresponding *loko* in pāda c of the reply in **169**. Pj II, however, interprets *upādāya* in the sense of "depending on," with an implicit primary clause: *kiṃ upādāya loko ti saṃkhaṃ gacchati*. On *upādāya* in this sense, DOP (s.v. *upādiyati*) gives as meanings "with, out of, because of; with reference to, in respect of; relative to, in comparison with." Spk I 96,17–18, commenting on the parallel verse of SN I 41,5, glosses the same line thus: *Upādāyā ti tāni yeva ca upādāya āgamma paṭicca pavattati*, "It occurs dependent on, contingent on, in dependence on them." The sutta itself, however, suggests that *upādāya* should be taken in the literal sense of "having clung to." For after the Buddha has replied with **169**, in **170** the yakkha asks: *Katamaṃ taṃ upādānaṃ yattha loko vihaññati?*, where *upādānaṃ* must surely refer back to *upādāya*.

766. Again, despite Pj II, it seems to me that *kismiṃ* should be taken as a simple locative in the sense of place.
767. Reading with Be *dhanadhaññādivasena*.
768. Norman finds problematic the use of *upādāya* as an absolutive with the object in the genitive plural, stating "we must assume that *upādāya* was interpreted as the instrumental of a noun *upādā*, which was extracted in the first place from *upādāya*" (GD 193). He seems, however, to have overlooked the use of *upādāya* as an absolutive with the genitive plural object in the definition of *rūpa*, for example, at MN I 53,13, SN II 4,1, and elsewhere: *Cattāro ca mahābhūtā catunnañca mahābhūtānaṃ upādāya rūpaṃ, idaṃ vuccati rūpaṃ*. The commentaries (such as Ps I 222,6 and Spk II 17,9) clearly construe *upādāya* here as an absolutive: *upādāyā ti upādiyitvā, gahetvā ti attho*.
769. According to DOP, *upādāna* has a dual meaning: "(1) taking as one's own, laying hold of, grasping; (2) material support or cause, fuel." DOP further remarks: "It is often difficult to determine which meaning is intended; both reinforce each other: previous grasping produces fuel, which is itself then grasped." Nevertheless, in the Nikāyas, except in reference to the fuel of a fire, *upādāna* seems always to be used to indicate the *subjective act* of clinging rather than the objective support of clinging. Thus it is more consistent with the Nikāyas to take *upādāya* in **168–69** and *upādāna* in **170** as referring to subjective clinging rather than to divide up the meaning, with *upādāya* taken as "in dependence on" and *upādāna* as "objective support for clinging." Both *upādāya* (as absolutive) and *upādāna* (as action noun) can thus represent the second truth, the cause of suffering.
770. *Sarūpena dassetvā ca adassetvā*. Literally "Having showed them and not showed them in their own nature."
771. See in this connection SN V 426,7–9: *Katamañca, bhikkhave, dukkhaṃ ariyasaccaṃ? 'Cha ajjhattikāni āyatanānī' ti'ssa vacanīyaṃ. Katamāni cha? Cakkhāyatanaṃ . . . pe . . . manāyatanaṃ. Idaṃ vuccati, bhikkhave, dukkhaṃ ariyasaccaṃ*; "And what, bhikkhus, is the noble truth of suffering? It should be said: 'The six internal sense bases.' What six? The eye base . . . the mind base. This is called the noble truth of suffering."
772. The seven consciousness elements are: eye-consciousness element, ear-consciousness element, nose-consciousness element, tongue-consciousness element, body-consciousness element, mind element, mind-consciousness element. The first five are based on the five sense bases, the latter two, according to the Abhidhamma commentaries, are based on the heart base. See CMA 144–48.

773. *Tāsaṃ vatthugocarabhedaṃ dhammāyatanaṃ gahitameva*: This is said because, according to the Abhidhamma system, the *dhammāyatana* or "mental phenomena base" includes the heart base (*hadayavatthu*)—the material basis for the mind element and mind-consciousness element—as well as material and mental phenomena that can be cognized only by mind-consciousness, not by sense consciousness. See in this connection Vibh 82 (§167): "What is the mental phenomena base? The feeling aggregate, the perception aggregate, and the volitional activities aggregate; whatever form is invisible, non-impinging, included in the mental phenomena base; and the unconditioned element." (*Tattha katamaṃ dhammāyatanaṃ? Vedanākkhandho, saññākkhandho, saṅkhārakkhandho, yañca rūpaṃ anidassanāppaṭighaṃ dhammāyatanapariyāpannaṃ, asaṅkhatā ca dhātu.*) See too CMA 286–87. On the heart base as the material support for the mind element and the mind-consciousness element, see Vism 447,27–34, Ppn 14.60.

774. Pj II explains that the Buddha's reply excludes the world-transcending states of consciousness (included in the mind base) along with their mental factors and the unconditioned element (all included in the mental phenomena base) because these states of consciousness, with their factors and their object, nibbāna, pertain to emancipation rather than to affliction.

775. Reading with Be and Ce *upāyanidassanena*, as against Ee *upādāya nidassanena*.

776. As I understand it, the sense here is this: "Even if you were stream-enterers, once-returners, or non-returners, I would declare this to you for the sake of achieving arahantship." It is puzzling that Pj II explains the verb *akkhāmi*, an indicative, as if it were an optative.

777. There is a Skt parallel to **173–75**, Śag 10.1–3; see Appendix 2. I take it that the question is asked about the trainee in general, without distinguishing whether it is a stream-enterer, once-returner, non-returner, or one on the path to arahantship. The four floods are the flood of sensual desire, the flood of [craving for] existence, the flood of ignorance, and the flood of views. DN III 230,11–12 merely enumerates them. DN III 276,19–21 includes them among the things that are to be abandoned.

778. *Upacārappanāsamādhinā iriyāpathaheṭṭhimamaggaphalehi ca susamāhito*. "Absorption" refers to full jhāna, "access" to the stage of concentration leading up to jhāna.

779. *Sabbato catutthamaggasampayuttāya samucchedaviratiyā virato*. On the three types of abstinence, see p. 760. It is peculiar that Pj II says that the eradication-abstinence of sensual perception

occurs on the occasion of the fourth path, the path of arahantship. Normally in the texts sensual lust is eradicated by the third path, the path of the non-returner, and it would seem this path also eradicates all perceptions and thoughts connected with sensual lust.

780. *Viratto ti pi pāṭho. Tadā kāmasaññāyā ti bhummavacanaṃ hoti.* Since in Pāli indirect cases for feminine nouns are often identical, *kāmasaññāya* can be understood either as an ablative (with *virato*, "abstaining *from* sensual perception") or as a locative (with *viratto*, "dispassionate *in regard* to sensual perception").

781. *Sagāthāvagge pana kāmasaññāsū ti pi pāṭho* (see SN I 53,20). Neither of the variant readings mentioned here has come down in the printed editions of the Sagāthāvagga now available to us, but they may have been found in manuscripts known to the commentator. Śag 10.3 reads *viraktaḥ kāmasaṃjñābhyo rūpasaṃyojanātigaḥ*, "one dispassionate toward sensual perceptions, who has overcome the fetter of form."

782. Whereas the three lower paths eradicate the five lower fetters, the fourth path eradicates the five higher fetters: desire for the form sphere, desire for the formless sphere, conceit, restless, and ignorance (*rūparāga, arūparāga, māna, uddhacca, avijjā*). The Nikāyas usually describe the three lower stages of realization in terms of the specific fetters eliminated by each, but the attainment of arahantship simply as "the destruction of the influxes" (*āsavakkhaya*) rather than the eradication of the higher fetters. See, for example, MN I 35,35. The Pāli parallel at SN I 53,20 has *rūpasaññojanātigo*, which is in agreement with the reading at Śag 10.3.

783. *Tatratatrābhinandinītaṇhāsaṅkhātāya nandiyā tiṇṇañca bhavānaṃ parikkhīṇattā nandībhavaparikkhīṇo so tādiso khīṇāsavo bhikkhu.* I translate in compliance with Pj II, but I am not sure that Pj II captures the original intention. I am inclined to understand *nandībhava* as an inverted compound meaning "delight in existence." This seems to be confirmed by Pj II 469,14 and Dhp-a IV 192,7–8, which gloss *nandībhavaparikkhīṇaṃ* (respectively at **637** and Dhp 413) as *tīsu bhavesu parikkhīṇataṇhaṃ*, "one who has destroyed craving for the three types of existence." On the three types of existence, see Appendix 3.

784. I read with Be *nandīparikkhayena saupādisesaṃ, bhavaparikkhayena ca anupādisesaṃ nibbānathalaṃ samāpajja paramassāsappattiyā. Nibbānathalaṃ* is preferable to Ce and Ee *nibbānaphalaṃ* ("the fruit of nibbāna"), since "high ground of nibbāna" fits the metaphor of not sinking in the deep. I take *nibbānathalaṃ samāpajja* to apply to both *saupādisesaṃ* and *anupādisesaṃ*.

785. Jayawickrama (PBR 1977, 143) thinks it probable that stanzas

176–77 "were interpolated from an earlier source," though he admits the Triṣṭubh meter testifies to their antiquity. As already noted (p. 108), **177** occurs as an independent hymn of praise at SN I 33 (§45).

786. *On akiñcana,* see pp. 58–59.
787. The two kinds of sensual pleasures are sensual objects and sensual lust. For the three types of existence, see Appendix 3.
788. Reading with Be *tesaṃ pathe santavihāre kamanenāp'etaṃ vuttaṃ.* Ce is similar, but Ee *tesaṃ pathe cha sattavihāre kamanenāp'etaṃ vuttaṃ* seems wrong.
789. See note 730.
790. *Mahantānaṃ guṇānaṃ esanena mahesiṃ.* See note 573, and pp. 1170–71.
791. Ce and Ee read *nipuṇatthadassigahaṇaṃ na dussati;* Be *nipuṇatthadassiggahaṇaṃ nidasseti.* Neither reading works well and thus my rendering is conjectural.
792. Resolving *nipuṇatthadassiṃ* here as *nipuṇatthe dassetāraṃ.*
793. With Ce and Ee I read *anuppage. Anuppage* (Ee *anupage*) occurs at Sp V 1098,9 in the sentence *tattha tattha paviṭṭhānaṃ āmisakhādanatthāya anuppageyeva sannipatitānaṃ kākānaṃ oravasaddaṃ,* where both Sp-ṭ III 299 and Vmv II 179 gloss the word as "morning" (*anuppage evā ti pāto va*).
794. The sutta also occurs at SN 10:12 (I 213–15), with a very similar commentary at Spk I 316 foll.
795. Dhammika 32 lists *eṇimiga* under *eṇeyyaka* and tentatively identifies it with the blackbuck.
796. *Mahārājasantikā varaṃ labhitvā.* This, it seems, is a different king from the subject of this story, perhaps his predecessor.
797. Reading with Be and Ce *thālipākañca.* DOP sv *thālī*: "*thālipāka* a pot of food, a dish of food used as an oblation." Spk-ṭ I 279 says that the king, in the hope of securing his release, first gave him half the deer.
798. I read here with Ce *svāhaṃ bhavantampi muccheyyaṃ, kathaṃ jīveyyaṃ.* Be and Ee read *svāhaṃ bhavantampi jīyeyyaṃ,* "I would lose you."
799. Reading with Be and Ce *mūlakandaṃ.* See DOP sv *kanda,* which identifies *kandamūla* as a radish.
800. I here follow Be: . . . *gantvā tassa yakkhassa bhavanaṃ pāvisi. Tena vuttaṃ "āḷavakassa yakkhassa bhavane" ti.*
801. *Calakkakudhamahāusabhasamīpe.* Spk-ṭ does not offer any help. DOP, sv *cala,* offers a conjecture for *cala(k)kakudha*: "having a tremulous or quivering hump?"
802. DOP: "The tree Butea frondosa (with orange-red blossoms); its blossom."
803. Reading with Be and Ce *–vibhiṃsana–,* as against Ee *–vihesikā–.*

804. *Kumbhaṇḍa*: a kind of demon.
805. Reading with Be *uttarisāṭakaṃ*.
806. *Buddhapañhā buddhavisayā*. But instead of *buddhapañhā*, Spk (Be) I 286 has *puṭṭhapañhā*, "questions asked," which Spk-ṭ I 286 glosses: *Sammāsambuddhena puṭṭhapañhā. Yasmā buddhavisaye puṭṭhapañhā, tasmā buddhavisayā va honti*. "Questions asked by a perfectly enlightened buddha. Since the questions asked are in the domain of a buddha, they are therefore the domain of a buddha."
807. I read here with Be *–byāmappabhānaṃ paṭighāto*. Neither Ce nor Ee include *–byāma-* in the compound, but Spk, both Ce and Be, have *–byāmappabhādipaṭighāto*.
808. *Paccanīkasāto*. See SN I 179. Spk I 264,15–17: *"sabbaṃ setan" ti vutte "sabbaṃ kaṇhan" ti ādinā nayena paccanīkaṃ karontass'ev'assa sātaṃ sukhaṃ hotī ti paccanīkasāto*; "One whose enjoyment or pleasure comes from taking a contrary position. So when it is said, 'It's all white,' he would say, 'It's all black,' and so forth."
809. *Su* is an indeclinable interrogative particle, from Vedic *svid*. See PED sv *su*[3].
810. *Kathaṃjīviṃ jīvatan ti vā pāṭho. Tassa jīvantānaṃ kathaṃjīvin ti attho*. Where the dominant reading, *kathaṃjīvijīvitaṃ*, has the noun *jīvitaṃ* as the subject, this reading has *jīvataṃ*, a present participle in the genitive plural.
811. With Ee I read *lokasannatiñ*, as against Ce *lokasantatiñ* and Be *lokasanthutiñ*. Spk (Ce and Be) have *lokasantatiñ*. Because of the graphic similarity between *t* and *n* in the Sinhala script, *t/n* confusion is not uncommon in Sri Lankan manuscripts and editions. In support of *sannati*, see SED sv *saṃnati*, "subjection or submission to, humility toward," and the verb *saṃnamati*, "to bend down, to bow before or to." Dhp 303 (quoted just below), which says being honored everywhere (*tattha tatth'eva pūjito*) is a benefit of faith, seems to confirm *lokasannatiñ*.
812. I interpret this sentence in Pj II 231,25–29 (= Spk I 328,7–11) with the aid of Spk-ṭ I 281, which elaborates on the four reasons the treasure of faith is best: *Paralokaṃ gataṃ anugacchatī ti anugāmikaṃ. Aññehi na sādhāraṇan ti anaññasādhāraṇaṃ. Sabbasampattihetū ti sabbāsaṃ sīlasampadādīnaṃ lokiyalokuttarānaṃ sampattīnaṃ hetu. Anatthāya hoti anupāyapaṭipattito. Tasmā anugāmikattā anaññasādhāraṇattā sabbasampattihetubhāvato hiraññādivittanidānattā ca saddhāvittameva seṭṭhaṃ*.
813. The text of Sn uses *purisa*, usually a gender-specific word for a man as contrasted with *itthi*, a woman, but I have rendered it "a person," which captures the intention, as the commentarial explanation shows. Reflecting the Indian cultural bias, the commentary describes "a man" as superior (*ukkaṭṭha*).

814. On Soṇa, see Vin I 179 foll., AN III 374 foll.; on Raṭṭhapāla see MN II 54 foll. Spk-ṭ I 281 explains that Mahāpaduma was a king who was the son of the queen Padumavatī. He first enjoyed the happiness of kingship and afterward, having become a paccekabuddha, he enjoyed the happiness of nibbāna.

815. The verse is untraced. Ee reads *saccavācena udakaṃ hi gādhati;* Ce *saccena vācenudakaṃ hi gādhati;* Be *saccena vācenudakampi dhāvati.* Spk-ṭ I 282 explains: *udakapiṭṭhiyaṃ abhijjamānāyaṃ pathaviyā viya dhāvati gacchati;* "one runs on the surface of water without dividing it, as if it were earth." The text available to this author obviously had *dhāvati* rather than *gādhati.*

816. An allusion to AN I 128–30, where "one with two eyes" is a householder who looks after both his temporal and spiritual welfare.

817. *Paññājīvino jīvitaṃ, taṃ vā paññājīviṃ jivataṃ.* The alternative glosses refer back to the two alternative readings of the line.

818. In one Chinese parallel to this sutta, SĀ 1326, after the Buddha has answered Āḷavaka's first four questions, the yakkha asks questions that correspond to **168** and the Buddha answers as in **169**. The yakkha next asks questions that correspond to **173**, and the Buddha answers as in **174–75**. This exchange takes place at T II 364c23–365a7. Finally, at 365a09 Āḷavaka asks the questions that correspond to **183** and at 365a12 the Buddha asnwers as at **184**. The other Chinese parallel, $SĀ^2$ 325 (T II 482c08 foll.), does not include this interpolation and is, in this part of the sutta, closer to the Pāli.

819. *Atthayuttipucchā.* Spk-ṭ I 284 glosses: *Paññādiatthasamadhigamassa yuttiyā kāraṇassa pucchā;* "questions about the means, method, for achievement of the benefit, wisdom and so forth."

820. I omit *kiṃ pana,* in Ce and Ee, and instead read with Be *yasmā pana.*

821. Readings of **186**c, in both sutta and commentary, vary between *sussūsā labhate paññaṃ* and *sussūsaṃ labhate paññaṃ.* The former is found in the sutta in Ce and Ee, the latter in Be and all three editions of Pj II. The commentary treats *sussūsā* as a truncated instrumental of *sussūsāya,* but Jayawickrama (PBR 1977, 146) says that the word "is to be taken as a shorter instrumental singular (Vedic) and not as a contraction of the Pāli *sussūsāya.*" *Sussūsaṃ* is somewhat problematic. In relation to *paññaṃ, sussūsaṃ* may be the first member of a split compound meaning "the wisdom consisting in a desire to learn." Pj II uses the compounds *sussūsapaññā* and *sussūsanapaññā,* which suggests that it adopts this interpretation. However, a gloss in Pj II employs an explicit instrumental, *sussūsāya sakkaccaṃ paññādhigamūpāyaṃ suṇāti,* "through a desire to learn one

carefully listens to the method for achieving wisdom." This suggests that Pj II takes *sussūsā*, understood as a truncated instrumental, to be the definitive reading.

822. The Little Apprentice (Cūḷantevāsī) is the protagonist of Ja I 120–22. I read the name of the elder monk with Pj II (Be), which agrees with Spk (Be and Ce), as against *Milakkhāmahātissa* in Pj II (Ce and Ee). The three postures are sitting, walking, and standing. He did not lie down to sleep but slept in the sitting posture.
823. Giving is the first of the four means of attracting and sustaining a retinue (*saṅgahavatthu*). The other three are pleasant speech, beneficial conduct, and equality of treatment.
824. Despite the reading *damo* in Spk I (Be), the gloss in Spk-ṭ supports *dhamma*: *Tattha "ime kusalā, ime akusalā" ti ādinā te atthe yāthāvato dhāraṇato upadhāraṇato dhammo.*
825. Here the two expressions are respectively *sussūsaṃ labhate paññaṃ* and *sussūsanapaññaṃ*.
826. I read with Be *saccā bhiyyo kittippattikāraṇaṃ vā* as against Ce and Ee *saccā bhiyyo kittippattikāraṇaṃ saccaṃ*. The final word seems redundant. Spk 256–57 (Ce) is in agreement with Pj II (Be) on this.
827. Reading with Be and Ce, as well as Spk (Ce), *sussūsanapaññāpadesena* as against Ee *sussūsanapaññāpadena*. To add to the medley, Spk (Be) has *sussūsā ti paññāpadesena*.
828. All three editions of Pj II, as well as Spk (Be), read here *sussūsaṃ labhate paññaṃ*, as against Spk (Ce) *sussūsā labhate paññaṃ*, but I translate following my preferred reading of the sutta.
829. The four qualities mentioned at **188–89** refer back to **186–87**. *Truth* (*sacca*) occurs in all three places in the Pāli text: **187**c, **188**c, and **189**c. *Generosity* (*cāga*) in **188**c and **189**c clearly corresponds to giving (*dadaṃ*) in **187**d. As to the equivalence of wisdom (*paññā*) in **186**c and *dhamma* in **188**c, Spk-ṭ I 287 comments (on the parallel, SN 1:12, I 214–15): "Wisdom is called *dhamma* because of *bearing up* and *examining* entities in accordance with actuality" (corrected to read: *ime kusalā, ime akusalā ti ādinā te atthe yāthāvato dhāraṇato upadhāraṇato dhammo, paññā*). Although the equivalence of *dama* and *dhamma* raises the suspicion that a corrupt reading has been passed down, almost all versions of the sutta have *dhammo* in **188**c and *damā* in **189**c. Spk I 287 explains that wisdom is designated self-control "because it controls the defilements, or controls body, speech, and so forth" (*kilese, kāyavācādike vā dametī ti damo, paññā*). *Steadfastness* (*dhiti*) in **188**c is indicated by the expressions "dutiful" and "one with initiative" (*dhuravā uṭṭhātā*) in **187**ab, and equated with patience (*khanti*) in **189**d.

Thus the correlations can be shown schematically as follows:

(1) **187**c: truthfulness = **188**c and **189**c: truth.

(2) **186**c: wisdom = **188**c: *dhamma* = **189**c: self-control.

(3) **187**d: giving = **188**c and **189**c: generosity.

(4) **187**ab: dutifulness, initiative = **188**c: steadfastness = **189**d: patience.

830. *Ekamekaṃ padaṃ atthuddhārapaduddhārapadavaṇṇanānayehi vibhajitvā*. Spk-ṭ expands on this: "*Each individual term*: each term such as 'wisdom' and so forth. *Extraction of the meaning* is, for example, extracting the meaning 'wisdom' thus: 'Wisdom is called "wisdom" in this place and "*dhamma*" in that.' *Extraction of terms* is extracting synonymous terms, for example: 'wisdom, understanding,' and so forth. *Commenting on the term* is discussion of the term, for instance, 'Wisdom is what understands, *dhamma* is what sustains, taming is what tames.'"

831. Here all three editions of Pj II read *sussūsaṃ labhate paññaṃ*, but Spk (Ce) I 257,18–19 has *sussūsā labhate paññaṃ*.

832. Although the commentary explains *attha* as the visible benefit (*diṭṭhadhammikaṃ dasseti*) and *samparāyika* as the benefit in future lives, it seems the two words should be understood simply as an adjective and a noun bearing a single significance, namely, the good pertaining to future lives. For this reason my translation departs from the explanation of the line in Pj II.

833. Ee *vicakkhaṇe*, Be *kiccatthe*, Ce *payojane*. Spk I 292 (Be) has *vicakkhaṇe*, but Spk I 334,25 (Ee) *ācikkhane*. Ee notes still more variants. Spk-ṭ I 287 glosses *vicakkhaṇe* with *sapayojanatāya*, "with purpose."

834. Spk-ṭ I 287: "Of the deities who had assembled to hear the Dhamma" (*dhammassavanatthaṃ sannipatitadevatāhi*).

835. *Satapuññalakkhaṇaṃ*. Spk-ṭ I 288: "Because he had accumulated merits through 100,000 eons, by way of those merits he had a hundred marks of merit, marks produced by his many merits."

836. So Be. Ce and Ee have "Hattha-Āḷavaka."

837. Kāyavicchandanikasuttaṃ.

838. The story of Nandā, Nanda's sister, is at Mp I 363–65 and Dhp-a III 112–19 (BL 336–39). She is declared foremost of meditators among the bhikkhunīs at AN I 25,23. Both commentaries state that because of her exceptional beauty she was also called Rūpanandā and Janapadakalyāṇī, the same name as Nanda's sister. Thus it is open to question whether the two were distinct or the narrative tradition has created multiple identities.

839. The word *rūpa* can mean *material form*, the first of the five aggregates; *visible form*, the object of the sense of sight; and *beauty*. Here all three meanings are involved. In translation,

therefore, I slide from one to the other, depending on the dominant nuance. The "danger in form" is depicted most graphically at MN I 88–89.

840. Be has here and below *abhipatthitaṃ*; Ce has *abhinanditaṃ* in both places; Ee has *abhinanditaṃ* here but *abhipatthitaṃ* below. Thī 19 has the second couplet thus: *asubhāya cittaṃ bhāvehi, ekaggaṃ susamāhitaṃ* (= **341**cd). The lines here assigned to Thī are addressed to the bhikkhu Kulla at Th 394, and to the bhikkhunī Khemā at Ap II 548 (v. 354). In both places Be has *abhinanditaṃ*.
841. Except for the gender of *upasantā*, the verse is identical with **342**.
842. *Catuppamāṇike hi lokasannivāse*. See AN II 71,10–15: "Bhikkhus, there are these four kinds of persons found existing in the world. What four? One who takes form as the criterion, whose confidence is based on form. One who takes voice as the criterion, whose confidence is based on voice. One who takes stringency as the criterion, whose confidence is based on stringency. One who takes Dhamma as the criterion, whose confidence is based on Dhamma."
843. This refers to the thirty-two characteristics of physical excellence and the eighty minor features.
844. The Pāli *tasmiṃ rūpe chandarāgo tanuko ahosi* literally means, "her desire and lust for that form diminished," but I do not think the text intends to imply that Nandā had sexual passion for the illusory woman; rather, it was fascination with her beauty.
845. Reading here with Be and Ce *kamaṃ*. Ee *kammaṃ* should be corrected.
846. Reading with Be and Ce *dhātuso*, as against Ee *dhātuyo*.
847. The physician in King Bimbisāra's court.
848. Dhp 223. The story is at Dhp-a III 302–15 (see BL 3:99–107). What follows is a very short summary of this background story.
849. "Constant meals" (*niccabhattāni*) are meals that she would provide every day at her home. While the number was constant, the bhikkhus would change by rotation.
850. Dhp 147. The story is at Dhp-a III 104–9 (BL 2:330–34).
851. Suyāma is the ruler of the Yāma heaven.
852. According to the background story, this took place on the fourth day after her death.
853. *Desantare rūpantarapātubhāvo*. Viewed in the light of the Abhidhamma theory of phenomena as momentary, a material object does not actually move from one position to another. When the object of gross perception is seen to move, what

happens at the micro-level is that discrete material phenomena belonging to the same series arise and perish in rapid succession at slightly different locations along a given trajectory.

854. On how the three characteristics are concealed and how they become apparent, see Vism 640,1–12, Ppn 21.3–4, along with note 3 to Ppn 21.4.

855. *Saviññāṇaka-aviññāṇaka*. Literally "that with consciousness and that without consciousness." The reference is respectively to a living body and a dead body.

856. The explanation of the thirty-two parts by way of color, etc., is at Vism 249–65, Ppn 8.83–138. The method of non-concern (*avyāpāranayena*) is elaborated at Vism 353–63, Ppn 11.47–80. The "method of non-concern" demonstrates that each part of the body is unconcerned with its relationship to the surrounding parts. As illustrated by the case of head hairs: "The inner skin that covers the skull does not know, 'Head hairs grow on me,' nor do the head hairs know, 'We grow on inner skin that envelops a skull.' These things are devoid of mutual concern and reviewing."

857. Pāli texts distinguish two aspects of the skin: the *chavi*, the outer skin, which corresponds to the epidermis, and *camma*, the inner skin. Since modern anatomy distinguishes three layers of skin—the epidermis, the dermis, and the hypodermis—I assume the *camma* includes both the dermis and the hypodermis. The word *taca* is generally used for the skin as a whole, but also sometimes refers specifically to the *camma*: "The *taca* is the *camma* that envelops the whole body. Outside it is what is called the *chavi*, which is black, brown, or yellow in color. . . . The *taca* is always white, as becomes evident when the *chavi* is destroyed by contact with fire or the impact of a blow or some other cause" (Vism 251,20–25, Ppn 8.93).

858. It seems to me that a clause has dropped out from this sentence. The point the author is making is that if the epidermis were removed from the body, the body's repulsive nature would become apparent; but in the sentence as it now stands, this conclusion is not explicitly stated but only implied by the next sentence. I have added the implied clause in brackets.

859. I read here with Ce and Ee *chaviyā rāgarañjito* as against Be *chavirāgarañjito*.

860. Be has *nhārusamuṭṭhitāni*, Ce and Ee *nahārusamotthatāni*. I believe the correct reading should be *nhārusamotatāni*. See PED *samotata*, "strewn all over, spread," and Ja V 167,1, *samotataṃ jambuhi vetasāhi*, with the gloss at Ja V 168,6–7: *Samotatan ti ubhayatīresu jamburukkhavetasarukkhehi otataṃ vitataṃ*.

861. *Abbhantarakuṇapāni*: The primary meaning of *kuṇapa* is a

corpse, but the texts use the word to refer to the organs and tissues of the body, which in their loathsomeness are taken to be comparable to corpses.

862. *Anādiyitvā*. See DOP *ādiyati*[2], "attends to, takes notice of, shows respect to."

863. I omit here the passage in which Pj II identifies the organs mentioned in the verses. These should already be clear from the translation.

864. This excludes the arahant, who has no further need for training.

865. A more formal explanation of the three kinds of full understanding is at Vism 606–7, Ppn 20.3. Here full understanding of the known (*ñātapariññā*) is explained as "the understanding that occurs by observing the specific characteristics of such and such phenomena," that is, seeing the distinct characteristics of each of the five aggregates, twelve sense bases, and so forth, or more broadly, of all "name and form" together with their conditions. Full understanding as scrutinization (*tīraṇapariññā*) is "the understanding consisting in insight with the general characteristics [impermanence, suffering, non-self] as its object that occurs in attributing a general characteristic to those same phenomena." And full understanding as abandoning (*pahānapariññā*) is "the insight with the characteristic as its object that occurs as the abandoning of the perception of permanence, [pleasure, and self] in those same phenomena." The commentarial scheme of the three kinds of full understanding seems to be based on such passages as Nidd I 37–38 commenting on **778**. See pp. 1034–35.

866. I read with Be *attanā matassa sarīrassa samānabhāvaṃ karonto*. Ce and Ee are missing *matassa sarīrassa*, which seems to leave a gap in the sentence.

867. Be *sabhaṃ* is no doubt a typographical error that should be corrected to *samaṃ*.

868. *Evaṃ sekhabhūmiṃ dassetvā idāni asekhabhūmiṃ dassento*. The previous verses describe the stage of a disciple in training (particularly one at the lower three stages of realization); the present verse shows the arahant, one who has completed the training.

869. *Taṇhāsaṅkhātavānābhāvato nibbānaṃ*. The word *vāna* is a homonym that can mean either "weaving" or "jungle, woods." Without further elaboration, it is sometimes difficult to determine whether a comment is explaining nibbāna as "absence of weaving" (that is, of craving as weaving one existence to the next) or as "absence of the jungle" (that is, of craving as entan-

gling one in the various realms of existence). Here I take Pj II to be explaining nibbāna as the absence (*nir*) of weaving (*vāna*). A fuller version of this etymology is at Sv II 465,3–5 (= Ps II 175,17–20, and Spk I 196,21–23): "That craving is called 'weaving' because it weaves together, stitches together, existence with existence, or kamma with its fruit. Nibbāna is that which has departed from this weaving" (*sā pan'esā taṇhā bhavena bhavaṃ, phalena vā saddhiṃ kammaṃ vinati saṃsibbatī ti katvā vānan ti vuccati; tato vānato nikkhantan ti nibbānaṃ*). The derivation of *nibbāna* accepted by modern scholars is from the verb *nibbāti* or *nibbāyati*, "to go out," referring to the going out of a fire. These verbs and their prefixed form, *parinibbāyati*, are common in the Nikāyas.

870. This explanation differs from the previous one, it seems, in that the first explanation sees the phrase "one who has expunged desire and lust" as applying to the bhikkhu who has already passed through the path and fruit of arahantship, while the second sees it as applying to the bhikkhu at the moment he obtains the fruit of arahantship immediately following the path.
871. *Tena idamassa pahīnaṃ, idañcānena laddhan ti dīpeti.* That is, he has abandoned desire and lust, and he has obtained the state of nibbāna.
872. Reading with Be *aññatarā duggatitthī matapatikā.*
873. This incident forms the background to AN 5:55 (III 67–68), which, however, ends with different verses.
874. The verse is cited at Mil 211–12 as one side of a dilemma that King Milinda asks Nāgasena to solve: "When the Buddha spoke this verse in praise of wandering without an abode, why did he also encourage laypeople to build and offer monasteries to the Sangha?"
875. *Taṃ nānuppaveseyya.* Pj II apparently takes *anuppavecchati* to be from *anuppavesati*, but PED sv *pavecchati* suggests the verb is a mutation of *payacchati* by way of **payecchati*. See too SED sv *pra-yam* > *prayacchati*, "to offer, present, give, grant, bestow."
876. Pj II here offers two alternative ways of taking *muninaṃ*, either as an accusative (= *muniṃ*) or as a genitive plural (glossed by the locative plural *munīsu*).
877. The three kinds of peace are *sammutisanti, tadaṅgasanti*, and *accantasanti*. The "conventional peace" correlated with the sixty-two views probably refers to the mistaken views of liberation held by non-Buddhist ascetics. "Peace in a particular respect" is correlated with insight because insight temporarily removes defilements. But nibbāna alone is the ultimate peace.
878. *Pamāya bījan ti yaṃ tesaṃ vatthūnaṃ bījaṃ abhisaṅkhāraviññāṇaṃ,*

taṃ pamāya hiṃsitvā vadhitvā, samucchedappahānena pajahitvā ti attho. Some manuscripts read the absolutive as *pahāya,* but while *pajahitvā* occurs in the explanation, the gloss *hiṃsitvā vadhitvā* supports *pamāya.* See PED *pamāya*[2] and SED *pra-mṛṇ* > *pramṛṇati,* "to crush, destroy," *pramṛṇa,* "destroying, crushing."

879. *Abhisaṅkhāraviññāṇaṃ.* See Mp-ṭ II 166: "Volitionally active consciousness is consciousness coarisen with kamma" (*abhisaṅkhāraviññāṇan ti kammasahajātaṃ viññāṇaṃ*). This consciousness is called the seed because it gives rise to a new set of aggregates, the newly arisen sentient being, at the beginning of a new life.

880. *Sineha* means both "moisture" and "affection." The word play is hard to replicate in English.

881. See p. 1214 and Appendix 3. Pj II evidently understands *takkaṃ pahāya* to mean that the muni has abandoned unwholesome thoughts, but I think it more likely the expression means that the muni has gone beyond the range of thought. Having passed into nibbāna, he has become *atakkāvacaro.*

882. I read with Be *puggalo* as against Ce and Ee *bālo.*

883. The encounter is at MN I 170–71 and Vin I 8. The Ājivakas were a sect contemporary with the Buddha. The background story here is based on Ps II 189–91 and Thī-a 220–22.

884. Ps II 190,17 says that she sang: "Do not cry, son of a meat carrier, son of a deer hunter!" At Thī-a 221, her name is given as Cāpā.

885. At SN I 35,10 he is said to have been one of seven bhikkhus who attained full liberation after being reborn as nonreturners in the Aviha pure abode.

886. *Adhimuttan ti vuttaṃ hoti.* This seems a strange comment. *Adhimutta* generally signifies that one is *intent upon* or *disposed to* something that one has not yet acquired, and thus indicates a stage lower than actually being liberated (*vimutta*). Yet here the purport is clearly that the muni has attained the destruction of craving. Spk II 243,16–17, commenting on the same line, consistently uses *vimuttaṃ*: "*Liberated in the destruction of craving*: liberated in nibbāna, designated the destruction of craving, through the liberation that takes this as its object" (*taṇhakkhaye vimuttan ti taṇhakkhayasaṅkhāte nibbāne tadārammaṇāya vimuttiyā vimuttaṃ*).

887. *Vibhāvanattho hi ettha vā-saddo ti.* Pj II takes *vā* here to be the emphatic *eva,* with the initial vowel elided and the final vowel lengthened on account of liaison with *api.*

888. Revata was the younger brother of Sāriputta. The story of the Buddha's visit to him in the acacia forest is told at Dhp-a II 191–93 (BL 2:211–14). The reference to Revata as a "builder" is based on this portion: "As soon as the Elder Revata learned

that the Teacher was approaching, he created by ma Fragrant Chamber for the Blessed One, and likewise for t monks five hundred pinnacled residences, five hundred covered walks, and five hundred night quarters and day quarters. The Teacher spent an entire month there as his guest" (see BL 2:212). In the Dhp-a version of the story there are *two* old bhikkhus who complain about Revata and his dwelling place.

889. *Vikubbanādhiṭṭhānappabhedena vā paññābalena.* This second interpretation must refer to Revata's ability to work wonders of psychic power. On *vikubbana*, the ability to work wonders, see Paṭis II 210,13–30.

890. See Appendix 3.

891. *Vibhāvanattho hi ettha vā-saddo ti.* See note 887.

892. Jayawickrama (PBR 1977, 35) believes that pādas cde are an interpolation made under the influence of **71**abc. If these pādas are removed, he says, we then obtain a four-line stanza like the others in this poem. On the eight worldly conditions, see Appendix 3.

893. This may be an allusion to the distinction drawn at Nidd II 105 between "alone in the way designated the going forth" (*pabbajjāsaṅkhātena*) and "alone by separation from a group" (*gaṇāvavassaggaṭṭhena*). See pp. 1088–89.

894. The verse is Dhp 176. The story of Ciñcā, based on this verse, is told at Dhp-a III 178–81 (BL 3:19–22). In brief, Ciñcā regularly went at night in the direction of the Jetavana monastery, telling people she had an appointment with the Buddha. After several months she tied a block of wood to her belly, concealed it beneath her dress, and in the midst of the assembly accused the Buddha of making her pregnant. Just then mice gnawed away the ropes binding the block to her belly, so that the block fell, exposing her as a fraud.

895. Norman (GD 200) takes *ogahane* to mean "in the midst of oppression." Pj II, however, glosses as *manussānaṃ nhānatitthe.* Jayawickrama renders accordingly as "at a bathing place."

896. I follow Ce here: *ṭhapitindriyaṃ, avikkhittindriyaṃ alolindriyan ti pi.* Ee omits *alolindriyaṃ,* while Be has *ṭhapitindriyaṃ, rakkhitindriyaṃ, gopitindriyan ti pi,* "one whose faculties are steady, protected, guarded."

897. Pāli *ṭhitatto,* a compound of *ṭhita,* firm, steady, and *atta,* self. Compounds ending in *atta* occur throughout Sn. They do not signify the existence of a substantial self but are mere conventional expressions.

898. Four wrong courses of action are mentioned at AN II 18,14–18: deeds motivated by desire, hatred, delusion, and fear.

899. Pj II 266,10–11 adds: *Yogavibhāgena hi upayogatthe karaṇavacanaṃ*

hati, "In grammar, by the separation of union, tal case conveys the meaning of an accusative." cause, in its gloss, Pj II 266,8–10 construes jigu- accusative (*pāpakāni kammāni gūthagataṃ viya a ca jigucchati*), but here and elsewhere in canon- hati occurs with the object in the instrumental— at MN III 300,33, AN IV 375–76. So too at Vin I 88,5: *so tena pāpakena kammena aṭṭīyati harāyati jigucchati.*

900. *Ettha ca vikappe vā samuccaye vā vāsaddo daṭṭhabbo.* I do not see that either a disjunction or conjunction is relevant here. I take *vā* as representing *va* (= *eva*), lengthened due to *sandhi* with *pi.*
901. Dhp-a III 170–76 (BL 3:14–18) has a somewhat different version of the story.
902. *Tacapañcakakammaṭṭhānaṃ adaṃsu.* Literally "They gave him the meditation subject with the skin as fifth." This meditation subject consists of the first five of the thirty-one (or thirty-two) parts of the body: head hairs, body hairs, nails, teeth, and skin. It is traditionally taught as part of the ordination ceremony.
903. See note 392.
904. *Saṃyatatto.* This is another compound with *atta* as its second member, in this case preceded by *saṃyata*, hence meaning "with a controlled self."
905. A similar story is related at Dhp-a IV 98–101 (BL 3:252–53). That version says that at the end of the discourse both the brahmin and his wife attained the fruit of a non-returner.
906. *Puthuka.* See SED sv *pṛthuka*: "rice scalded with hot water and then dried over a fire and ground in a mortar."
907. Reading with Be *bhojanaṃ* as against Ce and Ee *bhājanaṃ.*
908. The Pāli word *agga* can mean either "top" or "best, foremost." In line with the story, Pj II explains it in the former sense, but the original intention is probably that it is the best.
909. *Paradattūpajīvī.* Literally "one living on what is given by others."
910. The three seasons in northern India: the hot season, the rainy season, and the cool season. At AN I 145,14–18, the Buddha says that in his youth he, too, had three mansions, a different one for each season.
911. Pj II evidently takes the locative *yobbane* as representing a young woman, the object of sexual desire, glossed *bhadrepi yobbane vattamāne kvaci itthirūpe.* It seems to me, however, that *yobbane* refers to his own state of youth. Norman and Jayawickrama likewise translate in this latter sense.
912. For the canonical source, see Ud 21–24. See too Dhp-a I 115–22 (BL 1:220–23) and Ud-a 168–78.
913. This was Nanda's intended bride. Her name means "the coun-

try belle." It is uncertain whether this was a proper name or a sobriquet. She eventually became a bhikkhunī; see pp. 633–36.

914. With Ce and Ee I read the absolutive here as *ukkiledetvā* (as against Be *uggiletvā*). See DOP sv **ukkiledeti*, "moistens, softens; treats with an emollient." The explanation at Ud-a 172,14–22 may be clearer: "But when Nanda had a lustful mind, why did the Blessed One tell him to look at the celestial nymphs? To make it easier to remove the defilements. For as a skillful physician, treating a person with swollen humors, first softens his humors with moisture and drinks, etc., and then afterward removes them completely with emetics and purgatives, so when Nanda's lust was swollen, the Blessed One, skilled in taming persons to be trained, first softened it by showing him the nymphs. But he wished to remove it completely with the medicine of the noble path."

915. *Bhatakavādena*. Ud-a 173,24–27 explains that he was called thus because he was living the spiritual life in order to enjoy the celestial nymphs, who were to be like his wages.

916. See SN IV 157,6–10. Though all three editions of Pj II read *rūpamadādi–*, on the basis of the sutta I would correct this to *rūpamayādi–*.

917. See pp. 1073–74.

918. Spk I 17,35–18,5: "*In the sense of sweeping downward*: in the sense of leading downward. For this leads downward those who come under its control; it causes them to be reborn in a bad destination, such as in hell; or it does not allow one to go upward, to nibbāna, but it makes one go downward in the three realms of exisence, the four modes of generation, the five destinations, the seven stations for consciousness, and the nine abodes of beings."

919. Spk III 2,21–24: "The eye is whipped up among various objects, which may be blue and other colors. When unrestrained and flowing down, the eye goes along a toxic journey by becoming a cause for the arising of defilements; thus 'ocean' has the sense of whipping up."

920. On the four "bodily knots," see Appendix 3. For elaborations, see Dhs 252–53 (§§1140–44).

921. *Sucivatattā sundaravatattā ca subbato*. The text uses the expression *subbato*, literally "one of good observance," which I render in accordance with its implied sense as "an ascetic." This statement is intended to explain in what sense the monk is called "one of good observance."

922. *Aññā eva hi ayaṃ jāti, pūjaneyyavatthu liṅgaṃ*. The sense seems to be that in this case, veneration is not determined by seniority but by whether the person has the form (*liṅga*)—

specifically, the robe—of a monastic. As the text says, even a lay non-returner should show respect to a newly ordained novice.

923. *Lakkhaṇārammaṇūpanijjhānena*. "Close meditation on the characteristics" (*lakkhaṇūpanijjhāna*) is a commentarial designation for insight meditation, in which the focus is on the three characteristics of impermanence, suffering, and nonself. "Close meditation on the object" (*ārammaṇūpanijjhāna*) is a designation for serenity meditation, in which there is sustained attention to a single object.
924. A Skt version of the Ratana Sutta is at Mvu I 290–95 (see Jones 1949, 1:242–45). Both Mvu and the Pāli commentaries explain that the verses were spoken on account of the plague in Vesālī. For a comparison of the two versions by Ānandajoti, see http://www.ancient-buddhist-texts.net/Buddhist-Texts/C1-Ratanasutta/Ratanasutta.htm.
925. As in the case of the Metta Sutta, Pj II (Ee) includes only the first few sentences of the commentary on the Ratana Sutta, which is also included in Khp. Thus, starting here, bracketed page numbers refer to Pj I (Ee).
926. *Alattakapaṭalabandhujīvakapupphasadisaṃ*. I base this rendering on DOP sv *alattaka*, "red juice, lac," and *alattakapaṭalavaṇṇa*, "(colored) like a layer of lac; (or with the red color of lac)." The *bandhujīvaka* flower is said to be red.
927. *Evaṃ te nicchavitāya vā līnacchavitāya vā licchavī ti paññāyiṃsu*. Word plays are involved here that cannot be reproduced in English. *Nicchavi* means "skinless," and *līnacchavi* means "adhesive skin." The Licchavis were the ruling community of Vesālī.
928. The Licchavis of Vesālī, together with the people of Videha, a neighboring realm, constituted the Vajjī confederacy, one of the largest and most powerful of the old kshatriya republics before it fell to the aggressive kingdom of Magadha.
929. *Tassa punappunaṃ visālīkatattā vesālī tveva nāmaṃ jātaṃ*. A legendary explanation of the name of the city, deriving it from *visāla*, "large."
930. The text uses the word *rājāno*, plural for king. Since Vesālī was a republic, unless the text is being anachronistic, the "kings" must have actually been kshatriyas who formed an elite council. The "king" (*rājā*, a singular) referred to just below must have been the head of the council rather than a monarch.
931. Six contemporaries of the Buddha, who propagated their own teachings in the Ganges plain. See p. 241 and pp. 914–15.
932. With Be and Ce I read here *dhajapaṭākāpuṇṇaghaṭakadaliādīni ussāpetvā*.

933. They are mentioned at DN II 258,18. Sv II 688,19–21 says they were powerful nāgas who lived at the foot of Mount Sineru and could not be lifted up even by the supaṇṇa birds.
934. *Pokkharavassaṃ vassi*. PED, sv *pokkharavassa* (literally "lotus-leaf shower"), says: "A portentous shower of rain, serving as a special kind of test shower in which certain objects are wetted, but those showing a disinclination toward moisture are left untouched, like a lotus-leaf."
935. Reading with Be and Ce *amanussesu gatamattesu manussānaṃ gattesu rogo vūpasanto*.
936. *Apare pana vadanti: ādito pañc'eva gāthā bhagavatā vuttā, sesā parittakaraṇasamaye Ānandattherena*.
937. Here Pj I *bhūtaṃ bhūtato* should be corrected to *bhūte bhūtato*, which is found in the sutta itself.
938. Happiness is the causal root of concentration; concentration is the causal root of wisdom.
939. On the "eight inopportune conditions that are not occasions for living the spiritual life" (*aṭṭha akkhaṇā asamayā brahmacariya-vāsāya*), see AN IV 225–28.
940. The three disasters were famine, evil spirits, and plague. Pj I includes here another sentence that rejects the reading *mānusiyaṃ pajaṃ*, on the grounds that a meaning in the locative case would not be appropriate.
941. The reference is to AN 11:15, V 342.
942. These are the names of other sacrifices. See p. 795.
943. I follow Ce, which includes *dīpapūjañca*, not in Be and Ee.
944. *Taṃ hi vittiṃ janetī ti vittaṃ*. There is a word play here between *vittiṃ* and *vittaṃ*.
945. *Te hi sobhanena kammena irīyanti gammantī ti saggā, suṭṭhu vā aggā ti pi saggā*. These are word plays that derive *sagga* from *so* + *ga* and from *su* + *agga*.
946. *Ratanan ti ratiṃ nayati*. Another word play.
947. Reading with Be *atappakaṃ* as against Ce and Ee *anappakaṃ*. Because of the graphic similarity between *t* and *n* in the Sinhala script, *t/n* confusion is not uncommon in Sri Lankan manuscripts and editions. The Sinhala-script SHB commentaries to DN, MN, SN, and AN consistently gloss *paṇīta* with *atappaka*. *Atappaka* is supported by Ps-ṭ II 41, which explains the gloss *atappakaṭṭhena paṇītaṃ* at Ps IV 63,25 thus: *Atappakaṭṭhenā ti uḷāratarabhāvena jhānasamāpattiyā atittikarabhāvena*.
948. The seven gems of a wheel-turning monarch are described at DN II 172–77 and MN III 172–76.
949. Reading *muddhāraṃ* with Ce and Ee as against Be *muṇḍāraṃ*.
950. *Sīhamukha*. PED says only "an ornament at the side of the nave of the king's chariot."

951. On "uposatha" as the name for a class of elephants, Sv-ṭ I 187 says: "'Uposatha' is a mere designation for bull elephants included in the ninth class of elephants, assigned conventionally without reference to any activity" (*navamahatthinikāyapariyāpanne hatthināge kiñci kiriyaṃ anapekkhitvā rūḷhivasena samaññāmattaṃ uposatho ti*). In the Nikāyas it seems "uposatha" is the proper name of the monarch's elephant.
952. See Nidd I 261, quoted at p. 1175.
953. These are the four continents of ancient Buddhist geography. They are not peculiar to our world system, for every world system is supposed to have these same four continents; see AN I 227,28–34.
954. *Sobhanānaṃ atthitā hotu*. Pj I derives *sotthi* from the prefix *su–* (glossed by *sobhana*, "beautiful") and *atthi* ("there is"), or its abstract form, *atthitā*, existence. Thus *sotthi* is "the existence of good" or safety.
955. I do not translate a few sentences in Pj I about the relationship between "gem" and "gemness," the exact sense of which is hard to convey in English.
956. *Buddhaguṇena*. One would have expected a plural here, *buddhaguṇehi*, which I would have rendered "the excellent qualities of the Buddha." Similarly below we find *dhammaguṇena* and *saṅghaguṇena*.
957. Reading here with Be *atappakaṭṭhena* as against Ce and Ee *anappakaṭṭhena*. See note 947.
958. "Sakyamuni" as a designation for the Buddha Gotama appears to be relatively late, and its occurrence here suggests the relative lateness of the Ratana Sutta. Elsewhere, the term occurs at Ap I 41 (v. 499a), Ap I 42 (v. 515a), Bv 65 (v. 9c), Pv 82 (v. 700c), Vin I 310,30, Vin V 86,10. In several instances it is unclear whether it functions as an epithet or as a name. At Nidd II 189, where it occurs along with the names of the six previous buddhas, it is clearly a name. In the Mahāyāna sūtras, Śākyamuni virtually replaces Gautama as the Buddha's name.
959. *Anubuddhapaccekabuddhasaṅkhātesu vā buddhesu seṭṭho ti buddhaseṭṭho*. Those "awakened after him" (*anubuddha*) are disciple arahants. *Buddhaseṭṭho* should not be understood to mean "supreme among buddhas," since all buddhas are considered equal by way of their wisdom and virtues.
960. The Pāli *samādhimānantarikaññamāhu* should be resolved: *samādhim ānantarikaṃ yam āhu*. At DN III 273,7 it is said that "concentration of mind without interval is the one thing hard to penetrate" (*ānantariko cetosamādhi, ayaṃ eko dhammo duppaṭivijjho*). On this Sv III 1056,28–31 says: "Elsewhere it is the fruition immediately after the path that is called

'concentration of mind without interval.' But here what is intended by 'concentration of mind' without interval is the path that immediately follows insight, so called because it immediately follows insight or because it yields its own fruit without interval" (*ānantariko cetosamādhī ti aññattha maggānantaraṃ phalaṃ ānantariko cetosamādhi nāma, idha pana vipassanānantaro maggo vipassanāya vā anantarattā attano vā anantaraṃ phaladāyakattā ānantariko cetosamādhī ti adhippeto*). The tenet that the fruit immediately follows the path hinges on the Abhidhamma presentation of "path" and "fruit" as momentary occasions of experience occurring in a fixed sequence. This understanding is fundamental to the commentarial system, based on the Abhidhamma, but is not apparent in the Nikāyas.

961. By coincidence, *sataṃ* can be either genitive plural of *santa*, "good [person]," or the number "hundred." The former explanation of the commentary depends on taking *sataṃ* in the former sense; the alternative, as the number. The former explanation is certainly the one intended, as is clear from the next line in the verse as well as the canonical verse of homage to the Sangha: "the four pairs of persons, *the eight types of individuals*, this is the Blessed One's Sangha of disciples" (*cattāri purisayugāni aṭṭha purisapuggalā esa bhagavato sāvakasaṅgho*).

962. The three types of stream-enterers are at SN V 204,3–4, AN I 233,12–19, Pp 15 (§§31–33), etc. The five types of non-returners are at SN V 69,22, SN V 201,14–19, AN I 233,26–36, Pp 16–17 (§§36–40), etc. The distinction between arahants as dry-insighters (*sukkhavipassaka*) and those who make serenity their vehicle (*samathayānika*) is commentarial. The canonical texts usually distinguish between arahants liberated by wisdom (*paññāvimutta*) and arahants liberated in both respects (*ubhatobhāgavimutta*), on which see MN I 477,25–36, Pp 14 (§§24–25). The two dichotomies are not identical.

963. *Bhagavā sobhanena gamanena yuttattā, sobhanañca ṭhānaṃ gatattā, suṭṭhu ca gatattā suṭṭhu eva ca gadattā sugato, tassa sugatassa.* Word plays are involved here, elaborated at Vism 203–4, Ppn 7.33–35.

964. *Sabbepi te vacanaṃ suṇantī ti sāvakā.* Ee is missing *vacanaṃ*, mentioned in a note but included in Be and Ce. The word *sāvaka*, "disciple," is derived from *sāveti*, the causative of *suṇāti*, to listen to, to hear. Thus disciples are so called because they are "caused to hear" the teachings of their teacher.

965. See MN III 255–57, AN II 80–81. Gifts are said to be "purified" either through the giver (when the giver is of great virtue), through the recipient (when the recipient is of great virtue),

or through both. To be "purified" means that the gift is productive of great fruits (Ps V 76,6: *mahapphalabhāvena visujjhati, mahapphalā hoti*). In the fourth case, when neither the giver nor the recipient is of great virtue, the gift is still meritorious but not productive of great fruit (*na taṃ dānaṃ vipulapphalan ti brūmi*).

966. *Nikkāmino ti kāye ca jīvite ca anapekkhā hutvā paññādhurena viriyena sabbakilesehi katanikkhamanā*. So Ce and Ee, but Be reads the last word as *katanikkamanā*. This is unlikely to be a typographical error, since the reading is the same at Pj I 146 (VRI). Pj evidently derives *nikkāmino* from *nikkhamati*, "to depart, to renounce," though *nikkāma* suggests the intended meaning is absence (*nir*) of desire (*kāma*), and I translate based on this understanding. See Pj II commentary on **1131** at p. 1323.

967. *Ito bahiddhā*: a stock expression used to denote ascetics outside the Buddha's Teaching.

968. *Nānappakārampi amaratapaṃ karontānaṃ*. The split compound *amaraṃ tapaṃ* occurs at SN I 103,19 (with the wrong reading *aparaṃ tapaṃ*). Spk I 169,18–20 explains the term as meaning "devotion to self-mortification, stringent austerity practiced for the sake of the immortal state" (*amaratapaṃ amarabhāvatthāya kataṃ lūkhatapaṃ, attakilamathānuyogo*). See CDB 411, note 263. See too **249**d: *ye vāpi loke amarā bahū tapā*.

969. *Mudhā ti avyayena kākaṇikamattampi vyayaṃ akatvā*. *Vyaya* (from *vi* + *i*, like the more familiar *vaya*) means both "disappearance, decay, ruin, loss" and "spending, expense, outlay, disbursement." See PED and SED sv *vyaya*. Hence *avyaya* means "without expense," that is, for free.

970. *Bahujanapaccakkhena sotāpannasseva guṇena*. A global search for *bahujanapaccakkh** in CST4 turns up only this passage and its parallel in Pj I. Thus it is hard to determine exactly what is meant by this expression.

971. The passage is at Pp 16 (§§31–33), where the three occur from lowest to highest. The Pāli names for the three in the order given here are *ekabījī, kolaṃkola,* and *sattakkhattuparama*.

972. Reading with Be and Ce *sotāpattimaggañāṇena*, as against Ee *sotāpattiñāṇena*.

973. See pp. 1236–37.

974. *Sotāpattimaggo hi nibbānaṃ disvā kattabbakiccasampadāya sabbapaṭhamaṃ nibbānadassanato dassanan ti vuccati*. This qualification is added because, in the commentarial view of the path process, it is actually the mind-moment called *gotrabhū* ("change-of-lineage") that first sees nibbāna. However, unlike the path, *gotrabhū* does not eliminate defilements and thus does not "accomplish the task to be done upon seeing nibbāna." For a discussion, see Vism 672–75, Ppn 22.5–14.

975. Pj I 188,8 explains *su* here as "an indeclinable in the role of a mere line filler" (*padapūraṇamatte nipāto*).
976. *Sati kāye vijjamāne upādānakkhandhapañcakasaṅkhāte kāye vīsativatthukā diṭṭhi sakkāyadiṭṭhi*. This derivation correctly resolves *sakkāya* into *sat* + *kāya*. See too As 348,9–11: *Sakkāyadiṭṭhī ti vijjamānaṭṭhena sati khandhapañcakasaṅkhāte kāye; sayaṃ vā satī tasmiṃ kāye diṭṭhī ti sakkāyadiṭṭhi*.
977. *Taṃ paññācikicchitaṃ ito vigataṃ, tato vā paññācikicchitā idaṃ vigatan ti vicikicchitaṃ*. The definition of doubt (*vicikicchā*) as absence of a cure is common in the commentaries, for example, *vigatā cikicchā ti vicikicchā* at As 259,9 and Vism 471,10, Ppn 14.177.
978. See Appendix 3. The source is Dhs 231 (§1008).
979. Apparently these were practices by which an ascetic would imitate the behavior of a cow or a dog. See MN 57, where the Buddha speaks to such ascetics.
980. *Sabbampi . . . amaratapaṃ*. See note 968.
981. This is an allusion to the three "rounds" into which the twelve links of dependent origination are classified: the round of defilements (*kilesavaṭṭa*), from which arises the round of kamma (*kammavaṭṭa*), which in turn produces the round of results (*vipākavaṭṭa*). See Vism 581,9–14, Ppn 17.298; CMA 300–301.
982. Parallel to its treatment of the verses (see note 95), Be numbers this section of the commentary 234. I follow Ee, which treats this as a verse of eight lines. Ce does not number the sections of the commentary. The Skt parallel, v. 7, does not include pādas ef, *catūh'apāyehi . . . abhabbo kataṃ*, which suggests they are a late addition. The mention of four planes of misery also suggests lateness. The four Nikāyas consistently speak of only three bad destinations: the hells, the animal realm, and the realm of afflicted spirits. The asura realm, in the older texts, is not expressly assigned to either the good destinations or the bad ones.
983. I read *ekacce cha chābhiṭhānānī ti paṭhanti*. The alternative reading states that there are two sets of six deeds which the noble disciple is incapable of doing. The first consists of the five heinous deeds (matricide, etc.), together with acknowledging another as one's teacher; the second consists of violating the five precepts, again with the sixth as acknowledging another as one's teacher. For violation of the five precepts as the "five enmities" (*pañca verāni*), see SN II 68–69, AN IV 405–6, and AN V 182–83.
984. I am unsure of the source for this. The purport, it seems, is that the village children who are noble disciples would not catch live fish but would only pick up fish that had already died.

985. Here and below I have expanded slightly the cryptic shorthand references the text makes to several rules of the Pātimokkha. These are Saṅghādisesa 6 and Pācittiya 5.

986. The rules alluded to here are Pācittiyas 4 and 7. Idle chatter and harsh speech as such are not violations of Pātimokkha rules but infractions of two of the four verbal courses of unwholesome kamma.

987. Pj I 192,2–5 adds: *vanappagumbo, svāyaṃ vanappagumbe ti vutto. Evampi hi vattuṃ labbhati "atthi savitakkasavicāre, atthi avitakkavicāramatte, sukhe dukkhe jīve" ti ādīsu viya.* Norman points out (GD 204) that Pj I is here explaining *vanappagumbe* "as a masculine nominative singular of an *–a* stem in *–e*, i.e., an Eastern form, a so-called Māgadhism, and giving other examples from the canon."

988. *Phussitāni aggāni assā ti phussitaggo, sabbasākhāpasākhāsu sañjātapuppho ti attho.* Norman conjectures that *phussitagge* "may stand for *phassitagge* . . . or it may have arisen by analogy with *phusati,*" with *–ss* for the sake of the meter. It is hard to see, however, how either of these participles from *phusati* fits the context. The Skt parallel, v. 14, has *puṣpitāgrā* (= Pāli *pupphitagge*), which is more appropriate. *Phussitagge* may be an old reciter's error that has persisted through time. I translate on the assumption that *pupphitagge* is the correct reading. Just below, in fact, Pj I 192,15–16 has the gloss *supupphitaggasākho . . . pagumbo,* "a thicket whose branches have full flowering crests."

989. *Paṭhamasmiṃ gimhe, citramāse ti attho. So hi paṭhamagimho ti ca bālavasanto ti ca vuccati.* It may sound contradictory to call this season both "summer" and "spring," but in northern India the year is divided into three major seasons: the hot season, from mid-March until mid-July; the rainy season, from mid-July until mid-November; and the cool season, from mid-November until mid-March. The early part of the hot season would be called spring, and the later part summer. The month of Citra runs from mid-March until mid-April, followed by Visākhā, from mid-April to mid-May, the month in which the Theravāda tradition celebrates the Buddha's birth, enlightenment, and parinibbāna.

990. Pj I 192,23–24 adds that in *paramaṃhitāya,* the nasal *–ṃ–* is inserted for the sake of euphony (*ettha ca gāthābandhasukhatthaṃ anunāsiko*).

991. This verse is without a parallel in the Mvu version, which again suggests that it is a late addition. See Jayawickrama 1977, 105.

992. *Paṇītādhimuttikehi icchito "aho vata mayampi evarūpā assāmā" ti, varaguṇayogato vā varo.* Pj I is here playing upon two senses

of the word *vara* (both from the verb *varati, vuṇāti* = to wish, to choose): (1) excellent and (2) a wish (boon, favor). See PED *vara*[1] and *vara*[2]. Perhaps the English word "choice" can capture this dual meaning: what is chosen and also what is considered of prime quality, like "choice Ceylon tea."

993. *Nibbedhabhāgiyavāsanābhāgiyavaradhammadāyi*. Mp-ṭ I 59 explains the distinction between *vāsanābhāgiya* and *nibbedhabhāgiya* as follows: "*Habituation* means the cultivation of merit. What occurs in this section of habituation 'partakes of habituation.' Or it 'partakes of habituation' because it causes one to partake of habituation. *Penetration* is the act of penetrating, the splitting of the mass of greed and other defilements. What occurs in this section of penetration 'partakes of penetration.' Or it 'partakes of penetration' because it causes one to partake of penetration." Put more simply, a teaching that "partakes of habituation" enjoins wholesome practices that permeate one's mind with wholesome qualities, leading to a good rebirth and serving as long-range supporting conditions for the attainment of nibbāna; a teaching that "partakes of penetration" enjoins practices that lead directly to the destruction of defilements and the realization of nibbāna.

994. "The group of five" (*pañcavaggiya*) were the five ascetics to whom the Buddha gave his first teachings (SN V 421; Vin I 10–13). "The fortunate group" (*bhaddavaggiya*) was a group of young men who became bhikkhus early in the Buddha's career (Vin I 23–24). The matted-hair ascetics (*jaṭila*) were the former fire ascetics to whom the Buddha taught the Fire Sermon (SN IV 19–20, Vin I 34–35).

995. The thirty pāramīs are obtained by taking the ten pāramīs at three levels: basic (*pāramī*), intermediate (*upapāramī*), and supreme (*paramatthapāramī*). Only perfectly enlightened buddhas fulfill the ten pāramīs at all three levels, hence thirty pāramīs in all.

996. This explanation refers to the four *adhiṭṭhāna*, on which see MN III 245–46.

997. *Navalokuttaradhammaṃ*. The four paths, the four fruits, and nibbāna.

998. *Dhīrā ti dhitisampannā*. From this gloss it appears that Pj II is explaining *dhīra* in the sense of "steadfast," but I follow Norman and Jayawickrama, who both take the word here in its other sense of "wise."

999. Norman (GD 205) assumes that *tathāgata* in all three verses refers to the Buddha, and thus in the second and third verses he sees an implicit "and." In my translation I have followed Pj II, which takes the word as an adjectival compound qualifying all three objects of veneration, each in its own way. The

compound *tathāgata* is ambiguous in that it can be taken to mean either "thus come" or "thus gone." Pj II explains it in both ways in relation to the Buddha but solely as "thus gone" in relation to the Dhamma and the Sangha. For this reason I render it "thus gone" in relation to all three. Jayawickrama, too, in his translation ascribes "thus gone" to each of the three objects of veneration.

1000. I read with Be and Ce *buddhādīhi tathā avagato*. The reading of Ee seems confused here.

1001. A parallel version of this story is at Dhp-a III 445–48 (BL 3:174–76).

1002. *Sippaṃ*. This must refer to the performance of the sacrifices, rituals, and ceremonies of the Vedas and Brāhmaṇas.

1003. The bracketed page numbers are again those of Pj II (Ee).

1004. *Āmagandha*. Literally "raw smell," referring especially to the smell of fish and meat. By extension, it is applied to food that gives off such a smell, to the fish and meat themselves, hence "carrion."

1005. I read with Be *tesu pasīditvā* as against Ce and Ee *te isī disvā*, "having seen those rishis."

1006. *Vacchagiddhinī gāvī viya*. See Vin I 193,14–15.

1007. *Isipabbajjaṃ pabbajitvā*. This means that, without formally taking ordination in a particular sect, he leaves the home life, adopts an ascetic lifestyle, and leads a contemplative life deep in the forest.

1008. I pass over Pj II's glosses of the words for these food items. I rely on DOP and Norman for my renderings.

1009. This is stated at MN I 369,4–10.

1010. On the distinction between teachings based on persons and based on qualities, see p. 72.

1011. Though the text says *kāmapaṭisevanasaṅkhātesu kāmesu*, it is clear that by *kāma* Pj II here intends sexual pleasure, as in the third precept.

1012. *Natthikadiṭṭhī ti "natthi dinnan" ti ādidasavatthukamicchādiṭṭhisamannāgatā*. The allusion is to the common canonical formula for the tenfold wrong view. See Appendix 3.

1013. *Durannayā*: Norman renders this "hard to fathom," but while DOP recognizes this as one meaning of the term, it includes a second meaning, "intractable," which matches Pj II's explanation and better fits this context. The same word occurs below in **251**d in a positive sense, as describing the Buddha, where the literal sense "hard to lead" is more appropriate.

1014. *Adānasīlā na ca denti kassaci*: It seems that this line could be taken to be describing one type, "Those of a non-generous nature who do not give to anyone," but just below Pj II classifies them as two factors distinguished on the basis of temperament and conduct.

1015. *Adinnapubbaka* was the soubriquet of a brahmin, the miserly father of Maṭṭhakuṇḍalī, whose story is told at Dhp-a I 25–36 (see BL 1:159–65) and Vv-a 322–30. This brahmin, however, was converted by the Buddha after the death of his son and attained realization of the Dhamma; thus he could not have been reborn in the spirit realm. I therefore take the expression as descriptive of a miserly family, not a sobriquet of a particular person. The *nijjhāmataṇhikapetā* constitute a subgroup in the spirit realm.

1016. Pj II offers two ways of resolving *paresamādāya*: (1) *paresam ādāya*, "having taken [that which belongs] to others," with *paresam* as genitive plural in relation to *ādāya*, in other words, stealing the belongings of others; and (2) *pare samādāya*, "having captured others," with *pare* as accusative plural object of *samādāya*. I translate on the basis of the first alternative, also preferred by Norman and Jayawickrama. Pj II, in its enumeration of kinds of "carrion" in the verse, seems to lean toward the second.

1017. *Ye lokantarikandhakārasaṅkhātaṃ . . . tamaṃ vajanti*. This refers to the dark regions between worlds "where even the light of the sun and moon, so powerful and mighty, does not reach"; see SN V 454,17–20. These regions, according to the texts, are infernal states inhabited by beings who are unaware of each other's existence.

1018. *Evaṃ pana sundarataraṃ siyā "na macchamaṃsānaṃ anāsakattaṃ na macchamaṃsānānāsakattaṃ na sodheti, maccan" ti*. Pj II is suggesting that instead of taking *anāsakattaṃ* ("not-eating," or "fasting") as an independent term, it should be taken in conjunction with "fish and meat." This would require that *macchamaṃsaṃ* be changed into the genitive plural *macchamaṃsānaṃ*, which is then abridged for metrical reasons as *macchamaṃsāna* and joined to *anāsakattaṃ*, yielding *macchamaṃsānānāsakattaṃ*.

1019. I read with Ce and Ee *parattha tapena saṅgahitattā* as against Be *amaratapena saṅgahitattā*.

1020. *Amarā ti amarabhāvapatthanatāya pavattakāyakilesā*. This seems to construe *amarā* as an independent noun, but as Norman explains (GD 207), it should be seen as part of a split compound, together with *tapā* and separated by *bahū*. Hence I keep the full compound in the lemma.

1021. *Yaññamutūpasevanā*: Norman renders this line as "the performance of sacrifices at the proper season," taking the two components as indicating one practice, but I follow Pj II and Jayawickrama in taking *yañña* and *utūpasevanā* separately.

1022. Reading with Ce and Ee *lepena* as against Be *kilesena*.

1023. According to the commentaries, whenever the Buddha ordains someone by the "Come, bhikkhu!" utterance, through the Buddha's spiritual power and the candidate's own past merits, his appearance instantly changes into that of a monk equipped with robes and bowl. This idea is not found in the canonical texts.

1024. I read with Be *sāvakapāramiñāṇaṃ* as against Ce and Ee *sāvakañāṇaṃ*. Sp-ṭ I 308 and Vmv I 62 define *sāvakapāramiñāṇaṃ* thus: "*The knowledge of a disciple's perfection*: all the world-transcending and mundane knowledge to be obtained by the chief disciples" (*sāvakapāramiñāṇan ti aggasāvakehi paṭilabhitabbaṃ sabbameva lokiyalokuttarañāṇaṃ*). See too Mp-ṭ III 201.

1025. Since these hermit-bhikkhus are already in the Buddha's presence, it is hard to see why they should need to "come through the sky" (*ākāsenāgantvā*) to venerate him. I assume that the phrase has been inserted here by a mechanical repetition of the earlier statement about Tissa.

1026. Sv I 270–71 has a slightly different list of eight.

1027. Ce and Ee *assamuṭṭhikā*, Be *asmamuṭṭhikā*. See DOP *assa*[1] (= Skt *aśman*) a stone. This rendering is supported by the commentarial explanation *pāsāṇa*.

1028. *Dantaluyyakā*. *Luyyaka* is from *lunāti*.

1029. Be adds here *khāditvā*, "having eaten," which though absent in Ce and Ee seems necessary to complete the meaning. In all three editions *khāditvā* occurs in the parallel statement about the next class of hermits.

1030. The verses are also at Ja III 196,10–23, with commentary at Ja III 196–97.

1031. *Sayhāni kammāni anādiyantan ti evaṃ bhāsitvāpi ca sayhāni kātuṃ sakkānipi tassa kammāni anādiyantaṃ karaṇatthāya asamādiyantaṃ*. *Kātuṃ sakkāni* is evidently intended as the gloss on *sayhāni*, but the parallel at Ja III 196,12 has *seyyāni kammāni*, glossed *vacanassa anurūpāni uttamakammāni*, "supreme deeds that accord with his words."

1032. *Atītānāgatehi padehi*. This probably refers to reminders of past favors done and promises of future favors.

1033. *Vyañjanacchāyāmatten'eva piyaṃ*. Literally "endearing only through a mere shadow of the expression."

1034. Pāda a in all editions reads *na so mitto yo sadā appamatto*. Everywhere else in the Nikāyas *appamatta* has a positive sense, "heedful" or "diligent." Here, however, we find a rare (perhaps unique) negative use of the word, which I render "alert" to distinguish it from the positive sense. This false friend is "alert" only in looking out for one's faults. It is also possible the text has been corrupted here.

1035. *Katamadhurena upacārena sadā appamatto viharati*. A global search through CST4 does not turn up any other occurrences of *katamadhur** either in the Tipiṭaka or the commentaries. Hence my rendering is a guess based on a literal rendering "with what task?"

1036. Ja III 193,10 glosses *randhamevānupassī*, not glossed by Pj II, thus *chiddaṃ vivarameva passanto*.

1037. Ja III 196–97 treats this verse as a further elaboration on good friendship, which may be a more satisfactory explanation than the one given by Pj II. It says that here the "state productive of joy" refers specifically to good friendship; for friendship with a wise and good friend produces joy, brings praise, and is a cause for bodily and mental happiness in this world and the next.

1038. Ja III 197,6–7 explains one's personal duty (*porisaṃ dhuraṃ*) as fourfold: giving, virtuous behavior, meditation, and good friendship.

1039. Be alone repeats the question here, *kīdiso payogo payuñjitabbo*.

1040. In citing the lemma as *dhammapītirasaṃ pivaṃ niddaro hoti nippāpo*, Pj II inverts pādas c and d of the text.

1041. Since the Maṅgala Sutta also occurs as Khp 5, and is commented upon by Pj I, Pj II (Ee) includes only the first few sentences of the commentary on the Sn version of the discourse. Thus from here on, bracketed page numbers refer to the commentary on the sutta in Pj I (Ee).

1042. This is likely an allusion to the Rāmāyana.

1043. The word *maṅgala* signifies what is auspicious, often referring to lucky signs. Since English does not have a convenient noun corresponding to "auspicious," I resort to "blessing," which fits the discourse if taken in the sense of "a thing conducive to happiness or welfare" rather than as "help and approval from God."

1044. *Diṭṭhamaṅgaliko nām'eko puriso*. The two to follow are the *sutamaṅgaliko puriso* and the *mutamaṅgaliko puriso*. The three terms *diṭṭha, suta,* and *muta* are often mentioned as a group in Sn; see note 60. A set of four terms, *diṭṭha, suta, muta,* and *viññāta*, covers all possible objects of experience, respectively, the seen (objects of sight), the heard (objects of hearing), the sensed (objects of the other three physical senses), and the cognized (objects of reflective consciousness). At **1086**a the four occur together.

1045. Readings of this term vary, though all agree it is a kind of bird. I follow Ce and Ee, which have *bhāsamānasakuṇaṃ*, perhaps a myna bird or parrot. Other Sinhala manuscripts have *vācasakuṇaṃ*, "a speech bird," and *vātasakuṇaṃ*, "a wind bird." Be has *cātakasakuṇaṃ*.

1046. These are personal names that suggest prosperity and good fortune.
1047. *Kappakolāhala, cakkavattikolāhala, buddhakolāhala, maṅgalakolāhala, moneyyakolāhala.* Ja I 47–48 describes three commotions: *kappakolāhala, buddhakolāhala,* and *cakkavattikolāhala.*
1048. *Muttasirā.* PED takes this to mean that they are confused, but Vism-mhṭ II 47 explains this to mean that the bands of their topknots are loosened (*sikhābandhassa muttatāya muttasirā*).
1049. This alludes to Nālaka's discourse with the Buddha in III,11.
1050. The passage from here until the explanation of the first verse is taken from Pj II 300.
1051. In Pāli "there is everything" is *sabbam atthi,* which on this explanation was contracted to form the city name Sāvatthī. Perhaps this etymology would work better in a dialect that had *savvam atthi.*
1052. *Anāthānaṃ piṇḍo etasmiṃ atthi.* His actual name was Sudatta, but because he generously supported orphans, widows, and other destitute people, he was generally known as Anāthapiṇḍika.
1053. The story of how he purchased Jeta's Grove and constructed a monastery there is told at Vin II 158–59.
1054. The point is that, while the noun *devatā* is feminine in gender, it does not necessarily mean that the deity was female. The femine suffix *–tā,* added to *deva,* was originally an abstract ending (like English –ness or –ship), but the word *devatā* had lost its abstract meaning and came to refer to any deity.
1055. Here the page numbering resumes from Pj I.
1056. *Dibbantī ti devā, pañcahi kāmaguṇehi kīḷanti, attano vā siriyā jotantī ti attho.* DOP sv *dibbati* confirms this double meaning of *dibbati*: "sports, amuses oneself, plays (with dice), gambles; is bright, shines." The word *deva* is originally derived from *diva,* sky, heaven.
1057. Vibh 494–95 (§1021). See too pp. 1261–62.
1058. *Manuno apaccā ti manussā. Porāṇā pana bhaṇanti – manassa ussannatāya manussā. Manassa ussannatāya manussā.*
1059. See pp. 688–89.
1060. *Balanti assasantī* [Ee *anantī*] *ti bālā, assasitapassasitamattena jīvanti, na paññājīvitenā ti adhippāyo.* Pj II here explains *bālā* on the basis of the verb *balanti,* glossed *assasanti* ("breathe"). See SED sv *bal*².
1061. *Paṇḍantī ti paṇḍitā, sandiṭṭhikasamparāyikesu atthesu ñāṇagatiyā gacchantī ti adhippāyo.* The verb *paṇḍati* (in SED but not in PED) is probably artificial, devised to explain *paṇḍita.*
1062. The monks Kokālika, Kaṭamorakatissa, Khaṇḍadeviyāputta, and Samuddadatta were allies of Devadatta in his conflict with

the Buddha; see Vin II 196,27–28 and Vin III 171,3–5. The story of Kokālika (or Kokāliya) is told at III,10. On Ciñcā, see note 894.

1063. Apart from the parallel passage to this one in Pj I, it seems no other mention of Dīghavida's brother is found in the Pāli Canon or its commentaries. DPPN refers only to this passage.

1064. The verses are at Ja IV 240–41, commented on at Ja IV 242. On the ambiguous line *dunnayo seyyaso hoti*, Ja IV 242,7–9 explains: "*He is hard to guide to the good*: He takes the bad way to be better, that is, he takes transgression of the five precepts to be better. Or else [the line means] he is hard to guide toward beneficial behavior; he is hard to guide, cannot be guided." In the verses, Sakka addresses Akitti as "Kassapa," perhaps his clan name.

1065. For details on these, see DPPN.

1066. The story of Sumana is essentially the same as at Dhp-a II 40 foll. (BL 2:123 foll.). Mallikā was the wife of King Pasenadi. She was the daughter of the chief garland-maker of Kosala. Shortly after she made an offering of porridge to the Buddha, Pasenadi met her, fell in love with her, and brought her to the palace, where he appointed her chief queen.

1067. Be includes his name, Bimbisāra.

1068. Be has here *dvattiṃsamahāpurisalakkhaṇāsītānubyañjanapaṭimaṇḍitaṃ*, "adorned with the thirty-two marks of a great man and the eighty minor features." This phrase is not in Ce or Ee.

1069. Reading with Ce *bālasevanapaccayabhayānaṃ parittāṇena*.

1070. *Tāsaṃ phalavibhūtivaṇṇanāyaṃ vuttanayen'eva*. The expression *phalavibhūti* occurs at Pj I 222,20.

1071. *Navaṅgaṃ satthu sāsanaṃ*. The reference is to the ninefold classification of the Buddha's teachings: discourses, mixed prose and verse, expositions, verses, inspired utterances, quotations, birth stories, wonders, and questions-and-answers (*suttaṃ, geyyaṃ, veyyākaraṇaṃ, gāthā, udānaṃ, itivuttakaṃ, jātakaṃ, abbhutadhammaṃ, vedallaṃ*).

1072. The "miracle" by which he simultaneously emitted water and fire from his body. See Paṭis I 125–26.

1073. His descent at Saṅkassa after spending three months in the deva world. See pp. 1203–4.

1074. The six are: (1) the unsurpassed sight, (2) the unsurpassed hearing, (3) the unsurpassed gain, (4) the unsurpassed training, (5) the unsurpassed service, and (6) the unsurpassed recollection. See AN III 325–29.

1075. Mahākappina had been the king of a city named Kukkuṭavatī in a frontier region. When he learned about the Buddha, he abandoned his kingdom and went forth. His wife, the queen, followed him and became a bhikkhunī. The story is at Mp I

318–24. Mahākappina became the foremost exhorter of the bhikkhus.

1076. *Agārikabāhusaccaṃ*. Literally "the learning of a layperson"; a secular branch of learning, such as grammar, astronomy, medicine, or any of the other esteemed subjects of study.

1077. Reading with Ce *agāriyavinayo ca anagāriyavinayo ca* [Be: *agārikavinayo ca anagārikavinayo ca*]. This is missing in Ee.

1078. *Catupārisuddhisīlaṃ*. The four are: restraint according to the Pātimokkha, restraint of the sense faculties, purification of livelihood, and reflection on the use of the requisites. See Vism 15–16, Ppn 1.42.

1079. Here and in the following verses I do not translate the commentary on terms, which merely resolves compounds and defines words with synonyms.

1080. In the compound *puttadārassa*, *putta* means "son(s)," but Pj II allows it to represent both sons and daughters. I follow Pj II in rendering it by the gender-neutral term "children."

1081. These are probably the twenty kinds of women with whom one can legitimately have sexual relations, mentioned at Sv III 1048–49, Ps I 199, etc. These include not only wives in the proper sense but concubines, temporary partners, and so forth.

1082. The commentator adds that in the following summary, "wife and children" are comprised under the word "wife."

1083. Pj I is alluding here to three of the four *saṅgahavatthu*, which I render "means of attracting and sustaining a retinue." On the four, see AN II 32. I do not know why the fourth, equality of treatment, is omitted.

1084. Walshe apparently thinks bees collect honey, for he renders this line: "He gathers wealth just as the bee gathers honey." The text, however, reads *bhamarasseva irīyato*, which I render very literally.

1085. The list of items to be given, as found for example at MN III 205,7–8, AN II 203,19–20, and AN V 271–73, consists of: food, drink, clothes, vehicles, garlands, fragrances, ointments, bedding, dwelling places, and lamps.

1086. I follow Be and Ce *subuddhipubbikā*. Ee has *santuṭṭhipubbikā*, "preceded by contentment."

1087. Ee is missing *kāyavacīmanosucaritakammāni*, found in Be and Ce.

1088. *Sampattavirati, samādānavirati, samucchedavirati*. This analysis is made elsewhere in the commentaries, for instance, at Ps I 203–4, Spk II 149–51, It-a II 55, and Paṭis-a I 224–25.

1089. *Ariyasāvakassa pañca bhayāni verāni vūpasantāni honti*. The five "perils and enmities" are the transgressions of the five precepts. On this see AN IV 406,1–20, AN V 183,1–18.

1090. *Harītakaṃ vā āmalakaṃ vā*: "yellow myrobalan or emblic myrobalan." These are commonly used in Indo–Sri Lankan ayurvedic medicine.

1091. With Be and Ce reading *ābādhiko*, omitted in Ee.

1092. See Appendix 3.

1093. I read with Ee *bhāvitakāyasīlacittapaññānaṃ*. Be and Ce have *–vacī–* in place of *–sīla–*, but see SN IV 111,19, and for the negative *abhāvitakāyā, abhāvitatsīlā, abhāvitatcittā, abhāvitapaññā*, see AN III 106,4.

1094. The verses (slightly different) occur with the background story at Ps II 16–17. When the Buddha was living at the Indasāla cave on Mount Vedisaka, an owl would accompany him part way through the woods when he went on alms round. One evening the owl descended from the mountain and paid homage to the Buddha and the Sangha. The Buddha smiled. Ānanda asked for the reason and the Buddha explained that by these acts of veneration, the owl would be reborn among devas and humans and in the end become a paccekabuddha named Somanassa. The name means "joy."

1095. *Tapas* is an Indian religious concept meaning "religious austerity, bodily mortification, penance, severe meditation, special observance" (SED). The Buddha rejected *tapas* as bodily mortification but did not entirely reject the idea of religious austerity. Instead, he reconceptualized *tapas* as energy (*viriya*), so called because it "burns up" (*tapati*) unwholesome qualities.

1096. So Ce. Ee has *Kumārakapañhesu* [Be: *Kumārapañhe*], "The Boy's Questions," a short catechism included in Khp. The text, however, merely mentions the four noble truths, while its commentary treats them succinctly, so the reading in Be and Ee is likely to be faulty or the reference mistaken.

1097. *Tam pi pañcagativānena vānasaññitāya taṇhāya nikkhantattā nibbānan ti vuccati.* This etymology of nibbāna involves a word play that derives nibbāna from *vāna*, which I here take in the sense of "jungle," with the prefix *nir-* indicating absence. At p. 645, I took nibbāna as "absence of weaving" (based on *vāna* as meaning "weaving"). See note 869.

1098. *Diṭṭhadhammasukhavihārādihetuto.* The context suggests that this must mean the arahant's dwelling at ease after realizing nibbāna.

1099. On the eight worldly conditions (*lokadhamma*), see Appendix 3. The source is AN IV 156–59.

1100. I follow a variant cited in a note in Ce, *asekkhakkhandhādilokuttamabhāvāvahanato*. The aggregates of one beyond training are the arahant's collections of good behavior, concentration, wisdom, liberation, and knowledge and vision of liberation. See AN III 134,24–28, etc.

1101. Pj I 155,3 explains that the letter *–m–* (in *sabbatthamaparājitā*) should be understood as a mere liaison consonant (*ma-kāro c'ettha padasandhikaraṇamatto ti viññātabbo*).

1102. Pj I 155,10 explains that the nasal stop (in *sotthiṃ*) is inserted for the sake of euphony (*anunāsiko c'ettha gāthābandhasukhatthaṃ vutto ti veditabbo*). Thus the nasal stop does not mean that *sotthiṃ* is an accusative object of *gacchanti*; the commentary treats it as an adverb of manner.

1103. The bracketed page numbers now return to those of Pj II (Ee).

1104. Spk I 302 gives slightly different accounts of the past kammas responsible for their rebirth as yakkhas. It says that, under the Buddha Kassapa, Sūciloma was a monk who arrived from afar and, with his body soiled by sweat and dirt, laid down on a bed belonging to the Sangha without respectfully covering it with a bedsheet. Khara had been a lay follower who laid down on carpets belonging to the Sangha without covering them with his own upper robe. He also took the Sangha's oil and used it to anoint his own body. Nothing is said about them being reborn in hell on account of such kamma. Rather, it seems they were immediately reborn as yakkhas.

1105. While in the translation of I,7 I rendered *samaṇaka* "low ascetic," since there the brahmin addresses the Buddha in pejorative terms, I here render the word "sham ascetic" in compliance with the commentarial gloss *samaṇapaṭirūpakattā pana samaṇako hoti*, "one who has only the outward form of an ascetic is a sham ascetic."

1106. I read with Be *Uragasutte*, as against Ce and Ee *Abhayasutte*. Be is certainly correct here. Nine kinds of thoughts are distinguished in the commentary to the Uraga Sutta (see p. 375), but neither the Abhaya Sutta (at SN V 126) nor its commentary analyzes the kinds of thoughts.

1107. Despite the variant *vaṅkaṃ* appearing in some manuscripts, *dhaṅkam* (< Skt *dvāṅkṣam*) must have been the reading known to the commentators, for both Pj II and Spk I 304,7 gloss the word with *kākaṃ*, crow, which they would not have done if *vaṅkam* was the reading.

1108. *Evaṃ kusalamanaṃ akusalavitakkā kuto samuṭṭhāya ossajantī ti pucchati.* This explanation separates *mano* and *vitakkā* and treats *mano* as the accusative object of *ossajanti*. I part with Pj II here and take *manovitakkā* to be a compound with the object of *ossajanti* merely implicit, namely, *oneself*, the very source from which the thoughts arise. *Manovitakke* is clearly a compound in the line *samodahaṃ bhikkhu manovitakke* at SN I 7,18, where Spk I 37,31–32 glosses *manovitakke ti manamhi uppannavitakke*. So too Ja III 120,17, *athopi me āsi manovitakko*, glossed *evaṃ me manovitakko uppanno*.

1109. In the Skt the two verses are inverted, so that Śag 11.2 corresponds to **272** and Śag 11.3 to **271**. In the simile, Skt has *kumārakā dhātrīm ivāśrayante*, "as children depend upon a wet-nurse," which is mirrored by the Chinese of SĀ 1324 (T II 363c22): 猶如新生兒，依倚於乳母.

1110. *Attabhāvaṃ sandhāy'āha*. The word *attabhāva* occurs in the texts in at least three senses, not always distinguishable: the physical body, individual existence, and the existing individual, the person, understood as the collection of five aggregates. Here the last seems to be intended.

1111. *Tadaññaṃ pakatiādikāraṇaṃ paṭikkhipanto*. The mention of *pakati* (Skt *prakṛti*) may be an allusion to the Sāṅkhya system.

1112. Readings of this clause vary. I follow Ce: *ādikāya kamānugāminiyā paññāya anukkamamānā*.

1113. While Pj II calls this the Kapilasutta, Sn titles it the Dhammacariyasutta.

1114. The verse is at Ja V 257,17–18 with the commentarial explanation immediately following: "One who speaks more than this to another who does not accept his advice is like a slave in the presence of his master; for a slave keeps on speaking whether or not his master accepts his word."

1115. Reading with Be and Ce *Yasojo*.

1116. There is a word play in the Pāli here, since the word *vaṇṇa* means both "praise" and "color." Thus because he spoke praise (*vaṇṇaṃ kathesi*) of the Buddha, he has gained this color (*īdisaṃ vaṇṇaṃ paṭilabhi*).

1117. So Ce and Ee, but Be says she was also reborn in the great hell.

1118. Pj II sees here two objects of *na jānāti*, taking *akkhātaṃ* (= that which has been declared by the bhikkhus) as distinct from *dhammaṃ buddhena desitaṃ*. It seems to me, however, that in the text *akkhātaṃ* also describes *dhammaṃ buddhena desitaṃ*, "the Dhamma declared and taught by the Buddha." Norman, too, renders it in such a way: "the doctrine even when proclaimed [and] taught by the Buddha."

1119. I here follow Norman (at GD 213), who takes *bhāvitattānaṃ* as an accusative singular. Pj II offers two alternative interpretations. On the first, *vihesaṃ* is taken as a present participle, in which case *bhāvitattānaṃ* is explained as a genitive plural doing service for an accusative plural, *bhāvitatte*. On the second, *vihesaṃ* is taken as an accusative noun, with the present participle supplied by *karonto*; in this case *bhāvitattānaṃ* serves as a true genitive plural, so the meaning would be "creating trouble for those who are self-developed."

1120. For *purakkhata* PED has only "honored, esteemed, preferred," but the gloss, *purakkhato pesito payojito*, indicates *purakkhata* can also indicate motivation.

1121. Be has *sesapabbajitānaṃ bhāvitattānaṃ* "the remaining monastics who are self-developed," but I follow Ce and Ee, which do not have *sesapabbajitānaṃ*.

1122. Pādas cd read: *Saṃkilesaṃ na jānāti, maggaṃ nirayagāminaṃ*. I follow Norman, whose rendering, "he does not know that defilement [is] the road which leads to hell," posits identity between *saṃkilesa* and *maggaṃ nirayagāminaṃ*. Pj II takes the two terms as linked by an implicit conjunction *ca*. Jayawickrama follows the commentary: "he does not know the defilement [now] and the path leading to a woeful state."

1123. With Ce and Ee I read *sāṅgaṇo puggalo*, as against Be *sampuṇṇo puggalo*.

1124. With Be I read *abhūtaguṇapatthanākārappavattāya pāpikāya icchāya*. Ce and Ee have *–pattāya* instead of *–pavattāya*.

1125. At Vibh 276 (§513) "gifts of bamboo" (*veḷudāna*) is the first in a list of items that constitute wrong livelihood. The purport is that by making such gifts to laypeople, one expects to receive support from them.

1126. At Vibh 277 (§514) resorting to the place of prostitutes (*vesiyāgocaro*) is the first in a list of wrong resorts for a bhikkhu.

1127. The three verses in the text, **281–83**, are also at AN IV 172,6–11.

1128. The incident is related at AN IV 204–6, Ud 52, and Vin II 236–37.

1129. This incident is related at Ud 24–27. A group of five hundred bhikkhus headed by Yasoja came to visit the Buddha. The Buddha spent the entire night sitting in meditation together with them. Several times during the night Ānanda urged the Buddha to greet the visitors, but the Buddha kept silent. Finally, the Buddha emerged from meditation and told Ānanda that he and the five hundred bhikkhus had all been sitting in imperturbable concentration (*āneñjasamādhi*). Ud-a 185,14–16 identifies this as the concentration of the supreme fruit (of arahantship) based on the fourth jhāna, though some say it was based on a formless jhāna (*āneñjasamādhinā ti catutthajjhānapādakena aggaphalasamādhinā, arūpajjhānapādakenā ti pi vadanti*).

1130. I omit here a passage that merely comments on the various terms used to signify advanced age and on how the brahmins exchanged greetings with the Buddha.

1131. *Porāṇānaṃ brāhmaṇānaṃ brāhmaṇadhamme*. Norman has "brahmanical lore," and Jayawickrama "brahmanic custom." The word *dhamma* means not only the Buddha's teaching but the unchanging principle of goodness and truth. Each community has its own particular *dhamma*, its way of embodying and enacting this principle of goodness. The discussion here concerns the way appropriate for a brahmin.

1132. *Desakālādidhamme chaḍḍetvā yo brāhmaṇadhammo, tasmiṃyeva.* The sense, it seems, is that the brahmanical *dhamma* is to be explored in its ideal form, distinct from the particular practices that have been established by custom as obligatory for a brahmin.

1133. *Jatumāsaka.* DOP: "a coin made of or marked with lac."

1134. Pj II alludes here to AN 5:192, III 223–30, which distinguishes five types of brahmins: the one like Brahmā, the one like a deva, the one who remains within the boundary, the one who has crossed the boundary, and the caṇḍāḷa brahmin. The *one like Brahmā* (*brahmasama*), after completing his studies, goes forth into homelessness and develops the four divine abodes. The *one like a deva* (*devasama*) marries a brahmin woman and subsists by wandering for alms; after raising children he goes forth into homelessness and develops the four jhānas. The *one who remains within the boundary* (*mariyāda*) marries a brahmin woman, settles on his property, begets children, and does not go forth into homelessness. The *one who crosses the boundary* (*sambhinnamariyāda*) couples with a woman from any caste and indulges in sexual intercourse for pleasure as well as procreation. The *caṇḍāla brahmin* (*brāhmaṇacaṇḍāla*) couples with a woman from any caste, including an outcast woman, and earns his living by all kinds of work, even occupations unsuitable for a brahmin.

1135. Pj II 316,15 says that in addition to the reading *vijjācaraṇapariyeṭṭhiṃ acaruṃ*, there is also a reading *vijjācaraṇapariyeṭṭhuṃ acaruṃ*, meaning, "They practiced to seek knowledge and conduct."

1136. Reading with Ce and Ee *brāhmaṇadvāre*, as against Be *brāhmaṇā*.

1137. Reading with Ce and Ee *rocentāpi*, as against Be *karontāpi*.

1138. Pj II glosses *nāssu gacchanti* with *n'eva gacchanti*. This indicates that *nāssu* here should be understood as *na* + *assu* < Skt *sma*, which (as Norman points out, GD 216) "can be linked with a present tense to give a past sense." See too PED *assu*[3], DOP *assu*[7].

1139. The verse reads: *Aññatra tamhā samayā, utuveramaṇiṃ pati; antarā methunaṃ dhammaṃ, nāssu gacchanti brāhmaṇā.* Norman translates: "Brahmins did not indulge in sexual intercourse at any other time except at the cessation of the menstrual period." And Jayawickrama: "Leaving aside that time after the ceasing of menstruation, in between the brahmins did not, indeed, indulge in sexual intercourse." Both evidently take *utu* to mean the time of menstruation. But *utu* refers to two distinct periods in a woman's monthly cycle—the menstrual period and the period of fertility. See DOP sv *utunī*:

"menstruating; liable to menstruate; in the (subsequent) fertile period, fertile." The usage in relation to menstruation is seen in such texts as Vin II 271,34–37, where it is said that bhikkhunīs who were *utunī* sat down and lay down on covered furnishings and soiled the lodging with blood. But the application to the period of fertility is seen at MN I 266,4, which says that conception takes place when the parents have intercourse, "and the mother is fertile" (*mātā ca utunī hoti*). AN III 226,15–19 says that a brahmin does not go to his wife (for intercourse) when she is not fertile because his purpose is not to enjoy sensual pleasure but to beget children. Thus, since the intention of the brahmins in this verse is to beget offspring, it seems that here *utu* must mean not the time of menstruation but the fertile period, when the woman is most likely to conceive.

1140. *Uddissa ariyā tiṭṭhanti, esā ariyāna yācanā*. The line is at Ja III 354,18. The accompanying commentary explains that when the noble ones (the buddhas, their disciples, and renunciant bodhisattas) need anything, they do not break out into speech but indicate what they need by standing still in the course of their alms round. Their lay supporters, it is said, then understand what they need.

1141. Milk, curd, whey, butter, and ghee (*khīra, dadhi, takka, navanīta, sappi*). See Vin I 244,34.

1142. *Nānappakārakaṃ sukhaṃ edhittha pāpuṇi, sukhaṃ vā edhittha sukhaṃ vuḍḍhiṃ agamāsi*. This offers two alternative ways of taking *sukhaṃ edhittha*: with *sukhaṃ* either as the object of *edhittha* or as an adverb relative to *edhittha*.

1143. This is the fourth of the five types of brahmins. See note 1134.

1144. Reading with Ce and Ee *jhānappamaññānibbānasukhāni*, as against Be *jhānasāmaññanibbānasukhāni*.

1145. *Abhijjhāyiṃsū ti "aho vat'idaṃ amhākaṃ assā" ti taṇhaṃ vaḍḍhetvā abhipatthayamānā jhāyiṃsu*. An etymological explanation of *abhijjhāyiṃsu* from *jhāyiṃsu*, "contemplated," with the prefix *abhi–* from *abhipatthayamānā*, "desiring."

1146. *Nimittatthe hi etaṃ bhummavacanaṃ*. The locative term is *tattha*.

1147. *Āsaṃsāyaṃ hi anāgatepi vattamānavacanaṃ icchanti saddakovidā*.

1148. *Rathesabho ti mahārathesu khattiyesu akampiyaṭṭhena usabhasadiso. Rathesabha* is literally "chief bull of chariots." My rendering follows PED. According to SED *ratha* can also mean "a warrior, a hero, a champion."

1149. The explanations of the following sacrifices are far from clear to me in all respects. I thank Petra Kieffer-Pülz for help in deciphering this passage. A parallel at It-a 94 has been translated by Masefield (2008, 237–40).

1150. The horse sacrifice (*aśvamedha*) is discussed by Keith 1914, cxxxii–cxxxvii. Here are a few highlights: "As revealed in the later texts the sacrifice is essentially one of princely greatness. The steed for a year roams under guardianship of a hundred princes. . . . If the year were successfully passed the steed was sacrificed with a ritual of extreme elaboration, though even these texts show that there was no real holocaust of victims on a scale indicated by the numbers mentioned, as the wild ones were set free. . . . There are also as central features the lying of the chief queen reluctantly with the horse . . . the laying of importance on the power of the sacrifice to redeem sin."

1151. *Dvīhi pariyaññehi*. SED, sv, *pariyaj*, says on *pariyajña*: "a secondary or accompanying rite (which precedes or follows another in any ritual)."

1152. Discussed by Keith 1914, cxxxvii–cxl. He writes (cxxxviii): "There can be no doubt that the ritual is a mere priestly invention to fill up the apparent gap in the sacrificial system which provided no place for man. On the other hand, the Yajurveda texts recognize only a symbolic slaying of a whole host of human victims who are set free in due course and only animal victims are offered. The ritual does not help to decide whether the form was substituted later for a real sacrifice or was a mere priestly invention, and the decision on this matter can only be given by other considerations."

1153. *Sammam ettha pāsantī ti sammāpāso*. See SED *śamyā*, "a wooden pin or peg . . . a sacrificial vessel," and *paś*[3], "to fasten, bind."

1154. Spk-ṭ I 157, commenting on a parallel passage at Spk I 146,1–3, says: "A *yāga* is to be performed for just a few days without the sacrificial posts; a *satrayāga* is to be performed over many days with the sacrificial posts" (*ayūpo appakadivaso yāgo, sayūpo bahudivasaṃ sādheyyo satrayāgo*). The passage is also at Mp-ṭ II 271.

1155. *Sarassatinadiyā nimuggokāsato pabhuti paṭilomaṃ gacchantena*. In this connection Spk-ṭ I 157 says: "In the past, it is said, a king, while performing the *sammāpāsa* sacrifice, was submerged (swallowed up?) in a fissure made in the earth along the bank of the Sarasvatī River. The blind foolish brahmins who followed in succession had the idea, 'This is one's path leading to heaven,' and so they started the *sammāpāsa* sacrifice there." This passage, too, is at Mp-ṭ II 271.

1156. *Vājamettha pivantī ti vājapeyyo*. PED defines *vāja* as "a strength-giving drink" and *vājapeyya* as "a soma offering." SED explains *vājapeya* as "one of the seven forms of the Soma-sacrifice (offered by kings or Brāhmans aspiring to the highest position)."

1157. Spk-ṭ I 157 (= Mp-ṭ II 271) says: "The objects of offering consist of seventeen units of bullion, units of gold, cattle, buffaloes, and so forth" (*hiraññasuvaṇṇagomahiṃsādi-sattarasakadakkhiṇassa*).

1158. *Natthi ettha aggaḷā ti niraggaḷo*. DOP sv *aggala, aggaḷa,* merely describes this as the name of a brahmanical sacrifice. Perhaps the idea of "unbolted" suggests "without limitation or restriction." *Aggaḷa* also designates the door panel. In either case we would have a house that is open, not closed with a bolt or a door panel.

1159. Pj II 324,22 says that, in place of *viyāpanne,* there is an alternative reading *viyāvatte,* glossed with *viparivattitvā aññathābhūte,* "having been transformed and become different." SED has among the meanings of the Skt *vyāvṛtta,* "turned away from, turned back, gotten rid of, split asunder."

1160. *Puthū vibhinnā khattiyā*. Norman renders "khattiyas were split wide apart." Though he does not have a note, he apparently interprets *puthu* in the sense of Vedic *pṛthak,* "spread out, far and wide." I follow Pj II, which has *bahū* in the gloss, thus identifying *puthu* with Vedic *pṛthu*.

1161. Reading with Be and Ce *patiṃ bhariyā'vamaññatha*. Ee has *pati,* but an accusative is needed.

1162. SN IV 247 mentions five powers of a woman: beauty, wealth, relatives, sons, and virtue.

1163. The point of this, it seems, is that the caṇḍāla brahmin, the lowest of the five types, arises in the world only after the ancient brahmin way of virtue has totally collapsed and unrighteous ways prevail, while in this discourse the Buddha develops his teaching only up to the point where unrighteous ways begin to spread. In the Doṇa Sutta, however, he discusses all the types of brahmins and therefore includes the caṇḍāla brahmin. There the caṇḍāla brahmin is described thus (AN III 229,6 foll.): "He takes a wife by buying and selling as well as a brahmin woman given to him by the pouring of water. He couples with a brahmin woman, a khattiya woman, a vessa woman, a sudda woman, and a caṇḍāla woman, and a woman from a family of hunters, bamboo workers, chariot makers, or flower scavengers. He couples with a pregnant woman, a woman who is nursing, a woman in season and out of season. His brahmin wife serves for sensual pleasure, amusement, and sensual delight, as well as for procreation. He earns his living by all kinds of work [including those unsuitable for a brahmin]."

1164. The title in the root text is Nāvāsutta, but Pj II comments on it under the alternative title Dhammasutta.

1165. See note 1024.

1166. *Upadhāraṇasamatthatāya dhīro puriso*. Pj II is apparently explaining *dhīra* here on the basis of the action noun *upadhāraṇa*, "upholding, bearing in mind."

1167. *Paramasukhumatthapaṭivedhatāya nipuṇo*. There is a word play here between two nuances of *nipuṇa*: in relation to the subject of knowledge, it designates *astuteness* of understanding; in relation to the objective domain of knowledge, it designates that which is *subtle* and hard to discern. Here the subjective sense is relevant. The objective sense is seen in the description of the Dhamma as *gambhīro . . . nipuṇo paṇḍitavedanīyo* (MN I 167,31).

1168. I follow Be here, which reads *anugacchanto*, as against Ce and Ee *anugacchante*, an accusative plural, which would be describing those swept along by the stream. While this makes sense, I understand pāda c of the text, *so vuyhamāno anusotagāmī*, to be descriptive only of the man who stepped into the river.

1169. In the term analysis, Pj II explains that because the pronoun *so*, indicating the man, occurs in pāda c, the syllable *so* in pāda d is an indeclinable, a strengthened interrogative particle *su*. Thus on this account, *kiṃ so* means *kiṃ su* (*sokārena tassa narassa niddiṭṭhattā nipātamatto sokāro, kiṃ sū ti vuttaṃ hoti*).

1170. Pj II glosses *nijjhāpetuṃ* with *pekkhāpetuṃ*.

1171. MN I 45,3–10. The passage (abridged) states: "Cunda, it is impossible that one who is himself sinking in the mud could rescue another who is sinking in the mud; so too it is impossible that one who is himself untamed, undisciplined, unpeaceful, could tame another, discipline him, and lead him to peace." The passage is cited by Nidd I 23, commenting on *na hi aññamokkhā* at **773**b (see p. 1026), and again at Nidd II 84, commenting on **1064**.

1172. *Vedagū ti vedasaṅkhātehi catūhi maggañāṇehi gato*. When the Buddha uses *vedagū* in a discussion with brahmins or with reference to brahmins, to bring out the word play, I render it as "Veda-master." When no such allusion is apparent, as here, I render it "knowledge-master." The commentaries interpret *veda* in the expression as the knowledge in the four world-transcending paths, from stream-entry through arahantship.

1173. *Sotāvadhānūpanisūpapanne ti sotaodahanena ca maggaphalānaṃ upanissayena ca upapanne*. Pj II here distinguishes two prerequisites for realization, taking *sotāvadhāna* and *upanisā* as a *dvanda* compound. I take *sotāvadhāna* to be itself the *upanisā*. Thus there is a discrepancy between my rendering and the explanation in Pj II. Norman also renders the line as if a single prerequisite is being mentioned: "if they have the ability to listen attentively." Jayawickrama, however, follows the commentary: "who are gifted with ready attention and potential means." AN I 198,27–30 seems to support the identity between *sotāvadhāna* and *upanisā*: *Anohitasoto, bhikkhave, anupaniso hoti, ohitasoto saupaniso hoti. So saupaniso samāno abhijānāti ekaṃ dhammaṃ, parijānāti ekaṃ dhammaṃ, pajahati ekaṃ dhammaṃ, sacchikaroti ekaṃ dhammaṃ.* ("One who does not lend an ear does not have a supporting condition; one who lends an ear has a supporting condition. One who has a supporting condition directly knows one thing, fully understands one thing, abandons one thing, and realizes one thing.")

1174. *Tattha kiṃsīlo ti kīdisena vārittasīlena samannāgato.* I follow Be and Ce, which have *vārittasīlena*, as against Ee *cārittasīlena*. The commentaries distinguish between *vārittasīla*, "good behavior as restraint," and *cārittasīla*, "good behavior as positive action."

1175. See AN III 317–19, on the six proper occasions for going to see an esteemed bhikkhu.

1176. *Thaddhabhāvakaraṃ mānaṃ vināsetvā. Thambha*, the word rendered here as "pride," literally means "stiffness." The connection between the two is reflected in the English idiom "stiff with pride."

1177. Reading with Ce and Ee *bhāvanaṃ*, as against Be *kathānaṃ*.

1178. Reading with Ce and Ee *dhammaṃ patvā vattanto*, as against Be *dhammaṃ vattanato*.

1179. *Samathavipassanāpaṭisaṃyuttān'ev'ettha tacchāni, tathārūpehi subhāsitehi nīyetha nīyeyya. Taccha* (Skt *tathya*) is an alternative adjective based on *tathā*.

1180. In brief, that consisting in the use of requisites, in the postures, and in insinuating talk. For a detailed explanation, see pp. 1123–24.

1181. See Vibh 427 (§924.22): "The three blemishes are the blemishes of lust, hatred, and delusion" (*rāgakasāvo, dosakasāvo, mohakasāvo ime tayo kasāvā*). Another three (at §924.23) are blemishes of body, speech, and mind.

1182. See p. 72.

1183. *Etañca sutamayañāṇaṃ viññātasamādhisāraṃ, tesu viññātesu dhammesu yo samādhi cittassāvikkhepo tathattāya paṭipatti, ayam assa sāro.* Pj II apparently takes *sutaṃ* as the subject of the line, qualified by *viññātasamādhisāraṃ* as a *bahubbīhi* compound. I take *viññāta* to be a truncated noun, a parallel subject with *sutaṃ*, both qualified by *samādhisāraṃ*. The point, it seems, is that well-spoken words are fulfilled by being understood, and the words learned and understood are fulfilled by *samādhi*. Norman renders "learning [when] understood is the essence of concentration." This, I believe, inverts the intended meaning. Lines **330**cd seem to support my interpretation.

1184. I read *santi* with Be and Ce, as against Ee *khanti*. Ee itself has *santi* in the citation at p. 336,4. Norman points out (at GD 221) that PDhp 330 has *khānti* for *santi*, and Udāna-v 19.1 has *kṣānti*. In Pāli texts, too, *khanti* and *soracca* are often paired, for instance, at DN III 213,2, AN I 94,25, and Dhs 286 (§§1348–49). Hence, as Norman suggests, "This may be an example of a vocabulary replacement by near-synonyms, but it may be an early example of the *s/kh* alternation." While there is a strong case for *khanti* being the original word, I translate from the texts, whose reading *santi* here is supported by the commentary.

1185. *Santisoracce samādhimhi ca saṇṭhitā hutvā*. Pj II takes *santisoracca* to be a *tappurisa* compound. In translating the comment, I follow its analysis, but in rendering the verse I follow both Norman and Jayawickrama, who treat the compound *santisoraccasamādhi* as a three-term *dvanda*.

1186. *Āsaṃsāyaṃ bhūtavacanaṃ*. The point, it seems, is that while the verb *ajjhagū* is an aorist (a past tense), the statement expresses *the anticipation* of future attainment; that is, those who possess the requisite qualities are expected to reach the core of learning and wisdom. Compare this with the use of the present by way of anticipation, as mentioned at p. 794.

1187. *Santiyā soraccanti santisoraccaṃ, nibbānārammaṇāya maggapaññāy'etaṃ adhivacanaṃ*. Pj II here treats *santisoraccaṃ* as a *tappurisa* rather than as a *dvanda* compound. However, it is clear that in the text *santi, soracca,* and *samādhi* are intended as parallel terms joined in a *dvanda* compound. Just below, I use "gentleness of peace" to maintain consistency with the commentarial explanation.

1188. I translate literally, but I cannot visualize how rooms with a story above them could be described as having peaks (*kūṭāgāragabbha*).

1189. The canonical account is at SN V 269–70.

1190. Both Be and Ce have *karīsabhūmiyaṃ ṭhitaṃ*, which would mean "standing on excrement ground." Ee has *karañjabhūmiyaṃ*, where *karañja* is a kind of tree. Perhaps the correct reading should be *kharibhūmiyaṃ* or *kakkhaḷabhūmiyaṃ*, "solid ground."

1191. See p. 1047.

1192. *Etaṃ nānappakāresu visayesu visaṭavitthiṇṇavisālattā visattikaṃ bhavabhogataṇhaṃ*. Although *visattikā* is actually based on *visatta* (Skt *viṣakta* < *viṣañj*), "attached to, stuck on," the commentaries explain it as though it were based on *visaṭa* (Skt *visṛta* < *visṛ*), "diffused, spread out."

1193. Sp V 1004–10, commenting on Vin I 82.

1194. Here I would read *dappaṃ* with a Burmese manuscript cited in a note in Ee. Ce and Ee have *jappaṃ*, Be *madaṃ*.

1195. It strikes me as odd that Sāriputta would be called "the torchbearer of humankind" (*ukkādhāro manussānaṃ*) when it is the Buddha who is so often said to bring the light of wisdom, as in the stock response after a discourse: "The Blessed One has made the Dhamma clear in many ways, as though he were . . . holding up a lamp in the darkness so those with good eyesight can see forms." I suspect the introductory verses were originally intended as a dialogue between Rāhula and an unspecified inquirer, with the Buddha as the subject. Once, however, the tradition arose that the Buddha spoke the entire sutta, the "the torchbearer of humankind" had to be someone else and thus the title was given to Sāriputta, Rāhula's preceptor.

1196. *Nekkhammādhimuttattā*. See DOP sv *adhimuccati*, where *adhimutta* is defined as "inclined to; applying oneself to; believing in; set on." The past life story of Rāhula is told in detail at Mp I 251–59.

1197. *Paccaye ti gilānappaccaye*. Although *paccaya* normally applies to all four requisites, since three—robe, almsfood, and lodging—are mentioned separately, Pj II identifies *paccaya* here with requisites in time of illness, the fourth requisite.

1198. These austere practices, and those mentioned just below, are all described in Vism 59 foll., Ppn 2.2 foll.

1199. On the three types of contentment, see pp. 762–64.

1200. Pj II 343,5–8 remarks that the imperative verb "be," not included in the text, should be connected with the other lines as well: *Tattha saṃvuto pātimokkhasmin ti ettha bhavassū ti pāṭhaseso. Bhavā ti antimapadena vā sambandho veditabbo, tathā dutiyapade.*

1201. *Sabbaloke anabhiratasaññī hohi*. The allusion here is to the meditation subject called "non-delight in the entire world" (*sabbaloke anabhiratasaññā*), explained at AN V 111,5–7 thus: "As to engagements and clinging, mental standpoints, adherences, and underlying tendencies about the world, a bhikkhu dwells abandoning them without clinging to them" (*bhikkhu ye loke upādānā cetaso adhiṭṭhānābhinivesānusayā, te pajahanto viharati anupādiyanto*).

1202. *Saviññāṇake aviññāṇake vā kāye*. That is, a living body or a corpse. See pp. 638–39, 641–42.

1203. The reference is to MN 147, the Cūḷarāhulovāda Sutta.

1204. Vaṅgīsasuttaṃ is the title in the text of Sn itself.

1205. *Aggāḷave cetiye ti āḷaviyaṃ aggacetiye*. This derives the name of the shrine from *agga*, "chief, foremost," and *āḷava*, based on Āḷavī.

1206. It may seem odd that a male and female wanderer would beget children, but apparently not all wanderers in the Buddha's time observed celibacy. Spk I 285,6–10 says that this female wanderer traveled over Jambudīpa challenging others to debate. She lost a debate with a certain male wanderer. She coupled with him and from their union Vaṅgīsa was born.

1207. *So satasahassakappaṃ pūritapāramī abhinīhārasampanno.* Spk I 285,3–5 says that during the time of the Buddha Padumuttara, he saw a disciple who possessed inspired ingenuity (*paṭibhānasampannaṃ*), presumably in composing poetry. He gave alms and then made the aspiration to achieve a similar status under a future buddha. To achieve this goal he fulfilled the pāramīs for 100,000 eons.

1208. *Tacapañcakaṃ kammaṭṭhānaṃ.* See note 902.

1209. *Upajjhāyo vajjāvajjādiupanijjhāyanena evaṃ laddhavohāro.* Pj II here derives *upajjhāya*, preceptor, from *upanijjhāyati*, "to consider, to contemplate" (or, more likely, from the causative form *upanijjhāpeti*). This is an "edifying etymology." The word is actually derived from *upa + adhi + eti*, and is related to "recitation" or "study." See SED sv *upādhyāya*, "a teacher, preceptor (who subsists by teaching a part of the Vedas or Vedaṅgas)."

1210. *Thirabhāvaṃ patto ti thero.* Technically, the designation *thera*, "elder," is given to one who has completed ten years (marked by rains retreats) as a bhikkhu.

1211. *Tādisañca akhīṇāsavānampi hoti khīṇāsavānampi pubbaparicayena.* This is the basis for what come to be called the *vāsanā*, the habitual formations. See notes 748 and 993.

1212. The participle *parinibbuta* is used to designate both one who has attained nibbāna and one who has passed away as an arahant. Thus when the text says *nigrodhakappo nāma thero . . . aciraparinibbuto hoti*, it means that Nigrodhakappa had recently passed away *as an arahant*. And when it says that Vaṅgīsa wondered, *parinibbuto nu kho me upajjhāyo udāhu no parinibbuto*, it does not mean that Vaṅgīsa was uncertain whether his preceptor had died but whether he died as an arahant.

1213. For *saṇṭhāpana* as "manner of adjustment," see Ja I 304,2–3, *rattavākamayaṃ nivāsanapārupanaṃ saṇṭhāpetvā ajinacammaṃ ekasmiṃ aṃse katvā*: "having adjusted his lower robe and upper robe made of red bark, having put his antelope hide over one shoulder."

1214. *Anomapaññan ti omaṃ vuccati parittaṃ lāmakaṃ, na omapaññaṃ, anomapaññaṃ, mahāpaññan ti attho.*

1215. *Abhinibbutatto ti guttacitto apariḍayhamānacitto vā.* Pj II comments in this way because the participle *nibbuta* often describes one who has attained nibbāna. If Vaṅgīsa had intended the term in this sense, it would follow that he did not have any doubts about his teacher's fate and thus would have had no reason to question the Buddha on this matter. Hence the commentator explains the word in a merely provisional sense.

1216. *Daḷhadhammadassī.* The suffix *–dassī* usually means "a seer of," but Pj II explains it on the basis of the causal verb *dasseti*, to show, and thus I render it "one who shows." Norman renders the expression "seer of what is firm by nature," but Jayawickrama also follows the gloss of Pj II with "you who point out the immutable state." I follow Pj II in taking it as a vocative addressed to the Buddha (*daḷhadhammadassī ti bhagavantaṃ ālapati*), not as a description of Nigrodhakappa.

1217. By glossing *parinibbutaṃ vedaya* with *parinibbutaṃ ñatvā*, Pj II treats *vedaya* as an absolutive. However, in my translation of the verse, I follow both Norman and Jayawickrama, who take *vedaya* to be a causative imperative, "make known." Thus Norman renders "tell [us]" and Jayawickrama "inform us."

1218. On the four "knots" (*ganthā*) see Appendix 3. Formal definitions are at Dhs 252–53 (§1140–44).

1219. That is, as a way of praising the Buddha in order to make him speak about Kappa's fate.

1220. *Mayaṃ hi vipassinaṃ sabbadhamme yathābhūtaṃ passantaṃ bhagavantaṃ jānantā eva upāgamamhā.* Pj II glosses the text's *jānaṃ* with *jānantā eva*, in agreement with the plural finite verb *upāgamamhā* (Be *upāgamumhā*). This suggests that Pj II takes *jānaṃ* to qualify the speaker, Vaṅgīsa, who uses the polite plural when speaking to the Buddha. Both Norman and Jayawickrama, however, take *jānaṃ* to qualify the Buddha. Thus Norman has "We have come to one who sees by insight and knows," and Jayawickrama "you who . . . know." Nevertheless, I follow Pj II here.

1221. This is a reference to the Buddha's "brahmā-like voice, like the karavīka bird" (*brahmassaro hoti karavīkabhāṇī*), one of the thirty-two marks of a great man.

1222. *Dhonan ti dhutasabbapāpaṃ.* DOP says that *dhona* is "probably the past participle of *dhovati*, or possibly of *dhunāti*." By using the past participle *dhuta*, Pj II here relates it to *dhunāti*.

1223. The obscure expression *saṅkheyyakāro* is glossed by *vīmaṃsakāro* and explained by *paññāpubbaṅgamā kiriyā*.

1224. This is said with reference to the Buddha's ability to foretell future events and declare the destiny of those who pass away. For the cases cited here, see Dhp-a III 79,2–5 and III 45,15. Translations of the stories of Santati and Suppabuddha are at BL 2:312–16 and BL 2:291–93.

1225. *Mā mohayī ti mā no akathanena mohayi jānaṃ jānanto kappassa gatiṃ.* It may be puzzling that Vaṅgīsa pleads with the Buddha, the one who brings wisdom and light, not to delude him, when the Buddha's task is just the opposite: to enlighten others. I take this to be poetic irony, used to impart a sense of urgency to his appeal.

1226. *Sutaṃ pavassa*, literally "rain down what is heard." Pj II says that, besides this reading (adopted by Be and Ce of Sn), there is also the reading *sutassa vassa* (adopted by Ee of Sn), glossed "pour down the rain of the aforementioned sound base (*saddāyatana*)."

1227. *Yathā vimutto ti kiṃ anupādisesāya nibbānadhātuyā yathā asekhā, udāhu saupādisesāya yathā sekhā ti pucchati.* The expression *upādisesa* is used in the Nikāyas in two senses. In some passages, such as DN II 314,14–315,7, and AN IV 378–81, it signifies *a residue of grasping*, and thus describes the stage of a non-returner as contrasted with that of an arahant. Elsewhere, most explicitly at It 38, the *saupādisesā nibbānadhātu* is contrasted with the *anupādisesā nibbānadhātu*. Here the nibbāna element with residue remaining is that achieved by arahants while alive; the element of nibbāna without residue is that achieved with their passing away. In this case the "residue" refers to the five aggregates, which persist for the living arahant but utterly cease when the arahant passes away. Since Kappa has already passed away, *saupādiseso* in the verse must refer to the residue of grasping that remains for the non-returner, while *nibbāyi* refers to nibbāna without residue. Thus Vaṅgīsa is in effect asking whether Kappa passed away as a non-returner or as an arahant.

1228. For the three types of craving, see Appendix 3.

1229. On the five aggregates of Dhamma and the five eyes, see Appendix 3.

1230. *Isisattama* is explained here in two ways: the first takes *sattama* as the superlative of *sant*, hence as meaning "the best"; the second, as the ordinal number "seventh," indicating that Gotama is the seventh of the buddhas starting from Vipassī. The former is certainly the correct explanation.

1231. Pj II says that besides the reading *tataṃ māyāvino*, there is also a reading *tathā māyāvino*, "one of such deceit," meaning that Māra approached the Blessed One many times with many tricks.

1232. *Upādātabbaṭṭhena idha upādānan ti vuttaṃ.*

1233. Mahāsamayasuttaṃ. Not to be confused with DN 20, also called Mahāsamayasuttaṃ.

1234. *Nimmitabuddhena*. See pp. 841–42.

1235. See DN III 92,23–30, which explains how the people gathered and appointed a king to preserve order and prevent transgressions.

1236. *Ghoratapo*. Sv-ṭ I 476,19 explains *ghoratapa* as "one who practices austerities that are terrible because of their difficulty" (*ghora-tapo ti dukkaratāya bhīmatapo*).

1237. *Jātisambheda* refers to marriage between those of different castes or clans.

1238. *"Sakyā vata bho kumārā" ti udānaṃ udānesi*. So Ce and Ee. Be has a fuller exclamation. There seems to be a triple word play here between *sakya* meaning "capable," *saka* meaning "one's own" (because they took their own sisters as wives), and *sāka* meaning "teak," the trees in the forest where the city was built.

1239. I follow Be here. Ee has the last two names as Sukkodana and Sukkhodana, Ce as Sukkodana and Asukkodana.

1240. *Pisācillikā*. Sp-ṭ III 259 explains that goblins themselves are called "little goblins"; it cites another view that *pisācillikā* are "the children of goblins."

1241. Attadaṇḍasutta, IV,15.

1242. Respectively, at Ja IV 207–11, Ja III 174–77, and Ja I 208–10.

1243. *Pubbahetuṃ*. Presumably this refers to past merit that enables them to be immediately transformed into monks, complete with bowls and robes, as soon as the Buddha said: "Come, bhikkhu."

1244. Of these kinds of birds, *haṃsa* is defined as both goose and swan; for *koñca*, DOP has "probably a heron or crane"; for *cakkavāka*, DOP says merely "the *Cakra* bird (the ruddy sheldrake?)"; for *karavīka*, DOP has "a sweet-voiced bird, probably the Indian cuckoo"; and for *pokkharasātaka*, PED has "a species of crane, Ardea Siberica." On *hatthisoṇḍaka*, the Pācityādi-yojanā, a Vinaya subcommentary, says (at II 34): "They are birds with the features of an elephant, for they have a trunk (a beak?) similar to the trunk of an elephant."

1245. Ja no. 536, V 412–56. The theme of this Jātaka is the lustfulness and deceitfulness of women.

1246. SN I 26–27 = DN II 253. The verses cited in part just below are from this source.

1247. *Attajjhāsayena nu kho jāneyya, parajjhāsayena, aṭṭhuppattivasena, pucchāvasena*. This alludes to the four sources for the origination of a teaching posited by the commentaries. See p. 71.

1248. *Yaṃnūnāhaṃ nimmitabuddhaṃ māpeyyaṃ*. The sequel will make clear what is meant by a "mind-created buddha."

1249. *Manomayiddhiyā abhisaṅkharitvā nimmitabuddhaṃ māpesi*. On the *manomayiddhi* see DN I 77 (= MN II 17–18): "From this body he creates another body having material form, mind-made, complete in all its parts, not lacking any faculties. Just as, if a man were to draw out a reed from its sheath . . . or a sword from its scabbard . . . or a snake from its slough, so from this body he creates another body having material form, mind-made, complete in all its parts, not lacking any faculties."

1250. This resolution of the complex *bahubbīhi* compound *maṅgala-dosavippahīno* takes *maṅgaladosa* as an internal *dvanda* compound representing two separate items—*maṅgala* and *dosa*—rather than as an internal *tappurisa*, "defects of blessings."

1251. Penetration of the four truths, identified here with *dhamma*, occurs by a breakthrough (*abhisamaya*) that acts upon each noble truth in its own way: the truth of suffering by full understanding; the truth of its origin by abandoning craving; the truth of cessation by realization of nibbāna; and the truth of the path by developing the noble eightfold path. This is already indicated in the Buddha's first discourse at SN V 422–23, and at SN V 436, §29. For a more technical account, see Vism 689–91, Ppn 22.92–97. The four breakthroughs occur with the attainment of each of the four paths but are completed only by the path of arahantship.

1252. See Appendix 3.

1253. See Appendix 3.

1254. Norman renders pāda c "completely released from the fetters." However, *saṃyojaniyehi* does not denote the fetters themselves but the things that arouse the fetters. On the distinction between *saṃyojana* and *saṃyojaniyā dhammā*, see particularly SN IV 89, SN IV 163–65, and SN IV 281–83.

1255. *Upadhīsū ti khandhūpadhīsu*. On the four "acquisitions," see Appendix 3.

1256. *Nibbānapadābhipatthayāno ti anupādisesaṃ khandhanibbānapadaṃ patthayamāno*. Because Pj II takes the bhikkhu being described as an arahant, it interprets the aspiration for nibbāna here as the arahant's wish to reach "the nibbāna element without residue remaining," where the five aggregates cease. According to its apparent sense, however, the verse is not describing an arahant but a trainee (*sekha*), who has "rightly understood the Dhamma" (*sammā viditvā dhammaṃ*) without yet having fully comprehended it.

1257. See Appendix 3.

1258. *Na sandhiyethā ti na upanayhetha na kuppeyya*. Norman (at GD 227) suggests that *sandhiyetha* < *sandhayatha*, meaning "reflect upon" and then "resent."

1259. Ee *kāmabhavo* should probably be corrected to *kammabhavo* as in Be and Ce. See Vism 571,8–21, Ppn 17.250.

1260. Be *patirūpaṃ* here should certainly be corrected to *appatirūpaṃ*, the reading in Ce and Ee. "Improper search" and "proper search" refer to the quest to obtain the requisites, such as robes, food, and lodgings.

1261. *Yathābhūtañāṇena, catusaccadhammaṃ vā maggena viditvā*. The knowledge of things as they really are is taken to represent the "tender stage" of insight knowledge, starting from "discrimination of name-and-form" (Mp III 229,9–10: *nāmarūpaparicchedañāṇaṃ ādiṃ katvā taruṇavipassanā*). Its objective sphere is conditioned things seen as impermanent, suffering, and nonself. At the culmination of insight, the path emerges, penetrating nibbāna and cutting off defilements.

1262. *Sabbadvāravisevanaṃ hitvā*. Presumably, the three doors of action—body, speech, and mind—are intended. For *visevana*, see the use of *visevitāni* in relation to the taming of a horse at MN I 446,6.

1263. *Parinibbuto ti kilesaggivūpasamena sītibhūto*. *Parinibbuto* might also have been rendered "attained to nibbāna," with reference to the "nibbāna element with a residue remaining," but I chose to follow Pj II in rendering the word according to its metaphorical rather than doctrinal usage.

1264. This explanation is intended to reconcile the description of the bhikkhu as *saddho* with the claim that he is an arahant, who as such would no longer be dependent on faith. The statement cited is made by Citta the Householder (at SN IV 298,15), who says he does not depend on faith in the Buddha about the four jhānas because he can attain them himself. It is also made by Sāriputta (at SN V 221,1–4), who says that he does not depend on faith in the Buddha about the five faculties ending in the deathless, for he has known this for himself.

1265. On "the fixed course of rightness" (*sammattaniyāma*) as the world-transcending path, see note 481.

1266. *"Idaṃ ucchijjissati, idaṃ tath'eva bhavissatī" ti*: The two statements are intended to epitomize the annihilationist view (*ucchedadiṭṭhi*) and the eternalist view (*sassatadiṭṭhi*), respectively.

1267. *Dosavisesanamev'etaṃ*. Since *paṭigha* is used as a synonym of *dosa*, its mention here does not indicate a third factor additional to *lobha* and *dosa* but highlights an aspect of *dosa*.

1268. *Saṃsuddhajino ti saṃsuddhena arahattamaggena vijitakileso*. Norman translates *saṃsuddhajino* as a *dvanda* compound, "purified and victorious," though in relation to **84** he explains the suffix *–jino* as from *–jña* with a euphonic vowel (see GD 174–75). Jayawickrama renders the term "the conqueror of utmost purity," which seems to assume a reading *saṃsuddhijino* not attested to in any edition.

1269. *Vivattacchaddo ti vivaṭarāgadosamohachadano*. *Vivattacchaddo* (so Ce and Ee; Be *vivaṭṭacchado*) usually describes a buddha. The precise meaning of the term is obscure. Norman discusses it at length at GD 228–29; he renders it "with deceit removed," which I find unsatisfactory. I follow Nidd II 204 (on **1147**); see pp. 1325–26. *Vivattacchadda* also occurs without comment at

378c (*vivattacchaddāsi*), in the origin story of III,7 (p. 252), and in a verse cited by Pj II in the origin story of IV,9 (p. 1106).

1270. I read with Be and Ce *na hi'ssa sakkā te dhammā yathā ñātā kenaci aññathā kātuṃ*. Ee has *na hi'ssa sakkā te dhammā tathā ñātā kenaci aññātā kātuṃ*, "it is not possible for anyone to make those things unknown after they have been thus known."

1271. Through the four world-transcending paths.

1272. *Aticca suddhipañño ti atīva suddhipañño, atikkamitvā vā suddhipañño*. On *kappa*, see pp. 63–64. In *kappātīto*, *atīto* is the past participle of *acceti*[2], here part of a *bahubbīhi* compound. *Aticca* is an absolutive of the same verb. Pj II construes *aticca* in two ways: first, as conjoined with *suddhipañño* to form an "absolutive syntactical compound" *aticcasuddhipañño* (see Norman 1993, 218–19), which Pj II glosses with *atīva suddhipañño*; and second, as an uncompounded absolutive referring back to *kappātīto*.

1273. This alludes to the traditional temporal analysis of the twelve factors in the formula of dependent origination. See Vism 578, Ppn 17.284–87.

1274. *Parāyaṇan ti gatito paraṃ ayanaṃ gativippamokkhaṃ parinibbānaṃ*.

1275. Apparently Pj II takes *sabbaṃ ñāṇaṃ* and *dhammaṃ* to be the objects of *pakāsesi*. In my rendering of the verse I follow Norman and Jayawickrama in taking *sabbaṃ ñāṇam* to be the object of *avecca* and *dhammaṃ* to be the object of *pakāseti*. Pāda c has *vivattacchaddāsi*. *Vivattacchaddo* occurred in **372**a; see above, note 1269.

1276. *Na te atthi ācariyamuṭṭhi*. See DN II 100,2–4: "I have taught the Dhamma, Ānanda, without distinction of inside and outside. The Tathāgata, Ānanda, does not have a teacher's closed fist in regard to teachings." (*Desito ānanda mayā dhammo anantaraṃ abāhiraṃ karitvā. Natth'ānanda tathāgatassa dhammesu ācariyamuṭṭhi.*)

1277. *Kāmarūpī*. The word occurs at Ap I 31 (v. 376c) with reference to the deity Varuṇa, glossed at Ap-a I 239,24: "He can create whatever sensual pleasure he desires" (*yadicchitakāmanimmānasīlo*). DOP, sv *kāma*, however, provides a meaning that better fits the present context: "having the ability to assume any form at will." See too note 290.

1278. I read with Be and Ce *padumesu sikkhitā*. Ee *padume susikkhitā* should probably be corrected accordingly. The full verse (1028) is at Vv 96.

1279. *Vijitapāpadhammo*. Or possibly, "defeated evil qualities."

1280. Pj II 369,16 accepts the received reading of the verb *ajjhagamā* and comments: *ajjhagamā ti adhiagamā, gato ti vuttaṃ hoti*. Norman (GD 230) adopts von Hinüber's suggestion that we read here "an historically correct perfect form *jagāma*," which "not only corrects the metre, but also gives a better sense, since we need a translation 'went away,' which a form from *adhigam–* would not give."

1281. *So yakkho rañjanaṭṭhena rājā*. The derivation of *rājā* from *rañjana* is playful rather than literal. Vessavaṇa is one of the four divine kings (*cātummahārājano*). He rules over the yakkhas in the north.

1282. The Aṭṭhakavagga and Pārāyanavagga, respectively the fourth and fifth chapters of Sn. The incident described here is related at AN IV 63, though there only the Pārāyana is mentioned.

1283. Reading with Ce *mahākaṇṭhaṃ*, as against Ee *mahakkhandhaṃ*. Be has *mahantaṃ gīvaṃ*, which may have originally been a gloss on *mahākaṇṭhaṃ*.

1284. Reading *vikālo* with Be and Ce, missing in Ee.

1285. Mp-ṭ II 162 explains *muṭṭhihatthapādake* thus: *pādatalato yāva aṭaniyā heṭṭhimanto, tāva muṭṭhiratanappamāṇapādake*; "from the bottom of the feet up to the bottom of the frame, with the feet measuring a *muṭṭhiratana*." The point is that the lay followers observed the uposatha precept of "abstaining from high or luxurious beds."

1286. With a koṭi equal to ten million, this would make the population of Sāvatthī at the time 180,000,000, about twenty times the present population of New York City.

1287. *Ito bahiddhā*. A stock expression referring to ascetics following disciplines other than the Buddha's Dhamma.

1288. During the Buddha's time, the word *tittha* (Skt *tīrtha*), literally a ford for crossing a river, was used to designate a system of spiritual practice, probably in the sense that it provides the means for "crossing the river" of saṃsāra. The creator of a system was called a *titthaṅkara*, literally "a ford-maker," and those who adopt a system were known as *titthiya*, "those using the ford," more freely rendered here as "sectarians." Often in the Nikāyas we encounter the expression *aññatitthiyā paribbājakā*, "wanderers belonging to other sects."

1289. The six teachers contemporary with the Buddha—Pūraṇa Kassapa and the other five—are often mentioned in the Nikāyas, most notably at DN I 52–59, where their individual doctrines are described. See too pp. 241 and pp. 914–15. MN I 523,4, refers to three leaders of the Ājīvikas (or Ājīvakas), namely, Nanda Vaccha, Kisa Saṅkicca, and Makkhalī Gosāla; the last is also included among the six teachers. Pj II apparently takes Nanda, Vaccha, and Saṅkicca as three teachers, dividing Nanda Vaccha into two and omitting Makkhalī

Gosāla. For a fuller discussion of this problem, with references, see DPPN sv Nanda 13.

1290. Nātaputta, known to his followers as Mahāvīra or the Jina, was the most prominent Jain teacher of antiquity, contemporary with the Buddha. His followers were called Nigaṇṭhas. The Ājīvikas (or Ājivakas) were the followers of Makkhali Gosāla.

1291. Be is missing *diṭṭhiṃ*.

1292. My understanding of this verse differs from that of the commentary and thus there is a dissonance between my translation of the text and Pj II. Pj II regards *vādasīlā* and *vuddhā* as belonging together. However, since they occur in different pādas, it seems more likely that their referents are different, so that the brahmins given to debate are not necessarily identical with the elder brahmins. The commentary interprets *api brāhmaṇā santi keci* to refer to certain middle-aged and young brahmins, while I translate on the supposition that *vuddhā* in pāda b qualifies *brāhmaṇā* in pāda b.

1293. Pj II bases its gloss on the reading *taṃ no vada*, which I follow, but it notes that there is a variant reading, *tvaṃ no vada*. Ee reads *tvaṃ no vada*, while Be and Ce adopt the primary reading.

1294. The editions of Pj II follow their respective editions of the text here, Ce and Ee reading *dharatha*, and Be *caratha*.

1295. The reference is to Pācittiya 37, which states: "If a bhikkhu should consume hard or soft food at the wrong time, he commits a Pācittiya offense" (*yo pana bhikkhu vikāle khādanīyaṃ vā bhojanīyaṃ vā khādeyya vā bhuñjeyya vā, pācittiya*). The "wrong time" is defined as the time following midday until the arrival of the next dawn (*vikālo nāma majjhanhike vītivatte yāva aruṇuggamanā*). See Vin IV 84–85.

1296. I here follow Be *suṭṭhu gahitacitto*, as against Ce and Ee *suṭṭhugatacitto*.

1297. I read with Be *atappakaṭṭhena paṇīto dhammo* as against Ce and Ee *anappakaṭṭhena paṇīto dhammo*. The ten subjects of talk (*dasakathāvatthu*) are fewness of desires, contentment, solitude, disentanglement, arousing energy, good behavior, concentration, wisdom, liberation, and the knowledge and vision of liberation. See MN III 113,21–26, AN III 117,8–12, AN IV 352,8–12, etc.

1298. *Vādaṃ paṭiseniyanti virujjhanti, yujjhitukāmā hutvā senāya paṭimukhaṃ gacchantā viya honti*. Pj II is evidently deriving the verb *paṭiseniyanti* from the noun *senā*, "army," with the prefix adopted from *paṭimukhaṃ*, "opposition." Norman calls attention to the contrast between *usseneti* and *paṭisseneti* at AN II

214–15. In NDB 589 I translated these, respectively, as "pick up" and "push away." According to the sutta, a monk "does not pick up" (*na usseneti*) when he does not adopt any view of a personal entity. He "does not push away" (*na paṭisseneti*) when he does not retaliate against those who abuse him. Mp III 209,4–5 glosses "*He does not push away*: He does not become hostile and reject through quarrels and arguments" (*na paṭissenetī ti paṭiviruddho hutvā kalahabhaṇḍanavasena na ukkhipati*). DOP suggests that *usseneti* is a denominative from *ud* + *seṇi* (= Skt *śreṇi*).

1299. Pj II refers here to the formulas for reflecting on the four requisites (robe, almsfood, lodging, and medicinal requisites) (see MN I 10, AN III 388). *Pabbāsavādisu* in Ee should be corrected to *Sabbāsavādīsu*.

1300. *Varapaññassa tathāgatassa sāvako sekho vā puthujjano vā, nippariyāyena vā arahā*. The use of *nippariyāyena* here implies that "in the direct sense" only the arahant is a true disciple of the Buddha. I follow Pj II in taking *varapañña* in the compound to be an epithet of the Buddha rather than an adjective describing the disciple.

1301. In the Pāli text, the couplet about not killing living beings is stated first, followed by the couplet about putting down the rod. I have inverted the two couplets, as Pj II itself does in construing the verse. The three aspects of purified abstinence from the destruction of life (*tikoṭiparisuddhā pāṇātipātāveramaṇi*) are not killing with one's own hand, not asking others to kill, and not approving of killing by others.

1302. These refer to the line numbers of the Pāli text; in the translation they are the first and second lines. See respectively p. 419 and p. 577.

1303. This is said because, if the second couplet is construed as grammatically distinct, it would require a finite verb, which Pj II supplies by suggesting the addition of *vatteyya*.

1304. *Abrahmacariyaṃ*. On the meanings of *brahmacariya*, "spiritual life" or "pure conduct," see p. 396. Many laypersons observe the precept of complete abstinence on the uposatha days, but here it is recommended as a permanent observance.

1305. I here translate the commentary according to the order of the original, though in the translation of the text I had to invert the couplets to accord with normal diction.

1306. *Pāṭihāriyapakkha*. Apparently even as far back as the time of the commentators there were different interpretations of this expression. Other commentaries offer still other interpretations than those offered here. See CDB 480, note 573, and NDB 1642, note 387. Norman translates as "a special day of the fortnight," while Jayawickrama avoids the ambivalence by leaving the expression untranslated.

1307. Āsāḷha normally corresponds to June–July and Kattika to October–November. The rains retreat usually falls between July and October.

1308. I follow Ce *na puññena hāyitabbaṃ*, which seems preferable to Ee *na puññena bhāsitabbaṃ*. Be has *sabbaṃ vā pana puññakāmīnaṃ bhāsitabbaṃ*, "or all may be stated for those desiring merit."

1309. At Vin I 246,15–17 these are specified as mango juice, rose-apple juice, plantain juice, banana juice, honey juice, grape juice, lotus-root juice, and *phārusaka* (a berry?) juice.

1310. *Sattavaṇijjā, satthavaṇijjā, visavaṇijjā, maṃsavaṇijjā, surāvaṇijjā.* These five are specifically prohibited for the lay follower at AN 5:177, III 208.

1311. Jayawickrama (at PBR 1978, 5–6) compares the Pāli version and the Skt parallel of Mvu II 198–200.

1312. See pp. 1174–77.

1313. On *āyatana* as "a place for the production of" (*sañjātiṭṭhāna*), see Sv I 124,30–125,8: *kambojo assānaṃ āyatanaṃ, gunnaṃ dakkhiṇāpatho ti sañjātiyaṃ pavattati, sañjātiṭṭhāne ti attho.*

1314. See note 122.

1315. He had been a friend of the future Buddha during the time of the Buddha Kassapa. He became a non-returner and was reborn in the brahma world. See MN 81 and SN 1:50.

1316. The three kinds of bodily misconduct are taking life, taking what is not given, and sexual activity. The four kinds of verbal misconduct are false speech, divisive speech, harsh speech, and idle chatter. Wrong livelihood for a renunciant comprises improper ways of obtaining the requisites, such as scheming, persuasion, flattery, posturing, etc.

1317. The three factors of bodily good conduct, four of verbal good conduct, and right livelihood.

1318. In the account at Mvu II 198, the Bodhisatta went to Rājagaha *after* leaving Āḷāra Kālāma rather than directly from Kapilavatthu.

1319. This is Mount Vulture Peak.

1320. But see CDB 473, note 556.

1321. There is no prose record of this encounter in the Nikāyas, but at Vin I 37,17–30 Bimbisāra speaks of the five aspirations he formed in his youth, which had just come to fulfillment with the Buddha's arrival in his realm and his own realization of the Dhamma. This suggests that an earlier encounter took place between Bimbisāra and the Buddha. The meeting is often referred to in later sources, such as Ja I 66.

1322. Pj II does not comment on **412**. When there are occasional gaps in my numbering of the commentary sections, this is either because the commentary does not comment on the verse (since all the terms are already clear) or because it merely offers routine word glosses that I thought need not be translated.
1323. *Monatthāya paṭipannattā appattamunibhāvopi muni icceva vutto. Lokiyā hi amonasampattampi pabbajitaṃ munī ti bhaṇanti.*
1324. Though this line is not shown as a direct quotation, it seems to be the conclusion reached by the king's ministers.
1325. The allusion is to AN III 44,5–10: "Based on the Himalayas, great sāl trees grow in five ways: (1) in branches, leaves, and foliage; (2) in bark; (3) in shoots; (4) in softwood; and (5) in heartwood."
1326. *Kosalesu niketino*. Norman renders "[belonging to] one who is indigenous among the Kosalans." Jayawickrama has "domiciled in the land of the Kosalans." DOP, sv *niketi(n)*: "having a home; (one) who has a long connection with." The word probably alludes to the status of the Sakyans as a vassal state of Kosala, but in a way that bolsters their relationship to Kosala. Mvu II 199,15 has *dhanavīryena sampanno kośaleṣu nivāsito* and Saṅghabhedavastu 95,22 reads *ākīrṇā dhanadhānyena kausalā iti viśrutāḥ*. The Chinese parallel lacks such a line but instead reads: 有國大王治今在雪山北，父姓名為日生處名釋迦, "There is a country ruled by a great king, in the north, by the Himalayas. My father's family name is Ādicca (the Sun), my native land is the Śākyans." In this version not only is there is no reference to Kosala but the Buddha's father is elevated to the status of a "great king" (大王), perhaps under the influence of the evolving Buddha legend. In the Pāli, *rāja* is a vocative addressed to Bimbisāra.
1327. On the Buddha as Ādiccabandhu, Kinsman of the Sun, see **540**d, **915**a, and **1128**b.
1328. Pj II glosses *daṭṭhu* with *disvā*, indicating it is an absolutive.
1329. *Taṃ paramatthanekkhammaṃ nibbānāmataṃ sabbadhammānaṃ aggaṭṭhena padhānaṃ patthento padhānatthāya gamissāmi*. The explanation here plays upon two meanings of *padhāna*: (1) as "striving," synonymous with energy (*viriya*) and effort (*vāyāma*), the usual meaning in Buddhist discourse; and (2) as chief, the meaning that prevails in general Indian usage. Hence Pj II says that the Bodhisatta wishes to go for the purpose of *padhāna* (in the sense of striving) in order to attain *padhāna*, the foremost of all things, namely, nibbāna.
1330. *Cattāri pubbanimittāni disvā*. The old man, a sick man, a corpse, and a renunciant.
1331. At Mvu II 199–200, the verses include King Bimbisāra's request

to the Bodhisatta to return to him after attaining enlightenment, followed by the Buddha's promise to do so.

1332. Despite the connection established by the word "striving," since this discourse depicts the Buddha when he is immersed in his ascetic practices, the events related could not have followed immediately after those depicted in the previous sutta, when he was just about to embark on his practice of striving.

1333. *Nadiṃ nerañjaraṃ patī ti lakkhaṇaṃ niddisati. Lakkhaṇaṃ hi padhānapahitattāya nerañjarā nadī. Ten'eva cettha upayogavacanaṃ.* For *lakkhaṇa* in this sense, see SED sv *lakṣaṇa*, where among the meanings given is "aim, goal." On *pati* as used here, see SED, sv *prati*: "as a preposition, with usually preceding accusative, in the sense of toward, against, to, upon, in the direction of." Thus the point Pj II is making is that the accusative *nadiṃ nerañjaraṃ* is used with *pati* because the Nerañjarā River was his destination for the purpose of striving.

1334. *Viparakkammā ti atīva parakkamitvā. Jhāyantan ti appāṇakajjhānam anuyuñjantaṃ.* See MN I 243–44, where the Buddha describes how, after he went forth, he meditated by stopping the in-breaths and out-breaths through his mouth, nose, and ears.

1335. Reading here with Ce and Ee *sādhento* and below *sādhetvā*, as against Be *sāvento* and *sāvetvā*.

1336. *Bhagavatā eva pana paraṃ viya attānaṃ niddisantena sabbamettha evaṃjātikaṃ vuttan ti ayam amhākaṃ khanti.* This is one of the few places in Pj II where the author explicitly asserts his own opinion.

1337. Reading with Ce and Ee *muttajjhāsayaṃ*.

1338. Here Pj II alludes to Dhp 112cd, 111d, and 113d, respectively.

1339. Since the body of an adult male weighing 70 kg contains about five liters of blood, a *nāḷi* must be approximately 1.25 liters.

1340. Three of Māra's armies in **436** become Māra's three daughters in SN 4:25 (I 124–27). Kāma (sensual desire) appears under the name Ragā (Lust), whereas Aratī (Discontent) and Taṇhā (Craving) maintain the same names. They are referred to at **835**a.

1341. Following Be, I omit *āvahati*, which seems superfluous here.

1342. The couplet, *saṅgāme me mataṃ seyyo, yañce jīve parājito*, is also at Th 194cd.

1343. On *subbatā* as "disciplined," from *su* + *vata*, see note 601.

1344. *Siyā nu kho añño maggo bodhāyā ti ādīni.* The allusion here is to MN I 246,30 where the Bodhisatta abandons his practice of self-mortification and seeks another path to enlightenment.

1345. Ja I 71,31–33 says that Māra's army extended twelve yojanas in front, so too to the right and left, and behind to the boundary of the world sphere; upward it reached to a height of nine yojanas. It is hard to imagine how the elephant could be so much larger than the entire army, but Ja I 72,2 confirms this measurement.

1346. I follow Be *so ca kho tejen'eva, na kāyena*. Ce and Ee have *so ca kho ten'eva kāyena*, "and that is just by this body." However, it seems that the battle will be one of spiritual force, not a physical battle.

1347. Reading *yakkhaṃ* with Ce and Ee. Be has *pakkhaṃ*, which might be understood as "faction."

1348. The incarnation in which the future Buddha Gotama fulfilled the perfection of giving. His story is told in Jātaka no. 547.

1349. Dhp 153–54. The commentaries consider these verses to be the first utterance of the Buddha after his enlightenment. See Dhp-a III 127–28.

1350. The prose introduction of SN 4:24 (I 122–24) states that Māra had trailed the Buddha for seven years without success in his efforts to tempt him. The dialogue in verse represents Māra's final, and unsuccessful, attempt to lead the Buddha astray. According to Spk I 185,7–8, the seven years were six years prior to the enlightenment and one year afterward (*satta vassānī ti pure bodhiyā chabbassāni, bodhito pacchā ekaṃ vassaṃ*). Spk quotes **446** in commenting on *satta vassāni*. SN 4:24 ends with the verses about the crow that mistook a rock for a piece of meat. Jayawickrama comments (PBR 1978, 9): "It is quite probable that Sn 446 is a versification of a passage corresponding to that at SN I 122 while the next two stanzas were perhaps taken from the same source as SN." These stanzas are not included in the Lalitavistara parallel, while the parallel at Mvu II 240 moves from the counterpart of **445** to the counterpart of **449**.

1351. Reading with Ce and Ee *aṅgulehi*. Be has *kusalehi*, "by those who are skilled."

1352. The verse is also at SN I 122, in connection with the passing away of the monk Godhika, where it seems misplaced. Instead of the line about the lute, *vīṇā kacchā abhassatha*, Mvu 240,16 reads: *vināsaṃ gacchi ucchriti*, "His pride went to destruction." Jayawickrama (PBR 1978, 12) asserts that this "probably expresses the original idea that may have existed prior to the importation of the *vīṇā* from the developed legend, which speaks of his daughters as playing instrumental music as a part of their wiles."

1353. *Attajjhāsayato c'assa uppatti*. See p. 71 on the four origins of a discourse.

1354. *Lokagaru*: alternatively, "the world teacher," *garu* being the Pāli counterpart of Skt *guru*.

1355. *Tena nesaṃ hīnādhikajanasevitaṃ vuttiṃ pakāsento uddhata-dīnabhāvaniggahaṃ karoti.* Ps I 13–14 and Spk-ṭ II 3 explain this expression in identical terms: "*Their practice is resorted to by both inferior and superior people*: There are bhikkhus who are elated and proud, vain about their social class, and those who consider walking for alms to be the lowest way of life because in lay life they did not have to depend on others. By addressing both of them as 'bhikkhus' he restrains their elation by showing that this is the practice resorted to by inferior people, the destitute who have reached the lowest state of misery and subsist by walking for alms among other families. Again, he prevents dejection by showing that this practice is resorted to by superior people, by the buddhas and others who have gone forth from superior wealthy families such as khattiyas to purify their livelihood."

1356. Reading *ce* with Be and Ce as against Ee *ve*.

1357. These passages, as understood by the commentaries, refer not to the actual utterance but to the psychological and volitional factors responsible for speech.

1358. Reading with Be and Ce *–niddesavacanaṃ* as against Ee *–nidassanavacanaṃ*.

1359. Neither Ce nor Ee include the disjunction *vā* found in Be.

1360. *Pāpassa akaraṇaṃ, kusalassa upasampadaṃ.* An allusion to Dhp 183ab.

1361. On *mantāvacana*, Spk-ṭ I 251 says: "Thoughtful speech is speech uttered with reflection. For a wise person of restrained speech does not speak words that lead to harm." (*Mantāvacanan ti mantāya pavattetabbavacanaṃ. Paññavā avikiṇṇavāco hi na ca anatthāvahaṃ vācaṃ bhāsati.*)

1362. *Liṅgavacanavibhattikālakārakādīhi sampattīhi ca samannāgataṃ vācaṃ.* The compound is resolved and explained at Spk-ṭ I 251: *Liṅgaṃ itthiliṅgādi vacanaṃ ekavacanādi. Paṭhamādi vibhatti atītādi kālaṃ.*

1363. The meaning of this passage is stated more clearly below at p. 1001. For *sussavana* in the sense of "good information," something good to hear, see Ja I 61,7, where the future Buddha reflects on the verse spoken to him by Kisā Gotamī: *Ayaṃ me sussavanaṃ sāvesi, ahaṃ hi nibbānaṃ gavesanto carāmi, ajj'eva mayā gharāvāsaṃ chaḍḍetvā nikkhamma pabbajitvā nibbānaṃ gavesituṃ vaṭṭati.*

1364. The Pāli word *uttama* normally means "best," but since it precedes "second, third, fourth," here it evidently means "first (in sequence)."

1365. On Vaṅgīsa, see II,12.

1366. *Tattha paṭibhāti man ti mama bhāgo pakāsati. Paṭibhātu tan ti tava bhāgo pakāsatu.* This is a very literal translation of Pj II's explanation. The verb *paṭibhāti* and noun *paṭibhāna* are almost impossible to render satisfactorily into English. The unprefixed verb *bhāti*, "to shine," is here glossed with *pakāsati*. The prefix *paṭi–* can convey a reflexive sense. *Paṭibhāti* has an unspecified subject, and the person to whom it occurs is the object in the accusative case. *Paṭibhāti* thus suggests that a flash of illumination arises that enables a person (set in the accusative case, as if an object of the action) to grasp the significance of an idea or event, thereby making it "one's share" (*bhāga*). Perhaps an English parallel would be: "It dawns on me" or, more colloquially, "I get it." The Buddha's reply, *paṭibhātu taṃ vaṅgīsa*, would mean literally "Then let it shine on you, let it dawn on you." This is to be understood as an invitation to speak, hence I render it: "Then express your inspiration, Vaṅgīsa."

1367. *Amata* (Skt *amṛta*) means both "not-dead" (= deathless) and "ambrosia," the nectar of the gods. See PED sv *amata* and SED *amṛta*. The latter also gives "anything sweet, a sweetmeat."

1368. The explanation here presupposes that the three nouns—*sacce, atthe*, and *dhamme*—are all locatives and *āhu* an aorist of *honti* (= *ahū*). But *āhu* should probably be taken instead as a perfect meaning "[they] said." Based on the work of Lüders, Norman suggests (1969, note to 1229) that *atthe* and *dhamme* were originally nominatives in an Eastern dialect that had the nominative singular in *–e*. When transposed into Pāli they were mistaken for locatives. I follow Norman in my rendering of the line, and thus there is dissonance between my translation and the explanation of Pj II.

1369. Pj II takes *khemaṃ* to be an adjective qualifying *vācaṃ* and thus tries to explain why the Buddha's speech is secure. However, I take *khemaṃ* to be an epithet for nibbāna, set off in the accusative for metrical reasons.

1370. Designated by Pj II as the Pūraḷāsasuttaṃ but by the text as the Sundarikabhāradvājasuttaṃ. A partly parallel sutta, but with very different verses, is SN 7:9 (I 167–70), at the end of which Sundarikabhāradvāja becomes a monk and attains arahantship.

1371. This is the third Bhāradvāja to appear in Sn. The previous two were Kasibhāradvāja (in I,4) and Aggikabhāradvāja (in I,7). Apparently the Bhāradvājas were a clan of high-ranking brahmins.

1372. This is a free rendering of *nārāyanasaṅkhātabalopi* (so Be; Ee has *nārāyanasaṅghātabalopi*). Vibh-a 397,31–35 is helpful here: "One Tathāgata has the strength of ten six-tusked elephants. Just this is also called the strength of Nārāyana (*nārāyanasaṅkhātabalan ti pi idameva vuccati*). That is equal to the strength of 1,000 kotīs of ordinary elephants and 10,000 koṭīs of men. This is the Tathāgata's bodily strength" (*idaṃ tāva tathāgatassa kāyabalaṃ*).

1373. Reading with Ce and Ee *sabbaso kāyapaṭijagganaṃ na karonti eva*. Be omits *na*.

1374. *Parittamattampi sikhaṃ adisvā*. This refers to the tuft of hair that brahmins retained.

1375. *Na brāhmaṇo no'mhi*. Pj II explains *na* as a negation and *no* as serving for emphasis. See DOP *no*[5].

1376. *Jātivādasamudācāraṃ*. Since a person's social class in ancient India was determined by birth, the word *jāti* meaning "birth" comes by extension to mean caste or social class.

1377. On the three kinds of full understanding, see pp. 1034–35.

1378. *Mantā jānitvā ñāṇānuparivattīhi kāyakammādīhi carati*. Pj II explains that *manta* of the text represents *mantā*, with the final vowel shortened because of the meter (*chandavasena rassaṃ katvā*). Although it may seem that Pj II glosses *mantā* with *jānitvā* and thus takes it as an absolutive, just below it equates *mantā* with *paññā*, which suggests it actually takes *mantā* as a truncated instrumental. This suggestion is reinforced by the explanation *tāya c'esa carati* ("and he lives by means of that"). See too note 744.

1379. See note 131.

1380. Ee prints the brahmin's question as prose, but the Buddha's reply consists only of a single couplet. One would expect the verse of reply, in the Pāli, to consist of four lines. Quite likely textual corruption has set in here. The question recurs at **1043**, with a reply at **1044**, commented on by Nidd II 46–48 at pp. 1246–47. It seems to fit better there, where the Buddha directly answers it.

1381. *Yaññamakappayiṃsūti ma-kāro padasandhikaro*. Pj II explains *–m–* here as a liaison consonant, and thus takes *yañña* as an accusative plural shortened from *yaññe*. Norman (at GD 245) conjectures that *yaññam* may be the accusative plural from *–aṃ*, shortened to *–am* before a vowel.

1382. According to Pj II, *puthū* in pāda b can be taken in apposition either to *yaññaṃ* or the people who perform the sacrifice. Nidd II 47, commenting on **1044**, allows *puthū* to be taken with the recipients as well.

1383. *Antagū*, literally "one gone to the end, one who has reached the end."

1384. *Catūhi ca maggañāṇavedehi kilese vijjhitvā gatattā vedagū*. Norman suggests that *vedagū* may actually be from *vedaka*, a follower of the Vedas. However, SED lists *vedapāraga* as "one who has gone to the further end of the Veda," and *vedāntaga* as "one who has gone to the end of the Veda or who has complete knowledge of the Veda." Thus it does not seem unreasonable to accept *vedagū* as it stands.

1385. All editions here read *paramatthayogagambhīraṃ*, but it would seem that *paramatthayaññagambhīraṃ* makes better sense. Nothing shows that at this point the Buddha has taught him the supreme yoga; the conversation is still about a sacrifice productive of merit.

1386. Although Ee represents the first words of this line of verse *tasmā ti ha*, Pj II rephrases this with *tasmā pana iha*, which suggests that *tasmātiha* should be understood as *tasmā-t-iha*, with *t* as a liaison consonant.

1387. *Idāni ito pubbaṃ atthen'atthikapadaṃ parapadena sambandhitabbaṃ*. That is, *atthena atthiko* should be taken as the subject of the verb *abhivinde* in pāda d.

1388. The reading on which Pj II first comments is *yattha hutaṃ*; the alternative reading is *yathā hutaṃ*.

1389. The reference is to MN 93 (II 152–53).

1390. Again, the text here ascribes a new meaning to an old concept, which Pj II makes explicit by identifying the Vedas with the knowledge of the four paths, or in this case, as the "end of the Vedas" (*vedanta*), the knowledge of the path of arahantship.

1391. Rāhu is an asura or titanic spirit said to periodically take possession of the moon and sun.

1392. Following the commentarial interpretation, the line *samo samehi visamehi dūre* would be translated: "Equal to equals, far from unequals." I render the lemma here to accord with the commentarial interpretation, but I translate the text according to my understanding of the intended meaning. The line, as I see it, involves a word play. *Sama* means both "equal" and "righteous, virtuous," while *visama* means both "different, unequal" and "unrighteous, unvirtuous." The verse can thus be read as asserting that the Buddha is an equal of the righteous but far from the unrighteous. See SN I 7,25: *caranti visame samaṃ*; SN I 48,26: *ariyānaṃ samo maggo, ariyā hi visame samā*; and AN III 285,16–17: *ariyasāvako visamagatāya pajāya samappatto viharati*.

1393. The discussion of this last point is not entirely clear to me. The Pāli (following Ce and Ee) reads *vyāmāsītianantappabhāhi yuttā honti*. *Asīti* (= eighty) is clearly a distinct type of aura, but what "eighty" qualifies is left unstated, and I therefore assume it refers to the number of fathoms (one *vyāma* being the median height of a man). The sequel seems to be saying that while the aura is fixed in extent for those buddhas who have an aura a fathom or eighty fathoms wide, those who have a boundless aura can regulate its extension.

1394. *Aṭṭhamakassa paññā adhikā*. "The eighth" refers to one who has attained the path of stream-entry, the lowest of the eight noble persons.
1395. Reading with Be and Ce *taṇhādiṭṭhinivesanaṃ*. Ee has *taṇhādiṭṭhisevanaṃ*, "the resort of craving and views."
1396. *Dhammaṃ c'aññāsī ti sabbañca ñeyyadhammaṃ aññāsi*. Pj II is apparently taking *dhammaṃ* as an accusative plural in *–aṃ*, representing Skt *dhammān*.
1397. See pp. 1034–35.
1398. I follow Pj II here, which glosses *paravediyan ti parehi ñāpetabbaṃ*. This evidently takes *vediya* in a causal sense. Jayawickrama also renders it in this sense ("propounded by others"), though Norman takes it as passive ("which can be known by others").
1399. *Upādānakhaye vimutto ti nibbāne nibbānārammaṇato vimutto, nibbānārammaṇavimuttilābhī ti attho*. The reference is to the commentarial tenet that the path and fruit take nibbāna as their object. Though I translate the locative as such, it seems that the locative is being used here with an instrumental sense.
1400. *Accantakhayassa samucchedappahānass'etaṃ adhivacanaṃ*. On "abandoning by eradication," see p. 363. On the two nibbāna elements, see note 747.
1401. See AN IV 195; Dhp 241–43.
1402. On readings of the text, see note 135. Both Ce and Ee read the lemma as *yo attanā attānaṃ nānupassati*. Be has, in both text and lemma, *yo attano attānaṃ nānupassati*, "who does not see a self of himself." *Attan* is used in Pāli in both ontological and reflexive senses.
1403. The gloss in Pj II 410,25–27—*ñāṇasampayuttena cittena vipassanto attano khandhesu aññaṃ attānaṃ nāma na passati, khandhamattameva passati*—can be understood to support either reading mentioned in the preceding note. The gloss may be trying to accommodate *both* readings. Since the commentaries occasionally gloss *attan* in the texts with *citta*, the instrumental expression *ñāṇasampayuttena cittena* may be an attempt to explicate *attanā* with an expression that better accords with the tenet of non-self. On the other hand, *attano khandhesu* may be attempting to do the same with a genitive reading *attano* in the text, taken as a reflexive possessive pronoun.
1404. *Mohantarā ti mohakāraṇā mohapaccayā, sabbakilesānametaṃ adhivacanaṃ*. The explanation here is hard to follow. See DOP sv *dosa*[2], where *dosantara* is explained as "inwardly hostile, motivated by ill-will." Assuming *mohantara* to be parallel to this, it should mean "inwardly deluded, having delusion within."
1405. The text has *ettāvatā yakkhassa suddhi*, and Pj II glosses:

yakkhassā ti purisassa. Normally, *yakkha* denotes a demonic being, sometimes capable of spiritual understanding, as in I,9, I,10, and II,5. This use of *yakkha* might point back to a more archaic meaning of the word. Norman here leaves *yakkha* untranslated. Jayawickrama, following the commentary, renders it "of a being."

1406. The text has *Brahmā hi sakkhi*. Norman translates "For Brahmā is [my] witness." This seems to miss the point, which, as I understand it, is: "You—the Buddha—are Brahmā himself appearing directly before me" (*paccakkhameva hi tvaṃ brahmā*). Jayawickrama catches the intention with his rendering: "You, indeed, are Brahmā manifest." See **508** and its commentary below.

1407. In the text I translate *sīmantānaṃ vinetāraṃ* as "one who has removed the boundaries," but here I add "the ends of" to accommodate Pj II's explanation; see next note.

1408. *Sīmā ti mariyādā sādhujanavutti, tassā antā pariyosānā aparabhāgā ti katvā sīmantā vuccanti kilesā, tesaṃ vinetāran ti attho. Sīmantā ti buddhaveneyyā sekkhā ca puthujjanā ca, tesaṃ vinetāran ti pi eke.* The word *sīmanta* does not occur elsewhere in the canon or commentaries. Norman renders it "boundaries and limits," Jayawickrama has "(defilements) that violate propriety." I think it more likely that *sīmanta* has a unitary sense, simply a boundary. See SED sv *sīman*, where *sīmanta* is defined as "a boundary, limit," and *sīmānta* as "a border, boundary." *Vinetā* can mean either "one who removes" or "a guide, leader." The dual meaning allows for the two explanations.

1409. *Moneyyasampannan ti paññāsampannaṃ, kāyamoneyyādisampannaṃ vā*. On the three kinds of sagacity, bodily and so forth, see pp. 1036–37.

1410. For other derivations of the name Rājagaha, see Ps-ṭ II 102.

1411. Vmv I 142: "*Vasantavana*: woods for playing, for in the springtime it is mostly used for play; hence it is called 'springtime woods'" (*vasantavanan ti kīḷāvanaṃ, vasantakāle kīḷāya yebhuyyattā pana vasantavanan ti vuttaṃ*).

1412. *Vadaññū ti yācakānaṃ vacanaṃ jānāmi*. It appears that Pj II takes *vadaññū* to be a compound of *vada* + *jña*. But as Norman points out (GD 251–52), the word is actually from Skt *vadānya*, which SED sv *vad* defines as "bountiful, liberal, munificent." SED also gives "speaking kindly" as a meaning of *vadānya*, but that meaning is not relevant here.

1413. *Yācayogo ti yācituṃ yutto*. Norman states (GD 252): "Because of the idea of giving to *yācanakas* [or *yācakas*, supplicants], we get a mixture of *yāc-* and *yāj-*." Some texts read *yājayogo* rather than *yācayogo*. While for the brahmins, *yājayoga* meant "devotion to sacrifice (in the literal sense)," for the Buddhists it meant "devotion to charity."

1414. On the four ways of "purifying" gifts: through the donor, through the recipient, through neither, and through both, see MN III 256–57, AN II 80–81.

1415. *Vadaññun ti vacanaviduṃ, sabbākārena sattānaṃ vuttavacanādhippāyaññun ti vuttaṃ hoti.* Again, *vadaññū* is being derived from *vada* + *jñā*. See note 1412.

1416. Reading with Ce and Ee *na nipannā* as against Be *nādhimuttā*.

1417. Pj II glosses *vitareyya* in **495**b with *taritvā,* thus taking it as an absolutive. This may be justified by the presence of *caranti* as the finite verb of the sentence.

1418. I read here with Ce and Ee: *Bhavābhavāyā ti sassatāya vā ucchedāya vā. Atha vā bhavassa abhavāya bhavābhavāya, punabbhavānabhinibbattiyā ti vuttaṃ hoti.* Be has *punabbhavābhinibbattiyā,* which may be a typographical error.

Pj II obviously takes *bhavābhava* to be a compound of *bhava* + *abhava*, but I follow Norman, who explains the term (at GD 253) as a "rhythmical lengthening for *bhavabhava* = repeated existence, various existences." Jayawickrama also takes it in this sense. Ps II 74,17–19, commenting on *bhavābhava* at MN I 109,23, says: "In regard to *bhavābhava*: in regard to *repeated existence*, or in regard to inferior or superior states of existence; for a superior state of existence, which marks improvement, is called *abhava*" (*bhavābhave ti punappunabbhave, hīnapaṇīte vā bhave, paṇīto hi bhavo vuddhippatto abhavo ti vuccati*). So too, Ps IV 28,20–22, commenting on *itibhavābhavahetu* at MN II 238,15, says: "*For the sake of such bhavābhava*: based on such means of doing merit as teaching, I will experience bliss *in this or that state of existence*" (*itibhavābhavahetū ti evaṃ imaṃ desanāmayaṃ puññakiriyavatthuṃ nissāya tasmiṃ tasmiṃ bhave sukhaṃ vedissāmi*).

1419. This verse, which is not in the printed editions of the text, differs from the previous verse only in replacing *susaññatattā* with the synonymous *susaṃvutattā*.

1420. The text has *yathātathā idaṃ*, which Pj II glosses: *ye ettha khandhāyatanādisantāne* ***yathā idaṃ*** *khandhāyatanādi* ***tathā jānanti****, yaṃsabhāvaṃ taṃsabhāvaṃyeva sañjānanti aniccādivasena jānantā.*

1421. Ee *cha-sattavihārasatiyā* should be corrected to *chasatatavihārasatiyā*, as in Be and Ce. On the "six constant dwellings," see DN III 250,14–20, DN III 281,1–8, and AN II 198,24–29.

1422. *Saraṇaṃ bahūnan ti bahūnaṃ devamanussānaṃ bhayavihiṃsanena saraṇabhūto.* This explanation is contingent on equating Pāli *saraṇa*, "refuge," with Skt *śaraṇa*[1], "killing, slaying" (from *śṛī* > *śṛṇāti*, "to crush, to break"), rather than, correctly, with Skt *śaraṇa*[2] (from *śri* > *śrayati, śrayate*, "to approach, resort to [for help or refuge]"). For the contrast, see SED, p. 1056c and p. 1057a. Similarly Pj I 16,10–13 playfully derives the word "refuge" in the "going for refuge" formula from the verb *hiṃsati* meaning "to injure": *Saraṇagamanādīsu hiṃsatī ti saraṇaṃ, saraṇagatānaṃ ten'eva saraṇagamanena bhayaṃ santāsaṃ dukkhaṃ duggatiṃ parikkilesaṃ hiṃsati vidhamati nīharati nirodhetī ti attho.*

1423. Text has *ken'attanā gacchati brahmalokaṃ*, which Pj II glosses *ken'attanā ti kena kāraṇena*. The reflexive use of instrumental *attanā* is common in Pāli, but apart from **477**a, **756,** and **1119**, there is almost no explicit discussion in Sn of the opposition between views of *attā* and the Buddha's teaching of *anattā*. I therefore think it unlikely that the brahmin asked his question with the view of an *attā*, a substantial self, as the underlying premise. The Buddha's reply does not challenge such an assumption, and Pj II evidently takes *attanā* in a simple reflexive sense. I have translated the line in compliance with the comment that takes *attanā* as equivalent to *kāraṇena*, "cause, means." Jayawickrama treats *attanā* as the reflexive pronoun in his rendering of the line: "With (the aid of what) does one go to the world of Brahma oneself?" Norman, however, translates it as if the speaker had assumed a metaphysical entity: "With what self does one go to the Brahma-world?"

1424. According to the Abhidhamma and commentaries, the meditation on loving-kindness (as well as compassion and altruistic joy) can lead to the three lower jhānas of the sutta scheme, and to four jhānas of the Abhidhamma scheme. The latter recognizes five jhānas by dissecting the second jhāna into two: a second, in which *vicāra* is present without *vitakka*, and a third, in which both *vitakka* and *vicāra* are absent.

1425. *Bāhirapabbajjaṃ upādāya vuccati*. That is, a "going forth" or renunciation outside the Buddha's teaching.

1426. The Pāli word for council hall being *sabhā*, Pj II interprets the name "Sabhiya" as "one born in a council hall." A similar but more elaborate background story is related in the Skt parallel in Mvu III 389–94, where the protagonist is called Sabhika (see Jones 1956, 3:389–94). The parallel verses are at Mvu III 394–401 (see Jones 1956, 3:394–401). Another parallel, preserved in Chinese in the *Abhiniṣkramaṇa Sūtra, is at T III no. 190, 833b8–835b22, translated by Beal (1875).

1427. The following is not in the Mvu parallel. In this version, Sabhika simply travels over "the sixteen great provinces" (of India) seeking a wise man and poses the questions on his own when he meets the Buddha.

1428. *Uddiṭṭhā ti uddesamatteneva vuttā, na vibhaṅgena.* Discourses (*suttas*) are sometimes distinguished into *uddesa*, meaning the brief (*saṅkhitta*) statement of the subject, and the elaboration (*vitthāra*) and analysis (*vibhaṅga*). Often these two elements occur in a single discourse, with the *uddesa* introducing the topic, followed by the *vibhaṅga* or analysis.

1429. *Ye te ti idāni vattabbānaṃ uddesapaccuddeso.* I could not find a dictionary meaning for *paccuddesa*, which may occur only in this passage. Here I take *uddesa* to be the general characterization of them as "ascetics and brahmins, leaders of sanghas, leaders of groups," and so forth, and *paccuddesa* to be the specification of them individually, as "Pūraṇa Kassapa, Makkhali Gosāla," and so forth.

1430. The six rival teachers are described in similar terms at DN I 47–49, MN II 2–4, and SN IV 398–99. Their doctrines are identified at DN I 52–59.

1431. Reading with Ce and Ee *lābhasampannā*. Be has *lābhaparivārasampannā*, "possessing gains and retinues."

1432. *Sādhavo ete santo sappurisā.* The statement is almost redundant.

1433. The word means "filling," in this case, filling the auspicious number of a hundred.

1434. Since Kassapa was a brahmin clan name, according to this account he must have been born as a slave in a brahmin household of the Kassapa clan, and thus, disguising his origins, he took the clan name of the family he had served. Needless to say, such accounts should be regarded with a dose of skepticism; it seems their purpose is to discredit the teachers outside the Buddhist fold.

1435. This is Mahāvīra, the Jina, the best known historical proponent of Jainism.

1436. *Appaccayan ti appatītataṃ, domanassan ti vuttaṃ hoti. Appaccaya* here does not mean "without a condition" (*a* + *paccaya*), but "not being pleased," a negation of *patītatā*, the state of being pleased.

1437. *Rattaññū ti ratanaññū, "nibbānaratanaṃ jānāma mayan" ti evaṃ sakāya paṭiññāya lokenāpi sammatā, bahurattividū vā. Rattaññū* is from *ratta*, night, used to signify a length of time (as in the expression *dīgharattaṃ*, "a long time"); to this is added the suffix *ññū* from the verbal root *ñā*, to know. By folk etymology, however, Pj II transmutes *ratta* into *ratana*, gem, which it equates with nibbāna. The etymologically correct meaning is "knowers of nights," an idiom meaning "of long standing."

1438. See SN I 69,1–7, where this is said about a khattiya, a serpent, a fire, and a bhikkhu.

1439. *Balavatiyā vicinanto kicchati yeva, na sakkoti sanniṭṭhātun ti vecikicchī*. This explanation involves a word play, deriving *vicikicchā* (doubt) from the word fragments *vici* and *kiccha* (in *vicinanto kicchati*).

1440. Although this would amount to about 4,200 miles, longer than the breadth of India, Pj II explains that he did not travel in a straight line but had wandered off in various directions to ask other teachers his questions.

1441. See pp. 620–21.

1442. *Manasicchasī ti manasā icchasi*. Elsewhere asking a question "with the mind" clearly means formulating the question mentally, without verbalizing it, as a test of the Buddha's psychic powers (see below, where at **1017** we find *manopañhe apucchatha* and at **1024** *manasā pucchite pañhe*), but here, I believe, the Buddha is simply inviting him to ask the questions that have been on his mind.

1443. *Idāni yehi dhammehi attamano, te dassento āha: pamudito pītisomanassajāto ti*. This is said because, while the words *attamano* and *udaggo* are simple adjectives, *pāmojja*, *pīti*, and *somanassa* are understood in the commentaries to represent real *dhammas*, concrete factors of experience.

1444. Mvu III 395,7 has *suvrataṃ* in place of Pāli *surata*. The verse of reply in Mvu does not use either word. For a discussion of the ambiguity in the readings, see Levman 2014, 219–21. The Chinese has 伏 in the question at T III 834a19 but 調 in the reply at 834a26. Both correspond to *dānta*.

1445. *Vibuddho, buddhaboddhabbo vā*. *Vibuddha* is not in PED, but see SED sv *vi-budh*, where *vibuddha* is defined as "awakened, wide awake; expanded, blown." See too pp. 1208–9 and note 1456.

1446. *Bhinnakileso paramatthabhikkhu, so ca nibbānappatto hoti*. This is an edifying etymology that playfully explains *bhikkhu* on the basis of *bhinna*, past participle of *bhindati*, to break up.

1447. *Parinibbānagato kilesaparinibbānaṃ patto*. This alludes to the distinction between two types of *parinibbāna*, *kilesaparinibbāna*, the full extinction of defilements, and *khandhaparinibbāna*, the full extinction of the aggregates. These correspond respectively to the *saupādisesanibbānadhātu* and the *anupādisesanibbānadhātu*, the elements of nibbāna with and without a residue (of the aggregates) remaining. Since the Buddha is here describing a living bhikkhu (not one deceased), *parinibbānagato* must be taken in the former sense.

1448. *Vipattisampattihānivuddhiucchedasassataapuññapuññabhedaṃ vibhavañca bhavañca vippahāya*. See in this connection MN III 244,20–21: "He does not act, does not intend, either for existence or nonexistence. Not acting, not intending, he does not cling to anything in the world. Not clinging, he is not agitated. Being unagitated, he personally attains nibbāna."

1449. *Samitapāpattā samaṇo*. See note 576.
1450. Where the Pāli has *ussadā*, the Skt has *utsanno*, an adjective understood in a positive sense, and the Chinese has 諸縛, "bonds" or "ties." Levman 2014, 222–28, discusses the variants. By the time of the commentaries, a set of seven *ussada* had been established.
1451. Pj II here distinguishes two types of development: development of the objective resorts (*gocarabhāvanā*), which comes about by contemplating the three characteristics; and development by habituation (*vāsanābhāvanā*), which comes about by mindfulness and clear comprehension. *Vāsanā* is literally the perfuming effect of certain fragrances. Mindfulness and clear comprehension impart a habitual disposition, or "fragrance," to the faculties. On *vāsanā*, see note 748.
1452. *Nibbijjha ñatvā paṭivijjhitvā parañca lokaṃ*. With its reading *nirvidhya imaṃ paraṃ ca lokaṃ*, Mvu III 396,2 corresponds to the Pāli. The Chinese, however, at 834a28 has 厭離此世及後世, where 厭離 corresponds to Pāli *nibbijja*, absolutive of *nibbindati*. *Nibbijja* as an alternative reading is noted in Ee. The verse is quoted at Nidd I 244, with the reading of the line *nibbijjh'imaṃ parañca lokaṃ*.
1453. *Buddho nāma buddhisampanno kilesaniddāvibuddho ca*. On *vibuddha*, see note 1445.
1454. *Tattha kappānī ti taṇhādiṭṭhiyo. Tā hi tathā tathā vikappanato kappānī ti vuccanti*. On *kappa*, see pp. 63–64.
1455. *Viceyyā ti aniccādibhāvena sammasitvā*. On the ambiguity of *viceyya*, see GD 257. Mvu III 396,4 has *kalpāni vikīrya kevalāni*, which Jones renders "who has scattered all false fancies." The Chinese at 834a29 takes *kalpa* in the sense of eon, reading 於諸劫中勤苦修, "diligently practiced ascetic cultivation for eons."
1456. *Imāya lokuttaravipassanāya cutūpapātañāṇabhedāya buddhiyā sampannattā imāya ca vigatarajāditāya kilesaniddā vibuddhattā tāya*. Pj II is offering here two explanations of *buddha*, one based on *buddhi* as the faculty of understanding, the other based on *vibuddha*, "awakened," from the sleep of defilements. The verbal root *budh* originally meant both "to awaken" and "to know, to understand, to discern." Thus it would be shortsighted to insist that *buddha* must mean "Awakened One" and to dismiss "Enlightened One" as an error—a common trend today in both scholarly and popular circles. In the Nikāyas, the Buddha's *sambodhi* is most often depicted as *an attainment of knowledge and understanding*, not as an awakening from sleep. The latter imagery, while occasionally used by the commentaries (whose practice is to draw out all nuances of a word), is notably absent in the Nikāyas, and thus there is almost no justification for an exclusive insistence on "the Awakened One" as the

correct translation of *buddha*. "The One Who Has Understood" would probably be closer to the dominant sense recognized by the Buddha's contemporaries.

1457. *Kappāni viceyya kevalānī ti anekepi saṃvaṭṭavivaṭṭakappe amutrāsin ti ādinā nayena vicinitvā ti attho*. In this explanation, *kappa* is taken as a cosmic eon, the most common meaning of the word, as found in the stock passage on recalling past lives at DN I 81, MN I 22, etc.

1458. *Brahmabhāvaṃ seṭṭhabhāvaṃ patto paramatthabrāhmaṇo bāhitasabbapāpo hoti*. On this playful etymology of *brāhmaṇa*, see note 576.

1459. Pj II consistently takes *tādi/tādī* in an elevated sense, as one "unalterable by worldly conditions" (*lokadhammehi nibbikārattā*). This sense is ascribed to *tādī* as far back as the Niddesa; see pp. 1073–74. However, since the word occurs in nine verses here, it is more likely it here simply means "one like that, one who fits this description." See my discussion of the word at pp. 59–60.

1460. Like the Pāli, Mvu III 396,18 has *brahmā*. The Chinese translation at 834b9 has 是名為聖梵行人, "he is called a practitioner of the noble spiritual life (that is, a *brahmacārin*)."

1461. *Samaṇo pavuccate tathattā ti tathārūpo samaṇo pavuccatī ti*. On this etymology of *samaṇa*, see note 576. Pj II is evidently glossing *tathattā* as if it were a compound of *tathā* + *attā*. DOP resolves the term in just that way, though with a question mark in parentheses. Norman does not comment on the word but translates it as "rightly," apparently taking it as the ablative of *tathatta* (= Skt *tathatva*). The parallel verses of Mvu have the ablative *tathatvāt*. I follow Norman in taking this to have been the original meaning. Along the same lines, Jayawickrama renders the word "on account of that nature." See BHSD sv *tathatā* and *tathatva*. The Chinese 得此證者 means "one who has realized this."

1462. *Rajānaṃ vigamena virajo*. Mvu III 396,20 has *virato*, the Chinese at 834b10 has 無惱, "without distress," which may reflect an original close to the Pāli or may even correspond to *vighāto*.

1463. *Ninhāya . . . tamāhu nhātako ti*. Pāli *nhātaka* = Skt *snātaka*, on which SED says: "one who has bathed or performed ablutions, i.e., a Brāhman who, after performing the ceremonial lustrations required on his finishing his studentship as a Brahmacārin under a religious teacher, returns home and begins the second period of his life as a Gṛihastha (householder)." The highest of *snātakas* is the *vidyāvratasnātaka*, one who is completely versed in the Vedas and religious observances (SED sv *vidyā*).

1464. *Taṇhādiṭṭhikappehi kappiyesu devamanussesu kappaṃ na eti*. It is hard to see how this relates to the sense of "bathed." It is possible lines of the original have been lost or wrongly allocated. The Chinese at 834b13 has 一切天人不能穢, "he cannot be defiled by any devas and humans." While I cannot reconstruct the original, this clearly relates more closely to the theme of bathing than the Pāli and Skt.

1465. There is a folk etymology here of *nāga* from *na* + *āgu* (not + crime). See too note 472.

1466. Presumably the two are liberation of mind (*cetovimutti*) and liberation by wisdom (*paññāvimutti*), which jointly constitute the fruit of arahantship. For the distinction between them, see AN I 61,6–14.

1467. The double explanation in Pj II indicates that there were alternative ways of reading pāda a here, either *khettāni viceyya kevalāni* or *khettāni vijeyya kevalāni*. The three editions all have *viceyya*, but the first explanation suggests the commentator was also familiar with a text that had *vijeyya*. Despite the gloss, Pj II does not cite a variant for *viceyya*. Norman's comment that no known edition reads *viceyya* in the first line is no doubt a typo that should be corrected to *vijeyya*, as in Norman 1992, 146. Norman 2004, 79, comments on the ambiguity: "This doubtless goes back to an earlier version of the sutta where, in a dialect where both *-c-* and *-j-* became *-y-*, the word appeared in the ambiguous form **viyeyya*." Mvu III 398,19 has *saṃyama*, while the Chinese, which takes the verse to be explaining how one is a "field of merit" (福田 = *puññakkhettaṃ*), at 834b22 has 諸刹一一分別知, "one analytically knows each land." This seems to be based on a reading corresponding to Pāli *khettāni viceyya kevalāni*.

1468. All three editions read *yañca brahmakhettaṃ chaḷāyatane cakkhāyatanādidvādasāyatanabhedaṃ*. This may be an ancient copyist's error that should be corrected to *dvādasāyatanesu cakkhāyatanādichaḷāyatanabhedaṃ*. I translate on the assumption that this is the correct reading. In a note Ce points out that there are only six bases and two bases respectively in the form realm and the formless realm. According to Vibh 474 (§994) and Vibh 476 (§996), in the form realm there are only the eye base, ear base, and mind base and their objects—visible form, sound, and mental phenomena; and in the formless realm there are only the mind base and mental phenomena.

1469. *Khettajina*. I follow Norman in taking this word to be derived from Skt *kṣetrajña*, with *jina* obtained from *jña* by the insertion of a euphonic vowel. In rendering *maggajina*, however, I deferred to the commentary (see note 594). Pj II's two readings of the absolutive, as "having conquered" (*vijeyya*) and "having examined" (*viceyya*), are apparently intended to cover both possibilities, as "field-conqueror" and "field-knower," respectively. While Norman renders *khettajina* as "field-knower," Jayawickrama chooses the alternative and renders it "the winner of the field." The parallel verses at Mvu III 398,14 and Mvu III 399,2 have *kṣetrajño*. See too Bhagavadgītā 13.1: *idaṃ śarīraṃ kaunteya kṣetram ity abhidhīyate; etad yo vetti taṃ prāhuḥ kṣetrajña iti tadvidaḥ.*

1470. *Kosānī ti kammāni vuccanti, tesañca lunanā samucchedanā kusalo hoti.* Norman says that "the presence of the word *lunanā* in the cty implies that it was commenting upon a text which has the absolutive of the root *lu-*, i.e., **lunitvā* or **lavitvā*." However, Pj II quotes and comments on the text as if it has the reading found in all editions, *viceyya*. On this edifying derivation of *kusala*, see As 39,3–4: *te akusalasaṅkhāte kuse lunanti chindantī ti kusalā*, and Vism-mhṭ II 106: *āyatiñca anudahanena vināsanato kuṃ siyantī ti kusā, rāgādayo, te viya attano nissayassa lavanato chindanato kusalaṃ.*

1471. Where the Pāli here has *viceyya* as in the previous verse, Mvu III 399,3 has *vicārya*, absolutive of *vicārayati*, "to examine," and the Chinese at 834b24 has 分別, "to distinguish, to analyze," which supports *viceyya*.

1472. That is, the volitions of the five jhānas (according to the Abhidhamma fivefold division of jhāna), and the volitions of the four formless attainments.

1473. The word is again *kosāni*. DOP lists five meanings of *kosa*. Those relevant here are: (1) "a treasury, a storehouse," and (2) "a case, a covering, a sheath, a covering membrane, a pouch."

1474. This is an attempt to derive the noun *paṇḍita* from an artificial verb *paṇḍati*, which the commentaries interpret as meaning "to move." Thus Pj I 124,25–26 has: *paṇḍantī ti paṇḍitā, sandiṭṭhika-samparāyikesu atthesu ñāṇagatiyā gacchantī ti adhippāyo.* "The wise pundits are those that move; the purport is that they proceed along the course of knowledge toward the good in this life and future lives." Saddanītippakaraṇa (CST4) takes *paṇḍa* to be synonymous with wisdom and also connects the verb *paṇḍati* to *gacchati*, "goes": *Ettha paṇḍā ti paññā. Sā hi sukhumesupi atthesu paṇḍati gacchati dukkhādīnaṃ pīḷanādikampi ākāraṃ jānātī ti "paṇḍā" ti vuccati. Paṇḍito ti paṇḍāya ito gato pavatto ti paṇḍito. Atha vā sañjātā paṇḍā etassā ti paṇḍito. Paṇḍati ñāṇagatiyā gacchatī ti pi paṇḍito.* The Skt and Chinese versions of this verse do not match well with the Pāli.

1475. *Asatañca satañca ñatvā dhammaṃ. Asataṃ* and *sataṃ* here are genitive plurals. Norman observes (GD 260–61) that the verse would be more coherent if in place of the absolutive *ñatvā* there were a verb related more directly to *muni*. He proposes that the verse may originally have had **mutvā*, and that *ñatvā* entered as a gloss that replaced the original.

1476. *Catūhi maggañāṇavedehi kilesakkhayaṃ karonto gato, so paramatthato vedagū nāma hoti.* The word *veda* is from the verbal root *vid*, meaning "to know" and "to experience." Both *vijjā*, "clear knowledge," and *vedanā*, "feeling," are derived from this root. Thus the Buddha's reply shifts the meaning of *veda* from brahmin scriptures to the knowledge attained by the arahant. The word play is hard to replicate in English, but to translate *veda* by "wisdom" obscures the verse's role as a rejoinder to the brahmins. For the Buddha, a true Veda-master is one who has gone to the destruction of defilements by means of knowledge. In the third line, *veda* reappears in *vedanā*, feelings that may be painful, pleasant, or neutral. Here a Veda-master is one who has removed attachment to feelings. The prefix *vīta–* in *vītarāgo* is based on the participle *ita*, which also means "gone," and thus echoes the suffix *–gū* in *vedagū*. Mvu III 397,20 has *vedako*.

1477. *Anuvicca papañcanāmarūpaṃ*. I follow here Pj II, which just below treats *papañcanāmarūpaṃ* as a *dvanda* compound, divisible into *papañcaṃ* and *nāmarūpaṃ*: *taṇhāmānadiṭṭhibhedaṃ papañcaṃ tappaccayā nāmarūpañca*.

1478. Where the Pāli has *rogamūlaṃ* in pāda b, Mvu III 398,2 has *rāgabhūtaṃ*, and in pāda c, where the Pāli has *–rogamūlabandhanā pamutto*, Mvu III 398,3 has *rāgamūle bandhanapramukto*.

1479. *Sabbesaṃ rogānaṃ mūlabandhanā, sabbasmā vā rogānaṃ mūlabandhanā, avijjābhavataṇhādibhedā, tasmā eva vā papañcā pamutto hoti*. The comment offers alternative ways of resolving the compound *sabbarogamūlabandhanā*, according to whether *sabba* is joined with *roga* or with *bandhana*.

1480. The verse playfully derives *viriyavā* from *virato*, "abstained." Mvu III 398,8 takes a different route, deriving *vīryavān* from *virajo*, "dustless."

1481. *Viriyavāso viriyaniketo*. The gloss supports reading *viriyavāso* in the text, as against Ee *viriyavā so*.

1482. All three editions of Pj II (as well as of the text) read *dhīro* here, but it would make better sense to read *vīro*, as proposed by Norman (GD 262). Confusion between the two words is not uncommon in the texts. Confirmation of *vīro* is obtained from Nidd II, which cites the verse when commenting on *vīraṃ* at **1096**a, *vīra* at **1102**b, and *vīro* at **44**c. The Chinese, too, at 834c12 has 精進人, "a vigorous man."

1483. There is an evident mismatch here between the first three pādas, which contain no pun or explanation suggesting "thoroughbred," and the subject of the verse, *ājāniyo*. It is likely, as Norman suggests, that *ajāni* from **536**b originally occurred in this verse.

1484. *Ariyo pana bāhusaccena nissutapāpatāya ca paramatthasottiyo hoti.* The etymology depends upon a word play that connects *sottiya* (Skt *śrotriya*, based on the root *śru*, to hear, to learn) with *nissuta* (Skt **niḥsruta*, a prefixed form of the past participle *sruta*, from the root *sru*, to flow, to stream). The word play works in Middle Indo-Āryan dialects in which all sibilants are identical but vanishes in Skt, which distinguishes *ś* and *s*. SED sv *śrotavya* defines *śrotriya* as "a Brahman versed in the Veda."

1485. Another folk etymology that derives *ariya* from *araṇīya*.

1486. The two attachments (*dve ālayāni*) are craving and views.

1487. The three types of wrong perception are sensual perception, malevolent perception, and aggressive perception. See Vibh 420 (§911).

1488. *Pāpakehi ārakattā ariyo hoti anaye ca anirīyanā*, reading as in Ce and Be. Ee has *anayena ca aniriyanā*. More playful etymologies of *ariya* are involved here.

1489. Pj II 433,23 adds that the locative case of the text (*caraṇesu*) is used in the sense of cause (*nimittatthe bhummavacanaṃ*). Thus, on this interpretation, one is "accomplished *because of* good conduct."

1490. Pj II connects *sabbadā* with the verb *ājānāti*, but I take the word order to be determined by metrical requirements and thus see *sabbadā* as belonging with *kusalo*. In this I follow both Norman and Jayawickrama.

1491. *Paribbājayitvā ti nikkhāmetvā niddhametvā.* Though I adopt Ee's reading of *parivajjetā* for the text, I translate the lemma in Pj II as it has come down in the three editions. *Paribbājetvā* may have been substituted for *parivajjetā* (or *parivajjetvā*) due to a failure to grasp the word play, which, as Norman points out (GD 263), only works in a dialect where *–bb–* > *–vv–*.

1492. *Osaraṇānī ti ogahanāni titthāni, diṭṭhiyo ti attho.* Norman renders *osaraṇāni* as "heresies" and Jayawickrama as "havens (of heretical views)." *Osaraṇa* is from the verb *osarati*, "to descend upon, to enter." DOP defines *osaraṇa* as "approach, entrance," and *ogahana* as "a bathing-place, a ford." These are metaphors for the views of non-Buddhist teachers.

1493. See SN IV 286–87, where the view of a personal entity (*sakkāyadiṭṭhi*) is said to underlie all the sixty-two views of the Brahmajāla Sutta.

1494. *Yadetaṃ itthī puriso ti saññakkharaṃ vohāranāmaṃ. Saññakkhara* occurs only in this passage.

1495. Text reads *antagū'si pāragū dukkhassa*, which might also have been construed: "You have gone to the end [of suffering] and gone beyond suffering." Mvu III 401,2 has *antako'si duḥkhasya pārago'si dharmāṇaṃ. Sabbadhammāna pāraguṃ* occurs at **167**b and **699**d, *pāraguṃ sabbadhammānaṃ* at **1105**c and **1112**c.

1496. Different orthographies suggest different renderings. If printed *nāganāgassa*, without hiatus (as in Be and Ee), the expression would be interpreted as a compound meaning "the nāga of nāgas," which is Norman's rendering. But Pj II's explanation calls for a hiatus to be inserted, yielding two words, *nāga nāgassa*, the orthography in Ce. On this reading, *nāga* is a vocative directly addressed to the Buddha, while *nāgassa* should be connected with *tassa te . . . bhāsato*, as part of the genitive absolute. I have translated on this second interpretation.

1497. I read with Ce and Ee *sabbaṃ pasādena ca takkāya ca bhaṇati*. Be has *namakkārakaraṇaṃ* for *takkāya ca*. I am uncertain whether *takkāya* is here a masculine dative or a feminine instrumental. Both would be irregular.

1498. *Anusāsaniyā satthavāhatāya ca*: The second explanation depends on a word play between *satthar* as "teacher" and *sattha* as "caravan."

1499. Māra as the defilements, the aggregates, death, and the malevolent deity.

1500. *Liṅgaṃ vijahitvā āgatena*: This seems to mean one who has discarded the marks that defined him as an ascetic belonging to another sect; for example, going naked or wearing just a loincloth, carrying a trident, covering the body with ashes, wearing the hair in a topknot, and so forth.

1501. Anālayo 2011b includes a translation of the parallel, EĀ 49.6 (at T II 798a25–800b26), along with a comparative study between this version and the Pāli version. The two differ considerably, and the verses so prominent in the Pāli version are almost entirely absent in the EĀ parallel.

1502. *Gaṅgāya pana yā uttarena āpo, tāsaṃ avidūrattā uttarāpo ti pi vuccati*. Though Pj II uses the word *gaṅgā*, the river intended, as will be seen, is not the Ganges but another of the five great rivers. This river is also distinct from the Mahī River that originates in Madhya Pradesh and flows into the Arabian Sea.

1503. *Gandhamādanakūṭaṃ sānumayaṃ*. The meaning of *sānu* here is unclear, but Ja III 172,20 glosses *sānūni* with *paṃsupabbate*, so I take it to be soil.

1504. *Pariṇāhena tigāvutapamāṇā udakadhārā hutvā*. Since a gāvuta is a quarter of a yojana, three gāvutas would be roughly 4.5 miles.

1505. Ce and Ee: *vijjhaṃ nāma tiracchapabbataṃ paharitvā*. Be: *viñjhaṃ nāma tiracchānapabbataṃ paharitvā*.

1506. *Duvidhā cārikā turitacārikā, aturitacārikā ca*.

1507. Sv I 239,22–24 says: "The quick tour is when he sees people capable of being enlightened even at a distance and goes suddenly in order to enlighten them" (*bodhaneyyapuggalaṃ disvā tassa bodhanatthāya sahasā gamanaṃ*). This formulation is also at Ps II 148,30–31 and elsewhere in the commentaries.

1508. The explanation of the Buddha's epithets that follows is based on Vism 198–212, Ppn 7.4–64. Despite the commentaries, I do not take the initial *itipi* as suggesting reasons for the epithets but simply as a way of opening an oral report.

1509. *Ārakattā, arīnaṃ arānañca hatattā, paccayādīnaṃ arahattā, pāpakaraṇe rahābhāvā ti imehi tāva kāraṇehi so bhagavā arahan ti veditabbo.* These explanations are all based on word plays on *arahaṃ* that cannot be replicated in English.

1510. The passage is at Paṭis I 122,14–24. Taking the sets that may not be familiar, the four nutriments are at DN III 228,3–5; the seven stations for consciousness at DN III 253,9–26 (see pp. 1303–5); the eight worldly conditions at DN III 260,6–7; the nine abodes of beings at DN III 263,9–30; the ten bases are probably the ten *kasiṇāyatana*, which are at DN III 268,20–27. See Appendix 3 for enumerations.

1511. These terms—*āsaya, anusaya, carita, adhimutti*, etc.—are analyzed at Vibh 388–91 (§§813–27). See too Paṭis I 123–24.

1512. On *aḍḍhuḍḍhāni* (Skt *ardhacaturdha*) as three and a half, see DOP sv *aḍḍha*.

1513. According to DOP *nahuta* can mean either 10,000 or a very vast number (as at **677**).

1514. I read with Be *vimokkhantikañāṇavasena buddho*. Ce and Ee have *-nāmavasena* for *-ñāṇavasena*, but Vism 209,18 has *–ñāṇavasena*. Vism-mhṭ I 235 (= Sp-ṭ I 260) explains the term thus: "Emancipation is the supreme path [the path of arahantship], which is completely emancipated from obstacles. Its end is the supreme fruit. Because it must be gained when the former has been gained, it is called 'the knowledge pertaining to the end of emancipation.' This is the entire buddha-knowledge together with the omniscient knowledge." (*Sabbaso paṭipakkhehi vimuccatī ti vimokkho, aggamaggo. Tassa anto aggaphalaṃ, tattha bhavaṃ tasmiṃ laddhe laddhabbato vimokkhantikañāṇaṃ, sabbaññutaññāṇena saddhiṃ sabbampi buddhañāṇaṃ.*) See too note 1853.

1515. *Bhagyavā bhaggavā yutto, bhagehi ca vibhattavā; bhattavā vantagamano, bhavesu bhagavā tato.* These derivations involve word plays. For more on the epithet *bhagavā*, see pp. 1086–87.

1516. Vism 198–212, Ppn 7.4–67.

1517. I read with Ce and Be *attano atthabhūtena sīlena*. Ee's *attabhūtena* should probably be corrected.

1518. *Taṃ sutvā tathattāya paṭipannena adhigantabbāya abhisambodhiyā vā ādikalyāṇo*. This alludes to the complete enlightenment (*abhisambodhi*) of a sammā sambuddha.

1519. Sp-ṭ I 286 explains: "Because it leads to being untainted by worldly conditions; for by means of six-factored equanimity one in the state of impartiality [is not tainted] by things desirable and so forth" (*tādibhāvāvahanato ti chaḷaṅgupekkhāvasena iṭṭhādīsu tādibhāvassa lokadhammehi anupalepassa āvahanato*).

1520. *Nāthappabhavattā ca pabhavasuddhiyā ādikalyāṇo, atthasuddhiyā majjhekalyāṇo, kiccasuddhiyā pariyosānakalyāṇo.* Sp-ṭ I 286 treats *nāthappabhavattā* in purely grammatical terms, but *nātha* is often used as an epithet for the Buddha; hence the sense is that the Dhamma is good in the beginning because it originates from the Buddha. Sp-ṭ explains *atthasuddhi* to mean the Dhamma's emancipating nature because it is without defilement (*nirupakkilesatāya niyyānikatā atthasuddhi*), and *kiccasuddhi* to mean the purity of its function, that is, its being good to practice (*suppaṭipattisaṅkhātakiccassa suddhiyā*).

1521. The fourfold depth: *atthagambhīratā, dhammagambhīratā, desanāgambhīratā, paṭivedhagambhīratā.* These are explained in relation to *paṭiccasamuppāda* at Sv 493–94. For an English translation, see Bodhi 1995, 64–67.

1522. This is a reference to the four kinds of analytical knowledge (*paṭisambhidā*)—of meaning, doctrine, language, and ingenuity (*attha, dhamma, nirutti, paṭibhāna*)—on which see Vism 440–43, Ppn 14.21–31.

1523. *Brahmabhūtehi.* The meaning will be explained just below.

1524. This refers to the origin story to the allowance for certain drinks to be consumed after midday, at Vin I 245 foll.

1525. Reading with Ce and Ee *savitānaṃ maṇḍapaṃ karoti,* as against Be *setavitānamaṇḍapaṃ karoti,* "made a white-canopied pavilion."

1526. I use the more familiar Skt names of the three Vedas. The Pāli reads *tiṇṇaṃ vedānan ti irubbedayajubbedasāmavedānaṃ.*

1527. *Saha nighaṇḍunā ca keṭubhena ca sanighaṇḍukeṭubhānaṃ.* Pāli *nighaṇḍu* (Skt *nighaṇṭu*) is said to be "a collection of difficult and obsolete words, which formed a basis for instruction in the mode of expounding the Veda" (Roth, cited in D'Alwis 1863, lxx, note 3).

1528. Perhaps this is said with reference to the *kavi* who preside at Vedic rituals. DOP defines *keṭubha* as "the science of the (Vedic) rituals, the rules concerning the rites," which seems to be supported by Pj II. No cognate Skt word is found in SED. Sv-ṭ I 379,20–23, commenting on *keṭubha* as *kiriyākappavikappo,* says: "The procedure for carrying out acts is so called because it is by this means that an act—characterized as utterance of speech and so forth—is prescribed. Since this has many divisions through distinctions of connections between letters and terms, the meanings of terms, and so forth, it is called 'the division in the procedures for carrying out acts.'"

(*Vacībhedādilakkhaṇā kiriyā kappīyati etenā ti kiriyākappo, so pana vaṇṇapadasambandhapadatthādivibhāgato bahuvikappo ti āha kiriyākappavikappo ti.*)

1529. D'Alwis 1863, lxx, note 3, refers to Sāyana's definition of the brahmanical *śikṣā* as "the science of the pronunciation of letters, accents, etc."

1530. *Itihāsapañcamānan ti athabbanavedaṃ catutthaṃ katvā itiha āsa itiha āsā ti īdisavacanapaṭisaṃyutto purāṇakathāsaṅkhāto itihāso pañcamo etesan ti itihāsapañcamā*. Since the stock description of a learned brahmin in the Nikāyas always refers to *three* Vedas it is possible that historical lore (*itihāsa*) is "the fifth," not of the Vedas but of the auxiliary branches of learning, along with the lexicons, rules of ritual, phonology, and etymology.

1531. Sv-ṭ I 380,4–6: "One who states those same Vedas by way of terms is a philologist. Grammar is the science of words, by which one explains and expounds each word and its meaning." (*Te eva vede padaso kāyatī ti padako. Taṃ taṃ saddaṃ tadatthañca byākaroti byācikkhati etenā ti byākaraṇaṃ, saddasatthaṃ.*)

1532. Sv I 248,1–8 is clearer on this: "A science consisting of 12,000 works explaining the marks of great men, the buddhas and so forth, wherein there were 16,000 verses called 'buddha hymns,' by which it could be determined that those possessing certain marks are buddhas; those with other marks are paccekabuddhas; those with still other marks are the two chief disciples, the eighty great disciples, a buddha's mother, a buddha's father, the chief male lay supporter, the chief female lay supporter, and a wheel-turning monarch."

1533. I read with Ce and Ee *mahādānaṃ* as against Be *mahāyajanaṃ*.

1534. *Pubbe katādhikārattā*. The expression means that one has established strong supporting conditions for realization by serving previous buddhas, making offerings to them, and practicing their teaching.

1535. Reading with Ce and Ee *kappasahassehipi*. Be has *kappasatasahassehipi*, "even in 100,000 eons."

1536. This seems to be an attempt to rationalize the absence of any description of the marks of a great man in the Vedas as they were known in the age of the commentaries.

1537. Pj II 449,1–5 mentions different meanings of the word *gati*: as the five realms of existence, as a dwelling place, as wisdom, and as diffusion. It asserts that in this passage *gati* has the sense of outcome (*niṭṭhā*).

1538. *Catūhi acchariyadhammehi saṅgahavatthūhi ca lokaṃ rañjanato rājā*. This is a playful derivation of *rājā* from *rañjati*. On the four means of attracting a retinue, see Appendix 3.

1539. *Catūhi sampatticakkehi vattati, tehi ca paraṃ vatteti*. The expression likely refers to the four *iddhis* of a wheel-turning monarch, mentioned at MN III 176–77: he is extremely handsome, has a long life span, enjoys good health, and is loved by brahmins and householders.

1540. "Wheel-turner" (*cakkavattī*) is a qualifier because it specifies what kind of king is intended.

1541. *Atha vā vivatto ca vicchaddā cā ti vivattacchaddā, vaṭṭarahito chadanarahito cā ti vuttaṃ hoti.* This is an alternative resolution of the compound. On *vivattacchadda*, see note 1269.

1542. *Evaṃ purimapadadvayass'eva hetudvayaṃ vuttaṃ hoti.* That is, the absence of the round is the cause for his being designated an arahant, and the removal of coverings is the cause for his being designated a sammā sambuddha.

1543. On the four kinds of self-confidence, see MN I 71–72 and AN II 8–9. The second self-confidence is that of claiming without fear of contradiction that he has destroyed all the influxes, which testifies to his arahantship. The first self-confidence is that of claiming he is fully enlightened to all things, which testifies to his buddhahood. The third and fourth kinds of self-confidence are, respectively, claiming without fear of contradiction that what he declares to be obstructions are truly obstructive, and claiming without fear of contradiction that the practice of his teaching leads to emancipation from suffering. According to Pj II, these testify to his removal of the coverings.

1544. Sīlakkhandhavagga-abhinavaṭīkā II 211 says: "*The first*—the term 'arahant'—*accomplishes the eye of the Dhamma*, a designation for the knowledge of the lower three paths and fruits; for the term is an indication that the Blessed One has destroyed the defilements, which are the enemy, and that he has destroyed the spokes of the wheel of saṃsāra. *The second*, the term 'perfectly enlightened buddha,' *accomplishes the eye of a buddha*, a designation for the knowledge of the inclinations and latent tendencies of beings and the knowledge of the inferior or superior conditions of their faculties. For these two kinds of knowledge are not fully obtained by disciples and paccekabuddhas. *The third*, the term 'one who removes the coverings,' *accomplishes the universal eye*, a designation for the omniscient knowledge; for it is an indication of the abandoning of all defilements along with their habitual formations."

1545. *Sīhāva ekacarā.* The text here echoes **166**a, which also compares the Buddha, in his love of solitude, to a solitary lion.

1546. See Mil 167–69. The wording of the actual text is slightly different, though the point is the same.

1547. I have passed over the commentary to **548–53**, which offers mere glosses on the terms. The meanings should be clear enough in the translation.

1548. Anālayo writes (2011b: 50) that a comparison of the Sn version with the EĀ version "suggests that the ideas that flattery will cause the Buddha to praise himself, and that such praise in turn then becomes the central means of converting an eminent Brahmin, probably reflect later developments."

1549. *Anujāto tathāgatan ti tathāgatahetu anujāto, tathāgatena hetunā jātoti attho.* See in this connection MN III 29,8–13: "Bhikkhus, if, rightly speaking, one could say of anyone: 'He is the son of the Blessed One, born of his breast, born of his mouth, born of the Dhamma, created by the Dhamma, an heir in the Dhamma, not an heir in material things,' it is of Sāriputta that one could rightly say this."

1550. The passage alludes to the four tasks with respect to the four noble truths: fully understanding the truth of suffering; abandoning its origin; realizing its cessation; and developing the path.

1551. *Bujjhitabbaṃ bujjhitvā buddho jāto'smī' ti yuttena hetunā buddhattaṃ sādheti.* Alternatively: "Having been enlightened about that to which one should become enlightened, I have become an enlightened one."

1552. *Sallakatto ti rāgasallādisattasallakattano.* Perhaps we should read the last word in the compound as *kantano*. See DOP sv *katta*, *kantana*. On the seven darts, see Appendix 3.

1553. Pj II alludes here to **436–42**.

1554. That is, they are ordained solely by invitation from the Buddha, with no need to undergo the procedure by a quorum of bhikkhus.

1555. While all three editions of text read *yattha* ("where"), all three editions of Pj II read *yathā* ("how, because") in the lemma.

1556. See note 1025.

1557. *Onītapattapāṇin ti pattato onītapāṇiṃ, apanītahatthan ti vuttaṃ hoti.* For a more detailed discussion of this expression, see CDB 1418, note 135, and 1441, note 290.

1558. In Ee the two couplets making up this verse occur in inverted order. I follow Be and Ce, in which the order of the couplets conforms to the following verses as well. The verses are also at Vism 367–68, Ppn 11.102.

1559. See Vism 368,33–369,4, Ppn 11.109: "The earth element is a condition for the other three as a foundation, the water element as cohesion, the fire element as maintaining, and the air element as distension."

1560. Reading with Be and Ce *niruddhato pabhuti sattānaṃ*. Ee *niruddhapakatisattānaṃ* should probably be corrected.

1561. Pj II is quoting Nidd I 30–31 here. For the full passage, see pp. 1029–30.

1562. *Saṅkhāradukkha-vipariṇāmadukkha-dukkhadukkhehi saṃyutaṃ*. The three kinds of *dukkha* are at Vism 499,14–21, Ppn 16.35. In brief, *dukkhadukkha* comprises painful bodily and mental feeling; *vipariṇāmadukkha* comprises pleasant feeling, which is painful when it changes; and *saṅkhāradukkha* comprises neutral feeling, or all conditioned things, "because they are oppressed by rise and fall."

1563. *Pariḷāha*, which in relation to people usually means either a bodily fever or the "fever of passion."

1564. *Tena tāni phalāni pāto pāto niccakālaṃ patanti, nesaṃ pāto patanato bhayaṃ hoti, patanā bhayaṃ hotī ti attho*. Following Norman (see GD 270), I take *niccaṃ* to be the preferred reading. Pj II, it seems, is trying to explain the verse on the basis of both *pāto* and *niccaṃ*. Ja IV 127,3 has *phalānamiva pakkānaṃ, niccaṃ patanato bhayaṃ*. The paraphrase at Ja IV 128,6–8 clearly supports *niccaṃ*: *pakkānaṃ phalānaṃ pakkakālato paṭṭhāya "idāni vaṇṭā chijjitvā patissanti, idāni patissantī" ti patanato bhayaṃ niccaṃ dhuvaṃ ekaṃsikameva bhavati*.

1565. *Na so labbhā mayā*. In Sn I rendered this following the gloss in Pj II. Here I translate it literally.

1566. *Pajappan ti taṇhaṃ*. See DOP *jappa*[1] and the contrast between *jappati*[1], "speaks, prattles, mutters," and *jappati*[2], "desires, longs." DOP does not list a noun *jappa* corresponding to *jappati*[2] but suggests that the latter may actually be identical with *jappati*[1]. In that case *jappati* would be one verb with two nuances.

1567. *Nibbuto*, implying that the subject has attained nibbāna.

1568. Anālayo, in his comparative study of all MN suttas with their non-Pāli parallels, remarks (2011a: 572) that apart from the Sn version, "so far no parallel of this discourse appears to have been identified."

1569. *Nemittikaṃ*. This word usually means "one who drops hints (for gain)" or "one who interprets signs or omens," but here it means "arising from a cause, based on attributes" (DOP).

1570. *Jappe ti vede*. Though Pj II seems to identify *jappa* with the Vedas themselves, recitation of the Vedas must be intended. See DOP sv *jappa*.

1571. *Kammanā ti dasavidhena kusalakammapathakammanā*. Apparently the sense here is not that one has been born a brahmin because of one's kamma in previous lives but that one is a brahmin by reason of one's present action. The Buddha's reply supports this second interpretation.

1572. The allusion is to the threefold good: the good pertaining to this present life, the good pertaining to future lives (a fortunate rebirth), and the supreme good or nibbāna.

1573. Where the verses use the single word *jāti*, I have rendered this word variously, according to context, as "birth," "social class/caste," and "kind." Its use to define social status was natural in a social system where the family into which one was born determined one's social class.

1574. The words *upādiṇṇa* and *anupādiṇṇa* are here used in a technical sense that I try to convey by rendering them as "sentient" and "non-sentient," respectively. Literally they mean "clung to" and "not clung to."

1575. I pass over Pj II's comments on **602–6**, which merely explain the types of beings referred to or give examples of each.

1576. *Brāhmaṇo khattiyo ti nānattavidhānapariyāyaṃ vokāraṃ, taṃ vokārañca manussesu samaññāya pavuccati, vohāramattena vuccati.* On *vokāra*, "classification," Ps-ṭ II 201 says: "Classification is the act of classifying. The point is that different kinds are not classified through an [inherent] distinction" (*vokāran ti vokaraṇaṃ, yena visiṭṭhatāya na vokarīyati jātibhedo ti attho*).

1577. I pass over Pj II's glosses of the terms designating the various means of livelihood, which are already incorporated into the translation.

1578. *Yvāyaṃ catunnaṃ yonīnaṃ yattha katthaci jāto.* The four *yonis* usually designate four modes of birth—from the womb, eggs, moisture, and spontaneous birth (MN I 73,3–15)—but here the expression clearly refers to the four castes: khattiyas, brahmins, vessas, and suddas.

1579. I read with Ee *brāhmaṇassa saṃvaṇṇitāya mātari*, as against Be and Ce *brāhmaṇasamaññitāya mātari*.

1580. Ps-ṭ II 202: "By this, a special position somewhere among the four kinds of genealogy is delineated. Hence he says: 'there too specifically.' Thus, having explained the meaning of the expression 'one of [good] genealogy and maternal origin' in general terms by way of a specific position, he next says 'this one [is well born on both sides]' to state the meaning by way of a specified explanation, without bringing in a general explanation." The point seems to be that the sentence beginning "Whether one is born anywhere" describes what is meant by descent in general, by referring both to one born in any of the four castes as well as to one specially born into a brahmin family. In contrast to this, the next sentence, beginning "But the descent spoken of by the brahmins," refers exclusively to a good descent as recognized by the brahmins.

1581. *Brāhmaṇehi brāhmaṇassa parisuddhauppattimaggasaṅkhātā yoni kathīyati.*
1582. *Bhovādi nāma so hoti.* Literally "he is just a sayer of *bho.*" *Bho* (the vocative of *bhavaṃ*, meaning "honored sir") was the word the brahmins used to address each other and other respected persons. Thus the brahmins would address the Buddha as *bho Gotama.*
1583. *Sace hoti sakiñcano.* At GD 274, Norman discusses the alternative readings *sa ve* and *sace.* Be and Ce of Sn, all three editions of Pj II, and MN (Ce) have *sace.* Confusion between the consonants *c* and *v* is common in the manuscripts. On *kiñcana* as an impediment or defilement, see p. 58.
1584. On this edifying etymology of *brāhmaṇa*, see note 576.
1585. Ce and Ee: *Na paritassatī ti taṇhāya na bhāyati.* On how *paritassati* conveys the sense of both fear and craving, see note 696.
1586. Pj II concludes its comments on each verse with this sentence. I omit the repetition except at the end.
1587. *Pāṇiādīhi pothanañca.* This must be intended as a gloss on *vadha–* in the verse. On the ten bases of insult, see Appendix 3.
1588. Ps III 437,19–21 comments: "When [patience] has arisen once it is not called a powerful troop, but it becomes such when repeatedly arisen."
1589. *Vatavantan ti dhutavatena samannāgataṃ.*
1590. See Vism 15–16, Ppn 1.42.
1591. Sensual objects and sensual lust.
1592. *Dhammojapaññāya medhāviṃ.* Ps III 438,9 has instead: *medhāvin ti pakatipaññāya paññavantaṃ* ("Intelligent: wise through natural wisdom").
1593. See pp. 428–29.
1594. *Nābhisaje ti yāya girāya aññaṃ kujjhāpanavasena na laggāpeyya. Khīṇāsavo nāma evarūpameva giraṃ bhāseyya.* The explanation plays on the double meaning of *abhisajati*: (1) becomes attached; (2) takes offense. Pj II must be taking *abhisaje* as a causative, hence either "to cause to become attached" or "to cause offense, to hurt." See note 466.
1595. *Aṭṭha vatthūni.* See Appendix 3.
1596. *Amatogadhamanuppattan ti amataṃ nibbānaṃ ogahetvā anuppattaṃ.* It seems that in Pāli two words distinct in Skt have been conflated, creating an ambiguity. The Skt participle *gāḍha* (from root *gāh*) means "dived into, bathed in, deeply entered" (see SED sv *gāh*), from which comes *avagāḍha*, "immersed, plunged into." *Gādha* (from root *gādh*) means "offering firm standing-ground, shallow," or as a noun, "ground for standing on in water." I take *ogadha* here to be based on *gādha* rather than *gāḍha*. For support I would appeal to the verse beginning *yāva na gādhaṃ labhati nadīsu* at SN 2:15 (I 47–48). Norman too

takes this option, rendering the line "arrived at the firm foundation of the death-free." Pj II, it seems, relates *ogadha* to *gāḍha*, which Jayawickrama follows with his "reached immersion in immortality."

1597. *Ubho ti dvepi puññāni pāpāni ca chaḍḍetvā ti attho*. This does not mean that the arahant is "beyond good and evil," a common misconception. Evil is contrasted here not with "good" but with "merit," wholesome kamma capable of ripening in the round of rebirths. Since arahants have eradicated all defilements, they do not create fresh kamma, but from a moral point of view all their actions are good.

1598. *Vimalan ti abbhādimalavirahitaṃ*. This probably alludes to AN II 53,5–13, which speaks of four impurities on account of which the sun and moon do not shine: clouds, mist, smoke-and-dust, and Rāhu, lord of the asuras.

1599. *Nandībhavaparikkhīṇan ti tīsu bhavesu parikkhīṇataṇhaṃ*. Pj II takes the compound as a *bahubbīhi* built upon an inverted *tappurisa* (that is, as equivalent in sense to *bhavanandīparikkhīṇaṃ*). Dhp-a IV 192,7–8 glosses the expression in the same way as Pj II does here, but Ps III 439,22 takes it as a *bahubbīhi* built upon a *dvanda*: *nandībhavaparikkhīṇan ti parikkhīṇanandiṃ parikkhīṇabhavaṃ*. So too does Pj II 215,1–3, on which see note 783.

1600. As 168,8–13: "*Twofold jhāna*: the contemplation of the object and the contemplation of the characteristics. Of these, 'contemplation of the object' is the eight meditative attainments, in which one contemplates the object, the earth kasiṇa and so forth. Insight, the paths, and the fruits are called 'contemplation of the characteristics.'"

1601. Here Pj II resolves the compound *kāmabhavaparikkhīṇaṃ* into a *bahubbīhi* built upon a *dvanda*: *taṃ parikkhīṇakāmañceva parikkhīṇabhavañca*.

1602. *Taṇhāya ceva bhavassa ca parikkhīṇattā taṇhābhavaparikkhīṇaṃ*.

1603. *Nibbutaṃ*, which implies attainment of nibbāna.

1604. *Kiñcanan ti yass'etesu ṭhānesu taṇhāgāhasaṅkhātaṃ kiñcanaṃ natthi*. This explanation plays upon the original meaning of *kiñcana* as "something," and its derivative meanings, as a possession and as an impediment.

1605. Presumably the Māras of the defilements, the aggregates, and the malign deity. The Māra of death is conquered only with the arahant's parinibbāna.

1606. *Ajānantā no pabruvanti jātiyā hoti brāhmaṇo ti, ajānantā yeva evaṃ vadanti*. On *no* as an emphatic particle, see DOP *no*[5].

1607. *Idāni nippariyāyameva jātivādaṃ paṭikkhipanto kammavādañca niropento*. Up to this point the Buddha had been indirectly indicating that one is not a brahmin by birth. Now he explicitly says so, contrasting *jātivāda* with *kammavāda*, the doctrine of determination by birth with the doctrine of determination by action.

1608. Here the word *kamma* seems to pivot in meaning from present action to kamma as the capacity of action to bring forth results that reflect the ethical quality of the original deed, including one's birth into a specific social class. Thus, at least as seen by the commentator, at this point the verse seems to confirm the standpoint of the brahmins that a person is born into a brahmin family as a result of good kamma in past lives. Ps-ṭ II 204 says: "*In a respectable or despised family*: in a khattiya family and so forth, which are respectable; in a caṇḍāla family and so forth, which are despised."

1609. In my rendering of this verse, I no longer translate kamma as action but leave the word in the original, since I believe the purport here switches from kamma as immediate action serving as the basis for class designation to kamma as the moral determinant of one's mode of rebirth and social class.

1610. Though the verse does not use the word *kamma*, what lurks in the background is kamma understood in the sense of present action. It is by present action—by austerity and so forth—that one becomes a true brahmin, not by birth into a brahmin family. The verse also occurs at Th 631, affirming the arahant Sunīta, a former outcast, as the true brahmin.

1611. I read with Ce and Ee *seṭṭhena seṭṭhaṭṭhena brahmabhūtena kammunā*. Be does not include *seṭṭhena*.

1612. *Yasmā etaṃ brāhmaṇamuttamaṃ, yasmā etaṃ kammaṃ uttamo brāhmaṇabhāvo ti vuttaṃ hoti.*

1613. DPPN suggests that the distinction between the two Kokālikas rests on a literary fiction: "There seems to be great confusion in the stories of these two men— if they were really two. In the Jātaka Commentary, for instance, the introductory stories of several of the Jātakas refer to the Takkāriya Jātaka for details of Kokālika, obviously having in mind Devadatta's partisan; but the introductory story of the Takkāriya Jātaka is identical with that related elsewhere of Cūḷa Kokālika." The Chinese parallel of SN 6:10, SA 1278, at T II 351b13, identifies this Kokālika as a companion of Devadatta (有瞿迦梨比丘，是提婆達多伴黨).

1614. See note 392.

1615. The *Mahāprajñāpāramitopadeśa (大智度論) relates a different background story to Kokālika's slander of the chief disciples. As recounted at T XXV 157b5 foll., Kokālika accused them of having had sex with a woman. See Dharmamitra 2009, 261–63.

1616. Spk-ṭ I 216: "Boils start outside and then split the bones, but these first split the bones and then rose up."

1617. The highest of the pure abodes (*suddhāvāsa*) and the highest plane in the form realm.

1618. I omit a section explaining the relations between measures of volume culminating in twenty measures (*vīsatikhāriko*) of sesamum seed.

1619. *Pāṭhavasena.* This apparently refers to lines of the text that are cited for elucidation by the commentary.

1620. *Gāthādvayameva pana mahā-aṭṭhakathāyaṃ vinicchitapāṭhe natthi.* The Mahā-aṭṭhakathā was one of the old Sinhala commentaries, no longer extant. This statement implies that the Mahā-aṭṭhakathā commented on the other verses. On the nature and function of the Mahā-aṭṭhakathā, see Endo 2013, 33–45.

1621. Ee *uttamattena* should probably be amended to *uttamatthena*, as in Be and Ce.

1622. DOP explains *kali, kalī*: "the losing number of dice; . . . the die causing one to lose, the extra die, the losing die; bad luck; defeat, disaster." *Kaliyuga* means "the last and worst of the four ages; the present age."

1623. *Sugatesū pi suṭṭhu gatattā, sundarañca ṭhānaṃ gatattā sugatanāmakesu buddhapaccekabuddhasāvakesu. Sugata,* literally "well gone," is used most often as a unique epithet of the Buddha. In that context I render it "the fortunate one." Here, however, it is applied to all who have "gone well" along the eightfold path and realized "the good state," nibbāna.

1624. The verse occurs also at Ud 45, in a different context. It is recited as a rejoinder to the wanderers of other sects who try to defame the Buddha and his monks by accusing them of murdering the woman wanderer Sundarī. *Abhūtavādī* would normally mean "a speaker of untruth," but since this term is paired with "one who, having done [evil], says, 'I didn't do it'" (*yo vāpi katvā na karomi c'āha*), *abhūtavādī* probably refers to one who ascribes a nonexistent transgression to others.

1625. The verse is also at SN I 13,13–16.

1626. Ce and Ee have *turitavatthugāthā*. Be has *vāritavatthugāthā*, which might be rendered "verses of restraining." The expression seems to be unique to this passage. It is obscure but is not explicated elsewhere in the commentaries.

1627. The word *guṇa* is sometimes used to indicate multiples, as in the expressions *diguṇa*, "twofold," *catugguṇa*, "fourfold," and so forth.

1628. See note 1412 on *vadaññū*.

1629. I pass over the glosses of words whose meanings are already clear in translation.

1630. *Bhūnahu bhūtihanaka, vuḍḍhināsaka.* See Ps III 211,4–5: *bhūnahuno ti hatavaḍḍhino mariyādakārakassa.* Neither commentary seems to have correctly understood the term, which is equivalent to Skt *bhrūṇahan*, based on *bhrūṇa*, an embryo (from *bharati*, "to bear, to carry"), with suffix *han* (> *hu*), a killer; thus it means "one who kills an embryo." It seems to function here as an imprecation rather than a literal accusation. See Norman 2004, 80–81.

1631. *Ayosaṅkusamāhataṭṭhānaṃ tiṇhadhāramayasūlamupeti*. The place of arrival is *āhataṭṭhānaṃ*, in the accusative case; the other terms—*ayosaṅkusam*, *tiṇhadhāram* and *ayasūlam*—are *bahubbīhi* compounds describing the place.

1632. At MN III 182,34, AN I 141,1.

1633. I read *khīla* with Ce instead of Be and Ee *khila*. As DOP points out, the two words are often confused.

1634. *Ayogahaṇena c'ettha tambalohaṃ, itarena ayoguḷaṃ veditabbaṃ*. Pj II glosses *ayo*, which normally means iron, with *loha* and *tambaloha*, which mean copper. This may be on account of Dhp 371c: *Mā lohaguḷaṃ gilī pamatto*, "Do not be a heedless one who swallows the copper ball." See too AN IV 131–32.

1635. I read with Ce and Ee: *agginisamaṃ jalitan ti samantato jalitaṃ sabbadisāsu vā samañ jalitaṃ aggiṃ*: Be has *ginisampajjalitan ti samantato jalitaṃ sabbadisāsu ca sampajjalitaṃ aggiṃ*. This seems less acceptable, since Pj II is explaining the unusual formation *agginisamaṃ jalitan*.

1636. At MN III 183,26, AN I 141,30.

1637. MN 130. AN 3:36 is also known as the Devadūta Sutta.

1638. I read with Ce and Ee: *vitthataṃ hotī ti attho, vikatan ti pi pāṭho*. Be has *vitataṃ hotī ti attho. Vitthatan ti pi pāṭho*.

1639. Norman (GD 283) explains that "the singular *kumbhiṃ* in pāda a refers to the name of the hell, while the word *tāsu* [a plural] in pāda c refers to the pots in that hell."

1640. *Kilissatī ti bādhīyati. Kilijjatī ti pi pāṭho, pūti hotī ti attho*. Ee reads *kilijjati* in the text but *kilissati* in the lemma. Since Pj II mentions *kilijjati* as an alternative, *kilissati* must have been the primary reading available to the commentator.

1641. This is a gloss on the unusual term *ārajayārajayā*. DOP explains the word as from the imperative of *ārajayati*, causative of *ārañjati*, "pierces, scores, marks."

1642. *Āracayāracayā ti pi pāṭho, āviñchitvā āviñchitvā ti attho*.

1643. Pj II explains that "brown and spotted" should be connected with "dogs" in the following line (*sāmā sabalā ti etaṃ parato soṇā ti iminā yojetabbaṃ*). I follow DOP in my rendering of *kākola* as "ravens."

1644. *Paṭigiddhā ti suṭṭhu sañjātagedhā hutvā, mahāgijjhā ti eke*. All three editions of Pj II read *paṭigiddhā* in the lemma, but Ce and Ee and the Thai edition of Sn all have *paṭigijjhā*. "Large vultures" may be explained by the fact that Pāli *gijjha* means "vulture." Since Pj II does not cite an alternative reading in Sn, I assume its author and those he cites had *paṭigiddhā* in their source.

1645. Jayawickrama (PBR 1978, 13–17) argues on the basis of

language, style, meter, content, and relationship to parallel versions that the *vatthugāthā* portion of the sutta is considerably later than the discourse to Nālaka, the more archaic core of the sutta. He concludes that "the two parts of the sutta known as Nālaka Sutta in Sn are in reality two independent poems differing in age, brought together at a subsequent date which, most probably, coincided with that of the final collation of Sn." Nevertheless, the figure of Nālaka connects the two sections, which suggests they are not totally independent.

1646. Parallel versions of the story of Asita are common in Buddhist literature. In the Pāli tradition the story is also at Ja I 54–55. Skt versions are at Mvu II 30 foll. (see Jones 1952, 2:27 foll.) and the Saṅghabhedavastu (Gnoli 1977, 1:52–55). The Abhiniṣkramaṇa Sūtra preserves the story in Chinese at T III 619c23 foll. (see Beal 1875, 56 foll.).

1647. *Ānandajāte ti samiddhijāte vuddhippatte. Patīte ti tuṭṭhe. Atha vā ānandajāte ti pamudite. Patīte ti somanassajāte.* The first gloss on *ānandajāta*, as "successful, flourishing," is problematic; the second, as "exultant," conveys the expected meaning.

1648. The narrative account of Asita's visit to the Bodhisatta is at Ja I 54–55.

1649. A fuller version of this story is at Dhp-a I 264–72; see BL 1:314–19.

1650. The seven vows, at SN I 228, were: "As long as I live (1) may I support my parents; (2) may I respect the family elders; (3) may I speak gently; (4) may I not speak divisively; (5) may I delight in giving and sharing; (6) may I speak the truth; and (7) may I be free from anger, but if I do get angry may I dispel it quickly."

1651. Reading with Ce and Ee *pāricchattakapaṭicchandabhūtāya*. Be has *–paṭicchannabhūtāya*. Though I could not find another instance of *paṭicchanda* in the Pāli Canon or its commentaries, SED sv *prati* has *praticchanda*, defined as "a reflected image, any image, likeness, a substitute." This fits the context where the trumpet-flower tree (*citrapāṭalī, cittapāṭali*) in the asura realm corresponds to the pāricchattaka tree in the Tāvatiṃsa heaven (see SN V 238,15).

1652. This statement of self-recrimination involves a word play between the noun *surā* meaning liquor and *sura*, meaning god (synonymous with deva). The asuras are so called because they are anti-gods (*a* + *sura*), but Pj II here playfully explains the word on the basis of the statement *na dāni mayaṃ suraṃ pivimhā, asuraṃ pivimhā*, "Let us now not drink liquor, let us drink non-liquor." Therefore "we are no longer gods but we have now become non-gods" (*na dāni'mhā surā, asurā dāni jātamhā*).

1653. *Atītānāgate cattālīsakappe anussaritum̩.* The verb *anussarati* usually means to recollect the past or a topic of meditation but is here extended to the future. At Ja I 54,31–32, it is explicitly said that Asita could "recollect"—or "bring to mind"—forty eons both in the past and in the future (*tāpaso atīte cattālīsa kappe, anāgate cattālīsā ti asīti kappe anussarati*). The verb is used in relation to the future in the poem itself, where at **692**b Asita says: *Nāhaṃ kumāre ahitaṃ anussarāmi.*

1654. *Seḷantī ti mukhena usseḷanasaddaṃ muñcanti.* Norman renders *seḷanti* (Be *seḷenti*) as "shout," but Jayawickrama has "whistle." DOP defines *usseḷana* as "whistling."

1655. *Mārisā ti deve āmanteti, nidukkhā nirābādhā ti vuttaṃ hoti.* Sv III 698,27 says: "*Mārisa* is a term of affection, an expression particularly used by the deities" (*mārisā ti piyavacanametaṃ, devatānaṃ pāṭiyekko vohāro*). SED sv *māriṣa* relates the word to *mādṛiś*, "like me, resembling me."

1656. *Sekhāsekhabhūmiṃ pāpuṇissāma.* The "plane of trainees" comprises the three lower stages of realization: stream-entry, once-returning, and non-returning. The "plane of those beyond training" is arahantship.

1657. Respectively, *marū pamoditā* in **681**d and *kalyarūpo* in **680**c.

1658. See AN II 95–99. The four are those practicing for the well-being of themselves and others, for their own well-being but not that of others, for the well-being of others but not for their own well-being, and for the well-being of neither.

1659. *Sirikaṇha,* in Skt, would be Śrīkṛṣṇa, but it is doubtful that the Buddhist texts identify Asita with the divine charioteer of the Bhagavadgītā. Pj II glosses *jaṭi* with *jaṭilo,* indicating he was a matted-hair ascetic.

1660. I read here with Be *ahatthapāsagataṃ sandhāya,* as against *hatthapāsagataṃ sandhāya* in Ce and Ee.

1661. I follow Ce and Ee, which read *disvā punavacanaṃ na dussati.* Be has *tasmā puna vacanaṃ "disvā" ti.*

1662. Since the feet are the lowest part of the body and the head the highest, this gesture symbolizes the Bodhisatta's superiority to Asita.

1663. *Paramavisuddhadassī ti nibbānadassī. Taṃ hi ekantavisuddhattā paramavisuddhaṃ.* The text itself seems to be using the expression *paramavisuddhadassī* to refer to *the quality* of the Buddha's sight (or vision), but Pj II takes it to refer to *the object* of his sight.

1664. *Dhammamaggan ti paramadhammassa nibbānassa maggaṃ, dhammaṃ vā aggaṃ saha paṭipadāya nibbānaṃ.* The alternative explanations are based on two different ways of resolving *dhammamaggaṃ.* The first takes it as the *tappurisa* compound, *dhamma + maggaṃ,* the second as *dhammam + aggam.* I take it in the second sense. I here read *paṭipadāya* with Be, as against Ce and Ee *paṭisambhidāya*, "with analytical knowledge."

1665. The fifth of the five kinds of commotion (*kolāhala*). See pp. 737–38.

1666. Reading *vivarati* with Be as against Ce and Ee *vicarati*.

1667. A Skt version of the Buddha's conversation with Nālaka is at Mvu III 382, 386–89; see Jones 1956, 3:379, 384–88. Here Nālaka belongs to the Kātyāyana clan. After his ordination he is referred to as the Venerable Kātyāyana. It is uncertain whether Mvu intends to identify him with Mahākaccāyana, the foremost expositor of brief sayings.

1668. *Aññātametan ti viditaṃ mayā etaṃ*. Pj II evidently takes *aññātametaṃ* to be resolvable into *aññātaṃ me etaṃ*.

1669. I read *yada* with Be as against *yadi*, "if," in Ce and Ee.

1670. Pj II glosses text's *taṃ taṃ* with *tasmā taṃ*. Hence I render **699**c: "therefore I ask you."

1671. See p. 601.

1672. *Uttamaṃ padan ti uttamapaṭipadaṃ*. Since the Buddha will explain the practice for munihood, Pj II seems correct in taking *pada* to be a metrical shortening of *paṭipadā*.

1673. Ce and Ee: *Vyavasānatthe nipāto*. Be: *Byavasāyatthe nipāto*. SED has for *vyavasāya*: "settled determination, resolve, purpose"; and with the verb *karoti*, "to make up one's mind."

1674. *Paramasallekhaṃ*. The word *sallekha* seems to have been adopted by the Buddha from the ascetic culture of his time and used in the sense of the obliteration of defilements; see the Sallekha Sutta (MN 8).

1675. *Samānabhāgan ti samabhāgaṃ ekasadisaṃ ninnānākaraṇaṃ*. Here all three editions agree on *samānabhāgaṃ*, as does the Skt parallel at Mvu III 387,6. Sn (Ee) alone has *samānabhāvaṃ*. The meaning is not affected.

1676. *Sabbepi sataṇhanittaṇhatāya tasathāvare pāṇe*. See note 696.

1677. The Vinaya commentaries mention six methods of killing: with one's own hand (including a weapon held in one's hand), by command, by a missile (such as an arrow or a bullet shot from a gun), by a stable object (such as poison), by magic power, and by psychic power. See Sp II 439–40.

1678. Pj II refers here to three of the four aspects of purified moral conduct recognized in the commentaries. The fourth, proper use of the requisites, is stated in the next verse.

1679. Reading with Be and Ce *avirodhento*. Ee has *avirādhento*, "not failing in."

1680. Reading with Be and Ce *tadanusārena ca*, as against Ee *tadanusāren'eva*.

1681. An allusion to the reflection on the use of almsfood; see note 394.

1682. On the three kinds of contentment (*santosa*), see pp. 762–63.
1683. An elder known for his modesty, spoken of at Ps II 139,25 foll., Mp I 76,2, etc. It is said that although he was an arahant, he did not want people to know this.
1684. *Evamettha uppaṭipāṭiyā yojanā veditabbā*. This is said because the verse puts *nicchāto* before *aniccho*, whereas Pj II explains *aniccho* to precede *nicchāto* in sense. The past participle *nibbuto* is often used to denote one who has attained nibbāna, but here it obviously describes one still in training.
1685. On these practices, see Vism 60–61, Ppn 2.4–8.
1686. *Nesajjikaṅgaṃ*. The practice of sleeping in the sitting posture. Pj II probably goes too far in seeing the expression *āsanūpagato* as signifying this ascetic practice.
1687. I follow Be here: *So anuppannassa jhānassa uppādanena uppannassa āvajjanasamāpajjanādhiṭṭhānavuṭṭhānapaccavekkhaṇehi ca jhānesu pasuto anuyutto*. Ce and Ee are missing *samāpajjana*. Pj II refers to the five stages in the mastery of the jhānas, on which see Vism 154–55, Ppn 4.131–36.
1688. See pp. 407–14.
1689. *Na vācaṃ payutaṃ bhaṇe*. The phrase also occurs at AN I 199,12 glossed at Mp II 314,1-2: *saccālikapaṭisaṃyuttaṃ vācaṃ na bhaṇeyya*; "one should not speak words that mix lies with the truth." Mvu III 388,1 has here *na vācā prepsutāṃ bhane*. *Prepsā* is a desiderative of *pra* + *āp*, meaning "wish to obtain, desire, longing for," and *prepsu* "wishing to attain, desirous of obtaining" (SED).
1690. *Chinnakatho viya hutvā*. The expression suggests that he is acting as if he were observing a vow of silence.
1691. *Obhāsaparikathānimittaviññattipayuttaṃ ghāsesanavācaṃ na bhaṇeyya*. These types of insinuation are considered violations of right livelihood for a bhikkhu. See Vism 40–43, Ppn 1.113–22.
1692. The words of the text are: *Alatthaṃ yadidaṃ sādhu, nālatthaṃ kusalaṃ iti*. *Sādhu* and *kusala* are being used virtually as synonyms.
1693. *So tādī nibbikāro hutvā*. Here the text itself seems to use *tādī* in the sense of "impartial" preferred by the commentaries. See pp. 59–60.
1694. From the explanation that follows, Pj II seems to understand *rukkhaṃ vupanivattati* as a simile, taking *-v-* to represent *iva*. I think it more likely that *-v-* is the emphatic *eva*, so that the line is saying that whether or not the monk receives almsfood, he simply returns to the tree where he has been staying. Norman adopts the literal interpretation of the line, "he goes back to the very [same] tree," but Jayawickrama accepts the simile, translating, "he returns *as though* going back from a tree." If

"from a tree" were intended, we would have expected the ablative *rukkhā* rather than the accusative *rukkhaṃ*. Mvu III 388,5 has *rukṣatvaṃ vinivartaye*, "he returns to the tree."

1695. The reference is to the four modes of practice at AN 4:161–63, II 149–52. The "other two" are the modes of painful practice with quick superknowledge, and pleasant practice with sluggish superknowledge.

1696. *Na pāraṃ diguṇaṃ yanti, nayidaṃ ekaguṇaṃ mutaṃ*. The couplet is enigmatic. Pj II's interpretation is questionable. Since the verse constitutes a whole, I would read pādas cd in the light of pādas ab, thus as meaning that one does not "go beyond" by adopting two modes of practice, yet there is not just a single mode of practice valid for all. Norman, at GD 297, offers still another interpretation: "There are two extreme paths [= the two *antā* rejected by the Buddha], but these (two paths) do not constitute two ways of getting to nibbāna—in fact, neither works, so one cannot even get there once." Mvu III 389,2 is partly similar to the Pāli, but with the lines inverted: *na pāraṃ dviguṇāyati nāpi caivaṃ guṇāyati, uccāvacā pratipadā śrāmaṇyena prakāśitā*. Note the use of *śrāmaṇyena* (the abstract noun meaning "recluseship' or "the ascetic life") in place of *samaṇena*. Jones 1956, in 3:388, note 1, says the verse would be "a little more intelligible by the change of *caivaṃ* to *caikaṃ* (*ca-ekaṃ*)," which would correspond more closely to the Pāli.

1697. *Yassa ca visatā natthi*. *Visata* is from *visṛta* (also represented by *visaṭa*), "gone in various directions, dispersed . . . stretched out, spread, extended" (SED). Here it is a participle functioning as a noun. Mvu III 388,10 has *yasyātra saritā nāsti*. At AN II 211,31–32, craving is described by both *saritā* and *visaṭā*: *taṇhā jālinī saritā visaṭā visattikā*. In this same sutta the 108 "currents of craving" (*taṇhāvicarita*) are elaborated.

1698. *Nirāmagandha* is the absence of *āmagandha*, "carrion," polluted food, on which see II,2. Where the Pāli has *brahmacariyaparāyaṇo*, "with the spiritual life as one's support," Mvu III 388,16 has *vṛkṣamūlaparāyaṇo*, "with the root of a tree as one's support."

1699. The thirty-eight meditation subjects differ from the forty subjects only in that the latter adds the light kasiṇa and the limited space kasiṇa. The suttas mention ten kasiṇas but the last two—the space kasiṇa and the consciousness kasiṇa—seem to be identical with the base of boundless space and the base of boundless consciousness, the first and second formless meditations. Hence the Vism adds two more to make an even forty.

1700. See note 183.

1701. Text has *upetaṃ atthasaṃhitaṃ*. Pj II glosses: *upetaṃ atthasaṃhitaṃ, atthupetaṃ dhammupetañca hitena ca saṃhitaṃ*. This seems to connect *upetaṃ* with both *attha* and *dhamma* and *saṃhitaṃ* with *hitena*. Pj II may be treating *atthasaṃhita* as a *dvanda* compound, which would be contrary to its normal usage, where it means "connected with meaning, beneficial," as in the standard description of right speech as *atthasaṃhita*, for example at MN I 180,4. The four noble truths, it is said at SN V 438,16, are taught because they are *atthasaṃhita*.

1702. Mvu III 389,9 has: *nirvāṇaṃ sākṣātkuryāya jānanto bahu bhāṣati*, "knowing, he speaks much for the realization of nirvāṇa."

1703. See the passage from Nidd I 131 at p. 1103. The same passage is at Paṭis II 195,1–7.

1704. The distinction in the Pāli is between *monaṃ arahati*, where *monaṃ* is identified with *moneyyapaṭipadā*, and *monaṃ ajjhagā*, where *monaṃ* is identified with *arahattamaggañāṇa*.

1705. The Mvu version does not have a concluding story but simply ends with the final verse.

1706. The story of Migāra's conversion is related in Dhp-a I 400–407 (see BL 2:70–75).

1707. See DPPN *mahālatā-pasādhana*. The story is at Dhp-a I 410–17 (see BL 2:77–82).

1708. The uposatha can fall on either the fourteenth or fifteenth day of the fortnight. On this occasion it fell on the fifteenth, which, as the text asserts, was a full-moon night.

1709. *Sattatiṃsabodhipakkhiyadhammā*. Pj II affixes *dhammā* to the expression to bring it into accord with the inquiry about *ye te kusalā dhammā*. I do not translate *dhammā* here because the first explanation signifies the thirty-seven factors themselves as *dhammā*, not teachings about them.

1710. Similar definitions, with minor differences, are found elsewhere. Sv III 883,29–31 offers a fivefold definition of *kusala*: "The wholesome should be understood as fivefold: in the sense of being healthy, blameless, originating from wholesomeness, being without distress, and having pleasant fruits" (*ārogyaṭṭhena, anavajjaṭṭhena, kosallasambhūtaṭṭhena, niddarathaṭṭhena, sukhavipākaṭṭhenāti pañcadhā kusalaṃ veditabbaṃ*).

1711. *Kā upanisā, kiṃ kāraṇaṃ, kiṃ payojanaṃ kimatthaṃ tumhe te dhamme suṇāthā ti vuttaṃ hoti*. Elsewhere *upanisā* is glossed as "cause" or "condition" (*sa-upanisan ti sakāraṇaṃ sappaccayaṃ*), as at Spk II 53,19–20; and still elsewhere, as "decisive-support condition" (*upanissayapaccaya*; see Vism 535–37, Ppn 17.80–84), as at Mp IV 162,7.

1712. *Yāvadeva dvayatānaṃ dhammānaṃ yathābhūtaṃ ñāṇāya.*
1713. *Yadetaṃ lokiyalokuttarādibhedena dvidhā vavatthitānaṃ dhammānaṃ vipassanāsaṅkhātaṃ yathābhūtañāṇaṃ.*
1714. *Kiñca dvayataṃ vadethā ti ettha pana sace, vo bhikkhave, siyā, kiñca tumhe, bhante, dvayataṃ vadethā ti ayamadhippāyo, padattho pana "kiñca dvayatābhāvaṃ vadethā" ti.* The purport (*adhippāya*) expands the bare phrase of the text to set it in context, while the term meaning (*padattha*) simply explains the meaning of the words without supplying the broader context. In this case it glosses *dvayataṃ* with *dvayatābhāvam.*
1715. Pj II refers here to the seven purifications, elaborated in Vism on the basis of MN 24. The third and fourth are respectively purification of view (by comprehending the specific characteristics of the five aggregates—see Vism chap. 18) and purification by overcoming doubt (by comprehending conditionality—see Vism chap. 19). The fifth is purification by knowledge and vision of what is the path and what is not the path (see Vism chap. 20).
1716. Pj II explains *sati vā upādisese* differently from the commentaries to the main Nikāyas. Thus Sv III 805,26–27 glosses *sati vā upādisese* at DN II 314,14 with *upādānasese vā sati aparikkhīṇe,* "if there is a residue of clinging that has not been exhausted" (so too Ps I 301,33 on MN I 62,36). Spk III 175,31 has *gahaṇasese upādānasese vijjamānamhi,* "if a residue of grasping, a residue of clinging, is found." These commentaries thus take *upādisesa* to signify the remainder of *subjective clinging* that still remains in the non-returner, while Pj II takes it to refer to the aggregates that a non-returner will acquire in the next existence. It-a I 169,14–18, it seems, combines both.
1717. *Pubbe vuttaṃ asamatthatāya anuggahetvā. Anuggahetvā* should be understood as the negative absolutive of *uggaṇhāti,* not as the positive absolutive of *anuggaṇhāti.*
1718. A similar but more concise explanation of the purpose of adding verses is at p. 883.
1719. *Sāsavakammapaccayā.* This is a narrow interpretation of *upadhi* that seems to miss the point. In commenting on the line *upadhīnidānā pabhavanti dukkhā* at **1050**c, Pj II offers a more satisfactory explanation of *upadhi* in a context similar to the present one: "The various sufferings such as birth and so forth originate based on acquisition such as craving and so forth" (*upadhinidānā pabhavanti dukkhā ti taṇhādiupadhinidānā jātiādidukkhavisesā pabhavanti*).
1720. Both Be and Ce include *vā;* Ee has it in parentheses. The first alternative takes *nirodha* to be the result of *virāga;* the second takes *virāga* and *nirodha* to be synonyms.
1721. *Dukkhassa jātippabhavānupassī ti vaṭṭadukkhassa jātikāraṇaṃ "upa-*

dhī" ti anupassanto. Pj II does not clarify the syntactical relationship between *jāti* and *pabhava.* The verse recurs at **1051**, but Niddesa comments only on *pabhavānupassī.* I take *jāti* and *pabhava* to function as a *dvanda* in which the two members are near-synonyms, joined by *anupassī* to create a complex *bahubbīhi.*

1722. *Bhavagāmikammasambhāra-avijjāpaccayā.* The syntactical relationship between the two major parts of this complex compound is not clear. Hence my resolution of the compound is conjectural.

1723. Pj II takes *jāti, maraṇa,* and *saṃsāra* as separate items, but I take *jātimaraṇasaṃsāraṃ* to mean "the wandering on in birth and death," or "the wandering on consisting of birth and death."

1724. I take *itthabhāvaññathābhāvaṃ* to be a complex *bahubbīhi* compound qualifying *jātimaraṇasaṃsāraṃ.*

1725. Pj II apparently takes *avijjāyeva* as resolvable into *avijjā-y-eva,* and thus explains *gati* as a condition (*paccayabhāvo*). It seems to me, however, that *avijjāyeva* should be resolved into *avijjāya eva,* that is, as the instrumental followed by *eva.*

1726. *Vijjāgatā ca ye sattā ti ye ca arahattamaggavijjāya kilese vijjhitvā gatā khīṇāsavasattā.* Apparently Pj II is trying to derive *vijjā* from the verb *vijjhati,* to pierce.

1727. *Puññāpuññāneñjābhisaṅkhārapaccayā.* For formal definitions of these terms, see Vibh 153–54 (§226).

1728. Be adds *asaṅkhatañca niccādito ñatvā,* "and having known the unconditioned to be permanent and so forth." This last phrase is not in Ce or Ee.

1729. *Kammasahajāta-abhisaṅkhāraviññāṇapaccayā*: This is mentioned because the discourse is exploring the origin of the suffering of saṃsāra, and it is the volitionally active consciousness, which creates kamma, that is responsible for producing a new existence within saṃsāra.

1730. That is, in the usual sequence of dependent origination, where name-and-form and the six sense bases come between consciousness and contact. In the Abhidhamma system only mental phenomena are comprised under the "association condition" (*sampayuttapaccaya*). Name-and-form is mentioned in §15, on the true and false (see **756–57**), while the six sense bases are implied by §16, on happiness and suffering (see **760–61**).

1731. Ee *eva honti* should be corrected to *eva na honti,* as in Be and Ce. Without *na* the statement becomes self-contradictory.

1732. This refers respectively to pleasant, painful, and neutral feeling. See MN I 303,3–6: *Sukhā kho, āvuso visākha, vedanā ṭhitisukhā vipariṇāmadukkhā; dukkhā vedanā ṭhitidukkhā vipariṇāmasukhā; adukkhamasukhā vedanā ñāṇasukhā aññāṇadukkhā.* ("Pleasant feeling, friend Visākha, is pleasant when it persists, painful when it changes. Painful feeling is painful when it persists, pleasant when it changes. Neither-painful-nor-pleasant feeling is pleasant with knowledge, painful without knowledge.")

1733. *Mosadhamman ti nassanadhammaṃ*. See note 1747.

1734. *Phussa phussā ti udayabbayañāṇena phusitvā phusitvā*. Pj II's explanation seems contrived. The expression *phussa phussa* can simply mean that one contemplates any feelings that occur through contact.

1735. Sn (Ee) has *evaṃ tattha virajjati*, as against Be and Ce *evaṃ tattha vijānāti*, which I follow. Both Norman and Jayawickrama translate from the Ee reading. All three editions of Pj II, however, have *vijānāti*, and the syntax of the explanation—*evaṃ tā vedanā vijānāti, tattha vā dukkhabhāvaṃ vijānāti*—with the object as accusative, indicates that this was the reading available to the commentator. The parallel verse at SN IV 205,5 has *virajjati*, which Spk III 74,24 confirms by putting the object in the locative plural: *evaṃ tāsu vedanāsu virajjati*.

1736. Though the subject of this section is clinging, by mentioning existence, birth, and death, the verses complete the sequence on dependent origination. Thus at this point the discourse has covered all the links of the usual sequence except name-and-form and the six sense bases.

1737. *Ārambhapaccayā ti kammasampayuttaviriyapaccayā*. Among the meanings of *ārambha* given in DOP, the ones relevant here are "undertaking, initial effort, exertion." Often *ārambha* is used in a commendable sense, as in the expression *viriyārambha*, "the arousing of energy," used to describe one who makes right effort. Here, however, it is used in a negative sense, perhaps to mean the initiation of actions motivated by greed, hatred, and delusion.

1738. Pj II does not comment on **746**c, where the editions vary between *vikkhīṇo jātisaṃsāro* and *vitiṇṇo jātisaṃsāro*. *Vikkhīṇo jātisaṃsāro* often occurs elsewhere and thus I take it as the established reading.

1739. *Sattā rūpūpagā, vedanūpagā, saññūpagā, saṅkhārūpagā*. This method of interpretation—which correlates the four types of nutriment with four of the five aggregates—seems to be unique to Pj II. I cannot find a parallel in any other commentary.

1740. See pp. 1269–70.

1741. *Iñjita* is the past participle of *iñjati*, "moves, stirs; is moved, is disturbed," functioning as a noun meaning "movement, agitation."

1742. *Ejaṃ vossajja*. For *ejā* (from *ejati*) DOP has "motion, disturbance, agitation, emotion." The connection with craving is supported by DN II 283,21, where Sakka, ruler of the devas, tells the Buddha: "Impulse, Bhante, is a disease, a boil, a dart. Impulse drags this person around toward the production of this or that state of existence" (*ejā, bhante, rogo, ejā gaṇḍo, ejā sallaṃ, ejā imaṃ purisaṃ parikaḍḍhati tassa tass'eva bhavassa abhinibbattiyā*).

1743. AN II 33,22–30: "When those devas who are long-lived, beautiful, abounding in happiness, dwelling for a long time in lofty palaces, hear the Tathāgata's teaching of the Dhamma, for the most part they are filled with fear, a sense of urgency, and terror thus: 'It seems that we are actually impermanent, though we thought ourselves permanent.'"

1744. Pj II explains text's *tadam* as a contraction of *taṃ idaṃ*.

1745. I read the sentence with Ce: *nikkilesasaṅkhātā subhabhāvā, dukkhapaṭipakkhasaṅkhātā sukhabhāvā, accantasantisaṅkhātā niccabhāvā ca anapagamanena paramatthato saccan ti yathābhūtaṃ sammappaññāya sudditthaṃ*.

1746. The text has *yena yena hi maññanti tato taṃ hoti aññathā*. The couplet is also at **588**, though in a different context. See too Ud 32, with *maññati*. Ud-a 209,26–210,7, commenting on the verse, says: "*In whatever way one conceives it*: When one asserts these five aggregates, which are an illness, to be a self or the belongings of a self, whatever people conceive through views, conceit, and craving *as the basis* for such assertions—form, feeling, and so forth—or whatever *the mode* in which people conceive them, as eternal and so forth, *it turns out otherwise*: the five aggregates that are the basis of the conceiving turn out otherwise than the way they are imagined by oneself; [in other words] they are not a self and not the belongings of a self. This means that because one cannot exercise mastery over them, they do not admit of 'I'-making and 'mine'-making."

1747. *Taṃ mosadhammaṃ nassanadhammaṃ hoti*. Since *mosadhamma* is glossed with *nassanadhamma*, it appears that Pj II takes *mosa* to signify impermanence. In this it follows Ps V 59,25, which has *mosadhamman ti nassanasabhāvaṃ* and *amosadhamman ti anassanasabhāvaṃ*. But *mosa*, according to PED, is the *guṇa* form of *musā*, false, which immediately precedes it. See too *mosavajjaṃ* at **819**d and **866**c, and *mosavajje* at **943**a, meaning false speech. Norman renders *mosadhamma* as "a false nature," and Jayawickrama as "a deluding element."

1748. *Tacapañcakamattaṃ*. See note 902.

1749. There is a word play here between *magā* and *maggā*. *Magā* (Skt *mṛgā*) means "animals" or "brutes," but *magga* (Skt *mārga*) is "path." Both words are from the same verb, *maggati* (Skt *mṛgyati, mṛgayate*), "to track, to hunt for, to seek," one being the object of the quest, the other the means to reach the object. Pj II offers two glosses on the line. The first (*magabhūtā janā . . . akovidā*), based on the reading *magā*, is likely to be the original. The second (*maggāmaggadhammassa . . . akovidā*), based on *maggā*, alludes to the fifth of the seven purifications, "knowledge and vision of what is the path and what is not the path" (*maggāmaggañāṇadassana*). I read with Be *saccadhammassa vā akovidā* as against Ce and Ee *sabbadhammassa vā akovidā*, "unskilled in the Dhamma of the all (or: in all phenomena)."

1750. *Māradheyyānupannehi*. *Anupanna* is past participle of *anupajjati*, "follows, accompanies, enters with" (DOP). The *sandhi* form here must be governed by the meter, as the gloss *tebhūmaka-vaṭṭaṃ anupannehi* indicates.

1751. The story is also at Dhp-a 284–85 (to Dhp 216); see BL 3:88–89. The origin story behind the parallel in the Chinese translation, *Arthapada no. 1 (Bapat 1951, 1–11), though much more elaborate, is basically similar.

1752. See Appendix 2 for a Skt version of the verses. Except for the last verse, the two are very similar.

1753. *Manāpiyarūpāditebhūmakadhammasaṅkhātaṃ vatthukāmaṃ*. Since agreeable sense objects are absent in the formless plane of existence it is odd that Pj II mentions "the three planes." Norman points out (GD 308) that the singular *kāmaṃ* in pāda a is "surprising," especially in view of the plural forms used in the following verses. He suggests this may be an example of a masculine accusative plural in *–aṃ*. The commentary on the rest of this verse offers little more than word glosses.

1754. *Nimmitā kāmā animmitā kāmā paranimmitā kāmā*. These terms, it seems, refer to the sensual pleasures conjured up according to wish by the beings in the fifth and sixth sense-sphere heavens.

1755. This elaborate gloss construes *kāmayānassa* as a *bahubbīhi* compound composed of *kāma* and *yāna*. The word is actually a present participle of the *–āna* type.

1756. Nine reasons are actually mentioned here. The passage mirrors SN IV 324,25–325,3, which mentions only eight. The additional factor in the above passage is "undear relatives take them."

1757. *Sabbaṃ lokaṃ visaritvā ṭhitattā loke visattikāsaṅkhātaṃ taṇhaṃ*. See note 1192.

1758. *Vikkhambhanato vā samucchedato vā*. The former is usually explained as the meditative absorptions, the latter as the world-transcending paths. The commentaries mention still another method, "abandoning in a particular respect" (*tad-aṅgappahāna*). This method would seem to be covered by reflections on the defects in sensual pleasures, but the Niddesa subsumes this method under "suppression." See pp. 363–64.

1759. The textual source for these similes is MN I 130–33, with elaborations at MN I 364–66.

1760. Niddesa mentions first the ten recollections, elaborated in Vism chaps. 7 and 8, followed by the eight meditative attainments (the four jhānas and the four formless attainments).

1761. Pj II (following Niddesa) reads the line in two ways: one—the common reading—with *abalā*, a nominative plural subject; the other with *abalaṃ*, an accusative singular object. The Skt parallel, Śag 40.5, has *abalaṃ vā balīyāṃso mṛdnaṃty enaṃ parisravāḥ*, with *abalaṃ* as accusative singular object: "Those more powerful crush the weakling or obstacles [crush] him." Norman (at GD 310) suggests that *abalā* here may mean women. While SED does include "a woman" as one meaning of feminine *abalā*, the line may not intend anything so specific but simply be a generalization about the weakness of those overcome by sensual desire.

1762. *Vikkhambhanasamucchedavasena*. "Suppression" by way of the jhānas, "eradication" by way of the world-transcending path.

1763. *Pāragū ti yopi pāraṃ gantukāmo sopi pāragū; yopi pāraṃ gacchati sopi pāragū; yopi pāraṃ gato, sopi pāragū*. Nidd I-a I 82,27–83,2: "One settled in insight knowledge who *wishes to go beyond* to nibbāna is called 'gone beyond' because he will certainly go there. By way of aspiration in the preliminary portion and by possession of insight, he too is said to have 'gone beyond.' One possessing the path who *is going beyond* to nibbāna is also said to have 'gone beyond.' And one who has completed the task by the path, who is settled in the fruit, and *has gone beyond* to nibbāna is said to have 'gone beyond.'"

1764. The story is also at Ja IV 375. The origin story behind Arthapada no. 2 (Bapat 1951, 16–17), though very different in details, also tells how King Udayana abused a meditating monk.

1765. I read with Ce and Ee here: *Kosambiyaṃ gaṅgātaṭe udakavanaṃ nāma udenassa uyyānaṃ*.

1766. All three editions read *bahunābhichanno*, which Pj II and Niddesa follow in their comments. I translate on the basis of this reading, but Ee notes a variant *bahunābhichando* in Burmese manuscripts. The Chinese (at T IV 176a24) reads 多所願, which, as Bapat notes (1951, 13), "supports the Pāli reading *bahunā'bhichando*."

1767. *Mohana*, as explained by the commentary, seems to be the objective basis or external manifestion of the internal state of *moha*, delusion.

1768. Pj II offers two ways of construing the verse. One takes the subject to be the objects of attachment, in which case *te duppamuñcā* means these objects are "hard to let go of" and *na hi aññamokkhā* that others cannot let go of them on one's behalf. The second takes the subject to be the beings who are attached to the objects, in which case *te duppamuñcā* means "they let go with difficulty," and *na hi aññamokkhā* that they cannot be freed by others. Niddesa also allows both construals. I have opted for the second, though the text itself can support either.

1769. Since there is no finite verb here, this verse and the next form a single unit of meaning, but for ease of comprehension I treat them as distinct. From the gloss it seems that Pj II takes *va* of the text to be a short form of *vā*.

1770. These explanations are based on different derivations of *avadāniyā*. See my note on *vadaññū*, note 1412.

1771. According to MN III 289–90, what should be fully understood are the five aggregates subject to clinging; what should be abandoned are ignorance and craving for existence; what should be developed are serenity and insight; and what should be realized are clear knowledge and liberation.

1772. These are free renderings guided by the explanations. The text reads: *ṭhitiparittatāya vā appakaṃ jīvitaṃ, sarasaparittatāya vā appakaṃ jīvitaṃ.*

1773. Several of these verses are quoted at Vism 238. See Ppn 8.39, which includes a long note on the verses.

1774. *Paññatti paramatthiyā.* The line is obscure. Normally, in the commentarial system, concepts (*paññātti*) and things that exist in the supreme sense (*paramattha*) are mutually opposed. Nidd I-a I 151,18 foll. gives two explanations. (1) *Paramatthiyā* is based on *paramā ṭhiti*, "supreme persistence," and the line means that there is no "supreme persistence" of beings because it is merely their name (a concept) that endures. (2) *Paramatthiyā* is based on *paramo attho*, "supreme meaning," and the line means that one is described as "dead" (a concept) on the basis of an actually existent phenomenon, the dissolution of the life faculty. I adopt the second alternative.

1775. Ee prints these lines as prose, while Be and Ce print them as verse. There are differences in the readings. I follow Ce, which has *bhaṅgabyā* in pāda b (as does Ee; Be has *gandhabbā*); *pabhāvitā* in pāda c (as does Ee; Be has *pabhāvikā*); and *pabhavakā* in pāda d (Be has *pabhāvikā*; Ee *pabhāvitā*). The *–m–* in *kadācimaddasuṃ*, according to Nidd I-a I 154,15, is a mere liaison consonant (*ma-kāro padasandhivasena vutto*).

1776. *Dhitisampannāti dhīrā. . . . Dhī vuccati paññā.*

1777. Norman (GD 142) explains *bhavābhava* as involving a rhythmical lengthening of the middle vowel, hence as resolvable into *bhava + bhava*, "existence after existence."

1778. I translate following Nidd I-a I 159,26–27, which takes *kammabhava* as the "round of kamma" (*kammavaṭṭa*) and *punabbhava* as "the round of results" (*vipākavaṭṭa*). "Kamma existence" is thus the activity that creates the kamma leading to a new existence in the future, while "renewed existence" (or "rebirth existence," *upapattibhava*) is the life experience (including rebirth itself) resulting from past kamma. On this distinction, see Vism 571–72, Ppn 17.250–53.

1779. On the 108 currents of craving and these sets of views, see Appendix 3.

1780. The six bases (*vatthu*), the physical bases of mental processes, are the eye, ear, nose, tongue, body, and heart; the six doors (*dvāra*), the media through which the mind gains access to objects, are the eye, ear, nose, tongue, body, and the mind-door; the six objects (*ārammaṇa*) are forms, sounds, odors, tastes, tactile objects, and mental phenomena. On the distinction between bases and doors, see CMA 144–45.

1781. See **1042** and AN III 399–402, where six bhikkhus offer their own interpretations of the two ends.

1782. *Nirupādāno jātavedo'va parinibbāti*. The simile plays upon the double meaning of *upādāna* and *parinibbāti*: of *upādāna* as the sustenance of a fire (its fuel) and as clinging (to the five aggregates); and of *parinibbāti* as "goes out" (of a fire) and "attains nibbāna" (of an arahant).

1783. See AN I 273. "Sagacity" renders *moneyya*. I think "sagacity" works better here than "munihood," my usual rendering of *moneyya*.

1784. See MN I 302,1–5, where it is said that the bodily activity (*kāyasaṅkhāra*), as in-and-out breathing, ceases in the fourth jhāna; the verbal activity (*vacīsaṅkhāra*), as thought and examination, ceases in the first jhāna; and the mental activity (*citta-saṅkhāra*), as perception and feeling, ceases with the attainment of the cessation of perception and feeling.

1785. *Pariggaha*, it seems, can refer to either the object possessed or the subjective act of taking possession. As a consequence of desire, the subjective acts of taking possession are likely intended. At AN IV 400,27 both aspects of *pariggaha* fit the context: "In dependence on attachment there is possession; in dependence on possession there is miserliness" (*ajjhosānaṃ paṭicca pariggaho, pariggahaṃ paṭicca macchariyaṃ*).

1786. *Brahmabhūtena attanā viharati*. This may be an allusion to the Upanishads, which proclaim the identity of the *ātman* with *brahman*. But since the idea of a neuter impersonal *brahman* seems to be absent in the Nikāyas, *brahma* here may simply have the sense of "holy," as in *brahmacariya*, without reference to the Upanishads.

1787. This refers to the story of Ciñcā, who also defamed the Buddha. See p. 657.

1788. The story of Sundarī is at Ud 43–45 and Dhp-a III 474–78 (see BL 3:189–91). A connection between the story and the theme of this sutta is not apparent in the discourse itself. Yet Niddesa also alludes to this incident in its exegesis, and the Arthapada (see Bapat 1951, 22–30) says this discourse originated from the commotion set off by the murder of Sundarī. Thus, even if the Sundarī incident was not the actual historical origin of this sutta, the tradition connecting the two must be very old, likely preceding the division of the schools.

1789. *Yaṃkiñcideva bhaṇati.* According to Ud-a 259,2–3 she replied: "I am coming back after spending the night pleasuring the ascetic Gotama alone in his Fragrant Cottage." See too Dhp-a III 475,12–13.

1790. Contrary to the Pāli commentaries, the Chinese text apparently takes the expression corresponding to *saccamanā vadanti* in a positive sense. The first couplet (at T IV 177b28) might be rendered: "Those with hostile minds speak of the other's faults, while those whose minds have understood the truth say what is good" (邪念說彼短, 解意諦說善).

1791. This evidently alludes to the attempt by the sectarians to blame the Buddha for the murder of Sundarī. Niddesa mentions Sundarī in its comment on **781**a: "How could one transcend one's own view?"

1792. Here and just below the orthography of Be should be corrected to follow Ce: ". . . *pātukaroti akārako'mhī ti.*"

1793. See Appendix 3.

1794. The full verse occurs in Sn as **661**, but in relation to the present origin story it is also found at Ud 45,10.

1795. This comment on the line shows that the tradition connecting the sutta with the murder of Sundarī goes back as far as the Niddesa. It is strange, however, that the sectarians are criticized here not for committing murder but for being attached to their view, certainly a minor fault compared to instigating murder. This, in my view, casts suspicion on a connection between the story and the sutta.

1796. *Ātumānaṃ* is an alternative formation of the accusative of *attan*, represented by *attānaṃ* in the paraphrase. Pj II glosses *pāvā* with the present indicative *vadati*, Niddesa with *pāvadati*. Norman (at GD 315) proposes, on a suggestion from Richard Gombrich, that "it would probably be best to take it as the imperfect of *pra + vac*, which would be *prāvak*(*t*)."

1797. On the meaning of these practices, see Vism 60–61, Ppn 2.4–11. The passage is not saying that the austere practices and the undertaking of energy are bad behavior. The point, rather, is that in the technical sense these are classified under *vata* but not under *sīla*.

1798. *Taṃ nissito kuppapaṭiccasantiṃ*. *Kuppa* is the opposite of *akuppa*, which occurs in the expression *akuppā cetovimutti*, "unshakable liberation of mind," a designation of arahantship (see MN I 298,11–25). See too Th 364: *sacchikatvā akuppataṃ, pappuyya paramaṃ santiṃ*, "having realized the unshakable, one may attain supreme peace." The expression *kuppapaṭiccasanti* is unusual—Bapat calls it "curious"—and I suspect it results from textual corruption. Since the word *kappa* plays such an important role in this chapter, perhaps *kappa–* had been corrupted by a transmission error to *kuppa–*. The parallel verse of the Arthapada (T IV 177c12) has nothing corresponding to this but reads: 自見行無邪漏，不著想何瞋憙. This has a straightforward meaning: "He sees that his own conduct has no evil influxes. For one unattached to perceptions, how can there be aversion or joy?"

1799. *Idaṃsaccābhinivesa*. The dogmatic insistence on a speculative view as truth.

1800. These are ascetic practices observed in the Buddha's time. By the first three one imitates the manner of a goat, a cow, or a dog (see MN I 387–88); the next is sitting in the midst of four fires at midday with the sun overhead; the "rocky precipice" may be standing or sitting at the edge of a precipice; the squatter's exertion is remaining in the squatting position; and the last, obviously, is sleeping on thorns.

1801. While out of context *niccheyya* may be either an absolutive or an optative, the list of synonyms—*nicchinitvā vinicchinitvā vicinitvā*, etc.—makes it clear that here it should be taken as an absolutive.

1802. *Dhona* is probably the past participle of *dhovati*, "to wash." It can function as a personal noun *dhona*, "one who is cleansed," and as feminine, the noun *dhonā*, "cleansing," which Niddesa identifies with *paññā*. The commentaries, however, derive *dhona* from *dhunāti*, "to shake off," and hence as synonymous with the past participle, *dhuta*, "shaken off." The austere practices, *dhutaṅga*, are thus taken to be means of "shaking off" defilements.

1803. I follow Norman here in taking *upeti vādaṃ* to refer to disputes or debates. See PED *vāda*[3]: "discussion, disputation, argument, controversy." Niddesa and Pj II, however, seem to take the couplet to be saying that it is impossible to describe the arahant, "one uninvolved." The disjunction between my translation and their comments becomes especially apparent in relation to the next line.

1804. *Attaṃ nirattaṃ na hi tassa atthi*. There is a word play in both Pj II and Niddesa. It is uncertain whether such a pun is intended by Sn itself. *Atta* (< *ātta*) is the past participle, masculine plural, of *ādiyati*, "to take up," and *niratta* the past participle of *nirassati*, "to reject, to cast away, to dismiss." Hence the original sense of the line is: "For him there is nothing taken up or rejected." This is confirmed by **785**d, which describes one attached to views thus: *nirassatī ādiyatī ca dhammaṃ*, "he rejects and takes up a teaching." But by a phonetic coincidence, *atta* is a homonym of the word meaning "self" (Skt *ātmā*) and *niratta*, as the negation of this, suggests the denial of self (along the lines of annihilationists, who repudiated personal survival of death). Hence the commentaries read into the dichotomy of *atta* and *niratta* the contrast between affirmation of a self (the eternalist view) and repudiation of a self (the annihilationist view). See in this connection MN I 8,17–18, where both the affirmation "I have a self" and the denial "I have no self" are said to be views that appear to be true and accurate (*atthi me attā ti vā'ssa saccato thetato diṭṭhi uppajjati; natthi me attā ti vā'ssa saccato thetato diṭṭhi uppajjati*).

1805. See Dhp-a IV 187–89 (BL 3:304–5).

1806. Two *hatthas* are roughly half a meter, hence forty meters.

1807. *Tacapañcakakammaṭṭhānaṃ ācikkhi*. See note 902.

1808. The background story in the Arthapada Sūtra (Bapat 1951, 34), though different in details, suggests a common origin. A certain brahmin student named Māgha had died. His fellow students put his body on a couch and placed it at the crossroads outside Sāvatthī, telling people: "Those who saw Māgha will all attain liberation. Those who now see his corpse will also attain liberation. Later, those who hear his name will also gain liberation." The monks heard about this during their alms round and reported it to the Buddha, who spoke the discourse.

1809. Apparently the expressions *suddhaṃ paramaṃ arogaṃ* refer to the *attā*, the self, regarded as eternal and immutable. See the statements of eternalism at DN I 31, beginning *rūpī attā hoti arogo paraṃ maraṇā saññī ti naṃ paññapenti* (translation in Bodhi 2007b: 76–77). Sv I 119,9 glosses *arogo* with *nicco*, "permanent." Similar declarations are made about the self at MN II 228–29. Ps IV 16,18, commenting on this passage, also glosses *arogo* with *nicco*.

1810. Reading *cakkhuviññāṇena* with Ce, and so too in all repetitions of this phrase below.

1811. *Cakkhuviññāṇaṃ*. I assume the correct reading should be *cakkhuviññāṇena*.

1812. *Diṭṭhī hi naṃ pāva tathā vadānaṃ*. On *pāva*, see note 1796. *Vadānaṃ* is the accusative singular of a reflexive present participle of the *–āna* type. I believe the gloss, *vadanti*, in all three editions of PJ II should be corrected to *vadantaṃ*, as suggested in a note in Pj II (Ee).

1813. On the triad, *diṭṭha-suta-muta*, see pp. 142–43. Since *diṭṭhe*, etc., are locatives, Pj II interprets them as objects of wrong knowledge. It is likely, however, that these are truncated instrumentals, and I translate them as such in the text. While Pj II follows Niddesa in taking the past participles to refer to objects of the different senses, it is possible that *diṭṭha* was originally intended in the sense of a view (*diṭṭhi*), *suta* in the sense of learning (*suti*), and *muta* in the sense of thought or knowledge. At **839**a, we find *na diṭṭhiyā na sutiyā na ñāṇena*, "not by view, nor by learning, nor by knowledge."

1814. The comment, following Niddesa, explains *attañjaha* on the basis of *atta* as both "self" and the past participle of *ādiyati*. See note 1804.

1815. Niddesa gives examples of each belief, which I omit here. They are mentioned at pp. 735–37.

1816. *Anibbāhakabhāvaṃ*. See PED sv *nibbāhati*, "to lead out, carry out, save from." Some manuscripts cited in Ee have *anibbānavāhakabhāvaṃ*, "a nature not leading to nibbāna."

1817. Pāda c of the stanza reads: *vidvā ca vedehi samecca dhammaṃ.* By its gloss of *vedehi* with *catūhi maggañāṇavedehi*, Pj II again appears to be reconceptualizing the four Vedas of the brahmins with knowledge as understood by the Buddha. See too p. 923 and note 1476.

1818. Apparently these were ascetic and devotional observances.

1819. The same list of doctrinal principles was cited in connection with the enlightenment of a paccekabuddha; see note 405. In relation to the present passage Nidd I-a I 229–30 comments: "*These things should be directly known* (*abhiññeyyā*): the phenomena of the three planes (the desire realm, form realm, formless realm), which should be known in their specific nature or by the superior knowledge illuminating them by comprehension of their specific characteristics. *These things should be fully understood* (*pariññeyya*): things to be known by comprehension of their general characteristics (impermanence, suffering, non-self) and to be known pervasively by completion of the task." This explanation connects *abhijānāti* here with *nāmarūpavavatthāna* and *paccayapariggaha*, the subjects of Vism chaps. 18 and 19 respectively, and *parijānāti* with the knowledges from *sammasanañāṇa* on up, discussed in Vism chap. 20 and following.

1820. *Tesu sabbadhammesu mārasenaṃ vināsetvā ṭhitabhāvena visenibhūto*. There is a word play here by which *visenibhūta* ("apart from the crowd") is derived from *vināsetvā*, "having destroyed," and *senā*, "army" (of Māra), thus as the absence (*vi–*) of the army (*senā*).

1821. There is an ambiguity in the Niddesa here, since the subject of the verb in **793**d, *kenīdha lokasmi vikappayeyya*, is evidently not the muni himself, who is the object described by the accusative forms in **793**c, *tameva dassiṃ vivaṭaṃ carantaṃ*. Yet Niddesa's explanation states that because the muni has abandoned the two kinds of *kappa*, someone else cannot conceive or categorize him (*vikappayeyya*). Nidd I-a I 233,1–2 indicates that this is indeed the intended meaning: *idha loke taṇhākappena vā diṭṭhikappena vā koci vikappeyya*.

1822. I translate here from Ee. Be may make better sense: *paramattha-accantasuddhi-adhigatattā anaccantasuddhiṃyeva akiriyasassata-diṭṭhiṃ accantasuddhī ti na te vadanti*. ("Because they have achieved supreme ultimate purity, they do not assert the view of non-doing or eternalism, which is not ultimate purity, to be ultimate purity.")

1823. This is an allusion to the doctrine of "purification through saṃsāra" (*saṃsārasuddhi*), ascribed to Makkhali Gosāla at DN I 53–54. According to this view, migration in saṃsāra has a fixed limit, so "both the foolish and the wise, having roamed and wandered [for a fixed time], will make an end to suffering." At DN I 52–53 Pūraṇa Kassapa advocates the doctrine of not-doing (*akiriya*), which holds that there is no such thing as evil deeds and meritorious deeds.

1824. The four, as explained by Niddesa just below, are the clusters of defilements to be eradicated by the four world-transcending paths.

1825. *So ca kāmarāgābhāvato na rāgarāgī, rūpārūparāgābhāvato na virāgaratto*. The text, **795**c, reads *na rāgarāgī na virāgaratto*. This appears to present a paradox. Dispassion (*virāga*) is often held up as the ideal; in several suttas it is explicitly identified with nibbāna (AN II 34,26, It 88,6). Yet here the practitioner is extolled as one who is not attached to it. Pj II and Niddesa offer their own solutions to the paradox. A simpler explanation, consonant with Pj II on **813**d, would simply be that, having attained dispassion, there is no way he could become attached to it.

1826. *Yato evaṃvidhassa idaṃ paran ti kiñci idha uggahitaṃ natthī ti*. The text, **795**d, reads: *tass'īdha natthī paramuggahītaṃ*. The gloss in Niddesa suggests that *paramuggahītaṃ* should be resolved *paraman ti uggahītam*, "grasped as supreme." This seems to differ from the paraphrase in Pj II. I prefer the Niddesa explanation, which refers back to *paramaṃ* in the opening line of the sutta.

1827. This parable of the blind men and the elephant is also at Ud 68–69.

1828. *Api ca kho pana asañjātaṃ uparūpari diṭṭhimpi lokasmiṃ na kappayeyya*. The idea, it seems, is that one should not create new views that add to those already in circulation.
1829. *Samāpattiñāṇādinā ñāṇena*. This may have been said as a precaution because the Buddha himself formulated his Dhamma on the basis of knowledge—knowledge of the four noble truths, dependent origination, etc. Thus here the commentary is cautioning against views based on misinterpreted meditative experience, perhaps with an oblique allusion to the Buddha's first meditation teachers, who based their teachings on the third and fourth formless attainments, respectively.
1830. There is an allusion here to the four "wrong motives" (*agati*) for taking a course of action (at AN II 18): desire, aversion, delusion, and fear.
1831. *Attaṃ pahāyā ti attadiṭṭhiṃ pahāya. Attaṃ pahāyā ti attagāhaṃ pahāya*. This comment on the line construes *attaṃ*, actually a past participle of *ādiyati*, "to take," as the accusative of *attā*, "self." See note 1804.
1832. *Attaṃ pahāyā ti taṇhāvasena diṭṭhivasena gahitaṃ parāmaṭṭhaṃ abhiniviṭṭhaṃ ajjhositaṃ adhimuttaṃ pahāya*. This comment, which employs a chain of synonyms meaning "grasped," is presumably based on the more literal understanding of *attaṃ* as the past participle of *ādiyati*.
1833. Niddesa (Be) has *ñāṇena* in its citation of the lemma and in the explanations to follow, as against *ñāṇe* in Sn, Pj II, and Niddesa (Ce and Ee). I follow the latter.
1834. Reading with Ee *saññādhipateyyatā*, as against Be *saññāvikappayeyyatā*, Ce *saññāvikappayatā*.
1835. Pj II may here be trying to exclude the Buddha's teachings from the class of things that should not be "embraced" (*paṭicchitāse*). But see MN I 260–61: "Bhikkhus, purified and bright as this view is, if you adhere to it, cherish it, treasure it, and appropriate it, would you understand that the Dhamma has been taught as like a raft, for the purpose of crossing over, not for the purpose of grasping?"
1836. See pp. 59–60.
1837. On these types of craving and views, see Appendix 3.
1838. See too Dhp-a III 317–20 (BL 3:108–10).
1839. The attainment of complete nibbāna by laypeople is extremely rare in the canonical texts. It is recorded only of those ready to enter monastic life or of those on the verge of death.
1840. The background story in the Arthapada Sūtra (Bapat 1951, 50) is quite different. It tells of a brahmin who died at the age of 120 and a child who died at the age of seven. The families of both performed the funeral ceremonies on the same day and in the same manner, prompting the Buddha to speak these verses.

1841. Niddesa here repeats its explanation of the line "for the wise say this life is short" in **775**.

1842. *Jarasāpi miyyatī ti jarāyapi miyyati. Jarasā* is an instrumental based on Vedic *jaras*. Pj II glosses it with the feminine instrumental *jarāya*.

1843. *Vinābhāvaṃ santamev'idan ti. Nānābhāve vinābhāve aññathābhāve sante saṃvijjamāne upalabbhiyamāne*. Norman (GD 324) suggests *vinābhāvaṃ santam* may be an accusative absolute construction.

1844. *Māmako*. The word is based on *mama*, "mine," implying "one who belongs to me" or "one who takes as 'mine.'" I follow the commentary and render it as "my follower." Norman renders it "one of my followers." There are no significant comments on **807**.

1845. *Sāmaggiyamāhu tassa taṃ, yo attānaṃ bhavane na dassaye. Sāmaggi* usually means "concord, harmony," but Pj II here glosses it with *patirūpam*. The explanation by Pj II and Niddesa seems to construe *bhavana* as equivalent to *bhava*, but this may be reading too much into the line. I take the original sense of this couplet to be simply that he should not dwell in a fixed residence but should instead adopt the life of homeless wandering. The verse should hang together, and thus I see the first couplet as determining the meaning of the second. The Chinese at T IV 179a16 is more straightforward: 欲行止意觀意，已垂諦無止處: "If he wishes to cultivate serenity and insight, being inclined to truth, he should not settle in a fixed place." See Bapat 1951, 52.

1846. See note 1825.

1847. The text reads *yadidaṃ diṭṭhasutaṃ mutesu vā*. I understand the difference in the cases to be determined by the meter and thus I do not treat the three terms as syntactically different. Niddesa joins them into a *dvanda* compound: *diṭṭhasutamutesu*.

1848. *Na hi so rajjati no virajjati*. See note 1825.

1849. This syntactical pattern of conceiving (*maññanā*) forms the framework of MN 1, the Mūlapariyāya Sutta, which includes the seen, heard, sensed, and cognized among the twenty-four bases of conceiving.

1850. *Tissametteyyā nāma dve sahāyā sāvatthiṃ āgamaṃsu*. Pj II takes *Tissametteyya* to be a *dvanda* compound, names of two different people, yet the sutta itself uses the singular, *āyasmā Tisso Metteyyo*, which treats these as two names of one person. Niddesa explains Tissa as the elder's personal name (*tassa therassa nāmaṃ*) and Metteyya as the elder's clan (*tassa therassa gottaṃ*). Pj II, however, construes even this statement in a way that supports its background story. DPPN also seems perplexed about the names, listing Tissa (8) as "the personal name of Metteyya, friend of Tissa (7)," so that one friend is named Tissa and the other Tissa Metteyya. It is more likely that here a single name has been severed to fit a traditional background story. The Pārāyanavagga has a Tissa Metteyya, a disciple of Bāvari, but he seems to be a different person. The background story to the Arthapada parallel is completely different.

1851. The explanation devolves on the synonymity of *ubhaya*, "both," and *mithu*, "a pair, a couple." It is from the latter that *methuna* is derived.

1852. I read with Ce *bhaggakaṇṭako ti*. Nidd I-a I 211: "The 'thorn' is defilements in the sense of piercing" (*kaṇṭako ti vinivijjhanaṭṭhena kilesā eva*).

1853. *Vimokkhantikametaṃ buddhānaṃ bhagavantānaṃ bodhiyā mūle saha sabbaññutaññāṇassa paṭilābhā sacchikā paññatti yadidaṃ bhagavā ti*. Nidd I-a I 213: "*The end of emancipation*: The path of arahantship is emancipation; the fruit of arahantship is the 'end of emancipation.' A name pertaining to the end of emancipation is one that occurs with the occurrence of the end of emancipation. Omniscience is *being* accomplished by the path of arahantship; it *has been* accomplished with the achievement of the fruit of arahantship. Therefore omniscience occurs at the end of emancipation. A name indicative of that is one pertaining to the end of emancipation. *A designation accruing to the buddhas, the blessed ones, along with realization, with the obtaining of the omniscient knowledge at the foot of the bodhi tree*: A designation arisen with the realization of the fruit of arahantship or with the realization of all phenomena, together with the obtaining of omniscient knowledge at the aforesaid moment at the foot of the great bodhi tree." See too note 1514.

1854. The distinction is between *pariyattisāsana* and *paṭipattisāsana*.

1855. *Suttaṃ, geyyaṃ, veyyākaraṇaṃ, gāthā, udānaṃ, itivuttakaṃ, jātakaṃ, abbhutadhammaṃ, vedallaṃ*. This is the early ninefold division of the Dhamma.

1856. Reading with Ee *attabhañjanena* as against Be and Ce *atthabhañjanena*, "by injuring what is beneficial." Niddesa supports Ee in its elaboration of the simile: *niraye attānaṃ bhañjati*.

1857. *Puthu kilese janentī ti puthujjanā*. Word plays are involved here that are hard to replicate in English.

1858. *Tāsu satthānī ti kāyaduccaritādīni. Tāni hi attano paresañca chedanaṭṭhena satthānī ti vuccanti*. The use of *satthāni* in this sense, and the explanation, seem contrived relative to the context, but it is hard to propose an alternative. The Chinese parallel (at T IV 179b23) has 漏戒懷恐怖, which seems to mean "one of corrupt behavior harbors fear (or danger)." Bapat renders the line thus: "A man with leaky conduct bristles with dangers."

1859. *Mahāgedho ti mahābandhanaṃ*. This *gedha* should be

distinguished from *gedha* meaning "greed." *Gedha* in this sense is at AN I 154,1. See too DOP *gedha*²: "thick, dense, entangled, or a thicket." Niddesa makes the sense clear with its synonyms: *mahāvanaṃ mahāgahanaṃ mahākantāro*, etc.

1860. *Svāssa* (< *so assa*) *musāvādajjhogāho mahāgedho ti veditabbo.* The gloss replaces the rare *mosavajja* with the more familiar *musāvāda*.

1861. This is the stock canonical definition of false speech.

1862. The list of punishments follows MN I 87,9–20, AN I 47–48, etc.

1863. Though much shorter, the background story in the Arthapada Sūtra (Bapat 1951, 62–63) centers around a debate. A boastful sophist claims that he can defeat the Buddha in debate. When the Buddha arrives in town, the sophist comes out to debate the Buddha, but when he sees the Buddha's spiritual power he is overcome by dread and cannot utter a word. The Buddha then speaks this discourse. In a note, Bapat writes: "The Sanskrit version of the sūtra, says Hoernle, is a translation of some Prakrit original, which differs from the Pāli version, and the order of Sn verses 825-827 is not followed in the same. The portions found in it are very fragmentary and correspond to only fragments of the Pāli stanzas."

1864. DPPN describes him as "an Elder who possessed the knack of saying 'the wrong thing.'" He is censured by the Buddha at MN III 208,28–31, AN III 322–23, and elsewhere.

1865. *Abhājanabhūto*. At Mp II 186,31 and Mp III 16,19 the word occurs as a gloss on *abhabbo*, meaning "incapable." *Mukhabandha* (or *mukhabandhana*), "binding of the mouth," occurs elsewhere in the commentaries, for instance, at Sv I 97,1–2 in connection with a mantra: *Hanusaṃhananan ti mukhabandhamantena yathā hanukaṃ cāletuṃ na sakkonti, evaṃ bandhakaraṇaṃ*. ("*Lockjaw* is using the mouth-binding mantra to prevent people from being able to move their jaw, thus binding it.")

1866. The Niddesa offers two derivations of the rare word *kathojja*, defined by DOP as "discussion, dispute." It is derived from *kathā* + *ujja*; the latter is equivalent to Skt *udya*, from the root *vad*, to speak. The first derivation is straightforward, using a string of synonyms: *Kathojjaṃ vuccati kalaho bhaṇḍanaṃ viggaho vivādo medhagaṃ*. The alternative explanation, *anojavantī sā kathā kaṭhojjaṃ vadanti*, relates the suffix *–ojjaṃ* to *ojā*, nourishment.

1867. Pj II paraphrases *na h'aññadatth'atthi pasaṃsalābhā* as *na hi ettha pasaṃsalābhato añño attho atthi*. Thus *aññadatth–* here is not *aññadatthu* with the last vowel elided, but *añño attho*, with *–d–* as a liaison consonant. Norman also points out that *kathojjaṃ* after *virame* is an instance of the ablative in *–aṃ*.

1868. The explanation in Pj II, *tuṭṭhiṃ vā dantavidaṃsakaṃ vā āpajjanto hasati,* and just below in Niddesa, *so tena jayatthena tuṭṭho hoti haṭṭho pahaṭṭho attamano paripuṇṇasaṅkappo, atha vā dantavidaṃsakaṃ hasamāno,* shows that the verb *hassati* (in text) was considered ambiguous, taken to represent either Skt *harṣati,* "to rejoice, to exult," or Skt *hasati,* "to laugh." I give precedence to the former. Norman has "he laughs," Jayawickrama, "he rejoices," and Paññobhāsa, "he is mirthful."

1869. *Yā unnatī sā'ssa vighātabhūmī ti.* Unfortunately neither Pj II nor Niddesa offers more than word glosses on this interesting statement, which corresponds to the familiar adage: "Pride goeth before a fall."

1870. The line—*pubbeva natthi yadidaṃ yudhāya*—is obscure. I am not sure that Pj II and Niddesa have caught the original intention. Literally the words mean: "In the past indeed there was not this which is for a fight." Norman renders it: "Already indeed there is nothing [left] to fight against [here]." Jayawickrama has: "for nought exists herein to combat as of yore" (taking *va* as standing for *iva* rather than *eva*). Paññobhāsa has: "The one for battle has never been here." The Arthapada parallel lacks a counterpart to this line.

1871. On this verse, Pj II merely offers the word gloss, *paṭisenikattā ti paṭilomakārako,* which construes *paṭisenikattā* as the nominative singular of the agent noun. Niddesa, just below, apparently takes *paṭisenikattā* as a plural, connecting it with the plural verb *kareyyuṃ.* Pj II, however, is more likely to be historically correct.

1872. See note 1826.

1873. *Sabbe dhammā sabbākārena buddhassa bhagavato ñāṇamukhe āpāthaṃ āgacchanti.* Although in the Nikāyas there are hints that the Buddha is omniscient in a qualified sense (see AN II 25,1–4), this statement exceeds anything that can be found in the more archaic texts.

1874. It seems that in this passage the word *attha* is being used in two senses, as "good, benefit" and as "meaning." I thus render it differently in different expressions. The distinction between an implicit discourse, whose meaning needs to be interpreted, and one of explicit meaning (*neyyo attho* and *nīto attho*), traceable to AN I 60,18–20, was to become a major theme in Buddhist hermeneutics.

1875. The same passage is at Paṭis II 195–96. As the Niddesa is considered older than Paṭis, it is likely the latter adopted it from the Niddesa, unless both received it from a common source.

1876. The story is also at Dhp-a I 199–202 (BL 1:274–76) and Dhp-a III 193–97 (BL 3:31–35). The Arthapada parallel, no. 9, relates the same origin story, with the brahmin named Mākandika (see Bapat 1951, 68–72). Bapat refers to fragments of a surviving Skt version of this sūtra edited by Hoernle (in JRAS 1916, 709–32). There is a parallel to the story of the Buddha's meeting with Māgandiya (there also called Mākandika) at Divyāvadāna 515–21 (story no. 36).

1877. The Pāli here reads: *rattassa hi ukkuṭikaṃ padaṃ bhave, duṭṭhassa hoti anukaḍḍhitaṃ padaṃ; mūḷhassa hoti sahasānupīḷitaṃ; vivattacchaddassa idam īdisaṃ padaṃ*. The verse occurs with this reading at Mp I 436 and Vism 105, accompanied by an explanation. Vism-mhṭ I 118 explains "arched" as "without contact in the middle" (*ukkuṭikan ti asamphuṭṭhamajjhaṃ*). Dhp-a I 201 and Dhp-a III 195 offer a different reading, according to which the forceful footprints are ascribed to the hating type and the dragged footprints to the deluded type: *duṭṭhassa hoti sahasānupīḷitaṃ, mūḷhassa hoti avakaḍḍhitaṃ padaṃ*. Though I translate from Pj II, the reading in Dhp-a seems to match the two character types better. The Arthapada, at 180a26–27, has 婬人曳踵行，恚者斂指步，癡人足踝地，是跡天人尊. According to Bapat (1951, p. 71, note 6), the Skt fragment supports this reading. Divyāvadāna has still another reading: *raktasya puṃsaḥ padamutpaṭaṃ syān nipīḍitaṃ dveṣavataḥ padaṃ ca; padaṃ hi mūḍhasya visṛṣṭadehaṃ suvītarāgasya padaṃ tvihedṛśam*.

1878. *Udakūpasaṭṭhaṃ*. Literally "sprinkled with water," the rite of marriage. Be lacks this expression.

1879. The incident is recorded at SN I 124, where it is situated one year after the Buddha's enlightenment. However, Ja I 78–79 and Dhp-a III 195–96 assign the encounter to *the fifth week* after the enlightenment. This seems more cogent, given that the encounter is said to have occurred at the foot of the goatherd's banyan tree (*ajapālanigrodhamūle*). All other texts that speak of the Buddha as dwelling at this site place his sojourn there soon after the enlightenment (*paṭhamābhisambuddho*); see DN II 267,22–23, SN V 167,5–6, SN V 185,4–6, SN V 232,15–16, Ud 3,7–8, and Vin I 2,29. No texts speak of him as ever returning to this place at a later time.

1880. Both lines must be speaking of Māgandiya's daughter, the first metaphorically, the second literally.

1881. Norman translates "What sort of view, life lived *according to* virtuous conduct and vows," apparently to capture the nuance of the Ce and Ee reading *diṭṭhigataṃ sīlavatānujīvitaṃ*. Be has *diṭṭhigataṃ sīlavataṃ nu jīvitaṃ*. I follow Niddesa and Pj II, both of which treat the line as a series of parallel terms: *diṭṭhiñca sīlañca vatañca jīvitañca*.

1882. Neither Pj II nor Niddesa resolves *bhavūpapattiṃ*, but I take it to be a *dvanda*. Often in the Niddesas, we find *upapat-*

tiṃ and *bhavaṃ* juxtaposed in a series of near-synonyms, for instance, at Nidd I 70: *gatiṃ . . . upapattiṃ . . . paṭisandhiṃ . . . bhavaṃ . . . saṃsāravaṭṭaṃ ādiyanti;* and Nidd I 227–28: *kiṃ gatiṃ . . . kiṃ upapattiṃ . . . kiṃ paṭisandhiṃ . . . kiṃ bhavaṃ . . . kiṃ saṃsāraṃ . . . kiṃ vaṭṭaṃ upeyya upagaccheyya gaṇheyya parāmaseyya abhiniveseyyā ti – anūpayo so upayaṃ kimeyya.*

1883. I translate the Niddesa passage as it has come down, but it looks as if the passage merges its comment on the following verse with this one. It does not have a separate exegesis of the next verse—the only omission in the entire work.

1884. The former gloss takes *anuggahāya* as an absolutive, the alternative as an optative participle.

1885. *Yānī'māni diṭṭhigatāni tehi tehi sattehi vinicchinitvā gahitattā vinicchayā ti ca attano paccayehi abhisaṅkhatabhāvādinā nayena pakappitāni cā ti vuccanti.* It seems this explanation interprets *pakappitāni* by establishing *kappita* and *abhisaṅkhata* as synonyms and explicating the prefix *pa–* by *paccaya.*

1886. *Suddhimāhā ti ettha vuttaṃ āha-saddaṃ sabbattha nakārena saddhiṃ yojetvā purisavyattayaṃ katvā "diṭṭhiyā suddhiṃ nāhaṃ kathemī' ti evamattho veditabbo. Yathā c'ettha, evaṃ uttarapadesupi.* In the Pāli the negative *na* is widely separated from the verb *āha,* hence Pj II points out that they should be conjoined. "Making a change of persons" (*purisabyattayaṃ katvā*) is said to indicate that the verb *āha,* though third person in form, should be taken as first person in sense, indicated by the gloss *kathemi.*

1887. The tenfold right view and the ninefold learning will be explicated by Niddesa just below.

1888. The orthography in both Be and Ee should be corrected to *kammassakata-saccānulomikañāṇaṃ.* The former is the right view of ownership of one's kamma, the latter the preliminary knowledge of the four noble truths—through learning and insight—prior to direct penetration by the right view of the path.

1889. Again, this second explanation construes *anuggahāya* as an optative participle rather than as an absolutive.

1890. *Amarāvikkhepadhammo ti evaṃ maññāmi.* The allusion is to the endless evaders or "eel-wrigglers" among the sixty-two views, explained in the Brahmajāla Sutta; he refers specifically to the fourth type of evader, described at DN I 27,9 as stupid and confused (*ekacco samaṇo vā brāhmaṇo vā mando hoti momūho*). Since the Buddha negates both sides of a dyad, it seems to Māgandiya that he fits into this category.

1891. Though I follow the text in using the ablative forms *ito ajjhattasantito paṭipattito dhammadesanato,* perhaps a genitive "of this" makes better sense in English. Jayawickrama so renders it:

"of this (inward tranquility) you have not gained the minutest perception."

1892. Reading with Be *so samānādīsu*. In Ee the hiatus in *sa mānādīsu* should be closed.

1893. At SN 22:3, III 9, the householder Hāliddakāni asks Mahākaccāna to explain this verse, which the elder interprets as a metaphor for the relationship between consciousness and the five aggregates. Niddesa explicates the verse by quoting SN 22:3 in full.

1894. See p. 921.

1895. Pj II is apparently commenting on a text that has the reading *diṭṭhiyāyako*, preserved in Sn (Be). But Niddesa comments as if the reading were simply *diṭṭhiyā*. I assume that is the more archaic reading.

1896. Niddesa here illustrates this by quoting **529** (of the Sabhiya Sutta).

1897. For the distinction between one liberated in both respects (*ubhatobhāgavimutta*) and one liberated by wisdom (*paññāvimutta*), see MN I 477–78 and Pp 14, §§24–25. For the distinction between one who makes serenity the vehicle (*samathayānika*) and one who makes bare insight the vehicle (*suddhavipassanāyānika*, an alternative name for the "dry-insight practitioner," *sukkhavipassaka*), see Vism 587–88, Ppn 18.3–4. The canonical source for this distinction may be the distinction made between one who develops insight preceded by serenity (*samathapubbaṅgamaṃ vipassanaṃ bhāveti*) and one who develops serenity preceded by insight (*vipassanāpubbaṅgamaṃ samathaṃ bhāveti*), on which see AN II 156–57, Paṭis II 91–100. In the canonical scheme, both serenity and insight are needed; the distinction lies in the priority of their development. The "one who makes serenity the vehicle" does not necessarily become "liberated in both respects." One who attains arahantship by gaining the four jhānas or even access concentration, without the formless meditations, still emerges as "one liberated by wisdom." It is attainment of the formless meditations that marks one as "liberated in both respects." It is not at all certain that the verse itself intends to distinguish the two types of arahant. It is more likely that both pādas are simply describing the arahant in different ways.

1898. See AN I 66,10–13: "It is, brahmin, because of adherence to lust for sensual pleasures . . . that householders fight with householders. It is because of adherence to lust for views . . . that ascetics fight with ascetics."

1899. The Arthapada parallel is no. 15, 子父共會經, Pitṛputrasamāgama, "The Meeting of Father and Son." The origin story tells of the Buddha's first meeting with his father in Kapilavastu after his attainment of buddhahood. In this version, after King Suddhodana acquires the Dhamma-eye, he asks the Buddha questions like those in the opening verse of the Pāli version. This is followed by the Buddha's reply.

1900. Falsehood, divisive speech, harsh speech, and idle chatter.

1901. This explanation devolves on two meanings of *kukkucca*, literally "misdeed": (1) agitated behavior with the hands and feet; and (2) regret over past wrongdoing. See DOP. In the second sense it is one of the five hindrances, but as interpreted here the word can bear both meanings.

1902. *Āpāthakajjhāyī va hotī ti sammukhā āgatānaṃ manussānaṃ jhānaṃ samāpajjanto viya santabhāvaṃ dasseti*. Nidd I-a II 269: "*Meditates in public*: among people who have come into his presence, he displays a peaceful manner as if he had entered jhāna."

1903. Niddesa elaborates upon each of these. I have translated only the case of impudence in regard to the Sangha. For details, see pp. 574–75.

1904. *Na saddho ti sāmaṃ adhigatadhammaṃ na kassaci saddahati. Saddhā* is usually praised as a virtue, but Niddesa takes the expression here to be describing one who has known the Dhamma through direct experience and thus is not dependent on faith.

1905. *Na virajjati*. Pj II and Niddesa take this to be referring to an arahant, who has already eradicated lust (*rāga*).

1906. Reading *atthe ca ñāye ca*, with the parallel at Nidd II 251, as against *attatthe ca ñāyatthe ca*.

1907. The verse is a riddle built up of word plays.

1908. The text has *aviruddho ca taṇhāya, rasesu nānugijjhati* (so Be and Ce; Ee has: *aviruddho ca taṇhāya, rase ca nānugijjhati*). Pj II paraphrases: *virodhābhāvena ca aviruddho hutvā taṇhāya mūlarasādīsu gedhaṃ nāpajjati*. Both Norman and Paññobhāsa render pāda c: "He is not opposed to craving." This cannot be correct, for it runs contrary to what is said elsewhere in the Nikāyas about *taṇhā*. I thus follow the gloss in Pj II, which construes *taṇhāya* with pāda d. Niddesa interprets the couplet in a similar way (see below). Jayawickrama also follows this: "not hostile, and does not covet delights with craving for them."

1909. The text here has *bhikkhave*, as if directly quoting the Buddha, but it does not repeat the word in the rest of the passage, as is characteristic of sutta style, and thus I do not treat it as a scriptural citation.

1910. Here all three compilations (*piṭaka*) are mentioned, which suggests the Niddesa was composed after the Abhidhamma was established as a distinct collection. For other references to the Abhidhamma in the Niddesa, see note 25.

1911. See Appendix 3.
1912. *So imaṃ visatādibhāvena visattikāsaṅkhātaṃ mahātaṇhaṃ atari*. See note 1192.
1913. See note 403.
1914. *Ye keci bhovādikā*. See note 1582.
1915. The Arthapada parallel is no. 10. The origin story begins with a contest in which the Buddha defeats the six heterodox teachers in a display of miraculous powers. He then preaches and converts many people to the Dhamma. Some, however, wonder why renunciants engage in quarrels and disputes. To dispel their doubts, the Buddha creates a double of himself, who poses the questions (as in the Pāli commentary), which the Buddha himself answers.
1916. The text reads *ye vāpi* [Be: *cāpi*] *lobhā vicaranti loke*, which seems to personify *lobha* by making it a plural subject of the verb *vicaranti*. Pj II tries to solve this problem by taking *lobhā* to represent *people* who wander about motivated by greed and overcome by greed (*lobhahetukā lobhenābhibhūtā vicaranti*). The question then becomes about the greed of those people (*tesaṃ so lobho ca kutonidāno*). I translate closer to the line's literal meaning.
1917. Reading with Ce and Ee: *Ye samparāyāya narassa hontī ti samparāyanāya honti, parāyanā hontī ti vuttaṃ hoti*. Apparently Pj II here, and Niddesa below, do not take *samparāya* in the usual sense, as referring to a future life, but in a more immediate sense conveyed by *parāyana*. I translate according to the usual meaning of *samparāya*, but by following the commentaries this line might also have been rendered "which a person has for support."
1918. *Sahajātā saṃsaṭṭhā sampayuttā ekuppādā ekanirodhā ekavatthukā ekārammaṇā*. This is the formal definition of coarisen mental factors in the Abhidhamma. See Kvu 337–38, CMA 76–77.
1919. The six channels for loss of wealth (*cha bhogānaṃ apāyamukhāni*), with analysis and verses, are at DN III 182–85. Four sources for loss of weath and four for gathering of wealth are mentioned at AN IV 283–84.
1920. On the basis of Be and Ce, Ee's *natthi tassa dhammesu ñāṇaṃ* should probably be corrected to *natthi tassa dhammesu aññāṇaṃ*.
1921. In the gloss on **867** Pj II says the "pleasant and unpleasant" comprise the two types of feelings *as well as* the objects on which they are based. But here, since it will be said that the "pleasant and unpleasant" are dependent on contact, the terms must be restricted to the two kinds of feelings; the objective bases for these feelings are excluded because they are not themselves caused by contact.
1922. Pj II adds that a change of gender is made here (*liṅgavyattayo ettha kato*). This is said because it takes *vibhavaṃ bhavañca*

etampi yaṃ atthaṃ to be functioning as a neuter nominative expression (glossed *vibhavo bhavo cā ti yo esa attho*); but if the nouns are taken as objects of *pabrūhi*, there should be no problem with gender.

1923. *Ettha ca sātāsātānaṃ vibhavabhavavatthukā vibhavabhavadiṭṭhiyo eva vibhavabhavā ti atthato veditabbā*. That is, the question concerns *the views* of eternal existence and annihilation based on observation of the arising and vanishing of the pleasant and unpleasant. I use different renderings each for *bhava* and *vibhava* to capture their different nuances with respect to processes and with respect to views. Pj II here echoes SN II 17,10–13: "For one who sees the origin of the world as it really is with correct wisdom, there is no [notion of] nonexistence in regard to the world. And for one who sees the cessation of the world as it really is with correct wisdom, there is no [notion of] existence in regard to the world."

1924. That is, sensory contacts depend on the associated mental factors that constitute the "name body," and on the sense base (sense organ) and sense object that constitute the "form body." It is from these that the corresponding types of consciousness arise. The meeting of sense base, sense object, and consciousness constitutes contact. According to the Abhidhamma system on which the commentaries rely, the relationship of association (*sampayuttapaccaya*) pertains only to coexistent mental factors (including *citta*), not to the relationship between mental factors and "form" or material phenomena.

1925. The five kinds of sensory contact alone are specified because contact without external sensory cognition exists in the formless meditative attainments.

1926. Contact also pertains to *nāma*, but since the passage is explaining its origin, and contact is not self-generated, contact itself is excluded from the explanation.

1927. "The base consisting of form" (*vatthu rūpaṃ*) is the heart-base (*hadayavatthu*). "Mental phenomena that partake of form" (*dhammā rūpino*) are the material constituents of the mental phenomena base (*dhammāyatana*), that is, types of matter that are classifed as "not visible, not involved in sensory impingement, included in the mental phenomena base" (*anidassanaṃ appaṭighaṃ dhammāyatanapariyāpannaṃ*). These are the female and male sex faculties, the life faculty, nutritive essence, bodily and verbal intimation, the space element, etc. (see Dhs 226, §984)

1928. See note 1785.

1929. *Icchāya asantyā asaṃvijjamānāya natthi anupalabbhamānāya*. This confirms the Be and Ce reading of the text as the locative absolute, *icchāy'asantyā*.

1930. The explanation here hinges on two meanings of the verb *vibhāveti,* "to be made to vanish," and "to recognize, to clearly understand." Accordingly the past participle *vibhūta* can mean "vanished" and "recognized." It seems here the first two ways (*ñātavibhūtena, tīraṇavibhūtena*) correspond to the meaning "recognized," the second two ways (*pahānavibhūtena, samatikkamavibhūtena*) to the meaning "made to vanish."

1931. It is puzzling that both Pj II and Niddesa gloss *kathaṃ sametassa* with words that mean practice and behavior (*kathaṃ paṭipannassa kathaṃ iriyantassa kathaṃ vattentassa*, etc.) rather than attainment. *Sameta* is the past participle of *sameti*, which means "to come together, to meet, to arrive at" (see PED and SED), and this suggests attainment rather than procedure. I thus translate the text on the basis of the standard meaning of *sameta* as "attained" rather than the glosses here.

1932. The four alternatives in Pāli are: (1) *na saññasaññī*, (2) *na visaññasaññī,* (3) *nopi asaññī*, (4) *na vibhūtasaññī*. Norman (GD 343) succinctly states the commentarial explanation thus: "He is, then, in the fourth jhāna, and is at the stage where, having overcome perceptions of form completely, he is about to enter the sphere of unbounded space." The verse is enigmatic, and it is hard to determine whether the commentaries have captured the original purport. The Arthapada parallel, at T IV 181c13, has 不想想，不色想，非無想，不行想. Here 不想想 matches *na saññasaññī*, and 非無想 matches *nopi asaññī*. The other two phrases differ from the Pāli. 不色想 would be *na rūpasaññī*, and 不行想 might be *na saṅkhārasaññī*. Bapat renders 不色想 as "nor with consciousness of the formless," but there is only one negation here and thus the meaning must be "not percipient of form." Similarly, he renders 不行想 as "nor with consciousness inactive," but again the line has only a single negation and so must mean not percipient of activities or not with active perception.

1933. Although this statement is phrased as though it were a canonical quotation, the statement does not occur in the Nikāyas themselves. The first part of the quotation, in the Nikāyas, introduces the attainment of the three *vijjās* or the six *abhiññās*, not the formless meditations.

1934. *Saññānidānā hi papañcasaṅkhā ti. Papañcāyeva papañcasaṅkhā.* The line is discussed at Ud-a 372–73, which enumerates five kinds of *papañca*: lust, hatred, delusion, views, and conceit. The perception of beauty is the cause of the *papañca* of lust, a ground for resentment the cause of the *papañca* of hatred, the influxes the cause of the *papañca* of delusion, feeling the cause of the *papañca* of craving, perception the cause of the *papañca* of views, and thinking the cause of the *papañca* of conceit.

Ps I 111 quotes the line and explains that inverted perception is the basis for misconceivings (*maññanā*), the latter being a synonym for *papañca*: *Saññāvipallāso maññanānaṃ padaṭṭhānaṃ. Saññānidānā hi papañcasaṅkhā ti.*

1935. The text has *yakkhassa suddhiṃ idha paṇḍitāse udāhu aññampi vadanti etto*. On this use of *yakkha*, see note 1405. At **478** the Buddha uses *yakkhassa suddhi* with reference to himself, so it seems unlikely that the expression here implies a subtle affirmation of self, though such a nuance is not impossible.

1936. *Yakkhassā ti sattassa narassa mānavassa posassa puggalassa jīvassa jāgussa jantussa indagussa manujassa*. It is hard to render all these synonyms into English.

1937. The use of *samayaṃ* here is problematic. The word normally means "occasion, time," but with a prefix, as *abhisamaya*, it means "attainment, realization, breakthrough." In the commentaries *samaya* also means a system of thought, a philosophy. For lack of a better interpretation I treat it as short for *abhisamaya*. Just below, Niddesa apparently derives it from Skt *śam*, "to be calm," hence as "calmness, tranquility."

1938. *Anupādisese kusalā vadānā ti anupādisese kusalavādā samānā.* Elsewhere *anupādisesa* is used to indicate either the arahant's elimination of all residue of clinging or the nibbāna element reached with the breakup of the body, which is "without residue" of the five aggregates. Here, as construed by the commentaries, it designates the annihilation of an existing being. The term thus establishes a polarity betweeen eternalism and annihilationism, the two philosophical extremes rejected by the Buddha.

1939. *Te sattassa samaṃ upasamaṃ vūpasamaṃ nirodhaṃ paṭipassaddhinti vadanti*. Apparently the accusative nouns here are offered as glosses on *samayaṃ*, which is being derived from the Skt root *śam*. I am not sure whether this is intended as a word play or as a serious gloss, but *samaya* is from the verb *sameti*, "to attain, to realize," from which the participle used earlier, *sameta*, is derived. It has no connection with *śam*.

1940. This seems to be an allusion to the annihilationists of the Brahmajāla Sutta, who at DN I 34–35 speak of four separate selves associated with each of the four formless attainments (see Bodhi 2007b: 79–81). Each says with respect to that particular self: "Since this self is annihilated and destroyed with the breakup of the body and does not exist after death, at this point the self is completely annihilated" (*so kho bho attā yato kāyassa bhedā ucchijjati vinassati, na hoti paraṃ maraṇā, ettāvatā kho bho ayaṃ attā sammā samucchinno hoti*).

1941. The verb *sameti* may have been used deliberately to set up a contrast with those who have attained (*sameta*) what they take to be the foremost purity of the spirit, and with those who assert the attainment (*samaya*) without residue remaining, which—as interpreted by Niddesa and Pj II—signifies annihilation. Although I translate *bhavābhavāya na sameti dhīro* in compliance with the commentaries, *bhavābhava* here may actually refer to the duality of views about eternal existence and annihilation. Since the preceding verse established a dichotomy of theories, and the present verse says that the muni does not enter a dispute, *bhavābhava* would seem to echo this dichotomy. On how inclining neither to existence nor annihilation leads to liberation, see MN III 244,21–25: "He does not choose, does not intend, either for existence or nonexistence. Thus he does not cling to anything in the world. Not clinging, he is not agitated. Without agitation, he pesonally attains nibbāna."

1942. The Arthapada parallel, no. 11, explains that this discourse originated at the Great Gathering, in a way similar to the Pāli version, with details as in the commentary to II,13. But in this version, the doubt arose in the mind of a brahmin student named Měngguān (猛觀). To dispel his doubt, the Buddha created a double of himself who posed the questions that the real Buddha answered. See Bapat 1951, 95–97.

1943. *Sādhurūp'amhā*. Literally "We are in good form."

1944. *Tā purimaḍḍhena vuttamatthaṃ pacchimaḍḍhena paṭivyūhitvā ṭhitā. Tena vyūhena uttarasuttato ca appakattā idaṃ suttaṃ "cūḷavyūhan" ti nāmaṃ labhati*. This explains the use of the word *vyūha* in the title. For *vyūha* (also spelled *byūha*), PED has: "(1) the array or arrangement of troops in particular positions, order of parade or battle; (2) a heap, collection." It is also possible the word here refers to the alignment of forces in the battles between those of divergent views.

1945. Both Ce and Ee abridge the lemma, as shown here, while Be cites it in full: *sandiṭṭhiyā c'eva na vīvadātā. Saṃsuddhapaññā kusalā mutīmā ti*. The reading itself, and the explanation based on it, seem self-contradictory, for which reason I prefer the Ee reading *sandiṭṭhiyā ce pana vīvadātā*, recognized by Pj II as an alternative. Norman does not discuss the problem. Both Norman and Jayawickrama translate on the basis of the Ee reading. Paññobhāsa accepts the primary reading and renders "even though they are not immaculate." The commentarial explanation (just below) accords better with the alternative reading. On *sandiṭṭhi* as meaning "one's own view," see the expression *sandiṭṭhiparāmāsī* at MN I 43,24 and elsewhere.

1946. Pj II adds: *Ettha ca tathiyan ti, tathivan ti* [Be: *kathivan ti*] *dvepi pāṭhā*. The meaning is not affected. Be's *kathivan* is unintelligible and almost certainly an error.

1947. I read with Be and Ce: *Yasmiṃ pajā no vivade pajānan ti yamhi sacce pajānanto pajā no vivadeyya*. For *pajā no* Ee has *pajāno* in the text, lemma, and comment, probably to avoid the disparity of gender between the feminine *pajā* and the participle *pajānaṃ*. This, however, makes the line self-contradictory. *Pajānaṃ* might be understood as a metrical shortening of the feminine participle. A note in Pj II (Ce) suggests reading *pajānantī* for *pajānanto* in the comment. Niddesa supports the reading in Be and Ce but glosses the line in the plural (see below).

1948. The text and Pj II use the singular verb (*vivade, vivadeyya*); Niddesa has the plural (*kalahaṃ kareyyuṃ*).

1949. By glossing *anussaranti* with *anugacchanti*, it seems Pj II takes *anussaranti* to correspond to Skt *anusṛ* (see SED), "to go after, to follow," rather than Skt *anusmṛ*, "to recollect." The gloss in Niddesa supports this supposition: *udāhu takkena saṅkappena yāyanti nīyanti vuyhanti saṃharīyanti*.

1950. *Takkapariyāhataṃ vīmaṃsānucaritaṃ sayaṃ paṭibhānaṃ vadanti*. This is mentioned as the basis for several views among the sixty-two views: eternalism at DN I 16,19–20, partial-eternalism at DN I 21,16, dialectical skepticism at DN I 23,35, and the view of spontaneous origination at DN I 29,10. At MN I 68,18–20, the Buddha himself is accused of teaching on the basis of mere reasoning, a criticism he rejects.

1951. *Diṭṭhigatāni janetvā sañjanetvā nibbattetvā abhinibbattetvā "mayhaṃ saccaṃ tuyhaṃ musā" ti, evamāhaṃsu*. "Speculative views" (*diṭṭhigatāni*) usually refers to the sixty-two views of the Brahmajāla Sutta. See Appendix 3.

1952. *Diṭṭhe sute sīlavate mute vā*. Norman (GD 346) explains these as nominative singular forms in an Eastern Prakrit.

1953. All three editions read *suddhibhāvasaṅkhātaṃ vimānaṃ*, but the context seems to require just the opposite: *suddhi-abhāvasaṅkhātaṃ vimānaṃ*. Ee notes that one Burmese manuscript had this reading. I translate on the basis of this reading.

1954. *Sayameva sāmaṃ manasābhisitto*. *Abhisitta* (from *abhisiñcati*) refers to the rite by which a king is consecrated ruler, as in the expression *rājā khattiyo muddhābhisitto* (or *muddhāvasitto*), "a head-anointed khattiya king."

1955. I read the gloss in Pj II with Ee *te aparaddhā*. Be and Ce have *ye aparaddhā*, which puts failure to reach purity on the side of the antecedent rather than the consequence. Niddesa supports Ee on this.

1956. *Titthaṃ vuccati diṭṭhigataṃ. Titthiyā vuccanti diṭṭhigatikā*.

1957. The Arthapada parallel, no. 12, was also spoken on the occasion of the Great Gathering, in response to a doubt arisen in a brahmin student named Făguān (法觀), "One Who Contemplates the Dharma."

1958. In this context what is meant by *vivāda* is philosophical disputes rather than disputes over possessions and privileges.
1959. *Khantiṃ akubbamāno chandaṃ akubbamāno pemaṃ akubbamāno rāgaṃ akubbamāno.* Although all editions of the text, Pj II, and Niddesa read the object as *khantiṃ*, the gloss in Pj II (*diṭṭhasutasuddhīsu pemaṃ akaronto*) and the Niddesa explanation cited here suggest that the object may originally have been *kantiṃ*, "liking, attachment," which corresponds more closely to such words as *chanda, pema*, and *rāga*. Jayawickrama (PBR 1976, 142) points out that the citation of the line in the Bodhisattvabhūmi has *dṛṣṭaśrute kantim asamprakurvan*. Jayawickrama retains *khantiṃ* in his edition of Sn but translates the line thus: "not forming any attachment to the seen and the heard."
1960. *Niyāmāvakkantiṃ*: attainment of the path of stream-entry.
1961. As in the text, I read here with Ee *tapūpanissāya jigucchitaṃ vā*. Be and Ce have *tamūpanissāya* in their editions of Niddesa as well as in the text. However, as Norman points out (GD 350), the explanation in Niddesa (*tapojigucchavādā tapojigucchasārā tapojigucchanissitā*) points to *tapūpanissāya* as the correct reading. This is further confirmed by Nidd I-a II 367, cited just below in note 1964. Jayawickrama is ambiguous: he reads *tamūpanissāya* but translates "Depending either on it (austerity), which is despised . . ." Paññobhāsa, taking *tamūpanissāya* as a *sandhi* of *tamo upanissāya*, renders "Depending upon ignorant darkness," but there is no exegetical support for this and it is not idiomatic. *Jigucchitaṃ* can be understood as a past participle used as a noun.
1962. *Amaratapaṃ*. See note 968.
1963. Norman suggests amending the text of Sn to read *uddhaṃsarasuddhim*. He translates: "They speak of purity by means of continuing further." This, however, is not supported either by Niddesa or Pj II. At MN II 232,14–16 we find: *sabbe pi'me bhonto samaṇabrāhmaṇā uddhaṃsarā āsattiṃyeva abhivadanti*, glossed by Ps IV 21,18–19: *Uddhaṃsarā ti uddhaṃ vuccati anāgatasaṃsāravādo, anāgataṃ saṃsāravādaṃ sarantī ti attho.*

    We should read with Be and Ce *bhavābhavesu avītataṇhāse suddhimanutthunan ti vadanti kathentī ti*. Ee is missing *suddhim* here. DOP lists two homonyms for *anutthuṇāti, anutthunāti*: (1) [related to BHS *anustanayati*] "wails, deplores, laments (for)"; (2) [also *anutthavati*] "praises, speaks of repeatedly." The former is at **586** and **827**. The gloss in Pj II, *vadanti kathenti* (with more synonyms in Niddesa), indicates that the second meaning is intended.
1964. Nidd I-a II 367,18–20: "*Who assert austerity and scrupulousness*: whose doctrine is revulsion toward evil by means of austerity, physical torment, and so forth. *Who take austerity and scrupu-*

lousness as the essence: who take the essence to be revulsion by means of that austerity."

1965. Reading with Ce: *Saṃvedhitañcāpi pakappitesu, taṇhādiṭṭhīhi c'assa pakappitesu vatthūsu saṃvedhitampi hoti.* Ee's *taṇhā diṭṭhi c'assa* should be corrected in accordance with this.

1966. As in text, so in Pj II and Niddesa we should read with Ce and Ee *sadhammapūjā* as against Be *saddhammapūjā*.

1967. *Bāhitapāpattā brāhmaṇo*. Again, an "edifying" etymology of *brāhmaṇa* from *bāhita*. See note 576.

1968. Pj II does not clearly gloss *tumassa*. It is a by-form of *attā* in the genitive singular. The derivation is *ātmā* > *ātuma* > *tuma*.

1969. *Tattha tathaddasā so,* Norman translates "[saying] he saw reality there," and Paññobhāsa, "who has seen 'reality' there." Here, however, *tath–* is a truncated form of *tathā*, an adverb, not an accusative object, thus indicating the manner in which he sees. Pj II glosses with *tath'eva naṃ addasa*.

1970. I read with Ee *pakappitaṃ diṭṭhi purekkharāno ti pakappitaṃ abhisaṅkhataṃ saṇṭhapitaṃ diṭṭhiṃ purakkhato purato katvā carati.* Be and Ce differ slightly.

1971. Pj II (Be) *Saṅkhā ti saṅkhāya jānitvā ti attho.* Ce and Ee have *saṅkhanti*. Norman (GD 354) writes that *saṅkhaṃ* is a present participle explained as an absolutive, but he admits *saṅkhā* may be accepted as the reading, in which case it is a truncated absolutive. That is how I take it. Niddesa just below confirms the absolutive with its string of synonyms: *saṅkhāya jānitvā tulayitvā tīrayitvā vibhāvayitvā vibhūtaṃ katvā*.

1972. Be *uggahaṇanti maññe,* Ce *uggaṇhanti maññe,* Ee *uggahaṇan-ta-m-aññe*; the last is supported by Pj II (Ce). The Ce reading, evidently a normalization, is metrically deficient. Norman suggests reading *uggahaṇantam,* understood as a middle-voice imperative, but the exegetical tradition does not support this. Niddesa uses the present tense verb: Be *uggahaṇanti maññe* and Ce *uggaṇhanti maññe*. Thus on these readings the *–m–* can be understood simply as a liaison consonant.

1973. This explanation is given because, from an analytical perspective, it is impossible to abandon occasions of defilements that occurred in the past.

1974. *Sa sabbadhammesu visenibhūto*. This expression, it seems, plays on two meanings of *dhammā*: doctrinal teachings—glossed as the sixty-two views—which conforms to the overarching theme of this sutta; and phenomena in the broad sense, elaborated by way of the seen, heard, and sensed. The expression occurred earlier in **793**a, where again it is connected with the seen, heard, and sensed.

1975. The parallel in the Arthapada is no. 13. The first part of the background story, which actually has no apparent connection with what follows, is a parallel to the Hemavata Sutta (I,9); see Bapat 1951, 114–21. The verses originate after a brahmin named Dōulè (兜勒 = Tuvaṭaka?) gives rise to doubts about the double created by the Buddha. The double then questions the Buddha, who responds. The parallel verses begin at T IV 184b12.

1976. Two explanations are given because the term *santipadaṃ* can be understood as either the definitive state (*pada*) of peace or as the practice (*paṭipadā*) leading to peace.

1977. Niddesa treats *mahesi* as a compound of *mahā* and *esī*, from the verb *esati*, "to seek." The word is actually the Pāli counterpart of Skt *maharṣi*, from *mahā* and *ṛṣi*.

1978. Niddesa glosses the indicative verb *nibbāti* with the causative *nibbāpeti*.

1979. *Papañcā ti saṅkhātattā papañcā eva papañcasaṅkhā*. See too **874**d: "concepts due to proliferation originate from perception." MN I 111,32–112,13 explains how *papañcasaññāsaṅkhā* originate and assail a person. While the sutta does not analyze the expression itself, the exposition suggests the compound can be understood as *saññā* (perceptions and ideas) and *saṅkhā* (notions and concepts) arisen through mental proliferation based on the raw data of sensory experience. Ps II 75,5 equates *saṅkhā* with "a portion" (*koṭṭhāso*) and *papañcasaññā* with perceptions or ideas associated with the "proliferations" arisen through craving, conceit, and views (*taṇhāmānadiṭṭhipapañcasampayuttā saññā*). It is unclear to me why the commentaries gloss *saṅkhā* with *koṭṭhāsa*.

In the present verse, I would interpret *papañca* as the activity of mental proliferation and the conceit "I am" as the primal concept born of proliferation, the "root" that in turn gives rise to all the other products of *papañca*.

1980. The text has *mantā*, expanded into *mantāya* in the lemma. *Mantā* might be an agent noun in the nominative singular, "a thinker," but Pj II treats it as a truncated instrumental, *mantāya*. Niddesa equates *mantā* with *paññā* and also treats it as a truncated instrumental. Hence I render "by reflection." See notes 744 and 1378.

1981. Here I translate the lemma following Pj II, though my understanding differs. Pj II sees two things that are to be stopped, *mūlaṃ papañcasaṅkhā* and *asmī ti*. Niddesa too interprets the text in this way. However, since the text itself does not include a conjunctive (*ca* or *pi*), it seems that the original point was that the notion "I am" is *itself* the root of concepts due to proliferation. This supposition is confirmed by SN IV 202, where "I am" is the starting point for a series of more elaborate speculations: "'I am' is a conceiving (*maññita*); 'I am this' is a conceiving; 'I shall be' is a conceiving; 'I shall not be' is a conceiving; 'I shall consist of form' is a conceiving; 'I shall be formless' is a conceiving; 'I shall be percipient' is a conceiving; 'I shall be nonpercipient' is a conceiving; 'I shall be neither percipient nor nonpercipient' is a conceiving." The same is repeated for proliferations (*papañcita*). On the expression *mūlaṃ papañca-saṅkhāya*, see the Niddesa passage just below.

1982. Where the text reads *tāsaṃ vinayā sadā sato sikkhe*, the paraphrase in Pj II has *vinayāya*, taking *vinayā* to be a truncated dative of purpose. The gloss in Niddesa also confirms this (see below). The normal dative occurs at **974**b, where we find *yesaṃ satīmā vinayāya sikkhe.*

1983. *Asmī ti rūpe asmī ti māno asmī ti chando asmī ti anusayo.*

1984. The gloss here explicates *vinayā* at **916**d with a string of datives: *vinayāya paṭivinayāya pahānāya vūpasamāya paṭinis-saggāya paṭipassaddhiyā*. Apparently Niddesa, like Pj II, takes *vinayā* as a truncated dative.

1985. Niddesa is not particularly helpful with this line, *nātumānaṃ vikappayaṃ tiṭṭhe*. It merely provides a string of synonyms without explanation: *attānaṃ kappento vikappento vikappaṃ āpajjanto na tiṭṭheyyā ti: nātumānaṃ vikappayaṃ tiṭṭhe*. The brief explanation in Pj II suggests that *ātumānaṃ* (= *attānaṃ*) should be taken in the reflexive sense rather than the metaphysical sense, that is, as "oneself" rather than "the self."

1986. Be has *sabbakilesūpasamavasenapi*. Ce and Ee lack *sabba*.

1987. This second construal takes *bhaddaṃ* as an adjective in apposition to *paṭipadaṃ*, and subsumes *paṭipadaṃ* under *te*, glossed with *tava*.

1988. The full list of unsuitable shows is at DN I 6,11–18, translated at Bodhi 2007b: 55. The last items mentioned, going to see military displays, are prohibited by Pācittiya 50.

1989. The text repeats the preceding passage, from "whether he has entered among the houses," but in the mode of abstinence.

1990. An abridgment of the standard formula of reflection on the use of food, in full at note 394.

1991. Niddesa mentions here a long list of illnesses found at AN V 110,1–12.

1992. Reading with Be *paramatthagaruko*. Ce has *sadatthagaruko*. Both readings must have been known to the author of Nidd I-a II 405, who writes: *Paramatthagaruko ti uttamatthagaruko. Sakattha-garuko ti vā pāṭho.*

1993. A common pericope used in the Nikāyas in the explanation of *jāgariya*.

1994. Niddesa mentions a large number of games. These are also at DN I 6–7, translated at Bodhi 2007b, 55–56.

1995. *Āthabbaṇikamantappayogaṃ*. At the time the Nikāyas were compiled the Atharva Veda was apparently not granted full status as a Veda, since only three Vedas are mentioned. The Atharva Veda contains a large number of incantations directed to various ends, such as long life, good health, wealth, etc.

1996. For some reason, this explanation seems to distinguish this kind of "buying and selling" (*kayavikkaya*) from that prohibited by Nissaggiyapācittiya 20 of the Pātimokkha. However, abstaining from buying and selling is included in the standard list of monastic *sīlas* mentioned in the Nikāyas. The five *sahadhammikas* are fellow bhikkhus, bhikkhunīs, sikkhamānās (female trainees), sāmaṇeras (novice monks), and sāmaṇerīs (novice nuns).

1997. *Ītiṃ uppādenti, upaddavaṃ uppādenti, rogaṃ uppādenti, pajjarakaṃ karonti, sūlaṃ karonti, visūcikaṃ karonti, pakkhandikaṃ karonti.* The terms are commented on at Nidd I-a II 335, Sp-ṭ II 227–28, and Vmv I 195.

1998. *Amaravitakka.* Nidd I-a II 418,14–16: "The thought of one who undertakes self-torment, thought connected with self-torment, for the sake of immortality. For they believe that when suffering is worn away by the squatter's practice and other ascetic observances, the self will be blissful in the future."

1999. *Parānudayatā paṭisaṃyutto vitakko.* Nidd I-a II 418,24–32: "Thought connected with worldly affection that resembles true sympathy. When one's supporters are delighted or sorrowful, one is doubly delighted and sorrowful with them. When they are happy or miserable, one is double happy or miserable with them. One undertakes various tasks and duties on their behalf and, to accomplish them, one transgresses a rule or oversteps the bounds of self-effacement. Worldly thought connected with such intimate bonding or with undertaking such tasks is what is intended here as 'thought connected with solicitude for others.'"

2000. While Be reads *puthujanānaṃ* in the citation and lemma, as against Ce *puthuvacanānaṃ*, the explanation of the lemma does not employ the standard trope on the *puthujjana* but instead supports *puthuvacanānaṃ*.

2001. *Rāgassa santattā santo . . . sabbākusalābhisaṅkhārānaṃ santattā samitattā vūpasamitattā vijjhātattā nibbutattā vigatattā paṭipassaddhattā santo upasanto vūpasanto nibbuto paṭipassaddho ti – santo.* Niddesa here explains the text's *santo* as if it were derived from Skt *śam*, but in that case a plural subject *santā* would be needed to match the verb *karonti*. *Santo* is from the root *sat* in its extended meaning, "the good ones."

2002. See pp. 837–38. The Arthapada parallel, no. 16, originates from King Virūḍhaka's massacre of the Sakyans.

2003. *Attadaṇḍā bhayaṃ jātaṃ attano duccaritakāraṇā jātaṃ*. Both Pj II and Niddesa apparently take *attadaṇḍa* here to mean *attano daṇḍaṃ*, "one's own punishment," or "punishment due to oneself." But *atta* is actually a past participle of *ādiyati* and *attadaṇḍā* a *bahubbīhi* compound meaning "those who have taken up the rod," who have embraced violence. See DOP, sv *ādiyati*, *attadaṇḍa*[1]. See too the gloss on *attadaṇḍesu*, p. 963, which is also at Dhp-a IV 180,5–7: *hatthagate daṇḍe vā satthe vā avijjamānepi paresaṃ pahāradānato aviratattā attadaṇḍesu janesu*.

2004. These are the ten courses of unwholesome conduct, elaborated at MN I 286–87, AN V 264–66, etc.

2005. The text elaborates on the torments of hell, as described at MN III 166–67 and MN III 182–86.

2006. Niddesa mentions a variety of countries, among them Taxila, Java, and Tambapaṇṇī (Sri Lanka). Others are hard to identify.

2007. I have selected only a few representative items from the long list of austere practices that are mentioned here. They are found in full at MN I 77–78, MN I 307–8, MN I 342–43, AN I 295–96, etc.

2008. Niddesa quotes here at length from MN II 108–10.

2009. *Tannimittaṃ hatthisikkhādikā anekā sikkhā kathīyanti uggayhanti vā*. The two glosses on *sikkhānugīyanti* in Pj II—explained even more elaborately in Niddesa—suggest the authors were uncertain whether to take the expression as resolvable into *sikkhā anugīyanti* or *sikkhā uggayhant* (in the latter case with *–n–* presumably serving as a liaison consonant). Norman says (GD 363): "The fact that the commentaries give two explanations . . . seems to indicate that the pāda was not fully understood." He proposes the line is not an integral part of the verse, but "an instruction to the reciter which has become embedded in the text . . . an interpolation, although clearly it is a very old one." The Arthapada does not have a corresponding line, which supports Norman's supposition.

The trainings mentioned in pāda a should likely be connected with the last pāda, where "training" is indicated by the optative verb: *sikkhe nibbānamattano*. The following verses can then be seen as detailing the training. Norman renders the line, "At that point the precepts are recited," and Jayawickrama has: "Recounted in song is the training therein." I believe Paññobhāsa was misled by the layout in Be into his rendering, "Therein training rules are recited which are ties in the world," which wrongly identifies *sikkhā* with *gathitāni*. *Yāni loke gadhitāni* should be seen, rather, as a relative clause completed by *na tesu pasuto siyā*.

2010. Nidd I-a II 433,18–20 glosses this in a way that allows two meanings to *kāmaṃ*, as an emphatic and as sensuality: *Kāmañca te upadhiparikkhayāyā ti ekaṃsena te paṇḍitā kāmakkhayāya kāmakkhepanatthaṃ dānāni denti.*

2011. Here *ākāsa* is Skt *ākarṣa*, "attraction, fascination." See SED sv *ākṛṣ*. The verb in Niddesa is *ākassati* (= Skt *ākṛṣyate*).

2012. Pj II apparently takes all the nouns here—*gedhaṃ, mahogho, ājavaṃ, jappanaṃ, ārammaṇaṃ*, and *pakappanaṃ*—as parallel objects of *brūmi*, metaphorical terms referring back to *ākāsaṃ* in the preceding verse. In contrast, Niddesa (see below) takes *mahogho* as a metaphor for *gedhaṃ* and *jappanaṃ* as a metaphor for *ājavaṃ*. I invert the relationship, taking *ājavaṃ* as the metaphor.

2013. *Thale tiṭṭhati brāhmaṇo*. On this expression, a metaphorical description of the arahant, see SN IV 157,9, SN IV 175,3, AN II 5,13, and AN IV 12,31–13,7.

2014. These are the view of the personal entity, doubt, seizing upon good behavior and observances, lust, hatred, delusion, and conceit. They are mentioned on p. 1058, Nidd I 62 commenting on **790**.

2015. Pj II may be taking *dhammaṃ* as an accusative plural (Skt *dharmān*). Niddesa does not offer a direct gloss on *dhammaṃ* but instead states the principles that are known: "All conditioned things are impermanent," etc.

2016. On this explanation of *vedagū*, see Pj II comment on **529** (p. 923).

2017. *Nājjhetī ti nābhijjhāyati*. See SED sv *ādhyai*, "to wish or pray for anything for another," and the cognate noun *ādhi*, "care, anxious reflection, mental agony, anxiety; hope, expectation." The first derivation in Niddesa explains *nājjheti* on the basis of Skt *na ādhyāyate*. The second apparently sees *nājjheti* as a contraction of *na* + *jāyati* and thus relates it to the "peaceful muni" who is not born, does not grow old, and does not die, described at MN III 246,18–26.

2018. I here follow Be, which accords better with Niddesa: *Tattha aniṭṭhurī ti anissukī. Aniddhurī ti pi keci paṭhanti*. Ce and Ee have: *Tattha anuddharī ti anissukī. Aniṭṭhurī ti pi keci paṭhanti*. For *niṭṭhuri(n)* DOP has "harsh, rough, cruel; (according to commentaries) resentful, spiteful." See too SED sv *niṣṭhura*. DOP gives "not proud" for *anuddharī*.

2019. The "all" (*sabba*) is brought in to account for the word *sabbadhi*, "everywhere."

2020. *Yasmā nisaṅkhariyati nisaṅkharoti vā, tasmā nisaṅkhitī ti vuccati.*

2021. *Viyārambhā ti vividhā puññābhisaṅkhārādikā ārambhā*. See p. 1005, where Pj II explains *ārambha* as "energy associated with kamma" (*kammasampayuttavīriya*).

2022. *Therapañhasuttan ti pi vuccati*. Norman points out (GD 366) that Dharmānanda Kosambī identified this sutta with the text named Upatisapasine mentioned in King Aśoka's Calcutta-Bairāṭ Edict. Upatissa was the given name of Sāriputta. The Arthapada parallel, no. 14, also explains this discourse as originating from the Buddha's descent after spending three months in the heaven of the Thirty-three, where he went to teach the doctrine to his mother. For a translation, see Bapat 1951, 130–49. The parallel verses start at T IV 186b14.

2023. What follows is an extremely compressed account of the events leading up to the twin miracle, the twin miracle itself, the ascent to heaven, and the return to the human realm. The story is related in full at Dhp-a III 199 foll. (see BL 3:35 foll.).

2024. Dhp-a III 225 (see BL 3:53): "When the rains retreat was over and the Pavāraṇā ceremony had been held, the Teacher told Sakka: 'Great king, I will return to the human realm.' Sakka then created three ladders, one of gold, one of jewels, and one of silver. The feet of these ladders rested against the gate of the city Saṅkassa, and their tops against the summit of Mount Sineru. On the right side was the ladder of gold for the deities, on the left side the ladder of silver for Mahābrahmā and his entourage, and in the middle the ladder of jewels for the Tathāgata. . . . The deities descended on the ladder of gold, Mahābrahmā and his entourage on the ladder of silver, and the Perfectly Enlightened One himself descended on the ladder of jewels."

2025. Pj II here relates in summary form the story told at Ja I 405–7.

2026. Since the origin story says that the Buddha had just descended from the Tāvatiṃsa heaven, it is puzzling that Pj II relates the descent from Tusita mentioned here to his conception in his mother's womb. Perhaps there was some uncertainty about exactly where the Buddha spent this rains retreat, whether in the Tāvatiṃsa heaven (the dominant view) or the Tusita heaven (implied here). Just below, the Niddesa will state that he had spent the rains retreat in the Tāvatiṃsa heaven but descended from Tusita to enter his mother's womb. For a discussion of the problem, see Anālayo 2014, 162–64.

2027. *Tusitā gaṇi-m-āgato ti tusitakāyā cavitvā mātukucchiṃ āgatattā tusitā āgato gaṇācariyattā gaṇī, santuṭṭhaṭṭhena vā tusitasaṅkhātā devalokā gaṇī āgato tusitānaṃ vā arahantānaṃ gaṇī āgato*. In relation to the latter two explanations, Be has *gaṇiṃ āgato* for *gaṇī āgato* in both places, with *–m–* functioning as a liaison consonant. Norman (GD 367) remarks that the *sandhi* "has doubtless been extracted from **957**b where *gaṇiṃ* is grammatically correct." The last two explanations offered by Pj II depend on a word play between *tusita* as the name of this particular class of devas and its literal meaning "contented."

2028. DOP: "Probably the Indian cuckoo."

2029. *Visaṭṭho ca viññeyyo ca mañju ca savanīyo ca bindu ca avisārī ca gambhīro ca ninnādi ca.*

2030. Both Pj II and Niddesa are trying to explain *yathā* in **956**b. Neither, I believe, does so successfully. The problem could be solved by taking the first couplet of **956** to be linked syntactically to **955**, in the way shown in my rendering of the text.

2031. Compare the following with the description of the paccekabuddha at pp. 420–22. The descriptions differ only in the details particular to the Buddha.

2032. I read with Ce and Ee: *atthi pañhena āgaman ti atthiko pañhena āgato'mhi, atthikānaṃ vā, pañhena atthi āgamanaṃ vā*. I have modified the punctuation. The alternative explanations revolve around the meaning of *atthi*. On the first it is the masculine singular of *atthin*, from *attha* in the sense of need; on the second, it is a truncated genitive plural; and on the third it is the verb (= Skt *asti*) meaning "is." Norman discusses the problem at GD 367 but cites only the first explanation in Pj II. The second explanation, it seems, can be rejected because the same form occurs at **1043**, **1105**, **1112**, and **1118**, where a plural reference does not fit.

2033. I read *sissānaṃ*, in Be but not in Ce or Ee.

2034. Nidd I-a II 441,29–31: "*A buddha as one who has opened up*: a buddha because of blossoming like a lotus flower through the blossoming of his various excellent qualities" (*vikasitāya buddho ti nānāguṇavikasanato padumamiva vikasanaṭṭhena buddho*).

2035. See note 1853.

2036. Nidd I-a II 440,32: "Pupils are said to be 'bound' in that they live in dependence on their teacher" (*sissā hi ācariyapaṭibaddhavuttittā baddhā ti vuccanti*).

2037. In translating this verse I have inverted the line order to accord best with normal English syntax. I begin with pāda d and the second half of pāda c, and only then come to pādas a, b, and the first half of c.

2038. Bhikkhus, bhikkhunīs, sikkhamānās, sāmaṇeras, sāmaṇeris, upāsakas, and upāsikās.

2039. *Anoko ti abhisaṅkhāraviññāṇādīnaṃ anokāsabhūto*. Pj II seems to be alluding to the explanation of *oko* and *anokasārī* at SN III 9–10.

2040. *Mūlampi tesaṃ palikhañña tiṭṭhe*. This is a unique instance of the absolutive *palikhañña* (< *palikhaṇ* + *ya*) in the canonical texts. Pj II glosses it with *palikhaṇitvā*. Niddesa employs a string of synonyms beginning with the standard absolutive:

palikhaṇitvā uddharitvā samuddharitvā uppāṭayitvā samuppāṭayitvā pajahitvā, etc. *Pali-* here is an Eastern form of the prefix *pari-*.

2041. I accept Norman's suggestion that in pāda d the hiatus should be removed, so that we would read: *addhābhavanto abhisambhaveyya*. Norman, who discusses the word at GD 371–72, takes the long vowel in *addhā* to be governed by the meter but possibly also resulting from Skt influence. Pj II evidently reads *addhā bhavanto* as two words, glossed *ekaṃsen'eva abhibhaveyya*, in this respect following Niddesa. This seems to assign a double duty to *addhā*, first as an indeclinable affirmative, and second as a prefix of *bhavanto*, reconceived as *abhibhavanto*. The line, and the word *addhābhavanto*, is also discussed in a recent paper by von Hinüber (2015, 219–27). Von Hinüber argues that *addhabhavati* is an artificial formation that arose through a misunderstanding of the archaic Vedic usage of *anubhavati* in the sense of "to encompass." That meaning, however, does not work well in the present passage, where the equivalence of *addhabhavati* and *abhibhavati* upheld by the commentaries makes better sense.

2042. Like Pj II, Niddesa here glosses *addhā* as if it were separate from *bhavanto*, taking it as an indeclinable expressing affirmation. But just below in the paraphrase it has *abhisambhavanto* and *abhibhavanto* (or *adhibhavanto*), thus apparently taking *addhābhavanto* as one word. Since I take *addhābhavanto* as one word, I do not translate *addhā* separately as an affirmative. The commentaries may not have recognized that the long *ā* was governed by the meter and thus felt obliged to explain *addhā* as the indeclinable word of affirmation.

2043. Ee: *Athappiyaṃ vā pana appiyaṃ vā addhā bhavanto abhisambhaveyyā ti piyāppiyaṃ sātāsātaṃ sukhadukkhaṃ somanassadomanassaṃ iṭṭhāniṭṭhaṃ abhisambhavanto vā abhibhaveyya abhibhavanto* [Ce and Be: *adhibhavanto*] *vā abhisambhaveyya*. I understand the use of two related verb forms here, differing only in prefixes, to be an attempt to mirror the apparent redundancy of *addhā bhavanto abhisambhaveyya*.

2044. *Janavādadhammāyā ti janavādakathāya*. Niddesa's comment is clearer.

2045. *Saṅgahavatthu*. See Appendix 3.

2046. *Paribhogadhātu*: an item used by the Buddha himself.

2047. Be *dhammakaraṇaṃ* should probably be corrected to *dhammakarakaṃ*, as in Ce and Ee. Elsewhere *dhammakaraka* means a water vessel (used with a strainer), but here it must mean "one who practices the Dhamma."

2048. The figure in Be is probably more accurate: *avasesāpi soḷasādhika-soḷasasahassā*. Ce and Ee have *avasesāpi soḷasasahassā*, which leaves the sixteen chief pupils unaccounted for.

2049. Stanza **976**c has *ākiñcaññaṃ patthayāno*, which Pj II glosses: *ākiñcaññan ti akiñcanabhāvaṃ, pariggahūpakaraṇavivekan ti vuttaṃ hoti*. While Pj II's explanation may be valid, we cannot exclude the possibility that the text is referring to *ākiñcaññāyatana*, the third formless meditative state. The advice to Upasīva at **1070–74** and Posāla at **1115** suggests that some of Bāvari's pupils were familiar with the meditative state of nothingness.

2050. Pj II takes *purā* here as an indeclinable referring to time, which I adopt in the translation. But *purā* can also be the ablative of *pura*, meaning city (as in **1012–13**). Norman does not comment on the ambiguity but renders *purā kapilavatthumhā* as "from the city of Kapilavatthu." Jayawickrama has "in times of yore."

2051. *Sabbābhiññābalappatto ti sabbaṃ abhiññāya balappatto vā sabbā vā abhiññāyo balāni ca patto*. The explanation offers alternative resolutions of the compound.

2052. *Vimutto ti ārammaṇaṃ katvā pavattiyā vimuttacitto*. This may be an oblique allusion to the cognitive process of the path of arahantship, which takes nibbāna as object.

2053. *Varabhūrimedhaso ti uttamavipulapañño bhūte abhiratavarapañño vā*. The second explanation, it seems, takes *bhūri* as synonymous with *bhūta*.

2054. *Manasāyeva pucchathā ti ime satta pañhe citten'eva pucchatha*. In other words, do not ask them verbally but only in the mind. This will be a test of the Buddha's superknowledge.

2055. *Pubbavāsanavāsitā*. On *vāsana* (or *vāsanā*), see notes 748 and 993. Jayawickrama remarks that "the doctrine of *vāsana* is apparently alien to early Buddhism" and takes this as evidence for the later origin of the *vatthugāthā*. Since texts that use the word *vāsanā* are not earlier than the second century B.C.E., he regards this as the lowest limit for the composition of the *vatthugāthā* (PBR 1976, 154–55).

2056. Reading with Ce, Ee: *māhissatināmikaṃ purimanagaran ti vuttaṃ hoti*.

2057. Pj II does not gloss *ath'assa gatte disvāna, paripūrañca byañjanaṃ*, but *ca* in pāda b implies that *gatte* should be taken as an accusative plural with a singular sense. Just below, however, in **1019**c, *gatte* is a locative singular.

2058. *Manopañhe apucchatha*. In accordance with Bāvari's instructions, Ajita is asking the questions with his mind. In the paraphrase, *katamāni tāni'ssa gatte tīṇi lakkhaṇānī ti pucchati*, *gatte* again functions as a locative singular. On the two hidden characteristics, see pp. 252–53.

2059. *Paññāvacanaṃ* should perhaps be changed to *pañhavacanaṃ*.

2060. Reading with Be and Ce *ekarasaṭṭhabhāvamupagatattā*. In the world-transcending path these factors have "a single flavor" because they occur with a single object (nibbāna) and have a single function (the eradication of defilements). On *ekarasaṭṭha*, see Paṭis I 28–30, which speaks of the faculties, powers, and enlightenment factors all occurring "with a single flavor."

2061. While Sn calls each section a *pucchā*, "[a set of] questions," Pj II designates each section a sutta. Thus in Sn the first section is called *Ajitamāṇavapucchā*, but in Pj II it is called *Ajitasuttaṃ*. For a Skt parallel to Ajita's verses, see Appendix 2. Within the ascriptions of the text, the sixteen inquirers are designated *āyasmā*, "venerable," but the word is likely being used proleptically. When they address the Buddha, they sometimes call him *bhagavā*, but never *bhante*. In Sn *bhante* occurs only ten times, all in standard canonical prose passages. The more common direct address the inquirers use is *mārisa*, which in Sn occurs ten times, nine in the Pārāyanavagga; the other is at **814**b, used by the bhikkhu Tissa Metteyya.

2062. Pj II (Ee) has *Ki'ssābhilepanaṃ brūsī ti kiṃ assa lokassa abhilepanaṃ*. Norman (GD 382) thinks it more probable that *ki'ssābhi-* is < *kissu abhi* < *kiṃ su abhi-* and suggests the orthography *kissābhilepanaṃ*.

2063. The word *bhaya* has both subjective and objective meanings, referring to either fear or the cause of fear, a dangerous condition. Niddesa glosses *mahabbhayaṃ* by a register of terms that signify peril or danger rather than fear, for which other synonyms would have been used. I therefore translate *mahabbhayaṃ* as "great peril" rather than "great fear."

2064. As Norman points out (GD 383), the meter of pāda b is incorrect. He suggests that *pamādā* might be omitted, but the Skt follows the correct meter with its reading, *pramādān na prakāśate*; the Skt does not have anything corresponding to *vevicchā*. Niddesa, however, comments on *vevicchā*, which must therefore be old.

2065. On stream (*sota*) as a metaphor for craving, see **355**ab (*taṇhaṃ . . . Kaṇhassa sotaṃ*).

2066. Reading with Be and Ce *samannesamānā*. Ee should be corrected accordingly.

2067. *Gati*. DOP gives five meanings: (1) movement; (2) path, way; (3) sphere [of movement]; (4) destination; (5) one's career; (6) where one goes after death. It is hard to determine exactly which is intended here, but I have opted for (3).

2068. The Skt parallel has an additional pair of verses here, Śag 39.7–8 (see Appendix 2), which in Sn occur in the Questions of Udaya as **1110–11**. Since that exchange continues the discussion about the cessation of consciousness, it seems to fit better with the Questions of Ajita, as it does in the Skt version.
2069. The seven trainees (*sekha*) are those who have attained the four paths and the three lower fruits. The arahant, who has attained the fourth fruit, is "one beyond training" (*asekha*).
2070. *Bhinnattā bhikkhubhāvaṃ patto*. There is a word play here between *bhikkhu* and *bhinnattā*, "demolished."
2071. These were accessories adopted by non-Buddhist ascetics.
2072. *Mantā na lippatī ti paññāya na lippati*. I follow Pj II, which takes *mantā* to be a truncated instrumental. Norman again takes it as the agent noun *mantar*. See notes 744, 1378, and 1980.
2073. At AN 6:61, III 399–402, six monks discuss the meaning of **1042**, which they each interpret in a different way. When they present their views to the Buddha, he says they have all spoken well but his intention was this: "Contact is one end; the arising of contact is the second end; the cessation of contact is in the middle; and craving is the seamstress. For craving sews one to the production of this or that state of existence."
2074. The different interpretations here are drawn from AN 6:61.
2075. *Lepa*, an adhesive, is that by which one "gets stuck," *lippati*.
2076. See Appendix 3.
2077. The same question is posed at **458**, where it seems out of place, since the Buddha does not answer it. Pj II here glosses *akappayiṃsu* with *pariyesanti*, which is hard to explain. In relation to **458**, the word was glossed *saṃvidahiṃsu akaṃsu*, which seems more suitable.
2078. These were sects of ascetics contemporary with the Buddha. The Ājīvakas were followers of Makkhali Gosāla, who taught a doctrine of determination by destiny; the Nigaṇṭhas were the Jains; *jaṭilas* were matted-hair ascetics; and *tāpasas* were unaffiliated hermits.
2079. In **1043**d, *puthū idha loke*, the exact reference of *puthū* is ambiguous. I connect it with the subject, but Niddesa offers three alternatives.
2080. See p. 891 and p. 1114.
2081. *Catasso upādinnadhātuyo upadhī*. Nidd II-a 22,5–6: "These are just the four primary elements—earth and so forth—originating from kamma, acquired through kamma."
2082. This differs from the usual fourfold explanation of *upadhi* found in the commentaries, as sensual pleasures, as the aggregates, as defilements, and as volitional activities. See p. 397.
2083. *Dukkhassa jātippabhavānupassī ti vaṭṭadukkhassa jātikāraṇaṃ upadhī ti anupassanto*. See note 1721. In explicating the expression

dukkhassa jātippabhavānupassī, the Niddesa, if I understand it correctly, associates *jāti* with *dukkhassa* and takes *pabhavānupassī* as a separate term, thus as "contemplating the origin of suffering [such as] birth." I differ and take *jāti* and *pabhava* to be parallel terms.

2084. The expression *diṭṭhe dhamme* (or *diṭṭhe'va dhamme*) is normally used in the Nikāyas to mean "in this very life" as contrasted with future lives. Pj II offers this as an alternative gloss, but its primary gloss, *diṭṭhe dukkhādidhamme*, takes *diṭṭhe dhamme* literally as "things (teachings, principles) that are seen." Niddesa also offers both explanations. I have adopted the second one, which seems to fit better with *anītihaṃ*.

2085. This is the standard verse of homage to the Dhamma.

2086. See AN I 189,8–10, though the order of terms is slightly different here.

2087. Apparently Pj II sees *ca* in pāda a as a true conjunction indicating two objects, and it thus separates *tañ*, which it identifies with the Buddha's statement, from *dhammamuttamaṃ*. I do not find this convincing, but see *ca* as a mere metrical filler. Neither Norman nor Jayawickrama follows Pj II here.

2088. *Uddhaṃ adho tiriyañcāpi majjhe*. Norman translates this as if four terms were indicated, separating *tiriyañ* from *majjhe*: "across, and also in the middle."

2089. The text reads: *etesu nandiñca nivesanañca, panujja viññāṇaṃ bhave na tiṭṭhe*. Pj II paraphrases: *Etesu nandiñca nivesanañca, panujja viññāṇan ti etesu uddhādīsu taṇhañca diṭṭhinivesanañca abhisaṅkhāraviññāṇañca panudehi, panuditvā ca bhave na tiṭṭhe, evaṃ sante duvidhepi bhave na tiṭṭheyya*. Pj II proposes two ways of construing *panujja*, as imperative *panudehi*, and as the absolutive *panuditvā*. Niddesa glosses *panujja* exclusively with a series of imperatives (*nuda panuda jaha pajaha*, etc.). I find this problematic, since *panujja* is clearly an absolutive (< *panudya*). Further, contrary to Pj II, I understand *viññāṇaṃ* to be the subject of *tiṭṭhe*, not the object of *panujja*. I elaborate on this point in the following note.

2090. Norman and Jayawickrama both follow Pj II and Niddesa in their translations, taking *viññāṇaṃ* to be the object of the absolutive *panujja*. It seems to me, however, on doctrinal grounds that *viññāṇam* should be seen as the subject of *bhave na tiṭṭhe*. Thus I render the line: "consciousness would not persist in existence." But when rendering the commentary, to bridge the disparity, I put "one" in brackets. My reading of the verse is consonant with such passages as SN II 102,26–28: "If there is no lust, no delight, no craving [in regard to the four nutriments], consciousness is unestablished, not coming to growth there" (*natthi rāgo natthi nandī natthi taṇhā, appatiṭṭhitaṃ tattha viññāṇaṃ avirūḷhaṃ*). A similar point is made by SN III 53,20–26: "If a bhikkhu abandons lust [for the five aggregates], through the abandoning of lust the basis is cut off and there is no establishment of consciousness" (*bhikkhuno rāgo pahīno hoti, rāgassa pahānā vocchijjatārammaṇaṃ patiṭṭhā viññāṇassa na hoti*). At SN III 124,12–13, the Buddha declares that the monk Vakkali, who expired as an arahant, "attained final nibbāna with consciousness not established" (*appatiṭṭhitena viññāṇena Vakkali kulaputto parinibbuto*).

Pj II (and Niddesa) may have thought that since Mettagū is the implicit subject of the relative clause (*yaṃ sampajānāsi*) and of the absolutive (*panujja*), he must also be the subject of *na tiṭṭhe* in the main clause and thus it made *viññāṇaṃ* an object of *panujja*. However, while taking *viññāṇaṃ* to be the object of *panujja* (along with *nandiṃ* and *nivesanaṃ*) may avoid a grammatical glitch, a doctrinal problem would then crop up owing to the unusual injunction to dispel *viññāṇa*. The Nikāyas consistently assert that it is craving and related defilements that are to be dispelled, not *viññāṇa*, while the suttas cited just above state that it is *viññāṇa* that is "unestablished" and that therefore "would not persist in *bhava*." I translate the line accordingly, even though in doing so I depart from the commentaries.

2091. I cite the lemma as I translate the text, which differs from the explanation given just below by Niddesa. See the preceding note.

2092. It seems that Niddesa is here glossing *panujja* by a register of imperatives, which would be problematic, since *panujja* is not an imperative form. In an online discussion Lance Cousins remarked: "I don't think Niddesa intends to interpret *panujja* as an imperative. Rather it is giving an explanation: 'having dispelled' implies a prior instruction to dispel: 'whatever you understand thoroughly, <you should dispel>. Having dispelled it . . .'" I doubt that Cousins is correct about this. Pj II 591,15 explicitly ascribes the imperative sense to *panujja*: *panujja-saddassa "panudehī" ti.*

2093. Since Niddesa does not specify the subject, I have used the alternative "[it/one]," where "it" represents consciousness and "one" represents the person.

2094. *Aṭṭhitan ti sakkaccaṃ, sadā vā. Aṭṭhitan* is a negative past participle used adverbally.

2095. *Sattannaṃ dhammānaṃ bāhitattā brāhmaṇo*. Compare with the explanation of "bhikkhu" at p. 1045 and p. 1238 as one who has demolished (*bhinna*) these same seven things. Here, there is a different word play involved, a derivation of *brāhmaṇa* from *bāhita*. See note 576.

2096. The commentaries often gloss *kiñcana* with *palibodha,* impediment, as Nidd II-a 27,15–16 does here: *Rāgakiñcanan ti rāgapalibodhaṃ. Dosakiñcanan ti ādipi es'eva nayo.* Thus, on this interpretation, *akiñcana* might have been rendered "one without impediments." See too pp. 58–59.

2097. I read with Be here: *nāhaṃ sahissāmī ti ahaṃ na sahissāmi na sakkhissāmi, na vāyamissāmī ti vuttaṃ hoti.* Ce and Ee have *nāhaṃ gamissāmī ti, ahaṃ na gamissāmi, na sikkhāmi* [Ce: *na sikkhissāmi*]. Niddesa (Ee) has *n'āhaṃ samīhāmi,* but Be and Ce have *nāhaṃ sahissāmi.* Norman (GD 389) prefers *sahissāmi.*

2098. Niddesa supports this statement by quoting the same canonical passages cited on p. 1026, but omitting the citation of **1064** itself.

2099. *Santo* can be either the present participle of *atthi,* "is, exists," or the past participle of *sammati,* "becomes peaceful," functioning as an adjective. Since the Buddha follows up his request by offering to teach the state of peace (*santiṃ*), it seems self-evident that *santo* was intended as "peaceful." Pj II, however, bypasses the apparent meaning and glosses it only as *samāno,* an alternate form of the present participle from *atthi.* Niddesa, in contrast, glosses it in both ways, with *samāno* and *upasanto vūpasanto.* This is an interesting case where the commentary not only neglects the apparent meaning of a term but favors the term's less likely meaning over a better gloss offered by a more ancient exegetical text.

2100. Pj II glosses *nattamaho*—apparently unique to this verse—with *rattindivaṃ.* In this it follows Nidd II, which glosses *nattaṃ* with *ratti* and *aho* with *divaso.*

2101. The text has *virato kathāhi.* Niddesa first explains *kathāhi* as a truncated form of *kathaṃkathā* (literally "how-how"), which normally means doubt or perplexity. It then takes *kathāhi* as the ablative plural of *kathā,* "talk," and relates it to the thirty-two kinds of pointless talk (*dvattiṃsa tiracchānakathā*).

2102. Norman renders *saññāvimokkha* as "release from perception," which takes the first term of the compound as an ablative. I understand the compound to mean that these meditative attainments are *accompanied by perception*; they thus stand in contrast to the two higher attainments, the base of neither-perception-nor-nonperception and the cessation of perception and feeling. In the former perception is so refined that its function is no longer discernible; in the latter it has utterly ceased. In this connection MN II 229,31–230,3 says: "Some make assertions about the base of nothingness, immeasurable and imperturbable; [for them] 'there is nothing' is declared to be the purest, supreme, best, and unsurpassed of those perceptions—whether perceptions of form or of the formless, of unity or diversity." (*Yā vā pan'etāsaṃ saññānaṃ parisuddhā paramā aggā anuttariyā akkhāyati yadi rūpasaññānaṃ yadi arūpasaññānaṃ yadi ekattasaññānaṃ yadi nānattasaññānaṃ, 'natthi kiñcī' ti ākiñcaññāyatanam eke abhivadanti appamāṇaṃ āneñjaṃ.*) The future Buddha attained the base of nothingness under Āḷāra Kālāma, his first teacher, but finding it insufficient he left to continue his quest.

2103. In the text, I read *vimutto* with Be and Ee as against Ce *dhimutto* (= *adhimutto*). Pj II does not gloss the word. Nidd II glosses *adhimutto tatrādhimutto tadadhimutto*. Despite this, it seems this meditator has already attained the base of nothingness, which would correspond better to *vimutto*. In contrast, *adhimutto* suggests resolution on attaining it.

2104. *Saññāvimokkhā vuccanti satta saññāsamāpattiyo*. The seven attainments are the four jhānas and the lower three formless attainments.

2105. *Adhimuttivimokkhena adhimutto*. The purport of this expression, apparently, is to explain *vimokkha* as *adhimutti*, thus indicating that the meditator has not yet attained the base of nothingness but is merely intent on it. I can see no reason, however, for denying that this meditator has actually attained the base of nothingness.

2106. *Pūgampi vassānan ti anekasaṅkhampi vassānaṃ, gaṇarāsin ti attho*. For *pūga*[1] PED gives "heap, quantity." The word is not completely distinct from *pūga*[2], meaning "corporation, guild."

2107. Be and Ce read the verb here as *bhaveyya*, Ee *vibhaveyya*. On the basis of Niddesa, I take the correct reading to be *caveyya*, a use of the active optative to gloss the rare middle-voice verb *cavetha*. The verb *cavati* is usually joined with *upapajjati* to signify death and rebirth. Here, however, Pj II offers two interpretations: either as complete annihilation or as death preceding a new rebirth. It is hard to determine the original intention.

2108. The passage is describing the practitioner who, as a human being, had become a trainee (*sekha*) and then taken rebirth in the base of nothingness, the third of the four formless realms. Since he attains the formless meditations, he is said to have been earlier "naturally" (*pakatiyā*) liberated from the form body (*rūpakāya*). By reaching the fourth path, the path of arahantship there, he becomes an arahant and is said to be liberated from the mental body (*nāmakāya*). Although I render *nāmarūpa* as "name-and-form," I felt that to render *nāmakāya* here as "name body" would obscure the intended meaning.

2109. Pj II and Niddesa construe being liberated from the mental body as the attainment of arahantship and thus take the expression *nāmakāyā vimutto* as designating one who, having attained arahantship, continues to live on as "one liberated in both respects" (see MN I 477,26–29, Pp 14, §24). Perhaps, though, *nāmakāyā vimutto* refers to one who, after having already attained arahantship in the base of nothingness, attains final nibbāna in that realm.

2110. I read with Ce *tadaṅgasamatikkamā,* as against Be *tadaṅgaṃ samatikkamā.* On this interpretation, the sage is first temporarily liberated from the form body by attainment of the formless meditations, which suppress the defilements as well as the experience of the body. Then subsequently, with the attainment of arahantship, he is liberated from the mental body.

2111. Pj II here rearranges the syntax of the verse in a way contrary to the intended meaning. The original line, *santi loke munayo janā vadanti,* says: "people say there are munis in the world"; the paraphrase makes this say: "people in the world say there are munis." Niddesa simply glosses the words in their original sequence without making any rearrangements.

2112. The pāda **1078**a, *na diṭṭhiyā na sutiyā na ñāṇena,* is identical with **839**a. This dialogue has a flavor similar to that of several suttas in the Aṭṭhakavagga.

2113. See p. 1061, Pj II and Niddesa commentary on **793**.

2114. *Kotūhalamaṅgalādinā.* Mp III 302,20–22: "The belief in auspicious sights and sounds, 'This will happen on account of that,' which is designated superstition" (*kotūhalamaṅgaliko ti "iminā idaṃ bhavissatī" ti evaṃ pavattattā kotūhalasaṅkhātena diṭṭhasutamutamaṅgalena samannāgato*).

2115. This exact statement is untraced, but statements about abandoning craving—or desire and lust—for the six sense objects are numerous in the Nikāyas.

2116. *Sabbaṃ taṃ takkavaḍḍhanaṃ.* Although Pj II and Niddesa take *takka* here to be identical with *vitakka,* in the sense of distracting thoughts, it is possible that *takka* was intended in the epistemological sense as one of the criteria of belief rejected as inadequate, for example, at AN I 189,9. See too the expression dismissive of the rationalists at DN I 16,19–21, etc.: *ekacco samaṇo vā brāhmaṇo vā takkī hoti vīmaṃsī, so takkapariyāhataṃ vīmaṃsānucaritaṃ sayaṃ paṭibhānaṃ evamāha,* "an ascetic or a brahmin is a thinker or investigator, who declares his own insight that has been hammered out *by thought* and encompassed by reflection." The Dhamma, in contrast, is called *atakkāvacara,* "beyond the range of thought."

2117. Niddesa cites here in full the entire passage from the Mahāsatipaṭṭhāna Sutta, which at DN II 308–9 defines "things with a pleasing and agreeable nature" as the sixfold sets of internal sense bases, external sense bases, consciousness, contact, feeling, perception, volition, craving, thought, and examination.

2118. *Accutan ti niccaṃ dhuvaṃ sassataṃ avipariṇāmadhammanti – nibbānapadamaccutaṃ*. While the Nikāyas speak of nibbāna as *accutaṃ* and *dhuvaṃ*, the use here of the terms *niccaṃ*, *sassataṃ*, and *avipariṇāmadhammaṃ* to describe nibbāna seems innovative.

2119. *Diṭṭhadhammābhinibbutā*. Both Pj II and Niddesa take *diṭṭhadhamma* here to mean "those who have seen the Dhamma." Hence Pj II equates the term with *viditadhamma* and Niddesa treats it as a truncated nominative plural, *diṭṭhadhammā*, glossed *ñātadhammā tulitadhammā tīritadhammā vibhūtadhammā vibhāvitadhammā*. I understand the term as equivalent to *diṭṭh'eva dhamme*, simplified to fit the meter, and thus in the text I render it "in this very life." Hence I translate the lemma following my understanding rather than in compliance with the commentaries. Norman, who translates the term "in the world of phenomena," evidently shares my understanding, but Jayawickrama, following the commentary, has "by their realization of the teaching." The arahant is often described as *diṭṭh'eva dhamme . . . nibbuto sītībhūto*, which supports "quenched in this very life" (see MN I 349,1–2, AN II 211,25–26, and AN V 65,3).

2120. Here all three editions read *nirāsaso so uda āsasāno*.

2121. *Paññakappī*. Pj II, following the lead of the Niddesa, interprets *kappa* in the sense of "thought," but as a suffix the word can also mean "similar to," as in the expression *khaggavisāṇakappa*, a meaning that works better here.

2122. *Yathāyidaṃ nāparaṃ siyā ti yathā idaṃ dukkhaṃ puna na bhaveyya*. The line on its own is opaque. Norman renders "so that this [misery] may not occur again." Jayawickrama takes it as describing *dīpaṃ*: "that island the like of which shall never be." The commentaries support Norman's rendering, and I follow him in sense.

2123. *Anāparan ti aparapaṭibhāgadīpavirahitaṃ, seṭṭhan ti vuttaṃ hoti*. DOP explains *anāpara* as "*a* + *apara*, with rhythmical or metrical lengthening."

2124. The explanation in Niddesa is ambiguous, since *vāna* is a homonym meaning either "weaving" or "jungle." Both are used in the commentaries in playful etymologies of nibbāna. For *vāna* as weaving, see note 869, and as jungle, note 1097.

2125. *Itipi so bhagavā*. An allusion to the canonical verse of homage to the Buddha.

2126. *Sahajanettā ti sahajātasabbaññutañāṇacakkhu*. *Sahaja* is literally "coarisen," but the word seems to be used to mean what comes along at birth. Norman, following Pj II, translates *sahajanetta* simply as "omniscient one." Jayawickrama takes *bhagavā* and *sahajanetta* together and renders "Exalted One of inborn vision."

2127. See note 1786.

2128. *Yamahaṃ jātijarānaṃ pahānabhūtaṃ dhammaṃ idh'eva jāneyyaṃ.* It appears that Pj II takes *idha* in relation to *vijaññaṃ*, which requires that *idha* be transposed syntactically from pāda e to pāda d of this five-line verse. Niddesa, however, takes *idha* to belong with *vippahānaṃ*. This is preferable both by way of meaning and syntax.

2129. *Jātijarāya idha vippahānan ti idh'eva jātijarāya maraṇassa pahānaṃ vūpasamaṃ paṭinissaggaṃ paṭippassaddhiṃ amataṃ nibbānan ti.* Unlike Pj II, Niddesa retains *idh'eva* in the same syntactical position as *idha* of the text.

2130. As in relation to **424**, here too Pj II glosses *daṭṭhu* with the normal absolutive, *disvā*.

2131. Sn **1098** reads *uggahitaṃ nirattaṃ vā, mā te vijjittha kiñcanaṃ.* Compare with **787**, *attā nirattā na hi tassa atthi* (commented on at pp. 1051–52).

2132. Niddesa here interprets "home" (*oka*) as the five aggregates to which craving becomes attached. In this respect it resembles Mahākaccāna's interpretation of **844**. See note 1893.

2133. These include not only the states of greater India but regions beyond the subcontinent.

2134. *Ādānataṇhaṃ.* Strictly speaking, this is probably a *dvanda* compound combining "taking" and "craving." The explanation in Niddesa, however, can justify my rendering, which treats *ādāna* as a function of *taṇhā*: *tāya taṇhāya rūpaṃ ādiyanti upādiyanti gaṇhanti parāmasanti abhinivisanti.*

2135. Māra as the five aggregates is one of the four kinds of Māra recognized by the commentaries. In the formula of dependent origination, these are acquired at birth (*jāti*), which is conditioned by kammically active existence (*bhava*) in the previous life, which is in turn conditioned by clinging (*upādāna*).

2136. All editions read *paññānubhāvanijjhātaṃ*, but a search through CST4 does not turn up any other occurrences of **nijjhāta** at the end of a compound. The abstract noun in the ablative, *nijjhātattā*, occurs several times in Nidd II in a string of synonyms indicating calmness, but this does not fit here. With a Burmese manuscript noted in Ee, I thus read *paññānubhāvena jātaṃ*.

2137. The first couplet of each verse is also in the verses cited at Nidd I 383. See p. 1215.

2138. *Etameva ca aññāvimokkhaṃ avijjāpabhedanasaṅkhātaṃ nibbānaṃ nissāya jātattā kāraṇopacārena avijjāya pabhedanan ti pabrūmi.* See DOP sv *upacāra*[3] where the word is explained as "extended application, non-literal application, figurative use, secondary meaning." The point is that nibbāna itself is the unconditioned state in which ignorance is perpetually absent, while arahantship, as the conditioned event by which ignorance is broken up, arises on the basis of nibbāna.

2139. Verses **1108–9** are also at SN I 39, §4.

2140. This verse and the following one seem to fit in better with the dialogue with Ajita and would be a natural sequel to **1037**. In the Śag counterpart to the Ajita Sutta, that is precisely where they are found; see Appendix 2, Śag 39.7–8. This discrepancy suggests that in the Pāli version of Sn the pair of verses has been misplaced.

2141. At Paṭis I 120–35 these knowledges are described at length. The omniscient knowledge (*sabbaññutañāṇa*) and the unobstructed knowledge (*anāvaraṇañāṇa*) are actually two names for the same knowledge; the *asaṅgam appaṭihatam anāvaraṇañāṇaṃ* as well refers to this knowledge. The mention of these knowledges, as well as other passages, suggests an affinity between the Niddesa and Paṭis.

2142. Nidd II-a 58,11–12: "*One's form body is abandoned*: the form-sphere body of the one who obtains the formless meditative attainment. *By overcoming it in a particular respect*: transcended by abandoning in a particular respect. *By abandoning it through suppression*: abandoned by suppression by obtaining a formless jhāna." On the distinction between these types of abandoning, see p. 363.

2143. *Vimuttan ti ākiñcaññāyatanādīsu adhimuttaṃ*. Such is the reading in all three editions of Pj II, but the treatment of the line in Niddesa suggests there was an ambiguity about the reading. See note 2150 just below.

2144. *Tapparāyaṇan ti tammayaṃ*. The meaning, it seems, is one who is heading toward rebirth in that realm.

2145. Nidd II-a 59,6–15: "Human beings are different in body (*nānattakāyā*) because there are no two people whose bodies are exactly alike. Even twins of the same complexion and figure differ in the way they look around, etc. People are different in perception (*nānattasaññino*) because in some cases their rebirth perception (*paṭisandhisaññā*) has three roots, in others two roots, and in still others it is rootless. The devas mentioned are the six sense-sphere devas. The beings in the lower world are certain yakkhas and spirits outside the fourfold plane of misery."

2146. Nidd II-a 59,28–60,6: "These are the devas of Brahmā's assembly, Brahmā's ministers, and the great brahmās. Their bodies are different in pervasion according to their respective level, but their perception is the same because they all have the perception pertaining to the first jhāna. The beings in the four planes of misery also belong to this group. [Their bodies are different] but they all have a [rebirth] perception that is a rootless unwholesome resultant."

2147. Nidd II–a 60,8–16: "The radiance given off by their bodies streams off, flickering like the flame of a torch. Hence they are called deities of streaming radiance. Those who develop to a limited degree the second and third jhānas of the fivefold scheme are reborn as devas of limited radiance. Those who develop them to a middling degree are reborn as devas of measureless radiance. Those who develop them to a superior degree are reborn as devas of streaming radiance (*devā ābhassarā*). All are included here by mentioning the best. In each plane, their bodies all have the same pervasion (*ekavipphāro va*), but their perception is different in that some are without thought but with examination alone (*avitakka-vicāramattā*), while others are without thought and without examination (*avitakka-avicārā*)."

2148. Nidd II–a 60,17–24: "They form a single mass through their glory, the beauty of their bodily radiance. Their radiance does not flicker like that of the devas of streaming radiance. Beings are reborn as devas of limited glory, measureless glory, and refulgent glory by way of the inferior, middling, and superior quality of the jhāna—the third in the fourfold scheme and the fourth in the fivefold scheme. The devas of refulgent glory (*subhakiṇhā*) are identical in body and identical in perception because they all have the perception pertaining to the fourth jhāna (in the scheme of five jhānas). The devas of great fruit (who are reborn through the fifth jhāna of the fivefold scheme) come under the fourth station of consciousness. The nonpercipient beings do not have consciousness and thus are not included."

2149. Niddesa quotes at length here the passage on the Buddha's ability to know in advance the rebirth of beings, at MN I 74–77.

2150. Ce reads *adhimuttaṃ tapparāyaṇaṃ ti*; Be has *dhimuttaṃ tapparāyaṇan ti* where *dhi-* is apparently a metrical shortening of *adhi-*. Thus both versions, in the lemma as well as in the gloss, adopt *adhimuttaṃ* over *vimuttaṃ*, which is found in all three printed texts of Sn. Ee of Niddesa, however, has *vimuttaṃ* both in the verse citation and in §587 (p. 250). The expression *vimokkhenadhimuttaṃ* (so Ce; Be *vimokkhena dhimuttaṃ*) in the register of terms suggests that even the authors of Niddesa were uncertain what was intended in the original. Whereas *vimutta* normally means "liberated, released," either temporarily or permanently, *adhimutta* means "resolved on, intent on."

Thus, while both are prefixed forms of *mutta*, "freed," there is a substantial difference in their meanings. The same ambiguity is also at **1072**.

Nidd II-a 69,30–70,5 tries to bridge the two terms by explaining *vimokkha* in terms of *adhimuccana*: "In what sense should 'emancipation' be understood? In the sense of being resolved upon. And in what sense are they resolved upon? In the sense of emancipating thoroughly from the adverse phenomena and in the sense of emancipating thoroughly by way of delight in the object. What is meant is [the mind's] occurrence on the object without constraint, free from apprehension, similar to the way a little boy sleeps in his father's lap, his body completely relaxed." (*Kenaṭṭhena vimokkho veditabbo ti? Adhimuccanaṭṭhena. Ko ayaṃ adhimuccanaṭṭho nāma? Paccanīkadhammehi ca suṭṭhu vimuccanaṭṭho, ārammaṇe ca abhirativasena suṭṭhu vimuccanaṭṭho, pitu aṅke vissaṭṭha-aṅgapaccaṅgassa dārakassa sayanaṃ viya aniggahitabhāvena nirāsaṅkatāya ārammaṇe pavattī ti vuttaṃ hoti.*)

2151. These are seven of the traditional thirteen austere practices (*dhutaṅga*).

2152. The elision here should be filled in with the remaining six meditative attainments.

2153. The elision here should be filled in with all the items under the rubric of "resolved upon" just above.

2154. *Itī ti padasandhi padasaṃsaggo padapāripūrī akkharasamavāyo byañjanasiliṭṭhatā padānupubbatāpetaṃ itī ti.*

2155. On the three kinds of devas, see pp. 1261–62.

2156. Reading with Ce and Ee *bhagavā devo c'eva isi cā ti devisi*. Be is missing *devo*.

2157. *Avasiyapavattasallakkhaṇavasena vā tucchasaṅkhārasamanupassanāvasena vā ti dvīhi kāraṇehi suññato lokaṃ passa*. These will be elaborated by Niddesa below.

2158. Reading with Be *uddharitvā* as against Ce and Ee *uttaritvā*. Both Be and Ce have *uddharitvā* and *samuddharitvā* in the gloss on the word in Niddesa.

2159. The first verse cited here and the first couplet of the second verse are at Th 716–17ab.

2160. *Rūpesū ti rūpahetu rūpapaccayā*. Pj II explains the locative *rūpesu* as having an instrumental sense.

2161. *Atthamaññāyā ti pāḷiatthamaññāya. Dhammamaññāyā ti pāḷimaññāya*. Here the word *pāḷi* is being used in its original sense, as a designation for the canonical text.

2162. Just above Pj II said that Piṅgiya did *not achieve* arahantship but the stage of non-returner, and below it will say that he attains arahantship after he returned to Bāvari. Thus in ascribing arahantship to the sixteen, Pj II must be speaking proleptically.

2163. *Ñāṇagamanen'eva godhāvarītīraṃ gantvā*. Perhaps what is meant is that he traveled by psychic power.

2164. *Nibbano*, from *nir* + *vana*. Literally "without the jungle," where "jungle" (*vana*) symbolizes craving.

2165. *Saccavhayo ti "buddho" ti saccen'eva avhānena nāmena yutto*. Thus *saccavhaya* does not mean "whose name is truth" but one *truthfully named* as "Buddha."

2166. This alludes to the doctrine that the fruit arises in immediate succession to the path. The adoption of this doctrine by Niddesa does not imply that the work recognizes the "cognitive process" (*cittavīthi*) precisely as it developed in Abhidhamma circles. The tenet that the fruit directly follows the path may have been held in a more general form at the time the work was composed.

2167. The story of the monk Vakkali is told at SN 22:87, III 119–24. Āḷavi Gotama is mentioned only here. By "send forth faith" (*pamuñcassu saddhaṃ*) is meant establishing firm faith and trust.

2168. *Muñcassu pamuñcassu sampamuñcassu adhimuñcassu okappehi*.

2169. *Adhideve abhiññāyā ti adhidevakare dhamme ñatvā*. I take the prefix *adhi-* here to be just a referential term. Norman (GD 407) cites the Critical Pāli Dictionary, which "takes the word as an indeclinable phrase made from *adhi* + locative singular or accusative plural of *deva* = 'concerning the gods.'"

2170. I interpret *kaṅkhīnaṃ paṭijānataṃ* differently from Pj II. The verb *paṭijānāti* can mean either "to make a claim" to something or "to admit" something. Pj II takes it to mean that they claim to be without doubt (*kaṅkhīnaṃyeva sataṃ nikkaṅkhamhā ti paṭijānantānaṃ*). I understand it to mean that they *admit their doubt*. This makes better sense, for the Buddha can resolve doubt only for those who admit their doubt, not for those who consider themselves wise. Though it does not gloss *paṭijānataṃ*, Niddesa seems to support my interpretation (see just below). Norman has "those who are in doubt, [and] admit it," which corresponds to my reading. Jayawickrama follows the commentary: "those with doubt who were claiming (that they were free from doubt)."

2171. *Vivattacchaddo sambuddho*. See note 1269.

2172. The corresponding verse at the beginning of Pj II reads the last word in pāda b as *lokanissaraṇesinā*, but in this concluding verse the corresponding word is *lokanittharaṇesinā*. This is preferable, for the Buddha, as *lokanātha*, is better conceived as one seeking *to rescue* the world than as one seeking *to escape* from it.

2173. This colophon is similar to the one at the end of Vism. I base this translation on Ñāṇamoli's rendering of the colophon to Ppn, with slight modifications.

Pāli-English Glossary

This glossary consists primarily of terms with doctrinal significance; they are arranged according to the order of the Pāli alphabet, on which see p. 21. Preference is given to nouns over cognate adjectives and verbs. Preference is also given to positive forms over negations, though the latter are included when they are more prominent than their positive base. Compounds are included only when their meaning is not immediately apparent from their members. Distinct meanings of a single term are indicated by an enumeration, with semicolons as separation. Different renderings intended to capture distinct nuances of a word are separated by commas, without enumeration. Homonyms are listed separately. Terms that signify a numerical set are cross-referenced to Appendix 3. Square brackets are used when I am filling in a definition, parentheses when I add an explanatory comment.

Pāli	English
akālika	immediate (without an interval of time)
akiñcana	owning nothing
akusala	unwholesome
agāriya	a layperson
aggi	fire. *See* Appendix 3 (under 11).
accaya	a transgression [of the monastic rules]
accuta	imperishable (said of nibbāna)
ajjava	honesty, rectitude
ajjhāsaya	inclination of the mind

Pāli	English
aññā	final knowledge [entailing arahantship]
atimāna	arrogance
atta	taken up
attabhāva	(1) the person, personal existence, personhood; (2) the body
attā	self
attha	(1) meaning; (2) benefit, good; (3) purpose, goal
atthaṅgama	passing away
adhikāra	(1) a basis, a foundation; (2) service; (3) a governing word
adhigama	achievement [of a stage of realization]
adhiṭṭhāna	mental determination
adhippāya	purport [of a statement]
adhimutti	conviction, resolution
adhivacana	designation
anattā	non-self
anabhirati	dissatisfaction
anaya	misery
anāgāmī	a non-returner
anāgāriya	a homeless one
anādāna	not taking
anāvila	unsullied
anāsava	without influxes
anigha	untroubled
anicca	impermanent
animitta	markless (a state of concentration)
anītika	without adversity
anītiha	no matter of hearsay
anukampaka	compassionate
anupassanā	contemplation
anupādisesa	without residue remaining (said of nibbāna at death of arahant)
anuvyañjana	minor features [of physical excellence]
anusandhi	sequence [of a teaching]

PĀLI	ENGLISH
anusaya	latent tendency. *See* Appendix 3 (under 4).
anussati	recollection
anussava	oral tradition
aneja	without impulse (description of an arahant)
apāya	the plane of misery (the bad realms of rebirth)
apekkhā	anxious concern
appagabbha	courteous
appanā	absorption [concentration]
appamāda	heedfulness
appicchatā	fewness of desires
abhijjhā	longing, covetousness
abhiññā	(1) direct knowledge; (2) super-knowledge. *See* Appendix 3 (under 5).
abhinibbuta	quenched
abhinīhāra	undertaking (the resolution for enlightenment)
abhilepana	an adhesive
abhisaṅkhārā	volitional activities
abhisamaya	the breakthrough [to realization of the path]
amata	the deathless (said of nibbāna)
amanussa	a spirit (literally, a nonhuman being)
arati	discontent
arahatta	arahantship
arahant	*untranslated*: one fully liberated from the round of rebirths
ariya	noble, a noble one
arūpa	formless [meditative attainment or realm of existence]
alasabhāva	indolence
avijjā	ignorance
aviññāṇaka	insentient (literally, without consciousness)
aviparīta	undistorted

Pāli	English
avihiṃsā	harmlessness
Avīci	*untranslated*: the lowest hell realm
asaṃkuppa	unshakable (said of nibbāna)
asaṃhīra	immovable (said of nibbāna)
asaṅkhata	unconditioned (said of nibbāna)
asaṅkheyya	an "incalculable" (an extremely long period of cosmic time)
asammoha	non-delusion
asubha	unattractive [nature of the body]
asekha	one beyond training (said of an arahant)
asoka	sorrowless
assāda	gratification
ākāsa	space, the sky
ākiñcañña	(1) nothingness (as a meditative state); (2) ownerlessness
āghāta	resentment
ājānīya	a thoroughbred (said metaphorically of an arahant)
ājīva	livelihood
Ājīvaka	an adherent of an ascetic sect headed by Makkhali Gosāla
ādiccabandhu	Kinsman of the Sun (an epithet of the Buddha)
ādīnava	danger
ānantarika	without interval
ānisaṃsā	benefit
ānubhāva	spiritual might
āpatti	an offense (a transgression of the monastic rules)
āpo	water [element]
āyatana	a sense base. *See* Appendix 3 (under 12).
āyu	vitality
ārammaṇa	object [of meditation]
āvaraṇa	obstruction [of the mind]
āsaya	interest, wish, inclination

Pāli	English
āsava	influx. *See* Appendix 3 (under 4).
āhāra	nutriment. *See* Appendix 3 (under 4).
iñjita	agitation
ito bahiddhā	outside here (outside the Buddha's Teaching)
iddhi	spiritual power, spiritual potency
iddhipāda	a base of spiritual potency. *See* Appendix 3 (under 4).
indakhīla	a gate post
indriya	a faculty (spiritual or sensory). *See* Appendix 3 (under 5).
iriyāpatha	posture. *See* Appendix 3 (under 4).
isi	a rishi (an ascetic sage)
issā	envy
īti	adversity
ugghāti	elation
uccheda	annihilation (often compounded with *–diṭṭhi* or *–vāda*)
uju	upright
uṭṭhāna	initiative
udāna	joyful or inspired utterance
uddhacca	restlessness
unnati	pride
upacāra	access [concentration]
upaddava	disaster
upadhi	acquisition. *See* Appendix 3 (under 4).
upanāha	hostility
upanissaya	support, supporting condition
upapatti	rebirth
upaya	involvement
upavāda	criticism, blame
upasama	peace
upasampadā	full ordination
upassagga	calamity
upādāna	clinging. *See* Appendix 3 (under 4).

Pāli	English
upāsaka	lay follower (male)
upāsikā	lay follower (female)
upekkhā	equanimity
uposatha	*untranslated*: day of religious observance (the full-moon and new-moon days)
uppatti	origin [of a sutta]. *See* Appendix 3 (under 4).
uppāda	arising
ussada	swelling. *See* Appendix 3 (under 7).
eka	one, alone
ekagga	one-pointed (a quality of the concentrated mind)
ekabījī	a one-seed attainer (a type of stream-enterer)
ekāyanamagga	one-way path
ejā	impulse
okappana	trust
okāsaloka	the cosmos
obhāsa	radiance
ogha	flood. *See* Appendix 3 (under 4).
ottappa	moral dread
ovāda	an exhortation
kaṅkhā	doubt, perplexity
kataññutā	gratitude
kathaṃkathā	perplexity
kathojja	an argument (in a debate)
kappa	(1) eon; (2) mental construct, mental construction
kamma	action, deed (in technical sense untranslated)
kammaṭṭhāna	meditation subject
kammantā	an occupation
karuṇā	compassion
kalaha	a quarrel

Pāli	English
kalyāṇamitta	a good friend
kasiṇa	*untranslated*: a type of meditation object, usually representing an element or a color
kahāpaṇa	*untranslated*: a certain coin
kāma	sensual desire, sensual pleasure
kāmaguṇa	strands of sensual pleasure (pleasant forms, sounds, etc.)
kāmarūpī	able to assume any form at will
kāya	the body
kāla	time, proper time
kiñcana	"something," an impediment
kibbisa	wickedness
kilesa	a defilement
kukkucca	regret
kusala	(1) wholesome; (2) skilled, skillful
kusīta	lazy
kuhaka	a schemer
kuhana	scheming
kevalī	a consummate one (said of an arahant)
koṭi	*untranslated*: ten million
kodha	anger
kopa	irritation, anger
kolaṃkola	a family-to-family attainer (a type of stream-enterer)
kolāhala	a commotion. *See* Appendix 3 (under 5).
kosajja	laziness
khaggavisāṇa	a rhinoceros horn
khaṇa	(1) a moment; (2) an opportunity
khattiya	*untranslated*: the administrative-warrior caste
khanti	patience
khandha	aggregate. *See* Appendix 3 (under 5).
khila	barrenness. *See* Appendix 3 (under 3).
khema	security

Pāli	English
gaṇa	a group
gati	destination [of rebirth]. *See* Appendix 3 (under 5).
gantha	knot. *See* Appendix 3 (under 4).
gahaṭṭha	a householder
gārava	reverence
gāvuta	a unit of length (about 1.5 miles)
gihī	a layman
guṇa	excellent quality
gharāvāsa	the household life
cakkavatti	a wheel-turning monarch
cakkavāḷa	a world sphere
cakkhu	the eye
cakkhumā	"One with Vision" (epithet of the Buddha)
caṇḍāla	*untranslated*: a low type of outcast
caraṇa	conduct, good conduct
carita	temperament
cāga	(1) generosity; (2) relinquishment
cārikā	a tour
citta	the mind
cetanā	volition
cetiya	*untranslated*: a memorial shrine, often containing relics of holy beings
cetokhila	mental barrenness. *See* Appendix 3 (under 5).
chanda	desire (both wholesome and unwholesome)
jaṭila	*untranslated*: an ascetic wearing matted hair
jappā	hankering
jarā	old age
jāgariya	wakefulness

Pāli	English
jāti	(1) birth, production; (2) caste, social class
jina	conqueror (epithet of the Buddha or an arahant)
jeguccha	morally repulsive
jhāna	*untranslated*: meditative absorption
ñāṇa	knowledge
ṭhitatta	inwardly firm
takka	thought, reasoning
taṇhā	craving. *See* Appendix 3 (under 3 and 108).
tadaṅga	in a particular respect
tapo	austerity
tasathāvara	the frail and the firm
tādī	(1) one who is impartial; (2) such a one
tāpasa	a hermit
tiṇṇa	crossed over (the metaphorical flood—see *ogha*)
titthakara	a "ford-maker" (founder of a spiritual system)
titthiya	an adherent of another [non-Buddhist] sect
tīraṇa	scrutiny
tejo	fire [element]
thambha	pride, obstinacy
thina	dullness
dakkhiṇā	an offering
dakkhineyya	one worthy of offerings
daṇḍa	the rod (as a metaphor for violence)
danta	tamed
daratha	distress

Pāli	English
dassana	vision, perspective, seeing
dāna	giving, a gift
diṭṭha	seen
diṭṭhi	view
diṭṭhigata	speculative view. *See* Appendix 3 (under 62).
diṭṭhigatika	a theorist
diṭṭhe dhamme	in this very life
dukkarakārikā	difficult practice of austerities
dukkha	suffering, pain
duggati	a bad destination [of rebirth—see *gati*]
duccarita	misconduct
dussīla	immoral
deva	*untranslated*: a deity
devatā	a deity
desanā	a teaching
domanassa	dejection
dosa[1]	hatred
dosa[2]	fault
dhamma	(1) *untranslated*: the Buddha's teaching; (2) any teaching; (3) a mental quality; (4) thing (in general), a phenomenon; (5) righteousness
dhātu	(1) realm; (2) element. *See* Appendix 3 (under 3, 4, and 18).
dhiti	steadfastness
dhīra[1]	wise
dhīra[2]	steadfast
dhutaṅga	an austere practice
dhura	(1) a burden; (2) a vocation
dhona	cleansed [of evil]
nandī	delight

PĀLI	ENGLISH
nāga	*untranslated*: (1) a dragon-like being; (2) a cobra; (3) a large bull elephant; (4) epithet for the Buddha or an arahant
nāmarūpa	name-and-form
nikati	fraudulence
nikūṭa	culmination [of a teaching]
niketa	an abode
nikkāma	desireless
Nigaṇṭha	a Jain ascetic
nighāti	dejection
nindā	blame
nipaka	judicious
nipuṇa	(1) subtle; (2) astute
nippariyāya	direct [mode of teaching]
nibbidā	disenchantment
nibbuta	quenched, attained to nibbāna
nibbedha	penetration
nimitta	mark, sign
nimmita	emanated, (mind-) created
niyata	fixed in destiny
niyāma	fixed course (the noble path)
niyyāna	outlet
niyyānika	emancipating
niratta	rejected
niraya	hell
nirāsa	wishless, desireless
nirodha	cessation
nivāta	humility
nivāraṇa	a barrier
nivissavādī	a dogmatist
nivesana	(1) residence; (2) attachment
nisaṅkhati	activation
nissaya	dependency, a support
nissaraṇa	escape
nissita	dependent
nīvaraṇa	a hindrance. *See* Appendix 3 (under 5).

Pāli	English
nekkhamma	renunciation
pakappanā	formulation
pagabbha	impudent
paccakkha	directly cognized
paccaya	(1) a condition; (2) a material requisite [of monastic life]. *See* Appendix 3 (under 4).
paccavekkhaṇa	reviewing
paccūsasamaye	the time just before dawn
paccekabuddha	*untranslated*: one enlightened for himself
pajā	the population [of sentient beings]
paññā	wisdom
paṭikūla	repulsiveness
paṭigha	aversion
paṭiññā	(1) a promise, a vow; (2) an acknowledgment; (3) a claim
paṭippassaddhi	subsiding
paṭibhāna	ingenuity
paṭivedha	penetration
paṭisandhi	conception (at rebirth)
paṭisambhidā	analytical knowledge. *See* Appendix 3 (under 4).
paṭisallāna	seclusion
paṇidhi	(1) resolution; (2) wish
paṇīta	sublime
paṇḍita	a wise person
patiṭṭhā	foundation, foothold
patthanā	(1) aspiration; (2) longing
pathavī	the earth
pada	a state
padhāna	striving
papañca	proliferation [of mental activity]
pabbajita	one who has gone forth, a monk
pabbajjā	going forth [into homelessness]
pamāṇa	(1) measure; (2) a criterion [of knowledge]

Pāli	English
pamāda	heedlessness
payoga	effort
paramattha	the supreme goal
parābhava	downfall
parāyaṇa	a support
pariggaha	(1) a possession; (2) discernment [of conditions]
pariccheda	delimitation
pariññā	full understanding. *See* Appendix 3 (under 3).
paritassitā	agitation
parideva	lamentation
parinibbāyati	attains final nibbāna (with the passing away of an arahant)
parinibbuta	attained to nibbāna (either during life or by passing away)
paribbājaka	a wanderer
pariyatti	scriptural learning
pariyāya	(1) a way [of exposition]; (2) indirect [mode of exposition]
pariyuṭṭhāna	obsession [by a defilement]
parissaya	obstacle
parovara	from top to bottom, far and near
palibodha	impediment
paḷāsa	insolence
Pavāraṇā	*untranslated*: the ceremony that ends the three-months rains retreat
paviveka	solitude
pasaṃsā	praise
pasāda	(1) confidence; (2) clarity
pahāna	abandoning
Pācittiya	*untranslated*: a class of offenses against the monastic rules (those that can be cleared by confession)
pāṭihāriya	(1) a wonder; (2) a counteractive measure
pāṇa	a living being

Pāli	English
Pātimokkha	*untranslated*: the code of monastic rules
pāpa	evil
pāra	beyond [the round of birth and death]
pāramī	*untranslated*: a virtue to be perfected to attain enlightenment
Pārājika	*untranslated*: a class of offenses against the monastic rules (those that entail expulsion from the Sangha)
piṇḍapāta	almsfood
pīti	rapture
pīḷana	oppression
puggala	a person
puñña	merit
puthujjana	a worldling
punabbhava	renewed existence
pubbayoga	past exertion, prior meditation practice
purisa	a person
purekkhāra	preference
pūjā	veneration, honor, offering
pesala	well behaved
pesuṇa	slander
porāṇā	the ancients (early commentators)
phala	a fruit [of the path]. *See* Appendix 3 (under 4).
phassa	contact
bala	a power. *See* Appendix 3 (under 5).
bāla	a fool
bāhusacca	much learning
bījā	a seed
bojjhaṅga	a factor of enlightenment. *See* Appendix 3 (under 7).
bodhi	enlightenment

Pāli	English
bodhisatta	*untranslated*: an aspirant for buddhahood
brahmacariya	spiritual life
brāhmaṇa	a brahmin (either by caste or spiritual attainment)
bhagavā	the Blessed One (an epithet of the Buddha)
bhaya	(1) peril; (2) fear
bhava	(1) a state of existence; (2) coming-to-be
bhāvanā	development
bhāvitatta	self-developed
bhikkhu	a fully ordained monk
bhikkhunī	a fully ordained nun
bhūta	(1) a being; (2) what has come to be
bhūmi	ground, stage
makkha	denigration
magga	the path (especially the four world-transcending paths). *See* Appendix 3 (under 4).
maṅku	humiliation
maṅgala	a blessing, an auspicious sign
maccu	death
macchariya	miserliness. *See* Appendix 3 (under 5).
mada	vanity, intoxication, infatuation
maddava	mildness
manasikāra	attention
manussa	a human being
mano	mind
manta	sacred hymn [of the Vedas]
mantā	reflection
mamattā	taking things as "mine"
mamāyita	thing taken to be "mine"
maraṇa	death
mahāpurisa	the Great Man (the future Buddha)
mahesi	great rishi (an epithet of the Buddha)

Pāli	English
mātikā	an outline
māna	conceit
māyā	hypocrisy
micchādiṭṭhi	wrong view
mitta	a friend
middha	drowsiness
mucchā	infatuation
muta	sensed (an object of the physical senses)
muditā	altruistic joy
muni	*untranslated*: a sage leading an ascetic life
musāvāda	false speech
mūla	a root [of mental states and actions]
mettā	loving-kindness
methuna	sexual intercourse
medhaga	strife
moneyya	munihood (the state of a sage)
mosa	falsity
moha	delusion
yakkha	(1) *untranslated*: a demonic being; (2) the spirit
yañña	a sacrifice
yoga	bond, yoke
yogakkhema	security from bondage
yojana	a unit of length (about six miles)
yojanā	the construing [of a passage]
yoni	(1) the womb; (2) a mode of generation. *See* Appendix 3 (under 4).
ratana[1]	a gem. *See* Appendix 3 (under 3).
ratana[2]	a cubit: a measure of height, approximately sixteen inches
rati	delight
rāga	lust
rūpa	(1) material form; (2) visible form

Pāli	English
lakkhaṇa	(1) a characteristic of things; (2) the major bodily marks of a buddha
laggana	fastening
lūkha	stringency, stringent
lepana	an adhesive
loka	world
lokuttara	world-transcending. *See* Appendix 3 (under 9).
lomahaṃsa	terror
vañcana	cheating
vaṭṭa	the round [of birth and death, saṃsāra]
vaṇṇanā	explanation [of either terms or their meaning]
vata	observance (undertaken as a rite or an ascetic practice)
vatthu	(1) base, object; (2) a legal case; (3) a story
vanatha	desire
vavatthāna	delineation [of name-and-form, etc.]
vasala	an outcast
vācā	speech
vāda	(1) a doctrine, an assertion; (2) debate [about doctrines]
vāyo	air [element]
vāsana, vāsanā	a habitual formation, habituation
vikkhambhana	suppression
vikkhepa	distraction
vighāta	distress
vicakkhaṇa	astute
vicikicchā	doubt. *See* Appendix 3 (under 8).
vijjā	clear knowledge. *See* Appendix 3 (under 3).
viññatti	intimation
viññāṇa	consciousness
viññāta	cognized
vitakka	thought. *See* Appendix 3 (under 9).

Pāli	English
vitatha	unreal
vitta	a treasure
vinaya	(1) discipline; (2) removal
vinicchaya	a judgment [about disciplinary issues and views]
vinibandha	bondage
vipatti	a defect, a failure
vipallāsa	an inversion [of views, thought, and perception]
vipassanā	insight
vipāka	result [of kamma]
vippaṭisāra	remorse
vibhava	(1) non-existence; (2) vanishing
vimutti	liberation
vimokkha	emancipation
viraja	dust-free
virati	abstinence
viriya	energy
vivattacchadda	with coverings removed (said of the Buddha)
vivāda	a dispute
viveka	seclusion. *See* Appendix 3 (under 3).
visattikā	attachment
visaya	objective domain
visalla	free of darts
visuddhi	purification
visenibhūta	remote
visesa	a distinction (excellence in meditation practice)
vihiṃsā	harming (as a thought or intention); aggression
vihesā	harassment
vītarāga	one devoid of lust
vīthi	a process [of consciousness]
vīra	a [spiritual] hero
vedagū	(1) a Veda-master; (2) a master of knowledge (said of the Buddha)
vedanā	feeling

Pāli	English
vera	enmity
vevicchā	avarice
vessa	*untranslated*: the mercantile and agricultural caste
vokāra	a constituent (the aggregates constituting a sentient being)
vohāra	a conventional expression
vyasana	ruin, disaster
vyākaraṇa	(1) prediction [of future buddhahood]; (2) declaration [of attainment]
vyāpāda	ill will
vyārosanā	anger
saupādisesa	with a residue remaining (said of nibbāna during life)
saṃyojana	fetter. *See* Appendix 3 (under 10).
saṃvara	restraint
saṃvega	a sense of urgency
saṃsagga	bonding
saṃsāra	*untranslated*: the round of repeated birth and death
sakadāgāmī	a once-returner
sakkāya	the personal entity (the assemblage of five aggregates). *See* Appendix 3 (under 20) for twenty views about.
sagga	heaven
saṅkappa	intention, thought
saṅkilesa	defilement
saṅkhata	conditioned
saṅkhā	a designation
saṅkhāta	comprehended
saṅkhārā	(1) volitional activities; (2) conditioned things
saṅga	a tie
saṅgaṇikā	company
saṅgītikārakā	the compilers [of the canonical texts]
sacca	truth. *See* Appendix 3 (under 4).

Pāli	English
sacchikiriyā	realization
saññatatta	self-controlled
saññā	perception
saṭhatā, sāṭheyya	deceitfulness
sati	mindfulness
satipaṭṭhāna	establishment of mindfulness. *See* Appendix 3 (under 4).
satta	a [sentient] being
sattakkhattuparama	a seven-times-at-most attainer (a type of stream-enterer)
satthā	a teacher
saddhā	faith
santati	continuity [of mind]
santi	peace
santuṭṭhi	contentment
santosa	contentment
santhava	intimacy
sandiṭṭhika	directly visible, pertaining to the present life (said of the Dhamma)
sapadānacārī	one who walks on alms round without skipping houses
sabbaññutā	omniscience
samaññā	a designation
samaṇa	an ascetic
samatha	serenity (meditation practice aimed at concentration)
samaya	(1) an occasion; (2) a philosophical system; (3) an attainment
samādhi	concentration
samāpatti	a meditative attainment. *See* Appendix 3 (under 8).
samuggahita	(1) grasping; (2) what is grasped
samuccheda	eradication [of defilements]
samudaya	origin [of suffering, etc.]
sampajañña	clear comprehension
sampatti	excellence, success
samparāyika	pertaining to future lives
sampasādana	placidity

Pāli	English
sambādha	confinement
sambodhi	enlightenment
sammasana	exploration [of conditioned things as impermanent, etc.]
sammādiṭṭhi	right view
sammuti	an opinion
sayambhū	self-accomplished (said of buddhas and paccekabuddhas)
saraṇa	a refuge. *See* Appendix 3 (under 3).
salla	dart. *See* Appendix 3 (under 7).
savana	hearing, listening [to the Dhamma]
saviññāṇaka	sentient (literally, with consciousness)
sassata	eternalism (often compounded with *–diṭṭhi* or *–vāda*)
sahāya	a companion
sākacchā	discussion
sāta	pleasant
sāmaggī	concord
sārambha	(1) rivalry; (2) instigation
sāvaka	a disciple
sāsana	the Teaching [of the Buddha]
sikkhā	a training. *See* Appendix 3 (under 3).
sikkhāpada	a training rule
siddha	accomplished
sineha	(1) affection; (2) moisture
sibbinī	the seamstress (a metaphor for craving)
sīla	good behavior, behavior. *See* Appendix 3 (under 4).
sīlabbata	good behavior and observances
sukkhavipassaka	a dry-insight meditator
sukha	pleasure, happiness
sugata	the Fortunate One (an epithet of the Buddha)
sugati	a good destination (see *gati*)
suñña	empty
suññata	emptiness

Pāli	English
suta	(1) what is heard; (2) learning
sudda	*untranslated*: the caste of laborers and servants
suddhāvāsa	a pure abode (realm for rebirth of non-returners)
suddhi	purity
supaṇṇa	*untranslated*: a kind of supernatural bird
subhāsita	well-spoken [speech]
suvaca	amenable to advice
sussūsa	a desire to learn
suhajja	a friend ("dear to one's heart")
sekha	a trainee
soka	sorrow
sotāpatti	stream-entry
sotāpanna	a stream-enterer
sotthi	safety
sotthiya	a learned scholar
somanassa	joy
soracca	gentleness
sovacassatā	being amenable to advice
havya	an oblation
hiri	moral shame
hetu	a cause

Bibliography

I. Pāli versions of the Suttanipāta consulted

Burmese-script Chaṭṭha Saṅgāyana Tipiṭaka edition. Vipassana Research Institute electronic version 4.0. Online at http://www.tipitaka.org/cst4.

Roman-script edition, edited by Dines Anderson and Helmer Smith. Oxford: Pali Text Society, 1913. Reprint 1997.

Sinhala-script edition, Buddha Jayanti Tripitaka Series, volume 25. Online bilingual version (Pāli-Sinhala) at http://www.aathaapi.net/tipitaka/29.OTSPKN_Sutta_Nipatha.pdf.

II. Previous translations of the Suttanipāta consulted

Jayawickrama, N. A., trans. 2001. *Suttanipāta: Text and Translation*. Kelaniya, Sri Lanka: Post-Graduate Institute of Pāli and Buddhist Studies.

Norman, K. R., trans. 2006b. *The Group of Discourses*. 2nd edition. Lancaster: Pali Text Society.

Paññobhāsa, Bhikkhu, trans. 2012. *The Aṭṭhakavagga* (*Sutta Nipāta 4*), Pali, with English translation. n.p. Path Press.

Saddhātissa, H., trans. 1994. *The Sutta-Nipāta*. London: Routledge Curzon.

Ṭhānissaro Bhikkhu. 1997a. "The Atthaka Vagga: The Octet Chapter." Online version see http://www.accesstoinsight.org/lib/authors/thanissaro/atthakavagga.html.

———. 1997b. "The Parayana Vagga: The Chapter on the Way to the Far Shore." Online version see http://www.accesstoinsight.org/lib/authors/thanissaro/parayanavagga.html.

III. Versions of the Paramatthajotikā consulted

A. Paramatthajotikā I

Burmese-script Chaṭṭha Saṅgāyana Tipiṭaka edition. Vipassana Research Institute electronic version 4.0. Online at http://www.tipitaka.org/cst4.

Roman-script edition, edited by Helmer Smith from a collation by Mabel Hunt. *The Khuddakapāṭha together with its Commentary, Paramatthajotikā I.* Oxford: Pali Text Society. 1915. Reprint 2005.

Sinhala-script edition, edited by Acharya Welipitiye Dewananda Thera, finally revised by Mahagoda Siri Ñāṇissara Thera. Colombo: Simon Hewavitarne Bequest Series, 1922.

B. Paramatthajotikā II

Burmese-script Chaṭṭha Saṅgāyana Tipiṭaka edition. Vipassana Research Institute electronic version 4.0. Online at http://www.tipitaka.org/cst4.

Roman-script edition, edited by Helmer Smith. 2 vols. *Sutta-Nipāta Commentary being Paramatthajotikā II.* Oxford: Pali Text Society. Vol. 1. 1916, reprint 1989. Vol. 2. 1918, reprint 1997.

Sinhala-script edition, edited by Siryagoda Sumaṅgala Thera and Mapalagama Candajoti Thera, finally revised by Mahagoda Siri Ñāṇissara Thera. Colombo: Simon Hewavitarne Bequest Series, 1920.

IV. Versions of the Niddesa consulted

A. Mahāniddesa

Burmese-script Chaṭṭha Saṅgāyana Tipiṭaka edition. Vipassana Research Institute electronic version 4.0. Online at http://www.tipitaka.org/cst4.

Roman-script edition, edited by L. de la Vallee Poussin and E. J. Thomas. London: Pali Text Society. Part I first published 1916. Part II first published 1917. Combined reprint 1978.

Sinhala-script edition, Buddha Jayanti Tripitaka Series, volume 33. Online bilingual version (Pāli-Sinhala) at http://www.aathaapi.net/tipitaka/35.OTSPKN_Maha_Niddesa_Pali.pdf.

B. Cūḷaniddesa

Burmese-script Chaṭṭha Saṅgāyana Tipiṭaka edition. Vipassana Research Institute electronic version 4.0. Online at http://www.tipitaka.org/cst4.

Roman-script edition (Cullaniddesa), edited by W. Stede. Oxford: Pali Text Society. First published 1918. Reprint 1988.

Sinhala-script edition, Buddha Jayanti Tripitaka Series, volume 33. Online bilingual version (Pāli-Sinhala) at http://www.aathaapi.net/tipitaka/36.OTSPKN_Chulla_Niddesa_Pali.pdf.

V. Other works consulted

Anālayo. 2010. "Paccekabuddhas in the Isigili-sutta and its Ekottarika-āgama Parallel." *Canadian Journal of Buddhist Studies* 6: 5–36.

———. 2011a. *A Comparative Study of the Majjhima-nikāya*. Taipei: Dharma Drum Publishing.

———. 2011b. "The conversion of the Brahmin Sela in the Ekottarika-Āgama." *Thai International Journal of Buddhist Studies* 2: 37–56.

———. 2014. *The Dawn of Abhidharma*. Hamburg: Hamburg University Press.

———. 2015. "Pratyekabuddhas in the Ekottarika-āgama." *Journal of the Oxford Centre for Buddhist Studies* 8:10–27.

Bapat, P. V. 1951. *Arthapada Sūtra Spoken by the Buddha*. Santiniketan, India: Visva-Bharati. Online English translation, with Pāli parallels, at http://mbingenheimer.net/tools/bibls/Bapat.1951.Arthapadasutra.pdf.

Beal, Samuel. 1875. *The Romantic Legend of Sākya Buddha from the Chinese-Sanscrit*. London: Trübner. Online version at https://archive.org/details/romanticlegendof00ahbi.

Bodhi, Bhikkhu, trans. 1995. *The Great Discourse on Causation: The Mahānidāna Sutta and Its Commentaries*. 2nd edition. Kandy, Sri Lanka: Buddhist Publication Society.

———, trans. 2000. *Connected Discourses of the Buddha* (*Saṃyutta Nikāya*). Boston: Wisdom Publications.

———, ed. 2007a. *A Comprehensive Manual of Abhidhamma* (*Abhidhammattha-saṅgaha*). 3rd edition. Kandy, Sri Lanka: Buddhist Publication Society.

———, trans. 2007b. *Discourse on the All-Embracing Net of Views: The Brahmajāla Sutta and Its Commentaries*. 2nd edition. Kandy, Sri Lanka: Buddhist Publication Society.

———, trans. 2012. *Numerical Discourses of the Buddha* (*Aṅguttara Nikāya*). Boston: Wisdom Publications.

Brough, John. 1962. *The Gāndhārī Dharmapada*. Reprint 2001. Delhi: Motilal Banarsidass.

Burlingame, Eugene Watson. 1921. *Buddhist Legends*. 3 volumes. Cambridge, MA: Harvard University Press.

Collins, Steven. 1982. *Selfless Persons: Imagery and Thought in Theravāda Buddhism*. Cambridge: Cambridge University Press.

Cone, Margaret. *A Dictionary of Pāli*. Oxford: Pali Text Society, part 1 (a–kh) 2001, part 2 (g–n) 2010.

D'Alwis, James. 1863. *An Introduction to Kachchāyana's Grammar of the Pāli Language*. London: Williams and Norgate.

Dhammika, S. *Dictionary of Flora and Fauna in the Pāḷi Tipiṭaka*. Unpublished manuscript.

Dharmamitra, Bhikshu. 2009. *Nāgārjuna on the Six Perfections*. Seattle: Kalavinka Press.

Edgerton, Franklin. 1953. *Buddhist Hybrid Sanskrit Dictionary*. Reprint 2004. Delhi: Motilal Banarsidass.

Endo, Toshiichi. 1997. *Buddha in Theravāda Buddhism*. Dehiwala, Sri Lanka: Buddhist Cultural Centre.

———. 2013. *Studies in Pāli Commentarial Literature: Sources, Controversies, and Insights*. Hong Kong: Centre of Buddhist Studies, University of Hong Kong.

Enomoto, Fumio. 1989. "Śarīrārthagāthā, A Collection of Canonical Verses in the Yogācārabhūmi," in *Sanskrit-Texte aus dem buddhistischen Kanon: Neuentdeckungen und Neueditionen Folge 1*. Göttingen: Vandenhoeck and Ruprecht.

Fronsdal, Gil. 2016. *The Buddha before Buddhism: Wisdom from the Early Teachings*. Boulder, CO: Shambala Publications.

Geiger, Wilhelm. 1994. *Pāli Grammar*. Revised and edited by K. R. Norman. Oxford: Pali Text Society.

Gnoli, Raneiro, ed. 1977. *The Gilgit Manuscript of the Saṅghabhedavastu*. Rome: Istituto Italiano per il Medio ed Estremo Oriente. Online Sanskrit text at http://prajnaquest.fr/downloads/BookofDzyan/Sanskrit%20Buddhist%20Texts/sanghabhedavastu_vol_one_1977.pdf.

Hinūber, Oskar von. 2015. "The Verb *addhabhavati as an Artificial Formation." *Journal of the Pāli Text Society* 32: 213–27.

Horner, I. B., trans. 1938–66. The *Book of the Discipline* (*Vinaya-Piṭaka*). 6 vols. London: Pali Text Society.

Jayawickrama, N. A. 1976–78. "A Critical Analysis of the Suttanipāta." Serialized in *Pāli Buddhist Review*: 1.2 (1976): 75–90; 1.3 (1976): 136–63; 2.1 (1977): 14–41; 2.2 (1977): 86–105; 2.3 (1977): 141–58; 3.1 (1978): 3–19; 3.2 (1978): 45–64; 3.3 (1978): 100–113.

Jones, Dhivan Thomas. 2014. "Like the Rhinoceros, or Like Its Horn? The Problem of Khaggavisāṇa Revisited." *Buddhist Studies Review* 31.2: 165–78.

———. 2016. "'That bhikkhu lets go both the near and far shores': meaning and metaphor in the refrain from the Uraga verses." *Journal of the Oxford Centre for Buddhist Studies*, pp. 71–107.

Jones, J. J., trans. 1949–56. *The Mahāvastu*. 3 vols. London: Luzac.

Keith, Arthur Berriedale. 1914. *The Veda of the Black Yajus School entitled Taittiriya Sanhita*. Cambridge, MA: Harvard University Press. Online version at https://archive.org/details/vedablackyajuss00keitgoog.

Levman, Bryan Geoffrey. 2014. *Linguistic Ambiguities, the Transmissional Process, and the Earliest Recoverable Language of Buddhism*. PhD dissertation, University of Toronto.

Macdonell, Arthur A., and Arthur Berriedale Keith. 1912. *Vedic Index of Names and Subjects*. London: John Murray. Online version at https://archive.org/stream/vedicindexofname01macduoft/vedicindexofname01macduoft_djvu.txt.

Malalasekera, G. P. 1937–38. *Dictionary of Pāli Proper Names*. 2 vols. Reprint 1960. London: Pali Text Society.

Masefield, Peter, trans. 2008–9. *The Commentary on the Itivuttaka* (*Itivuttaka-aṭṭhakathā*). 2 vols. Oxford: Pali Text Society.

Monier-Williams, M. 1899. *Sanskrit-English Dictionary*. Reprint 2005. Delhi: Motilal Banarsidass.

Müller, Max. 1860. *A History of Ancient Sanskrit Literature*. London and Edinburgh: Williams and Norgate.

Ñāṇamoli, Bhikkhu, trans. 1960. *Minor Readings and the Illustrator of Ultimate Meaning* (*Khuddakapāṭha and Paramatthajotikā*). Reprint 2005. Oxford: Pali Text Society.

———, trans. 1956. *The Path of Purification* (*Visuddhimagga*). 5th edition. 1991. Kandy, Sri Lanka: Buddhist Publication Society.

——— and Bhikkhu Bodhi, trans. 1995. *The Middle Length Discourses of the Buddha: A Translation of the Majjhima Nikāya*. Boston: Wisdom Publications.

Norman, K. N., trans. 1969. *Elders' Verses* I (trans. of Theragāthā). London: Pali Text Society.

———. 1983. *Pāli Literature*. Wiesbaden: Otto Herrassowitz.

———. 1992. *Collected Papers* 3. Oxford: Pali Text Society.

———. 1993. *Collected Papers* 4. Oxford: Pali Text Society.

———. 2001. *Collected Papers* 7. Oxford: Pali Text Society.

———. 2004. "On Translating the Suttanipāta." *Buddhist Studies Review* 21.1: 68–83.

———. 2006a. *A Philological Approach to Buddhism*. 2nd edition. Lancaster: Pali Text Society.

———. 2006b. *The Group of Discourses* (*Sutta-nipāta*). 2nd edition. Lancaster: Pali Text Society.

Nyanaponika Thera. 1977. *The Worn-Out Skin: Reflections on the Uraga Sutta*. Reprint 2009. Kandy, Sri Lanka: Buddhist Publication Society. References are to the BPS online edition: http://www.bps.lk/olib/wh/wh241.pdf.

Premasiri, P. D. 1972. *The Philosophy of the Aṭṭhakavagga*. Kandy, Sri Lanka: Buddhist Publication Society.

Pruitt, William, ed., and K. R. Norman, trans. 2001. *The Pātimokkha*. Oxford: Pali Text Society.

Rhys Davids, T. W. and William Stede. 1921–25. *Pali-English Dictionary*. Reprint 1999. Oxford: Pali Text Society.

Salomon, Richard. 2000. *A Gāndhārī Version of the Rhinoceros Sūtra*. Seattle: University of Washington.

Ṭhānissaro, Bhikkhu. 2007. *The Buddhist Monastic Code*. 2 vols. Valley Center, CA: Metta Forest Monastery. Revised edition.

———. 2016. "Truths with Consequences." *Insight Journal*. https://www.bcbsdharma.org/issue/2016.

Thapar, Romila. 1997. *Aśoka and the Decline of the Mauryas*. Delhi: Oxford University Press.

Waldschmidt, Ernst. 1951. *Das Mahāparinirvāṇasūtra, Text in Sanskrit und Tibetisch, verglichen mit dem Pāli nebst einer Übersetzung der chinesischen Entsprechung im Vinaya der Mūlasarvāstivādins, auf Grund von Turfan-Handschriften herausgegeben und bearbeitet*. Volume 2. Berlin: Akademie Verlag.

Index of Subjects Discussed in the Commentaries

This index lists significant references only, and only to subjects discussed in the commentaries. Themes dealt with in the Suttanipāta itself are highlighted in the Thematic Guide to the Verses (p. 93). I generally give preference to noun forms over adjectives, even though the item referred to occurs in the text as an adjective rather than as a noun. The Pāli word is usually given in the singular. I do not include a Pāli word after English terms that do not bear a technical sense.

Abandoning (*pahāna*), 362–64, 1510 n. 1758, 1511 n. 1762, 1554 n. 2142
Abstinence (*virati*), 759–60, 1386 n. 494, 1415–16 n. 779, 1466 n. 1301
Acquisitions (*upadhi*), 397–99, 844, 848, 929, 1002–3, 1024, 1057, 1252–53, 1256
Adhesion (*abhilepana, lepana*) 1081, 1082, 1233, 1234, 1243
Affection (*sineha*), 429–30, 482, 776
Aggregates (*khandha*): five, 358–60, 397, 525, 699, 919, 1003, 1029–30, 1509 n. 1746, 1553 n. 2135; three (of training) 491, 812, 1186–87; five (of arahant) 464, 1170, 1254
Agitation (*iñjita*), 1006–7, 1241–42, 1248–49
Alms round, 407–14, 481, 497–98, 855–56, 987, 991, 992–94
Alone (*eka*), 420–22, 649, 1088–89, 1093, 1207–8
Altruistic joy (*muditā*), 493
Amenable to advice, being (*sovacassatā*), 572, 766
Anger (*kodha*), 365–67, 384, 540, 1119–20, 1141
Arahant, 414, 695–96, 705–6, 769–70, 839–41, 1127, 1257, 1306–7, 1496 n. 1597; brahmās as, 840–41; Buddha as, 934–35; com-

Contentment (*santuṭṭhi, santosa*), 446, 447, 573–74, 762–64, 822, 992, 1213–14, 1381 n. 446
Courteous (*appagabha*), 574–75, 1124–25
Coverings removed (*vivattacchadda*), 846, 944–45, 1062, 1325–26
Craving (*taṇhā*), 372–73, 488, 543, 1005, 1118, 1119, 1171, 1197–98, 1245, 1281–82, 1284, 1292, 1318–19; attachment to world, as, 543, 1017–18, 1279; for existence, 1031, 1032, 1071, 1130, 1179, 1243, 1264; for tastes, 480–81, 1129, 1179; full understanding of, 1275–76. *See too* Desire; Lust; Sensual pleasure; Taking as "mine"

Dart (*salla*), 379, 817, 956, 1016, 1037–38, 1192–95
Death (*maraṇa*), 642, 644, 660–61, 953–56, 1007, 1077–79; realm of, 832, 1293–94, 1325; recollection of, 409
Deer in forest, simile of, 439–42
Defilements (*kilesa*), 358–61, 377–78, 379, 516, 649, 777–78, 1018–19; eight, 1023, 1270–71; seventeen, 1023, 1242, 1381 n. 450; three grades, 1183–84
Delusion (*moha*), 376, 469, 1192, 1193
Dependent origination (*paṭiccasamuppāda*), 967, 1435 n. 981, 1507 n. 1730, 1508 n. 1736, 1553 n. 2135
Desire (*chanda*, *vanatha*), 378–79, 1138, 1139, 1278. See too Craving; Lust; Sensual pleasure
Devas, 356–57, 519–20, 537, 543–44, 620, 678, 737–38, 739, 740–41, 742, 804, 839–42, 860, 979–82, 1205, 1206, 1396 n. 577, 1410 n. 730, 1442 n. 1054, 1509 n. 1743
Dhamma: bad, of 539–40; brahmins, of, 787–92; comprehension of, 488–89, 845, 1008–9, 1130, 1185, 1237; delight in, 809–10; directly visible, 949, 1253–54, 1323–24; excellence of, 522, 854, 704–5, 938–40, 1288, 1317, 1323; gem, as, 691–93; knowledge of, 1130, 1185; learning of, 547, 764–65, 767–68, 804–6; love and hate toward, 538–39; means to happiness, 623; praise of, 522, 854; realization of, 1060–61, 1517 n. 1819; wheel of, 355, 589–90, 946–47, 986
Dhamma body (*dhammakāya*), 394, 395, 1269
Discipline (*vinaya*), 586–58, 753
Disputes (*vivāda*), 1040–41, 1051, 1095–1103, 1135–37, 1149–55, 1157–58, 1166
Divine dwellings (*brahmavihāra*), 582, 1390 n. 526, 1390–91 n. 529, 1393 n. 545

Index of Proper Names

Index of Pāli Words Discussed in the Notes

This index is arranged in the order of the Pāli alphabet. Preference is given to the stem forms of nouns (with *ī* for nouns of the *–in* class) unless there is a cogent reason to retain an inflected form.

About Wisdom Publications

Wisdom Publications is the leading publisher of classic and contemporary Buddhist books and practical works on mindfulness. To learn more about us or to explore our other books, please visit our website at wisdompubs.org or contact us at the address below.

Wisdom Publications
199 Elm Street
Somerville, MA 02144 USA

We are a 501(c)(3) organization, and donations in support of our mission are tax deductible.

Wisdom Publications is affiliated with the Foundation for the Preservation of the Mahayana Tradition (FPMT).

Thank you for supporting Wisdom!

Please visit wisdompubs.org/books/pali-canon to read suttas from the Pāli Canon online.